Deblicquy Site, Bathurst Island

Red Bay

L'Anse Aux Meadows

L'Anse Amour Burial

Debert Site

Augustine Burial Mound

Cliché-Rancourt Site

Rideau Canal

Snake Hill Cemetery

Thedford II Site

Arviat

Kitigaaryuit (Kittigazuit)

Lower Fort Garry

Gowan Site

Stampede Site

Old Crow

Bluefish Cave

Keatley Creek Site

Wally's Beach/ St. Mary's Reservoir

Head Smashed In Buffalo Jump

Kwäday Dän Ts'inchi

Haida Gwaii

Namu

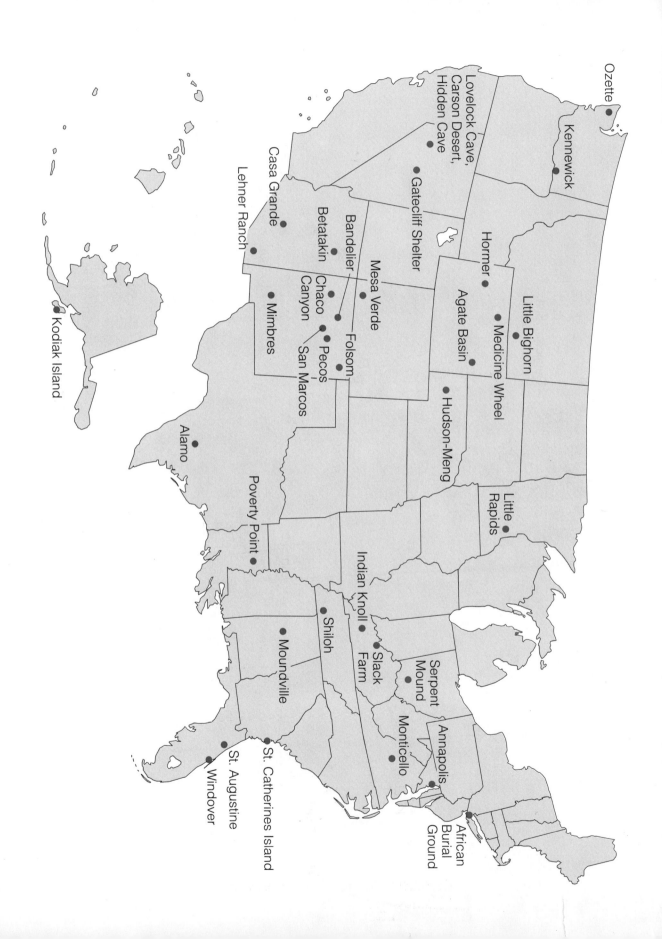

Ozette

Kennewick

Lovelock Cave,
Carson Desert,
Hidden Cave

Casa Grande

Lehner Ranch

Gatecliff Shelter

Betatakin

Bandelier

Hormer

Little Bighorn

Agate Basin

Mesa Verde

Medicine Wheel

Chaco
Canyon

Mimbres

Folsom

Pecos

San Marcos

Hudson-Meng

Kodiak Island

Alamo

Little
Rapids

Poverty Point

Indian Knoll

Shiloh

Moundville

Slack
Farm

Serpent
Mound

Monticello

Annapolis

Windover

St. Augustine

St. Catherines Island

African
Burial
Ground

Archaeology

FIRST CANADIAN EDITION

David Hurst Thomas
American Museum of Natural History

Robert L. Kelly
University of Wyoming

Peter C. Dawson
University of Calgary

NELSON EDUCATION

NELSON / EDUCATION

Archaeology, First Canadian Edition

by David Hurst Thomas, Robert L. Kelly, Peter C. Dawson

Associate Vice President, Editorial Director:
Evelyn Veitch

Editor-in-Chief, Higher Education:
Anne Williams

Senior Acquisitions Editor:
Scott Couling

Marketing Manager:
Heather Leach

Developmental Editor:
My Editor Inc.

Photo Researcher and Permissions Coordinator:
Mary Rose MacLachlan

Content Production Managers:
Carrie McGregor/Karri Yano

Production Service:
Lachina Publishing Services

Copy Editor:
Kelli Howey

Proofreader:
Lachina Publishing Services

Indexer:
Lachina Publishing Services

Senior Production Coordinator:
Ferial Suleman

Design Director:
Ken Phipps

Managing Designer:
Katherine Strain

Interior Design:
Lachina Publishing Services

Cover Design:
Dianna Little

Cover Image:
© Peter Christopher/Masterfile

Compositor:
Lachina Publishing Services

Printer:
Courier

Library and Archives Canada Cataloguing in Publication Data

Thomas, David Hurst
    Archaeology/David Hurst Thomas, Robert L. Kelly.—1st Canadian ed./Peter C. Dawson

Includes bibliographical references and index.
ISBN 978-0-17-610306-4

    1. Archaeology. I. Kelly, Robert L. II. Dawson, Peter C., 1965- III. Title.

CC165.T46 2008   930.1
C2007-904700-9

Brief Contents

v

Contents

CHAPTER 2   Archaeology, Anthropology, Science, and the Humanities   28

CHAPTER 3   The Structure of Archaeological Inquiry   57

CHAPTER 5   Doing Fieldwork: Remote Sensing and Geographic Information Systems   120

CHAPTER 6   Doing Fieldwork: Why Archaeologists Dig Square Holes   143

CHAPTER 7   Geoarchaeology and Site Formation Processes   166

CHAPTER 8   Chronology Building: How to Get a Date   190

CHAPTER 9   The Dimensions of Archaeology: Time, Space, and Form   225

CHAPTER 15 Understanding Key Transitions in World Prehistory   403

CHAPTER 16 Historical Archaeology and Industrial Archaeology: Insights into Canada's Rural, Urban, and Industrial Past   436

CHAPTER 17 Archaeological Ethics and Indigenous Archaeology: Exploring Ways to Protect, Respect, and Share Canada's Diverse Cultural Heritage   469

To Kate, for constantly reminding me that the present is as important as the past; and to Liam, who has given me a future to look forward to.

—P.C.D.

Preface

Archaeology, First Canadian Edition, is a user-friendly introduction to archaeology: what it is, who does it, and why we should care about it. This text addresses archaeological methods and theory, and yet it departs in some important ways from the standard introductory textbook.

Students say they sometimes don't bother reading the introductory textbooks they've purchased—whether the books are about archaeology, chemistry, or whatever. There are several reasons for this paradox: The instructor covers exactly the same material, using the same examples as the text—so why bother reading what you can get condensed in a lecture? Or their textbooks are deadly dull, written in arcane academic jargon that nobody (including the professor) really understands. Still others convey that they take an archaeology course just because it sounds like a fun way to fulfill a distribution requirement—but the text actually has nothing to say to them.

Archaeology's approach, writing style, and broad, up-to-the-minute coverage of the discipline distinguishes it from other introductory texts, and aims to satisfy both instructors and students alike.

Personal Examples, High-Interest Topics

In most archaeology texts, the approach is fairly encyclopedic and dispassionate. After all, modern archaeology is a specialized and complicated academic discipline, with plenty of concepts, several bodies of theory, and a huge array of analytical methods—all things students should learn about. But perhaps the best way for students to begin to understand archaeology (or any subject, for that matter) is through a few well-chosen, extended, personalized examples—stories that show how archaeologists have worked through actual problems in the field and in the lab. So that's the approach taken in this text.

Writing an introductory textbook is not easy. The book must provide a solid foundation for students who intend to become professional archaeologists. This requires a thorough review of the discipline, including all its major concepts and jargon. But it must also be written for the many students who will *not* become professional archaeologists. Accordingly, many of the book's topics were chosen with the non-professional in mind.

As it turns out, these are the very subjects that the budding career archaeologist should know. Most chapters, for instance, include sidebars titled *Archaeological Ethics,* which touch upon sensitive subjects that influence both the professional archaeologist and the public (who pays for most of the archaeological research in Canada and the United States). Many archaeological texts avoid these sensitive issues, such as the excavation of the dead, repatriation of artifacts, and working with descendant communities. But these are the issues that often matter most to students and to instructors, and therefore, in this text they have received the coverage they deserve.

Why a Canadian Edition?

By nature, introductory textbooks tend to paint disciplines with a broad brush so that important concepts and ideas are not lost in huge amounts of detail. Producing a Canadian edition narrows the width of that brush just a little, thereby drawing attention to the unique ways that archaeology has developed (and continues to develop) as a discipline in Canada, as compared to the United States and other areas of the world. In addition to providing a solid foundation in archaeology, students will now see how politics, ethics, geography, and relations with indigenous societies have shaped the practice of archaeology in Canada. The result is the emergence of a uniquely Canadian perspective on many important concepts, methods, and issues encountered in the discipline.

Aids to Learning

Archaeological Ethics These sidebars address critical ethical issues, such as the relationship between industrial development and archaeology, the selling of artifacts in electronic auction houses, the excavation of human remains, and the ownership of sacred sites. The Canadian edition includes an entire chapter (Chapter 17) on ethical issues and their logical outcome—indigenous archaeology. This chapter and the accompanying sidebars could easily form the basis of writing assignments or group discussions for students. Reviewers were enthusiastically unanimous in their support for these sidebars: "Keep them at all costs," wrote one.

Looking Closer These features cover ancillary topics in each chapter. For example, in the first chapter, a *Looking Closer* box discusses how archaeology developed as a discipline in Canada; in the chapter dealing with fieldwork, a *Looking Closer* sidebar describes how Parks Canada archaeologists search for submerged sites in Gwaii Haana, British Columbia. Many of these sidebars are exclusive to the Canadian edition, and highlight uniquely Canadian examples. Some tell students what sort of equipment they need for survey and excavation, what courses they might take, or how they can help promote archaeology in their own communities. Others look at the lighter side of archaeology, such as how sites get their names, or they give personal glimpses into fieldwork—for example, what it's like to do survey or ethnoarchaeology. Still others discuss the origins and usage of terms such as "Eskimo" and "Inuit" or "Native American" and "First Nations."

In His/Her Own Words and Profile of an Archaeologist Beginning in Chapter 1, *In His/Her Own Words* biographies recount the history of archaeology in Canada and the United States. *Profile of an Archaeologist* elements also emphasize the diversity of today's working archaeologists and illustrate the varied ways in which archaeologists can make a living.

The above features combine with the following learning aids to help students master this complex, fascinating discipline:

* Chapter Outlines at the beginning of each chapter.
* Bulleted Chapter Summaries at the end of each chapter.
* Running glossaries in each chapter (with glossary terms defined at the bottom of the page on which the term is introduced) plus an alphabetized Glossary at the end of the text.
* Photographs and figures that were carefully chosen or created to give students a visual sense of a case study and to act as integrated pedagogical aids to the text.
* Additional Readings at the end of each chapter, including articles and books that will be comprehensible to students taking an introductory course.
* Online Resources at the end of each chapter to remind students of resources available—including practice quizzes and exercises—on the text's Web site.
* A chapter-by-chapter bibliography that provides an easy way to find references and additional reading on each chapter's subjects. Despite the absence of in-text citations, students will still be able to locate material discussed in the text, as well as additional readings, in a chapter's bibliography. Page references for the few longer quotes that appear are noted in the relevant bibliographic entry.

A Distinctive Approach

The following strategies all contribute to a full, up-to-date exploration of the field:

Discussions of archaeological objects in context
You'll notice that there is no chapter on "archaeological objects"—stone tools, ceramics, metals, architecture, and so forth (and what archaeologists can do with them). This encyclopedic approach tends to encourage students to simply memorize a laundry list of techniques without context. Instead, discussions of things like stone tools and ceramics have been embedded and contextualized in other substantive examples. For example, pottery—its manufacture and basic constituents—is discussed in Chapter 13, which deals with using petrographic analysis to track down trade networks. This presentation ensures that students learn about these basic archaeological objects in ways that carry significance for them—so that they see why, for instance, it might be useful to know where a sherd's temper comes from.

Coverage of key methods/technologies topics To reflect the growing importance of certain methods and technologies, the Canadian edition includes detailed discussions on geographic information systems (GIS) technology (Chapter 5) and trapped-charge dating methods, such as optically stimulated luminescence (Chapter 8). Chapter 18 discusses exciting advances in the use of computer modelling, laser scanning, and virtual reality for reconstructing, interpreting, and preserving archaeological sites. Examples of these approaches are provided, including new computer reconstructions of the Temple site of Phimai, and Thule Inuit whalebone houses from the Canadian High Arctic.

Focus of chapter on neo-evolutionary approaches Chapter 15 focuses on the ways in which different archaeological paradigms can help to provide a more complete understanding of two key transitions in world prehistory: the origins of agriculture and the origins of the state. This is done for two reasons. First, given that this introductory course may very well be the only archaeology class that a student ever takes, at least some appreciation for world prehistory must be conveyed (even if the course focuses on methods). Second, students should understand that different paradigms are not simply different stories about the past, but rather are different perspectives that contribute to our understanding of the past. Too often, students see debates about different theoretical paradigms as an academic Super Bowl—winner takes all, and the loser goes home with its tail between its legs. Emphasizing the compatibility of various paradigms is a much preferred approach—even if those paradigms sometimes appear to conflict.

Balanced Coverage: Depth, Breadth, Theory

The text is not encyclopedic, but it does cover the field in a comprehensive manner. Given the background knowledge that a first- or second-year university student brings to an introductory course, this text strikes a first-rate balance among the different directions that archaeologists can take. By providing extended discussions of theoretical paradigms, the nature of science (what it can and cannot do), the humanities, and the intellectual process of learning about the past, this text aims to be

both one of the most readable and "intellectual" available. Students will learn a little about the Enlightenment, the origins of postmodern perspectives, and evolutionary thinking in these pages. And students can apply the topics in this textbook—especially those in the first three chapters—to virtually any area of study.

Geographic Coverage

The Canadian edition expands the geographic coverage from western North America to include most provinces and territories in Canada. The Canadian arctic receives a little more attention because it is an area that Dawson knows best. The inclusion of information from the Canadian north is also timely, as this region has recently captured the attention of the international community as a locus for the study of climate change, and its effects on plant and animal populations—including people. Nevertheless, the Canadian edition continues to draw upon work in other areas of the world, including Central and South America, Egypt and the near East, Madagascar, France, Australia, Micronesia, to name only a few. Although the text is focused, it is not provincial—and should thereby inspire classroom discussions or research projects from around the world.

Organization of the Text

This text is constructed so that various ideas build upon one another. Each archaeologist teaches his or her introductory course differently, but many chapters cross-reference material discussed in other chapters (and each instance of this is noted within the text).

Chapter 1 begins with a discussion of Kwäday Dän Ts'ìnchi and Kennewick Man—a purposeful selection, because this textbook makes an explicit point of discussing the ethical matters that confront archaeology, and highlighting the different social and political environments that archaeologists working in Canada and the United States sometimes encounter. These examples are thus used to set the tone (and the subject of archaeological ethics is returned to in detail in Chapter 17). The remainder of Chapter 1 addresses the history of archaeology in Canada and the United States, with an emphasis on individuals in both countries who have defined the field.

In Chapters 2 and 3, we relate archaeology to the rest of anthropology and wrestle with the diversity of theoretical paradigms evident in contemporary archaeology.

This diversity is introduced not as the interbraided stream that it really is—with all its side channels, backwaters, eddies, and periodic flash floods—but rather in terms of simple dichotomies: Science and humanism, adaptive and ideational approaches, processual and postprocessual archaeology. The discussion of paradigms and of low-, middle-, and high-range theory in Chapter 3 should help to organize the rest of your course. This somewhat simplified presentation provides an easy entry into the diversity of contemporary archaeology. And, rather than come down on the side of processual or postprocessual archaeology, the text takes a centrist position that characterizes the majority of working archaeologists today: There is something to be gained from looking at prehistory through both of these paradigms, each which is well suited for answering a particular kind of question.

Chapters 4 through 6 provide the nuts and bolts of archaeology, explaining how archaeologists go about doing surface survey, using remote sensing equipment, and excavating sites. Students are given some sense of how much fun fieldwork can be, but also are introduced to issues such as sampling bias, how a survey's on-the-ground procedures can bias results, the cost of dating methods, and the utility of GIS to a postprocessual perspective.

Chapter 7 discusses the field of geoarchaeology, with a decided emphasis upon site formation processes. This chapter also covers archaeological stratigraphy, beginning with the law of superposition, and shows students how a site's stratigraphy can be "read" to provide a context to the artifacts contained there.

Chapter 8 covers dating methods used in prehistoric and historic archaeology. The major purpose of this chapter is not to write an encyclopedia of available methods, but instead to provide enough information about key techniques so that students can relate dating technology to ancient human behaviour.

Chapter 9 discusses various archaeological concepts—types, cultures, and phases—that help construct large-scale patterns in space and time. In this chapter, the authors strive to help the student see the world as an archaeologist views it, as an ever-changing spatial and temporal mosaic of material culture.

The next chapters consider how archaeologists go about breathing some anthropological life into this spatial and temporal mosaic—how they actually use material remains to infer something about past human behaviour.

Chapter 10 is about middle-range theory—how it is different from standard analogy and how archaeologists construct it through taphonomic, experimental, and ethnoarchaeological research. It is intended to convince students that archaeologists don't just make stuff up, but instead give plenty of thought to how they infer ancient behaviour from material objects and their contexts.

Chapter 11 recounts how archaeologists reconstruct diet from faunal and floral remains and how they infer hunting strategies and symbolic meanings attributed to the natural world.

Chapter 12 considers what can be learned—about diet, disease, and workload—from human skeletal remains and explores the relatively new field of molecular archaeology.

Chapter 13 shows how archaeologists can reconstruct social and political systems of the past and looks at gender, kinship, and social hierarchies.

Chapter 14 presents how archaeologists address the symbolic meanings once attached to the material remains; here, the nature of symbols, and what archaeologists can realistically hope to learn about them, is examined.

After describing (and rejecting) unilineal thinking about evolution, Chapter 15 addresses two major evolutionary transitions in human history: the origins of agriculture and the origins of the state.

Chapter 16 explores historical archaeology and industrial archaeology, especially those aspects that set these fields apart from prehistoric archaeology—the ability to uncover "hidden history," the ability to provide a near-forensic analysis of historical events, and the ability to present alternative perspectives on Canadian and American history. The inclusion of a section on industrial archaeology is entirely unique, and gives coverage to an area of archaeology that is rarely addressed in introductory textbooks.

Chapter 17 examines ethics in archaeology, and the rise of indigenous archaeology in which First Nations and Inuit communities are actively engaged in all aspects of archaeological research. This chapter also covers the drafting of ethical principles for archaeological research by various national and international organizations, as well as issues relating to the reburial and repatriation of human remains and artifacts.

Chapter 18 looks at the future of archaeology, such as the role of high-tech approaches to archaeological interpretation and heritage preservation (computer modelling, virtual reality), and the ways in which archaeologists apply their knowledge to contemporary problems. The chapter concludes by discussing the increased involvement of indigenous peoples in the archaeology of themselves and by posing the question of whether we are on the brink of another revolution—one that might produce an entirely new form of archaeology.

Supplemental Materials

This text also comes with a strong supplements program to help instructors use their class time most effectively and to aid students in mastering the material.

Instructor's Manual with Test Bank (0176105107): The instructor's manual offers chapter outlines, learning objectives, key terms and concepts, and lecture suggestions. The test bank consists of 40–60 test questions per chapter, including multiple-choice, true/false, and essay questions.

Instructor's Resource CD-ROM (0176105115): The instructor's resource CD-ROM includes:

* An electronic version of the Instructor's Manual with Test Bank.
* ExamView Computerized Test Bank: Tests can be created, delivered, and customized in minutes with this easy-to-use assessment and tutorial system. ExamView offers both a Quick Test Wizard and an Online Test Wizard that guide instructors step-by-step through the process of creating tests, and its unique WYSIWYG capability allows users to see the test they are creating on the screen exactly as it will print or display online. Tests of up to 250 questions can be built, using up to 12 question types. Using ExamView's complete word-processing capabilities, instructors can enter an unlimited number of new questions or edit existing questions.
* PowerPoint Lecture Slides: A chapter-by-chapter slide show providing an overview of chapter content; also available as a download from the Web site.

Companion Web Site: The companion Web site includes the following for each chapter of the text: tutorial practice quizzes, Internet links and exercises, flashcards of the text's glossary, crossword puzzles, essay questions, and much more.

Also available: ***Doing Fieldwork: Archaeological Demonstrations CD-ROM*** (0155059297): Granted that students can learn field techniques only from actually participating, this CD shows professional archaeologists involved in various digs (many of which are referenced in the text), illustrates field techniques, gives students perspective about what they're learning, reinforces concepts and techniques via live examples, and encourages students to participate in a dig themselves. The presentation is organized by the main techniques that one uses on a dig. Users are taken through each step automatically or can navigate to any point via the navigation bar. Students review illustrations and video clips of each technique. After reviewing a step in the dig process, students are taken to "Check points," which are concept questions about each step of the dig. Students can see the answers, receive their score, and e-mail the score to the instructor.

Who Helped Out?

I wish to extend my gratitude to many people for their assistance in the development of this first Canadian edition of *Archaeology:*

Ariane Burke, Université de Montréal
Aubrey Cannon, McMaster University
Claude Chapdelaine, Université de Montréal
David Blower, Golder Associates
Dianne Newell, University of British Columbia
E. Leigh Syms, Manitoba Museum
Andrea Freeman, University of Calgary
Gerry Oetelaar, University of Calgary
Jerimy Cunningham, University of Calgary
J. M. Mailol, University of Calgary
Mark Skinner, Simon Fraser University
Marty Magne, Parks Canada
Natasha Lyons, University of Calgary
Rudy Reimer, McMaster University
Richard Levy, University of Calgary
Julie Ross, Government of Nunavut
Sandra Peacock, University of British Columbia
Scott Raymond, University of Calgary
Max Friesen, University of Toronto

Ted Litherland, IsoTrace—University of Toronto
Brian Kooyman, University of Calgary
A. Kate Peach, FMA Associates

I am also thankful to the numerous reviewers, whose thoughtful and helpful comments helped shape the manuscript:

B. A. Nicholson, Brandon University
Jill Taylor-Hollings, Lakehead University
Lisa K. Rankin, Memorial University
   of Newfoundland
Stephen A. Davis, Saint Mary's University
Franca Elise Boag, University of Alberta
Andrea Freeman, University of Calgary
Haskel Greenfield, University of Manitoba
Susan Blair, University of New Brunswick
Yin-Man Lam, University of Victoria
Michael MacKinnon, University of Winnipeg
Jean-François Millaire, University of Western
   Ontario
John R. Triggs, Wilfrid Laurier University

Last but certainly not least, I would like to express my thanks to my colleagues at the University of Calgary, and across Canada, who helped with suggestions, comments, criticisms, and produced content for the textbook. Special thanks to Natasha Lyons for all of her help with the research, and to A. Kate Peach for her many useful suggestions and editorial comments.
—Peter C. Dawson

Keeping in Touch with the Author

This textbook is an opportunity to become more available to both instructors and students. Knowing what you think about this text and about archaeology—what you like and what you don't care for—is invaluable information that can only help to improve future editions. And so I encourage you to contact me at the e-mail address below; provided that I'm not off on some remote dig somewhere, I'll get back to you right away.
P. C. D.
Calgary, Alberta
pcdawson@ucalgary.ca

About the Authors

Peter Dawson was introduced to archaeology as an undergraduate by Dr. Richard "Scotty" MacNeish, who managed to lure him away from his original major (zoology). He has worked in the American Southwest, the provinces of Alberta, Ontario, and Manitoba, and the territories of Nunavut [Northwest Territories], and Yukon. In addition to excavation, he has conducted ethnoarchaeological fieldwork in the Canadian Arctic. This work focused on understanding the impact of Euro-Canadian architecture on Inuit families, and how current northern house designs might be improved to accommodate their distinctive lifestyles and cultural values. He is currently using computer modelling to study traditional Inuit architecture, and conducting archaeological research into the origins of the Caribou Inuit. He has published numerous articles and book chapters, and has been the recipient of several prestigious teaching awards. Dr. Dawson has been a faculty member in the Department of Archaeology at the University of Calgary, Alberta, since 2001.

David Thomas has served since 1972 as Curator of Anthropology at the American Museum of Natural History in New York City. A specialist in Native American archaeology, Thomas discovered both Gatecliff Shelter (Nevada) and the lost 16th/17th century Franciscan mission Santa Catalina de Guale on St. Catherines Island, Georgia. Since 1998, he has led the excavation of Mission San Marcos near Santa Fe, New Mexico. A founding trustee of the National Museum of the American Indian at the Smithsonian since 1989, he has published extensively, including 100 papers and 30 books—most recently, the best-selling *Skull Wars: Kennewick Man, Archaeology, and the Battle for Native American Identity.* As an archaeologist, Thomas likes "old stuff," including his 1961 Corvette, his 120-year-old house, and the Oakland Raiders.

Robert Kelly began collecting arrowheads in farmers' fields when he was 10 years old and has participated in archaeological research since 1973 when he was a high school sophomore. He has worked on excavations in North and South America and conducted ethnographic research in Madagascar. He is currently conducting research into the Paleoindian archaeology of Wyoming's Bighorn Mountains. A former president of the Society for American Archaeology and a past secretary of the Archaeology Division of the American Anthropological Association, Kelly has published nearly 100 articles and books, including the 1996 *Choice* Magazine Outstanding Academic Book *The Foraging Spectrum: Diversity in Hunting and Gathering Societies.* Dr. Kelly has been a professor of Anthropology at the University of Wyoming since 1997.

1 Meet Some Real Archaeologists

OUTLINE

Archaeologists and bioanthropologists search a high alpine ridge in Tatshenshini-Alsek Provincial Park, Northern British Columbia, for the remains of Kwäday Dän Ts'inchi—meaning "long ago person found" in the Southern Tutchone language spoken by his First Nations descendants.
Source: Sarah Gaunt—CAFN

Preview

This book is about what archaeologists want to learn, how they go about learning it, and what they do with what they have learned. These tasks require archaeologists to piece together a picture of the past from scraps of bone, rock, pottery, architecture, and other remains that are hundreds, thousands, or tens of thousands of years old. And, as we will see, the very nature of archaeology carries with it some serious ethical dilemmas.

In this book, we will look at some of the perspectives that characterize today's archaeology: scientific and humanistic, objective and subjective, ecological and ideational. Sometimes these approaches coexist, sometimes they clash. As we discuss these various archaeological perspectives, you should keep a couple of things in mind: First, no archaeologist fits perfectly into any of these named categories, and second, there is more than one way to do good archaeology.

This chapter looks at how archaeology has evolved in Canada and the United States. Archaeology is a relatively young discipline, still going through some growing pains. In order to illustrate the unique ways that archaeology has developed in these two countries, as well as define how modern archaeologists practise their craft, we begin with two examples that illustrate some of the ethical dilemmas that archaeologists face today.

Introduction

On August 14, 1999, three men hunting Dall sheep in Tatshenshini-Alsek Provincial Park in Northern British Columbia met another hunter on the edge of a remote glacier. On the surface, such an encounter might not seem out of the ordinary. What made this one unique, however, were their age differences. The fourth man was perhaps as old as 300 years, and had travelled through this region a mere two centuries after Columbus had made his historic voyages to North America. The three modern hunters had noticed some small pieces of wood that were obviously out of place in the treeless and rugged environment they were travelling through. Further examination had revealed other artifacts, including the body of their ancient counterpart. Following a two-day hike out of the Park, they commendably described their find to government archaeologists working for the Heritage Branch of the Yukon Territorial Government. Government officials immediately contacted members of the Champagne and Aishihik First Nations (CAFN), in whose traditional territory the find had been made. CAFN Elders named the individual "Kwäday Dän Ts'inchi," meaning "long ago person found" in their Southern Tutchone language. So began the investigation of what would become one of the most unique finds in the history of Canadian archaeology.

Who Was Kwäday Dän Ts'inchi?

Once news of the discovery had been made, archaeologists and biological anthropologists flew to the scene by helicopter to begin removing the remains of Kwäday Dän Ts'inchi, as well as recover the artifacts that were found in association with him. Had it not been for the remoteness of the setting, the procedure might have looked similar to an episode of a popular forensic detective show on television. The unique conditions of the glacier meant that soft tissues such as skin and hair had been well preserved. Scientists dressed in white Tyvek suits and sterile latex gloves cautiously

2

approached the recovery area downwind to reduce risks of contamination. The remains were carefully lifted and wrapped in sterile synthetic hospital wraps, followed by a layer of clear plastic sheeting. The bundles were then gently placed in rigid plastic containers and flown directly to Whitehorse, where they were stored at minus 17°C. Accompanied by a conservator and a representative of CAFN, the remains were then flown to the Royal British Columbia Museum in Victoria, B.C., for study.

Forensic and archaeological analysis revealed that Kwäday Dän Ts'inchi was male, and had been about 20 years old at the time of his death. Among the objects he had carried that fateful day were a knife/hand tool in its sheath and a leather pouch containing a modest meal of salmon (Figure 1-1). He wore a hat (which remarkably still held its shape) over his shoulder-length hair, and a fur cloak sewn from the small pelts of Arctic ground squirrels. It is difficult to speculate what Kwäday Dän Ts'inchi was doing on the glacier that day. Perhaps he was travelling between communities, or hunting Dall sheep like the hunters who discovered him. Whatever the circumstances, he obviously found himself unable to continue his journey. He died lying slightly on his right side, with his right arm outstretched forward of his head, forearm flexed so that his head rested on his wrist or hand. Sometime after being frozen into the glacier, his body had slipped into a crack, forcing the fur garment up and around his neck. Segments of Kwäday Dän Ts'inchi's body, including his head, right arm, and lower leg, were never recovered. They had likely melted out of the glacier long ago, only to be carried away by melt water, or scavenging animals. All of this

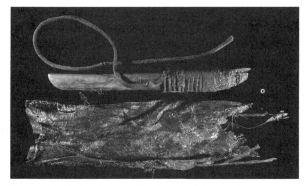

Figure 1-1 The hand tool and leather pouch found with the remains of Kwäday Dän Ts'inchi.

Source: Yukon Government Heritage Branch

information is the product of a remarkable collaborative partnership between the CAFN and archaeologists, forensic anthropologists, cryo-biologists, glaciologists, and cultural anthropologists (to name only a few!). The recovery and analysis of human remains in other areas of North America, however, has been much more contentious.

Who Controls Human Remains?

A mere four years prior to the discovery of Kwäday Dän Ts'inchi, two college students watching hydro-plane boat races on the Columbia River in Washington State made a similar find. Unlike Kwäday Dän Ts'inchi's well-preserved body, these were skeletal remains, and they would prove to be far older—and much more controversial. The skeleton was recovered and analyzed by James Chatters, an archaeologist who was asked by the coroner of the nearby town of Kennewick to examine the finds. Methods similar to those used to study Kwäday Dän Ts'inchi revealed that this individual was a 45-year-old male who had died 9400 years ago. So-called "Kennewick Man" is one of the oldest human skeletons ever found in the Americas. Even more intriguing, the skull did not look like any other Native American skull; some even thought it might be European! It is not, but the suggestion titillated the media, who created sensationalist stories of how Europeans, rather than the ancestors of American Indians, first colonized the Americas. Soon, archaeologists and biological anthropologists interested in studying the finds found themselves in a legal battle with several tribes from the Kennewick area over who "owned" the find.

Why was the study of Kennewick man so much more contentious than that of Kwäday Dän Ts'inchi? This is a complicated question for which there is no single answer. One reason may lie in the different ages of the remains themselves. Kwäday Dän Ts'inchi lived between 1670 to 1850 cal A.D., making him more of a direct ancestor to living First Nation groups in northern British Columbia. Therefore, determining who rightfully controls his remains is more clear-cut. In contrast, the greater antiquity of Kennewick Man makes it difficult for Native American groups to establish a definitive historical link. We have to keep in mind that archaeological discoveries often have real economic and political consequences for indigenous societies. Establishing that Kwäday Dän Ts'inchi is a direct ancestor of the CAFN, for example, proves they have used the area for a long time, presumably strengthening their land claims within the province. With such issues at stake, it is therefore not surprising that the study of human remains can sometimes be litigious.

Another reason may have to do with the laws that govern archaeology in both countries (we'll examine these in greater detail in Chapter 17). In the United States, the 1990 Native American Graves Protection and Repatriation Act (NAGPRA) provides for the repatriation of Native American human remains to their culturally affiliated tribes. In the case of Kennewick Man, several Native American groups claimed that Kennewick was their ancestor, and cited NAGPRA in their request to have the remains turned over to them. This placed them in conflict with scientists, eight of whom filed a lawsuit arguing that handing over the bones would actually violate NAGPRA—not only because the skeleton was not affiliated with the modern tribes, but also because it might not even be Native American. The scientists also claimed that their First Amendment rights would be violated if the government kept them from studying the remains. Currently, no legislation such as NAGPRA exists in Canada. Because ethical relationships between scientists and First Nations are less legalistically bound, Canadian archaeologists have tended to be more proactive in developing collaborative relationships with Aboriginal communities. Soon after the discovery of Kwäday Dän Ts'inchi, for example, government officials were quick to hold meetings with representatives of the CAFN to explore ways of dealing with the find. In contrast to the Kennewick situation, Elders from the CAFN explained to the media that they favoured scientific study of the remains and artifacts. Many felt that it was important to get as much information as possible from this person, whoever he was. Members of the CAFN even identified with the predicament of the young man, pointing out that falling into crevasses remains one of the biggest dangers in the area today. As one person explained, "In the springtime, there is old snow hiding these crevasses—you are walking along, and you are gone."

Because scientists and the CAFN had a mutual interest in studying the remains, a collaborative partnership agreement was formed among provincial archaeologists, the Royal British Columbia Museum, and the CAFN. Archaeologists and museum people were responsible for coordinating research on the human remains, while the CAFN were responsible for studies relating to the artifacts, traditional knowledge, and cultural concerns. Unlike Kennewick, the agreement stipulated that that Kwäday Dän Ts'inchi and his artifacts would be returned to the CAFN for final disposition. His remains were cremated and flown by helicopter to the site where he had originally been found. In July 2001, Kwäday Dän Ts'inchi was honoured at a Potlatch ceremony.

Kwäday Dän Ts'inchi and Archaeology in North America

The study of finds like Kwäday Dän Ts'inchi raises important questions that we will address throughout this book. How did archaeologists know, for example, that his remains were between 330 and 150 years old? How did they figure out what kinds of dried fish he carried in his leather pouch? How were they able to determine what had happened to his body following his death? Which of the First Nations in British Columbia and Yukon Territory was he related to? Answering questions like this is what archaeologists do: They reconstruct the human past from the crumbling remains that survive.

But finds like Kwäday Dän Ts'inchi and Kennewick Man raise some interesting ethical questions. What gives archaeologists the right to poke into the past, the right to study the dead? Who owns the past, anyway? And who gets to decide? This is also what archaeologists do—they make difficult ethical and moral decisions about the past and how it affects the present. How these concerns are addressed sometimes varies in Canada and the United States. For example, Canada has a larger population of First Nations and Inuit peoples, many of whom live in close proximity to major urban centres. Land claims and the desire for self-governance have meant that Canadian aboriginal groups have become concerned about who has access to archaeological resources. The Inuit, for example, now largely regulate archaeology in the newly created territory of Nunavut, in Canada's Arctic. The discipline of archaeology in both countries is also currently experiencing some growing pains. With more than 10,000 practising archaeologists in the United States and Canada, archaeology harbours a host of diverse and sometimes conflicting perspectives. Some believe that archaeology is a science, pure and simple; others argue that archaeology must be responsive to humanistic concerns.

Looking Closer
Indian or First Nations, Eskimo or Inuit?

What's in a name? A great deal, as it turns out. In 1939, the Supreme Court of Canada ruled that "Eskimos" (aboriginal peoples living in the northern portions of Canada) were, in fact, "Indians" in the eyes of the Canadian constitution. The legal case came about because of a dispute over whether the government should assume fiscal responsibility for the Inuit of Northern Quebec. Diamond Jenness, a noted Canadian anthropologist, explained to the court that important cultural differences separated the two groups. However, the judge was more compelled by government lawyers, who explained that Indians and Eskimos exhibited "the same dependence on fish and game for subsistence, the same lack of organization for agricultural or industrial production, the same exchange of wealth by way of money, the same poverty, the same ignorance, the same unhygienic mode of existence." While offensive by today's standards, these remarks ignored the linguistic and cultural diversity of Canada's aboriginal peoples. The Canadian constitution currently recognizes three distinct categories: Indian, Inuit, and Métis.

The name "Indian," of course, is a legacy of 15th century European sailors who believed they were in India when, in fact, they had arrived in North America. While some aboriginal people consider the term "Indian" offensive, others use it as a self-designation. The name "First Nations" is now used more widely. First Nations societies are the most culturally heterogeneous of the three categories, speaking more than 50 different languages across Canada.

The singular "Inuk" and the plural "Inuit," meaning "person" and "people," respectively, have almost totally replaced the term "Eskimo" in Canada. We now know that the Inuit represent a separate movement of people into the arctic regions of Canada, and that they have a separate history. Inuit groups are more culturally homogeneous than First Nations, speaking a single language with regional dialects across the country.

The third category of Métis emerged during the fur trade period in Canada, and is the product of unions between male fur traders (primarily French Canadian) and First Nations women. They speak a language called "Michif," which is a mixture of French, English, and First Nations languages. During the 19th century, Métis groups forged a common identity and lifestyle on the western Plains of Canada. Attempts to create a separate Métis Nation, however, were crushed by federal government forces in 1870 in Manitoba, and again in 1885 in Saskatchewan. Almost 100 years later, the Métis were recognized as one the aboriginal people of Canada in the Canadian constitution. It should be noted, however, that Métis also has an increasingly broader connotation, because some Métis live beyond the confines of the western Plains—for example the Labrador Métis Nation, which has its own land-claims issues and whose members speak English and Inuktitut.

In this textbook, we will refer to aboriginal peoples in the United States as "Native Americans." The categories of "First Nations," "Inuit," and "Métis" are used when discussing aboriginal peoples of Canada.

We will explore how science-based and humanistic approaches to archaeology have developed in both Canada and the United States. Archaeologists agree that science-based approaches require high standards of evidence, and methods for making inferences about the past call for continual examination. Science in this sense is self-correcting, making the approach essential to most inquiry (including archaeology). But even scientific inquiry is susceptible to cultural biases. Alternatively, humanistic approaches downplay scientific standards of evidence to explore new ideas and perspectives and to examine the biases and larger agenda of science. The ongoing dialogue about the ethics of archaeology will ultimately benefit scientific

Figure I-2 Archaeology today confronts both scientific and ethical challenges. Yet there are many signs that archaeology need not be antagonistic to indigenous peoples. Natasha Lyons, a graduate student in archaeology, consults with Donald Uluadluak, an Inuit Elder from Arviat, Nunavut.

Source: Dr. Peter Dawson

perspectives by pinpointing some biases that may hold us back from achieving a more complete understanding of humanity's shared past.

Archaeologists often say that we study the past in order to avoid repeating it, and that understanding where humanity has been helps us to chart the future. But the Kennewick case points up the dilemma buried in both aphorisms. By claiming the skeletal remains as their own, the Native American tribes asserted that no scientific studies should be conducted. The tribes believed that they already understood their own past and resented attempts by non-aboriginal scientists to probe the remains of their ancestors. While the case of Kwäday Dän Ts'inchi reveals that not all aboriginal people agree with this position, many do, and this underscores the important point that archaeology is not just about the dead; it is also about the living. How can we justify "studying the past to create a better tomorrow" if the very act of conducting research offends the living descendants of the ancient people being studied? Our position will be that archaeologists must work closely with indigenous peoples and descendant communities to achieve the goals of a scientific archaeology (as in Figure 1-2, which shows a working example of this compromise).

Rather than sweep the ethical dilemmas that confront modern archaeology under the rug, we will highlight them in the "Archaeological Ethics" boxes that appear in Chapters 2 through 17. And, after we learn something more about the practice of archaeol-

ogy, in Chapter 17 we will return to the issue of ethics in archaeology to explore its implications for archaeology in Canada and the United States.

We now turn to a brief history of archaeology. This will help set the stage for an understanding of modern archaeological approaches explored in Chapters 2 and 3.

The Western World Discovers Its Past

Most historians ascribe the honour of "first archaeologist" to Nabonidus (who died in 538 BC), the last king of the neo-Babylonian Empire (see "Looking Closer: A.D./B.C./B.P. . . . Archaeology's Alphabet Soup"). A pious man, Nabonidus's zealous worship of his gods compelled him to rebuild the ruined temples of ancient Babylon and to search among their foundations for the inscriptions of earlier kings. We are indebted to the research of Nabonidus's scribes and the excavations by his subjects for much of our modern picture of the Babylonian Empire. Though nobody would call Nabonidus an "archaeologist" in the modern sense of the term, he remains an important figure for one simple reason: *Nabonidus looked to the physical residues of antiquity to answer questions about the past.* This may seem like a simple step, but it contrasted sharply with the beliefs of his contemporaries, who regarded tradition, legend, and myth as the only admissible clues to the past.

For archaeology to become an intellectual field, scholars first had to recognize the idea of "the past." A major contribution of the Renaissance (circa A.D. 1300 to 1700), particularly in Italy, was the distinction between the present and the past. Classical Greeks and Romans recognized only a remote past, which they reified through myth and legend. Because Europeans of the Middle Ages likewise failed to distinguish between themselves and ancient populations, it fell to Renaissance scholars to point to the differences between classical and medieval times.

Petrarch (1304–1374), perhaps the most influential individual of the early Renaissance, defined an intellectual tradition that continues to be important in today's archaeology. Beyond his considerable talents as poet and linguist, Petrarch also provided strong impetus for archaeological research. To him, the remote past was an ideal of perfection, and he looked to antiquity for moral philosophy. Of course, to imitate classical antiquity, one must first study it. In a real sense, Petrarch's approach led to a rediscovery of the past by those in the Western European intellectual tradition. Petrarch's influence can best be seen in the work of his close friend Boccaccio, who wrote extensive essays on classical mythology, and also in that of Giovanni Dondi, who is generally credited with the first systematic observations on archaeological monuments.

But it remained for the 15th century Italian scholar Ciriaco de' Pizzicolli (1391–1455) to establish the modern discipline of archaeology. After translating the Latin inscription on the triumphal arch of Trajan in Ancona, Italy, he was inspired to devote the remainder of his life to studying ancient monuments, copying inscriptions, and promoting the study of the past. His travels took him into Syria and Egypt, throughout the islands of the Aegean, and finally to Athens. When asked his business, Ciriaco is said to have replied, "Restoring the dead to life"—which today remains a fair definition of the everyday business of archaeology.

Archaeology and Society

From the beginning of Renaissance Europe's interest in the past, however, it was clear that not everyone wanted the dead to be restored to life. In 1572 Matthew Parker, Queen Elizabeth's archbishop of Canterbury, formed the Society of Antiquaries, devoted to the study of Anglo-Saxon law and writings.

At the same time, Parliament upheld English Common Law, said to have been granted by William the Conqueror upon his conquest of England in 1066. English Common Law was based on the laws and customs of the Anglo-Saxons. Unfortunately, British kings had persistently claimed that their authority to rule—the "divine right of kings"—originated in their descent

Looking Closer

A.D./B.C./B.P. . . . Archaeology's Alphabet Soup

In anything written by archaeologists, you'll encounter a blizzard of acronyms that refer to age. Let's clear the air with some concise definitions of the most common abbreviations:

- **B.C.** ("before Christ"): For instance, 3200 B.C.; note that the letters follow the date.
- **A.D.** (anno Domini, meaning "In the year of the Lord") indicates a year that falls within the Christian era (that is, after the birth of Christ). Given the English translation of the phrase, archaeologists place the "A.D." prior to the numerical age—we say the Norman Invasion occurred in "A.D. 1066" rather than "1066 A.D." The earliest A.D. date is A.D. 1; there is no A.D. 0 because this year is denoted by 0 B.C., and double numbering is not allowed.
- **A.C.** ("after Christ"): Basically the same as A.D., except that it's written A.C. 1066 (with the abbreviation written before the number). This usage is confusing, and hardly anybody uses it anymore. Neither do we.
- **B.P.** ("before present"): Many archaeologists feel more comfortable avoiding the A.D./B.C. split altogether, substituting the single "before present" age estimate (with A.D. 1950 arbitrarily selected as the zero point; we'll explain why in Chapter 8). By this convention, an artifact from the Hastings battlefield would be dated 884 B.P. (1950–1066 = 884).

Note that all the abbreviations used so far are capital letters. Just in case you're not confused enough, you may also run into a date written in lowercase, such as 3200 b.c. This convention denotes that a date was derived by radiocarbon methods and reflects radiocarbon years rather than calendar years (we'll explain the difference in Chapter 8). So the term "3200 b.c." would be read "3200 radiocarbon years before Christ." We find this usage confusing and won't employ it here.

from the legendary King Arthur (who probably lived about A.D. 500, but no one really knows). King James therefore asserted that Common Law did not apply to the Anglican Church or the King, because it originated with William rather than with Arthur. But the Society of Antiquaries used ancient documents to demonstrate that William the Conqueror did not actually create English Common Law—instead, he had simply allowed it to stand and to be fused with his own ideas of justice. This was a problem for King James, for in English Common Law the people had the right to rebel against an unlawful and unjust king. King James saw that meddling with this particular piece of the past had too much potential to start riots in the streets, and so he ordered the dissolution of the Society of Antiquaries. The study of the past will often be controversial.

But the die was cast, and the Society for Antiquaries was only the first of many British scholarly societies interested in the past. Of course, many private collectors were concerned only with filling their curio cabinets with *objets d'art*, but the overall goal of British antiquarianism was to map, record, and preserve national treasures. By the late 18th century, members of Europe's leisure classes considered an interest in classical antiquities to be an important ingredient in the "cultivation of taste," hence the non-scientific bent implied in the term "**antiquarian.**"

The Discovery of Deep Time

Archaeological research until the 18th century proceeded mostly within the tradition of Petrarch—that is, concerned primarily with clarifying the picture of classical civilizations. This lore was readily digested by the 18th- and early-19th-century mind, because nothing in it challenged the Bible as an authoritative account of the origin of the world and humanity.

A problem arose, however, when very crude stone tools like that shown in Figure 1-3 were discovered in England and continental Europe. About 1836, a French customs official and naturalist, Jacques Boucher de Crèvecoeur de Perthes (1788–1868), found ancient axe heads in the gravels of the Somme

Figure 1-3 Boucher de Perthes found Paleolithic handaxes like this in the Somme River gravels.
Source: American Museum of Natural History

River. Along with those tools, he also found the bones of long-extinct mammals. To Boucher de Perthes (as he is more commonly known), the implication was obvious: "In spite of their imperfection, these rude stones prove the existence of [very ancient] man as surely as a whole Louvre would have done."

But few contemporaries believed him, in part because prevailing religious thought held that human beings had been on earth for only 6000 years. Why? Some 200 years before Boucher de Perthes' discoveries, several scholars had calculated the age of the earth as no more than about 6000 years. Perhaps the most meticulous of these calculations was that of James Ussher (1581–1656), Archbishop of Armagh, Primate of All Ireland, and Vice-Chancellor of Trinity College in Dublin. Using Biblical genealogies and correlations of Mediterranean and Middle Eastern histories, Ussher concluded in 1650 that Creation began at sunset on Saturday, October 22, 4004 B.C. His effort was so convincing that the date 4004 B.C. appeared as a marginal note in most Bibles published after 1700.

antiquarian Originally, someone who studied antiquities (that is, ancient objects) largely for the sake of the objects themselves—not to understand the people or culture that produced them.

This reckoning, of course, allowed no chance of an extensive human antiquity; there simply wasn't enough time. Therefore, the thinking went, Boucher de Perthes must be mistaken—his rude implements must be something other than human handiwork. Some suggested that the "tools" were really meteorites; others said they were produced by lightning, elves, or fairies. One 17th-century scholar suggested that the chipped flints were "generated in the sky by a fulgurous exhalation conglobed in a cloud by the circumposed humour," whatever that means.

But customs officials have never been known for their reserve, and Boucher de Perthes stuck to his guns. More finds were made in the French gravel pits at St. Acheul (near Abbeville), and similar discoveries turned up across the Channel in southern England. The issue was finally resolved when the respected British paleontologist Hugh Falconer visited Abbeville to examine the disputed evidence. A procession of esteemed scholars followed Falconer's lead and declared their support in 1859; the idea that humans had lived with now-extinct animals in the far distant past was finally enshrined in Charles Lyell's 1863 book *The Geological Evidences of the Antiquity of Man.*

The year 1859 turned out to be a banner year in the history of human thought: Not only was the remote antiquity of humankind accepted by the scientific establishment, but Charles Darwin published his influential *On the Origin of Species.* Although Darwin mentioned humans only once in that book (on nearly the last page he wrote, "Much light will be thrown on the origin of man and his history . . ."), he had suggested the process by which modern people could have risen from ancient primate ancestors. In the beginning, though, Darwin's theory (which had to do with the transformation of species) was unconnected to the antiquity of humanity (which was a simple question of age). We'll come back to Darwin's contributions in Chapter 15.

Nonetheless, the discovery of deep time—the recognition that life was far more ancient than Biblical scholars argued and that human culture had evolved over time—opened the floodgates. British archaeology soon billowed out across two rather divergent courses. One direction became involved with the problems of remote geological time and the demonstration of long-term human evolution. Others continued the tradition of Petrarch and focused on classical studies, particularly the archaeology of ancient Greece and Rome, a field

now known as **classical archaeology.** This philosophical split has continued into modern times, although some signs hint that these fields are coming back together.

Archaeology and Native North Americans

Across the Atlantic, North American archaeology faced its own vexing issues of time and cultural development. How, 19th-century scholars wondered, could regions such as the Valley of Mexico and Peru have hosted the civilizations of the Aztecs and the Inkas while people in many other places—such as the North American West—seemed impoverished, even primitive? When did people first arrive in the New World? Where had these migrants come from, and how did they get here?

Speculation arose immediately. One idea held that Native Americans were one of the Lost Tribes of Israel. Another suggested that Indians came from Atlantis. Others said they were voyaging Egyptians, Vikings, Chinese, or Phoenicians.

Gradually, investigators came to realize the considerable continuities that existed between the unknown prehistoric past and the Native North American population of the historic period. As such knowledge progressed, profound differences between European and American archaeology became more apparent. While Europeans wrestled with their ancient flints—without apparent modern correlates—American scholars saw that living Native Americans were relevant to the interpretation of archaeological remains. In the crass terms of the time, many Europeans saw Native Americans as "living fossils," relics of times long past.

New World archaeology thus became inextricably wed to the study of living Native North American people. Whereas Old World archaeologists began from a baseline of geological time or classical antiquity, their American counterparts developed an anthropological understanding of Native America. The **ethnology** of American Indians became an important domain of Western scholarship in its own right, and Americanist archaeology became linked

classical archaeology The branch of archaeology that studies the "classical" civilizations of the Mediterranean, such as Greece and Rome, and the Near East.

ethnology That branch of anthropology dealing chiefly with the comparative study of cultures.

with anthropology through their mutual interest in Native North American culture.

Let us stress an important point here: As Europeans refined the archaeology of Europe, they were studying their own ancestors (Anglo-Saxons, Celts, Slavs, Franks, and so forth). But New World archaeology was a matter of Euro-Americans digging up somebody else's ancestors. This fundamental difference explains the following elements peculiar to New World archaeology:

- The racist theories about indigenous peoples that dominated the thinking of early 19th-century North American scholars,
- The form of antiquity legislation in North America, and
- The fact that many contemporary Aboriginal people still do not trust conventional Western scholarship to interpret their past.

We'll return to these issues in later chapters.

Founders of Americanist Archaeology

We are now prepared to look more closely at how Americanist archaeology is currently practised. Although many other terms—such as "scientific archaeology," or "anthropological archaeology"—are used, we prefer Robert Dunnell's phrase **Americanist archaeology** because it is descriptive, yet it contains the many perspectives that constitute American archaeology today. Let us also emphasize that archaeologists working in the Americanist tradition practise their craft around the world, and not only in North America.

The history of Americanist archaeology (all history, really) is a commingling of tradition and change—illustrated here by a few individuals whose lives and careers typify archaeology of their time. These individuals were by no means the only ones practising archae-

Americanist archaeology The brand of archaeology that evolved in close association with anthropology in the Americas. It is practised throughout the world.

The Canadian Institute An organization, founded in 1849 by Sir Sandford Fleming, dedicated to the advancement of science. It exists today as the Royal Canadian Institute, and is the oldest scientific society in Canada.

ology over the last 150 years. However, their stories demonstrate stages in the growth of Americanist archaeology and show how goals and perspectives have changed.

The Development of Archaeology in Canada

Although the term "Americanist Archaeology" denotes approaches used by archaeologists throughout North America, it is important to recognize that archaeology developed along distinct lines in Canada. For one thing, Canadian archaeology appears to have emerged much more slowly as an academic discipline. By the end of the 1960s, for example, there were only 10 professional archaeologists working in Canada. William E. Taylor Jr., one of Canada's most eminent archaeologists, quipped that during this period a national meeting of archaeologists could have been held in the back of a station wagon! Add Canadian geography to the mix, and you have small numbers of researchers nibbling away at a complex archaeological record covering an extremely large and ecologically varied landmass.

Archaeology also began under different circumstances in Canada, where the spectacular earthen mounds that captured the interest of the American Philosophical Society and the American Antiquarian Society were largely absent. Because of this, 19th-century learned societies like **The Canadian Institute** rarely concerned themselves with the origins of North America's aboriginal peoples, or solving the mystery of the mound builders. In the United States, these issues played an important role in developing agencies like the Bureau of American Ethnology, which had active programs of archaeological research. Instead, a belief that the cultural traditions of many First Nations and Inuit societies were fast disappearing diverted government funding away from archaeology and toward the collection of ethnographic and linguistic data. Acquiring archaeological data was seen as less crucial because it could be left safely in the ground.

The Canadian Institute eventually developed into a multi-disciplinary research organization with a growing regional archaeology collection. In 1884 the Institute hired Canada's first professional archaeologist (see "David Boyle: Antiquarian Schoolteacher Extraordinaire," below), who was given a meagre research budget and a starting salary of $400 a year. The Bureau of American Ethnology, in startling contrast, employed more archaeologists who earned up to 10 times as much!

In addition to poor funding, before the 20th century there were no academic departments at Canadian universities where one could receive training in archaeology. Initially, officers of the Geological Survey of Canada (GSC) such as Harlan Ingersoll Smith and John William Wintemberg were responsible for archaeological research in Canada. Prior to joining the Anthropological Division of the GSC, Smith had gained experience in archaeology and ethnography through his close association with Fredrick Ward Putnam at the Harvard Peabody Museum, and his participation in the Jessup North Pacific Expedition organized by Franz Boas. While at the GSC, Smith initiated some of the first systematic attempts to sketch out the archaeology of Canada as a whole. Smith supervised the professional development of Wintemberg, who had received earlier training in archaeology through his close friendship with David Boyle at the Provincial Museum. Wintemberg eventually landed himself a job at the Victoria Memorial Museum (later the National Museum of Canada), where he worked as a research archaeologist for many decades. Although sickly throughout much of his life, Wintemberg was an active fieldworker. Among his accomplishments was an extensive survey of the north shore of the Gulf of St. Lawrence, where he attempted to define the geographic extent of Iroquois culture. Wintemberg practised a kind of early functional-processual archaeology to aid his analysis of the archaeological materials he excavated. In order to determine how various artifacts were made, for example, he consulted with native people, and conducted experiments (assisted, no doubt, by his earlier career as a craftsman). Both Wintemberg and Smith did exemplary work, but were largely self-taught.

It was not until 1926 that Thomas McIlwraith founded the first anthropology department at the University of Toronto. By 1948, J. Norman Emerson had established the first academic program to train archaeologists in Canada. The expansion of Canadian universities during the 1950s soon resulted in additional departments of anthropology. The absence of Canadian Ph.D.s in archaeology meant that faculty had to be imported from Europe and the United States. However, newly minted Canadian archaeolo-

gists soon began to appear. Many took up jobs created by recent heritage legislation enacted to protect cultural resources, and by extensive programs of archaeological research in the provinces and territories initiated by the National Museum in Ottawa. As more funding became available following the 1960s, archaeologists fanned out across Canada, in an attempt to construct detailed chronologies and cultural histories of this vast country. In the process, many also became interested in understanding how First Nations and Inuit peoples had adapted to the different ecological regions in which they lived, both past and present.

Archaeology in Canada has received an additional boost in recent years, thanks in large part to the cultural resource management (CRM) industry. Many graduates of archaeology programs at Canadian universities are finding work in the northern and western parts of the country, where mining and oil and gas development are accelerating at breakneck speed. Aboriginal populations, which are larger in Canada than in the United States, now control access to many areas where such development is occurring. As a result, archaeologists are working in closer association with First Nations and Inuit than ever before. Documenting traditional environmental knowledge is also becoming as important as archaeology in Canada, where archaeologists are quietly filling the vacant core left behind by cultural anthropologists, whose numbers studying aboriginal groups have dwindled in recent years. Jane Kelley and Ron Williamson, two archaeologists who are interested in the future of archaeology in Canada, suggest that this may integrate archaeology more solidly into the wider field of anthropology. The future of the past in Canada seems bright.

David Boyle: Antiquarian Schoolteacher Extraordinaire

David Boyle (1842–1911) was Canada's first professional archaeologist (shown in Figure 1-4). Boyle developed an interest in archaeology while teaching at a small school in Elora, Ontario. Although he received no formal training in archeology, Boyle set up a small museum of artifacts he had discovered while on natural history field trips with his classes. Soon after his 30th birthday, Boyle decided that he needed a change. So, he quit his teaching job and moved to Toronto, where he established a small bookshop.

Figure 1-4 David Boyle (1842–1911), an antiquarian archaeologist from Elora, Ontario, worked hard to professionalize archaeology as a discipline in Canada.

In 1884, Boyle joined the Canadian Institute, now known as the Royal Canadian Institute. At this time, the teaching of science at Canadian universities was limited primarily to medicine and the natural sciences. As a learned society, the Canadian Institute attempted to contribute to the cultural life of Canadian cities by advancing art, engineering, and the physical sciences. The 19th century was an important time in the history of Canadian archaeology. The industrialization of eastern Canada, the westward expansion of railways, and the settling of the Prairie Provinces accelerated the discovery of new and exciting archaeological sites and artifacts. Boyle was concerned that, in the absence of a proper museum in Canada, many of these interesting finds would be sent to institutions in other countries. He succeeded in convincing the Canadian Institute that it should set up such a museum, and hire him as curator. The Institute already had a small museum, and Boyle quickly set to the task of describing and classifying the objects in its small collection. The closure of his bookshop in 1888 out of "financial necessity" transformed Boyle from a part-time to full-time professional archaeologist.

Eager to emulate the research projects of the Smithsonian Institution in the United States, the Canadian Institute encouraged Boyle to conduct archaeological fieldwork in various regions of Ontario. In 1885, Boyle began by circulating a pamphlet originally written by the noted engineer and railway builder Sand-ford Fleming. The pamphlet asked interested parties to answer a series of questions on earthen mounds, artifacts, petroglyphs, and aboriginal place names. The response rate was extremely high, and Boyle used the information to recommence the recording of archaeological sites in the province.

The publication of E.G. Squire's *Aboriginal Monuments of the State of New York* in 1851 also stimulated interest in archaeology among Canadians. Newspapers even called on the new Dominion Government of Canada to establish a Department of Archaeology and Ethnology, with an annual budget of $25,000. This initially angered Boyle, who was concerned that artifacts might end up in a national repository in Ottawa rather than the museum he had laboured so hard to create. While the department was never created, Boyle managed to extract a small research budget from the Liberal government of the time. He used the money to fund a wide variety of archaeological excavations throughout Ontario.

While his methods of excavation were unsophisticated by today's standards, Boyle carefully and systematically recorded what he found. Unlike areas of Europe and the southwestern United States, deeply stratified sites were practically non-existent in Ontario. As a result, Boyle was unable to place his finds into a chronological sequence. Instead, he used evolutionary schemes similar to those of European Paleolithic archaeologists to organize his collections in accordance with broad developmental changes. Boyle was also a strong supporter of public archaeology. He designed portable exhibits of his finds and regularly displayed them at events such as county fairs. Furthermore, he published his discoveries in a popular journal called *Archaeological Report.* By communicating his research to a wider audience, Boyle recognized that he could deepen their interest in archaeology.

Boyle also established lines of communication with American archaeologists such as William Henry Holmes of the Smithsonian, and Fredrick Ward Putnam of Harvard, keeping them advised of his work. His American colleagues regularly cited his work, much of which was incorporated into the mainstream of North American archaeology at the time. Closer to home, Boyle's efforts to preserve Ontario's heritage earned him enormous respect. As a consequence of this, he soon became Canada's most recognized archaeologist. Attempts were subsequently made to lure Boyle to the University of Toronto, but a suitable arrangement could not be made. This was unfortunate, as it caused Canadian universities to lag behind their American counterparts in developing academic programs of anthropology. When David Boyle died in 1911, Dr. Rowland B. Orr, a physician who was a longtime collector, succeeded him at the Ontario Provincial Museum.

David Boyle's contributions to Canadian archaeology are impressive, and the fact that he was self-taught makes him representative of archaeology's roots in Canada (see "The Development of Archaeology in Canada," above). Boyle also typifies North American archaeology's ancestry because he was an antiquarian, more interested in the objects of the past than in reconstructing the lives of the people who produced them, or in explaining the past. We should not hold this against Boyle's generation because, frankly, you can't move toward understanding the past until you have some idea of what the past was like. Antiquarians like Boyle helped lay the groundwork for the archaeology that was to follow.

Diamond Jenness: One of Canada's First Academic Archaeologists

A rock in Endurance crater on the planet Mars bears the name of one of Canada's most important anthropologists and archaeologists. To many, the Canadian north is as cold and distant as any Martian landscape. But to Diamond Jenness, the Arctic and its people were practically a second home (Figure 1-5). Diamond Jenness (1886–1969) was born in Wellington, New Zealand. After finishing his schooling, Jenness moved to England where he attended Balliol College at Oxford University. While at Oxford, Jenness led an expedition to New Guinea in 1911, where he studied the d'Entrecasteaux islanders. Following his return to New Zealand in 1912, young Jenness was offered a position on the Canadian Arctic Expedition by Edward Sapir, head of the newly founded anthropology division of

Figure 1-5 Diamond Jenness at Bernard Harbor, July 1916, during the Canadian Arctic Expedition.

Source: Diamond Jenness at Bernard Harbour, Northwest Territories (Nunavut) © Canadian Museum of Civilization, George H Wilkins, July 1916, 51236

the Geological Survey of Canada. Jenness would become the expedition's ethnologist.

The opportunity to assert Canadian sovereignty and discover new land in the Arctic was the principal motivation for the Canadian government's full financial support of the Canadian Arctic Expedition. As a result, scientific knowledge was likely only a secondary goal for Vilhjalmur Stefansson, the expedition's leader, and Canadian Prime Minister Robert Borden. In late July 1913, the expedition's three ships sailed from Nome, Alaska toward Canadian arctic waters. The *Karluk* was the main ship of the expedition, and it became perilously trapped in pack ice during the expedition's first winter. The ship began to drift westward and was eventually crushed by ice. Eleven members of the expedition were killed in the disaster, and the survivors marooned on Wrangle Island off the mainland of far northeast Siberia! Luckily, Stefansson had sent Jenness and two other members of the crew ashore at Barrow, Alaska, prior to the wreck. The research originally slated to Henri Beauchat, a French ethnographer who had been killed in the *Karluk* disaster, fell squarely on the shoulders of Jenness who, at the tender age of 27, had no arctic or northern experience whatsoever.

Jenness more than rose to the task, spending four years learning the ways of the Inupiat Eskimo and Copper Inuit, recording songs on wax cylinders, and collecting poems and legends. He even wrote an entire monograph on Inuit string figures—with diagrams! Jenness also did much for the development of North American archaeology while on the expedition. In the few weeks in June 1914, he managed to excavate 60 semi-subterranean house ruins at Kaktovik, Alaska with the help of Inupiat Eskimo assistants. He collected more than 2000 artifacts and kept detailed notes about the locations of his finds, making it the first systematic archaeological excavation ever conducted in the North American Arctic. These experiences gave Jenness a taste for arctic archaeology that stayed with him for the rest of his career.

The isolated circumstances of the Canadian Arctic Expedition meant that Jenness and his colleagues had no idea that World War I had begun in their absence. Upon his return, he promptly joined the Canadian artillery, where he served as a gunner from 1917–1919. After the war, Jenness was employed by the National Museum of Canada, where he undertook archaeological investigations near Cape Dorset, on Baffin Island. Analyzing the data led Jenness to define a culture older than Inuit, which he named Dorset. In 1926, Jenness identified another arctic culture in Alaska he called Old Bering Sea, which led to the discovery that the ancestors of North America's arctic peoples were migrants from Northeast Asia. Jenness went on to become the chief of anthropology of the National Museum of Canada, a position he would retain until his retirement in 1948.

Diamond Jenness represents the beginnings of change in Canadian archaeology and anthropology. Unlike David Boyle, who was self-taught, Jenness received academic training in his discipline. He also felt comfortable pulling double duty as an ethnologist and archaeologist, which is a characteristic feature of Canadian archaeology at this time. In the absence of stratified sites in regions like the Canadian Arctic, Jenness and his contemporaries found ethnological data extremely useful for classifying artifacts and constructing culture histories. However, Canadian archaeology during this period was more substantive than theoretical, because archaeologists like Jenness were committed to understanding the past for its own sake. During the same time period, American archaeologists such as A. V. "Ted" Kidder were developing

potsherd Fragment of pottery.

stratified sites Archaeological sites with deep deposits of artifacts, owing to their repeated occupation.

methods of stratigraphic observation, and using them to construct the first regional cultural chronologies in the Americas. They were also interested in using archaeological data for anthropological purposes.

A. V. "Ted" Kidder: Founder of Anthropological Archaeology

Although he was born in Michigan, the life and career of Alfred V. Kidder (1886–1963), shown in Figure 1-6, revolved about the academic community of Cambridge, Massachusetts. Kidder's father, a mining engineer, saw to it that his son received the best education available. First enrolled in a private school in Cambridge, Kidder then attended the prestigious La Villa, in Ouchy, Switzerland, after which he registered at Harvard. Kidder soon joined an archaeological expedition to northeastern Arizona, exploring territory then largely unknown to the Anglo world. The southwestern adventure sealed his fate.

When Kidder returned to Harvard, he enrolled in the anthropology program and in 1914 was awarded the sixth American Ph.D. specializing in archaeology—and the first with a focus on North America. Kidder's dissertation examined prehistoric southwestern ceramics, assessing their value in reconstructing culture history. Relying on scientific procedures, Kidder demonstrated ways of deciphering meaning from one of archaeology's most ubiquitous items, the **potsherd** (a fragment of pottery). Urging accurate description of ceramic decoration, he explained how such apparent minutiae could help determine cultural relationships among various prehistoric groups. Kidder argued that only through controlled excavation and analysis could inferences be drawn about such anthropological subjects as acculturation, social

Figure 1-6 A. V. Kidder, an archaeologist of the American Southwest and the Maya region, advocated multidisciplinary field research.

Source: Faith Kidder Fuller

organizations, and prehistoric religious customs (see "In His Own Words: The Pan-Scientific Approach to Archaeology" by A. V. Kidder).

In 1915, the Department of Archaeology at the Phillips Academy in Andover, Massachusetts, was seeking a site of sufficient size and scientific interest to merit a multiyear archaeological project. Largely because of his anthropological training, Kidder was selected to direct the excavations. After evaluating the possibilities, he decided on Pecos Pueblo, a massive prehistoric and historic period ruin located southeast of Santa Fe, New Mexico. Kidder was impressed by the great diversity of potsherds scattered about the ruins and felt certain that Pecos contained enough stratified debris to span several centuries. Kidder excavated at Pecos for 10 summers.

The excavations at Pecos were consequential for several reasons. Kidder modified the stratigraphic method of digging used by other archaeologists to construct a cultural chronology of the Southwest. He went beyond the pottery to make sense of the artifact and architectural styles preserved at Pecos. His intensive artifact analysis, done before the advent of radiocarbon dating or tree-ring chronology (methods that we discuss in Chapter 8), established the framework of Southwestern prehistory, which remains intact today.

Kidder then joined the Carnegie Institution of Washington, D.C. as director of the Division of Historical Research. He launched an ambitious archaeological program to probe the Maya ruins of Central America. Kidder directed the Carnegie's Maya campaigns for two decades, arguing that a true understanding of Maya culture would require a broad plan of action with many interrelated areas of research. Relegating himself to the role of administrator, Kidder amassed a staff of qualified scientists with the broadest possible scope of interests. His plan was a landmark in archaeological research, stressing an enlargement of traditional archaeological objectives to embrace the wider realms of anthropology and allied disciplines. Under Kidder's direction, the Carnegie program supported research by ethnographers, botanists, geographers, physical anthropologists, geologists, meteorologists, and, of course, archaeologists.

Kidder even proved the potential of aerial reconnaissance by convincing Charles Lindbergh, already an international figure, to participate in the Carnegie's Maya program. Early in 1929, Lindbergh flew Kidder throughout British Honduras, the Yucatán peninsula, and the Petén jungle of Guatemala. Beyond discovering new ruins, the Lindbergh flights also generated a wealth of previously unavailable ecological data, such as the

In His Own Words

The Pan-Scientific Approach to Archaeology

by A. V. Kidder

Teamwork is a requirement of all modern archaeology. Kidder fully anticipated this modern trend with his "pan-scientific" approach at Chichén Itzá (Yucatán, Mexico) in the 1920s:

In this investigation the archaeologist would supply the Prehistoric background; the historian would work on the documentary record of the Conquest, the Colonial, and the Mexican periods; the sociologist would consider the structure of modern life. At the same time studies would be made upon the botany, zoology, and climate of the region and upon the agriculture, economic system, and health conditions of the urban and rural, European mixed and native populations. It seems probable that there would result definite conclusions of far-reaching interest, that there would be developed new methods applicable to many problems of race and culture contacts, and that there would be gained by the individuals taking part in the work a first-hand acquaintance with the aims of allied disciplines which would be of great value to themselves, and through them to far larger groups of research workers.

boundaries of various types of vegetation. Today, the interdisciplinary complexion of archaeology is a fact of life. But when Kidder proposed the concept in the 1920s, it was revolutionary.

In addition to his substantive Maya and Southwestern discourses, Kidder helped shift Americanist archaeology toward more properly anthropological purposes. Unlike many of his contemporaries, Kidder maintained that archaeology should be viewed as "that branch of anthropology which deals with prehistoric peoples," a doctrine that has become firmly embedded and expanded in today's Americanist archaeology. To Kidder, the archaeologist was merely a "mouldier variety of anthropologist." Although archaeologists continue to immerse themselves in the nuances of potsherd detail and architectural specifics, the ultimate objective of archaeology remains the statement of anthropological universals about *people.*

James A. Ford: A Master of Time

Born in Water Valley, Mississippi, James A. Ford's (1911–1968) major research interest centred on the archaeology of the American Southeast. While Ford (shown in Figure 1-7) was attending Columbia, Nels Nelson retired from the Department of Anthropology at the American Museum of Natural History, and Ford was chosen as the new assistant curator of North American archaeology.

Ford came of age during the Great Depression, part of an archaeological generation trained literally on the

Figure 1-7
James A. Ford helped develop the technique of seriation to sort out cultural changes over time.

Source: American Museum of Natural History and Junius Bird

job. As the Roosevelt administration created jobs to alleviate the grim economic conditions, crews of workmen were assigned labour-intensive tasks, including building roads and bridges and general heavy construction. One obvious make-work project was archaeology, and thousands of the unemployed were set to work excavating major archaeological sites. This program was, of course, an important boost to Americanist archaeology, and data from government-sponsored Depression-era excavations are still being analyzed and published.

Ford worked at Poverty Point, a Louisiana site explored 40 years earlier by C. B. Moore. Poverty Point is a large, 160-hectare site that dates to the first and second millennia B.C. It contains a number of large earthen mounds, one in the shape of a bird that is close to 20 metres high and 215 metres wide. Lying before this mound, like a gigantic amphitheatre, is a set of concentric $1^1/_2$-metre-high earthen semi-circles, 1 kilometre in diameter. We still don't fully understand their purpose. After mapping these and the site's other mounds, Ford launched a series of stratigraphic excavations designed to define the prehistoric sequence.

Ford's objective was to learn what Poverty Point had to say about the people and culture who lived there, a considerably more ambitious goal than that of C. B. Moore, who dug primarily to unearth outstanding examples of artwork. Ford continually asked the question, What does archaeology tell us about the people? As he excavated the mounds, he tried to recreate the social and political networks responsible for this colossal enterprise. In this regard, his approach typified the overarching anthropological objectives of mid-20th-century Americanist archaeology (see "In His Own Words: The Goals of Archaeology" by James A. Ford).

The unprecedented accumulation of raw data during the 1930s was a boon for archaeology, but it also created a crisis of sorts: What was to be done with all these facts? Ford and his contemporaries were beset by the need to synthesize and classify and by the necessity to determine regional sequences of culture chronology. Unlike Kidder and the others working in the American Southwest, Ford did not have access to deep, well-preserved refuse heaps; southeastern sites were more commonly shallow, short-term occupations. To create a temporal order, Ford relied on an integrated scheme of surface collection and classification.

Ford refined techniques to place the various stages of pottery development in sequential order, a process known as seriation (which we discuss further in Chapter 8). The central idea is simple: By assuming that cultural styles tend to change gradually, archaeologists can chart the relative popularity of a style, such as pottery decoration, through time and across space. By fitting the various short-term assemblages into master curves, Ford developed a series of regional ceramic chronologies. Although sometimes overly simplistic, Ford's seriation technique was sufficient to establish the baseline prehistoric chronology still used in the American Southeast.

Ford then synthesized his ceramic chronologies into patterns of regional history. Early on, when excavating the hundreds of prehistoric mounds throughout the Southeast, they lacked a system for adequately dating their finds. Using seriation along with other methods, Ford helped bring temporal order to his excavations,

and he rapidly moved to synthesize these local sequences across the greater Southeast. He proposed the basic division between the earlier Burial Mound Period and the subsequent Temple Mound Period, a distinction that remains in use today.

North American Archaeology at Mid-20th Century

The biographies of these forebears provide a sense of how Americanist archaeology developed during the first half of the 20th century. You have no doubt noted that none of them are women. Nonetheless, women such as Madeline Kneberg (1903–1996), Frederica de Laguna (1906–2004), H. Marie Wormington (1914–1994; see Figure 1-8), and Florence Hawley Ellis (1906–1991) were, in fact, contributing—but because they were commonly excluded from traditional communication networks, their contributions

In His Own Words
The Goals of Archaeology

by James A. Ford

The study of archaeology has changed considerably from a rather esthetic beginning as an activity devoted to collecting curios and guarding them in cabinets to be admired for their rarity, beauty, or simple wonder. Students are no longer satisfied with the delights of the collector and are now primarily interested in reconstructing culture history. In recent years methods and techniques have progressed rapidly, and there are indications which suggest that some phases of the study may develop into a truly scientific concern with general principles. This trend seems to be due more to the kinds of evidence that past human history offers than to any planned development. For centuries the perspective of the study of history was narrowed to a listing of battles, kings, political situations, and escapades of great men, an activity which is analogous to collecting curios and arranging them in cabinets. Such collections are fascinating to those

who have developed a taste for them, but they contribute little towards the discovery of processes which are always the foremost interest of a science. The evidence that survives in archaeological situations has made it impossible to study prehistory in terms of individual men, or even in terms of man as an acculturated animal. When the archaeologist progresses beyond the single specimen, he is studying the phenomena of culture.

I join a number of contemporaries in believing that archaeology is moving in the direction of its establishment as a more important segment of the developing science of culture than it has been in the past. This does not mean that such objectives as discovering chronological sequences and more complete and vivid historical reconstructions will be abandoned; rather these present aims will become necessary steps in the process of arriving at the new goal.

Figure 1-8 Marie Wormington, a female pioneer in American archaeology.

Source: Denver Museum of Nature and Science

are more difficult to find. Today, this is no longer true—in fact, half of all American archaeologists are women.

North American archaeology began as a pastime of the genteel rich such as C. B. Moore, but through the years it developed into a professional scientific discipline. As trained practitioners, most archaeologists after Moore's time have been affiliated with major museums and universities; others have joined the private sector, working to protect and conserve America's cultural heritage. This institutional support not only encouraged a sense of professionalism and fostered public funding, but also mandated that public repositories would care for the archaeological artifacts recovered. The 20th-century Americanist archaeologist is not a collector of personal treasure: All finds belong in the public domain, available for exhibit and study.

We can also see a distinct progression toward specialization in our target archaeologists. Scholars knew virtually nothing about North American prehistory in the early 19th century. But by the end of that century, so

culture history The kind of archaeology practised mainly in the early to mid-20th century; it "explains" differences or changes over time in artifact frequencies by positing the diffusion of ideas between neighbouring cultures or the migration of a people who had different mental templates for artifact styles.

much archaeological information had already accumulated that no single scholar could know everything relevant to Americanist archaeology. Although Diamond Jenness became the leading authority on Arctic archaeology, and the ethnography of Canada's native peoples, he knew little about the finds being made by his contemporaries in Peru, Central America, and the American Southwest. By the mid-20th century, archaeologists like James Ford were forced to specialize in specific localities within limited cultural areas. Today, it is rare to find archaeologists with extensive experience in more than a couple of specialized fields.

Possibly the greatest change, however, has been the quality of archaeologists' training. Although an educated man, David Boyle was untrained in archaeology; his fieldwork methods were based on personal trial and error. Archaeologists such as A. V. Kidder were members of the first generation of professionally trained archaeologists, and they studied under North America's most prominent anthropologists. From then on, Americanist archaeologists were, almost without exception, well versed in anthropology.

Although archaeologists by mid-century wished to transcend mere cultural chronology, in truth classifying artifacts and sorting out their patterns in space and time left little time for more anthropological objectives, such as reconstructing society. Most archaeologists by mid-century were involved in what is called **culture history.** Their main goal was to track the migrations and development of particular prehistoric cultures by documenting how material culture changed over time and space. Differences in artifact frequencies between sites were attributed to the presence of different cultures; changes in artifact frequencies over time, such as the types of pottery found in different layers of earth at a site, were attributed to the diffusion of ideas from other cultures or the replacement of one culture by another. Archaeologists tried to explain changes by relating them to climatic change, for example, or to some vague ideas about cultural development. But for the most part, artifact changes were "explained" by the diffusion of ideas or the influx of a new people.

However, by the 1950s, the basic prehistory of North America was so sufficiently well understood that some archaeologists were ready to move beyond simple documentation to more in-depth reconstructions of prehistory and even to efforts at explaining prehistory.

Revolution in Archaeology: An Advancing Science

Beginning in the 1940s, a succession of scholars challenged orthodox archaeological thinking, urging explosive change and demanding instantaneous results. Two such crusaders were particularly influential in shaping modern archaeological thought.

Walter W. Taylor: Moses in the Wilderness

Educated first at Yale and then at Harvard, Walter W. Taylor (1913–1997), shown in Figure 1-9, completed his doctoral dissertation late in 1942. After returning from overseas military service, he published in 1948 an expanded version of his dissertation as *A Study of Archeology*. It was a bombshell. Greeted with alarm and consternation by the archaeological community, the book was no less than a public call for revolution. Taylor blasted the archaeological establishment of the day. Few liked Taylor's book, but everybody read it.

Taylor launched a frontal attack on the elders of Americanist archaeology. This assault was particularly plucky, as Taylor was himself a wet-behind-the-ears newcomer, having published little to establish his credentials as an archaeologist, much less a critic.

A Study of Archeology blasted A. V. Kidder, among others. Kidder repeatedly maintained that he was an anthropologist who had specialized in archaeology. But Taylor probed Kidder's publications to determine how well his deeds conformed to his stated anthropological objectives and boldly concluded that they did not. He could find in Kidder's research no cultural synthesis, no picture of life at any site, no consideration of cultural processes, no derivation of cultural laws—no anthropology at all, in Taylor's opinion.

These were serious charges, considered blasphemous by most archaeologists of the time. But Taylor supported his case with a line-by-line dissection of Kidder's published record. Kidder's research at Pecos and elsewhere in the American Southwest was said to be full of "apparent contradictions," merely "description for its own sake." Taylor claimed that Kidder was incapable of preparing a proper site report (a charge that was a bit over the top), much less of writing the anthropology of the prehistoric Southwest.

Taylor turned to Kidder's prestigious research into the archaeology of the Maya and, once again, accused him of failing to live up to his own goals. Granting that Kidder began his investigations with anthropology in mind, Taylor concluded that "the road to Hell and the field of Maya archeology are paved with good intentions." Taylor deduced that the Carnegie Institution, under Kidder's direction, "has sought and found the hierarchical, the grandiose. It has neglected the common, the everyday." Kidder, Taylor declared, had been blinded by the "pomp and circumstance" of Classic Maya archaeology, the grand temples and ceremonial centres. According to Taylor, Kidder merely skimmed off the sensational, the spectacular, the grandiose—and forgot all about the Maya people themselves: How did they live? What did they do? What did they believe?

In 1948, Taylor was indeed archaeology's angriest young man. Kidder and other luminaries were accused of compiling **trait lists,** an account of the presence or absence of particular kinds of artifacts at different sites to no real purpose; of classifying artifacts and describing them, but for the mere sake of classification and description. Taylor pointed out that whereas Kidder and his generation claimed to be anthropologists, they failed to do anthropology (at least according to Taylor). Though careful not to deny the initial usefulness of their strategies, Taylor urged archaeologists to get on with the proper business of anthropology: finding out something about ancient

Figure 1-9 Walter W. Taylor in Coahuila, Mexico in 1937; Taylor advocated that archaeologists focus less on grand temples and more on the lives of common people.
Source: Courtesy of Walter W. Taylor

trait list A simple listing of a culture's material and behavioural characteristics, for example, house and pottery styles, foods, degree of nomadism, particular rituals, or ornaments. Trait lists were used primarily to trace the movement of cultures across a landscape and through time.

people. Chronology, to Taylor, was merely a stepping-stone, a foundation for more anthropologically relevant studies of human behaviour and cultural dynamics.

Taylor's prescription was his so-called **conjunctive approach** to archaeology. By this, Taylor meant combining ("conjoining") a variety of lines of evidence to create a picture of what the past was like and to discuss the functions of artifacts, features, and sites. From his critique, we can see that Taylor would have scrutinized the artifacts and features of a single Maya centre, inferred their functions, and then written a comprehensive description of the people who once lived there. Taylor urged archaeologists to forsake the temples for the garbage dumps, for it was there that the lives of everyday people were recorded.

Taylor proposed that archaeologists quantify their data, rather than merely create trait lists, and that they test hypotheses that would progressively refine their impressions (too often, Taylor asserted, initial observations were taken as gospel). He also argued that archaeologists must excavate less extensively and more intensively (too many sites were just "tested" then compared with other remote "tests" with no effort to detect patterning *within* sites). Archaeologists must recover and decode the meaning of unremarkable food remains (the bones, seed hulls, and rubbish heaps were too often simply shovelled out) and embrace specialties in the analysis of finds (zoological, botanical, and petrographic identifications were too often made in the field and never verified). Taylor also argued that we should write more effective and detailed site reports (too often only the glamorous finds were illustrated, with precise proveniences omitted).

In perusing Taylor's propositions nearly six decades after he wrote them, we are struck by how unremarkable they now seem. Where is the revolution? Today's archaeologists do quantify their results; they do test hypotheses; they do excavate intensively; they do save food remains; they do involve specialists in analysis; and they do write detailed site reports.

But archaeologists did not do these things routinely in 1940, and this is what Taylor was sputtering about. Oddly, though, Taylor himself never carried through and actually implemented the conjunctive approach.

Maybe the time just wasn't right. Nonetheless, Taylor's suggestions of 1948 embody few surprises for today's student—testimony to just how far archaeological doctrine and execution have matured since Taylor wrote *A Study of Archeology.*

Lewis R. Binford: Visionary with a Message

Americanist archaeology's second angry young man is Lewis R. Binford (1930–) (Figure 1-10). After a period of military service, Binford enrolled in 1954 at the University of North Carolina, wanting to become an ethnographer. By the time he moved on for graduate education at the University of Michigan, however, Binford was a confirmed archaeologist.

As a young professional, Binford was a man on the move—literally. He taught a year at the University of Michigan, then moved on to the University of Chicago, to the University of California at Santa Barbara, down the coast to UCLA, on to the University of New Mexico, and then to Southern Methodist University (in Dallas).

The mid-1960s was a hectic time for archaeology. Baby-boom demographics and the GI Bill inflated university enrollments. Campuses were the focal point of waves of social and political confrontation that rolled across the nation. Clashing opinions over the war in Vietnam and civil rights created a revolutionary atmosphere.

Archaeology was firmly embedded in this intellectual climate. Everyone, including archaeologists, was primed for change.

Figure 1-10   Lewis R. Binford (right) at Tulugak Lake in Alaska in 1999 with a Nunamiut friend, Johnny Rulland. Binford helped develop the "new archaeology" of the 1960s.

Source: Courtesy of Lewis R. Binford, photo by Grant Spearman

conjunctive approach As defined by Walter W. Taylor, using functional interpretations of artifacts and their contexts to reconstruct daily life of the past.

Binford fit into this cultural climate. He could lecture, sometimes for hours, with the force and enthusiasm of an old-time southern preacher, and he rapidly assumed the role of archaeological messiah. His students became disciples, spreading the word throughout the land: as the study of cultural change, archaeology has obvious relevance to modern problems. To fulfill this role, archaeology must transcend potsherds to address larger issues, such as cultural evolution, ecology, and social organization. Archaeology must take full advantage of modern technology by using scientific methods and sophisticated, quantitative techniques. Archaeology must be concerned with the few remaining preindustrial peoples in order to scrutinize firsthand the operation of disappearing cultural adaptations. And archaeology must be concerned with the methods we use to reconstruct the past. In the 1960s, this became known as the **new archaeology.**

The new archaeology (an odd term, since it is now quite old to all of us—and especially to today's student) became associated with a new way of studying the past and doing archaeology. The plan for it was set forth in a series of articles published through the 1960s and early 1970s, many by Binford and his students.

Binford asked why archaeology had contributed so little to general anthropological theory. His answer was that, in past studies, material culture had been simplistically interpreted. Too much attention had been lavished on artifacts as passive traits that "blend," "influence," or "stimulate" one another. Echoing Taylor, Binford proposed that artifacts be examined in terms of their cultural contexts and interpreted in their roles as reflections of technology, society, and belief systems.

Binford also underscored the importance of precise, unambiguous scientific methods. Archaeologists, he argued, should stop waiting for artifacts to speak up. They must formulate hypotheses and test these on the remains of the past. Binford argued that, because archaeologists always work from samples, they should acquire data that make the samples more representative of the populations from which they were drawn. He urged archaeologists to stretch their horizons beyond the individual site to the scale of the region; in this way, an entire cultural system could be reconstructed (as we discuss in Chapter 4). Such regional samples must be generated from research designs based on the principles of probability sampling. Random sampling is commonplace in other social sciences, and Binford insisted that

archaeologists apply these scientific procedures to their own research problems.

Binford's mostly methodological contributions were gradually amplified by projects designed to demonstrate how the approach fosters the comprehension of cultural processes. Intricate statistical techniques were applied to a variety of subjects, from the nature of Mousterian (some 150,000 years old) campsites to the patterning of African Acheulian (500,000 years old) assemblages. He proposed new ideas, rooted in the field of human ecology, to explain the origins of plant domestication. These investigations were critical because they embroiled Binford in factual, substantive debate. Not only did he advocate different goals and new methods, but he also gained credibility among field archaeologists through these substantive controversies—he argued about specifics, not just theory. And Binford conducted his own ethnographic fieldwork among the Nunamiut Eskimo, the Navajo, and the Australian aborigines, testing the utility of archaeological concepts and methods on the trash of living peoples.

In Taylor-like fashion, Binford lambasted archaeology's principles, accusing them of retarding progress in the discipline. And yet his reception was quite different from Taylor's. Whereas *A Study of Archeology* languished on the shelf, Binford was hailed as "the father of the new archaeology." Taylor was the unwelcome harbinger of impending change, but Binford was the architect.

Binford and his students set off a firestorm that quickly spread throughout the archaeological community. A 1970s generation of graduate students and young professionals was greeted with the inquisition, "Are you a new archaeologist, an old archaeologist, or what? Make up your mind!"

Today, the new archaeology of the 1960s has transformed into what is termed processual archaeology. In subsequent chapters, we explore the tenets of this position and also examine how yet another wave of archaeological criticism—postprocessual archaeology—finds fault with Binford's approach and suggests some alternative directions.

---

new archaeology An approach to archaeology that arose in the 1960s emphasizing the understanding of underlying cultural processes and the use of the scientific method; today's version of the "new archaeology" is sometimes called processual archaeology.

Looking Closer
Did the New Archaeology Catch On in Canada?

 While Lewis Binford and his students were championing the new archaeology, Canadian researchers held more of a "middle of the road" position, continuing to focus primarily on chronology and culture history. Why were Canadian archaeologists in the 1960s busy doing the work that their American colleagues had done decades earlier? It may be because the ideas of anthropologist Franz Boas had been institutionalized into Canadian archaeology years earlier, through the appointment of a former student (Edward Sapir) to the Geological Survey of Canada. The approaches used by Boas argued against making generalizations about cultural processes. Fifty years later, Binford was making the opposite case. Within the Boasian tradition, however, the responsibility of archaeology was to explore the time dimension of historic aboriginal groups by figuring out their culture histories. With so few archaeologists working in a country as large as Canada, cultural history dominated Canadian archaeology well into the 1960s. This may have effectively watered down the influence of the new archaeology in Canada.

The importance of culture history at this time is apparent in the research of such important archaeologists as Richard S. MacNeish, James V. Wright, and Richard Forbis. MacNeish, for example, was an American archaeologist who worked for the National Museum in Ottawa from 1949 to 1963. Known as "Scotty" to his friends, he was a tireless fieldworker who established some of the first cultural chronologies for such areas as the Mackenzie River (Nunavut and Yukon territories) and southeastern Manitoba. Interestingly, MacNeish also became concerned with making archaeology more rigorous through the scientific method. Like Binford, he felt strongly that archaeologists needed to move beyond simple culture

history and begin to study underlying cultural processes. In 1963, he was given the opportunity to put his vision of archaeology into action. Eric Harvey, a Calgary billionaire with a passion for the past, invited MacNeish to lunch at the Calgary Curling Club. If MacNeish would head it up, Harvey offered to fund the creation of a department of archaeology at the University of Calgary.

In many ways, the very idea of a department of "archaeology" went against the Boasian intellectual tradition in Canada, where archaeology was simply one of a group of integrated subdisciplines in anthropology. In order to train archaeologists in the methods of science, MacNeish put together courses in soils, geology, physics, zoology, botany, and so on. On the surface, this might look like the beginnings of the new archaeology. It wasn't, however, because MacNeish parted company with Binford on a number of critical issues. MacNeish's primary criticism of the new archaeology was that it ignored cultural specifics in favour of broad generalizations. To MacNeish, the "big" theories of culture change promoted by Binford and his students were practically impossible to test.

Bruce Trigger, perhaps the most important historian of the discipline, argues that culture history and processual archaeology effectively constitute two sides of the same coin in Canadian archaeology. Trigger argues that these two approaches coexist in a way that defines the way archaeology is currently practised in this country. As mentioned previously, this likely stems from both Canada's size and ecological diversity. However, as Canadian archaeologists begin to work in closer association with First Nations and Inuit peoples, approaches that are more humanist and post-colonial are gradually supplementing those that are strictly science-based approaches. We will explore this transition in greater detail in Chapter 2.

Bruce G. Trigger: Canadian Historian of World Archaeology

While many of his contemporaries have led the charge forward into the future of the discipline, Canadian archaeologist Bruce Trigger is notable for his insistence that archaeologists should take the time to look back (Figure 1-11). In Kingsley Amis's novel *Lucky Jim*, there is a noteworthy moment when the head of the history department in a fictitious English provincial university answers the telephone with the presumptuous words: "HISTORY SPEAKING." Had Trigger ever chosen to utter this phrase into his own phone, there probably isn't an archaeologist alive who would have disputed it. Trigger's immense knowledge and understanding of archaeology was nothing short of remarkable. Why is the history of archaeology important? Simply put, the best way to understand the current direction of a discipline is to know its past.

Bruce Graham Trigger was born in 1937 in Preston, Ontario, and completed his doctoral degree in archaeology at Yale. Although Trigger's first academic job was at Northwestern University, he soon returned to Canada, where he took up a position in McGill University's Department of Anthropology. It was at McGill that Trigger would spend his academic career, writing more than a dozen and a half books, many of which went into multiple editions. While Trigger's contributions to the archaeology of Nubia and Canada alone would be enough to place him among the most influential archaeologists, the publication of his book *A History of Archaeological Thought* in 1989 solidified his position as the preeminent historian of the discipline. In the book Trigger charts the development of archaeology, from antiquarianism and paleolithic/evolutionary archaeology, through culture history and the rise of the new archaeology, to the emergence of postprocessual archaeology. Trigger discusses the sheer variety of approaches used by archaeologists, such as "processual," "postprocessual," "critical," and "feminist," in a way that is both balanced and impartial.

Trigger's work made many of us see the intellectual history of our discipline in a completely new light. For one thing, Trigger's analysis reveals that the development of theory in archaeology is influenced by the social and political climate in which it is practised. Thus, the new archaeology, with its emphasis on environmental and technological determinism, is very much a reflection of the unbridled technological optimism of the 1960s, as epitomized in such events as Expo '67, and the race to the moon. Trigger also made us realize that a single unified body of theory has never existed within archaeology. Instead, different theories compete with one another, which accounts for the complexity of the discipline. Finally, Trigger points out that we shouldn't confuse the simple accumulation of archaeological data with the advancement of theoretical approaches to understanding the human past. In the recently revised version of *A History of Archaeological Thought*, published shortly before his

Figure 1-11 Professor Bruce G. Trigger.
Source: Courtesy of McGill University

untimely death in 2006, Trigger argues that there is still much basic analytical work to be done if archaeology is ever to attain a unified theoretical approach. He believed that this is something all archaeologists should strive for, even though it is potentially unachievable.

It is important to note that Trigger exemplifies many aspects of Canadian archaeology. As a noted Egyptologist, Trigger demonstrates that many Canadian archaeologists work abroad and make substantial contributions to archaeology in other areas of the world. His recognition of the importance of ethnography in the interpretation of archaeological data, his sensitivity to the plight of Canada's First Nations, and his recognition of the need to involve them in archaeological research have also emerged as defining features of Canadian archaeology in the 21st century.

Archaeology in the 21st Century

So, what about today? Who is a mover and shaker of the 21st century?

Perhaps in another 50 years or so, hindsight will suggest one person who truly captures the spirit of these times. But right now, we do not detect a single, defining trend that dominates Americanist archaeology; instead, the discipline has several branches, each growing and intersecting in interesting ways. Many of these diverse approaches result from new techniques and perspectives; others arise from the nature of employment in archaeology. Some archaeologists still work in museums and universities, but many more are employed in federal agencies and private archaeology firms (companies that arose as a response to federal legislation passed in the 1960s designed to protect the nation's archaeological resources—more about these in Chapter 17).

Prior to the 1970s, most Canadian and American archaeologists were white and male. Today, equal numbers of men and women, and more minorities, including Native North Americans, are actively involved in the archaeological profession. Throughout these pages, we will meet some archaeologists who exemplify those trends (in boxes labelled "Profile of an Archaeologist"). For now, we wish to present one more archaeologist as a way to introduce modern archaeology.

Aubrey Cannon: Archaeology Comes of Age

Aubrey Cannon of McMaster University (shown in Figure 1-12) is an excellent example of a Canadian archaeologist working in the 21st century. As an undergraduate student at Simon Fraser University in the late 1970s, Cannon excavated shell **midden** sites on Canada's west coast, analyzed the faunal remains they contained, and studied the new archaeology of Lewis Binford and Michael Schiffer. After graduation, Cannon spent several years analyzing ethnographic data collected by Brian Hayden (Simon Fraser University) in the Maya highlands. The purpose of this work was to correlate material culture patterns with information on the social, economic, and demographic characteristics of living households. Hayden and Cannon found generally weak correlations at the level of individual households, but discovered that collective averages of households displayed strong patterns of material culture that were indicative of their status. For example, things like the presence of luxury goods, the size of houses, and their architectural complexity seemed to be good predictors of whether a group of households was wealthy or poor in the archaeological record. These types of material cultural generalizations are essential for reconstructing social organization in the past, and are a hallmark of processual archaeology. Hayden and Cannon argued that residential corporate groups, consisting of families that lived close together and cooperatively engaged in economic activities like food production, were better than households as the focus of archaeological analysis. Their ethnoarchaeological studies also documented patterns in the disposal of household garbage, which provides important clues for selecting archaeological excavation strategies.

Following this, Cannon began his Ph.D. in Cambridge in 1983 under the supervision of Ian Hodder. As we will see in the next chapter, Hodder rejected many of the tenets of the new archaeology in favour

midden Refuse deposit resulting from human activities, generally consisting of sediment; food remains such as charred seeds, animal bone, and shell; and discarded artifacts.

Figure 1-12   Aubrey Cannon, professor of anthropology, McMaster University.

Source: Paul Ewonus, Department of Anthropology, McMaster University

of a more subjective and interpretive approach to understanding the past. Influenced by the post-processual archaeology of Hodder, Cannon began a study of variability in Victorian grave monuments. While studying tombstones might not seem like the kind of thing an archaeologist would do (many have tended to study what's under them), Cannon arrived at some remarkable conclusions.

It had long been recognized that Victorians in 19th-century England liked to give their relatives "a good send-off" when they died. This often meant an extravagant funeral, topped off with a monumental headstone. However, Cannon recognized a cyclical pattern to Victorian mortuary behaviour. Ostentatious headstones had declined in frequency through time, being gradually replaced by more modest ones. This process had culminated in the regulation of monument sizes by the British clergy toward the end of the 19th century. Remarkably, Cannon found that the mortuary behaviours of other cultural groups followed a similar cycle of elaboration, decline, and regulation. Cannon showed that mortuary behaviour can be a form of competitive display that follows a pattern typical of other forms of fashion. Styles first adopted by elite members of society are copied by lower social classes, which encourage elites to adopt new and more elaborate styles. Eventually fashions reach a point where

they are available to everyone. The fashion is then abandoned or regulated out of existence. These are the patterns that emerged in Victorian society as individuals used funerary trappings to advertise their status. This is an excellent example of an interpretive rather than science-based approach to archaeology.

Like many archaeologists, Cannon is now comfortable using approaches derived from both processual and post-processual archaeology. Like a processual archaeologist, Cannon is interested in developing and applying cross-cultural generalizations. At the same time, he is also interested in understanding how things like human agency, cultural experiences, and contingent circumstances are played out in the archaeological record. The methodologies Cannon uses in his research are those of a scientist. For example, he collects core and auger samples from coastal shell midden sites, and studies the fish bones, shell, and other materials they contain to reconstruct the pre–European contact histories of peoples on the Northwest Coast. However, science is a moving target in the 21st century, and archaeologists are finding ever newer science-based techniques to boost the amount of information that can be squeezed out of an archaeological site. In researching the archaeological sites in the Namu area on the central coast of British Columbia, for example, Cannon, his students, and colleagues have applied AMS radiocarbon dating, stable isotope analysis, ancient DNA analysis, palaeo-ethnobotany, and archaeoparasitology toward better understanding variability in pre-contact settlement and subsistence economies. New research continues to raise questions and to provide inspiration for further analyses and field investigation.

Back in the day, archaeologists properly devoted twice as much time in the lab as in the field. In the 21st century, the ratio now is on the order of between ten and a hundred to one! Studying cultural landscapes using science-based and humanistic approaches is revealing exciting new insights, yielding more data with less site destruction, and ensuring a continuing basis for expanding knowledge and understanding.

Conclusion: Archaeology's Future

Archaeology has a vibrant, lively future. The field enjoys enormous public interest, as shown by the popularity of places such as Mesa Verde National Park, television programming, and related university and college courses. This level of public support suggests that more, not less, archaeology will be needed in the future.

Archaeology in Canada and the United States has evolved from a pastime of the wealthy to an established scientific discipline. But with these changes has come the realization that studying the human past raises numerous ethical issues. Nobody can practise archaeology in a political or cultural vacuum. As we learn more about how archaeologists go about studying the past, we will also confront, in each of the following chapters, some of the ethical issues facing archaeology today.

Summary

- Archaeology today is a lively field that contributes enormously to an understanding of the human condition and confronts serious ethical dilemmas.

- The beginnings of an interest in the past can be traced back to the 6th century B.C. Babylonian king Nabonidus, who looked at the physical residues of antiquity to answer questions about the past.

- In North America, archaeology began as the pastime of antiquarians, the curious and the wealthy, who lacked formal training.

- As archaeology emerged as a formal discipline, it began to develop differently in Canada and the United States. For example, it took longer for professional archaeology to develop in Canada because of poor funding and an absence of academic departments of anthropology.

- Early on, archaeology was necessarily concerned with description and with culture history, constructing chronologies of material culture and relating these to the diffusion of ideas and the movements of cultures; but it also drew upon a variety of fields, especially the natural sciences, to help recover and reconstruct the past.

- By the 1950s, archaeology began to move beyond description and chronology to more focus on the reconstruction of past lifeways.

- This trend continued in the 1960s, with the addition of efforts to employ a scientific approach aimed at discovering universal laws and to develop theories to explain the human history uncovered by archaeology.

- Today, archaeology is a diverse field that covers both prehistoric and historic archaeology. The number of archaeologists has grown dramatically since the 1960s, and the field today is diverse, representing many different theoretical perspectives and acknowledging the need to communicate results to the public.

Additional Reading

CANADIAN RESOURCES

Beattie, Owen, Apland, Brian, Blake, Erik W., Cosgrove, James A., Gaunt, Sarah, Greer, Sheila, Mackie, Alexander P., Mackie, Kjerstin E., Straathof, Dan, Thorp, Valerie, and Troffe, Peter. (2000). The Kwäday Dän Ts'inchi discovery from a glacier in British Columbia. *Canadian Journal of Archaeology 24*(1–2), 129–147.

Kelley, Jane H. and Williamson, Ronald. (1996). The positioning of archaeology within anthropology: A Canadian historical perspective. *American Antiquity 61*(1), 5–20.

Richards, Michael P., Greer, Sheila, Corr, Lorna T., Beattie, Owen, Mackie, Alexander, Evershed, Richard P., von Finster, Al, and Southon, John. (2007). Radiocarbon dating and dietary stable isotope analysis of Kwaday Dän Ts'inchi. *American Antiquity 72*(4), 719–734.

Smith, Pamela Jane, and Mitchell, Donald (Eds). (1998). Bringing back the past: Historical perspectives on Canadian archaeology. Hull, Quebec: Canadian Museum of Civilization Paper/Archaeological Survey of Canada, 158.

Williamson, Ronald, and Bisson, Michael S. (Eds). (2006). *The Archaeology of Bruce Trigger: Theoretical Empiricism.* Montreal and Kingston, London, Ithaca: McGill–Queen's University Press.

OTHER RESOURCES

Chatters, James C. (2001). *Ancient Encounters: Kennewick Man and the First Americans.* New York: Simon and Schuster.

Daniel, Glyn, and Renfrew, Colin. (1988). *The Idea of Prehistory.* Edinburgh: University of Edinburgh Press.

Patterson, Thomas. (1995). *Toward a Social History of Archaeology in the United States.* Fort Worth: Harcourt Brace.

Thomas, David Hurst. (2000). *Skull Wars: Kennewick Man, Archaeology, and the Battle for Native American Identity.* New York: Basic Books.

Trigger, Bruce. (1999). *A History of Archaeological Thought.* (2nd ed.). Cambridge, England: Cambridge University Press.

Willey, Gordon R., and Sabloff, Jeremy A. (1993). *A History of American Archaeology.* (3rd ed.). New York: Freeman.

Online Resources

For court documents on the Kennewick case, visit the Society for American Archaeology's website, *http://www.saa.org/,* and click on government affairs.

For more information on Kwäday Dän Ts'inchi, visit the B.C. government's website, *http://www.tsa.gov .bc.ca/archaeology/kwaday_dän_ts'inchi/index.htm.*

For information on the origins of provincial and national museums in Canada, visit the Canadian Museum of Nature's website, *http://nature.ca/.*

COMPANION WEBSITE

Visit *http://www.archaeology1ce.nelson.com* to access a wide range of material to help you succeed in your introductory archaeology course. These include flashcards, Internet exercises, Web links, and practice quizzes.

RESEARCH ONLINE
WITH INFOTRAC COLLEGE EDITION

From the Student Companion website, you can access the InfoTrac College Edition database, which offers thousands of full-length articles for your research.

2 Archaeology, Anthropology, Science, and the Humanities

Inuit students assist with the excavation of a semi-subterranean house feature on the western coast of Hudson Bay, Nunavut.

Source: Dr. Peter Dawson

Preview

In this chapter we consider how archaeologists relate to the broader approaches of anthropology, science, and the humanities. The concept of culture has long been critical in anthropology and, as you will see, the anthropological use of the term takes on quite a different meaning from its everyday use. We will also explore the adaptive and ideational perspectives, two rather different ways of studying culture.

These contrasting perspectives also condition the contrast between scientific and humanistic approaches. These opposing yet complementary research strategies are each important to understanding diversity and universals among humanity.

Introduction

Some 50 years ago, archaeologist Philip Phillips declared, "Archaeology is anthropology or it is nothing." Today, Americanist archaeology remains a subfield of anthropology. Thomas and Kelly, the American authors of this textbook, have both earned multiple degrees in anthropology, and both work in departments of anthropology. On the other hand, Dawson, the Canadian author of the textbook, earned undergraduate and graduate degrees in anthropology but works in a department of archaeology. There are currently three Canadian universities with stand-alone archaeology departments. It must be stressed, however, that the existence of these separate departments reflects administrative decisions made by universities. Archaeology is still considered a subfield of anthropology in Canada.

A diversity of perspectives and goals characterizes archaeology in the 21st century. In fact, there are few U.S. departments of archaeology (the most prominent is at Boston University). Outside of the United States and Canada, however, archaeology is often more closely aligned with the humanities, such as history, classics, or art history (and it sometimes appears in these departments in U.S. and Canadian Universities). But the boundaries between these various archaeologies and their former affiliations are crumbling. Many classical archaeologists, for instance, are turning to anthropology as a source of ideas. And although many North American archaeologists remain committed to a scientific approach, others look to the humanities

for insight. Americanist archaeology is surely changing, but we believe that it will always remain closely aligned with anthropological thinking.

In this chapter, we examine the broader anthropological context of archaeology. We will also explore how scientific and humanistic perspectives condition archaeological approaches to the past. Although we draw a dichotomy between science and humanism, you should know that most archaeologists are a bit of both; many U.S. archaeologists, for example, receive funding for their research from the National Science Foundation and the National Endowment for the Humanities, while Canadian archaeologists receive their funding primarily through the Social Sciences and Humanities Research Council of Canada (SSHRC).

So, What's an Anthropological Approach?

Everyone thinks they know what anthropologists do: They study native people and fossils and chimpanzees. They grin from the pages of *National Geographic* magazine, make chit-chat on late-night talk shows, and show up on the Discovery Channel. They are Richard Leakey, Jane Goodall, and Don Johanson. Some people think that the late Stephen Jay Gould was an anthropologist (actually, he was a paleontologist and a brilliant historian of science).

But this is a limited vision of anthropology. The truth is that few people seem to know what anthropologists actually do, what anthropologists share, what makes them anthropologists at all. Anthropology is tough to pin down because anthropologists do so many different things.

So, what makes an anthropologist an anthropologist?

The answer is surprisingly simple: All anthropologists believe that the best understanding of the human condition arises from a global, comparative, and holistic approach. It is not enough to look at a single group of Americans, Chinese, or Bushmen to find the keys to human existence. Neither is it enough to look at just one part of the human condition, as do economists, historians, political scientists, and psychologists. Looking at only part of the picture gives you just that—part of the picture.

What holds anthropology together is its dogmatic insistence that every aspect of every human society, extant or extinct, counts. For a century, anthropologists have tried to arrive at the fullest possible understanding of human similarities and diversity. Because of this broad-brush approach, anthropology is uniquely qualified to understand what makes humankind distinct from the rest of the animal world. This is not to say that all anthropologists study everything: Margaret Mead never excavated an archaeological site, and Richard Leakey never interviewed a native Lakota speaker. The Renaissance anthropologist—the individual who does everything—has passed into folklore. Today, nobody can hope to do everything well.

So anthropologists specialize, and archaeologists are anthropologists who specialize in the deceased. But archaeologists still draw upon each of the other subfields of anthropology (not to mention several other sciences). Before examining how modern archaeology articulates with the rest of anthropology, we first must see just how anthropologists have carved up the pie of human existence.

anthropology The study of all aspects of humankind—biological, cultural, and linguistic, extant and extinct—employing an all-encompassing holistic approach.

biological anthropology A subdiscipline of anthropology that views humans as biological organisms; also known as *physical anthropology.*

Kinds of Anthropologists

The basic divisions within anthropology reflect the very nature of human existence. **Anthropology** embraces four primary fields of study: biological anthropology, cultural anthropology, linguistic anthropology, and archaeology (all shown in Figure 2-1). Although these are not wholly independent divisions, they do divide the discipline into manageable domains of study.

Biological Anthropology

Biological anthropologists (also known as physical anthropologists) study humans as biological organisms. One major concern is the biological evolution of humans. How did *Homo sapiens* come into being? To answer this question, biological anthropologists have pieced together an intricate family tree over the past century, working largely from fossil evidence and observation of living primates.

A second focus of modern physical anthropology is the study of human biological variability. No two human beings are identical, even though we all are members of a single species. The study of inherited differences has become a strategic domain of scientific investigation and also a matter of practical concern for educators, politicians, and community leaders.

Yet a third area of biological anthropology is bioarchaeology, the study of the human biological component of the ancient past. Archaeology overlaps with biological anthropology in that archaeologists often encounter human skeletal remains and work with biological anthropologists in their recovery and analysis. (We devote Chapter 12 to bioarchaeological inquiry.)

Each year, roughly 12 percent of the 250–300 anthropology Ph.D. degrees granted in the United States are awarded in biological anthropology. This healthy percentage indicates that, although biological anthropology remains a fairly small subfield of anthropology, it has a remarkable ability to adapt to changing technologies and an increasingly diverse academic environment. Spectacular recent fossil finds, the progress in studying human DNA, the expansion into forensic and medical studies, and advances in evolutionary anthropology have all given biological anthropology a very visible academic and public profile.

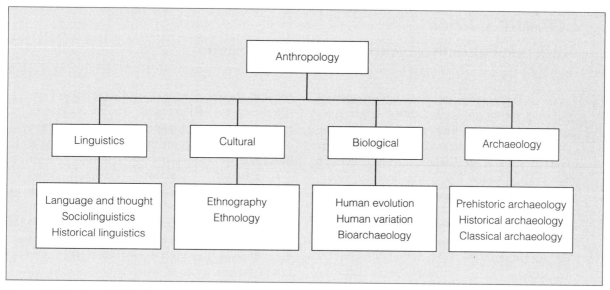

Figure 2-1 The four subfields of anthropology and their areas of study.

Cultural Anthropology

Cultural anthropologists describe and analyze the culture of human groups in the present and relatively recent past. Cultural anthropologists commonly employ the method of **participant observation,** gathering data by personally questioning and observing people while living in their society. Anthropologists study rituals, kinship, religion, politics, art, oral histories, medical practices—anything and everything that people in contemporary societies do, say, or think.

Conventionally, cultural anthropologists who describe present-day cultures on a firsthand basis are termed **ethnographers,** and their descriptions are called **ethnographies** (we mentioned in Chapter 1 that the comparative study of cultures is termed ethnology). About 60 percent of the Ph.D.s in anthropology are awarded to cultural anthropologists. Archaeology overlaps with cultural anthropology in that some archaeologists conduct research with living peoples to understand the relationships between behaviour and material remains (see Chapter 10), and all archaeologists look to ethnographic research for ideas about how to interpret the things they find in sites.

Linguistic Anthropology

Anthropological linguists evaluate linguistic behaviour in detail: how sounds are made, how sounds create

languages, the relationship between language and thought, how linguistic systems change through time, the basic structure of language, and the role of language in the development of culture. Anthropological linguists also use language to chart historical relationships and track ancient migrations between now-separate, but linguistically related, populations. Today, many linguists study the process whereby people acquire second languages and work with native peoples to revive dying languages.

The field of linguistic anthropology is shrinking; in 2001, **linguistic anthropology** accounted for only 1

cultural anthropology A subdiscipline of anthropology that emphasizes nonbiological aspects: the learned social, linguistic, technological, and familial behaviours of humans.

participant observation The primary strategy of cultural anthropology in which data are gathered by questioning and observing people while the observer lives in their society.

ethnographers Anthropologists who study one culture and write detailed descriptions of that culture's traditions, customs, religion, social and political organization, and so on.

ethnographies The descriptions of cultures written by ethnographers.

linguistic anthropology A subdiscipline of anthropology that focuses on human language: its diversity in grammar, syntax, and lexicon; its historical development; and its relation to a culture's perception of the world.

Looking Closer
Academic Funding for Anthropology in Canada

 Every year, Canadian anthropologists of varying stripes and career stages apply for funding from agencies such as the Social Sciences and Humanities Research Council of Canada (SSHRC) and the Natural Sciences and Engineering Research Council of Canada (NSERC). *Cultural anthropologists, archaeologists,* and *linguistic anthropologists* typically apply for academic and research funding through SSHRC, and only occasionally through NSERC. This is because these three sub-branches of anthropology are aligned more closely with the social sciences and humanities than with science and engineering. There are exceptions, however. Dr. Matt Boyd, a geoarchaeologist from Lakehead University, has received funding through NSERC to reconstruct the early landscape associated with Glacial Lake Agassiz, the largest of several proglacial lakes formed in central Canada during the late Pleistocene. Boyd is interested in understanding the impact that late-glacial environments had on the earliest human populations in North America. Using the approaches of science, such as geoarchaeology, to accomplish this task means that Boyd's research was fundable through an NSERC research grant.

Boyd's research demonstrates that the multidisciplinary nature of anthropology can sometimes make it difficult for researchers to figure out which funding agencies they should be applying to.

For instance, the complex and diverse field of *biological anthropology* examines a wide variety of issues concerning the relationship between human biology and culture. Techniques such as skeletal biology, DNA analysis, and stable isotope analysis are methods of science. However, these approaches are frequently brought to bear on such topics as childhood growth and development in Third World nations, human population movements, and the reconstruction of past and present diets. Because they use the *methods* of science to investigate the *issues* of social science, such projects could be funded through either SSHRC or NSERC. As a result, some projects occasionally fall through the cracks.

Students enrolled in graduate anthropology programs at Canadian universities usually apply for funding from SSHRC to assist with their Masters and Ph.D. dissertation research work. Upon completion of a Ph.D., young scholars will frequently apply for a post-doctoral fellowship. This funding allows newly minted professors to turn their dissertation research into peer-reviewed articles in books and academic journals. It also provides them with an opportunity to establish a program of research, while they seek out work either in government or as a tenure-track assistant professor at a college or university. Once a position has been secured, faculty members will then spend the rest of their careers in the hunt for larger

percent of all Ph.D.s in anthropology (down from 7 percent in 1970). Archaeology overlaps with linguistics when language helps reconstruct when and from where modern populations migrated.

Archaeology

Archaeology accounts for about a quarter of the doctoral degrees awarded in anthropology. Most archae-

ologists also attempt to understand human culture, but their technology and field methods differ radically from those of ethnologists and linguists. Because archaeologists commonly study extinct cultures, they work at some disadvantage. Lacking living, breathing informants, archaeologists have formulated a powerful array of techniques for gleaning relevant information from the material remains of the past. As we will see, these methods sometimes give archaeologists information that living, breathing informants probably never would (or could) have told them.

archaeology The study of the past through the systematic recovery and analysis of material remains.

research grants, funded through the various programs of SSHRC, NSERC, and a host of other national and international funding agencies.

Obtaining research funding is extremely challenging regardless of whether you are applying for a student fellowship or a large multi-year research grant. Applications for funding are usually vetted by a committee of established academics, and require strong support through letters of recommendation and external peer reviews. There are always more applicants seeking funding than there is money to support their research. Consequently, it is fair to say that most granting committees are looking for reasons *not* to fund applications, rather than the other way around. As a result, success rates at all levels are usually low. Recent statistics from SSHRC (2005–2006), for example, are presented in Table 2.1.

As you can see, the relatively low success rates indicate that the quest for funding among graduate and newly minted Ph.D.s is extremely competitive. A similar pattern is revealed for statistics on university faculty applying for SSHRC Standard Research Grants to support their research. In 2005–2006, for example, 218 archaeologists and anthropologists submitted 110 project applications, requesting a total of $15,416,751. Of these applications, only 40 percent (44) were successful. As we saw in Chapter 1, the development of archaeology in Canada was somewhat hindered by a lack of research funds. While anthropology has seen substantial gains since the 1960s, we still lag behind our colleagues in the United States in terms of access to research dollars. This will hopefully change as public awareness of the importance of anthropological research increases.

TABLE 2-1 Breakdown of SSHRC Funding for Anthropology (2005–2006)

DOCTORAL FELLOWSHIPS	NO. OF APPLICANTS	GRANTS AWARDED	SUCCESS RATE
Anthropology	160	45	28.1%
Archaeology	69	16	23.2%
Linguistics	111	19	17.1%

POST-DOCTORAL FELLOWSHIPS	NO. OF APPLICANTS	GRANTS AWARDED	SUCCESS RATE
Anthropology	34	8	23.5%
Archaeology	18	8	44.5%
Linguistics	18	6	33.3%

The future of archaeology is bright indeed. Archaeology is a strong element of many graduate programs in anthropology, and undergraduates often find archaeology to be the most lively and exciting program within anthropology. This excitement is due, in part, to the dazzling assortment of new ways to explore the past that we discuss in this text.

Archaeology is also the subfield of anthropology most capable of delivering jobs to undergraduates. Americanist archaeology is expanding, especially in such areas as historical archaeology, heritage programs, and cultural resource management programs.

Look for archaeology to continue making significant contributions to the overall mission of anthropology.

The Culture Concept in Anthropology

We have already said that a global, comparative, and holistic perspective tends to unite the diversity within anthropology. But even more than that, it is the concept of culture that brings together the subfields of anthropology.

A dozen academic disciplines purport to study culture (or at least cultural behaviour): economics, sociology, linguistics, political science, history, cultural geography, psychology, and so forth. "Classical" historians, for instance, might investigate Greek, Roman, or Byzantine culture; their interest centres on the cultural characteristics of each particular society. But one does not expect to find classical historians discoursing on the general nature of culture; if they did, they would cease to be classical historians and would become anthropologists. This overarching conception and investigation of culture traditionally forms the central theme melding so many diversified (and sometimes conflicting) concerns into the anthropological perspective.

What Is Culture?

Nearly 50 years ago, Alfred Kroeber and Clyde Kluckhohn compiled more than 200 distinct definitions of culture. Since that time, the number of definitions of culture must have tripled.

Do these definitions have anything in common?
Absolutely.

Suppose we begin with the classic definition offered by Sir Edward Burnett Tylor (the person considered by many to be the founder of modern anthropology). Tylor's definition of culture appeared in 1871 on the first page of anthropology's first textbook and remains one of the clearest:

> Culture . . . taken in its wide ethnographic sense is that complex whole which includes knowledge, belief, art, morals, law, custom, and any other capabilities and habits acquired by man as a member of society.

Culture in Tylor's sense is *learned*—from parents, peers, teachers, leaders, and others. Note that culture is not biological or genetic; any person can acquire any culture. And under the anthropological definition, all peoples have the same amount of culture. Someone who can recite Shakespeare and who listens to Beethoven's *Moonlight Sonata* is no more (or less) cultural than someone who reads *Reader's Digest* and prefers Flatt and Scruggs' *Foggy Mountain Breakdown*. If a baby born to European parents in Europe were raised in China, that individual's appearance would come from its genes (as moderated by environmental factors), but he or she would speak Chinese and act and think as other Chinese do.

Culture creates very different conceptions of life, of what is proper and what is not. Tribal people in New Guinea think it laughable that American women wear earrings, but they think it normal to wear bone or shell nose ornaments for ceremonies. Cultures change over time in part by changes in **enculturation,** the process whereby an individual learns their culture as a child. Material factors (such as nutrition) and historical factors (such as contact with other peoples) affect this process. Given that archaeology is concerned with how cultures change over time, the concept of learned culture is essential to archaeology.

Culture is also shared. By this, we mean that although each person is an individual with their own particular values and understandings, human groups share some basic ideas about the world and their place in it. Shared ideas, rather than individual variations on them, are the traditional focus of anthropology.

Many Euroamerican homes, for instance, are divided into multiple rooms, including a living room, a smallish kitchen, family room, and bedrooms. The main entry often opens directly into the living room. This pattern is considered normal and comfortable by most Euroamericans.

But, according to George Esber (Miami University), when Apache people were given the chance to design their own homes, they preferred a single large living area that included the kitchen, with only the bedrooms and baths separate. These large living areas could accommodate large social gatherings. In order to cook for so many people, Apaches also preferred kitchens with an almost industrial capacity, including large cabinets to accommodate large cooking pots. In this case, different ideas about life result in different social behaviours that result in different material remains. By delving into material remains, then, archaeology investigates and expands anthropology's concept of culture.

Finally, culture is *symbolic*. Consider the symbolism involved in language: There is no reason that the word "dog" in English means "a household pet," any more

---

culture An integrated system of beliefs, traditions, and customs that govern or influence a person's behaviour. Culture is learned, shared by members of a group, and based on the ability to think in terms of symbols.

enculturation The process whereby individuals learn their culture.

than do "chien," "perro," or "alika" (French, Spanish, and Malagasy). And there is no reason why dogs are necessarily pets. Indeed, in many places in the world, such as Micronesia and Southeast Asia, dogs are feast foods. Many Americans consider this disgusting, and some Vietnamese immigrants in California have wound up in court over it. But neither the idea of "pet" nor "food" is inherent in a dog—they are symbolic meanings that cultures give to dogs (the same is true for guinea pigs, which are eaten in highland Peru). Symbolic meanings such as these affect which bones wind up in ancient middens.

Virtually all human behaviour is symbolic to some degree, and this symbolism can create considerable misunderstanding. When North Americans talk, for example, they tend to stay about an arm's length away from each other. Latin Americans stand much closer, often touching one another. As a result, Latin Americans sometimes see North Americans as cold and distant, whereas North Americans often feel their southern neighbours are too intimate or aggressive. Such symbolic meanings of behaviour condition what we do, which in turn affects the material traces of those behaviours (such as the structure of houses and public places). Again, archaeology studies the concept of culture by studying these material traces.

So, culture is learned, shared, and symbolic; it provides you with a way to interpret human behaviour and the world around you; and it plays a key role in structuring the material record of human behaviour—which archaeologists recover.

How Do Anthropologists Study Culture?

To oversimplify a bit, anthropologists study culture in two basic ways. An **ideational perspective** focuses on ideas, symbols, and mental structures as driving forces in shaping human behaviour. Alternatively, an **adaptive perspective** isolates technology, ecology, demography, and economics as the key factors defining human behaviour. Let's examine each perspective.

Culture as Ideas

According to anthropologist Roger Keesing (1935–1993), the basic theme of the ideational perspective in anthropology is that culture is a complex set of conceptual designs and shared understandings that underlie the way people act. Culture, in this sense, is principally what humans learn, not what they do or make. This perspective emphasizes ideas, thoughts, and shared knowledge and sees symbols and their meanings as crucial to shaping human behaviour. It encompasses material culture insofar as material things manifest symbolic ideas.

The ideational theorist insists on "getting inside a person's head" to seek out the shared meanings of a society. According to the ideational view of culture, one cannot comprehend human behaviour without understanding the symbolic code for that behaviour. Moreover, according to this view, our interpretation and, in fact, the symbolic meaning(s) that we give to things heavily influence our perception of the world around us.

Culture as Adaptation

An adaptive perspective is primarily concerned with "culture as a system." Social and cultural differences are viewed not as reflections of symbolic meanings, but rather as responses to the material parameters of life, such as food, shelter, and reproduction. Human behaviours are seen as linked together systemically, such that change in one area, say technology, will result in change in another area, such as social organization. Leslie White (1900–1975) pioneered the investigation of cultural systems, and archaeologists have reworked White's reasoning to suit the study of extinct cultural systems. Following White's lead, Lewis Binford (discussed on page 20) defined the cultural system as a set of repetitive articulations among the social, technological, and ideological aspects of culture. These three facets are, in White's terminology, "extrasomatic," meaning "outside the body" or "learned," as noted above. And it is the cultural system—technology, modes of economic organization, settlement patterns, forms of social grouping, and political institutions—that articulates the material needs of human communities with their ecological settings.

In the adaptive perspective, culture keeps societies in equilibrium with their ecosystems. Adaptive prime

ideational perspective The research perspective that defines ideas, symbols, and mental structures as driving forces in shaping human behaviour.

adaptive perspective A research perspective that emphasizes technology, ecology, demography, and economics in the definition of human behaviour.

movers are those elements of technology, subsistence economy, and social or political organization most closely tied to life's material needs: food, reproduction, and shelter. Archaeologists working with the adaptive perspective link cultural behaviours largely to the environment, demography, subsistence, or technology. They see ideational systems as secondary.

Let's look at an example of how these two perspectives produce different but complementary understandings of cultural behaviour.

An Example: The Kwakwak'awakw Potlatch

The Kwakwak'awakw (see "Looking Closer: Who Are We?" by Gloria Cranmer Webster) are a Native American tribe that lives on the coast of British Columbia. Prior to extensive European contact, they were hunter-fishers, living primarily by fishing for salmon and halibut, hunting sea mammals, and gathering shellfish. Importantly, they were quite dependent on a few large salmon runs in the fall to provide them with nearly all their food for the long winter. They once lived in villages that consisted of many large, decorated houses built of cedar planks and that often housed several related families. They had a social hierarchy in which some families could claim a higher rank (and perhaps a greater share of resources) than other families. Slaves were occasionally taken in raids between villages. Many modern Kwakwak'awakw still live in their original territory and, although many are commercial fishermen, others are carpenters, computer programmers, lawyers, and teachers.

The element of Kwakwak'awakw life that has most fascinated anthropology for the last century is the **potlatch** (Figure 2-2 shows a contemporary artist's rendering). The potlatch is an example of competitive feasts, a social custom found in many societies. The term comes from Chinook, a Northwest Coast **trade language,** and means "to give." Potlatches varied in size, from small affairs between families to huge feasts between villages—the kind the Kwakwak'awakw called "doing a great thing."

Figure 2-2 Artist's rendering of a late-19th-century Kwakwak'awakw (Kwakiutl) potlatch ceremony (painting by Will Taylor).

Source: American Museum of Natural History

The potlatch existed when James Cook explored the northwest coast of North America in 1778. Taking some American sea otter pelts with him across the Pacific, Cook discovered that the Chinese valued them highly. A lively transpacific trade began: the Europeans supplying blankets, beads, metal pots, and axes to the Native Americans in exchange for pelts to be taken to China and elsewhere. The influx of so many European goods increased the size and significance of potlatches. One in 1921 included motorboats, sewing machines, gramophones, musical instruments—even a pool table!

Potlatches accompanied high-ranking marriages between villages (like those between Europe's royal houses), funerals, and the raising of totem poles. And all of them involved ambitious, status-hungry men who battled one another for social approval by hosting massive, opulent feasts. These feasts proceeded according to culturally dictated rules. One chief functioned in the role of host, inviting neighbours to his village for the festivities. The host parcelled out gifts of varying value: boxes of candlefish oil, baskets of berries, stacks of blankets, animal skins. As the chief presented each gift, the guests responded with a great

potlatch Among 19th-century Northwest Coast Native Americans, a ceremony involving the giving away or destruction of property in order to acquire prestige.

trade language A language that develops among speakers of different languages to permit economic exchanges.

degree of (culturally prescribed) dissatisfaction, for they could not insinuate that their host was generous.

There were bonfires, magic tricks, and singing at potlatches, and ranking families displayed valuable family heirlooms such as carved dishes. There were elaborate dances (such as the cannibal dance, in which members of the audience might be bitten) and others where birds and whales were portrayed by wooden masks whose hinged mouths would dramatically open wide to reveal a human face peering up from the throat.

And there was food, lots and lots of food. Men drank fish oil from shovel-sized spoons, spilling it all over themselves. Guests would "eat themselves under the table" and crawl groaning into the forest, only to vomit and return for more. The more food one gave away, the greater one's prestige.

The feasting extended beyond simple gluttony. A high-ranking member of the host village would give away blankets, slaves, canoes, food, and other things to a high-ranking man from a rival village. One particularly important item was "coppers"—hammered, shield-like sheets of European copper, often with designs embossed or painted on their surfaces. These copper sheets had names, such as "Killer Whale," "Beaver Face," and "All Other Coppers Are Ashamed to Look at It." Late 19th-century potlatching sometimes culminated in the outright destruction of property—hosts threw coppers into the sea and burned food, clothing, money, and canoes.

The logic behind this conspicuous consumption was this: The more goods given away or destroyed, the greater the host's prestige. The guest chief would belittle the host's efforts, but he knew that to regain prestige he would eventually have to give an even grander feast.

So, what was this all about?

The Potlatch as Ideational Message

What was the symbolic message of the feasts? What did the participants think was happening?

For the person giving the feast, the objective was prestige. Hosts obtained the dispersed goods through hard work, but also by giving smaller potlatches within their own villages. Traditionally, the value of goods given in those potlatches had to eventually be returned (not the exact gifts, but their equivalents) plus a little bit more. It was investment banking.

By giving away all the collected goods to a visitor or by destroying them, a host insulted his guests by symbolically saying, "This is how powerful I am. I can give all this away and it does me no harm. You can't do this." And through association with this man, village members also gained prestige. For them, a successful potlatch truly was "doing a great thing."

To the non-Kwakwak'awakw, the images of killer whales, huge spoons, bears, and boxes of candlefish oil seemed bizarre and chaotic. Indeed, the Canadian government found potlatches to be barbaric and wasteful and banned them in 1885 (a ban that was not

Looking Closer
Who Are We?

We are not the Kwakiutl, as the white people have called us since they first came to our territory. The only Kwakiutl ... are the people of Fort Rupert. Each of our village groups has its own name.... The language we speak is Kwakwala. The name Kwakwak'awakw refers to Kwakwala speakers and accurately describes who we are. To call all of us who live in a specific cultural area "Kwakiutl" is like calling all indigenous people of the Americas "Indians." No longer is either acceptable.

by Gloria Cranmer Webster (Kwak-wak'awakw), a historian and former director of the U'mista Cultural Centre (Alert Bay, British Columbia)

lifted until 1951). This is because white Canadians did not share in Kwakwak'awakw culture. They did not know the stories and legends that "made sense" of the masks and symbols—stories and legends that every Kwakwak'awakw child knew. White Canadians saw no good purpose to potlatching; instead, they saw only a material chaos and waste that stood in the way of converting the Kwakwak'awakw to Christianity and a system of Western values.

But imagine if we could bring a 19th-century Kwakwak'awakw man to an American football game. Costumed men smash into one another below. The observers in the stands scream, some literally calling for blood; many have their faces (and bodies) painted in garish colours, wear horned masks, and wave giant pointing puppet hands in the air. Observers drink to excess, and fights may break out in the bleachers. A streaker dashes down the visiting team's side of the field. Based on who wins the contest, supporters celebrate far into the night and enjoy increased status—until the next game.

Would the Kwakwak'awakw have understood? Or would he have thought he was in the presence of madness?

There was even more to the potlatch than the search for prestige. Many cultures contain rituals or festivals in which prohibited behaviours are demonstrated by symbolically indulging in them, by temporarily inverting the social order. During Halloween, for example, American children are allowed to dress (and act) like ghouls and make demands of adults—behaviour that is normally banned. The potlatch involved the excessive consumption of food among a people where table manners were normally as precise and rigorous as those at a Victorian banquet or a Japanese tea ceremony. Stanley Walens argues that the potlatch was a way of enforcing such behaviour by demonstrating what happens when people do not control their hunger: they turn into cannibals and become like killer whales that swallow people whole.

The Potlatch as Adaptive Strategy

A different interpretation of the potlatch arises when we look at the potlatch from the adaptive perspective. How did the loss of so much personal property serve useful ecological, technological, or economic purposes?

Recall that the Kwakwak'awakw depended on salmon for their winter food supply. Some villages were located on streams with large, reliable salmon runs; others were on streams of smaller, less reliable runs. These less-fortunate villages tried to ally themselves with the larger, more fortunate villages—villages they could count on for assistance in years of poor salmon runs. Through alliances cemented by potlatching, the large villages also alleviated the possibility that smaller villages might, under desperate conditions, try to attack them. They therefore fought wars of "property" in addition to (or instead of) wars of "blood." Through the potlatch system, the less fortunate villages were invited to potlatches hosted by their more prosperous neighbours. Although visitors were required to endure seemingly endless barbs and slights, they departed with full bellies—and, more important, with a powerful ally.

And what if some villages sustained a continued subsistence catastrophe? Some research suggests that the potlatch helped shift population from less productive to more productive villages: economically prosperous villages could boast of (and demonstrate) their affluence at the potlatch ceremonies, thereby inducing guests to leave their impoverished situations and join the wealthier, more ecologically stable village. More people meant more labourers and bigger, more elaborate feasts that would allow a chief to outcompete his rivals. In other words, the drive for individual prestige held a material significance for the rank-and-file villagers.

Potlatches also allowed villagers to judge the leadership capacity of a man vying for prestige. If he gave a poor potlatch, then it was apparent that he did not have much backing or clout and therefore was not capable of establishing intervillage ties—social ties that were critical in times of poor salmon runs, storms, harsh winters, or warfare. If people wanted to have a better chance of "making it" through bad times, then they should want to be part of a village that had ties to neighbours who could, and would, help in times of need.

Which Perspective Is Better?

In a word, neither. The differences between these two perspectives on culture are a lot like the differences between any two cultures themselves, such as Kwakwak'awakw and European culture. Each perspective looks at the world in a different way, highlighting some aspects and downplaying others; each makes mistaken interpretations here and finds insights there. The adaptive perspective recognizes that humans must respond to the material conditions of their environments, and the ideational perspective shows how they do this through particular symbolic behaviours. The adaptive perspective cannot account for the particular way in which the potlatch was conducted, and the ideational perspective cannot account for why the potlatch occurred where and when it did or what goods were given away. Hence, we need both adaptive and ideational perspectives to understand human diversity and history.

Scientific and Humanistic Approaches in Archaeology

Anthropologists also distinguish between scientific and humanistic approaches. This struggle is between two incompatible views of the world (culture again!) and consequently is a disagreement about which tools are best for any particular task. This difference is critical to understanding the two major flavours of modern archaeology (which we will discuss in Chapter 3).

What's a Scientific Approach?

Science (from the Latin "to know") refers, in its broadest sense, to a systematic body of knowledge about any field. Although the era of modern science is generally considered to have begun in the Renaissance, the origins of scientific thought extend far back in human history. The **archaeological record**—the documentation of artifacts and their contexts recovered from archaeological sites—has preserved examples of early **scientific reasoning:** astronomical observations, treatment of disease, calendrical systems, recipes for food and drink. Cave paintings and carvings in bone or stone are often cited as early instances of systematizing knowledge.

Science as a distinct intellectual endeavour began in the 17th century with work in mathematics, astronomy, and physics by such luminaries as Galileo, Newton, Kepler, Pascal, and Descartes. Sir Francis Bacon codified the scientific method in his book *Novum Organum* (1620). Darwin's 19th-century consideration of evolution added a biological component to the scientific picture.

Today, pure science is divided into the physical sciences (including physics, chemistry, and geology), the biological sciences (such as botany and zoology), and interdisciplinary sciences, such as biochemistry (which understands life processes in terms of chemical substances and reactions) and anthropology (which aims to understand humans as biological and social beings).

So, what exactly is science? A good definition is hard to pin down; perhaps it is easiest to simply list some key characteristics. Lawrence Kuznar (Indiana-Purdue University at Fort Wayne) provides several:

- *Science is empirical, or objective.* Science is concerned with the observable, measurable world and has nothing to say about the non-material world. Questions are scientific (a) if they are concerned with the detectable properties of things, and (b) if the result of observations designed to answer a question cannot be predetermined by the biases of the observer.
- *Science is systematic and explicit.* Scientists try to gather information in such a way that they collect all data that are relevant to a problem, and they aim to do this in such a way that any trained observer under the same conditions would make the same observations.
- *Science is logical.* It works not only with data, but with ideas that link data with interpretations and with ideas that link other ideas themselves together. These linkages must be based on previously demonstrated principles, otherwise an argument is a house of cards.
- *Science is explanatory and, consequently, predictive.* Science is concerned with causes. It seeks theories—explanatory statements that allow one not only to predict what will happen under a specified set of conditions, but also to explain why it will happen. The goal of science is to develop theories that can be criticized, evaluated,

science The search for universals by means of established scientific methods of inquiry.

archaeological record The documentation of artifacts and other material remains, along with their contexts recovered from archaeological sites.

scientific reasoning Accepted principles and procedures for the systematic pursuit of secure knowledge. Established scientific procedures involve the following steps: define a relevant problem; establish one or more hypotheses; determine the empirical implications of the hypotheses; collect appropriate data through observation and/or experimentation; compare these data with the expected implications; and revise and/or retest hypotheses as necessary.

and eventually modified or replaced by other theories that explain the data better.

- *Science is self-critical and based on testing.* Many people think that science requires white lab coats, supercomputers, and complex equations. Although science might entail these things, it is really about honesty. Scientists propose hypotheses, tentative ideas about the world or explanations of previous observations. Then they say, "Here is my idea, here is the evidence that will prove it wrong, and here is my attempt to collect that evidence." Scientists acquire understanding not by proving that an idea is right, but by showing that competing ideas are wrong. Consequently, scientists always ask themselves: How do I know that I know something? They are professional skeptics, always looking for biases in their data, always testing their methods and prevailing ideas against competing ones.

- *Science is public.* A scientist's method and observations and the arguments linking observations with conclusions are explicit and available for scrutiny by the public. The source or political implications of ideas are unimportant; what matters in science is that the ideas can be tested by objective methods. Taken together, these characteristics of science combine to produce the scientific method, an elegant and powerful way to understand the workings of the material world—and to conduct archaeology.

Archaeologists have been doing scientific research for a long time. Consider, for example, how scientific methods were used to solve the "mystery" of the Moundbuilders.

How Science Explains Things: The Moundbuilder Myth

When Europeans arrived on the North American continent in the 16th century, they of course met Indians. And in so doing, they confronted a serious issue: Who were these people? This was an important question, for in its answer lay the answer to another question: Did Europeans have the right to take the land?

Later, as colonial Americans began to expand westward through Indian lands, they discovered thousands of mounds and earthworks, especially in the Ohio River and Mississippi River valleys. Some of these mounds were modest, a metre or so high and a few metres in diameter. Others were enormous: Monk's Mound at the site of Cahokia, in Illinois, just across the Mississippi River from St. Louis, stands nearly 20 metres high and covers as many hectares as the largest pyramid in Egypt. Some were conically shaped; others were truncated pyramids. Some were "effigy mounds," fashioned in the shape of animals such as serpents and birds (Figure 2-3 shows an example); still others were precise geometric embankments that enclosed many hectares.

Colonial farmers levelled the mounds with plows, and the curious dug into them. Many contained human skeletal remains, but it was the remarkable artifacts that really caught the eye: copper and antler headdresses; stone pipes beautifully carved into birds, frogs, bears, and other animals; sheets of mica, intricately cut into hands and talons; carved shells; massive log tombs; beautiful spear points; incised pottery; copper ornaments; and polished stone disks (Figure 2-4 shows an etched disk from Alabama). We now know that mounds were constructed as early as 3500 B.C. in the southern Mississippi River valley and that the practice was fairly widespread in the eastern United States by 1000 B.C. In the early 16th century, the Spanish explorer Hernando de Soto and other explorers saw mounds being made and used as burial grounds and as foundations for priestly temples in the southeastern United States, but elsewhere the practice had ceased hundreds of years earlier.

But the colonists knew nothing about de Soto's observations, and so they devised a variety of hypotheses to account for the mounds. Some argued that the Moundbuilders were the ancestors of living Indians, but the "race" had degenerated. Others believed that the Moundbuilders had migrated to Mexico, where they became the Toltecs and Aztecs.

But the favoured interpretation was that the Moundbuilders were a superior race that had been wiped out by the Indians. Some scholars claimed that this earlier race was Viking; others said Moundbuilders were actually Egyptians, Israelites, Chinese, Greeks, Polynesians, Phoenicians, Norwegians, Belgians, Tartars, Saxons, Hindus, Africans, Welsh, and Atlanteans from the lost continent of Atlantis. A 19th-century Ohio reverend suggested that God had created the Serpent Mound in southern Ohio to mark the site of Eden.

Figure 2-3 Aerial photo of Serpent Mound, an effigy mound in Ohio.
Source: Ohio Historical Society

Anyone, it seemed, could have been the Mound-builders—except the ancestors of American Indians. Instead, scholars saw the Indians as late-coming marauders, destroyers of what was obviously a magnificent civilization. The human bones in the mounds were evidence of great battles fought on the monu-

ments. In various mounds, stones allegedly incised with Hebrew, Chinese, Celtic, Runic, Phoenician, or other languages were proffered as evidence that the Moundbuilders were, in fact, Europeans—or at least not Indians. And thus, the myth of a Moundbuilder civilization arose.

This was a handy idea, because it gave colonists a sense of superiority and the right to avenge the Moundbuilders by dispossessing Native Americans of their land. Handy, but was it true?

A President's Attention

From its beginning, the Moundbuilder myth attracted scrutiny at the highest levels of American society. One of the most notable was Thomas Jefferson (1743–1826), author of the Declaration of Independence, third president of the United States—and the first scientific archaeologist in America.

Jefferson was described by a contemporary as "an expert musician (the violin being his favorite instrument), a good dancer, a dashing rider, and proficient in all manly exercises." He was an inventor, an avid player of chess (avoiding cards), an accomplished horticulturalist, scientist, distinguished architect, and a connoisseur of French cooking.

Jefferson was also curious about the origins of Native Americans. Fascinated by Indian lore since boyhood and trained in classical linguistics, Jefferson

Figure 2-4 An etched slate from Moundville, Alabama. Artifacts such as these convinced 19th-century scholars that the Moundbuilders were a superior culture.

Source: Peabody Museum, Harvard University

believed that Native American languages held valuable clues to the origins of the people. Jefferson collected linguistic data from more than 40 tribes and wrote a treatise on the subject. From his linguistic studies, Jefferson sensed an Asiatic origin for Native Americans (a conclusion that few scholars would argue with today).

Jefferson's contribution to Americanist archaeology was presented in his only book, a response to a number of questions sent to him by French scholars. It appeared as a limited French edition in 1784 and as a widely distributed American edition in 1787. *Notes on the State of Virginia* dealt, in part, with the aborigines of Virginia, their origin, and the question of the mounds. Jefferson listed the various Virginian tribes, relating their histories since the settlement of Jamestown in 1607 and incorporating a census of Virginia's current Native American population. In it, Jefferson argued that Native Americans were in no way mentally or physically inferior to the white race and rejected all current racist doctrines used to explain Indians' origins. (He later argued for intermarriage between Europeans and Native Americans, a practice he did not support between Europeans and Africans, although he probably fathered children with one of his slaves.) He reasoned that Native Americans were wholly capable of having constructed the prehistoric earthworks of the United States.

Archaeological Ethics
Who Owns the Past?

 Many Inuit and First Nations groups are beginning to challenge archaeological interpretations of their past, and even the rights of others to access archaeological sites and artifacts for research. The reasons for this may stem from the scientific perspective that archaeologists sometimes use when interpreting the archaeological record. This is very different from the humanistic point of view expressed by many Inuit and First Nations peoples. Let's look at an example.

In 1992, several archaeologists working in Canada's High Arctic were denied permission to excavate by the Inuit community of Resolute Bay. Dr. James Helmer and Dr. Genevieve LeMoine had hoped to begin archaeological fieldwork on a nearby island that summer. Instead, they met with Elders, Hamlet Council members, and even the mayor of Resolute Bay in an attempt to find out why permission had been denied. Many Inuit in the community expressed concerns about how archaeology had been practised in the North. For example, some thought that artifacts were sold rather than studied, believing that archaeological research was motivated by profit. Others had misconceptions about the destructive nature of archaeological excavation, explaining that tourists visiting the north want to see old houses rather than holes in the ground. Perhaps most importantly, many saw archaeology as unnecessary, explaining that Inuit Elders already knew all that was needed about the past.

Rightly or wrongly held, these perceptions indicate that archaeologists have done a poor job communicating their work to aboriginal people. They also demonstrate that indigenous societies interpret and understand the past in a fundamentally different way. Professional archaeologists commonly use the tools of Western science and philosophy to create rigorous, objective, and intrinsically interesting interpretations of the past. However, these explanations often have little relevance to indigenous people, who rely on oral histories passed down from one generation to the next. In fact, many First Nations and Inuit see a "scientific" approach as denigrating their own indigenous versions of history. Take the peopling of the Americas, for instance.

As early as 1589, the Jesuit missionary José de Acosta wrote in *Historia Natural y Moral de las Indias* that Indians had walked to the New World via a land route that connected the New World with Asia. Even though de Acosta knew nothing of northern lands, his ideas were, remarkably, more or less correct. Biological, archaeological, and linguistic data today demonstrate without a doubt that the ancestors of First Nations peoples migrated from Asia, via a land bridge that spanned the Bering Strait, at least 13,500 years

Then Jefferson took a critical step: He proceeded to excavate a burial mound located on his property. Today, such a step seems obvious, but Jefferson's contemporaries would have rummaged through libraries and archives rather than dirty their hands with bones, stones, and dirt to answer intellectual issues. This is why Jefferson is often said to be the founder of American archaeology (some paleontologists claim Jefferson to be the founder of their field as well).

Jefferson's account described his method of excavation, the different layers of earth, and the artifacts and the human bones that he encountered. He then tested the **hypothesis** that the bones resulted from warfare. Noting the absence of traumatic wounds (such as

those made by arrows), and the interments of children, Jefferson rejected the idea that the bones were those of soldiers who had fallen in battle. Noting that some remains were scattered, he surmised that the burials had accumulated through repeated use. And he saw no reason to doubt that the ancestors of Native Americans had constructed the mounds.

Although many years later another future president, William Harrison, would argue that the mounds were built for defensive purposes, few archaeologists today

---

hypothesis A proposition proposed as an explanation of some phenomena.

---

ago. In 1988, The Assembly of First Nations in Canada wrote a document titled *A Declaration of the First Nations* that summarized an entirely different view. It stated "We the Original Peoples of this land know the Creator put us here. The Creator gave us our spiritual beliefs, our languages, our culture, and a place on Mother Earth, which provided us with all our needs. We have maintained our freedom, our languages and our traditional from time immemorial." Native leaders see archaeological theories like the Bering Strait hypothesis as depriving them of their spiritual beliefs, and stripping them of their cultural heritage. In addition to contradicting traditional beliefs, the Bering Strait theory also implies that indigenous Canadians are simply immigrants to the New Word, just like Europeans. Many Aboriginal leaders are concerned that such an idea undermines the legitimacy of Native land claims. This likely explains why Native peoples feel they have such a vested interest in who "owns" the past.

So, how do we reconcile the rationalist explanations of the past, offered up by archaeologists, with the traditional beliefs of First Nations and Inuit? Dr. Robert McGhee of the Canadian Museum of Civilization explains that there are three possible responses:

1. Archaeologists could simply dismiss theories of the past that are based on spiritual beliefs in favour of

those that are based in science. Choosing this path, however, means further marginalizing the beliefs and cultural values of indigenous peoples.

2. Archaeologists could abandon the topic of North American prehistory altogether, and accept the rights of First Nations and Inuit to study their own past in their own way. However, excluding others from researching histories can sometimes lead to the misrepresentation of the facts, because individuals know that their interpretations cannot be contradicted. Examples of this include the distortions of history created by Nazis in Germany, and by Stalin in the Soviet Union.

3. Archaeologists can accept that the past can be shared and used in different ways. Within this view, the past can be used to maintain traditional values, provide people with a sense of their cultural identity, and used in a professional capacity to construct a scientific history that best fits the available facts.

McGhee sees the third option as the most promising. In later chapters, we explore how indigenous peoples trained as archaeologists are using both scientific and humanistic approaches to interpret the past.

would modify Jefferson's conclusions: Some mounds might have been defensive, but the majority were not, and there is no reason to attribute them to someone other than the ancestors of Indians.

The Myth Gains Momentum

Nonetheless, Jefferson did not come out strongly on either side of the Moundbuilder debate and, in 1799 (as president of the American Philosophical Society), he distributed a pamphlet calling for the systematic collection of information on the mounds. Others were not so silent. Ignoring the fact that conquest, racism, forced movements, poverty, and disease had forever altered Native American communities, 19th-century scholars were convinced that Indians were not capable of building the mounds. In 1820, Caleb Atwater reasoned in *Antiquities Discovered in the Western States* that, because living Indians had not buried their dead in mounds, or constructed earthworks, or made artifacts of metal, they could not possibly be the descendants of the Moundbuilders. Instead, Atwater attributed the mounds to Hindus. Josiah Priest came to a similar conclusion in his 1833 best seller, *American Antiquities and Discoveries in the West*.

Some of these scholars actually did dig into mounds, but it was not until 1848 that the systematic compilation that Jefferson desired finally appeared.

The Surveyor and the Doctor

Ephraim Squier (1821–1888) was a Connecticut civil engineer, surveyor, journalist, and, later in life, a politician intent on making a name for himself (he advocated the radical idea of building a canal across Central America). Like many educated people of the time his interests were wide ranging, but the Moundbuilders held a special fascination for him.

Edwin Davis (1811–1888) was an Ohio physician. He was intrigued by the mounds, especially those near his hometown of Chillicothe. Unlike Squier, he was content to live a calm life with his family near his hometown.

With Squier's ambition and Davis's money, the two gentlemen formed an alliance to study the mounds. Although the two came to dislike one another intensely, their names will forever be wed in American archaeology because of their 1848 monograph *Ancient Monuments of the Mississippi Valley*—the first publication by the newly formed Smithsonian Institution.

Squier and Davis claimed that they did not seek to "sustain" any particular hypothesis, but only "to arrive at truth" and to avoid "speculation." True to this intent, the book devotes its first 300 pages to meticulous description. Squier and Davis defined six kinds of earthworks: defensive enclosures, sacred enclosures (including effigy mounds), altar mounds, burial mounds, temple mounds, and "anomalous mounds." They based this classification on others' reports, as well as on their own investigations of some 200 sites, primarily in the Ohio River Valley. The volume contains more than 200 beautiful illustrations of artifacts, mound cross-sections, and maps of earthworks (like that shown in Figure 2-5). Squier embellished some of the maps—completing earthen walls that had been destroyed by erosion or making his circular and rectangular earthworks a bit neater than reality. Still, his survey work recorded some remarkable features. And since most of the sites have now been obliterated by the plow or have disappeared beneath cities, *Ancient Monuments* is archaeology's only record of them.

Only in the final pages of their monograph did Squier and Davis allow themselves to speculate. The Moundbuilder population, they wrote, "was numerous and widely spread" as was "evident from the number and magnitude of the ancient monuments and the extensive range of their occurrence." It was also homogeneous in customs and habits, and was "sustained by the great uniformity which the ancient remains display." They described the Moundbuilders as agricultural peoples because agriculture, they assumed, was necessary to a "large population, to fixedness of institutions, and to any considerable advance in the economical or ennobling arts."

Although Squier and Davis claimed no commitment to the Moundbuilder hypothesis, they nonetheless pointed out the differences between the Moundbuilders and American Indians. The art in the mounds, they claimed, was "immeasurably beyond anything which the North American Indians are known to produce." They saw differences in burial practices, skull form, warfare, and defensive structures. They even argued for a difference in subsistence, the Moundbuilders being agriculturalists, the Indians only hunters (despite the fact that they taught maize horticulture to the colonists).

In the end, Squier and Davis suggested that the Moundbuilders were related to the "semi-civilized"

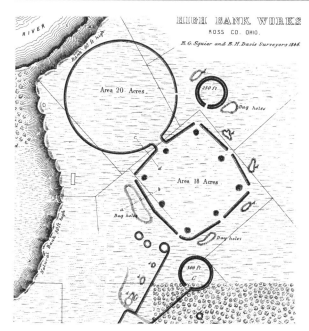

Figure 2-5 A portion of one of Squier and Davis's maps—showing a mound group in Ohio.

Source: From Squier, E. G. and Davis, E. H., (1848). *Ancient Monuments of the Mississippi Valley. Smithsonian Contributions to Knowledge, (1),* Washington, DC, 51.

nations of Mexico and Central America (such as the Aztecs), thus providing more fodder for supporters of the Moundbuilder hypothesis. By 1873, the president of the Chicago Academy of Sciences thought it "preposterous" that Indians could have built the mounds. And in his 1872 book, *Ancient America,* J. D. Baldwin considered any relationship between the Moundbuilders and Indians to be "absurd."

The Engineer and the Entomologist

During the Civil War, at the Battle of Shiloh, a young Union captain had raised his right arm to give an order to fire when a Confederate minie ball took it off at the elbow. A lesser man's career would have ended there, but John Wesley Powell (1834–1902) went on to explore the West, mount the first expedition down the Colorado River through the Grand Canyon, and hold several important posts in the federal government.

After the war, Powell's western explorations brought him into close personal contact with many Native Americans, an experience that many East Coast scholars could not claim. It is telling, then, that Powell held a different, and much higher, opinion of Indians.

Powell was intrigued by Native Americans and the evidence of their history. Before the Civil War, he had even tested a few mounds himself. (We wonder if those at Shiloh—one of which is pictured in the opening of this chapter—caught his eye.) He concluded that close ancestors of Native Americans had built the mounds, although he thought they had done so soon after European contact.

Powell found himself in a position to pursue the Moundbuilder issue when, in 1879, he became head of the newly formed Bureau of Ethnology (later the Bureau of American Ethnology, which was placed within the Smithsonian), as well as the U.S. Geological Survey. Because the Moundbuilder issue was of such public interest, Congress insisted that the Bureau of Ethnology spend $5000 a year—one-fifth of the Bureau's budget—on mound exploration. Powell looked for someone to head up the bureau's new division of mound studies and finally settled on Cyrus Thomas.

Born in Tennessee, Thomas (1825–1910) spent his early career as a lawyer and merchant, and then served as an entomologist for geographical surveys. He was Illinois state entomologist from 1874 to 1876 and a member of the U.S. Entomological Commission from 1874 to 1882. The study of insects may seem an odd background for an archaeologist but, as an educated man, Thomas was as qualified as any of his predecessors or contemporaries to do archaeology (recall that Nels Nelson, a member of the first trained generation of archaeologists, was born in 1875).

Through the Bureau of Ethnology, Thomas began his own program of survey and excavation. Over the next 12 years, and with the aid of local affiliates, he compiled data on some 2000 sites in 21 states, finally publishing a 700-page report in 1894. In the beginning, Thomas was a proponent of the Moundbuilder hypothesis. But unlike Squier and Davis, Thomas began with an explicit question: "Were the mounds built by the Indians?"

Thomas took each claim made previously as evidence of a separate Moundbuilder race and evaluated it. Did the Indians have the knowledge of moundbuilding? Thomas pointed out that earlier scholars overlooked Spanish and French explorers' reports that described mound construction and use in the southeastern United States (see Figure 2-6).

Figure 2-6 Mounds in use among southeastern Indians as illustrated in the account of Jacques Le Moyne, a 16th-century French explorer.

Source: Wiley, G., and J. Sabloff, 1980. *A History of American Archaeology*, 2nd ed. San Francisco: W. H. Freeman and Company

Was the Moundbuilder culture older than Indian culture? Thomas made an error here when he discounted some earlier efforts to date the mounds—for example, by counting the rings of trees growing on their tops—and concluded that the mounds had been built after European arrival.

What about those tablets inscribed with Hebrew or other scripts? Thomas showed that the circumstances of the discovery of each of these tablets made them all suspect; indeed, even Squier and Davis had written the tablets off as hoaxes (as indeed they were). And what about the copper objects? Indians had no smelting technology, but Thomas's examination of the artifacts led him to conclude (correctly) that the copper was a raw metal that is not smelted and is found naturally in the Great Lakes region. Mining and shaping such native copper required little more than a stone hammer.

Thomas quietly but definitively concluded that "the author believes the theory which attributes these works [the mounds] to the Indians to be the correct one." There was no lost race of Moundbuilders. They had not been overrun by Native Americans. There was no justification for Europeans to seek revenge. The myth that had helped perpetuate a racist attitude toward Native Americans was simply that—a myth.

inductive reasoning Working from specific observations to more general hypotheses.

Sadly, by 1894, the truth about the Moundbuilders had come too late. The Indian Wars were officially over, virtually all Native Americans were confined to reservations, and a change in racist attitudes toward Native Americans was still decades away.

The Scientific Method

The history of the Moundbuilder myth provides a simple example of some characteristics of the **scientific method,** which we can reduce to six simple steps:

1. Define a relevant problem.
2. Establish one or more hypotheses.
3. Determine the empirical implications of the hypotheses.
4. Collect appropriate data through observation and/or experimentation.
5. Test the hypothesis by comparing these data with the expected implications.
6. Reject, revise, and/or retest hypotheses as necessary.

We admit that this is an ideal process only, and in hindsight we can see that scientific research often does not proceed neatly through each of these steps—although that remains the goal of scientists today.

The Role of Inductive Reasoning

The first two tasks (Steps 1 and 2) are to define a relevant question and translate it into an appropriate hypothesis. The idea is to get beyond a simple description of the known facts and create a hypothesis to account for them. Such hypotheses are generated through **inductive reasoning,** or working from specific facts or observations to general conclusions. The facts as known serve as premises in this case; the hypothesis not only should account for the known facts but also should predict properties of as-yet-unobserved phenomena.

Unfortunately, no rules exist for induction (just as there are no rules for thinking up good ideas). Some hypotheses are derived by enumerating the data, isolating common features, and generalizing to unobserved cases that share these features. At other times, archaeologists turn to analogies, relatively well-understood ethnographies that seem to have relevance to poorly understood archaeological cases. Judgment, imagination, past experience, and even guesswork all have their place in science. It does not matter where or how one derives the hypothesis. What matters is how well the hypothesis accounts for unobserved phenomena.

It is, of course, entirely possible that several hypotheses apply to the same data. Scientists work their way systematically through the various possibilities, testing them one at a time. This method of **multiple working hypotheses** has long been a feature of scientific methods. Most scientists assume that the simplest hypothesis is the most likely to be correct (an idea referred to as "Occam's razor"). Thus, they begin with the simplest hypothesis and see how well it holds up against some new data. If it fails the test, scientists will then try the next least complicated hypothesis, and so on.

The Moundbuilder hypothesis was based in part on a set of facts and in part on cultural biases: 19th-century scholars could not reconcile what they found in mounds with what they knew of Native American culture. Squier and Davis (as well as Jefferson) were scientists in the tradition of Francis Bacon. They believed that when a sufficiently large number of facts were collected—when 200 mound sites were mapped and probed for artifacts—the meaning of those facts would become apparent. This is why Jefferson called for a systematic collection of data; he knew that too little was known even for the kind of legitimate speculation that could advance scholars to Step 2 in the process. In a sense, this means that 19th-century scholars jumped from Step 1 to Step 4. But such data collection is only the beginning of the scientific process.

Jefferson, Squier, and Davis worked in the inductive phase (Steps 1 and 2) of Moundbuilder research. Because no one knew much about the mounds, the first order of business was to gather some facts: How many mounds were there? What sort of variability was present among the mounds? What exactly was in the different types of mounds? How old were they? What were they made of? From these data, Squier and Davis inductively derived a conclusion: The living Indians of the United States were not descendants of the Mound-builders.

Science Is Self-Correcting

Squier and Davis, as it turned out, were completely wrong; but the beauty of the scientific method is that it is self-correcting. Science insists that we always ask: Do we really know what we think we know? Squier

and Davis thought they were at Step 6 in the process, but in hindsight we can see that they had only inductively formulated a hypothesis. It was left to others to test this idea, to take their conclusion and treat it as a hypothesis. This is how science sometimes proceeds, by backtracking and rethinking things that others thought was over and done with. And that was the case here. Even in Squier and Davis's day, other investigators found facts that contradicted their Mound-builder hypothesis. John Wesley Powell was one; Cyrus Thomas was another. Although Thomas never used the rhetoric of science, he was indeed testing Squier and Davis's hypothesis that Indians were not the descendants of the Moundbuilders.

How does one accomplish Steps 4 and 5—that is, test a hypothesis? Once a hypothesis is defined, the scientific method requires its translation into testable form. Hypotheses can never be tested directly because they are abstract statements. The key to verifying a hypothesis is simple: you don't. What you verify are the logical material consequences of hypotheses (the empirical implications established in Step 3).

Deductive reasoning is required to uncover these logical outcomes. A deductive argument is one for which the conclusions must be true, given that the premises are true. Such deductive arguments generally take the form of "if ... then" statements: If the hypothesis is true, then we will expect to observe the following outcomes. Bridging the gap from *if* to *then* is a tricky step.

In the "harder" sciences, these bridging arguments derive directly from known mathematical or physical properties. In astronomy, for instance, the position of "unknown" stars can be predicted using a chain of mathematical arguments grounded in physics. The classic deductive method begins with an untested hypothesis and converts the generalities into specific predictions based on established mathematical and/or physical theory. These are sometimes called **bridging arguments.**

multiple working hypotheses A set of hypotheses that are tested against the empirical record from the simplest to the most complex.

deductive reasoning Reasoning from theory to account for specific observational or experimental results.

bridging arguments Logical statements linking observations on the static archaeological record to the dynamic behaviour or natural processes that produced it.

But how do archaeologists bridge this gap? Where is the well-established body of theory that allows us to transform abstract hypotheses into observable predictions?

Although Thomas was never explicit about this, we can see in his reasoning the simple bridging arguments he employed for his version of Step 5. For example, *if* American Indians did not know about mound building, *then* there should be no explorer accounts of mound building by Indians (or evidence should be found that those people whom explorers observed building mounds were not Indians). Or, *if* the mounds were built by a long-vanished race, *then* they should be considerably older than the known age of Indian culture. And, *if* the metal artifacts in mounds were signs of a "superior" Moundbuilder culture, *then* the manufacturing technology associated with them should have been absent from later Indian culture. In doing this, Thomas laid out the criteria whereby he could claim the Moundbuilder hypothesis to be false. (We will return to a discussion of these bridging arguments in archaeology when we discuss middle-range research in Chapters 3 and 10.)

For Thomas, "testing" meant collecting data, analyzing it, publishing it, and openly evaluating it against the competing hypotheses. The **testability** of a hypothesis is critical. An idea is testable if the hypothesis' implications can be measured in some fashion *with the same results by different observers.* That is, the observation has to be independent of whoever is doing the observing. We have to know that you would make the same observations that we would make.

Science Is Reiterative

The process we have sketched out, commonly called the *scientific method,* is really more of a cycle because it is repetitive, as shown in Figure 2-7. Step 6 (testing, rejecting, or revising the hypothesis) normally leads back to Step 1 (redefining the problem at hand). Figure 2-7 shows the same process with more emphasis on the kinds of reasoning that researchers use to move through the steps.

Scientific cycles commence in the world of facts—in the Moundbuilder example, the amassed data from hundreds of excavations and maps plus contemporary accounts plus bogus artifacts. Through the process of induction, these facts are probed, and hypotheses are devised to account for what is already known. But because hypotheses are general declarations, they cannot be tested against further facts until they are translated into their logical consequences, through the judicious use of bridging arguments.

The scientific cycle thus begins and ends with facts. But these newly discovered facts themselves will suggest new hypotheses, and, once again, inductive reasoning will lead from the world of facts to the world of abstraction, initiating a new cycle of investigation. As a method, science implies a continual spiral in knowledge.

Scientific thinking applies at many different levels, from "small" questions such as, "What's this red stain in the soil?" or "What was this stone tool used for?" to "big" questions such as, "Why did humans switch from hunting and gathering to agriculture?" or "What is human nature?" Sometimes the cycle plays out over the course of a day, sometimes over the course of many lifetimes (as it did in the Moundbuilder controversy).

The scientific process is often not explicit. And since science is a human venture, it is subject to false starts, dead ends, preconceived notions, and cultural biases. A scientific approach does not always deliver the right answer on the first try or even the second or third. It tends to make halting, stumbling progress, often by taking two steps forward and one step back. Sometimes we can see what we have learned only in hindsight. But we generally find, in the end, that we have learned something. And that is what science is all about.

Science Is Not Infallible

Although philosophers of science rarely agree on many points, they do generally agree that (1) there is no single right way to do science, and (2) a scientific approach cannot guarantee truth. It is clear, for instance, that the Moundbuilder hypothesis was not drawn directly and inductively from sterile archaeological facts. This idea was widespread well before anyone knew much about the mounds because the myth facilitated and justified what colonists wanted all along—seizure of Indian land. Science is unavoidably embedded in the scientist's culture and hardly free of cultural biases. The social, cultural, and political context of archaeology influences its theories.

Because of these biases, some archaeologists reject scientific methods in archaeology. The argument often

testability The degree to which one's observations and experiments can be reproduced.

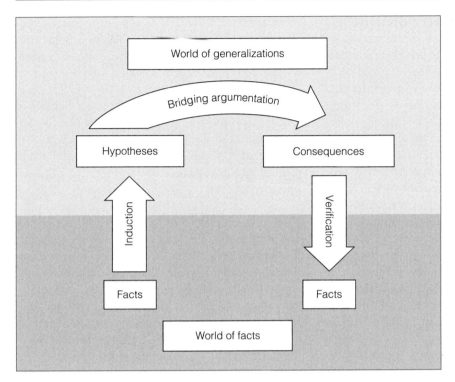

Figure 2-7 The scientific cycle.
Source: After Kemeny (1959:86)

goes like this: Because archaeology is not precise in the same sense as are the physical sciences, then the methods of science are inappropriate (or even harmful) when applied to the study of humans. Although these claims contain some truth, most blatant attacks on the scientific methods are directed at exaggerated caricatures that depict science as claiming infallibility (a claim rejected by even the most "scientific" of archaeologists).

Science offers no ironclad assurance that application of its methods will necessarily result in the absolute, final truth about anything; rather, scientists claim only that scientific methods provide a means to determine, more or less, whether the evidence favours the validity of a hypothesis. And, as we saw in the Moundbuilder example, careful, honest, scientific analysis can help reveal and shatter cultural biases and, indeed, arrive at the truth. Nonetheless, these observations about the nature of science have led some archaeologists to another approach.

What's a Humanistic Approach?

In general, **humanism** tends to emphasize the dignity and worth of the individual. Humanistic-style inquiry begins with the premise that all people possess a

capacity for self-realization through reason. Unlike the purely scientific approach, which stresses objectivity and independent testing, humanists believe that their scholarship should proceed in precisely the opposite direction: By stressing the intuitive and subjective, humanists seek strength and understanding in the very biases that science seeks to circumvent.

Virtually all modern archaeologists, whether "humanist" or "scientific," subscribe to the basics of science. All of us believe in careful scholarship, in generalizations backed by firm data, in honesty, and in giving full consideration to "negative" evidence (data that run contrary to a hypothesis' predictions).

But archaeologists are not emotionally or politically neutral data-gathering machines. Archaeologists will always make moral or ethical judgments about the past (and particularly about its use in the present). This occurs because archaeologists are "historically situated," meaning simply that archaeologists are products of the times in which they live. This is why

humanism A doctrine, attitude, or way of life that focuses on human interests and values. In general, a humanistic approach tends to reject a search for universals and stress instead the importance of the individual's lived experience.

many archaeologists bring a humanistic perspective to their understanding of the past and, in this section, we will see why most archaeologists are both scientists and humanists.

The primary distinction between scientific and humanistic approaches occurs over the issue of **objectivity.** If you believe that archaeology is "mostly objective," then you probably lean more toward the scientific side. You probably see a clear-cut separation between the observer and what is observed—the "facts" of archaeology. And you probably search for an inherent regularity to cultural behaviour (which you might term "laws"). You probably believe that the world out there can be known in a manner more or less independent of your ability to perceive and engage it. Finally, you likely are more inclined to take an adaptive perspective on human cultural behaviour, looking for explanations in factors that are "outside" the culture—that is, in the environment, in biology, in technology, or in demography.

But if you think that archaeology is "mostly subjective," then you likely are more comfortable with humanistic perspectives, which emphasize that the observer and the observed can never really be separated, that our knowledge of the past mostly depends on who is doing the observing. You probably mistrust conventional science and feel more comfortable with an ideational perspective. You may be more interested in empathetic approaches, more connected with what people think rather than with what they do. You are probably more intrigued by human languages, cultural values, and the artistic achievements of other cultures.

Humanistic Archaeology at a Dakota Village

We can explore the basics of humanistic perspectives in archaeology by looking at Janet Spector's study of a Dakota site in Minnesota.

Spector (retired, formerly a professor of anthropology at the University of Minnesota) is a specialist in the archaeology and ethnohistory of the Great Lakes region. Spector was interested in excavating a site that would allow her to examine the activities of men and women and that also would reveal the nature of early

contacts between the Dakota and Europeans. Eventually, she encountered the Little Rapids site in Minnesota, which had been occupied by the Eastern Dakota (or "Sioux"; see "Looking Closer: Sioux or Dakota?") sometime in the early to middle 1800s. Spector decided to work there because a number of documentary sources that depicted life at sites like Little Rapids (shown in Figure 2-8) could help with interpretation of the site; likewise, the site could supplement the information contained in the historical documents.

Involving Dakota People in Dakota Archaeology

The work at the Little Rapids site was done according to standard archaeological procedures: In her excavation and analysis, Spector was a scientist. But as she wrote her site report, she felt something was lacking. She came to realize that, as a relatively privileged non-Indian university professor, she was in danger of doing something that had bothered her for years: Inadvertently, she was excluding exactly the people she wished to learn about.

Once she recognized the problem, Spector began talking to Dakota people. Initially, she encountered some resentment toward the "anthros," as the Indians called them; throughout Indian Country, many Native American people question whether archaeologists can really be trusted. But after months of discussion and site visits, Spector enlisted several Dakota people to help her understand the archaeology of their ancestral site. Excavations began again at Little Rapids, this time with the hands-on participation of members of the Wahpeton Dakota community.

Figure 2-8 Dakota village (engraving by Seth Eastman, 1853).
Source: American Museum of Natural History

objectivity The attempt to observe things as they actually are, without prejudging or falsifying observations in light of some preconceived view of the world—reducing subjective factors to a minimum.

NEL

Tribal members helped by providing Dakota names for various plants and animals, and some crew members learned the rudiments of the Dakota language as they dug. During lunchtime, Dakota people led discussions about their culture and history. On Fridays, the project historian helped the groups work through the strengths and limitations of the available documentary evidence. "For the first time in my archaeological career," Spector wrote, "a project felt right. We worked as an interdisciplinary, multicultural team."

The dig proceeded in a standard scientific fashion, and the crew fell into the rhythm typical of all digs. Arrive early, split into small teams, dig, write notes. Get together at lunch and talk about the finds. Work all afternoon digging or doing labwork, then finally knock off for the day.

But Spector came to see archaeology in a different light. Although she continued to dig according to standard scientific procedures, the style of her archaeology changed. Spector found herself trying to transcend the detail of the archaeological and written records. "I sometimes imagine being transported into the past by a bilingual, bicultural, bi-temporal guide— a Dakota person willing and able to explain to me his or her view of the area's politics, tensions, and interactions." She encouraged students to speculate about what had taken place on this or that part of the site, why artifacts had been left where they were found, how the 19th-century Dakota people felt living there: "Did they watch the darkening skies some days as we did, hoping to finish our work before a thunderstorm struck? Was their community life, like ours, punctuated by summer romances and interpersonal tensions, or were such relationships a product of our particular time and place only?"

Eventually, Spector located a part of the site that she had interpreted as a dance area. After some excavation there, Spector's team applied for permission from the Minnesota Intertribal Board for further testing in the suspected dance area. A non-Dakota Indian board member objected strongly. Spector found that "to them, a dance area—even a suspected one—was sacred and, like a burial place, should not be disturbed." Respecting these views, Spector shifted the excavation. More and more, archaeologists are conflicted by episodes like this. Spector noted: "Do I wish we might have had a chance to follow these tantalizing leads? Yes. Would I knowingly dig in sacred areas? No."

Archaeology in the Active Voice

When it came time to publish the results, Spector wrestled with the meaning of what she had found. Although conducted according to standard scientific procedures, the Little Rapids project had also been strongly conditioned by Spector's changing perceptions of archaeology. The dig itself was part of the story, and so was the world around it.

In the fall of 1991, as Spector was writing up the Little Rapids materials, the Atlanta Braves baseball team made it to the World Series. Three months later, professional football's Washington Redskins played in the Super Bowl. That year, Indian people across the country protested the use of Indian images as sports

Looking Closer
Sioux or Dakota?

The term "Sioux" (pronounced "sue") is French pronunciation of a fragment of the Ojibwa word "nadoweisiw-eg." This name is a derogatory term, meaning "little snakes," and implies "enemy." The Chippewa used it to refer to their western "Sioux" neighbours (and to distinguish them from the Iroquois, who were the "true snakes," or major enemy). Although "Sioux" remains in common use, many contemporary tribal members resent its use and prefer the more specific, indigenous terms "Dakota," "Nakota," and "Lakota," which refer to three mutually intelligible dialects of the "Dakota Sioux" language.

In Her Own Words
What This Awl Means

by Janet Spector

The women and children of Inyan Ceyaka Aton-wan (Little Rapids) had been working at the maple sugar camps since Istawicayazan wi (the Moon of Sore Eyes, or March). At the same time, most of the men had been far from the village trapping muskrats. When Wozupi wi (the Moon for Planting, or May) came, fifteen households eagerly reunited in their bark lodges near the river. . . .

One day some villagers brought their tanned furs and maple sugar to the lodge of Jean Baptiste Faribault. He lived among them a few months each year with his Dakota wife, Pelagie. In exchange for furs and maple sugar, Faribault gave them glass beads, silver ornaments, tin kettles, and iron knives, awl tips, axes, hatchets, and hoes for their summer work. . . .

Mazomani (Iron Walker) and Hazawin (Blueberry Woman) were proud of their daughter, Mazaokiyewin (Woman Who Talks to Iron). The day after visiting Faribault, they had given her some glass beads and a new iron awl tip. The tip was the right size to fit into the small antler handle that Hazawin had given Mazaokiyewin when she went to dwell alone at the time of her first menses. Mazaokiyewin used the sharp-pointed awl for punching holes in pieces of leather before stitching them together with deer sinew. Though young, she had already established a reputation among the people at Inyan Ceyaka Aton-wan for creativity and excellence in quillwork and beadwork.

Mazaokiyewin's mother and grandmothers had taught her to keep a careful record of her accom-plishments, so whenever she finished quilling or beading moccasins, she remembered to impress a small dot on the fine awl handle that Hazawin had made for her. When Mazaokiyewin completed more complicated work, such as sewing and decorating a buckskin dress or pipe bag, she formed diamond-shaped clusters of four small dots which symbolized the powers of the four directions that influenced her life in many ways. She liked to expose the handle of this small tool as she carried it in its beaded case so that others could see she was doing her best to ensure the well-being of their community.

When she engraved the dots into her awl handle, she carefully marked each one with red pigment, made by boiling sumac berries with a small root found in the ground near the village. Dakota people associated the color red with women and their life forces. Red also represented the east, where the sun rose to give knowledge, wisdom, and understanding. Red symbolized Mazaokiyewin's aspirations to these qualities.

When the designated day in Wasuton wi arrived, Mazomani led the people in the medicine dance near the burial place of their ancestors. Members of the medicine lodge danced within an enclosed oval area, separated from the audience by a low, hide-covered fence. . . .

One hot day following the dance, Mazaokiyewin gathered together all of the leatherwork she had finished since returning to Inyan Ceyaka Atonwan after the spring hunting and sugaring seasons. . . .

mascots, highlighting tensions between themselves and the dominant Euroamerican community. To Spector, this was a repetition—150 years later—of the initial confrontation between Indians and Euro-peans evident in the archaeological record at Little Rapids.

Maybe if the American public knew more about Indian cultural roots and sensibilities, she thought, they would better understand why being consid-ered a sports mascot is so offensive to Indian peo-ple, why so many Native Americans object to the way movies, television, and pop culture portray them.

Spector felt a growing need to communicate with others what she had learned about this abandoned Dakota site. She wanted to highlight women's activi-

Now, Mazaokiyewin eagerly anticipated the quilling contest and feast called by a woman of a neighboring household to honor a family member. Mazaokiyewin knew she had produced more beaded and quilled articles than most of the community's young women, and she looked forward to bringing recognition to her parents and grandparents. . . .

She started uphill carrying the miniapahatapi (skin water bags) carefully, but near the quilling-contest lodge she slipped on the muddy path where water had pooled in the driving rain. As she struggled to regain her footing without dropping the bags, the leather strap holding her awl in its case broke, and the small awl dropped to the ground. It fell close to one of the cooking fires outside the lodge entrance.

Mazaokiyewin did not miss her awl that day, because as soon as she entered the lodge with the water, the host of the contest took her hand and escorted her to the center of the crowd. The host had already counted each woman's pieces and distributed a stick for each. Mazaokiyewin had accumulated more sticks than all but three older women. The host then led the four to the place of honor in the lodge and gave them their food first to honor their accomplishments. Later, the results of this contest would be recorded for all to see on the hides lining the walls of the lodge. This pleased Hazawin and Mazomani.

The heavy rain that day had scattered debris over the village, and on the day after the quilling contest and medicine dance, people joined together to clean up the encampment. Using old hides and baskets, they carried off loads of fallen branches, wet fire ash and charcoal, and the remains of the feast to the community dump above the slough. Somehow, Mazaokiyewin's small awl was swept up and carried off with other garbage from the quilling contest. It disappeared in the dump as the villagers emptied one basketload after another on top of it.

Later, the loss of the awl saddened Mazaokiyewin and Hazawin, but they knew the handle was nearly worn out, and both realized it was more a girl's tool than a woman's. Mazaokiyewin was almost a woman ready to establish her own household, no longer a child of her mother's lodge. It was time to put aside her girl-tools, she knew, but she had intended to keep this awl. Its finely incised dots and engraved lines showed how well she had learned adult tasks, and she took as much pleasure in displaying it as her mother did in watching others admire it. . . .

The following day, they packed the equipment that the family would need over the next several months. As they assembled their hide-working tools, they spoke again of Mazaokiyewin's missing awl. They realized that their feeling of loss was not simply about that one small tool. Instead, as fall approached and they prepared to leave Inyan Ceyaka Atonwan, they had troubling premonitions about the future.

Source: Janet D. Spector, *What This Awl Means: Feminist Archaeology at a Wahpeton Dakota Village.* (1993). St. Paul: Minnesota Historical Society Press. 19–29. Used with permission.

ties and the relationship between men and women, but she also wanted to draw Dakota voices and perspectives into her story.

One particular find captured her imagination: the deer antler handle of an awl, and its iron tip found nearby (shown reassembled in Figure 2-9). From her ethnohistoric research, Spector knew that 19th-century Dakota women used such awls for working hides into moccasins, bags, and clothing. Although buried for more than a century, this particular awl was remarkably well preserved, with traces of red pigment still evident in the decorations along the edge. Because it was not broken or worn out, Spector felt that someone must have lost it, rather than deliberately thrown it away. She became intrigued with the woman who once had owned it.

Figure 2-9 The awl from Little Rapids.
Source: American Museum of Natural History, drawing by Diana Salles

This simple yet elegant artifact symbolized for Spector what she was learning by doing archaeology at Little Rapids. She was concerned that the strictly scientific, "lifeless" format of the standard archaeological report failed to communicate much about the people who had lived at Little Rapids, and she sought another way to convey what she had learned from the site.

The answer came in describing the awl.

From her archival reading, Spector learned that Dakota women kept count of their accomplishments on their implements in the way that men kept war records. In their ambition to excel, women recorded the number of robes and tipis they completed by incising dots along the handles of their elk antler tools. For Spector, such a realization "provided a kind of access to the people at Little Rapids that [she] had never before imagined possible," and this had an effect on how she finally decided to describe the awl.

Archaeologists, of course, describe things all the time. Using the standard archaeological typologies and language, such awls would be grouped into a series of carefully defined, objective categories according to size, material, shape, and so on. Spector had done such classifications many times. But she gradually realized that bland, impersonal typologies did not describe Native American life in the way that she wanted to, for they minimized the role of actual living, breathing people.

So Spector took a different approach. She wrote an imaginative reconstruction of Mazaokiyewin, the young Dakota woman who Spector envisioned as the owner of the awl—which was lost in a rainstorm and later swept up and discarded in the dump (see "In Her Own Words: What This Awl Means" by Janet Spector). Although Spector made up the specific circumstances about the awl, Mazaokiyewin was a real person (a grandmother of one of the Dakota women who worked on the excavation). Such narratives, though uncommon, are one way of injecting more humanistic perspectives into archaeology, of trying to see things in a different light—specifically, from that of the Dakota, rather than the Euroamerican perspective.

Conclusion: Scientist or Humanist?

So, should Americanist archaeology declare a preference for a scientific or humanistic perspective? Archaeologist Steve Lekson (University of Colorado) sees it this way: "I divide scientific and humanistic approaches by method: scientific approaches build knowledge that is external and cumulative while humanist approaches seek knowledge that is internal and historical. The former depersonalizes, the latter is highly personal. The two are compatible and co-exist in each of us—think of Leonardo da Vinci, artist and scientist."

When archaeologists wish to seek and understand patterns and regularities in prehistoric cultures, they are scientists. When they wish to understand the history and culture of particular past societies, they are humanists. When archaeologists wish to test their ideas about the past, they are scientists. When they wish to present their results in a way that will be meaningful to the public, they are humanists. So archaeologists will be more one than the other, at different times, depending on their objective.

But there is more. We noted earlier that cultures have their own unique views of the world. We also pointed out that a hallmark of science is its ability to correct itself, to ask if the current "view" of the world is correct. Where do we get new ideas, new thoughts, new insights? One place is through other cultures: By taking humanistic approaches that ask us to step into another culture's shoes and see the world differently, we discover new ideas, new insights, and new ways of understanding the past. This is why a humanistic approach is critical to a scientific approach.

But at the same time, the scientific method is critical for checking whether the conclusions derived from humanistic approaches are correct. A humanistic approach is good at generating ideas, but it is less useful for testing those ideas; that's where science comes in. Good archaeologists know that they need a humanist in their hearts, and a scientist in their hands.

Summary

- Anthropologists believe that a true understanding of humankind can arise only from a comparative and holistic perspective.

- Biological anthropology views people as biological organisms, focusing on human evolution and diversity in human biology.

- Cultural anthropology is interested in understanding variation in traditions, customs, religion, kinship—the non–biologically driven components of human behaviour.

- Linguistic anthropology focuses on variation in the specific cultural behaviour of language, looking at the historical development of language, the relationship between language and thought, and the evolution of sound systems.

- Archaeology can be thought of as a branch of cultural anthropology, but it is primarily concerned with using past societies to further document the range of human cultural behaviour and with understanding how human societies change over time.

- Culture unifies these diverse fields. Culture is a learned, shared, and symbolically based system of knowledge that includes traditions, kinship, language, religion, customs, and beliefs.

- Two major strategies of research characterize contemporary anthropological thinking: The ideational perspective deals with mentalistic, symbolic, cognitive culture; it sees culture as primarily an instrument to create meaning and order in one's world. The adaptive perspective emphasizes those aspects of culture that most closely articulate with the environment, technology, and economics, and sees culture as the way that humans adapt to their natural and social environment.

- Archaeologists draw upon both ideational and adaptive perspectives, and no single anthropological school dominates contemporary archaeology.

- For more than a century, archaeology has been firmly grounded in a scientific perspective, which provides an elegant and powerful way of allowing people to understand the workings of the visible world. The goal of science is to develop ideas that can be criticized, evaluated, and eventually modified or replaced by ideas that explain the archaeological data better.

- Scientific ideas must be testable; hypotheses must predict consequences that are measurable in the material world.

- All archaeologists believe in certain scientific fundamentals: in honest and careful scholarship, in generalizations backed by firm data, and in full disclosure and consideration of evidence that runs contrary to a hypothesis.

- Many archaeologists also believe in humanistic approaches—those that incline archaeologists to look for holistic syntheses of the cultural patterns of the past, for the role of the individual, for the feelings and thoughts of the long dead.

- For decades, archaeologists have prided themselves on their ability to straddle the fence between scientific and humanistic perspectives.

Additional Reading

CANADIAN RESOURCES

McGhee, Robert. (2004). Between Racism and Romanticism, Scientism and Spiritualism: The Dilemmas of New World Archaeology. In *Archaeology on the Edge, New Perspectives from the Northern Plains,* Brian Kooyman and Jane Kelley (Eds). Occasional Paper No. 4. Calgary: Canadian Archaeological Association.

Wylie, A. (2002). *Thinking from Things: Essays in the Philosophy of Archaeology.* Berkeley: University of California Press.

OTHER RESOURCES

Harris, Marvin. (1968). *The Rise of Anthropological Theory.* New York: Thomas Y. Crowell.

Horgan, John. (1996). *The End of Science: Facing the Limits of Knowledge in the Twilight of the Scientific Age.* Reading, MA: Addison-Wesley.

Kuznar, Lawrence. (1997). *Reclaiming a Scientific Anthropology.* Walnut Creek, CA: Altamira.

Mcgee, R. Jon and Williams, Richard L. (2004). *Anthropological Theory: An Introductory History.* (3rd ed). New York: McGraw Hill.

Watson, Patty Jo. (1995). Archaeology, anthropology, and the culture concept. *American Anthropologist 97,* 683–694.

Online Resources

Visit *http://www.sshrc-crsh.gc.ca/* to learn about the Social Sciences and Humanities Research Council of Canada, and the Canadian researchers and institutions it currently funds.

COMPANION WEBSITE

Visit *http://www.archaeology1ce.nelson.com* to access a wide range of material to help you succeed in your introductory archaeology course. These include flashcards, Internet exercises, Web links, and practice quizzes.

RESEARCH ONLINE WITH INFOTRAC COLLEGE EDITION

From the Student Companion website, you can access the InfoTrac College Edition database, which offers thousands of full-length articles for your research.

3   The Structure of Archaeological Inquiry

Archaeologists conduct excavations
on the shores of Lake
Minnewanka, Banff, Alberta.
Source: Courtesy of FMA Heritage Resources
Consultants Inc.

Preview

T his chapter sets out the theoretical baseline for the rest of the book, as follows:

- Theory at the middle level is what links these archaeological data to human behaviour. Sometimes archaeologists generate these links by conducting controlled experiments, sometimes by observing living peoples to see how behaviour is translated into the archaeological record.
- High-level (or "general") theory aims to answer larger "why" questions.
- Paradigms provide the overarching frameworks for understanding the human condition.

We conclude the chapter by showing how these various concepts fit together into a model of archaeological inquiry.

Paradigms apply to all intellectual inquiry about human beings; it is not restricted to archaeology. We will concentrate on two kinds of paradigms—cultural materialism and postmodernism—to see how these paradigms translate into research strategies that archaeologists pursue. We understand that many students are put off by obscure discussions of various "-ologies" and "-isms," but it's important that you understand these basic theoretical points. We'll try to minimize the jargon; in the coming chapters, we think you'll recognize the importance of understanding these basic theoretical concepts.

Introduction

We all use the term **theory** in a number of different ways. In the more casual, popular usage, a theory is simply an idea. Sometimes "theory" is a put-down, referring to an untested explanation that the speaker believes to be clearly false. For example, some might speak of Erich Von Dähniken's goofy *Chariots of the Gods* "theory," in which he argues that major accomplishments in prehistory, such as construction of the

pyramids, were performed or directed by extraterrestrial beings.

A theory may also be a set of untested principles or propositions—in other words, theory as opposed to practice. Thus a new invention to harness solar energy might work "in theory" (that is, on paper), but would require extensive field testing before one could decide whether it was a successful design. If the solar device functioned as expected, the theory would be valid; if the device failed, scientists would consider the theory behind it invalid.

Although both usages are common, neither has much to do with scientific theories, which are statements that purport to explain observed, empirical

---

theory An explanation for observed, empirical phenomena. It is empirical and seeks to explain the relationships between variables; it is an answer to a "why" question.

---

phenomena. Theories are answers to "why" questions. These questions occur at different levels; we will call them low-level, middle-level, and high-level. We distinguish the different levels not by complexity or difficulty, but by their functions in the process of archaeological inquiry.

Low-level theories help make the observations that emerge from hands-on archaeological fieldwork. Although you may be accustomed to thinking of such observations as self-evident data or facts, we will see why even the baseline facts of archaeology are themselves really the results of theories.

Middle-level theory (or, more commonly, "middle-range theory") links archaeological data with the relevant aspects of human behaviour or natural processes (for example, the actions of water or animals) that produced them. This is the unique realm of archaeology because it moves from the archaeologically observable (the "facts") to the archaeologically invisible (human behaviour, cultural beliefs, or natural processes of the past). Here the archaeologist answers questions such as, "*Why* do we think that this stone tool was used for scraping wood (and not hides)?" or "*Why* do we know that these bones came from an animal hunted and butchered by humans, and not killed and eaten by lions?"

Then there is **high-level (or general) theory,** which seeks answers to larger "why" questions, such as *why* did hunter-gatherers become agriculturalists? *Why* do some societies fight whereas others cooperate? *Why* did some societies evolve stratified social and political systems whereas others remained egalitarian? These are the sorts of questions that we really wish to answer; they are the reason we do archaeology. Low-level and middle-level theories are steps toward the creation of high-level theory.

We also need the concept of **paradigm,** which provides the overarching framework for understanding some research problem (in our case, the human condition). Paradigms are not specific to archaeology, but apply to intellectual inquiry in general. A paradigm is a lot like "culture" because (as we explained in Chapter 2) just as culture provides you with some idea about what is (or is not) acceptable behaviour, a paradigm also guides a researcher's path of inquiry. Your paradigm defines what will or will not be an interesting question. Paradigms also define what will (or will

not) be acceptable data by drawing our attention to some facts and blinding us to others. In so doing, paradigms not only define questions, but also direct a researcher to particular answers. In this chapter, we will introduce two major research paradigms in Americanist archaeology.

Levels of Theory

Before we can explore these different levels of theory and paradigms in more detail, we must first address the concept of data. Although many may think of data as a straightforward concept—scientists collect data and then explain them—data are actually much more complex. Data do not lie out there waiting for us to pick them up like Easter eggs on the lawn (as James Ford—introduced in Chapter 1—used to say). In fact, data are as dependent on theory as theory is on data.

What Are Data?

Low-level archaeological theory defines what constitutes archaeological data. But what, exactly, are archaeological data? To answer this question, we will introduce an archaeological site that crops up later in this text.

Gatecliff Shelter is a prehistoric **rockshelter** in Nevada where people camped now and again beneath a shallow overhang over a period of some 7000 years (Figure 3-1). Thomas found Gatecliff in 1970, and he worked there with an interdisciplinary team that, throughout the 1970s, excavated the deposits in the shelter.

---

low-level theories The observations and interpretations that emerge from hands-on archaeological field and labwork.

middle-level (or middle-range) theory Hypothesis that links archaeological observations with the human behaviour or natural processes that produced them.

high-level (or general) theory Theory that seeks to answer large "why" questions.

paradigm The overarching framework, often unstated, for understanding a research problem. It is a researcher's "culture."

rockshelter A common type of archaeological site, consisting of a rock overhang that is deep enough to provide shelter but not deep enough to be called a cave (technically speaking, a cave must have an area of perpetual darkness).

Figure 3-1 Gatecliff Shelter, late in the excavation: removing deposits through a bucket brigade method.

Source: American Museum of Natural History, photo by Dennis O'Brien

Gatecliff was discovered by old-fashioned, dogged fieldwork (see Chapter 4 to find out how). The excavation was "vertical"—in some places nearly 12 metres deep, with cultural deposits stacked up within a floor area of about 28 square metres. Buried within Gatecliff Shelter were thousands of cultural objects— that is, artifacts: projectile points made of chipped stone, bone awls, basketry made of willow splints, grinding stones, small pieces of slate incised with enigmatic geometric designs, woven sagebrush bark mats, stone scrapers, shells and turquoise used as

ornaments. Gatecliff also contained objects not made by humans—**ecofacts**—which are items relating to the natural environment, such as bighorn sheep bones, charcoal, piñon nut hulls, and pollen. We also encountered **features**—pits, hearths, rodent burrows—which are cultural and non-cultural things that archaeologists measure, draw, photograph, and sample, but that they cannot take home in a bag.

The point here is simple but important: After nearly a decade of excavating at Gatecliff, Thomas excavated no data at all. Why would any right-thinking archaeologist waste a decade digging holes that produce no archaeological data?

Thomas found no data at Gatecliff because archaeologists do not excavate data. Rather, they excavate objects. **Data** are *observations made on those objects.* Those observations are critical to making *interpretations* of the objects. Observations answer one or more questions that will permit the archaeologists to make interpretations: Is this grubby little black thing a piece of pottery? To answer that question, we need to ask if it contains the characteristics of pottery: Does it contain clay and temper (material added to the clay to give it strength)? Does it look as though it had been fired (heated)? If the answers are yes, then we "interpret" the grubby little black thing to be a piece of pottery.

Cleaning this piece of pottery off, we might observe that the convex surface (the pot's outer surface) is covered with white paint, with remnants of a black design on top of the white paint. This observation might allow us to further "interpret" the piece as belonging to a particular kind of pottery, perhaps one called Chupadero Black-on-white (a kind of pottery found in the American Southwest).

ecofact Plant or animal remains found in an archaeological site.

feature The nonportable evidence of technology; usually fire hearths, architectural elements, artifact clusters, garbage pits, soil stains, and so on.

data Relevant observations made on objects that then serve as the basis for study and discussion.

Likewise, we might look at a small black circle of earth that we've just uncovered, make observations on its properties (its diameter, depth, and fill), and interpret it, depending on the exact observations, as nothing more than a filled-in rodent burrow or, alternatively, as an ancient posthole, filled with the decayed remains of a post.

Data, therefore, are observations that allow us to make interpretations. They tell us *why* something is what we think it is. And this means that the observations we make on objects, as well as the interpretations of those observations, *are all theory-driven*. This is why it is important to understand the different levels of theory in archaeology.

Low-Level Theory

Low-level theory begins with archaeological objects; it then generates some relevant facts or data about those objects. Some data consist of physical observations. For example, "Artifact 20.2/4683 is (a) made of obsidian, (b) 21.5 mm long, and (c) weighs 2.1 grams." This statement contains three pieces of data—observations made on an archaeological object (the number 20.2/4683 is the item's unique catalog number for identification—more on that in a later chapter). Other observations might be contextual: "Artifact 20.2/4683 was found in unit B-5, 56 cm below the surface." Why are these theoretical statements? Because each of them is actually based on a "why" question: Why do we know that something is obsidian? Because the stone has certain characteristics that fit a definition of obsidian (a dark volcanic glass) and that clearly differentiate it from other stone types, such as chert or quartzite. Why do we know the length, weight, and provenience? Because these measurements were made using digital instruments whose ability to measure things reliably is based on theories from the field of electronics.

Another example: While excavating, a student comes upon a curving red band in the sediment. On the concave side of the red band are some black flecks that turn out to be charcoal. The student calls to her crew chief, "I've got a hearth over here!" How did she know it was a hearth? The charcoal was a clue, but archaeological sites often contain scattered charcoal.

This student apparently knows that sufficient heat has a predictable effect on sediments with high iron content: The iron is oxidized (bonded with oxygen) and turns red. She may be unaware of the theory that accounts for the oxidation and colour change, just as someone making measurements may be unaware of the theory of electronics that permits them to measure a projectile point's length with a digital caliper. But both of these observations are nonetheless based on theories. Likewise, the ability to identify an animal bone as bison rather than deer, or as a femur rather than a humerus, is based on evolutionary theory.

We refer to this area of archaeology as "low-level" theory, not because it is simple or unimportant (indeed, evolutionary theory is anything but simple and is incredibly important to many fields), but because archaeologists normally give little thought to the theories that stand behind basic observations such as those we've described here. We record that we found something—a hearth or bison femur—without presenting the geochemical or evolutionary theory that gives us the ability to identify something as a hearth or a bison bone.

We can make an infinite number of observations on any single archaeological object. Many of these are made on the object itself: length, width, thickness, weight, angle measurements, material, colour, curvature, chemical composition, manufacturing techniques, and so forth. Others might be observations on the object's context; that is, where it was found in a site. Overall, the important dimensions of low-level theory are the classical ones in archaeology: form and context.

Low-level theory is critical because it allows archaeologists to know that their data are comparable. However, these basic observations can become the focus of scrutiny if, for instance, archaeologists try to determine when humans began to use fire intentionally (perhaps some hundreds of thousands of years ago). In this case, what constitutes an *intentional* hearth becomes of more than passing interest. The same is true when archaeologists try to determine whether some chipped stones are tools or simply rocks that Mother Nature has broken in fortuitous ways (more than one archaeologist has been fooled). When archaeologists give this sort of attention to inferences made from observations, they move into the realm of middle-level theory.

Middle-Level Theory

Archaeological theory at the middle level links some specific set of archaeological data with the relevant aspects of human behaviour or natural processes that produced them. At this middle level, we make a critical transition by moving from the archaeologically observable (the low-level theoretical facts) to the archaeologically invisible (relevant human behaviours or natural processes of the past). How, you might wonder, does this transition actually take place?

First, remember that the archaeological record is the *contemporary* evidence left by people of the past. Strictly speaking, the archaeological record is composed only of static objects—the artifacts, ecofacts, and features that have survived the passage of time. Those objects are the products of two things: human behaviour and natural processes. Our job is to infer the long-gone behaviour and processes from the static results—the objects we recover from archaeological sites. For example, Figure 3-2 shows a large scatter of bison bone at a site in Wyoming. All that the archaeologist can record is the kind of bones that are present and their arrangement. But how does the archaeologist infer from these observations whether people killed these bison? (You may think the answer is straightforward but, in Chapter 10, we will show you that it is not.)

Archaeologists conducting research at the middle level seek situations in which they can observe (1) ongoing human behaviour or natural processes and (2) the material results of that behaviour or those processes. This requires that archaeologists step out of their excavation trenches and turn to experimental archaeology, ethnoarchaeology, or taphonomy. We'll discuss these fields in much more detail in Chapter 10. For now, we will briefly introduce them, so that you can see how they contribute to the goal of inferring behaviour and natural processes from archaeological remains.

In **experimental archaeology**, we use controlled experiments to determine the effect of one archaeologically invisible variable on an archaeologically observable one. For example, archaeologists sometimes conduct controlled experiments in which they manufacture their own stone tools. In doing so, they study specific stoneworking techniques (which are

Figure 3-2 The Horner site in Wyoming. The bones are those of dozens of bison: How would we know if these animals had been hunted?

Source: University of Wyoming, Frison Institute

obviously not directly visible archaeologically) to learn how different tool manufacturing methods are translated into archaeologically observable evidence (such as flaking scars, breakage patterns, and by-products). For similar reasons, archaeologists conduct intensive studies of pottery manufacture, house-construction methods, ancient agricultural technologies, and hunting and gathering techniques, to name but a few areas.

Some archaeologists conduct middle-level research as **ethnoarchaeology**, in which they observe ongoing, present-day societies (as shown in Figure 3-3) to see how behaviour translates into the archaeological record. Research with living hunter-gatherers, for instance, shows that people butcher animals in different ways depending on several variables, such as the size of the animal, the distance from the kill site back to the camp, the number of people available to carry the meat, and so forth. Under some conditions, hunter-gatherers may bring the entire carcass back to camp. Under other conditions, they may leave some of the less-useful portions behind; and sometimes they return with only the meat, leaving all the bones behind. Such behaviours result in distinctly different arrangements and assortments of bones left at the kill

experimental archaeology Experiments designed to determine the archaeological correlates of ancient behaviour; may overlap with both ethnoarchaeology and taphonomy.

ethnoarchaeology The study of contemporary peoples to determine how human behaviour is translated into the archaeological record.

Figure 3-3 Kelly (in middle) conducting ethnoarchaeological research in Madagascar.

Source: Robert Kelly, photo by Jim Yount

sites and at the residential camps. Such patterns give archaeologists tools with which to interpret the animal remains in archaeological sites.

Taphonomy studies the role that natural processes play in the formation of an archaeological site. This includes the effects of climate, rivers, soil formation, plants, and animals on archaeological sites. The aim is to distinguish the patterns caused by natural processes from those produced by human behaviour. Humans butcher animals that they kill, for instance, but carnivores also kill animals; other animals die of old age and are eaten by scavengers, or simply decay. To tell the difference between bones resulting from these different processes, we need to understand not only how hunter-gatherers butcher game, but also how carnivores consume a carcass, how carcasses decompose, and how natural factors, a river for example, affect a carcass.

High-Level Theory

High-level (or general) theory is archaeology's ultimate objective; low- and middle-level research are necessary steps to attain this goal. High-level theory goes beyond the archaeological specifics to address the "big questions" of concern to many social and historical sciences. High-level theory applies to all intellectual inquiry about the human condition, raising questions such as: Why did we humans become cultural animals? Why did hunter-gatherers become agriculturalists? Why did social stratification arise? Why did human history take the particular course it did in the New World as opposed to the Old World? Why did aboriginal hunter-gatherers in California not take up agriculture? Why did large civilizations develop in some parts of the world and not in others?

Some general theories stress environmental adaptation, some emphasize biological factors, and some involve only cultural causality; others try to combine these. In Chapter 15, we will look at some of the general theories that archaeologists have offered as answers to some big questions.

Paradigms

Paradigms provide the overarching framework for understanding "how the world works" that each researcher brings to a particular question or problem. This is the most abstract and yet the most important of our concepts.

As we said above, paradigms are a lot like culture—both are learned, shared, and symbolic. Archaeologists sharing the same paradigm can converse with one another and leave a lot unstated; an archaeologist following another paradigm might have to ask many questions, seeking definitions of basic concepts and terms. Like culture, your paradigm influences how you view humanity, how you frame your questions about the present and the past, and how you interpret the answers that you receive to these questions. It consists of some *a priori* notions of which variables are

taphonomy The study of how organisms become part of the fossil record; in archaeology it primarily refers to the study of how natural processes produce patterning in archaeological data.

Looking Closer
Maggots, Moose Bone, and Middle-Range Research

 As an undergraduate student at the University of Toronto, Dawson assisted Dr. Max Friesen (University of Toronto), then a Master's student at the same institution, with an unforgettable experiment in taphonomy. At the time, Friesen was interested in seeing if it was possible to identify different agents of bone breakage within an assemblage of mammoth bone, recovered from the controversial site of Old Crow, in Yukon Territory. Dr. William Irving, the site's principal investigator, had always maintained the bones had been broken through human agency. As the site had originally been radiocarbon-dated to somewhere around 27,000 years old, this was a significant interpretation because it suggested that humans had been in northern North America much earlier than previously thought (for the complete story, see "Looking Closer: Re-dating an Ancient and Controversial Bone Tool from Yukon Territory" in Chapter 8).

Friesen felt that a variety of natural agents might also have been responsible for the patterns of bone breakage observed at the site. These included large Pleistocene carnivores, such as *Arctodus simus* and *Arctodus pristinus,* commonly known as the short-faced bear. Given that much of the broken mammoth bone had been re-deposited by the Old Crow River, it was also possible that the rafting of ice, caused by dynamic spring breakups, had broken mammoth bones deposited along the banks of this large northern river. Natural taphonomic agents such as these have one thing in common—they fracture bone through force of pressure. Humans, on the other hand, use rocks (hammer stones) to break large bones through direct percussion. This is often done to retrieve the protein-rich marrow that is found within the medullary cavities of long bones. Friesen hypothesized that if forces of pressure and percussion produce distinctive fracture morphologies in bone, then it should be possible to determine whether the mammoth bone recovered from Old Crow had been broken by natural versus human agents.

Friesen decided to conduct an experiment, in which he would break two samples of bone: one by pressure, and one by percussion. Friesen began by establishing some controls. First, moose bone would be used as an analogue for mammoth bone. Friesen obtained a sample of 20 long bone elements from road kills recovered near a necropsy pit, close by Algonquin Park in Northern Ontario. Next, a large vise, used to split interlocking patio stones, was employed to simulate taphonomic agents that break bone through force of pressure, and 10 of the 20 bones were broken. The remaining 10 elements were then broken percussively, using an anvil stone and a large rock. Friesen subsequently spent many hours in the lab, quantifying and statistically comparing the breakage patterns produced by his experiments. His results led him to conclude that the breakage patterns produced by both techniques were equally complex, and almost indistinguishable.

The moose-bone experiment brings to mind an article entitled "Performance Practice, Experimental Archaeology, and the Problem of the Respectability of Results," in which Randall A. Rosenfeld tells the "melancholy" tale of the late Dr. Robert Ball, of Dublin. It was Dr. Ball's contention that side-blown Irish Bronze Age horns were really musical instruments. To test his hypothesis, he attempted to produce a distinct sound on a large trumpet. Unfortunately, he burst a blood vessel during the attempt, and died a few days later; this was considered "The first and only fatality known to experimental archaeology." One of the side effects of Friesen's bone breakage experiment was the unanticipated force with which moose bones blew apart when subjected to pressure from the large vise. In the process, Dawson and Friesen found themselves covered in an unpleasant mixture of rotting moose marrow and maggots. While not fatal, the experiment did prove somewhat unpleasant.

relevant and which are not. And, like culture, a paradigm can give you both correct and incorrect answers. Paradigms are not open to direct empirical verification or rejection; they simply turn out to be useful or not.

Just as all humans participate in a culture, all archaeologists operate within a paradigm, whether they are aware of it or not. Without a paradigm, nothing would make sense. So, although a paradigm can give us an inaccurate bias, our goal cannot be to free ourselves of any paradigm. Instead, we simply must be aware of the paradigm we are using.

The central message of anthropology is that there is value in other ways of being human and in other cultures. Extrapolating that lesson to paradigms, you should ask not, "Which paradigm is best?" but rather "Which paradigm will be most useful for the kind of theory I am trying to construct or for the problem I am trying to solve?"

Paradigms in Archaeology

We are going to characterize North American archaeology in terms of two paradigms—the **processual** and the **postprocessual**—which define what modern Americanist archaeology is all about. However, our presentation of these paradigms is necessarily abstract and a simplification of the field of archaeology. No archaeologist falls neatly into either category; some, in fact, achieve the difficult posture of straddling the two.

Paradigms sometimes are categorically opposed to one another, in other cases they overlap, and most are embedded in still more-abstract frameworks of thinking. Processual archaeology is embedded within **cultural materialism,** and postprocessual archaeology is embedded within **postmodernism.** We will present the basics of cultural materialism and sketch its importance to archaeology's processual paradigm. We then look at the premises of postmodernism to see how it gave rise to archaeology's postprocessual paradigm.

Cultural Materialism

Although its roots extend back at least a century, modern cultural materialism is largely associated with the late Marvin Harris (1927–2001), a cultural anthropologist, who gave it its name.

Harris argued that anthropology is a science, and its knowledge should therefore be acquired through public, replicable, empirical, and objective methods. Armed with such methods, the cultural materialist aims to formulate theories to scientifically explain the evolution of differences and similarities in human societies. Rival theories are judged by the same criteria, based on their power to predict outcomes and to admit independent testing. Cultural materialism posits that environmental, technological, and economic factors—the *material* conditions of existence—are the most powerful and pervasive determinants of human behaviour. By explicitly (and exclusively) embracing a scientific framework to examine the effects of material factors on human societies, cultural materialists reject humanist, ideational approaches and advocate the adaptive view of culture discussed in Chapter 2.

Cultural materialism focuses on behavioural events, which must be distinguished from mental events because they are observed in different ways. Modern human behaviour is available to the scientific community in a form that can be observed, measured, photographed, and objectively described. We observe human thought, the events of the mind, only indirectly. Although distinct relationships exist between behaviour and thought, we must demonstrate these associations, not assume them. This is obviously true for archaeology—given that the people who left the

processual paradigm The paradigm that explains social, economic, and cultural change as primarily the result of adaptation to material conditions; external conditions (for example, the environment) are assumed to take causal priority over ideational factors in explaining change.

postprocessual paradigm A paradigm that focuses on humanistic approaches and rejects scientific objectivity; it sees archaeology as inherently political and is more concerned with interpreting the past than with testing hypotheses. It sees change as arising largely from interactions between individuals operating within a symbolic and/or competitive system.

cultural materialism A research paradigm that takes a scientific approach and that emphasizes the importance of material factors—such as environment, population density, subsistence, and technology—in understanding change and diversity in human societies.

postmodernism A paradigm that rejects grand historical schemes in favour of humanistic approaches that appreciate the multiple voices of history. It seeks to see how colonialism created our vision of the world we occupy today; it eschews science and argues against the existence of objective truth.

objects behind are long dead—and it is also true for cultural anthropology, because we must still infer ideas from speech and other behaviours.

Although behaviour is symbolic—actions carry meaning to the one doing the action and to those observing it—cultural materialists concentrate on the observable outcomes. Within these guidelines, cultural materialist research covers an array of topics, among them warfare, marriage, dietary patterns and food taboos, settlement and demographic trends, and the origin and evolution of gender roles. It contains within it a wide variety of sub-paradigms—some that take an explicitly evolutionary approach and others that are more ecological.

Cultural materialists use three fundamental concepts in their approach: infrastructure, structure, and superstructure. **Infrastructure** denotes those elements considered most important to satisfying basic human needs: food, shelter, reproduction, and health. These demographic, technological, economic, and ecological processes are assumed to lie at the causal heart of every sociocultural system. The infrastructure mediates a culture's interactions with the natural and social environment through the following two mechanisms:

- *Mode of production* refers to the technology, practices, and social relations employed in basic subsistence production (especially food and other energy production), given the specific technology used.

- *Mode of reproduction* concerns the technology, practices, and social relations employed for expanding, limiting, and maintaining population size (specifically, demography, mating patterns, fertility, natality, mortality, nurturing of infants, medical controls, contraception, abortion, infanticide).

At the next level, the sociocultural system's **structure** is made up of those interpersonal relationships that emerge as behaviour. It includes the **domestic economy**, which is the organization of reproduction and basic production, exchange, and consumption within camps, houses, apartments, or other domestic settings. This entails information on family structure, division of labour, enculturation, age and sex roles, hierarchies, and sanctions.

A society's structure also includes the **political economy**, which is the organization of reproduction, production, exchange, and consumption within and between bands, villages, chiefdoms, states, and empires. It includes political organizations, factions, clubs, associations, corporations, division of labour, taxation, tribute, political socialization and education, social divisions and hierarchies, discipline, police/military control, and warfare.

Finally, **superstructure** refers to a society's values, aesthetics, rules, beliefs, religions, and symbols, which can be behaviourally manifested as art, music, dance, literature, advertising, religious rituals, sports, games, hobbies, and even science.

The Principle of Infrastructural Determinism

Distinguishing cultural materialism from other approaches is the **principle of infrastructural determinism.** This principle has two tenets: (1) human society strives to meet those needs most important to the survival and well-being of human individuals (primarily sex, sleep, nutrition, and shelter); responses to these needs occur directly in the realm of infrastructure; and (2) the infrastructure determines the rest of the sociocultural system. To cultural materialists, *change in the sociocultural system is largely a product of change in the infrastructure.*

Though clearly interrelated, the infrastructure, structure, and superstructure influence one another differentially, and cultural materialists assign causal priority to the modes of production and reproduction (as indicated by the size of the arrows in Figure 3-4).

---

infrastructure In cultural materialism, the elements most important to satisfying basic human survival and well-being—food, shelter, reproduction, health—which are assumed to lie at the causal heart of every sociocultural system.

structure The behaviour that supports choices made at the level of the infrastructure, including the organization of reproduction, production, exchange, family structure, division of labour, age and sex roles, political units, social organization, and warfare.

domestic economy The organization of reproduction and basic production, exchange, and consumption within camps, houses, apartments, or other domestic settings.

political economy The organization of reproduction, production, exchange, and consumption within and between bands, villages, chiefdoms, states, and empires.

superstructure A group's values, aesthetics, rules, beliefs, religions, and symbols, which can be behaviourally manifested as art, music, dance, literature, advertising, religious rituals, sports, games, hobbies, and even science.

principle of infrastructural determinism Argument that the infrastructure lies at the causal heart of every sociocultural system, that human society responds to factors that directly affect survival and well-being, and that such responses determine the rest of the sociocultural system.

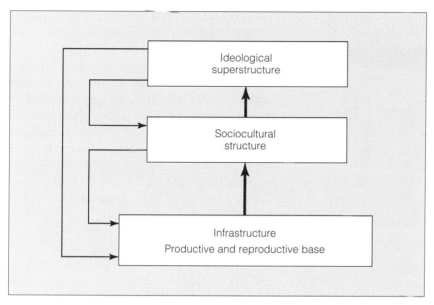

Figure 3-4 How the cultural materialist views causality.

would have evolved differently. However, the important point is that *significant* changes in human society result from those factors that directly influence the infrastructure—subsistence and the extraction of energy from the environment.

Cultural materialists argue that their paradigm is better than alternatives in conforming to the canons of acceptable scientific explanation. One can therefore discredit their strategic principles only by providing alternative principles that produce better and more scientifically acceptable theories.

Technological, demographic, ecological, and economic processes become the independent variables, and the structure and superstructure become second- and third-level responses. Cultural materialists argue that different modes of production and reproduction foster quite distinctive ideological systems. Hunter-gatherers think differently than farmers, who in turn view the world differently than industrialists. *To cultural materialism, infrastructure is the key to understanding the growth and development of all cultures.*

Cultural materialists see such causality as probabilistic, however: Not all hunting and gathering societies have precisely the same sociocultural structure or superstructure. Some sociocultural traits in a given society arise from arbitrary, historically contingent events. And feedback flows among the three components (as shown by the smaller arrows in Figure 3-4). However, as scientists, cultural materialists look past arbitrary or historical events to seek overarching generalities that we can test.

Stating that structure and superstructure are causally dependent on infrastructure does not mean that determinations are transmitted in a single direction; as anthropologist Leslie White put it, the influences are *reciprocal* but not necessarily *equal.* No component is a passive recipient. Without input from domestic, political, and ideological subsystems, the observable modes of production and reproduction

Processual Archaeology: Materialism at Work in Archaeology

The processual paradigm is cultural materialism applied to the study of the past. It includes the new archaeology of Lewis Binford and others, and it also extends to brands of evolutionary archaeologies practised by a large segment of Americanist archaeologists today. For now, it is important only that you understand the basics of the processual paradigm and how they differ from those of postprocessual archaeology (these differences are summarized in Table 3-1).

If you recall our discussion of Walter Taylor and Lewis Binford in Chapter 1, you will see how processual archaeology grew out of dissatisfaction with the increasingly sterile cultural-historical and largely descriptive archaeology of the 1950s. Processual archaeologists correctly noted that culture history, as a paradigm, was inadequate for the description of ancient lives, as well as for the explanation of how cultures operated in the past. The "new archaeologists" of the 1960s retained the chronology-building tools perfected in cultural-historical archaeology, but they rejected the rest in favour of the processual paradigm.

The processual paradigm has several key characteristics:

1. *Processual archaeology emphasizes evolutionary generalizations, not historical specifics, and it*

TABLE 3-1 Some Contrasts between Processual and Postprocessual Archaeology

PROCESSUAL ARCHAEOLOGY	POSTPROCESSUAL ARCHAEOLOGY
Emphasizes evolutionary generalizations and regularities, not historical specifics; it downplays the importance of the individual.	Rejects the search for universal laws and regularities.
Views culture from a systemic perspective and defines culture as adaptation.	Rejects the systemic view of culture and focuses on an ideational view of humanity's extrasomatic means of culture.
Explanation is explicitly scientific and objective.	Rejects scientific methods and objectivity.
Attempts to remain ethically neutral; claims to be explicitly non political.	Argues that all archaeology is unavoidably political.

downplays the importance of the individual. In the early days of the processual paradigm, archaeologists viewed history as the opposite of science, as description rather than explanation. But the processual paradigm is scientific, not historical. It focuses on regularities and correlations. An interest in developing cultural (as opposed to biological) evolutionary theory directed the processual paradigm away from ideology and history and toward environmental change, population growth, food production, trade, and conflict over limited resources as the forces driving cultural evolution.

In its early days, processual archaeology was interested in particular historical sequences, but primarily as data sets that would allow them to test or develop ideas about cultural evolutionary theory. Put another way, processual archaeologists saw particular historical sequences as individual "experiments" from which one could construct theory and law-like generalizations. Early processual archaeologists did not consider culture history by itself to be important.

As part of the processual paradigm's focus on historical regularities and correlations, Binford and others rejected "great man" explanations of history—these are explanations that attribute major changes in economy or social or political organization to a single person who had a "great idea." For example, archaeologists once thought that the origin of agriculture was a product of one of these great ideas, a hypothesis that has been disproven.

2. *Processual archaeology views culture from a systemic perspective and defines culture as humanity's extrasomatic means of adaptation.* Because culture provides the nonbiological system through which people adapt to their environment, processual archaeology could (and, briefly, did) tap into a much larger body of established external theory, often called **general systems theory**. The theoretical premise here is that various complex entities—thermostats, computers, glaciers, living organisms, and even human societies—are most profitably viewed as systems composed of multiple parts that interact in a limited number of predictable ways. Depending on the application, the general rules governing all systems (such as positive feedback, negative feedback, and equilibrium) could explain the behaviour of the major parts of any system—regardless of the specifics of that system. (Although many processual archaeologists today still look at the interconnections among things, they no longer seek to explain human societies in the sterile terms of general systems theory.)

Processual archaeology focuses attention on technology, ecology, and economy and takes an adaptive rather than ideational perspective on culture. Processual archaeology tends to focus on behaviour rather than on the cultural ideas, values, and beliefs that stand behind that behaviour. Religion and ideology are seen as "epiphenomena"—cultural add-ons with little long-term explanatory value. Thus, the processual paradigm agrees with the principle of infrastructural determinism.

general systems theory An effort to describe the properties by which all systems, including human societies, allegedly operated. Popular in processual archaeology of the late 1960s and 1970s.

3. *Explanation in processual archaeology is explicitly scientific.* Procedures in processual archaeology depended on deductive models grounded in the hard sciences (math, chemistry, physics) and emphasized the importance of being objective. By objective, we mean that processual archaeologists believed that they could see the world "as it really is," and not through a filter that coloured their perception of the world.

Initially, the processual paradigm championed the view that predicting events (even those in the past) is equivalent to explaining them. More recent approaches, however, stress the interplay between induction and deduction, the relative objectivity of observations, and the probabilistic nature of explanation in the social sciences.

4. *Processual archaeology attempts to remain ethically neutral and claims to be explicitly non-political.* Processual archaeology tries to provide evidence about the past that is deliberately disconnected from the present. Politics of the present, processual archaeologists argue, should have nothing to do with the study of the ancient past. Archaeology should avoid subjectivity, and its conclusions should not be influenced by modern politics. Processual archaeology is not interested in passing moral judgments on people of the past.

However, processual archaeology does wish to be relevant to the modern world and to provide an understanding of cultural evolution that is useful in directing the world's future. Archaeology should influence politics, but politics is not to influence archaeology.

Roughly half of Americanist archaeologists today pursue the processual paradigm in one form or another (although many of these agree with some tenets of the postprocessual paradigm, as discussed below). Why does the paradigm of cultural materialism hold such appeal to archaeologists? One reason is that cultural materialism emphasizes technology, economy, environment, and demography—those aspects of human existence that leave the clearest traces in the archaeological record. But cultural materialism may also be popular because it suggests that the world and cultural change result from orderly processes—an idea that the postmodern paradigm challenges.

Postmodernism

Postmodernism is a world apart from cultural materialism. Although "postmodernism" is more often used to describe literary and artistic styles, it helped structure the late 20th-century format of the social sciences as well. Just as cultural materialism informs processual archaeology, postmodernism underlies the postprocessual paradigm of Americanist archaeology.

Most new paradigms, whether in the sciences or the arts, are responses to the perceived excesses or failures of a previous paradigm. To understand postmodernism, therefore, you need to understand how it was a response to a set of European philosophical, political, and ethical ideas that reigned from the 17th through 19th centuries—an exciting period known as the **Enlightenment.**

What Was the Enlightenment?

The Enlightenment, or "Age of Reason," was a shift in Western thought in the 17th and 18th centuries when thinkers tried to develop objective sciences and universal standards for morality and law. The Enlightenment worldview held that rational (not religious) thought was the key to progress, and that technology, governed by rational thought, would free people from the control of nature and permit the development of moral and spiritual virtues.

Enlightenment thought saw the world as knowable through science. Scholars argued that scientific thought would always produce truth, and truth was always right (and good). This was a period of great optimism, when scholars threw off the fetters of religious dogma and made scientific discoveries that helped humanity control the perversities of nature.

To liberate humans from the perceived oppression of myth, religion, and superstition, Enlightenment

Enlightenment A Western philosophy that advocated ideas of linear progress, absolute truth, science, rational planning of ideal social orders, and the standardization of knowledge. It held that rational thought was the key to progress; that science and technology would free people from the oppression of historical traditions of myth, religion, and superstition; and that the control of nature through technology would permit the development of moral and spiritual virtues.

Archaeological Ethics
Excavating the Dead of World War I

Most people think that archaeologists study only very ancient sites, like Egypt's pyramids. But archaeologists also study the more recent past, including the two World Wars. A prominent element of this archaeology is the remains of the soldiers lost on battlefields.

As you might imagine, the looting and plundering of human burials is a problem the world over, but so is their professional excavation. We see both of these issues in the excavation of World War I's dead.

The "Great War," the "War to End All Wars," was truly a horror. Mechanized and chemical warfare brought death on a scale that was horrendous even to soldiers accustomed to cavalry charges into cannons. Tens of thousands of men died in the trenches along the western front in France and Belgium. Their bodies were often lost in seas of mud churned by shellfire; even if found, they were frequently buried in shallow, hastily dug graves.

The war ended in 1918, but its horrors continue as relic hunters plunder the buried trenches and bunkers in search of war memorabilia and jewellery. Looting is especially prevalent in Belgium, where some 50,000 British and untold numbers of French, German, African, Australian, Canadian, and Native American soldiers were lost (Choctaws served as codetalkers in World War I, just as Navajo did in the Pacific theatre in World War II).

In Ypres, a town in Flanders, collectors gather each month at a pub to buy and sell war memorabilia and swap stories. A British television program in 2000 showed looters brazenly bragging of what they had robbed from the dead: "This is something I've got which is very nice. It's a British officer's ring. Gold with a diamond. I always told my wife one day I'd come home with gold."

Many of the sites are patrolled by police, but they are few and they can hardly stop the looting that occurs under cover of darkness. Military memorabilia, stolen by those who did not fight in the war, is increasingly valuable on an international market. "It's not human, it's just greed," said one veteran.

To help stop the looting, in 1992 Ypres authorized a group of avocational archaeologists, who call themselves The Diggers, to remove burials from the trenches for proper burial. In two years they unearthed more than 100 burials, and their work continues. The Diggers are sanctioned by the Belgian government and are licensed by professional archaeologists. All remains and artifacts are turned over to the Commonwealth War Graves Commission for burial in military cemeteries.

Some veterans support The Diggers; others believe that their comrades should remain where they fell. But this option is not always possible. For example, The Diggers have worked at Boezinge, near the town of Ieper, where in 1915 the German army launched its initial gas attack. This land is now being developed, and the choice is to bulldoze the bodies, preserve the battlefield as a memorial, or professionally excavate and rebury the remains.

How should we treat these remains? Bulldozing them seems disrespectful, and preservation may not be feasible in a small, crowded nation. Professional excavation seems the logical solution. But the dead come from different nationalities and religions with different opinions and customs on treatment of the dead. Do we bulldoze, preserve in place, or excavate? How should the dead of recent wars be treated?

---

thinkers appealed to the ideas of linear progress, absolute truth, planning of ideal social orders, and the standardization of knowledge. They searched for order and believed that order in the physical and social world was natural and good. The period was characterized by great thinkers who saw world history as unfolding according to a great, orderly plan that involved and ensured continual improvement for humanity. John Locke (1632–1704) was an Enlightenment scholar; so were Immanuel Kant (1724–1804) and Thomas Jefferson (1743–1826). Sigmund Freud, Karl Marx, and Charles Darwin, all of whom saw society as improving (although for different reasons), were scholars of the late Enlightenment—a period that sociologists refer to as "modern." This gives us the "modern" in "postmodern."

What Is Postmodernism?

Serious cracks began to appear in this system of thought in the early 20th century, especially after World War I. The "Great War" showed many people that science and rational thought, which promised to produce a better society, could also produce the horrors of tank and gas warfare. Many young intellectuals felt betrayed, for the world was not as they thought it was.

The initial result was modernism, artistic and literary styles that shrugged off optimism, rationality, and ideals of progress (be careful not to confuse modernism with "modern," defined above). This artistic movement tried to see all perspectives simultaneously, as can be seen in the art style of cubism, best known through the work of Pablo Picasso. Novels and poetry by Gertrude Stein, Virginia Woolf, T. S. Eliot, Franz Kafka, and Ezra Pound eschewed straightforward narrative in favour of new literary techniques such as multiple narratives and stream-of-consciousness writing, as well as moral ambiguity.

Postmodernism arose from modernism in the latter half of the 20th century, especially after the 1960s. Postmodernism takes some modernist themes to an extreme. Andy Warhol was a postmodern artist, and Jorge Luis Borges and Thomas Pynchon were postmodern writers. Although modernists saw the fragmentation of knowledge as a tragic loss, they believed that art and literature could help people find some moral unity and coherence in the world. But postmodernism sees no forward movement to history, no "grand narrative," and no promise of a brighter future made possible by science. Indeed, postmodernism argues that there really is no truth and no coherence *except* that all understanding and meaning is "historically situated."

By "historically situated," postmodernists mean that our understanding of the world is not really truth, but rather only a product of the time in which we live. For this reason, postmodernism often seeks to understand how colonialism, a major social force of the past several hundred years, constructed the Western world's understanding of humanity. Some postmodernists try

to correct the previous worldview by documenting the multiple voices of history (especially those of colonized and oppressed peoples) and by showing how colonialism constructed our image of others. The idea is that each group has a right to speak for itself, in its own voice, and to have that voice accepted as authentic and legitimate. Such pluralism is an essential theme of postmodernism.

Deconstruction and the Maya

Just as science was the primary tool of the Enlightenment, **deconstruction** is the primary tool of postmodernism. Coined by French philosopher Jacques Derrida (1930–) in the 1960s, the term refers to efforts to expose the assumptions behind the allegedly scientific (objective and systematic) search for knowledge.

Here's an archaeological example. The Maya civilization flourished in portions of Central America and Mexico, reaching a zenith about A.D. 700. The Maya constructed magnificent centres with stone pyramids, surrounded by thousands of households. These complexes were the centre of a rich ceremonial life, places where kings recorded their exploits in hieroglyphics on stone monuments called **stelae** (Figure 3-5). The society ran according to a set of complex calendars and supported its agriculture with water storage systems. By A.D. 900, however, Maya civilization had collapsed; people abandoned the centres, which were gradually consumed by the jungle. Why?

Processual archaeologists proposed many explanations for the collapse of Maya civilization (the Maya people never disappeared; they are still there today). These fell into three major areas: war, environmental degradation, and the abuse of power by political elites. Anthropologist Richard Wilk (Indiana University) showed that these three explanations waxed and waned in popularity, as indicated by articles published in professional journals, in relation to major U.S. political events. Warfare as an explanation began in 1962, the beginning of the Vietnam War, and grew in

deconstruction Efforts to expose the assumptions behind the alleged objective and systematic search for knowledge. A primary tool of postmodernism.

stelae Stone monuments erected by Maya rulers to record their history in rich images and hieroglyphic symbols. These symbols can be read and dated.

Figure 3-5 Stela B at Copán, Honduras; erected A.D. 731 it depicts the ruler, 18-Rabbit.

Source: Charles & Josette Lenars/CORBIS

Many contemporary ethnographers see their task as analyzing a culture the way a literary critic reads a book or poem. They reject the goal of discovering scientific truths in favour of composing elegant and convincing interpretations about the target culture. According to one postmodern critic, ethnography, or an archaeological report, is not an empirical account; it is instead a species of fiction. As part of this approach, many anthropologists adopted a *reflexive* viewpoint, focusing more on what the anthropological endeavour says about the anthropological process and less on ethnographic descriptions of other cultures.

An extreme form of postmodernism even suggests that objectivity is impossible and that truth is subjective and relative (mediated by one's cultural identity and background and influenced by who is seeking the knowledge and for what purpose). If these premises are accepted, then science becomes merely one way of telling a story about the world around us, and there are no criteria for determining the validity of any competing story. Some critics argue that in postmodernism "anything goes," and hence there are no real gains in knowledge. Most postmodernists, however, adhere to a weaker version of this thesis, seeing the effects of cultural biases as difficult, but not impossible, to remove.

Postprocessual Archaeology: Postmodernism at Work in Archaeology

Although it had forerunners in the United States and elsewhere, the formal postprocessual paradigm arose largely in Great Britain and Europe, nurtured by archaeologists such as Ian Hodder (formerly Cambridge, now Stanford University). Adherents today can be found on both sides of the Atlantic. We can perhaps best characterize postprocessual archaeology by contrasting it with processual archaeology. We will list some of these characteristics below, but we caution that postprocessual archaeologists, like their processual colleagues, have ameliorated the initial, extreme position in recent years.

1. *Postprocessual archaeology rejects the processual search for universal laws.* The postprocessual paradigm holds that universals of human behaviour simply do not exist and that scientific explanations are inadequate because they downplay historical circumstances in their search for universals. Processual archaeology

popularity until the end of that war. During the ecology movement of the mid-1970s, explanations that focused on environmental degradation became prominent. After 1976, in the aftermath of the Watergate fiasco and historic resignation of Richard Nixon, abuse of government power was the favoured explanation.

Wilk argues that by deconstructing archaeological thinking about the Maya collapse, we can see the degree to which modern political events affected the views of archaeologists working on this problem. There is nothing new in suggesting that archaeologists are products of their own culture: People who consider themselves scientists (like Wilk) have always tried to discover biases, remove their effects, and move on. What is new in postmodernism is that deconstruction is often the *goal* of research.

saw the particulars of history—such as cultural ideas about men and women or specific religious beliefs—as playing no significant role in the grand scheme of history. Postprocessual archaeologists see the grand scheme, if it exists at all, as uninteresting; instead, they see the trajectory of particular societies as heavily influenced by that society's particular cultural ideas. For some postprocessual archaeologists, archaeology should be more closely allied with history (as it is in Europe) than with anthropology (as it is in the United States).

In fact, postprocessual archaeology often emphasizes the role of the individual in human society. We do not mean that postprocessual archaeology aims to see particular individuals in archaeology—for example, to find the name of the person who made a particular pot. Instead, postprocessual archaeology argues that large social change results from individuals going about their daily lives. In this view, societies are not animated solely by change from the "outside" (such as environmental change). More specifically, postprocessual archaeology tends to see social tension—for example, competition between men and women, elites and non-elites, or regional groups—as especially important in generating social change. This has prompted some to observe that the postprocessual world is a sad one indeed, where individuals prosper only by exploiting one another and where cooperation is mere pretense.

2. *Postprocessual archaeology rejects the systemic view of culture and focuses on an ideational perspective.* Postprocessual archaeology discredits the systems approach as a "robotic view of humans." Postmodernism in general distrusts any deterministic perspective that reduces individual humans to the status of a historical droid, not significantly different from conditioned laboratory rats.

Postprocessualists argue that the systemic view of human society suggests a coordinated, uniform organism responding only to outside pressures, mainly the environment and demography. But, postprocessualists argue, a society is composed of conflicting individuals, groups, families, and classes, whose goals are not necessarily identical and whose interests and actions are often in conflict with the adaptive success and functional needs of the cultural system as a whole. How can we reconcile a vision of society as a well-oiled machine of checks and balances with the fact that specific individuals with interests that are maladaptive for others, such as dictators, often control a society?

Whereas processual archaeology is grounded in the adaptive perspective of culture, postprocessual archaeology follows the ideational perspective we discussed in Chapter 2. As a result, many postprocessual archaeologists pursue humanistic approaches, seeking explanations that consider human thoughts, emotions, and symbolic meanings. A culture's understanding of the environment, for instance, affects the way that the culture interacts with it—meaning that cultures could respond differently to similar environmental pressures. In Figure 3-4, postprocessual archaeologists might reverse the size of the arrows. For example, during the Dust Bowl days of the 1930s, the federal government instituted livestock reduction programs as a way to drive prices up and move the nation out of the Depression. But in the American Southwest, Navajo sheepherders actually *increased* production as their land degraded. Why? The Navajo view the natural and cultural worlds as not only mechanically but also spiritually linked. To them, if land is not productive, then supernatural forces will punish them by degrading the land. Navajos, therefore, responded to Dust Bowl conditions by raising more, not fewer, sheep. Sheep can be very destructive to land, however, and so the Navajo response only exacerbated the conditions brought on by climate change. (And they were horrified when the federal government arrived to kill their sheep.) This example suggests that we cannot understand different cultural approaches to environmental change without understanding different cultures' ideas about the relationships between humans and land.

As a result, postprocessualists tend to look at artifacts differently than do processual archaeologists. Processual archaeologists tend to look at the things, such as the pot shown in Figure 3-6, in terms of functions: Was the pot used for cooking? Food or water storage? Is it a serving vessel? But postprocessual archaeologists remind us that things also carry symbolic meanings: Did this pot "stand for" women, or hospitality, or the Raven clan? Thus, postprocessualists argue that we cannot understand what artifacts mean simply by looking for their functions; we also must consider their symbolic meanings. Consider, for example, what a Dodge minivan versus a Porsche convertible tells you about your neighbour.

It is understandable, then, that postprocessual archaeology has become more firmly entrenched in historical rather than prehistoric archaeology, because historical documents provide us with some access to the symbolic meanings of objects.

3. *Postprocessual archaeology rejects objectivity and explicitly scientific methods.* Given the importance of the ideational perspective, many postprocessual archaeologists argue that objectivity is impossible. They argue that we all see the world through a cultural lens; we can never see the world "as it really is." Postprocessual archaeologists argue that we should therefore drop any pretense of objectivity, because our understanding of the past is merely a construction in the present. Knowledge is not

Figure 3-6 A Maya polychrome vessel (Tikal, Guatemala, A.D. 350–400); processual archaeology focuses on its function, postprocessual archaeology on its meaning.

Source: Stuart Rome, Drexel University

absolute, postprocessualists argue, but only relative to the culture that produced it. This view argues that there are "many pasts" and no way to judge which is better. Today, many postprocessual archaeologists have backed away from this extreme position, although it still forms a major criticism of research conducted under the processual paradigm.

Having posited that objectivity is impossible, postprocessualists argue that the kind of science practised by processual archaeology is impossible, because it required a strict separation of data and theory. Even though many processual archaeologists admit that the notion of science practised early on in processual archaeology was limiting, many postprocessualists still distrust science in any form.

4. *Postprocessual archaeology argues that all archaeology is political.* Although processual archaeologists wished to be "relevant" to modern society, they considered themselves politically neutral. This was a derivative of their view of scientific objectivity: They believed they saw the world as it actually was, uncoloured by any political or personal agenda.

But postprocessual archaeology argues that all research is inescapably political. The Moundbuilder researcher Ephraim Squier, for example, was a confirmed polygenist—that is, he believed that humankind included several "races," each having separate instances of creation and separate capacities for progress. In his opinion, demonstrating that someone other than the Indians built the mounds showed that the Indians did not originate in the same act of creation as did those of European ancestry. This belief probably clouded his interpretation of the evidence. Likewise, postprocessualism argues that a cultural evolutionary view of the past is based on Western notions of progress and hence is potentially (and some would say fundamentally) racist.

Postprocessual archaeologists place the political implications of their research front and centre. For many, this means that the study of the *presentation* of the past, in museums, scientific publications, and popular media, is as critical as the study of the past itself, if not more so.

Is Postmodernism All That New?

Despite their claims of "newness," the basic concerns of processual and postprocessual archaeology have deep historical roots. In Chapter 2, we presented the process of understanding the mounds as an example of archaeology-as-science. Although it might have seemed a curious choice, we selected this example to make a simple point: Though lacking in all the jargon, the process of figuring out who the Moundbuilders were employed all the fundamentals of scientific inquiry. Although we described the "new archaeology" as concerned with conducting archaeology as a science, the truth is that the canons of science were with us long before the new archaeology came along.

We make a similar point here: Some of the key ideas and concerns of postprocessual archaeology have been kicking around for a long time. To demonstrate that point, we turn to one (particularly colourful) nineteenth-century archaeologist—Adolph Bandelier (1840–1914).

Adolph Bandelier: Scientific Humanist or Humanistic Scientist?

Born in Switzerland, Adolph Francis Bandelier came to America at the age of 8 and grew up in Highland, Illinois. He worked in the family banking and mining businesses, but it was American Indians that fascinated him. In 1880, when he was 40 years old, the newly founded Archaeological Institute of America hired him to explore Ancestral Pueblo ruins in the Southwest (see "Looking Closer: Anasazi or Ancestral Pueblo?"). An intrepid explorer, he travelled thousands of kilometres, often unarmed and ill-equipped, on foot and horseback, working under the most adverse conditions. At one point, Bandelier was erroneously reported dead at the hands of Geronimo and his Apache warriors in southern Arizona.

But when he arrived at Pecos Pueblo (where Alfred Kidder would later excavate) in 1880, he wrote, "I am dirty, ragged, and sunburnt, but of good cheer. My life's work has at last begun." Most archaeologists today understand just how he felt.

The Scientific Bandelier

Bandelier knew the basics of Pecos history from documentary research. Founded in the distant past, Pecos Pueblo had grown to 2000 inhabitants by the time the Spanish explorer Coronado passed through in 1540. It was a flourishing trade centre, straddling the border between the farming Pueblo world to the west and the buffalo hunters of the high plains. Out of Pueblo country came turquoise, pottery, maize, cotton blankets, and marine shells (imported from the Pacific Coast). From the plains to the east came hunters, such

Looking Closer
Anasazi or Ancestral Pueblo?

For more than 60 years, archaeologists have used the word "Anasazi" to denote the last prehistoric (ca. A.D. 200–1600) culture centred on the Four Corners area of northwestern New Mexico, northern Arizona, southwestern Colorado, and southern Utah. Generally, archaeologists consider the Anasazi to be ancestors of modern Pueblo groups in New Mexico and the Hopi peoples of northwestern Arizona.

But over the past several years, some Pueblo people have expressed concern over use of this term. "Anasazi" comes from a Navajo word meaning "ancient enemy." Why, Puebloan peoples ask, should their ancestors be known by a non-Puebloan term, especially one that means "enemy"? (Recall that this is very similar to the problem that the Lakota/Dakota people face, discussed on page 51.) Although archaeologists have offered a number of substitutes, many today prefer the term "ancestral Pueblo" to "Anasazi."

Figure 3-7 The circular ruin of Tyuonyi (New Mexico).
Source: David H. Thomas

as the Comanche, bringing bison meat, fat, and tanned hides; flint cores for tool making; and wood for bows. A Franciscan mission was established, but the native population began dying out, and by 1838 the site was deserted.

From this sketchy background, Bandelier concluded that the lengthy archaeological record at Pecos could provide an important baseline to long-term cultural development in the American Southwest. He mapped the ruins, measured wall thickness and room dimensions, collected samples of artifacts and building materials, and photographed the site.

Bandelier also conducted ethnography, working first at Santo Domingo Pueblo, on the banks of the Rio Grande, but later switching to Cochiti Pueblo. Here he recorded details about Pueblo customs and beliefs, religious ceremonies, and daily life. Though he had no formal training in such things, he even recorded the Keresan language as well as myths, legends, and origin tales.

Bandelier spent the next decade of his life exploring and describing nearly 400 major archaeological ruins throughout the American Southwest and northern Mexico. His *Final Report* describing this fieldwork is an 800-page monument to his focus on detail and accuracy; it is still a source of baseline information about the archaeology of the American Southwest. So great were his contributions that, two years after his death in 1914, President Woodrow Wilson designated the archaeological site of Tyuonyi (near Santa Fe) and the surrounding region "Bandelier National Monument," one of the nation's first national monuments, shown in Figure 3-7.

The Postmodern Bandelier

Bandelier was a scientist, but he was also deeply concerned about popular perceptions of the American Indian. He was annoyed with the success of James Fenimore Cooper (the author who had piqued Nels Nelson's interest), whose five-volume *Leatherstocking Tales*

(1823–1841) celebrated both the American wilderness and the basic frontier life that played out there.

Many romantic authors of the 19th century, such as Cooper, rejected the Enlightenment's optimism and believed that science, art, and European social institutions corrupted humankind from its natural, or primitive state—which was seen as morally superior to the civilized state. He idealized the American Indian as a heroic yet sadly vanishing species, creating an image of Indians as the "noble savage," full of innate simplicity and virtue.

In truth, though, most of what Cooper knew about Indians was distorted or false. In *The Last of the Mohicans* (1826), for instance, Cooper appropriated the name "Uncas" for his title character. Although Uncas was a historical figure—a 17th-century chief of the Mohegan (Mohican) people—the fictionalized Uncas was transplanted and sanitized into a "good Indian," a noble and loyal friend of the colonist. And Cooper convinced generations of Americans that, with the death of the fictional Uncas, the Mohican people became extinct. In truth, the Mohegan people survive today, many still residing in Uncasville (in southeastern Connecticut).

Bandelier detested inaccuracy and romantic sentimentality. He ridiculed Cooper's superficial knowledge of American Indians and stewed about the impact the "cigar-store red man" was having on the American public. In the late 1880s, as Bandelier was preparing the manuscript describing his scientific explorations, he decided to write his own novel.

Originally published in German (as *Die Koshare*) in 1890, *The Delight Makers* was based on Bandelier's extensive knowledge of ethnography and history— what he called "the sober facts"—to create a rich description of Pueblo life projected back into the past. The book is a tale about the pre-contact (that is, before the arrival of Europeans) people living at Tyuonyi and, in the title role as "delight makers," Bandelier featured the **Koshare** (ko-*shar*-ee), individuals who are members of a powerful secret society whose functions include performing as a kind of clown.

The story begins on a sparkling June day at Tyuonyi in A.D. 1450. Okoya, an adolescent boy, is confronted by his younger brother, Shyuote, who complains about the older boy's cynical attitude toward the Koshare. This worries Okoya. He had confided these inner thoughts to his mother, and yet his father is a Koshare, and Shyuote is pledged to become one.

Okoya's doubt about the Koshare escalates into accusations of witchcraft. The dissidents perform their own rituals, but little happens except that much-needed rain does not fall. Navajo intruders side with the anti-Koshare forces and threaten to murder Okoya's grandfather, a war chief. As the Koshare search for evidence of heresy, antagonism within Tyuonyi intensifies. When the grandfather's scalped corpse is found, a revenge-driven blood feud breaks out with the neighbouring Pueblo group (although it was Navajo interlopers who did the deed). As the Pueblo people fight it out, the Navajos destroy Tyuonyi. But thanks to heroism, many escape. The story ends when the Pueblo fugitives begin building a new village.

Why did Bandelier write this particular tale?

In the first place, he thought it a more accurate portrayal of Indians than any that existed at the time. Reacting against the sentimentality of Cooper, Bandelier drew on his years of experience in the Southwest to describe Puebloan society, ceremonies, and customs. But Bandelier also stepped out of his role as scientific observer. He adopted an *empathetic* approach to prehistory and attempted to describe ancient daily Pueblo life from the inside, from the perspective of the participants.

Bandelier interrupted his basic storyline with asides about nature, the human condition, or general characteristics of "The Indian" ("The reader will forgive a digression . . . ," "This tradition was told me by . . . ," and so forth). By jumping in—as first-person author—Bandelier shifted the narrative and made his own reflexive comments.

Ethnographer, literary critic, and professor of English Barbara Babcock (University of Arizona) highlights Bandelier's postmodern penchant for "deconstruct[ing] stereotypes of the savage, past and present." In *The Delight Makers,* Bandelier employed both the authoritative tone of the ethnographer and the insider view of the Cochiti Indian. In postmodern fashion, Bandelier struck up a dialogue between himself (Anglo-American ethnologist) and his Cochiti friends (the "informants"). To deconstruct Cooper's noble savage, Bandelier felt obliged to step out of his

Koshare An English rendering of a Keresan (one of the Pueblo Indian languages) word that refers to ritual clowns in Rio Grande Pueblo society.

In His Own Words
Robert McGhee and the L'Anse-Amour Burial

Dr. Robert McGhee is currently curator of Arctic Archaeology at the Canadian Museum of Civilization. In 1973, he and James Tuck of Memorial University of Newfoundland were conducting archaeological survey work along the Labrador coast of the Strait of Belle Isle. The two archaeologists made a remarkable discovery—half hidden in the fir thickets that cover the landscape, a cairn of rocks and boulders capping a burial pit. McGhee and Tuck cleared away the brush, carefully mapped the positions of the rocks, and began their excavation. To their astonishment, the skeleton of a small child was revealed about $1\frac{1}{2}$ metres below the arrangement of boulders. Analysis of the bones revealed that the child was male, and about 12 to 13 years of age at the time of his death.

The bones were stained with an earth pigment called red ochre, and a flat rock rested on the back of the child, who had been placed face down in an extended position. Included with the burial were a variety of artifacts, including eight chipped stone knives or spear points, a carved antler pestle for grinding the paint, a decorated bone pendant, and a whistle or flute made from hollow bird bone. An ivory walrus tusk had been placed in front of the child's face, and a harpoon and crescent-shaped object, both made from ivory, were found under his chest. Radiocarbon dates indicated that the burial was between 7000 and 7500 years old. Other examples of burial ceremonialism on the west coast of Newfoundland were known at the Port-au-Choix site, where individuals had been placed into small pits with grave goods. But the burials at Port-au-Choix were 4000 years old. For McGhee and Tuck to have found evidence for the ceremonial treatment of the dead 3000 years earlier was indeed truly remarkable. But what did it all mean?

McGhee decided to explore this question by stepping outside of his role as a scientific observer. Like Adolph Bandelier in *The Delight Makers*, he used an empathic and reflexive approach to try to understand the L'Anse-Amour burial. McGhee wrote a fictional story, based on archaeological fact, in which he speculated about the fate of the young boy. In the story, the child is portrayed as a loner who encounters a large brown bear while out walking with his dog. The boy wounds rather than kills the bear with his spear, which is seen as a bad omen by others in the group. Soon after, the sky turns crimson and hazy with the smoke of forest fires. This reminds older people of a time when forest fires drove away caribou, and even the porcupines and hares that they often rely on during times of famine.

role as objective scientist and bring something of the complexity of real American Indian lifeways to the greater American public. He could not do this through pages of archaeological detail, but he could do it through a novel. Bandelier used his own intimate knowledge of the past and present to educate the public about the "true" nature of Native Americans to give a voice to a people who at that time were rarely heard in American society.

Bandelier: A 19th-Century Scientist "In Full Ritual Undress"

But there is even more to *The Delight Makers*. Babcock suggests that Bandelier was motivated by a reflexive concern with himself as observer, and, according to Babcock, *The Delight Makers* was his attempt to come to terms with something he saw at Cochiti that deeply disturbed him.

They recall suffering through a harsh winter, and then travelling to the coast in springtime only to find that there was no pack ice. This delayed the arrival of the harp seal, which caused more hardship. That night, the shaman has a vision in which he sees bears setting fire to the North Country, out of revenge for their fallen comrade. Many feel that the actions of the child might bring about a return to those bad days remembered by the elders. The drastic actions that are next taken are described in these excerpts from McGhee's story:

> As the young men slid into the hole I could see the kid in their midst, drooping and unresisting. His face and body had been painted red, and on a cord around his neck he wore the whistle that I had made for him last year and that he always carried.
>
> The old man was shouting orders, people moved about gathering wood to build two fires in the bottom of the pit, one on either side of the young men. A flame was brought from the village and the fires set alight. The smoke hung in the pit before rising straight in a single column into the still air, and the figures in the pit moved about as if in a fog. They had been told what they had to do, and I knew what was happening without having to watch.
>
> When I turned back it was over, and the kid lay belly-down on the sand between the two fires, the harpoon line still looped around his neck. The shaman was telling the young men to leave the body face down because the ghost would be less dangerous that way. Someone passed a rock down into the pit, and placed it on the kid's back. It was then that the first gust of rain came on the wind blowing from the sea.
>
> For the last while they have been carrying rocks from the streambed and piling them on the mounds of sand where the pit was filled in. I have seen this once before, when I was young with a painted face, and I know how they feel—frightened at what they have done, maybe a little ashamed of their foolishness, but not sure that it was a foolish thing to do. He was an ugly kid who probably would never have been a good hunter, and next winter we will meet the caribou and most of us will live.

McGhee is a scientist, but he is also interested in making archaeology accessible to the public. Adopting just a scientific approach would not have allowed him to explore how people living on the west coast of Newfoundland more than 7000 years ago may have dealt with the emotional dimensions of uncertainty, fear, and death.

The Koshares entranced Bandelier. He described them as "hideous, often obscene clowns or jesters [who] endeavor to provoke merriment by performances which deserve decided reprobation." Bandelier and his contemporaries were clearly confused and conflicted over Koshares. Year after year, Bandelier returned to Cochiti to observe what he once called those "disgusting creatures . . . in full ritual undress." In his diary he wrote:

During [the dancing] the skirmishers kept acting around them. One of [the Koshares], who was particularly fond of rolling in the dust, was at last dragged about and through the lines [of dancers] by his companions till he was completely naked. There an exhibition of obscenity hard to describe took place. [Numerous sexual acts were] performed to greatest perfection . . . to the greatest delight of the spectators (certainly over a hundred), men, women, girls and boys. . . . I was terribly ashamed, but

In His Own Words

Bruce G. Trigger (1937–2006)—Memories of a Graduate Student

by Jerimy Cunningham, Ph.D.

As we saw in Chapter 1, Bruce Trigger is a significant figure in Canadian archaeology. Professor Trigger was very interested in the process of archaeological inquiry, and had much to say about both processual and postprocessual archaeology. In this section, a former graduate student recalls what taking a class with Professor Trigger was like at McGill University.

As one of his last graduate students, I have to say that I found my weekly meetings with Bruce Trigger (Figure 3.8) to be awe-inspiring events. Because of the relatively small number of archaeology graduate students at McGill University, most courses in the department were one-on-one weekly meetings. In Professor Trigger's courses, carefully prepared lists of readings and official-looking course syllabi were diligently prepared at the start of each semester to fulfill the department's administrative requirements and then would disappear, never to be consulted again. In their place emerged tailor-made courses that would move from issue to issue with an astounding fluidity. Reading assignments would appear organically out of the issues that arose each week, often pulled directly from Trigger's vast library.

The meetings themselves also seemed to have a certain rhythm. My carefully prepared notes, for example, would be presented in a short summary, as an assessment at the beginning of each meeting. Trigger would then listen encouragingly through the first few minutes and then slowly tilt back in his chair into a comfy repose. Right on cue, his eyes would gradually roll closed, and he would drift into what appeared to be a fitful nap. I doggedly continued my presentation—as any diligent graduate student faced with this situation would do—despite the fact that anyone witnessing our meeting would have to conclude I was speaking entirely to myself. As my presentation drew to

a close, Bruce's eyes would flutter open, he would lean forward in his chair, fix me with a penetrating if slightly scandalized stare, and then pose the sort of uncomfortably direct question that erased any doubt that he had missed a single word I'd said. My response would spark the direction of our discussion, and over the next two and a half hours I would be treated to an expertly guided tour of more than three centuries of archaeology's intellectual history. The meetings would wrap up in the same reliable manner. Bruce would highlight an issue he saw at the core of our discussion and then jump to his feet, suggesting that he knew "an interesting book" we could read on that subject for the following week. Fetching the book would usually require him to stand on a chair in a darkened corner of his office, digging among ancient off-prints and priceless texts on Egyptology until it was located. The "interesting book" inevitably was the most forceful counterargument to whatever position I favoured during our discussions.

In his own words (Trigger 2006), Trigger noted that he would often play devil's advocate for conflicting positions in order to reinforce to his students that archaeology required a broad set of theoretical tools. In many ways, this dialectical approach to the art of teaching also reflects Trigger's unique brand of scholarship. As a specialist in Egyptology, the Huron, comparative civilizations, archaeological theory, and the history of archaeology, Trigger's scholarship spanned an immense breadth. This gave him an incredible ability to find value in research trends that often had fallen off the radar in contemporary archaeological practice. During the heady days of the new archaeology, for example, Trigger opposed its positivism and ecological determinism and inspired many archaeologists who would later become leading figures in postprocessual archaeology. As post-

Figure 3-8 Jerimy Cunningham stands with Dr. Bruce Trigger, after receiving his Ph.D. in Anthropology at McGill University, Montreal.

Source: Dr. Jerimy J Cunningham

interests, Trigger published *A History of Archaeological Thought*, which showed in intricate detail how both power and knowledge had combined to produce modern archaeology. Finally, as postprocessual archaeology's particularism reached its highest level of popularity, Trigger generated a breakthrough comparative study of ancient civilizations that underlined the importance of studying cross-cultural regularities.

This struggle to widen archaeology's theoretical vision seems to have had some impact on archaeology in Canada. Canadian archaeology has always sat somewhat outside core debates in archaeology. Conventional wisdom would suggest that this is because a relatively small number of Canadian archaeologists were too preoccupied with the need to outline basic culture history to engage in theoretical debate. While this is certainly true for vast areas of the country, some areas, such as Southern Ontario and the Northwest Coast, have received enough research to risk entanglement in disciplinary polemics. In these cases, however, Trigger's dialectical approach seemed to have served as an important inoculation against leaping into too-hasty dogmatisms. In this way, the core theme of Trigger's teaching transcends those of us who were lucky enough to work directly with him.

processualism gained a wider prominence, the hyper-relativism that it occasionally championed prompted a series of critiques in which Bruce asked whether academic responsibility had been completely abandoned. What is unique about this process of providing a coherent synthesis of archaeology by combining and resolving contradictory arguments was that it often took the form of highly ambitious research programs. In response to processual archaeology's devaluation of history, for example, Trigger produced his landmark ethnohistories of the Huron. In the 1980s, as polarized positions fought to define archaeology either as a science or as a complete manifestation of political

nobody seemed to take any concern about it. . . . The naked [Koshare] performed masturbation in or very near the center of the plaza, alternately with a black rug and with his hand. Everybody laughed. I went home.

Bandelier was both repulsed and intrigued by the lewd conduct of the Koshares. Even today, much of the public misunderstands the Koshare. But anthropologists understand them as an example of ritual clowns, who mediate between the spiritual and material worlds. Like cannibal dancers at a Kwak-wak'awakw potlatch, they invert accepted ways of living and demonstrate how to live by showing how ludicrous an opposite way of living would be. But for Bandelier, these scandalous clowns destroyed the boundary between sacred and secular, between dignified and obscene, terror and delight.

Babcock suggests that Bandelier wrote *The Delight Makers* over a seven-year period in which he tried to come to terms with the Koshares. Bandelier remained precise and literal in his scientific writings. But in his novel, Bandelier could let his imagination run free, allowing him to confront another culture in a way denied him by sterile scientific reporting; this is why he can let Okoya doubt the Koshares. It was another approach to understanding, and it is perfectly valid because science does not care where ideas come from, only how they are evaluated.

Archaeology Today

At this point, you may be asking yourself if there is anything new about archaeology. If Cyrus Thomas was doing science long before Binford was born, and if Bandelier was writing postmodern novels more than a century ago, did archaeologists fool themselves into thinking that they had hit on something novel in processual and postprocessual archaeology?

Yes and no. Elements of scientific and postmodern thought can be found throughout the history of archaeology. But several things changed along the way. For one, we've learned a great deal about basic world prehistory. One hundred years ago, for example, we did not know when people first occupied the New World, when the first agricultural economies began, or how old humanity was. With a better understanding of the world's basic prehistory, archaeologists have moved on to investigate other topics, and this has led some archaeologists to new research paradigms.

Other changes have taken place as well. With more fieldwork came greater understanding of how archaeological sites form and a greater appreciation for how difficult it is to infer human behaviour from archaeological remains. The initial optimism of processual archaeology—that everything about the past was knowable if we were just clever enough to figure out how to get at it—has given way to the more sobering realization that some aspects of the past may lie forever beyond our grasp.

The relationship between archaeologists and indigenous peoples also changed as indigenous people gained a greater voice and archaeologists realized that they could not ignore other perspectives on the past. Perhaps as a result of these indigenous voices, archaeologists saw that their work, whether they liked it or not, existed within a political context that they simply could not ignore.

Processual-Plus

Considerable tension still exists between those who call themselves processualists and those who prefer the postprocessual label. But much intellectual change occurs through the process of "thesis–antithesis–synthesis." An analogy to a clock is useful here. One paradigm pulls the clock's pendulum far to one side. In response, another paradigm pulls it to the opposite side. And in the end, it comes to rest in the middle. In recent years, many (perhaps the majority) of Americanist archaeologists have listened to debates between hard-core processual and postprocessual archaeologists and found a middle road that Michelle Hegmon (Arizona State University) calls "processual-plus."

Few archaeologists subscribe to the extreme postmodern idea that we cannot know anything true about the past. And many still feel that material factors such as technology, subsistence, and environment play critical roles in how human societies have changed. But few seek universals; instead, many seek generalities, patterns that point to how material factors may constrain or channel, but not determine, cultural change.

These same archaeologists also recognize the importance of other factors. All archaeologists know that artifacts carried symbolic meanings for people in the past and that humans respond to their situations in terms of cultural understandings of the world. Likewise, few see the details of history (and prehistory) as minor matters whose effects can easily be subtracted to discover the evolutionary processes behind them. History is a product of evolutionary processes, but it is also the result of myriad contingencies—environmental disasters, particular political decisions, cultural views, and so on—that are as integral to a culture's particular history as any evolutionary process. Archaeologists today are as interested in history as they are in cultural evolutionary theory.

And most archaeologists recognize that all of history is, indeed, the result of the actions of individuals and, in one way or another, an understanding of individual actions and motivations for those actions is critical to understanding the larger cultural evolutionary processes at work. Especially important has been a trend to look at gender, at the roles that men and women played in ancient societies (we'll return to this topic in Chapter 13).

Most archaeologists today recognize the links between politics and their research. Although few approach their research for purely political purposes, most archaeologists at least understand the political context of their research. The Archaeological Ethics boxes discuss these issues, and we will return to this sensitive subject in Chapter 18.

The Structure of Archaeological Inquiry

A century of archaeological practice has taught us a great deal about how archaeologists need to go about doing archaeology. So, what did we learn from this?

Figure 3-9 presents a model of the process of archaeological inquiry. This synthesis is similar to the model of the scientific cycle (described in Chapter 2), but is presented in a format specific to archaeology.

Notice that the entire process of archaeological inquiry takes place within a box labelled "Social, Cultural, Political Context." This arrangement recognizes that no scientist can step outside his or her culture—should we try that, we would cease being human, and our ability to analyze and understand the world would disappear. Still, we cannot ignore how our cultural context affects our understanding of the past. By constantly checking ourselves, over time, we should be able to distinguish between what is cultural bias and what is actually true.

The dotted line surrounding the "Paradigm" box symbolizes this interplay between one's research agenda and cultural context. As emphasized above, both paradigm and culture provide (often vague)

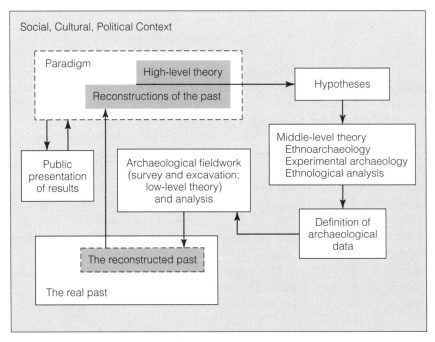

Figure 3-9 A model of archaeological inquiry.

understandings of the world, and each points the researcher toward a question's answers. These biases are not necessarily wrong. For example, Richard Wilk's analysis suggests that it was the Vietnam War that encouraged 1960s researchers to consider war the primary cause of the Maya civilization's collapse. Although Wilk's hypothesis was true, this does *not* mean that war was *not* the cause.

Paradigms provide specific guidelines for high-level theory—general statements such as "Agriculture occurs when a human population grows to the point where it exceeds the natural carrying capacity of the local environment." But paradigms can also generate more specific claims about a region's prehistory, such as "In the Mimbres Valley of southern New Mexico, there was a change in social organization as evidenced by a shift from pithouse to pueblo villages about A.D. 1000." Both statements are linked to the overarching paradigm by directing researchers to measure some variables (such as demography and changing social organization) and to set other variables (such as religion) aside. Propositions like this statement occur to archaeologists operating within a materialist paradigm.

In contrast, someone operating within a post-processual paradigm might say, "Agriculture originated from the need to create goods to give away at competitive feasts" or "In the Mimbres Valley a new symbolic order appeared about A.D. 1000, as evidenced by an art style involving painted naturalistic designs on bowls that are ritually killed and placed in human burials."

Testing Ideas

In either case, the next step is to construct hypotheses designed to test the various propositions—to see if our ideas might actually be true. For each hypothesis, we would frame one (or more) if . . . then statements that build upon the research proposition and predict some currently unknown aspect of the archaeological record. This is how we test ideas. Figure 3-9 shows this as "Hypotheses" resulting from high-level theory.

Take, for example, the question relating population growth and agriculture. Suppose we already know that in our research area, an agricultural economy began by 2000 B.C. We might hypothesize thus: If our proposition is true—that is, if population is the driving force behind agriculture—then signs of population

growth and subsequent pressure on the food base should appear prior to 2000 B.C.

This is where the Hypotheses lead to Middle-Level Theory (as shown in Figure 3-9). Testing the proposition requires some way of inferring population numbers from archaeological data. We can't measure population directly, of course—the people in question died a long time ago—so we need a bridging argument to infer changes in population over time from archaeological variables. To do so, we might have to survey existing ethnographic data or conduct our own ethnoarchaeological research to find correlates between population size and things that an archaeologist could record, for example house or village size.

We also need a way to measure "stress" on the food base. Perhaps we can find ethnographic evidence demonstrating that people use certain types of foods only under conditions of stress (such as those foods that are more difficult to harvest or that are less nutritious). On the other hand, we may need to conduct experiments, such as gathering foods with aboriginal technologies and measuring the efficiency with which they are collected. Such research might tell us that very small seeds are less efficiently harvested than large seeds and therefore that their use might signal subsistence stress.

Once we have adequate middle-level theory, we can define what constitutes relevant archaeological data (shown at lower right in Figure 3-9). If we believe that house size is the best variable, we will need to measure a sufficient number of houses from sites that date to various time periods before and after 2000 B.C.—to see if there is evidence of population growth *before* the appearance of an agricultural economy. If we decide that decreasing seed size is a good way to show that an ancient population was approaching an environment's carrying capacity, then we must recover and measure seeds from the appropriate archaeological sites (in Chapter 11, we discuss how archaeologists do this).

This background work done, we can state the general hypothesis in a more specific way: If agriculture appears because population exceeds carrying capacity, then (1) house size should increase before 2000 B.C., and (2) seeds found in trash associated with those houses should become smaller through time.

This brings us to the fun part, the archaeological fieldwork (shown in the centre of Figure 3-9) to collect the data necessary to test our hypothesis. We must design such fieldwork to generate adequate samples of house floors and seeds from the right time periods. Low-level theory is required to identify house floors (through the presence of postholes, packed clay floors, hearths, and so forth) and to identify seeds (we'll discuss fieldwork much more in the following chapters).

Reconstructing the Past

Testing such hypotheses requires that we reconstruct the past, that we say something about what actually happened back in time (as shown at the lower left in Figure 3-9). Perhaps we will find that houses became larger over time (or maybe not); perhaps we learn that seeds became smaller through time (or maybe not). Notice that in Figure 3-9, the dotted line enclosing "The reconstructed past" is itself inside a larger box labelled the "The real past." We did this to emphasize, first, that we cannot hope to reconstruct the complete past. Although we are always improving our ability to recover and extract better information from material remains, a complete picture of the past will always elude us. There was, to be sure, a real past made up of real people who lived real lives and who died real deaths; but our reconstructed past will never be an exact duplicate.

As the postprocessual critique makes clear, our experiences in the present heavily colour our vision of the past. The particular hypothesis used here as an example looks to demography (rather than religion or social change) to explain a change in subsistence. The upshot of this hypothesis is that, to reconstruct the past, we will focus on some issues and downplay others. Had we hypothesized a religious cause to agricultural origins, we would have sought very different data during our fieldwork. For example, we might have looked for evidence of how plants were used in different rituals, and that might have led us to excavate religious structures rather than houses.

Now we return to our original propositions to see whether we confirmed or falsified them. Did the fieldwork and ensuing analyses find evidence of population growth and resource stress prior to 2000 B.C., or did it not?

At this point, the archaeologist presents the results to a public audience. This presentation begins with scientific monographs or papers that other archaeologists will scrutinize. But modern archaeologists also know that results need to be conveyed to a broader public through books or magazine articles written in lay terms, public lectures, television presentations, museum exhibitions, or even novels (like *The Delight Makers*). In this way, the public can learn from and comment upon the research. From all of this professional and public feedback, the archaeologist may revisit the research propositions and commence the process all over again. And, through this recursive process (shown at left in Figure 3-9), archaeologists may find such a lack of fit between their ideas and the empirical archaeological record that they may discard their paradigm for another.

In truth, few archaeologists can do every step in the process; instead, almost everyone specializes. Some focus their careers on middle-level theory, doing experimental or ethnoarchaeological research. Others concentrate on the public side, presenting their research and that of others to a broader audience. Others work mostly with theory, and still others spend most of their time doing fieldwork. It's even more important, then, that archaeologists understand what role they are playing in the whole process.

Conclusion: Processualist or Postprocessualist?

Although there will always be competing paradigms in archaeology, we believe that Americanist archaeology works best when it sees paradigms as tools, rather than dogmatic religions. If you look at the field that way, then archaeologists should be able to draw what is useful from each paradigm, rather than be forced to ally themselves unwaveringly with one way of viewing the world.

And, indeed, one sees relatively few hard-core processualists or diehard postprocessualists these days. Most are processual-plus archaeologists, refusing to reduce the past to mechanical processes, but still believing in the power of scientifically tested ideas. Most contemporary archaeologists agree that multiple ways exist to learn about the past and that some aspects of the past will remain unknown. However, most would also agree that we can accept a certain amount of ambiguity and yet still learn something real about, and from, the past. And in the following chapters, we show you how archaeologists go about doing exactly that.

Summary

- Low-level theory involves the observations that emerge from archaeological fieldwork; this is how archaeologists get their "data," their "facts."

- Middle-level (middle-range) theory links archaeological data with human behaviour or natural processes; it is produced through experimental archaeology, taphonomy (the study of natural processes on archaeological sites), and ethnoarchaeology (the study of living peoples to see links between behaviour and material remains).

- High-level ("general") theory provides answers to larger "why" questions.

- Paradigms are frameworks for thinking that interrelate concepts and provide research strategies. They apply to intellectual inquiry in general and are not specific to archaeology.

- Two major paradigms in modern Americanist archaeology are processual and postprocessual archaeology; they are derived, respectively, from cultural materialism and postmodernism. The former takes a scientific approach and focuses on the material factors of life; the latter emphasizes humanistic perspectives and symbolic meaning.

- Processual and postprocessual approaches to prehistory have existed within archaeology for a long time. Individual archaeologists emphasize one more than the other, and some move back and forth between the two. They have different purposes and should not be confused.

- A model of archaeological inquiry shows how the different levels of theory, paradigms, and the public presentation of results help to ensure that our understanding of the past continually improves over time and overcomes the biases presented by the archaeologist's particular cultural context.

Additional Reading

CANADIAN RESOURCES

Hodder, Bruce. (2006). Triggering post-processual archaeology and beyond. In *The Archaeology of Bruce Trigger: Theoretical Empiricism*. Ronald Williamson and Michael Bisson (Eds). McGill–Queen's University Press: Montreal.

Trigger, Bruce. (2006). *A History of Archaeological Thought*. Cambridge: Cambridge University Press.

OTHER RESOURCES

Binford, Lewis R. (1983). *In Pursuit of the Past*. London: Thames and Hudson.

Harris, Marvin. (1979). *Cultural Materialism: The Struggle for a Science of Culture*. New York: Random House.

Hodder, Ian. (1999). *The Archaeological Process: An Introduction*. Oxford: Blackwell.

Hodder, Ian. (Ed.). (2001). *Archaeological Theory Today*. Oxford: Blackwell.

Johnson, Matthew. (1999). *Archaeological Theory: An Introduction*. Oxford: Blackwell.

Online Resources

COMPANION WEBSITE

Visit *http://www.archaeology1ce.nelson.com* to access a wide range of material to help you succeed in your introductory archaeology course. These include flashcards, Internet exercises, Web links, and practice quizzes.

RESEARCH ONLINE WITH INFOTRAC COLLEGE EDITION

From the Student Companion Website, you can access the InfoTrac College Edition database, which offers thousands of full-length articles for your research.

4

Doing Fieldwork
Surveying for Archaeological Sites

Parks Canada archaeologists excavate at Gwaii Haanas, British Columbia.
Source: Courtesy of Dr. Marty Magne

Preview

Now the fun begins. In the next few chapters, you will get a glimpse of what it's like to actually do archaeology. For many in the discipline—ourselves included—fieldwork is why we became archaeologists in the first place. That said, we must begin this introduction to archaeological field techniques with two important warnings:

- There is no one "right" way to look for and excavate sites (but there are plenty of wrong ones).
- Nobody ever learned how to do proper archaeological fieldwork from a book (including this one).

Despite recent advances, archaeological fieldwork remains as much art as science. All we can do here is examine some common techniques, list some archaeological standards and principles, and give you a sense of what it feels like to participate in an archaeological exploration.

Introduction

Every archaeologist addressing a general audience is eventually asked the same question: "How do you know where to dig?"

There are many answers. We've known about some **archaeological sites,** such as Egypt's pyramids, for centuries—they were never lost. The locations of other sites have been handed down through the generations, preserved in oral and written traditions. For example, archaeologists identified the site of Tula in northern Mexico as the prehistoric Toltec capital by tracing and testing Aztec traditions. Sites are sometimes deliberately discovered in large-scale systematic surveys, during which large regions are scanned for the remains of previous habitation. And some of the most important archaeological sites in the world were found by accident, hard work, and luck.

archaeological site Any place where material evidence exists about the human past. Usually, "site" refers to a concentration of such evidence.

Good Old Gumshoe Survey

In Chapter 3, we mentioned Gatecliff Shelter in Nevada, where both Thomas and Kelly excavated in the 1970s. But before we could dig at Gatecliff, of course, the site had to be found. How did that happen?

Gatecliff was found by a fortunate combination of happenstance, hard work, and luck, a process that James O'Connell (University of Utah) calls old-fashioned "gumshoe survey."

In the summer of 1970, Thomas was in central Nevada's Reese River Valley conducting systematic archaeological survey (a technique we discuss later in this chapter). Basically, this fieldwork entails mapping and collecting archaeological stuff found on the ground. The survey went well, but it could not answer all the questions. Thomas needed to know, for example, something about prehistoric subsistence and the chronology of different artifact types. Such information can only come from buried sites, where food remains (bones and seeds) might be preserved and where artifacts can be dated. Rockshelters and caves often contain the necessary buried deposits but, despite the Reese River crew's best efforts, they could not locate one.

At the end of the first field session in Reese River, Thomas assembled the crew for steak dinners in the town of Austin, about an hour's dusty ride away. Austin is a pocket-sized Nevada mining town with fewer than 250 citizens, a picturesque little desert dive. Writer Oscar Lewis described it as "the town that died laughing," and William Least Heat Moon called it "a living ghost town: 40 percent living, 50 percent ghost and 10 percent not yet decided."

When two dozen grubby archaeologists come to such a town for steaks and beverages, word gets around quickly. Thomas soon found himself talking with the waitress's husband, Gale Peer, a mining geologist who had prospected central Nevada for 40 years. There are few places Gale Peer had not been, so Thomas asked if he knew of any caves or rockshelters.

Indeed, Mr. Peer did know of a cave—in Monitor Valley, about 20 kilometres east of Austin. He had not been there in years, but the details were fresh in his mind.

"You take the main dirt road south in Monitor Valley, then turn west, up one of the side canyons. I don't remember which one. As you drive along, oh, let's see, maybe 10 or 15 miles, there's a large black chert cliff. At the bottom of the cliff is a cave. Some time, a long time ago, the Indians painted the inside of the cave. There are pictures of people and animals, plus a lot of writing I don't understand. Top of the shelter's caved in. Maybe in an earthquake. There's not much of the cave left. Drive out there when you get a chance. I'd like to know what's in that cave." He sketched a map on his business card.

This is the essence of gumshoe survey—hanging out in coffee shops, bars, and gas stations, listening to those who know more about the landscape than you do.

Searching for Gatecliff

The next summer Thomas and his crew returned, hoping to find the cave that Mr. Peer had described. They knew that the rockshelter was several kilometres up a canyon, on the north side—but there were 15 such canyons.

Beginning at the southern end of Monitor Valley, the crew drove up and down each side canyon, working their way northward. They were hampered by

spring snow and washed-out roads—typical fieldwork conditions in central Nevada.

Each of the canyons had potential. The crew would see something, stop the truck, and skitter up the hillside. But each time, the "something" turned out to be a shadow, an abandoned mine shaft, or just a jumble of boulders.

After a week, Thomas came to Mill Canyon, just the next one on the list, with no greater potential than the ten canyons they had already combed. The road was a little worse than most and, even in four-wheel drive, the truck lurched down a steep ridge into the rocky canyon. Finally, as the crew moved up the flat canyon bottom, a black cliff loomed ahead, riddled with small caves and rockshelters.

As had happened many times before, the shelters were empty, unless you count coyote scats and packrat nests. Finally, the crew spied a dim shadow where the black dolomite formation was swallowed up beneath the Mill Canyon bottomland.

The paintings were invisible until you stood right in the mouth of the shelter. But there they were, just as Mr. Peer had said: small human figures, painted in red and yellow. On the other wall were cryptic motifs in white and black. And, yes, the roof had caved in years before. One boulder dwarfed the pickup.

There was nothing "archaeological" on the surface, but a small test pit turned up telltale signs that people had once lived in the shelter: several pieces of broken bone, a few of them charred, and a dozen stone flakes (probably debris from resharpening stone knives or **projectile points**).

Across the campfire that night, the crew assayed the finds. The rock art was intriguing; only two similar sites were known in central Nevada. The stones and bones were suggestive, but the shelter seemed hardly the deep site they were seeking. Thomas named the site after the rock formation, Gatecliff, in which they found it (see "Looking Closer: How Do Archaeological Sites Get Their Names?").

On the strength of this meagre evidence, they decided to dig some—a good decision, it turned out,

projectile points Arrowheads, dart points, or spear points.

because the deposits inside Gatecliff Shelter proved to be 12 metres deep, making it one of the deepest rock-shelters in the Americas. And the strata were spectacularly layered, not jumbled up like most sites in the area. Flash floods had periodically inundated the shelter, the surging waters laying down thick layers of rock-hard silt. This flooding occurred at least a dozen times, separating the deposits into clean occupational "floors."

This meant that Gatecliff had what textbooks—including this one—describe as "layer-cake stratigraphy." Sandwiched between these sterile flash-flood deposits was a wonderful 7000-year record of human activity and environmental change in Monitor Valley.

Looking Closer
How Do Archaeological Sites in Canada Get Their Names?

Human beings spend an inordinate amount of time naming things, and archaeologists are no exception to this rule. Naming sites has traditionally been considered the archaeologist's prerogative. But sites are given different names for different reasons. In 1993, Dr. James Helmer asked an Inuit Elder to recommend a name for an archaeological site he had discovered on Little Cornwallis Island in the Canadian Arctic. The Elder suggested *Tasiarulik*, an Inuktitut word meaning "place of many small lakes," which is an apt description of the setting. Some archaeological site names have humorous stories attached to them. The site of Migod in the barrenlands of the Canadian North, for example, is located above a small but deep back eddy pool, caused by a submerged rock band jutting out from the site. Lake trout congregate here, where the fast-moving Dubawnt River leaves Grant Lake, Nunavut. When archaeologist James V. Wright was testing the site in 1973, a crewmember caught a particularly large trout—and exclaimed the name that Wright gave to the site!

As archaeological activity in Canada increased following the end of World War II, it became obvious that simply assigning a name to a site was not good enough. Consequently, a coding system was developed that enabled Canadian archaeologists to make reference to their sites in publications, and catalogue their finds in a way that was universally consistent. Dr. Charles E. Borden, a British Columbia archaeologist and professor of German studies, developed this system in 1952. Borden joined the German Department at the University of British Columbia (UBC) in 1939, but became interested in archaeology after the war with Germany made it difficult for him to obtain research materials. In 1949 Borden took up an appointment in the Department of Sociology and Anthropology at UBC, where he made many important contributions to Canadian archaeology. Borden's system is elegant in its simplicity, and has been used by the Sites Office at the Canadian Museum of Civilization since 1956. Here's how it works:

A grid system, based on the National Topographic Map series published by the Government of Canada, overlies a map of Canada. Each unit within the grid is represented by a double-lettered block, which provides the site designation and looks like this: JgKm-1. The capital letters "J" and "K" represent latitude and longitude. The lower-case letters "g" and "m" represent intervals along the dimensions of the grid, which are expressions of latitude and longitude in degrees and minutes. The sizes of these grid units change as one moves north because the distance between the degrees of longitude changes as the meridians converge at the pole. The number that follows the double-lettered block designation denotes the archaeological site—usually one of many found within the block. These sites are numbered according to the sequence in which they were discovered.

So, an archaeological site can have different names for different purposes. The site of "MiGod" is named for a great fish story, while its Borden number, KkLn-4, tells other archaeologists where the site is located, and how many sites were discovered before it.

The University of California (Davis) began the research, followed by the American Museum of Natural History, which dispatched five major expeditions to Gatecliff Shelter. The National Geographic Society supported part of the fieldwork, shot an educational film, and wrote a book about the site. The *New York Times* and *The New Yorker* magazine published stories about Gatecliff. There was television and radio coverage. Even a United States congressman became involved in preserving the site.

Gatecliff Shelter was on the map—and all because a waitress's husband in Austin, Nevada remembered an interesting place from years before. In fact, many important sites have been found by ranchers, cowboys, sheepherders, farmers, geologists, and amateur archaeologists—anyone who spends a lot of time wandering about outdoors.

Archaeology Is More Than Just Digging Sites

Archaeologists feel lucky to find sites like Gatecliff Shelter, which was a marvellous place to dig. But as John Hyslop (1945–1993) worked his way up and down the Andes Mountains, he wasn't looking for a place to dig. Hyslop was surveying the ancient Inka road (Figure 4-1). Though they did not have wheeled vehicles, the extraordinary Inka civilization of the 14th and 15th centuries still created thousands of kilometres of roads connecting coastal and highland cities from Ecuador to northern Chile. Although excavation would have been possible at many of the places he recorded, Hyslop knew that his Inka Road survey would, in itself, produce a huge quantity of valuable details about ancient road building and engineering, as well as about Inka economy. In fact, Hyslop wrote an important book, *The Inka Road System,* based strictly on his survey results—without ever digging at all.

This is an often forgotten point about archaeological reconnaissance. Sometimes archaeologists survey to find good places to dig (this is why Thomas was looking for Gatecliff Shelter). But other times, the archaeological survey itself is a way to generate archaeological data on a regional scale. In the following sections, we will examine a few ways developed by archaeologists to systematize the survey process. As you will see, archaeologists can learn plenty without ever lifting a shovel.

Figure 4-1 Inka road survey.

Source: American Museum of Natural History

The Fallacy of the "Typical" Site

Survey is important because of the problem of representation. Suppose you spend seven years digging a site like Gatecliff (which we did). You recover plenty of artifacts from the stratified and well-dated sediments. But what do all these ancient things mean in human terms?

The first thing to remember is that nobody lives in just one place—not now and certainly not millennia ago. To understand the past, therefore, we need to examine the range of places in which ancient peoples lived their lives. This is why many archaeologists employ the **systematic regional survey** as a way of recording the full range of human settlements, rather than just seek out a "typical" site.

To see why this is so, take a look at the map of the **seasonal round** of the Western Shoshone people of the central Great Basin (Figure 4-2). Produced by

systematic regional survey A set of strategies for arriving at accurate descriptions of the range of archaeological material across a landscape.

seasonal round Hunter-gatherers' pattern of movement between different places on the landscape timed to the seasonal availability of food and other resources.

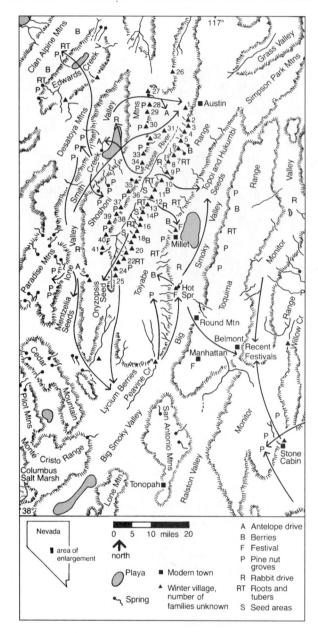

Figure 4-2 Julian Steward's reconstruction of the seasonal round of the Western Shoshone and Northern Paiute people (Nevada), projected for the mid-19th-century period.

Source: After Steward 1938, figure 8.

because of their intimate relationship with the natural environment, they were able to work out a seasonal round that allowed them to travel from one habitat to another to harvest local wild foods as they became available.

Look closely at the map. The numbered triangles in the Toiyabe and Shoshone mountain ranges are winter villages, inhabited seasonally to hunt bighorn sheep and to exploit the piñon nuts that grow there. These nutritious nuts ripened in the late summer and early autumn and were stored for the winter, along with buffalo berries and currants available in the low foothills. Other kinds of sites (denoted by letters) occur at lower elevations and along the Reese River; the Shoshone lived there during the summer to gather ricegrass seeds and roots, catch rabbits, and hunt antelope. In upland areas they gathered berries, tubers, and hunted bighorn sheep. They did other things at other places on the landscape for ceremonial purposes or in pursuit of specific foods.

Steward based this reconstruction on what Shoshone people told him between 1925 and 1936. Because most of the mapped sites were abandoned sometime in the 19th century, Steward's native consultants were often recalling events of 50 years ago. Despite the fact that Steward's consultants most likely did not recall everything, the map nonetheless demonstrates the native peoples' intricate and complex seasonal round. This seasonal round also provides examples of what archaeologists call a *settlement pattern*—the distribution of sites across a landscape—and a *settlement system*, which describes the movements and activities inferred from the sites that make up the settlement pattern (a seasonal round is one type of settlement system).

This map also illustrates the fallacy of the typical site. Suppose that an archaeologist had a chance to locate and excavate just one of Steward's Shoshone sites. Which one should he or she choose? Winter village sites are of interest because they represent the lengthiest occupation and probably contain remains of a great variety of activities. But winter village sites are almost always located on windswept ridges (where the wind blows the snow away), and all that is preserved are stone tools and ceramics.

Would it be better to seek out one of the small upland shelters where hunters briefly camped while pursuing bighorn sheep? The preservation in these shelters is often good, and the chances are excellent

ethnographer Julian Steward (1902–1972), this map charts the cultural landscape of the Shoshone, a people who survived by hunting antelope and bighorn sheep and by collecting various plant foods.

This ecological adaptation depended on a precise exploitation of Great Basin environments. The prehistoric Shoshone were nomadic hunter-gatherers and,

for finding remains of sandals, snares, pieces of bows, arrows, food bones, seeds, and fire-making apparatus. But these small shelters represent only a minor portion of the overall Shoshone pattern. Women were probably not included in such small hunting parties, and men conducted only a limited range of activities there. Perhaps one might choose to excavate a seed-gathering camp, an antelope drive, or a place where women gathered berries.

The difficulty is clear: No matter which site we select, we will miss a great deal, and the archaeologist will come away with a biased image. Let's suppose, for example, that you decided to excavate a piñon-gathering camp in the Toiyabe Range. You would probably conclude that the economy was based on harvesting piñon nuts, the camp contained between 12 and 24 people, and the men made lots of stone tools and repaired their weapons. You might also conclude that the women spent a great deal of time collecting piñon nuts and grinding them into meal, sewing hide clothing, and making basketry.

But now suppose that someone else decided to excavate the scene of a *fandango* (or festival site, denoted by "F" on Steward's map). The ensuing reconstruction would probably suggest a grouping of 200 to 300 people who subsisted on communal hunting of jackrabbit and antelope and who spent a great deal of time dancing and gambling.

In other words, you would have reconstructed a hardworking society composed of extended families, whereas your colleague would have seen a more exuberant people living in large aggregations and particularly concerned with ritual and feasting.

In truth, of course, the same people produced both sites throughout the course of a single year, as part of the Western Shoshone's seasonal round. Our point is simple: Neither site is typical.

This is not just a problem for archaeologists who study nomadic hunter-gatherers. Agricultural peoples also do not live their lives in one location. They create residences in one place, field houses near outlying crops, check dams in the arroyos, hunting camps in the mountains, and maybe ritual centres in yet another place. This holds true for your daily life as well. Trying to reconstruct your life from just one of the places you use would present a very biased view.

The goal of archaeological survey is not just to find deep sites full of interesting artifacts. Instead, survey can document the range of archaeological remains that occur across a landscape to avoid a biased image of the lives of ancient peoples.

We do this by looking at the distribution of sites across a region. Decades ago, archaeologists often ignored surface sites because they lacked the contextual relations necessary to establish solid cultural chronologies. But such sequences, although important, are only part of the puzzle. Surface sites provide unique data regarding past human–land relationships. In the next section, we consider the surface archaeology of the Carson Desert in western Nevada to illustrate how archaeologists implement this regional perspective.

Surface Archaeology in the Carson Desert

The Great Basin is best known for vast stretches of sagebrush and arid mountain ranges, but it also contains a number of substantial wetlands. Julian Steward's Depression-era research documented the lives of those Shoshone and Paiute people who lived in areas *without* wetlands. So, without much ethnographic data, archaeologists in the 1970s debated how the wetlands were incorporated into the seasonal round of the region's native peoples.

One hypothesis held that the wetlands provided a permanent, sedentary home for hunter-gatherers; an opposing one held that the wetlands served as but one element in a broader seasonal round. Both of these hypotheses were grounded in the materialist paradigm and focused on food. The first hypothesis argued that wetlands provide abundant, high-quality foods; it also assumed that people would become sedentary (that is, stay in one location year-round) wherever food was abundant. The latter hypothesis viewed wetland food resources as lower quality and more difficult to gather than others, such as piñon and large game. And in contrast it assumed that hunter-gatherers became sedentary when the lack of food elsewhere forced them to do so. Expressed as research questions, the hypotheses were: Did prehistoric peoples settle down and focus exclusively on the wetlands, or did they incorporate the mountains' resources into a more diversified seasonal round?

One of the Great Basin's largest wetlands lies in the Carson Desert, about 100 kilometres east of Reno, Nevada. A large basin filled with sand dunes and alkali

In His Own Words
Surveying Late Ice Age Landscapes of Southeastern Quebec

*by Dr. Claude Chapdelaine, Département d'Anthropologie,
l'Université de Montréal*

In order to know where to look for archaeological sites, archaeologists need to understand what the environment and landscape of an area would have looked like thousands of years ago. This is especially the case in Canada, where Paleoindian groups camped and hunted along the ancient shorelines of large pro-glacial lakes, which have long since drained away. Dr. Claude Chapdelaine, (Département d'Anthropologie, l'Université de Montréal) has conducted extensive walking surveys along what used to be the paleo-beaches of the Champlain Sea, near the Canada–U.S. border. In the following section, Dr. Chapdelaine outlines his recent research, which illustrates how an understanding of Late Glacial environments and landscapes led him to discover the evidence for the earliest human occupation in the province of Quebec.

During the summer of 2003, while excavating at the Clichée-Rancourt site, we found the first fluted point fragments for the entire province of Quebec, pushing back the initial period of human occupation in our research area, and for the entire province, to between 12,500 and 12,000 calBP. It is a jump back in time of more than 4,000 years, from the Middle Archaic to the Early Paleo-Indian Period in our study area. At the end of our fourth field season at the site in 2006, we had uncovered a total of seven fluted point fragments, four proximal bases and three distal ends, a dozen channel flakes of distinct fluted points, a few bifaces, end scrapers, side scrapers, gravers, a rare unifacial awl, and more than a hundred utilized flakes made of red Munsungun chert, from a source located 175 kilometres away in northeastern Maine. This

assemblage is distributed over four separate areas. It is thus a small hunting camp where several activities were carried out, including curating projectile points, scraping with available flakes to maximize the longevity of the well-made scrapers, and thinning some bifaces based on the recovery of more than 3,000 small flakes. How can we explain the presence of this hunting group up north at the end of the Late Ice Age?

The Cliché-Rancourt site is located on a sandy terrace overlooking Lac-aux-Araignées in the Mégantic Lake area, which is the source of the Chaudière River flowing north to the Quebec City area. The drainage is very good and the site is about 12 metres above the actual lake level, making it suitable for occupation soon after deglaciation of the area. The ecological position of the site, viewed in a larger geographic perspective, is part of a narrow 100-kilometre-long corridor at an altitude ranging between 300 and 450 metres above sea level (m asl), crossing the Appalachians. This corridor allowed animals and humans to travel from the Chaudière River to the Kennebec River. The Cliché-Rancourt site, at an altitude of 418 m asl, therefore occupies a key area after crossing the lowest mountain passes at 430 m asl, making the crossing from the Kennebec hydrographical system to the Mégantic Lake area a moderate undertaking.

The Mégantic Lake area was one of the first to be deglaciated in southeastern Quebec, and the large mountain pass allowed caribou herds to cross from the Dead River basin to the receding postglacial Chaudière Lake as early as 13000 calBP. With the discovery of the Cliché-Rancourt site, it is thus argued that the same mountain pass also served as a major entrance route for human groups. At the estimated time of occupation by Paleo-Indian hunters at Cliché-Rancourt (between 12,500 and 12,000 calBP based on the style of fluted points), Mégantic Lake probably had a shape similar to its present configuration. The ice-free Chaudière River drained the postglacial Chaudière Lake into the Champlain Sea, starting around 13,100 calBP. Although the environmental conditions at that time have no modern analogues, it is accepted that climate during the Younger Dryas (also referred to as "The Big Freeze") was colder than before and that an open vegetation, similar to the tundra, was prevailing in Northern New England, the Maritimes, and the Mégantic Lake area. The exploitation of barren ground caribou in this northern environment during the late summer and fall months is the most logical explanation for the presence of Late Ice Age hunters on this well-drained terrace. The terrace upon which the site is located is situated between two lakes, in an area that is ideal for observing herd movements and intercepting caribou herds before their migration toward southern latitudes.

It is well known that early Paleo-Indian groups were very mobile, selecting a particular lithic raw material source, usually a high quality chert or flint, that might be very far from habitation sites. At least 95 percent of the total debitage associated with the early Paleo-Indian occupation at the Cliché-Rancourt site has been identified as red Munsungun chert, to which the hunters of Cliché-Rancourt

Figure 4-3 Seven fluted points from the Cliché-Rancourt site.

Source: Dr. Claude Chapdelaine, Département d'Anthropologie, Université de Montreal

seem to have had direct access. With a detailed analysis of the Cliché-Rancourt lithic assemblage, we hope to determine if they were returning from the quarry, or were heading toward it and therefore making a detour to encounter caribou herds in a newly recognized hunting territory.

After five years of testing and excavating the Cliché-Rancourt site, named in honour of the land owners, we have assigned the Cliché-Rancourt hunters to the Middle Phase of the Early Paleo-Indian Period, which is dated between 12,500 and 12,000 calBP—it is, for the moment, the unique site of this oldest chapter in Quebec prehistory.

flats (Figure 4-4), the Carson Desert is also the terminus of several large rivers. These create a vast, slightly alkaline wetland. This wetland is host to many species of plants and animals that provided ancient peoples with food and various kinds of raw material for clothing, houses, and tools: cattail, bulrush and other plants, fish (especially tui chub), muskrats, and other small mammals. Piñon pine nuts grow in the piñon-juniper forest of the Stillwater Mountains that form the eastern edge of the Carson Desert, and foragers could find tubers, seeds, bighorn sheep, and other game there as well. Previous research suggested that people had lived in this region off and on for more than 9000 years.

In the late 1970s, we were excavating Hidden Cave, a site located at the south end of the Stillwater range, which overlooks the Carson Desert. The site was used primarily between 5000 and 1500 years ago as a place to cache hunting gear and as a cool escape from the desert's extreme summer heat (Figure 4-5). Hidden Cave is an intriguing site, but remember the "fallacy of the typical site": Because we knew that people had lived in the Carson Desert for at least 9000 years, we assumed that Hidden Cave documented only a portion of the region's prehistory. And furthermore, a specialized cache cave obviously gives us only limited insights about the lives of the people who had lived in this area—like trying to reconstruct someone's life by looking at only their safe deposit box or back porch. (We'll have more to say about Hidden Cave in Chapter 11.)

To understand ancient life in the Carson Desert, we therefore needed to explore the regional archaeological record: What kind of archaeological remains are found near the marsh, in the dunes, in the low foothills of the Stillwater Mountains, and, higher in the mountains, in the piñon-juniper forest? Put simply, we hypothesized that if the wetland was exploited by a sedentary population, then we should find evidence of large, year-round populations living near the marsh. There should be little evidence of use of the mountains, except perhaps by hunting parties seeking bighorn sheep. People should have made far less use of the dunes and alkali flats, because their economic potentials are low compared with that of the wetland.

But on the other hand, if the wetlands were just one stop on a broad-scale seasonal round, then we should find evidence of more transient use of the wetlands and a more intensive use of the mountains.

With this in mind, we generated some archaeological expectations for each hypothesis. Because we would rely strictly on surface archaeology, where organic remains are not preserved, we focused on stone tools (pottery is rare in this region) and the waste flakes from their manufacture and resharpening. We'll talk more about these kinds of artifacts in Chapter 10.

Figure 4-4 Students collecting a site found during survey in the Carson Desert.
Source: Robert Kelly

Figure 4-5 Archaeologists excavating inside Hidden Cave (Nevada). Without the 500-watt quartz-halogen landing lights (evident on the left), the excavation area would be pitch black. Note also the respirators and hard-hats—often required equipment for working inside such enclosed cave environments.

Source: American Museum of Natural History; photo by Dennis O'Brien

The point is this: Long before we took to the field, we had a good idea of what we should find *if* one hypothesis was correct and the other was incorrect. For example, if a sedentary population had used the wetlands, then we expected to find dense scatters of waste flakes and broken tools (the remains of villages occupied for years at a time) in the wetland. In the uplands, we expected to find only evidence of hunting activities, evidenced by small campsites containing broken projectile points.

But if the second hypothesis was correct, then we expected to find smaller, less-dense settlements on the valley floor and evidence of hunting, but also tuber, seed, and piñon gathering in the mountains, as shown by the **manos** and **metates** (grinding stones) used for processing seeds and nuts.

Some Sampling Considerations

So, you can see that the fieldwork needed to test our hypotheses required that we explore the character of archaeological evidence across the region. But what should that region be? And did we need to search every square centimetre of it? Given the practicalities of desert archaeology, it was obvious that we could

not look everywhere. We must *sample,* but capricious and biased sampling methods can lead the archaeologist astray. What if we looked only in places where we thought sites would be located? Not being Great Basin hunter-gatherers, we would surely not see the landscape as past foragers did. We would undoubtedly overestimate the importance of some places and overlook others, generating a biased image of the region's archaeology.

The best way to ensure unbiased results is through judicious use of **statistical sampling.** We'll cover only the basic principles of this large and complex subject here. (But note that any student contemplating a career in archaeology will need to take several statistics courses, because statistical analysis is as indispensable to archaeologists as their trowels.)

To acquire a statistical sample, you must first define the **statistical population** that you wish to characterize. In biology, "population" refers to a group of organisms of a single species that is found in a circumscribed area at a given time. Cultural anthropologists also commonly use the term "cultural population" to denote a specific society, and archaeologists often speak of archaeological populations, such as "Ancestral Pueblo populations" or the "Shoshone-speaking population."

mano A fist-sized, round, flat, hand-held stone used with a **metate** for grinding foods.

metate A large, flat stone used as a stationary surface upon which seeds, tubers, and nuts are ground with a mano.

statistical sampling The principles that underlie sampling strategies that provide accurate measures of a statistical population.

statistical population A set of counts, measurements, or characteristics about which relevant inquiries are to be made. Scientists use the term "statistical population" in a specialized way (quite different from "population" in the ordinary sense).

But statisticians use the term "population" to refer not to physical objects but to data, which are, as you will recall, *observations made on objects*. The difference is subtle yet important. A defined group of people, such as Shoshone Indians or American males, could make up a biological or sociocultural population, but they are not a statistical population. Only measurements made on variables—such as stature, daily caloric intake, or religious beliefs—could constitute a statistical population. A statistical population consists of a defined set of observations of interest.

The population of interest to us in our project was the observations we could make on the stone artifacts and waste flakes found in the archaeological sites of the wetlands and dunes of the Carson Desert and the piñon-juniper forests of the Stillwater Mountains.

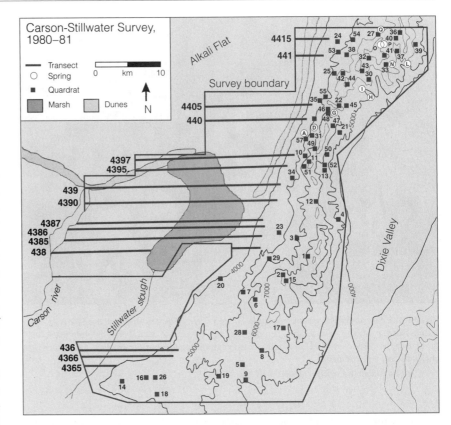

Figure 4-6 Map of the Carson Desert and Stillwater Mountains (Nevada), showing the locations of survey transects, quadrats, and spring surveys.

Source: Robert Kelly, "Prehistory of the Carson Desert and Stillwater Mountains," University of Utah Anthropological Papers, No. 123, 2001.

Statistical sampling also requires that we define a relevant sample universe, the archaeological sites that will provide the sample population. Because the research question concerned the relationships between sites on the valley floor, in particular those in the wetland and those in the mountains, our **sample universe** had to contain both of these regions.

The result was a sample universe—a survey area—of some 1700 square kilometres that looks like the head of a large, barking dog (shown in Figure 4-6). The size and shape of a survey area is a result of the research question and practical considerations. In this case, the survey area's odd shape was a product of the need to encompass the wetland, dune area, and alkali

sample universe The region that contains the statistical population and that will be sampled. Its size and shape are determined by the research question and practical considerations.

flats, as well as the northern Stillwater Mountains, where there is a piñon-juniper forest today, and the southern mountains, which are covered primarily by sagebrush. But we also needed to avoid (1) the town of Fallon, (2) a large wildlife refuge that lies in the dog's "mouth," and (3) up in front of the dog's ear, a large naval bombing range that contained unexploded ordinance. (Fallon is home to one of the U.S. Navy's elite fighter pilot schools. Watch the film *Top Gun*, and you'll catch some glimpses of the Carson Desert and Stillwater Mountains beneath the screaming F-14s.)

Because soil formation in deserts is often slow and vegetation is sparse, many archaeological remains still lie on the surface, where people dropped or discarded them hundreds or even thousands of years ago. Doing surface archaeology in such places means that you simply spot an artifact, plot its location in your field notes, pick it up, and label it—no digging!

But who could survey all 1700 square kilometres? That could take lifetimes! This is where statistical sampling theory helps out, providing a set of methods that allows us to characterize a population without having to record data on every item in that population. We draw upon the same set of methods and theory that pollsters use to take the nation's political pulse by interviewing only a thousand people.

You begin by randomly selecting those sites that will be included in the sample. The word "random" here is critical, for it specifically means that *each site has an equal chance of being selected for the sample.* If there were 100 sites, say, then each site must have a $1/100 = 1$ percent chance of being included in the sample. If the sample is not selected in a random manner, then some sites may be overrepresented and others underrepresented in the sample. And that would bias the final results.

Random sampling provides the only way for archaeologists to collect meaningful negative evidence. This is important because, in addition to knowing what activities took place where, archaeologists want to know which activities did *not* occur in a particular area or biotic community. As you will see, the requirement for negative evidence imposes severe yet necessary requirements on survey fieldwork.

Randomly selecting the samples also permits us to analyze the results statistically. Because statistical analysis generally requires a random sample, archaeologists who use a biased sampling design will never know if their results are meaningful or not.

Getting the Sample

Once we had decided on the sample universe, the next task was to select the sample. The first step here is to decide on the **sample fraction.** What portion of the sample population would be included—1 percent of the sites? 5 percent, 10 percent, 50 percent? Archaeologists are somewhat hampered in this regard because the size of the sample depends on characteristics of the population being sampled. For example, if there is a lot of variation, say, in the number of projectile points in sites (some have a few, others have many), then we would want a larger sample than if there were only a small amount of variation. The problem is that archaeologists rarely know much about the populations they are sampling; this is especially true when undertaking survey in a new region.

One solution to this problem is to start with a small uniform sample across the region and then use the

findings from that sample to decide whether some regions need more intensive sampling. And so, in 1980 we began with a 1 percent sample of the entire region and then increased the sample fraction in particular areas the following summer.

The second step is more pragmatic: How do you actually acquire the sample? Ideally, we would take all the sites in the sample universe, give each one a number, and then randomly select some portion of those numbers and examine those sites. But we don't know anything about the region—we don't know how many sites there are, let alone their locations. This means that we have to sample the landscape in order to sample the sites.

We could just go out and start walking across the land, but it would be hard to keep track of how much land we covered and hence difficult to compute the sample fraction. And we would almost certainly bias the sample by avoiding areas that were hard to reach or unpleasant to walk across.

We solved this problem by using randomly selected **sample units.** Sample units can be many different shapes, although squares, circles, and transects (long, narrow rectangles) are the most commonly used; all three were employed in this survey. The choice of which to use depends somewhat on the research questions, but also on practical considerations.

In the mountains, we used 500×500-metre squares (we called them quadrats) as the sample unit. Kelly selected this size because Thomas's previous experience in other Nevada surveys showed that they were a manageable size, given the exigencies of survey in the desert mountains and the number of crew members he had.

We located these squares randomly using the UTM grid (Universal Transverse Mercator). What is the UTM grid? Simply put, mapmakers divide the world into a grid of 1×1-metre squares; each intersection in that grid has north and east coordinates. Look at a standard USGS topographic map, and you will see these coordinates written in small, black numbers

sample fraction The percentage of the sample universe that is surveyed. Areas with a lot of variability in archaeological remains require larger sample fractions than do areas of low variability.

sample units Survey units of a standard size and shape used to obtain the sample, determined by the research question and practical considerations.

along the map's margins. (And many maps today include 1 × 1-kilometre blocks of the UTM grid drawn in black lines.) These numbers provide a handy, pre-existing way to sample a landscape.

We randomly selected sets of north and east coordinates (by putting the UTM coordinates in a hat—nothing fancy here!). Each set of north and east coordinates defined the northwest corner of a 500 × 500-metre sample square; for example, the coordinates of Quadrat 36 were 4416000 North, 407500 East. We then located these squares on the appropriate topographic map and drew them in. We selected a number of units from pre-defined portions of the mountains to ensure that survey units were spread throughout the extent of the Stillwater Mountains.

We also drew 500-metre-radius circles around all the active springs in the northern mountains. Water is obviously critical for hunter-gatherers living in a desert environment. In the Stillwater Mountains, water is mostly present as springs that create a small seep or a short creek. Only one "stream" exists in the Stillwaters; jokingly labelled "Mississippi Canyon" on USGS maps, it trickles only a few hundred metres before disappearing beneath rock and sand. In his Reese River Valley survey, Thomas found that sites tended to occur within about 450 metres of a water source, so we chose to survey a 500-metre radius around a sample of the springs. These 500-metre-radius circles were then completely surveyed for sites.

On the valley floor (defined as all land below 1340 metres in elevation), we used 100-metre-wide transects (instead of 500-metre squares) to sample the area. We chose this width because we had 10 to 12 students working on the project, and this meant that they could be spaced about 10 metres apart—an interval that previous experience told us was the maximum distance surveyors should be apart to avoid missing small sites.

We located the first transect by randomly selecting a UTM north coordinate from near the north end of the valley survey and used that line to define the middle of the 100-metre transect width (that is, the transect extended 50 metres north and 50 metres south of the random UTM north coordinate). To increase the sample to the desired fraction, we then selected additional transects at 10-kilometre intervals south of the first. Later, additional transects were selected by placing them between these existing ones. It may seem that these later transects were not randomly selected,

but they actually were, given that their locations were predicated on that of the first—and it was randomly selected.

Why didn't we use our 500 × 500 quadrats on the valley floor? Quadrats are fairly easy to locate on the ground in areas with topographic relief. Plotted on the map, we could see that the southeast corner of Quadrat 36, for example, could be reached by walking up a particular canyon, then, where the canyon makes a turn to the south, going north up a small draw to the ridge top.

But the Carson Desert is flat, with only 1 to 2 metres of elevation over vast stretches. We could have spent hours just trying to locate the corner of a survey unit through triangulation with a compass (this was before GPS units were available—more on those under "GPS Technology and Modern Surveys" later in this chapter). We used transects because we could locate them on the ground where they crossed a road or two-track on the map (using the truck's mileage gauge from some known point, such as an irrigation canal or a permanent USGS marker). Once we found the transect, we spread out over the 100-metre width and walked due east or west with the help of a compass. We didn't use transects in the mountains because there are few roads and hence few entry points. This meant that surveyors might have had to walk many kilometres in straight lines across steep, rocky terrain before they could reach a point where a vehicle could pick them up. One long day on an experimental transect in the mountains showed us how impractical they were in that environment!

Doing the Work

We completed the Carson-Stillwater survey in two summers. As we've already said, in the first summer we took a 1 percent sample of the entire sample universe. This meant surveying a total of about 17 square kilometres—35 quadrats in the mountains (8.75 km^2) and about 82 kilometres of transects (8.2 km^2). We found that archaeological remains were most dense and variable in the piñon-juniper forest of the mountains and in the dune area (the dog's "nose") and southern portions of the valley floor (the dog's "chin"). Site density and variability was somewhat less in the wetland region of the valley floor and in the unforested portion of the mountains.

This is why, during the second summer, we pursued a **stratified random sample,** which takes the sample universe and stratifies it into sub-universes. We eventually divided the sample universe into five strata: the wetland, the dune area to the west of the wetland, the south valley, the northern Stillwater Mountains, and the southern Stillwater Mountains. As a result of the first summer's survey sample, we sampled some of these areas more intensively than the others.

As mentioned above, the first summer's survey team consisted of 10 to 12 student archaeologists and volunteers. When surveying the transects, surveyors walked at 8- to 10-metre intervals, winding their way through the sagebrush and greasewood. A similar procedure was used on the quadrats but, because these units were 500 × 500 metres, we made five 100-metre-wide passes across them; we used the same procedure for the spring surveys, but with up to 10 such passes.

When someone found a site, each crew member marked his or her place on the line (so they'd know where to resume surveying) and then gathered together. We located the site on a sketch map of the quadrat and then sketched a map of the site itself. Most sites were unglamorous scatters of flakes, but occasionally we found rock art on scattered boulders and once a standing **wickiup** (a conical log structure) that had been built sometime in the early 20th century, judging from the enamel pots hanging in a tree and the steel axe cuts on the logs.

For each site, we filled out a form that asked for a variety of information—the site's location and topographic setting; distance to water; the type and density of surrounding vegetation; evidence of disturbance by people or erosion; potential for buried deposits; estimates of site age and size; outcrops of stone suitable for making tools; structures or features such as hearths; slope; and general comments. We photographed each site and collected a large sample of the stone tools and waste flakes.

We gave each site a field number, but eventually each site was assigned a permanent **Smithsonian number**—a cataloguing system that most states use to keep track of their sites. (In most states, these numbers are given out by the state's historic preservation office—we'll talk about these more in Chapter 17.) For example, one site found in our survey acquired the number 26CH798: The 26 stands for Nevada, because it is the 26th state alphabetically (excluding

Alaska and Hawaii, which acquired statehood after this system was in place; they are now 49 and 50). The CH stands for Churchill County, and 798 means it was the 798th site recorded in that county.

After two summers, we had surveyed 57 quadrats, 8 springs, and 260 kilometres of transects—about 47 square kilometres, or a sample fraction of the total survey universe of about 3 percent. But some strata were sampled more intensively than others: Table 4-1 shows how the sample was distributed across the five strata. We recorded 160 sites and collected some 10,400 stone tools and more than 70,000 manufacturing and resharpening waste flakes. We analyzed these over the next several years.

What We Learned

Recall that the original research question concerned two different hypotheses about the role of wetlands in the ancient hunter-gatherer seasonal round. The first hypothesis held that wetlands had been the focus of a sedentary settlement system, predicting that the highest site density should be in the wetland. But our survey found that the highest site densities are found in the dunes, the south valley region, and the northern forested portion of the mountains.

The first hypothesis also predicted that sites in the wetlands should contain evidence of long-term habitation. But the archaeological survey recovered stone tools and evidence of stone tool manufacturing techniques suggesting that wetland sites were short-term camps. This evidence is more in line with the second hypothesis, which argued that the wetland was but one stop on a complex seasonal round (and, in fact, the sites in the dune region contained tools and waste flakes that suggested even more transient stays than those in the wetland).

stratified random sample A survey universe divided into several sub-universes that are then sampled at potentially different sample fractions.

wickiup A conical structure made of poles or logs laid against one another that served as fall and winter homes among the prehistoric Shoshone and Paiute.

Smithsonian number A unique catalogue number given to U.S. sites; it consists of a number (the state's position alphabetically), a letter abbreviation of the county, and the site's sequential number within the county.

TABLE 4-1 Sampling Fractions of the Survey Strata and Predicted Site Densities, Carson Valley Survey (1970–1975)

REGION	SIZE (km²)	QUADRATS	SPRINGS	TRANSECTS (km)	SAMPLE FRACTION	SITES	SITE DENSITY (sites/km²)
Piñon-juniper forest	150	23	5	-	6.5	41	4.2
Unforested mountains	820	34	3	-	1.3	12	1.1
Wetland	305	-	-	133	3.4	30	2.9
Dunes	243	-	-	93	3.8	57	6.1
South valley	53	-	-	34	6.4	20	5.9
Total	1571	57	8	260	2.7*	160	3.4*

Source: Kelly 2001, Table 6-1

Looking Closer
Surveying the Drowned Landscapes of Gwaii Haanas

Archaeologists have argued that the ancestors of First Nations peoples entered the New World sometime before 12,500 B.P. Small groups of related nuclear families likely moved southward into the continent along one of two proposed routes. Initially, archaeologists hypothesized that travel had been undertaken through an ice-free corridor, formed during periods when the great ice sheets that covered North America had not coalesced. Others suggested that these pioneering families had moved along the coastlines of Alaska and the Northwest Coast, which would have been un-glaciated by 13,000 B.P. Archaeologists have spent many decades searching for early sites in order to resolve this issue.

Daryl Fedje is an archaeologist with Parks Canada who has spent a great deal of time searching for early archaeological sites in the Gwaii Haanas archipelago. This National Park and Haida heritage site is located at the southern end of Haida Gwaii, also known as the Queen Charlotte Islands, in British Columbia. The islands that make up the archipelago are covered by lush rainforests, which make the search for archaeological sites tremendously difficult. Furthermore, extremely rapid sea level changes have occurred in Gwaii Haanas over the past 13,000 years. The geographic distribution of glacial ice has produced complex patterns of sinking, and upward movement of the earth's crust at different times, and in different places. A sea level history constructed by Fedje and his associates summarizes these astonishing changes. From 13,000 to 10,500 B.P., sea levels were much lower than today. Sea levels then rose very quickly, from 10,500 to 9000 B.P., when they reached levels that are 16 metres higher than today. These high levels remained stable from 9000 to 5000 B.P., and began to fall from 5000 B.P. to the present. The changing positions of the coastline associated with these fluctuations make searching for archaeological sites in Gwaii Haanas like looking for a needle in a haystack!

Fedje and his associates were able to reduce the size of this particular haystack by applying the sea level history data to their archaeological survey methods. Experience taught Fedje that the best places to search for early sites would be old shoreline locations that date to between 9000 and 5000 B.P. The sea level histories for Gwaii Haanas suggested that landforms of this age would be found between 15 and 20 metres above the modern high-tide mark, and range anywhere from 100 metres to 2 kilometres inland. The fact that sea levels were stable during this period meant that these landforms might also contain more than

The second hypothesis, however, also suggested that the piñon forests should have been included in the seasonal round. But although we found evidence of hunting there, evidence for plant collecting, in the form of grinding stones, was almost nonexistent.

Some areas of survey, such as the alluvial fans, are excluded from this table, and the areas covered by open water are excluded from the wetland total (* indicates values calculated from entire survey region).

In sum, neither hypothesis seemed to provide an adequate reconstruction of ancient life in the Carson Desert and Stillwater Mountains. We have come full circle in the research cycle and now are back at the beginning, proposing new hypotheses that take into account what we learned.

But maybe the survey's conclusions are completely wrong. Maybe the site densities and contents that we recorded are unknowingly biased. Is there reason to think that survey tells us anything valid?

Does Sampling Actually Work? The Chaco Experiment

Samples are supposed to give us an accurate picture of what a population is like. Given that we didn't know—and still don't know—the actual population of sites in the Carson Desert, how do we know that the survey actually did what it was supposed to do?

To test the accuracy of survey methods, we need to do a sample survey in an area where archaeologists have already conducted a 100-percent survey—that is, where the population is already known. Few such surveys have been conducted: After all, why do a survey

four millennia of cultural deposits. In a region where dense rainforest severely reduces the visibility of archaeological sites, such a density of human occupation increased the likelihood of discovery. Armed with accurate altimeters and GPS units, Fedje and a team of archaeologists set out to test areas targeted by their sea level history reconstruction. A total of 17 new sites were located, all of which dated to the mid to early Holocene.

But were there sites in the area that were even older? The low sea levels that characterized periods before 9000 B.P. meant that the landmass of Haida Gwaii would have been more than twice its present size. These unknown landscapes would have been "drowned" as sea levels began to rise in later periods. Any sites that might be present would now be under metres of water, and may be located many kilometres from the present coastline. Fedje and his associates used a remote sensing technique called *swath bathymetric imaging* to map the lakes, rivers, terraces, and estuaries of this now submerged region. Swath imaging uses radar waves to produce images of objects and was recently used by NASA's Magellan spacecraft to map the surface of Venus. Fedje used his model of the drowned landscape to target high-potential landforms where archaeological sites might be expected. Bucket sampling on one such landform 55 metres below the sea surface has produced one stone tool thought by Fedje to represent terrestrial use of this area.

Although this work is extremely challenging, underwater surveys of drowned landscapes on the Northwest Coast is exciting and may provide further evidence to support the idea of a coastal migration route into the New World by its earliest human inhabitants.

Figure 4-7 Parks Canada archaeologist Daryl Fedje excavates inside a cave in Haida Gwaii, British Columbia.

Source: Courtesy of Dr. Marty Magne

to approximate the population if the population is already known?

Sample surveys were one of the methodologies advocated by the new archaeology of the 1960s. Early on, therefore, archaeologists asked themselves whether this method actually worked: Did a survey sample adequately characterize a region's surface archaeology? Concerned with this, James Judge (Fort Lewis College), Robert Hitchcock (University of Nebraska), and James Ebert (Ebert & Associates, Albuquerque) conducted a test of survey methods against the known archaeology of Chaco Culture National Historical Park, located in Chaco Canyon in northwestern New Mexico.

Figure 4-8 Pueblo Bonito, photo by Charles Lindbergh, 1929.
Source: Charles A. Lindbergh, courtesy of the School of American Research

Today Chaco Canyon is smack in the middle of nowhere, but in the 11th century Chaco was the place to be in the American Southwest. Beginning about A.D. 700, early Ancestral Pueblo people began constructing their distinctive multiroom apartment complexes that would give their descendants, the Pueblo Indians of New Mexico, their popular name. By A.D. 1050, Chaco was the centre of a complex, centralized social and political system based on maize horticulture. The canyon contains many sites; among them are nine large pueblos, known to archaeologists as "Great Houses," made of beautifully shaped and coursed stonework that are virtually impossible to miss as one enters the canyon. Pueblo Bonito (Spanish for "beautiful town"), for example, contains more than 600 rooms and is four stories high in places (Figure 4-8). It holds more than 24 kivas (round semi-subterranean ceremonial structures), one more than 20 metres in diameter. America would not witness a larger apartment building until the 19th century and the Industrial Revolution.

Chaco Canyon was the centre of a vast sociopolitical system. Although the Ancestral Pueblo people used no wheeled vehicles or beasts of burden, roads radiate out from the canyon like spokes on a wheel (we'll return to these in Chapter 5). Some run for 50 kilometres. People brought massive pine trunks for roof beams from mountains 80 kilometres away. Turquoise, shell bracelets, copper, iron pyrite, conch shells, and macaws in the Great Houses point to a vast trade network.

Although the reasons are still unclear, by A.D. 1150 Chaco's power and population began to decline. People moved elsewhere and, by A.D. 1350, the canyon was all but abandoned.

Chaco became a national monument in 1907, and in the 1970s it was the focus of a long-term National Park Service–sponsored research project. For inventory purposes, this project conducted a 100-percent survey of the 50-square-kilometre monument with archaeological crews walking over every hot, dusty square centimetre. They found 1130 sites and, of these, 621 could be pigeonholed into a "cultural phase," a period of time based on architecture and pottery types (we'll talk about this term in Chapter 9). These phases were Archaic sites (sites that are older than 100 B.C.), Basketmaker II (100 B.C.–A.D. 400), Basketmaker III (A.D. 400–700), Pueblo I (A.D. 700–900), Pueblo II (A.D. 900–1100), Pueblo III (A.D. 1100–1300), Navajo sites (late, but the actually age is uncertain), and multicomponent sites (sites with evidence of occupation during two or more of the phases).

Later, in 1975, Judge, Ebert, and Hitchcock resurveyed the monument, although this time from the comfort of an air-conditioned office. They used several different sampling strategies—regularly spaced and randomly spaced transects and quadrats, with both stratified and unstratified samples (using ecological zones as the strata). They selected a 20-percent sample in all the experiments, plotted the selected transects or quadrats on maps of the monument, and tallied which sites were "found."

Their experiment showed that archaeological survey sampling really does work. Table 4-2 shows the results of their regularly spaced transect sample. Notice that the frequency of sites generated by the survey sample mirror the actual frequency of sites. For example, using the sample alone, we could say that half the datable sites in Chaco Canyon are Navajo sites—and we would be right. The sample survey also would lead us to claim, correctly, that site density (and perhaps population as well) grew between Pueblo I and Pueblo II times and then declined during the

Pueblo III period. The point is this: We can draw the same conclusions from the 20-percent survey as we can from the 100-percent sample—and it would have required only one-fifth the work!

Judge, Ebert, and Hitchcock found little difference between the systematic transect and random transect designs. Transects, in fact, appeared to be better indicators of site density and population attributes for the monument as a whole. The quadrat sample provided better indicators of population attributes within ecological zones, that is, when using a stratified sample. Judge and his colleagues urged archaeologists to take a small initial sample of an unknown region and use that as the basis for a second sampling strategy applying a stratified sample and different sample fractions in the strata. And that's just what we did in the Carson Desert survey.

But there is more. Although the Chaco experimental surveys were notable for what they found, they were also notable for what they *missed*—namely, most of the Great Houses. How could this be? Once in the valley, most archaeologists could find Pueblo Bonito blindfolded—if only by walking into one of its massive two- or three-storey-high walls. Missing Pueblo Bonito would be like walking across a college campus and not seeing the football stadium. What good is a survey that misses a 600-room pueblo?

Sample surveys are very good at recording the general character of a region, but they are less useful for finding unique or rare sites. In fact, even (relatively

TABLE 4-2 Actual and Predicted Site Frequencies from the Systematic Interval Transect Sample in Chaco Canyon National Monument

SITE TYPE	ACTUAL	ACTUAL FREQUENCY (%)	INTERVAL TRANSECT COUNT	INTERVAL TRANSECT FREQUENCY (%)
Archaic	5	0.8	-	-
Basketmaker II	3	0.5	1	0.8
Basketmaker III	67	10.8	12	9.0
Pueblo I	38	6.1	6	4.5
Pueblo II	53	8.5	12	9.0
Pueblo III	40	6.4	11	8.3
Navajo	317	51.0	69	51.9
Multicomponent	98	15.9	22	16.5
Total	621	100.0	133	100.0

Source: Judge, Hitchcock, and Ebert 1971

large) 20-percent surveys are likely to miss rare items, like Pueblo Bonito. Note in Table 4-2 that the transect sample also missed all the Archaic sites as well—because they are rare (only five in the survey area). Surveys are not designed to find rare sites—that takes common sense, open eyes, and some plain old gumshoe survey.

Quality Control in Surface Survey

The Chaco experiment demonstrates that survey sampling can be quite effective. But the quality of a survey is affected by factors other than the attention given to the sampling strategy. In fact, the on-the-ground implementation of survey itself affects what you recover.

Any archaeologist can tell you that crews are not as effective when working in a driving rainstorm or oppressive summer heat. In the Carson Desert, where afternoon temperatures could reach 43° Celsius, we began work before sunrise, and we tried to complete the day's survey by 2 p.m. (although this wasn't always possible)—partly out of a concern for the crew's safety but also because we knew that the quality of data collection would be compromised.

The interval between surveyors is another variable whose effect on survey results is difficult to determine. In doing survey, especially in desert regions, archaeologists often record "sites" and "isolates"—sites are clusters of material; isolates are artifacts that occur by themselves. How do we separate isolates from sites? Is this one projectile point an isolate, even though a scraper and a potsherd lie 20 metres away? Or do the three items together constitute a site? The answer depends partly on understanding how surveyors actually go about doing survey.

As a surveyor is walking across the survey unit, he or she will find something—a flake or projectile point or pottery sherd. The surveyor will stop, flag the item, and then take a few steps around, looking a bit more intently than otherwise. If the surveyor finds nothing within a few seconds, he or she will collect, label, and map the item as an isolate. If the surveyor finds more cultural items, he or she will call out that they've found a site. The crew will then assemble on the location and complete the site form and collection.

One of the Chaco researchers, James Ebert, conducted an experiment to find out how this survey behaviour affects the way archaeologists record surface archaeology. During a survey in southwestern Wyoming, he planted washers and nails in one survey unit. Some were painted buff (the same colour as the surrounding sand), and others were painted black. Ebert mapped the locations of each washer and nail and then turned a survey crew loose on the unit.

The crew found only two-thirds of the "artifacts," and slightly more of the black- than buff-coloured items. Of greater interest was the fact that the surveyors found washers and nails placed near one another at a much higher frequency (80 percent) than washers and nails planted by themselves (22 percent). Why? Surveyors look a bit more intensely after they find an item. If they find another, they'll look even more intensely until they decide that they have a site, at which point they and the entire crew really scour the surface. As a result, the artifact recovery rate goes up when artifacts occur near one another. But if a surveyor sees nothing within a few seconds' glance after finding an artifact, he or she will move ahead with the survey. As a result, artifacts that occur in less-dense scatters could be systematically underrepresented in a surface survey.

Two points arise from this observation. First, artifacts that were discarded or lost *individually* have a smaller chance of being discovered later. The implication is that surveys do not recover many isolated items, even though Ebert's surveyors walked at 5-metre intervals. We could lessen this problem by having surveyors walk at 1- or 2-metre intervals—although this would greatly increase the cost and time required for the survey.

So, What's a Site?

Ebert's experiment raised a second problem. Archaeologists speak all the time about sites, but many would be hard-pressed to define what "site" actually means. In the Carson Desert, we defined a site as five pieces of cultural material within approximately 50 square metres. Often geography places a boundary on a site's edges, for example, a riverbank or a steep slope. But sometimes, artifact scatters are more or less continuous, and the archaeologist has to make a judgment call. For example, Figure 4-9 is a map of Quadrat 36 in the Stillwater Mountains. We recorded ten sites in

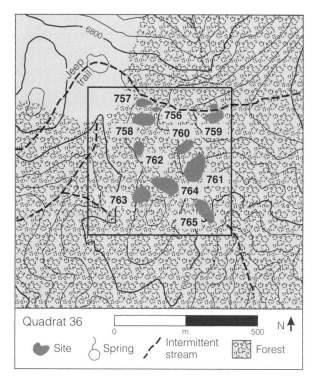

Figure 4-9 Topographic map of Quadrat 36 in the Stillwater Mountain survey. Sites are shown as numbered patches. Is there one site here, or ten?

Source: Robert Kelly, "Prehistory of the Carson Desert and Stillwater Mountains," University of Utah Anthropological Papers, No. 123, 2001.

many of the "sites" on the valley floor were actually conglomerates of unrelated material produced through **deflation,** the geologic process whereby fine sediment is blown away by the wind and larger items—mostly stone artifacts, in this case—are left behind. This process results in archaeological remains—which originally might have been discarded at different times in the past throughout an accumulating dune—being eventually left together on the same surface after the sand was blown away. This process produces a dense scatter of debris that is not a site in the traditional sense of the term, but a number of isolated items brought together through a geologic process. Many of the sites we recorded in the Carson Desert were, in fact, nothing more than such geologic aggregates of cultural material.

Finally, even if we could define sites "correctly," what would they be? We tend to think of sites as discrete behavioural entities. But sites, especially surface sites, are not necessarily the archaeological equivalent of the ethnographer's village, hamlet, or foraging camp (although sometimes they are). Sites can result from multiple occupations over decades, or even hundreds or thousands of years, and archaeologists have to be wary of all the natural processes that go into the formation of a site (we'll discuss more of these in Chapter 7).

Is There a Solution?

One way around this problem is to dispense with the notion of "site" altogether. Instead of using sites as our unit of data collection, current technology allows us to use the artifacts themselves. Some archaeologists have done this by intensively surveying their sample units and plotting every single item found using an electronic **total station,** also known as an electronic distance meter (EDM). This device uses a beam of infrared light to obtain X, Y, Z coordinates relative to a known point. Total stations can obtain accurate locational data over distances of a kilometre or more, and they make the precise mapping of large areas practical.

this quadrat; but it's possible that another archaeologist might have recorded eight sites, or five, or just one big one.

Figure 4-10 illustrates the problem with defining a site on the ground. All four boxes in this figure contain the same hypothetical scatter of artifacts, consisting of two artifact concentrations with a light scatter between and around them. In A, the dashed line indicates that an excruciatingly careful archaeologist has found everything and categorized it all as one site. In B, surveyors did not recover the isolated items at the same rate as clumped remains (as Ebert's experiment suggests might happen), and so the archaeologist decided that there were two sites. In C, another careful archaeologist found the same scatter that was recorded by A, but this archaeologist felt that the two scatters were sufficiently distinct to call them two sites. In D, the same artifact distribution is recorded, but the archaeologist felt that all items had to be considered part of one site or the other.

The problem is even more complex when we factor in geology. In the Carson Desert, it was clear that

deflation A geologic process whereby fine sediment is blown away by the wind and larger items—including artifacts—are lowered onto a common surface and thus become recognizable sites.

total station A device that uses a beam of light bounced off a prism to determine an artifact's provenience; it is accurate to +/- 3 millimetres.

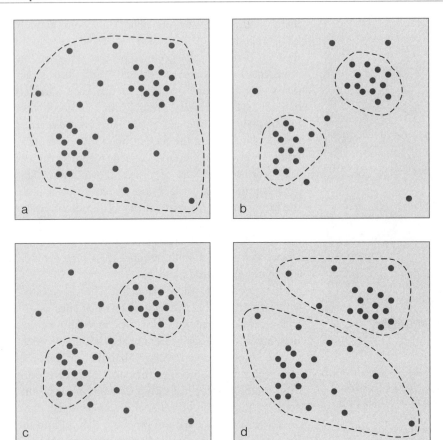

Figure 4-10 A hypothetical artifact scatter showing four site-definition scenarios.

In essence, the archaeologist treats the entire survey unit as if it were one large site. He or she can then use a variety of statistical methods to look for patterns in which artifact types are physically associated—do projectile points occur near scrapers, or are potsherds found near hearths? Alternatively, the archaeologist could define clusters of artifacts—that is, sites—based on tightly mapped artifact distributions rather than on decisions possibly made by a hot, tired, and hungry surveyor in the field.

This approach, however, is not practical when dealing with very large regions. It would have been impractical, for example, to try to plot all artifacts within the 1700-square-kilometre Carson Desert survey area (even if the technology to do so were available in the early 1980s, which it was not). An alterna-

tive is known as **non-site archaeology,** which focuses not on the analysis of materials from within a batch of artifacts collected from a single site, but on *regional* patterns in artifacts—patterns manifested on a scale of kilometres or hectares.

In the Carson Desert, we never analyzed a single site. We never tried to reconstruct the daily activities that transpired at a site, because we began with the assumption that the sites in our sample were merely different-sized samples of a more or less continuous distribution of archaeological debris. Thus, we analyzed the data in terms of the five sample strata. For example, we compared what we found in the piñon-juniper forest *as a whole* to the other four strata. In this way, it did not matter if Quadrat 36, mentioned above, contained one or ten sites—we added the artifacts from this quadrat's sites to everything else found in the piñon-juniper zone for analysis. In this way, we looked for large-scale patterns in artifact distribution that were more meaningful, in terms of our research questions, and more reliable than a fine-grained interpretation of any single site.

non-site archaeology Analysis of archaeological patterns manifested on a scale of kilometres or hectares, rather than of patterns within a single site.

Archaeologists will never completely dispense with the notion of "site" because the concept is critical from an administrative point of view. All state archaeological databases record archaeology in terms of sites, and researchers receive permits to work on particular sites. But all archaeologists today have a more realistic and sober understanding that, under many conditions, sites are *samples* and are rarely equivalent to something that might make immediate intuitive sense to us, such as a "village" or "camp."

What about Things That Lie below Ground?

So far, the archaeological surveys that we have discussed recorded only evidence that is visible with a pedestrian survey. In places like the Carson Desert, important archaeological remains have lain on a stable desert surface for millennia. But in many other places, artifacts may be washed away or deeply buried (as at Gatecliff Shelter). In Grand Teton National Park in Wyoming, for example, you can walk over an area south of Jackson Lake known as "the potholes," a land surface that mammoths tread upon some 14,000 years ago. But 3 kilometres north, that same ancient land surface is buried beneath 30 to 40 metres of **glacial till** and outwash sediments. And at the south end of the park, that land surface doesn't exist at all—it was eroded away thousands of years ago.

This issue cropped up in the Carson Desert project after we finished our survey in 1981. Two years later, and about 300 kilometres away, torrential rains and heavy snows began falling across the headwaters of the Humboldt River, which eventually drains into the Carson Desert. The heavy precipitation kept up until the Carson Desert—that barren basin of sand dunes and alkali flats—had become a 64-kilometre-wide lake.

During the summer of 1986, the floodwaters began to recede. As they did, they stripped away the tops of dunes and exposed hundreds of human burials and archaeological sites containing shallow houses (Figure 4-11 shows an example), storage pits, bones, stone tools, beads, and grinding stones (we discuss these sites and burials in Chapters 11 and 12). When the U.S. Fish and Wildlife Service (the agency that manages the Carson Desert's wetland) plotted the newly exposed finds, their maps showed that our survey crews had literally walked right over some of these

sites. We missed them because there was no surface indication of what lay buried below. However, the kinds of projectile points found in the wetland strata of the survey and in the newly exposed sites were the same: The survey had, in this regard, accurately characterized the wetland's archaeology.

Still, it is clear that surface archaeology documents only what lies on or near the ground surface. Surface and subsurface material often correlate, but you can never be absolutely certain about what lies below.

Shovel-Testing

Archaeologists working in the eastern United States, Europe, and elsewhere confront this problem all the time, because these areas witness considerable soil buildup, and artifacts rarely lie on the undisturbed ground surface. In agricultural regions, archaeologists do **plow-zone** archaeology, walking through plowed fields after spring tilling (and especially after a rain) because the plow will turn up shallowly buried archaeological remains.

In other areas, archaeologists use a procedure known as **shovel-testing.** Survey crews carry small shovels and sometimes a backpacked screen with them. As the crew moves across a survey unit, each member stops at a predetermined interval, digs a shallow hole and screens the dirt back into the hole, looking for evidence of buried archaeological remains. It is slow going, and it obviously cannot locate remains that are more than a foot or two deep.

Looking for more deeply buried remains, some archaeologists use backhoe trenches or hand or mechanical soil augers, but the former can be very expensive (as well as destructive) and the latter very slow. We normally use them in areas that previous research suggests are good places to prospect for buried remains. In other cases, archaeologists use natural exposures, such as arroyos or riverbanks, that sometimes expose deeply buried deposits.

---

glacial till The mixture of rock and earth pushed along the front and sides of a glacier.

plow zone The upper portion of a soil profile that has been disturbed by repeated plowing or other agricultural activity.

shovel-testing A sample survey method used in regions where rapid soil buildup obscures buried archaeological remains; it entails digging shallow, systematic pits across the survey unit.

Figure 4-11 An archaeological crew excavating a semi-subterranean house pit in the Stillwater Marsh (Nevada). Surface survey missed dozens of sites like this because they were not visible beneath sand and saltgrass.

Source: Robert Kelly

In Chapter 5, we will discuss some high-tech ways to "see" below ground. Here, we consider a way in which surface survey was combined with a subsurface sampling strategy to find Mission Santa Catalina, a Spanish Franciscan mission lost in Georgia's Sea Islands for more than 300 years.

How to Find a Lost Spanish Mission (Part I)

At its 17th-century zenith, Spanish Florida had three dozen Franciscan missions, each a satellite settlement heavily dependent on the colonial capital at St. Augustine. To the west lived the Timucuan, Apalachee, and Apalachicola Indians; to the north, toward St. Catherines Island, lay the province of Guale. Although a dozen 16th- and 17th-century missions once existed in the present state of Georgia, archaeologists and historians had not identified one

such mission site when Thomas began his search for Santa Catalina.

Many historians and archaeologists felt that the lost mission of Santa Catalina lay along the western margin of St. Catherines Island, a 567-hectare tract 80 kilometres south of Savannah. Unlike the other so-called Golden Isles, St. Catherines Island has not been subdivided and suburbanized. The Georgia-based, not-for-profit St. Catherines Island Foundation owns the island and regulates a comprehensive program of research and conservation. This enlightened and progressive land management policy ensured that Mission Santa Catalina was not destroyed beneath the crush of condos and fast-food joints that typify the southern barrier islands.

The Survey: Stage One

In 1974, when we first visited St. Catherines Island, the combined French, English, and Spanish historical documentation supplied only vague geographic clues and, although several first-rate archaeologists had previously worked on the island, none had successfully located this important mission site.

Virtually uninhabited, St. Catherines Island is today blanketed with dense forest, briar patches, and almost impenetrable palmetto thicket. When we began our search for Santa Catalina, we were overwhelmed by the vastness of the area involved. We knew so little about the landscape that we could not overlook any portion of St. Catherines Island.

By its nature, archaeological fieldwork is slow and tedious—and nobody could (or should) excavate an entire island—so we began by random sampling. Taking the island's size into consideration, Thomas figured that 30 east–west transects, each 100 metres wide, would provide a 20-percent sample of the island (Figure 4-12). This sample would allow us to charac-

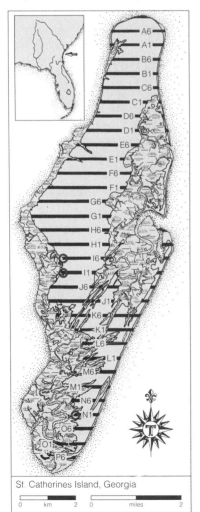

Figure 4-12 Systematic transect research design used to derive a 20-percent regional randomized sample on St. Catherines Island (Georgia). All surveyed transects (the darker stripes) have a letter + number designation. Occurrences of 16th- and 17th-century Spanish ceramics have been circled.

Source: © American Museum of Natural History

terize the island's archaeology and help search for the lost mission of Santa Catalina de Guale. But recall that sampling, even with a relatively large 20-percent sample, is not always good at finding rare sites—and there was only one Santa Catalina de Guale.

In surveying, the idea is to walk in the straightest line possible, climbing over rocks and deadfalls, walking along the sides of steep ridges—looking even in places where you really don't expect to find anything. In Nevada's wide-open spaces, it is fairly easy to keep your bearing even if you don't have a compass: Just keep walking toward that peak, mesa, or other landmark in the distance. But on densely vegetated St. Catherines Island, it was impossible to see past the palmetto bush a metre in front of you (Figure 4-14). The entire crew was experienced in desert survey and carried compasses, but even then, some veered off their paths as they wound their way through bushes and briars. Palm-sized orb spiders hung down from Spanish moss–draped oaks; an occasional scream told others that someone had taken one in the face. Fortunately, orb spiders are not dangerous. But the cottonmouths and canebrake rattlesnakes are, and the crew quickly learned about tides and alligators.

In Nevada we could see sites on the ground—but on St. Catherines, most of the sites are buried. We searched for them partly by using probes—metrelong, sharpened steel rods. We would push the probe down into the ground every few steps and see if we hit something. This was effective because St. Catherines Island is one huge sand dune—there is no natural stone on the island. Eventually, we learned to tell the difference between the feel of a tree root and rock or shell—the last two suggesting a buried archaeological site. We recorded 135 sites, ranging from massive shell middens to isolated shell scatters. We investigated each site with several 1-metre-square test units (see Chapter 5); we excavated more than 400 such test pits.

The Survey: Stage Two

The surface survey and testing told us that 16th- and 17th-century Spanish ceramics occurred only at 5 of the 135 archaeological sites, all but one along the western perimeter of the island. The ruins of Mission Santa Catalina almost certainly lay buried in a target area the size of 30 football fields along the southwestern margin of the island.

But 30 football fields is still a huge area to dig with dental pick and camel hair brush. Moreover, although

Archaeological Ethics
Professional and Avocational Archaeologists

 Avocational archaeologists are individuals interested in archaeology, but who have little or no formal academic training in archaeological methods and theories. In Canada, avocational archaeologists outnumber professional archaeologists by about 5 to 1. As a result, they play an essential role in promoting public awareness about the importance of archaeology. Unlike looters, who destroy archaeological sites in their quest for artifacts, these dedicated people help to promote and protect heritage resources across Canada. Many amateur archaeologists began to form organizations such as the Ontario Archaeological Society during the 1950s. These societies acted as watchdogs to curtail the increasing destruction of historic and pre-contact resources by urban, commercial, and industrial development. While initially self-funded, many archaeological societies in Canada now flourish because of growing membership (both amateurs and professionals) and access to government funding.

Avocational societies promote archaeology in a number of different ways. Many prepare their own newsletters and publish web pages that highlight the archaeological research being done near their communities. The Ontario Archaeological Society even publishes its own peer-reviewed academic journal, called *Ontario Archaeology*. Avocational archaeology societies also promote public education by providing opportunities for members to actively participate in archaeological digs. For many years, the *Manitoba Archaeological Society* has run successful public archaeology programs at historic and pre-contact sites along the banks of the Red River. Associations like the *Archaeological Society of Alberta* arrange public tours of sites that are off the beaten track, such as bison jumps, medicine wheel sites, and petroglyphs (rock art). Professional archaeologists are often invited to give public lectures on national and international archaeological research at monthly society meetings. In fact, the Ontario Archaeological Society was formed in 1950 by members of the public who had been inspired by the lectures of J. Norman Emerson, one of Canada's first professional archaeologists!

The most important roles played by avocational archaeology societies, however, are that they discourage the illegal excavation of archaeological sites, and promote the advancement of ethical practices in archaeology. In some cases, professional archaeologists

our confidence was growing, we had to admit almost complete ignorance of what we were looking for. Did Santa Catalina survive merely as heaps of 16th- and 17th-century garbage? Or could we realistically hope to find buried evidence of buildings as well? Clearly, it was time to scratch the surface.

Looking around for better ways to find the needle hidden in this haystack, Thomas learned from Kathleen Deagan about her successful search for 16th-century St. Augustine. She and her students used a gasoline-powered posthole digger and excavated hundreds of round holes on a grid system. Following her lead, we did the same on St. Catherines Island for the area that the survey had identified as most likely to contain the mission. With the noisy, nasty auger, two people could dig a metre-deep hole in less than a minute. The power auger threw up a neat doughnut of dirt that was hand-sifted for artifacts. Hundreds of such holes were dug.

Once the field-testing was complete, we identified all materials recovered and plotted the distribution in a series of simple maps. Since then, a number of readily available computer programs have greatly assisted the data conversion process. But even using the hand-plotted maps, the power-auger data allowed us to focus further field evaluation on a single 100 × 100-metre square in the overall sampling grid where diagnostic mission-period artifacts were found.

train society members so that they can work collaboratively to record and protect archaeological sites across Canada. An excellent example of this is the SCARP (Saskatchewan Centennial Archaeology Research Project) program, set up by the *Saskatchewan Archaeological Society* to celebrate the 100th anniversary of the province. The objectives of this project are to increase the level of reporting of archaeological sites in the province. Avocational archaeologists and members of the general public have been asked to report to the Saskatchewan Archaeological Society cultural features such as stone circles (tent rings), medicine wheels, cairns, petroglyphs, and glacial erratics associated with native oral histories. The society acts as a sort of clearinghouse for this information, which it then passes on to the provincial government's professional archaeologists. The Society helps members of the public fill out site forms and write reports on the cultural features they discover. In this way, the SCARP program provides interested citizens with a way of making a real contribution to provincial archaeology. Think about becoming a member of an avocational archaeological society in your own province or territory!

Figure 4-13 Public archaeology is an exciting way to introduce people to archaeology. Avocational archaeology societies often run public excavations, such as this one in Manitoba.
Source: Donalee Deck, Parks Canada

Although this area contained absolutely no surface evidence to distinguish it from the surroundings, judicious use of surface and subsurface sampling had narrowed the search from an entire island to a relatively small area. And this is indeed where we eventually discovered the remarkably well-preserved ruins of Mission Santa Catalina de Guale.

In Chapter 5, we complete the Santa Catalina story by showing how remote sensing technology helped find the invisible mission site. By using a combination of proton magnetometers, ground-penetrating radar, and soil resistivity techniques, we pinpointed actual buildings inside the mission complex—before we ever excavated them.

GPS Technology and Modern Surveys

Surveys today are also assisted by **global positioning system** (GPS) technology. This system did not exist when we surveyed St. Catherines Island and the Carson Desert, but we certainly wish that it did. We had to use triangulation, pacing, and topography to locate sites on maps—and all that took time. Additionally,

global positioning system Hand-held devices that use triangulation from radio waves received from satellites to determine your current position in terms of either the UTM grid or latitude and longitude.

Figure 4-14 Systematic archaeological survey on St. Catherines Island (Georgia).

Source: American Museum of Natural History, photo by Dennis O'Brien

we've since discovered that, in the heat of the day, a lot of mistakes can be made.

GPS technology has changed all that. The GPS consists of 27 satellites (24 active ones and 3 spares) that circle the earth in 12-hour evenly distributed orbits at an altitude of about 14,000 kilometres. These orbits repeat the same ground track (because the earth turns beneath them) twice each day. Each satellite carries a computer and very accurate atomic clocks.

Hand-held GPS units operate by picking up the continuously broadcast signals from at least four satellites. The GPS receiver triangulates a position fix using the interval between the transmission and reception of the satellite signal.

The global positioning system is funded and controlled by the U.S. Department of Defense. It was originated, and continues primarily, to provide continuous, worldwide position and navigation data to U.S. and allied military forces. But legitimate commercial and scientific applications were recognized early in the system's development, and it was decided to allow access to GPS signals within certain constraints. The satellite signals were originally coded (and used a practice called selective availability, because the coding function could be turned on and off by the military), so that real-time locational data

were (often wildly) inaccurate. This was to prevent a hostile military power from using the GPS as a free, super-accurate, targeting computer.

In the 1980s, GPS units cost thousands of dollars, were bulky and heavy, and required a car battery for their power. And they were not terribly accurate. But today you can buy a cell phone–sized GPS unit at discount stores for about $150. And a few years ago the military turned off selective availability, so now the field archaeologist can get 5-metre accuracy within seconds with an easily portable and affordable unit. Most units give locations using the UTM coordinates mentioned above (or latitude and longitude, but UTM coordinates are easy to use). Expensive devices can even give subcentimetre accuracy.

GPS technology has not only made fieldwork easier—calculating a location is as easy as pushing a button—but it also permits survey sample units to be odd shapes. We used squares, circles, and transects in the Carson Desert and on St. Catherines Island in large part because they are easier to locate on a map and on the ground. Hence, they make it possible to keep track of how much land we surveyed. But with a GPS, a surveyor's individual line of survey can be tracked. A crew could wander anywhere across the landscape and, at the end of the day, plot out the covered area. It would not matter if they walked a square, circle, or some shapeless blob. The archaeologist can calculate the area surveyed and keep a running sample fraction tally. No archaeologist would undertake fieldwork today without a GPS unit.

Full-Coverage Survey

We have spent most of this chapter discussing and advocating survey sampling. But there are instances in which you may not want to sample a region at all, times when you really need to look at the whole thing. Research in southern Mexico's Valley of Oaxaca provides an example.

The Valley of Oaxaca Archaeological Survey

For more than a century, explorers and archaeologists have celebrated the monumental ruins at Monte Albán (*mon*-tay al-*bahn*), overlooking Oaxaca (wa-*ha*-kuh) City in the highlands of southern Mexico. Literally "white mountain," Monte Albán is an extraordinary concentration of pre-Columbian architecture atop an artificially flattened mountain summit (Figure 4 15).

Beginning in 1931, Alfonso Caso and several other Mexican archaeologists undertook 18 field seasons of excavation. They determined that Monte Albán was founded shortly after 500 B.C., the mountaintop settlement reaching its maximum physical size around A.D. 700.

Along the edge of the plaza, which covered nearly four football fields, rose low masonry pyramids. Stepped platforms at either end hid tombs and served as foundations for palaces and temples, a complex of buildings that housed the ruling families and provided formal spaces for these rulers to meet with high-ranking government officials and ambassadors from afar. Nearby was a ballcourt for ritual ball games, which were important throughout Mesoamerica. The main plaza served as the centre of government for the city and the region.

Caso's Monte Albán project explored more than 170 tombs in the vicinity of the sprawling central plaza, the perimeter of which was decorated with carved stone monuments depicting sacrificial victims killed, and sometimes mutilated, by the rulers of Monte Albán.

The discoveries in Tomb 7 grabbed headlines around the world. Sometime during the decline of Monte Albán, a very powerful leader had been buried in a tomb constructed earlier. Inside was one of Mesoamerica's greatest treasures: gold, shell, turquoise, jet, crystal, and carved jaguar bones. This was one of the richest caches ever discovered in the New World.

Today, many tourists travel to Oaxaca to view first-hand the partially restored ruins of Monte Albán, and local Aeromexico flights sometimes circle the site, dipping wingtips so that the passengers can catch an aerial view of the fabled sacred city of the Zapotecs.

Figure 4-15 The central plaza at Monte Albán (Oaxaca, Mexico).
Source: David H. Thomas

What's Outside Monte Albán?

But the potential of Oaxacan archaeology was hardly exhausted by the excavations at Monte Albán. Spectacular as it may be, Monte Albán is only a single site. In 1971, another team of archaeologists undertook a decade-long regional survey to determine how Monte Albán fit into the regional landscape of Oaxaca. They began with a complete mapping of Monte Albán, estimating a total population between 25,000 and 30,000. The archaeological reconnaissance project soon expanded into a systematic **full-coverage survey** of the hinterlands—covering the entire Valley of Oaxaca.

The main players—Richard Blanton (Purdue University), Gary Feinman (Field Museum), Laura Finsten (McMaster University), Linda Nicholas (Field Museum), and Stephen Kowalewski (University of Georgia)—selected this area for several good reasons. First, the cultural chronology for the Valley of Oaxaca was fairly well understood—a critical factor for anybody designing a regional survey. Second, the physical land conditions were conducive to the regional surface survey: The land surface over the past 3000 years had been relatively stable (meaning that most sites remained visible from the surface), and vegetative ground cover was relatively thin and sparse. Third, settled villages were established in the Valley of Oaxaca beginning about 1500 B.C., creating huge quantities of archaeological debris—readily datable remains that could be observed simply by walking along.

The Valley of Oaxaca Settlement Pattern Project established a set of systematic protocols to ensure that data were collected in standardized format. The survey crews consisted of three or four trained people, each familiar with the basic ceramic sequence of the area. They covered all terrain in the survey area by systematically walking 25 to 50 metres apart while searching for archaeological materials. Unlike some regional survey projects, the Valley of Oaxaca research design called for the surveyors to walk in a zigzag pattern, checking all suspicious features along either side of the survey line. Through geological studies, interpretation of aerial photographs, and field inspection of geological cuts, the researchers determined where

full-coverage survey Performing 100-percent coverage of a large region; used where topography and archaeological remains make it feasible and where the relationships between specific sites (as opposed to types of sites) are the subject of interest.

soil erosion or buildup had occurred (thereby modifying the dimensions of the sites encountered).

The idea here was the same that was used when surveying a sample quadrat in the Carson Desert: Find *everything archaeological* by looking even in places where nothing is expected to be. As Stephen Kowalewski has learned from his experiences in Oaxaca and the red clay country of Georgia, this survey strategy also ensures an up-close appreciation of "alluviation, erosion, mesquite thickets, manzanillo thickets, palmetto thickets, copperheads, pine forests, precipices, cities and their dumps, salt marshes, mean dogs, and meaner land owners."

Sites were usually recognized from surface scatters of potsherds and/or building stones. Once found, sites were plotted on aerial photographs and mapped by the crew leader, while others took notes and made sherd collections. Time-diagnostic sherds were analyzed on-site, enabling the crew to map the distribution of each archaeological phase separately while still in the field.

In the course of 10 years, the archaeologists spent five field seasons on the Oaxaca survey. They searched about 2100 square kilometres completely, resulting in about 2700 places being recorded as containing archaeological remains. But these field-numbered sites were not very meaningful units, because they often lumped together numerous components (evidence of occupation at a site during a particular time period; we'll discuss this concept further in Chapter 9). These 6353 components, defined and mapped right in the field, became the basic units of analysis for the Valley of Oaxaca survey. For each such unit, the investigators recorded 97 substantive variables, such as environmental zone, soil characteristics, degree of erosion, predominant vegetation, current land status, present irrigation (if any), artifact types, and building materials. In addition, the survey teams located 2000 pyramidal mounds, 9000 residential terraces, and 124 tombs. Overall, the Valley of Oaxaca personnel feel satisfied that they found most occupations, even the small ones, in this huge area.

The massive database from the Oaxaca survey has enabled archaeologists to understand the nature of ancient Zapotec society. Using the number of size-specific components and the variable ceramic densities, for instance, it was possible to estimate human population sizes through time and develop a quantitative model of settlement location and land use. These models, in turn, helped archaeologists understand the dynamics behind the evolution of one of America's ancient civilizations.

The Case for Full-Coverage Survey

The Valley of Oaxaca survey employed the full-coverage technique, an alternative to the random sampling designs discussed earlier. This technique involves large-scale, 100-percent reconnaissance of an archaeological region. Many specific research designs exist for such surveys, but the single common denominator is the systematic examination of contiguous blocks of terrain, surveyed at a uniform level of intensity.

By "region," most archaeologists usually mean something ranging anywhere from a few dozen to several thousand square kilometres. This is not just a matter of semantics: Define too large a region, and a satisfactory survey becomes too expensive. Define too small a region, and you will end up with an incomplete view of the cultural system you are trying to understand.

The question of "How big?" depends on what the project is trying to find out. To answer this question correctly requires the ability to estimate—*before the survey starts*—the expected spatial limits of the system being studied, so that the overall scope of the survey region can be adequately defined as early as possible.

We would, of course, like to have 100-percent coverage of the Carson Desert and St. Catherines Island to ensure that rare items are included. But when can the expense and effort of full-coverage survey be justified?

The full-coverage approach seems most appropriate to areas (1) with a highly visible archaeological record and (2) where the topography is not too formidable. Arid or semiarid environments are ideal for both full-coverage and sample surveys because of the optimal surface visibility. When these conditions are not met, full-coverage survey can become too expensive.

For the same reason, full coverage of regions is most appropriate when the main objective is finding relatively large, dense concentrations of artifacts—that is, in places where the nature of ancient residential patterns is reasonably clear from the surface evidence. This will most frequently be true for ancient societies that built substantial houses and public buildings, had high population densities, and produced large amounts of nonperishable material culture (for example, pottery).

In such cases, a full-coverage survey can treat a region as if it were a single site. It can better examine the relationships between different settlements and settlement types because it will have a large sample of those relationships. And, perhaps most importantly, the full-coverage survey can talk about *specific relations between specific communities, rather than about types of relationships between types of communities.*

The Special Case of Cultural Resource Management

Full-coverage survey is becoming increasingly common in archaeology for several reasons. We will look at one of them here and consider yet another in Chapter 5.

As you will learn in Chapter 17, most archaeology done in the United States today is part of a field called "cultural resource management," whose archaeological surveys are conducted to clear the way for roads, pipelines, dams, and other projects so that the sites can be excavated before the bulldozers move in, or so that the project can be redirected and the sites avoided.

Two aspects of these projects are important. First, the survey area is defined by the construction project, not a research question. This can lead to some survey universes that have even odder shapes than a dog's head. A fibre-optic cable survey area, for example, may be 50 metres wide and 500 kilometres long. It is often challenging, but archaeologists do try to devise research questions that can be addressed with such a sample.

Second, these areas are often surveyed in their entirety, 100 percent. The objective is not to sample, but to make sure that no significant site will be destroyed. Significant sites may be very rare, like Mission Santa Catalina. As you have seen, sample surveys are not very good at finding rare sites. If Thomas had not suspected that a Spanish mission lay on St. Catherines Island, the mission might still remain undiscovered. Instead, finding rare sites often requires a full-coverage survey.

As a result of these two factors, culture resource management surveys often have a different character than purely research-driven surveys, although, to be sure, the culture management surveys contribute enormous amounts of data that are useful to a range of research questions. At any rate, because most U.S. fieldwork is done through cultural resource management, many surveys undertaken today are full-coverage surveys.

Conclusion

We began this chapter with a discussion of "gumshoe survey," looking around for a good site to excavate by talking with lots of people, none of whom may be archaeologists. This is a good way to find rare or spectacular sites because those are the kinds of places that non-archaeologists will remember. Few would note, or even notice, small scatters of potsherds or stone flakes.

But archaeologists aren't just interested in the big, spectacular sites. They are interested in whole range of human settlement, in everything from big spectacular pueblos to the small scatter of a single broken pot. Sample surveys arose in the 1960s as a way not to find

sites, but to adequately characterize a region's archaeology. Spectacular sites are always informative, but they are much more informative when we know something about their regional context. And sample survey provides that context.

Although a 100-percent sample is always preferable, because it alone can guarantee the discovery of rare sites, such surveys are usually too expensive, and, as we have shown here, most research questions can be addressed with a far smaller sample. In addition, even a 100-percent survey may miss sites that lie deeply buried. What archaeology needs is a way to see below ground, and, as you will see in Chapter 5, we have some ways to do precisely that.

Summary

- Archaeological sites are found in different ways, and there is no single formula. Luck and hard work are the major keys; other sites are found through systematic regional survey.

- Settlement pattern archaeology transcends the single site in order to determine the overarching relationships among the various contemporaneous sites used by societies. The regional approach precludes assuming single sites as typical of a given culture; instead, the emphasis is on variability among sites within the settlement pattern.

- In some places, archaeological remains have simply lain on stable ground surfaces rather than becoming buried by sand, silt, and gravel. We can sample such areas using one or more probability-based sampling designs to minimize bias in recovering settlement pattern data.

- Sometimes these archaeological surveys record the distribution of archaeological sites. In other cases, the concept of "site" is not used at all, particularly when archaeological artifacts are distributed across broad areas. The Carson Desert is an example of non-site archaeology.

- Experimental studies show that survey sampling does indeed work—it can accurately characterize a

region's archaeology. But survey sampling is not good at finding those rare sites that so often play an important role in understanding a region's prehistory. These are found by gumshoe survey.

- Many factors enter into an archaeologist's understanding of just what the survey data mean. Both the survey and natural geologic processes act together to create sites. Where one or both of these are demonstrably significant factors, archaeologists should adopt the non-site approach.

- Judicious use of survey sampling can help locate a rare buried site whose existence, if not its exact location, is already known.

- Sometimes, the full-coverage technique—large-scale, 100-percent reconnaissance—is better than random sampling designs. These entail the systematic examination of contiguous blocks of terrain, surveyed at a uniform level of intensity. Full-coverage surveys are necessary when trying to ensure that no rare but significant site will be missed—for example, in surveys undertaken in advance of a construction project.

- Full-coverage survey is also useful (1) when the research question concerns complex settlement systems and seeks to explain their changes through time; (2) when a surface archaeological record is clearly visible; and (3) when addressing questions regarding specific relations between specific sites.

- Above all, remember that there is no one right way to do survey or to sample a region. The survey unit shape, the sampling fraction, and the collection

policy all depend on the question the archaeologist seeks to answer, the time and resources available, the topography, and the specific character of the archaeology (for example, ephemeral surface scatters of stone flakes or deeply buried sites with no surface indications).

Additional Reading

CANADIAN RESOURCES

Borden, Charles E. (1952). A uniform site designation scheme for Canada. In *Anthropology in British Columbia, 3*, Victoria: British Columbia Provincial Museum: Department of Education, 44–48.

Fedje, Daryl W. and Mathewes, Rolf W. (2005). *Human History and Environment from the Time of Loon to the Time of the Iron People.* Vancouver: UNB Press.

Fedje, Daryl W. and Christian, Tina. (1999). Modeling Paleo-Shorelines and Locating Early Holocene Coastal Sites in Haida Gwaii. *American Antiquity (64)*, 635–652.

OTHER RESOURCES

Banning, E. B. (2002). *Archaeological Survey.* New York: Kluwer Academic/Plenum.

Drennan, Robert D. (1996). *Statistics for Archaeologists: A Commonsense Approach.* New York: Plenum Press.

Madrigal, Lorena. (1995). *Statistics for Anthropology.* Cambridge: Cambridge University Press.

Orton, Clive. (2000). *Sampling in Archaeology.* Cambridge: Cambridge University Press.

Thomas, David Hurst. (1986). *Refiguring Anthropology.* Prospect Heights, IL: Waveland Press.

Online Resources

Visit *http://www.ontarioarchaeology.on.ca/* for information on the Ontario Archaeological Society, one of many avocational archaeology societies in Canada that you can join.

COMPANION WEBSITE

Visit *http://www.archaeology1ce.nelson.com* to access a wide range of material to help you succeed in your introductory archaeology course. These include flashcards, Internet exercises, Web links, and practice quizzes.

RESEARCH ONLINE
WITH INFOTRAC COLLEGE EDITION

From the Student Companion Website, you can access the InfoTrac College Edition database, which offers thousands of full-length articles for your research.

5

Doing Fieldwork
Remote Sensing and Geographic Information Systems

Doing archaeological survey the old fashioned way: The 1967 Glacial Lake Agassiz Survey Crew: Left to right, Morgan Tamplin, Steven Baker, Les Leonoff, Patrick Carmichael; Gary Dickson in back.

Source: Photo courtesy of Laboratory of Anthropology, University of Manitoba

Preview

Generations of archaeologists have longed for some magical x-ray machine that would allow us to peer beneath the earth's surface without digging. Today, that dream has almost come true. Remote sensing technology comprises a battery of different geophysical methods that provide cost-effective ways of doing archaeology in a noninvasive, nondestructive manner. It's often possible to learn much about the extent and contents of a site before excavation; sometimes, these new techniques can even acquire the necessary information and obviate the need for any excavation at all.

Those same archaeologists who longed for ways to see below the earth's surface also wished to search for spatial patterns in their data quickly and reliably. They previously did so by laboriously compiling data on paper maps. Geographic information systems are a new way to compile and analyze spatial data at multiple scales of resolution—from that of a single site to an entire continent to, conceivably, the world. It allows more rapid input and analysis of locational data, and it permits entirely new perspectives on the archaeological record.

Introduction

Modern archaeology has much in common with modern medicine. It was not long ago that a slipped disk or blown-out knee—both common archaeological ailments—meant immediate and sometimes radical surgery. And surgery was often more painful than the injury itself. Although your knee joint bounced back pretty quickly after the cartilage was removed, the muscle tissues and nerves needed months to recover from the centimetres-long incision required to access the injured area. Here was a classic case of the cure being almost worse than the disease.

Modern medical technology has changed all that. CAT scan and MRI technology today allow the physician to map afflicted areas in detail without any nasty exploratory surgery or damage to the patient. And when surgery is warranted, techniques like arthroscopy and laser microsurgery permit physicians to trim, cut, excise, and repair even gross damage with only the slightest incision. Today's noninvasive medicine minimizes tissue damage and surgical intervention.

Americanist archaeology has undergone a parallel revolution. In the good old days, archaeologists didn't have much choice but to dig in order to determine the extent of a site or to locate a buried structure. At Colonial Williamsburg, for example, the architectural historians who conducted the first excavations in the 1930s used an extraordinarily destructive method known as cross-trenching, which entails digging parallel trenches a shovel blade in width and throwing up the dirt on the unexcavated space between. The strategy was designed to disclose foundations for restoration, but the workers paid little attention to the artifacts and none whatsoever to their context. To archaeologists at mid-century, the greatest technological revolution was the advent of the backhoe as a tool of excavation.

Americanist archaeology today views its sites differently. A new conservation ethic suggests that we dig less and save more of our archaeological remains for the future. No ethical archaeologist would ever dig all of a site just because it's there. We always try to save something for future archaeologists, who will have new questions and technology that we cannot even imagine.

Augmenting this more ethical approach is an array of remote sensing techniques for doing relatively non-destructive archaeology. Using the archaeological equivalents of CAT scan and ultrasound, archaeologists can now map subsurface features in detail—without ever excavating them. And when it does become necessary to recover samples, we can execute pinpoint excavations, minimizing damage to the rest of the site.

Remote Sensing: Data at a Distance

Remote sensing refers to an array of photographic and geophysical techniques that rely on some form of electromagnetic energy—it might be raw electricity, light, heat, or radio waves—to detect and measure some characteristics of an archaeological target. This greatly enhances our ability to see, quite literally, given that the human eye can detect less than 1 ten-millionth of the entire electromagnetic spectrum.

Most of these techniques were initially designed to measure geophysical features on the scale of hundreds of metres or even kilometres. Yet to be effective in archaeology, such measurements must be scaled down to the order of metres or even centimetres. As you will see, researchers have made this advance in several of these technologies.

High-Altitude Imagery

The first aerial photograph was taken from a balloon suspended over Paris in 1858, and not too long afterward a few archaeologists were taking aerial photos of their sites, primarily with cameras attached to crewless balloons.

But it was World War I that opened up the possibilities of aerial photography for archaeology. Airplanes developed into a reliable technology during this war,

remote sensing The application of methods that employ some form of electromagnetic energy to detect and measure characteristics of an archaeological target.

and future British archaeologist O. G. S. Crawford (1886–1957) saw the potential in aerial photography when he analyzed aerial photographs of German military units. In fact, during the war itself, German military aviators photographed ruins in the Sinai from biplanes.

Taken with sunlight at an oblique angle, black and white photographs show shadows alongside slight undulations in the ground surface that point to shallowly buried walls not discernible on the ground. Soon after World War I, Crawford used aerial photography to locate networks of Roman settlements in Britain. And about the same time a French Jesuit priest, Père Antoine Poidebard (1878–1955), used aerial photography to find Roman-age settlements in the deserts of Syria. Since these early efforts, archaeologists have used everything from balloons and airplanes to the Space Shuttle and satellites to take aerial photographs and "sense their sites remotely."

In the Western Hemisphere, Charles Lindbergh (1902–1974), the famous American aviator-explorer, took some of the earliest archaeological aerial photographs. Two years after his 1927 nonstop transatlantic solo flight, Lindbergh undertook "goodwill tours" throughout Mexico, Central America, and the West Indies. Working closely with archaeologist A. V. Kidder, Lindbergh photographed important Maya archaeological ruins at Chichén Itzá (Mexico) and Tikal (Guatemala). He also did extensive photographic reconnaissance at Chaco Canyon, New Mexico. These photographic records have proven invaluable to archaeologists working in these areas today. Let's look at what they did for Chaco Canyon.

The Ancient Roads of Chaco Canyon

As mentioned in Chapter 4, Chaco was the centre of a vast social and political network between A.D. 1050 and 1150. During this time, two distinct kinds of sites appeared in the region. Throughout the Four Corners area, numerous smaller pueblo sites dotted the landscape. But huge sites—the Great Houses such as Pueblo Bonito (pictured in Figure 4-8)—appeared in Chaco Canyon and a few other places on the Colorado Plateau. The Great Houses were centrally located amid a cluster of smaller sites, defining a "community." By A.D. 1100, the Great Houses had developed into large, formal ancestral Pueblo towns.

In 1970–1971, archaeologist R. Gwinn Vivian (Arizona State Museum) was mapping what he thought was a series of ancient canals in Chaco Canyon. As he began excavating, Vivian realized that the linear features were like no canals he'd ever seen. Instead of having a U-shaped cross-section, the Chaco "canal" appeared to be a deliberately flattened and carefully engineered *roadway*. Although some archaeologists working in Chaco had speculated about possible roads, they lacked the technology to trace these possibilities very far, and their ruminations were buried deep inside voluminous field notes, unavailable to Vivian.

Vivian described his curious find to Thomas Lyons, a geologist hired to experiment with remote sensing possibilities in Chaco Canyon. Together, Vivian and Lyons started looking at the available aerial photographs from the area. They compared one set taken in the 1960s with Lindbergh's 1930s series, which was taken before grazing was permitted at Chaco.

The more they looked, the more they saw unmistakable traces of a prehistoric road network. They commissioned new flights, and road segments were field-checked

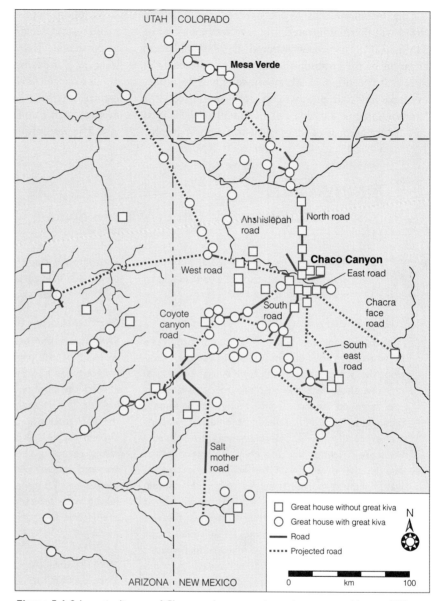

Figure 5-1 Schematic diagram of Chaco road system as it may have appeared by A.D. 1050.

against the aerial photographs. By 1973, Gwinn and Lyons had identified more than 300 kilometres of prehistoric roads (diagrammed in Figure 5-1). Amazingly, Lindbergh's photographs actually showed the famous Chacoan roads. But nobody recognized them as such until 1971, when archaeologists had a clue of what to look for (actually, Navajos living in Chaco Canyon had known about portions of the roads more than a century ago, although they, too, were unaware of their complete extent).

Aerial photography today is far more advanced than the simple black and white photographs obtained by hanging off the side of a biplane. Early photographic techniques were restricted to the visible portion of the electromagnetic spectrum, and cloud cover often hampered them. A variety of new photographic techniques allows film to capture portions of the electromagnetic spectrum that the naked eye cannot see and that are unaffected by cloud cover.

One technique that NASA used at Chaco in the 1980s was thermal infrared multispectral scanning, or TIMS. TIMS measures infrared thermal radiation given off by the ground; it is sensitive to differences as little as 0.1° centigrade. Although we've had the ability to make infrared photographs for some time—the Landsat satellite was doing it in the 1970s—TIMS is an advance because of the quality of the photographs.

All photographs consist of pixels, and an instrument cannot record anything smaller than the size of a particular technique's pixel. In earlier satellite imagery (for example, Landsat photos) the pixels were 30 metres on a side, and so these techniques could not record anything smaller than about 900 square metres. Such photos were of limited use to archaeology. The resolution of TIMS images still depends on

Looking Closer
Remote Sensing Imagery: Other Ways of Seeing

These are just a few of the remote sensing approaches that are available to archaeology today.

Aerial Photography

These are black and white or colour photographs taken from various elevations; the lower the elevation, the greater the resolution. Aerial photography can show features that are too indistinct or too large to discern from ground level. Photos taken over agricultural fields at different seasons are especially useful; plants growing over buried walls are browner because they are less vigorous due to the presence of buried stone or adobe walls. Likewise, buried trenches or houses contain looser, organic sediment and promote plant growth; these appear on the surface as greener plants. Taken at the right time of the year, aerial photos show buried walls and features as browner or greener circles, lines, and rectangles. Its drawback: It is limited to the visible light spectrum and is hampered by cloud cover or haze.

Colour Infrared Film (CIR)

CIR detects wavelengths at and beyond the red end of the light spectrum. In this way, it can detect heat (and was used at night in World War II to locate camouflaged tanks and artillery that retained more daytime heat than did the surrounding land). CIR can record differences in vegetation, because plant cover affects the heat reflected from the ground; if differences in plant cover suggest buried features as in standard aerial photography, then it can detect those buried features. But like aerial photography, CIR also needs light and cloudless skies.

Synthetic Aperture Radar (SAR)

SAR uses radar beams to locate buried features, working on the principle that hard buried surfaces reflect more energy than do softer surfaces, which absorb the energy. SAR works well when searching for linear and geometric features and when the background is dry, porous soils. In 1982, radar aboard the Space Shuttle penetrated the Saharan sands, revealing the presence of previously undiscovered ancient watercourses, along which ancient towns lie. Using airborne radar in Costa Rica (along with other methods), Payson Sheets found prehistoric footpaths, deeply buried by ash.

Landsat Multi-Spectral Scanner (MSS)

Used in the late 1970s, MSS images were taken from Landsat satellites and used the infrared spectrum (like TIMS) to construct false-colour images that track infrared radiation. However, the resolution was only about 80 metres.

SPOT

SPOT is a French-based satellite imagery system that can simultaneously record one or more bands of the electromagnetic spectrum. Some of its images have a resolution of only 2.5 metres and can be produced as three-dimensional images; it is unaffected by cloud cover and shadows.

the altitude at which the photos are taken. This can vary since the TIMS instrument is flown in NASA aircraft (and will eventually be placed in satellites). At 3000 metres, for example, the photos have a resolution of about 8 metres, but some projects have attained resolutions as small as 1–2 metres. These photographs can be quite useful to archaeology, and they are unaffected by cloud cover.

TIMS images are taken with a very complex kind of camera, and the data—the sensed infrared radiation—are transformed via a computer program into so-called "false-colour" images. False-colour images map the ground in terms of infrared radiation—rendering terrain in garish colours, such as red, blue, and purple. Because the Chacoan roads are more compacted than the surrounding soil (even if their compacted surface is buried), they should reflect more radiation than the surrounding sand.

And indeed they do. In false-colour images, the roads appear as clear, tan lines against a backdrop of red sand. The Chaco experiment proved that TIMS can detect features such as buried road systems, even if they are invisible to an archaeologist standing on top of them.

Today, analysis of aerial and high-altitude photographs has revealed possibly as much as *600 kilometres* of ancient roadways around Chaco Canyon. These roads are only 5 to 10 centimetres deep and yet sometimes 7 to 10 metres wide. Often they turn suddenly in doglegs and are occasionally edged by low rock berms. Sometimes they are littered with potsherds. Sometimes they are cut into the earth, and sometimes they were made by clearing away the surface rock and vegetation.

The longest and best-defined roads, probably constructed between A.D. 1075 and 1140, extend some 50 kilometres outward from Chaco Canyon. Sometimes the roads are just short segments, and it is unclear if they were intended to be segments, if they were unfinished, or if portions of the road have disappeared through erosion. In places the Chacoans constructed causeways, and elsewhere they cut stairways into sheer cliffs. The generally straight bearings suggest that the Ancestral Pueblo laid out the roads prior to construction, although archaeologists are unsure exactly how they did it.

Why did the Chaco people build these roads across the desert? This elaborate road system covered more than 250,000 square kilometres, and yet the Ancestral

Pueblo had no wheeled vehicles or even beasts of burden. Why are the roads so wide and so straight? What were they used for?

Although we don't have answers to these questions yet (but we'll return to them below), it is clear that archaeologists had unknowingly walked over the remains of the Chaco road system for decades. Their discovery had to come from data that were sensed remotely. Today, a battery of different, highly sophisticated photographic techniques helps archaeologists find buried remains (see "Looking Closer: Remote Sensing Imagery: Other Ways of Seeing"). Other techniques, used on the ground rather than in airplanes or satellites, also help archaeologists see below the ground.

How to Find a Lost Spanish Mission (Part II)

You'll remember from Chapter 4 that we used transect survey and power-auger testing to narrow down the location of Mission Santa Catalina to a 1-hectare area on St. Catherines Island, Georgia. One of the survey units in this area, Quad IV, was an undistinguished piece of real estate covered by scrub palmetto and live oak forest. The only evidence of human occupation was a little-used field road for island research vehicles. Although we could see aboriginal shell midden scatters here and there, Quad IV betrayed absolutely no surface clues as to what lay below.

At this point, we shifted our field strategy from preliminary subsurface testing to noninvasive, nondestructive remote sensing. Choosing the right method depends on what you expect to find. What, exactly, were we looking for? For more than a century, Santa Catalina had been the northernmost Spanish outpost on the eastern seaboard, and this historical fact implied considerable size and permanence. The 17th-century mission must have had a fortified church; some buildings to house soldiers and priests; plus enough granaries, storehouses, and dwellings for hundreds of Guale Indian neophytes.

We reasoned that the mission buildings were built by a wattle-and-daub technique (Figure 5-2). Freshly cut timbers were probably set vertically along the walls and reinforced with cane woven horizontally between the uprights. This sturdy wattlework was then plastered (daubed) with a mixture of marsh

Figure 5-2 Artist's reconstruction of the wattle-and-daub technique used to build Mission Santa Catalina. The upright wattlework is being daubed (plastered) with a mixture of marsh mud and organic fibres.

Source: After Boyd et al. (1951); courtesy of the University Press of Florida

mud, sand, and plant fibres (probably Spanish moss). Roofs were thatched with palmetto.

So constructed, wattle-and-daub buildings are biodegradable. If the roof does not burn, the roof's thatch will eventually rot and blow away. And once directly exposed to the weather, mud and twig walls will simply wash away. Archaeologists seeking such a dissolved mission would soon be out of business.

But thatched roofs often burn, and if that happened at Santa Catalina, the heat would have fired and hardened the daub walls, like a pot baking in a kiln. Fired daub, nearly as indestructible as the ubiquitous potsherd, thus became a key in our search for the mission.

So, how do you find chunks of burned mud buried beneath a foot of sand without excavating thousands of square metres?

proton precession magnetometer A remote sensing technique that measures the strength of magnetism between the earth's magnetic core and a sensor controlled by the archaeologist. Magnetic anomalies can indicate the presence of buried walls or features.

The Proton Magnetometer

It turns out that the marsh mud used in daub plaster contains microscopic iron particles. Normally, these are randomly oriented to all points of the compass. But when intensely heated, the particles orient toward magnetic north—like a million tiny compass needles. To pinpoint these magnetically anomalous orientations, we relied upon a **proton precession magnetometer.** The theory behind this device is complicated, but the principle is simple: Magnetometers measure the strength of magnetism between the earth's magnetic core and a sensor controlled by the archaeologist. If hundreds of these readings are taken across a systematic grid, a computer plotter can generate a magnetic contour map reflecting both the shape and the intensity of magnetic anomalies beneath the ground surface.

Many subsurface anomalies are archaeologically irrelevant magnetic "noise"—interference from underlying rocks, AC power lines, or hidden iron debris. The earth's magnetic field fluctuates so wildly on some days that the readings are meaningless, and electrical storms can hopelessly scramble magnetometer readings. Even minor interference, such as the operator's wristwatch or eyeglasses, can drive a magnetometer crazy.

But when everything works just right, the magnetometer provides the equivalent of a CAT scan, telling archaeologists what is going on beneath the earth's surface. Many archaeological features have characteristic magnetic signatures—telltale clues that hint at the size, shape, depth, and composition of the archaeological objects hidden far below. Shallow graves, for instance, have a magnetic profile vastly different from, say, a buried fire pit or a wattle-and-daub wall.

We worked with Ervan Garrison (now with University of Georgia) and a magnetometer team from Texas A&M University (Figure 5-3). As they were packing up their field equipment to work up the data in their lab, they shared a couple of hunches, based strictly on their raw magnetometer readings: "If we were y'all, we'd dig in three places: here, over yonder, and especially right here." We took their advice, exploring each of the three magnetic anomalies in the few days remaining in our May field season. One anomaly— "especially right here"—turned out to be a large iron barrel ring. Excavating further, we came upon another ring, and more below that. At about 3 metres down,

Figure 5-3 Ervan Garrison and Deborah Mayer O'Brien looking for Mission Santa Catalina (on St. Catherines Island, Georgia) using a proton magnetometer. She is holding the sensor, and he is recording magnetometer readings.

Source: American Museum of Natural History; photo by Dennis O'Brien

we hit the water table. Digging underwater, we encountered a well-preserved oak well casing.

Archaeologists love wells because, like privies, they can be magnificent artifact traps. After removing the bones of an unfortunate fawn (which had long ago drowned), we found an array of distinctive Hispanic and Guale Indian potsherds and a metal dinner plate dropped (or tossed) into the well. All artifacts were typical of the 16th and 17th centuries. We had indeed found Mission Santa Catalina, and we pressed on to see what else the magnetometer might have turned up.

Our second magnetic anomaly—the one "here"—was a small mound. We thought at first that it might be a grave or tomb. But after removing the overburden, we came across a burned daub wall that, as it fell, had crushed dozens of Spanish and Guale domestic artifacts: imported tin-enameled glazed cups, painted ceramic dishes, a kitchen knife, and at least two enormous pots for cooking or storage. Charred deer and chicken bones littered the floor, and dozens of tiny corncobs lay scattered about. This time, the magnetometer had led us to the kitchen (in Spanish, *cocina*) used by 17th-century Franciscan friars at Santa Catalina.

Finally, we began digging the "over yonder" anomaly, which proved to be a linear daub concentration more than 12 metres long—obviously the downed

wall of yet another, much larger mission building. Here excavations turned up none of the everyday implements and debris so common in the scorched *cocina*. Instead, we found human graves.

The search was over. We had discovered the church, the paramount house of worship at Santa Catalina de Guale. Our magnetometer survey had given us trustworthy directions to the buried daub walls and iron barrel hoops. Even without computer enhancement, the magnetometer had taken us to the very heart of Mission Santa Catalina.

Since the discovery of Santa Catalina, we have spent a decade excavating the church ruins. The lateral church walls were constructed of wattle and daub that, when encountered archaeologically, consisted of a densely packed linear rubble scatter; this is what the magnetometer "saw" in Quad IV. Beneath the nave and sanctuary of the church, we discovered the cemetery, where the Franciscans had interred 400 to 450 Christianized Guale Indians.

Soil Resistivity

Proton magnetometry was just one of the techniques used to locate and define Santa Catalina de Guale. **Soil resistivity survey** monitors the electrical resistance of soils in a restricted volume near the surface of an archaeological site. Perhaps partially because of its relatively low cost, soil resistivity survey has become a popular technique of geophysical prospecting over the past four decades.

The degree of **soil** resistivity depends on several factors, the most important of which is usually the

---

soil resistivity survey A remote sensing technique that monitors the electrical resistance of soils in a restricted volume near the surface of an archaeological site; buried walls or features can be detected by changes in the amount of resistance registered by the resistivity meter.

amount of water retained in the soil—the less water, the greater the resistance to electrical currents. Compaction such as occurs in house floors, walls, paths, and roads tends to reduce pore sizes and hence the potential to retain water; this registers as high resistance. In effect, when electricity is sent through the soil, buried features can often be detected and defined by their differential resistance to electrical charge (caused by their differential retention of groundwater).

The aggregation of fill in pits, ditches, and middens will also alter resistivity. Foundations or walls, particularly those in historic-period sites, generally have *greater* resistivity than surrounding soil, whereas the generation of humus by occupation activity increases the ion content of the soil, *reducing* resistivity.

After the initial discovery of the mission and a pilot resistivity survey, Mark Williams and the late Gary Shapiro returned to St. Catherines Island to conduct a more comprehensive study.

We measured soil resistance by setting four probes in line at 1-metre intervals, each probe inserted to a depth of 20 centimetres. We passed an electrical current between the probes and recorded the electrical conductivity between the two centre probes.

We took readings on east–west grid lines at 1-metre intervals. The line was then advanced a metre north or south, and another set of readings were taken. This procedure resulted in a gridded array of resistance values, recorded in the field on graph paper and eventually transferred to a computer. We also charted the locations of trees, backdirt (the piles of dirt created by excavation), roads, and other features that might influence resistance.

We conducted one of the preliminary resistivity surveys in a 15 × 15-metre area that straddled a test excavation of Structure 2 at Santa Catalina, initially located by the proton magnetometer survey. From our test excavations, we suspected that this building was probably the kitchen, but we had no idea of the building's configuration. Figure 5-4 shows the resistivity diagram of this area, clearly identifying the margins of the unexcavated building. Later, excavations confirmed the accuracy of the soil resistivity diagram.

ground-penetrating radar A remote sensing technique in which radar pulses directed into the ground reflect back to the surface when they strike features or interfaces within the ground, showing the presence and depth of possible buried features.

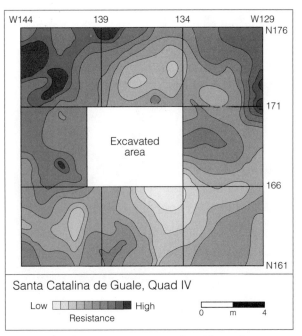

Figure 5-4 Soil resistivity contour map from Mission Santa Catalina (Georgia). The top of this map is oriented toward magnetic north; the buried kitchen building appears as a large square outline below right centre, oriented at 45° off north.

Source: Courtesy American Museum of Natural History

In some circumstances, archaeologists opt to use conductivity meters, which measure the inverse of what a resistivity meter measures—that is, how well sediment *conducts* electricity. A conductivity instrument, which looks like a 1- to 3-metre-long carpenter's level, is easy to use. The archeologist simply lays it on the ground along a grid line, pushes a button, and records the reading. Conductivity meters are useful when soil is completely dry, because resistivity meters require wet, but not saturated, soils. However, conductivity meters are expensive (about $17,000) and the data they generate are not as easily manipulated and analyzed as are resistivity data.

Ground-Penetrating Radar

Yet another method of geophysical prospecting is **ground-penetrating radar** (GPR). Although this method tends to be expensive, its cost is offset to some degree by its speed. But neither operating the radar equipment nor interpreting the results is simple, and the assistance of trained specialists is required.

GPR was first developed in 1910, but a significant peak in relevant articles coincided with the *Apollo 17* lunar sounding experiment in the early 1970s. Today, environmental engineering firms commonly employ GPR techniques to find buried rock or deep swamp deposits, or to search for caverns. GPR works well on snow-covered ground (one of the benefits of this method for Canadian archaeologists).

In GPR, radar pulses directed into the ground reflect back to the surface when they strike targets or interfaces within the ground (such as a change in the density of dirt, groundwater, buried objects, voids, or an interface between soil and rock). As these pulses are reflected, their speed to the target and the nature of their return are measured. The signal's reflection provides information about the depth and three-dimensional shape of buried objects.

With transducers (a device that converts electrical energy to electromagnetic waves) of various dimensions, a researcher applying GPR can direct the greatest degree of resolution to the depth of specific interest. A pulsating electric current is passed through an antenna, inducing electromagnetic waves that radiate toward the target and return in a fraction of a microsecond to be recorded. The dimensions of the transducer influence the depth and detail that are desired in any specific archaeological application. As the antenna is dragged across the ground surface, a continuous profile of subsurface electromagnetic conditions is printed on a graphic recorder. The location and depth of subsurface targets can be inferred from, and tested against, this graphic record.

Groundwater can pose a problem in GPR studies, because it changes the relative permeability of most sediments. Soils are good reflectors when they are associated with steep changes in water content, as occurs in coarse materials. Unsorted sediments, such as glacial till, will have a broad and varying capillary zone, and thus no clear reflection. GPR is generally ineffective over saltwater, in penetrating some clays, and at depths of more than about 30 metres below the surface. The maximum depth of penetration depends on the conductivity of the overlying deposit.

GPR works best when the soil resistivity is high, as in well-drained soils and those with low clay content. Subsurface wells, foundations, cellars, voids, cavities, and well-defined compacted zones, such as house floors, can provide clear radar echoes.

Why did we begin using GPR at Santa Catalina? Historical documents suggested that the Spanish had fortified the mission as a precaution against British attack, perhaps by building a stockade and moat complex to protect the buildings immediately adjacent to the central plaza. Yet, after three years of using magnetometer and resistivity surveys and limited test excavations, we had failed to locate any trace of defensive fortifications, such as palisades, bastions, or moats encircling the central mission zone. Given that these features might not have burned and because they could be as saturated with water as the surrounding sediment, they might have eluded the magnetometer and resistivity instruments. However, these features might have differed from the background sediment in terms of their compaction, and that suggested to us that GPR might help locate them.

We used the existing grid system, having cleared brush and palmetto from the transect lines before our survey. Initially, a number of systematic north–south transects were run at 20-metre intervals, followed by a series of east–west transects. Obvious anomalies were hand-plotted on the greyscale computer output, and additional transects were run across these target areas. We located significant anomalies on the ground by means of pin flags. We then ran a third set of transects at a 45° angle, to intercept buried anomalies at a different angle.

So, what happened? Directed by the radar profiles, test excavations led directly to the discovery of the palisade and bastion complex encircling the central buildings and plaza at Santa Catalina. Although this defensive network could surely have been located by extensive test trenching, the radar approach proved to be considerably more cost-effective and less destructive than conventional archaeological exploration.

Cerén: The New World Pompeii?

Remote sensing studies work best when we can calibrate instrumentation and imagery to local conditions and when field verification is possible. Such a situation existed at the site of Cerén, located in the Zapotitán Valley of El Salvador.

A bulldozer operator discovered the Cerén site in 1976 as he attempted to level a platform on which to build some grain storage silos. When he noticed that his bulldozer blade had uncovered the corner of a deeply buried building, the curious workman stepped down and looked around. When he found some old-looking pottery buried in the building, he stopped work and notified the National Museum in San Salvador. Unfortunately, when a representative of the museum arrived three days later, he dismissed the find as very recent construction and gave the heavy equipment operator his blessing to continue working. As an unfortunate result, several other ancient buildings were bulldozed.

Two years later, when Payson Sheets and his students from the University of Colorado arrived to conduct a survey of the Zapotitán Valley, townspeople told them of the unusual find and showed them where some of it remained. Sheets saw some adobe columns protruding from the disturbed area and expected to find bits of plastic and newspaper eroding out of the ruined building. Even when he found some Maya polychrome pottery (that Sheets knew dated to about A.D. 500–800), he too thought that the building was modern—the thatch roof was almost perfectly preserved, even though it was buried beneath nearly 5 metres of volcanic ash (Figure 5-5).

But after a few hours of excavation, Sheets found lots of ancient Maya artifacts—without any sign of historic-period material. Sheets worried: What if he announced these well-preserved buildings were prehistoric and they turned out to be recent? The whole issue turned, of course, on dating. Sheets collected some of the buried roof thatch for radiocarbon analysis (we'll discuss dating methods in Chapter 8). When the results of the tests came back, he no longer worried about embarrassing himself—all the thatch samples (and therefore the buried houses as well) were 1400 years old.

Figure 5-5 Adobe columns and flooring of Structure 1 at the Cerén site (El Salvador). This Maya house was buried instantaneously in about A.D. 590 by nearly 5 metres of volcanic ash from the nearby Loma Caldera. When archaeologist Payson Sheets and his crew excavated this house, they found all artifacts left in place. Even the thatched roof had been preserved.

Source: Payson Sheets

Large volcanoes and cinder cones, many of which are active, surround the Zapotitán Valley. The Cerén site, as it came to be known, was buried in about A.D. 590 by several metres of volcanic ash from the nearby Loma Caldera. Because the ash had cooled off considerably by the time it hit, nearly all the ancient agricultural features and cultural artifacts were miraculously preserved—crops still in the field, orchards, a central public plaza surrounded by adobe houses with artifacts left exactly as buried—even ancient Maya farmers' footprints!

But the ash that so preserved Cerén also completely obscured it. How could Sheets map a village buried beneath 5 metres of volcanic debris?

Sheets and his colleagues turned to GPR as a way to see what lay below the surface. The depositional conditions at Cerén were almost ideal for remote sensing. The overlying volcanic ash contained relatively little clay and there was only minimal soil formation. One of the radar antennas, using 300 MHz frequency radar energy, could penetrate 5 metres deep, and it could detect features as small as 45–50 centimetres. The resulting readout is shown in Figure 5-6.

But radar antennas are unwieldy and difficult to pull over rocky terrain. And to make matters worse, much of the ground surface at Cerén was a functioning maize field. Sheets found an innovative solution that used local technology: They loaded their GPR system into the back of an oxcart. Although it was an incongruous sight—a wooden cart laden with hundreds of kilograms of high-tech radar equipment, pulled by plodding oxen—it worked well.

Sheets mapped and reconstructed the entire ancient landscape at Cerén from the GPR results and then verified the reconstruction with test pits and broad excavations. By carefully working out the various radar signatures from the excavated houses, Sheets was able to map these unexcavated pre-Columbian houses precisely using remote sensing and associated computer modelling techniques. The population density of the buried zone was surprisingly high. On the day it was buried, Cerén was a prosperous farming village with closely packed domestic, civic, and religious buildings constructed on elevated platforms, with all intervening space between them taken up by agricultural crops (Figure 5-7).

Because of its extraordinary Pompeii-like preservation, the Cerén site is one of the most important places in Central America for studying ancient land-use practices. And GPR mapping proved to be a cost-effective method for discovering buried houses—some of which were excavated; the rest preserved for the future.

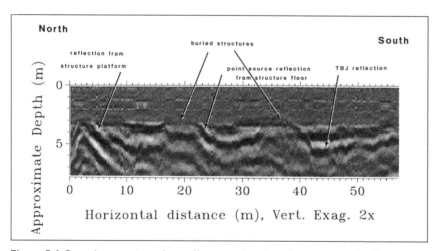

Figure 5-6 Ground-penetrating radar profile across three buried structures at the Cerén site.
Source: © Payson Sheets

Figure 5-7 Artist's reconstruction of the buried structures at the Cerén site. The domicile (Structure 1) appears in the centre, with the workshop on the right, and the storehouse on the left.
Source: Payson Sheets

In His Own Words
Jean-Michel Maillol and GPR in Northern Mexico

by Jean-Michel Maillol

One of the major challenges that archaeologists face is the challenge of locating buried architectural and cultural remains. In many cases, very little surface expression of an archaeological site is present. Even if some major features are exposed it is always very difficult to assess the full extent of a site. More recently, new challenges have appeared. Urbanization and land development, both in industrialized and in developing countries, are continuously threatening known and undiscovered cultural heritage resources. In addition, environmental awareness and regulations designed to protect existing resources make it increasingly difficult for archaeologists to rely on destructive excavation as the main investigation approach. To face all these challenges archaeologists are calling on an array of remote sensing techniques that allow them to map entire archaeological sites without ever touching or seeing their components. Here is an example of how I have used remote sensing techniques in my research.

Approximately 800 to 1300 years ago, in the arid valleys of present-day Northern Mexico, people of the Chihuahua culture lived in small agricultural villages. The typical dwellings consisted of round pit structures consisting of either "house-in-pits," with interior-wall support poles, or "pithouses," with support poles located outside the excavated floor area and anchored in the pit walls. The first archaeological excavations of these structures took place in the 1930s, and since then a number of these structures have been excavated in detail. However, a number of problems remain under investigation: spatial extent of these villages, pattern of organization of dwellings within each village, evolution in time of this pattern, and factors controlling the location of the settlements within the landscape. Since only very few structures have any remaining expression at the ground surface, only a few houses can be spotted and a meaningful analysis of the distribution of the dwellings would in principle require a complete stripping of the top ground layer over areas as large as 20,000 square metres. This is hardly a practical option, even if it were environmentally acceptable, which it definitely is not! The only possible alternative is to use remote sensing tools that allow the subsurface to be imaged without disturbance.

In 2005, I worked with Canadian researchers from the University of Calgary and the University of British Columbia, and Mexican colleagues from the National Institute of Anthropology and History, using a technique called ground penetrating radar (GPR) to create a solution to this problem. One of the most advanced ground-based remote sensing tools available to archaeologists, GPR works by sending pulses of high-frequency radiowaves through the ground. If heterogeneities are present in the subsurface, such as a pithouse floor or a wall, these waves bounce back to the surface and produce an echo. The echo is analyzed and mapped using computerized techniques that produce a three-dimensional representation of the subsurface.

The Potential and Limitations of Noninvasive Archaeology

It is clear from these examples that remote sensing can help archaeology in very significant ways. One drawback has been that remote sensing techniques are expensive, but the cost has been going down as the machinery becomes more widely available. And remote sensing can pay for itself, given that the alternative—hand excavation—is also costly. By targeting excavation efforts, remote sensing could actually reduce a project's cost.

But remote sensing cannot work everywhere—at least not yet. The different geophysical devices work

Data were acquired at four different archaeological sites following a dense survey grid consisting of 50-metre-long profiles spaced 0.50 metres apart, and the total area covered exceeded 35,000 square metres. Over the entire area, a 1.5-metre-thick "slice" of ground could be reconstructed and imaged using computer graphics. A very limited number of targeted test pits were dug to verify the remote sensing results. This is called "ground-truthing" in remote sensing terminology, and it is always necessary when a technique is used for the first time in a new area.

The remote sensing results went beyond expectations as the computed images clearly revealed the outlines and even some internal details of a large number of circular pit structures at every site. While only two to four houses were known at each site from previous excavation projects, the total count is now more than 70. Even more significantly, the limits of the villages can be clearly delineated, and the patterns of house distribution can be studied. In some cases, even the layout of postholes inside individual houses can be seen thus allowing some architectural analysis to be conducted.

These "subsurface pictures" now offer a view of the settlement habits of the Chihuahua culture people at a scale previously unattainable by traditional excavation or survey methods, and with almost no disturbance of the ground. They constitute a powerful tool for archaeology and for the protection and conservation of sites.

Figure 5-8 Jean-Michel Maillol conducting a GPR survey as part of a Canadian archaeology project in Northern Mexico.
Source: J M Maillol, Department of Geology/Geophysics, University of Calgary

best under certain conditions. In places where there is a lot of background noise—such as a high groundwater table, lots of background rock, or natural subsurface features—it is often difficult to pick out which anomalies in the magnetometer, resistivity, or GPR readings are worth investigating. And high-altitude imagery has to be ground-truthed (that is, verified with physical observation) to determine what the images are recording. But with increasing refinements to the technology, remote sensing has become an indispensable excavation tool.

For years, archaeologists considered only artifacts that they could hold in their hands or features that they could see with their eyes as sources of data.

Remote sensing changes that, provided that we can construct the requisite linkages between the larger things that archaeologists find—walls, structures, and features—and the way that they are remotely perceived by the sensors of geophysical machinery and remote imagery.

Geographic Information Systems

Archaeological data are inherently spatial, and archaeologists map things all the time. Maps show where things are, and, more importantly, how they relate to each other. Archaeologists use maps to plot the results of remote sensing, such as artifact distributions within a site and distributions of sites across a region, province, or even a continent.

But in their traditional form, maps are difficult to update with new information, and the resulting distributions are often unwieldy to analyze.

This all changed in the late 1980s with the advent of **geographic information systems (GIS),** computer programs designed to store, retrieve, analyze, and display cartographic data. GIS lets you view information—any geographically related information—visually. The most common programs in use today are ArcView and ArcInfo.

Every GIS consists of three primary components: a powerful computer graphics program used to draw a map, one or more external databases that are linked to the objects shown on the map, and a set of analytical tools that can graphically interpret or statistically analyze the stored data. Most U.S. states are in the process of putting all their site records into a GIS. Clearly, GIS is a basic skill that any student contemplating a career in archaeology should learn.

In true GIS format, the earth's various features are not depicted visually—as they would be on standard two-dimensional maps—but as digital information. Virtually every standard USGS topographic map is now available digitally (some high-end GPS units contain them already). The primary source of geospatial data in Canada is the Centre for Topographic Information (CTI) of Natural Resources Canada (NRCan). GIS resources are also made available by the Canadian Space Agency. In particular, satellite data from Radarsat have been used for both remote sensing and GIS applications. Data stored digitally, of course, can be manipulated and displayed in numerous ways.

In GIS, a database is composed of several themes, or layers. Envision a base topographic map—that's one theme. Now envision laying a clear sheet of Mylar plastic over that map (this is how we used to do it!). You will plot on the Mylar sheet all the archaeological sites you just found in a survey. This layer is another theme. Over the first Mylar sheet, we will lay another on which we will draw in all the water sources; this is a third theme. On yet another sheet, we will draw the distribution of different vegetation communities. On another, we will plot the results of high-altitude imagery. On still another, the region's different soils . . . you get the picture.

Mapping like this with physical sheets of paper or Mylar is unwieldy, and the resulting patterns are difficult to analyze statistically. However, by inputting all these different data digitally into a single **georeferenced** database, we can call up one or more of the layers and analyze the distributions. "Georeferenced" means that all the data are input using a common mapping reference, for example, the UTM grid system mentioned in Chapter 4. Because the data are digital, we can do spatial analyses in minutes that previously might have taken weeks or longer. Each of the data points are linked to a database, which can include complete information on that point. A site record, for example, might contain information on a site's artifacts—how many projectile points or potsherds were found there—plus other data such as its size, its slope, and the kind of architecture that was present.

We can ask myriad questions of this database. For example, we might ask, "How far away from water sources are pueblo sites found?" With a GIS database we can quickly *buffer* springs and streams at some standard distance, say 1-kilometre intervals. Think of this as drawing concentric circles around the springs with radii of 1 kilometre, 2 kilometres, 3 kilometres, and so on. Likewise, we would trace out land areas within 1, 2, and 3 kilometres from rivers and streams. We could then ask the program to tell us how many pueblo sites versus other kinds of sites are in the vari-

geographic information system (GIS) A computer program for storing, retrieving, analyzing, and displaying cartographic data.

georeferenced Data that are input to a GIS database using a common mapping reference—for example, the UTM grid—so that all data can be spatially analyzed.

ous buffers. We could also see if sites are more frequently associated with a particular kind of vegetation community or soil types—in fact, with any data set that has a spatial dimension to it.

In this fashion, GIS allows archaeologists to do many things that otherwise might be too time-consuming to tackle. GIS, for instance, can create a viewshed that shows what portion of a landscape is visible from a particular site. With such a capability, we could test the proposition that a site on a ridge top is a hunting stand or lookout. Obviously, the view from a hunting stand should encompass land where we would expect to find grazing animals or migrating herds of game.

The Predictive Capacity of GIS: The Aberdeen Proving Ground

GIS databases do require an *enormous* amount of time to construct. Although many archaeologists today record their data digitally and can download them to a GIS database, decades worth of archaeological data remain to be manually input. But the eventual time savings can be significant, because a GIS database can be used to predict site locations. This can be extremely cost-effective because it can help target surveys just as remote sensing techniques can help target excavations; it can also help prevent the needless destruction of archaeological sites. Konnie Wescott and James Kuiper (Argonne National Laboratory) developed such a predictive model for the Aberdeen Proving Ground in Maryland.

The Aberdeen Proving Ground consists of 16,000 hectares of land on the north end of Chesapeake Bay. Only 1 percent of the entire area has seen a traditional archaeological survey. This area is especially difficult to survey, because much of it is marsh and the sites are mostly ephemeral shell middens and scatters of ceramics and stone flakes. And a traditional survey could be dangerous, because unexploded ordnance litters the military proving grounds. Still, the Army wished to develop a plan that would help it take cultural resources—archaeological sites—into account as the proving ground developed. A predictive model would help the Army know where it was likely to encounter sites and allow it to plan construction in areas of low expected site densities.

Wescott and Kuiper developed a predictive model by using characteristics of 572 archaeological sites

outside the proving ground along the shores of Chesapeake Bay—sites that had been found by traditional archaeological surveys. They recorded many different variables that described the site locations—distance to water, topography, slope, soil type, and elevation.

A good predictive model will use the fewest number of variables possible so that noise is eliminated from the predictions. Wescott and Kuiper analyzed the data on the 572 sites to discover which variables were the best predictors of site locations. They found that a combination of type of nearest water (for example, bay shoreline, river shoreline, freshwater creek), elevation, topographic setting (for example, floodplain, hill slope, interior flat), and distance to water were sufficient to predict most of the known site locations.

They then went about creating a predictive model for the proving ground by creating several layers for the key variables. One layer created 300-metre buffers around water of different types. Another drew buffers (at 30, 150, and 300 metres) around water sources. A third blocked out the different kinds of topography. A fourth layer made use of a digital elevation model (DEM—a three-dimensional virtual model of a landscape) to block out elevations in 3-metre intervals. The layers are shown in Figure 5-9.

So far, all they had were some pretty maps (and they look even better in colour). What they really needed, however, was a map that shows where sites might be found and where they probably will not be found. Wescott and Kuiper used their four identified best predictors (type of water, elevation, topography, and distance to water) in order to define areas in the proving ground of high, medium, and low potential to contain sites. For example, they found that most shell midden sites (those composed mostly of discarded shells from meals) were found within 150 metres of fresh or brackish water; below 6 metres in elevation; and on terraces, bluffs, floodplains, or flats. By digitally overlaying the layers, the GIS developed a new map showing areas where all these criteria were met. This map is shown at the bottom of Figure 5-9, with known site locations plotted. Although the sample of known sites is limited, the predictive model seemed to work fairly well, especially for shell midden sites. With this map in hand, the Army can locate its new facilities on land with the least potential for disturbing archaeological sites.

Landscape Archaeology

GIS is a tool that opens up new ways to analyze spatial data. Partly because of this new ability, archaeology developed a new approach called **landscape archaeology.** Although the word "landscape" has a colloquial meaning, Carole Crumley (University of North Carolina) defines landscape as "the material manifestation of the relation between humans and their environments." Landscape archaeology allows us to return to the difference between processual and postprocessual paradigms and see how we can think about a landscape in different but productive ways.

In a sense, landscape archaeology has been around since the 1940s, when Gordon Willey (1913–2002) conducted the first archaeological settlement pattern study in Peru's Virú Valley. In this regard, landscape archaeology is similar to the settlement pattern archaeology we discussed in Chapter 4, but it adds a concern with how people use and modify their environment. Landscapes from the perspective of the processual paradigm are made of places with different economic potential. Fertile bottomlands are good places to grow maize; the uplands are places to gather nuts; the mountains to the east contain trees for houses, but good clay for pots is found to the west; turquoise for trade is found at the base of a far-off butte. The Carson Desert study is an example of a processual perspective on a landscape, because it focused on the economic use of a region's resources.

But postprocessualism adds to this economic vision of a landscape the social and symbolic meanings of land as well. Places on the landscape are often laden with meaning, sometimes linked to a culture's origin myths. A mountain may be sacred because it is where a mythical hero destroyed monsters in "the time before people." Directions may be associated with particular sacred beings, supernatural powers, or human emotions. The site of the World Trade Center is now a symbolically powerful part of the American landscape; so is Dealey Plaza in Dallas, where President Kennedy was assassinated.

GIS is not limited to one of these perspectives on the landscape. It fact, the following examples show how it can be a very powerful tool for both.

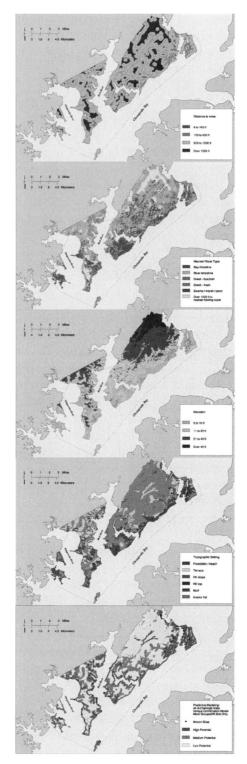

Figure 5-9 Wescott and Kuiper's GIS maps showing distribution of water type, elevation, topographic setting, and distance to water. The bottom map shows the distribution of known sites and areas of predicted high and low site potential.

Source: © Wescott and Kuiper and Taylor & Francis Publishing

landscape archaeology The study of ancient human modification of the environment.

Modelling an Economic Landscape: The Carson Desert Revisited

Following up on Kelly's Carson Desert research discussed in Chapter 4, David Zeanah (California State University, Sacramento) was interested in devising even better models for predicting the archaeology of the Carson Desert and Stillwater Mountains, and he turned to GIS models to do so. Specifically, Zeanah used ethnographic data to map out the territory of one Northern Paiute group, the Toedökadö, as it existed in the late 19th century. Their territory encompassed the Carson Desert, Stillwater Mountains, and some lands beyond. Zeanah divided the Toedökadö territory into 1-kilometre squares using the UTM system and then georeferenced this block of grid squares to the digitized topographic maps for the region.

Zeanah then developed a landscape model in which he defined 41 vegetation communities using modern range-management data. Each of these vegetation communities was made up of varying percentages of different plants, some of which were important food sources for people, such as ricegrass (*Oryzopsis hymenoides),* and some of which were important sources of food for animals. Using wildlife management data, Zeanah then graded each vegetation community in terms of its potential for key animal species, such as bighorn sheep.

Soil type and topography largely control the distribution of particular vegetation communities across a landscape. Using soil maps—again, georeferenced to the topographic maps—Zeanah could characterize each 1-kilometre square in terms of its vegetation community and game productivity (Figure 5-10). In this way, he created baseline "economic potential" maps of a range of food plants and game animals for the Northern Paiute's ethnographically known territory.

But the baseline maps were only the beginning. We know that climate has changed over time in the Great Basin and that such climatic changes affect the abundance and distribution of plants and animals. Can the GIS be altered to take those climatic changes into account?

Changes in precipitation and temperature change effective moisture, and that, in turn, affects plant productivity and the abundance and distribution of animals. Range-management data tell us that plant productivity responds in predictable ways to increases or decreases in effective moisture. Using what archaeolo-

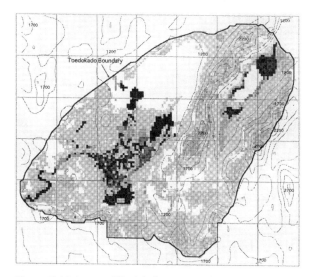

Figure 5-10 A map of Toedökadö territory showing the predicted productivity of ricegrass; the darker the square, the higher the productivity.

Source: © David Zeanah

gists already knew about changes in temperature and precipitation over time in the Great Basin, Zeanah altered the baseline model by increasing and decreasing a community's productivity by an appropriate percentage for each climatic period of the past. He could even shift the percentage of perennial or annual plants depending on whether the paleoclimatic data suggested a shift to summer precipitation (which favours annuals) or winter precipitation (which favours perennials). In addition, he could remove the piñon pine layer for the layers describing the landscape prior to 1500 years ago, because we know that piñon pine did not exist in the region before that date.

By massaging the data in this fashion, Zeanah modelled the changing effects of climate on the economic productivity of the region. His model thus predicts where we might expect to see archaeological evidence of prehistoric activities at different times in the past as a product of climatically induced changes in plant and animal abundance and distribution.

By making predictions based on an explicit model, archaeologists can evaluate the role of subsistence as opposed to some other factor in conditioning past human behaviour. Such predictions could then be tested by one of the survey strategies we described in Chapter 4. In fact, Zeanah chose to use 1-kilometre squares as the basic unit of map construction so that they could provide easy sample units for future field research.

Archaeological Ethics
Assessing the Visual Impact of Oil and Gas Development on Sacred Sites in Alberta

Archaeologists are very concerned about protecting cultural resources from the destruction occasionally caused by industrial and urban development. Over the past three decades, a whole industry based on the management of cultural resources has emerged in countries such as Canada and the United States. Take the province of Alberta, for example. Oil and gas development has become an important part of the provincial economy in recent years. When access roads, well pads, and pipelines are constructed in remote areas where archaeological sites might be present, cultural resource management (CRM) archaeologists are called in to assess the risks such developments may pose. In some cases, projects can simply be moved to alternate locations. When this is not possible, CRM archaeologists conduct salvage excavations. Archaeological sites, however, are impacted by development in different ways.

The Majorville Medicine Wheel in southern Alberta is an important spiritual site for local First Nations peoples. Medicine wheels are found throughout the Great Plains, and are large stone constructions usually laid out in the shape of a spoked wheel. Others, like the Minton Turtle Wheel in Saskatchewan, are built as effigies of important animals in First Nations mythology. Archaeologists aren't exactly sure what these mysterious rock structures were used for. Some have suggested that they functioned as astronomical calendars,

vision-questing sites, geoglyphs, Sundance lodges, or even monuments to deceased war chiefs. We do know that many indigenous communities consider these locations highly spiritual. For example, offerings are still left in the central stone cairn of the Majorville Medicine Wheel by First Nations, who visit the site during significant times of the year.

Like many medicine wheels, the Majorville site is located in an isolated upland area that offers a dramatic view of the surrounding landscape. It is also a location that contains valuable petroleum resources. Because of the spiritual nature of the site, visual impacts to the Majorville Wheel, such as wellheads protruding from the landscape, would be as detrimental as any physical destruction. How do archaeologists protect the nonmaterial integrity of sacred sites like these? Traditionally, CRM archaeologists had visited the Majorville site repeatedly to check on the visual effects of proposed developments. Could someone see a wellhead, for example, if they stood at the central cairn? However, recurring visits might eventually lead to physical damage, as the paths around the site began to wear. CRM archaeologists at Golder Associates Ltd., an international environmental consulting firm, came up with an extremely innovative way of solving this problem.

As anyone who has played a recent video game knows, computer graphics have progressed to the point that virtual worlds are almost indistinguishable

Zeanah used existing survey data (457 sites) to test the baseline model for 94 units of 1 × 1 kilometre. The baseline model ranked sample units in terms of how productive a unit was expected to be and thus how likely it was that archaeological remains would be found in that unit. Zeanah found that he could accurately predict the archaeological record of between 60 and 78 percent of the 94 sample units. The model worked best where sample units were predicted to offer very low or, alternatively, very high amounts of

food to a mobile, hunting-and-gathering population. These are very good results, especially for a first-generation model.

GIS and the Chacoan Roads
Zeanah's research was undertaken entirely within the processual paradigm, and it looked on the Carson Desert landscape purely from an economic point of view. To show how GIS can assist with a view of the landscape as a set of symbolically laden places, let's

from the real ones they depict. In 2002, Golder staff set out to conduct a terrain model and viewshed analysis to assess the potential visual impacts of developments proposed at different locations around the wheel site. To accomplish this, they had to construct a 3D computer model of the landscape surrounding the Majorville Medicine Wheel, and build a virtual model of the wheel itself. Viewshed analysis uses a geographic information system (GIS) to establish what can and cannot be seen from a specific location on the ground. The results were extremely impressive. Jason Harris, one of the CRM archaeologists, estimated that by using the computer model they could reduce the time required for two archaeologists to verify the visual impact of 37 well sites, access roads, and pathways the old fashioned way (by foot and truck) by two-thirds! In addition to being more cost-effective, the computer modelling approach further reduces physical impacts on the site by minimizing the number of "real world" visits, and allows for pre-disturbance planning of well site locations. Computer modelling and viewshed analysis also provide a means of figuring out how visual disturbances like wellheads can be camouflaged so that they

Figure 5-11
A still image of the computer model of the Majorville Medicine Wheel site, and its surrounding landscape in southeastern Alberta.
Source: C. Jason Harris

match the texture and colouring of the surrounding terrain.

In Chapter 18 we further explore how this type of "Xbox archaeology" can be used as an effective tool in archaeological analysis.

return to the Chacoan roads that we mentioned above and the question, "If the Chacoans had no wheeled vehicles or beasts of burden, what were these roads for?"

One hypothesis is that the Chaco roads functioned as we believe the Inka roads (also discussed in Chapter 4) functioned: as a way to move foods and goods across the landscape. The roads radiate outward from Chaco Canyon, so perhaps they were a way to provision the inhabitants of the canyon's Great Houses with maize, timber, and other supplies.

But as we pointed out above, landscape carries symbolic meanings as well as economic potentials. Perhaps the roads were not economic at all, but instead served some ceremonial function with symbolic meanings. In fact, the roads' tendency to cut straight across hills, rather than skirt around their bases, and to make inexplicable sharp turns in the middle of desert have led many to favour a non-economic interpretation.

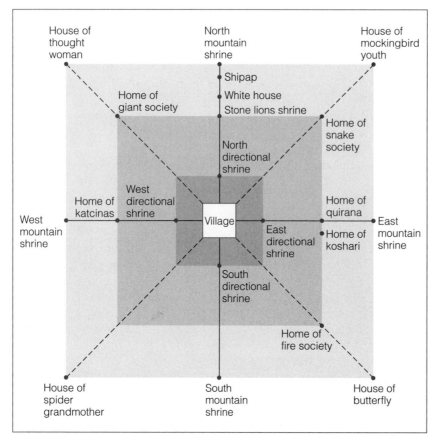

Figure 5-12 A schematic representation of the Keres symbolic landscape.

Source: Snead, J., and Preucel, R. "The Ideology of Settlement: Ancestral Keres Landscapes in the Northern Rio Grande." In W. Ashmore and A. B. Knapp (Eds.), *Archaelogies of Landscape: Contemporary Perspectives* (pp. 169–197). Oxford: Blackwell Publishers.

The likely descendants of the people who inhabited Chaco Canyon are the Keres, the Puebloan peoples who live along the northern Rio Grande in New Mexico in the pueblos of Cochiti, San Felipe, Santa Ana, Santo Domingo, and Zia. In traditional Pueblo theology, the world consists of several nested layers, surrounded at the edges by four sacred mountains. As James Snead (George Mason University) and Robert Preucel (University of Pennsylvania) describe them, these nested layers centre on a village, and different directions are associated with different powers, societies, and supernatural beings, as well as with maleness and femaleness (Figure 5-12). Direction is important in this view of the world (although the directions are not always the same, even for neighbouring pueblos).

This symbolic landscape is physically manifested by different kinds of shrines. For example, the shrine on Mount Taylor, the west mountain shrine for Laguna Pueblo, is a shallow pit where people still come to

pray. Directional shrines may be located closer to the villages and are often found in caves or near springs. One important directional shrine is two mountain lions carved from bedrock and surrounded by a circle of stones. Closer to the village are directional shrines that mark a village's boundaries. Located in the four cardinal directions, they are often keyhole-shaped stone structures with openings to the north or east. Other shrines are found within the village itself, especially in plazas where important dance rituals take place.

So, it is clear that in the Puebloan world the landscape has economic and symbolic meanings. Direction, in particular, seems to hold special symbolic significance in Pueblo religion. Although the ancient Chacoans probably did not share the Keres worldview exactly, they may have had a similar one, or at least one in which shrines marked significant places and directions on the landscape.

Working in a region just south of Chaco Canyon, John Kantner (Georgia State University) used a GIS to test whether the roads were linked to the economic or symbolic aspects of the desert landscape. He reasoned that if the roads were for purely economic purposes, then they should follow the path of least resistance between Pueblo villages; if they did not, then perhaps the roads fulfilled a more religious purpose that was driven by the ancient peoples' symbolic interpretation of the landscape.

Using a digital elevation model, Kantner asked the GIS to do a straightforward task: Find the easiest walking route between settlements that are connected by roads. The easiest walking route would be the one where a person gained the least amount of elevation in walking from one village to another. Although it would take an archaeologist many days to walk out the possibilities in the field or even to trace them out on topographic maps, the GIS could quickly calculate the "path of least resistance" for someone walking from one settlement to another.

Interestingly, Kantner found that the GIS did *not* predict the locations of the roads. In fact, some of the roads cross terrain that is substantially different from that predicted by the GIS. The Chacoan roads do not follow the path of least resistance.

Kantner had assumed that anyone as familiar with their landscape as the Ancestral Pueblo peoples would know the easiest way to walk from one settlement to another. But perhaps this assumption was wrong— perhaps people did *not* know or did *not* use the easiest paths between settlements. To test this hypothesis, Kantner asked whether there were any archaeological remains associated with the GIS-predicted paths.

In fact, he found that small stone shrines occur along the predicted footpaths; it appears that someone was using the predicted paths, and probably on a regular basis. In addition, large circular stone shrines, ones that required more effort to construct, were almost always found with the roads, not the predicted footpaths.

From this, Kantner concluded that the roads did not serve simply as part of Chacoan economy. Although food and goods may have been moved along the roads, this does not appear to have been their primary purpose. People probably moved food and goods along trails that followed the paths of least resistance between villages, footpaths that are marked only by small shrines today. But the formal roads' association with large shrines suggests that they performed some other role. Perhaps they were religious paths; some, in fact, lead directly to places on the landscape that figure prominently in modern Puebloan religion. Or perhaps they helped to integrate the small far-flung pueblos with the Great Houses in Chaco Canyon. We still don't know the purpose of the roads for sure, but GIS clearly casts doubt on the "economic hypothesis."

Conclusion: The Future of Remote Sensing and GIS

Archaeology today is pervaded by a new conservation ethic. Because only a finite number of sites exist in the world, we excavate only what we must to answer a particular research question, saving portions of sites, or entire sites, for future researchers. Remote sensing will never (and should never) completely replace excavation. But by giving archaeologists a cost-effective means of making observations on objects and features that have not yet been excavated, it will obviate the need for excessive excavation and permit archaeologists to preserve more of a site for the future. And that is important to any ethical archaeologist.

GIS has likewise become an important tool. One of archaeology's strengths is its ability to use spatial patterns to test hypotheses about ancient cultural behaviour. Although a high-powered, quantitative technique might seem to be most useful to processual archaeology, the examples we have cited here show that it can be useful to research conducted within the postprocessual paradigm as well. GIS is also extremely useful to federal and state agencies that must manage the archaeological sites on their properties. For these reasons, it is likely that GIS will become as indispensable to archaeologists as their Marshalltown trowels. However, these methods will never replace our trowels, or our need to excavate sites. And that realization brings us to the next chapter.

Summary

- In the days of C. B. Moore, archaeologists had no choice but to excavate large portions of sites to acquire data on the distribution of artifacts and features within the site. Even in the 1970s, archaeologists had no choice but to excavate.

- Today, a new conservation ethic alters how we view archaeological sites: They are nonrenewable resources that we need to use carefully so that future generations can bring better techniques and new questions to them.

- Important to carrying out this task are a variety of methods for doing noninvasive, and hence relatively nondestructive, archaeology.

- Using a variety of methods that provide the archaeological equivalents of CAT scans, archaeologists can often map subsurface features in detail without ever excavating them.

- When it does become necessary to recover samples, we can target excavations and hence minimize damage to the rest of the site.

- High-altitude imagery involves a series of techniques like taking photos from hot air balloons, airplanes, the Space Shuttle, or satellites that can see the ground in the electromagnetic spectrum invisible to the human eye and that betray subsurface features.

- Various geophysical prospecting techniques, such as proton magnetometry, soil resistivity, and ground-penetrating radar, are just a few tools that permit archaeologists to see under the ground before they excavate.

- Geographic information systems, or GIS, allow archaeologists to construct georeferenced databases. These permit us to graphically portray and statistically analyze spatial relationships between archaeological and other kinds of data or to create powerful models to predict regional patterns in the spatial distribution of archaeological data.

- Although high-tech, this new technology is not restricted to one paradigm; landscape archaeology, as an improvement of settlement archaeology or as a way to look at landscapes in more terms of rituals or symbols, are both enhanced by GIS.

Additional Reading

CANADIAN RESOURCES

Conolly, J., and Lake, M. (2006). *Geographical Information Systems in Archaeology.* Cambridge Manuals in Archaeology. Cambridge: Cambridge University Press.

Litherland, A. E., and Pavlish, L. A. (Eds). (2003). Physics and Archaeometry, 2003, Special issue of *Physics in Canada*, 59 (5).

Vaughan, C. J. (1986). Ground-penetrating radar surveys used in archaeological investigations. *Geophysics* 51(3), 595–604.

OTHER RESOURCES

Aldenderfer, Mark, and Maschner, Herbert (Eds.). (1996). *Anthropology, Space, and Geographic Information Systems.* New York: Oxford University Press.

Donoghue, D. N. M. (2001). Remote sensing. In D. Brothwell and A. Pollard (Eds.), *Handbook of Archaeological Sciences* (pp. 555–564). Chichester, England: John Wiley and Sons.

Wescott, Konnie L., and Brandon, R. Joe (Eds.). (1999). *Practical Applications of GIS for Archaeologists: A Predictive Modeling Kit.* London: Taylor and Francis.

Wheatley, David, and Mark Gillings. (2002). *Spatial Technology and Archaeology: The Archaeological Applications of GIS.* London: Taylor and Francis.

Online Resources

Visit *http://maps.nrcan.gc.ca/index_e.php* to see the Centre for Topographic Information at Natural Resources Canada. Examine topographic maps of Canada, and view some of the Centre's fascinating Cartographic Visualization projects.

COMPANION WEBSITE

Visit *http://www.archaeology1ce.nelson.com* to access a wide range of material to help you succeed in your introductory archaeology course. These include flashcards, Internet exercises, Web links, and practice quizzes.

RESEARCH ONLINE
WITH INFOTRAC COLLEGE EDITION

From the Student Companion Website, you can access the InfoTrac College Edition database, which offers thousands of full-length articles for your research.

6

Doing Fieldwork
Why Archaeologists Dig Square Holes

Julie Ross, Chief Archaeologist, Nunavut, using a total station to map archaeological features.
Source: Julie Ross

Preview

Ask most people what archaeologists do, and they'll tell you this: "They dig." And that's true. Despite what we have seen in the preceding two chapters about archaeological survey techniques and remote sensing technology, digging up old stuff remains at the heart of archaeology—and probably always will.

But excavation is a much more complex and sophisticated venture than throwing a shovel into a pickup and heading off for the mountains. Archaeologists are well aware of the fact that as they gather data from a site they are also destroying that site, because once a site is excavated it can never be excavated again. Therefore, it's essential that archaeologists record as much detail as possible, so that future archaeologists can reconstruct what earlier archaeologists did and use the records to answer new questions. This means that you dig slowly and take excruciatingly careful and detailed notes. Nonetheless, as Kent Flannery (University of Michigan) once said, "Archaeology is the most fun you can have with your pants on." And he's right, as anybody who has ever participated in a dig will tell you. Thomas joined his first archaeological expedition as a college junior; Kelly as a high school sophomore; and Dawson after his first year of university. We were all hooked from the start.

We warned earlier about the problems of learning archaeological field techniques from a book (even this one): You just can't do it. But in this chapter we describe common archaeological field methods, and we do hope to show you how fieldwork is done and what it really feels like.

Introduction

In Chapter 4, we talked about how archaeologists go about finding sites, such as Gatecliff Shelter. But locating sites is only the beginning, and actually excavating these sites can be far more time-consuming. Along with fields such as geology and paleontology, the science of archaeology destroys data as it is gathered—for once we excavate a site, nobody can ever dig it again. This is why archaeologists are compulsive about field notes—recording, drawing, and photographing everything we can about an artifact or a feature before removing it. This is also why we usually try to leave a portion of a site unexcavated for the future.

This chapter can be reduced to one simple point: An artifact's **provenience**—its location and context within a site—is the most important thing about that artifact; some might even say it is more important than the artifact itself. Here's one account that demonstrates that fundamental principle.

The Folsom Site and Humanity's Antiquity in North America

In Chapter 2, we discussed how 18th-century scholars were preoccupied with the question of where Native Americans came from. A closely related question was "How long have Native Americans been here?" As we saw in the Moundbuilder controversy, many scholars believed that American Indians arrived in the Western

provenience An artifact's location relative to a system of spatial data collection.

Hemisphere only shortly before European colonists. This matter was politically important because, if archaeology showed that American Indians were long-time inhabitants of the New World, then their claim to the land was strengthened. But if Indian people were only recent immigrants, their hold on the land could be minimized in favour of the Europeans.

And so, from the earliest colonial times, scholars debated the antiquity of humanity in the New World (and they still do). Some claimed that the discovery of apparently crude stone tools demonstrated that humans had been in the New World for thousands of years, since the last phase of the Ice Age, but others showed that these crude artifacts could be mere quarry rejects, unfinished pieces that the artisans deemed too flawed to complete. For some scholars (notably, most of them worked for the federal government), the lack of ancient tools similar to those that Boucher de Perthes had found in France (see Chapter 1) showed that Indians were recent arrivals in the New World.

Eventually, the argument over the antiquity of humanity in the New World came down to animals. 19th- and early 20th-century archaeologists had no way to date their sites absolutely. But they knew that the world had experienced a great Ice Age in the distant past. And they reasoned (quite accurately it turns out) that this Ice Age, more properly called the **Pleistocene,** had ended about 10,000 years ago. Scholars also knew that different kinds of animals lived in North America during the Pleistocene—mammoths, mastodons, a large species of bison, giant bears, ground sloths, horses, camels, and so on. Anybody who found artifacts in undisputed association with the bones of such extinct fauna would prove that humans had been in North America for at least 10,000 years. And thus, the quest relied heavily on context: seeking ancient artifacts in unquestionable association with the bones of extinct fauna.

In Chapter 4, we mentioned that some of the most important archaeological sites are found by non-archaeologists. A hard-rock miner found Gatecliff Shelter, and an ex-slave named George McJunkin (1851–1922) found the Folsom site—the place that proved the extent of human antiquity in the Americas (Figure 6-1).

The Black Cowboy

Born into slavery in 1851, McJunkin acquired his freedom at age 14. That year, he "borrowed" a mule that belonged to his former owner and left his home on a Texas plantation in search of work. By 1868, he was breaking horses for a Texas rancher and later held down a string of ranch jobs in Colorado and New Mexico. He became an expert cowboy and knew just about all there was to know about horses and cattle.

McJunkin also learned a lot about many other things. Although he never received a formal education, he taught himself to read and play the fiddle. He was curious about everything, especially natural history, and one of his prize possessions was a wooden box filled with rocks, bones, fossils, and arrowheads. McJunkin never married and lived most of his life as the only African-American in his community.

Early in the 1890s, McJunkin's talents were recognized by the owner of the Crowfoot Ranch, in northwestern New Mexico near the town of Folsom. Soon, McJunkin was ranch foreman and proved himself an able leader of men, as well as cowpuncher and wrangler.

One day in August of 1908, torrential rains fell on the Crowfoot Ranch, creating a flash flood that destroyed much of Folsom. (Many people were killed, but more would have died had not the local telephone operator, Sarah Rooke, remained at her post, calling people to warn them until the floodwaters claimed her life.) After helping to search for the dead, McJunkin began checking the Crowfoot's fences. Up Wild Horse Arroyo, he found a line that dangled across a now-deep, muddy gully. Pondering how to fix it, he spotted bones protruding from the walls of the arroyo, some 4.5 metres down the embankment.

McJunkin had seen plenty of cow bones in his day, and these were definitely not cow. The bones even seemed too large for bison. McJunkin returned to the site over the years to collect bones that he then stacked on his mantle at home. He would talk to anyone who showed an interest in them and showed the site to several interested townsfolk.

A Spear Point between the Ribs

Eventually, the site was brought to the attention of Jesse Figgins, director of the Colorado Museum of Natural History (now the Denver Museum of Nature and Science), who was looking for skeletons of the extinct Pleistocene bison, *Bison antiquus,* for a

---

Pleistocene A geologic period from 2 million to 10 thousand years ago, which was characterized by multiple periods of extensive glaciation.

Figure 6-1 The Folsom site in 1997. Wild Horse Arroyo runs through the middle of the photo; site excavators David Meltzer and Lawrence Todd are at the lower left.

Source: Robert Kelly

museum display. Sadly, McJunkin had died a few years before Figgins's arrival and so he did not live to see the day that his site made archaeological history.

Some of the townsfolk who had visited the site with McJunkin had occasionally found an artifact or two among the bones (now identified as ancient bison), but they did not document their finds, meaning that the context of these artifacts was unknown. And in 1926, Figgins's crew also found a beautifully made spear point with a distinct central groove or channel (what we now call a "flute"). But, unfortunately, they could not tell whether the artifact was found with the bison skeletons or had fallen from a later, higher level—meaning that the newest find still lacked the necessary context.

Figgins telegrammed the crew to leave any artifacts exactly where they were discovered, so that he could

personally observe them in place. And so, when excavators located similar spear points the following summer, they left the artifacts **in situ** (in place), so that their context could be recorded. One of these points lay between the ribs of a bison (Figure 6-2). Figgins sent telegrams to prominent members of the archaeological community, including the skeptical A. V. Kidder, who was excavating at Pecos only 160 kilometres away.

After joining other archaeologists at the excavation site, Kidder solemnly pronounced that the association between the spear points and the extinct bison remains was solid. There was no evidence that rodents had burrowed into the deposit, carrying later artifacts from higher in the ground down to the bison skeletons. There was no indication that streams had redeposited the artifacts on top of the remains. Everyone present saw undeniable evidence that the spear points had killed the extinct bison.

For the first time, the association between extinct fauna and human artifacts was confirmed: People had

in situ From Latin, meaning "in position"; the place where an artifact, ecofact, or feature was found during excavation or survey.

Figure 6-2 A fluted Folsom spear point lying between the ribs of an extinct form of bison at the Folsom site.

Source: Denver Museum of Nature and Science

been in the Americas since at least the end of the Pleistocene, some 10,000 years ago. Today, we know McJunkin's site as the Folsom site, and the distinctive spear points found there are called Folsom points—both named after the nearby town that had been nearly destroyed by the deadly flood that first exposed the site.

As you can see, context was everything at the Folsom site. And this is true for any site. In fact, other than "When's lunch?" what you'll hear most frequently on any archaeological dig is "Show me exactly where that came from."

Excavation: What Determines Preservation?

The exact procedures in any excavation depend on several factors, beginning with the kind of materials that have survived the passage of time. Some sites have wonderful preservation of organic materials, including basketry, leather, and wood; but in other sites, only ceramics, stones, and bones survive; and in the earliest archaeological sites, only the stone tools remain. Here are some examples that demonstrate the various conditions under which organic remains are preserved.

The Duck Decoys of Lovelock Cave

Lovelock Cave (Nevada) sits on a barren hillside, just north of the Carson Desert. But thousands of years ago, anybody sitting in the cave's mouth would have looked out upon a vast wetland, just a few kilometres away. Lovelock Cave was first excavated in 1912 (by Lewellyn Loud, a museum security guard at the University of California, who was sent by anthropologist Alfred Kroeber to gather museum specimens), and again in 1924, by Mark Harrington of New York's Museum of the American Indian. Like Hidden Cave (mentioned in Chapter 4), the dry and dusty interior of Lovelock Cave was used more for storage than habitation.

Loud and Harrington found several caches of gear. One that Harrington found, Pit 11, held a buried basket that contained 11 duck decoys. Cleverly crafted from tule reeds twisted to simulate the body and head of a duck, some had plain tule reed bodies and others were adorned with paint and feathers. As artifacts, the decoys are striking (Figure 6-3). Even *Sports Illustrated* extolled the creativity and craftsmanship of these prehistoric duck hunters.

Someone buried this basket of decoys in Pit 11 (in fact, they were interred beneath the pit's false bottom) intending, evidently, to use them on a later duck hunt. Although the person who buried the decoys never retrieved them, it was wise to cache them inside Lovelock Cave because they were perfectly preserved; they are usable even today. We now know from radiocarbon dating (discussed in Chapter 8) that these decoys were made about 2000 years ago.

The Houses of Ozette

Equally remarkable, yet strikingly different, preservation is seen at the site of Ozette on Washington's

Figure 6-3 A 2000-year-old duck decoy from Lovelock Cave, Nevada.

Source: National Museum of the American Indian

Figure 6-4 The archaeological site of Ozette on the coast of Washington.

Source: Ruth Kirk

Olympic Peninsula (Figure 6-4). Ozette was a major beachside village once occupied by the ancestors of the Makah people. In fact, some Makahs remained at Ozette into the 1920s, and their oral traditions helped lead Richard Daugherty (then at Washington State University) to the site in the first place.

Ozette was once a lively village stretching 1.5 kilometres along the Pacific Coast, home to perhaps 800 people who lived in massive split-plank cedar houses. They hunted; gathered berries in the forest; collected shellfish along the coast; and fished for halibut, salmon, and other fish. They even hunted killer whales.

Part of Ozette village lay along the bottom of a steep hill. Some 300 years ago, during an especially heavy rain (or possibly a tsunami), the hillside above the village became saturated and, with a roar, an enormous mudslide descended on the village, shearing the tops off five houses and burying their interiors. Some people escaped, but others were caught inside. Because the coast of Washington is so wet, the destroyed portion of Ozette remained waterlogged and was capped by a thick layer of clay by the mudslide.

The saturated dirt and the clay cap preserved entire houses with all their furnishings and gear. During the 1970s, Richard Daugherty excavated the houses, recovering some 42,000 artifacts, including baskets, mats, hats, halibut hooks, bowls, clubs, combs—even an entire cedar canoe. The archaeological team worked closely with the Makah people, and many of the artifacts from Ozette village are now on display at the Makah Cultural and Research Center in Neah Bay, Washington. These displays highlight the remarkable degree of preservation at this important waterlogged site.

The Ice Man of the Alps

Our third example demonstrates yet a different kind of archaeological preservation. In 1991, two skiers in the Alps came upon the body of a man lying in a pool of icy glacial water at 3000 metres. The body was so well preserved that the authorities thought at first he was perhaps a mountaineer who had perished in a blizzard a few years earlier. But today, we know this man as Ötzi, the "Ice Man," who died some 5300 years ago. His body was remarkably well preserved—even tattoos are clearly visible on his skin—because he froze shortly after he died, and a small glacier then sealed his body in the shallow depression where it had come to rest. Here he freeze-dried and lay undisturbed until the warmth of recent decades caused the glacier to recede, exposing his remains (Figure 6-5).

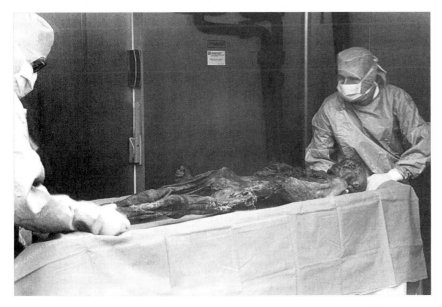

Figure 6-5 Ötzi, the "Ice Man" (above) and portions of some of his tools (below).

Source: South Tyrol Museum of Archaeology/www.iceman.it

discovered with Kwäday Dän Ts'inchi were made from organic materials that rarely preserve in the archeological record. These included his hat, fur cloak, and leather pouch containing what was probably dried salmon.

Scientists were able to study the contents of the European Ice Man's stomach, and determined that he had not eaten for at least 8 hours before his death and that his final meal had been barley, wheat, deer, and wild goat. Pollen analysis of the contents of his intestine suggests that he died in the spring.

Why did this 30-year-old man die at such a high elevation, far from any village or camp? An arrow point that penetrated past his shoulder blade suggests that he had been attacked shortly before his death. One of his hands also bears unhealed cuts, as though he warded off an assailant armed with a knife. One guess is that he was fleeing, stopped to rest in a depression away from the wind, and quietly passed away from his wounds.

Realizing the significance of the Ice Man, archaeologists scoured the site and recovered portions of his clothing—a belt to hold up a leather breechcloth and leggings, a coat of deerskin, a cape of woven grass, a leather fur-lined cap, and calfskin shoes, filled with grass. They also recovered tools, including a hafted copper axe, a bow and a quiver of arrows, bone points, extra bowstrings, a wooden pack frame, birchbark containers, a stone scraper, a hafted knife, and a net.

The degree of preservation associated with Ötzi, the "Ice Man," is similar to that of Kwäday Dän Ts'inchi, discussed in Chapter 1. Many of the items that were

The Preservation Equation

So, why were the Lovelock duck decoys, the houses of Ozette, and Ötzi the "Ice Man" so well preserved?

Decomposition is carried out by microorganisms that require warmth, oxygen, and water to survive. In each of the above cases, one of these was lacking: Lovelock Cave lacked moisture, the wet deposits beneath the clay cap at Ozette were anaerobic (oxygenless), and the Ice Man's glacial environment lacked warmth.

These different preservation conditions present the archaeologist with both opportunities and challenges.

At Ozette, for example, the waterlogged archaeological deposits were a muddy gumbo that was almost impossible to trowel or shovel. And because the wooden artifacts were saturated with water, a misplaced shovel stroke could slice them like a knife through butter. To cope with these conditions, Daugherty assembled a complex system of pressurized hoses to wash the mud away. By adjusting the water pressure, they could use fire hoses to clean off the massive house posts and wall planks, switching to a fine misting spray when exposing delicate basketry.

Likewise, sites such as Lovelock Cave offer a wealth of artifacts not normally found, but such sites tend to be extremely complex. They are favourite places for rodents and carnivores, whose actions can move artifacts up and down, making it difficult to sort out what belongs with what. This means that they require especially slow excavation.

And although the Ice Man contributed enormously to our knowledge of the past, his preservation now requires a sophisticated storage chamber (at Italy's South Tyrol Museum), where museum personnel control the temperature and humidity.

Preservation, of course, is only one factor conditioning how we excavate a site; other determinants include the site's depth, time and financial constraints, accessibility, and, perhaps most important, the research questions being pursued. We have excavated with backhoes, shovels, trowels, dental tools, and garden hoses. We even used a jackhammer once (to remove rooffall in Gatecliff Shelter).

Sometimes the archaeologist can rely on the latest technology; but other times, financial constraints or remote conditions require the use of less-elegant methods. Archaeologists excavate ancient Pueblo sites in New Mexico that contain well-defined room clusters very differently from high-altitude caves in Peru. Peeling off sequential levels of a Maya temple in Guatemala differs radically from excavating through seemingly homogeneous shell midden deposits in Georgia. Submerged sites, such as ancient shipwrecks, require their own special brand of archaeology.

There are many ways to excavate a site, and each is appropriate if it allows the archaeologist to achieve the project's research goals within the constraints of time, funding, and technology. The only important thing is that *the excavation techniques must record an artifact's context as precisely as possible.*

Principles of Archaeological Excavation

The key to maintaining information about an artifact's context is to record its provenience. Provenience means an artifact's location, but location is both hierarchical and relative.

Location is hierarchical because an artifact's provenience is simultaneously a particular country, a particular province or state in that country, a particular county in that province, a particular site in that county, a particular excavation unit in that site, a particular vertical level in that unit, and a particular position and orientation in that level. Obviously, the last levels in this hierarchy are more useful than the first levels. Figgins's excavators found some spear points at the Folsom site, but it was not until they were found in situ, lying between the bison's ribs, that their provenience became meaningful to a particular question. Of course, we can make use of artifacts whose proveniences are imprecise to answer some types of research questions, but nonetheless *the excavator's first goal is to record context by recording provenience as accurately as possible.*

Location is relative because we measure an artifact's position relative to a spatial system. We could use the UTM grid (mentioned in Chapter 4), or we could use a site-specific format. The key is to find a procedure that will allow a future archaeologist to reconstruct, in great detail, where you found things in the site.

So, how do we go about excavating a site so that we recover an artifact's provenience? Let's return to Gatecliff Shelter to see how this is done.

Test Excavations

From day one, Thomas wanted to learn two things: how long people had used Gatecliff Shelter, and whether the buried deposits could tell us about how human life had changed over time in this part of the Great Basin. The initial goal, then, was to decide if Gatecliff could help answer these questions. This meant that Thomas had to know what kind of historical record Gatecliff preserved. Was it a short or long record? Was it nicely stratified or a jumbled mess?

For this reason, the initial **test excavation** strategy was vertical, designed to supply, as expediently as possible, a stratified sequence of artifacts and ecofacts associated with potentially datable materials. Consequently, Thomas "tested" Gatecliff with two test pits (the French call them *sondages,* or "soundings"). Like most archaeologists, we dig metrically, typically in 1-metre squares for practical as well as scientific reasons: Squares much smaller would squeeze out the archaeologist, and larger units might not allow sufficient accuracy and would remove more of the site than necessary to answer the initial questions.

Test pits are quick and dirty because we must excavate them "blind"—that is, without knowing exactly what lies below. But even when digging test pits, archaeologists maintain three-dimensional control of the finds, recording the X and Y axes (the horizontal coordinates) and the Z axis (the vertical coordinate) for each one. This is one reason why archaeologists dig square holes. Provided the pit sidewalls are kept sufficiently straight and perpendicular, excavators can use the dirt itself to maintain horizontal control on the X and Y axes by measuring directly from the sidewalls. Here the horizontal provenience is relative to the sidewalls of the pit. (In some sites, this can become problematic if one is not careful: As test pits deepen, their sidewalls will slope inward, creating a "bathtub" effect that throws off the measurements.)

What about vertical control? At Gatecliff, Thomas dug the test pits in arbitrary, but consistent, 10-centimetre levels. Everything of interest—artifacts, ecofacts, soil samples, and so forth—was kept in separate level bags, one for each 10-centimetre level. The Z dimension for each level was usually designated according to distance below the ground surface: Level 1 (surface to 10 centimetres below), Level 2 (10 to 20 centimetres below), and so forth. This way, excavators measured vertical provenience relative to the ground surface. This also can be a problem, given that the ground surface can change over time and make it potentially difficult for future archaeologists to correlate their levels with those of a previous archaeologist. But every project requires trade-offs, and there is no point to investing much effort in a site before knowing if it will provide the necessary information. This is why test pits often record only minimal levels of provenience.

Expanding the Test Excavation

At Gatecliff, the test pits told Thomas that the site warranted a closer look, and he returned the next year to do just that. He first divided the site into a 1-metre grid system, oriented along the long axis of the shelter. The exact compass orientation of this grid was recorded (many archaeologists today routinely orient their grids to magnetic or true north, but sometimes pragmatics dictate otherwise). He assigned consecutive letters to each north–south division and numbered the east–west division (see Figure 6-6). By this method, each excavation square could be designated by a unique alphanumeric name (just like Bingo—A-7, B-5, and the ever-popular K-9). Other archaeologists use different systems, some numbering each unit according to the X and Y coordinates of the units' southwest (or some other) corner. In this system, a unit with the designation North 34 East 45 (or N34 E45) means that its southwest corner is 34 metres north and 45 metres east of the site's N0 E0 point.

At Gatecliff, the east wall of the "7-trench" (so named because it contained units B-7 through I-7) defined a major profile that exposed the site's stratigraphy. Stratigraphy, you will recall from Chapter 1, is the structure produced by the deposition of geological and/or cultural sediments into layers, or strata. The stratigraphy is a vertical section against which the archaeologist plots all artifacts, features, soil and pollen samples, and radiocarbon dates. (Some archaeologists use the term "stratification" to refer to the physical layers in a site, reserving "stratigraphy" only for the analytical interpretation of the temporal and depositional evidence.)

A vertical datum was established at the rear of the shelter. For all on-site operations, this **datum point** was arbitrarily assigned an elevation of zero. All site elevations from this point on were plotted as "*x* centimetres below datum," rather than below surface (given that the surface almost never has the same elevation across any given site). Using an altimeter and a U.S. Geological Survey topographic map, Thomas

test excavation A small initial excavation to determine a site's potential for answering a research question.

datum point The zero point, a fixed reference used to keep control on a dig; usually controls both the vertical and horizontal dimensions of provenience.

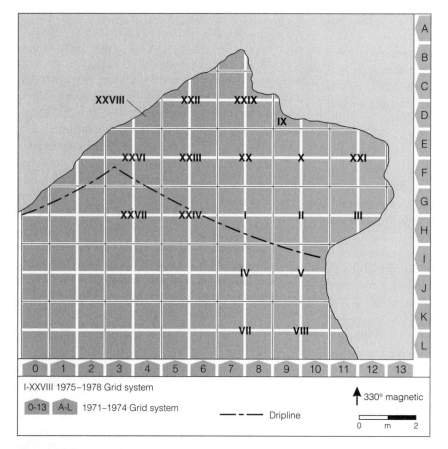

Figure 6-6 Plan view of the two grid systems used at Gatecliff Shelter. The alphanumeric system (consisting of letters and numbers) defined 1-metre excavation squares used in the first four seasons. Roman numerals designate the 2-metre squares used later, when large horizontal exposures were excavated.

Source: After Thomas (1983b: figure 8). Courtesy American Museum of Natural History

their elevation) based on the datum point. Incidentally, artifacts found in the test pit are brought into this system simply by determining the depth below datum of the ground surface at the test unit and plotting the test unit onto the master site grid.

This is how we did things in the 1970s. Today, however, we would have placed the datum many metres off the site in an area that would remain undisturbed by construction, natural processes, or future excavation. The datum would be an aluminum or brass cap marked with the site's Smithsonian or other identifying number, set in concrete or on top of a long piece of concrete reinforcement bar driven into the ground. Today, we would also use a GPS instrument to determine the datum's elevation and UTM location. Once the datum is tied into the UTM grid, a future archaeologist could recreate its location even if the marker were destroyed.

determined the elevation of this datum point to be 2319 metres above sea level. All archaeological features—fire hearths, artifact concentrations, sleeping areas, and the like—were plotted on a master site map, and individual artifacts found in situ were plotted in three dimensions—their X and Y coordinates based on the map, and their Z coordinates (that is,

natural level A vertical subdivision of an excavation square that is based on natural breaks in the sediments (in terms of colour, grain size, texture, hardness, or other characteristics).

arbitrary level The basic vertical subdivision of an excavation square; used only when easily recognizable "natural" strata are lacking and when natural strata are more than 10 centimetres thick.

strata (singular, "stratum") More or less homogeneous or gradational material, visually separable from other levels by a discrete change in the character of the material—texture, compactness, colour, rock, organic content—and/or by a sharp break in the nature of deposition.

How Archaeologists Dig

Despite what action-hero characters like Indiana Jones or Lara Croft might lead you to believe, archaeologists do not dash in, grab the goodies, and then run for their lives. We don't even mindlessly shovel dirt into a bucket. Instead, we excavate within horizontal excavation units in **natural levels** and **arbitrary levels.** Natural levels are the site's **strata** (singular, "stratum"), which are more or less homogeneous or gradational material, visually separable from other levels by a change in the texture, colour, rock or organic content, or by a sharp break in depositional character (or any combination of these).

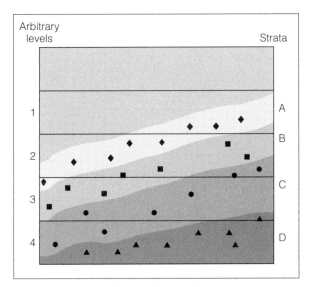

Arbitrary
levels   Strata

1   A

                                                   B

2

                                                   C

3

4   D

Figure 6-7 Hypothetical relationship between natural (A through D) and arbitrary (1 through 4) levels showing how arbitrary levels can potentially jumble together artifacts that come from different natural strata.

Archaeologists prefer to excavate in natural levels wherever possible. Figure 6-7 shows the main reason for this practice. In this hypothetical profile are four natural strata—A, B, C, and D—each containing a particular kind of artifact (denoted by the different symbols). If you imagine that each of these strata represents some unit of time, then you can see that there was a clear change in the kind of artifacts left behind at this site over the four time periods. But note that these strata slope. If we excavated them blindly using arbitrary levels—denoted by the solid lines and numbers 1, 2, 3, and 4—those levels would crosscut the various strata. Arbitrary Level 1 contains artifacts from only Stratum A; but Level 2 contains artifacts from three different time periods: Strata A, B, and C; Level 3 contains artifacts from all four strata; and Level 4, artifacts from Strata C and D. If we assumed that the arbitrary levels correlate to time, then the results of this method of excavation would suggest a very different—and erroneous—image of artifact change over time than that suggested by the natural strata.

Excavators at Gatecliff—most of them college students—excavated by natural levels wherever possible. Where these natural levels were thicker than 10 centimetres, they excavated in arbitrary levels no more than 10 centimetres in thickness within the natural

levels. (Today, when many archaeologists excavate in arbitrary levels, they excavate ones only 5 centimetres deep to maintain even greater control over provenience.)

Excavators carefully trowelled the deposit, then passed it outside the cave for screening (we'll have more to say about this later); artifacts and ecofacts found in the screen were bagged by level. Individual excavators kept field notes at this stage in bound, graph-paper notebooks. Good field notes record everything, whether or not it seems important at the time. Remember, the excavator's goal is to capture the detail that will allow a future archaeologist to "see" what the excavator saw as he or she was digging. Today, field notes employ standardized forms (unique to each excavation) so that excavators record the same detailed information for each level (Figure 6-8). Depending on how much he or she finds, it might take the excavator a week to complete this one form (but usually it is less than a day). This information will include the date, the excavator's name, a map of the unit showing where artifacts and features were found, and a detailed description of the sediments ("rock hard clay, grading from brown to reddish-orange" or "loose, and dusty, with a lot of packrat feces and cactus spines"). A geologist's Munsell soil colour chart is often used to record sediment colours.

The form will also include the level's beginning and ending elevations, observations on how this level was different from that above it ("there is more charcoal in this level"), whether any samples were taken (soil, carbon, plant materials), and so on. In addition, copious photographs (black and white, colour slides, and digital) are taken of all unit profiles, all significant finds in situ, and all features. Nowadays, some archaeologists make a video recording of all excavation units at the end of each day or during the excavation of important features and finds.

Expanding Gatecliff's Excavation

The vertical excavation strategy at Gatecliff was a deliberately simplified scheme designed to clarify chronology. By the end of the fourth field season, Trench 7 had reached a depth of 9 metres below the ground surface. We had learned a good deal about the cultural sequence of Gatecliff Shelter, but our vertical excavation strategy had also left us with a series of extremely steep and hazardous sidewalls. Even though

Juniper Cave (48BH3178) Excavation Form

Date: _____ / _____ /04

Excavators _____ Unit _____

Opening depths: SW _____   NW _____   NE _____   SE _____

Closing depths: SW _____   NW _____   NE _____   SE _____

Strata _____. Feature number (if any) _____. Describe level and sediment on back of form; show on map where excavated if less than entire unit; show rodent burrows, roots, rocks; note soil changes.

Total sediment weight (before screen) _____ kg After screen _____ kg

Screen size (circle):   1/4   1/8   1/16   Water screened?

Screen/piece plot total counts:

Debitage _____   Bone _____   Other (_____)_____

Samples taken (circle): C14   sediment   (weight): _____)   botanical   other

Number of level bags: _____   Artifact catalog numbers: _____

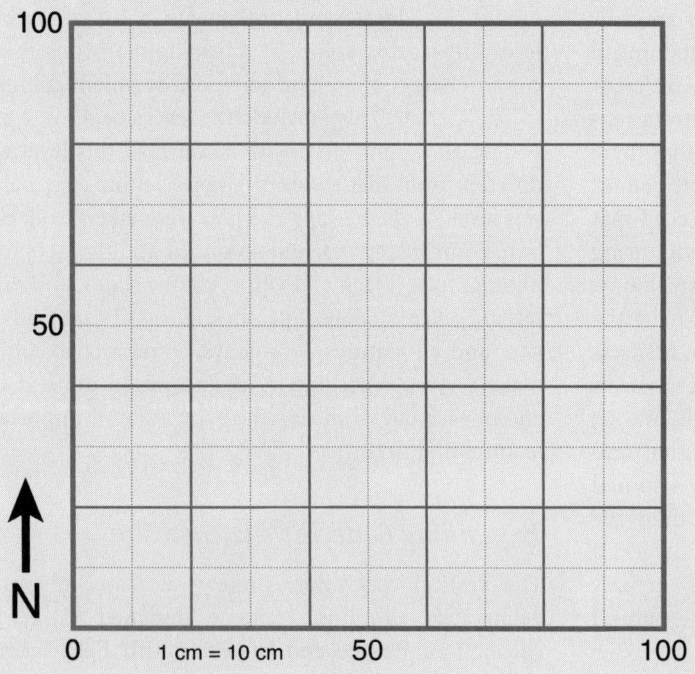

100

50

↑
N

0   1 cm = 10 cm   50   100

Crew chief form check: _____

Page _____ of _____

Figure 6-8 A typical excavation form.

the excavation was stairstepped to minimize the height of these sidewalls (see the terraces in Figure 3-1), they were still dangerous. Today, deep excavation trenches are heavily shored. Unshored walls higher than 4 feet are a violation of federal OSHA—Occupational Safety and Health Administration—regulations (similar regulations exist in Canada). And with good reason: More than one archaeologist has been nearly killed by collapsing profiles. Clearly, a change was in order for reasons of safety.

Change was required for conceptual reasons as well. The early excavations demonstrated that Gatecliff could contribute much more than mere chronology. The vertical excavation showed us that Gatecliff had witnessed something unique. Periodically, flash floods filled the shelter with thick beds of silt. Eventually, the shelter dried out, and people used it once again. The result was that layers of sterile silt neatly separated **living floors,** occupational surfaces, inside the overhang. This was a remarkable opportunity to study discrete living surfaces within a rockshelter environment.

Few archaeologists have such a chance, and so we shifted away from the initial chronological objectives to concentrate on recording the spatial distributions of artifacts and features on the living floors. The goal now was to reconstruct what activities took place in the shelter as indicated by the distribution of artifacts across the living floors sandwiched between the silt layers. With the stratigraphy suitably defined, extensive vertical sections were no longer necessary, and we concentrated on opening entire (horizontal) living surfaces.

We switched to 2 × 2-metre units, but excavated the living floors more slowly than in the previous vertical excavations, and excavators tried to recover and map all artifacts in situ. We excavated and screened features such as hearths separately, and soil samples were retained for laboratory processing. On master living floor maps we plotted artifacts, scatters of waste flakes from stone tool manufacture, concentrations of bone—anything found in situ.

This horizontal strategy required significantly more control within contemporary layers. A single excavator carefully worked each 2-square-metre unit, attempting to find as many artifacts as possible in situ. All artifacts, features, and large ecofacts were plotted onto the large-scale living floor maps for each surface. The result was a set of living floor maps that are rare among rockshelter excavations in the world (Figure 6-9).

Precision Excavation

This description of the Gatecliff excavation provides a general sense of what goes on at archaeological sites. But excavation has become an even more exact science since Thomas excavated Gatecliff in the 1970s. Given the importance of an artifact's context, archaeologists continue to devise ways to record provenience for more objects with greater precision.

For example, at Gatecliff we first used string line levels tied to the datum and tape measures to determine an **artifact's** vertical provenience (its depth below datum); we later switched to a more precise builder's level and measuring rod. We recorded horizontal provenience by measuring distances from two of a unit's sidewalls. But today, many archaeologists, ourselves included, use the total stations (mentioned in Chapter 4) to record provenience. New instruments still cost a pricey $5000, but they are necessary for state-of-the-art excavation.

How do total stations work? The devices are set up on a tripod over the site's datum. After workers input the correct data, the total station "knows" where it is on the grid system and which direction it is pointing. When an artifact is found, a glass prism is held on the artifact's location, and the total station is turned and aimed at the prism. Push a button, and the station shoots a beam of infrared light at the prism. By measuring the time it takes the light to bounce back, the total station calculates and records the artifact's X, Y, and Z coordinates—its provenience. This information is later downloaded to a database for mapping and analysis. Total stations take only a second or two to make measurements that are accurate to +/− 3 *millimetres.* And these instruments can be used at distances of hundreds of metres so that a site may need only one, rather than the several datums that other measurement systems may require (Figure 6-10).

Is That All There Is to It?

No, there is more to recording provenience than simply location. Today, archaeologists sometimes record not only an artifact's X, Y, and Z coordinates, but also which side of the artifact was "up" when it was found

---

living floors A distinct buried surface on which people lived.

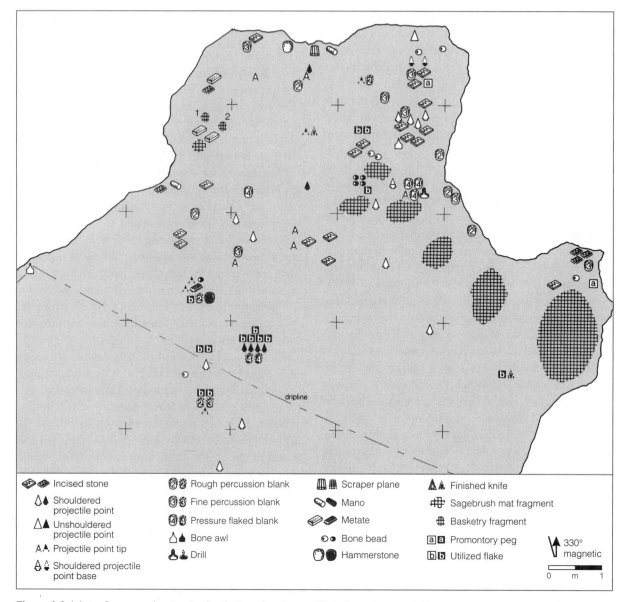

Figure 6-9 A living floor map showing the distribution of artifacts and hearths on Horizon 2 (deposited about A.D. 1300) at Gatecliff.

Source: Courtesy American Museum of Natural History

(sometimes we mark the object's "up" side with a dot in permanent ink), the compass orientation of its long axis, and its slope or inclination (recorded with a builder's angle finder or clinometer). We would also note whether the artifact is burned, has calcium carbonate or a particular kind of sediment adhering to it, or possesses other characteristics. Although this can make excavation mind-numbing, as we will see in Chapter 7 the resulting information is critical to

understanding how a site was formed and consequently for inferring what people did at a site.

Sifting the Evidence

Digging is just the beginning of excavation. No matter how carefully you excavate, it is impossible to see, map, and recover everything of archaeological inter-

Figure 6-10 Harold Dibble (centre) and Shannon McPherron (right) record data on site while excavating Pech de L'Azé IV in France; the student at the far left is using a total station.

Source: Robert Kelly

est; this is why we use sifters to find things that hand excavation misses. This is also the second reason why we excavate in square units—sometimes only .5 × .5 metres in size. If the excavator misses something, the sifting process can at least tie its provenience down to a particular level in a particular unit—a very small area of the site.

At Gatecliff, excavators removed deposit with a trowel and whisk broom or paintbrush, carefully sweeping it into a dustpan. When an excavator found an artifact in situ, he or she recorded the artifact's provenience; sometimes it was photographed in place and a sketch drawn in the field notes before the artifact was placed in a separate bag and labelled with an identifying number.

The dustpan of dirt was then poured into a bucket and tagged with a label identifying the unit and level. When the bucket was full, the day's "gopher" took it to the screening area, outside the shelter in the hot sun (the gopher is the person whose daily assignment was to "go for" this and "go for" that). Here the bucket was poured onto a screen with $^1/_8$-inch mesh (to give you some idea of the size, standard window screen is $^1/_{16}$-inch mesh), where workers sifted and carefully checked for any artifacts missed by the excavators, including stone tool manufacturing waste flakes, fragments of bone, and anything else of importance.

Although archaeologists agree that Marshalltown makes the only trowel worth owning, there are many opinions on screens. Many archaeologists manufacture their own, and so the design and workmanship of screens varies from dig to dig (a few are shown in Figure 6-11). Some are suspended from tripods, some are mounted on rollers, and others are driven by gas engines to speed things up. When Thomas dug Alta Toquima, a village located at 3600 metres in the mountains of central Nevada, he invented a "backpacker" design for the screens. At Gatecliff, we used the most common kind—a shaker screen mounted on two pivoting legs.

Exactly what kind of screen you use is far less important than the mesh. Many archaeologists prefer $^1/_8$-inch hardware cloth, but the choice of mesh size varies with the circumstances. The important point is that *screen size affects what you recover and how fast you can recover it.* Use $^1/_4$-inch mesh and you can process dirt faster, but you will lose a surprising number of important objects. Use $^1/_{16}$-inch mesh and the recovery rate goes up—but so does the time to process the dirt.

Thomas did an experiment some years ago to see how different screen sizes might affect the recovery of animal bones in archaeological sites. He built a three-decker screen with superimposed layers of $^1/_4$-inch over $^1/_8$-inch over $^1/_{16}$-inch mesh screens. He then ran a set of faunal remains recovered from a site through the screens.

As you might guess, he found that $^1/_4$-inch mesh was adequate for recovering bones of large animals such as bighorn or bison. But he also found that significant numbers of bones of medium-sized animals, such as rabbits and rodents, were lost. The $^1/_8$-inch mesh screen was better for recovering the bones of these small mammals. But, in fact, significant amounts of small mammal bones are even lost through $^1/_8$-inch screens! One needs $^1/_{16}$-inch mesh (or flotation; see

Archaeological Ethics
The Curation Crisis: What Happens to All That Stuff after the Excavation?

 Anyone who has ever watched the film *Raiders of the Lost Ark* likely remembers the scene in which the Ark of the Covenant is boxed up and wheeled off to be stored in a cavernous and run down government warehouse. Humanity is kept safe from harm because the crate containing the ark is indistinguishable from the millions of others that fill the building. In the real world, however, archaeologists have an ethical responsibility to ensure that the artifacts they collect are locatable and well looked after.

The implementation of heritage legislation, coupled with the rise of the cultural resource management (CRM) industry, has resulted in the discovery of thousands of new archaeological sites in Canada. These sites, and the artifacts they produce, are an important source of information for future generations of Canadians. Therefore, it is imperative that they be adequately maintained. Systems need to be in place to track, house, and protect artifacts and the sites where they are found. Currently, the Archaeological Sites Office, located in the Canadian Museum of Civilization, is responsible for managing official site inventories for the Yukon, Northwest Territories, Nunavut, and Prince Edward Island. Even though the remaining provinces and territories manage their own site inventories, ideas and information about how archaeological site databases can be better managed are exchanged through an informal association called the Archaeological Sites Inventory Group. This association was formed in 1999 and comprises members from every province and territory.

The Sites Office at the Canadian Museum of Civilization currently uses computer databases to manage site inventories. The simple DOS-based programs used 30 years ago have given way to sophisticated geographic information systems (GIS) that produce dynamic maps tied directly into site databases. The old adage "garbage in, garbage out" means that archaeological data have to be entered into these databases consistently and accurately so that the database can function properly as a management tool.

Attempts have also been made to link the artifact and site inventories of not-for-profit institutions like museums through something called the Canadian Heritage Information Network (CHIN). CHIN was created in 1972 to increase standards in collection management and make the information more accessible to researchers and the public. More than 1200 heritage institutions from across Canada are currently members of the CHIN network. Recently, CHIN has been promoting the idea of digitizing heritage information to make it available for future generations of Canadians. This approach is also being used in the Virtual Museum of Canada, where visitors can view more than 185 exhibits on Canada's cultural heritage without leaving their computer screens. Digitizing heritage content can be as simple as photographing an artifact using a digital camera. Or, it can be as complex as using laser scanning technology to capture 3D images of artifacts that can then be manipulated in virtual space. All of these techniques are designed to ensure that archaeological data are safeguarded for future generations.

Some archaeologists record the provenience of virtually every item that is found *in situ* when conducting excavations—a practice sometimes called piece-plotting. Others set a cut-off, recording provenience on everything found *in situ* that is larger than, say, 3 centimetres in any dimension. As we said before, there are always trade-offs. Recording the provenience of every item found *in situ* provides the archaeologist with a very accurate record of where you found things, but it takes much more time—meaning that less gets excavated (this is especially problematic if the site is threatened with destruction). How much you piece-plot depends on how much time you have for the excavation and the questions you need the data to answer.

Figure 6-11 A few of the innumerable sifter designs used by archaeologists.

simply poured onto a screen (usually $^1/_8$- or $^1/_{16}$-inch mesh) and sprayed with a garden hose until all the sediment is washed through. The screen will then be set aside and, once dry, searched. Kelly used water-screening at a site in the Stillwater Marsh in the Carson Desert (Figure 6-12). Because the site was located on a clay dune that contained no natural rock, he simply water-screened the deposits through $^1/_{16}$-inch mesh, dried what was left, and bagged it all. He saved literally everything—flakes from the manufacture of stone tools, burned pieces of mud, fish and bird bones, and shell fragments—and sorted it later in the field camp.

You should always use the finest mesh screen possible. But using very fine mesh during the excavation can slow everything down to the point where you do not excavate a sufficient sample of the site to say anything worthwhile. Dense clay deposits, for example, can clog even a $^1/_4$-inch screen quickly. For this reason, many archaeologists use a larger screen mesh in the field, but take bulk sediment samples from each level. These samples are processed in the lab and provide a sample of those items missed by the $^1/_4$-inch screens. If the deposit has a low clay content, the sediment below) to recover the remains of animals the size of, say, pack rats, small birds, and especially fish.

Water-Screening and Matrix-Sorting

Archaeologists sometimes use **water-screening,** especially when the artifacts and ecofacts are expected to be very small. As the name suggests, water-screening requires that plenty of water be available. The dirt is

---

water-screening A sieving process in which deposit is placed in a screen and the matrix washed away with hoses; essential where artifacts are expected to be small and/or difficult to find without washing.

Figure 6-12 Wet-screening in the Stillwater Marsh, Nevada.

Source: Robert Kelly

samples may simply be fine-screened. If they have a high clay content, they may be deflocculated (have the clay removed) by soaking the sediments in a solution of dishwasher detergent. After the clays are broken down, the slurry is poured through a fine screen (or often a set of screens), dried, and sorted by hand to separate stone from small stone tool waste flakes, shells, bits of ceramics, and bones. This is known as **matrix-sorting,** and, along with writing catalogue numbers on artifacts, it is often one of the first tasks a novice may be assigned in a lab.

Ideally, as with piece-plotted artifacts, we wish to record data from the screening process that will allow us to reconstruct the site in the most detail possible. Running dirt through a screen, believe it or not, is *not* enough. In some sites, we also weigh it: We've recorded how much each bucket of deposit weighs, keeping a running tally on the level's excavation form. After screening a bucket, we return the material

remaining in the screen to the bucket and weigh it again. (In most cases, the material that goes back into the bucket is unmodified rock.) By recording the before- and after-screening bucket weights, we record the frequency of rock in the deposits and determine the different densities of artifacts and ecofacts among a site's strata. These data help us understand how a site formed (more on that in Chapter 7) as well as changes in the intensity of site use over time.

Flotation

In some archaeological sites, like the upper parts of Gatecliff Shelter, the deposits are sufficiently protected from moisture that plant remains simply dry up and can be recovered by screening. But in other kinds of deposits, plant remains may be preserved only if they were burned and carbonized. These remains are often quite small and nearly impossible to collect by hand in the field.

The most common method of recovering such plant remains is **flotation,** a technique that is standard at most excavations.

Several procedures exist for floating archaeological samples, but all are based on the same principle: Dirt

matrix-sorting The hand-sorting of processed bulk soil samples for minute artifacts and ecofacts.

flotation The use of fluid suspension to recover tiny burned plant remains and bone fragments from archaeological sites.

doesn't float, but carbonized plant (and some animal) remains do. By using water flotation, archaeologists can float most burned plant remains out of samples of archaeologically recovered dirt.

In one of the earliest applications, Stuart Struever (retired, former president of the Crow Canyon Archaeological Center) floated soil samples from 200 features attributable to the Middle Woodland component at the Apple Creek site, Illinois. The samples were hauled to nearby Apple Creek, where they were placed in mesh-bottomed buckets and then water-separated by students who worked midstream. More than 40,000 charred nutshell fragments, 2000 carbonized seeds, and some 15,000 identifiable fish bones were collected in this manner. Standard dry screening techniques would have missed most of these.

While excavating at Salts Cave in Kentucky, Patty Jo Watson (Washington University) and her associates were not blessed with a nearby stream, so they improvised (Figure 6-13). The sediments to be floated were placed in double plastic bags and carried outside the cave. They first spread the samples (weighing a total of 680 kilograms) in the shade to dry. They then filled two 208-litre drums with water, and placed the dry samples in metal buckets whose bottoms had been replaced with window screen. They submerged the buckets in the 55-gallon drums (208 litres).

After a few seconds, the investigator skimmed off the charcoal and carbonized plant remains that had floated to the surface, using a small scoop made from a brass carburetor screen (cloth diapers work well, too). They spread the debris that floated to the top (called the light fraction) and the stuff that sank (the heavy fraction) on labelled newsprint to dry again. These flotation samples yielded carbonized remains of hickory nuts and acorns, seeds from berries, grains, sumpweed, chenopods, maygrass, and amaranth.

Today, flotation is not an expensive or even a particularly time-consuming process. Flotation techniques can (and should) be fitted to the local requirements. At Mission Santa Catalina, Thomas also used a converted 55-gallon drum, and one person could process dozens of samples each day. Some elaborate power-driven machines are equipped with aeration devices and use deflocculants or chemicals to remove sediment that might adhere to and sink carbonized plant remains. The technology is available to fit any budget.

But accuracy, not technology, is the issue. For a long time archaeologists saved only bone (and even then, just the large, identifiable pieces) but ignored plant remains. This frequently led archaeologists to overemphasize hunting and herding, thereby de-emphasizing the plant component of the economy. Now that flotation techniques have come into their own, we are discovering new things about the past. For example, from those seemingly innocuous burnt seeds of sumpweed, chenopods, maygrass, and amaranth that Patty Jo Watson and others collected through flotation, archaeologists made the important discovery that Native Americans had domesticated some indigenous plants of North America's eastern woodlands more than 4000 years ago—more than 1000 years before maize appeared on the scene. Those tiny bits of burnt plant material floating on the water turned out to be very important.

Figure 6-13 Patty Jo Watson (left) and Louise Robbins operating a flotation device constructed in a 55-gallon drum. Carbonized seeds and other plant remains are recovered as they float to the surface.

Source: Patty Jo Watson

Cataloguing the Finds

Excavating objects is just the beginning; in fact, excavation is only about 15 percent of a project—most of our time is spent in the lab analyzing the finds. And before the artifacts and field data can be analyzed, the objects must be catalogued. In many cases, the archaeologist assigns artifacts their catalogue numbers in the field, as they are excavated. We do this by printing up sheets of sequential catalogue numbers on peel-off return address forms (we've used the format 48BH3178/xxxx, where the 48BH3178 is the site's Smithsonian number and the xxxx is a sequential number, but others use more complex systems). When an artifact is found, it is piece-plotted and placed in a small Ziploc bag. The excavator peels a catalogue number off the sheet (ensuring that there can be no duplicate numbers) and places it inside the bag (in case the label peels off, it will still be in the bag with the artifact). A crew member then records the number in the total station's data log.

Back in the lab, the archaeologist catalogues the artifacts. Most archaeologists are fanatical about cataloguing their finds, because it's easy for one distracted

Profile of an Archaeologist
A Day in the Life of a Territorial Archaeologist

by Julie Ross, Department of Culture, Language, Elders, and Youth, Nunavut

The responsibilities of the Territorial Archaeologist for the Government of Nunavut are varied and range from administrative tasks to conducting fieldwork during the short Arctic summers. The key purposes of my position are to ensure that archaeological resources are managed according to legislated and professional standards and to enhance the status of archaeological research throughout Nunavut. The education required for the position is a minimum of a Masters degree with a specialty in Arctic archaeology.

As the Territorial Archaeologist for Nunavut, I work with many people of different affiliations. The most frequent correspondence is with environmental review boards, university researchers, archaeological consultants, Nunavut land claim organizations, Nunavut community members, federal, provincial, and territorial employees, and the general public.

The responsibilities of my job can be classified into four main tasks: issuing and monitoring archaeological permits, evaluating land use applications, managing databases regarding Nunavut's archaeological and paleontological resources, and conducting field projects in Nunavut. Each of these activities must be carried out while adhering to several pieces of policy and legislation including the: Nunavut Act, Nunavut Land Claim Agreement, Nunavut Archaeology and Palaeontology Sites Regulations, Historical Resources Act, and Territorial Land Use Regulations.

In order to conduct archaeological or paleontological investigations in Nunavut, it is necessary to hold a Nunavut Archaeology or Palaeontological Permit. These permit applications are submitted to the Territorial Archaeologist. I then send these applications out to different stakeholders for review and evaluate the applications. I also continually monitor the work conducted under previously issued permits. This is done to make certain that archaeological sites are treated with respect. It also ensures that the data relating to the archaeology of Nunavut are of a quality to allow for the protection and management of these resources and to ensure it for future generations. The regulatory aspect of my job can sometimes place me in conflict with people.

As the Territorial Archaeologist, I also provide comments and recommendations to several other licensing or permitting agencies regarding the protection and management of archaeological and paleontological resources. A large part of my job is to participate in

lab worker to mess up an artifact's record of provenience. The cataloguers work through the field bags, writing the catalogue number onto the artifact itself with an archival pen, and sealing the number with clear fingernail polish; numbered tags are sometimes tied to some artifacts, such as small beads. Some archaeologists pre-print the catalogue numbers on minute labels and glue them to artifacts with archivally stable glue. Even those items that were not found in situ or otherwise assigned a catalogue number in the field will be given a number in the lab. The catalogue number is what ties a particular artifact back to observations made in the field. Thus, although cataloguing can often take hundreds of person-hours, it is necessary to ensure that an artifact's original provenience, and consequently its context, is never lost.

Lab workers then enter the catalogued artifacts' information into a computer database, usually including rudimentary observations (such as weight, condition, colour), collection date, its provenience (for example, unit, level, X, Y, Z coordinates), and contextual data (for instance, stratum, inclination, orientation). A digital photo may be attached to the data

the evaluation of environmental impact assessments that are conducted to ensure the best practice is used when development and research projects are conducted in Nunavut. I am sometimes required to comment on hundreds of development or land use proposals over the space of a year.

In order to properly manage the cultural resources of Nunavut it is necessary to develop and manage databases about the archaeological and paleontological resources of the territory. Since Nunavut is a new territory, much of the data regarding its resources have been managed by other jurisdictions; many databases, such as an electronic artifact database, have to be developed or adjusted to suit Nunavut's management needs.

The Government of Nunavut also runs archaeological field projects during the summer. These field projects can be diverse and many are conducted at the request of local communities while others are conducted to assist other government departments. Some of the projects are designed specifically as an opportunity to promote archaeological awareness and train people who live in Nunavut.

Overall I find the position of Territorial Archaeologist a very interesting job. It is best suited for an

Figure 6-14 Julie Ross, Chief Archaeologist of Canada's largest territory, Nunavut.
Source: Julie Ross

archaeologist who is able to be involved in several projects at the same time and who has an interest in policy and legislation as well as the long-term preservation of the archaeological record. While there is a small research component in the position, this work is often guided by need as opposed to individual interest.

record. Copies are then made of the database so that the artifacts' all-important contextual data will not be lost.

Conclusion: Archaeology's Conservation Ethic: Dig Only What You Must

Archaeologists have traditionally protected their excavations against vandals and pothunters. Excavation often draws unwanted attention, and vandals have been known to attack sites during field season even during the night. On Thomas's first job in archaeology, a 24-hour guard (armed, appropriately enough, with bow and arrow) was posted to protect the open excavation units from looters. At Gatecliff, we tediously backfilled the site by hand every year to protect the archaeology from the curious public, and the public from the dangers of open-pit archaeology.

On St. Catherines Island, the problem is somewhat different. The only visitors are scientists, who realize the research value of archaeological sites and leave the excavations untouched. It is thus possible to open a few test units on several sites, process the finds, and then return next year to the more promising sites for more intensive excavation.

On strictly research projects—like our work at Mission Santa Catalina—the sites are not threatened by outside incursions, and one must adopt a conservative excavation strategy. Archaeologists never excavate more of a site than is needed to answer their research questions; extensive excavations are undertaken only in the case of sites threatened by development or erosion. Most archaeologists leave as much of a site intact as possible for later investigators, who undoubtedly will have different questions and better techniques. And, as we have seen, remote sensing technology and archaeological survey techniques sometimes provide archaeologists with low-impact ways of learning without digging at all.

Regardless of whether we use high-tech instruments or old-fashioned elbow grease, our personal responsibility for site conservation remains unchanged and fundamental. Archaeology is a destructive science. We said it at the beginning of this chapter and it is worth repeating: Sites can be excavated only once, and so it is imperative we do things right. Sometimes those sites have remarkable preservation and many, many kinds of materials are preserved; other times, only stone artifacts are preserved. This affects what kind of excavation techniques are used and how quickly the excavation can proceed. But how much or how little is found in a site does not change the fact that we must take any step necessary to ensure that provenience for virtually every artifact, ecofact, and feature is acquired during the excavation and recorded. We excavate in controlled units, sometimes as small as .5 × .5 metre, using a systematic grid system; we excavate in natural levels where possible, and, even if natural strata are present, in levels no more than 10 or even 5 centimetres thick; we record everything we can about an item before we pull it from the ground; and we assign catalogue numbers to everything found so that each item can be related back to information gathered on its context. Once we have this information in hand, we are prepared to move on to the next chore of archaeology: making sense of everything we have found.

Summary

- The guiding rule in all excavation is to record context, and this means recording provenience of the artifacts, features, and ecofacts. Diverse excavation strategies respond to different preservation conditions, constraints, and objectives.

- Preservation is enhanced in continuously dry, continuously wet, and/or very cold environments—any place where conditions prevent the existence of the microorganisms that promote decay.

- Initial tests of a site may employ a vertical strategy, designed largely for chronological control.

- In a horizontal strategy, designed to explore the conditions of past lifeways, the context of artifacts and ecofacts within excavation strata becomes critical; excavation proceeds with the goal of finding all artifacts in situ. When an excavator misses an artifact—and it turns up in the screen—a significant piece of information has been lost because that artifact can then be located only within the excavation square and level.

■ Archaeologists use screening, flotation, and bulk matrix processing to recover extremely small artifacts with some control on provenience.

■ All recovered materials are catalogued so that each item is permanently linked to its excavation record.

■ From test pit through full-scale excavation, archaeologists maintain exact records of the three-dimensional provenience of the objects being recovered and their context. The objective of archaeological records is to record the excavation in such a way that another archaeologist could "see" what the original excavator saw.

■ It's hard to overemphasize the importance of hands-on experience in archaeology. There is no substitute for personal field experience, and no textbook, computer simulation, or classroom exercise satisfactorily simulates the field situation.

Additional Reading

CANADIAN RESOURCES

K. R. Fladmark. (2006). *A Guide to Basic Archaeological Field Procedures.* Burnaby: Simon Fraser University Archaeology Press.

OTHER RESOURCES

Collis, John. (2001). *Digging Up the Past: An Introduction to Archaeological Excavation.* Phoenix Mill, Stroud, UK: Sutton Publishing.

Roskams, Steve. (2001). *Excavation.* Cambridge: Cambridge University Press.

ONLINE RESOURCES

Visit *http://www.museevirtuel.ca/English/index_noflash .html* to see digitized exhibits from museums across Canada at the Virtual Museum of Canada.

Visit *http://www.cci-icc.gc.ca/main_e.aspx* to learn more about the Canadian Conservation Institute.

Visit *http://objectdb.royalbcmuseum.bc.ca/* to view The Royal B.C. Museum objects database available online.

COMPANION WEBSITE

Visit *http://www.archaeology1ce.nelson.com* to access a wide range of material to help you succeed in your introductory archaeology course. These include flashcards, Internet exercises, Web links, and practice quizzes.

RESEARCH ONLINE WITH INFOTRAC COLLEGE EDITION

From the Student Companion Website, you can access the InfoTrac College Edition database, which offers thousands of full-length articles for your research.

7 Geoarchaeology and Site Formation Processes

Dr. Len Hills inspects nine mammoth footprints, perfectly preserved, identified at the St. Mary's Reservoir Site, Alberta (DhPg-8).
Source: Paul E McNeil

Preview

Every archaeological site is unique. Some sites are remarkably well preserved; others are not. Some sites lie on the surface, some are deeply buried, and others lie underwater. Some are frozen, others are dry. Each site that we have personally worked on has presented new challenges. But they all had one thing in common: dirt.

Although Americanist archaeology is firmly embedded in anthropology, it has a foot securely in geology as well. In fact, we can't do archaeology without also doing geology. Archaeological sites are created by human activities, but they also build up through many natural processes, including those that are commonly studied by geologists (and, especially, geomorphologists). The study of the dirt in and around archaeological sites has become an important subfield of archaeology, known as geoarchaeology.

Geologists first pulled together the major principles of stratigraphy. This chapter introduces the important concept of superposition, the simple operating principle behind the interpretation of archaeological sediments. We then discuss how geoarchaeologists contribute to our understanding and interpretation of archaeological sites, focusing on natural and cultural site formation processes.

Introduction

Michael Waters (Texas A&M University) defines **geoarchaeology** as "the field of study that applies the concepts and methods of the geosciences to archaeological research." In his opinion, geoarchaeology has two objectives: The first is to place sites (and the artifacts found in them) in a "relative and absolute temporal context through the application of stratigraphic principles and absolute dating techniques." We'll focus on stratigraphic principles here (and discuss dating techniques in Chapter 8).

Waters's second objective of geoarchaeology is "to understand the natural processes of **site formation,**" which includes all the human and natural actions that work together to create an archaeological site. In the past, many archaeologists worked with geologists to fulfill this need. But as important as these collaborations were, it became clear that archaeology needs geologists not only who are trained in **geomorphology,** the geological study of landforms and landscapes (rivers, sand dunes, deltas, marshes, glacial and coastal

environments, and so on), but also who understand the special brand of geology that applies specifically to archaeological sites. Rockshelter sediments—like those that filled the Stampede site in southeastern Alberta (see below)—are often foreign to traditionally trained geologists, as are the sediments that fill a collapsed pueblo room. Traditional geologists may also look at sediments on a broader temporal scale than is required for understanding the formation of archaeological sites.

---

geoarchaeology The field of study that applies the concepts and methods of the geosciences to archaeological research.

site formation The human and natural actions that work together to create an archaeological site.

geomorphology The geological study of landforms and landscapes, for instance, soils, rivers, hills, sand dunes, deltas, glacial deposits, and marshes.

Despite their different emphases, however, geological and geoarchaeological analyses share a common foundation, beginning with the law of superposition.

The Law of Superposition

Nicolaus Steno (1638–1686) is generally acknowledged as having formulated the **law of superposition,** which says that, in any pile of sedimentary rocks undisturbed by folding or overturning, the strata on the bottom were deposited first, those above them were deposited second, those above them third, and so on. This principle seems preposterously simple, but it was a critical observation in the 17th century. Why?

Steno was an anatomist (a curious background for one who would make a major contribution to geology). In dissecting a shark, he noticed that the teeth looked exactly like things that naturalists occasionally found in rocks, and that Steno's colleagues called "tongue stones." The tongue stones were, in fact, fossil shark teeth, but scholars of Steno's day commonly believed that fossils were stones that had fallen from the moon or had grown inside rocks; a contemporary of Steno attributed them to "lapidifying virtue diffused through the whole body of the geocosm," which isn't especially helpful.

But others, including Steno, held the then-radical notion that these odd "stones" were in fact ancient shark teeth. Left unsolved, however, was the perplexing question of how one solid, a shark's tooth, came to be inside another solid, a rock. In his *Preliminary Discourse to a Dissertation on a Solid Body Naturally Contained Within a Solid* (1669), Steno pondered this question. He concluded that at some point in time, one of them must not have been solid. But which one? Believing that all rock began as liquid, Steno postulated that rocks must have been laid down horizontally (a concept he termed the principle of original horizontality); any departure from the horizontal, Steno reasoned, must have resulted from later disturbance. He then argued that if a thing were already a solid when the liquid rock was laid down, it would force that liquid to mould itself around the existing

solid. Thus, Steno argued that fossils came to be inside solid rock because the fossils were older, and because the rock was originally laid down as a liquid. Conversely, if a solid formed after the rock had hardened, it would conform to voids and fissures already in the rock (thus crystals and mineral-filled veins conform to voids in the rock that contains them).

Working from these observations, Steno postulated that if rock were originally deposited horizontally as a liquid, then the oldest layer should be the deepest and progressively younger layers should lie above it. Although formulated as an aside, Steno's law of superposition became the foundation of all stratigraphic interpretation—whether we are talking about the Grand Canyon or Kidder's excavations at Pecos Pueblo. Here's an example of how it helps to place things in time.

Fossilized Mammoth Footprints in Alberta: The Law of Superposition in Action

A variety of large mammal species roamed around portions of North America toward the end of the last ice age. These included mammoths, mastodons, camels, horses, and an extremely large species of bison. Archaeologists have always wondered why so many of these creatures became extinct soon after the Pleistocene ended. Some have suggested that the changing post-glacial climate of North America may have played a role. In addition to climatic stress, it is possible that the presence of early human hunters further contributed to these extinctions. The evidence necessary to test such ideas is understandably rare in the archaeological record. So, imagine how surprised a group of researchers from the University of Calgary were when they came across the perfectly preserved footprints of mammoth, bison, and caribou in southern Alberta (see Figures 7-1 and 7-2).

The site in question is called Wally's Beach (Borden number DhPg-8), and it is located on the St. Mary's reservoir, northeast of Cardston, Alberta. Local resident Shayne M. Tolman noticed the footprints, along with stone tools and ancient horse bones, after water levels in the reservoir were dropped during construction of a spillway. He then commendably reported the site to government and university-based archaeologists. Brian Kooyman and Len Hills—both researchers at the University of Calgary—quickly put together a team to investigate the area. The combination of paleontological and archaeological remains required the

---

law of superposition The geological principle stating that, in any pile of sedimentary rocks that have not been disturbed by folding or overturning, each bed is older than the layers above and younger than the layers below; also known as Steno's law.

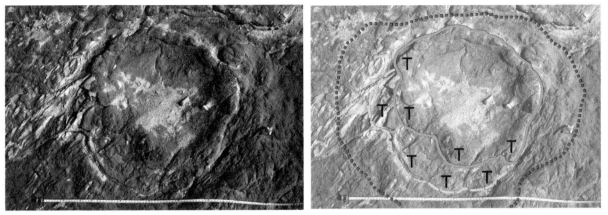

Figure 7-1 An individual track from the St. Mary's Reservoir Site. The dotted line indicates the extent of sediment deformation, the dashed line is the overstepped front foot track, and the solid line is the hind foot track. T indicates the impression of individual toes.

Source: Paul E McNeil

participation of geologists (Len Hills and Paul McNeil) and archaeologists (Kooyman). As a result, the St. Mary's reservoir excavations nicely demonstrate the interdisciplinary nature of many archaeological research projects. The site itself is 1.5 kilometres in length, and .5 kilometres in width, and follows the eastern bank of what would have been the St. Mary's river channel just after glaciation. Between 1.5 and 2 metres of sediment had been removed from the unprotected floor of the reservoir by wind erosion. This had revealed the ice age animal tracks, as well as stone tools associated with a Paleo-Indian culture known as Clovis.

How Were the Tracks Preserved?

Few sets of mammoth tracks have been discovered in North America. Wally's Beach was especially unique because it contained the first Pleistocene trackway ever found in Canada. Plant roots often leave etched marks on bone, and the presence of such etching on skeletal elements indicated that St. Mary's reservoir would have been a lush, grassy plain with low shrubs when Pleistocene animals frequented it. The mammoth tracks were circular in shape, and had raised lips around their edges, indicating the animals had been trudging through heavy mud when they were made. Soon

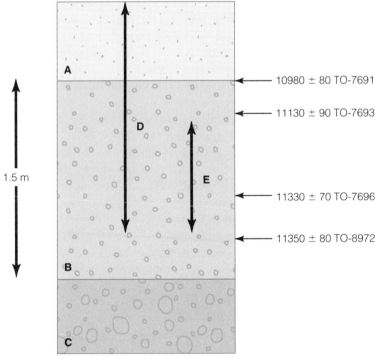

1.5 m

10980 ± 80 TO-7691

11130 ± 90 TO-7693

11330 ± 70 TO-7696

11350 ± 80 TO-8972

Figure 7-2 Simplified stratigraphic column of the track-bearing sediments at the St. Mary's Reservoir Site. **Layer A:** Well-developed paleosol containing only very rare tracks. **Layer B:** Aeolian sediments containing many extinct animal bones and tracks, used by the researchers to study Late Pleistocene mammoth populations. **Layer C:** Proglacial deltaic and lacustrine sands and gravels. **(D)** identifies the entire range of tracks recorded, while **(E)** indicates only those tracks used in the study.

Source: McNeil et al. (2005). Mammoth tracks indicate a declining Late Pleistocene population in southwestern Alberta, Canada. *Quaternary Science Reviews, 24*(10–11),1254.

after, the tracks appear to have been quickly covered over by wind blown (**aeolian**) silts and sands, thereby explaining their excellent state of preservation. A well-developed **paleosol** had then formed in the millennia that followed, effectively capping the deposit. Kooyman and Hills recorded more than 500 footprints. Some of these were so well formed that they showed the outline of the three or more toes mammoths typically have on their hind feet.

How Old Are the Mammoth Footprints?

Obviously, the team was interested in learning exactly how old these mammoth trackways were. But how do you date something like a footprint? In these situations, the *law of superposition* comes in very handy. As you recall, Steno's Law states that, all things being equal, undisturbed sedimentary layers overlying other layers are likely more recent in age. Let's look at a simplified stratigraphic column of the site containing the tracks (starting with, of course, the youngest layer on top [see Figure 7-2]).

The stratigraphy of the site revealed an absence of tracks in the proglacial deposits (Layer C). Tracks were also extremely rare in the well-developed paleosol (Layer A). Working from the bottom up, the proglacial and lacustrine sands and gravels (Layer C) *should* therefore be *older* than the layers containing the tracks and extinct animal bones (Layer B). Likewise, the well developed paleosol lacking the extinct animal bones and most of the tracks (Layer A) *should* be *younger* than the layers containing most of the tracks (Layer B). We now have a relative dating sequence for the mammoth footprints. AMS dating techniques were used to further pin down the age of the tracks. Remember that absolute dates for the layers can be obtained indirectly by radiocarbon dating the faunal materials they contain. In layer B, the lowest aeolian sediments with tracks contained a caribou (*Rangifer tarandus*) bone that was dated at 11,350 +/– 90 years B.P. The upper aeolian deposits, with the last of the track concentration, contained an extinct bison (*Bison antiquus*) bone that was dated at 11,130 +/– 90 years B.P. Therefore, because most of the tracks

used in the study (E) were sandwiched between these two dates, they must have been laid down during the roughly 200-year period that separates them. With the dating of the footprints, Kooyman, Hills, McNeil, and Tolman could go on with further research aimed at assessing whether the St. Mary's mammoth populations were expanding or in decline at the end of the Pleistocene (see "Looking Closer: Human Hunting and Megafauna Extinction: The View from Wally's Beach").

Reading the Dirt at the Stampede Site

The stratigraphy at Wally's Beach is relatively simple when compared with that of the Stampede site (DjOn-26), a deeply stratified, open-air site located along the north slope of the Cypress Hills near the town of Elkwater in southeastern Alberta. The site extends over a large area on both sides of a small stream that flows into a marshland located along the eastern end of Elkwater Lake. This important archaeological site was first discovered and tested in 1971 by Eugene Gryba, and was the subject of more intensive investigations from 2000 through 2006 as part of the SCAPE project. Funded by the Social Sciences and Humanities Research Council of Canada (SSHRC) through its Major Collaborative Research Initiatives grants program, the SCAPE project was designed to "Study Cultural Adaptations within the Prairie Eco-zone" throughout the Holocene. Gerald A. Oetelaar (University of Calgary) returned to the Stampede site to explore the potential of this deeply stratified site, and directed the Alberta component of this multidisciplinary project. In the section that follows, Oetelaar provides an in-depth overview of the Stampede site's stratigraphy. (See also "In Her Own Words: Geoarchaeology and SCAPE," by Andrea Freeman, University of Calgary, later in this chapter.)

Excavating the Stampede Site
by Gerald Oetelaar

By the end of the 2006 field season, the excavation pit at the Stampede site measured 9 metres north–south by 8 metres east–west and extended an astounding 6 metres below surface. Cultural remains occur at even greater depths (at least an additional 2 metres), but access to these materials unfortunately wasn't possible because of the elevated water table. Nonetheless, a

aeolian A geomorphic process whereby soil-forming material is transported and deposited by wind.

paleosol Old (fossil) soils formed over long periods of time that are buried underneath either sediments or volcanic ash.

remarkable 8000 years of human history are represented in the 6 metres of dirt excavated to date, with the possibility of another two or three millennia remaining buried below this level.

The law of superposition gives us the first geoarchaeological tool for reading the stratigraphy at this archaeological site. On the basis of this law, we know that the story begins at the bottom, with succeeding "chapters" lying above. With a few more tools, we can fill in the story of the site's geologic history even though some of the first chapters are still missing.

The Stampede sediments, like those of all archaeological sites, resulted from both *natural processes* and *human activities.* The first question we need to ask is, What are the possible ways in which materials at the Stampede Site—artifacts, bones, rocks, and dirt—came to rest where they were found by the archaeologist? The artifacts and a good portion of the animal bones entered the Stampede site through the activities of humans, but some of these materials were introduced through *natural processes.* Therefore, the geoarchaeologist must consider both *human* and *natural factors* in reading the stratigraphy at the site.

The Stratigraphy of the Stampede Site

The stratigraphic profile at the Stampede site includes a number of thin, dark levels separated from one another by thicker layers of lighter coloured dirt. The thin dark layers, of which 30 are exposed in the 6-metre profile, represent soils in the early stages of development. At the Stampede site, 19 of the 30 dark layers also contain cultural debris, suggesting that people camped at this location during episodes of soil development. In these instances, the land surfaces also represent "living surfaces" where the activities of humans contribute to the texture and colour of the buried soils. In addition to the organic matter contributed by plants, these living surfaces contain fire hearths, charcoal, burned bone, complete and broken tools of stone, bone, and shell, fire broken rock, flakes, and animal and plant remains. There are also indications that people built temporary shelters, dug pits, and otherwise contributed to the stratigraphic record at the site. At the Stampede site, the living surfaces are generally well separated by *sterile layers,* allowing archaeologists to study entire assemblages of tools used by the successive occupants of the site. Such opportunities are rare in Canada, where most sites

contain a 10,000-year record of human activities in some 30 centimetres of dirt. At sites with such compressed stratigraphy, it is not uncommon to find a 5000-year-old projectile point next to a Coke bottle from the 1950s!

A Word About Soils

The majority of the dark layers identifiable in the stratigraphic profile from the Stampede site are *incipient soils,* whereas the lighter-coloured layers represent sediments introduced through *natural processes.* Soils, by definition, are not depositional units; instead, they are *developmental sequences*—distinctive layers that develop in place. You can see these as dark bands in road cuts or pipeline trenches. Soils develop when a land surface remains stable for a period of time, allowing plant growth and displacement of minerals through the unconsolidated sediment. As the plants grow and die, they contribute organic matter to the mineral component of the sediment. This organic matter, as well as other mineral components in the dirt, is displaced through chemical and mechanical processes. With time, distinct horizons, normally identified as the A, B, and C horizons, will form within these depositional units.

The **A horizon** is the dark, humus layer found near the surface. Organic matter tends to accumulate in this horizon, whereas other minerals tend to be leached out of this layer through chemical and mechanical decomposition. The **B horizon** lies below the A horizon and this is where clays and other minerals accumulate as rainfall and snowmelt transport them downward through the profile. Still deeper lies the **C horizon,** a mineral horizon normally referred to as the parent material, or the sediments that were initially laid down on the stable land surface. (The preceding discussion is necessarily a basic description of soils, most of which are far more complex with subdivisions of each of these horizons—see Figures 7-3 and 7-4).

A horizon The upper part of a soil, where active organic and mechanical decomposition of geological and organic material occurs.

B horizon A layer found below the A horizon, where clays accumulate that are transported downward by water.

C horizon A layer found below the B horizon that consists of the unaltered or slightly altered parent material; bedrock lies below the C horizon.

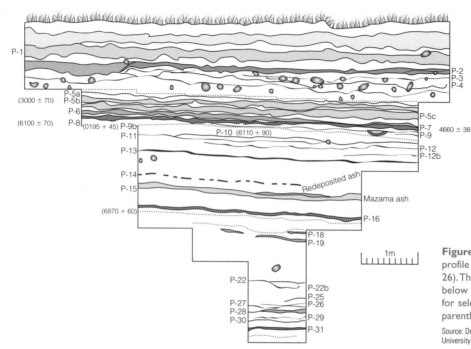

Figure 7-3 The master stratigraphic profile from the Stampede site (DjOn-26). The excavation extends 9 metres below the surface. Radiocarbon dates for selected layers are included in parentheses.

Source: Dr. Gerald A Oetelaar, Department of Archaeology, University of Calgary. E-mail: oetelaar@ucalgary.ca

Why Was More Dirt Deposited in Some Periods Than in Others?

The sequence of thin dark and thicker light layers in the stratigraphic profile at the Stampede site tells us that the sediments did not accumulate at a steady rate during the past 8000 years (see Figure 7-5). Instead, the influx of sediments was fairly rapid at some times, thus preventing the development of soils. At other times, very little sediment was introduced over a prolonged interval, allowing plants to grow and soils to develop on the stable surface. In fact, when one looks at the stratigraphic profile of the Stampede site, one notices that over the entire 6-metre interval the thin dark layers appear to be somewhat thicker and more closely spaced at certain depths, while they are thinner and more widely spaced at other depths. This aspect of the profile indicates that the rate of sediment influx fluctuated over the last 8000 years. What could cause such dramatic fluctuations in the amount of dirt being introduced into the site area?

One possible explanation lies in the site's location near the base of the steep north slope of the Cypress Hills. Furthermore, a small, spring-fed stream, which originates near the top of this upland, flows

Figure 7-4 An exposure showing the stratigraphy of the south wall of the Stampede site.

Source: Dr. Gerald A Oetelaar, Department of Archaeology, University of Calgary

within a relatively narrow channel that ends rather abruptly as the water reaches the base of the slope and flows out across the surface of a former meltwater channel. The sudden change in gradient causes the stream to discharge much of its sediment, thereby creating an alluvial fan. The Stampede site is, in fact, located on this alluvial fan. **Alluvial sediments** can accumulate very rapidly on these landforms, as we witnessed during the spring and summer of 2002. In late May of that year and again in mid-June, for example, late spring and early summer storms deposited approximately one metre of snow on the plateau of the Cypress Hills, as well as some 20 centimetres on the site. Warm weather a few days later caused the snow to melt within a few days. The sudden influx of water into the channel caused the stream to overflow its banks and to deposit a layer of alluvial sediment approximately 4 centimetres thick just east of the excavation. Such flood events were also identified in the stratigraphic profile as layers displaying a characteristic **fining upward sequence;** that is, layers that tended to grade from coarse sand to fine clay. These fining upward sequences are representative of flood events, because streams that overflow their banks first deposit the coarse sediments. As the velocity of the water diminished its carrying capacity decreased, allowing the smaller particles to be deposited. Differences in the frequency of thin dark layers in the profile at the Stampede site could thus reflect changes in the number or intensity of these flood events.

The amount of sediment deposited during any of these flood events could have increased as a result of beaver activity in the area. The small stream flowing through the site contains a series of beaver dams spaced at somewhat regular intervals upstream of the site. Exactly how long ago these dams were constructed remains uncertain, but there is evidence of beaver activity in the area extending back at least 9000 years. Beaver dams, however, can be breached, especially during rapid snow melts or violent thunder storms, and when this happens the sudden influx of sediment into the drainage basin increases quite dramatically. Exactly how much alluvial sediment could be added to the downstream areas will vary depending on the amount of sediment that had accumulated behind the dam and the number of dams that would have been breached as a result of the increased water flow.

The rate of sediment accumulation on alluvial fans also varies greatly from place to place depending on the arrangement and distribution of the distributaries (small channels) flowing across the surface. Thus, the differences in the rate of sediment accumulation could simply reflect the changes in the location of the distributaries relative to our 8×9-metre excavation block. In fact, the former channel of one such distributary was uncovered in the southern portion of our excavation, approximately 1.5 metres below surface. At times like these, when the distributaries were positioned close by there would be more sediment added to this portion of the alluvial fan with only very brief intervals of landscape stability. By contrast, when the distributaries were flowing farther away from this portion of the alluvial fan, sediment accumulation would be slower allowing for the development of soils.

A second possible explanation for the sudden influx of sediment at the Stampede site may relate to the fact that this area along the north slope of the Cypress Hills is prone to episodes of mass movement. In fact, one such landslide, which occurred some 9400 years ago, impeded the natural drainage in the area and contributed to the formation of Elkwater Lake. A more recent example of such mass movement occurred in May 1967, when slope failure introduced a substantial amount of sediment into the Battle Creek valley of the Cypress Hills. Both of these landslides involved a huge amount of **colluvial sediment,** but smaller episodes of mass movement have also been documented in the area. In this case, headward erosion by the small spring-fed streams undercuts the escarpment and eventually causes slope failure. At times such as these, a large amount of *colluvium* is introduced into the site area. At the Stampede site, a thick layer of unsorted gravel approximately 4 metres below surface appears to derive from one such event, which happened about 7500 years ago in this area. The introduction of such massive quantities of sediment into the stream basin can also increase the rate

---

alluvial sediments Sediments transported by flowing water.

fining upward sequence A layer of sediment that includes coarser materials (usually sand) at the bottom and finer materials (usually clays) at the top.

colluvial sediments Sediments deposited primarily through the action of gravity on geological material lying on hillsides.

Looking Closer
Human Hunting and Megafauna Extinction: The View from Wally's Beach

What role did early human hunters play in the extinction of Pleistocene animals? Some archaeologists speculate that it may have been a lethal combination of both climate change and the arrival of efficient and deadly human predators. Wally's Beach, in southern Alberta, provides some unique insights into this issue.

In nature, animal populations are expanding, declining, or stable. Research into the demographic structures of contemporary elephant species in Africa and Asia indicates that stable and expanding populations have large numbers of immature and juvenile individuals that more than replace the older animals that are more vulnerable to predation, disease, and death from old age. In contrast, elephant populations in decline are weighted more heavily (no pun intended) toward mature and old individuals because there are too few young to replace them.

McNeil, Hills, Kooyman, and Tolman attempted to reconstruct the population profile of the St. Mary's mammoth population using the trackways they had mapped and recorded. In order to assess the ages of individuals present at the site, they measured the diameters of complete tracks. These measurements were then broken down into four age classes, based on the life stages of living African elephants—yes, someone actually measured the foot lengths of living elephants as a function of age! The representation of each age class was then graphed as a percentage of the total number of tracks used in the sample. The results indicate that the age structure of the St. Mary's mammoth population closely matched that of a declining population (Figure 7-5).

These researchers carefully considered all of the potential preservational, temporal, and behavioural factors that might have biased their population reconstruction. Because adults are larger and heavier than juveniles, would their tracks preserve better because they make deeper footprints? This seemed unlikely because feet are directly proportional to body size, meaning that animals of different ages should exert the same amount of force per unit area when making footprints. If the St. Mary's trackways represented a single event in time, then short-term fluctuations in the population would have been another potential source of bias. However, AMS dating and the law of superposition indicate that mammoths had frequented this area over a period of some 200 years. Trackways

of sediment accumulation throughout the drainage and thus explain some of the variation seen in the profile from the Stampede site.

A third explanation for the changing rate of sediment deposition relates to the impact of climate change. The amount of sediment introduced into a drainage basin, including a small one, reflects, to some extent, the nature of the vegetation growing in the area. Hillslopes with very little vegetation are prone to erosion and thus contribute more sediment to the drainage basin than those that are heavily vegetated. Although human activities such as burning can cause changes in the plant cover, climate is generally invoked as the natural agent responsible for shifts in

vegetation; that is, vegetation cover tends to become sparser during prolonged episodes of drought. Thus, the intervals of increased sediment influx could represent episodes of increased aridity, whereas the dark layers would represent episodes of increased precipitation and, by extension, denser vegetation. At the Stampede site, the intervals with the lowest numbers of clearly defined soils date to the Hypsithermal, a documented episode of increased aridity on the Northern Plains.

Natural disasters also may have played an important role in the introduction of sediments to the Stampede site. Approximately 3 metres below surface, there is a layer of volcanic tephra approximately

made over such a long period would have captured such variation. Finally, male elephants tend to roam over large areas, while females stick close to water with juveniles. Could this aspect of elephant behaviour have biased the representation of age classes? Matriarchal herds should have frequented St. Mary's because it was adjacent to a water source. If this were true, then the age classes in an unstressed population should have expressed a greater tendency toward juveniles. Since this was not the case, the sample did not represent a biased sample of the total population.

Why might mammoth populations at St. Mary's have been in decline? Clearly, the retreat of glaciers and the warming climate would have severely altered the habitats of many ice-age animal species, especially in Canada and the northern regions of the United States. But not all regions of the continent would have experienced the same levels of climatic and biotic disturbance. Then why was the extinction of Pleistocene megafauna continent-wide? Kooyman, Hills, McNeil, and Tolman have suggested that no single factor can account for this. Rather, multiple factors probably conspired to produce this effect. The data from Wally's Beach demonstrate that mammoth populations were already in decline. Perhaps the arrival of human hunters delivered the final *coup de grâce*. . . .

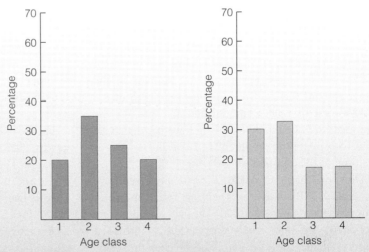

Figure 7-5 Mortality profiles of a declining elephant population (left) match that of the St. Mary's mammoth population (right).

Source: McNeil et al. (2005). Mammoth tracks indicate a declining Late Pleistocene population in southwestern Alberta, Canada. *Quaternary Science Reviews, 24*(10–11), 1257.

Marker Beds

10 centimetres thick. This ash deposit derives from the eruption of Mount Mazama some 6730 years ago. The eruption of this volcano in southwest Oregon created what is today Crater Lake and deposited a thick layer of ash that covered most of northwestern North America, including the Cypress Hills. Based on research conducted after the eruption of Mount St. Helens in May 1981, a 10-centimetre layer of ash has a devastating impact on the local vegetation for several years after the event. Therefore, this natural disaster would have denuded the hills of vegetation and increased the rate of erosion. In this context, it is interesting to note that the section of the profile above the Mazama ash contains a small number of widely spaced dark layers.

The Mazama tephra serves as a **marker bed,** which allows archaeologists to correlate deposits from a number of different sites. This volcanic ash, which consisted of silt-sized fragments of glass, was ejected into the air during the eruption of Mount Mazama. Within a few days or weeks, the ash cloud spread over a very large area and settled out of the atmosphere

marker bed An easily identified geologic layer whose age has been independently confirmed at numerous locations and whose presence can therefore be used to date archaeological and geological sediments.

over a period of several months to several years. Geo-logically speaking, the tephra represents a moment in time and allows researchers to correlate deposits across the site but also across a much larger region. In Alberta, for example, one can identify sediments and cultural deposits over the southern half of the province by using this marker bed. One can also relate paleoenvironmental data obtained from lake cores to the activities of humans at nearby sites by using such marker beds. Finally, we are able to reconstruct the topography of the site by examining the depth of the marker bed in excavations around the site. At the Stampede site, for example, this marker bed has been used to recreate the topography of the alluvial fan at the time of the eruption.

Thus, the dirt and rock of the Stampede site have provided SCAPE researchers with as much informa-tion of the site's history as have the artifacts that were recovered. In this case, geoarchaeology provided important clues as to the nature of the changing envi-ronments to which the ancient hunter-gatherers who used the Stampede site had to adapt.

Is Stratigraphy Really That Easy?

Unfortunately, no. The Stampede site has textbook stratigraphy precisely because it makes for nice photo-graphs and is relatively easy to understand. Some sites are like this. For example, the site of Cerén in El Sal-vador (discussed in Chapter 5) was caught by volcanic activity and "frozen" in time, buried so deep that very little happened to it until its discovery.

But, frankly, many archaeological sites can be geo-logical nightmares. Human and natural processes churn the sediments, moving things up or down. In Figure 7-6 you see a hypothetical scenario that makes this point. Hunter-gatherers first live in a temporary camp beside a stream at about 3000 B.C., leaving behind some artifacts on the surface, along with a hearth and some postholes from a windbreak that they built. The river overflows and deposits layers of silt over the camp. So far, so good.

But about 1000 B.C., people arrive who live in **pit-houses**—semi-subterranean homes with log roofs covered with sod. To make these houses, they dig into the previous campsite and throw the charcoal from the hearth of the 3000 B.C. temporary camp up onto the current land surface—thereby moving older mate-rial (the charcoal) upward in the stratigraphic sequence. And their habitation has cut down into the previous living surface, introducing "young" artifacts to older layers of earth. You can see that the law of superposition, blindly applied, would lead us astray here.

But we're not done. Suppose that, in A.D. 800, the nearby river is diverted and cuts an arroyo next to the pithouse. The hillside slumps, pushing part of the pit-house and its contents into the arroyo. People build a pueblo, like those in Chaco Canyon. A new hearth is made outside the walls, as well as a trash pit. Again, later materials move downward in the stratigraphic sequence.

Many years pass. The pueblo is abandoned, its roofs and walls collapse, and the rooms accumulate eolian deposits. A 19th-century farmer scavenges posts from the now-abandoned pueblo and uses them to build a fence. He digs a canal through the buried pithouse and pueblo trash pit. The canal is later abandoned and left as a dry ditch. If an archaeologist were to walk through this ditch, he or she would see pithouse occu-pation debris on one side and, at the same elevation, pueblo trash on the other. The law of superposition might suggest that they were of the same age, yet clearly, they are not.

Most archaeological sites are similarly complex. Let's turn to an archaeological example that shows how the law of superposition can mislead us if we do not consider the human behaviour that goes into the formation of a site.

Reverse Stratigraphy at Chetro Ketl

Florence Hawley Ellis (1906–1991) was a pioneer of Southwestern archaeology. Beginning in the 1920s, she embarked on a long-term research program in Chaco Canyon, focusing on the site of Chetro Ketl (*chee-tro ket-*tle), along the northern wall of the canyon. This three- to five-storey pueblo contained more than 500 rooms, although it was located only about a half-kilometre from the equally large Pueblo Bonito. On the cliffs behind Chetro Ketl are near-vertical steps cut

---

pithouse A semi-subterranean structure with a heavy log roof, cov-ered with sod.

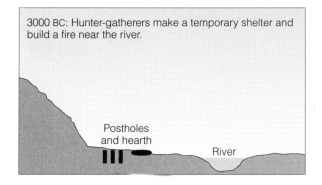

3000 BC: Hunter-gatherers make a temporary shelter and build a fire near the river.

Postholes and hearth

River

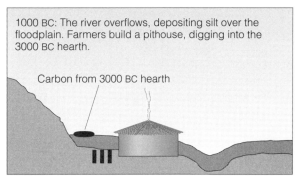

1000 BC: The river overflows, depositing silt over the floodplain. Farmers build a pithouse, digging into the 3000 BC hearth.

Carbon from 3000 BC hearth

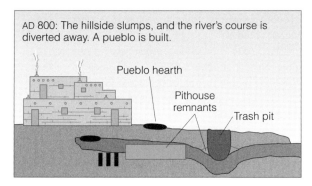

AD 800: The hillside slumps, and the river's course is diverted away. A pueblo is built.

Pueblo hearth

Pithouse remnants

Trash pit

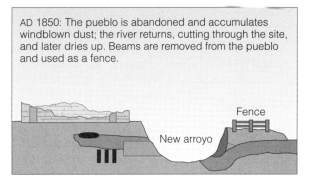

AD 1850: The pueblo is abandoned and accumulates windblown dust; the river returns, cutting through the site, and later dries up. Beams are removed from the pueblo and used as a fence.

Fence

New arroyo

Figure 7-6 The development of a hypothetical archaeological site over time, showing how cultural and natural processes affect a site's formation.

into the rock face that lead to one of the Chacoan roads. Excavating there in the 1920s, Hawley figured out that Chetro Ketl had been built in four major construction periods, beginning in A.D. 945 and continuing until A.D. 1116.

But Hawley was less successful in creating a ceramic chronology, a record of how pottery styles had changed over time (more on this in Chapter 9). She returned to the site again and again, excavating the huge refuse heap to the east of Chetro Ketl—archaeological sediments that reached nearly 6 metres deep in places. (She later conducted field school sessions nearby.)

Hawley recognized that two kinds of strata were present. Beginning at the bottom, she defined Strata 1 and 3 as household debris: daily sweepings containing ash, charcoal, and potsherds heaped in small, overlapping mounds. After examining comparable dumps in modern pueblos, Hawley decided that these sediments must have accumulated basketful by basketful, as trash was thrown out of individual homes daily.

By contrast, Strata 2 and 4 consisted of a mass of refuse, with a generalized gray colour signalling a mix-

ing of ash and charcoal throughout. Although these strata also consisted of stone, ash, and charcoal debris, they lacked the laminations and outlines of small basketloads.

But the kind of pottery contained in these strata seemed wrong. What Hawley knew to be the more-recent pottery turned up near the base of the trash mound. This material seemed to have been removed in bulk from some abandoned section of the pueblo, perhaps to make way for a new building to be constructed on the site of a previous dumping area.

In other words, part of the dump appeared to be upside down. Hawley stewed about this interpretation: "The suggestion looked far fetched, however, for this would place *half the mound* as re-dumped material." But eventually, tree-ring dating (which we will discuss in Chapter 8) confirmed that yes, indeed—the lower sediments were *younger* than the upper sediments. The stratigraphy violated the law of superposition: It was reversed.

Why was it upside down? Decades later, archaeologist Steven Lekson (University of Colorado) and others found out that the midden Hawley excavated at

In Her Own Words
Geoarchaeology and SCAPE

by Andrea Freeman, University of Calgary

The application of geoarchaeology can involve a wide spectrum of methods and techniques and can employ a variety of conceptions regarding human interactions with the natural environment. The SCAPE project (Study of Cultural Adaptations in the Prairie Ecozone) set out to employ geoarchaeological techniques in order to understand how prehistoric people settled and exploited the natural resources of the Canadian Prairies over a wide span of prehistoric time (9000 to 500 years B.P.).

The SCAPE project's team of scientists included specialists in plants, mapping, stratigraphy, soils, landscape formation processes, and archaeology. Together, our ultimate goal was to understand how prehistoric people adapted to changes in the natural environment over a span of prehistory. Prior to this project, the archaeological record seemed to indicate that there were times when the prehistoric bison hunters of the northern Plains did not occupy every part of the prairie landscape. In fact, it appeared that they occupied only the fringes of the Plains during a period of climatic change approximately 8000 years ago. A dry climatic period, it was hypothesized, forced both bison and the prehistoric people who hunted them to remain near the foothills of the Rocky Mountains, where abundant natural resources and water could be easily obtained.

Our group of scientists investigated a number of sites on the northern Plains that appeared to be occupied either continuously or nearly continuously throughout prehistory. The presence of these continuous occupations made us question the hypotheses previously presented. Because these sites contained occupations that spanned many thousands of years, some of the archaeological deposits were found well below the ground surface. Similarly, plant macrofossil and microfossil remains were also located metres below the ground. In order to sample deposits containing these artifacts and ecofacts, we employed a hydraulic coring rig called a Geoprobe© (Figure 7-7).

Geoprobe technology allows the scientist to push a metal tube tens of metres into the ground in order to retrieve samples of the underlying

Chetro Ketl was actually a deliberately constructed *architectural* feature. (Archaeologists have recognized these large earthen platforms at several of the major sites in Chaco Canyon, including at Pueblo Bonito.) The strata were layers of trash, deliberately hauled in for building purposes. When the ancient Chacoans looked around for easily excavated fill sediments, they turned to their own trash. Naturally, then, the first material they scooped up in baskets was the material on top of the trash mounds—material that had been thrown out the most recently. That recent material was the first to be placed down for the mound's base. As they dug deeper into the trash mound, they removed progressively older sediments and piled these on top of the younger trash.

In a way, the law of superposition was still correct—the material at the bottom had been deposited first, the material above that second, and so on. But because the ages of the artifacts in the layers of fill are in reverse order, archaeologists refer to this situation as **reverse stratigraphy.**

reverse stratigraphy The result when one sediment is unearthed by human or natural actions and moved elsewhere, whereby the latest material will be deposited on the bottom of the new sediment, and progressively earlier material will be deposited higher and higher in the stratigraphy.

sediment plus any artifacts or ecofacts contained in that sediment. Inside the metal tube is a plastic sample tube that allows the researcher to recover everything intact, keeping it in proper stratigraphic order. Coring equipment commonly used to dig holes in the ground around cities or oil wells often mixes up the stratigraphy. By keeping everything in correct stratigraphic position, the scientists can measure the changes in types and number of plants and in the cultural affiliations of different groups that occupied these unusual areas.

In addition to sampling on or near archaeological sites, geologists and geographers on the project utilized the Geoprobe to sample the surrounding landscape. We were able to measure changes in the processes that formed the landscape and reconstruct what each site might have looked like thousands of years ago. Reconstruction of the landscape, and of plants present on that landscape, helped us to determine there were always pleasant places to live on the Canadian prairies where people could find food, water, and other necessities of survival.

Figure 7-7 Researchers with the SCAPE project use a Geoprobe to sample the prairie landscape of Canada.

Source: Dr. Andrea Freeman

Site Formation Processes: How Good Sites Go Bad

The casual observer may think of the ground as stable and unchanging, and yet every archaeologist knows better. Sites are complex, and things can move around after they are buried. It's the job of the archaeologist to draw inferences about human behaviour from sites, but to do that we have to know how a site formed over time.

To accomplish this important task, we must always bear in mind that *the archaeological record is only the contemporary evidence left over from past behaviour.* Artifacts are the static remains of past dynamic behaviour. However, because both natural and cultural factors impinge on these remains to such a degree, the archaeological record is rarely a *direct* reflection of past behaviour.

The archaeological record is a contemporary phenomenon. Although the objects and their contexts might have existed for centuries or millennia, observations and knowledge about those objects and contexts are as contemporary as the archaeologists who do the observing. Archaeological strata are "leaky," and artifacts can move around quite a bit from where they were originally deposited.

To interpret the archaeological record more accurately, Michael Schiffer (University of Arizona) distinguishes between **archaeological** and **systemic contexts.** Artifacts, features, and residues were once part of an ongoing, dynamic behavioural system. Arrowheads were manufactured, used for specific tasks, broken, repaired, and then lost or deliberately discarded. Potsherds were once part of whole pots, which were manufactured and decorated according to prescribed cultural criteria. People used the pots for cooking or storage or ceremonial functions. The pots broke or were intentionally broken or discarded, perhaps as part of a ritual. Food bones and plant remains are the organic residues of a succession of activities—hunting or gathering, butchering or processing, cooking, and eating. While these materials are being manufactured and used, they exist in their systemic context. These items are part of the living behavioural system.

By the time such materials reach the archaeologist's hands, though, they have long since ceased to participate in this behavioural system. The artifacts, features, and residues encountered by archaeologists are recovered from their archaeological context, where they may continue to be affected by human action, but where they also are affected by the natural environment.

Formation Processes in the Systemic Context

Using Schiffer's distinction between systemic and archaeological context, we can discuss **formation processes,** how artifacts enter the archaeological record and how they are modified once they are there (Table 7-1). For our purposes, we will distinguish among four distinctive processes in the systemic context that influence the creation of archaeological sites: cultural deposition, reclamation, disturbance, and reuse.

archaeological context Once artifacts enter the ground, they are part of the archaeological context, where they can continue to be affected by human action, but where they also are affected by natural processes.

systemic context A living behavioural system wherein artifacts are part of the ongoing system of manufacture, use, reuse, and discard.

formation processes The ways in which human behaviours and natural actions operate to produce the archaeological record.

reclamation processes Human behaviours that result in artifacts moving from the archaeological context back to the systemic context; for example, scavenging beams from an abandoned structure to use them in a new one.

TABLE 7-1 Site Formation Process Summary	
SYSTEMIC CONTEXT	**ARCHAEOLOGICAL CONTEXT**
Cultural Deposition	Floralturbation (plants)
Discard	Faunalturbation (animals)
Loss	Cryoturbation (freezing)
Caching	Argilliturbation (wet-dry cycles)
Ritual interment	Graviturbation (hillslopes)
Reclamation	
Cultural Disturbance	
Reuse	

Cultural Depositional Processes

Cultural depositional processes constitute the dominant factor in forming the archaeological record. Following are the four primary ways in which artifacts enter the archaeological record:

- *Discard:* Tools, clothing, structures—everything eventually breaks or wears out and is discarded. When this happens, the object ceases to function in the behavioural system and becomes part of the archaeological context. This is one way that things enter the archaeological record.
- *Loss:* Other things are inadvertently lost, such as an arrow that misses its target or a necklace or pot left at an abandoned camp. In this case, the items are most likely small and still in usable condition.
- *Caching:* Still others are intentionally cached. The duck decoys we mentioned in Chapter 7 were intentionally buried in Lovelock Cave. They remained part of the archaeological record because the person who cached them never returned.
- *Ritual interment:* Burials and their associated grave goods are the most obvious example of ritual interment, but other examples include offerings left at a shrine or, alternatively, deliberate destruction and burial of a shrine or religious site.

Reclamation Processes

Part of the archaeologist's job is to figure out whether the artifacts entered the archaeological record through discard, loss, caching, or ritual interment. This task is made difficult because artifacts can move back and forth between the systemic and archaeological contexts. For example, artifacts can be *reclaimed*. Archaeologists frequently find artifacts that were scavenged by later peoples. Pueblo peoples, for example, believed that ancient stone arrow and spear points contained power. If they happened to encounter a point while out working, they might keep it and later make a ritual offering of it. In this case, the arrowhead has moved from a context where it was (perhaps) unintentionally lost to one in which it was intentionally interred. It has also moved from the context of an earlier time period to one of a later time period, as well as from a context that records its original everyday function to one that records another culture's ritual.

Whenever a discarded projectile point is resharpened, a potsherd picked up and used to scrape hides, or an old brick reused in a new fireplace, reclamation has occurred. The farmer who used roof beams to build a fence in our hypothetical scenario above was reclaiming older materials.

Likewise, all archaeologists must cope with the fact that nonprofessionals (amateur archaeologists and looters) often collect artifacts from sites. If we ignore this fact, we run the risk of misinterpreting archaeological data. In the Carson Desert, for example, we knew that local people had collected projectile points from sites in the wetland for decades. One man had more than 25,000 points in his collection. The walls of his dining room were covered with picture frames full of points, and he lined his driveway with large stone mortars and metates. The fact that our survey recovered relatively few projectile points from sites in the marsh probably reflected this reclamation process—otherwise known as looting—and not necessarily a lack of hunting.

Cultural Disturbance Processes

Reclamation processes are the transfer of materials from the archaeological to the systemic context. But the archaeological record is also heavily conditioned by transformations *within* the archaeological contexts. Disturbance changes the contexts of materials within the archaeological site itself. Examples include such diverse cultural mechanisms as dam building; farming; and construction of houses, pits, hearths, and so on. In the hypothetical example above, the movement of charcoal from the early hunter-gatherer hearth upward in the stratigraphic sequence was an instance of cultural disturbance.

Reuse Processes

In reuse process, an object moves through a series of different behavioural settings before it enters the archaeological record. This can entail the recycling of some objects. Potsherds, for example, are sometimes ground up and used as temper in manufacturing new vessels. Broken arrowheads are sometimes re-chipped into drills and scrapers. Beams from one building are sometimes pulled out and reused in another. The point here is that an object can be created for one purpose, but it can be modified and deposited in an entirely different context than are similar objects that are not reused.

The difference between reuse and reclamation has to do with whether the archaeological context is involved. If beams are taken from a currently occupied building, it is an instance of reuse, if they are taken from a building long abandoned, then it is reclamation. The distinction seems trivial and yet it tells us something about the potential difference in the age of the items being reused. Items that are reclaimed are probably moving from an archaeological context considerably older than the systemic context they enter; reused items, on the other hand, are probably moving between systemic contexts that are much closer in age.

This review of cultural formation processes shows that archaeologists need to be aware that human activities frequently move things from their original depositional provenience to another. This can make archaeological sites very complicated and difficult to interpret. And natural processes can complicate matters even more.

Formation Processes in the Archaeological Context

Once an object enters an archaeological context, a host of natural as well as cultural formation processes take place. These natural processes determine not only whether organic material will be preserved (as we discussed in Chapter 6), but also where objects will be found. In the hypothetical example above, a river and a landslide played major roles in creating the archaeological record. Following are a few major categories of natural site formation processes (Figure 7-8). This assortment of processes is only a brief introduction,

cultural disturbance processes Human behaviours that modify artifacts in their archaeological context; for instance, digging pits, hearths, canals, and houses.

reuse processes Human behaviours that recycle and reuse artifacts before the artifact enters an archaeological context.

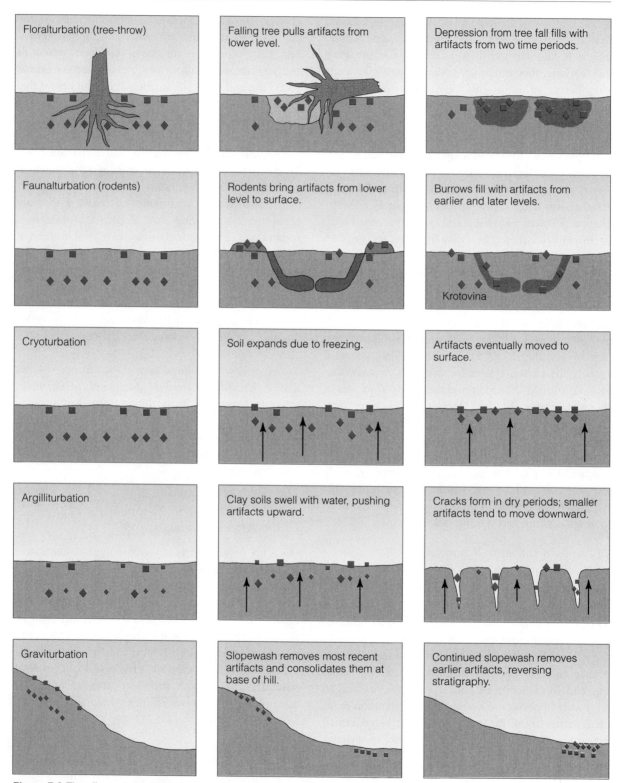

Figure 7-8 The effects of some natural formation processes on the distribution of artifacts in a hypothetical archaeological site.

and its purpose is to help you conceptualize just how complex an archaeological site can be. Additionally, this discussion shows that natural processes can both disrupt patterns that would otherwise tell us something about human behaviour and, at the same time, create their own patterns, which could be misinterpreted as the result of human behaviour. They warn us, then, that *there is no simple correspondence between the distribution of artifacts in a site and human behaviour* We'll give an example of how important an understanding of site formation processes can be, and we'll revisit this important aspect of archaeology in Chapter 10, as well.

Floralturbation

Anybody who has walked down a sidewalk knows what tree roots can do to concrete slabs. Roots do the same to buried ancient walls; and, by loosening soil, they also promote the downward movement of artifacts from their original stratigraphic context. But they can also move artifacts upward. When a large tree falls over, its roots pull up large amounts of sediment; we call this tree-throw. After hundreds or thousands of years, it can churn a site's sediments, pulling ancient materials up to more recent surfaces and creating holes that then fill with material of various ages.

Faunalturbation

Rodents and other animals often dig into sites, producing two major effects: First, burrowing rodents can push artifacts that were originally deposited in lower layers up to the surface. This can place old artifacts in a younger stratigraphic context. Second, burrowing can size-sort artifacts vertically, moving larger artifacts downward and smaller artifacts upward. For example, pocket gophers dig their burrows around any object larger than about 5 centimetres; anything smaller than this they push out of their burrows to the surface. The larger artifacts and rocks left behind might eventually tumble to the bottom of the burrows. Repeat this process over hundreds or thousands of years (and burrows), and you end up with a site where all the small artifacts and stones are near its top, and the large artifacts and stones are near its bottom. Someone applying the law of superposition blindly might conclude that people changed from using large to small tools over time. But that person would be wrong: The pattern tells us only about pocket gophers, not people.

Sometimes these burrows are filled with rock and earth washed or blown in from above, forming a feature called a **krotovina** (kro-toe-*vee*-na; the term comes to us from Russian soil science). If so, then archaeologists can excavate the burrow separately from the surrounding sediments. But if the burrows simply collapse, they can be difficult or impossible to see.

And burrowing animals are only one factor. Even the humble earthworm can obliterate the edges of features like burials, pits, and hearths, making them more difficult for the archaeologist to see and record.

Cryoturbation

In northern climates, freeze/thaw processes can move artifacts up in a stratigraphic sequence. As the soil freezes, it expands, pushing artifacts upward. As the soil thaws, soil particles move down first, partially or completely filling the void below artifacts, ensuring that the artifacts cannot move back down. Thus, freeze/thaw cycles move large artifacts upward (sometimes at a rate of several centimetres per year). This can create a site in which artifacts are vertically size-sorted, with the smallest artifacts at the bottom of the sediment and larger ones near the top (the opposite effect of burrowing animals). Cryoturbation also tends to orient buried artifacts vertically—that is, with their long axis pointing up and down.

Argilliturbation

A similar process happens in clay-rich soils that undergo wet/dry cycles. As these soils become wet, they expand and push larger artifacts upward for the same reason as cryoturbation. But as these soils dry, they form cracks—sometimes several metres in depth—down which artifacts can fall. Run this

floralturbation A natural formation process in which trees and other plants affect the distribution of artifacts within an archaeological site.

faunalturbation A natural formation process in which animals, from large game to earthworms, affect the distribution of material within an archaeological site.

krotovina A filled-in animal burrow.

cryoturbation A natural formation process in which freeze/thaw activity in a soil selectively pushes larger artifacts to the surface of a site.

argilliturbation A natural formation process in which wet/dry cycles in clay-rich soils push artifacts upward as the sediment swells and then moves them down as cracks form during dry cycles.

process over and over for hundreds or thousands of years, and a site's stratigraphy can become thoroughly churned.

Graviturbation

Archaeological materials deposited on hillsides eventually move downslope. This is accomplished through precipitation (slopewash), gravity (soil creep), or the slow movement of water-saturated sediments (solifluction). In any case, the result is that archaeological materials originally deposited on a hillside move downslope and eventually come to rest in a context completely different from the one where they were originally lost, discarded, cached, or ritually interred. This can also result in reverse stratigraphy, because the material closest to the surface will be the first to slide or tumble down the slope.

Some sites (like the Stampede site) have a high degree of stratigraphic integrity—meaning that artifacts are found where they were lost, discarded, cached, or ritually interred. Other sites are complex, with little stratigraphic integrity. In these sites, a range of cultural and natural formation processes have moved artifacts from their initial archaeological context. These processes do *not* make archaeology impossible, but it does mean, though, that one of our first tasks is to establish just how the artifacts got to where the archaeologists found them. Although how we do this is different for each site, the following case study shows how understanding a site's geologic context is essential to knowing what the site can, or cannot, tell us about ancient human behaviour.

An Ancient Living Floor at Cagny-l'Epinette?

The site of Cagny-l'Epinette sits on a gently sloping terrace in a broad river valley in northern France (Figure 7-9). French archaeologist Alain Tuffreau and his team had slowly and carefully excavated its 3 metres of sediments for many years. In the lower levels, in sediments that were some 200,000 to 300,000 years old, Tuffreau found artifacts as well as the bones of various large game animals. He interpreted Stratum I1

graviturbation A natural formation process in which artifacts are moved downslope through gravity, sometimes assisted by precipitation runoff.

Figure 7-9 The site of Cagny-l'Epinette, showing the distribution of artifacts and rock on a portion of Stratum I1.
Source: Shannon McPherron

as a living floor, a surface like those at the Stampede site, where our ancient human ancestors lived, made tools, and butchered animals. Tuffreau carefully mapped the locations of artifacts across Stratum I1 to look for clusters that could reconstruct where different activities took place and create a fuller picture of the past.

But there were a few troubling aspects to Level I1 at Cagny-l'Epinette. The artifacts found in Stratum I1 were separated by 11 to 64 centimetres of sediments. This could mean that (1) instead of one living floor, Cagny-l'Epinette preserved multiple floors, or perhaps (2) the artifacts had been deposited on one living floor, but had later been moved up and down by burrowing rodents. But it could also mean that the artifacts were deposited at widely different times through different formation processes.

Also troubling was the fact that the sediments of Stratum I1 were fluvial sands, deposited by a river. The fact that the deposit was mostly sand suggested that the river was usually slow moving, but the presence of some larger rocks pointed to periods of higher river energy. This could mean nothing more than that the river occasionally flowed over the terrace and created a pleasant sandy surface on which people later camped, made tools, and ate the game they killed along the river's banks. But many of the stone tools bore breaks that suggested they had been treated roughly, as if they had rolled along in a stream bed and been struck by other cobbles. Could the artifacts have been left by the same river that deposited the sand, and not by people?

The animal bones presented a third problem. As you will learn in Chapter 11, one way we know that animals were hunted is by the presence of distinctive breaks that form when fresh limb bones are broken open for their calorie-rich marrow. Another way is by the presence of cut-marks, where stone knives nicked bone as an animal was butchered. Oddly, the bones recovered at Cagny-l'Epinette bore very few such tell-tale characteristics. Perhaps they were the remains of animal carcasses that had floated downstream, and not the remains of game hunted by people. How could the excavators know for certain?

Determining the Effect of Formation Processes

All archaeologists dream of finding an undisturbed site. By this, they usually mean a site that Mother Nature has not thoroughly mixed up or that looters have not destroyed. But deep down, archaeologists know that *there is no such thing as an undisturbed site.* Even sites such as Cerén and Pompeii are not as pristine as they may first seem. As you learned in this chapter, a lot can happen between the time an artifact is deposited in the ground and when an archaeologist excavates it. Formation processes affect all archaeological sites to one extent or another. Our task is to figure out how these processes have affected a site in order to know what analytical use the site has.

Late in the excavation of Cagny-l'Epinette, Tuffreau was joined by Harold Dibble, Philip Chase (University of Pennsylvania), and Shannon McPherron (Max Planck Institute). The recovery strategy changed somewhat in order to collect data relevant to determining the kind and effect of formation processes on the site.

Recall from Chapter 6 that two observations we can make on artifacts found in situ are their inclination (the angle at which they are lying in the ground) and their orientation (the compass bearing of their long axis). The archaeologists at Cagny-l'Epinette collected this information in the later seasons not only from the artifacts and bones, but also from all unmodified stones found in situ. This information is important to understanding the site as a geological deposit, and that information, in turn, is essential to understanding the site as an archaeological deposit. What did it tell the archaeologists?

After compiling the data, Dibble and his colleagues discovered that the artifacts were oriented largely along two axes, perpendicular to one another. One of these axes was the same as the ancient stream that ran over the site. The other followed the slope of the terrace. And it was not only the artifacts that fit this pattern; unmodified rock and bone did, too. The inclination data were also intriguing. Artifacts, bone, and unmodified rock lay nearly, but not quite, flat—those that pointed in the same direction as the ancient stream had their "downstream" ends raised slightly above their "upstream" ends. What do these patterns mean?

First, the fact that the artifacts, bones, and unmodified rock all fit the same orientation and inclination patterns suggested that the same process was responsible for their deposition. Second, experimental studies show that when a river washes an object along, those objects eventually come to rest with their long axis pointing along the direction of the river's flow (Figure 7-10). This was true at Cagny-l'Epinette. At this site, a river probably deposited the rocks, bones, and artifacts. Some of these artifacts were apparently left exposed on the terrace's surface as the river's channel

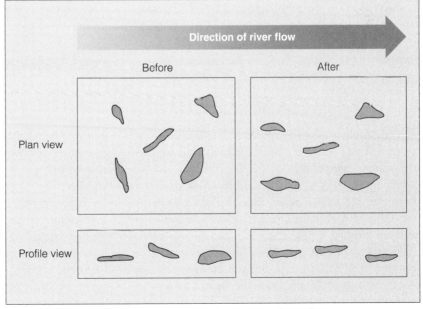

Figure 7-10 How artifacts become oriented to the direction of river flow.

Archaeological Ethics
Should Antiquities Be Returned to the Country of Origin?

 Many of the world's major museums contain artifacts that come from many different countries. The majority of these were acquired through legal channels. But some pieces have more checkered pasts. The Rosetta Stone, for example, is a large basalt tablet inscribed in three scripts, which allowed French linguist Jean-François Champollion to decipher Egyptian hieroglyphics. It was found by a French soldier in 1799 during Napoleon's conquest of Egypt. Fortunes change quickly in war, however, and by 1801 the Rosetta Stone was in the British Museum, where it is today.

Britain scored another "victory" in nearly the same year in Greece, one that has caused considerable consternation between these two countries.

The Acropolis is a limestone plateau that stands above modern downtown Athens. Temples and shrines adorn the plateau, and among them is the Parthenon, built between 447 and 438 B.C. and dedicated to the goddess Athena. It has been a sacred place in Greek culture for more than 2500 years and has served as a Catholic church and, during Turkish rule, as a mosque. A portion of the Parthenon was destroyed in 1687 when the Venetians bombed it; the damage might not have been so great had the Turks not been using the temple to store gunpowder.

The current problem began about 1800, when Thomas Bruce (better known as Lord Elgin) was British ambassador to Turkey. At that time, Turkey ruled Greece as part of the Ottoman Empire. Elgin removed statues and portions of the 75-metre marble frieze from the Parthenon, sending them to England aboard British military vessels. Elgin was later captured by the French and spent two years in prison, during which time the marbles were kept at his home, sometimes in the coal shed.

Elgin had spent most of his fortune removing the marbles and many other Greek art treasures. By 1816, he had lost his wife, contracted syphilis, and was deeply in debt. He sold the marbles to the British Museum for a fraction of what they cost him, and he died penniless in 1841.

Greece has been demanding the return of the marbles ever since. The late Greek minister of culture Melina Mercouri argued that they symbolize Greece itself, and many Greeks feel that the sculptures belong in Greece.

However, when he was director of the British Museum, Sir David Wilson countered that the museum acquired the marbles legally, had done nothing wrong, and that any such return—and most particularly that of the marbles—smacks of "cultural fascism." It is true that the museum purchased the sculptures legally; and Lord Elgin always claimed he had permission from the Turkish government to remove them.

But Greece points out that the Turks, as occupiers of Greece, did not have the right to give Greek patri-

shifted. While they were exposed, rainfall washed over them and, as a result of slopewash, they came to point downslope—perpendicular to the direction of the river's previous flow. By the time the river shifted to flow over the terrace again, these artifacts were sufficiently buried that their orientations were preserved and not affected by the river.

Fluvial geologists also know that stones on river bottoms tend to lie nearly, but not entirely, flat. The river removes sediment from the upstream ends of stones and then redeposits it beneath the downstream end. This is known as *imbrication,* and it results in stones lying with their upstream ends slightly lower than their downstream ends, or with the downstream end of one stone overlapping the upstream end of another.

These patterns strongly suggested that the artifacts in Stratum I1 were probably washed out of a site located farther upstream and then redeposited some unknown distance downstream. So, Level I1 of Cagny-l'Epinette is not the pristine living floor that archaeologists originally thought it was.

But neither is it completely useless. Cagny-l'Epinette still contains a record of what ancient

mony away. And, in fact, the surviving paperwork shows that Elgin had permission from the Turks only to draw, make casts, and do some small excavations. Some people claim that Elgin abused his political position and used bribes to remove the marbles from Greece. But the British Museum points out that Elgin probably saved these priceless treasures from the decay that political violence and pollution has visited upon the statues that remain on the Acropolis.

Britain argues that the marbles are now part of the world's—not just Greek—patrimony, and that they deserve to be in the British Museum, where many more people from around the world can enjoy them. The British Museum also points out that it is legally prevented from disposing of its holdings unless they are duplicates or worthless.

Finally, the British Museum claims that, if it returned the marbles to Greece, the floodgates would open, myriad countries would demand the return of art objects, major museums would be empty, and the world would have far less access to these cultural treasures.

Greece points out that it would be simple for England to pass a law to return the marbles, that pollution is now under control in Athens, and that conservation measures protect the sculptures (and that, in fact, the British Museum itself damaged them decades ago by using harsh cleaning solutions and chisels on them). The marbles themselves would be housed in a proposed museum at the base of the Acropolis, although construction of that museum is on hold since archaeological remains were discovered on its site.

Should treasures like the Parthenon's marbles be returned to their country of origin? Or should they be housed someplace where more of the world's people can enjoy them? Should we take into account the (often-nefarious) ways in which artifacts were acquired when making this decision, or are we opening up a tidal wave of litigation that will ultimately serve no one well? Do we consider whether the country of origin is capable of caring for artifacts by itself? Do we consider current national borders or those that existed at the time of the taking (do the sculptures go to Greece or Turkey . . .)? On the one hand, returning treasures to the country of origin would seem to encourage a balkanization of the ancient world that will not serve archaeology or humanity well. But on the other hand, consider this: Seeking to defend the British Museum's claim to the marbles, the Parliamentary Assembly of the Council of Europe passed a resolution stressing "the unity of the European cultural heritage." Does keeping the marbles in Britain achieve this goal better than keeping them in Greece?

humans did in northern France more than 200,000 years ago. That record is not as detailed as originally thought, but we now know what analytical utility this stratum in the site has. For example, the distribution of artifacts within the site is probably meaningless, for it does not reflect activity areas but only fluvial action and slopewash. But the site is still useful for making comparisons between the I1 artifact assemblage as a whole and those from other strata at the site, or from other sites. Likewise, the data from Stratum I1 could serve as a control, a background against which to compare data from other strata at the site to demonstrate that those other strata do indeed contain a living floor.

Conclusion

The important point of this discussion—and, in fact, this entire chapter—is that understanding the effects of site formation processes is the first step in knowing what an archaeologist can realistically accomplish with the information from a site. Archaeologists need to keep in mind all the processes that affect how artifacts and ecofacts enter the ground—and everything that can happen to them once they are there. In so doing, the archaeologist has to think of the site not only as a record of human behaviour, but also as a record of natural processes. He or she must think of the site as a geological record, as well as an archaeological record. Increasingly, archaeologists find that extremely careful and meticulous data, such as the orientation and inclination of plain old rocks as well as of artifacts, are needed to accomplish this goal. Thus, this realization of the importance of formation processes affects the way we go about excavating archaeological sites.

Summary

- Geoarchaeology applies the concepts and methods of the geosciences to archaeological research.

- Geoarchaeology uses stratigraphic principles to place sites in a chronological framework and studies the processes of site formation, which includes all the human and natural processes that work together to create an archaeological site.

- When dealing with stratigraphy, archaeologists rely on the law of superposition, which holds that (all else being equal) older geological strata tend to be buried beneath younger strata.

- But the law of superposition is only an organizing principle; in some instances, reverse stratigraphy can form in which the law of superposition is literally turned on its head.

- The stratigraphic record in some sites, such as burial mounds or pueblos, results from deliberate human activities: People systematically deposited strata as cultural features. But in many other sites, stratigraphy results from a complex interplay between natural and cultural deposition.

- You must understand the difference between an artifact's systemic and archaeological contexts in order to know how an artifact in the ground relates to the complex chain of human behaviour and natural processes that brought it there.

- Artifacts can enter the archaeological record through a variety of cultural depositional processes, including loss, discard, caching, and ritual interment.

- Once in the archaeological context, artifacts can continue to be moved and altered by a variety of natural site formation processes, including landslides, burrowing animals, earthworms, tree-throw, and the actions of water and climate.

- Geoarchaeologists use an understanding of site formation processes to determine how much artifact movement occurred during or after sedimentation. A range of methods and tests are used to accomplish this task.

Additional Reading

CANADIAN RESOURCES

Black, David W. (1992). *Living Close to the Ledge: Prehistoric Human Ecology of the Bliss Islands, Insular Quoddy Region, New Brunswick, Canada.* Occasional Papers in Northeastern Archaeology #6. Dundas, ON: Copetown Press.

Savage, Candice. (2006). Eight thousand years down. *Canadian Geographic Magazine,* Nov–Dec.

OTHER RESOURCES

Courty, M. A., Goldberg, P., and Macphail, R. (1989). *Soils and Micromorphology in Archaeology.* Cambridge: Cambridge University Press.

Davidson, D. A., and Simpson, I. A. (2001). Archaeology and Soil Micromorphology. In D. Brothwell and A. Pollard (Eds.), *Handbook of Archaeological Sciences* (pp. 167–178). Chichester, England: John Wiley and Sons.

Rapp, George, and Hill, Christopher. (1996). *Geoarchaeology: The Earth Science Approach to Archaeological Interpretation.* New Haven, CT: Yale University Press.

Schiffer, Michael B. (1987). *Formation Processes of the Archaeological Record.* Albuquerque: University of New Mexico Press.

Stein, Julie, and Farrand, William (Eds.). (1999). *Sediments in Archaeological Context.* Salt Lake City: University of Utah Press.

Waters, Michael R. (1992). *Principles of Geoarchaeology: A North American Perspective.* Tucson: University of Arizona Press.

Online Resources

COMPANION WEBSITE

Visit *http://www.archaeology1ce.nelson.com* to access a wide range of material to help you succeed in your introductory archaeology course. These include flashcards, Internet exercises, Web links, and practice quizzes.

RESEARCH ONLINE WITH INFOTRAC COLLEGE EDITION

From the Student Companion Website, you can access the InfoTrac College Edition database, which offers thousands of full-length articles for your research.

8 Chronology Building
How to Get a Date

Frederica de Laguna (left) and
Catherine McClellan excavating the
Parker Site on the Trent River,
Ontario, 1947.

Source: © Canadian Museum of Civilization, J433

Preview

This chapter is about dating archaeological sites—how archaeologists get a grasp on time. Here, you'll find a broad range of dating techniques: tree-ring dating, radiocarbon dating, thermoluminescence dating, and others that allow us to date organic material, rocks—even dirt itself. The chemical and physical underpinnings of these techniques can be mind-boggling, but you need to have at least a basic understanding of them in order to understand when you can and cannot use a particular technique.

You also need to understand the basis of these techniques in order to know just what the "date" is actually telling you, because dates in and of themselves mean nothing. Demonstrating the validity of associations between dates and human behaviour is the key issue in archaeological dating.

Introduction

The Fourth Egyptian Dynasty lasted from 2680 to 2565 B.C. The Roman Coliseum was constructed between A.D. 70 and 82. The Battle of the Little Big Horn took place on June 25, 1876. Each date represents the most familiar way of expressing chronological control—the **absolute date.** Such dates are expressed as specific units of scientific measurement—days, years, centuries, or millennia—but no matter what the measure, all such absolute determinations attempt to pinpoint a specific year or a specific range of years (the latter are sometimes referred to as chronometric, rather than absolute, dates). The advent of absolute dating was part of what revolutionized archaeology in the 1960s.

Absolute dating methods were not available in the early days of archaeology. Prior to the 1950s, most dates were instead **relative dates.** As the name implies, relative dates are not specific segments of absolute time but, rather, express relationships or comparisons: The stepped pyramid at Saqqara in Egypt is *earlier* than Khufu's pyramid; the historic settlement of Williamsburg is *later* than the pueblos of Chaco Canyon; Folsom spear points are *earlier* than Chupadero Black-on-white pottery. Relative dates are obviously not as precise as absolute dates, but prior to the 1950s they were the best that archaeology had.

Relative Dating

The keys to relative dating are (1) the law of superposition introduced in Chapter 7 and (2) the **index fossil concept.**

Developed in the early 19th century, the index fossil concept is often attributed to British geologist William "Strata" Smith (1769–1839), although it was in circulation throughout Europe at the time. Geologists of Smith's day wrestled with the problem of how to correlate the ages of widely separated exposures of rock. Smith observed that forms of life changed over time, and so different fossils characterize different rock strata. Thus, widely separated strata could be correlated and assigned to the same time period if they contained the same fossils. It seems like a simple idea,

absolute date A date expressed as specific units of scientific measurement, such as days, years, centuries, or millennia; absolute determinations attempting to pinpoint a discrete, known interval in time.

relative dates Dates expressed relative to one another (for instance, earlier, later, more recent, and so forth) instead of in absolute terms.

index fossil concept The idea that strata containing similar fossil assemblages are of similar age. This concept enables archaeologists to characterize and date strata within sites using distinctive artifact forms that research shows to be diagnostic of a particular period of time.

but it allowed Smith and others to make the first geological maps, and these radically altered the way that geologists conceived of the landscape. Now they could see broad patterns that told a story of ancient seas, mountain building, and ice ages.

The Index Fossil Concept in Archaeology

Archaeology faced a similar problem. The law of superposition could indicate which artifact types or styles were older than other forms in particular sites, but how could the individual site chronologies be chronologically related to one another? The index fossil concept provided the answer. In archaeology, however, artifacts replace fossils, and strata in widely separated sites that contain the same distinctive artifact forms—called **time-markers** in archaeology—are assumed to be of similar age.

The index fossil concept was introduced to archaeology by Swedish archaeologist Oscar Montelius (1843–1921). Trained in the natural sciences, Montelius switched to archaeology and became interested in Europe's Neolithic, Bronze, and Iron Ages. Working for the State Historical Museum in Stockholm, he travelled over Europe examining collections from various sites, paying special attention to objects in unmixed contexts, such as those from burials, hoards, and individual rooms.

Using hundreds of cases, Montelius divided the Bronze, Neolithic, and Iron Ages into chronological subdivisions, each with its own set of distinctive artifacts or artifact styles, such as particular kinds of axe heads, swords, or brooches. In some cases, Montelius had stratigraphic controls to help decide which artifact styles were earlier or later, and sometimes the artifacts appeared in contexts, such as Egyptian tombs, where documentary sources could provide the age. But he also employed assumptions about how styles change over time and arranged objects in sequences such that they formed, in his opinion, a "logical" progression from, say, small simple brooches to large, complex ones. This simple-to-complex assumption might work in paleontology because animal forms are linked through biological reproduction. But it is tenuous in archaeology because artifacts don't

reproduce; their shapes come from their makers' minds and not directly from "ancestral" artifacts.

Nonetheless, Montelius advanced archaeology by developing a way to create a chronology of artifact time-markers for Europe.

Time-Markers in the American Southwest

What Montelius could have really used, however, was a master sequence—a site with a deep stratigraphic profile that would permit the law of superposition to demonstrate the changing sequence of artifact types and styles. Nels Nelson, who was aware of European archaeology (and even helped excavate a cave in Spain), searched for just such a master sequence for the American Southwest during his excavation at Pueblo San Cristobal (New Mexico). Nelson knew that there were deep deposits at San Cristobal, and he hoped that a carefully controlled excavation into them would show whether certain artifacts could act as time-markers (Figure 8-1).

Selecting an area with minimal disturbance, Nelson isolated a block of debris measuring 3 feet by 6 feet wide and nearly 10 feet deep. Clearly, the midden had accumulated over a long interval, and several distinctive kinds of pottery were buried there. Because the dusty black midden lacked sharp stratigraphic divisions, Nelson personally excavated the block in 1-foot arbitrary levels, cataloguing the potsherds recovered by level. Imposing arbitrary levels on an undifferentiated stratigraphy seems almost pedestrian today, but in 1914 Nelson's stratigraphic method was revolutionary and immediately seized upon by New World archaeologists as a fundamental of excavation (for the record, however, Nelson got the idea of stratigraphic excavation from his European colleagues).

Nelson then applied the law of superposition to look for culture change within the midden column. All else being equal, the oldest trash should lie at the bottom, capped by more recent accumulations. Even though the dense midden lacked tangible stratigraphy, Nelson searched for time-markers in the form of distinctive pottery types.

Nelson thus applied the index fossil concept to the prehistoric ceramics of San Cristobal. Just as geologists learned to distinguish certain extinct life forms as characteristic of various rock strata, so too could archaeologists use distinctive artifact forms to characterize and correlate strata between archaeological sites. Pottery was a natural choice given that potsherds were

time-markers Similar to index fossils in geology; artifact forms that research shows to be diagnostic of a particular period of time.

Figure 8-1 General view across Nels Nelson's excavations at San Cristobal (New Mexico). The 700-year-old walls of this huge pueblo are clearly evident. Note also that no screens appear anywhere; sifting of archaeological deposits did not become standard practice until almost 50 years after this picture was taken.

Source: American Museum of Natural History

potsherds into obvious types and then plotted their distribution according to depth below the surface (we'll discuss the principles of creating types in Chapter 9). Table 8-1 summarizes his results: Column 1 contains the frequency of corrugated pottery, the most common everyday cooking ware. Because the relative frequency of corrugated potsherds remained more or less constant throughout the occupation of San Cristobal, Nelson rejected Column 1 as a potential time-marker. Column 2 tabulates the frequencies of biscuit ware, a dull whitish-yellow pottery that Nelson thought was traded into San Cristobal from elsewhere. But these frequencies did not change markedly throughout the stratigraphic column either, and he also rejected biscuit ware as a potential time-marker.

common cultural debris, and Nelson knew that ceramic styles varied considerably across the American Southwest.

More than 2000 potsherds turned up in the 10-foot test section at San Cristobal. Nelson first grouped the

Nelson then turned to the three remaining kinds of pottery—which he termed Types I, II, and III—and discovered, just as the Europeans had with their fossils,

TABLE 8-1 Potsherd Frequencies from Pueblo San Cristobal, New Mexico						
DEPTH BELOW SURFACE	CORRUGATED WARE	BISCUIT WARE	TYPE I: BLACK-ON-WHITE WARE	TYPE II: TWO-COLOUR GLAZE	TYPE III: THREE-COLOUR GLAZE	TOTAL
COLUMN NO.	1	2	3	4	5	
1st foot	57 (36.7)	10 (6.5)	2 (1.3)	81 (52.2)	5 (3.2)	155
2nd foot	116 (31.3)	17 (4.6)	2 (.01)	230 (62)	6 (1.6)	371
3rd foot	27 (15.3)	2 (1.1)	10 (5.7)	134 (76.1)	3 (1.7)	176
4th foot	28 (21.3)	4 (3)	6 (4.5)	93 (70.9)	0 (0)	131
5th foot	60 (17.3)	15 (4.3)	2 (.01)	268 (77.6)	0 (0)	345
6th foot	75 (18.6)	21 (5.2)	8 (1.9)	297 (73.8)	1? (.01)	402
7th foot	53 (23.1)	10 (4.3)	40 (17.5)	126 (55)	0 (0)	229
8th foot	56 (24.6)	2 (.01)	118 (51.9)	51 (22.4)	0 (0)	227
9th foot	93 (45.4)	1? (.01)	107 (52.5)	3 (1.4)	0 (0)	204
10th foot	84 (54.4)	1? (.01)	69 (44.8)	0 (0)	0 (0)	154
Total	649	83	364	1283	15	2394

Source: Nelson 1916.
Figures in parentheses are row-wise percentages.

that certain forms were associated with specific stratigraphic levels (Figure 8-2). The most ancient levels at San Cristobal contained a predominance of Type I painted pottery, black designs on a white background. Type I potsherds were most numerous at and below the 8-foot mark and only rarely recovered above 7 feet. Type II pottery—red, yellow, and grey potsherds ornamented with a dark glaze—occurred most com-

Figure 8-2 Examples of Nels Nelson's Types I (bottom), II (middle), and III (top) pottery from San Cristobal Pueblo.

Source: American Museum of Natural History; photo by Craig Chesek

seriation A relative dating method that orders artifacts based on the assumption that one cultural style slowly replaces an earlier style over time; with a master seriation diagram, sites can be dated based on their frequency of several artifact (for instance, ceramic) styles.

monly at and above the 7-foot mark. In other words, Type I potsherds characterized the lower strata, and the Type II potsherds characterized the upper deposits.

The Type III pottery, three-coloured glazed ware, was rare at San Cristobal and appeared only in the uppermost levels of Nelson's column. This made sense, given that Pueblo peoples were making three-coloured wares when the Spaniards arrived in New Mexico in the 16th century.

Nelson's arbitrary levels made possible the definition of three important ceramic time-markers. Not only did he document the specific ceramic changes at San Cristobal, but more important, his controlled stratigraphic excavation provided a master sequence with which to place other sites, strata, or features in the region into a relative chronological sequence. Alfred Kidder later applied Nelson's observations to Pecos Pueblo, using the presence of black-on-white ware to locate the original settlement.

The Next Step: Seriation

The index fossil concept was essential to the archaeology of the early 20th century. The law of superposition permitted archaeologists to produce a chronology of cultural change at a particular site, and the index fossil concept allowed archaeologists to date sites *relative* to one another. Given this discovery, archaeologists could date other Southwestern Pueblo sites based on the type of pottery found in them. A site with predominantly black-on-white pottery would be older than one that contained red glazed pottery. The archaeologist did not know *how much* older the first site was than the second, but he or she could nonetheless still place sites into a relative chronological sequence based on their ceramics. This was a tremendous advance for the time.

And this advance became the basis of **seriation,** a relative dating technique that was crucial to archaeology in the mid-20th century. First developed by European archaeologists in the late 19th century, the technique was introduced to the New World by Alfred Kroeber (1876–1960). Seriation is grounded in the same commonsense observation that guided Oscar Montelius: Styles change and new technologies arise over time. In ancient times just as now, most new ideas are slow to catch on, with only a few pioneers participating in the fad. Eventually, a new idea may become chic and replace earlier vogues, only to fall gradually into disuse and be replaced by the next "new thing."

The index fossil concept relied primarily on the presence or absence of distinctive kinds of artifacts. Seriation refined this by using changes in the *frequencies* of artifacts or styles to date sites relative to one another (paleontologists, by the way, do the same thing with fossils).

To get a sense of how seriation works look at Figure 8-3, which shows changes in lighting technologies in late 19th-century Pennsylvania. At mid-century, most houses were illuminated by candles and oil lamps; only a few households had gas lamps. But over the next 50 years, more and more families switched to gaslights. Those who could not afford such installations used kerosene lamps (made possible by the growing petroleum industry in Pennsylvania and elsewhere). By 1900, however, electric lights were replacing gaslights and, by 1940, gaslights had all but disappeared. By that year, virtually everyone used incandescent light bulbs—which by 1950 were already being replaced by fluorescent lamps.

The shape of such popularity curves, which James Ford termed "battleship curves" because they often look like a battleship's silhouette from above, is the basis for seriation. By arranging the proportions of temporal types into lozenge-shaped curves, one can determine a relative chronological sequence.

This phenomenon is evident in Nelson's potsherd counts from San Cristobal Pueblo (Figure 8-4 translates the frequencies from Table 8-1 into a seriation diagram). As we've already noted, when San Cristobal was first built, ceramics were most commonly decorated with black designs painted on a white background; corrugated ware was also fairly common. Moving up Nelson's stratigraphic column, however, two-colour glaze rapidly takes over in popularity, with black-on-white pottery fading out. In the top half of the column, three-colour pottery comes into use. The town dump at San Cristobal faithfully preserved these changes in ceramic "fashion."

Dating Sites with Seriation

This sequence can help archaeologists date other archaeological sites in the American Southwest. Instead of just using the presence or absence of a particular artifact type, we use frequencies of those different artifacts to place sites into a finer chronological sequence. For example, sites with high percentages of

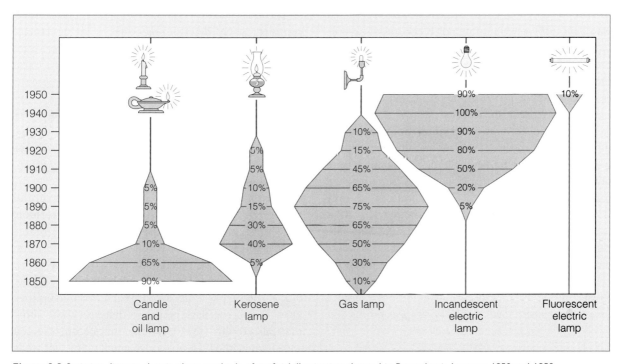

Figure 8-3 Seriation diagram showing how methods of artificial illumination changed in Pennsylvania between 1850 and 1950.

Source: Redrawn from Mayer-Oakes 1955, figure 15.

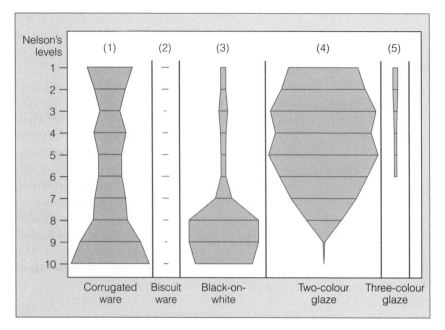

Figure 8-4 Seriation diagram based on Nelson's San Cristobal potsherd frequencies.

black-on-white ceramics would be older than sites with high percentages of two-colour glaze and small percentages of black-on-white pottery. These sites, in turn, would be older than sites with high percentages of two-colour glaze, small percentages of corrugated ware, and only trace amounts of black-on-white pottery. And these sites would be older than sites dominated by two-colour glaze with trace amounts of three-colour glaze.

We can use the seriation method based on a single master stratigraphy, or we can compile one analytically by linking several overlapping stratigraphies at different stratified sites. Thus, seriation takes the index fossil concept and refines it to permit a more fine-grained relative sequence. Nonetheless, seriation still cannot tell us *how old* a site or stratum is, only whether it is older or younger than another.

Seriation was a common technique in the mid-20th century, but today it is used mostly where absolute dating methods cannot be employed or are not sufficiently specific. And archaeologists still use the index fossil concept, but only as a rough guide. For example, excavations have shown that Folsom spear points, like

those found at the Folsom site mentioned in Chapter 6, date to around 10,300 to 10,900 years ago. If we excavated a site with Folsom points in it, we would gleefully tell our colleagues that "we had a Folsom site," and they would know that the site probably dated between 10,300 and 10,900 years. But we would *always* try to refine that estimate by using one of the absolute dating techniques mentioned below.

Absolute Dating

Absolute dating gave archaeology an incredibly powerful tool and helped shape it into the science that it is today. In this chapter, we will highlight only the most commonly used methods among the many techniques available. And we will give special attention to radiocarbon dating as a way to demonstrate the issues that archaeologists must consider when determining what a date actually means.

Tree-Ring Dating

Tree-ring dating, also called **dendrochronology,** was developed by Andrew E. Douglass (1867–1962), an astronomer interested in the effect of sunspots on the earth's climate. Douglass knew that trees growing in temperate and arctic areas remain dormant during the winter and then burst into activity in the spring. This results in the formation of the familiar concentric growth rings. Because each ring represents a single year, it's a simple matter to determine the age of a newly felled tree: just count the rings. Trees have alternating dark and light rings (Figure 8-5). The light rings are a year's spring/summer growth, and the dark rings are that year's late summer/fall growth (the darkness comes from the cell walls; when they do not grow quickly, the cell walls crowd together and take up a greater proportion of the ring's space).

tree-ring dating (dendrochronology) The use of annual growth rings in trees to assign calendar ages to ancient wood samples.

Figure 8-5 Cross-section of a ponderosa pine showing a detailed record of the tree's 108-year life span. Each year is represented by a light (summer) and a dark (winter) ring; evidence of fire scars is also preserved.

Source: American Museum of Natural History

For many tree species, the widths of the rings vary, and Douglass reasoned that the rings might preserve information about past climatic change. Because environmental patterning affects all the trees maturing in a given region, Douglass reasoned, year-by-year patterns of tree growth manifested as variable ring widths should fit into a long-term chronological sequence.

Douglass began his research on living trees, mostly yellow pines in central Arizona. He examined recent stumps and cores taken from still-living trees, counted the rings, and recorded the pattern of light and dark ring widths. He then extended this chronology backward in time by searching for an overlap between the early portion of young trees with the final years of growth of an old tree or stump. In doing so, he created a master sequence of tree rings extending back in time. But, all together, the stumps and living trees went back only about 500 years.

Douglass worked in the American Southwest, where arid conditions enhance preservation. Sampling ancient beams in pueblo sites, he slowly constructed a prehistoric "floating chronology," which spanned several centuries but was not tied into the sequence based on modern samples (Figure 8-6). Eventually, Douglass bridged this gap between the sequences of ancient and modern trees and gave Southwestern archaeology a reliable, year-by-year dating tool.

Year-by-Year Chronology Becomes a Reality

In August 1927, Douglass travelled to Betatakin, an impressive cliff dwelling in northeastern Arizona. He collected two dozen samples that placed the construction of Betatakin within a decade of A.D. 1270. Accuracy to this degree was stunning back

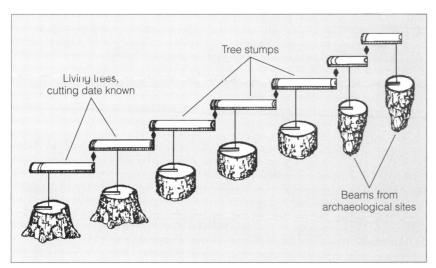

Figure 8-6 How a tree-ring chronology is built up by matching portions of tree-ring sequences from known-age living trees (lower left) to older archaeological samples; the diamonds indicate the portions of the sequences that overlap.

Looking Closer
Using Seriation to Examine the Origins of the Iroquois

The law of superposition can be used to measure changes in the frequencies of ceramic types when dealing with stratified sites. Unfortunately, many regions in Canada lack archaeological sites with such deeply stratified deposits. In these cases, it is possible to assemble chronological frameworks by referencing ceramic types to those used by living or historical societies. This is known as the *direct historical approach,* and it was used by Richard "Scotty" MacNeish to examine the development of Iroquoian culture in southern Ontario and Upper New York State.

During the late 1940s, the pre-contact origin and population movements of the Iroquois were not well understood. Many archaeologists felt that the Iroquois were descended from earlier cultures that had moved into Ontario from elsewhere. In the process, these interlopers displaced the ancestors of indigenous Algonquian-speaking groups. Linguistic evidence, for example, demonstrated that the languages spoken by Iroquoian peoples were most similar to the Siouan and Caddoan language families of the Great Plains. On the other hand, the languages of the Algonquian family, spoken by people who occupy the borders of Iroquoian-speaking areas of the Northeast, are clearly not related to Iroquoian languages. The eminent archaeologist Dr. James Griffin (University of Michigan) suggested to MacNeish that this would be an interesting question for him to examine through archaeology.

MacNeish contacted Dr. William Ritchie, an archaeologist in upstate New York, who provided him with a comprehensive list of all the major public and private collections of Iroquoian pottery. He then visited these collections and did detailed drawings and measurements on hundreds and hundreds of potsherds. The first step was to devise a way of identifying pottery types that were characteristic of the various historical Iroquoian groups. These included the Neutral-Wenro, Erie, Huron, Seneca, Cayuga, Susquehannah, Onondaga, Oneida, and Mohawk.

As we have seen, artifact types are simply "ideas" that appear, reach a peak in popularity, and decline through time. Put another way, artifact types have interrelated features that characterize certain groups living in certain time periods. On Iroquoian pottery, these features were reflected in decorative designs, and in the techniques used to apply them to vessels. MacNeish tabulated the frequencies with which different combinations of these variables appeared in the assemblages. Those combinations with high frequencies were identified as significant ceramic types. A second chart was then devised to link these newly identified types to ceramic assemblages from archaeological and historical sites of known age and group affiliation. This allowed MacNeish to turn his Iroquoian

then—and still is, compared with every other technique.

But we can be even more accurate with tree-ring dating. Jeffrey Dean of the University of Arizona's Laboratory of Tree-Ring Research collected further samples from Betatakin in the 1960s. The total collection grew to 292 individual beams, allowing Dean to document the growth of Betatakin literally room by room—his findings are summarized in Figure 8-8. (The samples, by the way, from both living trees and prehistoric beams are taken using a

hand or power drill equipped with a special bit that removes only a quarter-inch-diameter cylinder of wood, so the technique does not harm living trees and is minimally destructive of archaeological materials.)

Dean found that Betatakin was first occupied about A.D. 1250 by a small group who built a few structures that were soon destroyed. This occupation was probably transient, the rockshelter serving as a seasonal camping spot for people travelling to plant fields at some distance from their home.

ceramic types into index fossils. Once this had been completed, seriation could begin.

The direct historical approach involves tracing the history of a group back through time. In order to do this, ceramics from historically documented sites are connected to pre-contact sites using overlapping (seriated) pottery types. The pre-contact site with type frequencies that are most similar to the earliest dated historical site, for example, is likely ancestral to it. The next site in the sequence will display type frequencies similar to the pre-contact site previously tied to the historical one, and so on. MacNeish used this process to construct seriation diagrams for each Iroquoian group. The diagrams neatly ordered the archaeological sites according to their relative ages, and showed the appearance, florescence, and decline of pottery types for each group. Archaeologists could now date other pre-contact sites by comparing their ceramic types and their percentages to the seriation diagram.

The unbroken lozenge-shaped curves produced by MacNeish's seriation seemed to show that the Ontario Iroquois tradition had developed *in situ* out of an earlier cultural tradition called Owasco. While there were aberrant ceramic types that didn't seem to fit into the sequence, they were too small to support the idea of a population replacement. Instead, they seemed to represent outside influences pro-

duced through trade, the pottery traditions of women taken captive during raids, or copies of foreign vessels made by local potters.

Today, archaeologists remain divided over whether the Ontario Iroquois tradition was a local development, or the product of population migrations and displacements. Regardless, MacNeish's analysis of Iroquoian pottery types remains a classic example of how seriation and the direct historical approach were used by archaeologists in the mid-20th century—a time just prior to the advent of radiocarbon dating.

Figure 8-7 R. S. "Scotty" MacNeish (right) and William Taylor (left) in MacNeish's museum office, about 1955–1956.

Source: J1018/Canadian Museum of Civilization

The actual village at Betatakin was founded in A.D. 1267, when three room clusters were constructed; a fourth cluster was added in A.D. 1268. The next year, a group of maybe 20 to 25 people felled several trees, cut them to standardized length, and stockpiled the lumber, presumably for future immigrants to the village. Inhabitants stockpiled additional beams in A.D. 1272, but they did not use them until A.D. 1275, which signalled the beginning of a three-year immigration period during which more than ten room clusters and a kiva were added. Population growth at Betatakin

slowed after A.D. 1277, reaching a peak of about 125 people in the mid-1280s. The village was abandoned sometime between A.D. 1286 and A.D. 1300 for unknown reasons.

Methodology of Tree-Ring Dating

In practice, tree-ring dating works like this: The archaeologist digs up a sample of charcoal or wood of the appropriate species and that bears at least 20 rings. He or she then sends it to the appropriate lab—there are several around the world (such as the

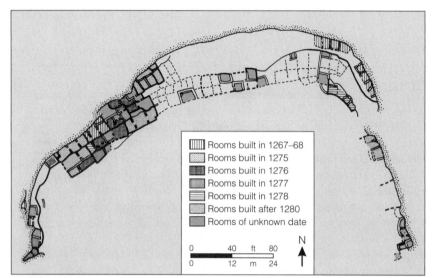

Figure 8-8 Floor plan of Betatakin and the construction sequence inferred by Jeffrey Dean from the tree-ring evidence.

Source: Redrawn from Dean 1970, figure 13.

University of Arizona's Laboratory of Tree-Ring Research)—with appropriate contextual data. There, an analyst will cut or sand the sample down so that the rings are easily visible, and the widths are then measured individually.

Now the hard work begins. Normally, the archaeologist will have some idea of how old the site is—perhaps less than 500 years old, or between 750 and 1000 years old. A lab analyst will try to match the sample to the appropriate portion of the regional sequence. This can be a slow, laborious process, because the analyst is looking for a segment of the master sequence that has the same order of variable-width rings as the archaeological sample—say, a pattern of four thick summer rings, followed by three thin ones, then three thick rings, two thin rings, and finally four not-quite-so-thick rings. Computer programs can assist in this task, but the matching often requires visual comparison because some samples have oddities, such as missing rings or partial rings, that only a trained technician can detect.

For tree-ring dating to work, the analyst has to make several adjustments and consider several factors. For example, trees grow more quickly when they are young than when they are old. Thus, absolute tree-ring width is a function of climate and a tree's age. But by using the estimated curvature of the ring on a sample, dendrochronologists solve this problem through a mathematical function that converts a tree's

rings into a standardized index that takes the tree's age into account.

Additionally, a sample's age is the age of the last (outermost) ring present on the piece. But if that ring is not present—if the outer portion of the sample was adzed off or burnt away—we still won't know what year the tree died. However, by looking for markings that are diagnostic of the outer edge of a tree— such as signs of bark or beetle activity—a trained analyst can determine whether the outermost ring on the sample was the tree's final ring. If so, then you have what is known as a *cutting date;* if not, then your date is only a maximum age (that is, we could say that a specimen was cut down after, say, A.D. 1225 but we would not be able to say *how many* years after).

Finally, the sample sent to the lab must also have at least 20 rings visible on it in order to increase the chance that the sample will match one and only one segment of the master sequence. A sample with few rings might match to several segments, leaving the archaeologist guessing which match is the correct one.

We can apply tree-ring dating to many species of trees as long as the species reflects climatic change. The most commonly used are piñon pine, ponderosa pine, Douglas fir, juniper, and white fir. Limber pine, bristlecone pine, oak, red cedar, and the giant sequoia are also useful. But some species are not suitable. Cottonwood, for example, grows only near water sources and taps into a more continuous supply of groundwater. As a result, its rings do not reflect local climate very well and, without climatically induced variation in ring width, we cannot link individual samples and build a chronology.

Additionally, because climate varies between regions, a tree-ring sequence is useful only for the region whose climate the tree rings reflect. A tree-ring sequence from northern New Mexico, for example, is not useful in the Mediterranean, or even in southern New Mexico.

Dendrochronological sequences have been developed in many areas, including the American Southwest, the Arctic, the Great Plains, the American Midwest, Germany, Great Britain, Ireland, New Zealand, Turkey, Japan, and Russia. In the American Southwest alone, more than 60,000 tree-ring dates have been established for some 5000 sites. Here the logs used to make pueblo rooms and pithouses allow the tree-ring sequence to extend back to 322 B.C.; using oaks preserved in ancient bogs, one sequence in Germany extends back to 8000 B.C.

Tree-ring dating has tremendous potential to provide absolute dates—to the year, in many cases—for archaeological sites, subject to the one important limitation of all dating methods: There must always be a clear-cut association between the datable specimen (the tree) and cultural behaviour (say, the construction of the building). At Betatakin, for example, Dean found that beams were scavenged from old rooms and incorporated into new rooms. In Alaska, archaeologists found that the driftwood used in some structures had apparently lain on the shore for a century before being used. In both cases, the tree-ring dates would be older (perhaps much older) than the cultural behaviour of interest.

Tree Rings and Climate

Dendrochronology also provides climatic data. Because tree-ring width is controlled by precipitation as well as temperature, trees preserve a record of past environmental conditions. Although tree metabolism is complex, analysts have made great progress in such ecological reconstructions. In the American Southwest, for instance, detailed models can tell us how much rain fell in, say, northwestern New Mexico, year by year, even season by season. For example, these data demonstrate that catastrophic floods occurred there in A.D. 1358. These detailed climatic reconstructions can provide archaeologists with fine-grained paleoenvironmental chronologies—provided the research focuses on an area with a dendrochronological sequence.

Radiocarbon Dating: Archaeology's Workhorse

In 1949, physical chemist Willard F. Libby (1908–1980) announced to the world that he had discovered a revolutionary new dating technique: radiocarbon dating. For his efforts, Libby deservedly received the Nobel Prize in chemistry in 1960. Although dendrochronology is a more precise technique, radiocarbon dating is more widely applicable and is the workhorse in archaeology's stable of dating methods.

How It Works

There are three principal isotopes of carbon—^{12}C, ^{13}C, and ^{14}C. The isotope ^{14}C (read this as "carbon-14") is of interest here, even though it is the rarest: only one ^{14}C atom exists for every trillion atoms of ^{12}C in living material. ^{14}C is produced in the upper atmosphere, where cosmic radiation creates neutrons that replace one of nitrogen's (^{14}N) protons to create ^{14}C. This ^{14}C is oxidated to form carbon dioxide, which is dispersed throughout the atmosphere by stratospheric winds. About 98 percent of all ^{14}C enters the oceans; plants take up much of the rest through photosynthesis. From plants, it enters herbivores, and then carnivores. So all organic life contains radioactive carbon (including you).

All radioactive isotopes are unstable and break down, or "decay," over time. ^{14}C breaks down through beta emissions (the emission of a negatively charged electron) back into ^{14}N. The amount a living organism loses through decay is replaced from the environment, so as long as an organism is alive, the amount of ^{14}C in it remains in equilibrium with the atmosphere. But once the organism dies, it ceases to take in ^{14}C, and hence the amount of ^{14}C in its body begins to decrease through decay.

But not very quickly. Libby calculated that after 5568 years, half of the ^{14}C available in a sample will have converted to ^{14}N; this is termed the **Libby half-life** of ^{14}C. (We have since learned that the actual half-life of ^{14}C is 5730 years—the so-called Cambridge half-life. To convert a date using the Libby half-life to one using the Cambridge half-life, simply multiply the Libby date by 1.03.)

What do we mean by "half-life"? Imagine a sample of charcoal that contains 100 atoms of ^{14}C (actually, it would contain much more, but let's keep it simple). After 5730 years, 50 of these atoms would have decayed into ^{14}N. After another 5730 years, half of the remaining 50 ^{14}C atoms (that is, 25 atoms) would

Libby half-life The time required for half of the carbon-14 available in an organic sample to decay; the standard is 5568 years, although it is known that the half-life is closer to 5730 years.

have converted to ^{14}N, leaving us with only 25 ^{14}C atoms. After another 5730 years (a total of 17,190 years), this amount would be halved again to about 12 ^{14}C atoms. As you can see, after a long time very few ^{14}C atoms remain. Theoretically, radiocarbon dating should extend far back in time, but current technology places a practical limit on it: Radiocarbon dating is good only for organic remains that are no more than about 45,000 years old.

Radiocarbon dating can be used on any organic material, although some are better sources of dates than others. Carbon, or charcoal, is perhaps the most common material dated in archaeology. After being collected in the field, the sample is sent to one of the world's 130 radiocarbon labs with appropriate contextual data. The archaeologist first examines the sample microscopically for intruding root hairs or other organic contaminants, and he or she will try to identify the wood species (see "Are All Organics Created Equal?" below).

The lab pretreats the carbon with one of several protocols, depending on its characteristics. The sample might, for instance, be physically crushed and dispersed in de-ionized water, then washed with hot hydrochloric acid to remove carbonates and then with an alkali wash (NaOH) to remove organic acids (these could make the date younger or older if not removed). Such pretreatment is important because even a small amount of contamination can greatly alter the measured date of a sample.

Once the sample has been pretreated, the lab counts the amount of ^{14}C in the sample by using a scintillation or ionization detector (devices akin to very sophisticated Geiger counters), which counts the number of beta emissions over a measured interval of time. The rate of emissions will be high if the sample is young and low if the sample is very old. By using an established equation, the lab converts the measured rate of beta emissions to an age.

What the Lab Can Tell You

The archaeologist who submits a sample will eventually receive a detailed report from the radiocarbon lab. Here's one date we received on a carbon sample from the Pine Spring site in southwestern Wyoming:

Beta-122584 6510 +/– 70 B.P.

The alphanumeric string records the laboratory and sample number: Beta Analytic (a radiocarbon lab in Florida) and sample number 122584 (in our reports, we always publish this number with the date so that another archaeologist could consult data in the lab's sample logbook). The second part estimates the age of the sample in radiocarbon years B.P. (before present—"present" being defined as 1950). Therefore, the radiocarbon lab told us this about the Pine Spring sample: A plant died and burned about 6510 radiocarbon years before A.D. 1950.

Why 1950? In radiocarbon dating, the present is defined as the year A.D. 1950—the year Libby invented the method. The reason for this is that "the present" keeps becoming the past, so we need a standard that keeps still. This means that a date of, say, 1000 B.P. obtained in the year 1960 is actually about 1058 years old in the year 2008 (add 58 years because 2008 is 58 years after A.D. 1950).

Why "radiocarbon years"? Labs measure samples in radiocarbon years, not calendar years. As we will see, radiocarbon dating has certain biases, and the laboratory date must be corrected to reflect actual calendar years. We'll return to this below.

Can You Handle the Uncertainty?

So far, so good. But remember that the lab report attached "+/– 70" to the age estimate. The decay process of ^{14}C is a statistical process, and the number of beta emissions is not constant over short periods (but the rate does average out over the half-life). For this reason, the lab measures the amount of beta emissions over several lengths of time and then averages those emissions to get an age. In Beta-122584, the number 6510 estimates the actual age of the sample; it is the mean of a number of measurements made by the lab.

That counting process also produces a standard deviation, read as "plus or minus," which estimates the degree of consistency among the counting runs. The standard deviation expresses the range within which the true date falls. We know from statistical theory that there is a 68-percent chance that the true date falls within one standard deviation on either side of the mean date. By both adding and subtracting 70 years from the age estimate, we know that there is a 68-percent chance that the true age of the carbon falls between 6440 (6510 − 70) and 6580 (6510 + 70) radiocarbon years B.P. If you want to be even more certain, statistical theory tells us that there is a 95-percent chance that the actual age falls within *two* standard deviations of the mean date, which in this case means between 6370 and 6650 radiocarbon years B.P.

The standard deviation must never be omitted from the radiocarbon date, because without it one has no idea how precise a date is. When archaeologists get a date back from a lab, they will first look at the mean date, but they will evaluate that date's utility by looking at the standard deviation. If it is very large, the date may be worthless (although it depends on the specific research question)

Are All Organics Created Equal?

The simple answer is no.

Bone, for example—and especially very old bone (>5000 years)—can create problems. Bone is very complex chemically and contains non-organic as well as organic components. In addition, it can be easily contaminated by younger carbon percolating in from the surrounding sediments. For these reasons, bones can give dates that are quite a bit older or younger than their actual ages. One way around this problem is to extract the amino acids chemically and date the carbon that is part of those organic molecules.

We also have to take care with plant remains. All plants take in carbon through the process of photosynthesis, but different plant species do it through one of three **photosynthetic pathways.** The first such pathway (discovered in experiments with algae, spinach, and barley) converts atmospheric carbon dioxide into a compound with three carbon atoms. This so-called C_3 pathway is characteristic of sugar beets, radishes, peas, wheat, and many hardwood trees. A second pathway converts carbon dioxide from the air into a complex compound with four carbon atoms. This C_4 pathway is used by plants from arid and semiarid regions, such as maize, sorghum, millet, yucca, and prickly pear. A third, the CAM pathway ("crassulacean acid metabolism"), is found in succulents, such as cactus.

The importance of these different photosynthetic pathways is that C_4 plants end up taking in *more* ^{14}C relative to the other isotopes of carbon than do C_3 and CAM plants. Because Libby developed radiocarbon dating before this diversity in photosynthesis was known, his system uses the photosynthetic process of C_3 plants as the standard. This can create problems.

Imagine a maize plant growing next to an oak; the maize, being a C_4 plant, will take in more ^{14}C than the oak, a C_3 plant. If both die at the same time, and both are later dated by an archaeologist, the maize sample will appear to be *younger* than the oak tree by 200 to 300 years, because the maize began the decay process with more radiocarbon than did the oak.

Fortunately, radiocarbon labs can correct this problem by measuring the ratio of ^{13}C to ^{12}C and using that value to normalize the resulting date on the sample. And this is why archaeologists should always try to identify the kind of plant that they are dating.

The Reservoir Effect

A second problem concerns the **reservoir effect.** Libby's method was based on the abundance of ^{14}C in the atmosphere, but some organisms obtain their carbon from sources whose carbon content may be significantly different from that of the atmosphere. Snails that live in lakes in areas of limestone will incorporate "dead" carbon (meaning that the carbon source is so old that no discernible ^{14}C remains) by incorporating the limestone's carbonate into their shells. If dated, a snail that died yesterday in such a situation can appear to be hundreds, or even thousands, of years old.

Similarly, this affects dating the remains of marine organisms that archaeologists find in coastal sites. Fish and shellfish take in carbon from the water, not the atmosphere. The ocean is another reservoir of carbon containing more "old" carbon than the atmosphere at any given time. Given that the radiocarbon method is based on an atmospheric standard, marine organisms also tend to date somewhat older than they actually are—by about 400 years, although the exact amount varies throughout the oceans. This creates an ancillary problem in dating skeletal remains of humans or animals who relied heavily on seafood, for their skeletons will reflect the isotopic composition of the foods they consumed—and hence they also would appear to be older than they actually are. Again, labs can correct this problem if they have background information on the sample.

photosynthetic pathways The specific chemical process through which plants metabolize carbon; the three major pathways discriminate against carbon-13 in different ways, therefore similarly aged plants that use different pathways can produce different radiocarbon ages.

reservoir effect When organisms take in carbon from a source that is depleted of or enriched in ^{14}C relative to the atmosphere; such samples may return ages that are considerably older or younger than they actually are.

Tree Rings Refine Radiocarbon Dating

In order to test the radiocarbon method, Libby had to calculate radiocarbon dates on material of known ages. He chose wood from the tombs of Egyptian pharaohs, because those burials were dated through documents. Although Egyptologists warned that the radiocarbon dates did not quite square with the historically derived dynastic chronology, Libby attributed this disparity to experimental error. But we now know that the effect is due to differential production of atmospheric ^{14}C over time.

The first investigator to find fault with the atmospheric assumption was Hessel de Vries of the Netherlands. In the 1950s, de Vries cut several beams from historical buildings and determined the age of the wood by counting the rings. When he dated the known-age specimens by radiocarbon assay, he found the ^{14}C dates to be 2 percent older than expected for the known-age wood. Scientists at the time generally dismissed the work, because the errors de Vries discovered were relatively small—just barely outside the limits of expected error.

But the spectre of larger errors finally inspired several radiocarbon labs to look more closely into the problem. In one landmark study, Hans Suess (University of California, San Diego) analyzed wood from bristlecone pine trees. Native to the western United States, bristlecones are the world's oldest living organisms (some living specimens are 4600 years old). Working from live trees to ancient stumps, investigators had already extended the bristlecone tree-ring sequence back nearly 8200 years (by the tree-ring technique discussed above). Suess radiocarbon-dated dozens of known-age samples and compared the results obtained by each method. When he did so, it became clear that significant fluctuations, now known as **de Vries effects,** occurred in the atmospheric ^{14}C concentrations. There were at least 17 such fluctuations over the past 10,000 years, produced, we believe, by pulses in sunspot activity.

This tree-ring research led to the discovery that the production of ^{14}C has not remained constant over time as Libby assumed. This is generally not a big problem for dates younger than about 3500 years; but it becomes progressively worse as we move farther back in time. In fact, a piece of carbon that gives a radiocarbon date of around 10,000 years is actually closer to 12,000 years old.

So the bad news is that *radiocarbon years are not the same as calendar years.* The good news is that we can fix the problem.

The fluctuations in ^{14}C are worldwide because the earth's atmosphere is so well mixed; studies made during aboveground testing of atomic bombs show that material released into the atmosphere is more or less evenly distributed throughout the atmosphere in a few years. We say "more or less" because Southern Hemisphere radiocarbon dates are 24 to 40 years too old compared with Northern Hemisphere dates (that is, a sample of carbon from South Africa will give a radiocarbon age that is 24 to 40 years older than a sample from Germany that is the same age). The land-to-ocean ratio is smaller in the southern than in the Northern Hemisphere, and this means that the oceans deplete the Southern Hemisphere's atmosphere of ^{14}C relative to the Northern Hemisphere. But 24 to 40 years is minor, and we can correct for it before calibration.

Using tree-ring chronologies from several places in the world, researchers have extended the calibration curve to 11,800 calendar years. Other methods push the calibration curve back even further, but they are still controversial. We can now convert radiocarbon dates into calendar dates through easy-to-use programs available online (by the way, this also takes care of the Cambridge/Libby half-life discrepancy mentioned above). And radiocarbon labs routinely provide the calibrated date along with the conventional radiocarbon age (see "Looking Closer: How to Calibrate Radiocarbon Dates").

In the Old World, calibration had an enormous effect. In areas where writing was invented quite early, historical records provide a firm chronology over some 5000 years. Radiocarbon dates for the Near East and Egypt were corrected and supplemented by independent historical records. Western European chronologies, however, lacked historical evidence and were therefore arranged according to radiocarbon determinations alone. Over the years, archaeologists interpreted these data as indicating that the early traits of civilization, such as metallurgy and monumental

de Vries effects Fluctuations in the calibration curve produced by variations in the atmosphere's carbon-14 content; these can cause radiocarbon dates to calibrate to more than one calendar age.

funerary architecture, were originally developed in the Near East and later diffused into Europe, first appearing in the Mediterranean region. Near Eastern peoples appeared to be the inventors, and the barbaric Europeans the recipients. This, in fact, was the conclusion that Oscar Montelius reached after he used the index fossil concept to construct European chronologies. In his day, the Near East was considered the "cradle of civilization."

Radiocarbon calibration changed much of that. Colin Renfrew (Cambridge University) showed that calibration shifted most European chronologies several centuries *earlier*, altering the temporal relationships between developments in Europe and those of the Mediterranean and Near East. Stonehenge, for example, formerly considered to be the work of Greek craftsmen who travelled to the British Isles in 1500 B.C., was under construction in 2750 B.C. and therefore predates even the Mycenaean civilization. Monumental temples were built on Malta before the pyramids of Egypt, and the elaborate British megalithic tombs are a full millennium older than those in the eastern Mediterranean. These "corrected" radiocarbon dates suggested that western Europe was not simply a passive recipient of cultural advances from the Mediterranean, and that the Near East was not the sole cradle of civilization.

Accelerator Dating: Taking Radiocarbon to the Limit

Some scholars see archaeology as an odd science because it progresses through unique and unrepeatable experiments. Digging remains our primary "experimental" method, and all archaeologists know that, as they dig, they are destroying data that no one has even yet thought of collecting. Before 1950, for example, archaeologists rarely saved charcoal—how could they have anticipated radiocarbon dating? This is why, today, we slowly excavate only that portion of a site necessary to answer a question, and it's why we compulsively save at least a sample of everything we find. We know that future technologies will allow us to learn things that we cannot even imagine now. New methods of radiocarbon dating demonstrate this fact.

Recall that labs obtain conventional radiocarbon dates by counting beta emissions. To do this effec-

TABLE 8-2 Recommended Sample Sizes for Radiocarbon and AMS Dating

	CONVENTIONAL (GRAMS)	AMS (MILLIGRAMS)
Charcoal	10–30	20–50
Wood	15–100	20–100
Dung	10–30	20–100
Peat	10–30	30–100
Seeds	n/a	20–50
Organic sediments	200–2000	2–10 grams
Bone/antler	200	2–10 grams
Shell	20–100	50–100
Pollen	n/a	15
Water	n/a	1 litre

Source: Beta Analytic Laboratory

tively, you need to submit a fairly large sample of carbon (see Table 8-2). Back in the 1970s, in fact, archaeologists sometimes said you needed a good "double handful" of carbon for a decent date. But often all we find are small, isolated bits of carbon; we can't simply combine them because we'd then risk combining carbon of vastly different ages—which will produce a standard deviation so large that the date may be useless.

The development of **accelerator mass spectrometry (AMS)** for radiocarbon dating in the 1980s changed this by drastically reducing the quantity of datable material required. Accelerator technology does not count beta emissions, as conventional technology does. Instead, it uses an electrostatic tandem accelerator and a technique known as mass spectrometry to count the *proportion* of carbon isotopes in a sample. Given that a single gram of modern organic material contains some 59 *billion* atoms of ^{14}C, a much smaller amount of material is required. In fact, AMS requires only a few milligrams of carbon—a sample about the size of a sesame seed.

accelerator mass spectrometry (AMS) A method of radiocarbon dating that counts the proportion of carbon isotopes directly (rather than using the indirect Geiger counter method), thereby dramatically reducing the quantity of datable material required.

Looking Closer
How to Calibrate Radiocarbon Dates

Let's calibrate the 6510 +/− 70 B.P. radiocarbon date mentioned in the text. We could calculate the calendar age simply by subtracting A.D. 1950 from 6510, given that B.P. in radiocarbon dating means "before A.D. 1950." This gives an answer of 4560 B.C. But recall that radiocarbon years are not the same as calendar years.

The first calibration curve used tree rings of known age that were removed one by one and then radiocarbon-dated. A curve was then statistically created to fit the resulting data points. From this curve, one can calculate a calendar age from a radiocarbon age. The figure shows a portion of the calibration curve and Beta Analytic's calibration of 6510 +/− 70 B.P. The radiocarbon age is on the *y*-axis, and the corresponding calendar age is on the *x*-axis. The black bar is one standard deviation on either side of the mean date; the clear bar is two standard deviations. To find the calibrated calendar age, draw a line from the mean date on the *y*-axis horizontally to the calibration curve, then drop down and intersect the *x*-axis. The radiocarbon date of 6510 B.P. converts to a calendar age of 5435 B.C., a difference of 875 years from the straightforward conversion. (We can convert the B.C. date to a calibrated B.P. date by adding 1950 to 5435, meaning that the tree that was burned to make our carbon sample died 7385 years ago.) By following the same procedure for the standard deviation, we can say that there is a 68-percent chance that the actual date lies between 5465 and 5345 B.C.—a span of some 120 years. That may not seem terribly precise, but for something that's over 7000 years old, it's about as good as it gets.

Some dates are more difficult to calibrate. The de Vries effects—those annoying "blips" in the curve—can cause a radiocarbon date to calibrate to more than one calendar date. Nonetheless, these dates are still "absolute" in that they point to a particular age range at a known level of probability. Sometimes those age ranges are large, sometimes they are small. Whether they are useful depends on your research question.

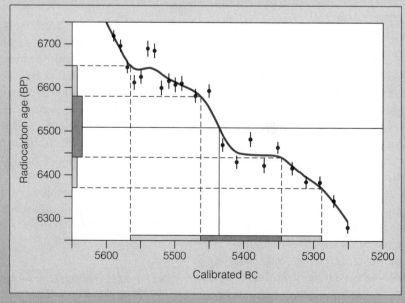

A portion of the calibration curve, showing how the radiocarbon date of 6510+/−70 B.P. is calibrated to a calendar age.

This new radiocarbon method allows archaeologists to test old ideas by allowing sites or objects to be dated that previously defied adequate dating. In some cases, AMS dating has corrected some significant errors. Following is one example.

How Old Is Egyptian Agriculture?

In 1978, Fred Wendorf (Southern Methodist University) and his research team made a remarkable discovery in southern Egypt, just west of the Nile River, in a series of small sites in Wadi Kubbaniya (a *wadi* is a dry stream drainage). The sites contained many stone tools (mostly blades fashioned from flint) and some large grinding stones. They also found the bones of fish, especially catfish and eel, and of waterfowl, wild cattle, hartebeest, and gazelle. They also found several hearths, from which they took some 30 charcoal samples that dated the site to between 17,000 and 18,300 years old.

None of the food remains were surprising in a site of this age. The evidence pointed to a hunting-and-gathering population that fished, hunted, and gathered plants along what was then a sluggish stream.

What was surprising, however, were four small grains of domesticated barley and one grain of wheat. In 1978, all evidence suggested that agriculture had begun about 10,000 years ago, far to the east in places such as Iran and Iraq. The evidence from Wadi Kubbaniya, however, suggested that agriculture in the Near East was 7000 to 8000 years *older*. This was indeed an important find.

But note that the few grains of wheat and barley were not themselves dated; instead, their age was based on their *association* with hearths that contained charcoal that was dated. In Chapter 7, you learned that objects, especially small objects like seeds, can move around quite a bit in archaeological sites. So the question was: Were the seeds deposited at the same time that the hearths were used?

Wendorf saw no obvious evidence that the seeds had been moved from a later level. But he knew that such evidence is often hard to see and that the best thing would be to date the wheat and barley themselves. But these small seeds, even if lumped together, would be too small a sample for the conventional radiocarbon method.

Wendorf is a cautious archaeologist, and he knew that his claim needed further testing. In 1978, AMS dating was just under development, but Wendorf knew that it could provide a test of the conventional radiocarbon dates. And so he submitted four barley seeds for analysis along with some charcoal from the hearths as a control (in fact, these were among some of the first archaeological samples dated with the new technique). As before, the charcoal yielded dates from 17,500 to 19,000 years old, but all the barley seeds were *less than 5000 years old*. The barley seeds (and presumably the lone wheat seed as well) were contaminants—seeds that had somehow worked their way down from a later level into an ancient site. Admirably, Wendorf quickly published a retraction of his earlier claim. Were it not for AMS dating, our understanding of the origins of agriculture might be quite different—and wrong.

By permitting archaeology to obtain reliable dates on extremely small samples, AMS dating also allows us to date objects that ethical considerations would otherwise prevent us from dating (see "Looking Closer: Re-Dating an Ancient and Controversial Tool from Yukon Territory"). AMS dating fulfilled the wishes of many archaeologists.

One wish, however, was not fulfilled. Archaeologists initially thought that AMS would push the radiocarbon barrier back to 100,000 or more years. Researchers keep trying, but for now AMS cannot reliably date anything that is older than about 45,000 years. For these sites, we need other methods.

Trapped Charge Dating

Those other methods are jointly known as **trapped charge dating,** which consists of three basic processes: thermoluminescence, optically stimulated luminescence, and electron spin resonance. Rare a decade ago, these techniques are increasingly common in archaeology today. Their age ranges are unknown, but they extend back to at least 300,000 years.

Their geochemical basis is complex, but we will keep the explanations simple. Working archaeologists need to understand both the potential and the limitations of these dating tools.

trapped charge dating Forms of dating that rely upon the fact that electrons become trapped in minerals' crystal lattices as a function of background radiation; the age of the specimen is the total radiation received divided by the annual dose of radiation.

Looking Closer
Re-Dating an Ancient and Controversial Tool from Yukon Territory

 AMS dating has changed our thinking about many important issues in archaeology, including the peopling of the Americas. In 1966, archaeologists made a startling discovery on the banks of the Old Crow River, in Canada's Yukon Territory. The artifact was found lying on the surface of the modern riverbed by archaeologist William Irving (University of Toronto) and paleontologist C. R. Harrington (Canadian Museum of Nature). The object had been made from a caribou tibia, and resembled tools that were used historically by First Nations peoples to remove the meat and fat from hides. However, conventional radiocarbon dates for the tool suggested that it was somewhere around 27,000 years old. At the time of this discovery, the vast majority of archaeologists accepted the Clovis tradition (11,500 years old) as the earliest identified culture in North America. The Old Crow caribou fleshing tool was significant because it suggested the existence of a much earlier, pre-Clovis culture.

The Old Crow River Basin is home to members of the Vuntut Gwitchin First Nation. For millions of years the Old Crow River has cut through the intermontaine basin, exposing fossil-bearing strata that date far back into the Pleistocene. Fossils and artifacts erode out of the basin and are redeposited along the banks of the Old Crow River. An area of the riverbank that researchers refer to as Locality 14N has produced the fossilized bones of a variety of mammoth, mastodon, and bison. Irving and his colleagues believed that humans had intentionally modified many of these bones. Some showed possible evidence of flaking, for example, while others seemed to have been split using large hammer stones. The caribou fleshing tool was somewhat unique in that it showed definite evidence of human manufacture. The "business end" of the tool had been whittled into the shape of a spatula using a sharp stone knife, and small notches had been carved along one edge to serve as "teeth."

Like many of the specimens recovered from Locality 14N, the fleshing tool was darkly stained due to chemical alteration. It seemed unlikely to Irving and Harrington that the flesher was recent. For one thing, the depth of the staining was comparable on both the worked and unworked surfaces of the tool, and chemical alteration made the tool far too brittle to use in its current condition. There were also few ethnographic examples of aboriginal groups using fossilized bone to make tools. Conventional radiocarbon dates of 27,000 B.P. +/− 2000 years on the fleshing tool seemed to support Irving and Harrington's claim that Old Crow was a pre-Clovis site. The dates were published in the prestigious journal *Science* in 1973, stimulating further multidisciplinary research in

The same principle underlies all three techniques: Over time, background gamma radiation (generated primarily by uranium, thorium, and a radioactive isotope of potassium) in sediment causes some electrons of the atoms of certain minerals, notably quartz and feldspar, to move to a different energy state. When this happens, some electrons are "trapped" in atomic imperfections in the minerals' crystal lattices (Figure 8-11). As time passes, an increasing number of electrons are trapped in this way.

Assuming that the radiation dose is constant over time, electrons become trapped at a constant rate. If we could somehow measure the number of electrons trapped in the crystal lattice, we would have an estimate of the *total* radiation dose the specimen has received over time. If we then knew the *annual* background radiation dose, we could calculate a specimen's age simply by dividing the first measure by the second. How might we calculate these values?

the Old Crow River Basin through the Northern Yukon Research Project.

Twenty years later, scientists decided to re-examine the caribou fleshing tool and other associated artifacts using AMS dating. The conventional radiocarbon date had been obtained using the inorganic or apatite fraction of the tool. Since the flesher had been dated, research has shown that the inorganic bone fraction is highly susceptible to diagenic exchange of carbon—meaning that the date could be faulty. Dating bone protein (proteinacious carbon) is now preferable. Unlike conventional radiocarbon dating, AMS dating techniques call for much smaller amounts of material. The original dating of the Old Crow specimens, for example, had required that the mammoth and bison bones recovered from 14N be entirely sacrificed. Luckily, the working tip of the caribou fleshing tool had been spared destruction for the purposes of museum display. Researchers removed a 0.3-gram sample from the tip of the fleshing tool using a clean miniature power saw. A weak solution of hydrogen chloride (HCl) was then used to remove inorganic materials from the sample. Finally, AMS measurements were made at facilities at Simon Fraser University and McMaster University.

Surprisingly, the AMS dates on the caribou fleshing tool revealed that it dated to 1350 B.P. +/– 150, making it almost 26,000 years younger than originally thought. AMS dating of artifacts at Local-

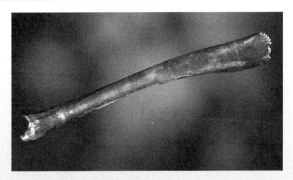

Figure 8-9 The infamous caribou fleshing tool recovered at the Old Crow site.

Source: © Canadian Museum of Civilization, S91-923

ity 14N has revealed that the evidence for human occupation in the northern Yukon 24,000 years ago or earlier is far from conclusive. Nevertheless, archaeologists such as the late Dr. Richard Morlan, of the Archaeological Survey of Canada, feel there are hints of the presence of humans in the unglaciated Old Crow Basin as far back as about 40,000 years ago. These sentiments are shared by the Vuntut Gwitchin, who believe that their ancestors have occupied the Old Crow Basin since time beyond memory, or the very beginning of time.

We figure the annual dose by burying a radiation-measuring device, called a **dosimeter**, in an archaeological site and retrieving it a year later. The device records how much radiation it was exposed to in a year's time.

To determine a specimen's total radiation dose, we need to measure the number of trapped electrons in that specimen. Obviously, you can't just count them. But several methods accomplish this task, and the three techniques are partially distinguished by the

methods used to determine the total radiation dose, as well as the kinds of material that they date. To understand *how* we can measure the total radiation dose, you must first understand *what* it is that trapped charge techniques measure.

> **dosimeter** A device to measure the amount of gamma radiation emitted by sediments. It is normally buried in a stratum for a year to record the annual dose of radiation. Dosimeters are often a short length of pure copper tubing filled with calcium sulphate.

In His Own Words

IsoTrace and the Use of AMS Dating in Canada

by A. E. "Ted" Litherland, University of Toronto

The IsoTrace Laboratory for radiocarbon dating grew out of a course in physics and archaeology aimed at third-year undergraduates at the University of Toronto given by Professors Ron Farquhar and Ted Litherland. In 1974, radiocarbon dating by beta ray counting was a highly developed science, using liquid scintillation counters or gas counters well shielded from the cosmic rays to reduce the background. Lecturing on atom counting for ^{14}C measurement, as a teaching tool, inevitably led to the question Why isn't this done? By chance, the low-memory high-current negative ion source, ideal for ^{14}C dating for atom counting, was just becoming available commercially at that time, and there were strong indications that the N^- ion was unstable.

The first successful tests on the degree of instability of the negative nitrogen ion and radiocarbon dating were done there in May 1977 and reported at a conference in France in late May. Atom counting turned out to be relatively easy for ^{14}C because it was found there was no sign at all of the ^{14}N ions using very much more sensitive equipment than was available earlier. ^{14}N ions have almost the same mass as the ^{14}C ions and are almost impossible to separate by mass spectrometry because they are many millions of times more abundant than the rare ^{14}C atoms. Nitrogen is the most common gas in the atmosphere.

At the University of Toronto, the idea of atom counting was supported strongly by the anthropologists and geologists, and so a proposal to build the IsoTrace laboratory was made in 1979. IsoTrace is an acronym for IsoTope and Rare Atom Counting Equipment. The generalization of ^{14}C dating to the measurement of other long-lived isotopes later became known as accelerator mass spectrometry, or AMS.

Dating using atom counting of ^{14}C demonstrates one of the great advantages of AMS when valuable artifacts are dated. The sample size needed is thousands of times smaller than for the beta ray counting method. In fact one-milligram samples of carbon, usually in the form of a graphite-like material, are all that is necessary to obtain a recent date to a precision better than ± 80 years and dates of material thousands of years old can be obtained with a precision of about ± 20 years.

Roelf Beukens of IsoTrace, and colleagues from Parks Canada, put the small sample requirement of atom counting to good use in dating the suspected Viking site at L'Anse aux Meadows, in Newfoundland. The archaeologists had found twigs at the site that had clearly been cut by metal implements. As the native peoples did not use metal at the time, this was considered to be key material for dating. Dating driftwood is not useful, as logs can float around the Arctic for thousands

The important thing to know is that electrons that are moved *out* of their orbits (that is, trapped) by background radiation are *returned* to their orbits by sufficient heat (500°C) or by exposure to even a few minutes of sunlight. Through the application of heat or light, the specimen has its clock reset to zero, so to speak, and the slow trapping process will begin again. So, strictly speaking, *trapped charge dating identifies the last time a specimen had its electron traps emptied.* Knowing this tells us how to apply the different techniques.

Thermoluminescence

Thermoluminescence (TL) measures the total radiation dose by heating a specimen rapidly to 500°C. Trapped electrons in quartz and feldspar crystals slip

> **thermoluminescence** A trapped charge dating technique used on ceramics and burnt stone artifacts—anything mineral that has been heated to more than 500°C.

of years, but twigs are not likely to survive for that length of time. Careful dating and the use of the best tree ring calibration of the radiocarbon clock gave a date of 997 ±8 A.D., which is quite consistent with the Norse sagas. As expected, other wood dates varied widely as driftwood is plentiful at the site.

Many radiocarbon dates in Canada are associated with the study of the rebound of the land after the ice had melted. This leaves shells and sea mammal bones on raised beaches, whose radiocarbon dates then give the age of the beach. However, the High Arctic has also been the home of several groups of people at different times, and Professor Max Friesen at the University of Toronto is studying their movements with the help of radiocarbon dating. One of the greatest controversies in the archaeology of the Canadian Arctic concerns the fate of the Dorset culture. Dorset peoples occupied the eastern Arctic before Inuit, the latter arriving from Alaska around 1200 cal A.D. Some archaeologists believe that

Figure 8-10 IsoTrace is located in the sub-basement of the McLennan Physical Laboratories, at the University of Toronto—about 10 metres underneath the walkway and the lawn on either side of it in the foreground of the picture above.

Source: Dr. W.E. (Liam) Kieser, University of Toronto

Dorset culture had died out long before Inuit arrived, however a suite of 12 IsoTrace dates on three sites from Victoria Island proved conclusively that Dorset had indeed survived there until at least 1200 cal A.D. Thus the two cultures, Inuit and Dorset, almost certainly came into contact.

free and move back to their orbits. When they do, they release energy in the form of light. Using special equipment, the lab measures the amount of light released as the specimen is heated; this gives us the needed measure of the total radiation dose. Like radiocarbon dating, trapped charge dating produces a mean date with a standard deviation.

Archaeologists have used TL to date ceramics. Imagine a ceramic pot, consisting of clay with some sand added to give the pot strength. The sand contains quartz and feldspar that have been slowly accumulating trapped electrons. When that pot is fired, however, those traps are emptied, and the pot's clock is reset. Eventually, the pot breaks and its sherds are discarded. Once those sherds become buried, the quartz and feldspars are exposed to gamma radiation and begin to collect trapped charges again. When the sample is reheated under laboratory conditions (a small portion of the specimen has to be destroyed for analysis), the intensity of the light emission measures the number

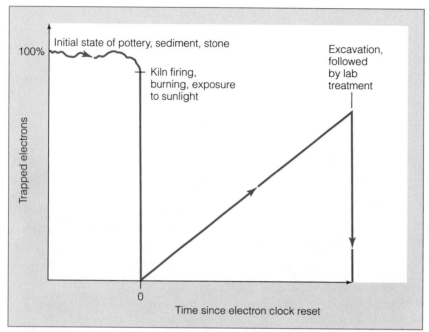

Figure 8-11 The process of setting an object's clock to zero in trapped charge dating. An object begins with some number of trapped electrons that is "reset" when the object is heated or exposed to sunlight. The object then slowly gathers more trapped electrons through time due to background radiation; its clock is again reset in the lab, where the number of trapped electrons is estimated to calculate the object's age.

of electrons that were trapped between the two episodes of heating—in the original fire and in the lab. The time between when a pot was fired and its burial is usually unimportant. (Museums use the method to detect ceramic forgeries, because TL can quickly distinguish between an ancient clay figurine and a 20th-century fake.) The method is also used to date burned stone artifacts, because heat resets the TL clock of the minerals in the stone. After the stone cools and is buried, its minerals are subjected to background radiation and electrons begin to be trapped again.

The artifact's context is therefore especially important, because what interests the archaeologist is the age of the artifact, which may or may not coincide with the events that trapped charge methods date. For instance, if a stone tool was accidentally burned 1000 years after its manufacture, TL will date the age of the

burning, not the age of the artifact's manufacture—and it is usually the latter that interests archaeologists. Nonetheless, by paying attention to context, trapped charge dating has the potential to rewrite prehistory, because it can date objects that radiocarbon cannot and because it can date objects that are beyond the range of radiocarbon.

For example, archaeologists Ofer Bar-Yosef (Harvard University) and Bernard Vandermeersch (University of Bordeaux) employed this technique to challenge our understanding of human evolution. The transition between **Neanderthals** and modern *Homo sapiens* was for many years based on the chronology of western Europe. There, *Homo sapiens* replaced Neanderthals about 40,000 years ago. But for various reasons, Bar-Yosef suspected that "archaic *Homo sapiens*" (called such because their skulls appear to be transitional between earlier hominids and biologically modern humans) appeared earlier in the Near East. Excavating the site of Qafzeh in Israel (Figure 8-12), Bar-Yosef and Vandermeersch found strata containing skeletal remains of archaic *Homo sapiens* along with stone tools, some of which had burned in hearths. Tests showed that these strata were beyond the range of radiocarbon dating and hence must be at least 45,000 years old—older than the western European counterparts.

But how much older? TL dating provided the answer. Dating a series of the burnt stone tools, Bar-Yosef found that the artifacts had burned some 92,000 +/– 5000 years ago, much earlier than the European chronology. The date's standard deviation might seem large, but note that it is only 5 percent of the mean date and, assuming that the tools were made by archaic *Homo sapiens*, it suggests that modern humans might be earlier in the Near East than in Europe.

Neanderthals (or Neandertals) An early form of humans who lived in Europe and the Near East about 300,000 to 30,000 years ago; biological anthropologists debate whether Neanderthals were in the direct evolutionary line leading to *Homo sapiens*.

Figure 8-12 The cave site of Qafzeh (Israel).

Source: Ofer Bar-Yosef

Optically Stimulated Luminescence

Another trapped charge dating technique, *optically stimulated luminescence,* is finding many uses in archaeology because it can date the most common material in archaeological sites: dirt. This technique relies on the fact that some of the trapped electrons are sensitive to sunlight as well as to heat.

Sand grains of quartz and feldspar have their clocks reset (referred to as bleaching) in a matter of minutes as they blow through the air and are exposed to sunlight; once buried, they begin accumulating trapped electrons again. *OSL therefore dates the time when the sands were buried.* Although OSL can be used on a variety of sediments, eolian sands are the best because they are more likely to have been sufficiently bleached by sunlight (and thus have their clocks reset) than alluvial sands.

Instead of measuring luminescence through the application of heat, OSL measures it by passing light of a particular wavelength over the specimen. This causes light-sensitive electrons to emit their own light as they return to orbit; the intensity of that light is a measure of the total radiation dose. This technique, by the way, requires some special handling, because the archaeologist must take soil samples in such a way that the samples are not exposed to sunlight—either by hammering a steel tube into sediments and capping it or by taking the sample in the dark under red light.

OSL offers enormous potential to archaeologists because it dates dirt itself, but we still have to be careful about contamination. Archaeology learned this lesson at Jinmium Rockshelter in Australia.

Named after a female character in an Aboriginal Dreamtime myth (who turned herself into stone to evade a lover), Jinmium Rockshelter is a lone block of sandstone that Native Australians used as a temporary shelter for thousands of years. While there, they painted its ceiling with pictures of kangaroos and other animals.

For years, all evidence suggested that people first occupied Australia about 40,000 years ago. And so the archaeological community was shocked when thermoluminescence dates on Jinmium's sediments dated them to as early as 175,000 years. What's more, red ochre, a stone commonly used to make red pigment, appeared in Jinmium sediments that TL dated to 75,000 years. If this date was true, Jinmium was the site of the world's oldest art!

But many archaeologists were skeptical, including Richard Fullagar (Australian Museum), who first dated the sediments. A new team, headed by Richard Roberts (La Trobe University), decided to try the then-new method of OSL on the shelter's sediments. Why? Simply put, some electrons have their clocks set quickly, after only a few minutes' exposure to sunlight. Others, however, require hours or even days of exposure. OSL measures the signal from the quick-bleaching electrons, and TL measures the signal from slow-bleaching electrons. This means that TL dates on sediments could be too old, because they might measure the signal from electrons that were not fully bleached—whose clocks were not fully reset—before they were slowly buried by the winds that carried sands into the shelter.

This turned out to be a problem at Jinmium Rockshelter. As the wind blew, the sandstone block eroded, grain by grain. Those grains had had their clocks reset millions of years ago. Deposited in the shelter's shade, the slow-bleaching electrons were not exposed to sufficient sunlight to have their clocks fully reset, and these contaminated the samples that the first team of archaeologists dated with TL. The problem is identical to combining carbon samples of different ages. Let's say that a hearth is really 1000 years old. And suppose that a burrowing rodent causes a 10,000-year-old piece of carbon to enter that hearth. If we dated a sample of the hearth's charcoal that contained both 1,000-year-old and 10,000-year-old pieces of carbon, the resulting date would be somewhere in between—and it would make the hearth appear to be much older than it actually is. The same is true with trapped charge dates on sediments: Even if only 1 or 2 percent of the grains in a sample were from the sandstone block, TL would produce misleadingly early dates.

So Roberts's team redated the sediments *grain-by-grain* using OSL. The OSL technique guaranteed that they were dating the last time the grain had its clock fully reset, and dating each individual quartz grain allowed them to discover some anomalously early dates. Grain-by-grain dating is the standard today, with a single OSL date actually being the result of 1000 dates on quartz grains from a single sample. Their redating, backed up by AMS radiocarbon dates as well, showed that human occupation at Jinmium was less than 10,000 years old, and the site's claim to fame in Australian prehistory fell by the wayside.

Electron Spin Resonance

Our final trapped charge dating method is **electron spin resonance,** whose primary archaeological application is the dating of tooth enamel.

Ninety-six percent of tooth enamel consists of the mineral hydroxyapatite, which contains no trapped charges when formed. Once the tooth is deposited in the ground, however, it accumulates charges from the background radiation. To measure those trapped charges, a portion of the specimen is exposed to electromagnetic radiation, which resets the electrons. In this case, the total radiation dose is proportional to the amount of microwave energy absorbed by the specimen.

electron spin resonance A trapped charge technique used to date tooth enamel and burned stone tools; it can date teeth that are beyond the range of radiocarbon dating.

potassium-argon dating An absolute dating technique that monitors the decay of potassium (K-40) into argon gas (Ar-40).

argon-argon dating A high-precision method for estimating the relative quantities of argon-39 to argon-40 gas; used to date volcanic ashes that are between 500,000 and several million years old.

ESR dating has also challenged our understanding of human evolution. As we noted above, the European chronology showed that modern humans rapidly replaced Neanderthals about 40,000 years ago. But when ESR was applied to tooth enamel of animals found in strata containing evidence of *Homo sapiens* and Neanderthals at Qafzeh in Israel, as well as at three nearby cave sites (Tabun, Skhul, and Kebara), the dates showed that *Homo sapiens* existed as early as 120,000 years ago, and Neanderthals as late as 60,000 years ago. This means that for a long period of time, perhaps as much as 60,000 years, modern humans and Neanderthals existed side by side—a different scenario than in western Europe, where they may have overlapped for much less time.

Trapped charge dating techniques can date objects that are beyond the range of radiocarbon dating. But we must remember that what we are dating is *the last time that the clock was reset*—by light in the case of OSL and by heat in the case of TL (neither seem to affect ESR measurements). Like radiocarbon dating, these techniques date accurately to a range of years, not a single year.

Potassium-Argon and Argon-Argon

Archaeologists have a variety of other radiometric dating techniques that, like radiocarbon dating, are based on the fact that radioactive isotopes decay at known rates. These include **potassium-argon dating** and its variant, **argon-argon dating.** *These techniques are useful for dating the age of the formation of a particular layer of rock itself.*

Because these radioactive isotopes have extremely long half-lives, they are useful only for dating materials that are hundreds of thousands or millions of years old—they cannot be used on rock that is less than 200,000 years old. For this reason, these are important dating methods for archaeologists who work in Africa and other places where early human remains are found. We will examine the particular method of potassium-argon dating, the technique used to establish the age of the Laetoli footprints (see Chapter 7), and its new variant, argon-argon dating.

Many rocks, including volcanic minerals, contain traces of potassium, which, like carbon, occurs naturally in several isotopic forms. One of these, potassium-40 or ^{40}K, decays slowly, with a half-life of 1.31 *billion* years, into argon-40 (^{40}Ar), an inert, stable gas—hence the name potassium-argon dating. By comparing the relative proportions of these potassium and argon isotopes in a sample, we can determine its age. As with radiocarbon dating, the principle is simple: The more ^{40}Ar in a sample relative to ^{40}K, the older that sample is.

For potassium-argon dating to work, there must have been no argon trapped at the time of rock formation. Like trapped charge dating methods, a rock's argon-accumulating clock must have been reset to zero such that all argon is the result of potassium decay. Fortunately, volcanic rock provides a comparable method for "zeroing out" the potassium-argon clock. During all major volcanic eruptions, high temperatures drive all gases—including ^{40}Ar—out of the microscopic rock crystals. Such episodes set the potassium-argon clock to zero, and all ^{40}Ar present in the ash today therefore accumulated since the ash was ejected from the volcano. In addition, all argon must be retained in the rock structure without loss to the atmosphere. Some rocks "leak" argon, and so care must be exercised in deciding which rock types to subject to potassium-argon dating.

This is why volcanic ash deposits are so useful. If an archaeologist finds human fossils or stone tools just *below* a layer of volcanic ash, the law of superposition tells us that the potassium-argon method will provide a *minimum* age estimate for the tools and fossils contained in the archaeological stratum below. Find fossils between two layers of volcanic ash deposits, and you bracket the age of the archaeological material (although you can't date the archaeological material itself). This is how the Laetoli footprints were dated.

The maximum age range of potassium-argon dating is theoretically the age of the earth. Although this method is not as precise as radiocarbon dating, its results are close enough, and it provides dates for some critically important early sites in Africa and elsewhere.

For example, potassium-argon dating was used to estimate the age of *Homo erectus,* an early hominid, in Asia. For decades, investigators believed that *Homo erectus* evolved exclusively in Africa, the earliest fossils being slightly less than 2 million years old (Figure 8-13). Then, sometime after 1.5 million years ago, *Homo erectus* expanded out of Africa, colonizing other parts of the Old World.

Thus, human paleontologists were shocked in 1971, when Garniss Curtis (then of the University of California, Berkeley) used potassium-argon to date the sediments associated with an infant *Homo erectus* skull from Mojokerto, Java. Because Java is a long way from Africa, most investigators thought that the Mojokerto skull should be much younger than a million years. But Curtis estimated that it was nearly twice that age—1.9 million years old. Most paleontologists rejected this extraordinarily ancient age because they were convinced that the only hominids in the world prior to 1 million years ago lived in Africa.

Both these early dates and the technique itself came under criticism. Although potassium-argon dating had been around for decades, the laboratory methods were cumbersome, and the process required a large sample that increased the chance for contamination (in a manner analogous to Jinmium's TL dates).

So Curtis teamed up with Carl Swisher (Institute of Human Origins, Arizona State University) to develop a new dating method. The argon-argon method simplifies the lab process and avoids the contamination problem by using small samples. The method works by irradiating the volcanic crystals. When a neutron penetrates the potassium nucleus, it displaces a proton, converting the potassium into ^{39}Ar, an "artificial" isotope not found in nature. The minute quantities of artificially created argon and naturally occurring ^{40}Ar are then measured to estimate the ratio of potassium to ^{40}Ar. This high-precision method also allows investigators to focus on single volcanic crystals, which can be dated one by one; thus, any older contaminants can be discarded.

In 1992, Curtis and Swisher used the argon-argon method to date some white volcanic pumice obtained from the matrix inside the braincase of the Mojokerto

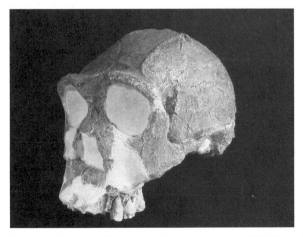

Figure 8-13 A 1.8-million-year-old *Homo erectus* skull (KNM-ER 3733, from Koobi Fora, Kenya).
Source: James Ahern

fossil. The result was virtually the same as the "old fashioned" potassium-argon date: 1.8 million +/– 40,000 years. These dates remain controversial, but received some support with the discovery of 1.75-million-year-old *Homo erectus* (some classify it as *Homo ergaster*) at the site of Dmanisi, in the country of Georgia. More to the point, dating techniques such as the argon-argon method will be increasingly important in evaluating fossil evidence in the years to come.

What Do Dates Mean?

These are just some of the ways that archaeologists can date sites—there are many others. It is important to keep in mind what materials the different techniques date, how far back in time they can extend, and what events the techniques actually date (summarized in Table 8-3), because these factors are necessary to answering the most important question of all: What do the dates mean?

We can never date archaeological sites by simple equivalences. The radiocarbon lab, for instance, takes a chunk of charcoal and tells you how long ago that tree died. By itself, this date says nothing important about your site. However, if we can show that the charcoal came from a tree used as a roof beam in a pueblo, then we have a date that matters.

In every case, you have to show that the dated event is contemporaneous with a behavioural event of interest—such as building a house, cooking a meal, killing a deer, or making a pot. We can drive this point home by examining a common issue of radiocarbon dating: the **old wood problem.**

How Old Are the Pyramids?

When most people hear the word "archaeology," they think about Egypt's pyramids (Figure 8-14). And with good reason: They are impressive structures, especially the three that stand watch over modern Cairo on the Giza plateau. One of these, the pyramid of Khnum-

old wood problem A potential problem with radiocarbon (or tree-ring) dating in which old wood has been scavenged and reused in a later archaeological site; the resulting date is not a true age of the associated human activity.

khuf ("the god Khnum is his protection"; often abbreviated to Khufu, or, in Greek, Cheops) is the largest in Egypt. Khufu began building his tomb soon after his reign began in 2551 B.C. Made of some 2,300,000 blocks of stone, each weighing an average of $2^1/_2$ tons, the pyramid measures 230 metres on a side and is oriented only 3 minutes and 6 seconds off true north. It contains several interior passageways and three chambers—one at the end of a tunnel cut into the bedrock deep below the structure. The burial chamber, in the centre of the pyramid, has several roofs above it; the Egyptians specifically engineered this roof to distribute the weight of the overlying rock outward and prevent the chamber from being crushed. The pyramid's exterior was originally covered in polished white limestone—making it a landmark that would have shone above the horizon for kilometres around (the limestone was scavenged by later pharaohs). At 146 metres, Khufu's pyramid remained the world's tallest building for 4440 years—until the Eiffel Tower was built in 1889! It is a remarkable piece of architectural engineering.

How old is it? The ages of the pyramids are based on historical documents—the hieroglyphs that cover the insides of tombs and temples (and that are found on papyrus used to stuff the bulls, crocodiles, ibexes, and other animals that were mummified and buried in the pyramids and other structures). The hieroglyphs give us the dates of the reigns of kings and document their accomplishments. The Egyptian civilization is probably one of the best dated in the world, and the pyramids on the Giza Plateau outside Cairo are among the oldest in Egypt.

But some speculate that the pyramids are actually thousands of years older, built by a civilization some 10,000 years ago. To check the ages based on historical documents, in 1984 a consortium of archaeologists, led by Shawki Nakhla and Zahi Hawass (The Egyptian Supreme Council of Antiquities), decided to date the pyramids through radiocarbon dating. But what could they date? The pyramids are made of stone, and the organic remains buried in them were often treated with tar and chemicals that make them unreliable for radiocarbon dates.

But Nakhla and Hawass knew of another source of carbon. Contrary to popular belief, the pyramids were put together with mortar. Workmen made this mortar by burning gypsum, apparently on the work platforms that were erected around the pyramid as it was being

TABLE 8-3 Summary of Absolute Dating Methods

TECHNIQUE	TARGET MATERIAL	RANGE OF ACCURACY	COMMENTS
Carbon-14	Any organic material; carbon is the most common.	To 45,000 B.P.	Requires calibration; calibration curve reliable only to about 11,000 years. Accelerator mass spectrometry permits dating of minute samples.
Thermoluminescence	Ceramics, burnt stone	Unknown, but perhaps back to 300,000 years	Dates the last time an object was heated to 500°C.
OSL	Quartz, feldspars in eolian sands	Unknown, but perhaps back to 300,000 years	Dates the last time sand was exposed to sunlight sufficient to empty the electron traps. Samples must avoid sunlight; lab must date individual grains.
Electronic spin resonance	Tooth enamel, burned stone tools, corals, shells	10,000 to 300,000 or more years	Dates when a tooth was buried. Electron traps reset by exposure to electromagnetic radiation in the lab.
Potassium-argon	Volcanic ash	200,000 to several million years	Dates the eruption that produced the ash. Needs large sample.
Argon-argon	Volcanic ash	200,000 to several million years	Dates the eruption that produced the ash. Needs large sample.

Figure 8-14 The pyramids at Giza.

Source: Charles & Josette Lenars/Corbis Canada

constructed. They mixed the resulting ash with water and sand and then slopped the mortar into the cracks between the massive blocks of stone. Inadvertently, pieces of carbon from the fires were caught in the mortar, trapped there for eternity.

In 1984 and 1985, the Egyptian's archaeological teams scrambled over the pyramids like ants on an anthill, looking for fingernail-sized bits of carbon. They found quite a few pieces, dated them using the AMS method, and then calibrated the dates.

They found not a shred of evidence that the pyramids were thousands of years older than the documentary sources indicate. But what they found still surprised them.

The radiocarbon dates on Old Kingdom (2575–2134 B.C.) pyramids were from 100 to 400 years *older* than the documentary dates suggested. And yet dates on later Middle Kingdom pyramids (2040–1640 B.C.) were not far off from their accepted ages. Why were the Old Kingdom dates "too old"?

The first explanation was the "old wood" problem: In desert (or high-altitude or arctic) environments, wood can lie around without decaying for a long time. In California's White Mountains, you can make a fire today from bristlecone wood, send a piece of the charcoal to a lab, and be told that your fire was 2000 years old. The wood is 2000 years old—but the fire that made the charcoal is not.

Egyptian archaeologists thought this "old wood" problem was unlikely. By Old Kingdom times, the Nile River valley had been occupied for millennia, and by a large population. Excavations near the pyramids reveal a community of stoneworkers, builders of the pyramids, that housed 20,000 people. All the Nile's people cooked over wood and used wood in house construction. And there is not much wood to begin with along the Nile; the floodplain is rich, but it's a narrow strip of green in a vast, treeless desert. For these reasons, the archaeologists postulated that there could have been no old wood lying along the Nile.

But perhaps Egyptians found another source of old wood. The Old Kingdom's construction projects at Giza were massive: three huge and several small pyramids, associated temples, boat docks on the Nile, the Sphinx, and the workers' quarters. These projects required massive amounts of wood—for construction; for ovens to bake bread for the workers; for levers, wedges, and sledges to move the stone blocks; for scaffolding; and for firewood to produce the mortar.

To get all the wood needed, it is likely that Khufu and other pharaohs raided older settlements or looted their predecessor's temples and tombs for wood—which Egypt's dry climate would preserve for hundreds, even thousands, of years. We know that pharaohs raided earlier temples and tombs for construction materials and jewellery. Perhaps for these Old Kingdom projects, they also sought out firewood. This may account for the early dates on Old Kingdom pyramids.

But then, why were the Middle Kingdom radiocarbon dates not "too old"? By Middle Kingdom times, Nakhla and Hawass reasoned, earlier construction projects had depleted the sources of old wood, and Middle Kingdom builders had to make do with the wood at hand—which would not have been very old.

The point here is that every absolute dating technique dates a particular event, but it is up to the archaeologist to decide how the age of that particular event is meaningful in terms of human behaviour.

The Check, Please

How an archaeologist excavates a site depends on several factors, one of these being cost. None of these dating methods is cheap. Right now, a standard radiocarbon date runs about $300 (including the $^{13}C/^{12}C$ calculation); an AMS date costs about $600. Bone dates can run as high as $850 per sample. Tree-ring dates are cheaper—the University of Arizona's Tree-Ring Lab charges about $25 per sample. TL and OSL dates may cost $800 a shot. There are no commercial rates for the other trapped charge and radiometric dating methods, but they have hidden costs. Because so much background data is required for their successful implementation, it is often necessary to finance a visit to the site by the specialist and to cover additional sediment and dosimetry studies.

Archaeologists try to get as many dates as they can for a site, but they always have to do so within budget limitations.

Dating in Historical Archaeology

As we pointed out in Chapter 1, historical archaeology is a rapidly growing subfield of archaeology. Sometimes, historical archaeologists work on sites whose

Archaeological Ethics
What's Wrong with Buying Antiquities? (Part I)

The small campsites of ancient arctic hunters dot coastlines throughout the Canadian North. During the 1970s, two 1000-year-old Thule Inuit culture figures disappeared from the National Museum in Ottawa (now the Canadian Museum of Civilization). Almost 30 years later, Dr. Douglas Stenton, Director of Heritage for the Territory of Nunavut, spotted them in a promotional brochure from an art gallery in Toronto.

The owner of the gallery had bought the two pieces from a collector, and had simply assumed that the deal they struck was legitimate. He had planned to sell the figurines for $4000, but quickly returned them to the museum after learning they had been stolen. Like the gallery owner, representatives from the Canadian Museum of Civilization were also shocked and embarrassed by the incident. In an interview with the *Nunatsiaq News*—an Iqaluit-based newspaper—a curator explained that museum security had been more lax in the 1970s, making thefts a more common occurrence. The curator assured the newspaper that it was unlikely such a theft could happen today, as security and collections management practices are now far stricter. What is truly amazing about this story is that Stenton was able to recognize and identify the wayward figurines. One clue that something was amiss lay in the fact that artifacts from the Canadian Arctic are generally quite rare on the antiquities market. Stenton also recognized the figures from photographs of finds made by Father Guy Mary-Rousselière, a well-known Catholic missionary who had conducted excavations for many years near Pond Inlet.

While there has always been a lively market in ancient artifacts, the Internet is now contributing to the problem. A recent search for Inuit artifacts on the popular auction site eBay revealed a posting describing "old Eskimo Inuit artifact tools" for sale. These objects included harpoons, spatulas, and snow knives (incorrectly labelled as "swords"). The artifacts were displayed in a glass-covered case and "guaranteed authentic" by the seller. Bidding started at US$16.95. The eBay site does have a policy designed to restrict or prevent the illegal selling of artifacts. The policy states that: "*Artifacts, cave formations (speleothems, stalactites, and stalagmites) and grave-related items that are protected under federal laws, such as The Federal Cave Resources Protection Act of 1988, and the Native American Grave Protection and Repatriation Act are not permitted on eBay.*" However, no mention is made of the antiquities policies of other nations, even though eBay is a site of international commerce. Regardless, the sheer volume of transactions that occur daily on eBay makes these policies practically impossible to enforce.

Why is it wrong to buy artifacts? Valuable information is lost every time an archaeological site is disturbed or destroyed for the purposes of selling artifacts. Archaeologists need to know where artifacts were found. As soon as a site is disturbed, this valuable provenience information is gone. Removing artifacts from sites without proper care can also damage or destroy them. Many provinces and territories in Canada have legislation that makes it illegal to disturb or loot an archaeological site. Strict fines and even jail terms await unscrupulous individuals who break the law. Buying artifacts is like buying drugs: The buyer is the only reason the business exists. And the business is the reason we are losing irreplaceable artifacts and information about the past every day.

Figure 8-15 These 1100–1170 A.D. Thule culture flat-bottomed figurines with human heads are made of sea mammal tooth.

Source: Werner Forman/Art Resource NY

ages are well known; for example, there is no question about when Jefferson's home at Monticello was built and occupied. But often they work on sites that are not documented, and these sites need to be dated.

Dendrochronology is sometimes used, but radiometric and trapped charge techniques are not. Even with small standard deviations, these methods are not sufficiently precise to be useful to historical archaeology. If we already know that a Spanish settlement in Florida was occupied sometime in the 16th century, a radiocarbon date on the site of A.D. 1550 +/– 25 would tell us that there is a 96-percent chance the site was occupied sometime between A.D. 1500 and A.D. 1600—and that's what we already knew.

For this reason, historical archaeology employs its own dating methods. These use documented changes in technology and styles of material culture to make fine-grained use of the index fossil concept and seriation. For example, before 1830, the metal fibres in nails ran crosswise to the nail's axis; after that, the fibres ran lengthwise. Examine the nails in a site, and you can tell if it dates to before or after 1830. Likewise, 19th-century glass often had a purplish cast, caused by sunlight reacting with magnesium oxide, but after World War I manufacturers stopped adding magnesium to glass. Purple glass is always older than A.D. 1917.

Often, this information is contained in industrial and other written documents. But sometimes, the archaeologist has to get creative. Kathleen Deagan knew that green and clear glass bottle fragments littered 16th-century Hispanic sites in Florida and the Caribbean and that these artifacts could be used as time-markers. The problem was that not a single complete bottle from this period survived anywhere. But rather than give up, Deagan turned to paintings, because bottles, it turns out, are frequently depicted in 16th-century Spanish art. By studying these dated paintings, Deagan constructed a chronological sequence of bottle forms. By reconstructing bottle forms from the glass fragments present on sites, she could use this chronological sequence to date the sites.

Pipe Stem Dating

One clever way to date Colonial-period American sites was developed in the mid-20th century by J. C. "Pinky" Harrington (1901–1998). Clay tobacco pipes and broken fragments turn up by the hundreds on many Colonial-era archaeological sites. These clay pipes held great potential as time-markers, because they generally broke within a year or so of their manufacture. And their shapes, decorations, stem lengths, and thicknesses changed markedly in the 17th and 18th centuries.

The difficulty in applying any of these observations to archaeological sites was that the fragile clay pipes rarely survived in a condition sufficiently complete to allow fruitful analysis. However, while working with the pipe collection from Jamestown, including some 50,000 small chunks of broken stems, Harrington observed that the early pipe stems had relatively large bores, which became smaller in the later specimens.

Measuring the stem hole diameters for 330 pipes of known age from Jamestown, Colonial Williamsburg (Virginia), and Fort Frederica (St. Simons Island, Georgia), Harrington found that the inside diameter changed through time. His resulting pipe stem chronology ran from A.D. 1620 to 1800 and was divided into five cultural periods. Fifteen years later, Lewis Binford reworked the original data to derive a statistical regression formula for estimating age from the size of pipe stem holes: $y = 1931.85 - 38.26x$, where x is the mean stem bore for a sample of pipe fragments and y is the projected mean date. By calculating the mean bore diameters of the pipe stems found in a site and plugging that value into the equation, we can come up with a pretty good estimate of the site's age.

Terminus Post Quem Dating

Dates in historical archaeology are generally of two types: They either define a temporal cutoff point (the site cannot be any older than a particular year) or they estimate a central temporal tendency (the site's "average" age). Let us explain how each works.

Kathleen Deagan and Joan Koch excavated an important cemetery named Nuestra Señora de la Soledad in downtown St. Augustine. They first classified the sherds into the various ceramic types commonly found on Spanish American sites. One such type, Ichtucknee Blue on White (Figure 8-16), is named for the surface decoration (blue designs on white background) and the Ichtucknee River in north central Florida (where the type was first recognized). The estimated age of Ichtucknee Blue on White ceramics ranges between A.D. 1600 and 1650.

Deagan and Koch could date each grave pit according to the concept of **terminus post quem (TPQ),** the date *after* which the object must have found its way into the ground. At Soledad, the TPQ indicates the first possible date that the latest-occurring artifact could have been deposited in that grave pit. So when a sherd of Ichtucknee Blue on White turned up in the grave fill at Soledad, excavators knew that this grave could not have been dug before A.D. 1600 (because Ichtucknee Blue on White did not exist before that date). Had the same grave pit contained a sherd of, say, San Luís Polychrome (with an associated age range from 1650 to 1750), then the TPQ date would be revised to 1650.

TPQ estimates the earliest possible date for the grave, based on the accuracy of the known date range for a particular artifact. When combined with the excavation data and documentary evidence about site usage, the TPQ estimates enabled Deagan and Koch to group the Soledad burials into three culture periods: 17th-century Spanish (TPQ: pre-1700), 18th-century Spanish (TPQ: pre-1762), and 18th-century British (TPQ: post-1762). Once this classification was established, they could look for cultural differences and similarities among burial assemblages: the Spanish-period burials, for example, were mostly shroud wrapped, whereas the British used coffins. The Spanish crossed the arms over the chest, whereas the British were interred with arms along the sides. Spanish burials were oriented toward the east, British toward the west, and so forth.

Mean Ceramic Dates

There is some disagreement about the utility of *terminus post quem* ceramic dating in historical archaeol-ogy. Many find the concept useful in providing a baseline for site chronology, but other archaeologists are less enthusiastic. They point to several complicating factors: for example, less is known about 17th-century Anglo-American ceramics, and status differences influence relative ceramic frequencies. In addition, there may be a considerable time lag between an artifact's date of manufacture and its date of deposition, making TPQ dating subject to gross error.

Stanley South (University of South Carolina) derived a provocative method to minimize these perceived problems. South's **mean ceramic date** approach emphasizes the mid-range or median age, rather than beginning and end dates for ceramic wares. Using Noël Hume's *A Guide to Artifacts in Colonial America,* South constructed a model based on selected ceramic types defined by attributes of form, decoration, surface finish, and hardness plus the temporal dates assigned by Noël Hume for each type.

Seventy-eight ceramic types were included in South's formulation. Canton porcelain, for instance, was manufactured between 1800 and 1830. The median date for this type is thus (1800 + 1830)/2 = 1815. Bellarmine Brown, a salt-glazed stoneware decorated with a well-moulded human face, ranges from 1550 through 1625; the median date is thus 1587. The mean ceramic date pools this information across a feature (such as a grave pit or house) or site to determine the median date of manufacture for each time-sensitive sherd and then averages these dates to arrive at the mean occupation date implied by the entire collection. Table 8-4 shows how South calculated the mean ceramic date for sediments filling the cellar of the Hepburn-Reonalds Ruin (North Carolina). The median date of each ceramic type is then weighted by multiplying each type's median date by the number of sherds found of that type. These products are then added and divided by the total number of sherds. Available historical records revealed that the building was probably still standing in 1734 and burned in 1776; the median historical date is thus (1734 + 1776)/2 = 1755. South's mean ceramic date came

Figure 8-16
Ichtucknee Blue on White plate: A.D. 1600–1650.

Source: American Museum of Natural History

terminus post quem (TPQ) The date after which a stratum or feature must have been deposited or created.

mean ceramic date A statistical technique for combining the median age of manufacture for temporally significant pottery types to estimate the average age of a feature or site.

TABLE 8-4 Applying the Mean Ceramic Date Formula to the Brunswick Hepburn–Reonalds Ruin

CERAMIC TYPE	MEDIAN YEAR OF MANUFACTURE	×	SHERD COUNT	=	PRODUCT
22	1791		483		865,053
33	1767		25		44,175
34	1760		32		56,320
36	1755		55		96,525
37	1733		40		69,320
43	1758		327		574,866
49	1750		583		1,020,250
44	1738		40		69,520
47	1748		28		48,944
53, 54	1733		52		90,116
56	1733		286		495,638
29	1760		9		15,840
Totals			1960		3,446,567
3,446,567 ÷ 1960 = 1758.4					

Source: South 1977a, Table 32. Used by permission of the author and Academic Press.

out to be 1758.4, only $3^1/_2$ years later than the median historic date. Moreover, the pipe stem date for this site is 1756, so substantial agreement exists among all three sources. In fact, South has found that the mean ceramic dates seldom deviate beyond a range of +/– 4 years from the known median historic date. Such agreement is nothing short of remarkable.

The mean ceramic date relies on two central assumptions: (1) that ceramic types are roughly contemporary at all sites where they occur, and (2) that the mid-range date of manufacture approximates the modal date of popularity. These are, of course, some fairly large assumptions, but the method still seems to produce useful age estimates on historical-era sites.

Conclusion

In Chapter 1 we pointed out that archaeology underwent a revolution of sorts in the 1960s. Walter Taylor's generation began that revolution in the 1940s and 1950s, but it was Lewis Binford's generation who brought about the transformation of archaeology. Binford, however, claimed that the widespread availability of absolute dating methods in the 1960s, notably radiocarbon dating, brought a huge change in how we do archaeology.

As you have seen, relative dating techniques helped to lift the fog of time that obscures the past. They were a significant advance because they helped to place objects and cultures into a historical sequence. Absolute dating techniques were an even more significant advance, because they could assign artifacts to a particular year or a specific range of years. Absolute dating techniques allow us to see not only the order of events, but the rate of change as well. Why did this permit Binford's generation to change archaeology?

One reason is that absolute dating techniques freed archaeologists to do other things with their data. Instead of spending time on seriation diagrams, an archaeologist could simply send a piece of carbon to a lab for a radiocarbon date.

But a more significant reason is that absolute dating techniques allowed archaeologists to control a major dimension of their data—age—in a more rigorous and absolute manner. Seriation was grounded in an often-unspoken theory of culture change—material items appear, grow in popularity, then disappear. No one knew, or really seemed to care, why this happened; all that mattered was that the technique provided a way to build a chronology. But for archaeologists to transcend chronology, they needed to know more. They needed to know how rapidly an item became prevalent, or how rapidly another replaced it. They needed to know how long a piece of material culture was used—50 years, 500 years, 5000 years? They needed to know whether an item first appeared in a particular region and then spread to others, or whether it had multiple centres of origin at the same time.

Relative dating methods could not answer these questions very precisely, and, in fact, relative dating methods tended to carry their own answers to them. Archaeologists relying on seriation, for instance, tended to see innovations as having only one centre and then spreading from there. They saw cultural change as gradual, rather than abrupt. Absolute dating methods permitted archaeologists to know when styles appeared, how quickly they spread, and whether there were multiple centres of innovation. These

methods opened the door to questions about past life-ways instead of focusing simply on chronology. This is why absolute dating techniques had a large effect on archaeological paradigms.

In recent years, technology has afforded us increasingly sophisticated ways to date artifacts, sites, and strata, and they show no sign of stopping. We can expect, then, that continual advances in dating methods not only will permit a greater understanding of the chronology of the past, but also will help create new paradigms, new ways of understanding the past.

Summary

- Contemporary archaeologists have a battery of techniques that can date objects of the past; these are divided into relative and absolute methods.

- Relative dating methods include use of index fossils and seriation. Called time-markers in archaeology, index fossils are artifacts with known dating orders that allow strata in different sites to be correlated; seriation refines this approach, placing sites or strata into a relative sequence based on changing frequencies of material culture. These techniques help understand the chronological order of culture change, but not the actual age.

- The advent of absolute dating methods helped usher in a new age of archaeology.

- Tree-ring dating (dendrochronology) enables archaeologists to establish the precise year of death for many species of trees commonly found in archaeological sites. This technique is limited to relatively small regions and in the American Southwest, where it is an important technique, dates only sites of the last 2000 years.

- Radiocarbon dating is a major radiometric technique that uses the known rate of decay of carbon-14 to determine the age of organics. It is useful for archaeological sites that are less than 45,000 years old.

- The atmospheric level of radiocarbon has changed over (at least) the last 20,000 years. Using correlations between tree rings and radiocarbon levels, archaeologists can calibrate dates—that is, convert radiocarbon years into calendar years—of the past 10,000 years.

- The accelerator (AMS) technique allows us to radiocarbon-date minute amounts of carbon.

- Trapped charge dating methods—thermoluminescence, optically stimulated luminescence, and electron spin resonance—date ceramics or burnt stone tools, eolian sediments, and tooth enamel, respectively. They date an object by calculating the amount of radiation an object was subjected to since the object's electron "clock" was last reset by heat (TL) or sunlight (OSL). These techniques date items tens of thousands of years old—beyond the range of radiocarbon dating.

- Potassium-argon dating and argon-argon dating are radiometric techniques used to date volcanic rock, especially ashes. These techniques are useful in places where archaeological sites are too old to use radiocarbon and trapped charge dating.

- Keep in mind that, by themselves, dating techniques tell us nothing about cultural activities. Radiocarbon dating, for example, tells us only when a plant or an animal died. In each case, the event being dated must be related to a behavioural (cultural) event of interest.

- Documentary evidence usually provides dates for historical sites. When such evidence is not available, known ages of particular artifact types can be used in various ways to create age-range or median ages for historical features or sites; these include TPQ and mean ceramic age dates.

Additional Reading

CANADIAN RESOURCES

Litherland, A. E., and Pavlish, L. A. (Eds). (2003). *Physics and Archaeometry, 2003,* Special issue of *Physics in Canada, 59* (5).

Nelson, D. E., Morlan, Richard, Voyel, J. S., Southon, J. R., and Harrington, C. R. (1986). New dates on Northern Yukon artifacts: Holocene, not Upper Pleistocene. *Science,* New Series 232, 749–751.

OTHER RESOURCES

Nash, Stephen E. (1999). *Time, Trees, and Prehistory: Tree Ring Dating and the Development of North American Archaeology, 1914–1950.* Salt Lake City: University of Utah Press.

Nash, Stephen E. (2000). *It's About Time: A History of Archaeological Dating in North America.* Salt Lake City: University of Utah Press.

Taylor, R. E., and Aitken, M. J. (Eds.). (1997). *Chronometric Dating in Archaeology.* New York: Plenum Press.

Online Resources

Visit *http://www.canadianarchaeology.ca/radiocarbon/card/card.htm.* The Canadian Archaeological Radiocarbon database (CARD) is a compilation of radiocarbon measurements that indicate the ages of archaeological and vertebrate paleontological sites in Canada, and other areas of North America.

COMPANION WEBSITE
Visit *http://www.archaeology1ce.nelson.com* to access a wide range of material to help you succeed in your introductory archaeology course. These include flashcards, Internet exercises, Web links, and practice quizzes.

RESEARCH ONLINE WITH INFOTRAC COLLEGE EDITION
From the Student Companion Website, you can access the InfoTrac College Edition database, which offers thousands of full-length articles for your research.

9

The Dimensions of Archaeology
Time, Space, and Form

A broken harpoon head sits on the
surface of a site in Canada's Arctic.
Source: Dr. Peter Dawson

Preview

I n the 19th century, archaeological sites were viewed as little more than mines in which to prospect for artifacts. But trained archaeologists, such as Nelson and Kidder, shifted their objectives to focus more on understanding the person behind the artifact rather than the artifact itself. And in the 1960s, archaeology further refined that focus, wishing not only to reconstruct what happened in the past, but to explain that past as well.

To achieve these objectives, archaeology analyzes how artifacts and features fall into changing patterns over space and time; this chapter shows how archaeologists identify those patterns. We first consider classification—the ways that archaeologists divide the many kinds of objects found into reasonable and useful artifact types. We then discuss the concepts of archaeological cultures, periods, phases, assemblages, and components—all of which are used to organize archaeological data into space–time systematics.

Introduction

The title of this chapter comes from an article by archaeologist Albert Spaulding (1914–1990), who pointed out that archaeology is about patterns in artifacts and features through time and across space. For example, the kinds of houses found in much of the American Southwest in 200 B.C. were semi-subterranean pithouses, usually round, and covered with heavy log roofs and a layer of sod. They were warm in the winter and cool in the summer. At the same time (200 B.C.), but in a different place—farther north toward the Great Basin—houses were more ephemeral, consisting of simple windbreaks or shade structures for summer houses and conical log structures for the winter. Returning to the Southwest, we see a dramatic change in house form around A.D. 700. At that time, many people made and lived in square, aboveground masonry homes—the familiar pueblos—rather than pithouses. Back in the Great Basin, however, people continued to live in the same sort of houses that they occupied in 200 B.C. Archaeologists have spent the greater part of the last century documenting such patterns in how material culture changes through time and across space; these patterns are what archaeologists seek to explain. How we go

about organizing data into meaningful spatial and temporal patterns is the subject of this chapter.

This organization is vital to the field, because archaeology's major strength is its access to tremendous quantities of time and space. Although many ethnologists study cultural evolution and culture change, they are restricted to short-term study if they deal exclusively with ethnographic evidence. And even if they include oral history or historical documents, ethnologists cannot go back in time more than a century or two. Archaeology, on the other hand, can address the entire complex history of humanity based on the things that people left behind, from 2.5-million-year-old stone tools in Africa to World War II destroyers on the bottom of Pacific lagoons. No other social science has so much time at its disposal.

Archaeologists also deal with worlds of "space." Many ethnologists study entire societies for years on end, but none can realistically employ the tools of ethnography to study an entire region such as the American Southwest, to say nothing of continents or hemispheres. So what archaeology loses in detail it makes up for by recording what the ethnologist cannot: patterns of human behaviour as they were manifested over vast reaches of space, far beyond the confines of a single community.

The goal of archaeology is to reconstruct and explain the past: What did people do, and why did they do it? But to reach this goal, we must first gain a firm grasp on artifact patterning in time and space. You must know the when and the where in broader terms before contemplating the how, the who, the what, and especially the why. Defining a spatial and temporal framework requires that archaeologists date the physical remains, classify archaeological objects into useful categories, and explore their distribution across time and space. In previous chapters we've discussed the fieldwork of archaeology. In this and succeeding chapters, we move into the other half of archaeology: the part that goes on after the excavation.

After the Excavation: Conservation and Cataloguing

Suppose that you've just completed a regional survey and have excavated a sample of the sites discovered. You did the survey and excavations by the book, dated the sites, studied the sites' formation processes, and so on. You've returned home with many, many carefully labelled bags full of bones, stone tools, ceramics, beads, and figurines. What happens to all the stuff now that the fieldwork is over?

The first step is to conserve the recovered materials. Once this meant little more than washing the artifacts off with water (but not things that water would obviously damage, such as basketry). But today, many archaeologists hesitate to wash some artifacts because even this simple operation might destroy some information. Stone and ceramic artifacts, for example, can contain pollen or residues of blood, plants, or other materials that can be identified and used to reconstruct tool use and diet (see Chapter 11)—but not if a scrupulous lab worker has thoroughly scrubbed the piece. In general, though, a simple cleaning is in order.

Other artifacts may require more attention, especially organic or metal artifacts recovered from wet deposits. Conservation on wooden artifacts recovered from the Ozette site (see Chapter 6) began as soon as excavators removed them from the muddy matrix, because wet wooden artifacts quickly crumble as they dry out. Richard Daugherty preserved Ozette's wooden artifacts by soaking them in vats of Car-

bowax—polyethylene glycol—melted and diluted with water. He needed huge vats to soak the houses' cedar timbers. Some of the artifacts, especially those made of hardwoods (which have small pores and soak up liquid slowly), had to soak for years.

And during an excavation near New York's Wall Street, archaeologists found several Revolutionary War–era cannons lying on the bottom of what was once the East River. The first task in preserving these artifacts was to replace the brackish water that had impregnated the metal with fresh water. Looking for watertight containers large enough to hold the bulky cannons, project directors Roselle Henn (U.S. Army Corps of Engineers) and Diana diZerega Wall (City College of New York) finally settled on metal coffins! The conservation of artifacts has become a significant specialty within archaeology.

It may also be necessary to reconstruct broken pieces. This is frequently done with pottery because ceramics are often found in pieces, and reconstruction obviously tells us more about vessel shape, size, and decoration. Piecing together a broken pot is like trying to put together a three-dimensional jigsaw puzzle where every piece is a different shape and there is no picture on the box. It requires a particular personality—somebody who can stay put for long hours—and a sculptor's eye. Some people can do this with ease, others are lucky if they get two pieces to fit.

The cataloguing procedure that actually starts at the excavation (and that we discussed in Chapter 6) continues in the lab after the field season is over. Every single item must be accounted for and its provenience retained through a catalogue. And the novice's first job in a lab is almost guaranteed to be cataloguing: writing all those minute numbers on artifacts or labels and entering the information into a database. This can take a great deal of time. In fact, for every week spent excavating, archaeologists generally spend three to five weeks or more cleaning, conserving, and cataloguing the finds. Sometimes it seems mindless, but cataloguing is essential because without the catalogue provenience is lost, and without provenience an artifact's value to future researchers is greatly reduced.

Archaeological Classification

Cataloguing and conservation are just the beginning because, at the end of those tasks, you are faced with thousands of artifacts that differ in terms of function, style, raw material, provenience, and condition. This is where the really time-consuming part of archaeology begins. Archaeologists spend far more time analyzing their finds than they do excavating them.

Archaeologists begin to get a handle on variability in artifacts through **typology,** the classification of artifacts into types. Even before cataloguing and conservation begins, an archaeologist will have begun to classify the objects. When things turn up in the sifter, the screener will sort the finds into simple categories of stone, bone, shell, ceramic, organic, brick, cloth, wood, metal, or some other category depending on the nature of the site. Sometimes, objects can't be identified and sorted in the field, so the on-site rule is always "When in doubt, send it to the lab."

In the lab, the catalogued artifacts are usually then further separated into even finer categories. The stone tool analyst might sort the stone artifacts into waste flakes and retouched pieces (flakes that have been chipped into tools) and then sort each of those into even narrower categories. Ceramics may be sorted into decorated and undecorated sherds, or into rim sherds (those that preserve a bit of the vessel's rim or mouth) and body sherds. And so forth.

But then what? How should you deal with all this stuff?

Here's a clue: The archaeologist's first responsibility is to simplify. Generations of archaeologists have found it unrealistic, even preposterous, to cope simultaneously with all the variability that turns up in even the simplest batch of archaeological objects. You could write a detailed paragraph on each artifact that you found. But although that might produce a wonderful descriptive catalogue, it would teach us little. Meaning lies not in endless data, but in patterns *within* those data. And patterns appear only when you isolate some aspect of the variation and ignore the rest (for the time being).

So you simplify to reveal meaningful patterns. Because archaeology's twin strengths are time and space, we first develop the categories necessary to reveal patterns in material culture through time and

space. Such patterning is known in archaeology as **space–time systematics.** And our first step in that direction is identifying types of artifacts.

Types of Types

Archaeology's basic unit of classification is termed a **type.** Be careful here, because "type," like "culture," is an everyday word appropriated by anthropology and reassigned a very specific, nonintuitive meaning.

Archaeologists can classify the same object in many different ways. Think about a familiar set of modern artifacts—say, a workshop of woodworking tools. Carpenters classify their tools by function—hammers, saws, planes, files, drills, and spokeshaves. But when insuring a carpenter's workshop, the insurance agent uses another classification, sorting these same tools into new categories, such as flammable and nonflammable, or perhaps according to replacement value: "under $10," "between $10 and $25," and so on. Should the carpenter relocate, the furniture movers will group these same tools into another set of divisions such as heavy or light, bulky or compact, or perhaps fragile or unbreakable. While storing the tools, the carpenter may classify them into "things my kids can touch" and "things my kids should not touch."

This discussion serves to make two important points. First, *types are abstractions* imposed by the archaeologist on a variable batch of artifacts. We saw in Chapter 2 how cultures classify the world differently. Dogs are considered food in some cultures, pets in others. There is nothing inherent in dogs that makes them "really" food or "really" pets. And there is nothing inherent in an artifact that makes it belong to one and only one type.

As we've said before, your analysis (and the types you create) will depend on your research question. Suppose, for instance, we wanted to learn whether everyone in an ancient society made pots, or if pots were made only by specialized potters. To do this, we might develop a way to classify pots into those made by novices and those made by experts, maybe by classifying pots according to the quality of their construction or painting. On the other hand, if we were interested in the household functions carried on in different rooms, then we might classify a site's ceramics into cooking vessels, water jars, serving vessels, and storage containers. We can classify the same object in many different ways.

typology The systematic arrangement of material culture into types.

space–time systematics The delineation of patterns in material culture through time and over space. These patterns are what the archaeologist will eventually try to explain or account for.

type A class of archaeological artifacts defined by a consistent clustering of attributes.

Do *not* think that our goal is always to classify things the way ancient peoples would have classified them. Archaeologists may divide stone scrapers into many different types based on their shape (to see if any could be useful time-markers), but ancient peoples may have recognized only two kinds: ones that were still useful and ones that were used up. Both classifications have their purpose, and both are valid.

And this brings us to our second point: We formulate a classification with a specific purpose in mind. Archaeology has no general, all-purpose classification. As Irving Rouse (Yale University) puts it, "Classification—for what?"

In Chapter 8, you saw one answer to this question: to create time-markers. At San Cristobal, Nelson sought distinctive types of pottery that he could use to assign strata or sites to a relative chronology. We began that discussion with some pottery types, such as biscuit ware and three-colour glaze pottery. Nelson was not concerned with the pots' functions, or quality, or anything else; he simply wanted to know if some types were earlier or later than other types. Another researcher might have a different purpose and create a different typology.

But where do such types come from? To answer this question, let's first consider three major types of types.

Morphological Types

Modern observers exploring the range of material remains left by an extinct group will encounter many unfamiliar artifacts. To make sense of the past using these remains, the first analytical step is to describe the artifacts carefully and accurately by grouping them into **morphological types.**

Emil Haury (1904–1992), an eminent Southwestern archaeologist, drafted one such description of some enigmatic stone disks (Figure 9-1) he recovered while digging at Ventana Cave, in Arizona:

> Discs—Of the twenty-four stone discs, twenty-two are centrally perforated. They were all made of schist, from 36 to 75 mm. in diameter and averaging 8 mm. in thickness. The customary way of producing them was by breaking and then smoothing the rough corners by abrasion. . . . Only one was well made. . . . Drill holes are bi-conical and not always centrally placed. Two were painted red. Next to nothing is known about these discs.

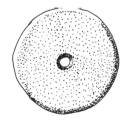

Figure 9-1 Two prehistoric stone disks excavated from Ventana Cave (Arizona).

Source: After Haury (1950:29)/American Museum of National History

Note that Haury did not speculate on how people used the discs; he simply illustrated and described the discs in enough detail so that other archaeologists could visualize the artifacts without having to view them firsthand. Such bald description is the primary function of a morphological type (sometimes termed a class in archaeological literature).

Morphological types have a second, basic property: They are abstract. Types are not the artifacts per se; they are the composite descriptions of many similar artifacts. This means that every morphological type must encompass a certain range of variability: several colours may have been applied; the quality of manufacture might vary; absolute size may fluctuate; and so forth.

Morphological types are purely descriptive. We ascribe no function to them at this point, and they don't necessarily have any chronological significance. No set rules exist for creating morphological types, although basic raw material (pottery, stone, shell, bone, and so on) is normally the first criterion, followed by shape. Morphological types help communicate what the archaeologist found without describing every single specimen.

morphological type A descriptive and abstract grouping of individual artifacts whose focus is on overall similarity rather than function or chronological significance.

Looking Closer
Harpoon Heads as Temporal Types in the Canadian Arctic

Harpoon heads are among the most important artifacts recovered by archaeologists working in Canada's Arctic regions. They are ubiquitous at many archaeological sites, and were used throughout the pre-contact and historical periods by Inuit, their Thule culture ancestors, and earlier Paleoeskimo groups. What makes harpoon heads so interesting is that their forms reveal much about *how* they were used, as well as *when* and *where* they were used. They also represent ingenious solutions to the challenges of hunting animals in open water and on sea ice.

Harpoons were multi-component technological systems designed so that the harpoon head would separate from the rest of the implement once the animal had been struck. The typical Inuit harpoon consisted of four basic components: harpoon head, foreshaft, socket piece, and shaft. The shaft was about 1 to 2 metres in length, and was usually fashioned from wood. If the harpoon was to be used for throwing, a socket piece was placed on the end of the shaft. A foreshaft was then inserted into the cup-shaped depression of the socket-piece, and then tipped with a harpoon head. This arrangement produced a loose and moveable fore-shaft that helped to ensure the separation of the harpoon head once the animal had been struck. "Throwing" harpoons were used to hunt seals and

other sea mammals in open water, or from the floe edge. If the harpoon was used for thrusting, a fixed or rigid foreshaft was used. With this arrangement, a slight backward tug was all that was needed to release the harpoon head once it entered the animal. Thrusting harpoons were used to hunt seals through breathing holes out on the sea ice. Most harpoon heads were drilled with one or two holes through which a line was fastened. Once the harpoon head separated from the fore-shaft, the hunter used this line to retrieve the animal before it sank or swam away. In some cases, a bladder was inflated and tied to the line so that the hunter could continue to track the movements of the animal if it submerged.

Because harpoons were so important to the livelihood of northern peoples, a great deal of time and energy was invested in their manufacture and decoration. The great morphological variability apparent in harpoon heads, for example, suggests that hunters were constantly experimenting with attributes that would increase their efficiency. In some cases, backward-facing barbs were used to ensure that the harpoon would remain firmly lodged inside the animal. In other cases, small spurs on the base were used to flip or "toggle" the harpoon head underneath the animal's skin. Some harpoons were self-bladed, while others had slots on their distal ends for inserting a small

Temporal Types

Temporal types are morphological types that have specific chronological meaning for a particular region. In other words, they are time-markers. If morphological Type B, for instance, occurs only in strata dating between A.D. 500 and A.D. 1000, then it can be elevated

to the status of a temporal type. This promotion is important because, when artifacts belonging to temporal Type B turn up in undated contexts, the time span from A.D. 500 to A.D. 1000 becomes the most plausible hypothesis for their age.

Functional Types

Functional types reflect how objects were used in the past. Functional types can crosscut morphological types. A set of stone scrapers, for instance, might have all been used to prepare hides (that is, they all had the same function), so they are a functional type. But some

temporal type A morphological type that has temporal significance; also known as a time-marker or index fossil.

functional type A class of artifacts that performed the same function; these may or may not be temporal and/or morphological types.

stone or iron endblade. There also seems to have been a great deal of variation in the number and placement of line holes. Arctic archaeologists have been able to use this variation to create typologies that organize ancient harpoon heads into discrete categories reflecting function, cultural affiliation, and time period. Let's look briefly at two examples.

The earliest sites in the Canadian Arctic belong to Paleoeskimo cultures such as Independence I (2300 B.C.) and Pre-Dorset (1800 B.C. to 700 B.C.). Paleoeskimo hunters entered the High Arctic with two types of harpoon heads: an open-socketed toggling variety, and a non-toggling variety (Figure 9-2). The toggling harpoon head had a foreshaft lashed into an open socket, which ended in two spurs. The non-toggling head ended in a conical spur, which was set into the end of the throwing shaft. In the Central and High Arctic, the non-toggling harpoon head was quickly replaced by toggling harpoon heads, although hunters in Greenland used both types. Pre-Dorset hunters utilized the toggling variety almost exclusively.

The Classic and Post Classic phases of Thule culture (A.D. 900 to A.D. 1600) are associated with harpoon heads that differ considerably from those used by Paleoeskimo hunters. The Thule Type 2 harpoon head, for example, is self-bladed, has two lateral barbs, and has a single asymmetrical spur on its base. The harpoon would have been attached to the foreshaft using an open socket at its base. The size and placement of the barbs suggest that they would have been easily broken. Therefore, it is likely that the Type 2 harpoon was intended for open-water hunting rather than breathing-hole hunting.

These and other harpoon heads are examples of *temporal types* because the groups of attributes that define them are restricted in time and space. However, their *morphological variation* also provides arctic archaeologists with valuable information about the lives of the people who used them.

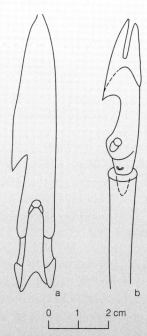

Figure 9-2 An open-socketed toggling Paleoeskimo harpoon (a) and non-toggling Paleoeskimo harpoon (b) from the Canadian Arctic.

Source: Schledermann, Peter. (1996). *Voices in Stone: A Personal Journey into the Arctic Past.* Calgary: Arctic Institute of North America, p. 50.

are big and others are small; some are thin and others are thick; some are made of chert, but others are of quartzite and obsidian; some are sharpened on the ends of stone flakes, others along their sides. But all these objects are the same with regard to their function. The remaining variability is (for now) irrelevant.

Functional types can also crosscut temporal types. Sometimes, pots are painted with distinctive designs for a limited period (like some of the pottery types that Nelson defined at San Cristobal). These distinctive styles of finish make the ceramics a temporal type. But all the differently decorated pots may be of the same functional type—they may all be cooking vessels, water jars, or seed storage pots.

Doing Typology

A good typology possesses two crucial characteristics:

- First, regardless of its final purpose, *a typology must minimize the differences within each created type and maximize the differences between each type.* If a lot of overlap and ambiguity occurs in the types, then they will not reveal any significant or meaningful patterning.

■ Second, the typology must be *objective and explicit*. This means that the result should be replicable by any trained observer. If it is not replicable, then your methods cannot be duplicated (and your work is therefore not scientific).

Once you've created your typology, you can focus on placing it in time and across space. The next section provides an example.

Paleo-Indian Projectile Point Typology in Southern Ontario

To show you how typology works, we're going to take you step-by-step through a classification of projectile points recovered from early and late Paleo-Indian sites in the Great Lakes Region of southern Ontario. Much of this will follow the work of archaeologists Brian Deller and Christopher Ellis (University of Western Ontario), both of whom have spent a great deal of time puzzling over the classification and interpretation of Paleo-Indian finds in this region of Canada.

The term "Paleo-Indian" refers to the earliest well-documented occupations of the Americas, which begin around 11,500 B.P. The archaeological remains associated with Paleo-Indian sites often have characteristic features, such as distinct artifact forms and raw material types. These attributes are used by archaeologists to group assemblages together, and are often taken to represent homogeneous social groupings, lifestyles, or ways of exploiting the environment.

Initially, it was thought that all Paleo-Indian groups shared a similar lifeway, focusing on the communal hunting of large gregarious animals such as caribou, muskox, bison, and mammoths/mastodon. These traditional interpretations, however, have been challenged by increasingly sophisticated reconstructions of past environments, which reveal that communal hunting was simply not possible in certain areas of northeastern North America. According to Deller and Ellis, archaeologists now recognize that the similarities apparent in Paleo-Indian assemblages reflect much more complex processes, such as group mobility, time allocated for certain tasks, and social interaction between groups.

Paleo-Indian archaeological remains were first discovered in the 1920s in New Mexico, in association with the remains of extinct bison. In the province of Ontario, Canada, isolated finds of Paleo-Indian projectile points were found as far back as 1906, when David Boyle included an illustration of one in an archaeological monograph. Of course, its age and significance were unknown to Boyle at the time. Most Paleo-Indian sites in Ontario have been found along strand lines and ancient beaches associated with pro-glacial lakes such as Lake Algonquin. These lakes no longer exist, having long since drained away as the great lakes such as Erie, Huron, Ontario, and Superior began to take shape following the end of the last ice age. While archaeological sites have been found in inland areas, most seem to concentrate along the edges of these earlier pro-glacial lakes. While this may reflect the biases of certain archaeological surveys, such locations would also have been rich sources of game, and provided easy access to fresh water. Furthermore, the winds blowing across these lakes likely afforded people relief from summer swarms of bugs.

The problem faced by archaeologists working in Ontario is that organic, and therefore dateable, materials such as bone are virtually absent from early and late Paleo-Indian sites. Paleo-environmental reconstructions reveal the existence of a boreal forest/sub-arctic environment during this time period, meaning that acidic soils appear to have broken down animal bone through chemical diagenesis. Equally problematic is the fact that most Paleo-Indian points have been recovered from single-component sites, rather than stratified sites where Steno's law of superposition can be used to assign relative dates. In the absence of radiocarbon dates and stratified sites, archaeologists have devoted much of their time to identifying temporal types (time-markers) that can be used to place Paleo-Indian artifact assemblages into organized frameworks. These frameworks provide a means of identifying and analyzing variation in tool form, and assemblage composition, across space and through time. As we will discuss in more detail later in this chapter, another term for this type of research is space–time systematics.

Choosing Criteria

Through their extensive archaeological research, Deller and Ellis have learned that Paleo-Indian projectile points were made from different types of stone, and that early and late Paleo-Indian groups in Ontario were very choosy about the raw materials they used. Many assemblages, for example, contain fine-grained cherts, some of which come from geological sources hundreds of kilometres away. Relying on non-local lithic materials meant that Paleo-Indian groups had to employ strategies to increase the transportability of the stone they used. The earliest stages of the **lithic reduction sequence,** for example, were often completed at the quarrying site to make the nodules easier to carry. Tools were also heavily re-sharpened and reworked, so that the working edges have more formalized shapes. Furthermore, these shapes appear to change through time. To illustrate, earlier points have a channel flake or "flute" that runs along the dorsal and ventral surface. They also tend to be lanceolate in shape, and have concave bases. The lower side edges of the point are also blunted through grinding, presumably so that the point wouldn't cut through the sinew used to haft (attach) it to the spear. Paleo-Indian points vary in other characteristics as well. The length of the point, for example, can differ because of the extent of re-sharpening, the skill of the manufacturer, and the type of raw material employed.

Defining Attributes

All of the characteristic features discussed above constitute *attributes,* which are measurable or observable qualities of an object. We could make an infinite number of observations and take an infinite number of measurements on a projectile point. There are no rules governing the number of attributes to record; in general, we try to use the fewest necessary to accomplish the purpose of the typology.

The two attributes of *size* and *concavity of the point base* are sufficient to create workable morphological types. But it is insufficient to just say "size" and "basal concavity." To define adequate attributes, we must explain precisely what we mean by the terms so that another observer could make identical observations.

Take *size.* We all know what *size* means, but it can be recorded in several ways. Measure the length of a projectile point and you know something about its size. The width also reflects size. Or you can weigh something to find its size. So, what size are we talking about?

Attributes that measure size, such as length, width, thickness, and flute length, are called *continuous variables.* When values are taken from a continuum, as with temperatures on a thermometer, they are defined as continuous variables. Attributes can also describe such things as shape, and are often measured using an indication of presence/absence. Such values are defined as *discontinuous variables* because they are taken from a defined set, as in "all spiders have eight

legs." Archaeologists working in the Great Lakes region have used continuous and discontinuous attributes to define three primary morphological types of early Paleo-Indian point types: Gainey, Barnes, and Crowfield. Figure 9-3 provides illustrations of these three types for you to compare.

Gainey Points

Gainey points are named after the archaeological site in Michigan where they were first encountered by archaeologists. They are the largest of the three types, especially in terms of thickness and base width. Gainey points generally have deep concave bases, roughly parallel sides, and a single flute. They also lack, or have only slightly flared, ears or "fish tails" on the edges of their bases.

Barnes Points

Barnes points are also named after a site in Michigan, where they were first discovered. They are small to medium in size, and fit between Gainey and Crowfield (see below) in terms of basal concavity, depth, thickness, and degree of expansion of the sides from the base. They have fishtails or basal ear-flaring, long single flutes, and have a maximum width at or just below the midpoint.

Crowfield Points

Crowfield points are extremely wide and thin, with shallow concave bases. Crowfield points lack fishtails and have slightly rounded basal corners. Multiple flutes are well executed—a remarkable feat, given the thinness of these distinctive points. The lateral edges of Crowfield points also expand from the base to a maximum width above the midpoint. Through re-sharpening, they sometimes take on a pentagonal, or 5-sided, appearance.

The attributes above have allowed archaeologists to group together and categorize various Paleo-Indian projectile points found in southern Ontario into these three morphological types. However, pay close attention and you will note that a trend is also reflected. As we move from Gainey to Barnes to Crowfield, morphology changes from large to smaller points with

> **lithic reduction sequence** A series of stages used by a flint knapper to sequentially remove flakes for the purposes of creating a finished tool.

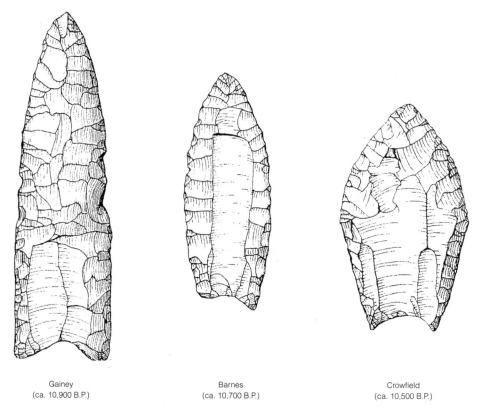

Gainey
(ca. 10,900 B.P.)

Barnes
(ca. 10,700 B.P.)

Crowfield
(ca. 10,500 B.P.)

Figure 9-3 Early Paleo-Indian point styles in southern Ontario.

Source: Ellis, Chris, and Deller, D. Brian. (1990). Paleo-Indians. In *The Archaeology of Southern Ontario to A.D. 1650*. Ellis, C., and Ferris, N. (Eds.). Occasional Publication of the London Chapter, OAS Number 5, pp. 40.

better fluting. These time trends have been noted in other areas of northeastern North America, where Gainey (ca. 10,900 B.P.), Barnes (ca. 10,700 B.P.), and Crowfield (ca. 10,500 B.P.) points have been found in reliably dated contexts. The fact that these *morphological types* represent different chronological time periods means that archaeologists can use them as time-markers, effectively elevating their status from morphological to *temporal types.* Consequently, an archaeologist who finds a Crowfield point in an undated context can infer that it dates to approximately 10,500 B.P.—the end of the early Paleo-Indian period.

Examining More Broad-Scale Changes in Projectile Points

Many of the stylistic trends mentioned previously continue into the late Paleo-Indian period in Ontario. Late Paleo-Indian (LPI) points, for example, share a number of attributes with early Paleo-Indian (EPI) ones, including a general lanceolate shape, absence of notches, grinding of the base and lateral edges, and excellence in manufacture. However, they also lack a number of attributes, the most important of which is fluting. The replacement of fluted with unfluted points occurs from west to east in North America, around 10,400 B.P. to 10,200 B.P. This timeline is based on the recovery of these point types in contexts reliably dated by carbon-14. Radiocarbon dates are generally lacking in the Great Lakes region for this transition, but many archaeologists feel that it occurred around the same time because of the presence of similar temporal types.

In addition to the loss of fluting, late Paleo-Indian points are now made on new types of raw materials, likely discovered by hunters as rock outcrops were exposed following the draining of glacial Lake Algonquin. As with EPI groups, a reliance on non-local raw materials means that the early stages of the lithic reduction sequence took place at lithic sources/quarries. LPI groups would then transport these cores and flake blanks to other locations for finishing. As a consequence, formal and highly retouched/re-sharpened tools dominate LPI archaeological sites located at some distance from these lithic sources. There is also an increase in variation in LPI projectile point forms, expressed across space and time.

Although many more specialized types have been identified, archaeologists working in eastern North America recognize two general classes of LPI points. These point types are illustrated in Figure 9-4.

Holcombe and Hi-Lo Points

The first of these classes includes thin points with concave bases, which expand from the base to the midpoint, or slightly above the midpoint. Holcombe points have shallow concave bases with small pointed ears, and rounded basal corners rather than fishtails. Instead of fluting, these points have short, often multiple, basal thinning. In many ways, Holcombe points resemble earlier Crowfield points, although they differ in their narrowness and absence of fluting. This has led some archaeologists to conclude that Holcombe

points developed directly out of Crowfield points, sometime after 10,400 B.P.

While Hi-Lo points are similar to Holcombe and other EPI points, they differ in several important ways. Hi-Lo points frequently lack tip impacts and are often extensively re-sharpened along their sides, suggesting their use as knives as well as spearheads. Hi-Lo points also appear to have been extensively recycled into a variety of other tool forms, including drills, gravers, side scrapers, and spoke shaves. Even though many of the distinctive attributes of Hi-Lo points seem to reflect their use as heavy-duty, multi-purpose tools, many researchers feel that there are enough similarities with Holcombe points to suggest that Hi-Lo developed directly out of Holcombe.

Lanceolate Points

The second class of LPI points is lanceolate in shape and lacks concave bases. They can be either stemmed or unstemmed, and vary in the degree of grinding and basal thinning, as well as in the degree to which their sides are parallel. Although rare in many parts of

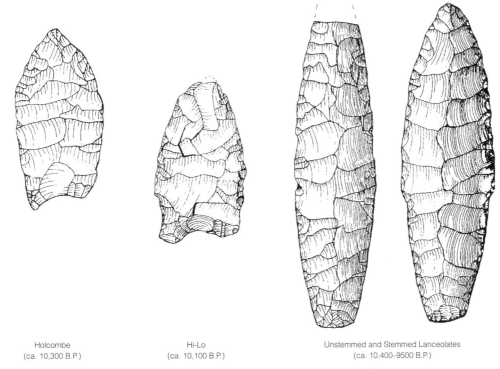

Holcombe
(ca. 10,300 B.P.)

Hi-Lo
(ca. 10,100 B.P.)

Unstemmed and Stemmed Lanceolates
(ca. 10,400–9500 B.P.)

Figure 9-4 Late Paleo-Indian point styles in southern Ontario.

Source: Ellis, Chris, and Deller, D. Brian. (1990). Paleo-Indians. In *The Archaeology of Southern Ontario to A.D. 1650.* Ellis, C., and Ferris, N. (Eds.). Occasional Publication of the London Chapter, OAS Number 5, pp. 40.

Looking Closer
The Frison Effect

Stone tools are important temporal types because they are ubiquitous in prehistoric archaeological sites. But stone tools are re-sharpened and, through re-sharpening, they not only become smaller, they also change shape. This can have an effect on tool typologies.

François Bordes (1919–1981) was a well-known French archaeologist whose groundbreaking research on stone tools influenced many archaeologists. (Bordes, a member of the French underground during World War II, also wrote several science fiction novels under the pen name of Francis Carsac.)

The stone tools found in Neanderthal cave sites especially intrigued Bordes. These assemblages, dating from 130,000 to 35,000 years ago, are referred to as *Mousterian,* after Le Moustier, the site where they were first found. Through experimentation, Bordes figured out how the tools were produced; using this information, as well as shape and inferred function, he divided Mousterian tools into 63 types, including a variety of points, scrapers, knives, handaxes, and denticulates (flakes with crenulated edges). He created this typology simply by laying out assemblages and then sorting them into morphological categories. This seat-of-the-pants typology was common in Bordes's day, though statistical analysis later supported his findings.

Bordes then looked at Mousterian sites and found something interesting: The 63 tool types co-occurred in set frequencies, creating four fundamental patterns. For example, the Mousterian of Acheulean Tradition contained many handaxes, denticulates, and backed knives, but only moderate numbers of scrapers; the Typical Mousterian contained few handaxes and backed knives.

Bordes found that none of the four assemblages was restricted in time; instead, they often seemed to alternate with one another throughout a site's strata. Bordes argued that the four assemblages reflected four different cultural groups of Neanderthals, just as different car and architecture styles reflected different groups of Europeans.

Bordes's typology did what a typology is supposed to do: It allowed Bordes to see a higher level of patterning that demanded explanation. Bordes's interpretation of the patterning assumed that the stone tools were in their final intended form. Different scrapers, for example, had different shapes because their makers had different ideas about what a "proper" scraper should look like.

But scrapers wear out, often quite quickly, and are rejuvenated by removing a few flakes along their edges. In the 1960s, George Frison (University of Wyoming) pointed out that stone artifacts can change their shape considerably over the course of their useful lives through such re-sharpening. Harold Dibble (University of Pennsylvania) decided to investigate whether the "Frison effect," rather than different mental templates, was responsible for at least some of the variation in Mousterian scraper types. Undertaking some experimental and archaeological studies, he eventually concluded that re-sharpening could account for some of Bordes's scraper types. For example, single-edge scrapers turn into "transverse scrapers" simply by re-sharpening.

Does this mean that Bordes's typology was wrong? Absolutely not. He saw and categorized morphological variation, and that process allowed him to see a higher level of patterning. Only his interpretation of the patterning may be wrong or at least incomplete, because some differences in tool form reflect not cultural differences but simply how heavily some tools were used. Strata with many transverse scrapers, for example, probably saw heavier use by Neanderthals than strata dominated by single-edge scrapers. Archaeologists proceed in exactly this way—they sort through variability, removing those parts that are explained by humdrum factors so that they can determine what are the more intriguing parts. Classification is an important first step in that process.

Ontario, these LPI point types are found throughout southern Quebec, northern New England, and the Maritimes, and may be more recent than Holcombe and Hi-Lo points.

Memorizing endless type names may seem meaningless, but dealing with these five descriptive names is many times better than coping with thousands of individual artifacts recovered from Paleo-Indian sites across northeastern North America. And that is the function of typology.

What Did the Typology Do?

In their studies of the early and late Paleo-Indian period in southern Ontario, Deller and Ellis used typology to organize jumbles of projectile points into groups based on measurable characteristics. But before the typology can be used to think in broader terms—those crucial dimensions of space and time—we must first ask if it has fulfilled the two necessary characteristics of typology.

Consider the first characteristic: minimizes the difference within and maximizes the differences between each type.

In the past, archaeologists accomplished this goal by simply placing artifacts on a table and sorting them into piles. However, most typologies today make use of statistical analyses (with names like cluster and discriminant analysis) that are designed to take a set of attributes and provide an objective measure of how well a typology accomplishes this goal. We've avoided statistical detail of EPI and LPI typology because it is beyond the scope of this book, but you can get a sense of where such an analysis might go by looking at Figure 9-5. In the graph, Gainey points (represented by triangles) and Barnes points (represented by circles and squares) are clearly different from each other—but why is this the case? Deller and Ellis used the attributes of length and width to infer that morphological differences existed between these projectile-point types. The formal shapes of each point type suggested to Deller and Ellis that they would change in different ways when subjected to re-sharpening. For

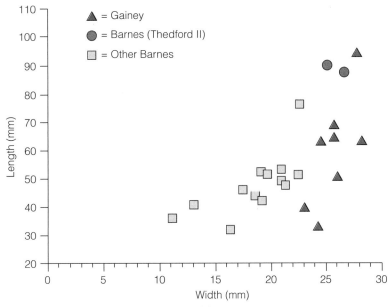

Figure 9-5 Plot of fluted point length by width.
Source: Deller, D. Brian, and Ellis, Chris. (1992). *Thedford II: A Paleo-Indian Site in the Ausable River Watershed of Southwestern Ontario.* Memoirs, Museum of Anthropology, University of Michigan, No. 24. p. 48, fig. 39.

example, a decrease in Barnes point width should occur as the overall length of the point was reduced. However, this trend should not be the case with Gainey points, as they are essentially parallel-sided. Deller and Ellis were able to confirm their inferences by plotting the attributes of length against width. Therefore, the typology meets the first criterion: it minimizes the differences within groups and maximizes the differences between groups.

The second characteristic was that the typology must be objective and explicit. The typology used by Deller and Ellis in their research actually makes use of many more attributes than simply length and width. By examining patterning in attributes, archaeologists working throughout northeastern North America have been able to organize the resulting projectile point types and their associated assemblages into flowcharts that illustrate spatial and temporal relationships among Paleo-Indian groups. To see how this typology is objective and explicit, let's take a hypothetically "unknown" projectile point and classify it according to the EPI/LPI criteria. For the purposes of this example, we have selected a sample of continuous and discontinuous variables (attributes).

Continuous Variables:
Length: 59.8 mm
Width: 26.1 mm
Thickness: 7.1 mm
Basal width: 25.2 mm
Basal concavity depth: 5.5 mm

Discontinuous Variables:
Position of maximum width: Roughly parallel sides
Fishtails: Only slight ear flaring
Pentagonal outlines: Absent
Shoulders: Absent
Pre-form tip preparations: Absent
Number of flutes: Single
Flute length: Shorter length

To type this point, a few definitions of these attributes are needed. Length is obvious, as are width and thickness. *Basal width* refers to the width of the point at its base, while *basal concavity depth* measures the distance from the centre of a line, drawn between the two ends of the point base, to its deepest point.

With respect to the discontinuous variables, most are also self-explanatory; *fishtails* refers to the flared ends present on some Paleo-Indian point types, *shoulders* denotes the projections found on the sides of points such as Crowfield, and *pre-form tip preparation* defines instances of deliberate tip narrowing, perhaps to permit the insertion of a device to aid in fluting the point.

The continuous variables for our unknown point indicate that it is fairly large, especially in terms of its thickness and base width. Our unknown point also has a deeply concave base. Turning to our discontinuous variables, the presence of roughly parallel sides, coupled with the absence of pre-form tip preparations and pentagonal outlines (a distinctive feature of re-sharpened Crowfield points), narrows things down further. Finally, our unknown point has a single flute of relatively short length.

If we use the EPI and LPI point typology discussed previously, it would appear that our mystery point shares more attributes with Gainey points than with any other point type. Using this typology, any trained student would classify this point as accurately as the most seasoned archaeologist. By using an explicit and objective typology, archaeologists know that, when they talk about a Gainey, Barnes, or Crowfield projectile point, each of them is talking about the same thing. The attributes we used are therefore objective and explicit. And that is what replicability is all about.

Therefore, the typology fulfills both of the essential characteristics: It sorts things using objective and explicit criteria into categories that minimize the differences within them, and maximize the differences between them.

Paleo-Indian Points as Temporal Types

We can further discern that our newly typed Gainey point roughly dates to between 11,000 and 10,700 B.P. This is because the morphological categories used in the EPI/LPI typology have been tested against independent evidence—specifically, other archaeological sites where identical point types have been recovered in securely dated contexts. Because the morphological categories of Gainey, Barnes, Crowfield, Holcombe, and Hi-Lo are restricted in time, they are elevated to the status of temporal types.

We began our discussion with the simplifying assumption that change through time reflects shifts in ancient peoples' "mental templates" for an idealized projectile point shape. Never mind what the artifacts meant to the makers, whether they were spear or arrow points, or how they were made. For now, we care only about whether some cluster of measurable attributes (which we call types) changed through time. This is why and how archaeologists have been able to create some projectile point time-markers for southern Ontario.

This is also why we must recognize that time-markers have distinct limitations. The trends identified in EPI and LPI point types show us what changes over time and what does not, which permits us to pose more interesting questions. For instance, although we now know that Hi-Lo points existed as heavily used, multi-purpose tools, we don't know why other point types weren't used in the same way. What are the functions of attributes such as fishtails and single versus multiple flutes? Do they reflect the stylistic displays of different social groups, the markers of competitive flint-knapping, or their use in different activities? Why were multiple flutes taken off Crowfield points, given that their thinness would have increased the likelihood of breakage during manufacture? All of these exist as untested hypotheses—yet they would have been impossible to deduce without first creating projectile point temporal types.

Space–Time Systematics

So far we have been talking only about the temporal dimension of archaeology, change in artifacts over time. We now shift and consider the spatial dimension of these temporal changes.

Americanist archaeology has adopted a relatively standardized framework for integrating the kind of chronological information just discussed into a regional framework. Gordon Willey (1913–2002) and Philip Phillips (1900–1993) initially set out this regional infrastructure in their influential book *Method and Theory in American Archaeology* (1958). Since then, the nomenclature has varied somewhat from region to region, some terms have been discarded because they reflect outdated theoretical paradigms, and others do not have quite the significance that they once carried. Nonetheless, the 50-year-old Willey–Phillips framework remains the most generally accepted system in the Americas.

Archaeological Cultures: Dividing Space

To begin, however, we must go back to before Willey and Phillips's day, to the early-20th-century concept of *culture areas*. Long before anthropology existed as a discipline in America, scholars recognized that not all Native American societies were alike. Some people were nomadic, others lived in large pueblos. Some hunted bison, others were maize farmers. Those in California relied heavily on acorns for their food; Northwest Coast peoples fished and hunted sea mammals. By the late 19th century, American anthropology had formalized these observations into culture areas (Figure 9-6), large regions defined primarily in terms of what people ate (which of course had a lot to do with the environment). The theory that attempted to explain these geographic patterns is no longer important to anthropology, but the culture areas left a legacy in that archaeologists who study the prehistory of North America tend to focus on one of these culture areas. They work on the Plains, or in the southeastern United States, California, or the Southwest.

Working with the prehistory of one of these regions, archaeologists quickly saw "sub-culture areas"—regions within a culture area whose material culture (such as house styles, settlement patterns, ceramics, or subsistence) differed from one another. These subdivisions of culture areas are called "tradi-

Figure 9-6 North American culture areas. Such areas were important to 19th-century anthropology, but are less so today.

tions," or *archaeological cultures*. Figure 9-7 shows the location of the three major archaeological cultures of the Southwest culture area: the Hohokam, Mogollon (*muh*-gee-own), and Anasazi. These three regions are distinguished from one another in terms of pottery and architectural styles.

However, these archaeological cultures are *not* the same as ethnographic cultures. If we could go back in time in, say, the Mogollon region and travel around, we would probably encounter several different languages, as well as different customs in different villages. In all likelihood, people in a village at the southern end of the Mogollon region considered themselves different from those who lived at the northern end. By drawing lines around areas on a map and labelling them archaeological cultures, we are simply drawing attention to spatial differences in the kinds of artifacts that are found in those regions. The *meaning* of these differences is another matter.

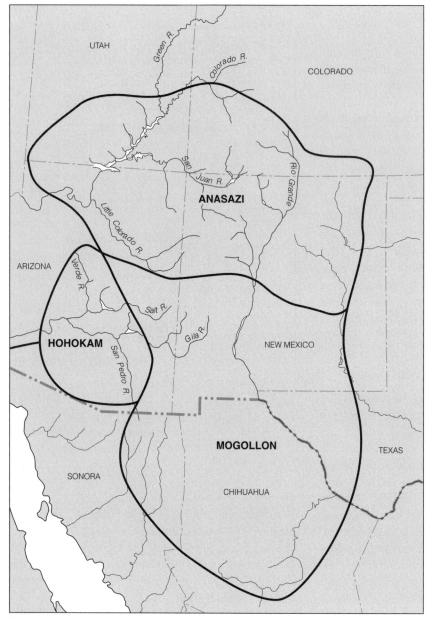

Figure 9-7 Southwestern archaeological cultures, or traditions. The theory that lay behind these areas is also outdated today, but the patterns that stand behind these traditions still demand explanation.

Source: From L. Cordell, *Prehistory of the Southwest*, p.15, 1984. Reprinted by permission of Elsevier.

Periods: Dividing Time

As archaeologists began to investigate the prehistory of regions, they also discovered that the Native Ameri-

period A length of time distinguished by particular items of material culture, such as house form, pottery, or subsistence.

can culture that ethnographers documented (and that formed the basis for maps of culture areas) had not always been there. The people who lived in the American Southwest some 5000 years ago, for example, were nomadic hunter-gatherers who never knew maize or built pueblos. As the chronologies of different culture areas were worked out, prehistory was organized into slices of time that were given different names.

Archaeologists divided prehistory into **periods** based on gross changes in easily observable archaeological remains, such as subsistence or house forms. These were sometimes labelled "stages," although that term is rarely used today (see Chapter 15). But the concept of periods is still used to organize archaeological thinking about time. For example, pick up a text on Southwestern archaeology and an early chapter will be on the "Paleo-Indian Period" (from 9000 to 5500 B.C.), a period of time in which the distinctive Pueblo archaeological cultures, such as the Mogollon, did not exist, and people were nomadic hunters of large game and gatherers of some plant foods.

The next chapter might be on the "Archaic Period" (from 5500 B.C. to A.D. 100). This is a time when people made heavier use of plant resources, began to develop distinctive region traditions in material culture, and experimented with agricultural crops, most notably maize. This may be followed by chapters that describe "Early Village" and "Pueblo" periods.

Major cultural transitions, such as the appearance of ceramics, settled life, or agriculture, were labelled *horizons.* These are analogous to (but should not be confused with) soil horizons and marker beds in that they form cultural "fault lines" that can crosscut archaeological cultures and culture areas. This kind of cultural horizon might have different ages in different regions. Maize, for example, was first domesticated in southern Mexico; over time people farther to the north adopted it, and it gradually spread to other people living still farther to the north. Thus, the agriculture horizon appears progressively later in time as we move from southern Mexico to the Great Lakes region (the northern limit of maize horticulture). This concept is not heavily used in archaeology today because of its association with an outdated evolutionary paradigm and because we now know that many transitions, including that from hunting and gathering to agriculture, were not as quick as the horizon concept assumed (see Chapter 15).

Nonetheless, like archaeological cultures, the concepts of periods and horizons helped to map out major spatial and temporal patterns in material culture. Periods and horizons record change over time; archaeological cultures record change over space. Knowing *how* and *when* material culture changed over time and space is an obvious first step toward explaining *why* those changes occurred.

Phases: Combining Space and Time

As archaeologists became increasingly familiar with the time-markers of a region, they observed that different regions in a culture area did not all change in lockstep with one another. Pottery, for example, may first appear at different times in different areas (forming a ceramic horizon that crosscuts different culture areas); likewise, from a common base, pottery styles may differentiate over time at different rates and in different ways in different regions. In other words, there are temporal and spatial changes in material culture of which periods and horizons were just first approximations.

A **phase** is a block of time that is characterized by one or more distinctive artifact types, a particular kind of pottery, housing style, and/or projectile point, for example. The phase has become the practicable and intelligible unit of archaeological study, defined by Willey and Phillips as "an archaeological unit possessing traits sufficiently characteristic to distinguish it from all other units similarly conceived . . . [and] spa-tially limited to the order of magnitude of a locality or region and chronologically limited to a relatively brief interval of time."

How do we construct phases?

Phases are defined by temporal types (like our Paleo-Indian points), items of material culture that show patterned changes over time. We have already seen how to derive temporal types: You group individual artifacts into morphological types, then test them against independent data (such as site stratigraphy, correlation with other known sites, or direct dating of the artifacts themselves). We recognize those types of artifacts that change systematically and observably through time as time-markers.

The next analytical step is to see how the time-markers themselves cluster to reflect site chronology. Here we have to define a few other terms that archaeologists commonly use.

Archaeological sites consist of **assemblages,** collections of artifacts recovered from some unit of provenience. We could talk about a site's stone tool or ceramic or projectile point assemblage. In this case, the provenience might be the site itself. We could also talk about the assemblage of a particular stratum in a well-stratified and carefully excavated site like the Stampede site (Chapter 7), where there could be many assemblages.

We might then analytically cluster these assemblages into **components.** A component is considered a culturally homogeneous unit within a single site. By "culturally homogeneous" we mean that, although the assemblages that go into a component might have been deposited during different years and by different individuals, they were deposited by people who were the same culturally. Some small archaeological sites may contain only one assemblage representing a single component; some could contain multiple assemblages that nonetheless still represent one component. Others

phase An archaeological construct possessing traits sufficiently characteristic to distinguish it from other units similarly conceived; spatially limited to roughly a locality or region and chronologically limited to the briefest interval of time possible.

assemblage A collection of artifacts of one or several classes of materials (stone tools, ceramics, bones) that comes from a defined context, such as a site, feature, or stratum.

component An archaeological construct consisting of a stratum or set of strata that are presumed to be culturally homogeneous; a set of components from various sites in a region will make up a phase.

Profile of an Archaeologist
A Cultural Resource Management Archaeologist

Figure 9-8 David Blower, Senior Archaeologist, Golder Associates.
Source: Courtesy of David Blower

David Blower is a senior archaeologist at an environmental assessment company in Calgary that provides cultural resource management services to western Canada, the Arctic, and the northern United States.

I began my archaeological career working in Ecuador and Peru. A rich archaeological heritage, mixed with the generosity of native peoples who were fascinated with "gringo arqueolgicos" like myself, made the experience an unforgettable one. I gained a lasting perspective on working in indigenous communities as an out-

sider, and learned that successful archaeology projects were built on mutual respect. My dissertation allowed me to pursue research questions that I found intrinsically interesting. Academic archaeology, however, is another kind of life with different expectations. . . .

In my early years as a cultural resource management (CRM) archaeologist I was often asked, "After working in South America, how can you work in CRM archaeology—and in Canadian CRM at that!" The answer is, "Well, there are many interesting places to work, but it isn't just the splendour of large-scale buildings, or the glitter of golden artifacts, that keeps archaeologists interested in doing their job." There is much more to "doing" archaeology than what can be seen on television; I doubt The Discovery Channel will ever do a show on a typical CRM archaeologist's day in the field. This is unfortunate, as it is just as exciting to find a single broken projectile point in a ploughed field in southern Ontario, or a scatter of lithic debitage in the oil sands of Alberta, as it is to stumble across monumental architecture in the jungle. The finds may appear to represent different scales of importance, but they don't. In many ways the methods and theories used in analysis and interpretation are quite similar, and the thrill of the hunt for information—and unlocking the secrets of the past—is just as interesting to archaeologists as the object itself.

may contain multiple assemblages representing several components. And some sites may be too badly mixed to sort out assemblages and define components at all.

Because defining archaeological components rests on the intangible factor of cultural homogeneity there can be no firm rules for their construction, but it helps if the strata are obvious from the stratigraphic profile, as at Gatecliff rockshelter in Nevada. Gatecliff's numerous strata of non-artifact-bearing silts separated the deposits into discrete living floors. During analysis, we could keep the floors dis-

tinct (as individual assemblages) or group them together on the basis of shared similarities. Although Gatecliff contained many living surfaces Thomas decided that it contained only five distinct cultural components, each incorporating the assemblages from one to six living surfaces. Components are thus site-specific—a given component is, by definition, from a single site.

Each component at Gatecliff is defined by its associated array of dates and its particular set of characteristic artifacts, including our much-analyzed pro-

CRM has made it possible for many archaeologists to work in their chosen profession after graduating with university degrees. Meeting the demands of development, within the parameters of historical/heritage resource legislation, requires a workforce of professionally trained archaeologists. The number of archaeologists making a full-time living at CRM is still comparatively small, but varies from province to province. Usually the CRM workforce comprises graduates with MAs and PhDs who fill the long-term positions as permit holders and project managers. Undergraduate students can also find work as seasonal contract workers. Obtaining a graduate degree, however, is key to long-term employment, as advancement potential within the profession is difficult without one.

I'd love to tell you that, as part of the job, my colleagues and I: a) collect more than our share of frequent flyer points, b) go to work in helicopters, c) drive expensive late-model trucks, d) get paid to drive ATVs, e) stay all-expenses-paid in hotels, and f) occasionally travel internationally, and it would all be true . . . but there is much more—or less, depending upon your perspective. For example, we spend 10- to 12-hour days walking through muskeg for two to three weeks at a time, occasionally winching ATVs from bogs, all the while looking for that high-potential landform where people may have camped or stopped to make stone tools, often never finding a single site. Many CRM archaeologists work alone; there are big jobs and smaller jobs, some with an expense account and some with only enough to get by. Not all CRM professionals work in a similar marketplace, and as such the types of projects, rates of pay, and financial support for fieldwork are not the same.

It's often said that the worst day in the field is better than the best day in the office. CRM archaeologists spend a lot of time writing reports and going to meetings. In fact, many spend more time on administrative duties than they do in the field doing archaeology. Once in the field, they live out of a duffle bag, eat more junk food than they should, and at times bemoan the fact that they are not at home leading a "normal" life. But it is on the best of days in the field that we hear the standard refrain: "They *pay* us to do this?"

CRM has its challenges, and rewards. There are trade-offs, and some might say that the smaller, independent-company archaeologists have more fun than their "corporate" counterparts who work in larger businesses; to each his own. We all work on parts of the bigger puzzle—and what is archaeology, if not looking for patterns and putting the puzzle together?

---

jectile points and artifacts such as incised slates and carved wooden pegs (used to construct snares to trap small mammals).

How do these observations help create phases? By comparing Gatecliff's components with those of other nearby sites we define the spatial and temporal range of particular artifact types, and from this comparison a regional chronology of phases is constructed. Briefly, assemblages (all items of one kind from one stratum or location) are grouped into site-specific components (differentiated in culture and in time). Components from nearby sites are grouped into phases. These building blocks therefore identify similarities across space and time.

To see how this works, consider the three hypothetical archaeological sites in Figure 9-9. These three hypothetical sites are located in the same geographic region—say, Montana. They have been carefully excavated and analyzed and, as is often the case, no single site contains the complete cultural sequence. The first site has Components A and B; the second site contains Component B plus a new component called C; and

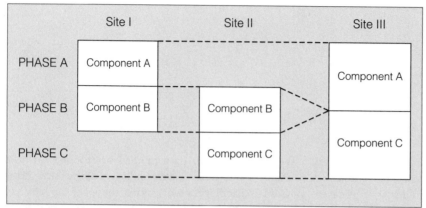

Figure 9-9 Relationship of archaeological sites to the analytical concepts of component and phase.

the third site has Components A and C but lacks Component B. By analyzing the temporal types shared among the components and comparing the absolute dates, a regional sequence of phases can be constructed from evidence at these three sites.

To give a more concrete example, archaeologists working in the central Great Basin divide the post–3550 B.C. era into five phases, each defined by one or more temporal projectile point types. You can see these in Figure 9-10, which shows how different morphological point types at Gatecliff sort out in time. These phases were defined on the basis of the analysis of assemblages from many stratified sites and the consistent association of particular morphological artifact types with particular spans of time.

For instance, the latest of these, the Yankee Blade Phase (named after a 19th-century silver mine in the nearby town of Austin) is typified by Desert Side-notched and Cottonwood Triangular points, as well as simple pottery. This phase began about A.D. 1300 and lasted until Euroamerican contact, about 1850 in central Nevada. The other phases were similarly defined, each composed of different kinds of artifacts (primarily projectile points) and spanning other episodes of time.

Phases: The Basic Units of Space–Time Systematics

The phase is archaeology's basic unit of space–time systematics, combining both spatial and temporal patterns in the material culture we dig up. Phases are defined by time, but also by space. There is no Yankee Blade Phase in Georgia, or New Mexico, or even Utah because the nature and tempo of change in material culture in these areas was not the same as in the central Great Basin. Even within the Great Basin, phases are not synchronous. Figure 9-11 shows some of the phase names used in the western and central Great Basin. Time and periods

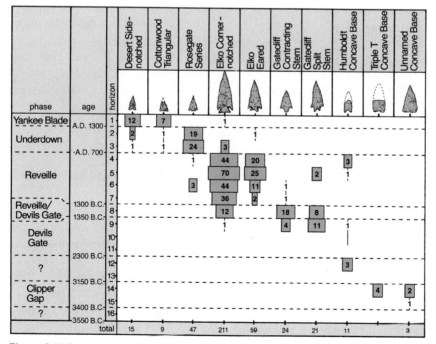

Figure 9-10 Relative proportions of selected projectile point types across the stratigraphic units of Gatecliff Shelter. Note how one or two extremely abundant temporal types deem to dominate most strata.

Source: After Thomas (1983b: fig. 66); Courtesy American Museum of Natural History.

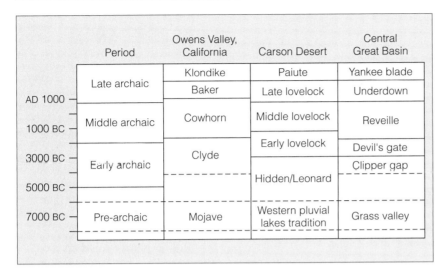

Figure 9-11 Space–time systematics: some of the phases used in three regions of the Great Basin, with period names. Dashed lines indicate phase boundaries that are not well dated.

Period		Owens Valley, California	Carson Desert	Central Great Basin
Late archaic		Klondike	Paiute	Yankee blade
		Baker	Late lovelock	Underdown
Middle archaic		Cowhorn	Middle lovelock	Reveille
Early archaic		Clyde	Early lovelock	Devil's gate
				Clipper gap
			Hidden/Leonard	
Pre-archaic		Mojave	Western pluvial lakes tradition	Grass valley

(Vertical axis markings: AD 1000, 1000 BC, 3000 BC, 5000 BC, 7000 BC)

appear at left, along the vertical axis; space appears along the horizontal axis. This diagram is one result of archaeologists' efforts to create space–time systematics. Each phase, or block, in this figure—Cowhorn, Early Lovelock, Grass Valley—is defined by particular artifact types that have particular temporal ranges in their particular regions.

We can see what the temporal boundaries are of, say, the Yankee Blade Phase, but you might be wondering where the geographic "edge" of the central Great Basin chronology is. At the town of Austin, in central Nevada? Or 160 kilometres east at Fallon in the Carson Desert? It's hard to say. Think of phases as analogous to pieces of a three-dimensional puzzle with very fuzzy edges. Neighbouring regions do not necessarily have the same phases, because they did not see the same progression of change in material culture.

The construction of phases allows archaeologists to synthesize reams of data into a series of (admittedly simplistic) time-slices that, in turn, can be compared and contrasted with similar schemes from neighbouring areas. They allow us to see, in a rough way, differences and similarities in the spatial and temporal scale of artifact change over time. Because we presume that artifacts reflect behaviour, phases are ultimately ways to track spatial and temporal change in human cultural behaviour. Phases are the first step toward developing ideas about regional patterns and trends—ideas that can be tested, refined, and expanded.

Phases can be as short as a few generations or thousands of years long. The length depends in part on the kind of archaeological remains involved and upon our contemporary knowledge of those remains. If pottery styles changed rapidly, then we can, with sufficient study of tightly controlled and well-dated stratigraphic excavations, develop short phases using seriation. Chronological control tends to be better for younger material, and so young phases tend to be shorter than old phases. One of the phases preceding the 550-year-long Yankee Blade Phase is the Reveille Phase, from 1300 B.C. to A.D. 700—some 2000 years. The Reveille phase is longer simply because the material remains used for its definition (including Elko series projectile points) continued to appear over a longer span of time than the remains used to define the Yankee Blade Phase (Desert Side-notched points, Cottonwood Triangular points, and pottery). Phases covering the most recent prehistory of the American Southwest may be only 25 to 50 years long.

The phase concept is vague, and deliberately so. Archaeology needs to impose a set of minimal units on time. The phase is that minimal unit. They allow archaeologists provisionally to define time, which is actually a continuous variable, as if it were a discrete set of temporally ordered points. When we discuss the Yankee Blade phase, we are treating the time span from A.D. 1300 to A.D. 1850 as if it were an instant. By definition, two components of the Yankee Blade phase are simultaneous, provided that "simultaneous" is understood to last 550 years.

But bear in mind that phases are always defined *provisionally*. As knowledge of the Yankee Blade phase expands, we may be able to recognize divisions within the phase—for instance, to distinguish an early Yankee Blade component from a late Yankee Blade component. When this happens, the initial phase is divided into *subphases*. This increasing subdivision reflects the amount of research accomplished on each phase and

Archaeological Ethics
What's Wrong with Buying Antiquities (Part II)?

 In Chapter 8, we argued that the buying and selling of artifacts promotes the destruction of archaeological sites. Like most archaeologists, we don't have a problem with the weekend collector who picks up arrowheads. Frankly, we'd rather they didn't do it, but we know that most of these people are well intentioned and not responsible for the massive loss of data that professional looting causes. We also understand that professional archaeologists don't "own" the past.

But there is another side to this. The serious collectors, the ones willing to shell out thousands of dollars for Mimbres pots or Etruscan statues, argue that if it were not for them, many of the world's treasures would never be recovered at all. Should we, they ask, let wonderful pieces of ancient art lie beneath the ground, not to be excavated until archaeologists get the time and funding? Given that archaeologists have to dig so slowly, that will take centuries! And in the meantime, aren't those pieces in harm's way, from the ravages of time and other countries' lax antiquities laws?

Wouldn't it be preferable, some collectors ask, to recover artifacts now, quickly, so that they do not deteriorate any more than they already have, and get them out where they can be enjoyed by people? The latter rings hollow if those precious objects are displayed only in a person's home or locked away in a private vault. But collectors counter that many private collections eventually end up in public museums. Indeed, they point out that the world's major museums own objects that were originally gathered by private collectors, at a collector's own expense. And they are right (look at the Parthenon marbles). Thus, collectors argue that any archaeologist who is proud of a museum but who criticizes collecting is a hypocrite.

We disagree. Had there been professional archaeologists around when Lord Elgin was removing the Parthenon's marbles, we'd like to think they would have raised hell about it. In addition, the needs of archaeology today are different than those of the past. Remember that for archaeologists today an artifact's provenience is as important as, if not more important than, the artifact itself. Looters don't record context, and so there is a big difference between 19th-century collecting and 21st-century looting.

This point was driven home on April 11, 2003, a few days after the U.S. military entered Baghdad. Although the Pentagon had assured several professional organizations that Iraqi cultural institutions would be protected, they left the Baghdad Museum unguarded, and it was looted. Some artifacts were wantonly smashed, and the computer and paper records were partially destroyed. Initially, the media reported that some 170,000 artifacts were stolen, but it turns out that museum personnel moved many of the museum's more significant items to safer locations in anticipation of the war. They moved gold artifacts, for example, to a bank vault.

underscores the degree to which our knowledge of the archaeological record is a contemporary phenomenon. This is why we leave the concept of phase vague, so that it can accommodate new findings and help us learn more, rather than place blinders on our ability to see new patterns in prehistory.

Conclusion: Space–Time Systematics and Archaeological Objectives

We began this chapter by pointing out that this search for patterning falls along three dimensions: space, time, and form (of artifacts). And this search leads to the construction of space–time systematics, a simplification of

An investigation headed by Colonel Matthew Bogdanos, USMC, concluded that 40 items were stolen from the main galleries, including the 4300-year-old Bassetki statue and the heads of Roman-era statues, as well as 3138 items from the old storage rooms and 10,337 items from a basement storage room. As of January, 2004, 4302 items had been returned, most through an amnesty program, but others were recovered through raids or customs inspections in Iraq, Jordan, Italy, Great Britain, and the United States. Some of these items were outside of Iraq within days of their theft.

Bogdanos's investigation found that some of the thieves did not know what they were doing. For example, the thieves took an entire shelf of fakes but overlooked some nearby genuine artifacts. Perhaps military personnel who, Bogdanos's evidence showed, used the museum as a firing position did some of this looting.

But the investigation also showed the presence of thieves with intimate knowledge of the museum. And they had inside help, given that some locked storage areas were opened with keys. These thieves were selective in what they took from the galleries, forgoing beautiful replicas for the most valuable genuine pieces. In the looted basement storage room, for example, the only room entered was that containing a huge collection of ancient gold and silver coins. Fortunately for Iraq, the thieves apparently dropped the keys to the cabinets and lost them in the unlit room (the electricity was off by this time; Bogdanos found the keys after hours of searching). The looters lit a fire in a desperate effort to find the keys, but they apparently only had time to abscond with the contents of 103 small plastic boxes that contained nearly 10,000 cylinder seals, pins, beads, pendants, and necklaces. The artifacts taken were so selective that many believe that, although the looting was carried out by Iraqis, it was orchestrated by wealthy, unscrupulous buyers in Europe, Japan, or the United States.

Other Iraqi museums were also hit, and archaeological sites were attacked by armed looters. Although some called for a "shoot first, ask questions later" approach to looters, one can hardly blame a poverty-stricken Iraqi farmer for exploiting an opportunity to make 10 years' worth of wages in a night of digging. Instead, it's the wealthy buyers in developed nations who are to blame. They are the ones that drive this destruction, who encourage a country to rob itself of its cultural patrimony and to destroy irreplaceable records of human history.

Iraq is a stark reminder of what is wrong with buying antiquities. If collectors truly wish to see the world's heritage protected (and do not simply want to add to their personal collections), then they should turn their financial resources to aiding those countries that need assistance in discovering, protecting, and displaying their cultural heritage.

the enormous variation in material culture over time and space into some meaningful patterns. You now have some sense of how we go about doing that. But the construction of space–time systematics is not the goal of archaeology, it is the means to an end. The goals of archaeology are to reconstruct and explain the past. How do space–time systematics help accomplish these goals?

Let us look at the case of Shoshone pottery to answer this question (Figure 9-12). Shoshone ceramics appear suddenly in many parts of the Desert West about A.D. 1300 (forming a ceramic horizon), and the Shoshone people made similar pottery until about 1860. Shoshone pottery thus implies certain limits: time (A.D. 1300–1860, the Yankee Blade Phase in the central Great Basin) and space (the Desert West).

With its temporal parameters estimated, Shoshone pottery becomes a useful time-marker. Sites containing

Figure 9-12 Shoshone ceramic vessel.

Source: Donald R. Tuohy/Nevada State Museum

these potsherds in the Desert West can be provisionally assigned to the A.D. 1300 to 1860 interval.

But we are nowhere near finished. In fact, we have just begun, for Shoshone pottery, taken as a time-marker, leaves many more questions unanswered. Was this pottery introduced by migrating Shoshone-speaking peoples? Or did the idea of pottery simply spread across the Desert West? Did the various peoples of the Desert West independently invent the idea of pottery? Or were the vessels traded in from neighbouring ceramic-manufacturing areas?

Each is a research question that could inspire years of investigation: Is it possible to document a population movement across the Desert West at A.D. 1300? If so, where did these newcomers come from? And what happened to the pre–A.D. 1300 inhabitants of the Desert West? Are there signs of trading activity or warfare in A.D. 1300?

Questions like this can pile up without end. Although we cannot reconstruct what happened in the past by looking only at time-markers, we also don't even know the relevant questions to ask or hypotheses to test until we know something about the when and the where of the past.

And reconstructing *what* happened in the past is itself but one step in the process. As we pointed out in Chapter 1, archaeologists today are equally interested in *why* prehistory took the particular courses that it did; we are interested in explaining the past as well as in reconstructing it. The time-marker Shoshone pottery tells us that distinctive potsherds occur in archaeological deposits dating from A.D. 1300 to A.D. 1860 across the Desert West. But viewed as a time-marker, Shoshone pottery tells us nothing about *why* pottery was introduced in A.D. 1300. For some reason, one segment of the Desert West cultural system changed, and people began manufacturing pottery. This complex issue can be studied only by pursuing related shifts in the lifeway, drawing evidence from the settlement pattern and demography, cultural ecology, social organization, and religion.

For example, let's say that we eventually conclude through research that the pottery was introduced through a migrating Shoshone population. The next question would be: Why did this population migrate in? What gave it the ability to replace the existing (pre–A.D. 1300) population? Did climate change to render the pre–A.D. 1300 adaptation untenable, thereby enabling the Shoshone to invade the Desert West? Did the ecological adaptation change to make ceramic vessels more efficient after A.D. 1300? Could it be that a ceramic-using population moved into the Desert West and intermarried with the previous inhabitants? Did population growth drive the migration, or was it warfare, or some environmental calamity?

By definition, we base our time-markers on selected aspects of shared culture; time-markers deliberately ignore much cultural behaviour. Obviously, questions such as diffusion, migration, invention, and adaptation are complex, reflecting changes in the underlying cultural systems. Time-markers, grounded only in shared behaviour, are patently inadequate for unravelling the mechanics of cultural systems.

In many respects, the space–time systematics of archaeology have been worked out, especially for North American archaeology, and they no longer preoccupy archaeology the way they did in the first half of the 20th century. Nonetheless, space–time systematics were and are a crucial first step in the archaeological process. It is only after documenting temporal and spatial change in selected artifacts that we can set about reconstructing what people actually did in the past. And in the following chapters, we will discuss how archaeologists go about doing exactly that.

Summary

- Archaeology's major contribution to anthropological knowledge is found in large-scale patterns in space and time. Although archaeology cannot recover the detail that ethnography can, it contributes to anthropology by studying the long-term temporal processes and vast spatial patterning that ethnology cannot record.

- After the excavation, archaeologists catalogue and conserve the artifacts recovered. This can be time-consuming and can require the help of trained specialists.

- The next task is to classify the artifacts in order to construct space–time systematics. This involves typology, the construction of a process to place artifacts into types. This process begins during the excavation, where artifacts may be sorted according to their raw material for the sake of convenience. Classification becomes more rigorous in the lab.

- Archaeologists create morphological types by relying on the shared aspect of culture. We assume that people made an item of material culture in a particular way because they shared a common idea of what a tool or object "ought" to look like. At this point, whether the final form was important to the maker or meaningful in any way is not significant to our analysis.

- The type is the basic unit of artifact analysis. It is an idealized construct that allows archaeologists to transcend individual artifacts so they can consider more generalized categories.

- Morphological types are descriptive and emphasize broad similarities. Temporal types monitor how artifacts change through time. And functional types group artifacts in terms of their function, regardless of their morphology.

- A typology groups artifacts in such a way that the differences within groups are minimized and the differences between groups are maximized.

- Types are based on criteria that are objective, explicit, and replicable.

- Spatial patterning in material culture helps define archaeological cultures or traditions, but these are not the same as ethnographic cultures.

- By seeking out clusters of temporal types we construct site components, which are culturally homogeneous units within a single site and can be synthesized into phases—archaeological units of cultural homogeneity that are limited in both time and space. Phases are the basic archaeological building blocks for regional synthesis.

- Space–time systematics is but one step toward the larger goals of reconstructing and explaining the past.

Additional Reading

CANADIAN RESOURCES

Deller, D. Brian, and Ellis, Chris. (1992). *Thedford II: A Paleo-Indian Site in the Ausable River Watershed of Southwestern Ontario.* Memoirs, Museum of Anthropology, University of Michigan, No. 24.

Ellis, Chris, and Ferris, Neal. (1990). *The Archaeology of Southern Ontario to A.D. 1650.* Occasional Publication of the London Chapter, OAS Number 5.

OTHER RESOURCES

Dunnell, Robert C. (1971). *Systematics in Prehistory.* New York: Free Press.

Lyman, R. Lee, and O'Brien, Michael. (2003). *W. C. McKern and the Midwestern Taxonomic Method.* Tuscaloosa: University of Alabama Press.

Lyman, R. Lee, O'Brien, Michael, and Dunnell, Robert C. (Eds.). (1997). *Americanist Culture History: Fundamentals of Time, Space, and Form.* New York: Plenum Press.

Whallon, Robert E., Jr., and Brown, James A. (Eds.). (1982). *Essays on Archaeological Typology.* Evanston, IL: Center for American Archaeology Press.

Online Resources

COMPANION WEBSITE

Visit *http://www.archaeology1ce.nelson.com* to access a wide range of material to help you succeed in your introductory archaeology course. These include flashcards, Internet exercises, Web links, and practice quizzes.

RESEARCH ONLINE WITH INFOTRAC COLLEGE EDITION

From the Student Companion Website, you can access the InfoTrac College Edition database, which offers thousands of full-length articles for your research.

10 Taphonomy, Experimental Archaeology, and Ethnoarchaeology

OUTLINE

Two Inuit hunters from Arviat, Nunavut, butcher a caribou.
Source: Dr. Peter Dawson

Preview

We have now explored how archaeologists locate and excavate sites, how they date those sites, and how they construct cultural chronologies. Now it is time to move a step up the theoretical ladder and examine the role of middle-range research in modern archaeology.

We have already discussed the various natural and cultural processes that combine to create the archaeological record. Low-level theory enables us to generate data from this record. Now, we can apply theory developed in middle-range research to relate these data to past human behaviours. If you flip back to the model of archaeological inquiry in Figure 3-9 (page 83), you'll recall that archaeologists sometimes put down their trowels, climb out of their trenches, and conduct research designed to give them the tools they need to interpret the data they have generated. That is what this chapter is about.

Here, we concentrate on three areas of middle-range research that we introduced in Chapter 3:

- Taphonomy studies the role that natural processes play in creating the archaeological record.
- Experimental archaeology uses controlled experiments to replicate the past under different conditions to look for links between human behaviour and its archaeological consequences.
- Ethnoarchaeology studies living societies to see how behaviour is translated into the archaeological record.

Introduction

Archaeologists are often compared to detectives, and this comparison is both appropriate and instructive. Both are concerned with what happened in the past, and both make inferences about the past based on recovered material remains. But, ideally, detectives deal with crime scenes that are found and sealed off as soon after the crime as possible. Imagine detectives confronted by a crime scene that is several thousand years old, in which nothing organic survives and burrowing rodents have jumbled the evidence. Even Sherlock Holmes would have a hard time making his conclusions stand up in court. And yet, this is what archaeologists deal with all the time.

Archaeologists also deal with the complication that, unlike detectives, they often recover objects whose function and meaning are unknown. Imagine if our detectives first had to figure out that the metallic cylinder lying on the floor was a spent cartridge (and not a piece of jewellery, child's toy, or the ever-popular ritual object). Detectives routinely use "common sense"—knowledge of their own culture, actually—to decide if something "doesn't look right" at a crime scene. Imagine how much more slowly investigations would proceed if those detectives first had to decide if the distribution of furniture in the room—a chair lying on its side, dishes strewn about the floor—was culturally normal or an aberration.

A complex suite of natural and cultural processes interact to create archaeological sites, and they make each site unique. And this means that archaeological interpretation is *never* straightforward; the low-level facts of archaeology cannot explain themselves. Middle-range research aims to provide archaeology with the tools needed to infer behaviour from the contemporary archaeological record.

Middle-Range Research: What Is It?

To develop such tools, archaeologists must observe behaviour and its material correlates simultaneously, but independent of one another. In an archaeological site, we have only the material remains. Behaviour must be inferred from those remains and thus it cannot be observed independent of them. Where, then, do archaeologists get the means to make these inferences?

Let's consider how archaeology's sibling discipline, geology, solved this problem. Like the archaeological record, the geological record consists of two things: objects and the relationships among them. A "geological fact" is a contemporary observation made by a geologist on objects from the geological record. Rocks do not speak, so how do geologists go from contemporary observations to meaningful inferences of the remote geological past?

Geologists addressed this question in the 18th century. A Scottish doctor and farmer, James Hutton (1726–1797), was also intrigued by geology. He formulated a simple principle that provides one of the cornerstones of modern geology. What became known as the **principle of uniformitarianism** asserts that the processes now operating to modify the earth's surface are the same as those of the geological past. It's that simple: Geological processes in the past and the present are assumed to be *identical.*

We know from modern observations, for instance, that as glaciers move their massive weight leaves striations—that is, scratches—on bedrock deposits. They also deposit rock and earth at their fronts and sides, often in distinctive formations called moraines. Study of modern glaciers shows that moraines and striations are formed only through glacial action.

Now suppose a geologist finds moraines and striated rocks in New England, where no glaciers exist today. Armed with knowledge of contemporary glacial processes, a geologist can confidently interpret those features as evidence of past glaciers.

The same logic applies to archaeology. Archaeologists recover the material remains of past human behaviour. And, like geologists, archaeologists must also look to the contemporary world to provide them with hypotheses that account for the formation and deposition of these physical remains. This is an important point: Observation of the contemporary world provides the information necessary to infer past human behaviour and natural processes from observations on archaeological objects.

Some Bones of Contention

Perhaps you are thinking that, sure, this makes sense—but shouldn't the meaning of remains still be relatively obvious?

To address this question, consider a simple problem in the interpretation of animal bones (also known as **faunal** remains) from archaeological sites. As we will discuss in Chapter 11, archaeologists study animal bones to learn about past diets, hunting and butchering practices, how animals were domesticated, the season in which the hunt occurred, and other related issues.

Most of these faunal studies begin by considering the relative frequencies of animal bones in a site. When analyzing the bones from Suberde, a 7th-millennium-B.C. Neolithic village in Turkey, Dexter Perkins and Patricia Daly observed that the upper limb bones of wild oxen were usually missing. Perkins and Daly suggested that the frequencies of the different bones resulted from how people had butchered the oxen. They must have first skinned the animals, then stripped the meat from the forequarters and hindquarters, and then thrown away the defleshed upper limb bones. Perkins and Daly presumed that the meat was piled on the skin and that the lower limb bones were used to drag the hide bearing the meat back home. Calling this the "schlepp effect," they believed their interpretation explained why only lower limb bones were discarded at the habitation site.

Now jump across Europe to England, where R. E. Chaplin analyzed the bones recovered from a late

principle of uniformitarianism The principle asserting that the processes now operating to modify the earth's surface are the same processes that operated long ago in the geological past.

faunal In archaeology, animal bones in archaeological sites.

9th-century-A.D. Saxon farm. The facts in this case also included a shortage of the limb bones of sheep and cattle, but Chaplin suggested that these bones disappeared because the carcasses were dressed and exported to market.

Across the Atlantic, archaeologists working on American Plains Indian sites also discovered that the upper limb bones of food animals were often missing. Theodore White decided that the bones were destroyed during the manufacture of bone grease. Relying on ethnographies of Plains Indians, White argued that the limb bones were pulverized and boiled to render their grease to make pemmican (a mixture of dried meat, fat, and berries), which was stored for the winter.

We could cite other examples, but the point should be clear: Three different teams made three different inferences from exactly the same archaeological facts—the lack of upper limb bones in habitation sites.

Archaeologists face such problems daily: several competing hypotheses accounting for the same body of facts. And all the hypotheses are reasonable.

Scientific protocol stipulates how to select among the competing hypotheses (and for the present, we will restrict our attention to the three target hypotheses). Each one is a generalized statement about human behaviour. But a contemporary archaeologist can never observe a Neolithic villager butchering a wild ox, and none of us will ever watch 19th-century American Plains Indians making bone grease. Archaeologists must therefore concentrate on finding the material *consequences* of activities like butchering Neolithic oxen or making bison bone grease.

We do this by constructing a series of logical if . . . then statements: *If* bone grease were manufactured from bison bones, *then* we should find artifacts X, Y, and Z and physical residues M, N, and O; bones should be distributed in patterns C, D, and E; and bone elements J, K, and L should be missing. Similarly, to test the second hypothesis, we must generate some if . . . then statements regarding the trading of meat and bones. Before we can do that, we need answers to some very specific questions: Which are the best cuts to trade? How far can meat be transported before it spoils? Is meat marketed only in the winter months? Are carcasses butchered in special ways so that certain cuts can be traded? Then we can

create arguments like "*If* these carcasses were being dressed for market, *then* we should see marks A and B on bones X and Y, and the site should include features G or H and implements K and L."

These if . . . then statements become *bridging arguments,* a concept we first mentioned in Chapter 2 (page 47) that translate hypotheses into specific expectations that can be tested using archaeological evidence. These bridging arguments are essential to testing ideas with archaeological evidence, and their construction is one of the most difficult things that archaeologists do.

But—we hope you are wondering—how do we know these things? Why do archaeologists surmise that making bone grease requires artifacts X, Y, and Z? And how do we know which bone elements are destroyed in the process? Hypothesis testing is only as robust as these if . . . then bridging arguments. If we generate incorrect implications, then our hypothesis testing will be worse than useless, because it will lead us to specious or erroneous conclusions. For instance, if we assume that the lack of limb bones *always* means that people were rendering grease from bones, we would make a completely incorrect inference if the lack of limb bones in a particular site was really the result of the schlepp effect.

Here is where the notion of middle-range research comes into play. Because the facts cannot speak for themselves, archaeologists must provide bridging arguments that breathe behavioural life into the objects of the past. Properly formulated, middle-range theory links human behaviour to empirical data that are archaeologically observable. Although it has been an important aspect of archaeological inquiry for more than a century, Lewis Binford's call for middle-range research served to focus additional attention on this neglected area of archaeology.

To create relevant bridging arguments, archaeologists must observe the workings of a culture in its systemic context, much as geologists defined their processes through observation of the contemporary world—such as streams carrying silt to a delta or the wind blowing sand across dunes. Geologists interested in glacial processes cannot study firsthand the massive continental glaciers that once covered portions of the Northern Hemisphere. But they can examine the effects that mountain glaciers today have on the landscape and use those observations to infer the past from geological traces.

Archaeologists do the same: They study modern analogies in order to understand the processes that created the archaeological record.

Analogy versus Middle-Range Theory

We used the term "analogy" in the previous paragraph, and you may be asking yourself if there is a difference between it and middle-range theory. The answer is that *middle-range theory is a particularly rigorous analogy.*

To see what we mean by this, let's first consider what a simple analogy is. An **analogy** notes similarities between two entities—for example, an archaeological feature and an ethnographic description of a similar feature—and infers from those facts that an *additional* attribute of one (the ethnographic feature) is also true of the other (the archaeological feature). Following Nicholas David (University of Calgary) and Carol Kramer (1943–2002), simple analogies take the following form:

- An archaeological object is characterized by attributes A, B, C, and D.
- The ethnographic analogy is characterized by A, B, C, and D and has the function or property E.
- Therefore, the archaeological object also has the function or property E.

For example, the first archaeologists to excavate ancient pueblo ruins in the American Southwest discovered many **kivas** in the settlements. Kivas are religious structures where native peoples of the American Southwest held various rituals. They are usually round and semi-subterranean, with massive log roofs that were covered by dirt. They were entered via a ladder placed in a central opening in the roof that also served as a smokehole.

Many kivas share certain features: an exterior, stone-lined vertical shaft that opens near the kiva floor, a central fireplace, and an upright stone slab (or a small masonry wall) between the fireplace and the shaft's opening. These features (shown in Figure 10-1) are probably functional. The fireplace provided light and warmth. The shaft provided ventilation, and the upright stone deflected wind blowing down the shaft and prevented smoke and embers from annoying the ritual's participants.

Along the wall opposite the ventilator shaft, archaeologists usually find a very small pit or simply a depression called the **sipapu** (a Hopi term meaning "place of emergence"). Unlike the fireplace, ventilator shaft, and deflector stone, the sipapu has no apparent material function. To interpret this recurrent feature, archaeologists turned to living Pueblo societies, such as the Hopi, who use kivas today for rituals.

Hopi kivas also contain this small, innocuous pit, and its size belies its cultural significance, for the sipapu symbolizes the place where the Hopi emerged from the underworld. In traditional Pueblo theology, the world consists of several levels, and oral histories recount stories of people moving from one level to the next by crawling through a small opening. The current world, the Hopi say, is the fourth world, with more worlds above it. The kiva's sipapu is a reminder of these stories, a portal through which the natural and supernatural worlds communicate. Archaeologists infer that sipapus in archaeological kivas had the same function as they do in modern kivas.

Does this inference fit the definition of an analogy? Let's put it into the David and Kramer definition:

- Archaeological kivas are semi-subterranean with entry through the smokehole; they have a central fireplace, a ventilator shaft, a deflector stone, and a small pit opposite the ventilator shaft.
- Hopi kivas are semi-subterranean with entry through the smokehole; they have a central fireplace, a ventilator shaft, a deflector stone, and a small pit (the sipapu) opposite the ventilator shaft. The sipapu represents the hole where the Hopi emerged into the current world; it allows communication between the natural and supernatural worlds.

---

analogy Noting similarities between two entities and inferring from that similarity that an additional attribute of one (the ethnographic case) is also true of the other (the archaeological case).

kiva A Pueblo ceremonial structure that is usually round (but may be square or rectangular) and semi-subterranean. They appear in early Pueblo sites and perhaps even in the earlier (pre-A.D. 700) pithouse villages.

sipapu A Hopi word that loosely translates as "place of emergence." The original sipapu is the place where the Hopi are said to have emerged into this world from the underworld. Sipapus are also small pits in kivas through which communication with the supernatural world takes place.

Figure 10-1 Looking down into an unroofed kiva at Mesa Verde National Park; note the square opening for the ventilation shaft (at the top of the photo), the upright stone between the ventilation shaft and the central hearth, and the sipapu—the small hole near the bottom of the photo.

Source: Robert Kelly

formal analogies Analogies justified by similarities in the formal attributes of archaeological and ethnographic objects and features.

relational analogies Analogies justified on the basis of close cultural continuity between the archaeological and ethnographic cases or similarity in general cultural form.

■ Therefore, the sipapus in archaeological kivas also represented the place where ancient peoples say they emerged from a previous underworld, and they also allowed communication between the natural and supernatural worlds.

Such analogies must be used cautiously. Why? Because just as we enumerated the similarities between the Hopi and the archaeological kivas, we can also list the *differences* between them: Hopi kivas are often square, not round; they are often placed in open plazas or streets between room blocks, rather than incorporated into blocks of residential rooms as they were at many prehistoric pueblos. We could list the similarities between Hopi and archaeological kivas and stack those up against the differences. But how similar do ethnographic and archaeological cases have to be for the analogy to hold true?

Formal and Relational Analogies

To answer this question, we must introduce you to two major kinds of analogy, which Alison Wylie (Barnard College) terms **formal** and **relational analogies.** Formal analogies rely on similarities in *form*—hence "formal" attributes—between the archaeological and ethnographic cases, regardless of whether the analogies come from the same culture. For example, we infer that stone projectile points, such as those you saw in Chapter 9, are in fact projectile points because they are so similar to the stone tips found on the projectiles of many ethnographically known peoples the world over. Formal analogies are, of course, strengthened (1) if many ethnographic cases demonstrate the same pattern and (2) if the archaeological and ethnographic cases have many attributes in common. But no rules exist to tell us *how many* ethnographic cases make a strong analogy, or *how many* similarities between the archaeological and ethnographic cases are needed to justify the analogy.

Relational analogies entail formal similarities, but the archaeological and ethnographic cases are related in some fashion. By "related," we mean that they both come from societies with similar settlement systems, economies, or environments—for instance, they may both be desert-adapted hunting-and-gathering societies or the ethnographic society that serves as an analogy may be a cultural descendant of the archaeological case.

In addition, relational analogies may entail "natural" relations; that is, a causal and hence *necessary* link between the attributes of an object or a feature and their interpretation. We'll come back to this aspect of relational analogies in a moment.

Our kiva example entails elements of both formal and relational analogies. There are formal similarities between the archaeological and Hopi kivas, and modern Hopi culture is clearly related to ancient Puebloan culture. Analogies such as this have been and always will be important to archaeological inference.

However, analogy entails certain risks. Suppose, for instance, you are studying a prehistoric horticultural and pastoral society in the deserts of Kenya. In the site you've excavated are many stone scrapers. You are interested in inferring who used these tools, men or women. As we will see in Chapter 13, inferring the activities of different genders from archaeological data is an extremely difficult task. Analogy is one option for making the inference.

Knowing that analogies are safer the closer they are in time and space to the archaeological case, you look around Africa for a contemporary society that is roughly comparable to the archaeological one—one that lives in a similar environment with a similar economy and a similar culture. Doing so, you encounter the ethnographic research of Steven Brandt and Kathryn Weedman (University of Florida) with several Ethiopian peoples. Among these people today are individuals who work cattle skins to manufacture bedding and bags. About a third of those who work hides use stone tools.

These seem to be wonderful sources for building an analogy, but which Ethiopian group should you use? If you pick the Gamo, you'll find that men do all the hide-working and tool manufacture. The Gamo-based analogy would imply that men also did all the hide-working in your archaeological society. But among the Konso, *women* do virtually all the stone-tool manufacture and hide-working (Figure 10-2), so the Konso analogy would obviously lead to a very different conclusion.

Like dynamite and backhoes, analogies are part of the archaeologist's toolkit but they must be used with caution.

Figure 10-2 Sokati Chirayo, a Konso woman in Ethiopia, working a hide with a stone scraper mounted in a wooden handle.
Source: Steven Brandt/Kathryn Weedman

Archaeological Ethics
The Ethics of Doing Ethnoarchaeology

Ethnoarchaeology does not come naturally to most archaeologists, who are more accustomed to dealing with the dead than with the living. We are used to thinking about whether our crews are well-fed, happy, and satisfied—but not about whether the site feels the same way.

But doing ethnoarchaeology means thinking about the ethics of working with members of another culture. Cultural anthropologists have thought about this quite a bit—in fact, the first line of the American Anthropological Association's Statement on Ethics reads: "Anthropologists' paramount responsibility is to those they study."

Anthropologists involve the host population in the project, seek the approval of those who participate, and avoid harm. For every house he measured, every settlement that he mapped, every photo that he took in Madagascar, Kelly explained his goals and asked permission. If the individual declined, he moved on.

Often, however, conflict arises between research goals and human decency. One cannot stand idly by while people are harmed, but an anthropologist also has a responsibility to the research and to the organization that sponsored it. Bram Tucker (Ohio State University) confronted such a problem during his research with the Mikea:

> In July 1998, I was living in Behisatse, a hamlet of six houses in the Mikea Forest. I was studying how the Mikea make a living in an unpredictable environment. Rainfall, the main source of water for wild and domestic plants and animals, varies unpredictably from 100 mm to 1500 mm each year. Mikea deal with this unpredictability by diversifying their economy, combining foraging with farming, herding, and producing hard goods for market. They forage in different microenvironments. They plant a mix of crops that do well in rainy years and those that do well in dry years.
>
> Some years, even the best economic strategies are ineffective, and the food supply is inadequate. This was the case in 1998. The maize crop germinated late because of insufficient rainfall, and then in February grasshoppers ate the withered stalks. Thieves ransacked manioc fields in the night. By March, the families at Behisatse were relying almost entirely on wild ovy tubers (Dioscorea acuminata). Ovy is an excellent food, but is prone to overharvesting. As the ovy patches near camp were depleted, foragers traveled increasing distances to find food, returning to camp each evening with barely enough to see them through the night.
>
> I was faced with an ethical dilemma. The curious scientist in me wanted to know how Mikea households cope with food shortage. But as their friend and honorary kinsman, I couldn't just watch them go hungry!
>
> My field assistant and I informed the camp elder that we planned to do something to help. The next day we visited a farmer friend in a distant village. I purchased 100 Kg of manioc, enough to feed everyone in Behisatse for a month and a half, for 40,000 Malagasy francs, about $7. The farmer said it would take a week to finish drying the manioc. During the following week at Behisatse, the adults continued to forage for ovy all day, leaving the children back at camp hungry. So, at each meal we prepared twice as much food as normal and invited the children to join us. Eventually our manioc gift arrived. Our friends continued to work hard and forage frequently, but they could now afford to rest a little without worry.
>
> I still learned a lot about how Mikea cope with food shortage. By the time our gift arrived, people were starting several alternative strategies, including planned movements to other locations and recalling debts from more prosperous acquaintances. But as field researchers, we become part of the communities we study. As such, we have a responsibility to help out when we can.

One way out of this problem is to determine the relative strength of the analogy. By increasing the number of formal similarities between an ethnographic and archaeological case, we increase the probability that the formal analogy is correct. Still, though, we wouldn't know if an analogy that relies on ten attributes is twice as good as one with only five. Even the best analogy is no more than a probability—and retains the chance that it could be wrong.

Drawing the analogy from an ethnographic case that is culturally related to the archaeological one improves the analogy, but what if recent events caused cultural discontinuity between the past and the present? And what happens with archaeological cases that have no clear ethnographic referent, such as the 10,000-year-old Folsom site we mentioned in Chapter 6?

Middle-Range Theory as Powerful Analogy

As we noted above, relational analogies can rely not just on cultural continuity but also on "natural" relationships, by which Wylie means causal linkages between attributes of a thing and the inference to be made from it.

We refer to analogies based on such causal linkages as middle-range theory. Middle-range theory is a special kind of analogy simply because it *is* theory. As you will recall from Chapter 3, theories explain things; they answer "why" questions. Middle-range theory tries to make an analogy more certain by explaining *why* there is a *necessary* relationship between an object's or feature's attributes and an inference made from those attributes. Relying on the principle of uniformitarianism, middle-range theory attempts to explain *why* an inference should necessarily be true.

This is hardly an easy task. In fact, this may be an archaeologist's most difficult chore. Consider the hypothetical example above in which the archaeologist wished to know if men or women used stone scrapers. What theory would *necessarily* link some observable attribute of a scraper—such as length, width, thickness, raw material, or context—to the gender of its user? It's hard to imagine.

Certainty may forever elude archaeological inference, but archaeologists have been able to make new and more secure inferences from archaeological remains by constructing their middle-range theories through.

Taphonomy

The word "taphonomy" (from the Greek term *tapho,* meaning "death" or "tomb") was coined by the Russian paleontologist I. A. Efremov; it refers to the study of how organisms become part of the fossil record. Archaeologists use the term to refer to the study of how natural processes contribute to the formation of archaeological sites. In Chapter 7, we discussed site formation processes—how human behaviour and natural processes affect the creation of the archaeological record. Taphonomy is an important aspect of the study of site formation processes because it considers how human behaviour and natural processes incorporate bones and plants into sites.

Taphonomists study some bizarre stuff. One might record how large animal carcasses decompose on an African savanna (Figure 10-3). How long does it take the carcass to disarticulate? Which bones separate first? Which ones are carried away by carnivores? And how far? Is decomposition in the rainy season the same as in the dry season? Others might examine lion kills and ask what telltale markings lions leave behind. How do these differ from the evidence that human hunters leave behind?

Another might find raptor nests along a cliff and collect their feces or vomit (many raptors eat prey whole and then regurgitate the bones and hair). What do rodent bones look like after they have passed through a raptor? Or what do fish bones look like that have passed through a dog? How about through a human? Depending on your perspective, taphonomic research is either gross or really cool.

In archaeology, taphonomy has expanded from paleontology's traditional concern with bones to include plant remains. What are the various ways that seeds, leaves, twigs, and pollen enter archaeological sites? Here you might study the feces of various herbivores, the plant-collecting behaviour of packrats (more on them in Chapter 11), or the way that wind or water carries leaves, pollen, and sediments.

Recall that taphonomy aims primarily at understanding how natural processes contribute to a site's formation. Although it's not easy, it's easier to infer natural processes from artifacts and ecofacts rather than human behaviour, because natural processes are more mechanistic and hence more predictable than human behaviour. This observation is useful to

Figure 10-3 Diane Gifford-Gonzales collecting data for a taphonomic study in Africa.

Source: Diane Gifford-Gonzalez, photo by Michael J. Mehlman

archaeology for two reasons: First, recall that data are *observations* on objects, and that archaeologists seek *patterns* in their data. Therefore, one strategy for understanding an archaeological site is first to *remove all the patterns that are the result of natural processes*. Once we do this, we know that the remaining patterns are the ones that need to be explained in terms of human behaviour. We saw this approach at the site of Cagny-l'Epinette (discussed in Chapter 7).

Second, understanding how a site formed is crucial to understanding not only the human behaviour that occurred at the site but also the *environmental context* of that behaviour. It can tell us if the climate was temperate or tropical, if a landscape was eroding away or

aggrading, if streams were running or were dry, if forest fires were prevalent, and so on.

In taphonomic research, archaeologists develop bridging arguments by simultaneously yet independently observing natural processes in action and their material results. By trying to explain *why* those natural processes produce the particular material results that they do, you move from simple analogies into middle-range theory. The Hudson-Meng bison **bonebed** provides an example of what taphonomic research can do for archaeology.

Taphonomy at the Hudson-Meng Bison Bonebed

The Hudson-Meng site lies in a low swale in windswept northwest Nebraska, where the remains of at least 500 bison are crowded into an area of about

bonebed Archaeological and paleontological sites consisting of the remains of a large number of animals, often of the same species, and often representing a single moment in time—a mass kill or mass death.

Figure 10-4 Students excavating a small portion of the Hudson-Meng site, Nebraska. A weatherport covers this excavation.
Source: Lawrence C. Todd

1000 square metres (Figure 10-4). Twenty-one spear points (or point fragments) were found among the remains. AMS dates indicate that the site is about 9500 radiocarbon years old.

Paleontologist Larry Agenbroad (Northern Arizona University) was the first to dig at Hudson-Meng, in the 1970s. Using the standard conventions of the day, he inferred human behaviour from *patterns* he observed in the faunal remains. One clear pattern was that the tops of the crania were missing. Mandibles were present along with some cranial fragments, but the top of nearly every single skull was missing. Agenbroad knew that modern Plains Indians often broke bison skulls open to remove the brains and use them in tanning hides. Using this as an analogy, he reasoned that the skull tops at Hudson-Meng were missing for the same reason and therefore that humans must have killed the animals.

Agenbroad then made several more inferences. How could people on foot, armed only with spears, have killed 500 bison? People without horses, Agenbroad decided, could not control a herd of 500 bison. So he inferred that there must be a low cliff nearby that is now buried beneath the sand that blows daily across western Nebraska. The hunters drove the bison over the cliff and then dragged some 500 of them to a processing area. And, calculating that 500 bison could produce nearly 10,000 kilograms of dried meat, Agenbroad inferred that the ancient hunters were a large group and that they had a sophisticated storage system.

So Agenbroad made inferences about (1) the presence of humans, (2) hunting strategy, (3) group size, and (4) food storage, all based on the patterning—the missing skull tops—evident in the skeletal assemblage. These inferences were all based on an analogy with historically known Plains Indians, one that had elements of both formal and relational analogies:

- It was a formal analogy because it relied on the similarity in bison skull form (the missing top of the cranium), and similarities between the site and ethnographically documented butchering practices.

- It was a relational analogy because it took a known practice of Plains Indians and extrapolated back in time to the ancestors of Plains Indians.

However, this is not middle-range theory, because Agenbroad did not try to explain the character of the skulls he found in light of what might happen to bison craniums butchered by known Plains Indian practices. The necessary bridging argument we mentioned above was assumed, not demonstrated.

From a taphonomic perspective, modern archaeologists look at the foundation of Agenbroad's inferences (the missing crania) and wonder: Could a natural process create the same pattern?

Hudson-Meng has always presented some troubling facts. For example, comparing it with similar bison kill sites, we might expect something closer to 150 points and point fragments, not just 21.

And why are there no cut marks on the bones? In the process of butchering 500 bison, it seems likely that a stone knife would occasionally have cut to bone as it sliced through tendons and meat. Archaeologists have encountered thousands of such telltale nicks at other kill/butchery sites, but only carnivore tooth marks appear on the bones at Hudson-Meng.

Finally, many of the skeletal remains are in anatomical position, lying in the ground as if the bison had simply died there and were buried undisturbed. If ancient hunters had butchered these animals, we'd expect them to have removed at least some of the meaty portions of the body, such as the upper rear leg (containing the femur).

Lawrence Todd (Colorado State University) and David Rapson (University of Wyoming) were bothered by these facts, and so they excavated a portion of the Hudson-Meng site using a battery of high-precision excavation techniques. They also applied the perspective of taphonomy, and began by asking this simple question: How do bison fall apart?

How Do Bison Fall Apart?

For years, taphonomists had studied the carcasses of large animals as they lay decomposing on North America's high plains, Africa's Serengeti, and elsewhere. Some of these animals had been shot; others had frozen to death or simply died of old age. Some

were ravaged by carnivores, others were undisturbed. Some died on hillsides, others in gullies. Some died in the winter or wet season, others in the summer or dry season. Sometimes the hide dried to form an armour-like case, holding the bones together years after death; sometimes the rotting carcass burst from the maggots within. In other words, taphonomists had documented what actually happens to a large animal carcass under a variety of natural circumstances.

Are there any patterns in how these large animal skeletons fall apart? Absolutely. Andrew Hill (Yale University) and Anna Behrensmeyer (Smithsonian Institution) found that the first joint to disarticulate is where the scapula attaches to the vertebral column, allowing the entire front limb to drop away. Then the caudal (tail) vertebrae-to-sacrum joint goes, followed by the scapula-humerus joint, and then the "elbow," where the humerus articulates with the radius and ulna. The last joints to disarticulate tend to be those of the vertebrae. Such documented sequences of natural disarticulation provide a baseline against which to judge the distinctiveness of human butchering practices.

Through time, the decomposing bison carcass eventually collapses into a flat pile of bones (Figure 10-5). The skull often ends up resting on its mandibles (the lower jaw). Carnivores may drag some limb bones away and, eventually, the entire skeleton lies flat on the ground—with the skull poking up above all the other bones.

Then what happens? The bones become a sediment trap, catching the blowing dust and sand. It takes 10 to 15 centimetres of sediment to cover the now-collapsed limb bones and rib cage, but 30 to 40 centimetres to cover the skull. This means that much of the skull is left sticking up above the ground surface after the rest of the bones are buried. And once leg bones, vertebrae, and ribs are buried—thus covering most of the irregular surface that trapped blowing sand—sediment accumulates less quickly, leaving the top of the skull exposed for a longer period of time than the rest of the skeleton.

Then the sun does its work. Sunlight is quite destructive of bone, and the exposed top of the skull quickly flakes away. Eventually, the top of the skull is destroyed and the rest is buried.

Taphonomy and Uniformitarianism

So the incomplete crania, the basis of Agenbroad's analogy, are readily explained by natural processes, not human behaviour. This is more than simple anal-

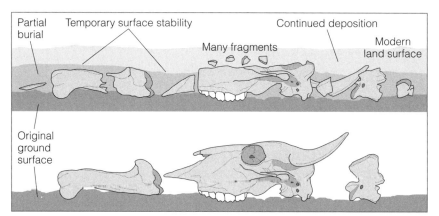

Figure 10-5 Todd and Rapson's reconstruction of how taphonomic processes, rather than human butchering, created the pattern of incomplete crania at the Hudson-Meng site. The animal dies and decomposes; as the body collapses into a pile of bone (bottom), it continues to trap sediment until it is mostly buried, although the skull's top remains exposed. The cranium weathers (top), and the small bone fragments that flake off are blown away by the wind.

ogy—it is middle-range theory, because we understand *why* bison bones disarticulate, become buried, and weather the way that they do. But this understanding is based on observations of modern animals. Can we trust these observations to explain archaeological remains?

The principle of uniformitarianism applies here, because ancient animals, like the bison that died at Hudson-Meng, had the same anatomy as the animals observed in taphonomic studies. Bison disarticulation is governed by the amount of cartilage and tendons holding bones together and the amount of muscle tissue around them. The more cartilage, tendon, and muscle in a joint, the more resistant that joint is to disarticulation. If skeletal disarticulation is largely a product of anatomy, and if bison anatomy has not changed over the past 10,000 years (and it hasn't), then modern observations are relevant to the interpretation of archaeological data.

Likewise, the effects of sunlight on bone are a product of the nature of bone and the nature of sunlight. And given that neither sunlight nor bone composition has changed over time, we have gone beyond analogy to explain *why* particular natural factors have particular predictable effects on bone. This is what qualifies the work as middle-range theory.

And, it suggests that humans played little role, if any, in the deaths of the 500 bison at Hudson-Meng. But if humans did not dispatch the 500 bison at Hudson-Meng—what happened? Todd and Rapson hypothesize that a summer storm sparked a massive prairie fire that drove the bison herd into the swale for protection (many of the bison lie with their heads to the southeast, which, using analogy with modern bison behaviour, suggests that they were responding to a northwest wind). None of the bones are burned, so these animals were not burned to death. But the fire could have jumped the swale and asphyxiated the bison by sucking up all the oxygen for a few critical minutes. This hypothesis remains to be tested.

And what of the 21 projectile points found there? As you have seen in previous chapters, archaeological sites are often reoccupied. In their careful excavations, Todd and Rapson found several thin soils containing a few archaeological remains *above* the bison. In fact, Agenbroad found fewer than 10 points *among* the bones. The spear points, then, were probably discarded or lost long after the bison had died, decomposed, and become buried, and a few points moved downward through rodent burrowing and sediment processes into the bonebed.

Experimental Archaeology

Taphonomy uses observations of modern processes to help make inferences from archaeological data. But what if this is impossible? What if we want to know the material effects of behaviours *that no longer exist?* This is especially relevant to human behaviours, because people did things in the past that they no longer do today. Understanding the material remains of these behaviours requires experimental archaeology.

Experimental archaeology is by no means new. Nearly 100 years ago, for example, Saxton Pope, a surgeon at the University of California Medical Center (San Francisco), began experimenting with archery methods. The poignant story began in 1911, when a starving, defeated Indian was found crouching in a slaughterhouse corral near Oroville, California. His

Looking Closer

Boundaries and Bones: Reconstructing Social Space at Head-Smashed-In Buffalo Jump

Anyone who has ever spent any time on a beach, or at a folk festival, knows that people can be quite territorial when it comes to space. In these situations, individuals commonly use such things as umbrellas, blankets, and coolers to define boundaries that separate themselves from others in the crowd. These boundaries are largely conceptual, because they lack physical barriers such as walls and partitions. Nevertheless, they are recognizable; the material objects and debris associated with peoples' activities define where others can and cannot sit. Transgressing these boundaries by taking over someone else's spot while they get a hotdog, or go to the bathroom, would inevitably lead to conflict.

Some of the conceptual barriers that separate the daily activities we engage in are permeable, and allow multiple activities to share a single space. For example, you may be able to read and do homework while your roommate watches television or plays video games. Others are more rigidly defined, and are used to separate activities that are considered incompatible. It is unlikely, for instance, that you would want to change the oil in your car and do your laundry in the same space. The study of this phenomenon is called *boundary theory,* and anthropologists and archaeologists use it to examine how humans strategically divide and use the spaces they occupy.

Head-Smashed-In Buffalo Jump is a UNESCO World Heritage Site located near Fort Macleod, Alberta (Figure 10-6). The name of the site comes from a Blackfoot legend in which a young boy, wishing to view the Bison Jump from a front-row seat at the base of the cliff, is crushed to death by falling bison. American humorist Dave Barry has written several columns for the *Miami Herald* about Head-Smashed-In. In one story, he describes calling the interpretive centre at the site and hearing the person on the other end of the phone answer, "Head-Smashed-In; How can I help you?" Barry lists this as one of the highlights of his life.

Junius Bird of the American Museum of Natural History first investigated the site during the 1930s. Since then, archaeologists working for Canadian universities and government agencies have carried out subsequent excavations. These include Dr. Richard Forbis, Dr. Brian Reeves, and Dr. Brian Kooyman of the University of Calgary, and Dr. Jack Brink, Archaeology Curator at the Royal Alberta Museum. One of the unique aspects of Head-Smashed-In is that the Blackfoot people play an active role in the site's interpretation and promotion to the visiting public.

Head-Smashed-In is a large and complex archaeological site that covers an area of nearly 600 hectares. Archaeologists believe that, with the exception of a short hiatus, the site was used almost continuously from 5700 years ago to the historic period. The development of communal bison hunting reflected at sites like Head-Smashed-In represents an important cultural development on the western Plains. Initially, hunters used stone-tipped spears launched from **atlatls** to kill bison. Taking animals individually, however, made it difficult to procure enough food for the entire group. In response, Plains aboriginal peoples combined their vast knowledge of bison behaviour with their equally vast knowledge of Plains topography to devise a means of dramatically increasing both their hunting success rates and the number of animals killed.

The Head-Smashed-In site comprises three different areas, each of which played an important role in the hunt. To the west of an 18-metre-high cliff is a large drainage basin, which naturally attracts bison because of the grasses that grow there. Hunters used long lines of stone cairns, called "dead men," to influence the movement of the bison herd toward the cliff. A buffalo runner would urge the herd to follow him by imitating the bleating noises of a buffalo calf. Other hunters would then circle round behind the herd, waving buffalo robes, shouting, and shooting arrows in order to scare the animals toward the direction of the cliff.

As the buffalo ran toward the edge of the precipice, the direction of the prevailing winds prevented the stampeding animals from smelling the kill site at the foot of the cliff. The animals at the front of the herd would have inevitably tried to stop as they approached the drop. However, they would have been prevented from doing so by the hundreds of animals following behind. In the mayhem, large numbers of animals fell to their deaths. Archaeological excavations at the cliff base have revealed accumulations of bone to a depth of 10 metres—a testament to both the success of this method of hunting, and the use of the site over many millennia.

Figure 10-6 Head-Smashed-In Buffalo Jump, a UNESCO World Heritage Site located outside of Fort Macleod, Alberta.
Source: Caroline Commins/Alamy

Brian Kooyman (University of Calgary) utilized boundary theory to explore how social space was structured at the site, and how activity areas combined to form these social spaces. Kooyman began by plotting the distribution of artifacts and bones on maps, level by level, to look for spatial patterning in the debris. What Kooyman found was extremely interesting. Primary butchering areas where animals were initially disarticulated had boundaries that were relatively impermeable to other types of activities. This makes sense, as tasks such as the re-sharpening of lithic tools might contaminate meat by introducing small, sharp pieces of debitage. The same was true for areas where concentrations of burned bone occurred. Plains groups commonly burned bone as a way of eliminating problems caused by rotting carcasses. Kooyman found that areas at Head-Smashed-In where concentrations of burned bone occurred were often located away from other sources of debris, suggesting the maintenance of a strong boundary,

perhaps as a means of reducing the danger of being severely burned. Secondary processing areas, where bones might be split and boiled for the extraction of marrow, were found to have much more permeable and complementary boundaries. Lithic re-sharpening flakes, as well as anvil and hammer stones, for example, were found mixed in with the faunal materials, likely reflecting the co-occurrence of secondary butchering activities such as the pulverizing and boiling of bones for grease. The same was true for hearth areas, which were commonly associated with lithic debris associated with stone tool production and maintenance.

Taphonomic agents obviously played a role in shaping the spatial distribution of artifacts and faunal material at Head-Smashed-In. However, they do not obfuscate the effects of human social behaviour as an agent of site formation. Identifying and interpreting such patterns via approaches like boundary theory demonstrates that social spaces can be identified at open-air sites and distinguished from patterns produced by natural taphonomic agents.

family may have been murdered, or perhaps they starved to death. Ishi (ca. 1860–1916) himself may have lost his will to live. He could neither speak nor understand English. The local sheriff locked him in the jail, because "wild" Indians were not allowed to roam about freely in those days.

Alfred Kroeber, a young anthropologist at the University of California, heard the story and recognized the Indian's language as Yahi, a native language of California. Kroeber named the man Ishi ("human" in Yahi) and brought him to San Francisco, where he stayed at the university museum, worked as an assistant janitor, and demonstrated arrow-making and fire-starting for museum visitors. Kroeber and his staff taught Ishi their culture, and the Indian revealed many secrets of his survival.

But Ishi soon developed a tubercular cough—which later cost him his life—and he was treated daily by Dr. Pope. Over their short association, Pope and Ishi found a common interest in archery. An odd combination: Pope, the urbane scholar paired with the Yahi Indian, hair singed in tribal custom, together shooting arrows through the parks of downtown San Francisco. Pope was a good student and, after Ishi's death, the doctor continued his research, studying bows and arrows in museum collections and often test-shooting the ancient specimens.

Pope wrote *Hunting With the Bow and Arrow* in 1923, describing his experiments in archery. The book provided baseline information for interpreting ancient finds and quickly became the bible of the bow-hunting fraternity (in fact, it is credited with reviving the sport of bow hunting in America).

From early studies such as Pope's, experimental archaeology expanded dramatically and has become an important way for archaeologists to reconstruct the past.

How Were Stone Tools Made?

Many prehistoric techniques died with their practitioners, and experimental archaeologists have been forced to rediscover them. Making stone tools is one such technique, and many archaeologists have experimented by manufacturing their own stone tools.

To make a stone tool, you must first locate and collect the appropriate raw materials—rocks that break with a glassy fracture such as obsidian, quartzite, or chert. This may require excavating into bedrock, because frost-fracturing and sunlight can ruin surface specimens. Some ancient peoples excavated major quarries into bedrock using only fire and wooden wedges.

If the stone is chert or quartzite, you might improve it by **heat-treatment**—burying large **flakes** or small **cores** in about 5 centimetres of sand, then burning a fire on top for a day or so. Ancient flintknappers learned that they could more easily chip and shape stone treated in this way. The problem is that, over the millennia, plenty has been forgotten about the detailed technology required to make good stone tools from a pile of rocks.

Fortunately, a school of experimentalists—many of them dedicated amateur archaeologists—has rediscovered some of this technology. One of the best known, Don Crabtree (1912–1980), spent a lifetime experimenting with stone tool manufacturing methods (Figure 10-7). One of his projects was to rediscover the techniques used to fabricate Folsom spear points.

Remember from Chapter 6 that Folsom points, such as those found at the Folsom site in New Mexico, date to 10,200–10,900 radiocarbon years ago. These exquisite points turn up in many sites on the Great Plains and in the Rocky Mountains where, mounted on spears or darts, they brought down game, including bison. Although the points are often only about 6 to 8 centimetres long, Crabtree counted more than 150 minute sharpening flakes removed from their surface.

The most distinctive property of Folsom artifacts are the **flutes**—wide, shallow, longitudinal grooves on each face of the point (Figure 10-8). Flutes are made by removing **channel flakes** from the point's base on both sides. Nobody is sure why these artifacts were

atlatl A spear thrower made from antler, bone, or wood and used to launch stone-tipped spears.

heat-treatment A process whereby the flintknapping properties of stone tool raw material are improved by subjecting the material to heat.

flake A thin, sharp sliver of stone removed from a core during the knapping process.

core A piece of stone that is worked ("knapped"). Cores sometimes serve merely as sources for raw materials; they also can serve as functional tools.

flute Distinctive channel on the faces of Folsom and Clovis projectile points formed by removal of one or more flakes from the point's base.

channel flake The longitudinal flake removed from the faces of Folsom and Clovis projectile points to create the flute.

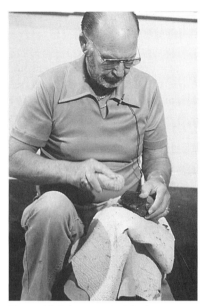

Figure 10-7 Accomplished flintknapper Don Crabtree uses a hammerstone to percussion-flake a block of obsidian.
Source: James Wood

Figure 10-8 Folsom-style spear points manufactured by Don Crabtree. Note the two large "fluting" flakes that were removed from the points at the bottom of the photograph.
Source: American Museum of Natural History

thinned in this fashion, but everybody agrees that fluting is an extraordinary feat of flintknapping.

The technical quality of Folsom points intrigued Crabtree. With enough practice, one can learn to quickly fashion many projectile points. But making Folsom points must have required hours, assuming that one understood how to do it in the first place. And in the 20th century, nobody did.

Archaeologists speculated for years how ancient peoples removed the channel flakes. And for 40 years, Crabtree tried every way he could think of to manufacture Folsom replicas. He eventually described 11 different methods he had tried to remove channel flakes. Most simply didn't work: Either the method was impossible with primitive tools or the resulting flute was different from those on the Folsom points. One method succeeded only in driving a copper punch through his left hand.

Crabtree eventually concluded that channel flakes could be removed in only two ways. In one experiment, he placed an antler shaft, known as a "punch," on the bottom of the unfinished artifact and then struck the punch with a sharp upward blow. Because placement of the antler punch was critical, this technique required two workers. A second technique was based on the 17th-century observations of Juan de Torquemada, a Spanish Franciscan friar who travelled through the Central American jungles in 1615. This method used a chest crutch to drive flakes off a core, and Crabtree wondered if it could also remove channel flakes off a Folsom point.

So Crabtree manufactured a chest crutch following Torquemada's description, padding one end and equipping the other with the end of an antler (Figure 10-9). He tied an unfinished experimental Folsom

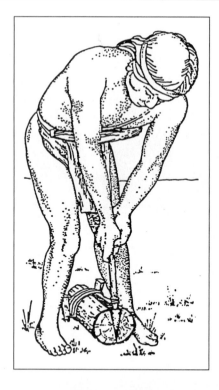

Figure 10-9
Conjectural reconstruction of the use of a chest crutch to drive off the central flute from a Folsom point.

point into a wood-and-thong vise, which he gripped between his feet. Bracing the crutch against his chest and pressing downward, he successfully detached perfect channel flakes, time after time. The resulting artifacts were almost identical to prehistoric Folsom points.

Crabtree's research unleashed an avalanche of experimentation in the fluting problem (it also had some unintended practical consequences; see "Looking Closer: Obsidian Blade Technology: Modern Surgery's Newest Ancient Frontier"). These efforts show that some ten different methods can successfully remove channel flakes and produce the distinctive flutes of Folsom points.

Experimental Archaeology and Uniformitarianism

Archaeologists have used replicative experiments in many different areas of archaeology. They have experimented with ways of moving enormous blocks of stone, such as the huge statues on Easter Island in the Pacific Ocean. They have experimented with ways to manufacture just about everything that is found in archaeological sites—stone tools, pottery, basketry, metal tools, houses, and so on. They've even built structures and then burned them down to see how destruction translates into archaeology.

But what do these experiments prove? Researchers found many ways to remove channel flakes from Folsom points, but which method was actually used in Folsom times? Where's the element of uniformitarianism?

Obviously, a variety of methods work. Crabtree demonstrated that it was *not impossible* to use a chest crutch to replicate Folsom points. But experiments show that other methods were also possible. None of the experimental flintknappers demonstrated conclusively how Folsom points were *actually made*. Replicative experiments often demonstrate only that a given technique could have been used in the past—that it was *not impossible.*

To determine which method or methods were used by Folsom flintknappers, further research is required to compare the characteristics of ancient Folsom points and the waste flakes from their manufacture with experimentally produced Folsom points and waste flakes. Because we know that stone breaks according to certain principles of fracture mechanics, we know that the characteristics of flakes produced today in experiments can help us infer what techniques were used in the past.

But even lacking this element, experimental archaeology can still teach us something about the past. For example, experimental archaeology has taught us three important things about Folsom spear point manufacture. First, regardless of which technique is used, it's difficult to flute points; it takes years of practice. Second, fluting results in a rather high breakage rate near the end of the manufacturing sequence, regardless of the technique. And third, fluting appears to have no specific function. In fact, after Folsom times, similar but unfluted spear points were made for another thousand years. Presumably, these were as effective as Folsom points.

This last point adds a new dimension to our understanding of Folsom spear points. Bruce Bradley, one of the world's premier flintknappers, suggests that fluting was part of a pre-hunt ritual. We don't know if Bradley is right, but the fluting experiments tell us that we need to consider other hypotheses to explain not only *how* people fluted their points, but also *why.*

Furthermore, the uniformitarian element of experimental archaeology often comes in the guise of telling us what *could* or *could not* have happened in the past. Although this may not pinpoint the precise technique that was actually used, it can provide powerful tests of hypotheses.

Here's another example.

Looking Closer
Obsidian Blade Technology: Modern Surgery's Newest Ancient Frontier

Should you try your hand at flintknapping, it won't be long until you've sliced your fingers. In his 50 years of flintknapping, Don Crabtree slashed himself in every conceivable way—across his fingers, through his palm, through a fingernail; one flake zipped right through his shoe.

Examining his cuts one day, Crabtree noticed that, although he still had scars from jagged-edged flint flakes, the wounds caused by obsidian had healed quickly and were almost invisible. He wondered about that.

Then Crabtree saw a friend slice himself while handling some newly made obsidian artifacts. The gash bled profusely, and a physician was summoned. But by the time the doctor arrived, some 20 minutes later, the wound had already begun to heal.

Curious, Crabtree used an electron microscope to compare some fresh obsidian flakes with new razor blades. Interestingly, he found that the fresh flakes were many times sharper than the best razor blades.

Recognizing the potential of such super sharp instruments for surgical applications, Crabtree worried that "the surgeon who pioneers the use of such blades may be accused of reverting to caveman tactics." But in 1975, when Crabtree himself faced major surgery, he managed to cajole his surgeon, Dr. Bruce A. Buck, into using obsidian blades Crabtree himself had fashioned:

The first surgery was when I had a rib removed and a lung section. The cut goes from right under the breast there, clear around back under the shoulder blade. So it's about an 18" cut. And you know I hardly have a scar. . . . And then I've had abdominal surgery four times, from my sternum down to the pelvis. . . . Then I had bilateral femur arteries of woven dacron tubing put in. . . . And there was no problem with sterilization. A fresh blade comes off sterile.

Not long thereafter, more assessments cropped up in medical journals reporting on successful experimental surgeries and speculating about additional applications. Everyone was impressed with the "exquisitely sharp" obsidian edge. It turns out that obsidian blades are as sharp as the newest diamond scalpels, were 100 to 300 times sharper than steel scalpels, and left a smaller cut with much clearer edges—meaning that obsidian blade incisions were quicker to heal and less likely to leave a scar than incisions made with a steel blade.

Several archaeologists now produce obsidian blades commercially for surgery, and these have been used in eye surgery, breast biopsies, bilateral vasectomies, facial plastic surgery, and nerve microsurgery.

Building the Pyramids

Swiss author Erich von Däniken has long argued that aliens from outer space built the world's prehistoric wonders, including the pyramids. Von Däniken looked at those engineering marvels (see Chapter 8) and asked, How is it possible that a primitive people working with the simplest of tools could have built structures of such astounding size and architectural sophistication? In fact, he asked, how could the Egyptians have even moved the large stones and statues without the aid of advanced technology?

This hypothesis can be tested using experimental archaeology: Can stones weighing several tons be moved using only the tools and materials that the ancient Egyptians had available to them? If not, then perhaps von Däniken's hypothesis has some merit. But if such stones *can* be moved with Egyptian technology, then his hypothesis is undermined.

Had von Däniken actually bothered to learn anything about Egyptian archaeology, he would have quickly discovered paintings within tombs that depict men hauling stones and statues. One shows 172 men pulling a statue of Djehutihotep (a Middle Kingdom noble) estimated to weigh some 58 tons (thus, each man is pulling about 300 kilograms). The statue rides on a wooden sledge accompanied by a man who pours a liquid onto the runway in front of the sledge—no doubt to ease the workmen's burden.

But does this method really work? Can it haul stone up ramps dozens of metres long? Maybe the Egyptian tomb painters just made it up.

More than a decade ago, experimental archaeology answered this question. Archaeologist Mark Lehner (Oriental Institute of the University of Chicago and Harvard Semetic Museum) and stonemason Roger Hopkins staged an experiment to see whether they could really move large blocks of stone in this manner. Working with Egyptian quarrymen and masons, they built a pyramid 6 metres high using ancient Egyptian technology. A TV crew from the series *NOVA* filmed the experiment, and so they had to complete the pyramid on a tight schedule—3 weeks.

Lehner experimented with several possible techniques to move and lift stone. One entailed the method depicted in Djehutihotep's tomb, but with the loaded sledge resting on wooden rollers. As the sledge was pulled, the workmen would pick up the rollers behind the sledge and move them to the front. Although this idea seemed sound, Lehner's experiment showed that, if the rollers were not placed perfectly, the sledge would veer off course. The same error happened if the rollers were not perfectly lathed. Lehner concluded that moving large stones over long distances with this method might have been more trouble than it was worth.

Another idea was that wooden levers helped to lift the stones up high. In this method, one side of the block is levered up, and planks are placed beneath it. Then the block's opposite side is levered up, and planks are placed below that side. The workers then repeated the process until they raised the stone to the desired height. This idea worked for small rises but, as the block rose higher, levering became difficult and the stone's balance became precarious.

Lehner then turned to ramps. Archaeologists have found remnants of ramps at several Egyptian sites, including the stone quarry beside the Giza Plateau. These ramps consist of two parallel retaining walls, the area between them filled with rubble and topped with a coat of sand or crushed gypsum. In this top layer the Egyptians set planed logs, perpendicular to the retaining wall, about 50 centimetres apart.

Egyptologists speculate on the kinds of ramps used by the ancient Egyptians. Some suggest a straight ramp—although, by the time the pyramid reached its peak, the ramp would have been hundreds of metres long. Other suggestions include ramps that formed a spiral up the sides of the pyramid or multiple ramps built at different levels during construction.

Lehner built his ramp with an incline of about 7 percent. He found that a 2-ton stone resting on a sledge could easily be hauled up by 20 men. Once the stone was on top of the pyramid, 4 or 5 men using levers could roll it. With this method, Lehner built his pyramid within the 3 weeks allotted for the task.

As in the Folsom fluting experiments, researchers found many ways to build a ramp, and perhaps the Egyptians used all of them. But the precise technique does not matter in this case. The principles involved in simple machines like levers and wedges have not changed from the days of the pharaohs; their capabilities today are the same as they were in the past. This is the important element of uniformitarianism that allows Lehner's experiments to test von Däniken's outlandish hypothesis. With no more than dirt ramps, wooden sledges, rope, and plenty of strong backs, the ancient Egyptians were well equipped to move the stones necessary to build their pyramids and temples. Aliens from outer space were not required.

What Were Stone Tools Used For?

In some cases, experimental archaeology can do more than show us what might or might not have been possible. Experiments can also help establish the unambiguous signatures of past human activities and contribute to archaeology's bridging arguments. Returning to stone tools, one promising direction of experimental study is determining the function of prehistoric stone implements.

As stone tools are used, the edges become damaged and dulled. Compare the edges of used and unused stone tools under a microscope, and you will see **microwear** consisting of minute striations, polish, pitting, and/or microflaking—all of which can reveal something about how the tool was used and what it was used on.

Given that few people use stone tools in their daily lives today, we must turn to experimental research. Microwear research was begun by the late Russian archaeologist Sergei Semenov, whose major work, *Prehistoric Technology,* was published in the Soviet Union in 1957. Many archaeologists followed his lead and

microwear Minute, often microscopic evidence of use damage on the surface and working edge of a flake or artifact; it can include striations, pitting, microflaking, and polish.

have conducted hundreds of experiments to find out what kinds of microwear result from a specific use. Some of the variables include the type of motion (cutting, scraping, boring), the length of time a tool is used, the material being worked (for example, meat, antler, bone, wood, hide), and the stone tool's raw material (chert, basalt, obsidian, and so on).

Ruth Tringham (University of California, Berkeley) studied with Semenov and was one of the first to follow up his research. She reproduced tools from British flint and used each in different ways on antler, bone, wood, skin, flesh, and plant fibre, carefully maintaining constant direction of force and counting the number of strokes. Some of the tools were hand-held, others were hafted to handles.

Tringham then examined and photographed the experimental tools under a low-power (40× to 60×) stereoscopic microscope. Tringham concentrated on the microflaking that occurs as stone tools are used and found that different kinds of use produce different kinds of microflakes on different parts of the tools. Cutting, for instance, produced a series of tiny uneven flake scars along both sides of the working edge. Scraping, however, produced flake scars only on the surface opposite that in direct contact with the worked material. Boring produced distinct trapezoidal flake scars, especially on the sides of the tool.

In addition, Tringham found that edge damage varied with the type of materials being worked. Soft materials such as skin and flesh produced only scalar-shaped scars, whereas hard materials such as antler and bone slowly crushed the edges, eventually dulling the tool so that it would no longer cut at all.

Tringham's experiments established the value of func-

tional analysis with low-power microscopy, and numerous investigators have followed her, taking advantage of the relatively inexpensive equipment and rapid rate of analysis.

Lawrence Keeley (University of Illinois) pioneered an alternative approach. He used high-powered microscopy (up to 400×) and focused on micropolishes rather than microflaking. He found that different worked materials produce different kinds of polish. Some polishes were pitted, some were not; some were extensive, others were present only on the high points of a tool's microtopography (Figure 10-10). Keeley's approach is now the most commonly used one in the analysis of stone tool wear patterns.

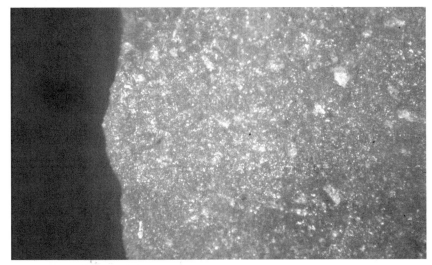

Figure 10-10 Comparison of tool use wear polishes. On the top is a photo taken of a tool's edge before use; on the bottom, the same tool edge after using it to scrape the inside of a hide (both photos taken at 200×).

Source: Doug Bamforth

But M. H. Newcomer (University of London) was skeptical of Keeley's ability to determine tool use from microwear analysis, and so Keeley agreed to a series of blind experiments to test his method's accuracy. Newcomer manufactured 15 tools of fine-grained black English flint. He then worked on a series of materials, such as pine wood, ox hide, and lamb meat, and replicated a range of simple activities, such as scraping, slicing, and boring.

Newcomer then turned the artifacts over to Keeley. The implements were cleaned using detergent, warm water, some chemicals, and an ultrasonic cleaning tank (this is now fairly standard in microwear studies because it removes even fingerprints and organic deposits from tool surfaces). Keeley then used his high-power method to study each piece, looking at (1) general tool size and shape, (2) type and placement of damage, (3) distribution and orientation of microscopic scratches, and (4) location and extent of polish.

How well did Keeley's method do? Table 10-1 shows some remarkable results. In 14 of 16 interpretations (because the right and left edges of Tool 14 seemed different, they were scored independently), he correctly identified the business end of the tool. Keeley contends that the only mistake should not be held against him. He admits to "simple human error" in the case of Tool 10: There is no doubt in Keeley's mind that, had he looked at the right area of the

TABLE 10-1 Results of Blind Testing in High-Power Microwear Analysis

			CORRECT INTERPRETATIONS		
TOOL NUMBER	USE BY NEWCOMER	INTERPRETATION BY KEELEY	AREA USED	ACTIVITY	MATERIAL WORKED
1	Whittling seasoned ash sapling (2 cm dia.) for 18 min.	Cutting (slicing, rather than whittling) wood (branch less than 4 cm dia.)	C		C
2	Chopping ash sapling (3 cm) on pine cutting board for 21 min.	Chopping wood	C	C	C
3	Sawing ash sapling (2.5 cm) for 12 min.	Sawing, possibly wood	C	C	C
4	Cutting raw lamb meat on cutting board for 44 min.	Cutting unknown material, possibly vegetable matter or meat	C	C	$\frac{1}{2}$ C
5	Scraping fat from raw pig hide for 31 min.	Unused			
6	Whittling seasoned pine for 14 min.	(1) Whittling wood (2) graving wood or bone (secondary source)	C	C	C
7	Drilling seasoned pine for 14 min.	Graving, planning, and scraping bone	C		
8	Cutting raw lamb meat on cutting board for 28 min.	Cutting meat	C	C	C
9	Unused	Unused	C	C	C
10	Cutting ox hide on cutting board for 23 min.	Cutting meat (guess) - wrong area of edge though to have been used (counts as wrong interpretation)			
11	Scraping ash sapling (1.5 cm) for 13 min.	Scraping antler (or possibly wood)	C	C	$\frac{1}{2}$ C
12	Cutting frozen lamb meat on cutting board for 23 min.	Cutting or sawing wood	C	C	
13	Cutting bracken fern for 26 min.	Slicing unknown material, but probably vegetable matter	C	C	C
14a	Right edge used to skin off rabbit then cut into strips	Cutting meat	C	C	C
14b	Left edge used to cut forefeet off rabbit at joint	Cutting meat, cartilage, bone (i.e., breaking joint)	C	C	C
15	Scraping ox bone for 11 min.	Scraping possibly hide, less likely antler	C	C	

Source: From Newcomer and Keeley 1979, table 1. Reprinted by permission of Elsevier.

implement's edge, he would have made the correct interpretation of its function. And Tool 5, used to scrape pig hide for 31 minutes, had no apparent wear, as fat will not damage flint.

Keeley's success fell off slightly when he reconstructed tool use (12 of 16 correct), but it is still not bad. His accuracy fell more when identifying the material being worked (10 of 16 correct), but look at some of the "misses": In conducting his butchering experiments, Newcomer had used a wooden cutting board, and Keeley felt that the wood and meat polishes confounded the interpretation of Tool 12. Similarly, Keeley misread the polish on Tool 7 as bone polish and that on Tool 11 as antler polish. But as it turned out, Newcomer had used extremely well-seasoned wood in both cases, at least 10 years old. Such hard wood would mimic the effects of antler.

All in all, these results are not bad, and they established the validity of Keeley's high-power microwear method, which has become an important method in the analysis of ancient stone tools.

Others have followed Keeley's example and conducted more experiments to refine his method. For example, experimental research shows that tools used for only a few minutes do not develop distinctive microwear (this may be why Keeley got the material worked by Tool 15 wrong—11 minutes was not enough time to develop the polish distinctive of bone). So, only microwear on heavily used tools can be fruitfully studied. Others have found that some microwears are difficult to distinguish, such as those produced by working hard wood versus bone (as Keeley found). And different kinds of stone—chert, quartzite, and so on—produce different kinds of polishes. In addition, archaeological objects may have seen multiple uses, with the latest form of wear masking an earlier form. Ancient peoples also re-sharpened stone tools when they became dull—an act that removes the microwear-bearing edges. Thus, only the tool's last use is available for the analyst. Tools were also dropped, trampled, and affected by geological processes—all of which can mask microwear traces. Because archaeological tools almost certainly go through more confusing life histories than Newcomer's experimental tools, Keeley's success rate is probably the best that the archaeologist should expect.

This experimental research is important, but it is still not quite middle-range theory because it does not tell us *why* microchipping and polish develop in the ways that they do. For example, what is it about chert

that results in one type of polish when working meat and another when working antler? The answer to this question would allow archaeologists to implement the principle of uniformitarianism and assume that processes observed in the present can be expected to be true of the past as well. Fortunately, some researchers, such as mechanical engineer Brian Cotterell (University of Sydney) and archaeologist Johan Kamminga (Australian National University), have investigated the micro-mechanics of stone tool wear. As research of this kind develops, experimental studies of use-wear will have an even more secure footing and play an even more important role in archaeological inference.

Taphonomy is good for understanding the role that natural processes play in creating patterns in data at archaeological sites. And experimental archaeology is useful for establishing how things might have been made in the past or for discovering "mechanical" relationships between behaviour and material remains, such as tool use and microwear. But how do we develop middle-range theory to study larger behavioural patterns of human behaviour?

Ethnoarchaeology

What if we wanted to know about ancient kinship, social, or political organizations that no longer exist? These questions were the sort that archaeology in the 1960s sought to answer, and they required the sorts of behavioural inferences that Walter Taylor and Lewis Binford sought.

Binford Takes Off for Points North

In the 1960s, the ways to infer social behaviour from archaeological remains were little more than simple rules of thumb that were often culturally biased. Archaeologists began to test them through ethnoarchaeology, with the understanding that if generalizations cannot cover *contemporary* behaviour, then they cannot be used to interpret the evidence of *ancient* behaviour.

Binford was concerned with this inferential problem and, to help solve it, he conducted significant ethnoarchaeological research in the 1970s among the Nunamiut Eskimo of Alaska. Binford's real interest lay in the Middle Paleolithic archaeology of Europe, especially France (see "In His Own Words: Why I Began

Doing Ethnoarchaeology" by Lewis R. Binford). Why would he study living Eskimos in Alaska if he were interested in the Middle Paleolithic archaeology of France?

Recall from Chapter 9 (see "The Frison Effect" on page 236) that the French archaeologist François Bordes argued that different stone tool Mousterian assemblages were a product of different Neanderthal cultures. These assemblages often alternated throughout the strata of some key French sites, and Bordes argued that this meant the caves were used alternately by different "tribes" of Neanderthals.

Binford saw things differently. He suspected that the different assemblages were the by-products of different activities, not different tribes. He argued that Bordes's inference (different tool assemblages = different Neanderthal tribes) needed to be evaluated. But we cannot evaluate an inferential argument using archaeological data, because the systemic context (the behaviour) cannot be observed independently of the archaeological data. Binford had to find a place where he could observe living hunting peoples and see what remains their activities left behind. The Nunamiut's Arctic environment was somewhat analogous to the French Middle Paleolithic environment, and the Nunamiut hunted large game (caribou and sheep), as had the Neanderthals. But Binford was not as interested in animal bones or the Nunamiut as he was in evaluating the concepts that archaeologists of the time employed to understand the past.

Binford accompanied Nunamiut hunters on their hunting trips, recording what they did at each locality and what debris was left behind. In so doing, he demonstrated that the same people—the same individuals, in fact—leave different kinds of tools and bones at different locations on a landscape. What Nunamiut hunters left behind was not just a product of their culture, but also of the season of the year, the distance back to camp, the availability of transportation, the amount of food already in camp, the weather, and other factors. Although culture plays a significant role in determining what kinds of artifacts are left behind, Binford demonstrated that archaeologists couldn't uncritically *assume* that a difference in artifacts reflects *only* a difference in culture. Other hypotheses, such as site function, have to be tested and discarded before inferring that different tool assemblages in a site's strata indicate use of the site by different cultures.

Ethnoarchaeology has frequently provided such cautionary tales. But ethnoarchaeology can also be a powerful tool for creating middle-range theory. It can do so (1) if it focuses on aspects of ethnographic data that are archaeologically observable, and (2) if it attempts to explain why a relationship between behaviour and archaeologically observable remains should necessarily hold true. As we will see, however, the principle of uniformitarianism is harder to implement in ethnoarchaeology than in taphonomy or experimental archaeology.

Ethnoarchaeologists have researched pottery and stone tool production, hunting and butchering, plant gathering, architecture, trash disposal, trade, and burial rituals in many kinds of societies all over the world. All these studies help archaeologists create better ways of inferring human behaviour from archaeological remains. Here we describe one such project conducted by Kelly in Madagascar.

Ethnoarchaeology in Madagascar

Kelly was trained as an archaeologist, with interests in the archaeology of western North America. He was particularly interested in how nomadism factored into peoples' lives. In some cultures, especially hunting-and-gathering societies, people are highly nomadic, moving as often as every week. In others, especially part-time farming cultures, people change their residence less frequently, perhaps only once or twice a year. Some people return seasonally to a settlement for several years in a row, and some stay year-round in sedentary villages.

Kelly was concerned with archaeology's ability to discern different levels of nomadism archaeologically, and so he looked for an ethnographic situation where he could see variation in nomadism and study its material consequences. He finally learned of the Mikea, a little-known society in the forest of southwestern Madagascar who grow maize and manioc, raise cattle, and do some hunting and gathering.

If you know anything about Madagascar, it probably has to do with lemurs leaping through a tropical forest, but such forests actually make up only a small part of Madagascar. The southwest part of the island, where the Mikea live, is drier and more open. It has distinct wet and dry seasons, and the wet season is blisteringly hot. The forest contains dense vine-covered thickets, stands of 5-metre-high cacti, and

In His Own Words
Why I Began Doing Ethnoarchaeology

by Lewis R. Binford

In 1967 I received funds to go to Europe for a year to work more closely with François Bordes in Bordeaux. My program for research was the following. If we could not study the chipped stone directly, perhaps we could study faunal remains and the horizontal distributions, on excavated archaeological floors, of both fauna and chipped stone. Then it might be possible to relate variability in the lithics to these other properties of the archaeological sites in question. I worked for a year in France, identifying and plotting all the stone tools and animal bones by anatomical part and by breakage pattern.

Thus began a series of disillusionments. I performed one correlation study after another—so many, in fact, that I needed a great steel trunk in order to carry all the papers back to the United States. I could tell you cross-correlations between any pair of Mousterian tool-types, between tools and bones, between bones and the drip-lines in cave sites, between almost any type of data you care to name. What I found, of course, was many new facts that nobody had seen before. But none of these new facts spoke for themselves.

My metal trunk was so big and heavy that I decided to return home by boat and that 5-day trip from Le Havre to New York gave me an opportunity for some disconsolate self-reflection. The whole project was obviously a total failure. What had I done wrong? What had I not done that I should have done? Could it really be that archaeologists simply cannot learn anything about the past? Where was I missing the real problem?

By the time we steamed into New York City, just before the New Year of 1969, some of the answers to these problems were suggested, at least in my thoughts. I prepared a research proposal to go to the Arctic in the spring of 1969 to live with a group of Eskimo hunters. My reasons for going there were little more specific at that stage than that it could hardly fail to be a good educational experience. If I was ever to be able to make accurate inferences from archaeological facts, I was convinced that I had to understand the dynamics of living systems and study their static consequences.

baobab trees. There are no rivers in the Mikea Forest and only a few wells. Bordering the forest on one side is the Mozambique Channel and on the other, a vast savanna.

Mikea live in four major kinds of settlements that differ in how long they are occupied (Figure 10-11). Many have houses in large, permanent villages of 1000 people or more located on the edge of the forest. Here they grow manioc and other crops and raise cattle, pigs, and chickens. These villages frequently host weekly markets that people attend from many kilometres around.

Some Mikea live most of the year in forest hamlets, in kin-related groups of about 40 people. Most people who live in these hamlets also maintain a house in the larger villages. Around these forest hamlets are **slash-and-burn** maize fields. As the arable land around the settlement becomes exhausted the hamlet is moved, about every 3 to 10 years.

Some Mikea who live in the villages also occupy seasonal hamlets in the forest during the growing season so that they can tend to their maize fields. These are much like forest hamlets, but they differ in that they are mostly occupied for a much shorter period of time—during the growing season.

> **slash-and-burn** A horticultural method used frequently in the tropics wherein a section of forest is cut, dried, and then burned, thus returning nutrients to the ground. This permits a plot of land to be farmed for a limited number of years.

Figure 10-11 Mikea habitations. Clockwise from upper left: A family sits around a hearth outside a lean-to in a temporary forest camp; a wattle-and-daub house in a permanent village (note the lack of trash); a house with shade structure in a forest hamlet; and a set of houses lacking shade structures in a seasonal hamlet.

Source: Robert Kelly

Finally, Mikea in the forest hamlets, and some who live in the villages, move away from their homes and into the forest during the dry season. These foraging camps are smaller and are occupied for up to 2 weeks. While in these camps, people collect tubers and honey and search tree hollows for estivating hedgehogs.

Kelly focused on the question, "Are the different lengths of stay reflected in the material remains left behind at these sites?"

Mikea Settlements from an Archaeological Perspective

Recall that ethnoarchaeology's first objective is to relate behaviour to archaeologically observable phenomena. Over time, the only thing that might remain of the Mikea settlements are features such as postholes, hearths, and pits, as well as scattered trash, such as burnt maize, bone fragments, and broken tools.

Accordingly, Kelly and his associates collected data on houses, features, and the distribution of trash in some 30 settlements; for some they recorded data over a 3-year period. They also counted the number of posts in houses and measured their diameters—an activity that amused their Mikea hosts (and once sparked an accusation of witchcraft). They mapped the settlements, showing the locations of houses and

features, as well as the placement of trash deposits. Through interviews, Mikea told the history of each settlement, how they were used, why they were abandoned, as well as other information. What did Kelly find out?

Trash Disposal

Ethnoarchaeologists often begin by observing what people do with their trash. In foraging camps, people unceremoniously toss ash from fires and other trash into bushes, only 1 to 2 metres away from the family hearth. In the forest and seasonal hamlets, trash is disposed in an arc some 3 to 9 metres in front of the house door. Unlike the foraging camps, hamlets were periodically swept clean. This meant that larger items would end up in the trash arc, whereas smaller pieces missed by the broom were trampled into the sand.

And as people occupied their hamlets for longer periods of time, they deposit their trash farther away from their house's door. For example, Kelly visited one settlement the year it was established and found that trash was deposited some 3 to 4 metres from the house. A year later, trash was deposited some 8 metres away. Why? Early in a settlement's life, bushes grow near the house, and they are a convenient place to toss trash. Eventually, however, the bushes are destroyed (for firewood, by children playing, and by goats and cattle foraging). As bushes disappear, trash is swept into bushes farther from the house. In hamlets occupied for several years, in fact, periodic cleanings create a second trash deposit, this time as a ring around the entire settlement.

The permanent villages exhibit a major change in the disposal of trash. Here one cannot simply sweep trash to the side of one's household, because this would mean sweeping trash into a neighbour's space. Consequently, people throw trash into pits next to the houses (the pits were excavated to make mud for the wattle-and-daub house) or they collect trash in baskets inside the houses and periodically dump it at the edge of the settlement, as much as 30 or 40 metres away.

By the way, this doesn't imply that Mikea settlements are filthy or reeking of rotting garbage. Much of the trash, in fact, is maize husks and other dry plant material. Any wet garbage—including almost all bones—is eaten by ever-hungry dogs and pigs.

House Posts

After trash, the next thing an ethnoarchaeologist might notice are houses. Other ethnoarchaeological studies have found, not surprisingly, that people invest more labour and care in houses that they expect to inhabit for a long time, and the Mikea were no different. But how is that investment reflected archaeologically?

In the villages, Mikea often build wattle-and-daub houses about 10 square metres in size. They first set posts upright in the ground, 75 centimetres deep (the length of an adult's arm), and then weave smaller saplings horizontally between these posts. They pack this lattice with coarse mud, smoothing the surface. The house has a door made of planks, usually with a lock, and one or two windows, with wooden shutters. The floors are packed clay. Most of these houses have thatch roofs that extend beyond the walls, forming a narrow veranda around the house. A wattle-and-daub house takes a month or more to build but, if the owner maintains the roof, the house will last 25 years or more.

In the forest hamlets, Mikea have more modest homes. About half the size of village houses, they are made of thinner posts not so deeply set and have roofs of baobab bark slabs and walls of bark, grass, or reeds. A cold wind blows nightly in the dry season, so the door is on the north wall, and the south wall is woven tightly. There is a hearth just inside and to one side of the door. Two to three metres outside the door is another hearth covered by a shade structure, the top of which serves to store dried corn and tools. These forest hamlet houses can be built in a week and need repair every year or so. Some are used for only a year.

The houses in seasonal hamlets look similar to those in forest hamlets, but they appear to a Westerner's eye to be shabbier. They are often shorter and have fewer shade structures outside the front door.

Because foraging camps are used in the dry season and it rarely rains at that time of the year, houses are rare in foraging camps; when they are present, they are no more than lean-tos or simple box-like structures, fashioned from whatever wood is handy and built in an hour or two.

As you might expect, the longer people intend to live in a house, the more time they invest in it. Foraging camps are the most transient of the four settlement types and contain the most ephemeral of shelters (when present at all—some families simply sleep by the fire), whereas the permanent villages contain the largest houses with the most substantial walls and roofs.

The amount of labour involved in each of these houses is reflected in a house's roof and walls, but these things disappear. However, the amount of labour is also reflected in the postholes. And these features are familiar to most archaeologists, because they are often all that remain of ancient houses. What can they tell us?

Plenty, and all of it is pretty commonsense. Although some of the wattle-and-daub houses are large, many of the reed or grass houses are about the same size. Nonetheless, the long wall of village houses contained *twice* as many posts as did the same wall in houses in seasonal hamlets; houses in forest hamlets fell between these two. In addition, the posts used in seasonal hamlets (those settlements used the least amount of time) had more variable diameters than the posts used in the more permanent settlements—especially the wattle-and-daub houses. In seasonal hamlets, people used whatever wood was handy, often scavenging poles from abandoned houses. Post diameters as well as consistency in post diameters reflect the fact that people are more selective about the wood they use when building houses that are more permanent.

Features Outside Houses

Recall from Chapter 3 that features are artifacts that can't be removed from a site—things like hearths, houses, pits, and postholes. In Mikea settlements, these outdoor features include different kinds of houses, fenced compounds, animal corrals, wash areas, cook houses, public troughs, drying racks, stores, wells, ceremonial enclosures, maize threshers, bellows, and storage bins and racks. The particular kinds of features found in a settlement are linked to the particular kinds of activities that take place in Mikea settlements and are not so useful to the development of universal middle-range theory. But differences in the

Looking Closer
Using Ethnoarchaeology to Assess Inuit Housing Needs

by Peter Dawson

Ethnoarchaeology has been used primarily as a tool for developing analogies to aid in the interpretation of archaeological data, but I believe that it can also be used to address problems in the contemporary world. Ethnoarchaeologists are uniquely trained to examine how material culture shapes, and is shaped by, human behaviour. Nowhere is this more apparent than in the relationship between "house form" and "culture." The floor plan of any house is a kind of *footprint* that spatially defines the activities people do, where those activities take place, and how family members interact with each other on a daily basis. Many homes in southern Canada, for example, are highly compartmentalized. This reflects the fact that Western families value privacy and prefer to keep activities separate from one another. Hence, families sleep apart in specific areas of the house, and conduct daily activities in specific rooms. But these conventions of family life vary cross-culturally. Some cultures, for example, emphasize communal living, and therefore sleep and conduct activities in only one or two spaces. As a result, the houses they build are often more open, with fewer walls and doors. This raises an interesting question: What happens when families from one culture are forced to inhabit houses designed by another cultural group? Do they conform to the ideas of family life that are reflected in the spatial organization of these dwellings? Or would such households retain their traditional patterns of activity and space use as a way of retaining their own family values and lifestyles?

Such a situation occurred in the Canadian Arctic following the end of World War II. Government administrators at the time felt that traditional houses such as *iglus* and skin tents were substandard, and were contributing to high instances of mortality in the Inuit population—especially among children. As one government report explained, Inuit children faced two stark choices:

"either gastro-enteritis in the shack, or pneumonia in the tent." In response, Inuit were moved from traditional camps into settled communities where they were provided with Euro-Canadian houses. The perception that new housing was urgently needed meant there was little time to consult with Inuit about their housing requirements. Consequently, the new houses built in the north were essentially the same as those used by Euro-Canadian families in the south.

Inuit families began to use their new houses as if they were traditional dwellings, almost immediately after moving in. For example, families would burn sea mammal oil lamps in houses to reduce heating and lighting costs, butcher seals in living rooms, store seal meat in bathtubs, and repair snow machine engines in kitchens. Government administrators felt that these activities damaged houses, and put the health of families at risk. In response, home economists were flown to the Arctic to educate Inuit in the "correct" ways to live in Euro-Canadian houses. Not surprisingly, these programs were largely unsuccessful.

Fifty years have now passed since the first government housing programs were introduced in the Canadian Arctic. I was therefore interested to learn if Inuit families had adopted the domestic practices of Western families, or if they continued to use their houses in traditional ways. I conducted ethnoarchaeological research in a small Inuit community called Arviat, located on the west coast of Hudson's Bay. I spent three months living with Inuit families, documenting the types of activities they carried out and mapping where these activities occurred within the house. The results were quite fascinating.

I discovered that the programmatic categories used to structure Euro-Canadian houses, such as living rooms, kitchens, bedrooms, and porches, are rarely adhered to by Inuit families (Figure 10-12). While this apparent mismatch between *intended* versus *actual* uses of space may appear arbitrary, it is, in fact, systematically matched to the spatial structure of the houses they inhabit. Inuit households, for example, lump most of their activities into one or two spaces within the house (i.e., living rooms, kitchens), and many express a preference for sleeping together as a family unit in living rooms. These rooms are typically integrated into the floor plan of the house, and are well connected to other areas of the house. Bedrooms, which were typically segregated and poorly connected, were either unoccupied or used as storage or work areas.

In many Inuit homes, the preparation and consumption of traditional foods like walrus, seal, and caribou are interactive processes that promote sharing and feelings of emotional closeness within the family. For these reasons, they were traditionally performed within the same space. Western kitchens, however, are inadequate for such purposes because they have been designed for cooking Western foods. Countertops cannot support the weight and size of traditional foods such as seal, beluga, and caribou. What's more, sinks are too small to catch the mess associated with butchering. This often means that traditional food is butchered and cooked on the porch outside the house, or in a canvas tent. Once prepared, it is then brought back into the house for consumption. When traditional food is eaten, tables and chairs are often removed to enlarge the kitchen space, and family members eat while seated on the floor. The use of small electric stoves to boil large pots of caribou meat also releases huge amounts of moisture into the air, causing construction materials to rot, and mould to form on surfaces. Such traditional practices reduce the life expectancy of houses—a critical issue because housing is in short supply in many arctic communities.

So why haven't Inuit families become more like Western families? The answer seems to be that

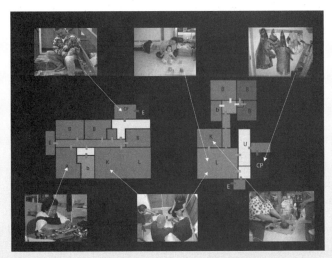

Figure 10-12 Mapping how Inuit families use space in Euro-Canadian style houses. (L) Living room; (K) Kitchen; (B) Bedroom; (b) Bathroom; (S) Storage Room; (U) Utility Room; (CP) Cold Porch.

Source: Dr. Peter Dawson

many traditional activities exist as important sources of cultural identity for Inuit families. In essence, performing them transforms Western-style houses into facsimiles of traditional houses, such as the *iglu* and hide tent. My ethoarchaeological observations about how Inuit families use space are currently being applied to design houses that better reflect the lifestyles and cultural values of Inuit families.

When it comes to northern housing, getting it right is important because well-designed houses last longer. More importantly, however, they foster feelings of security and well-being that strengthen cultural identities in the face of outside change. Is this really ethnoarchaeology? I believe it is, because it examines something that social-cultural anthropologists often ignore: the relationship between human behaviour and the material world in which we all live. It also provides an example of how the techniques of archaeology can be used to address important economic and social issues in the present.

range of diversity of features among the different settlement types are useful.

The more permanent a Mikea settlement is, the greater the range of features it contains. When people intend to stay in one place for years or plan to return to a settlement seasonally for several years, they invest more time in features that have a single purpose, rather than "making do" with temporary facilities. Washhouses, for example, are never found in foraging camps or seasonal hamlets: People are basically "camping" at both, and water is a rare commodity in dry season forest camps. People bathe back at the forest hamlet or village. Washhouses are also rarely found in forest hamlets—where the small, related community means that people can expect privacy without bothering to build a separate facility. However, washhouses are common in the densely populated villages, where privacy is more difficult, and where investment in a facility is worthwhile.

Table 10-2 summarizes these differences among Mikea settlements. In this table we related some archaeologically recoverable variables (trash distribution, postholes, features) to human behaviour (the length of occupation). Simply by recording the way trash is distributed, the range of features present, the number of postholes per house, and the variation in posthole diameter, we could place a new settlement into one of the four categories with a high degree of accuracy. This fulfills the first criterion of a middle-range study—it focuses on aspects of ethnographic data that are archaeologically observable. But does it explain why the relationship between behaviour and archaeologically observable remains is necessarily true? What do such ethnoarchaeological studies do for archaeology?

Ethnoarchaeology and Uniformitarianism

As we have pointed out, middle-range theory tries to *explain* patterning between behaviour and material remains. Such explanations depend on the principle of uniformitarianism. It is relatively easy to see how this principle applies in both taphonomy and experimental archaeology, because both study natural processes and mechanical relationships.

But the principle of uniformitarianism is tougher to apply in ethnoarchaeology, because human behaviour is anything but mechanical. We conducted our study of the Mikea within the materialist paradigm (explained in Chapter 3); more specifically, it relied upon a theoretical framework known as human behavioural ecology. One of the tenets of this framework is that, because people have many demands on their time, they make choices that maximize the utility of their decisions. Choices about what kind of house to build reflect this fact. Why would someone in a forest hamlet invest more than a month in building a wattle-and-daub house when one built in less than a week will suffice for the time that the hamlet will be occupied? The "extra" 3 weeks can then be put toward clearing another maize field, building a ceremonial enclosure, or some other task more important than house-building. Similarly, why take time to select just the right poles for a house in a seasonal hamlet that will be occupied for only a few months of the year? From a materialist perspective, the time would be better spent in clearing more fields, planting, weeding, or preparing for a celebration. In fact, the Mikea themselves said that the longer they intended to remain in a settlement, the more care they put into constructing houses and facilities such as maize-threshing bins and

TABLE 10-2 Summary of Differences in Mikea Settlements

SETTLEMENT TYPE	HOUSE SIZE	POST VARIABILITY	SECONDARY POSTS	DISTANCE TO TRASH (METRES)	FEATURE DIVERSITY
Villages	Various, but can be large	Low	Many, closely spaced	10–40+	High
Forest hamlets	Small	Low–Medium	Fewer, farther apart	4–9	Medium
Seasonal hamlets	Small	High	Fewer, farther apart	3–4	Medium–Low
Foraging camps	Lean-tos or "boxes," if present at all	n/a	n/a	1–2	Low

n/a = not applicable

outhouses. They also said they would be more selective in their building material, choosing poles of a particular diameter for posts and even searching out certain species of wood, such as ones known for their ability to resist destruction by insects.

These seem like logical choices, and several ethnoarchaeological studies have found similar patterns in trash disposal, house form, and feature diversity in other societies in the world. Combined with these other studies, the Mikea research helps form a strong formal analogy; combined with the theoretical framework of human behaviour ecology, it also contains elements that make it middle-range theory.

What about Culture?

But the issue of culture can make ethnographic analogies, even ones strong enough to qualify as middle-range theory, problematic. We have discussed, for instance, the disposal of trash among the Mikea as being simply a function of how long a settlement is occupied. The longer it is occupied, the farther away from a house trash is removed. But cultural ideas about trash may come into play.

Ian Hodder, a postprocessual archaeologist, conducted ethnoarchaeological research with the Moro and Mesakin in Sudan. Both groups raise various grains, as well as pigs, cattle, and goats. In both, families live in household compounds. But the Moro's compounds are relatively free of trash, whereas the Mesakin's are messier; in particular, the Moro keep pig bones out of the compounds.

Hodder argues that some of the difference between the two societies and the way they deal with trash lies in different ideas about women. Moro men see contact with women as potentially "polluting" their strength and authority. And, because Moro women take care of pigs, they are associated with these animals; men are associated with cattle. As a result, Moro men consider pig remains to be foul, and Moro women take care to remove pig bones from the trash and dispose of them separately. The Mesakin do not share the Moro's beliefs about women, and they treat pig bones the same as any other animal remains. Thus, Hodder argues that archaeologists need to consider the symbolic meanings of material culture in order to appreciate how it will be treated as trash.

But the "cultural" component is very difficult to study archaeologically. And this means that the principle of uniformitarianism will remain difficult to

implement in ethnoarchaeology. For some archaeologists, this means that ethnoarchaeology can provide us only with strong analogies, not middle-range theory.

For others, ethnoarchaeological studies conducted across a spectrum of societies provide archaeology with analogies that, taken together, suggest some important principles of human behaviour. These principles could *provisionally* be taken as uniform for the purpose of creating and testing hypotheses and allow ethnoarchaeology to act as middle-range theory to support archaeological inferences. Let's see how this might work.

Settlement Pattern Change in the Mimbres Valley

Specifics aside, the Mikea case suggests that more labour is invested in more-permanent rather than in more-transient houses. This could be reflected archaeologically in the use of more substantial building materials (such as wattle-and-daub or stone masonry rather than poles and grass), a larger number of posts, and more standardized posts. This information can be used to make archaeological interpretations.

Margaret Nelson and Michelle Hegmon (Arizona State University) have surveyed and excavated in the eastern Mimbres region of southern New Mexico for a number of years. (This is the region where we find the Mimbres pottery that we mentioned in Chapter 8.) The Mimbres region is far removed from Madagascar, but exhibits some similarities: Both regions are arid, and both are or were occupied by maize horticulturalists.

Nelson and Hegmon's survey found sites that contained two components, one dated to the Classic Mimbres Phase (A.D. 1000–1150), and the other to the Post Classic Phase (A.D. 1150–1300).

Nelson and Hegmon were interested in understanding the abandonment of regions. Although many archaeologists previously argued that people abandoned the Mimbres region after A.D. 1150, Nelson and Hegmon believed that the region was still occupied but that the settlement pattern had changed in such a way that it gave the region the *appearance* of having been abandoned.

Nelson and Hegmon found that during the Classic Mimbres Phase, people lived in large, pueblo villages. The houses were built of stone masonry, with roofs of heavy beams (Figure 10-13). Radiocarbon and tree-ring dating indicated that many of these villages were, indeed, no longer occupied after A.D. 1150.

Figure 10-13 Margaret Nelson (right) standing inside a Mimbres pueblo room; some postholes are visible on the floor.

Source: Margaret Nelson

But another kind of settlement was also in use during the Classic Mimbres Phase. Although people lived in large pueblo villages, they also used what Nelson and Hegmon term "farmsteads." These were small sites, consisting of only one or a few structures, usually open on one side and lightly constructed of a few, small posts, with few interior features. Nelson and Hegmon argue that a few members of the family occupied these sites during the growing season to care for the young maize plants. Located some distance from the villages, the field houses contained only minimal shelter requirements.

Nelson and Hegmon's careful excavation and extensive dating showed that, on some of these sites, someone modified the flimsy Classic Phase structures in farmsteads during the following Post Classic Phase. Added to the lightly constructed buildings were larger and more numerous posts, masonry walls, and more substantial roofs. Eventually, they formed small pueblos of some 6 to 12 rooms. Inside these small pueblo structures was also a greater diversity of features than was found in the Classic Phase field houses. From these data, Nelson and Hegmon argue that the Mimbres region had not been abandoned. Instead, during the Post Classic phase, people moved out of the large pueblos into smaller, dispersed communities and turned their field houses into permanent residences.

Nelson and Hegmon's Classic Phase field houses are analogous to Mikea seasonal hamlets, and their Post Classic Phase modifications are analogous to Mikea village house construction. Taken by itself, the Mikea case is only analogy—and a weak one at that, given that no cultural link exists between the Mikea and the prehistoric peoples of the American Southwest.

However, the Mikea study does highlight some necessary links between house size and construction elements—for example, large houses require larger support posts. Coupled with other ethnoarchaeological studies that reach similar conclusions, the Mikea data help form a strong formal analogy with elements of middle-range theory that provide a solid warrant for treating Nelson and Hegmon's interpretation as a viable hypothesis for further testing.

In this way, ethnoarchaeology will continue to play an important role in future archaeological inference.

Conclusion

Archaeology is all about making inferences from artifacts, ecofacts, features, and their contexts. Middle-range theory is what allows archaeologists to know that they really do know something about the past. It lies at the heart of archaeology, because archaeology is the study of the past based on material remains. As you have seen in this chapter, archaeologists go about constructing all-important middle-range theory through taphonomy, experimental archaeology, and ethnoarchaeology. It requires that archaeologists step out of their excavation trenches and conduct a different kind of research. Some archaeologists, in fact, have permanently hung up their trowels and devoted their careers to the development of middle-range theory. And this is good, because without middle-range theory, our inferences from archaeology would be little more than just-so stories, with no more credence behind them than silly ideas like aliens building pyramids. In the following chapters, we will see how archaeologists have put studies in taphonomy, experimental archaeology, and ethnoarchaeology to use in reconstructing the past.

Summary

- Because the "facts" of archaeology are incapable of speaking for themselves, archaeologists must follow geology's principle of uniformitarianism and study ongoing processes and their material remains.

- Analogy is one way to reconstruct the past but is limited in its utility to societies that have very close geographic and cultural counterparts (preferably ones with a historical connection) or to fairly low-level inferences.

- Middle-range research allows archaeologists to make better inferences from archaeological data by clarifying the basis for the inference; it is research designed to create bridging arguments that link human behaviour and/or natural processes to their material remains.

- The principle of uniformitarianism is critical in the development of middle-range theory because it is what allows confidence in a middle-range theory's ability to infer human behaviour or natural processes from archaeological remains.

- Analogies can be formal, relational, or a mixture of both. Formal analogies rely on similarities in form, and relational analogies rely on cultural continuity or causal linkages to justify their use in archaeological inference.

- Middle-range theory is a particular kind of analogy in that it attempts to demonstrate why a particular pattern in archaeological data can be unambiguously interpreted in a particular way.

- Taphonomy studies how natural processes help create the archaeological record; it helps weed out patterns that result from natural processes and thus helps define patterns that need to be interpreted in human behavioural terms. It also helps the archaeologist understand the environmental context of past human behaviour.

- Experimental archaeology studies things that can no longer be observed in action today, such as ancient technologies that are no longer practised.

- Replicative experiments are one class of experimental archaeology. They can help show what techniques could or could not have been used in the past.

- Experimental archaeology, such as stone tool use-wear studies, can also link human behaviour and material signatures.

- Ethnoarchaeologists study living societies, observing artifacts, features, and material remains while they still exist in their systemic, behavioural contexts. Ethnoarchaeology links human behaviour with archaeologically observable material remains.

- Of the three ways to develop middle-range theory, the principle of uniformitarianism is most difficult to implement in ethnoarchaeology.

Additional Reading

CANADIAN RESOURCES

Dawson, Peter. (2006). The relationship between "house form" and "culture" in Inuit society. *Etudes/Inuit Studies 30*(2).

Dawson, P. (1995). Unsympathetic users: An ethnoarchaeological examination of Inuit responses to the changing nature of the built environment. *Arctic, 28*(2), 71–80.

Kooyman, B. (2006). Boundary theory as a means of understanding social space in archaeological sites. *Journal of Anthropological Archaeology 25*, 424–435.

OTHER RESOURCES

Andrefsky, William. (1998). *Lithics: Macroscopic Approaches to Analysis.* Cambridge: Cambridge University Press.

Binford, Lewis R. (1978). *Nunamiut Ethnoarchaeology.* New York: Academic Press.

David, Nicholas, and Kramer, Carol (2001). *Ethnoarchaeology in Action.* Cambridge: Cambridge University Press.

Longacre, William A., and Skibo, James M. (Eds.). (1994). *Kalinga Ethnoarchaeology: Expanding Archaeological Method and Theory.* Washington, DC: Smithsonian Institution Press.

Schick, Kathy, and Toth, Nicholas (1993). *Making Silent Stones Speak: Human Evolution and the Dawn of Technology.* New York: Touchstone.

Online Resources

COMPANION WEBSITE
Visit *http://www.archaeology1ce.nelson.com* to access a wide range of material to help you succeed in your introductory archaeology course. These include flashcards, Internet exercises, Web links, and practice quizzes.

RESEARCH ONLINE WITH INFOTRAC COLLEGE EDITION
From the Student Companion Website, you can access the InfoTrac College Edition database, which offers thousands of full-length articles for your research.

11 People, Plants, and Animals in the Past

OUTLINE

The Stampede (1883), by Frederick Verner, depicts buffalo, or Plains bison, an important animal to the Blackfoot of Alberta. These animals covered the Plains in countless numbers, and provided food, clothing, shelter, and tools to Plains aboriginal groups.

Source: Frederick Arthur Verner, "The Stampede", 1883, oil on canvas, Collection of Glenbow Museum, Calgary, Canada, 55.28

Preview

Archaeologists have plenty of methods and techniques for reconstructing how people made a living in the past, and in this chapter we discuss a few of them.

We begin with faunal analysis, the identification and interpretation of animal remains recovered in an archaeological context. Animal bones not only enable the archaeologist to study ancient hunting methods and diet, but they also assist in reconstructing past environments. Of course, getting at the meaning behind the bones is neither easy nor straightforward. This chapter will provide you with the basics for understanding what we can do with a bunch of animal bones.

Plant remains are also valuable to archaeology. We have already seen how the study of tree rings provides archaeologists with a trustworthy way of dating specific events of the past—when a certain Pueblo dwelling was built, for example. We learned also that tree-ring analysis indicates something about past climates, environments, and the local history of forest fires. Archaeological plant remains—pollen, seeds, charcoal, and phytoliths—also tell us about what wild plants people collected, the crops they grew, the fuels they burned, and even the roles played by plants in rituals. Plant and animal remains can also tell us in what season of the year people occupied a site.

Introduction

So far, we have talked mostly about artifacts and features—objects created by humans and left behind. Archaeological sites also contain ecofacts—plant and animal remains; some of these are food refuse, left by humans, but sometimes similar remains enter sites through natural processes (as when plants and animals die on a site). As you'll recall, taphonomic studies figure out how plant and animal remains accumulate in archaeological sites. In this chapter, we are more concerned with what plant parts and animal bones tell us about human behaviour.

Formation processes are critical to inferences based on plant and animal remains. In fact, as you read this and later chapters, keep asking yourself: How do archaeologists know to interpret their data in one way rather than another? What middle-range research stands behind the inferences that archaeologists make? Could there be other interpretations? If so, how can we test those alternatives?

Archaeologists use many methods to recover and interpret animal and plant remains. So many, in fact, that we can present only a few here. Rather than blanket the field, we will introduce some of the major categories of data and provide a sense of how archaeologists go about interpreting them. We begin with archaeofaunas.

What's an Archaeofauna?

An **archaeofauna** consists of the animal bones recovered from an archaeological site. Archaeofaunas differ from paleontological assemblages because humans

archaeofauna The animal bones recovered from an archaeological site.

may have had a hand in their formation. Animal bones turn up in two major archaeological contexts:

- At a **kill** or butchering **site,** bones may lie more or less the way they were when the hunters left, affected by carnivore scavenging, weathering, and other natural factors.
- In camps and villages, we find bones where hunted animals were brought back or domesticated animals were butchered.

Sometimes a site's faunal remains number in the tens of thousands and include some animals killed on the site, some that were transported from kill sites elsewhere, and many noncultural remains (these are bones of animals that simply died in the site or that carnivores or raptors brought in after people abandoned the site).

After recovering an archaeofauna, archaeologists commonly perform a **faunal analysis;** the person who does this is a **zooarchaeologist** (also known as a **faunal analyst**). To show you how this is done, let's look at how one zooarchaeologist went about analyzing the archaeofauna of the Folsom component at Wyoming's Agate Basin site.

The Agate Basin Site

Sometime around 1916, rancher William Spencer was riding across the broken terrain of his ranch in eastern Wyoming. Visiting a spring, he noticed some large bones protruding from the edge of an arroyo (just as George McJunkin did at the Folsom site in New Mexico). His curiosity piqued, he returned to the spring several times, eventually collecting a number of large, beautiful spear points as well as bison bones from the site.

Years later, in 1941, Spencer met Robert Frison, a state game warden, at an informal gathering of history buffs under some cottonwood trees on the Cheyenne River, a short distance north of the Agate Basin site. Frison's job took him outdoors a lot, and he had visited many sites and developed quite an interest in Paleo-Indian artifacts. The following year, the men visited the site together and found more bison bones and spear points. Frison thought the points could be old, so he sent one to Frank H. H. Roberts at the Smithsonian Institution (Frison knew Roberts because Frison knew the man who had discovered the Lindenmeier Folsom site in Colorado, which Roberts had excavated).

The points intrigued Roberts, and so he conducted excavations at Agate Basin that summer and in the following years. Later, William Bass (then at the University of Kansas) excavated there, and then, in the 1970s, Robert Frison's nephew, archaeologist George Frison (see Chapter 9), and Dennis Stanford (Smithsonian Institution) worked there together. (See Figure 11-1.)

Frison and Stanford published a thorough report on their research, but there is always more that we can do with archaeological collections. For this reason, Matt Hill (Iowa State University) decided to take another look at Agate Basin's Folsom component archaeofaunas.

Let's begin with Hill's conclusions. About 10,780 radiocarbon years ago, a small group of Folsom hunters camped by the Agate Basin site in late March or early April. They killed at least 11 bison (*Bison antiquus*) and five pronghorn antelope (*Antilocapra americana*), probably not too far away from their camp. They partially butchered the bison at the kill site and, for the most part, brought entire limbs back to camp. The antelope were field-dressed at the kill site, and the nearly intact carcasses were carried back to the Agate Basin camp. Despite their success, the hunters may have had a hard time making ends meet. Unlike later hunter-gatherers on the Plains, these Folsom hunters seem not to have relied heavily on meat storage.

How did Hill extract all this information from a bunch of broken bones?

Identifying Bones

Hill began by identifying the bones from the Folsom component, working through the catalogued collection, piece by piece, and assigning each bone or bone fragment to a species, if possible.

"Identifying the bones" is more complicated than it might sound. Field archaeologists know, at least in a rough way, what mammal, bird, reptile, and fish bones look like, but far more detailed information is needed in faunal analysis. The first step is to assign each specimen

---

kill sites Places where animals were killed in the past.

faunal analysis Identification and interpretation of animal remains from an archaeological site.

zooarchaeologist (also faunal analyst) An individual who studies the faunal (animal) remains recovered from archaeological sites.

Figure 11-1 The Agate Basin site, showing the Folsom level under excavation in 1978.
Source: University of Wyoming, Frison Institute

to **element** (the anatomical part of the body). Is this bone a rib splinter, part of the pelvis, or a skull fragment? A femur, tibia, or calcaneus (the heel bone)? Identifying elements requires a solid working knowledge of comparative anatomy (Figure 11-2).

But conventional comparative anatomy classes are insufficient because they deal with whole bones—not the dirty fragments that archaeologists confront. Classroom experience helps, but you really learn faunal analysis by handling a lot of bones yourself.

The next step is to identify the specimens to **taxon** (kind of animal). One's success here depends on the condition of the specimen and the expertise of the analyst. The aim is to identify each bone to species, but sometimes the bones are so fragmentary that you can only identify them to higher-order groups, such as family or class. For instance, one can rarely determine whether a long bone fragment (that is, a small piece of one of the long limb bones, such as a femur shaft) came from a deer or a bighorn sheep—but anyone can tell that it's not a mouse bone. In this case, the analyst might be able to identify the fragment only to the order Artiodactyla (because deer and sheep are in different families, the next-broader level of classification is used). Identification to taxon, therefore, often means "narrowing down the possibilities," rather than identifying the exact species—although that is always preferred.

In other cases, the specimen might be so difficult to identify that you can only assign it to one of five standard animal **size classes.** Rodent- and rabbit-size animals are in size class 1; wolf- and pronghorn antelope–size animals are class 2; animals the size of mule deer and bighorn sheep are in size class 3; bison- and elk-size animals are in class 4; and in class 5 are large animals such as giraffes, hippos, and elephants.

element In faunal analysis, a specific skeletal part of the body—for example, humerus or sternum.

taxon In faunal analysis, the classification of a skeletal element to a taxonomic category—species, genus, family, or order.

size classes A categorization of faunal remains, not to taxon, but to one of five categories based on body size.

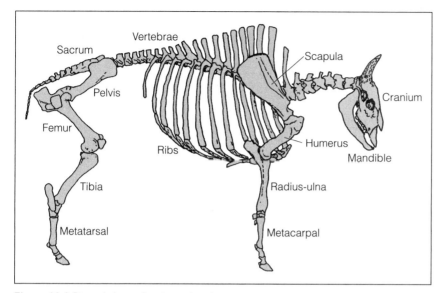

Figure 11-2 Bison skeleton showing major elements.

So, how did Hill know whether a scrap of bone was a piece of a bison femur, a pronghorn radius, a flat-headed peccary tibia, or a striped skunk skull? The zooarchaeologist makes these identifications through a **comparative collection.** The standard zooarchaeology lab commonly contains box after box of modern animal skeletons—everything from elephants to deer mice. Each box is labelled with the species, the individual's approximate age at death, its sex, and where and when it was collected. A comparative collection contains examples of young and old, as well as male and female, members of a species. These collections are put together by hunting or trapping the animals, picking up road kills (you need a licence to do these things in some provinces and territories in Canada, and most states), or acquiring carcasses from provincial, territorial, or state authorities (sometimes confiscated from poachers).

Once collected, the specimens are manually defleshed and cleaned. Sometimes the remains are buried and nature is allowed to take its course. Other methods include simmering the bones in a solution of detergent or placing the greasy bones in a colony of dermestid beetles, which, over a few weeks' time, will literally pick the bones clean of all tissue.

Using a comparative collection, Hill identified the archaeological bones to taxon. Measurements taken on some adult bones helped determine if the bone was from a male or female.

Hill eventually assigned all the Agate Basin bones to element and taxon (or size class). Most bones were bison or pronghorn, but other species included wolf, striped skunk, and frogs. Because there were only a few bones from most of these species, Hill focused on the bison and pronghorn.

Natural or Cultural?

Recalling the discussion of taphonomy in Chapter 10, you should be wondering how Hill could be certain (1) that the bison and pronghorn remains were deposited by humans and (2) that they were deposited during the same occupation of the site.

For one thing, the bones bore some stone tool cut marks (which we know how to distinguish from carnivore tooth marks), some were burned, and some of the larger ones had impact fractures—distinctive breaks that resulted when the Folsom people smashed the bones open to retrieve the fatty, calorie-rich marrow. Frison and Stanford also found a cluster of antelope bones, some of them burned, around a hearth.

A few of the bones did show evidence of carnivore gnawing. But tooth marks appeared on only a few bison humeri and femora, and on only three antelope specimens. So, the evidence pointed to humans as the agents responsible for the antelope and bison bones at Agate Basin.

Hill also thinks that the antelope and bison bones were deposited during the same occupation of the site. The Folsom assemblage is not large, nor is it widely dispersed; some of the remains, in fact, still lie in anatomical position. This is what we would expect to see in a one-shot use of the site. In addition, we might expect all the bones to be equally weathered, just as we saw at the Hudson-Meng site—an "instantaneous" herd death, where nearly all the skulls were weathered in the same way.

comparative collection A skeletal collection of modern fauna of both sexes and different ages used to make identifications of archaeofaunas.

To reach this conclusion, Hill took bone size into account. Because antelope bones are smaller than bison bones, they are more easily broken (by carnivores and also by hunters, who broke the bones for their marrow). Because they're smaller, sediment will cover antelope bones more quickly than the larger bison bones. So, even if all the faunal remains were deposited at about the same time, the bison bones should be slightly more weathered than the antelope bones. This was the case at Agate Basin, and Hill concluded that the bison and antelope bones in the Folsom component were animals killed by the same people during the same occupation.

What to Count?

To reconstruct human behaviour at Agate Basin, Hill needed to search for meaningful patterns in the bone data, and this required that he count the bones.

Zooarchaeologists count bones in two ways, depending upon their objectives. One method involves the **number of identified specimens,** or **NISP.** This count is simply the total number of bone specimens that are identified to a particular taxon. Table 11-1 shows the NISP for the Folsom component at the Agate Basin site. NISP is useful for comparing large numbers of collections from different sites, but it has a severe limitation in reconstructing human behaviour at a single site.

Table 11-1 suggests that bison were more important than pronghorn at Agate Basin. But what if the 1033 bison specimens came from a single highly fragmented skeleton, whereas each of the 297 antelope bones came from 297 different individuals? If this were the case, then antelope would be many times more important than bison at this site. Or, maybe the species were butchered in different ways, with certain bones becoming highly fragmented (and hence disappearing from the archaeological record altogether or turning into unidentifiable elements that are not included in the NISP counts).

number of identified specimens (NISP) The raw number of identified bones (specimens) per species; a largely outmoded way of comparing archaeological bone frequencies.

minimum number of individuals (MNI) The smallest number of individuals necessary to account for all identified bones.

TABLE 11-1 NISP Counts for the Folsom Component at the Agate Basin

COMMON NAME	SCIENTIFIC NAME	NISP
Bison	Bison antiquus	1033
Pronghorn antelope	Antilocapra americana	297
Wolf	Canis lupus	7
Coyote	Canis latrans	3
Red fox	Vulpes vulpes	1
Striped skunk	Mephitis mephitis	1
Flat-headed peccary	Platygonus compressus	1
Dog	Canis sp. (possibly domesticated)	5
Jackrabbit	Lepus cf. townsendii or californicus	10
Rabbit	Sylvilagus cf. nutallii or audubonii	4
Grouse	Centrocercus urophasianus	2
Frog	Rana pipiens	Few
Elk	Cervus elaphus (antler only)	2
Camel	Camelops sp. (possible tool)	1

Source: Hill 2001.

The "sp." in some scientific names means that the genus is certain, but the species is not. The "cf." in other cases means that the specimen compares very well with one or two species within a genus, but that the researcher is not certain of the species identification. Camel became extinct about 11,200 radiocarbon years ago, and there is no good evidence that humans ever hunted them; the specimen here might be a piece that a Folsom hunter picked up someplace or evidence of an animal that died at the site long before the hunters camped there.

Problems like this have led archaeologists to another way of comparing bone frequencies, called the **minimum number of individuals,** or **MNI.** Developed by paleontologists, MNI is the minimum number of individuals that is necessary to account for all the skeletal elements of a particular species found in the site. Suppose, for instance, that you excavated 100 fragments of bison bone from a site. The NISP equals 100, but what is the MNI? That is, what is the minimum number of individual bison required to account for those 100 bone fragments?

To figure this out, you must tabulate bone frequency by element (left femur, right tibia, hyoid, and so on) to determine the most *abundant* skeletal element. This process requires that you not only assign the specimens their correct *element,* but for those bones that come in pairs, to their correct *side* as well. If four right femurs show up in the 100 bone fragments, then you know that *at least* four bison account for the fragments.

But MNI has some limitations as well. When bones are fragmented, it is possible that the "four right femurs" are really fragments from the same upper leg bone. To eliminate this problem, you must compare the bone fragments, one by one, to see whether two fragments could have come from the same bone. In our hypothetical example, if we found that two of the four right femur fragments could have come from the same femur, then the MNI would only be three.

Calculating MNI also depends on how you divide your site. Agate Basin was probably occupied once by Folsom hunters for a few weeks. It is what archaeologists call a *fine-grained* assemblage, meaning that it hasn't become complicated by additional, overlapping occupations. But what if the site were *coarse-grained?* What if it had been repeatedly occupied over a long period of time such that the resulting assemblage is the result of many periods of use over decades—or even thousands of years? We could compute the minimum number of individuals for a coarse-grained assemblage, but this might have the unfortunate consequence of reducing hundreds of bone fragments to a very few MNI, perhaps just one or two individuals. This would obviously be a poor choice. Sometimes investigators calculate their minimum numbers based on stratigraphic breaks observed during excavation. Once again, however, the MNI per species depends on how fine one wishes to draw the stratigraphic boundaries.

Ultimately, the decision depends on the site's specific characteristics. In general, MNI is most useful and accurate when fine stratigraphic divisions are used and when bones are not overly fragmented. The Folsom component at Agate Basin meets these criteria.

Where did Hill go from here? Of the 1033 bison bones, Hill could identify 843 to element; likewise, he could identify 198 of the 297 antelope bone fragments to element. Although the antelope specimens were fragmented, Hill identified four right and one left humeri (upper arm bones). This might suggest an MNI of four (given that the single left humerus could be a match to one of the right humeri). But the single left humerus was not the same size as any of the right humeri, and so Hill concluded that *at least* five antelope were brought to the site.

Because they are larger and heavier, the bison long bones were more intact. Taking the humeri, radii, femora, and tibiae, Hill assigned each to a side and then decided, using a comparative collection, whether they were male or female (or indeterminate, because young, less-developed animals don't yet exhibit characteristics that allow assigning to a sex). He then com-

pared their sizes to see if the rights and lefts of each sex could possibly have come from the same animal, or whether the femora and tibiae, and the humeri and radii, could anatomically refit (that is, would they fit together in their usual anatomical positions; femora and tibiae, for example, articulate at the patella, the knee cap). If they did refit, then they could have come from the same animal (Figure 11-3).

From this comparison, Hill determined that there were *at least* four males, four females, and three immature bison brought to the site.

So now we know the minimum number of animals that Folsom hunters killed at the Agate Basin site: eleven bison and five pronghorn antelope.

Reconstructing Human Behaviour at Agate Basin

By looking at which specific elements were present, Hill found that elements of the **axial skeleton** (the head, mandibles, vertebrae, ribs, sacrum, tail) for both bison and pronghorn were rare compared with bones from the **appendicular skeleton** (everything else). Bison limb bones were also more common relative to the other bison bones, and antelope lower leg bones (especially for the front legs) and toes were rare.

What accounts for these patterns?

Viewed as food, bones function two ways—as a support for meat and as a container of marrow. Experimental research can quantify how much food value a bone represents in terms of these two entities. Bison long bones, for instance, rank high in both meat and marrow content, suggesting that hunters brought back only the high-utility portions of the bison and left the axial skeleton at the kill site.

The pronghorn skeletons at the Agate Basin site were more complete than the bison skeletons. Apparently, the antelope were gutted and then field-dressed by removing the feet and lower limb bones, which contain little marrow and have little meat wrapped about them. The hunters then carried the rest of the antelope back to camp as more or less complete carcasses. The

axial skeleton The head, mandibles, vertebrae, ribs, sacrum, and tail of an animal skeleton.

appendicular skeleton All parts of an animal excluding the axial skeleton.

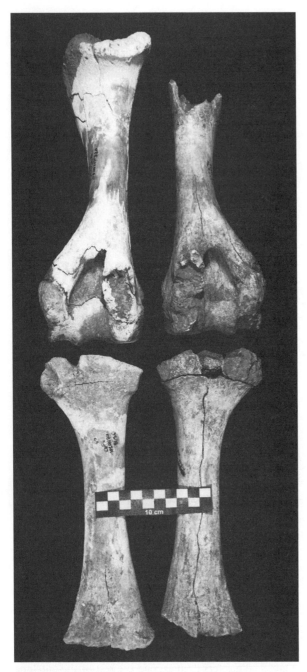

Figure 11-3 Anatomically refit calf bison humeri (top) and radii (bottom). Carnivore gnawing has removed the proximal (upper) end of the humerus on the right.

Source: Matt Hill

ribs and vertebrae may have been crushed for bone grease or consumed whole by dogs and carnivores, as suggested by taphonomic research.

Ethnoarchaeological studies suggest some other possibilities. Hunters consider several factors when deciding which parts of an animal to transport home: the distance back to camp, the number of hunters present, weather, terrain, and food needs of the household. If the animal is killed near camp, women and children might come out to help carry the entire carcass of a large animal back. If so, then the entire skeleton might end up in the camp, rather than at the kill site. If an animal is killed far from camp, the hunters might eat some of it immediately and then butcher the animal, bringing only meat and a very few bones back to camp. In this case, most of the skeleton would remain at the kill site.

Based on these ethnoarchaeological observations, Hill suggested that hunters at Agate Basin killed most of the animals individually, relatively close to camp. The smaller antelope were carried back with minimal field butchery. However, because the bison could not be carried whole, it is likely that the Agate Basin hunters (and perhaps their wives and children) ate some of the meat attached to the vertebrae and ribs at the kill site and then transported the legs—with their large meat packages and high marrow content—to camp using the lower limbs as convenient handles.

What Do Broken Toes Mean?

Although relatively rare at this site, some bison metapodials (portions of the foot), as well as bison and antelope phalanges (toe bones), had been broken open, presumably to extract the marrow. But foot bones do not contain much marrow, and they have no meat attached to them. Why did the hunters bother with toes, when they apparently had bison haunches and antelope tenderloin roasting on the fire?

Hill interprets the processing of the foot bones as evidence that, despite the eleven bison and five antelope, the Agate Basin Folsom hunters were experiencing some hard times. From paleoclimatic data, we know that the average annual temperature was some 11°C colder during Folsom times; perhaps late winter or early spring storms—which can strike with a vengeance on the high plains—made that day's hunt impossible. Or perhaps the meat stored in camp was frozen, leaving the camp's inhabitants with no choice but to extract marrow from low-utility elements, such as metapodials and phalanges.

Hill also concluded that these Folsom hunters were living more hand-to-mouth than did later hunter-gatherers on the high plains. The late winter and early spring is a tough season for hunter-gatherers, because game animals are lean (and lean meat is difficult to digest) and plants are not yet ripe. Many foragers survive the spring by relying on food stored from a previous fall hunt. But the data from Agate Basin suggest that these Folsom hunters lacked stored food, because they were hunting on a weekly or even daily basis during the spring that they occupied the site.

This interpretation depends on knowing that the Folsom hunters camped at Agate Basin in the spring. How did Hill know this?

In What Season Was Agate Basin Occupied?

Recall from the discussion of seasonal rounds in Chapter 4 that hunter-gatherers do not spend the entire year in a single camp or village. Folsom hunters moved across the landscape; so did the 19th-century Shoshone in Nevada and so do Mikea forager-horticulturalists. To understand what life was like in the past, we must pay attention to **seasonality,** the time of year that a site was used. This is important because only after we have identified the range of seasonal activities can we understand the entire seasonal round.

Hill determined the seasonality of Agate Basin by beginning with the knowledge that modern bison give birth during the last two weeks of April and the first two weeks of May. Hill assumed that bison in the past did likewise. This uniformitarian assumption seems justified because giving birth in the early spring is adaptive, allowing calves the maximum time to mature sufficiently to survive the next winter. Even considering the likelihood of climate change, it is highly likely that the birthing season of modern bison approximates that of their ancient cousins.

Bone development and tooth eruption in modern bison also follow quite predictable schedules (as they do for all animals, including humans). Young animals are most useful to archaeologists—indeed, once all their teeth have erupted, adults lose their value as seasonal indicators. The Agate Basin collection contained only a few young animals, but they were important in assessing the season of occupation. The teeth of the youngest bison showed that it was about 11 months old when it died. A second young bison had teeth that suggested an age of about 23 months. In other words, these two animals were just one month shy of their first and second birthdays, respectively. Assuming that these two bison were born in late April–early May, then they probably died in late March or early April. The presence of some fetal bison bones (either a late-

term fetus or a newborn) supports this inference. With this information, Hill concluded that Folsom hunters occupied Agate Basin at the tail end of winter or the beginning of spring.

Ancient DNA Analysis: A New Tool for Zooarchaeology

As we will see in Chapter 12, ancient DNA recovered from archaeological sites is currently being utilized to investigate aspects of human evolution, examine relationships between ancient and modern populations, determine kinship affiliation, and diagnose genetic and infectious diseases. However, ancient DNA is also being used to reconstruct the subsistence patterns of past human populations. In doing so, it is changing the way we do zooarchaeology. Dongya Yang, who runs the Ancient DNA Facility at Simon Fraser University, has recently been involved in two such studies. Both address an important issue in the archaeology of the Plateau and Northwest Coast regions of British Columbia—the relationship between salmon storage and the emergence of social complexity.

Salmon Utilization and the Emergence of Social Complexity

Archaeologists have long recognized the importance of salmon to the historical and pre-contact groups that inhabit the river systems and coastal regions of the Pacific Northwest. At some point in the past, people began to intensify their use of salmon species by developing more efficient mass-capture and storage techniques. This involved the use of dip nets, reef nets, and the drying of fish. Many archaeologists believe that the surpluses created by these techniques led to sedentism and the emergence of social hierarchies, where some families could claim higher rank than others. R. G. Matson of the University of British Columbia believes that economies based on salmon storage likely appeared on the Northwest Coast by 3500–3000 B.P. However, some researchers have suggested that salmon storage and sedentism extend much farther back in time, and that they may not necessarily be linked to population growth and social stratification.

seasonality An estimate of the time of year during which a particular archaeological site was occupied.

Groups living in interior and coastal regions of the Pacific Northwest used five key salmon species: Chinook, pink salmon, coho, sockeye, and chum. Ethnographically, sockeye and Chinook were preferred species because they have the highest fat and oil content. However, high oil content also meant that these species required much more labour to dry for storage. Conversely, while species such as pink salmon and coho were easier to dry they produced less oil, and therefore tasted less rich. Different salmon species also spawn at different ages. Pink salmon, for example, spawn in the first two years of life, meaning that they have smaller body sizes and therefore less consumable meat. In contrast, sockeye and Chinook species spawn after three years of age, and therefore tend to have larger body sizes with more meat.

Many Aboriginal groups on the Northwest Coast captured salmon species using a variety of different techniques. Pink salmon usually swim along the edges of rivers, making them easily accessible. Coho and other large species, however, swim in the deeper middle areas of a river, and therefore could be accessed only from specific locations along the river. Some native families would build wooden platforms that

Profile of an Archaeologist
Ariane Burke

A Professor of Anthropology at Université de Montréal

Figure 11-4 Dr. Ariane Burke of Université de Montréal.
Source: Dr. Ariane Burke

I started my career in classical studies, with a minor in linguistics. My desire to combine intellectual pursuits with a more active, "outdoors" lifestyle led me to pursue archaeology rather than linguistics. I moved on to take a master's degree in archaeological science with a specialization in archaeozoology at the University of Southampton. This course of study suited my taste for fieldwork and for doing research in the natural and social sciences, and left me with two abiding research interests: evolutionary ecology and prehistory.

The idea that humans are inseparable from their environment led me to adopt evolutionary ecology as an important theoretical framework in my own research. After a "gap year," during which I worked at the Bermuda Maritime Museum, I enrolled in anthropology at New York University (where I took an MPhil and PhD). I realized then that there was some method to my earlier madness—and that linguistics and archaeology can be integrated into the same field of study. I also learned the value of ethnographic analysis as a source of social models in prehistory. My dissertation research was narrowly focused on developing the use of dental microstructure as an archaeological tool. Teeth are essentially recording structures for an organism's life history; the analysis of tooth sections from horse remains found on Upper Palaeolithic archaeological sites in Southwest France enabled me to estimate their season of death, which in turn offered me the possibility of studying the occupational history of the sites as well as reflecting on prehistoric hunting strategies. Despite the specialized focus of this research, its broader application to the study of regional settlement patterns fit in well with my growing interest in evolutionary ecology.

Post-doctoral research carried out at the Canadian Museum of Civilization on material excavated from

extended out into the river to net these species. Wealthy families owned these structures, and had the necessary labour to process the oil-rich salmon species that were extracted using this technique. Common families, on the other hand, used pink salmon because they could be captured from the river's edge and required less labour to process for storage. Many archaeologists recognize that differential access to preferred resources is a hallmark of social inequality. The presence of status differences between families, therefore, might be reflected in how salmon species are distributed among houses at archaeological sites.

Case Study 1: Salmon Use and Social Hierarchy at Keatley Creek

The Keatley Creek site is a winter pithouse village located near the modern town of Lillooet, British Columbia (Figure 11-5). This site appears to have been occupied from 3500–1000 B.P. At its peak it is thought to have had a population of more than 1000 people. The pithouses vary in size, suggesting differences in status among occupants. There are also other types of specialized structures that may have been used to store food, or used in ritual activities. Archaeologists have

Bluefish Caves (Yukon Territory) enabled me to pursue this line of research further. I moved on to a position in anthropology at the University of Manitoba and began doing fieldwork in Crimea at the invitation of colleagues from Southern Methodist University (Texas) and the National Academy of Sciences, Ukraine. I was involved in collaborative research in Crimea for the following eight years, with the support of the Social Sciences and Humanities Research Council of Canada (SSHRC). My Russian didn't get any better over the years, but I did get the opportunity to analyze several faunal collections and become closely acquainted with the Neanderthal record of the Crimean Peninsula. I am apparently destined to travel farther and farther back in time, since my research is now very much focused on understanding the Neanderthal way of life.

I currently hold a position at Université de Montreal and with the support of the SSHRC have recently begun a survey program in Portugal, which will test the usefulness of predictive modelling (using geographical information systems) in archaeological survey design. My continuing interest in paleoethology (reconstructing the behaviour of prehistoric animals) as an archaeozoological tool is now being directed toward improving the design of predictive spatial models. I

have also begun a collaborative research program to develop models of hominid dispersals during the Middle Pleistocene with colleagues at Université de Montréal and McGill University, with the support of the Fonds québecois de la recherche sur la société et la culture.

It seems natural that I should adopt a landscape perspective over the years, given my early training and the directions my research has taken. The scale of my work has gradually shifted from occupational histories of individual sites to settlement systems, and from there to a consideration of regional land-use patterns. From my perspective, a landscape approach involves consideration of the mechanisms involved in human (or hominid) social integration as well as patterns of resource-use and movement between sites. This approach allows me to continue working within the framework of evolutionary ecology, adding elements of agency (consideration of hominids as social agents) and phenomenology as well as a humanist approach to the construction of social relations. Given my theoretical orientation and the type of research I am currently conducting, I consider myself lucky to be working within one of the few truly inter-disciplinary fields of research—paleoanthropology.

Figure 11-5 Pithouse depressions at the Keatley Creek site, after a brush fire removed surface vegetation. The largest depressions are about 20 metres in diameter.

Source: Dr. Brian Hayden

utilized salmon remains to test the idea that some households at the Keatley Creek site may have been of higher status than others.

Analysis of the fish bones recovered from pithouses and other features indicates that at least three species of salmon were stored and consumed at Keatley Creek. Vertebrae are often the best preserved of salmon bones. However, the morphology of salmon vertebrae does not allow for identification of these elements to species. As a result, radiographic (x-ray) analysis has been used to identify incremental growth lines on salmon vertebrae. These lines are laid down during slow periods of winter growth. Counting them provides a means of aging the salmon at the time of its death. This provides a way of separating pink salmon out from other species, because they spawn in their second year of life.

Analyzing salmon vertebrae from Keatley Creek showed a strong correlation between house size and the age distribution of the salmon species found within. Smaller houses, for example, contained higher percentages of pink salmon relative to other species. Remember that pink salmon have smaller body sizes and are not as oily as other species such as sockeye. Thus, the differential access to salmon species reflected in the pithouses seemed to support the idea that social hierarchies existed within the village.

Dongya Yang, along with Camilla Speller and Brian Hayden from Simon Fraser University, used ancient salmon DNA from Keatley Creek to test this hypothesis. One of the advantages of working with ancient DNA is that it provides a highly accurate way of identifying a specimen to the level of species. Identifying salmon vertebrae to species using growth rings is much more subjective and prone to error. Another disadvantage is that it cannot distinguish among three of the four salmon species that are present at the site. Remarkably, whereas the earlier radiographic studies had shown a preponderance of pink salmon, the DNA results indicated a complete absence! The majority of the remains identified to species were of sockeye. The DNA analysis did reveal differential access to preferred salmon species (Chinook) in some pithouses. However, the dramatic economic and social differences inferred from the distribution of salmon species in previous growth ring studies were not observed in the DNA study. This may change the way archaeologists think about social organization at Keatley Creek.

Case Study 2: Salmon Use and Early Sedentism at Namu

Archaeologists have always assumed that the storage of salmon and increasing sedentism on the Northwest Coast were directly linked to population increases and the development of stratified societies. The *Middle Period Marpole Culture* of southern Vancouver Island, for example, seems to show definite evidence of social hierarchies by 400 B.C. However, this idea would be undermined if earlier evidence for storage and sedentism existed among hunter-fisher-gatherers whose population levels were relatively stable over long periods of time. The site of Namu is located on the central coast of British Columbia. Aubrey Cannon of McMaster University and Dongya Yang decided to use ancient DNA analysis to look for evidence of storage in the early periods of Namu's occupation.

One fairly simple archaeological indicator of the practice of storage is the abundance of a particular resource relative to all others. Salmon was obviously one such resource at Namu. However, large amounts of salmon could indicate either intensive harvesting by seasonal aggregations of people or continuous, but less intensive, harvesting by people living at the site year round. The key difference is that groups who do the former eat their salmon fresh, while those who do the latter have to dry their salmon for storage (Figure 11-6). Each of these practices generates a different representation of body parts. Salmon consumed fresh, for example, have high proportions of crania, while salmon consumed dried contain higher proportions of vertebrae. This is because crania are removed during the drying process.

Aubrey Cannon believes that Namu was occupied year round by some portion of its population, who were dependent on the drying and storing of salmon to get them through the winter months. He has argued that this pattern remained fundamentally intact as far back as 5000 B.C. Previous zooarchaeological analysis revealed that vertebrae dominated the salmon remains recovered from the site. This weakly supported his idea of a storage-based economy at Namu. However, the overrepresentation of vertebrae relative to other elements might be explained by other factors, such as sampling error or the post-depositional destruction of other types of bone. Perhaps ancient DNA might further strengthen the weaker lines of evidence for storage.

Cannon and Yang's use of ancient salmon DNA showed a clear emphasis on pink salmon, followed by sockeye and chum. Remember from the Keatley Creek study that pink salmon are smaller and less oily than other species, so they would have been easier to preserve. If people had been aggregating at Namu only seasonally, then they would have harvested salmon for immediate consumption. As a result, we might expect them to have selected sockeye or coho over pink or chum, since relative fat and oil content is an important indicator of food preference. However, if they were living at the site year round, then we should see more use of pink salmon, which are easier to catch and preserve. Therefore, the focus on pink salmon species identified by the DNA analysis, coupled with the overrepresentation of vertebrae in the faunal assemblage, seems to support Cannon's hypothesis of year-round occupation of Namu and a salmon storage economy dating back as early as 5000 Cal B.C. This suggests that storage, sedentism, population growth, and social complexity may not necessarily be linked on the Northwest Coast.

Figure 11-6 A contemporary Aboriginal salmon-drying rack in the Fraser Canyon, near the Milliken Site. Such shelters were used to protect split and gutted salmon while drying in the canyon winds.

Source: K.R. Fladmark

The Future of DNA Analysis in Zooarchaeology

The work of Dongya Yang and the Ancient DNA Facility at Simon Fraser University is making important contributions to how archaeofaunas are used in archaeology. The species identifications provided by DNA analyses are far more accurate than identifications based on element morphology, or those derived from measurement of features such as growth rings in vertebrae and teeth. The drawback, of course, is the cost. DNA analysis is extremely expensive. As a result, most samples are substantially smaller than those done the old-fashioned way, using a zooarchaeological reference collection. The second problem has to do with contamination. As we will see in Chapter 12, the accidental mixing of archaeological samples with modern DNA can produce erroneous and inaccurate results. Extreme care must therefore be taken when obtaining samples for DNA analysis, both in the lab and in the field. Regardless, in situations where identifications to species are difficult because assemblages are highly fragmentary, DNA analysis provides a powerful tool.

These two examples, a Folsom camp in Wyoming and the use of DNA analysis to examine sequences of cultural development in British Columbia, show some of the ways archaeologists pursue faunal analysis and what it can contribute to our understanding of the past. Bones, however, are only half the story.

Studying Plant Remains from Archaeological Sites

A **paleoethnobotanist** is an archaeologist who specializes in recovering and identifying plant remains from ancient contexts, focusing on the world of plant–people interactions. Plant remains are particularly vulnerable to the biases of archaeological preservation. Some archaeological sites sometimes contain

paleoethnobotanist An archaeologist who specializes in recovering and identifying plant remains from ancient contexts, focusing on the world of plant–people interactions.

macrobotanical remains Readily recognizable plant parts.

coprolite Desiccated feces, often containing macrobotanical remains, pollen, and the remains of small animals.

palynology The technique through which the fossil pollen grains and spores from archaeological sites are studied.

well-preserved concentrations of **macrobotanical remains** (readily recognizable plant parts): caches of corncobs, pine nuts, a hearth's charcoal, or acorn mush adhering to the inside wall of a food bowl. For years, much of what we knew about ancient plants came from archaeological sites in arid climates, which had a far better chance of preserving them for study. The archaeological deposits inside Danger and Hogup caves (in Utah), for instance, consisted almost entirely of plant seeds, hulls, and chaff. In places, virtually no dirt was present, even though the deposits were more than 3 metres deep. From column samples of the fill, investigators reconstructed the vegetational history near both sites. Such studies can highlight the degree to which modern plant distributions can mislead the archaeologist studying the cultural ecology of even the fairly recent past.

In more humid climates, plant remains generally are preserved only when they have been burned and carbonized. For this reason, the most common method of recovering plant remains is flotation (as we discussed in Chapter 6). But plant remains are also sometimes preserved in waterlogged contexts (shipwrecks, mudslides, and wells), sun-dried adobe bricks, wattle-and-daub walls, and ceramics.

Archaeologists also find plant remains in curious places, such as inside ancient human stomachs (preserved through mummification) and in human **coprolites** (desiccated feces); this evidence of past diets is about as direct as one could hope for. Evidence of past plant consumption is also preserved in the chemistry of human bone (but we'll discuss this in Chapter 12). And it comes in a microscopic form, too, as pollen and phytoliths.

Palynology

Palynology, the analysis of ancient plant pollen and spores, has long been useful to the study of prehistoric ecological adaptations by helping to reconstruct past environments. The basics of palynology are easy to understand.

Most plants shed their pollen into the atmosphere, where the wind rapidly disperses it. Pollen grains— microscopic male gametes—are present in most of the earth's atmosphere; a single pine branch can produce as many as 350 million pollen grains. Pollen grains are tenacious and under the right conditions can preserve for tens of thousands of years, or even longer.

Determining what these pollen concentrations mean can be quite challenging, but the initial steps in extracting and identifying pollen are rather straight-forward. Sometimes pollen is recovered by core sampling, in which a circular tube is forced downward by a mechanical drilling rig into a sediment record. Lake bottoms are often good places to prospect for pollen.

We can also take pollen samples manually from archaeological stratigraphic profiles. The surface of the excavation profile is first scraped with a trowel (that has been cleaned with distilled water), and 0.2 to 0.3 litre of material is then extracted from the sediment with a clean trowel and placed in a sterile, sealable container. Samples are often taken at 5- or 10-centimetre intervals to provide a continuous record of the pollen rain throughout the period of deposition. The archaeologist takes the samples from the bottom of the profile to the top (rather than from the top to the bottom) so that the samples are not contaminated by falling dirt. The proveniences of the pollen samples are recorded in the same way that the archaeologists record the proveniences of artifacts and ecofacts. Pollen samples can also be taken from sealed deposits within architectural features (such as ancient floors or the fill found in pits), and they can be retrieved from artifacts such as grinding stones by washing the surfaces in distilled water. Occasionally, we find pollen in human burials, on the inside of ceramic vessels, trapped inside the weave of ancient baskets, or even adhering to the working surface of a stone tool. The analyst must always be certain that he or she has collected the sample from a recently exposed surface so that the modern pollen rain does not contaminate it.

In the laboratory, pollen grains are isolated from the soil matrix with repeated hydrofluoric acid baths and centrifuging (pollen survives the acid baths that destroy most everything else in the sample). A sample of the solution is then placed on a microscope slide, which is scanned at magnifications between 400× and 1000×.

Palynology is possible only because different plants produce pollen that look very different under a microscope. Pine pollen, for example, has two "wings" on it that carry it long distances on the wind. Elm pollen, on the other hand, is a lumpy round ball. This difference means that the individual grains can be identified, sometimes to species, and tabulated until the analyst records a statistically significant number, say about 400 to 500 grains per slide. (A skilled analyst can tabulate this number of pollen grains in 2 to 3 hours). The palynologist then converts the counts to percentages and creates a **pollen diagram** that shows the proportional shift in pollen frequencies between stratigraphic levels within a site.

Fluctuations in pollen percentages reflect changes in plant densities, and a primary application of palynology is to reconstruct past environments. Peter Mehringer's (Washington State University) research at the Lehner Ranch site shows how this works.

Reconstructing Past Environments at the Lehner Ranch Site

The question of when people first arrived in North America is still hotly debated. The people who made Folsom points were among the earliest peoples in the New World, but earlier still were people who made a different kind of fluted point, known to archaeologists as **Clovis** points. The name Clovis comes from an important site near Clovis, New Mexico where, a few years after the discoveries at the Folsom site, these distinctive spear points were found lying stratigraphically beneath diagnostic Folsom artifacts. Clovis artifacts date to about 10,900 to 11,200 B.C. and, at about a dozen sites, they are associated with the bones of extinct mammoths and mastodons.

One of those sites is the Lehner Ranch site in southern Arizona's San Pedro Valley, excavated by C. Vance Haynes (University of Arizona), among others. Here, Haynes found several distinctive Clovis fluted points and stone butchering tools in association with mammoth remains. It is hard to imagine mammoths plodding among the creosote and ocotillo of the southern Arizona landscape today. Clovis hunters clearly lived in an environment that was different from today's, and Peter Mehringer turned to the fossil pollen record to help Haynes reconstruct what that environment was like.

Figure 11-7 shows the pollen diagram from the Lehner Ranch site. Lehner has a complex stratigraphy, and Haynes could not find a single locality that

pollen diagram A chart showing the changing frequencies of different identified pollens through time from samples taken from archaeological or other sites.

Clovis The earliest well-established Native American culture, distributed throughout much of North America and dating 10,900 to 11,200 B.C.

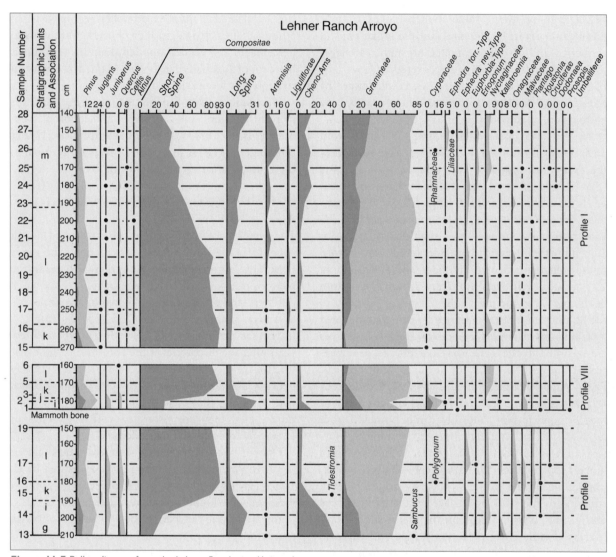

Figure 11-7 Pollen diagram from the Lehner Ranch site (Arizona).

Source: After Mehringer and Haynes (1966: fig. 8).

contained a continuous and unbroken pollen record. So, this diagram is a composite, showing the results of three separate but overlapping pollen profiles.

Pollen diagrams can look daunting, but don't let them put you off. Along the left edge is the sample number and, in the next column to the right, the stratigraphic unit, accompanied by the sample's depth. In this case, samples were taken at 10-centimetre intervals. Because this pollen diagram is a composite of three different profiles (shown at right), some of the stratigraphic units appear more than once. For instance, Unit K appeared at 260–270 cm in Profile I, 170–180 cm in Profile VIII, and 180–190 cm in Profile II.

Running along the top of the chart are the plant taxa—*Pinus* is pine pollen, *Juniperus* is juniper pollen, *Quercus* is oak, and so on. The horizontal scales below these are simply the percentages of the different kinds of plant pollen—for instance, artemisia constituted about 16 percent of the plants found at 160 cm in Profile I. The shaded areas show the changing frequencies of different pollen. For example, pollen of cheno-ams (chenopodiaceae and amaranthaceae, closely related plants of the goosefoot family and amaranth) is most common at the lowest levels of the site (look at Samples 13 and 14 in stratigraphic Units g and i). It becomes less common through time until stratigraphic Unit m (Samples 23 through 28), where it begins to pick up. The assumption is that pollen roughly mirrors the local abundance of the plant species producing it; thus, goosefoot and amaranth were common early in the sequence, then became less common and, later in time, returned.

To go further, you must recognize the difference between *local* and *regional* environments. Look around at any landscape, and you will see microenvironments that do *not* reflect the regional environment. A flowing spring in a desert, for example, might support a dense stand of spruce, aspen, and mountain mahogany. Analysis of pollen from sediments near such a spring would suggest that the environment was a dense forest, when in fact the regional environment is a vast sagebrush steppe. We need to understand what both local and regional environments looked like and, even more, we need to avoid confusing the two.

Mehringer had to cope with this potential difference between local and regional environments at Lehner Ranch. A distinctive "black mat" marker bed in the stratigraphy at Lehner Ranch suggests that the immediate area was a wet bog during late Clovis times

(Figure 11-8). Was that a local condition, or was it true for the larger regional environment? Pollen from composites (herbs such as ragweed and sagebrush) and cheno-ams (plants that prefer wetter conditions) dominates the pollen diagram, suggesting that the region was wetter. This pattern characterizes many post-Pleistocene pollen profiles from southwestern deserts, but it creates a problem because it could mask the presence of less-common yet ecologically sensitive indicators. Although the dominant cheno-am and composite pollen undoubtedly represent *locally* occurring species, they are insufficient for interpreting *regional* vegetation or climate.

To offset the high frequency of composite and cheno-am pollen, Mehringer applied a technique known as the *double fixed sum*. The dark profiles in the diagram are based on a standard summary for all pollen types identified, with the percentages based on the first 200 pollen grains encountered in each sample. A total of 25 such 200-grain sample counts are represented (for various reasons, some samples could not be run; note, for example, there is no Sample 4 in the diagram).

Figure 11-8 C. Vance Haynes (right) examines the "black mat" marker bed at the Lehner Ranch site as archaeologists Nicole Waguespack and Todd Surovell look on.

Source: Robert Kelly

Mehringer then made a second, 100-grain count (represented by the lighter areas). He computed the percentages for the second count by ignoring cheno-am and composite pollen, counting only the other, rarer pollen types. By comparing the results of both counts, one can study the gross frequencies of the dominants as well as fluctuations in the densities of the rarer but more environmentally sensitive species.

The pollen from stratigraphic Units i, j, and k at the Lehner Ranch reflect the climatic conditions that prevailed during Clovis times. Look carefully at the pollen frequencies of Samples 15 and 16 in Profile I, Samples 1, 2, and 3 in Profile VII, and Samples 13 and 14 in Profile II. The environment of the time these samples represent is "read" by moving across the diagram. Notice that the normal pollen count—the dark portions of the figure—shows a significant jump in short-spine *compositae* pollen in stratigraphic Unit k. The double-fixed-sum count shows slightly greater abundances of pine, oak, and juniper pollen. For trees such as pine, oak, and juniper to grow on the valley floor, the regional environment must have been slightly moister and/or cooler before and during the deposition of the lower part of Unit k. Somewhat later, during the deposition of upper stratigraphic Unit k and Unit l, a sharp increase in the *compositae* categories and a decline in tree pollen signal a shift to fully modern conditions.

Overall, the vegetation represented by the pollen spectra from Lehner Ranch suggests a desert grassland, which today occupies slightly wetter sites nearby. Mehringer and Haynes concluded that the climate at

Looking Closer
Palynology of Shanidar Cave: Why Formation Processes Matter

 Shanidar Cave (Iraq) was occupied sporadically over the past 100,000 years. In several seasons of excavation, Ralph Solecki (then of Columbia University) discovered several Neanderthal skeletons (one of which served as the inspiration for the shaman in Jean Auel's novel *The Clan of the Cave Bear*). One burial, Shanidar IV, was very fragile, and the entire block was removed in a plaster jacket, earth and all. The block was transported to an Iraqi museum, where it remained unopened for 2 years. Later, it was discovered that the Shanidar IV grave actually contained four individuals: three adults and an infant.

Whether Neanderthals intentionally buried their dead is a hotly contested issue. Some argue that they did not and hence lacked burial ritual—a key trait of modern humans. The palynology of Shanidar Cave played an important role in this debate.

Solecki took soil samples from the cave's strata as well as from within Shanidar IV. French palynologist Arlette Leroi-Gourhan (Musée de l'Homme, Paris) tested the Shanidar IV samples for pollen and—to everyone's surprise—found it preserved in surprising quantities; she found especially high amounts near the feet, the shoulders, and the base of the spine. Microscopic examination indicated that these three samples contained dense concentrations of at least seven species of brightly coloured wildflowers, including grape hyacinth, bachelor's button, and hollyhock.

Leroi-Gourhan suggested that the flowers had been woven into the branches of a pine-like shrub, which apparently grew nearby on the Ice Age hillside. She also concluded that the individuals found in the Shanidar IV grave were laid to rest between late May and early July, the time when the flowers would have been in bloom. These pollen data suggested that this Neanderthal burial took place as a formal interment, with a degree of planning and "humanness" that few were willing to grant Neanderthals at the time.

But scientists always ask themselves, "Do we really know what we think we know?" And in this case, the answer to that question focused on formation processes. Pollen is light, and it could have blown into the cave from the outside. Perhaps the pollen in the burial fill was simply what we call "background pollen rain."

But if the flower pollen was background rain, then it should have been present throughout the

the Lehner site 11,000 years ago was only slightly wetter and cooler than today, followed by a rapid shift toward drier conditions. As many palynology studies have found, only a small shift in temperature and/or precipitation was required to produce dramatic differences in the environment at the Lehner Ranch site. And with only slight changes in rainfall and temperature, mammoths, horses, tapirs, and a range of other animals disappeared from the southern Arizona landscape forever.

The main contribution of pollen analysis to archaeology is the reconstruction of environmental change. Pollen studies, properly applied, can also help archaeologists understand past human behaviour (see "Looking Closer: Palynology of Shanidar Cave: Why Formation Processes Matter"). And pollen also can play a role in figuring out what plants were important in prehistoric diet. An example from Nevada's Stillwater Marsh shows how and introduces other sources of paleoethnobotanical information.

What Plants Did People Eat in the Stillwater Marsh?

You will recall from Chapter 4 that after our survey of the Carson Desert (Nevada), high precipitation flooded the marsh and exposed dozens of archaeological sites and human burials. We discuss the burials in Chapter 12, and here we focus on the plant remains that were recovered from one site that we excavated in the wake of the flood.

Site 26CH1062 is not a particularly glamorous site (refer to Figure 4-9, page 107). It sits on a low clay

---

cave's deposits, not just the grave. Yet, it was not; the sediments outside the grave contained far less flower pollen than the burial pit. In addition, the pollen grains in the burial samples were clumped, which is how they would be deposited if the pollen had fallen from flowers that had been laid in the grave, rather than blown into the cave. And some pollen even lay in the form of the flowers' anthers, suggesting that the entire flower was once present. None of these patterns are what we'd expect if the pollen had simply blown into the cave.

But nothing is ever simple in archaeology. Perhaps the pollen came into the site as flowers, but does this mean that the flowers were laid in the grave by the hands of a grieving Neanderthal?

Jeffrey Sommer (University of Michigan) suggests another possibility: rodents. Solecki noted that Shanidar IV and, in fact, all the site's burials were riddled with rodent burrows. In fact, Solecki thought he could locate burials by tracing rodent burrows through the deposits.

Many of those burrowing rodents died in the cave, and their skeletons tell us that they were *Meriones persicus*, the Persian *jird*. These interesting creatures apparently store large numbers of entire flower heads, neatly clipped from their stems—including those of the species that Leroi-Gourhan had identified—in the side tunnels of their burrows. Sommers points out that the number of flower heads that this rodent routinely stores is more than enough to account for the amount of pollen that Leroi-Gourhan found.

Although it is not conclusive, an alternative explanation for the Shanidar burial "bouquets" is that they were placed there by the humble *jird*. And so the search for convincing evidence of ritual and religion among Neanderthals must continue.

Neanderthal skull as it was being exposed at Shanidar Cave (Iraq). This person was probably killed by rooffall inside the cave.
Source: Ralph Solecki

dune and consists of several pits, postholes, and at least two shallow houses that were perhaps little more than windbreaks. Radiocarbon dates show that the site was occupied at least twice, once about 1400 radiocarbon years ago and again about 1000 years ago. We water-screened all the deposits and recovered a large number of stone tools, manufacturing waste flakes, shells, and faunal remains. We floated soil samples from several of the features and retrieved many carbonized macrobotanical remains.

The macrobotanical remains were sent to paleoethnobotanist David Rhode, at Nevada's Desert Research Institute. Looking at the samples under a microscope at 15–40×, Rhode identified the various carbonized seeds and bits of burnt wood (using a comparative collection, much like those that faunal analysts use). Most of the charcoal was reed (*Phragmites australis*), greasewood (*Sarcobatus* sp.), and some willow (*Salix* sp.). Because these plants can be found today in the Carson Desert, we were not surprised that they turned up in the samples. They could have been used as firewood, in housing, or as tools.

The seeds were more interesting. Rhode found the carbonized seeds of several plants, including cattail, dock, seepweed, chenopods, pickleweed, silverscale, heliotrope, saltbush, and goosefoot. The inhabitants of the site could have gathered any of these as food, and all occur in the area today.

One of the most abundant seeds was that of bulrush (*Scirpus* sp.). The indigenous peoples of the Carson Desert, the Paiute, used bulrush (and many other wetland plants) as food. This makes sense, because experimental data show that bulrush seeds are an efficiently gathered and nutritious resource (we'll return to these kinds of foraging experiments in Chapter 15).

But *did* people collect bulrush seeds for food? And, if so, did they collect it in the Stillwater Marsh? It is possible that the bulrush seeds came in attached to bulrush plants that were used to build the temporary houses on the site or as material to make temporary containers. Any accidental burning of these artifacts could have toasted the seeds and left them behind for us to recover. Were bulrush plants, and not just their seeds, present on the site? To answer this question, we looked at another source of plant data in archaeological sites.

phytoliths Tiny silica particles contained in plants. Sometimes these fragments can be recovered from archaeological sites, even after the plants themselves have decayed.

Phytoliths

One important method of learning about plants in ancient sites is the analysis of microscopic plant opal **phytoliths,** literally, "plant stones." As plants take in water through their roots, they also take in silica, which is then deposited in mineral form between cells, within cell walls, or sometimes in the cells themselves (Figure 11-9). Phytoliths occur in members of the grass family, as well as in rushes, sedges, palms, conifers, and deciduous trees. When dead plant material decays, the almost-indestructible opal phytoliths—they can last for millions of years—are deposited in the ground.

Importantly, phytoliths take the shape of the cells in which they were deposited. Because different grasses have different cell shapes, their phytoliths also have different shapes. This means that we can identify the presence of certain kinds of plants long after those plants have decayed and disappeared.

Phytolith analysis is similar to pollen analysis: Both deal with plant remains at a microscopic level; samples for each are collected in the same way; and the same laboratory can be used for both analyses (although separate samples are needed for each, because the acid baths used to reduce a sample for pollen destroy phytoliths).

But there is an important difference. Although a plant produces a single form of pollen, phytoliths can vary within a single species, and not all plants produce phytoliths. Phytoliths are most useful for identifying the abundance of different kinds of grasses, although research continues to refine this ability and extend it to other plants.

Phytolith analysis was extremely useful in the Stillwater Marsh. We sent soil samples to Linda Scott Cummings (Paleo Research Labs, Colorado) and, as expected, she found that phytoliths were well preserved. Phragmites, a common marsh grass, probably accounted for most of the phytoliths, along with several other marsh grasses. What was most intriguing, however, was the complete *lack* of sedge phytoliths, which are produced by plants such as bulrush. This suggests that no bulrush plants decayed on the site. If they had, Cummings would have found their phytoliths in the soil samples.

Perhaps, then, there was no bulrush in the Stillwater Marsh 1000 years ago. But where did all those bulrush seeds come from? Perhaps a visiting Paiute brought some bulrush seed cakes from another wet-

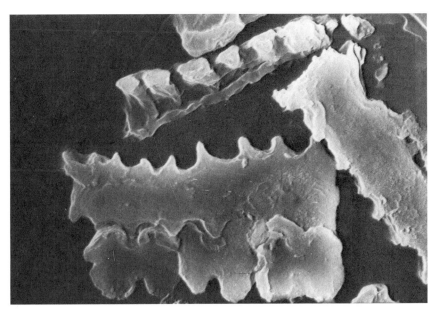

Figure 11-9 What a phytolith looks like under the microscope.

Source: Susan Mulholland

land, such as Walker Lake to the south or Winnemucca Lake to the west. This is a question about the regional environment. Although phytoliths can tell which plants were present on a specific site, pollen data are better for looking at regional patterns.

So, in addition to flotation and phytolith samples, we also took pollen samples from several of the features. These were sent to Peter Wigand, then at the Desert Research Institute, where he analyzed them using the protocols we described above. He found that the pollen in the samples was little different from the modern pollen rain of today; in fact, he found that sedge pollen was somewhat overrepresented in the samples: bulrush might even have been somewhat *more* abundant in the Stillwater Marsh of the past than it is today.

So, now we know (a) that burnt bulrush seeds were present on the site, (b) that bulrush plants were not on the site, but that (c) bulrush was abundant in the wetland at the time the site was occupied. Given that ethnographic data show that bulrush seeds were eaten by the Paiute, and experimental data indicate that bulrush is an efficiently gathered and nutritious food, we concluded that bulrush seeds were brought to the site to be eaten.

The macrobotanical remains were also interesting in what was *not* present. Completely missing were the seeds of upland plants such as ricegrass (*Oryzopsis*

hymenoides) or piñon (*Pinus monophylla*) pine nut hulls—both important food sources to the 19th-century Shoshone and Paiute in the Great Basin. This suggests that, when people lived in the Carson Desert, they got their plant food exclusively from the wetland and did not travel even a few kilometres into the low foothills to gather ricegrass, nor did they hike another 20 kilometres into the hills to gather piñon.

Site Seasonality

The seasonality of the Agate Basin site was determined using faunal remains, but at 26CH1062 we used the macrobotanical remains. Recall that we found bulrush seeds, along with cattail, seepweed, dock, chenopods, pickleweed, heliotrope, silverscale, saltbush, and goosefoot seeds. We know from ethnographic and experimental data that most of these seeds ripen in the mid- to late summer and into the early winter. Dock and heliotrope are gathered throughout the summer only. Late summer is therefore the only time when all of these are available, and that is probably the best estimate of when the site was occupied (although an occupation through the fall cannot be ruled out).

Wood Rat Nests

One important, if somewhat surprising, source of plant macrofossils is the ancient nests of **wood rats** (*Neotoma* sp.) that are found throughout the arid desert west (Figure 11-10). (Most people call these rodents pack rats, but the accepted scientific name is wood rats; they're the same critter.)

Wood rats are fascinating animals. They bring home extensive quantities of food and nest material,

wood rats (also pack rats) Rodents that build nests of organic materials and thus preserve a record, often for thousands of years, of changing plant species within the local area of the nest.

Figure 11-10 Wood rat midden in the Bighorn Mountains, Wyoming. The upper midden is a metre high.

Source: Steve Jackson

including wood, rock, bone, paper—anything that they can drag into a crevice or rockshelter. Archaeologists in the western United States know that wood rat nests are good places to look for organic artifacts—arrows, atlatl pieces, and basketry fragments are all incorporated into wood rat nests (as well as small tools or notepaper that a forgetful archaeologist might leave out overnight!).

Field studies demonstrate that pack rats do not travel more than 100 metres from their nests to collect materials. In contrast to pollen studies, wood rat nests reflect the *immediate* environment around their nests.

After collecting material, the rats build their nests in protected locations, such as crevices in cliffs or in cave mouths or rockshelters. This certainly helps to

Holocene The post-Pleistocene geological epoch that began about 10,000 radiocarbon years ago and continues today.

preserve the collected twigs and branches, but they do something else to the nests that guarantees their preservation: The rats urinate all over them. Their urine forms a lacquer-like covering on the nest that also promotes the preservation of organic materials—for thousands of years. As a result, researchers throughout arid North America use wood rat assemblages to reconstruct late Pleistocene and **Holocene** vegetational change.

Wood rat nests are often as hard as rock, and so you use hammers, chisels, saws, and pry bars to excavate them. (By the way, the nests have a strong smell. Some people hate it and others, oddly enough, like it.) After samples are taken from different levels in the nest, they are soaked in distilled water if they are covered with urine lacquer. After samples are dry, the analyst then sorts and identifies the materials. Specimens from each sample are radiocarbon-dated, and the resulting data help to reconstruct past environments.

Wood Rat Nests and Piñon in the Stillwater Mountains

We noted earlier that neither piñon pine nuts nor their hulls appear in sites in the Stillwater Marsh, and we suggested this meant that people did not travel to the mountains to collect them. But did people not collect piñon nuts because they did not need them, or because there was no piñon pine in the mountains 1000 or more years ago?

To answer this question, Peter Wigand and his colleague Cheryl Nowak studied a number of wood rat middens from several locations in western Nevada, including the Stillwater Range, which borders the Carson Desert. They found that evidence for piñon pine—in the form of branches, needles, and cones—did not appear in wood rat nests until about 1200 years ago in the Stillwater Mountains and considerably later in ranges farther west. So perhaps piñon was not present in the Stillwater Mountains, only 20–30 kilometres distant, in sufficient density to make a trip worthwhile at the time people occupied the marsh sites.

You will recall from Chapter 4 that research in the Carson Desert was aimed at understanding whether wetland food resources provided better returns and were preferred over those of the mountains. If we assume that the past environments of the Carson Desert and Stillwater Mountains were similar to the modern ones, then the data from 26CH1062 suggest that Native Americans eschewed piñon in favor of marsh plants. But the wood rat nest data suggest that the specific reason may be that piñon was not present in sufficient abundance to make a trip to the mountains worth the effort. This example shows that *it is essential that archaeologists make economic interpretations of subsistence data in light of paleoenvironmental reconstructions.* The former without the latter is almost useless.

Coprolites of Hidden Cave

Human coprolites are another source of information on prehistoric diet. Paleontologists first used the term "coprolite" (from the Greek *kopros* "dung" and *lithikos* "stone") about 1830 to describe fossilized dinosaur feces. Archaeologists use the term, but the feces we analyze are just desiccated, not fossilized. Coprolites are not common in the archaeological record, but they are, for obvious reasons, an excellent source of information on human diet.

Archaeologists find coprolites of many different kinds of animals, including humans, in dry archaeological sites. The archaeologist's first task is to identify which are human, and which belong to other species such as deer or mountain sheep. Believe it or not, some archaeologists have devoted time to identifying the criteria that distinguish human feces from, say, that of a coyote.

David Rhode, the same paleoethnobotanist who studied the macrobotanical remains from 26CH1062, also looked at human coprolites from Hidden Cave, a site that overlooks the Stillwater Marsh (see Chapter 4; Figure 4-5 on page 97). The cave's original opening was very small, barely large enough to crawl into and even though the cave opens into a large chamber, it was a lousy place to live or even to spend the night. It is dark and dusty and, if you made a fire for warmth or light, the chamber would soon fill with smoke. Thus, we were not surprised when we found no hearths, stone tool waste flakes, or bones left over from meals. People did not live in Hidden Cave; instead, they used it as a place to cache various kinds of gear—in pits between 3800 and 1500 years ago.

But there were also many quids—expectorated pieces of plants (such as cattail and bulrush) that people had chewed for their juices. And found nearby were bits of cordage, made from strips of bark rolled together. This suggests that people also used the cave

as a place where they could escape the summer afternoon's heat, passing the afternoon by chewing succulent stalks of bulrush and cattail in the cave's cool interior while rolling bark together to make cords to tie together bundles, repair sagebrush bark sandals, or repair torn baskets.

Many of the artifacts found in Hidden Cave were projectile points; these might suggest that men were the primary visitors to the cave (we'll deal with such gender assumptions in Chapter 13). Many coprolites were also found. Rhode decided to investigate the coprolites to see what the men who used the shelter were eating. He was surprised by what he found.

Rhode prepared the 19 coprolites by first soaking them in a solution of trisodium phosphate to reconstitute them (yes, really!). He then washed each specimen through fine mesh screens and dried the residue. Next, he examined and sorted this material under a microscope.

A small macrobotanical remain from each coprolite was AMS radiocarbon-dated. In so doing, Rhode found that the coprolites fell into two time periods: One batch dated between 3800 and 3400 B.P., the other from 1900 to 1500 B.P. All of the coprolites contained abundant evidence of plants, fish, and bird remains (people may also have eaten large mammals, but obviously their bones would not appear in coprolites).

Bulrush seeds were the most common seeds, some showing evidence of burning and milling (striations left from the action of grinding stones). Cattail pollen was also common. Rhode also found small feathers of waterfowl, as well as the bones of tui chub, a species of minnow that lives in the Stillwater Marsh. In fact, fish cranial (head) and caudal (tail) bones tell us that these small fish were eaten whole. Insects showed up too, as well as snails.

Curiously, only one coprolite contained a piñon pine nut hull. This coprolite, Number 167, also contained cattail seeds and pollen. This is interesting, because piñon nuts ripen in late September or early October, whereas cattail pollen is collected in July. Clearly, one of these resources must have been stored, and it was most likely the piñon. (By the way, this coprolite dated to 1740 B.P., again indicating that piñon was not present in the region until later in the region's history; but we don't know if it came from the Stillwater Mountains.)

All this was interesting, but then came the surprise. We can determine if a man or woman voided a coprolite depending on the abundance of the sex hormones estradiol, progesterone, and testosterone. This is done using a complex technique known as high-pressure liquid chromatographic analysis. After applying this technique, Rhode found that the coprolites' levels of sex hormones clearly indicated that women had voided the coprolites. We don't know if it was also women who cached the projectile points, spit out the quids, and spun cordage. But coprolite analysis clearly opens up new approaches to diet as well as new approaches to reconstructing the lives of men and women in the past.

In Her Own Words
Black Holes and Plateau Paleoethnobotany

by Sandra L. Peacock, University of British Columbia, Okanagan

Figure 11-11 Sandy Peacock, University of British Columbia, Okanagan.

Source: Sandra Peacock

I discovered my first "black hole" 15 years ago. It was a large, circular depression—about four metres across and a metre deep—with a prominent, raised rim that made it stand out in the surrounding grasslands of a valley I was surveying in the southern interior plateau of British Columbia. Excavations revealed a rock-lined basin filled with blackened sediments, burnt wood and charred plants, and copious amounts of fire-cracked rock (hence the nickname "black hole"). This particular black hole turned out to be almost 2000 years old. I was fascinated! In fact, black holes drew me into paleoethnobotany.

What are "black holes"? They are the remains of ancient earth ovens used by Plateau peoples—the Syilx, Secwepemc, Stl'atl'imx, Nlaka'pamux, and Tsilhqot'in First Nations—to pit cook a variety of wild root foods. Roots are a rich source of carbohydrate energy and they were harvested in large quantities, steamed in earth ovens, and stored for winter. The construction and repeated use of these ovens created permanent features on the landscape, massive basins and mounds up to eight metres in diameter. Hundreds of ovens dot traditional root-gathering grounds, marking more than 3000 years of continuous use.

As a paleoethnobotanist, I study people–plant relationships by analyzing plant remains from archaeological sites. So, you can see why I was drawn to black holes—they're ripe with paleoethnobotanical potential! They're highly visible and full

Lipid Analysis: Squeezing Fat from Ceramics

The analysis of faunal and macrobotanical remains, phytoliths, pollen, and coprolite analysis are fairly standard in archaeology's effort to reconstruct the past. But archaeologists and their associates in allied fields are always developing new techniques that extract even more information from archaeological remains and increase our ability to reconstruct the past. For example, some analysts are attempting to extract ancient blood from the microcracks in stone of charred plants to recover and identify. Further, there are plant use traditions shared by contemporary First Nations Elders to guide my interpretations of these ancient root-processing sites. This means I can blend perspectives from Western science and traditional ecological knowledge—two different but complementary ways of knowing—to produce a more complete picture of past plant use.

For example, I use scientific practices to identify plants found in the earth ovens. First, I collect samples of those blackened sediments and pour them into water, a technique known as flotation. This brings the lighter, charred plant materials to the surface, where they are skimmed off and set aside to dry. Back in the lab, I examine individual pieces under the microscope and look at the minute structures that provide clues to the plant's identity. My goal is to create a species list—a detailed accounting of the plant species present at the site including their scientific name, the parts found (wood, seeds, needles, etc.), and their provenience and frequency.

Creating such a list is an essential step in paleoethnobotany. But, it's just the beginning. The list might tell me whether I've recovered wood charcoal from different trees, or the seeds of wild berries. But it says nothing of the cultural use and significance of these species. For that, I turn to traditional knowledge systems, and specifically to the ethnobotanical evidence. Many of today's Elders remember helping their grandmothers harvest and prepare wild roots for pit cooking. Their stories and "recipes" have taught me a great deal about the plants I find in ancient earth ovens and about the ovens themselves. For instance, I've learned how to make my own earth oven to excavate the basin and heat the rocks, to choose Ponderosa pine for hot, smokeless fires, and to line the ovens with the branches of wild rose or Douglas-fir boughs to protect and flavour the food. I've also learned that Plateau peoples of the region name these plants (and hundreds of others) in their own languages, that prayers and protocols surround the harvesting and cooking of wild root foods, and that oral traditions passed between generations reinforce these practices. These insights challenge me to think about past people–plant relationships in new ways. Earth ovens are not simply "camp kitchens"; rather, they are symbols of a highly sophisticated system of wild plant food production developed by Plateau peoples over thousands of years.

A traditional teaching urges us to "listen to the plants whisper." This expression inspires me because it speaks to the practice of paleoethnobotany. We have much to learn from plants in the archaeological record and from the First Nations peoples whose ancestors created that record. But we need to ask the proper questions and be patient while searching for answers. Paleoethnobotanical truths, like many of life's lessons, often reveal themselves in subtle, fascinating ways.

As for my research—the black holes have not yet yielded all of their secrets. But I am listening.

tools and identify it to species. Another technique allows us to extract identifiable food residues from pottery.

The reconstruction of the plant component of ancient diets is more elusive than determining the role of meat. This is largely because of a substantial bias in preservation: Bone preserves better than plant remains. Macrobotanical remains are also more difficult to retrieve from archaeological sites. Flotation increases the recovery rate, but plant remains are still hard to come by: Water-screening allowed us to retrieve some 300,000 animal bones from 26CH1062 (mostly small fish bones, so the number is a bit exaggerated), but we collected only a few handfuls of macrobotanical remains. So archaeologists are always looking for new ways to retrieve information on plants from archaeological sites.

One promising way is to extract **lipids** from artifacts and even from sediments themselves. Lipids are those organic substances that resist mixing with water. This includes the fats, oils, and waxes that are found in both plant and animal tissues. Because they resist mixing with water, lipids have a tendency to remain where they were deposited (and even washing in the laboratory may not remove them).

Cooking vessels are a particularly good place to look for lipids, because the lipids are released from the plant or meat when heated and are absorbed into the fabric of the pottery. Cooking vessels often have a thick carbon residue inside, the result of many simmering stews, but the best place to look for lipids is actually in the walls of the pottery itself.

How do we identify lipids? Recall from our discussion of radiocarbon dating in Chapter 8 that there are three major kinds of carbon in the atmosphere—^{14}C, ^{13}C, and ^{12}C. Recall also that plants of different photosynthetic pathways take in these carbons in different amounts. Thus different classes of plants have different ratios of ^{13}C to ^{12}C, and the plant's fatty acids register this ratio.

The archaeological sample comes from a piece of the interior of a pot. The sherd is ground up and subjected to a laboratory process that separates the fatty acids in the lipid fraction. This extract is then subjected to gas chromatography and mass spectrometry. Without going into the details, these devices measure the ratio of ^{13}C to ^{12}C. Different ratios distinguish the fatty acids in the lipids of plants from those of animals; ongoing research shows that different plant taxa (and, to a lesser extent, different animal species) can be identified using this technique.

One of this method's pioneers, Richard Evershed (University of Bristol, England), has identified the lipids of leafy vegetables (perhaps cabbage) from pottery in Europe. He has also identified residues of milk and of meat. Looking at medieval pots from England, he found that the amount of lipids increased from the bottom to the top of the pot. This makes sense, because fats and oil rise to the top of a stew or soup as it cools, and upper portions of pots would therefore absorb more than the lower portions. In fact, on the inside bottom of some pots he found the fatty acid signature of beeswax. This was not part of a meal, but part of the manufacture of the pot: ethnoarchaeological research has found that many potters smear beeswax on the inside of a pot that is still warm from the kiln in order to season it.

Mary Malainey (Brandon University, Canada), along with colleagues Roman Przybylski and Barbara Sherriff, enhanced this technique by creating a comparative fatty acid "collection"—similar to a faunal analyst's or paleoethnobotanist's comparative collective—of some 130 plants, mammals, fish, and birds native to southwestern Canada. Malainey used lipid analysis to find evidence of meat, maize, plants (excluding maize), fish, and beaver residues on 200 potsherds from sites in southern Canada.

This technique works only with cooking pots, which could record a variety of different kinds of meals. The method holds great promise for reconstructing some elements of the diet that have otherwise proved elusive. There is even the possibility that lipids could be extracted from soil samples and help recover more information on plant foods, such as tubers and roots, that do not preserve well and are rarely found carbonized.

The Symbolic Meaning of Plants: The Upper Mantaro Valley Project

So far, we have been talking about plants, animals, and people from a strictly economic perspective: What did people eat in the past, and when did they eat it? But

---

lipids Organic substances—including fats, oils, and waxes—that resist mixing with water; found in both plant and animal tissues.

more can be done with plant and animal remains in archaeological sites. As discussed in Chapter 3, processual archaeology emphasizes the analysis of natural resources—such as plant remains—as a key to understanding how people coped with ecological issues of the past. But postprocessual archaeology encourages us to seek other things about the past, including not only how people interacted materially with their environment, but how they interacted with it symbolically as well. The Upper Mantaro Valley Project in Peru is one example.

The upper Mantaro Valley sits at 3300 metres above sea level in the central Andes of Peru. The intensively settled and cultivated valley floors are surrounded by rocky hillsides, supporting a few rocky fields, but mostly grasses, a few shrubs, and small trees (Figure 11-12). Thousands of years of intensive cultivation and herding have undoubtedly changed the character of these upland valleys, but nobody is certain just how. Although some investigators believe that the landscape was originally forested, pollen analysis sug-

gests that this area has been relatively treeless since humans first moved in, several thousand years ago.

The Upper Mantaro Archaeological Project excavated numerous house compounds from six archaeological sites spanning the period A.D. 500–1500 (divided into six phases: Pancán 1 through Pancán 4 and Wanka II and III). During the Wanka II phase, the population of the Upper Mantaro area aggregated into large, walled towns located on protected knolls just above the rolling upland zone. The archaeological evidence suggests that this was a time of fights between villages, with land use probably restricted to areas close to the walled settlements. After the Inka conquest during Wanka III times, the population was relocated into small villages on the valley floor. (The Inka often relocated conquered peoples as a way to control them.)

The researchers collected 6-litre soil samples from the floors, middens, pits, and hearths encountered in each excavation unit. The more than 900 samples contained thousands of pieces of charcoal and plant

Figure 11-12 Peaks in the Andes Mountains overlooking a homestead (lower right) on the puna in central Peru.
Source: Robert Kelly

fragments, recovered by both dry screening and flotation of the sediments. The recovered plant remains were classified into three simple categories: grass, stem (small-diameter twig fragments), and wood (pieces of mature wood). The wood category was further subdivided if the tree species could be identified.

Paleoethnobotanists Christine Hastorf (University of California, Berkeley) and Sissel Johannessen (U.S. Army Corps of Engineers) examined these flotation samples to analyze the changing patterns of fuel use in the central Andes of Peru. People can burn a number of different things in fires to cook food and to heat their homes. Grass, tied in tight bundles, small twigs, dung from herbivores, and, of course, mature wood can all be used. What does it mean if people use one source rather than another?

Hastorf and Johannessen found that grass, twigs, and mature wood were all used for fuel, and that mature wood was always the dominant fuel source. But it is the relative frequencies, rather than the absolute figures, that matter. Figure 11-13 graphs the ratio of wood to stems and wood to other (stems and grass) fuel sources for the six phases that cover the 1000-year-long sequence of the Upper Mantaro Valley. Prior to A.D. 1300 (during the Pancán phases), the relative proportion of mature wood fragments dropped; this means that, over time, people used more grass and stems as fuel rather than mature wood. Then, during Wanka II and Wanka III times, this trend reversed, with stem and grass remains decreasing again.

Hastorf and Johannessen also noted that the species composition of the mature wood shifted through time. Up to 40 different kinds of wood are present in the Upper Mantaro Valley samples, with no particular taxa being especially dominant. But the most common taxa did change in relative frequency through time. The five most popular wood types during the early Pancán phases (from yet-unidentified trees) dropped out entirely by Wanka II times. And beginning around A.D. 1300, new wood types appeared. One notable example is *Buddleia* sp. (known as *quishuar* in Quechua), a high-elevation tree that became the most popular fuel source during Inka (Wanka III) times.

What Explains Wood Use?

Let's work through the analysis step by step, following the arguments developed by Hastorf and Johannessen. First, we must consider whether the charcoal distributions on the diagram can be attributed to factors other than fuel use. Is it possible, for instance, that we are looking at changing patterns in the use of house construction materials, changing subsistence practices, or perhaps differential plant preservation through time?

Hastorf and Johannessen rejected all these possibilities. They noted that most of the charcoal comes from fire refuse accumulated over a span of several months or years. Although the possibility exists that some of the charcoal resulted from inadvertent fires (such as accidental burning of thatch roofs and roof beams), the investigators assume that the majority of the charcoal reflects intentional fuel use for heating and cooking. They also note that the composition of the house compounds (mud and stone), the general subsistence remains, and the depositional contents are basically constant throughout the 1000-year sequence. And there is little reason to believe that rates of preservation changed significantly through time.

Hastorf and Johannessen then moved to interpret the charcoal distributions strictly in terms of changing fuel use

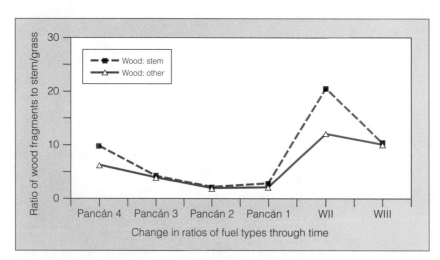

Figure 11-13 The changing ratios of wood to other fuel types through time in the Upper Mantaro area of Peru.

Source: After Hastorf and Johannessen (1991). Courtesy of Christine Hastorf

patterns. Beginning their paleoethnobotanical analysis in standard fashion, they first determined whether the archaeological patterning of fuel use revealed long-term shifts in the relationship between these highland people and their environment.

From this strictly economic perspective, the increased reliance through time on twigs and grasses during the Pancán sequence is just what one might expect in a relatively treeless landscape. Through time, the growing human population and more intensive agricultural land-use patterns made fuel wood scarce. It makes sense that, as people denuded their landscape of trees, they turned to less-desirable fuels, such as small shrubby plants, twigs, and grasses.

But if this is so, then why would this trend reverse during later Wanka times? Contrary to strictly ecological expectations, the archaeologically recovered plant remains show that the use of high-quality fuels actually *increased* after A.D. 1300.

Perhaps the evidence from settlement pattern archaeology provides a clue. Beginning in Wanka II times, an elite class began social and political consolidation of the area. Maybe this elite class mandated some sort of fuel management program, perhaps in the form of tree cultivating, resulting in a greater availability of mature wood sources. This scenario is certainly possible, because we know that tree cultivation was practised during Inka times.

Fuel, of course, has an important economic role in Andean life, especially at an elevation in excess of 3300 metres where the days, to say nothing of the nights, are cold. The increased fuel management/tree cultivation explanation provides a workable, rational answer in economic terms, but leaves several questions unanswered:

■ Why does the change take place in Wanka II times? Why not earlier (when the population first increased) or later (when the Inka took over and restructured the location of the production system)?
■ Why would cultivation be chosen to alleviate the fuel shortage? Why not simply go farther afield to gather fuel? Or why not just shift to lower-quality fuels?
■ And why do certain tree taxa show up during Inka times, when they were absent before?

At this point, Hastorf and Johannessen decided to explore explanations that went beyond conventional economic and ecological factors. They delved into the ethnographic and ethnohistoric records to document the relationships among Andean people, the upland forest, and traditional fuel sources. In so doing, Hastorf and Johannessen found that wood is more than simply fuel in the Andes. It also has an important symbolic dimension.

Collecting fuel was an important aspect of Inkan life, consuming up to 4 hours each day for some segments of the population. We know from documentary accounts that logs, kindling, and straw were also important tribute items in the Inka state.

But trees also had important, symbolic connotations in Andean cosmology. Certain sacred trees were planted at administrative sites. Others were symbolically linked with deities. In fact, the Inka burned *quishuar*, the wood that appeared during Wanka III times, in large quantities at festivals and ritually burned human figures carved of *quishuar* as sacrifices to the divine ancestor of the Inka dynasty. Trees were also symbolically associated with water, as well as with women, clouds, winter, and the moon.

From these and other ethnohistoric and ethnographic examples, Hastorf and Johannessen concluded that wood had strong symbolic as well as economic roles in Inka life, being used to cement social relations (perhaps because it was so important and so rare). Brothers-in-law, for instance, sometimes provided wood and straw to relatives at a wake (Figure 11-14).

Figure 11-14 Ethnohistoric sketch of an Inka man linking himself to his in-laws by presenting them with wood and straw fuel at a wake.
Source: Christine Hastorf

Relating Ideology to the Past

Hastorf and Johannessen supplemented their ecological perspective with a new appreciation of the cultural relationship between ancient Andean people and their environment. But why did the change take place in Wanka II times?

Hastorf and Johannessen argue that the ideology associated with the planting of certain trees could have been a factor in establishing the local political consolidation occurring at that time: The tree symbolized family continuity on the land, with the roots symbolizing ancestors and the fruits, the children. In fact, a ritual step in contemporary marriage ceremonies is termed "to bring the branch" and involves the bringing forth of ritual offspring. The dramatic increase in the use of *quishuar* might thus be attributed to its ritual significance of bringing social groups together into larger entities, rather than simply its mundane use as firewood.

These investigators believe that the act of planting trees—which could be interpreted as a purely economic response to a fuel shortage—was chosen from the other available alternatives because of cultural values concerning the ways in which cultivation and trees functioned as symbols of life and lineage, socially and politically.

Conclusion

This chapter has illustrated how archaeologists go about investigating the relationships among people, plants, and animals. From these remains we can determine what plants and animals people ate, what seasons of the year they were taken, and what sorts of tactics were used to hunt or gather them. They can help reconstruct trade relations. Often, archaeologists view information from plant and animal remains as evidence of ancient peoples' purely materialistic and mundane relations with their environment. And often, that is correct. But the final example from Peru suggests that our interpretations of the past may often be layered, and that material interactions with the environment may have symbolic importance as well.

Summary

- Plant and animal remains aid in the reconstruction of past diet and environments. Dietary reconstructions mean little without their environmental context.

- Faunal analysis—the study of animal remains in archaeological sites—can provide direct evidence of which species were hunted (or collected) for food, how many animals were killed, how they were captured, and what butchering methods were employed.

- Faunal remains can help establish the season of the year when a site was occupied using animal birthing and tooth eruption schedules.

- Plant remains are also powerful sources of data regarding ancient life. Flotation is the most commonly used method for recovering plant macrofossils from archaeological sites.

- Palynology—the study of pollen—is most useful in reconstructing past regional environments. Pollen diagrams enable us to document how local and regional vegetation has changed through time.

- The nests of wood rats can preserve millennia-long records of local environmental change.

- Macrofossils (intact plant parts) are important to paleoenvironmental reconstruction but are also direct evidence of which plant species were exploited, the season of site occupation, and plant processing technology.

- Phytoliths, small grains of silica that form inside plant stems, are less sensitive indicators of plants on a site, but can demonstrate which plant stems (as opposed to seeds) were present on a site.

- Coprolites (desiccated feces) provide evidence of what people ate. They are especially useful indicators of plants (because some seeds pass through undigested) and small animals (because their bones, feathers, or fur may also pass through). Coprolites also tell us what people ate in a single day and hence can point to food storage practices.

■ New methods such as the analysis of lipids on the insides of ceramic cooking vessels provide informa-

tion on plant use and on the roles of meat and cooking techniques.

■ People's interaction with the environment has an economic basis, but culture may frequently place layers of symbolic meaning on top of that interaction.

Additional Reading

CANADIAN RESOURCES

Cannon, A., and Yang, Dongya Y. (2006). Early storage and sedentism on the Pacific Northwest Coast: Ancient DNA analysis of salmon remains from Namu, British Columbia. *American Antiquity 71*(1), 123–141.

Speller, C. F., Yang, D.Y., and Hayden, B. (2005). Ancient DNA investigations of prehistoric salmon resource utilization at Keatley Creek, British Columbia, Canada. *Journal of Archaeological Science (32),* 1378–1389.

OTHER RESOURCES

Brothwell, D., and Pollard, A. (Eds.). (2001). *Handbook of Archaeological Sciences.* Chichester, UK: John Wiley and Sons.

Grayson, Donald K. (1984). *Quantitative Zooarchaeology: Topics in the Analysis of Archaeological Faunas.* Orlando, FL: Academic Press.

Pearsall, Deborah M. (2000). *Paleoethnobotany: A Handbook of Procedures.* New York: Academic Press.

Reitz, Elizabeth, and Wing, Elizabeth. (1999). *Zooarchaeology.* Cambridge: Cambridge University Press.

Sobolik, Kristin. (2003). *The Archaeologist's Toolkit, Volume 5: Archaeobiology.* Walnut Creek, CA: Altamira Press.

Online Resources

COMPANION WEBSITE
Visit *http://www.archaeology1ce.nelson.com* to access a wide range of material to help you succeed in your introductory archaeology course. These include flashcards, Internet exercises, Web links, and practice quizzes.

RESEARCH ONLINE WITH INFOTRAC COLLEGE EDITION
From the Student Companion Website, you can access the InfoTrac College Edition database, which offers thousands of full-length articles for your research.

12

Bioarchaeological Approaches to the Past

A 1st Pennsylvania Volunteer, 1813 (left) and a bioarchaeologist's sketch of a War of 1812 burial, from Fort Erie, Ontario.

Source: (skeleton) Courtesy of Archaeological Services, Inc. (infantry soldier) Military & Historical Image Bank

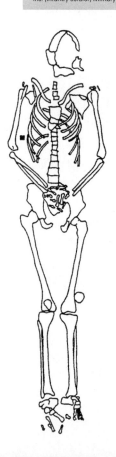

Preview

This chapter examines bioarchaeology, a specialty that straddles the fields of archaeology and biological anthropology. Bioarchaeologists study the human biological component of the archaeological record. Some bioarchaeologists study the origin and distribution of ancient diseases; others reconstruct human diets, analyze the evidence for biological stress in archaeological populations, and reconstruct past demographic patterns—all of this by exploring human bone, bone chemistry, and the DNA preserved in human tissues. Although this chapter is a bit heavy on chemistry and biology, the archaeological payoff is worth the effort.

The analysis of human remains today is a sensitive subject in many parts of the world. Handling, photographing, and sampling the physical remains of a once-living, breathing human being is upsetting to many First Nations and Inuit people (and, actually, to plenty of other North Americans as well). These concerns surfaced in the Kennewick case that we introduced in Chapter 1. Here, we discuss the astonishing amount of information that science can learn from human skeletal remains (and this chapter merely scratches the surface). In the process, we will demonstrate how scientists can conduct such studies in a respectful and sensitive manner. No skeletal remains of aboriginal or Native American people are portrayed in this or any other chapter.

Introduction

In Chapter 4, we described Kelly's archaeological survey project in the Carson Desert of western Nevada. We mentioned that the survey had failed to find many archaeological sites in the marsh because they were obscured by sand and vegetation. However, in the mid-1980s, the greatest floods the Carson Desert had witnessed in a millennium exposed many sites in the marsh.

But more was exposed than arrowheads and faunal remains. Kelly visited the marsh in the summer of 1986, while the Nevada State Museum was recording the new archaeological sites for the U.S. Fish and Wildlife Service (on whose lands most of the new sites were located). Many of the newly exposed sites were accessible only by airboat. Jetting up to the shore of one site, Kelly saw several human skulls rolling about in the wake. The flood had not only exposed many new sites, but dozens and dozens of human burials as well.

In 1987, after the floodwaters had receded, Kelly returned to the Stillwater Marsh to excavate one of the habitation sites (Site 26CH1062, which we mentioned in Chapter 11) and to survey the marsh for burials and human bone. By this point, Clark Spencer Larsen (Ohio State University), a noted **bioarchaeologist,** had joined the team. Bioarchaeologists like Larsen study the human biological component of the archaeological record. Larsen received graduate training in biological anthropology, with a focus on the human skeleton as a record of past human activity. But because he worked with skeletal remains recovered from archaeological sites, Larsen was fully aware of the complex nature of archaeological data as well.

bioarchaeology The study of the human biological component evident in the archaeological record.

Looking Closer
Bioarchaeology and the Snake Hill Cemetery Site

The War of 1812 was one of the bloodiest conflicts in Canadian history. The war resulted from tensions between Britain and the United States, due in part to the Napoleonic War. As Britain and France struggled to assert themselves, the newly established republic of the United States of America found itself firmly caught in the middle. Many of Britain's military actions were seen as a threat to American sovereignty. Escalating hostilities with Aboriginal peoples, who were once allies of the British, offered further cause for concern. President James Madison, enticed by the possibilities of expanding the lands of the new republic, felt the American people had no choice but to go to war. The Americans were woefully unprepared for the battles that soon raged, however, and were forced to rely heavily on local militiamen. The war eventually became concentrated along the border between Upper Canada and the United States. On July 3, 4000 American soldiers under the command of Major General Jacob Brown crossed the Niagara River into what is now Ontario, and captured British Fort Erie. Close to 1800 American and 2400 British soldiers were either killed or wounded over the next four months, making this one of the hardest-fought battles of the War of 1812. Following an arduous siege, the Americans eventually abandoned Fort Erie and retreated across the Niagara River.

Today, the Canadian side of the Niagara River is a peaceful location dotted with summer cottages, and the area where Fort Erie once stood is now a regional park. There are few visible traces of the bloody events that took place here two centuries earlier. This changed, however, when human remains turned up during the excavation of a basement foundation on a nearby lakefront property in 1987. Before any further development could take place, the Cemeteries Branch of Consumer and Commercial Relations recommended that the town of Fort Erie undertake steps to determine the extent of the cemetery. A Toronto-based archaeological consulting firm, Archaeological Services Incorporated, assembled an interdisciplinary team of historians, archaeologists, and bioarchaeologists to examine the remains. In addition to determining the extent of the cemetery, researchers were interested in identifying the nationalities of the individuals interred in the graves. Were they American or British? What types of injuries had they sustained through 19th-century warfare? Could anything be learned about their age, stature, sex, and daily lives? As it turned out, integrating historical records with archaeological and bioarchaeological information would provide a rare and fascinating glimpse into life and death during the War of 1812.

Archaeological investigation of the area revealed a total of 31 features. Of these, 28 appeared to be primary inhumations—meaning individuals who had been intentionally buried following death. The remaining three features were medical refuse pits containing the remnants of amputations (arms, legs) and such surgical waste as bandages and pins. Military doctors during the 19th century were faced with every kind of wound imaginable. This was almost entirely due to the fact that projectiles such as musketballs, cannon balls, shrapnel shot, and congrave rockets could induce complicated wounds in seconds. The most common way to treat such severe injuries was through amputation—often without anesthetic, or an understanding of infection. Infections often leave diagnostic traces on bone, and their low frequency in the Snake Hill Cemetery population indicates that many soldiers must have died before their wounds had healed. The presence of eight limbs in the medical waste pits demonstrates that amputation was seen as an effective form of battlefield medicine.

In addition to trauma sustained through warfare, bioarchaeologists such as Susan Pfeiffer (University of Toronto) were able to learn a great deal about the day-to-day lives of the soldiers through their bones. Evidence of herniated disks, collapsed vertebrae, and the eroded surfaces of vertebral plates, for example, signify that injuries sustained through heavy lifting and twisting were common. Some of these may have been caused by the daily drill routines that soldiers participated in. Brigadier General Winfield Scott, who shaped the army that eventually crossed the Niagara, was renowned for his particularly vigorous training regimes.

Dental evidence points toward a diet that was low in processed carbohydrates and sugar. This is also consistent with historical documents describing soldiers' rations of salt pork and hard tack (bread), along with a little alcohol and vinegar. The presence of pipe stem wear on teeth was a testament to the use of clay pipes for smoking tobacco.

Chemical and isotopic studies of the soldiers' bones, conducted by Anne Katzenberg (University of Calgary), revealed a diet rich in meat and fish. Nitrogen and carbon isotope ratios picked up from dietary water also indicated that most soldiers had originated from the northeastern part of the United States. In addition, several men had elevated lead levels in their bone chemistry, suggesting that they had worked in some lead-related occupation prior to military service. Such levels of lead poisoning are often associated with episodes of muscle weakness, abdominal pain, and nervous paralysis.

Finally, osteological studies of the bones indicated that most of the men had been young to middle-aged, and of taller than average height. This is consistent with remarks made by a captain in one of the Pennsylvania companies, who stated that he was interested in commanding only "Splendidly Big Men." Many of these taller individuals may have been in rifle companies, as riflemen were known for their height.

Injuries such as abdominal wounds do not leave traces on bone. In these cases, archaeologists used clothing and the spatial distribution of buttons to infer the nature of the injury. Archaeologists noted, for example, that certain articles of clothing were missing from some individuals. It is likely that shirts and/or pants were loosened or com-

Figure 12-1 The reburial of American soldiers from Fort Erie, with full military honours.

Source: Courtesy of Richard W. Roeller

pletely removed in order to facilitate medical treatment. There were also several instances in which clusters of buttons were recovered in the thorax and abdominal areas of the skeleton. These may represent the use of military garment fragments as wound dressings in the battlefield.

The various lines of evidence gathered from the site revealed that individuals interred in the Snake Hill Cemetery were American rather than British soldiers. It was likely the wish of most of these men that they be buried on the American side of the Niagara River. On June 30, 1988, at least some were granted this privilege. A repatriation agreement reached between the United States and Canada led to the transportation of these 28 individuals to the National Cemetery in Bath, New York, where they were afforded full military honours (Figure 12-1). A second agreement was also reached, stimulated by scientific interest in the isolated remains recovered from the medical refuse pits. These remains were divided between the Academy of Medicine in Toronto, and U.S. Army Medical Museum at the Armed Forces Institute of Pathology in Washington, D.C.

The Snake Hill site project brought the methods of bioarchaeology to bear on one small event of the War of 1812. Out of this has emerged a new understanding of both military and medical history.

A well-trained field archaeologist can tell the difference between human and animal bones. But few archaeologists are trained to go beyond such simple identification. When modern archaeologists expect to encounter human remains—as did Kelly when he approached the Stillwater Marsh—they involve a bioarchaeologist from day one. And if those remains are Native American, as they were at Stillwater Marsh, archaeologists likewise involve the appropriate American Indian community (or communities). And so, before proceeding further, we'd like you to know that all the data collection discussed in this chapter was approved beforehand by the local Native American community.

In 1987, we surveyed the previously flooded portions of the wetland, looking for new archaeological sites and keeping an eye open for all human remains. Along with the Nevada State Museum, we recovered the remains of more than 500 individuals. This was significant because the Stillwater finds *tripled* the number of human burials known from the entire state of Nevada. These remains were studied by Larsen and a team of bioarchaeologists he assembled to handle specific analyses.

Skeletal Analysis: The Basics

Larsen first had to confirm that all the bones collected by the survey team were in fact human. After all, the flood had washed out plenty of archaeological midden, scattering ancient and recent animal bone among the human remains. Although human bone is distinctive, archaeological skeletal remains are often fragmented and weathered, making them difficult to identify. We have seen surgeons who were unable to identify a bone scrap as a piece of a human femur. But archaeologists are accustomed to seeing things in their broken, dirty, smashed forms. Larsen learned how to identify bone through classes in human anatomy and **osteology**, but his real skill was acquired simply by handling thousands of human bone fragments. Figure

12-2 shows some of the major bones of the human skeleton, including ones mentioned in this chapter.

Bioarchaeologists working with bones from grave sites are accustomed to working with well-defined sets of remains, each from a single individual; this is why, unlike zooarchaeologists, bioarchaeologists are rarely concerned with issues of minimum number of individuals (MNI) or number of identified specimens (NISP).

Instead, bioarchaeologists are concerned with whether the human remains constitute a **burial population**, individuals who came from a specific area and who died over a relatively short period of time (as might be found in a historical-period cemetery). The Stillwater burials, however, derived from a 16-square-

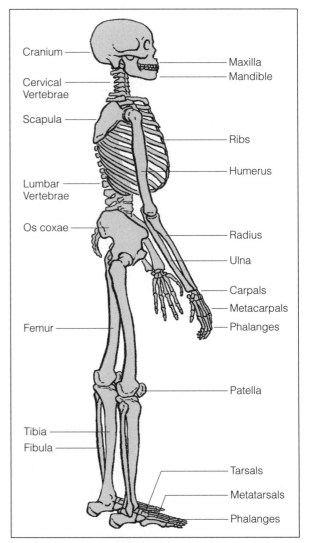

osteology The study of bone.

burial population A set of human burials that come from a limited region and a limited time period. The more limited the region and the time period, the more accurate will be inferences drawn from analysis of the burials.

Figure 12-2 Some major bones of the human skeleton.

Cranium
Cervical Vertebrae
Scapula
Lumbar Vertebrae
Os coxae
Femur
Tibia
Fibula
Maxilla
Mandible
Ribs
Humerus
Radius
Ulna
Carpals
Metacarpals
Phalanges
Patella
Tarsals
Metatarsals
Phalanges

kilometre area of marsh, not a single, well-defined cemetery. Few of the burials contained any grave goods (meaning that we could not use temporal types to place the burials within archaeological phases). And only a few of the burials could be dated by AMS radiocarbon determinations. Most of the projectile points found in the nearby sites could be assigned to temporal types, but these time spans were quite large (600 years for the Underdown phase and 1500 years for the Reveille phase). Although hardly ideal, these temporal types provided at least some rough parameters for the living population that this skeletal sample represented.

Good preservation conditions will provide the bioarchaeologist with a nearly complete human skeleton. But sometimes, only the hardest bones survive—parts of the skull, the central portions of the limb bones, and—the hardest portion of the human skeleton—the teeth. We've seen burials where nothing remained except for an eerie smile in the sand.

Ancient cultural practices can also mix human skeletal remains together and make it difficult to group skeletal remains by individual. Many eastern Native American tribes, for example, laid bodies out in a **charnel house,** where the body was allowed to decompose in the open. Eventually, the bones were cleaned of remaining flesh, bundled together, and ritually placed into a communal grave (these are known as **bundle burials**). Over time, the bones of various individuals would commingle. Careful excavation might be able to re-group bones by individual, but sometimes this is impossible. In other cases, as at the Stillwater Marsh, post-depositional processes scatter the once-intact burials. In fact, of the 500 individuals recovered, only 54 were encountered as intact primary burials. In this chapter, we focus on the analysis of those remains.

Determining Sex

After removing any nonhuman bones from the collection, Larsen assigned sex and age to the intact burials. How can we determine sex from bones? One obvious place where men and women differ is the pelvic area. Evolution designed women's hips (the hips are technically composed of two halves, the right and left os coxae or innominates) to birth children; as a result, the **sciatic** (sy-*a*-tik) **notch,** a U-shaped indentation in each os coxae's posterior (rear) portion, is wider in

women than in men. There is variation among the world's population in *how much* wider, but within a burial population, one can usually see a clear difference between those os coxae with wide and those with narrow sciatic notches.

Unfortunately, the os coxae are quite porous, making them some of the first bones to decompose. So if preservation is not excellent, the bioarchaeologist must look elsewhere.

The human skull also provides clues to a deceased individual's sex. Adult male skulls tend to be more robust than female skulls, with heavier brow ridges over the eyes, larger mastoid processes (two protrusions of bone on the bottom of the skull, one beneath each ear), and more rugged muscle attachments. Male skulls also tend to have squarer chins and eye orbits. A skilled bioarchaeologist can often "sex" a skull simply by its feel. Again, the world's populations vary in how robust or how gracile male and female skulls are, but within a burial population bioarchaeologists can usually detect discernible differences between *adult* male and female skulls. The sex of a child, however, is difficult to determine because the sexually distinctive characteristics of bone do not develop until young adulthood.

Larsen found that the Stillwater collection contained almost twice as many males as females, but sex could not be assigned to a large number of the burials (because some of the adult burials were poorly preserved or were missing key elements; others were the skeletons of children).

Determining Age

Age at death is next. Here, like a zooarchaeologist, Larsen used osteological standards based on comparative collections. Because the pattern and timing of crown formation and tooth eruption is consistent

---

charnel house A structure used by eastern North Americans to lay out the dead where the body would decompose. The bones would later be gathered and buried or cremated.

bundle burial Burial of a person's bones, bundled together, after the flesh has been removed or allowed to decay off the bones.

sciatic notch The angled edge of both halves of the posterior (rear) side of the pelvis; measurement of this angle is used to determine sex in human skeletons. Although its width varies among populations, narrow notches indicate a male and wider notches indicate a female.

among human populations, teeth are extremely useful for telling the age of younger individuals. Larsen determined age by recording which teeth had formed their crowns and/or erupted through the mandible or maxilla (the lower and upper jaw bones, respectively).

Patterns of bone fusion are also useful for determining age in skeletons of youths and young adults. At birth, many bones are actually several different pieces. The long bones, such as the femora or humeri, are made up of the central shaft and the two **epiphyses**—the ends that articulate with other bones. The epiphyses fuse to the shaft at known rates. For example, the proximal epiphysis of the radius ("proximal" refers to the end of a long bone that is closest to the body's centre, in this case, the end of the radius closest to the elbow; "distal" refers to the end of the long bone farthest from the body) completely fuses by about age 19, whereas portions of the scapula do not fuse until age 23. Noting to what extent various bones are fused can estimate an individual's age at the time of their death.

But most bones are fully fused by age 25 and, by that same age, most teeth have erupted. Therefore, other methods are required to age the skeletons of mature adults, and these are more difficult to implement. The first of these is bone wear. After age 30, bones begin to wear down. Much of the wear is related to a person's activity level (as well as diet). But some bones tend to wear no matter what. One particularly sensitive area is the **pubic symphysis,** the place where the right and left os coxae meet in a person's groin area. As the cartilage between the two halves erodes with age, the symphysis undergoes distinct changes. At age 20, for example, the symphysis has a distinct set of surface ridges that look like ocean waves. By age 35, these ridges have disappeared, and a rim has formed along the edge of the symphysis. By age 50, the rim has disappeared, and the symphysis looks like a shrivelled prune. But because the os coxae are among the first bones to decay, this useful method of determining skeletal age is not applicable to many archaeological skeletons.

epiphyses The ends of bones that fuse to the main shaft or portion of bone at various ages; most bones are fused by age 25. This fact can be used to age skeletons of younger individuals.

pubic symphysis Where the two halves of the pelvis meet in the groin area; the appearance of its articulating surface can be used to age skeletons.

Another method to age a skeleton uses the degree of tooth wear and loss. Because teeth wear down continually with age, bioarchaeologists have generated standardized tables (from non-industrial populations) to estimate age from the extent of tooth wear. But caution is required here too, because the rate of tooth wear and loss is strongly related to diet. People dependent on food processed on grinding stones will have higher rates of wear because of all the grit in their diet. And if their food is high in carbohydrates, people may also experience a higher rate of tooth loss from cavities (see "Cavities" later in the chapter).

Using these methods, Larsen determined that the Stillwater burials ranged in age from fetuses to individuals of more than 50 years old—but these age estimates have some limitations. Rarely can bioarchaeologists assign a specific age estimate to a skeleton; instead, because of the different indicators of age and slight error factors in the various methods, skeletons are placed into five-year age classes (0–5 years, 6–10 years, 11–15 years, and so on). It's also difficult to pin down the age of individuals older than about 50 years.

How Well Did the Stillwater People Live?

Eventually, Larsen derived the basics of the Stillwater population: He knew how many men, women, infants, and adolescents there were, and he knew these individuals' approximate ages. Now he could turn to questions he wanted to ask of this population. One of these was: How well did the people of Stillwater Marsh live? He did not ask this question out of idle curiosity. Instead, he wanted to use the Stillwater population to shed light on a major dilemma of anthropology.

Prior to the 1960s, many anthropologists assumed that the lives of ancient hunter-gatherers were, to use the words of 17th-century philosopher Thomas Hobbes (1588–1679), "nasty, brutish, and short." In this view, hunter-gatherers had to work excessively hard, lived hand-to-mouth with barely enough food, suffered from high rates of infant mortality, and lived short lives.

But research with the Ju/'hoansi of southern Africa's Kalahari Desert and other foragers in the 1960s suggested that hunter-gatherers actually had plenty of leisure time, an adequate diet, and low levels

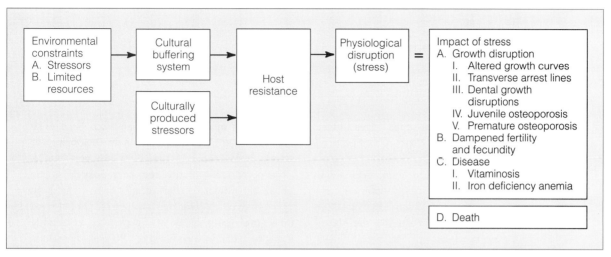

Figure 12-3 Environmental factors operate through and in conjunction with cultural behaviour to produce disease or malnutrition, which results in physiological disruption—some of which leaves material imprints on human bone.

of disease. Anthropologist Marshall Sahlins (University of Chicago) went so far as to label hunter-gatherers the "original affluent society." In the 1960s, this image of prehistoric peoples resonated with those seeking an alternative to the perceived excesses of modern industrial life.

Is one of these characterizations more accurate than the other? Both were based on ethnographic data, but the observers might have been predisposed to see hunter-gatherers in one way rather than the other. Larsen thought that the skeletal data of an archaeological population could provide a more objective assessment of the nature of the foraging lifeway. Larsen wanted to see whether the Stillwater foragers of 1000 years ago were closer to the "nasty, brutish, and short" or the "original affluent society" image of hunter-gatherers.

To do this, Larsen turned to **paleopathology,** the study of ancient disease. This specialization includes the identification of specific diseases, but few specific diseases can be identified from bones (syphilis [venereal and nonvenereal], tuberculosis, and leprosy are the major ones that leave distinctive lesions and other characteristics on bone). Broken bones, even if healed, are also easy to identify; unhealed breaks are usually evidence of trauma that was the immediate cause of death.

But bioarchaeologists can glean more from human skeletons if they look at human bone as being formed by complex interrelationships among the environment, behaviour, physiology, and cultural behaviour (see Figure 12-3). Larsen used this perspective to look

for *nonspecific* indicators of stress, particularly those caused by nutritional deficiencies and/or nonspecific infectious disease in the Stillwater burial population. Though challenging, the study of biological stress has become an important area of bioarchaeology.

Disease and Trauma at Stillwater

Larsen found little trace of specific diseases among the skeletal remains from Stillwater Marsh—no evidence of syphilis, tuberculosis, or leprosy. He did, however, find some telltale signs of iron deficiency anemia.

Iron is essential for adequate transport of oxygen by red blood cells. But sometimes iron is limited, perhaps by the lack of red meat in the diet (a primary source of easily absorbed iron), chronic diarrhea, or parasites (such as hookworm, which can cause internal bleeding and the loss of a body's iron stores). Regardless of the specific cause, whenever iron is limited, the body produces more red blood cells. Because red blood cells are produced in the marrow cavities of bone, these cavities enlarge. When this happens in the cranium, the surface of the skull takes on a spongy appearance, a characteristic known as **porotic hyperostosis.** The same phenomenon can happen to bone in the eye

paleopathology The study of ancient disease.

porotic hyperostosis A symptom of iron deficiency anemia in which the skull takes on a porous appearance.

Looking Closer
Hi-Tech BioArchaeology: Using 3D Imaging Technology to Reconstruct the Face of an Egyptian Mummy

Mummies—corpses that have been either intentionally or naturally preserved through the use of chemicals, or exposure to extreme cold, airlessness, or low humidity—have fascinated people for centuries. While mummies have been discovered in such widely diverse places as Peru and the Aleutian Islands, by far the most prolific practitioners of mummification were the ancient Egyptians. However, the great antiquity of many Egyptian mummies makes them extremely delicate, and therefore difficult to study. In an effort to overcome this, bioarchaeologists now employ non-invasive, high-tech imaging techniques such as computer tomography, more commonly known as CT scans. Using this technique, three-dimensional images of the internals of a human body can be constructed using a large series of two-dimensional x-rays, shot around a single axis of rotation. By leaving mummies intact, the age, sex, and health of ancient populations can be directly studied. Dr. Robert Hoppa is a Canada Research Chair and bioarchaeologist at the University of Manitoba, where he has established the Bioanthropology Digital Image Analysis Laboratory (BDIAL). Hoppa uses digital imaging technology to capture, process, and even print three-dimensional objects. In this case, he and his colleagues Heather Gill-Robinson (North Dakota State University), Jonathan Elias (Akhmim Mummy Studies Consortium), Frank Bender (Akhmim Mummy Studies Consortium), and Travis Allard (University of Manitoba) used three-dimensional computer imaging to reconstruct the face of an Egyptian woman who lived more than 2000 years ago.

Archaeologists estimate that the Egyptian site of Akhmim was continuously occupied for a period of 5000 years, making it among this country's most important sites. Not surprisingly, there are many necropolis areas located here, including the al-Hawawish Ridge Cemetery, a site where hundreds of mummies have been discovered since the 19th century, many of them belonging to priests connected with the cult of the god Min. A large component of the cemetery post-dates the Third Intermediate Period (1069–664 B.C.) in Egyptian history. During this poorly understood time, the governance of Egypt was constantly changing hands—from the Persian interlude (343–332 B.C.) to the Alexandrine/Ptolemaic period (332–30 B.C.), the latter brought about as a result of the conquering of Egypt by Alexander the Great. As native communities struggled to retain their autonomy under pressure from an ever-changing parade of dominators, many people were displaced. During this time, Akhmim had become an important focus for groups that were becoming increasingly resistant to outside rule. Hoppa and his colleagues undertook the facial reconstruction of a mummy recovered from Akhmim as a means of exploring ethnic diversity brought about by the widespread social and economic changes caused by these events.

The mummy in question was that of a 35- to 40-year-old woman named Ta-irty, or Ta-irty-bai, someone who had lived during these turbulent times. In 1885, Christian missionaries distributing bibles in Egypt purchased Ta-irty's mummy, along with four others, for $8 apiece. Ta-irty's mummy was nearly destroyed by fire in 1901, and it has resided in the Art Museum of the College of Wooster, in Ohio, ever since.

A CT scan was first made of Ta-irty's mummy at the Wooster Community Hospital in 2004. The Akhmim Mummy Studies Consortium CT-scanned Ta-irty's mummy at the Wooster Community Hospital in 2004. Image analysis revealed that she had been afflicted with spinal scoliosis, possibly the result of an improperly set fracture of her right femur, making one of her legs shorter than the other. As this aspect of the work continued, the CT scan images of the skull were forwarded to the University of Manitoba to produce an accurate 3D facial reconstruction of the mummy's skull. The first step involved the "virtual" removal of the bandages and skin from the mummy's skull. Computer technology meant that this could now be accomplished without ever touching the delicate subject. Skin, tissue, and bone produce distinctive greyscale values in the digital images that can then be edited out, leaving behind only the bone. Called *thresholding,* this technique was complicated by the large amounts of resin that had been used in the mummification process. In order to solve this problem, the researchers used pseudo-colouring to distinguish between resin and bone around the delicate facial areas such as the nose. Once the 3D model had been completed, it was then printed in three dimensions using a special printer. Unlike your standard desktop variety, this high-tech printer uses a plaster-based powder and binding solution to produce an accurate three-dimensional model of the imaged skull. The skull model then became the basis for the facial reconstruction (Figure 12-4). Modelling clay was first used to outline details of facial musculature. Next, a second layer of clay was applied, which served as skin. Although analysis of other Akhmimic mummies in ongoing, the researchers feel that the work on Ta-irty is an important first step toward examining ethnic diversity with an ancient population.

The results of the image analysis were truly fascinating, and revealed valuable information about the mummification process which in an earlier day would have required a destructive autopsy. The researchers were able to determine, for example, that Ta-irty's brain had been removed through her right nasal cavity, as was commonly practised in this region during Ptolemaic times. She also appeared to have suffered from some dental health problems while alive, as was indicated by several missing molars and wear patterns on many

teeth. The techniques used by Hoppa and his colleagues will inevitably be of benefit for studying mummies from other parts of the world, because the three-dimensional information they process is excellent for archival and research purposes and is gathered without damaging the subjects under examination.

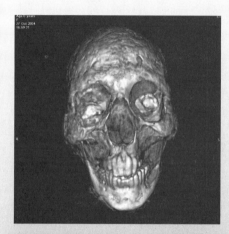

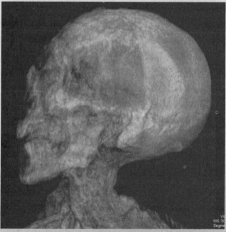

Figure 12-4 Three-dimensional images of the mummy Ta-irty, from Akhmim, one of ancient Egypt's greatest cities.

Source: Images courtesy of Akhmim Mummy Studies Consortium and Pinnacle Health System, Harrisburg, Pennsylvania

sockets (where it is known as **cribra orbitalia**). Larsen documented evidence of iron deficiency in only 4 of the 54 burials from the Stillwater Marsh.

The Stillwater group showed little evidence of physical trauma. Sheilagh Brooks (retired, University of Nevada, Las Vegas), who also studied the Stillwater materials, found only 18 individuals with bone breaks (all healed); 6 of these (5 males and 1 female) had broken noses. In general, then, the Stillwater population seemed to have been relatively healthy, suffering from a few broken bones (and perhaps the occasional fistfight).

These observations were made largely on adult skeletons, but many anthropologists will tell you that, to understand overall quality of life, you must look at the children. Because they are fragile, children's skeletons (especially those of the very young) are rarely well preserved, making it more difficult to find appropriate samples to study. But human bone has a "memory," and some childhood events leave a telltale record on the adolescent and adult skeleton.

Growth Arrest Features

Childhood growth may be periodically arrested because of disease, trauma, or malnutrition. Whenever this happens, the bones record the cessation of growth. In long bones, such as the tibia and femur, this growth arrest appears as a thin line of bone perpendicular to the bone's long axis. These lines are not visible on the outside of the bone, but they do appear in x-rays and are known as **Harris lines.** These lines form in childhood but disappear later in life, as the bone is remodelled as it grows.

Teeth likewise register the cessation of growth. Adult teeth form, of course, in the mandible and maxilla when children are quite young. When a child becomes severely ill or is malnourished, tooth growth stops. If the child recovers, growth starts up again, but the episode of growth arrest is forever encoded as shallow grooves, known as **enamel hypoplasias,** across the

front of the teeth (Figure 12-5). Because teeth grow at known rates, bioarchaeologists can measure the distance from the hypoplasia to the tip of the root to estimate how old a child was when the growth arrest event took place. Likewise, the width of a hypoplasia indicates the duration of the period of stress.

Enamel hypoplasias are permanent and therefore are more useful measures of stress than are Harris lines. For this reason, Larsen focused on enamel hypoplasias. (He could also analyze them without the cost of x-rays and with minimal disturbance to the bone.) Working with Dale Hutchinson (University of North Carolina), Larsen found that two-thirds of the individuals had hypoplasias, and that most of these occurred between the ages of 3 and 4. But the number of hypoplasias per tooth, and the average width of the grooves, was less than for other Native American populations. Larsen and Hutchinson concluded that the children of Stillwater Marsh had seen some hard times, but conditions were by no means as bad as they might have been.

The specific cause of the Stillwater hypoplasias, however, is more difficult to determine. They could have resulted from physical trauma to the face, parasitic infection, or malnutrition. We know that trauma was relatively rare (and restricted to adults), and the evidence for extensive infections was limited. Larsen and Hutchinson concluded that fluctuations in the food supply from the marsh—subject to the vagaries of local climate—most likely caused periods of malnutrition for young children.

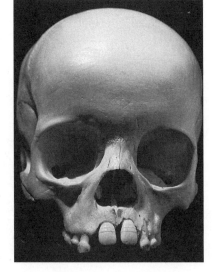

Figure 12-5
Enamel hypoplasias.
Source: Clark Larsen

cribra orbitalia A symptom of iron deficiency anemia in which the bone of the upper eye sockets takes on a spongy appearance.

Harris lines Horizontal lines near the ends of long bones indicating episodes of physiological stress.

enamel hypoplasias Horizontal linear defects in tooth enamel indicating episodes of physiological stress.

In fact, the young population might be especially hard hit by a fluctuating food supply. Among hunter-gatherers, children are often not fully weaned until they are 3, 4, or even 5 or 6 years old. This means that, if the 3- or 4-year-olds at Stillwater Marsh were in the process of being weaned during a severe winter or a lean spring, the child might very well suffer a limited period of malnutrition. That the individual survived to adulthood, however, demonstrates that this hard time was not insurmountable.

Workload

To this point, Larsen had discovered that the people who lived in the Stillwater Marsh enjoyed a relatively healthy life. But other skeletal data show that this life came at a cost.

As we said before, bones have a memory—they are a lifetime diary that records whether you lived life as a hotshot fighting forest fires or as a couch potato. Bones can be hard to read, but they do not lie.

Bioarchaeologists use a variety of ways to determine how much physical labour a person saw in his or her lifetime. When working with the Stillwater collection, Larsen relied on patterns of osteoarthritis and the study of bone biomechanics.

Osteoarthritis

Osteoarthritis is a joint disorder created by the loss of cartilage, often caused by mechanical stress. This condition appears as a bony growth (known as an **osteophyte**) that forms a lip around the edge of an articular surface of a long bone's epiphysis (for example, at the elbow or knee) or between vertebrae, as shown in Figure 12-6. When the cartilage disappears completely, the articular surfaces rub against one another, creating a polish known as **eburnation.** Eburnated joints are extremely painful to move.

Larsen found that *every single adult* skeleton in the Stillwater collection had osteoarthritis in at least one joint. In fact, this was the most severe osteoarthritis that Larsen had ever seen in any skeletal population. The people of Stillwater marsh may have lived a healthy life, but they apparently had to work—and suffer aches and pains—for it.

Males were slightly more osteoarthritic than females, and not in all the same places. Men suffered from osteoarthritis more in the hip, ankle, and foot; women, more in their lumbar vertebrae—their lower

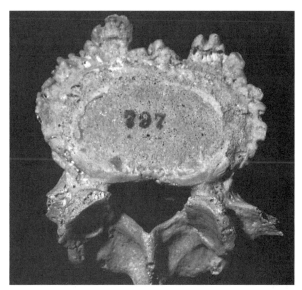

Figure 12-6 A vertebra with osteoarthritis.
Source: Clark Larsen

back. Larsen suggested that the males in the Stillwater population probably did more walking—and more difficult walking—than did women. This makes sense, because women probably foraged for plants, fish, and small game within a short distance of camps within the marsh itself, while the men probably traveled farther, into the rougher terrain of the Stillwater Mountains, in search of large game. The women were hardly taking it easy, though. They, too, had osteoarthritis that indicated they did a great deal of difficult walking, no doubt carrying children and gear when they moved camp. But men evidently did even more walking.

Why the high incidence of osteoarthritis in the lower backs of women? Larsen pointed to two likely factors: child rearing and food processing. Because hunter-gatherer children breastfeed until they are several years old, children must stay with their mothers. And if the Stillwater women were to complete their daily foraging tasks, they probably had to carry the

osteoarthritis A disorder in which the cartilage between joints wears away, often because of overuse of the joint, resulting in osteophytes and eburnation.

osteophyte A sign of osteoarthritis in which bones develop a distinct "lipping" of bone at the point of articulation.

eburnation A sign of osteoarthritis in which the epiphyses of long bones are worn smooth, causing them to take on a varnish-like appearance.

children with them (just as Ju/'hoansi women do). If so, then the Stillwater women probably carried children throughout most of their adult lives—with resulting strain on the lower back.

In addition, the seeds and tubers that women collected in the marsh were ground on metates. A lifetime of such seed grinding could have led women to overuse their lower vertebrae and given them a higher incidence of osteoarthritis there.

Biomechanics

Larsen also worked with Christopher Ruff (Johns Hopkins University) to transfer knowledge from civil engineering to the analysis of **long bone cross-sections.** Civil engineers know that the type of supports used in a building is a function of how much stress the building will place on the beams (which is largely a function of the building's height). Bones are the same, except that, unlike a building's support beams, bones change their cross-section over time as they respond to stress. Although the specifics are complex, the principle is simple: When femora are placed under heavy mechanical stress (for example, by routine walking over difficult terrain while carrying a heavy load), they tend to develop a more oval cross-section. The cross-sections of the femora of a couch potato, on the other hand, are more rounded.

Larsen and Ruff obtained cross-sections of the femora through CAT scans at the Veteran's Administration hospital in Reno, Nevada. Although the overall bone mass was relatively low in the Stillwater femora, bone strength was among the highest that Larsen and Ruff had ever seen. And, as was true for osteoarthritis, the femur cross-sections indicated that men did more—and more strenuous—walking than did women. This could be because the Stillwater folk, especially the men, were generally robust, with large, heavy bones. But when Larsen and Ruff looked at the cross-sections of the humeri (the upper arm), they

found no difference between men and women, and no real difference between the Stillwater and other populations of native North Americans. This suggests that the difference in men's and women's femoral cross-sections was produced by a difference in men's and women's behaviour and not simply by differences in the size of men and women.

In sum, the femur cross-sections and the patterns in osteoarthritis indicated that the people living at Stillwater Marsh walked a great deal to make a successful living. And men did more walking than women. Neither of these conclusions was particularly striking, but it was conclusive proof that the people who lived at Stillwater were nomadic and gave Larsen clearer ideas about differences in men's and women's lives.

Paleodemography

Still another way to judge quality of life is to examine patterns of mortality. **Paleodemography** reconstructs parameters such as life expectancy at birth, the age profile of a population, and patterns in the ages of death. Bioarchaeologists do this by constructing various sorts of **mortality profiles** for a prehistoric population based on the age and sex data of burials. Mortality profiles show at what age adult males, adult females, and children died.

Paleodemography works best with well-defined cemetery populations (that is, for a skeletal sample derived from the same biological population over a few years or decades). Available radiocarbon dates showed that most of the Stillwater burials dated to the Underdown phase, but this phase covers 600 years. This means that the Stillwater population is not an ideal candidate for a paleodemographic study.

Still, bioarchaeologist Sheilagh Brooks was able to derive some useful data from mortality profiles for the Stillwater burials. One of these profiles (Figure 12-7) shows the burial data sorted into 5-year age classes by sex. Note first that the 0–5 age category is composed entirely of "unknowns"; as we mentioned earlier, it is almost impossible to determine the sex of very young children.

Why did so many children die so young? Ethnographic data show that the mortality of newborns and toddlers is very high among hunting and gathering populations—50 to 60 percent of all children born in a foraging population do not survive to 5 years of age. The Stillwater mortality profile reflects this sad fact.

long bone cross-sections Cross-sections of the body's long bones (arms and legs) used to analyze bone shape and reconstruct the mechanical stresses placed on that bone—and hence activity patterns.

paleodemography The study of ancient demographic patterns and trends.

mortality profiles Charts that depict the various ages at death of a burial population.

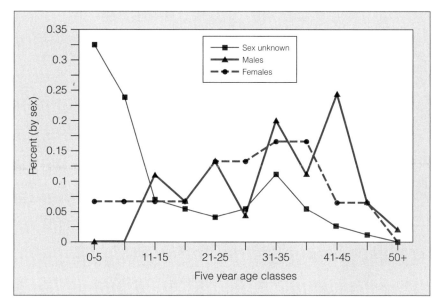

Figure 12-7 The Stillwater mortality profile.

Source: From data in Brooks et al., 1988

length varies from population to population, it is important that the bioarchaeologist apply the appropriate equation. Here, for instance, is the stature formula, which has an error factor of +/–3.5 centimetres, for ancient populations in central Mexico:

$$\text{living height} = (2.26 \times \text{femur length}) + 66.38$$

This equation tells us that, if a femur excavated in central Mexico measures 40 centimetres in length, it likely belonged to an individual who stood about 157 centimetres tall (5 feet 2 inches) give or take 3.5 centimetres. Different formulae are available for skeletons recovered from other parts of the world.

Height provides a useful measure of overall health, because it is closely related to diet. However, because different populations have different genetic capacities for height, it is best to use this variable as a measure of health when looking at data for one burial population across time. Larsen did not use height estimates for the Stillwater burials, because most of the burials dated to the same phase, and no good comparative population data were available.

However, Larsen did use height estimates to track health changes in another project that examined individuals who lived on St. Catherines Island and elsewhere along the coast of Georgia. Here he was interested in testing hypotheses about the effect of maize agriculture on a human population's health. He estimated the heights from skeletons of the hunting-and-gathering population (pre–A.D. 1150) and those of the agricultural population (post–A.D. 1150). Contrary to what you might expect, he found that the average agriculturalist male was 1 percent, and the average agriculturalist female 3 percent, *shorter* than their foraging ancestors. In this case, agriculture was a poorer diet than the previous hunting-and-gathering one, and it hit women harder than men. (If this makes you wonder why people switched from hunting and gathering to agriculture, turn to Chapter 15.)

Notice also that there are no strong peaks in female age at death. Girls may have had a slightly higher chance of dying at a young age compared with boys, and men may have had a slightly greater chance of surviving into their 40s than women. The female mortality profile shows an increase in deaths beginning at age 21, the early child-bearing years; this is also similar to other foraging populations. The male profile has several peaks and no distinctive pattern. Finally, notice that few individuals are assigned to the 46–50 and 50+ age categories; this reflects a shorter overall life expectancy. Although we might regard the late 40s as the prime of life, a 47-year-old person in Stillwater was an elder.

Stature

Measuring stature is yet another way to assess quality of life. Bioarchaeologists estimate stature with equations that relate the length of certain long bones to an individual's height. These equations were created, incidentally, from huge cadaver populations (composed of individuals who donated their bodies to science).

The femur is the best bone for computing stature (because tall people tend to have long femora and shorter people tend to have shorter femora). But because the relationship between height and femur

Profile of an Archaeologist
A Native American Archaeologist

Dorothy Lippert is an archaeologist with the Smithsonian Institution.

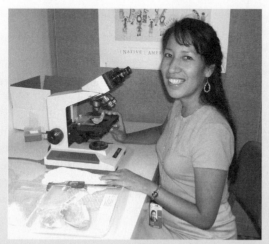

Source: Dorothy Lippert

Deciding to become an archaeologist was the easy part. I had no fixed ideas about what such a career would consist of other than that I would be participating in the scientific process of understanding our human past. I was unaware of the extent to which my own Native American heritage would play; in the beginning, I didn't realize that this part of my identity would so closely focus both my career and my beliefs about what we are meant to do as archaeologists. My reasons for choosing this discipline initially centred around a love of history and science, although I had little patience for understanding history as a simple

series of dates and even less for reducing science to sterile sets of data. Archaeology, for me, has always been a humanistic endeavour, one in which we come to know and respect people of the past in the same way we should people of the present day.

I find that archaeologists who are also Native American seem to have similar views of the discipline, particularly when talking about prehistoric archaeological work in North America. This is most likely because we know these people as our ancestors and in the course of practising archaeology it becomes our privilege and our responsibility to care for them and to speak about their lives. A common thread within indigenous cultures is a respect for our elders, and this permeates archaeology as it is practised by Native Americans.

In 2003, there were 11 Native Americans with doctorates in archaeology. It is my suspicion that this number reflects both the small numbers of Native Americans who hold doctorates in any subject as well as the emotional and scholarly hazards that archaeology holds for us. The impression that many tribal people have had up to now of archaeology is that it is something that is done to Native peoples by outsiders. Those of us who try to practise archaeology from a Native perspective are still caught by this impression and, in some people's eyes, have become outsiders ourselves. Tribal people have insinuated to me that I must not be truly Native if I can bring myself to prac-

Reconstructing Diet from Human Bone

The people who lived at Stillwater were hunter-gatherers. But can we go beyond this general statement to talk more specifically about what people ate? Following the old adage "You are what you eat," diet

caries Cavities.

can be reconstructed from human bone in several ways. We discuss how two of these methods were used on the Stillwater burial population below.

Cavities

Dental **caries** (cavities) can help differentiate between agriculturalists and hunter-gatherer populations. You might think that cavities happen to those who do not brush their teeth regularly or properly, but this is not

tise archaeology. I also have the added burden of having studied human osteology. Frequently, when I meet other Native people, I don't mention that I'm an archaeologist until late in the conversation, in hopes of forestalling a negative response.

Other Natives are more supportive, saying that it's about time that we (indigenous people) have started doing this work. Many understand just how difficult a career this can be and encourage me to continue. In their minds, as in my own, archaeology is a way to work for Native Americans, both the ancestors and present-day communities.

I think that many non-Native archaeologists are unaware of these kinds of reactions. Some seem convinced that archaeology done with a Native perspective will somehow be less scientific, as if their cultural heritage plays no role in their own studies. While I am a firm believer in maintaining scientific rigour in our analyses, I see no reason not to illuminate these studies with the cultural legacy that was maintained, sometimes at horrendous cost, by our ancestors. As Natives begin to participate fully in archaeology, I think the discipline will become broader in its approach and more open to combinations of different knowledge bases in order to understand a more human past.

When I speak with other Native Americans about the practice of archaeology, I find that we all tend to use this discipline to answer questions that are influenced by our cultural background. For instance, in my own studies of health and medical theory, I was interested in the ways that these were experienced by a small community whose inhabitants lived and died some 400 years ago. I could never quite see my research as the simple practice of collecting data; rather, I felt myself to be engaged in communication with these ancient ones. Their cold, white bones used my breath and mind to tell this world their long forgotten story. Through the practice of this science, I became their voice.

Even when reading archaeological reports and looking through pages of dry, scholarly text, I find that I am searching for the humanity of the people whose remains or material objects are being studied. I have also realized that this perspective is not limited only to indigenous archaeologists. There are a number of non-Natives who seem to intuitively approach our science with a very humanistic flair. I believe that in the years to come, more and more archaeologists will begin to appreciate just how much more fun it is if we see our discipline as dealing with fellow beings. Shakespeare summed it up well. "You are not stones, nor bones, but men." While archaeology frequently encounters both stones and bones, it is best if we keep in mind that what we are really meeting up with are human beings.

strictly true. Caries result when simple carbohydrates, especially refined sugar but also including starchy foods like maize or tubers, remain on your teeth. Bacteria that feed on the carbohydrates produce an acid as a by-product that dissolves tooth enamel. If you ate mostly meat, you would have few caries—regardless of whether you brushed your teeth.

The prevalence of caries, then, serves as an indicator of starchy diets (which, in ancient North America, generally means the consumption of maize). A skilled bioarchaeologist, in fact, can glance at a subject's teeth and make a good guess as to whether the person was an agriculturalist or hunter-gatherer—just by looking for caries.

The people at Stillwater Marsh were strictly hunter-gatherers; they did not grow or eat maize. Because their diet was low in simple carbohydrates (and obviously did not include refined sugar at all), only 3 percent of the Stillwater skeletons had dental caries—a remarkably low figure.

This is not to say that they were free of dental problems. The Stillwater folks lost many of their teeth by middle age, generally due to excessive tooth wear—a product of the grit in their diet from seeds and tubers ground on metates. They also suffered from abscesses, which appear as large voids in the mandibles and maxillas. In fact, some teeth had shallow grooves worn into their sides, where a person had habitually twirled a toothpick-sized twig to overstimulate the nerves and alleviate the pain of an abscess.

Bone and Stable Isotopes

Ancient diets can also be reconstructed by analyzing the carbon and nitrogen stable isotopes preserved in human bone.

We already encountered the concept of isotopes when discussing radiocarbon dating (in Chapter 8). Carbon, you will remember, has both stable and unstable isotopes. One stable form, ^{12}C, makes up about 99 percent of the world's carbon; ^{13}C is also stable but accounts for only about 1 percent. The unstable isotope, ^{14}C, most familiar to archaeologists because of its importance for dating, is extremely rare.

As we pointed out in Chapter 8, plants take in carbon through one of three photosynthetic pathways: C_3, C_4, and CAM. You will recall that the C_4 plants (such as maize) take in more ^{13}C and ^{14}C isotopes than do C_3 and CAM plants. Because human bones reflect the isotopic ratios of plants ingested during life, bioarchaeologists can reconstruct the dietary importance of certain classes of plants by measuring the ratio of carbon isotopes contained in **bone collagen,** the organic component of bone. A diet rich in C_4 plants (such as maize), for example, can produce bones with a significantly higher ratio of ^{13}C to ^{12}C than diets low in C_4 plants.

Nitrogen also has two stable isotopes, ^{14}N and ^{15}N. Some plants obtain their nitrogen from the air and others absorb nitrogen from the soil. These diverse mechanisms result in different ratios of ^{15}N to ^{14}N in various plants. Using this information, bioarchaeologists analyze a bone's stable isotope composition to determine which plants were eaten and which were not. In addition, we know that carnivores tend to lose

^{14}N through their urine, but they retain ^{15}N. This means that humans who consume large amounts of meat have a higher ratio of ^{15}N to ^{14}N than those who eat mostly plants. To complicate things further, marine plants tend to have ^{15}N to ^{14}N ratios that are 4 percent higher than terrestrial plants. These differences are passed up the food chain, and so marine mammals also tend to have higher ratios of ^{15}N to ^{14}N than terrestrial mammals. You can't interpret the values blindly, however, because of environmental differences. For example, hot desert soils tend to have higher nitrogen ratios than cool forest soils; so much so, in fact, that bones of desert-dwelling individuals with purely terrestrial diets can produce nitrogen values that, in another part of the world, would suggest a marine diet.

Control for these environmental factors, however, and differences in nitrogen values tell us whether people relied more heavily on marine than terrestrial foods or had more or less meat in their diets. Carbon and nitrogen values are measured relative to a known international standard.

Larsen submitted samples of human bone from 39 of the individuals recovered at Stillwater Marsh to Margaret Schoeninger (University of California, San Diego), one of the world's premier analysts of bone chemistry. With the human bone samples, Larsen also submitted several modern plant specimens and animal bones (identified to species) to act as controls.

The actual measurement of a bone's carbon and nitrogen isotope ratios is a complex process involving a mass spectrometer and need not concern us here. But Schoeninger's findings are not difficult to understand. To make her point, Schoeninger compared the results of the analysis of the Stillwater materials to two very different populations (Figure 12-7): the skeletal remains from Pecos Pueblo in New Mexico, a maize-dependent population, and the skeletal remains of a foraging population from Ontario that was heavily dependent on meat. In Figure 12-8, the horizontal axis plots the ratio of ^{13}C to ^{12}C—higher ratios are farther to the right (indicating more C_4 plants like maize in the diet), and lower ratios to the left (meaning fewer C_4 plants in the diet). Don't let the negative numbers confuse you. To make measurements comparable, Schoeninger reports the stable isotope values calibrated as deviations from an agreed-upon standard (the fossil *belemnitella,* in the Pee Dee limestone for-

bone collagen The organic component of bone.

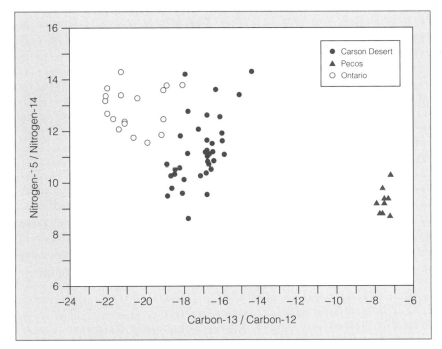

Figure 12-8 Stable carbon and nitrogen isotopes for the Stillwater burial population compared with those of Archaic Ontario hunter-gatherers and of Pecos Pueblo maize horticulturalists.

mation of South Carolina). The vertical axis plots the ratio of ^{15}N to ^{14}N; higher ratios are at the top (more carnivorous diet) and lower ratios are at the bottom (less carnivorous diet).

As Figure 12-8 shows, the Pecos population has a high ratio of ^{13}C to ^{12}C and a low ratio of ^{15}N to ^{14}N. This means that the Pecos population ate plenty of maize and very little meat. At the upper left part of the graph, the Ontario hunting population has a high ratio of ^{13}N to ^{14}N, with virtually no C_4 plants in its diet; this makes sense, because the Ontario foragers lived in an environment unsuitable for horticulture and relied primarily on fish, moose, and caribou (rather than plants) for food. The Stillwater ("Carson Desert") population lies between these two extremes, with very few C_4 plants in its diet, but a diet that was a mixture of plant and animal foods.

Schoeninger took her results even further. Remember that she also analyzed some modern plant samples, one of which was piñon pine. It turns out that piñon has a very low ratio of ^{15}N to ^{14}N. Schoeninger figured that if piñon was important to the Stillwater diet, then their bones should have a much lower nitrogen ratio than the graph indicates. Because they

do not, Schoeninger concluded that piñon could not have been an important component of the diet. Instead, by looking at the values for the other plant and animal control samples, Schoeninger concluded that a strictly marsh-based diet (that is, including no food plants from mountain environments) could readily account for the observed carbon and nitrogen isotope ratios in the Stillwater remains.

Note in Figure 12-8 that the Stillwater population has a greater *range* of nitrogen values than either the Ontario or Pecos populations. Schoeninger looked to see if this range was associated with an individual's age or sex. For example, if men spent time hunting large game then perhaps they ate more meat than women; or maybe children ate less meat than adults. However, there was no association between nitrogen values and age or sex.

Perhaps, then, there was a change through time, with the importance of meat increasing or decreasing. But, again, Schoeninger found no clear association between nitrogen values and the radiocarbon ages on the burials.

Consequently, Schoeninger suggested that the range of nitrogen values might be a product of dietary variability. Although bone chemistry is a lifelong average of one's diet, the period of youth and adolescence is particularly important because this is when bone collagen forms. If the foods available in the wetlands varied from decade to decade because of flooding, fires, climate change, or other factors, then perhaps people ate different suites of food over the years. In some years, perhaps jackrabbits were commonly roasted over the fire; in other years, bulrush seed cakes might have been the daily fare. If this dietary variability accounts for the differential nitrogen ratios, then it suggests that the Pecos farmers and Ontario foragers had far more monotonous diets than did the people living at Stillwater Marsh.

Lives of Affluence? or Nasty, Brutish, and Short?

We can now return to Larsen's original research question: Does the Stillwater burial population reflect human lives that were "nasty, brutish, and short" or those of an "affluent society"?

The answer, evident from these various analyses, is "Both" and "Neither." The people of Stillwater Marsh consumed a varied diet that probably went beyond their minimal nutritional needs. They were relatively healthy, generally free of serious disease, disorders, broken bones, and infections. This part seems to fit the "original affluent society" image.

But the Stillwater people also worked hard, and some had good reason to complain about aching knees and backs. Some youngsters suffered from periods of malnutrition, and a large proportion of the Stillwater children did not live to their fifth birthday. Nobody lived much beyond 50 years. These data conform more to the "nasty, brutish, and short" model.

Our objective, of course, is not to pigeonhole the Stillwater burial population; it is to learn what life was like for people in the past. We seek to understand the various factors that influenced their diet, their rates of infection and bone breakage, their workloads and their dental health. In some ways, the Stillwater population had a good life; in other ways, it was not so easy. The past can almost never be characterized in simple black-and-white terms.

Most of the time, bioarchaeologists analyze human skeletons to answer questions about human behaviour and quality of life. But recently developed technology now allows us to analyze the biology of ancient human populations in order to answer some old questions in new ways. The rest of this chapter explores the developing frontiers of archaeology at the molecular level.

---

molecular archaeology The use of genetic information in ancient human remains to reconstruct the past.

nuclear DNA Genetic material found in a cell's nuclei; this material is primarily responsible for an individual's inherited traits.

gene A unit of the chromosomes that controls inheritance of particular traits.

mitochondrial DNA (mtDNA) Genetic material found in the mitochondria of cells; it is inherited only from the mother and appears to mutate at a rate of 2–4 percent per 1 million years.

Archaeology and DNA: Tracing Human Migration

How was the world colonized? Are modern humans related to Neanderthals? When did Native Americans arrive in the New World?

In the past, archaeologists used artifacts alone to talk about ancient migrations and the historical relationships among the world's populations. But modern genetic technology provides another avenue to begin reconstructing the past. By using genetic material—DNA from human skeletal remains and living peoples—geneticists and archaeologists have joined forces to create a new approach to reconstructing the past known as **molecular archaeology.** As is so often true, this new approach raises as many questions as it attempts to answer.

A Little Background on DNA

Most of our genetic information exists as 46 chromosomes inside the nucleus of each cell in our bodies; this stuff, called **nuclear DNA** (deoxyribonucleic acid), makes each human being unique, and it's inherited from both of your biological parents. Your DNA contains the recipe for your biological composition, telling your body to create blue or green eyes, to be short or tall, to have straight or curly hair. A **gene** is a segment of a chromosome, one small piece of the recipe that codes for particular biological attributes; your body has about 50,000 genes.

Nuclear DNA is extraordinarily useful to the genetics of living populations, but it is not so useful to archaeology. Nuclear DNA degrades fairly quickly, and, by the time the human body decomposes, nuclear DNA is no longer intact (although sections of about 200 nucleotide base pairs can survive for thousands of years).

But another form of DNA, known as **mitochondrial DNA (mtDNA),** is found in the cells' mitochondria (organelles responsible for the cell's energy metabolism)—outside the nucleus. mtDNA contains only about 0.0006 percent of the genetic material of nuclear DNA, which would seem to limit its use, but mtDNA has three interesting properties. First, although it contains only a limited segment of the total genetic recipe, each cell contains thousands of copies of it (in contrast to just the two in the nucleus). This translates to a greater probability of retrieving

Archaeological Ethics
Should We Excavate and Analyze Human Remains?

In many places in the world, archaeologists have no qualms about excavating human skeletal remains. But in the United States, conducting research on American Indian remains is a sensitive issue indeed. In fact, archaeologists who do field research in the United States today generally excavate human remains only if they are in the way of a construction project that cannot be re-routed. And no archaeologist would excavate a burial without consulting at least the nearest tribe (in fact, such consultation is mandated by law if the excavation is on federal land). Sometimes this consultation works out well, as it did in Stillwater. But tribal attitudes change, and if the Stillwater remains were exposed today instead of nearly 20 years ago, it's possible that their excavation and analysis would be blocked. It has become increasingly difficult for bioarchaeologists to work with extant collections; those involved with the Kennewick case had to file a lawsuit to get access to that skeleton.

All of this raises major ethical questions. Some modern archaeologists believe that we should simply forgo the analysis of human skeletons and accept that as the price to be paid for showing respect and sensitivity to modern Native Americans who find the excavation and analysis of ancestral remains disrespectful. Many other Americans would agree with them.

Although many museums curate both Indian and non-Indian skeletal remains, the proportion of Native American skeletons often outweighs the non-Indian remains—reflecting, in large measure, the historical interest of American archaeology in excavating American Indian burial sites. And reburying non–Native American remains often seems to be the obvious, and respectful, thing to do. Those Civil War dead who are discovered today are sometimes studied, but always reburied.

Archaeologists have long curated Native American remains in museum collections, in case new techniques enable us to learn more about the past. And such breakthroughs do occur: Who, in 1965, would have thought that within two decades we would be extracting genetic material from 7000-year-old human skeletons? We've given you only a glimpse of what we can learn from human skeletons, and each year there are new techniques. There is so much more to learn.

Scientists wish to learn more about the past in order to increase our understanding of the history of humanity. This is a good thing. But Native Americans wish to see their ancestors, and themselves, treated with respect. This is also a good thing. Which should we choose?

Does science trump every other concern? Answer yes, and you appear ethnocentric.

Does one group of people have the right to shut the door on an area of knowledge? Answer yes, and you would seem to condone book burning.

What is knowledge worth? What is knowledge for? Every archaeologist, especially those who study human skeletal remains, must carefully consider these questions today.

---

mtDNA than nuclear DNA. But don't think that there are gobs of mtDNA just lying in archaeological sites: Its recovery is made possible through the technique of polymerase chain reaction (PCR), which enables researchers to create billions of copies of a very small sample of mtDNA, so that this genetic material can be more readily studied.

The second intriguing property of mtDNA is that you inherit yours *only* from your mother. Although mtDNA is present in the tail of sperm, after fertilization occurs the tail breaks off. This means that your mtDNA comes entirely from the ovum. If you are female, you pass along the same mtDNA to all your children. If you are male, none of the mtDNA that you inherited from your mother is passed on to your biological offspring. This makes it possible to define molecular "family trees" and to trace the movement of female lineages.

Finally, mtDNA seems to change in a particular way and at a particular rate that makes it potentially useful to archaeology. Briefly, although mtDNA is probably not completely free from the pressures of natural selection, it appears to be under less selective pressure than nuclear DNA. And because it is transferred from mother to offspring as a chunk, it does not recombine (as does nuclear DNA). Instead, mtDNA appears to change over time largely as a result of random mutations. Nuclear DNA can also change as a result of random mutation (this is, in fact, one of the main ways that new genetic material appears in a species). But compared with nuclear DNA, mtDNA mutates rapidly, about 2 to 4 percent every million years. Although this may seem awfully slow, it is *nearly 10 times* faster than nuclear DNA's mutation rate. *If* one is willing to assume that this rate of change has been constant through time, then differences in the mutations between related mtDNA samples can be used to estimate how much time has elapsed since the branches of the family tree diverged. For this reason, mtDNA is sometimes used as a "clock" to date the timing of human population movements in the remote past.

Prospecting for Ancient DNA

In 1984, Allan Wilson (1943–1991) and his student Vince Sarich (University of California, Berkeley) were the first to identify genetic materials from old tissue. When they cloned DNA from the 140-year-old skin of quagga—a recently extinct, zebra-like African beast—the Berkeley team showed the world that DNA could indeed survive after the death of an organism.

The next year, Swedish researcher Svante Pääbo (Max Planck Institute of Evolutionary Anthropology, Germany) cloned DNA from a 4400-year-old Egyptian mummy. This was the first time that anyone had applied PCR techniques to ancient humans. Not long after, Pääbo pushed the barrier back another 2600 years into the past by extracting ancient DNA from human brains preserved at the Windover site in Florida.

Some 7000 to 8000 years ago, ancient Native Americans at Windover buried their dead in a spring that flowed through an ancient limestone sinkhole. Water levels fluctuated seasonally, with a maximum depth of around one metre. At the bottom were several strata of peat—compact, dark brown organic material built up from the partial decay and carbonization of vegetation. The team of archaeologists, headed by Glen Doran (Florida State University), dug into these peat levels while pumps bailed out the encroaching water. Because peat deposits are anaerobic, Doran found many well-preserved skeletons, some still held in place by large stakes, probably placed there at the time of burial to keep the bodies from floating to the surface.

The low oxygen level and neutral pH of the peat bog were also perfect for preserving soft tissue. More than 60 well-preserved human brains turned up at Windover, including the one used by Pääbo in his pioneering extraction of ancient DNA. Geneticists were particularly excited about the number of burials, because it provided the first chance to examine gene frequencies across a prehistoric burial population.

Microbiologists were surprised to find how little the genetic makeup of the Windover population had changed during the thousand years that the burial ground was used, possibly a sign of ancient inbreeding. If this trend held for other early Native American populations, it would suggest that early Indian groups tended to stay put, perhaps explaining the remarkable linguistic diversity among the New World's indigenous peoples.

An African Eve?

The work at Windover signalled the birth of molecular archaeology as a viable way to explore the human past. However, as spectacular as the 8000-year-old brains from Windover might be, Wilson's research team at Berkeley had only begun to examine the possibilities in studying ancient DNA.

Wilson and his team collected mtDNA samples from around the world and compared the human data with that of chimpanzee (as a control). The most striking fact about mtDNA is how much of it we all share. At the molecular level, all living human groups share all but about 0.6 percent mtDNA. As you might expect, humans and chimpanzees share somewhat less; humans and horses share even less, and so forth. The 0.6 percent figure is important because it suggests a way to determine the relatedness among all living individuals and groups.

By examining the mtDNA from various modern human populations, Wilson could see what a close-knit species we really are. This was a surprise, because mtDNA is supposed to evolve fairly rapidly. Components of the modern global sample turned out to be remarkably alike—both within geographical populations and between continental groups. The result was a family tree for all of (surviving) humanity. Africa provided the longest branch on the tree, suggesting this is where human mtDNA began to differentiate. Those of African descent also showed the most variability among themselves and were the most distinct from other populations of the world. Wilson argued that this pattern is precisely what one would expect *if all modern humans had descended from a single population in Africa.*

These investigators went a step further, suggesting that all the genetic composition evident in living human populations could be traced to a single ancient African ancestor. Because mtDNA is passed down strictly through the maternal line, this fictive ancestor must have been female. She was quickly nicknamed Eve, after the biblical first woman and wife of Adam.

Even more controversial than Eve's African origin was the molecular clock that Wilson and his group derived. Because geneticists assume that mtDNA changes at a constant rate, the 0.6 percent figure is important for another reason: It provides a relatively precise way to gauge the first appearance of *Homo sapiens* (modern humans). Although this so-called **molecular clock** does not keep perfect time, it does suggest some genetic limits within which human evolution may have taken place.

Wilson's molecular clock suggested that Eve must have lived about 200,000 years ago. If so, then the first descendants of Eve (early modern humans) must have fanned out of Africa to supplant other hominids about this time. This theory, which has come to be known as the "out of Africa" hypothesis, had, it turned out, also been framed independently on the basis of the fossil evidence alone.

To call the Eve hypothesis controversial is an understatement. Some biological anthropologists, such as Milford Wolpoff (University of Michigan), see strong continuity between pre–200,000- and post–200,000-year-old skulls from various parts of the Old World. To these anthropologists, the skeletal data argue for continuity in various parts of the Old World (humans had not yet colonized the New World by this date) rather than recent replacement by a migrating population from Africa. (Although Africa is still the homeland of humanity, as we saw in Chapter 7, the question here is whether *all* modern humans derive from a later African expansion.)

Others charged that the Eve hypothesis was based on modern genetic distributions and that it needed to be tested by using DNA extracted from ancient bone. One particularly controversial area is whether the Neanderthals of Europe and the Near East are related to modern humans or if they are an evolutionary dead end. Looking at the skeletal biology, those biological anthropologists who see continuity between the Neanderthals and modern Europeans argue that Neanderthals are part of the human line. Others see skeletal differences too large to place Neanderthals in the ancestry of modern humans. Mitochondrial DNA has now been successfully extracted from three different sets of Neanderthal remains (and more efforts are underway), and *none* of these fall within the observed range of living human variation (but we have no mtDNA yet from Upper Paleolithic modern human skeletons with which to compare the Neanderthal data). This has not satisfied critics, who point to potential sources of error in the mtDNA extraction process and insist that, if Neanderthal maternal lineages are rare in modern humans, the relatively small number of samples could have missed them.

DNA will probably never replace human skeletal remains as the primary source of information about the human biological component of the archaeological record. But in conjunction with more traditional skeletal analyses, it will add new dimensions, questions, and knowledge to the complex story of human history. Research into the first colonization of the New World provides one example.

Skulls and DNA: Tracking the First Americans

The most consequential, if least dramatic, event in the history of the Americas came when that first human footprint appeared in the New World. Nobody knows exactly when this happened, or where. We do not know what these initial colonists of the New World wore, spoke, looked like, or thought. We do not know when they left their Asian homeland or what conditions they experienced along the way.

---

molecular clock Calculations of the time since divergence of two related populations using the presumed rate of mutation in mtDNA and the genetic differences between the two populations.

And yet there remains no reasonable doubt that the first Americans did indeed travel across a land bridge from Asia during the late Pleistocene; it is the timing and conditions surrounding their arrival (or arrivals) that remain incompletely known.

Clovis points, which we mentioned in Chapter 11, appeared in North America about 13,500 calendar years ago (about 11,500 radiocarbon years). Not so long ago the standard textbook account was that Clovis was the first and only migration and from this all native peoples of the New World descended. In this account, small numbers of people migrated from Asia via the Bering land bridge that formed between Russia and Alaska sometime during the height of the last glacial age, between 25,000 and 10,000 years ago. The standard account had these hunters walking from Asia into Alaska, migrating down the so-called ice-free corridor between the continental ice sheets that covered the Canadian Rockies on the west and much of Canada to the east.

A number of problems have risen with this scenario. First, it doesn't appear that the ice-free corridor was open until about 13,000 years ago—a little too late to allow Clovis through in order to be in the continental United States by 13,500 years ago. In addition, current studies suggest that, even when the corridor was open, it may have been uninhabitable—a vast wasteland of rock, sand, and lakes so laden with silt washing out from glaciers that they could support no fish or plant life.

Even more important, South America contains a number of sites that appear to be as old as, if not older than, Clovis. The best-known and -documented of these is the site of Monte Verde, in southern Chile (Figure 12-9). Like the Windover sites, Monte Verde is located in a wet peat bog, and so the preservation was remarkable. The excavator, Tom Dillehay (Vanderbilt University), found the remains of wooden structures, stone projectile points, hearths, pegs driven into the ground with leather straps still tied on, slabs of

Figure 12-9 Monte Verde (Chile); note the level of preservation in this wet site.
Source: Tom Dillehay

organic material identified as mammoth (or mastodon) meat, footprints, and other definitive evidence of human occupation.

Although the site's preservation is phenomenal, what makes it really special is that it appears to be 1000 years *older* than Clovis. If people came to the New World from Asia via Alaska and reached southern Chile by 14,500 years ago, then they had to pass through North America prior to this date. A handful of sites exist that *might* provide evidence of a pre-Clovis occupation of North America—sites such as Meadowcroft Rockshelter in Pennsylvania and some mammoth kill sites in Wisconsin. But none of these are as well demonstrated as Monte Verde, and some archaeologists still wonder why it is that, although Clovis appears in virtually all 48 contiguous states, evidence for a pre-Clovis occupation is almost impossible to find—despite the dogged efforts of many archaeologists.

Possibly the first migrants bypassed the interior of North America by migrating along the western coast. At first, this may have been to avoid the massive glaciers that covered much of northern North America. Once south of the ice sheets, however, they may have simply kept their maritime economy and continued to move along the coast all the way to Tierra del Fuego. Clovis people may have been a later migration from Asia or a population that eventually left the western coast and adapted to terrestrial hunting.

Testing the early coastal migration hypothesis means looking for early sites along the western coast. But this is harder than it sounds, for when the Pleistocene ended about 10,000 years ago, the massive continental glaciers melted, and sea levels rose, flooding the existing coastlines. Any sites deposited on the New World's western coast 14,000 or more years ago are now under water—150 metres deep in places—and thick layers of silt. Some archaeologists have tried dredging likely places on the sea bottom for artifacts, but they are looking for the proverbial needle in a haystack, and most have come up empty-handed.

Bioarchaeology and the Colonization

Frustrated with the difficulties of finding early archaeological sites, some have turned to bioarchaeological evidence. Christy Turner (Arizona State University) has conducted extensive studies of variability in human teeth. He knows what he is talking about: He's looked at some 200,000 teeth from 9000 individuals.

Focusing on the crown and root areas, Turner discovered that modern and pre-contact American Indian teeth are most similar to those of northern Asians. For example, individuals in both groups tend to have shovel-shaped incisors (incisors whose lateral edges curve to give the incisors a shovel shape) and three-rooted lower first molars. Examining geographic patterns in the frequency of different dental traits, Turner found three major groups: one that included all Native Americans from southern Canada to Tierra del Fuego (a group sometimes labelled "Amerind," for American Indians), another that included the Na-Dene (Athapaskan) speakers of northern Canada and central Alaska, and a third that included the Eskimo and Aleut. At the time, this grouping seemed to correlate with Native American language families.

Turner postulates an initial migration out of northeast Asia at the end of the Ice Age followed by two later migrations (oddly, he sees the Na-Dene arriving after the Eskimo-Aleut). Turner could not, however, place a date on these migrations.

The Skulls' Story

Recently, a new twist has been added to the story, this time using skulls rather than teeth. We have very few human remains that date to the New World's colonization era. In fact, for the entire New World, we only have about 40 skeletons that are 10,000 or more calendar years old; only a handful of these are Clovis-aged skeletons. Given two spacious continents and a period of 2000–3000 years, these 40 burials are not a good burial population. But some archaeologists and biological anthropologists still find it curious that a large number of these early skeletons have skulls whose shapes are distinctly different from those of later Native Americans. Kennewick, the case study that began this book (see Chapter 1), is one of those skeletons; another comes from Spirit Cave, a site in the Carson Desert, in Nevada (Figure 12-10).

The early skulls, such as those of Kennewick and Spirit Cave, are different from other Native American skulls because they are long and narrow, rather than round; they have a high-bridged nose and a gracile mandible, but prominent and square chins. Several studies conclude that, in a biological sense, the earliest Native Americans (including Kennewick) are more closely related to groups such as the Ainu, the native peoples of northern Japan, than to living Native Americans. (Some skulls from South America, in fact,

Figure 12-10 Facial reconstruction of Spirit Cave man by Sharon Long.

Source: Smithsonian Institution, photo by Chip Clark

appear to be more like those of Africans or Australians than later Native Americans.) Because skull shape largely reflects genes, the implication is that the earliest colonists of the New World came from a different Asian population than later migrants (who must have then genetically "swamped" the people who were already here).

mtDNA's Story

So, teeth and skull shape suggest that more than one migration occurred—perhaps even three or more. But when did these migrations begin? Here the geneticists jump in. They argue that the initial population moving out of northeastern Asia ran into a severe geo-

haplogroup Genetic lineages defined by similar genes at a locus on a chromosome.

graphic bottleneck as they passed across the Bering Strait into the New World, limiting the genetic diversity in the newly arrived population. This explains why Native Americans from Canada to southern South America are genetically similar. It also means that the differences between Asian and Native American populations must generally *postdate* the time when they separated at the Bering Strait. Thus measurement of the genetic distance between New World and Asian populations should estimate the time elapsed since these two groups separated, the age when someone first set foot in the New World.

Now we return to mtDNA. Recall that you inherit your mtDNA only from your mother. Using blood samples of living Native Americans from all over the New World, several studies have found that there are only five mtDNA lineages in the Americas, referred to as **haplogroups.** These are labelled A, B, C, D, and X. Three of these—A, C, and D—are found in northern Asia. Along with other evidence, such as Turner's dental records, this fact points to an Asian origin for Native Americans. And the fact that so few haplogroups are present among Native Americans suggests that the migration(s) entailed only small groups who brought a limited sample of their original population's genetic diversity with them. In fact, it is possible that 95 percent of all Native Americans came from a small number of Asian founding families.

What about the other two haplogroups? Haplogroup B appears today in south central China and coastal southern Asia. It is possible that it has simply disappeared in northern Asia. It's also possible, as some geneticists argue, that it points to a separate migratory wave from Asia. This could support the argument from the skulls—an early migration from southern China—but geneticists think that Haplogroup B came in a later, not earlier, migration.

Haplogroup X is more enigmatic. It is very rare among living Native Americans as well as Native American skeletal remains; it is most common among speakers of Algonkian languages, in northeastern North America, but it is also found in the 8000-year-old Windover burials. It's present in Asia (though very rare), as well as in Europe (where it is only slightly more common).

Some geneticists and archaeologists suggest that haplogroup X points to an ancient migration from *Europe,* in addition to ones from Asia. This seems implausible, because it would require a transatlantic voyage more than 8000 years ago; no land bridge ever connected North America and Europe. On the other hand, some geneticists ask: If haplogroup X points to an ancient migration from Europe, then shouldn't the more-common European haplogroups (such as H) be at least present among modern Native Americans? Because the European haplogroups do not appear among Native Americans, these geneticists suggest that haplogroup X is indicative of an extremely ancient (tens of thousands of years) shared genetic heritage between Native Americans and Europeans—perhaps dating back to the time of the African Eve. We simply don't know.

Can mtDNA Tell Us When the Colonization Occurred?

Recall that the molecular clock uses the number of differences due to random mutations between two geographically separated haplogroups to determine when they split apart. Using this principle, one study suggests that differences in the mtDNA of Native Americans and Asians point to a migration somewhere between 21,000 and 42,000 B.P. Another study at Emory University arrived at a migration time of between 22,000 and 29,000 years ago.

Archaeological data cannot support even the more conservative of these claims; possible pre-Clovis sites in North America range in age from 14,000 to 18,000 years old; and Monte Verde is at most 14,500 years old.

Could the geneticists be wrong? Can the mtDNA clock be used to date human migrations? Much can happen between the time one population splits off from another and goes its merry way.

Some critics, fellow geneticists among them, point out that the mtDNA studies depend on the critical, but unconfirmed, assumption that all the observed genetic diversity among New World populations began after these tribes crossed the Bering land bridge into the New World. But suppose the tribes had split up someplace in Asia, prior to arriving in America. If that happened, then the biological clock would have begun ticking before, and perhaps long before, colonization of the New World. Perhaps the population split between those people (or rather, their descendants) who would migrate to the New World and those who would remain in Asia did occur 21,000 or 29,000 or 42,000 years ago—but the actual migration occurred much, much later. In sum, mtDNA differences may record when populations diverged, but not necessarily when populations migrated.

On the other hand, maybe mtDNA cannot even record when populations split. Some researchers suggest that we really don't know the rate at which mtDNA mutates. Wilson's original research calculated the molecular clock's rate by dividing the difference between human and chimpanzee mtDNA by 5 million years, the assumed date of separation between the human and chimpanzee lines. But we now suspect that the split between the human and chimpanzee lines is older—that it occurred perhaps as much as 7 million years ago. If so, then the mtDNA clock might run *slower* than Wilson originally thought.

On the other hand, a recent study in Europe used the standard mtDNA clock to predict that haplogroup V (a haplogroup that appears in Europe but not in the New World) should appear in the Basque region of Spain about 10,000 years ago. However, analysis of nearly 100 human skeletal remains could not find that haplogroup in any individual that was more than 4000 years old. So, perhaps the clock runs *faster* than we think.

Maybe we've got the mtDNA molecular clock ticking too slowly or too quickly, or maybe the clock can speed up and slow down—given that we really don't know, it's best if mtDNA studies are verified by other methods.

The Guys Have Their Say

Recently, molecular archaeological studies have turned to the Y chromosome—genetic material that, unlike mtDNA, is inherited only through the male line. Like mtDNA, the Y chromosome also carries DNA that we don't think is under much pressure from natural selection and that mutates at a constant rate (at least, that's the assumption). Only a few Y chromosome haplogroups are known for Native Americans. One of these, haplogroup 10, also occurs in northern Asia. Both Asian and New World Y chromosomes contain a particular mutation (known as M242), suggesting that the mutation occurred before the migration. But the Native American haplogroup also contains another mutation, called M3, which does not appear in Asia. Using the hypothesized rate of mutation in the DNA of the Y chromosome, Mark Seielstad (Harvard School of Public Health) and his team propose that the split between the Asian and what would become the New World population occurred *no more* than 18,000 years ago. The

Looking Closer
Preparing Archaeological Remains for Ancient DNA Analysis

In Chapter 1, we discussed how bioarchaeologists, wearing gloves, masks, and Tyvek suits, carefully collected the remains of Kwäday Dän Ts'inchi for analysis. Such precautions are necessary in order to protect archaeological finds from contamination by modern DNA. Recently, Dongya Yang and Kathy Watt of Simon Fraser University's Ancient DNA Facility summarized factors that can adversely affect results in molecular archaeology. They have also outlined some basic protocols that archaeologists should follow when collecting specimens for ancient DNA analysis.

Chemical and physical degradation of ancient DNA can destroy most of the information-bearing portions of the DNA strand. As we have seen, PCR (polymerase chain reaction) is used to amplify the remaining information, essentially making billions of photocopies of the sequence-bearing strands in only a few hours. The problem is that PCR does not discriminate between ancient and modern DNA. This can result in errors as legitimate ancient DNA is quickly overwhelmed by contaminant DNA. Most people remember how genetic engineers in the movie *Jurassic Park* were able to extract dinosaur DNA from insects trapped in amber. Actual attempts at doing this, however, led to erroneous claims for positive PCR amplification of alleged Dino DNA because samples had been contaminated with modern DNA.

One misplaced touch can shed skin cells, each of which contain thousands of copies of mtDNA. In addition to excavators and laboratory analysts, other sources of contamination can include surrounding soils, modern pollen, and bacteria.

So, given that contamination often produces false positives in molecular archaeology, what kinds of controls should be put in place? Dongya Yang (Figure 12-11) and Kathy Watt suggest that rigid procedures need to be strictly followed both in the laboratory and in the field. A separate DNA laboratory kept clean of modern DNA, for example, should be used for sample preparation and analysis. Within the laboratory itself, DNA extraction areas should be separated from PCR areas. Air needs to be positively pressurized and filtered using UV-HEPA filters. Ultraviolet radiation must also be used to destroy any residual DNA on the surfaces of lab benches and equipment. Laboratory technicians should also wear hairnets, masks, gloves, and protective suits at all times—just like on the television show *C.S.I.*

How do archaeologists prevent contamination of the samples they collect? Yang and Watt recommend taking an ancient DNA sampling kit into the field. Such a kit consists of gloves, clean paper bags, aluminum foil, masks, hairnets, sealable plastic bags, bleach solution, and clean excavation tools such as trowels and dental picks. Archaeologists begin by selecting morphologically well-preserved

colonization of the New World, then, had to occur sometime *after* this date.

Although this date is more consistent with the available archaeological data, we cannot accept an estimate simply because it fits existing knowledge. If we did that, we would never learn anything new. As was the case with African Eve, we currently lack any kind of final, definitive word about the peopling of the New World based on genetic data. But the preliminary results are sufficiently intriguing to suggest that, whatever the answer may be, molecular archaeology provides a major new source of data regarding the

first Americans, as well as ancient migrations and population movements in general. If nothing else, these data will force archaeologists to reconsider whether they really do know what they think they know. And that, as we have said before, is what science is all about.

Conclusion

The study of human skeletal remains is about as close as archaeologists can get to studying the people

specimens. The less porous the material, the less likely it is to be contaminated. Therefore, Yang and Watt recommend selecting specimens in the following order: teeth, cortical bone, and, finally, spongy bone. If materials are wet, they should be allowed to dry naturally in a clean paper bag because moist conditions can create ideal conditions for bacterial growth—a source of modern DNA. A Dremel tool or hacksaw is often used to remove an appropriate amount of sample from the object for analysis. In order to avoid cross-sample contamination when cutting, Yang and Watt recommend cleaning tools after each cut using a bleach solution that will kill residual DNA. Once the sample is taken, it is placed into a plastic bag or vial and then sealed. The real challenge, however, comes when trying to extract ancient DNA from materials excavated many decades ago, as these are almost certainly contaminated with modern DNA. Knowledge of how the samples were handled, and by how many people, is useful information under these circumstances. The use of preservatives, for example, can also introduce contaminant DNA.

Finally, Yang and Watt recommend using a double-blind test in all ancient DNA studies. Using this technique, mock samples known only to the archaeologist are mixed in with the legitimate samples. The DNA laboratory should be able to distinguish between the two if there is no contamination.

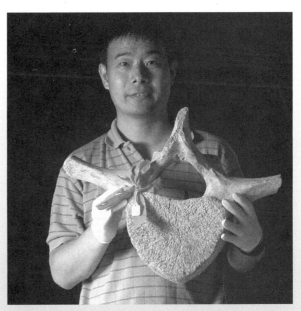

Figure 12-11 Dr. Dongya Yang, Simon Fraser University. Yang's previous and ongoing projects involve DNA analysis of archaeological remains of salmon, chicken, whale, northern fur seal, sturgeon, turkey, elk, rabbit, sheep, goat, cattle, horse, and water buffalo.

Source: Dr. Dongya Yang, Department of Archaeology, Simon Fraser University

Ancient DNA analysis holds great promise in archaeology. However, in order to reap its rewards, archaeologists need to stay vigilant and use great care when selecting, collecting, and interpreting sources of ancient DNA in the archaeological record.

of the past. Where burial populations are available, our knowledge of the past can grow by leaps and bounds. Through analyses of skeletal morphology and bone chemistry, we can learn a great deal about men's and women's workloads, diets, patterns of disease, trauma, and quality of life. And the field of bioarchaeology is really in its infancy: The field is producing new ways of analyzing bone every year and promises to expand our knowledge of the past considerably.

One of these areas is molecular archaeology, which promises to help reconstruct human migrations if we can figure out how genes can be used as clocks. This is an area of middle-range theory that will require considerable attention in the future.

Bioarchaeology deals with the material effects of people's lives on their bones and genes. Although the links between behaviour and bones are by no means direct or simple, in the following two chapters we move into elements of past human lives that are even more difficult to reconstruct: the realms of social and political behaviour and the meaning of symbols.

Summary

- Bioarchaeology is the study of the human biological component evident in the archaeological record; it examines the health and workload of ancient populations. This specialty requires expertise in the method and theory of both biological anthropology and field archaeology.

- We use characteristics of several bones, notably the pelvis and skull, to determine an individual's sex.

- An individual's age can be determined by tooth eruption; patterns of bone fusion, tooth wear, and bone wear are used to age individuals over the age of 25.

- Paleopathology is the study of those ancient diseases that leave skeletal traces. Iron deficiency, for example, leaves a distinctive spongy appearance on the skull and the interior of the eye orbits. In addition, growth arrest features, such as Harris lines and enamel hypoplasias, indicate childhood periods of severe disease or malnutrition.

- Bones respond to the routine mechanical stresses placed upon them; patterns of osteoarthritis and long bone cross-sections can point to different patterns of workload between the sexes or to changes through time.

- Paleodemography looks at patterns of death in a population, determining life expectancy, child mortality, and peaks in the age of death for men and women.

- Stature estimates can track changes in the quality of diet.

- Bioarchaeologists can also reconstruct diet: High frequency of dental caries indicates a diet high in simple carbohydrates and sugars. The ratios of carbon and nitrogen isotopes in bone can reconstruct the dietary importance of various kinds of plants and animals.

- Molecular archaeology uses data from living and ancient peoples to reconstruct population migrations. Especially useful is mtDNA and the genetic material in Y chromosomes. Although we still have much to learn about the rates at which DNA mutates, current studies suggest that DNA studies will someday be important to reconstructing the past.

Additional Reading

CANADIAN RESOURCES

Gill-Robinson, H., Elias, J., Bender, F., Allard, T., and Hoppa, R. (2006). Using imaging analysis software to create a physical skull model for the facial reconstruction of a wrapped Akhmimic Mummy. *Journal of Computing and Information Technology-CIT 14*(1), 45–51.

Pfeiffer, Susan, and Williamson, Ronald F. (1991). *Snake Hill: An Investigation of a Military Cemetery from the War of 1812.* Toronto: Dundurn Press.

Whitehorn, J. (1991). Fort Erie and U.S. operations on the Niagara Frontier, 1884. In S. Pfeiffer & R. F. Williamson (Eds.), *Snake Hill: An investigation of a military cemetery from the War of 1812* (pp. 25–61). Toronto: Dundurn Press.

Williamson, Ronald. (1991). Introduction. In S. Pfeiffer & R. F. Williamson (Eds.), *Snake Hill: An investigation of a military cemetery from the War of 1812* (pp. 21–25). Toronto: Dundurn Press.

Williamson, Ronald, and Pfeiffer, Susan. (1991). Conclusions. In S. Pfeiffer & R. F. Williamson (Eds.), *Snake Hill: An investigation of a military cemetery from the War of 1812* (pp. 295–303). Toronto: Dundurn Press.

OTHER RESOURCES

Jones, Martin. (2001). *The Molecule Hunt: Archaeology and the Search for Ancient DNA.* New York: Arcade Publishing.

Larsen, Clark Spencer. (1997). *Bioarchaeology: Interpreting Behavior from the Human Skeleton.* Cambridge: Cambridge University Press.

Larsen, Clark Spencer. (2000). *Skeletons in Our Closet: Revealing Our Past Through Bioarchaeology.* Princeton: Princeton University Press.

Larsen, Clark Spencer, and Kelly, Robert L. (editors and contributors). (1995). *Bioarchaeology of the Stillwater Marsh: Prehistoric Human Adaptation in the Western Great Basin. Anthropological Papers of the American Museum of Natural History 77.* New York.

White, Tim D. (2000). *Human Osteology* (2nd ed.) San Diego: Academic Press.

Online Resources

COMPANION WEBSITE
Visit *http://www.archaeology1ce.nelson.com* to access a wide range of material to help you succeed in your introductory archaeology course. These include flashcards, Internet exercises, Web links, and practice quizzes.

RESEARCH ONLINE WITH INFOTRAC COLLEGE EDITION
From the Student Companion Website, you can access the InfoTrac College Edition database, which offers thousands of full-length articles for your research.

13 Reconstructing Social and Political Systems of the Past

An earthen mound, located on the north bank of the Rainy River in Northern Ontario, is the largest pre-European human-made feature in Canada. The cut seen in the foreground was done by a curious bulldozer operator. The site is currently protected within the Manitou Mounds Provincial Park.

Source: Laurel Culture Burial Mound © Canadian Museum of Civilization, 71-2530

Preview

We now turn to some aspects of past human society that are more difficult to infer from archaeological data than the diet, activities, seasonality, and settlement patterns already discussed. In this chapter, we explore ancient social and political organizations—what they were and how archaeologists find out about them.

This chapter explores three key components of human society—gender, kinship, and social status—each of which entails its own interpretive problems and middle-range difficulties. What men and women did in the past is essential to understanding how a society operates, yet assigning specific artifacts to men and women is difficult. Kinship is a major structuring principle of human social organization, but it leaves ambiguous traces. The archaeological record reflects social status a bit more clearly, but many ancient societies may have been organized politically in ways that have no straightforward ethnographic analogies today. We also discuss trade—its role in political and social systems and how archaeologists track trade relations. Although we are entering a more difficult realm of archaeology, we will show that reconstructing past social and political systems is not impossible.

Introduction

Recall from Chapter 2 that Americanist archaeology is firmly situated within the broader field of anthropology. Right now, we must return to archaeology's roots in anthropology to define some terms and concepts.

Social Vocabulary

Social organization refers to the rules and structures that govern relationships between individuals within a group of interacting people. These relationships are never simple, because people belong to groups on many different levels; some of these crosscut one another, and others are hierarchically organized.

You, for example, simultaneously belong to one or more families (as a son or daughter, husband or wife, brother or sister) and to a town, a province, and a country. You are biologically male or female, and you may be a member of a sports club, political party, or community organization. Perhaps you hold a formal position in some of these groups. In other words, you play various roles in a variety of social groups.

Which identity is currently operating depends upon the situation.

Some social groups are residential, consisting of domestic families or households, territorial bands, or community-level villages. Residential groups tend to be physical agglomerations of people; they are face-to-face associations. Residential groups appear in the archaeological record as households and villages.

Other groups are nonresidential—associations of people that regulate some aspect of society. Nonresidential groups are groups in the abstract sense; in fact, some may never convene. Nonresidential groups are usually manifested archaeologically through the use of symbols, ceremonies, mythologies, or insignias of membership that appear as particular styles of material culture, such as ceramics, architecture, rock art, or

> **social organization** The rules and structures that govern relations within a group of interacting people. Societies are divided into social units (groups) within which are recognized social positions (statuses), with appropriate behaviour patterns prescribed for these positions (roles).

burials. In a sense, the residential group functions to regulate discrete spatial matters, whereas the nonresidential group binds these territorial units together.

A related concept is **political organization,** the formal and informal institutions that regulate a society's collective acts. Sometimes, control will rest primarily at the level of the residential group, but in other cases the nonresidential group exerts a powerful influence. The 19th-century Great Basin Shoshone and Paiute, for example, lived in nuclear families, three or four of which lived together in a residential group called a band. Such groups were ephemeral, and families would come and go in an ever-changing set of associations. Clusters of families would sometimes come together for a communal jackrabbit or antelope drive. When they did, one individual, recognized for his hunting ability, would take charge, but his authority would disappear when the drive was over. Shoshone families did not "do as they pleased," but neither did they participate in a formalized, permanent level of political integration above the family. This means that although behaviours such as murder and theft were considered antisocial, punishment varied depending on the particular circumstances and families involved.

Contrast this with 19th-century Tahitian society. At the time of European contact, Tahiti—an island in the South Pacific with a population of some 100,000—had a horticultural economy of taro, breadfruit, yams, and coconuts. People also raised pigs and chickens, caught fish, and collected shellfish. Families lived in small villages along the coast and in the island's interior.

Unlike Shoshone bands, the membership of Tahitian villages was more or less permanent, with several strong and overarching levels of control. Tahitian villages were organized into about 20 competing **chiefdoms.** A sacred chief (*arii rahi*) ruled each of these chiefdoms. Below the sacred chiefs were "small chiefs" (*arii rii*), and under the small chiefs were sub-chiefs (*raatira*). Below the sub-chiefs were the commoners (*manahune*). Sacred chiefs claimed to be descended directly from the gods, whereas commoners were said to exist only to provide for the needs of chiefs. A person from one of these four classes could not marry someone from a different class. Chiefs owned the land in their respective villages, and they had larger houses and canoes than commoners, as well as distinctive clothing. Some chiefs had craft specialists in their employ, and chiefs controlled communal fishing gear and village production.

The sacred chief also controlled the distribution of food and goods between villages. Periodically, he demanded tribute for special feasts and demonstrated his authority by redistributing food and goods to all who attended. The chief always retained some portion of the tribute for use by his household; chiefs also handed out punishments for social transgressions.

Clearly, the Great Basin and Tahiti provide extreme examples of social and political organizations. To understand such differences, we will restrict the present discussion to three broad areas of human social and political behaviour: gender, kinship, and social status.

From Artifact to Symbol

Before doing so, however, we must emphasize an important issue in middle-range theory. As you have seen, archaeologists use the physical residues of human behaviour to reconstruct past human activities. People butcher an animal and leave behind stone tools and some of the bones. They make, use, and break a pot, leaving the sherds behind in a trash midden. Natural processes then act on those remains. Discarded artifacts are sometimes reclaimed or recycled, meaning that they remain part of the cultural system long after fulfilling their original function. Archaeologists consider all these dimensions of artifact use and reuse when interpreting the archaeological record.

Now we add another dimension to our consideration of artifacts, an aspect that is especially important to understanding social and political organization. It may seem that archaeologists act as though artifacts reflect only human behaviour. But it is important to remember that artifacts are not just things, they are also *symbols*. Important life transitions, for instance, are often marked by material culture. In North American society of the 1950s and 1960s, getting your first car was not simply acquiring a mode of transporta-

political organization A society's formal and informal institutions that regulate a population's collective acts.

chiefdom A regional polity in which two or more local groups are organized under a single chief (who is the head of a ranked social hierarchy). Unlike autonomous bands and villages, chiefdoms consist of several more or less permanently aligned communities or settlements.

tion; the car you drove carried a symbolic meaning—it said something about your position in life. Similarly, thousands of years ago, a bow was a weapon for hunting, and it may also have been a powerful symbol of adulthood.

How an artifact enters the archaeological record is a product of how it was used. But because material culture carries symbolic meanings, people sometimes actively manipulate material culture to send culturally specific symbolic messages. Bringing flowers or a bottle of wine to dinner is a standard Canadian way to thank a host. But such a gesture would be meaningless to the Mikea (the forager-horticulturalists we discussed in Chapter 10), who instead expect guests to bring tobacco.

This fact—*that material culture reflects symbolic meanings as well as functional behaviours*—means that artifacts can be exceedingly difficult to understand. But archaeologists are making progress in using artifacts to infer ancient social and political organization, and this chapter provides several examples of how this works. We will return to this dimension of artifacts again in Chapter 14.

Archaeology and Gender

Anthropologists distinguish between sex and gender, and between gender roles and gender ideology. Sex refers to inherited, biological differences between males and females. Gender, on the other hand, refers to culturally constructed ideas about sex differences. Humans have only two sexes, male and female—but there can be more than two genders. Some societies recognize men who choose to live as women or women who choose to live as men as a third gender. In some Plains Indian tribes, for example, **berdaches** (also known as "two-spirits") were men who chose to live as women, performing women's traditional roles, and even marrying men (although marriage in this case did not imply a sexual relationship).

This leads us to the difference between gender *role* and gender *ideology.* **Gender role** refers to the different participation of males and females in the various social, economic, political, and religious institutions of a cultural group. These roles describe culturally appropriate behaviour for men and women. In some societies, women can play very public roles, for example, in politics; in others, women's public participation

may be limited (though their private participation may still be influential). **Gender ideology** refers to the culturally specific meaning assigned to terms such as "male," "female," "sex," and "reproduction." In some societies, men and women have a generally equal footing; in others, men are considered of greater importance; and in others, the activities of men and women are so differently valued that adult men and women interact very little. In traditional New Guinean societies, for example, men spend much of their leisure time in a communal men's house, rather than in their separate family homes.

These facts are important to understanding other societies, and they are important to understanding archaeological inference. Some years ago, recognition of gender ideology led Margaret Conkey (University of California, Berkeley) and Janet Spector (whom you met in Chapter 2) to argue that archaeology had a strong **androcentric** bias. Archaeologists at the time were mostly male, and they viewed the world largely in terms of men's activities and perceptions (and, in fact, in terms of white, middle-class, European male understandings of the world). Conkey and Spector saw this as a product of the reigning North American gender ideology, in which women's contributions were downplayed and women were supposed to stay home and not participate in the "important" activities of the public sphere. They documented several cases in which this gender ideology was projected onto the past, with males portrayed as stronger, more active, and more important than women, who were portrayed as weak, passive, and dependent. According to the archaeological interpretations of the day, men made things happen and women went along for the ride.

Conkey and Spector argued that archaeologists saw specific artifact forms as associated with one gender or the other: Hunting weaponry was always male, plant-collecting gear was always female. Men made

berdaches Among Plains Indian societies, men who elected to live life as women; they were recognized by their group as a third gender.

gender role The culturally prescribed behaviour associated with men and women; roles can vary from society to society.

gender ideology The culturally prescribed values assigned to the task and status of men and women; values can vary from society to society.

androcentric A perspective that focuses on what men do in a society, to the exclusion of women.

projectile points and stone tools; women made pottery and baskets. Archaeologists blithely assumed that a woman buried with a grinding stone *used* this artifact in life. But they assumed that a man buried with the same grinding stone had *manufactured* it.

Conkey and Spector found that most archaeologists failed to identify the sources for their assumptions and rarely tried to confirm or validate them. In other words, *the only middle-range theory operating here was the archaeologists' culturally biased view of gender roles.*

As an example, consider the site of Indian Knoll in western Kentucky, a one-hectare, 2.5-metre-deep shell midden along the Green River (Figure 13-1). This midden accumulated over a long period, from about 6100 to 4500 years ago. Indian Knoll was first excavated in 1916 by C. B. Moore and then in the 1930s and 1940s by William Webb (1882–1964). (Formally trained as a physicist, Webb was almost certainly the only archaeologist to help develop the atomic bomb.)

Indian Knoll is a **shell midden**—the remains of tens of thousands of shellfish meals are preserved there—but it was also a burial place. Between the two of them, Moore and Webb excavated some 1200 burials at the site. Men were generally buried with axes, fishhooks, and other tools; women were buried with beads, mortars, and pestles.

Also in some burials were beautifully polished stones, a few centimetres long, and somewhat triangular in cross-section, with the sides slightly convex. A hole was drilled neatly lengthwise down the middle of the stone. With these stones were often found pieces of whittled, slightly curved antler, with a neat hook at one end.

Moore was puzzled by these enigmatic objects. He thought the stones might have served to hold cords the appropriate distance apart when weaving fishing nets; the antlers he thought might be netting needles.

But having seen well-preserved examples from dry caves in Texas and Arizona, Webb recognized these artifacts as parts of atlatls, or spearthrowers. A wooden atlatl arm, perhaps a half-metre long, fit into one end of the drilled stone and the antler hook into the other; both were held in place by pitch or tree resin. The hook on the tapered end of the antler held the atlatl dart in place as the hunter took aim, and the

stone weight increased the centrifugal force of the weapon as the hunter swung the atlatl overhead, launching the dart. The wooden atlatl arm and accompanying darts would have long since decayed in the Indian Knoll midden, but the stone and antler remained.

Webb was curious about the distribution of these atlatls. Of the 76 burials that held atlatl weights, 31 were adult males, 13 were adult females, and 18 were those of children (sex could not be identified on the remaining 14 individuals). Why, Webb wondered, did people place hunting weapons in the graves of women and children? In 1946, he wrote "it is hardly to be supposed that infants, children, *and women* would have any practical use in life for an atlatl" (emphasis added).

Trying to explain this apparent conundrum, Webb noted that the people of Indian Knoll often buried these beautifully made atlatls intact; but they also sometimes intentionally broke the spearthrowers at the time of burial, as evidenced by the presence of all the fragments of an atlatl weight in grave fill. Adding this to the fact that the atlatls were buried with children and women, Webb argued that the artifacts reflected an intentional burial ritual rather than grave goods for use in the afterlife. We know that in some Native American societies, people cut their hair as a symbol of mourning. Perhaps thousands of years ago at Indian Knoll, the destruction and burial of atlatls carried a similar symbolic meaning—a way for men to express their grief for a deceased child, wife, sister, or mother in a culturally appropriate way.

Notice how Webb's argument is grounded in the assumption—by no means illogical—that atlatls were interred with adult males because they were tools used by men during their lifetime (hence they would need them in the afterlife). By this reasoning, of course, one must likewise assume that some of the women at Indian Knoll also hunted. But because Webb could not conceive of women as hunters, he searched for another explanation for the inclusion of atlatls in women's graves. Although his final explanation could still be right—why, otherwise, did people bury atlatls with children?—Webb's underlying logic demonstrates the importance of using caution to detect our own cultural biases, especially when it comes to matters of gender roles.

Before we look at how archaeologists reconstruct what men and women did in the past, let us pause to

shell midden The remnants of shellfish collecting; some shellfish middens can become many metres thick.

Figure 13-1 The site of Indian Knoll (Kentucky). In the days of WPA archaeology, a huge portion of the site was excavated, and hundreds of human burials were uncovered.

Source: William S. Webb Museum of Anthropology

consider whether this difficult task is even necessary. Do we really need to know whether men or women did the hunting, or plant gathering, or other tasks? Isn't this concern with gender simply an imposition of the *current* North American culture of political correctness? We don't think so; and the following ethnographic example demonstrates the importance of knowing what men and women did in the past.

Hunting in Africa's Rain Forest

Popularly known as "Pygmies," the BaMbuti are hunter-gatherers who live in the Ituri Rain Forest of central Africa. There, a number of different cultural groups such as the Efe, Aka, and Mbuti live in small temporary camps. They hunt a variety of animals and gather wild plants and honey in the forest. Nearly all these groups exchange meat for agricultural produce

with their neighbours, Bantu horticulturalists. They also sometimes work for them in their fields.

Years ago, Colin Turnbull (1924–1994) initiated a long-running debate in anthropology when he observed that some BaMbuti hunt individually with bows and arrows whereas other groups hunt communally with nets (Figure 13-2). Among net-hunters, women and children drive game (such as the duiker, a small antelope) through the forest into nets, where men club the animals (though in some groups women kill the netted game). Archers shoot monkeys and other prey that seek refuge in treetops, but they, too, hunt the duiker. Archers sometimes hunt communally, but they also hunt alone.

From an archaeological perspective, these two kinds of BaMbuti societies would differ in their hunting technology—one would leave behind nets and evidence of their manufacture; the other, projectile

Figure 13-2 A young Aka girl removes a blue duiker caught in a net.

Source: Barry Hewlett

points, bows, and arrows. Such differences in technology are precisely the sort of patterning that archaeologists seek to document and explain.

Why do the BaMbuti use different hunting methods? Turnbull attributed the difference to simple cultural preference; some groups, Turnbull argued, chose to use nets and other groups preferred the bow. But other anthropologists saw it differently. Some argued that Bantu horticulturalists introduced net hunting to the forest and that it had spread because it was more efficient than bow hunting; those who lived close to the Bantu had already benefited from this technology, whereas those living farther away had yet to acquire it. Others suggested that net hunting was a response to the crowding created by Bantu emigration; nets were a way to extract more food from limited portions of the forest. The bow hunters, on the other hand, worked in Bantu fields, receiving produce through their labour rather than by trading meat, and so they eschewed net hunting.

Others argued the inverse: that net hunting was less efficient than bow hunting and net hunters sacrificed efficiency for volume, using nets to harvest a surplus of meat for trade. Another explanation was that the thick undergrowth of the net hunters' environment made archery an impractical hunting technique there.

Anthropologists Robert Bailey (University of Illinois, Chicago) and Robert Aunger (University College, London) decided to test these competing hypotheses. Drawing upon ethnographic and environmental records, they found that (1) no significant differences exist between the environments of net hunters and those of archers, (2) net hunting is no more or less efficient than bow hunting, and (3) bow hunters did not live nearer to or trade more with Bantu peoples than net hunters. In other words, the evidence contradicted every available hypothesis.

Then Bailey and Aunger observed that whereas women participate in net hunts, they rarely hunt in the archer groups. So the question, perhaps, is not why some BaMbuti hunt with nets and others with bows and arrows, but rather *how women decide whether to participate in hunts.*

Recall that many BaMbuti trade meat with Bantu horticulturalists for produce; in fact, they can acquire up to 3 calories worth of agricultural food for every calorie of meat they trade. Some women also work as labourers for horticulturalists, and they receive some of the produce as payment. Bailey and Aunger argued that women decide to hunt or to work in fields depending on which activity gives them the greatest return for their effort. Testing this hypothesis, Bailey and Aunger found that net hunters live near Bantu with *small* gardens whereas bow hunters live near Bantu with *large* gardens.

In areas where gardens are small, Bantu women do not need BaMbuti women as labourers and, because they cannot work for produce, BaMbuti women help with the hunting. Presumably, as long as many people are available, net hunting is a better way to utilize this extra labour. Where gardens are large, Bantu women need assistance. They hire BaMbuti women, who apparently make a greater return as workers than as hunters. Without the extra labour, men hunt individually, with bows and arrows. The key to BaMbuti hunting technology, then, depended not on the hunting technology or environment alone, but also on women's choices.

This example demonstrates that options, decisions, and activities by both men and women condition the larger patterns in material culture that archaeology excels in revealing.

Reconstructing Male and Female Activities from Archaeology

One reason for archaeology's androcentric bias was the fact that for decades, the field was male-dominated. Another was that archaeologists were simply unaware of the extent to which their own culture affected the way they viewed and understood the world. We believed that, as true scientists, we could be objective about the past.

This attitude has changed significantly in recent years. Few modern archaeologists would blithely make such simplistic correlations as atlatl = male or pottery = female. We recognize the biases of past archaeological research and understand that knowing what men and women did in the past is not just politically correct; it is important to understanding prehistory.

Some feminist archaeologists believe that it is unnecessary to ascribe particular tasks to men or women in order to take a gendered perspective on prehistory. But others argue that we can't answer important anthropological questions unless we know, for a particular archaeological case, whether men or women used this or that artifact.

Can we reconstruct what men and women did in the past? If so, how?

These questions raise some difficult problems of middle-range theory. In Chapter 12, we explored one approach. Skeletal analysis can tell us something about the different mechanical stresses placed on men and women, but the cause of these stresses still requires some guesswork.

Stable isotope analysis can also point to differences in men's and women's diets. Following up Christine Hastorf's and Sissel Johannessen's research in the Upper Mantaro Valley (see Chapter 11), Michael DeNiro (University of California, Santa Barbara) analyzed bone samples from human skeletons dating to the different phases for carbon- and nitrogen-stable isotopes. He found no significant differences between men and women during the Wanka II phase, during which men and women apparently ate much the same foods. But analysis of human remains from the Wanka III phase (after the Inka had expanded into the Mantaro Valley) showed that half of the men had a considerably higher maize intake. DeNiro sees this as evidence that men participated in rituals (where maize beer was consumed) more often. If so, then not only did men participate in the public sphere of life more than women, but some men participated more than other men. This interpretation thus points out differences between men and women, as well as among men.

But human skeletal evidence can take us only so far. What about everything else found in archaeological sites? How would we know if a man or woman made or used a particular stone tool, pot, or basket? Because archaeologists lack an established method for objectively deriving this sort of information from material remains, most investigators are forced to rely on ethnographic analogy, with all its inherent limitations.

Were Ceramics Made by Men or Women?

Ceramic technology provides a case in point. There are two basic ways to make a pot. In the first method the potter constructs the vessel by hand, either by moulding the clay or by rolling it into a long "snake" and then coiling it up to build the pot's base and walls; the pot's walls are then smoothed by hand.

The other technique is to throw a lump of clay onto a wheel that is rotated manually by the potter (and today by a powered device). The potter then uses the spinning clay's centrifugal force to shape it by hand. The method used on a given pot is relatively easy to determine from characteristics of potsherds.

Working from this simple baseline, Prudence Rice (Southern Illinois University) surveyed ethnographic data from a variety of societies around the world and discovered that, when pottery is fashioned by hand, it is usually manufactured by women. By contrast, men usually manufacture pottery made on a wheel. Archaeologists can draw on this kind of strong analogy to infer past behaviour with a high (but not absolute) degree of certainty: If archaeological evidence shows that pottery was made by hand, then we infer that the pottery was *probably* made by women. By contrast, if we find evidence that pottery was made on the wheel, then we say that the potter was *probably* male.

As we cautioned in Chapter 10, this sort of analogy can be made stronger if we can actually *explain* the inferred pattern; but in this case, this explanation is not easy. There is, of course, no inherent reason why women could not have used the wheel to produce pottery (and, indeed, many female potters do so today). The uniformitarian assumption that we discussed in Chapter 10 fails in this case.

Perhaps the reason lies in the *purpose* of pottery made on the wheel versus that made by hand.

Archaeologists know that the wheel is associated with craft specialization and the marketing of pottery. Thus, it appears that when pottery moves from production for the residential group to production for the nonresidential group, the task shifts from women to men. *Why* this should happen, however, is much harder to say.

An alternative approach is to use an ethnographic analogy that is historically linked to the archaeological population being studied. Rosemary Joyce used this approach to create some deeper understanding of Maya men and women.

Gender in Maya Iconography

In previous chapters, we have mentioned the Maya civilization of southern Mexico and Central America (and we'll talk still more about the Maya in Chapter 15).

The Maya developed a remarkable art style and often depicted themselves on stone stelae, on polychrome (multi-coloured) pottery, in paintings and carvings on lintels inside temples and tombs, and in books called **codices,** which were long strips of paper, many metres in length when unfolded, made of pounded inner tree bark. (The Spanish considered them heretical and destroyed all they could find; only four survive today.)

The images commonly depict Maya wearing intricate, complex costumes. To the Western eye, these costumes appear flamboyant, even outlandish. But to the Maya, ways of dressing encoded immense amounts of cultural information. These figures rarely have overt sexual characteristics, in large part because of the elaborate costuming. Women are sometimes identified with a particular glyph, but not always.

Because we can read Maya hieroglyphic writing, we know much of what is going on in these images. And the images themselves tell us something about Maya sex roles. For example, women are often portrayed (especially on polychrome pottery) weaving, preparing maize for meals, and serving food to others. Joyce and others, notably Tatiana Proskouriakoff (1909–1985), used these images to discover that Maya iconog-

raphy displays women wearing three distinctive dress styles: a simple wrapped garment that covers the breasts, body, and legs, but leaves the arms bare; a woven *huipil,* a housecoat-like garment that covers the entire body; and, more rarely, a jade-bead skirt, often with a fish-monster-and-shell belt. Some interpret the latter to be individuals who are impersonating the male maize god, who is always depicted with such costuming.

Joyce used these clothing styles to identify women on the carved stelae, despite the lack of overt sexual characteristics. Women are seen holding and offering ceramic vessels, bundles of cloth, or paper and blood-letting instruments (the Maya believed that rulers had to sacrifice their blood, often by cutting their tongues, to communicate with the gods and renew the world). The remaining figures, the male ones, often hold weapons, shields, or scepters that represent double-headed axes—the instruments of war.

Although one might interpret the women in the images simply as servants, Joyce wondered if there was a deeper interpretation, and so she turned to ethnographic data gleaned from the codices, early Spanish observations, and modern ethnography.

The modern Maya participate in what anthropologists call a **cargo system,** in which a responsible, married man is selected annually to direct the ceremonial system (today this system is a combination of Catholicism and the indigenous religion). This individual is responsible for holding a number of feasts that accompany rituals; his wife, who acts as an assistant, takes on the title of "Mother of" the man's named position. Other elderly women are responsible for preparing food, tending to incense for purification ceremonies, and ensuring that everyone observes appropriate manners and protocol during the feasts. In this way, men and women occupy complementary roles in the important feasts of the cargo system.

Joyce argues that women depicted in the Classic Maya stelae may have occupied similar complementary, rather than subservient, roles. She points out that Maya ethnographers discuss the complementarity of men and women, and the need for rulers to "assert claims to represent in themselves the split and complementary totality that they would like to control." Joyce suggests that the pairing of male and female figures on stelae in culturally appropriate ways could symbolize a ruler's need to combine male and female elements to acquire and maintain political power. This could include not only a claim to male/female prerog-

codices Maya texts, long strips of paper, many metres in length when unfolded, made of the pounded inner bark of certain trees; these texts helped analysts interpret Maya hieroglyphics on stelae.

cargo system Part of the social organization found in many Central American communities in which a wealthy individual is named to carry out and bear the cost of important religious ceremonies throughout the year.

atives and powers, but might also extend to the right of male rulers to claim the products of female labour, such as weaving.

Interpretations such as this are impossible without adequate ethnographic analogy, and therefore they are subject to both the potentials and the pitfalls of such analogies (as we discussed in Chapter 10). For example, other archaeologists might point out that the cargo system is a poor analogy for interpreting Maya stelae because many of the women shown on stelae are often partners in marriages between royal families—marriages that created key military alliances, as they did in Europe. Thus, the purpose of women in these images is starkly different from that entailed in the cargo system.

One way to probe the strength of an analogy is to look for additional formal similarities between the analogy and the archaeological case, and there is at least one in this instance. Joyce found that women are often paired with men on stelae—sometimes on the "backs" of stelae (that is, the stelae's side that faces away from the largest public area), whereas male figures occupy the more public sides. Sometimes, the women are depicted in a lower position than their male counterparts.

Joyce points out that, when viewed from prominent vantage points in a ceremonial centre, women depicted on the stelae are more frequently to the left of the male images. Ethnographic data show an association between Maya women and left-hand and lower elevations, whereas men are associated with the right-hand and upper elevations. This ethnographic pattern may hold true for Maya stelae as well and, if it does, might strengthen the analogy.

Nonetheless, modern archaeologists still find it difficult to say much with certainty about gender roles in the past, let alone move beyond such relatively mundane activities to an understanding of gender ideology. Doing so may be limited to those instances where a close, historically linked analogy is available.

Archaeology and Kinship

Kinship refers to the socially recognized network of relationships through which individuals are related to one another by ties of descent (real or imagined) and marriage. A kinship system blends the facts of biological descent and relatedness with cultural rules that

define some people as close kin and others as distant kin, or not kin at all. These groupings are important because they strongly condition, and sometimes dictate, the nature of relationships between individuals.

Kinship may not seem very significant to you. We don't mean that you don't care about your family, but on a day-to-day basis most of the people you interact with are not kin. Instead, they are friends, teachers, representatives of the government, bosses, subordinates, and so on. But in the non-industrial world, most people interact on a daily basis with people who are kin. The same was true of much of the ancient world.

So, if you fail to understand a society's kinship pattern, you might misread a lot of their behaviour. For example, a woman from the island of Pingelap in Micronesia once casually listed the members of her household to Kelly: "That child there is my son, and that girl is my daughter. The young woman over there is my sister and the man next to her is her husband. Of course, my father over there [pointing to a man splitting open coconuts] is my mother's brother." If her last statement brings images of incest to mind, we assure you that you are wrong, and understanding the kinship system shows why.

Forms of Kinship

The world of kinship is incredibly complex; we will simplify matters here by concentrating on three basic forms of kinship. In Figure 13-3, the triangles stand for males and the circles for females. The equal sign (=) stands for marriage, the solid horizontal lines connect siblings, and the vertical lines indicate offspring. The square (indicating either sex) places you within the kinship diagram.

Bilateral descent should be familiar because it is the standard kinship in North America, as well as in many other industrialized nations. In bilateral descent, an individual traces his or her relatives *equally* on the mother's and father's sides. Although you might be closer to your mother's or father's side

kinship Socially recognized network of relationships through which individuals are related to one another by ties of descent (real or imagined) and marriage.

bilateral descent A kinship system in which relatives are traced equally on both the mother's and father's side.

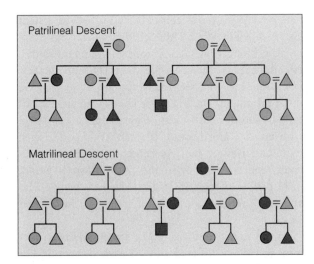

Figure 13-3 Patrilineal and matrilineal descent. The dark coloured circles (females) and triangles (males) show who belongs to one patrilineage (top) and matrilineage (bottom).

(because of geography, divorce, or personalities), neither side of the family is *a priori* more important than the other. Evidence of this is the fact that names applied to relatives on either side of the family are the same. Father's brother and mother's brother, for example, are both "uncles" (in English).

Kinship in cultures with bilateral descent tend to lack depth—meaning that few individuals know who their great or great-great grandparents are, much less their great-great grandparents' siblings' offspring's offspring. This is because *in bilateral descent, the nuclear family is the important economic unit.*

The next two kinds of kinship systems are strikingly different from bilateral descent because they privilege one side of the family over the other; these are *unilineal* descent systems. In **patrilineal descent,** the nuclear family may constitute the residential unit, but the most important group is the **patrilineage,** people to whom you are related *through the male line.* Figure 13-3 shows two hypothetical kin diagrams, one of which represents patrilineal descent, in which the shaded individuals belong to "your" patrilineage. These are all the people that are biologically related to

patrilineal descent A unilineal descent system in which ancestry is traced through the male line.

patrilineage Individuals who share a line of patrilineal descent.

you through a male—your father and his siblings, your father's father and his siblings, your father's brothers' children, and your father's father's brothers' children; we could extend the same to your great grandfather's and great-great grandfather's generation, and so on. These individuals are members of one patrilineage.

In patrilineal descent, you acquire your patrilineage from your father. The other people in the diagram belong to other patrilineages (societies with unilineal descent commonly forbid marriage between men and women of the same lineage). So, your mother belongs to a different patrilineage than your father and, consequently, a different patrilineage than you.

Patrilineal societies make up about 60 percent of the world's known societies. They are associated with a wide range of conditions, including hunting-and-gathering, agricultural, and pastoral societies. They are also associated with internal warfare—that is, war with close neighbours.

Keep in mind that patrilineages contain both males and females—because anyone biologically linked to you through a male is a member of your lineage (such as your father's brother's daughters). Your father's sister is included, but not her offspring. And don't think that members of patrilineal societies are confused about matters of human reproduction. They understand the biological facts of life completely, and they do not ignore "kin" on their mother's side. But in patrilineal descent, your mother's side is simply less important. This is because the lineage normally owns or controls land and other resources, not the nuclear family. The lineage makes decisions about whether to move a village, go to war, or dig irrigation ditches. Thus, although the nuclear family matters, it is secondary to the interests and concerns of the patrilineage.

This difference is reflected in kin terms. Men call their biological father by a term meaning "father," but they may also call their father's brother "father," and consequently, they may call their father's brother's offspring "brother" and "sister," rather than "cousins." In patrilineal descent your mother's brother's children belong to another lineage (*their* father's lineage), and so they are called by a term that we might translate as "cousin," but not "brother" or "sister." Your father's and mother's siblings are the same *kind* of relative in a bilateral descent system, but not in a patrilineal descent system.

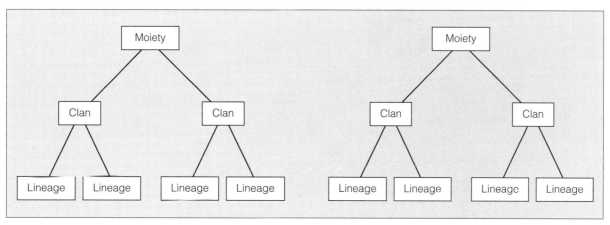

Figure 13-4 The relationships among lineages, clans, and moieties.

The bottom chart in Figure 13-3 contains the same biological facts as the top one, but they are now organized into a **matrilineal descent.** Here, you trace relatives through the female line, forming **matrilineages.** In matrilineal societies you get your lineage from your mother. Your lineage includes you, your mother, her siblings and her sisters' offspring, your mother's mother, her siblings and her sisters' offspring, and so on. As in patrilineal societies, nuclear families exist, but the primary unit is the matrilineage.

By now, you can probably guess why the Pingelapese woman said that her mother's brother was her father: In matrilineal societies, the mother's brother is a "fictive" father. The biological father, in fact, may have little to do with his biological offspring. Instead, he spends his time with his sister's children—because they are members of his lineage, and so it is they, not his biological offspring, who will inherit whatever resources, knowledge, or privileges he possesses.

Matrilineal societies are rare, composing only about 10 percent of the world's societies. They appear to be associated with horticulture, long-distance hunting, and/or warfare with distant enemies.

Finally, to complicate things even more, we need to note that lineages are sometimes clustered into **clans,** which is a set of lineages that claim to share a distant, often mythical ancestor (Figure 13-4). Clans, in turn, may be clustered into **moieties** (*moy*-i-tees; from the French word meaning "half"; in any society with moieties, there are only two). Moieties often perform reciprocal ceremonial obligations for each other, such as burying the dead of the other or holding feasts for

one another. We come back to these terms below, but first we must consider the visibility of such abstract groupings in the archaeological record.

Do Descent Systems Appear Archaeologically?

We return to Madagascar's Mikea (already discussed in Chapter 10), a patrilineal society who also practise **patrilocal residence**—a cultural "rule," commonly associated with patrilineal descent, in which a wife lives with her husband in his original village.

Recall that some Mikea live in forest hamlets of about 40 people. Figure 13-5 is a map of one Mikea hamlet, accompanied by the kinship chart of the families who lived there (the lines drawn through some of the symbols indicate deceased individuals). The diagram also indicates which families lived in which house. In some cases, young children (over the age of 10) and single, elderly individuals lived in small, separate houses.

---

matrilineal descent A unilineal descent system in which ancestry is traced through the female line.

matrilineage Individuals who share a line of matrilineal descent.

clans A group of matri- or patrilineages who see themselves as descended from a (sometimes mythical) common ancestor.

moieties Two groups of clans that perform reciprocal ceremonial obligations for one another; moieties often intermarry.

patrilocal residence A cultural practice in which a newly married couple live in the groom's village of origin; it is often associated with patrilineal descent.

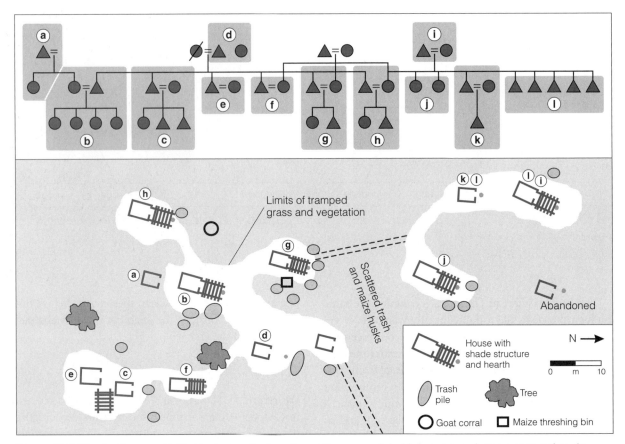

Figure 13-5 Mikea hamlet map with kinship chart; notice how the patrilineages are linked by marriage and yet are separated on the ground.

This figure demonstrates several facets of Mikea hamlets. First, the houses are arranged in a linear, north-to-south scatter, their doors facing north (recall from Chapter 10 that they are placed thus to avoid a cold southern wind at night). Second, the hamlet contains two clusters of houses, marked by trampled areas of vegetation around the houses, and an untrampled belt of vegetation and trash (mostly maize husks) between the two. A path (shown with dotted lines) connects the two clusters.

The kin diagram shows the presence of two patrilineages at this hamlet. On each side of the kin diagram is an older man and his wife, with their sons and their wives, and their unmarried children and grandchildren. Furthermore, these two patrilineages are linked by virtue of several marriages between the sons of one of the elder couples and the daughters of the other.

This is typical of Mikea forest hamlets. Members of two patrilineages live together, somewhat united by

marriage ties or a link through a woman. We say "somewhat" because there was always a palpable tension between these residential groups. For example, when Kelly gifted clothing to the hamlet depicted in the figure, one of the elder man's sons from the southern group insisted on taking charge of the distribution. And for the next two days, the northern group repeated accusations of stinginess and complained of an inappropriate distribution. Sharing (of tools and labour) occurred *within* each of these clusters, but was rarer *between* the two.

Finally, and most important, notice that the patrilineages map onto the ground: The northern cluster of houses contains men (and unmarried sisters) who belong to the same lineage, along with their wives and children. Likewise, the southern cluster contains brothers who belonged to another lineage, with their wives and offspring. The same social relationships mapped out in virtually every settlement we visited. Another ethnoarchaeological study conducted by Rob

Gargett (San Jose State University) and Brian Hayden (Simon Fraser University) found a similar pattern in Australian Aboriginal communities: The closer a social relationship is between two people or two groups, the closer they live to one another.

The difficulty, of course, is that archaeologically the Mikea hamlets appear simply as two clusters of houses. Although we might infer that each cluster represents a social grouping, we'd be hard pressed to say whether it was a patrilineage, matrilineage, or some other grouping, such as a clan or moiety. As with gender, we might have to fall back on a strong ethnographic analogy. Let's explore how this course of action might work in archaeology.

Looking for Matrilineal Descent

Anthropologists Melvin Ember and Carol Ember (Yale University, Human Relation Area Files) have devoted their careers to compiling and analyzing worldwide ethnographic data to find underlying patterns and correlations. Some of these relate human social organization to material culture and are useful to archaeologists.

We noted above that patrilineal societies may practise patrilocal residence. Likewise, matrilineal societies often practise **matrilocal residence,** in which the groom lives in the wife's village. The Embers found that people practising patrilocal residence tend to live in houses less than 60 square metres in size. Mikea houses fall comfortably within this range. The Embers also found that houses in matrilocal societies are larger, generally over 100 square metres in size. The reason for this difference appears to be that, in patrilocal societies, the residential group is the nuclear family (as among the Mikea), but in matrilocal societies, clusters of sisters often inhabit one large house, dividing it into interior spaces for each nuclear family. Iroquois longhouses are one example. The Iroquois often built enormous houses with dividing walls separating the interior space into units, each occupied by a sister, her husband, and their unmarried children.

So, where is the uniformitarianism here? For these observations to serve as middle-range theory to reconstruct the past, we must explain *why* residential units differ between matrilocal and patrilocal societies. Anthropologists don't have a good answer to this question (yet). But recall that matrilineal societies are often associated with long-distance hunting or external warfare. Warfare with distant neighbours takes

men away for long periods of time and, obviously, the men might not come back. The houses of matrilocal societies may reflect (and help create) bonds of assistance and cooperation between sisters while their husbands are away.

Can these observations help us infer kinship from archaeological remains?

Kinship at Chaco Canyon

To answer this question, we return to Chaco Canyon in northwest New Mexico. As you will recall from previous chapters, Chaco Canyon contains a number of large pueblos, or Great Houses, constructed between A.D. 900 and 1130. The Great Houses were connected to one another and to a vast network of pueblos outside the canyon by the road system that we described in Chapter 5. But Chaco Canyon also contains many smaller pueblos—these first appear about A.D. 700 (Figure 13-6)—and even older semi-subterranean pithouses.

Arguing from the Embers' cross-cultural patterns, Peter Peregrine (Lawrence University) suggests that Chacoan pueblo society practised matrilocal residence. Why? The pithouses, the earliest of the Chaco dwellings, average about 15 square metres in size, placing them well below the ethnographic range of matrilocal houses. The early small pueblos are not isolated houses, but clusters of rooms that abut one another. Although individual rooms were small, collectively they covered from 70 to more than 300 square metres. Using the Embers' cross-cultural data, Peregrine suggests that these pueblos may represent matrilocal residence. However, instead of a single large house divided into interior subdivisions, Peregrine argues the Chacoans built separate rooms, their side-by-side spatial arrangement reflecting a degree of social solidarity not seen in the earlier pithouse villages.

Not everyone agrees with Peregrine's inference, and contradictory data come from burials recovered from Pueblo Bonito in the early 20th century. Recall that women remain in their own village under a matrilocal residential pattern, with men coming from other villages. This means that women in such a village should

matrilocal residence A cultural practice in which a newly married couple live in the bride's village of origin; it is often associated with matrilineal descent.

Figure 13-6 A small pueblo in Chaco Canyon.
Source: Robert Kelly

genetically be more *similar* to one another than the men. Conversely, with patrilocal residence, the women should be genetically more *diverse* than the men.

In Chapter 12, we discussed how bioarchaeologists can use skeletal data to track population movements. These data can include not only measurements (like maximum cranial length and breadth or the height and breadth of eye orbits), but also some 200 nonmetric traits of the skull. The latter include the pres-

---

bilocal residence A cultural practice in which a newly married couple may live in either the village of the groom or the village of the bride.

status The rights, duties, privileges, powers, liabilities, and immunities that accrue to a recognized and named social position.

ascribed status Rights, duties, and obligations that accrue to a person by virtue of their parentage; ascribed status is inherited.

achieved status Rights, duties, and obligations that accrue to a person by virtue of what they accomplished in their life.

---

ence or absence of foramina (holes where blood vessels pass through bone), which in certain places (for example, above the eye orbits) also provide clues to genetic affinity.

Michael Schillaci and Christopher Stojanowski (University of New Mexico) analyzed the genetic traits of the Pueblo Bonito burial population specifically to determine post-marital residence patterns. Although the sample size was small, the female sample showed *greater* variation than did the male sample. Schillaci and Stojanowski suggested that, instead of matrilocal residence, the people of Pueblo Bonito practised patrilocal or **bilocal residence** (where the married couple resides either with the husband's or the wife's family). Bilocal residence, in fact, was common at the time of European contact among the eastern Pueblos who live along the upper Rio Grande and who might be descended from the people of Chaco Canyon.

Like gender roles and ideology, kinship is an element of past social organizations that is difficult to reconstruct. But our increasing ability to use genetic data and markers coupled with strong ethnographic analogies and ethnoarchaeological studies should eventually allow us to draw some secure inferences from the archaeological record.

Archaeology and Social Status

Status consists of the rights, duties, privileges, and powers that accrue to a recognized and named social position. In our own society, the status of "mother" is determined both by the duties she owes to her son or daughter and by the responsibilities she can legitimately demand of her children. Similarly, a child owes certain obligations to a parent and can expect certain privileges in return. As you will see, gender and age play important roles in status.

Two major ways of assigning status are through *ascription* and *achievement*. An **ascribed status** is assigned to individuals at birth, without regard to innate differences or abilities. Prince Charles, for example, has high status and expects to become king of England—not because of anything he has done, but simply because his mother is Queen Elizabeth II. His status and rights were ensured at birth.

Alternatively, many statuses are **achieved** and require that an individual possess certain admirable qualities or have accomplished certain tasks (the importance of these qualities and tasks being culturally defined). Rather than being assigned at birth, achieved statuses are earned through individual effort. A Shoshone man who proved to be a good hunter might achieve status as a leader in hunts, but upon his death no one would automatically fill his former position.

Egalitarian Societies

The concept of status allows us to bridge from the level of the individual to that of the entire society. A society is termed **egalitarian** when there is no fixed number of positions of status; instead, the number of valued statuses is equal to the number of persons with the ability to fill them. No one individual wields complete authority over another. The important feature, then, is that *members of egalitarian societies generally have equal access to critical, life-sustaining resources.*

The social system of the 19th-century Great Basin Shoshone people was generally egalitarian, with leadership by those individuals believed to be the most capable of supervising others. Anthropologists call such small-scale egalitarian societies **bands.** Authority was restricted to particular, short-term circumstances. A good hunter, for instance, might assume a temporary position of leadership when a group decided to hunt bighorn. An accomplished dancer might take charge of communal gatherings. Or the opinion of a gifted naturalist might convince others of the medicinal attributes of particular plants. But these individuals would have no authority outside their area of expertise. The key to leadership here is experience and social standing; such a social position is *not* inherited in an egalitarian society. Gender and age are the primary dimensions of status in egalitarian communities.

Ranked Societies

Ranked societies limit the positions of valued status so that not everyone of sufficient talent can actually achieve them. Such a social structure entails a hierarchy in which relatively permanent social stations are maintained, *with people having unequal access to life-sustaining resources.* Gender and age still play a role in the division of labour in ranked societies. But ranked societies tend to have economies that redistribute goods and services throughout the community, with those doing the redistributing keeping some portion

for themselves. This creates one or more ranked social tiers to the society. Many tribes of the American Northwest Coast (see Chapter 2) were ranked societies, as was Tahitian society (mentioned above). Localized residential kin groups (such as a patrilineage) control resources, and major economic goods flow in and out of a regional centre.

Death and Social Status

The categories "egalitarian" and "ranked" define a social spectrum of statuses that can be inferred from analyses of material culture. Mortuary remains are one important source of information on extinct political systems. For the past three decades, many archaeologists have used ethnographic data to show that *societies that have important social distinctions among living individuals will have material distinctions among the dead.*

Death, in a sense, is a period of separation and reintegration for both the deceased and those they leave behind. The deceased are separated from the living and must be properly integrated into the world of the dead. Social ties existed between the living and the once-living, and the ceremonial connections at death reflect these social relations. Mortuary rituals reflect who people were and the relationships they had with others when they were alive. Therefore, they should reflect the person's degree of social status in a society.

Rank and Status at Moundville

We can examine the ranking of social status at Moundville, one of the best-known and most intensively investigated ceremonial centres in the United States. Sprawling across 300 acres, Moundville overlooks Alabama's Black Warrior River. Three thousand

egalitarian societies Social systems that contain roughly as many valued positions as there are persons capable of filling them; in egalitarian societies, all people have nearly equal access to the critical resources needed to live.

band A residential group composed of a few nuclear families, but whose membership is neither permanent nor binding.

ranked societies Social systems in which a hierarchy of social status has been established, with a restricted number of valued positions available; in ranked societies, not everyone has the same access to the critical resources of life.

people once lived here, and for centuries Moundville was the largest centre in the American Southeast (Figure 13-7).

This complex of about 30 earthen mounds was a bustling ritual centre between about A.D. 1050 and 1450. Like most **Mississippian** political units, this maize-based society engaged in extensive trade, and their skilled artists worked in stone, ceramics, bone, and copper. Moundville contains 20 major ceremonial mounds—large flat-topped earthen structures designed to function both as artificial mountains (elevating elite residences and possibly temples above the landscape) and as mortuary areas. A stout bastioned palisade protected Moundville's large central plaza. This suggests that warfare was probably a recurring feature of life at Moundville (Figure 13-8).

Moundville was a major participant in the "Mississippian tradition," a term referring to the hundreds of societies that thrived between about A.D. 800 and 1500 throughout the southeastern United States. In their heyday, the Mississippian elite presided over breathtaking ceremonial centres (as at Moundville) that were invested with power by the thousands of people who lived in smaller nearby farmsteads.

The ubiquitous C. B. Moore conducted archaeological investigations at Moundville in 1905 and 1906, digging into both platform mounds and village areas. The Alabama Museum of Natural History then excavated at Moundville from 1930 through 1941. Over a half-million square feet of the village areas at Moundville were uncovered during this 11-year

Figure 13-7 Moundville (Alabama), looking southwest over Mound E; Mound A is in the centre of the clearing.
Source: The University of Alabama, Moundville Archaeological Park

period, in part by workers in the Civilian Conservation Corps. The more than 3000 excavated burials from Moundville provide a unique database for studying Mississippian social structure.

The Symbolism of Grave Goods at Moundville

Christopher Peebles (Indiana University) and Susan Kus (Rhodes College) took advantage of this database and analyzed Moundville's burials with an eye toward reconstructing Moundville's political organization. They began with the grave goods, many of which display the distinctive symbols characteristic of what archaeologists call the **Southeastern Ceremonial Complex.**

During the Mississippian period, artifacts that bore striking stylistic similarities appear in a number of sites and several large centres, including Moundville, across the southeastern United States from Oklahoma to Florida. These artifacts include conch shell gorgets and cups, copper plates, ceremonial axes and batons, effigy pipes, and flint knives—many decorated with one or more of a set of symbols, such as the "forked eye," the cross, the sun circle, the hand and eye, and the bi-lobed arrow (Figure 13-9). The distribution of these items parallels a trade network of exotic items, as well as basics such as food and salt. But the similarities in the motifs imply more than simple trade; a higher degree of social interaction was at work.

Mississippian A widespread cultural tradition across much of the eastern United States from A.D. 800–1500. Mississippian societies engaged in intensive village-based maize horticulture and constructed large, earthen platform mounds that served as substructures for temples, residences, and council buildings.

Southeastern Ceremonial Complex An assortment of ceremonial objects that occurs in the graves of high-status Mississippian individuals. Ritual exchange of these artifacts crosscut the boundaries of many distinctive local cultures.

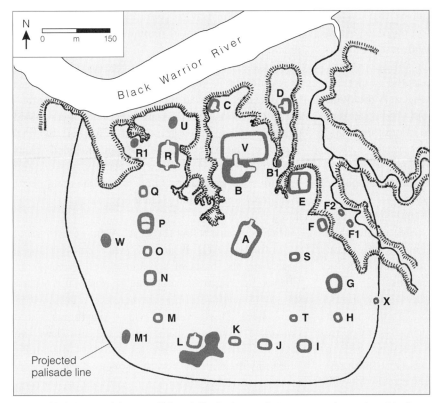

Figure 13-8 A map of the site of Moundville; the letters designate mounds mentioned in the text.

Source: From *Archaeology of the Moundville Chiefdom*, edited by Vernon James Knight, Jr. and Vincas P. Steponaitis, published by the Smithsonian Institute Press, Washington, D.C.; copyright © 1998 by the Smithsonian Institution. Used by permission of the publisher.

structed animal effigy vessels or parts of animals (such as canine teeth, claws, and shells). The local symbols probably functioned as status items within Moundville whereas the ceremonial complex symbols designated the rank of individuals in the overall region.

Each burial mound at Moundville contained a few high-status adults, as indicated by their grave goods. These included copper axes, copper gorgets, stone disks, various paints, and assorted exotic minerals—such as galena (cubes of natural lead), mica (paper-thin sheets of translucent silicate minerals), and sheet copper. Copper and mica items often depict scalloped circles, swastikas, and the "hand–eye" motif (an open hand with an eye in the palm). Presumably, individuals buried with these artifacts had statuses and reputations recognized throughout the entire Moundville cultural system. Each mound also contained some presumably lower-status individuals who were buried with only a few ceramic vessels. Other commoners were buried in cemeteries away from the mounds with no burial goods (or, at least, none that preserved).

By correlating the presence of higher- and lower-status symbols, Peebles and Kus could infer that social status was ascribed at Moundville. Some infants and children—clearly too young to have accomplished anything noteworthy in life—were buried with lavish grave goods. These children must have been important because of who they were at birth, not because of what they had done in their short lives. This is clear evidence of a ranked society.

Two Axes of Social Patterning

On the basis of ethnographic evidence, Peebles and Kus predicted that the Moundville population may have been subdivided along two major social axes, which they termed the superordinate and subordinate.

Whatever the Southeastern Ceremonial Complex really was—and archaeologists still debate it—it cross-cut the boundaries of many widely separate residential groups. At each major site are artifacts that bear local symbols. At Moundville, these artifacts are specially con-

Figure 13-9 An image in the Southeastern Ceremonial Complex style, pounded in copper. Note particularly the forked eye motif around the eye, which probably represents a symbolic association with peregrine falcons, known for their keen vision and skill as hunters (from Spiro, Oklahoma).

Source: American Museum of Natural History

The subordinate division recognizes that certain symbols and the energy expended on mortuary ritual reflect the statuses of age and sex. With respect to age, the older the individual, the greater the opportunity for lifetime achievement, and hence the higher the deathbed rank can be. This means that at Moundville (along the subordinate axis, at least), adult burials should be more lavish than those of children, and children should be accompanied by more grave goods than infants. And because the subordinate division is also graded by gender, men and women should not be expected to have equivalent grave goods.

The superordinate division at Moundville is a partially hereditary ordering based on criteria other than age and sex. Among the elite—people whose status was assigned at birth—some individuals will be infants, some children, and the rest adults.

Peebles and Kus predicted that the statuses should form a pyramid-shaped distribution. At the base of the pyramid are the commoners, whose statuses are determined strictly by sex and age. The next step up the social ladder, the next rank, consists of those few individuals with ascribed status. Finally, at the top will be the paramount individuals, those who enjoy all the emblems of status and rank available in the society.

Quantitative Distribution of Moundville Grave Goods

This model was tested by performing a statistical analysis of the grave goods of 2053 of the best-documented burials from Moundville. This analysis uncovered three distinct clusters and subclusters, represented by burials that contained similar kinds of grave goods (and diagrammed in Figure 13-10). The seven burials of Cluster IA—the supreme division—are presumably chiefs, those individuals enjoying the highest of statuses and the ultimate political authority. All males (we think; these are based on Moore's field assessments), the elite were buried in Mounds C and D, small mortuary mounds in a secluded area to the north of the plaza, and were accompanied by a lavish array of material culture, including numerous ceremonial complex–adorned artifacts. Infants and human skulls (of individuals presumably sacrificed for the occasion) were buried as part of the Cluster IA ritual. Distinctive artifacts in these graves were large axes of copper—a metal too soft to have allowed the implements to function as chopping tools. These, then, must have served primarily as symbols, a cultur-

ally meaningful way to communicate an individual's high status and a visual reminder of the reasons for differences in people's ranks.

Cluster IB burials, both children and adult males, were interred in the mounds surrounding the plaza and in cemeteries near mounds. They also had a number of ceremonial complex artifacts plus mineral-based paints included in their grave goods. Cluster II, the final cluster of the superordinate division, included adults and children buried in cemeteries near the mounds and beneath what were charnel houses near the main plaza; their grave goods included chest beads, copper gorgets, and galena cubes.

Hierarchically below the Level A elite are those of subordinate Levels B and C (who enjoyed status largely on the basis of sex and age differences). In Cluster III, for instance, stone ceremonial axes are found only with adult males, whereas infants and children have "toy" vessels, clay "playthings," and unworked freshwater shells. Unworked bird claws and deer and turtle bones were found only with adults. The individuals in the lowest segment, Level C, were mostly buried away from the mounds and major ceremonial areas at Moundville. But some of the burials in this cluster were individuals buried as retainers and isolated skulls placed at the bases of large posts.

Burial context appears to clarify the nature of ranking in the Moundville society. The most elite were buried in a sacred area and accompanied by symbols of their exalted status. The Moundville elite also apparently lived in larger, more complex dwellings than did the commoners. Elite membership was conditioned by genealogy and, because social position was inherited within the elite, even children occupied such social positions.

Farther down the ladder, the villagers' graves also reflected their social status in life at this level, positions conditioned largely by sex and age distinctions rather than by inheritance. Their less glamorous grave goods were distributed in a different way. Graves contained pottery vessels, bone awls, flint projectile points, and stone pipes, all of which were distributed mostly to older adults. Peebles and Kus infer that these individuals were required to achieve—rather than inherit—their social status. Over half of the Moundville graves contained commoners buried with no grave goods at all.

Peebles and Kus suggested that Moundville conformed to a chiefdom model, a society similar to that

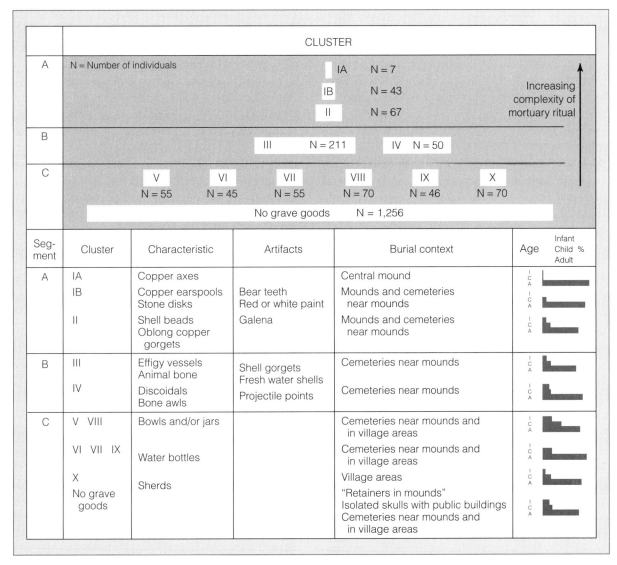

Figure 13-10 The hierarchical social clusters represented in burials at Moundville.

Source: After Peebles and Kus (1977: fig. 3).

of Tahiti and characterized by a status framework with fewer valued positions, although they saw no direct evidence for a redistributive economy.

How Well Did the Elite Eat?

Similar forms of social organization have been recognized at other Mississippian sites in Tennessee, Georgia, Oklahoma, and the lower Illinois Valley. In all cases, burial populations served as the source of inference. The burial goods reflect some clear status differences between men and women and among classes.

Some individuals clearly had different access to exotics. Did this difference also extend to some of the more basic necessities of life? For example, did the elite eat better than the commoners?

If the elite were better off than commoners, then we would expect that they had more nutritious diets, which might include eating more meat. In fact, through a faunal analysis of the trash associated with elite residences on Mounds G and Q (on opposite sides of the plaza, as shown in Figure 13-8), Ed Jackson and Susan Scott (University of Southern Mississippi) found evidence of many animals, including deer, turkey, bobcat, cougar, fox, bear, falcon, bison, and shark. The faunal remains indicated that those living on the top of the mounds ate the choicest cuts of meat from a wide variety of game—including imported items, such as bison and shark. The elite did indeed have access to resources that the commoners did not.

Bone chemistry, as you now know, can also tell us something about what people ate at Moundville. Margaret Schoeninger, the analyst who examined the Stillwater skeletal remains, also studied a sample of male and female remains from both low- and high-status burials. Her analysis suggested that there was little difference in the amount of maize and fish that people ate, but that men ate more meat than women, and that high-status men ate more meat than low-status men. These differences did fit the predictions, but they were not large and, although high-status men may have eaten the most meat, it does not seem that women and low-status men ate inadequate amounts of meat.

Did these differences in diet create significant differences in the quality of life? Mary Lucas Powell (University of Kentucky) hypothesized that, if the elites limited commoners' access to critical resources, then the elite should be taller, live longer, and show less evidence of caries, growth arrest features, iron deficiency (such as cribra orbitalia—see Chapter 12), infectious disease, and trauma than commoners.

In a nutshell, Powell could find no significant differences between the elite and the commoners. It appears that, although differences in social status allowed the Moundville elite to live well, the commoners did not lead lives of want. However, both of these analyses are hampered by the fact that some of the highest-status burials were excavated by Moore in the early 20th century. We have his notes and the grave goods, but Moore did not save the human skeletal remains, and so the highest stratum of the Moundville hierarchy is not available for biological study.

Kinship at Moundville

Despite the differences in rank, Moundville was still an integrated society. And it may have been bonds of kinship that provided the integrating factor and that prevented extreme differences between the elite and the commoners. Indeed, although chiefdoms are internally ranked, their members commonly understand that everyone is ultimately, albeit sometimes distantly, a relative of the chief, who might even use kinship terms to refer to his followers.

To help reconstruct Moundville's social organization, Vernon Knight (University of Alabama) employed an ethnographic analogy with the 19th-century Chickasaw, the Native Americans who lived in the vicinity of Moundville at the time of European contact. Knight noted that there are two major classes of mounds at Moundville. Some of the mounds contain burials; others were residential mounds, with evidence for wattle-and-daub or thatch structures on their flat tops.

These mounds alternate around the square Moundville plaza so that each residential mound is paired with one and sometimes two burial mounds, forming eight burial/residential mound groups. Knight saw in this pattern a parallel to Chickasaw society.

The ethnographic data are limited, and Chickasaw society had undergone profound changes because of European contact, but Knight found that the ideal Chickasaw village had sets of houses arranged around a square plaza, just as the mounds at Moundville form a square plaza. In Chickasaw society, each set of houses belonged to a matrilocal clan that was the political and land-owning unit. In addition, the clans were grouped into moieties, and each moiety lived on opposite sides of the square village layout. The highest ranking clan of each moiety was located on opposite sides of the north end of the square plan, with lower ranking clans to the south. Thus, Chickasaw villages spatially mirrored the kinship structure.

Knight wondered if this kinship pattern extended back to the inhabitants of Moundville. Perhaps, he suggested, each of the eight residential/burial mound units represents the high-ranking home of the leader of eight clans. Knight pointed out that the Moundville plaza can be neatly bifurcated by a line passing through Mound B at the north end of the plaza, through the central Mound A, and then between smaller burial mounds K and J (refer to Figure 13-9). Extrapolating from the Chickasaw analogy, the resulting halves might represent two moieties, each comprising four clans. Note also that the most elite burials were recovered in Mounds C and D; although these are not the largest mounds, they are located at either side of the north edge of the plaza.

But Moundville and Chickasaw villages exhibit crucial differences:

- In the Chickasaw camp layout, a large fire hearth in the centre of the village structurally and symbolically united the two moieties. There was, however, no central mound or ceremonial structure.
- Knight points out that 19th-century Chickasaw society was not a chiefdom and did not possess a central individual who was the uniting focus of the social and political organization. In Moundville, the large Mound B, at the north end of the site, might have been the home of the chief—the highest ranking individual—and evidence of a tier in the social organization that was not present among the Chickasaw.

In sum, Knight's analysis of the layout of Moundville's mounds, along with bioarchaeological and faunal analyses, supports a conclusion that Moundville was a chiefdom.

Trade and Political Organization

In our discussion of Moundville, we mentioned the Southeastern Ceremonial Complex, a social phenomenon that included an extensive trade network. All societies—from egalitarian bands to chiefdoms to modern states—exchange goods, ideas, and services. The geographic scale of trade tells us something about the nature of the nonresidential group that a population participated in and about how far-flung were their political, economic, and kinship connections.

In archaeological sites in the Great Basin, for example, archaeologists frequently find beads made of the shells of *Olivella, Haliotis,* and *Dentalia*—marine organisms that live along the coasts of California and Oregon. Obviously, they point to some sort of interaction between people on either side of California's Sierra Nevada.

The California shell beads in Great Basin sites are not numerous. They appear as personal ornaments in some burials, but they are not exclusively associated with men or women, the old or the young. Many are found in residential sites where, because they are small, they were probably lost as they fell off clothing or a necklace. It is more difficult to say if the beads indicate exchange of goods between the peoples of the Great

Basin and California or were simply the personal belongings of people (wives or husbands? emigrants?) who moved from California to the Great Basin.

Anthropologists have found that, as societies change from egalitarian bands (like the Great Basin Shoshone) to ranked societies (such as those of Tahiti or Moundville), the formal trade of **exotics** becomes an integral part of the economy. Exotics are artifacts made of raw material or in a style that indicates contact with the people of a distant region. Members of the elite trade or give away exotics at competitive feasts (such as the potlatch; see Chapter 2) as a way to communicate and maintain the social order. Exotic artifacts, therefore, are symbols of status and prestige—visual reminders of an individual's social, political, or religious connections to a larger world. As such, they are signs of power and, consequently, of social and political organization as well.

Tracing Exotics

Archaeologists have several methods to determine which objects are locally produced and which are non-local. In some cases, it is fairly easy to determine which objects are *not* locally produced or acquired. Recall that at Moundville, for example, some of the elite burials contained copper axes. This copper is not smelted, for smelting technology did not exist in North America prior to European contact. Instead, the copper was extracted in its raw form. We know that this kind of copper deposit, known as native copper, is not found around Moundville. In fact, native copper occurs only in the southern Appalachian Mountains and near the Great Lakes. The copper artifacts at Moundville have been traced to a geological deposit in the southern Appalachian source. Likewise, the galena cubes have been traced to geological sources in Missouri and Wisconsin.

Human societies create many different kinds of trade systems, but they tend to be of two major types. The first is **direct acquisition,** wherein you go to the natural source of a raw material and extract the material

---

exotics Material culture that was not produced locally and/or whose raw material is not found locally.

direct acquisition A form of trade in which a person/group goes to the source area of an item to procure the raw material directly or to trade for it or finished products.

Looking Closer
Mississippian Influences North of the 49th Parallel

 Archaeologists working in Canada have been interested in understanding the effects of the Mississippian expansion on the social evolution of Late Woodlands cultures north of the 49th parallel. Many feel that cultures in the Great Lakes region of Ontario and southern Manitoba were "Mississipianized" through population movements and participation in long-distance trade with groups in the Upper and Middle Ohio Valley (Figure 13-11). This may have stimulated the transition from mobile hunting and gathering to horticulture and semi-sedentary village life, and the evolution of tribal forms of social organization.

Early investigations of mound sites in southern Manitoba revealed the presence of Mississippian culture traits on the northern plains of Canada. Many of these discoveries suggested that a culture bearing the Southeastern Ceremonial Complex existed in this region when the Mississippian cultural tradition was at its peak (A.D. 800–1500). This complex is sometimes referred to as the Southern Cult, and it consists of distinctive artifacts, iconography, ceremonies, and mythology that are found throughout the Mississippian world.

Some of the most interesting Mississippian traits include a group of miniature mortuary vessels. These small ceramic pots are globular in shape, and decorated with motifs of thunderbirds, turtles, lizards, salamanders, and broken arrows—all designs that are synonymous with the Southeastern Ceremonial Complex. The thunderbird motifs, for example, more closely resemble Mississippian Thunderbirds to the south than they do depictions seen in Algonkian pictographs from the Canadian boreal forest. Other aspects of these pots look similar to those made by historical plains groups. This has led archaeologists to speculate that plains potters gradually fused these Mississippian motifs with their own stylistic innovations through time.

Mississippian-like pots are known almost exclusively from mortuary mounds distributed in an arc across the northeastern plains. With the exception of a single fortified plains horticultural village site on the James River in Minnesota, these unique ceramics have rarely been found in residential sites. The distribution of mound sites appears to overlap with the seasonal movements of bison herds. Based on this limited information, Leigh Syms (Manitoba Museum) has suggested that these mortuary vessels can be linked to nomadic Siouan bison hunters who moved seasonally between the plains and the Aspen Parkland. He defined this as the Devils Lake–Sourisford burial complex, with a date range of A.D. 900 to 1400. These dates make it more or less contemporaneous with the Mississippian cultural tradition (A.D. 800–1500).

The Devils Lake–Sourisford burial complex represents the first real synthesis of mortuary behaviour on the northeastern plains that is reminiscent of the Mississippian cultural tradition. But how did these traits get here? This is a difficult question to answer, because we still know comparatively little about the archaeology of southern Manitoba, North Dakota, and Saskatchewan during the Mississippian Climax. Evidence from the Lovstrom and Lowton sites in southwestern Manitoba suggests that middle Missouri farmers, linked to the Mississippian cultural tradition, may have expanded into these areas around A.D. 950. It is possible that the coalescence of these new arrivals with local groups introduced Mississippian-like ceramic styles, mortuary behaviour, and horticulture onto the northeastern plains.

While there is definite evidence for Mississippian contacts in southwestern Manitoba, the evidence is less clear in the Great Lakes Region of Ontario. Archaeologists have debated the degree to which contacts with the Mississippian world influenced the development of Ontario Iroquois culture. Some archaeologists, for example, have conceptualized Iroquoian economic and social evolution in terms of the core–periphery model mentioned above. Within this model, Mississippian sites in areas like Illinois and Ohio are "cores" that influenced the social and political development of peripheral groups like the Iroquois through trade, exchange, and possibly migration. Some archaeologists believe that these core–periphery contacts eventually transformed the Iroquois from hunter-gatherers to sedentary horticulturalists who farmed maize, beans, and squash. The emergence of fortified villages with longhouses, the development of tribal forms of social organization, ideology, and many aspects of their material culture are all seen as the result of either direct or indirect contact with Mississippian groups. Other archaeologists argue that there is little archaeological evidence at Iroquoian sites to support the levels of interaction necessary to bring about such changes. Instead, they suggest that the evolution of Iroquoian societies was stimulated more by interaction between local groups, and that contact with southeastern Mississippian centres was sporadic and limited.

The social formations of Late Woodland groups in Ontario and Manitoba fall somewhere between egalitarian foragers and ranked societies such as chiefdoms. Archaeologists characterize these as tribal societies. Tribes differ from nomadic hunter-gatherers in that they tend to practise horticulture, live in semi-sedentary villages, and are much

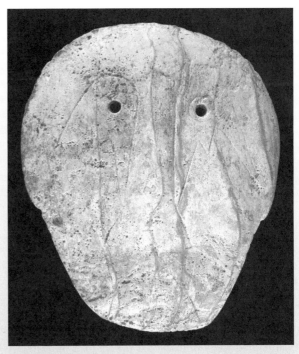

Figure 13-11 Shell gorget recovered from turn-of-the-century excavation of Calf Mountain Burial, located near Darlingford, Manitoba. The artistic motif, and perhaps the item itself, originated in the lower Mississippi Valley.
Source: University of Alberta

more competitive (more on this in Chapter 15). To what extent did participation in Mississippian trade and exchange networks facilitate these changes? While we may never know for sure, the presence of Mississippian traits north of the border demonstrates that people living in different areas of North America were not isolated from one another. This is an important fact that archaeologists must keep in mind when reconstructing social and political systems in the past.

yourself, exchange goods or services for it or for a finished artifact, or receive an artifact or raw material as a gift. Direct acquisition might entail a special trip or it may be embedded into a foraging excursion or a visit to relatives.

The second major type is **down-the-line trade,** in which people acquire a particular raw material or an artifact fashioned from that raw material from their neighbours, who have immediate access to the raw material. These people then trade it to others who live still farther away from the source, who may in turn trade it to people living still farther away. Down-the-line trade usually exhibits a steady decline in the frequency of artifacts made of a particular material in sites farther and farther away from the raw material's source. Occasionally, an unexpectedly high density of the raw material at a site distant from the source may signal that the site is a secondary trading centre.

Down-the-line trade can move raw materials long distances. For example, archaeologists have found incised Gulf Coast shells in sites along the Missouri River in Montana.

Nobody knows how the copper axes made their way to Moundville—perhaps they were gifts sent between ranking elites—but they clearly signal that only a few people had the authority and power to acquire them or to merit receiving them as gifts. Although the copper axes had no material function—they would have made poor cutting implements—they were powerful symbols of the "connections" an elite individual had and perhaps of his ability to draw upon social, economic, military or religious sanctions should anyone contest his hold on power.

Above we mentioned that the copper axes at Moundville were traced to geological sources in the southern Appalachian Mountains. Archaeologists do this primarily by "fingerprinting" an object and comparing it with similar fingerprints of known geologic

sources of the raw material. Several different methods can do this; we'll focus on three here—one used to trace obsidian and two used to trace ceramics to their sources.

Fingerprinting Obsidian

Obsidian—the volcanic glass that makes such impressively sharp implements—occurs naturally only in geologic deposits of the western United States. So, why do obsidian artifacts appear in **Hopewell** burial mounds and sites in Ohio and Illinois?

You will recall from Chapter 2 that Squier and Davis mapped and studied the earthworks of the eastern United States, especially along the Ohio River Valley and its tributaries. We now know that some of the flat-topped pyramid mounds—such as those at Moundville—belong to the Mississippian period. But other mounds—geometric earthworks and some effigy mounds—are earlier, belonging to the Hopewell culture. "Hopewell" refers to a particular archaeological culture found in the Midwest, especially the Ohio River Valley, between 200 B.C. and A.D. 400. Hopewell peoples were predominantly hunter-gatherers, although they also cultivated indigenous plants and small amounts of maize. They lived in small, sedentary villages.

Hopewell culture is best known for its elaborate mortuary rituals, which suggest the beginnings of a ranked society. Many goods appear in elite Hopewell graves, including copper ornaments, incised pottery, carved mica, ceramics, and obsidian. The fact that obsidian is found almost exclusively in burials of Ohio Hopewell sites, rather than in middens, suggests that obsidian played something other than a purely functional role in Hopewell society. (We'll talk more about Hopewell in Chapter 14.)

Squier and Davis recorded small numbers of obsidian spear points in five Hopewell mounds, and more have since turned up in Tennessee, Illinois, and elsewhere. At the time, Squier and Davis thought that the obsidian probably came from Mexico or perhaps the American Southwest. But this was simply a guess. Early in the 20th century, several archaeologists proposed the Rocky Mountains as the source—specifically the obsidian outcrops in Yellowstone National Park. More than a century after Squier and Davis first reported on the obsidian, James Griffin (1905–1997) used the then-new technique of neutron activation analysis to source the obsidian in the Ohio Hopewell

---

down-the-line trade An exchange system in which goods are traded outward from a source area from group to group, resulting in a steady decline in the item's abundance in archaeological sites farther from the source.

Hopewell A cultural tradition found primarily in the Ohio River Valley and its tributaries, dating from 200 B.C.–A.D. 400. Hopewell societies engaged in hunting and gathering and in some horticulture of indigenous plants. They are known for their mortuary rituals, which included charnel houses and burial mounds; some central tombs contained exotics. They also constructed geometric earthworks as ceremonial enclosures and effigy mounds.

mounds to Obsidian Cliff in Yellowstone National Park, some 2400 kilometres away. Because some questions have been raised about the accuracy of Griffin's method, Richard Hughes (Geochemical Research Laboratory, California)—one of the world's leading authorities on obsidian sourcing—used the current sourcing method, **energy dispersive x-ray fluorescence (XRF)**, to test Griffin's findings.

How can XRF trace obsidian artifacts to their geologic source? Many geological deposits form slowly—over years, decades, thousands, or even tens of thousands of years. But obsidian deposits are produced during a single lava flow, and hence they are created in a geologic instant. A volcano could produce multiple flows, but because each flow forms quickly, it usually has a unique chemical "fingerprint." This fingerprint appears as particular amounts of trace elements—like zinc, rubidium, strontium, and barium. Different flows contain different amounts of these elements. If we can fingerprint samples from all geologic sources of obsidian—a formidable but not impossible task—and then fingerprint obsidian artifacts, we should be able to match up an artifact with its source.

XRF allows us to accomplish this goal. The analyst shoots an x-ray beam onto a piece of obsidian, causing the electrons to become excited and emit fluorescent x-ray energies. Because different trace elements emit different levels of energy; the analyst can measure the spectra of energy emitted from the piece of obsidian and, from this, determine the proportion of each trace element present—defining the sample's distinctive trace element fingerprint. Comparing the sample's trace element composition statistically with all known sources allows the analyst to find the best match and, presumably, the geologic source of an artifact. XRF is a very useful technique because it is nondestructive, works well on very small samples (down to 1 millimetre in diameter), takes only minutes to complete, and is relatively inexpensive.

Hughes's analysis confirmed that most Hopewell obsidian came from Obsidian Cliff in Yellowstone National Park. But he also discovered that some obsidian, especially that found in Illinois and Indiana Hopewell sites, came from Bear Gulch in southeast Idaho.

Griffin had assumed that all the obsidian in Hopewell sites had come from one place and that there was no obsidian in sites between the Hopewell culture area and the Rocky Mountains. For these rea-

sons, he suggested that the Midwest obsidian was obtained in a "one-shot" visit by Hopewell people to the source itself—in other words, through direct acquisition. But we now know that obsidian from the Yellowstone region appears in small quantities on other Hopewell-age sites in Wisconsin, Iowa, Illinois, and Indiana. Instead of direct acquisition, high-ranking Hopewell individuals might have used down-the-line trade to acquire obsidian—its shiny black surfaces serving to remind people not of vacations to Yellowstone, but of the important social ties some individuals had to other high-ranking persons in distant Hopewell communities.

Fingerprinting Ceramics

To understand how archaeologists can fingerprint ceramics and trace them to their point of origin, we must first expand upon our earlier discussion of pottery manufacture.

The first step in making a pot, of course, is to acquire the clay. Clays occur as geologic deposits, usually water-laid, and different sources have different grain sizes and mineral composition. The mineral composition of the clay determines to some extent the kind of pottery that you can make from it. Potters use clay that is nearly pure kaolinite, for example, to manufacture fine porcelains.

After it is acquired, the clay is dried and pounded to remove any impurities. The potter then mixes in water and kneads the mixture to remove air bubbles. Clay's most important characteristic is that it is plastic; it can be modelled into shape. But as clay dries, it shrinks and then, when fired, it expands. Both processes can potentially crack the vessel.

Thousands of years ago, potters found that these problems could be alleviated by adding **temper** to the clay. Temper can be one of many kinds of materials: plant fibre, seed chaff, ash, ground-up shell or rock, sand, or even ground-up bits of old broken pots (sometimes called grog). The temper acts to hold the clay in place, gives the vessel strength, and prevents excessive shrinkage or expansion. After the temper is added, the potter shapes the pot and then fires it in an

energy dispersive x-ray fluorescence (XRF) An analytical technique that uses obsidian's trace elements to "fingerprint" an artifact and trace it to its geologic source.

temper Material added to clay to give a ceramic item strength.

oven or an open-air fire, at temperatures in excess of 1000°C if possible.

If we could characterize the mineral composition of clays and tempers for both pots and likely geologic sources—as XRF does for obsidian artifacts and geologic sources—then we could fingerprint a pot (and, if sand or crushed rock were used, its temper) and trace both to their geologic sources. Archaeologists do this with several techniques, including **instrumental neutron activation analysis** (or **INAA,** an improvement over the technique Griffin used on the Hopewell obsidians).

Likewise, minerals in the clay and in the pot's temper can also be identified through **petrographic analysis** (explained below).

Archaeologists have used these techniques to determine the sources of pottery in many different places in the world, and we draw upon a case from the islands in Micronesia to show how this is done.

Tracing Pottery in Micronesia

Micronesia comprises some 2500 islands in the western Pacific. Some of these are "high" islands—the tops of extinct, partially subsided volcanoes. These can reach elevations of several hundred metres and are primarily made of basalt and related volcanic stone. The others are "low" islands—atolls that form as coral grows up around the rim of an extinct, submerged volcano. As the coral breaks the surface of the sea, it catches sand, which eventually allows plant life to take hold. The habitable portions of some atolls are only a half-kilometre long and 180 metres wide. People inhabited most Micronesian high islands and atolls at least 2000 years ago.

None of these islands is very large. Although Micronesia's islands are spread over an oceanscape the size of the continental United States, the total landmass of the islands is only about the size of the state of Rhode Island. But Micronesians were expert mariners who used detailed knowledge of the wind, sun, currents, waves, swells, birds, and fish to sail across hundreds of kilometres of open ocean in out-

rigger canoes. A lively trade existed among many of the islands, especially between high islands and atolls.

The high islands have sources of clay for ceramic vessels. But, being only coral and sand, atolls have no clays suitable for pottery. Because pottery is found in archaeological sites on the atolls, it must have been imported from one of the high islands. If we knew which ones, then we could begin to reconstruct Micronesia's trade networks.

Micronesians fashioned their pottery by hand, and they used shell, sand, and (more rarely) grog temper. Because the high islands formed through separate geologic events, the bedrock geology of each is unique. And, given that the clays and some of the sands are derived from the bedrock, their mineral compositions should also be distinctive of each high island. This can be tested through petrographic analysis of the temper and neutron activation analysis of the clays.

The first step is to show that each high island's sands and clays are unique. If they are, then a fingerprint of the clay and temper of an atoll's pottery should indicate on which high island that atoll's pottery was made. If two or more islands' clays are the same, however, then it won't be possible to assign one atoll's pottery to a particular high island.

William Dickinson (University of Arizona) studied the sand tempers of several of the high islands as well as the temper found in pottery on several atolls, including Ulithi and Fais, located near the high island of Yap. To conduct petrographic analysis, you cut a thin section of the pottery and grind it to about 30 microns in thickness so that the minerals are translucent. This section is mounted on a slide, and the various minerals identified beneath a polarizing microscope at 25–400×. To make source identifications, the analyst must also take samples of the temper and identify its mineral composition. Sometimes a temper is distinguished by the presence or absence of key minerals, but normally the fingerprint consists of a particular combination of a standard range of minerals (feldspars, hornblendes, and so on) and different kinds of sand (for example, calcareous beach or volcanic sands).

Dickinson discovered that the sand tempers of different high islands have different mineral compositions (in addition, people on the high islands of Yap and Palau made grog-tempered ceramics). Comparing the tempers of ceramics on various high islands with

---

instrumental neutron activation analysis (INAA) An analytical technique that determines the trace element composition of the clay used to make a pot to identify the clay's geologic source.

petrographic analysis An analytical technique that identifies the mineral composition of a pot's temper and clay through microscopic observation of thin sections.

those recovered from potsherds of Ulithi, Fais, and other atolls, Dickinson found that the ceramics on the atolls were all made using temper from the high island of Yap. Although it's possible that the temper was imported, the lack of clays on atolls suggests that people on Yap most likely made the pottery and traded it to those folks living on the atolls.

Christophe Descantes (University of California, Berkeley), Hector Neff (California State University, Long Beach), and Michael Glascock (University of Missouri) followed up on Dickinson's analysis by using INAA to study sherds from several high islands and atolls. Neutron activation analysis identifies a sherd's trace elements, those in the temper and the clay combined, by bombarding a potsherd with neutrons generated by a nuclear reactor. This produces radioactive isotopes of the elements. These isotopes immediately begin to decay (some have *very* short half-lives) and emit gamma radiation of different energy levels. By measuring the spectrum of gamma radiation, an analyst can identify the concentrations of 30 or more isotopes. This provides the trace element fingerprint of a sherd. (This technique is destructive, and it leaves the tested sherd radioactive. But where people made ceramics, potsherds are usually abundant and the archaeologist can afford to sacrifice some.)

Although the high islands have different geologic histories, it is possible that two widely separate islands could produce similar clays and tempers. But a statistical analysis of the trace element compositions of the various islands' sherds showed that most of the high islands—Yap, Palau, Chuuk, Kosrae, and Pohnpei—can be distinguished from one another.

The archaeologists then used INAA to analyze sherds from the atolls of Fais, Satawal, and Ulithi. What did they find out? In a nutshell, the trace element compositions of sherds from the atolls were all similar to pottery from Yap; none were similar to pottery of Palau, Chuuk, Pohnpei, or Kosrae. In other words, they reached the same conclusion that Dickinson had, based on analysis of the sherds' tempers alone.

What do these analyses tell us about the relationship between the high island of Yap and the surrounding atolls?

Around the year A.D. 1400, Yap had extended its influence and political control to many outer atolls, as well as to Palau. A system of ranking on Yap was mediated in part by *rai*, large perforated limestone disks. Many of these are less than a metre in diameter but, during the early 19th century, some *rai* were quite large, up to 2 metres in diameter. These were transferred as part of competitive feasts similar to those held on the American Northwest Coast (see Chapter 2; *rai* are sometimes referred to as "stone money," but they are not directly comparable to currency). Interestingly, these stone disks were not produced on Yap, but were imported from Palau, some 245 kilometres to the southwest.

Yap also obtained exotic goods through a trade network, called *sawei*, between Yap and its outlying atolls (Ulithi is fairly close to Yap, but Satawal lies hundreds of kilometres to the east). This exchange system reflects a political organization that included Yap, Palau, and several atolls. The smaller atolls sent woven-fibre mats, sennit rope, and shell valuables to Ulithi, which then sent the goods to Yap. In return, Yap sent taro, yams, sweet potatoes, and bananas to Ulithi, where they were distributed to the smaller atolls. Yap also sent timber for building the oceangoing canoes necessary for this trade to continue.

Some describe this exchange network as a tribute system, but specialists disagree over the equality of the trade. Indeed, if an atoll expressed reservations about sending goods to Yap, Yapese sorcerers would threaten to bring typhoons down upon it (a considerable threat to an island whose highest point is only about a metre above sea level). But such threats were probably not necessary, because the atolls seem to have received more material support from Yap than vice versa. And they could seek refuge on Yap should a storm or drought strike their atoll. The petrographic and INAA analyses of the ceramics confirm that the *sawei* system is ancient and it both reflects and helped construct a political system that tied Yap with outlying atolls.

Conclusion

In reconstructing social and political organizations, archaeologists remember that artifacts were not just utilitarian items, but also carried symbolic meanings—meanings that could be manipulated and that played a role in how those artifacts eventually ended up in an archaeological context. Sometimes these symbolic meanings reflect elements of social and political organization—such as gender roles, kinship

Looking Closer
One of These Things Is Not Like the Other: Using Neutron Activation Analysis to Study Moche Craft Specialization

Many anthropologists and archaeologists have linked craft specialization to the emergence of social complexity in world prehistory. Elites often engage in the consumption of prestige goods in order to legitimize and overtly display their positions in society. These prestige goods are usually produced by craft specialists, who dedicate themselves to the production of such items as ceramic vessels, jewellery, figurines, statuary, and woven cloth. In order to become experts at their craft, these individuals have to be supported by others in society. This is something that is not seen among hunter-gatherers and many small-scale food-producing societies. The emergence of state-level organization among groups such as the Moche of Northern Peru demonstrates that craft production served a major urban function, and is therefore a key component to understanding the evolution of social complexity in human societies.

The Moche civilization flourished in northern Peru between A.D. 100 and A.D. 800. Many archaeologists believe that rather than existing as an empire it consisted of a series of autonomous polities integrated through common ideas, expressed in such things as iconography. One of the most important areas of craft specialization was the production of textiles. These textiles were woven from fine cotton, and used to make ornate clothing for the ruling elite. Ceramic spindle whorls are ubiquitous at many Moche sites, and were used to spin the cotton. Spindle whorls have been found in large numbers at the Moche site, a large urban centre that is the "type" site for this archaeological culture. For many years now, Claude Chapdelaine (Département d'anthropologie, Université de Montréal) and his colleagues have been investigating this fascinating site. Chapdelaine was especially interested in determining where these spindle whorls were manufactured. It seemed likely that they were made at the Moche site, since they were recovered in great numbers during excavations. However, were they

being produced by a single workshop, or were there other workshops elsewhere in the surrounding area? Neutron activation analysis provided Chapdelaine with a technique that could be used to address this important question.

Neutron activation analysis involves the irradiation of archaeological materials, such as ceramics, in a SLOWPOKE (an acronym for safe low-power kritical experiment) nuclear reactor. Unlike nuclear reactors made infamous by Sellafield-2 and Chernobyl, SLOWPOKE reactors are low-energy, pool-type nuclear reactors used primarily for research, designed by Atomic Energy of Canada Limited. The archaeological sample is shot inside the core of the reactor, where it is bombarded with neutrons, producing a radioisotope. The excess energy absorbed by the sample's atoms is eventually emitted as beta and gamma rays, relative to the half-life of those atoms. The chemical composition of the sample is determined using the gamma ray spectrum produced by the irradiated sample. This process often yields a periodic table–like list of elements, the relative concentrations of which are used to construct a distance matrix and *dendrogram*, which illustrates how similar or dissimilar the chemical compositions of two or more objects are. The analysis of the Moche spindle whorls was carried out using a Canadian SLOWPOKE reactor housed at the Nuclear Engineering Laboratory of the École Polytechnique of Montréal. The use of neutron activation analysis allowed Chapdelaine and his colleagues to assess the extent to which all spindle whorls recovered at the Moche site were made of clay from a single source, and manufactured at a single workshop. Homogeneous results would indicate that the whorls were being made of clay from a single deposit, while heterogeneous results would suggest the use of multiple clay sources at different workshop locations.

First, a distance matrix and dendrogram were used to determine whether Moche whorls were manufactured from local or non-local clay sources

(Figure 13-12). The results revealed that most were made from local clays. One grouping of whorls, however, showed no indications of being made from local clays. What's more, the whorls were made from clays unlike those found at the Moche site's only known ceramic workshop. This suggested that other clay sources might have been used to manufacture spindle whorls in other, yet to be discovered ceramic workshops. The existence of other workshops could be explained away if ceramic craft specialists at the known workshop had simply used clays from a variety of different sources. However, previous research had revealed that Moche ceramists consistently used clay from a specific source. Therefore, it seemed more reasonable to assume that Chapdelaine's results indicated the presence of other specialized ceramic workshops at the Moche site.

A second line of evidence for the existence of other workshops was sought by comparing the morphology of the whorls to their chemical compositions. One would expect, for example, that different workshops would produce whorls following specific ideas defining how they should be manufactured, and how they should look. However, results showed that there was no significant relationship between the chemical composition of the clays used to manufacture a whorl and its morphology. Consequently, if different ceramic workshops did exist at the Moche site, the craft specialists they employed obviously shared the same ideas regarding manufacturing techniques and appearance.

Identifying the possible existence of other workshops at the Moche site demonstrates how neutron activation analysis can be used as a tool for examining craft specialization—a key component of social complexity. Although fairly basic artifacts, spindle whorls nevertheless played an important role in Moche society because they

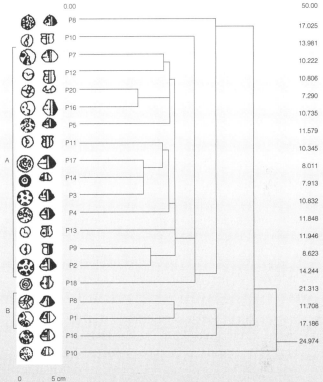

Figure 13-12 Dendrogram illustrating similarities and differences between groups of spindle whorls recovered from the Moche site, Northern Peru.

Source: In Chapdelaine, Millaire, and Kennedy, 2001. Compositional Analysis and Provenance Study of Spindle Whorls from the Moche Site, North Coast of Peru, *Journal of Archaeological Science 28*, p. 800.

provided inhabitants with woven fabrics, which were used to identify and reinforce status differences. Elsewhere, archaeologists have used neutron activation analysis to trace the movements of such artifacts as ceramic pots and lithic tools. It has even been used to analyze a lock of Napoleon Bonaparte's hair, to test the assertion that he was slowly poisoned by his captors while held prisoner by the British on the Island of St. Helena. So, the next time you see a bumper sticker that reads "Nuke the Whales," consider crossing out the word "whale" and replacing it with "artifacts"!

systems, trade networks, and political connections. However, it's hard to construct middle-range theory that allows us to infer social and political organization from archaeological remains, and it may forever require well-supported ethnographic analogy. However, new techniques—analysis of physical and chemical properties of artifacts and the use of genetic markers in human skeletal remains—give archaeology ways to test various hypotheses and continue to improve its reconstruction of the past.

In the following chapter, we go into an even more difficult area of archaeology: the analysis of symbols, concepts, and abstract thought. As you will see, reconstructing social and political organization is a walk in the park compared with trying to draw inferences from symbolic systems.

Summary

- This chapter dealt with social and political systems of the human past, defining what they were and how archaeologists study them.

- The basic social unit is the *group* (both residential and nonresidential); how that group operates is a matter of gender, kinship, and status.

- We separated sex, which is a matter of biology, from gender, which is culturally based interpretations of biology.

- Ethnographic research demonstrates that the sorts of patterns archaeologists are best at finding—large temporal and spatial differences in material goods, especially technology—can be related to different divisions of labour, which are a product of male and female decision making. Thus, knowing what men and women did is important to understanding larger social and economic patterns.

- But inferring what men and women did is difficult. Bioarchaeological analyses provide some clues as to differences in workload and diet, but strong empirical generalizations or historically linked ethnographic analogies are often needed.

- Kinship refers to the socially recognized network of relationships through which individuals are related to one another by ties of descent (real or imagined) and marriage. Like gender, kinship too plays a role in understanding the choices that people made in the distant past.

- Social groupings are reflected "on the ground" in terms of house spacing and placement. Genetic distance studies of human skeletal remains provide clues to post-marital residence.

- Status refers to the rights, duties, and privileges that define the nature of interpersonal relations. Social statuses are apportioned according to culturally determined criteria.

- A key element in political organizations is the difference between *ascribed* statuses, which are parcelled out to individuals at birth without regard to the characteristics of those receiving status, and *achieved* status, which comes from what one accomplishes in life.

- A society is *egalitarian* if achieved status is the common (or only) means whereby an individual acquires a high position; people in egalitarian societies have equal access to important resources.

- In a *ranked* society, ascribed status places people at birth into a ranked order of privilege; ranked societies exhibit a hierarchy, and its members have unequal access to basic resources.

- Egalitarian and ranked societies are often studied through patterning in mortuary remains on the assumption that treatment in death reflects status in life.

- Trade networks reflect the geographic scale of nonresidential groups, economic patterns, and political authority. Trade is established by determining whether artifacts were made or obtained locally and by determining the source of raw materials for artifact manufacture.

- Obsidian, clay, and temper sourcing studies can demonstrate the geographic scale of an economic and/or political organization.

Additional Reading

CANADIAN RESOURCES

Chapdelaine, C., Millaire, J.-F., and Kennedy, G. (2001). Compositional analysis and provenance study of spindle whorls from the Moche Site, North Coast of Peru. *Journal of Archaeological Science, 28,* 795–806.

Syms, L. (1979). The Devils Lake–Sourisford burial complex on the Northeastern Plains. *Plains Anthropologist, 24*(86), 283–308.

OTHER RESOURCES

Ember, Melvin, and Ember, Carol. (1995). Worldwide Cross-Cultural Studies and Their Relevance for Archaeology. *Journal of Archaeological Research, 30,* 69–94.

Galloway, Patricia (Ed.). (1989). *The Southeastern Ceremonial Complex: Artifacts and Analysis.* Lincoln: University of Nebraska Press.

Nelson, Sarah M. (1995). *Gender in Archaeology: Analyzing Power and Prestige.* Walnut Creek, CA: Altamira Press.

Parker Pearson, Michael. (1982). Mortuary Practices, Society and Ideology: An Ethnoarchaeological Study. In Ian Hodder (Ed.), *Symbolic and Structural Archaeology* (pp. 99–113). Cambridge: Cambridge University Press.

Sinopoli, Carla. (1991). *Approaches to Archaeological Ceramics.* New York: Plenum Press.

Smith, Bruce D. (Ed.). (1990). *The Mississippian Emergence.* Washington, DC: Smithsonian Institution Press.

Steponaitis, Vincas P. (1983). *Ceramics, Chronology, and Community Patterns: An Archaeological Study at Moundville.* New York: Academic Press.

Online Resources

COMPANION WEBSITE

Visit *http://www.archaeology1ce.nelson.com* to access a wide range of material to help you succeed in your introductory archaeology course. These include flashcards, Internet exercises, Web links, and practice quizzes.

RESEARCH ONLINE WITH INFOTRAC COLLEGE EDITION

From the Student Companion Website, you can access the InfoTrac College Edition database, which offers thousands of full-length articles for your research.

14 The Archaeology of the Mind

First Nation red ochre pictographs/ rock paintings found on a rock face in the McIntyre Bluff of British Columbia.

Source: © All Canada Photos/Alamy

NEL

Preview

As cultural beings, humans construct the world in which they live. By "construct" we mean that they physically alter the world—through farming, construction, trash disposal, logging, mining, and so forth. In addition, human cultures interpret their world symbolically, which leads to different approaches to the physical world. In this chapter, we will concentrate on these symbolic meanings. Some archaeologists have attempted to infer the symbolic meanings of specific artifact forms, and others have tried to reconstruct concepts and perceptions about how the ancients viewed the world and the place of humans in it.

As you might guess, symbolic approaches in archaeology raise some difficult issues, with both scientific and humanistic perspectives being applied. Although a huge range of human behaviour falls under the category of "symbolic," we will concentrate on investigations of ritual and religion, iconography, and the interpretation of prehistoric rock art.

Introduction

When processual archaeology gained prominence in the 1960s, it generated numerous studies of prehistoric demography, settlement patterns, subsistence, technology, and the human use of landscapes, plants, and animals. These important approaches relied heavily on rigorous scientific methods. The focus was heavily materialistic, because processual archaeologists believed that subsistence behaviour provided the infrastructure for the rest of the cultural system (see Chapter 3).

At the outset, processual archaeologists were optimistic that they could study *all aspects* of the human condition from archaeological data. But most processual archaeologists remained lukewarm toward **cognitive archaeology** throughout the 1970s and 1980s. For many, the archaeological record relating to "ideas" seemed too shaky and ambiguous to be approached in an explicitly scientific, objective manner. And cultural materialists assumed that the cognitive aspects of culture—including religion—were "epiphenomena," mere dependent variables deriving from the more critical technological and economic basics; as such, they were unimportant to understanding the past.

The appeal of cultural materialism to Americanist archaeology is fairly easy to understand. This is a research strategy that places priority on just those things that archaeologists are most confident in recovering from their sites—evidence about past environments, technologies, and economies.

But some archaeologists felt that such heavy-handed materialism dehumanized the past. They argued for an "archaeology of the mind" that emphasizes the values, ideas, and beliefs that make us all human. To be sure, any archaeology of the mind will have a more postprocessual than processual flavour, because such an approach will necessarily be concerned with recovering *meanings* (rather than law-like statements or generalizations about human behaviour). Today, much of cognitive archaeology remains

> **cognitive archaeology** The study of all those aspects of ancient culture that are the product of the human mind: the perception, description, and classification of the universe; the nature of the supernatural; the principles, philosophies, ethics, and values by which human societies are governed; and the ways in which aspects of the world, the supernatural, or human values are conveyed in art.

interpretive, but as we will demonstrate, such symbolic approaches can indeed lend themselves to scientific testing as well—if appropriate linkages can be made between the interpretations of ancient symbols and those human behaviours that can be more directly inferred from the archaeological record.

All humans interact with their world through their cultural perception of it, and modern archaeologists can ill afford to overlook the power of symbols. Take food, for example. Economic decisions might appear to be rather straightforward: Eat this food because it is nutritious and efficiently gathered, harvested, or hunted, and avoid that food because it is not. Although such decisions do heavily condition subsistence practices, we also face an ever-changing background of cultural information about what is/is not edible. As we pointed out in Chapter 2, some societies consider dogs to be food, even prestigious feast foods. Yet people in other cultures are repulsed by the idea of eating their "pets." And some animals may be highly valued in particular cultures not because of their nutritional content, but because of their symbolic meaning. Native peoples of New Guinea hunted cassowary birds not for food, but because their feathers were highly valued gifts that were given away at feasts.

Symbolism goes beyond food to permeate all arenas of human life. We saw in Chapter 11, for example, that even something as apparently mundane and utilitarian as firewood was symbolically loaded for the Inka. And Chapter 13 explained how kinship involves the differential imposition of symbolic ideas about kin onto biological relationships. Male and female tasks also differ among societies, depending on what symbolic value a culture gives to different tasks. In industrial societies, advertising tells us that clothing, houses, cars, hairstyles, tattoos, beer—virtually everything, in fact—carries symbolic meaning.

Humans live in a material world, and nobody can avoid the realities of survival. But people also live in a culturally constructed world, and material decisions are always made against a backdrop of symbolic meanings. This is why a number of archaeologists have turned to an ideational emphasis in their research, examining the active role of symbols in shaping the economic, social, and even technological structure of societies.

What's a Symbol?

The ability to use symbols goes to the essence of what it means to be human. Language is made possible by symbols; so are stories, art, and poetry. For anthropologists such as Clifford Geertz (Princeton University) and David Schneider (1918–1995), symbols shape the way that people see, understand, and feel about the world. We discussed the symbolic element of human culture in Chapter 2; now we consider symbols in more detail.

To most anthropologists, a **symbol** is an object or act (verbal or nonverbal) that by cultural convention stands for something else *with which it has no necessary connection.* Consider a simple symbol that is familiar to many Canadians: a red circle with a red line running diagonally through it. With a capital "P" in the centre of the circle, the symbol tells us "No parking"; with a cigarette in the middle, it means "No smoking." (The "P" and the cigarette, by the way, are not symbols but signs, because they do have a connection to what they signify—the word "parking" itself and the visual image of a cigarette.) Virtually all Canadians understand that a red circle with a diagonal line through it forbids whatever is in the circle.

But is there is any *necessary* connection between a red circle with a line through it and prohibition of a certain behaviour? No. In fact, this symbol might just as easily mean the opposite: Parking *is* allowed here, smoking *is* permitted here. If you were not enculturated into the meaning of the symbol, you would have no way of deducing the symbol's meaning merely from the symbol itself—*because there is no necessary connection between a symbol and the thing it stands for.* Some anthropologists suggest that a few basic symbols might have an inherent meaning genetically programmed into our consciousness; the colour red, for example, might carry the meaning of danger. But the vast majority of the symbols we use have no such "natural" meaning. (And if you think they do, rent a car in Paris and figure out the "natural" meaning of French road signs.)

This is why symbols are so powerful. A simple symbolic act can be made to carry enormous amounts of information. And, in fact, the same symbol can carry

symbol An object or act (verbal or nonverbal) that, by cultural convention, stands for something else with which it has no necessary connection.

different meanings under different situations. Consider a simple wink of the eye. In one situation, it can signal a playful conspiracy between two people against a third; in another, the same gesture is flirting (or harassment). But in another culture, a wink might mean nothing more than that a person has something irritating his or her eye.

Because symbols have no necessary connection to their culturally assigned meaning, they can be used in different ways. Much of the humor, pathos, and poignancy in literature and the arts come from the playful or artful use of symbols (such as the use of the red prohibition circle in the film *Ghostbusters*). This is another way in which symbols are powerful.

But their essential qualities make symbols difficult to study archaeologically. If there is no necessary connection between a symbol and what it stands for, then how can an outsider know the meaning of a particular symbol? How would you know that a red circle with a line through it *prohibits* rather than *permits* a behaviour? Deciphering these messages is difficult enough in an ethnographic context, where one has ready access to language, informants, and observable behaviour. But it is manifestly more difficult—and some would say impossible—to understand symbolic behaviour in an archaeological context, where the physical symbol survives, but its meaning does not.

Consider, for example, the rock art shown in Figure 14-1. This is one of the thousands of images found at La María, a complex of rockshelters in Patagonia (a region of southern Argentina). The central figure is a guanaco, a wild camelid once hunted by native peoples of the region. Along the guanaco's back and haunches is a series of white dots, and other white dots are on the body. In the upper right is a hand silhouette, created when the artisan placed his or her right hand on the wall and then blew paint over it. Between the hand and the guanaco runs a red, white, and black line, immediately below which is a line of red dots.

What do these images mean? Was the hand painted as part of ritual? Or is it little more than

graffiti "tagging"? What do the lines and dots represent? Are they representations of a hunting fence or drive line? Is it a map? Does the guanaco "mean" guanaco? Or is it a symbol that stands for something else, like a lineage? What about the dots on the guanaco? Is this hunting or fertility magic or an appeal to a supernatural being represented by the figure? We have no easy answers to these questions.

To interpret symbols, anthropologists might look at the various ways a particular symbol is used and its (possibly varied) contexts. They might see which symbols are consciously manipulated and which are not; which can be used for humour, and who finds them funny. They might see if some symbols are exclusively used by or associated with women or men. By viewing a symbol's use in a variety of circumstances, we can construct an understanding of what the symbol means. This approach, however, requires the living context of the symbol, which archaeologists do not have.

This means that ancient symbolic systems may remain forever silent as to their specific, detailed meanings. But many contemporary archaeologists think it's worthwhile to examine human behaviour as a system of meanings rather than simply as acts that meet material needs. Recall, for example, our discussion in Chapter 10 of the different treatment of pig bones in African societies. In the following two

Figure 14-1 A panel of art from a rockshelter at La María, in southern Patagonia. The central figure is a guanaco, a wild camelid.

Source: Robert Kelly

Looking Closer
Exploring the Symbolic Dimensions of Circumpolar Architecture

by Peter Dawson

The semi-subterranean whale-bone houses built by peoples of the Thule culture are among the most distinctive archaeological features in Canada's arctic regions. These enigmatic dwellings were constructed using the skeletons of large baleen whales that were either hunted from skin boats called *umiaqs,* or scavenged from the carcasses of naturally stranded whales. The use of whale bone as a construction material represents an ingenious architectural adaptation to life in the driftwood-poor regions of the Canadian Arctic. While may of these dwellings have been excavated, archaeologists still know relatively little about how they were built because few have ever been discovered intact. What we do know indicates that families began by excavating a house pit into the tundra using bone pickaxes. This pit was then furnished with a flagstone floor, and a raised sleeping platform was placed at the rear. A framework of whale bone was then erected over the house pit, and covered with hide and cut sod blocks. A person entered the dwelling through a narrow underground passage designed to trap warm air in the house and keep cold air outside.

Archaeologists have long suspected that the use of whale bone in Thule architecture may have been at least partially symbolic. In many parts of the world, for example, metaphor and symbolism are used to convey important cultural ideas and themes through architecture. Houses can stand for human body parts, animals, landforms, and supernatural creatures. Among the Yupik Eskimo of Western Alaska, entrance passages and roof vents were viewed as portals through which hunters accessed the hunted, and the living contacted the dead. Similarly, the Inupiat of the Alaskan North Slope tell stories in which objects lost at sea miraculously reappear within the passage, items thrown into the tunnel are later found inside landed whales, and drowned men are lured back from the sea through the house's *katak* or roof vent. The suggestion here is that entrances functioned as transitional boundaries separating land from sea, birth from death, and danger from safety. In other stories, shamans were able to reanimate the whale bones framing entrance tunnels so that they moved back and forth like scissors. Then, in deadly competition, contestants would jump in and out of the tunnel until the loser was cut in half. Many Alaskan whaling societies believed that women enticed the whales harpooned by their husbands through the entrance passage during the spring hunt. In the process, it is said that their domestic houses were transformed into actual "living" whales. There are also stories like The Raven and the Whale, in which the trickster raven flies into the jaws of a surfacing whale. Inside he finds a brightly lit *iglu* in which a young woman sits on a sleeping platform tending a lamp. Such stories imply that Thule whale-bone houses may have functioned as metaphors for actual *living* whales as well.

Working with Dr. Richard Levy, an architect and planner with the Faculty of Environmental Design at the University of Calgary, I used virtual reality and computer modelling to search for evidence of architectural symbolism in Thule whale-bone architecture. We began by building several three-dimensional computer models of different whale bone houses using archaeological data from a well-preserved Thule winter house in the Canadian High Arctic (Chapter 18 explains how this was done). Once completed, we placed the models in a virtual world where objects would behave as they would in the real world. Just like in a video game, where the laws of physics can cause a racing car to crash, or a building to blow up, our whale-bone house would collapse if it were not built properly. If Thule architects simply wanted to build the sturdiest structure possible, then using whale bone in a symbolic fashion might result in roof designs that were suboptimal. Finite element analysis provided us with a way of testing the stiffness of different roof designs, and their ability to deflect the stresses produced by such factors as wind, and the weight of sod block and snow insulation. Finite element analysis is a computer simulation technique used in engineering analysis to show how close a structure is to collapsing when subjected to stress. While engineers use finite element analysis on bridges and cars, we decided to try it out on our whale-bone house models.

One of the things that would have made whale bone a desirable building material is the tremendous spanning potential of certain elements. Lower jaw bones (mandibles) are among the longest elements, and were used extensively by Thule architects because they could easily span the width of most house pits. Although the upper jaws (maxillae) were slightly shorter, their spanning potential could be increased if they were left attached to the skull. The first Thule house model (House 4) we analyzed had a hemispherical-shaped roof that was self-supporting, and made almost exclusively from mandibles. The second house (House 8) was shaped more like a kidney bean, and had been roofed using two self-supporting domes of whale bone made from mandibles. What made this house unique, however, was the fact that three whale skulls, likely with their maxillae left attached, had been intentionally placed over top of the entrance passage! For someone sitting on the sleeping platform, this created the impression that a person entering the house was emerging from the mouth of a whale (Figure 14-2).

Finite element analysis revealed that House 4 optimizes the use of whale-bone elements to a higher degree than House 8. In fact, the use of the whale skulls and maxillae, combined with their placement over the entrance passage, would have noticeably weakened the overall structure of House 8. Given these disadvantages, why would Thule architects have used whale skulls and maxillae in this way? Perhaps they were trying to use the architecture of their houses to communicate the importance of whaling symbolically. The roof design used in House 8 certainly conveys the idea that "houses" and "whales" were one and the same. We may never know for sure, but techniques like computer modelling allow us to approach symbolism in the archaeological record in a new and exciting way.

Figure 14-2 Computer reconstruction of a Thule whale-bone house with hide and sod covering removed (left). Inside the model, looking toward the entrance tunnel from the sleeping platform (right). Note the use of whale skulls over the opening of the tunnel.

Source: Dr. Peter Dawson

examples, we will explore some of the potential and limitations involved with attempting an archaeology of the mind.

The Peace Pipe as Ritual Weapon

Writing in the late 1970s, archaeologist Robert L. Hall (University of Illinois, Chicago) used the calumet—the peace pipe—to demonstrate how a cognitive approach could broaden the horizons of archaeological investigations.

Hall focused on the Hopewell culture (mentioned in Chapter 13). Hopewell "culture" probably included many different peoples speaking different languages and living various ways, from the lower Mississippi to Minnesota, and from Nebraska to Virginia. But during Hopewell times (between 200 B.C. and A.D. 400), these diverse people apparently shared a unifying set of symbols that may indicate a common set of religious beliefs. Archaeologists referred to this common set of symbols found over a wide area as the **Hopewell Interaction Sphere.**

To understand what was going on, let's first consider whether the Hopewell people shared a common religion. Broadly speaking, anthropologists consider **religion** to be a specific set of beliefs about one's relation to the supernatural. Religion is a society's mechanism for relating supernatural phenomena to the everyday world—a set of rituals that enlists supernatural powers for the purpose of achieving or preventing transformations of state in humans and nature—in other words, to make sure that good things happen and bad things do not. In some religions, individuals use rituals to influence the course of events; in others, they help novices find their path in a world that they see as beyond their control. All living cultures have some form of religion, and we suppose that was true of past societies as well.

Religious beliefs are manifested in everyday life as **ritual,** a succession of discrete behaviours that must be performed in a particular order under particular circumstances—such as saying prayers at certain times of the day accompanied by particular acts or gestures. Rituals are fundamentally religious acts because they are the mechanisms by which individuals attempt to intercede with the supernatural.

This particular definition of religion is especially relevant to archaeology because of archaeology's emphasis on ritual. Rituals are behavioural acts that often entail material culture and therefore can be represented in the archaeological record. The analysis of past ritual behaviour is thus archaeology's major contribution to the study of religion.

Some of the highly standardized Hopewell artifacts are perhaps indicative of rituals. One particularly intriguing artifact is the stone platform pipe, some examples of which are shown in Figure 14-3. Hopewell artists fashioned these from pipestone, often ornamenting them with carved mammals, birds, or reptiles that rest on a straight or curved base. The pipes were probably used to smoke tobacco (which is indigenous to the New World; the earliest evidence of tobacco in the eastern United States dates to about A.D. 100).

The effort taken to carve these pipes suggests that whatever rituals the pipes were involved in were a critical aspect of Hopewell ceremonial life. Hundreds of pipes were found in the so-called Mound of the Pipes at Mound City, near Chillicothe, Ohio. Some think that this mound was a monument to a master carver of sacred pipes.

What were the pipes used for? What did they signal to their users?

To try to explain these pipes, Hall looked to historical and ethnographic data. He was especially intrigued by the fact that the "peace pipe" used historically to establish friendly contact almost always took the form of a weapon. He then reasoned that all cultures engage in certain culturally dictated customs whose exact meaning and origin may be lost in time. For example, the rite of toasting with drinks in Western culture originally was the sloshing and spilling together of two persons' drinks to reduce the possibility that one planned to poison the other. But how many of us who have toasted friends realize the origin of the custom? Or saluting, a custom that stems from the act of raising visors on armored helmets in order to expose the faces of the two persons encountering each other?

Hopewell Interaction Sphere The common set of symbols found in the midwestern United States between 200 B.C. and A.D. 400.

religion A specific set of beliefs about one's relation to the supernatural; a society's mechanism for relating supernatural phenomena to the everyday world.

ritual A succession of discrete behaviours that must be performed in a particular order under particular circumstances.

Figure 14-3 Hopewell effigy pipes. The bowl for tobacco is on the animals' backs. These would have been placed on the end of a wooden stem and may represent the hook on the end of an atlatl.

Source: American Museum of Natural History

Hall suggested that, although the original functions of the gestures lost their practical significance, the acts survive as elements of etiquette or protocol.

Hall applied similar reasoning to the Hopewell platform pipes by calling upon ethnographic data. Throughout historical times in the eastern United States, Indian tribes observed the custom of smoking a sacred tribal pipe. When the pipe was present, violence was ruled out. Moreover, the peace pipe usually was made in the shape of an atlatl (like those that appear in Figure 14-4)—a weapon that was a forerunner to the bow and arrow used in historical times. The Pawnee peace pipe, for instance, looked like an arrow, and the Osage word for calumet translated as "arrowshaft." Hall suggested that the weaponlike appearance resulted from a specific ceremonial custom. Could it be that, at least during the period of European contact, the peace pipe symbolized a ritual weapon?

Hall then projected his idea back into ancient Hopewell times. Suppose that the distinctive Hopewell platform pipes were also ritual weapons—but made before these people knew of the bow and arrow. At the time, the most common Hopewell weapon was the atlatl (the spearthrower—discussed in Chapter 13).

Hall suggested that the distinctive Hopewell platform pipe symbolically represented a flat atlatl, decorated with an effigy spur. Hall observed that the animal on the bowl was almost always carved precisely where an atlatl spur would be. And the curvature of the platform seemed to correspond to the curvature of the atlatl.

These correspondences led Hall to conclude: "I see the Hopewell platform pipe as the archaeologically visible part of a transformed ritual atlatl, a symbolic weapon which in Middle Woodland times probably had some of the same functions as the calumet of historic times, itself a ritual arrow."

Hall went on to propose that the importance of the Hopewell pipe might well extend beyond mere symbolism—that the platform pipe was not merely one of many items exchanged between groups, but that "it may have been part of the very mechanism of exchange." Adaptively oriented research on eastern United States prehistory has conventionally defined the Hopewell Interaction Sphere primarily in economic and environmental terms. Perhaps, by maintaining relationships between large-scale networks of ritual trading partners, far-flung Hopewell communities joined economic forces, looking to one another for support in lean years.

Hall suggested that a shift away from strictly materialistic thinking—toward a more cognitive approach—could generate a broader understanding of the Hopewell lifeway. Reasoning from Native American ethnographic analogies, Hall contended that peace pipe rituals served to mediate interaction over a vast area of eastern North America. By promoting a common set of symbols—perhaps linked to some common religious ideas—the Hopewell Interaction Sphere tended to reduce regional differences and promote contact and communication between discrete groups.

We pointed out that interpretations of the symbolic meanings of artifacts are difficult to test *directly*. But it would be possible to test the *implications* of Hall's conclusions by assessing whether the archaeology of the Hopewell Interaction Sphere supports the social and political ramifications of Hall's interpretation of the stone pipes. For example, is there evidence of conflict in Hopewell sites? If it is present, how does it

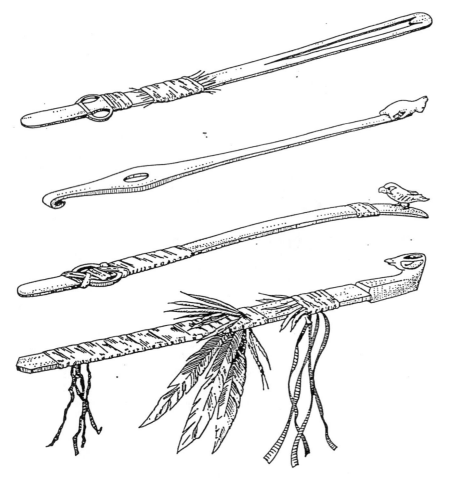

Figure 14-4 Some representations of atlatls in aboriginal North American art.

Source: American Museum of Natural History

Exploring Ancient Chavín Cosmology

In Chapter 11, we discussed the Chavín culture of the central Andes. Specifically, we looked at the faunal remains recovered from Chavín de Huántar and learned what these finds could tell us about subsistence and trade.

But to most archaeologists, the term "Chavín" conjures up much more than llama bones. Archaeologists commonly consider Chavín to be Peru's first highland civilization because of its stratified social and political organization and its achievements in metallurgy, weaving, monumental architecture, irrigation systems, and stone sculpture. Chavín was the first Andean civilization.

Chavín also left a lasting legacy in Andean **cosmology.** By cosmology we mean a culture's understanding of how the world works, how it originated and developed, how the various parts fit together, what laws they obey, and, especially, the place of humans in the natural and supernatural worlds. A glimpse of a culture's cosmology can often be found in its **iconography**—its art forms or writing systems (such as Egyptian or Maya hieroglyphics) that symbolically represent ideas about religion or cosmology.

The iconography at Chavín de Huántar established the tone of subsequent central Andean cosmology. All deities of the succeeding generations in the central Andes looked more or less like the gods in the temple at Chavín de Huántar. Archaeologists Richard Burger and George Miller (whose faunal analysis of Chavín de Huántar we discussed in Chapter 11) have explored the nature of Chavín cosmology, looking in particular at the distinctive Chavín iconography that appeared over a wide area of the central Andes nearly 2500 years ago.

relate to the distribution of stone pipes and their source areas? Or how does the distribution of pipes across the Hopewell Interaction Sphere relate to evidence for subsistence stress (from faunal, macrobotanical, and human skeletal remains)? In other words, *if we treat symbolic interpretations as hypotheses, it is possible to test them by linking them to phenomena that are more archaeologically accessible.* To see how this might work, let's return to an example that we have used before, the Chavín culture of Peru.

cosmology The study of the origin, large-scale structure, and future of the universe. A cosmological explanation demonstrates how the universe developed—both the totality and its constituent parts—and also describes what principles keep it together.

iconography Art forms or writing systems (such as Egyptian or Maya hieroglyphics) that symbolically represent ideas about religion or cosmology.

Figure 14-5 One of the carved stone heads on the temple at Chavín de Huántar that represent a shaman's transition from human to jaguar.

Source: Robert Kelly

crested eagle, monkey, serpent, and cayman (alligator). These creatures are native to the cloud forests and rain forests of the *eastern* Andean slope, if not the floodplains of Amazonia itself—located several hundred kilometers to the east, on the other side of the Andes. These same animals play a prominent role in the mythology and religious symbolism of modern people of Amazonia, but they were utterly foreign to the inhabitants of Chavín de Huántar.

Why were the major animals of Chavín religious art drawn from outside the local highland environment?

Animal Symbolism in Chavín Iconography

Chavín de Huántar has given its name to one of the Americas' most famous art styles—Chavín. Chavín iconography is derived from stone sculptures at Chavín de Huántar, some examples of which appear in Figures 14-5 and 14-6. This art style was reproduced in many villages in the central Andes on locally made ceramics, textiles, goldwork, and stone.

You will recall from Chapter 11 that the community of Chavín de Huántar depended on a range of animals for food, including wild deer, vicuña, llama, and guinea pigs. These were local beasts, probably encountered by local residents on a daily basis.

But the local highland animals of Chavín de Huántar are conspicuously absent from the thousands of known temple sculptures, ceramics, and textiles that display the widespread Chavín style. Instead, the Chavín style drew inspiration for its stylized fangs and talons, feathers and scales from the jaguar,

Where Did Chavín Cosmology Come From?

Archaeologists have proposed several hypotheses to explain this puzzling aspect of Chavín cosmology. The first is that the climate was radically warmer and more humid during Chavín times. If so, then maybe the lowland complex of animals—the jaguar, the cayman, the crested eagle, and so forth—could have once lived in the highlands around Chavín de Huántar.

Figure 14-6 A stone carving of a jaguar outside the temple at Chavín de Huántar.

Source: Robert Kelly

But this hypothesis is not correct. Several lines of evidence demonstrate that the climate was similar to the modern pattern during the Chavín time period (900–200 B.C.), and remember from Chapter 11 that the animal bones recovered from Chavín de Huántar belong to the same species as modern highland animals—camelids, deer, and so forth. Paleoenvironmental change cannot explain the nature of Chavín iconography.

Another hypothesis was championed by Peruvian archaeologist Julio Tello (1880–1947), discoverer of Chavín civilization and first excavator at Chavín de Huántar (in the 1930s), and later by American archaeologist Donald Lathrap (1927–1990). Plants indigenous to Amazonia—including manioc, bottle gourd, hot peppers, and possibly peanuts—all appear at Chavín de Huántar. Tello suggested that immigrants from the tropical forest introduced the lowland plants and animals to Chavín de Huántar. Lathrap attributed the migration to population pressure in the lowland Amazonian or Orinoco basins that forced the early Chavín folk into the Andean highlands. According to Lathrap, the heavy Amazonian component of Chavín religious art displayed homage and deference to the ancient homeland and subsistence regime that was responsible for the initial success of the Chavín elite.

But this hypothesis also seems to be incorrect. In the first place, the lowland crops are impossible to grow in the Andean environment. Their presence suggests trade or some other kind of contact between Chavín de Huántar and Amazonia, but they could not have been plants brought with and grown by an immigrant population. Burger also hypothesizes that, if a tropical forest people had moved wholesale into the Andes, their ceramic traditions should show a direct relationship to the Amazonian homeland. But the earliest ceramics at Chavín de Huántar show a conspicuous lack of Amazonian characteristics; the pottery looks local rather than imported. It also is clear that the basic high-altitude mixed agricultural subsistence pattern practised by the pioneer population at Chavín de Huántar was not Amazonian at all; it had developed in place—in the highlands—at least a thousand years earlier. The ceramic and subsistence evidence make it unlikely that a tropical forest group

oracle A shrine in which a deity reveals hidden knowledge or divine purpose.

was responsible for the lowland iconography evident on the earliest buildings at Chavín de Huántar.

For these reasons, Burger advocates a third hypothesis to explain the Amazonian elements of Chavín cosmology. Chavín de Huántar occupies a strategic gateway position, in a corridor that extends from the Pacific coast, to the highland Andes, and down to the lowland rain forest to the east. Burger argues that Chavín's religious leaders deliberately imported Amazonian symbolism, perhaps in the belief that the exotic lowland people had especially powerful esoteric knowledge. This interpretation, supported by ethnographic and ethnohistoric documentation, suggests that shamans and healers may have made pilgrimages to the distant lowlands—viewed as the powerful source of sacred knowledge, medicinal plants, and other ritual necessities. In fact, in many parts of the world anthropologists have found that people who live outside dense forests often ascribe magical powers or sacred knowledge to their neighbours who live in the forests. Burger argues that the Chavín people imported religious knowledge from the remote, exotic tropics to the Andean highlands.

Analysis of Chavín iconography provides some of the details, explaining the cult's remarkable success. Early sculptural evidence suggests that Chavín ideology held that priests had the ability to turn themselves into mythical beasts, in order to intervene with supernatural forces. Temple sculptures clearly demonstrate that, employing hallucinogenic snuff and beverages, Chavín shamans could transform themselves into jaguars or crested eagles. Specially designed drug paraphernalia—stone mortars, bone trays, spatulas, miniature spoons, and tubes—all seem to be part of the Chavín ritual toolkit. Use of similar artifacts can be documented among modern South American people.

Burger believes that this analogy—based on 16th-century ethnohistoric sources—may explain the singular success of the Chavín cult in uniting previously unrelated cultures throughout the Andean highlands and along the Peruvian coast.

The historical documents also provide a hypothesis for how this religious network might have operated 2000 years earlier. At the centre of the religion was a large ritual complex featuring an **oracle,** accessible only to certain cult specialists. Based on the oracle's secret projections, cult members were able to provide "insider information," offering favourable intervention with the natural elements, protection against disease, and specialized knowledge concerning auspicious times for planting and harvesting.

Under this regional religious system, local communities could establish "branch shrines" by pledging support for the religion. If the pledge was accepted a local priest was assigned, but in return local communities allotted agricultural lands to produce tribute and promised public labour for farming and herding. In effect, these local branches supported the religion's headquarters with large quantities of cotton, corn, dried fish, llamas, guinea pigs, raw materials (such as gold and obsidian), and manufactured goods (such as fine cloth).

Burger suggests that this ethnohistoric cult provides a workable model of the distinctive regional organization that characterized Chavín civilization. He hypothesizes that the oracle cult centre was located at the archaeological site of Karwa, which unfortunately was looted during the 1970s. Iconographic elements—particularly stylized felines and raptorial birds—woven into textile fragments recovered from tombs at Karwa show unmistakable ties to the sculptures at Chavín de Huántar. Despite the nearly 650 kilometres separating the two sites, the complex elements of Chavín cosmology seem to have been transported intact, without simplification or misrepresentation.

The Role of Cosmology in Andean Civilization

This model suggests that Chavín iconography was a widespread religion subdivided into a number of localized branches, each sharing in the major elements of Chavín iconography—probably reflecting major deities—but complemented by distinctive localized elements. According to this view, the Chavín religion maintained its characteristic regional flavour, but also demonstrated a willingness to incorporate motifs and symbols significant to local constituencies.

Burger emphasizes that the longstanding interest of archaeologists in Chavín iconography has led to a deep understanding of how this distinctive civilization came to be. Had this research taken place within a strictly materialistic framework, Burger suggests, the direction would have been much different and considerably more restricted. He stresses that interregional exchange and tribute in the form of gifts to the religious centre, rather than local agricultural production, contributed to the development of Chavín civilization.

The spread of Chavín elements (500–250 B.C.) across the central Andes happened at a turbulent time, following the collapse of many early coastal political systems. An unprecedented amount of contact occurred between distant and unrelated groups, producing a previously unknown degree of sharing of ideology and technology, reinforced by the actual movement of goods and people. For Burger, Chavín culture was a forerunner of the many later attempts in Andean history to create single social entities out of a diversity of local cultures.

So, why did Chavín succeed where earlier attempts failed?

Relying on historical evidence from the 16th-century regional ceremonial complex, Burger argues that Chavín was a large-scale religion, transcending political and ethnic boundaries. Chavín ideology and rituals were sufficiently powerful to support a hierarchical organization, with officials overseeing local cult activities and monitoring deviation among local congregations. Although regional diversity was evident throughout the reach of the Chavín cult, a central authority exerted its power and extracted tribute from smaller communities. Thus, Chavín religion spread not because of political expansion, but because of the extension of a powerful shared cosmology, rendered visible in ritual objects and manifested through the growth of complex interregional exchange networks.

Civilization (a term we discuss in Chapter 15) had appeared in the central Andes by about 400 B.C. According to Burger, the centres of the Chavín horizon rivalled the classic Greek cities in size and beauty, with massive public structures of finely cut and polished masonry, and the settlements were home to a complex society, differentiated by both social status and economic activities.

Burger argues that this power came from the original priests of Chavín de Huántar, who focused the growing Chavín mythology on the mysterious rather than the mundane. It was these mysterious animals of the lowlands that ultimately determined the long-term success of Chavín society and economy.

One message of Chavín art may have been that the prosperity and well-being of the community depended on maintaining the favour of forces alien to the local habitat and daily experience—forces redolent of the powers of the distant and mysterious tropical forest. The mediation of this relationship required the services of ritual specialists. This explanation suggests

Looking Closer

Mapping Culture: How Traditional Place Names Encapsulate Inuit Knowledge about Landscapes

Human beings spend a great deal of time naming places on the land. Even so, most of us don't give much thought to why a street, park, or mountain is named what it is. For many First Nations and Inuit in Canada, however, place names are very significant, and can actually influence how an individual thinks about, and interacts with, the landscape. This is because place names often reference important historical and mythological events, individuals, and activities that are known to have occurred there. To a person travelling along a path or trail, the names of places are like pages in a book, each one telling a different story or providing a different set of instructions. The maps of Canada that most of us are familiar with contain named places that were assigned by explorers such as Samuel Hearne (Coppermine) and Sir Martin Frobisher (Frobisher Bay). As such, they are essentially meaningless to First Nations and Inuit. In the Canadian Arctic, for example, places were occasionally named after the financial backers of 19th-century expeditions. By way of illustration, British Naval Captain John Ross named the northernmost point of mainland Canada the Boothia Peninsula, after Felix Booth, a well-known London gin distiller. The Inuit inhabiting this area no doubt had their own name for it, and would have likely been astounded to learn that their land had been renamed in Booth's honour. Thankfully, times are changing in arctic cartography. Nowadays, more and more traditional Inuktitut names are replacing European ones on maps of northern Canada. Canada's newest and largest northern territory is now called Nunavut, the capital of which is no longer Frobisher Bay, but Iqaluit. Similarly, the name Coppermine, given by Samuel Hearne to the mighty river he travelled in the 18th century, is now known as Kugluktuk.

The Inuit Heritage Trust (IHT), mandated under the Nunavut Land Claims Agreement, has developed a program of place name collection and documentation. IHT is seeking to inventory traditional place names from across Nunavut so that the names of places can be changed to reflect the culture of the Inuit, who lived in this land long before the arrival of Europeans. Luke Suluk is currently president of IHT, as well as a member of the Historic Sites and Monuments Board of Canada (Figure 14-7). He has been intimately involved in the collection of traditional place names since he was a young boy. Suluk sees the recording of place names as filling two important roles. First, it revitalizes the Inuit language. Second, the place name tells a story that allows Inuit and non-Inuit to gain an understanding of the significance of the location. IHT has been collecting traditional place name information from Elders across Nunavut. As much information as possible is typically gathered about a particular location, including a geographic description, the meaning of the name, and how the word is pronounced in languages such as Inuktitut and English. When completed, the maps are reviewed by IHT before being passed on to Canadian federal government agencies for the official name change.

Suluk explains that the names themselves enhance Inuit knowledge of an area. Most features

---

that Chavín ideology—heavily emphasizing the exotic tropical forest fauna—ritually reinforced the wealth and power of Chavín de Huántar society.

Current evidence suggests that social stratification may have first appeared in the highlands in association with long-distance exchange—offering local leaders an unparalleled opportunity to control and manipulate the existing socioeconomic system. Burger argues that tribute supplied to regional ceremonial centres by travellers and pilgrims could have been a major source of wealth and power for newly emerging elites.

Religious ideology seems to have played a central role in promoting and legitimizing these profound sociopolitical transformations, suggesting that many

on the landscape, for example, are named for their use. A place may be named as a good campsite, or as a location where certain types of animals are abundant. In other instances, the name of a place may describe its shape or physiographic characteristics. In this way, a person travelling across the landscape can navigate by knowing the names of the places s/he passes. Suluk describes a hypothetical situation in which he might become lost while hunting out on the land. He explains that it is possible for him to radio someone in the community who knows traditional place names. If he describes the shape of a hill, or the bend in a river, such an individual is often able to reconstruct the landscape in their head, and then give directions to Suluk to help him return to his camp, or the community where he lives.

Figure 14-7 Luke Suluk scans the horizon for caribou at the mouth of the McConnell River, on the southwestern coast of Hudson Bay.
Source: Dr. Peter Dawson

Even more remarkably, traditional place names serve as a record for documenting how the arctic land and seascapes are changing—perhaps as a result of global warming. Suluk explains that it is very interesting to compare what Inuit see today with the names people gave to those places in the past. Suluk lives in the Inuit community of Arviat, on the western coast of Hudson Bay. Near Arviat is a place Inuit residents call *Qikiataarjuk*. Even though the name means "small island" in Inuktitut, today the land is one long point on the coast. Suluk points out that no one knows how old some of these traditional names are, so it is difficult to say how long ago these changes occurred. Regardless, keeping the language of Inuktitut alive in Canada's Arctic may be one of the ways by which researchers can monitor climate change. Suluk's comments also demonstrate that the use of traditional place names provides an important key for understanding how indigenous societies perceived and understood the landscapes where they lived.

of the key ingredients for social complexity existed in the central Andes prior to the Chavín horizon. Although it remains a hypothesis to be tested, it was perhaps the power of Chavín's symbols—rather than a change in food resources, climate, or population density—that played a key role in the development of the Andes' first civilization.

Blueprints for an Archaeology of the Mind

Note that the two examples we have discussed so far share a couple of things. First, neither tries to interpret the exact meaning of the various symbols involved. Hall does not tell us what the raptors or other animals carved in stone on Hopewell pipes "mean." Neither do Burger and Miller attempt to explain what the jaguars, caymans, or crested eagles symbolized to those who participated in the religion and iconography of the central Andes some 2500 years ago.

Archaeologists simply cannot make the inferential leap from an ancient symbol to its past meaning based strictly on the symbol itself. Instead, we can speak in only general terms about what the symbols imply about a level of human interaction that is different from a purely material interaction with their environment.

Second, both examples rely upon solid ethnographic and ethnohistoric data. Hall's idea that Hopewell pipes were part of a peace pipe ritual was based on copious ethnographic data on such rituals among many eastern North American peoples. Likewise, Burger and Miller would have been hard pressed to generate a viable hypothesis to account for Chavín iconography without access to a rich historical and ethnographic record of the Andes Mountains.

Good researchers will always need to draw upon imagination to propose testable hypotheses. But ancient symbolic systems always pose the danger that imaginations can run amuck. Without some solid means to check the results of symbolic studies, archaeologists will always be in danger of what Kent Flannery and Joyce Marcus (University of Michigan) call "a bungee jump into the Land of Fantasy."

Likewise, Colin Renfrew (Cambridge University) warns of the pitfalls inherent in "new-age archaeology," insisting that cognitive archaeology proceed within the framework of acceptable scientific method. One must recognize that, at best, archaeology can capture only certain, limited aspects of ancient ideas. Renfrew discourages attempts to reconstruct "worldviews" or "totalities of thought"—emphasizing the

notable lack of success among ethnographers who have tried to do this (and they work with living people, whose totality of thought is very much intact).

Marcus and Flannery also suggest that cognitive archaeology can follow relatively rigorous methods, *provided ample historical and ethnographic documentation is available.* In fact, they warn that if such data are lacking, "far less success should be anticipated."

So, what do we do with truly ancient symbolic systems that have no such historically linked ethnographic data? Do we simply shrug our shoulders and turn to some other problem? To answer this question, let's examine how archaeologists have studied one of the earliest symbolic systems, the Upper Paleolithic cave art of western Europe.

Upper Paleolithic Cave Art

You will recall from Chapter 12 that the lineage that would eventually become *Homo sapiens* split from the rest of the primate lineage more than 5 million years ago. But the earliest evidence for artistic expression appears only in the last 90,000 years and does not become widespread until the last 40,000 years.

The **Upper Paleolithic** (40,000–10,000 B.C.) in Europe is distinguished by the appearance of a complex technology of stone, bone, and antler as well as wall art, portable art objects, and decorated tools—an example of which appears in Figure 14-8. Archaeologists sometimes call this an artistic "explosion," and the metaphor is appropriate. Only a handful of objects from the preceding 5 million years can be called art (and many of these may not be artifacts at all). But many, many Upper Paleolithic sites contain engraved, carved, or sculpted objects, and caves occupied by Upper Paleolithic peoples often contain wall paintings.

Cave paintings occur in 200 French caves, and still more are found in Spain. Much of the painting dates to the **Magdalenian** phase (16,000–10,000 B.C.). However, a new site, Grotte Chauvet, was discovered in France in 1994, and AMS radiocarbon dates on the paintings themselves (the black paint is charcoal, and fat or blood is sometimes used as a binder) and some torch marks on the walls date to 24,000–30,000 B.C.

Upper Paleolithic wall paintings have intrigued archaeologists for more than a century. More than simple line drawings, these are masterworks created

Upper Paleolithic The last major division of the Old World Paleolithic, beginning about 40,000 years ago and lasting until the end of the Pleistocene (ca. 10,000 B.C.).

Magdalenian The last major culture of the European Upper Paleolithic period (ca. 16,000–10,000 B.C.); named after the rockshelter La Madeleine, in southwestern France. Magdalenian artisans crafted intricately carved tools of reindeer bone and antler; this was also the period during which Upper Paleolithic cave art in France and Spain reached its zenith.

Figure 14-8 Carved from reindeer antler, this bison probably served as the end of an atlatl and is an example of the artistic work that typifies the European Upper Paleolithic.

Source: American Museum of Natural History

the descent into the darkness require a rope, but carbon dioxide also accumulates at the pit's base, making breathing difficult.

Upper Paleolithic artisans clearly intended to place their art in difficult places to access. And this remoteness strongly suggests a connection between the art and religious ritual, a suggestion supported by the occasional finds of bear teeth or ochre-covered flint blades stuffed into cracks in the cave walls; perhaps these were offerings of some sort.

The content of the art is also intriguing. Human beings rarely appear and, when they do, they are poorly executed in comparison with the marvellous animal figures. Also, Upper Paleolithic art contains no actual "scenes." Although images often overlap, no one has identified a "story" or landscape. And whereas the cave art provides vivid evidence documenting the range of animals living in Ice Age Europe, certain animals are emphasized, especially horses, aurochs (wild cattle), bison, ibex, stags, and reindeer, with occasional mammoths, bears, rhinoceros, and large cats. The ancient artists sometimes painted some images on top of (or partially overlapping) previous paintings, suggesting that the act of making the art was more important than the final product itself.

What accounts for the particular forms that the art takes and the locations where these forms were painted?

by talented artisans who knew animal anatomy and behaviour well. Careful shading shows the contours of animals' shoulders and haunches. Stags lower their heads to bugle in the rutting season. Some animals may be pregnant. Many of the images were painted with brushes, and hand silhouettes by the hundreds cover some cave walls.

The paintings are deliberately dramatic. The artists understood the principles of perspective, and they sometimes employed the natural topography of cave walls to bring the animals to life. As you walk down one dark, narrow passage in the French cave of Lascaux, for example, two bulls appear to be running toward and to either side of you—a trick made possible by clever use of the cave's contours.

Upper Paleolithic paintings sometimes turn up in the most obscure of places, difficult to locate even with modern equipment. The art is often found in the deepest recesses of caves, some at the very ends of passages, showing that a cave's entire passable extent was explored. Imagine entering one of these caves with only a reed torch or stone lamp burning tallow as your source of light. There are pits, pools, and rivers to avoid, narrow passageways to crawl through, and jutting rocks to duck under; and, remember, you have to find your way outside again. At Lascaux, cave art even appears at the base of a deep pit. Not only does

Art or Magic?

Various 19th-century scholars viewed Upper Paleolithic cave art romantically, as an early expression of a growing human sense of beauty and perfection. This "art-for-art's-sake" perspective stressed what humans could accomplish in the leisure time that technology could bring. So viewed, the animals had no particular meaning; they were simply artistic expressions of the things that people saw around them. The lack of scenes or stories in the art was taken to be evidence that the artistic sense was in a rudimentary stage of development.

David Lewis-Williams (University of Witwatersrand, South Africa) points out the circularity in this approach: An innate aesthetic sense is inferred from beautiful art, and the presence of beautiful art is evidence of this innate sense. The art-for-art's-sake approach likewise fails to explain why the artists chose such remote locations. If art was something done in leisure time for public enjoyment, why decorate remote, dangerous reaches of caves?

Other anthropologists suggested that the cave art involves **sympathetic magic,** grounded in the principle that "like controls like." In the late 19th century, Salomon Reinach (1858–1932) proposed that the images were intended to promote the fertility of game animals, thus ensuring an abundant food supply for Upper Paleolithic hunters: If you draw pregnant animals, then the real animals will become pregnant and the food supply will be ensured. Abbé Henri Breuil subsequently developed a similar line of thought, suggesting that the images were a form of sympathetic magic designed to guarantee the success of a hunt: If you kill the stylized animal on the wall, you will also kill the real animal out in the valley.

It is true that the artists drew some animals with spears thrust into them (although only a few may represent pregnant animals). But whereas bison and horse are the most frequently depicted animals, most of the bones recovered from Upper Paleolithic caves in Europe are red deer and reindeer. If this art represents sympathetic magic, then it was not very successful.

The sympathetic magic interpretation assumes that the animals are literal and that they have no symbolic meaning. But other scholars view the Upper Paleolithic cave paintings as a structured code, drawing upon a theoretical paradigm known as **structuralism.** Briefly, structuralism argues that humans understand reality as paired oppositions. The concept of "life," for example, is meaningless without the opposite concept of "death." Likewise, the concept of "male" means

nothing without the opposing concept of "female." From a structuralist perspective, culture—and its material expressions, such as art—is played out in terms of such paired oppositions. So viewed, the task of the archaeologist becomes discerning and interpreting these pairs of oppositions.

Following this paradigm, French archaeologists André Leroi-Gourhan (1911–1986) and Annette Laming-Emperaire (1917–1978) argued that Upper Paleolithic cave imagery contained binary oppositions that "stand for" male and female (although Laming-Emperaire backed away from this interpretation later in her life). Criticizing what she saw as simplistic, off-the-cuff interpretations, Laming-Emperaire advocated a more systematic approach to cave art. She sought to identify not merely the animals represented in the images, but also where in a cave particular images were found (the entrance, middle chambers, the rear), their positions (ceiling, wall, and so on), signs of use, archaeological remains, and associations among images. In other words, Laming-Emperaire did what a good archaeologist should do: She systematically analyzed both the contents and the contexts of the images.

It remained for Leroi-Gourhan to complete the work begun by Laming-Emperaire. Rejecting previous ethnographic analogies and earlier models of cognitive evolution, Leroi-Gourhan instead assumed that the minds of Upper Paleolithic people were every bit as complex as those of modern people. Collecting systematic, quantitative data from 66 French caves, Leroi-Gourhan's maps suggested that the various cave elements clustered into four major set of images:

- Small herbivores (horse, ibex, stag, reindeer, and hind)
- Large herbivores (bison, auroch)
- Rare species (mammoth, deer, ibex)
- Dangerous animals (cat, bear, rhinoceros)

Working in the structuralist paradigm, Leroi-Gourhan associated the small herbivores with "maleness" and the large herbivores with "femaleness." He also defined two major groupings of abstract signs—a set of "narrow" symbols (such as rows of dots, arrow-like representations, and straight lines) that he believed were "male," and a second set of "wide" symbols (rectangles, upside-down Vs, and some curvilinear symbols) that he associated with "female." In this way, the abstract symbols and the animal portrayals were viewed as complementary.

sympathetic magic Rituals in which doing something to an image of an object produces the desired effect in the real object.

structuralism A paradigm holding that human culture is the expression of unconscious modes of thought and reasoning, notably binary oppositions. Structuralism is most closely associated with the work of the French anthropologist Claude Levi-Strauss.

Leroi-Gourhan then looked for patterning in the placement of images within cave settings. Dividing the caves into entrances, central areas, peripheral areas, and back areas, he discovered that stags (a male sign) tended to appear in cave entrances. Male signs and images (stags, horses, and ibex) were also in the peripheral areas, whereas dangerous animals and carnivores appeared mostly in the backs of the caves. The central areas contained both male and female signs (along with horses, bison, and aurochs).

To some, the presence of a male sign at the entrance might suggest that the caves were regarded as "male" places, a stag being the equivalent of an ancient "No women allowed" sign. But Leroi-Gourhan reversed the argument, suggesting instead that the caves were considered female (whether this means that only women or men entered the caves is unknown). Keep in mind that structuralism arrays the world into oppositions: If there is a male, there must be a female. Leroi-Gourhan pointed out that central areas contain male elements placed around female elements (with male elements also found in peripheral areas and at the entrance). Where is the female to balance the male? It must be the cave itself.

Armed with these inferences, Leroi-Gourhan could now interpret the "meaning" of the caves: This is where Upper Paleolithic people dealt with the oppositions and contradictions that, according to structuralist thinking, are the inevitable consequence of thinking as a human. Inside the caves, they used symbols drawn from the world of nature to create and communicate a cosmology that explained life's fundamental oppositions: Male and female, nature and culture, human and supernatural, life and death.

But some empirical problems plague Leroi-Gourhan's analysis. Sometimes he used an image to determine whether a portion of a cave was "central" or "peripheral," and in others he reversed the process, assigning an indistinct painting to a particular species depending on where it was located. Both are instances of circular reasoning. And the associations that formed the baseline of his analysis have not held up as more caves are investigated. Eventually, his ideas collapsed under the very empirical standards that he had constructed; that's often how science progresses.

Of greater interest (at least today) are the ways in which Leroi-Gourhan interpreted the symbols. To pursue his structuralist paradigm, Leroi-Gourhan needed to define binary oppositions, the most prominent of which were male and female symbols. In so doing, he was required to jump from the symbol to its meaning. Because symbols take on meaning only from culture, there is always the danger that archaeologists will draw upon their own culture, rather than that of the ancient people to whom these symbols meant something. This was clearly a problem with Leroi-Gourhan's interpretation of abstract symbols of the Upper Paleolithic. Living in a world where Freudian psychology was popular, Leroi-Gourhan interpreted "narrow" and "wide" symbols as representing male and female genitalia. We see here how a paradigm affects the way that we understand the world. It is unlikely that, in a pre-Freudian world, Leroi-Gourhan would have proposed that lines = penises and rectangles = vaginas.

How did Leroi-Gourhan attribute different animal species to men and women? Like most symbolic anthropologists, he looked for associations in the symbols, focusing on bison and horses. In a limited number of cave paintings and engravings, he found women depicted next to bison and men painted next to horses (although the interpretation of some figures as men or women is dubious, as is the contemporaneity of the juxtaposed images). There were also opposite associations—men with bison and women with horses—or ambiguous ones, such as men *and* women with bison *and* horses.

Recall that the same symbol can be employed in many different ways even in the same culture. Do the opposite or ambiguous associations suggest that Leroi-Gourhan is simply wrong—that bison do not really "stand for" female and horses do not "stand for" male—or are they plays on the symbolic meanings of bison and horses? Maybe the men with bison are berdaches (see Chapter 13), and the women with horses are what the Lakota called "manly-hearted women."

Or maybe all of this is just a product of Leroi-Gourhan's imagination and culture. Maybe the bison and horses and other animals had different meanings in different caves at different times in the past. Maybe the images are **totems,** symbols of different clans (as Laming-Emperaire eventually concluded).

totem A natural object, often an animal, from which a lineage or clan believes itself to be descended and/or with which lineage or clan members have special relations.

That Leroi-Gourhan was influenced by Freud and structuralism does not automatically mean that his interpretation of the symbols in the paintings is wrong. *The problem is that we cannot assess whether he was right.*

The most secure way to go from symbols to their meanings is by using some historical or ethnographic information, as Burger and Miller did with Chavín art and Hall did with Hopewell platform pipes. But given that we lack any associated ethnographic data for the Upper Paleolithic, we must ask if there is anything we can do with this art other than admire its beauty and mystery.

Shamanism?

David Lewis-Williams offers an alternative explanation of Upper Paleolithic cave art that, although still speculative, is more firmly grounded in middle-range theory. In brief, Lewis-Williams argues that Upper Paleolithic cave art is evidence of shamanic trances. His explanation does not rely on an interpretation of the images' symbols, and he tries to explain multiple aspects of the art, including the particular abstract elements, as well as the locations of images in caves and their association with animal images.

Lewis-Williams begins by pointing out that virtually all hunting and gathering societies known to anthropology practise a form of religion that involves shamanism. **Shamans** are individuals (often men, but including women in some societies) who claim to be able to access supernatural powers, spirits, or deceased individuals and tap into the power and influence that they offer to the world of the living. They often do this through trances, brought on by the use of psychotropic drugs or by fasting, dehydration, and sensory deprivation. Shamans culturally interpret the visions seen while in an altered state of consciousness as communication with the supernatural world.

The Lakota, for example, performed **vision quests** in which men would lie for days on a mountaintop

shaman One who has the power to contact the spirit world through trance, possession, or visions. On the basis of this ability, the shaman invokes, manipulates, or coerces the power of the spirits for socially recognized ends—both good and ill.

vision quest A ritual in which an individual seeks visions through starvation, dehydration, and exposure; considered in some cultures to be a way to communicate with the supernatural world.

until starvation, dehydration, and exposure brought about visions. These visions were a way for men to communicate with the supernatural world and locate their source of power. Africa's Ju/'hoansi used trances, sometimes brought on by hours of physically and emotionally draining dancing, as a way to contact the ghosts of deceased individuals and perform healing rituals on gravely ill members of the band.

After several decades of study, Lewis-Williams argues that much (though by no means all) of the world's rock art is the result of shamanism. The art is a record of what a shaman saw while in a trance—a way to understand and interpret the meaning of the vision. How can Lewis-Williams say this? If anything is archaeologically inaccessible, it would seem to be what somebody saw in a trance thousands of years ago!

Lewis-Williams relies on cross-cultural psychological and neurological research to bolster his argument. According to this research, when individuals go into a trance, they go through three levels of consciousness, each with distinctive "visual" aspects. In the first stage, a person sees dots, grids, zigzags, nested curves (like rainbows), and meandering lines. These may flicker, vibrate, merge, and break apart. Known as entoptic (from the Greek word meaning "within vision") phenomena, these images appear even with your eyes closed, because they are a product of the optical nervous system. Because they are a function of the brain's hard-wiring, and given that all people everywhere (and we assume in the past, too) have the same neurology, all people should see the same entoptic images. Lewis-Williams thus injects the important element of uniformitarianism, which you will recall is essential to middle-range theory.

In the second, deeper stage of trance, a person's mind tries to make sense of the entoptic images by converting them into forms that are culturally meaningful (meaning that the particular images become culturally biased). Just as a 19th-century Lakota might see horses with riders on them, teepees, mountains, and bison, the mind of an Upper Paleolithic shaman would convert abstract images into things familiar to them, including animals such as aurochs and reindeer.

Those slipping into the third and final stage of trance will sense that they are moving through a tunnel or a vortex, with entoptic images swirling around them and merging into culturally intelligible ones.

Again, this experience seems to be universal, generated by human neurology.

Shamans in many hunting and gathering cultures talk about reaching the "other side" by moving through a hole or cave, an experience sometimes described as "dying." Upon reaching the third stage, a person is often unable to recognize any stimulus outside the visions. The images become more vivid and, although they may merge with one another and with abstract images, a person senses that they are nonetheless real. At this point, the person has entered an altered state of consciousness, and he or she no longer understands that they are viewing images. Instead, they see themselves as having become part of the image.

But does an understanding of the neurological basis of trance (and dreams) help us understand Upper Paleolithic rock art? Let's look at one especially well-known site that Lewis-Williams has studied: the French cave of Lascaux.

The Cave of Lascaux

Found by schoolboys in 1940, Lascaux is perhaps the most famous of all the European caves (see "Looking Closer: The Discovery of Lascaux"). The Paleolithic artists who painted the images inside Lascaux some 17,000 years ago would not recognize the outside of the

cave today. The schoolboys entered the cave through a sinkhole, then crawled down a long rubble-filled tunnel. Today, however, those lucky few who can enter Lascaux (it is closed to regular public visitations) walk through two airlock doors, then step into an antibacterial footbath (to remove any microbes brought from the outside), all the time listening to the hum of an expensive ventilation system designed to maintain the cave's humidity and preserve the paintings inside.

But the inside of the cave remains much as the Paleolithic artists left it. You first enter the Hall of the Bulls, whose ceiling sparkles with calcite (see Figure 14-9). You are struck immediately by the immense aurochs and horses, painted in red and black, that circle the roof; at 5 metres long, the bulls are the largest in all of European cave art. Smaller stags are present, some with many-tined antlers, as well as a bear. Many of the paintings take advantage of the cave's natural topography to accentuate a raised head or shoulders. One peculiar animal has two horns sprouting, unicorn-like, from its head. This painting is well executed, and Lewis-Williams suggests that the artist intended to create an ambivalent species.

A narrow, natural ledge about 1.5 metres above the floor seems to form a ground line for the animals (something rarely seen in Paleolithic art). But because the ledge is too narrow to stand on, the ancient

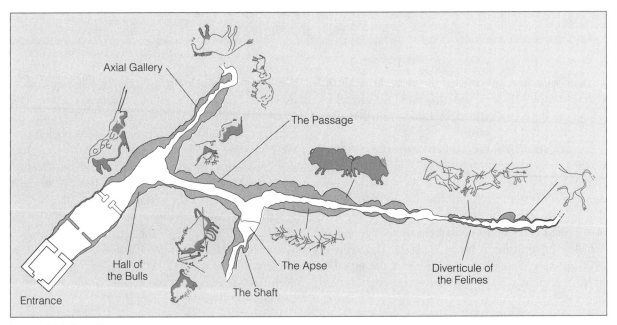

Figure 14-9 Map of Lascaux.

Looking Closer
The Discovery of Lascaux

Like so many major archaeological discoveries, Lascaux was found by accident. And it wasn't even a person who found it, but a dog.

Lascaux is located in the beautiful Dordogne region of southern France, a limestone karst topography rich in caves and rockshelters, many of which our human ancestors inhabited. In the 1940s, however, this region saw many refugees, people who were fleeing from the advancing German army. Life was hard and dangerous, but boys still found time to explore the hillsides and look for buried treasure.

In early September, several boys were hiking through the hills around Lascaux. The eldest was 18-year-old Marcel Ravidat (nicknamed "Jailbird" after a character in the novel *Les Miserables*). His dog, Robot, became lost, but the boys eventually found him in a shallow pit. Farmers once dumped animal carcasses there, and the dog was no doubt intrigued by lingering odours. Bending down to scoop up his dog, Ravidat also became intrigued when he felt cold air rising from a small hole in the pit's bottom.

The boys had heard rumours of a tunnel that connected a 16th-century manor house to the Montignac castle, a tunnel that locals said contained treasure (of course). Ravidat decided that the hole was an entrance to the tunnel and, on September 12, 1940, he returned with three other boys—Simon Coencas, Georges Agniel, and Jacques Marsal—to explore it. Using improvised tools, they dug down, eventually breaking into a cavern. As their homemade paraffin lanterns lit the way, the boys crawled down a long pile of rubble. At the bottom, they found a pool of water surrounded by low gleaming white walls. They explored farther.

The boys thought they were in a tunnel, and so they were stunned when they saw a vividly painted horse in the flickering lights. Holding their lights higher, they could see that the entire ceiling was painted. Reindeer, horses, a bear, and abstract markings covered the walls; bulls circled the ceiling. The boys just stood and stared. It was better than treasure.

They explored the cave over the next few days, finding more passages and images. Ravidat undertook the dangerous climb down into the well, where he found the now-famous bird-man image. The boys guessed that the images were old, but they had no idea that they were looking at some of the world's oldest art.

artisans must have constructed platforms to reach the ceiling. Beneath these paintings is room for groups of people to have participated in rituals; whether they did so, however, is unknown.

Moving straight ahead, you enter the narrow Axial Gallery, which slopes more deeply into the earth. Many horses are on the walls here, with some aurochs and stags. Two of the horses have what appear to be spears or darts shooting toward them. A long line of black dots appear beneath a large stag in a bellowing posture; a horse faces the stag. Lewis-Williams sees these dots as evidence of the merging of abstract and representational images that occurs in trance.

Near the end of the Axial Gallery is one of the most intriguing images in Lascaux. Painted on a jutting piece of rock is a life-size image of a horse, upside-down and apparently falling through the air. This image is not entirely visible until you walk around the bulge in the wall, single file. Several flint blades, covered in ochre and jammed into a crack, were found near this horse image. Walking around the "falling" horse, you encounter another horse, this one upright, and then the end of the passage.

Retracing your steps, you move back through the Hall of the Bulls and to the left. Passing through a low opening, you enter the Passage—this one longer than the Axial Gallery. The original opening was even smaller than it is today, and Upper Paleolithic artisans had to crawl through it.

In the Passage, the walls bear no calcite and the stone is softer. More horses and bulls are painted and

The boys informed a local schoolteacher, who brought word to Abbé Henri Breuil (1877–1961). Breuil was a priest, but he was also a scholar of Upper Paleolithic cave art (he taught for a while at the Collège de France). He had found and explored several caves, and professionals acknowledged his expertise with the title "the Pope of Prehistory." He would later explore and document the art in Lascaux, which he called the "Sistine Chapel of Prehistory."

But with a war on, there was little to be done immediately. Breuil advised the boys to pitch camp near the mouth of the cave and protect it. To their credit, the boys did exactly that. They faithfully guarded the cave, leading visitors through to prevent destruction and living in a conical log hut (after their tent burned down) heated by a wood stove through the winter of 1940–41.

But the war intensified. In the summer of 1942, Ravidat joined a resistance group, and Marsal was captured by the German army and sent to a labour camp. Coencas lost his parents, though he himself was saved by the French Red Cross. Agniel returned home to help support his parents.

And so Lascaux, the greatest of the French caves, sat until 1947, when work finally began again at the site. In 1948, it was opened to visitors, and Marsal became a guide. A ventilation system was installed in 1958 but, by 1963, the steady stream of visitors had brought in more humidity and microorganisms than the system could handle, and a green fungus began to cover the paintings. The cave was closed to the public and remains closed to this day, although the fungus has been removed. Only a few people are allowed to visit the site each week, and the waiting list is several years long.

Fortunately, the French government constructed an astonishingly precise replica of the Hall of the Bulls only 200 metres from the real cave. Lascaux II opened to the public in 1983, and a reunion meeting there in 1986 brought the four friends together at the cave again.

Lascaux continues to figure prominently in analyses of Upper Paleolithic cave art, and its magnificence is enjoyed by the tens of thousands who visit Lascaux II each year. And it all began with a lost dog.

engraved on the walls, although they are not as well preserved as in other parts of the cave. Images are piled up on top of one another, and the art here seems to be less "composed" than in the Axial Gallery and the Hall of the Bulls.

About 15 metres down the Passage, you encounter the Apse on your right, a small domed chamber with walls covered in engravings and a few paintings. Many different species are present—horses, bison, aurochs, ibex, deer, and perhaps even a wolf and lion. These images also overlay one another, producing a confusing jumble. Many engraved lines cut through the images.

Behind the Apse is the "Shaft" or "Well," a 5 metre-deep pit. Stone lamps were found at the bottom—turned upside down, as if the users meant to extinguish them. At the bottom of the pit is one of the oddest images of Upper Paleolithic art, which we show in Figure 14-10: A bison, his head lowered in defensive posture, appears to have a spear through the body. Some interpret the lines emanating from its belly to be entrails. In front of the bison is a stick figure of a man, his penis apparently erect, who appears to be falling backward from the bison's blow. The figure only has four fingers, however, and his head looks more like that of a bird. Beneath the man is a long vertical line, with what appears to be a bird perched on its top. The meaning of this image is the source of endless speculation.

Climbing out of the Shaft (which today is covered by a grid and accessed by a ladder), you return to the Passage and continue moving down its length. The walls contain more images for the next 15 metres or

Figure 14-10 Bison and "falling man" in Lascaux. It is not known if these images were painted at the same time (as a "scene") or at different times.

Source: Charles & Josette Lenars/CORBIS Canada

images appear in many caves and were used over thousands of years.

We do not know the specific meanings of these world-famous images (and, in truth, we probably never will). Lewis-Williams thinks that this art is somehow related to altered states of consciousness, but the images themselves could not, of course, have been produced while the artist was in a trance state, because one would need to be fully conscious to mix the paints, negotiate the cave's twists and turns with a stone lamp, and build scaffolding where needed. But Lewis-Williams thinks that the paintings at Lascaux and elsewhere provide firm evidence of Upper Paleolithic people trying to come to terms with understanding the meaning of altered states of consciousness—dreams and trances.

He sees the larger chambers, like the Hall of the Bulls, as places where communal rituals may have taken place, with people seeking assistance from a spirit world that existed belowground. Although the floor of Lascaux was damaged before it was investigated, the floors at Grotte Chauvet contain many human footprints, some 25,000 or more years old. Some of the prints are big and some are small, telling us that people of all ages visited even more remote portions of this cave.

Lewis-Williams also suggests that the distribution of art within a cave may parallel the stages of trances. In the front chamber are animals that figured in the lives of Upper Paleolithic people. Here, too, we find some abstract signs—the rectangles, wavy lines, and rows of dots that are apparent in early stages of trance. Deeper inside the cave, the narrowing passageway mimics the movement into the deeper states of trance. Lewis-Williams suggests that the falling horse at the end of the Axial Gallery is not falling at all, but it is instead an artist's representation of the vortex that one senses in the deeper stages of trance.

so, and then the images cease as the passage narrows and the ceiling drops. You encounter the two charging bison that we mentioned above—the ones that appear to be running toward and around you. After dropping to your knees and crawling along the cave floor, you encounter the Diverticule of the Felines, with its soft clay walls. If you are a small person, you are crouching; a larger person might be lying on his stomach.

Here there are aurochs and horses and bison, but also large cats—panthers or cave lions. Spears appear to pierce some of them, others are cut by lines or geometric markings or have lines emanating from their mouths and anuses. The images are well composed but seem to have been more hastily engraved than others in the cave. This section of the cave was perhaps rarely visited, because otherwise its soft clay walls would not have survived so well.

What Does All This Mean?

Leaving Lascaux, you might turn to look at the Hall of the Bulls one last time, trying to imagine how the scene would appear in the flickering light of a stone lamp. Something significant obviously transpired in these dark places. The aurochs, bison, and horses painted on Lascaux's walls and ceilings were not the fleeting whimsy of a Paleolithic artist. The same

Farther into the cave, we see "confused" images, such as those in the Apse and the Diverticule of the Felines. These, Lewis-Williams suggests, may represent the merging of abstract and natural images in the deeper stages of trance or efforts by one shaman to bond with the power of another by drawing an image over that drawn by another shaman. Although rare in Upper Paleolithic art (and absent at Lascaux), occasional animal images take on human characteristics. They walk on two feet, sometimes hold their front legs in a human way, or turn to stare at the observer with an eerily human gaze. These might record instances where observers entered the deepest stages of trance and were unable to see the difference between themselves and animals.

Lewis-Williams suggests that vision quests may have been held in the deepest cave recesses. Without food or water, the total darkness and silence of a cave is a perfect medium for the production of visions. Perhaps people of the Upper Paleolithic saw caves as one place to access the spirit world.

Recall that some images make use of the bumps and contours of a cave's wall; Lewis-Williams believes this is more than a clever artistic trick. Shamans in hunting-and-gathering cultures often speak of a strong yet permeable membrane between themselves and the spirit world. Lewis-Williams suggests that the nature of trance would have suggested that portions of the spirit world lie belowground. By mimicking the vortex of trance, caves are the closest a person could come to the spirit world; the rest of the journey had to be made through trance. If the cave wall is the membrane between this world and the spirit world, then paintings and engravings were perhaps ways to access that spirit world. By using the cave's contours, the artist makes the painting more a part of the cave wall itself and, in so doing, increases its power. The flints, teeth, and bones left shoved into cracks may also have been similar efforts to break through the membrane and contact the spirit world.

In sum, Lewis-Williams argues that Upper Paleolithic art is not art for art's sake; nor is it fertility or hunting magic. Instead, he argues that the art reflects humanity's effort to come to grips with the perception that their quotidian life was not all that made up existence, to answer the question "What is the meaning of life?" And that fact gives us, the denizens of the 21st century, a strong link to the artisans who painted bulls on the ceilings of caves by torch light thousands of years ago.

Conclusion

An archaeology of the mind attempts to move beyond the more easily accessible matters of diet and settlement patterns to religion, ritual, and cosmology. People respond to their world through culture, an integrated set of symbolic meanings that are communicated through material culture. But given that there is no necessary link between symbols and their meanings, the development of reliable middle-range theory is almost impossible, and so this crucial area of human behaviour often eludes archaeologists. Successful efforts rely upon historically linked ethnographic analogies, but these are limited to the more recent prehistory of regions with good ethnographic data. More ancient symbolic systems must be studied in ways that make use of uniformitarian elements of human neurology or perhaps a few symbolic universals (though these remain to be demonstrated).

Summary

- Although processual archaeology was initially optimistic that all aspects of the human condition were available for archaeological investigation, the proponents of processual approaches during the 1970s and 1980s were lukewarm, if not outright hostile, toward efforts to interpret symbols and construct an "archaeology of the mind."

- Modern cognitive archaeology aims to study the perception, description, and classification of the universe; the nature of the supernatural; the principles, philosophies, and values by which human societies are governed; and the ways in which aspects of the world, the supernatural, or human values are conveyed in art.

■ Studying these ancient modes of thought requires the interpretation of symbols, objects, or acts (verbal and nonverbal) that by cultural convention stands for something else *with which it has no necessary connection*. This means that, without some ethnographic context, there is no obvious way to connect a symbol to its meaning.

■ Archaeologists attempt to understand past religions—the specific set of beliefs based on one's ultimate relation to the supernatural. Such religious beliefs are manifested in everyday life through rituals—behaviours such as prayer, music, feasting, sacrifice, and taboos. As such, ritual is a material manifestation of the abstract idea of religion and archaeology's easiest portal to the study of ancient religions.

■ Archaeologists also attempt to understand cosmology. This encompasses how past cultures explain their universe—how it originated and developed; how the various parts fit together and what laws they obey—and express their concern with what the future of the universe holds.

■ Where archaeologists have some ethnographic data available that are closely related to the archaeological case, they may be able to extrapolate backward from the present to the past. Even these cases, however, harbour the chance that a symbol meant something different in the past than it does in the present.

■ Iconography, a culture's expression of abstract ideas in art and writing systems, can also be used to reconstruct the religious and other ideas that stand behind the art.

■ The study of ancient symbols runs the risk of becoming a free-for-all, with any interpretation being as valid as another. It is perhaps especially important, then, that the study of ancient iconography and other manifestations of a culture's cosmology and religion adhere to the canons of scientific analysis.

■ In instances where ethnographic data are not available, the archaeologist must be more restrained in his or her interpretations and focus not on the specific meaning of particular symbols, but look to the more general character of thought itself.

Additional Reading

CANADIAN RESOURCES

Dawson, P., and Levy, R. M. (2006). Constructing a 3D computer model of a Thule whalebone house using laser scanning technology. *Journal of Field Archaeology 30*(2005), 443–455.

Steinbring, Jack. (1998). Aboriginal rock painting sites in Manitoba. *Manitoba Archaeology Journal, 8*(1, 2), 153.

OTHER RESOURCES

Bahn, Paul. (1998). *The Cambridge Illustrated History of Prehistoric Art.* Cambridge: University of Cambridge Press.

Hall, Robert L. (1997). *An Archaeology of the Soul: North American Indian Belief and Ritual.* Urbana: University of Illinois Press.

Von Hagen, Adriana, and Morris, Craig. (1998). *The Cities of the Ancient Andes.* London: Thames and Hudson.

Online Resources

COMPANION WEBSITE

Visit *http://www.archaeology1ce.nelson.com* to access a wide range of material to help you succeed in your introductory archaeology course. These include flashcards, Internet exercises, Web links, and practice quizzes.

RESEARCH ONLINE WITH INFOTRAC COLLEGE EDITION

From the Student Companion Website, you can access the InfoTrac College Edition database, which offers thousands of full-length articles for your research.

15 Understanding Key Transitions in World Prehistory

The interior of a Northwest Coast plank house, Nootka Sound, painted by John Webber, 1878. By about 1500 years ago, Northwest Coast societies were living in large multi-family plank houses similar to these. There is good archaeological evidence to support the idea that these groups were ranked societies. This level of social complexity was likely achieved through an economy based on stored salmon, which was used to support other seasonal resources. Many archaeologists believe that the seeds of more complex societies lie within such groups, which are often referred to as "complex hunter-gatherers."

Source: Historical Picture Archive/CORBIS Canada

Preview

This chapter will introduce two milestones in the long-term evolution of human culture and, simultaneously, examine the role that paradigms play in interpreting the past.

Before considering these milestones, we will consider unilineal evolution, a now-defunct paradigm through which early anthropologists attempted to explain cultural evolution. We then concentrate on how archaeologists have tried to explain the origins of agriculture and the origins of civilization (and the "state"), each a major transition in long-term human history. As we examine the paradigms and explanatory theories used by archaeologists to understand these transitions, we emphasize two points. First, whereas each paradigm or theory contributes something to our understanding of these transitions, no single paradigm appears to give a complete accounting. Second, we emphasize the importance of differentiating between the specific processes at work, which can vary tremendously from case to case, and the general conditions that engender cultural change, which may be more universal.

Introduction

Archaeologists consider many kinds of questions, from small ones, such as "Is this a potsherd?" to big ones, such as "What is human nature?" Answering the broader questions of cultural evolution is one of archaeology's most significant contributions to anthropology. In this chapter, we illustrate the different ways that archaeologists approach two of archaeology's perennial "big" questions: the origins of agriculture and the origins of a form of political organization that anthropologists call the "state."

Earlier, we emphasized that archaeologists approach their research from both scientific and humanistic points of view. This is more than a simple difference in taste, because the study of human history requires its own particular blend of methods and theories. Laboratory scientists can always repeat their experiments, changing one variable while holding others constant, to determine what effect a particular variable has on the outcome. But archaeology (and the other historical sciences) cannot do this. The Inka civilization of the high Andes Mountains, for exam-

ple, existed only once and will never happen again. One cannot rewind history and replay it with one different variable—say, by changing the Andean Mountains to a desert—to see what happens.

Humanistic research directs us to the "when," "how," and "what" questions of prehistory. This research defines the particular processes and events at work in a given case. But to answer "why" questions, archaeologists benefit from a more comparative approach, one that looks for patterns among specific historical sequences that point to the general *conditions* of cultural change. To understand, for example, why civilizations and states evolved (terms we will define below), we can compare what happened in Egypt, China, Mexico, and other places where such forms of human organization first appeared. Doing this helps define how sequences of development were similar or different, leading us to suggest hypotheses that might explain general patterns in human cultural evolution.

Throughout this exercise, you should keep in mind a distinction between "necessary" and "sufficient" conditions of change. "Necessary conditions" must exist for a particular change to occur; "sufficient conditions" are the minimal ones needed for a change to occur. A basic knowledge of plant reproduction, for instance, is *necessary* for an agriculturalist (because you can't farm unless you know that plants come from seeds). But, as we demonstrate below, such knowledge is apparently not *sufficient* to inspire all foragers to transform themselves into agriculturalists. Other conditions must be in place for this economic change to occur.

Evolutionary Studies

Why did agriculture begin where it did? Why did farming not appear in other places? Why did large states—with their magnificent architecture, artwork, writing, and calendars—appear in some places and not in others?

A century ago, Western scholars answered these questions with a paradigm known today as **unilineal cultural evolution.** Before going any further, you must understand that *anthropology discarded unilineal cultural evolution a long time ago.* So, why bring it up at all? Evolutionary frameworks have been around since before the days of Charles Darwin, some with strong racist overtones. So, at the outset, we want to be clear about which evolutionary paradigms we are endorsing, and which we believe must be avoided.

Unilineal Cultural Evolution

The 19th century was an exciting time for European intellectuals. Recall from Chapter 1 that Boucher de Perthes was retrieving stone artifacts from France's river gravels and claiming a great antiquity for them. By the second half of the century, it was clear that Europe, as well as the New World, had an ancient history. What, European scholars asked themselves, had the past been like?

At the same time, several European countries had established themselves as major colonial powers. In their colonies in Africa, Asia, and the Americas, west Europeans encountered people who were strikingly different from themselves. Why, Europeans asked, were the peoples of the world so diverse?

They found answers to both questions in the paradigm of unilineal cultural evolution. To understand

why, we must remember the degree to which 19th-century scholarship in the West depended on Enlightenment philosophy (see Chapter 3)—especially the notion of progress. Recall that Enlightenment thinking held that progress resulted from increasingly "rational" thought, which allowed people to acquire the wealth and leisure time necessary to control nature and improve themselves morally. "Progress," in the Enlightenment sense, meant moving not only toward material perfection, but toward moral and spiritual perfection as well.

Enlightenment philosophy viewed the human past as a record of the march toward perfection. By the mid-19th century, archaeology had demonstrated that Europeans had passed through several stages in their progress to modernity (enshrined in the now-famous Stone, Bronze, and Iron Ages). But archaeology was a fledging science, lacking adequate methods to reconstruct the details of the past. Stratified sites showed technological change but, without the necessary middle-range theory, the archaeological record remained silent on matters such as kinship, politics, or social organization.

But this hardly stopped Western scholars, who attempted to reconstruct the past using an Enlightenment-era version of the **comparative method.** Today, this term refers to the testing of hypotheses against a range of human societies, but in the 19th century, the "comparative method" translated cultural diversity into a neat, evolutionary sequence, in which *different living peoples represented different stages in humanity's march of progress.* The comparative method argued that people were different because some had made more progress than others, and that consequently the world's different peoples provided living snapshots of the past.

Although Enlightenment philosophy held that all people shared the same capacity for progress, it seemed clear that some had done better than others. Why?

unilineal cultural evolution The belief that human societies have evolved culturally along a single developmental trajectory. Typically, such schemes depict Western civilization as the most advanced evolutionary stage; anthropology rejects this idea.

comparative method In Enlightenment philosophy, the idea that the world's existing peoples reflect different stages of human cultural evolution.

Darwin and the Origin of Species

With the Bible to guide them, many 19th-century scholars believed that the diversity of animal life arose in the biblical act of Creation. But just as the archaeological record showed that human societies had changed through time, the paleontological record likewise reflected multiple significant changes in animal life through the ages. Initially, scholars attributed this diversity to the biblical flood, but growing evidence suggested that many changes were gradual, not catastrophic. Was species diversity really a product of a one-time act of creation, or was something else involved?

With the publication of *On the Origin of Species* in 1859, Charles Darwin (1809–1882) provided a new way to understand biological diversity. Darwin's revolutionary volume suggested that, because the world's food supply is inherently inadequate, the young of any species must struggle to survive. Most don't make it. The survivors who live to foster the next generation do so because of fortuitously favoured characteristics. Consequently, through the process of **natural selection,** some physical characteristics are passed along to the next generation, and others are not. (Exactly how this happened was mysterious because genetics was all but unknown at the time.) The evolutionary process, being gradual and continuous, eventually gives rise to new species as individuals appear with characteristics that permit them to inhabit a new environment or a new niche. Darwin's ingenious argument thus introduced the notion that organisms descend from a common ancestor, and it provided evidence that the earth and its various life forms are dynamic and ever-changing.

Although the word "evolution" will always be associated with Darwin, he used the word "evolved" only once in the first edition of *Origin*. And although Darwin would later write about humans (in *The Descent of Man*), in *Origin* he mentioned humans only once—on nearly the last page (see Chapter 1). Nevertheless, the far-reaching implications of his work were hardly lost on scholars of ancient human history.

natural selection The process through which some individuals survive and reproduce at higher rates than others because of their genetic heritage; leads to the perpetuation of certain genetic qualities at the expense of others.

Lubbock's Pre-historic Times and Social Darwinism

Darwin's neighbour in Kent, England was the banker and statesman John Lubbock (1834–1913), later known as Lord Avebury. He was also an armchair anthropologist and, in 1865, he published the 19th century's most influential archaeology textbook, *Pre-historic Times, as Illustrated by Ancient Remains, and the Manners and Customs of Modern Savages.* In it, Lubbock married the Enlightenment's comparative approach with a rudimentary (and not entirely correct) understanding of natural selection.

Lubbock used the Enlightenment's comparative method to illustrate the life of the "paleolithic" (Old Stone Age) and "neolithic" (New Stone Age) people by reference to contemporary "primitives"—meaning the native peoples of Africa, Asia, and Australia. Lubbock argued that modern primitives were to archaeology as modern pachyderms were to paleontology. Although Lubbock made no specific analogies between particular living peoples and archaeological cultures, the implication was clear: Contemporary "primitives" were living approximations of what Europeans used to be.

Although not the only (or even the first) scholar to suggest this, Lubbock was highly influential. In fact, others soon expanded his argument, suggesting that living "primitives" were not merely "like" the past—they were in fact *living relics of prehistory.* Australian Aborigines were said to be lineal descendants of Neanderthals, and Eskimos were the descendants of the Magdalenians (the people who produced the Upper Paleolithic rock art of Europe). Using the comparative approach, these scholars barely needed archaeology. If you wanted to know what the past was, just find a living people who approximated the archaeological culture and describe them. There was no need to infer anything from archaeology, because the past still existed!

So, why did some people *appear* to be "back in the past" while others had apparently made so much progress?

Remember that scientific paradigms exist within a social context; for the 19th century, this meant colonialism. European scholars were unable to escape the belief in racial inequality that colonialism fostered. In 19th-century **social Darwinism,** cultural evolution became an extension of biological evolution by sug-

TABLE 15-1 Morgan's Three Phases of Human Cultural Evolution

PHASE	SUBPHASE	HALLMARK	EXAMPLE
Savagery	Lower	Subsistence of fruit and nuts	None survived into historical period.
	Middle	Fish, Fire	Australian aboriginals, Polynesians
	Upper	Bow and arrow	Athapaskan tribes of Hudson's Bay Territory
Barbarism	Lower	Pottery	Eastern Native American tribes
	Middle	Animal Domestication; construction with adobe, brick, and mortar; irrigation	Pueblos
	Upper	Iron smelting	Grecian tribes of the Homeric Age and Germanic tribes of the time of Caesar
Civilization		Phonetic alphabet; literacy records	Ancient civilization: Greece and Rome. Modern Civilization: Britain

gesting that both people and social forms compete for survival, with the richest and most powerful becoming the "fittest." Lower socioeconomic classes were seen as "the least fit" of industrial European society, and "primitive" peoples were the "least fit" people of the 19th-century world.

Social Darwinists argued that human societies varied in their "evolutionary" status from highly evolved groups (the Europeans) to those who differed only slightly from the advanced apes. Cultural differences, they believed, were grounded in biological differences. Today, of course, we know that culture has nothing to do with biology, because any person can be enculturated into any culture.

Lubbock, however, argued that through the process of natural selection, humanity was improving biologically, culturally, intellectually, and spiritually. Left alone, capitalist societies would prosper and improve. In fact, Lubbock concluded on an upbeat note: "The future happiness of our race, which poets hardly ventured to hope for, science boldly predicts."

The downside, of course, is that the world's "primitives" were doomed. In Lubbock's view, these people had not evolved sufficiently, and no degree of remedial education could repair the damage done by millennia of natural selection. Although neither Darwin nor Lubbock advocated exploitation of these populations, both believed that "primitive" peoples were condemned to extinction. Thus, the paradigm of unilineal evolution provided "scientific" justification for British colonization of the world.

Lewis Henry Morgan's Ancient Society

Across the Atlantic, one of the best known of the unilineal theorists was Lewis Henry Morgan (1818–1881), a Rochester lawyer-turned-ethnologist. He lived at a time when Americans saw United States history as all about progress and destiny, when they considered its westward expansion both inevitable and laudable.

In *Ancient Society* (1877), Morgan divided the progress of human achievement into three major phases—savagery, barbarism, and civilization (Table 15-1), a unilineal scheme that defined a kind of evolutionary ladder. The bottom rung was for the primeval, rudimentary, and primitive; the top rung belonged to Western civilization (particularly that of western Europe), with other groups and cultural practices arrayed between these two extremes. In this view of unilineal evolution, all peoples were thought to pass through the same stages—the ascending rungs of the evolutionary ladder—if they were intellectually capable of doing so. As the author of anthropology's first textbook, Edward Tylor (see Chapter 2), wrote, "The institutions of man are as distinctly stratified as the earth on which he lives. They succeed each other in

social Darwinism The extension of the principles of Darwinian evolution to social phenomena; it implies that conflict between societies and between classes of the same society benefits humanity in the long run by removing "unfit" individuals and social forms. Social Darwinism assumed that unfettered economic competition and warfare were primary ways to determine which societies were "fittest."

series substantially uniform over the globe, independent of what seem the comparatively superficial differences of race and language."

But even top-rung Western civilization was not the evolutionary peak. Recall that Enlightenment thought was grounded in progress—technological, cultural, moral, *and* spiritual. Above the elite classes of Europe on the evolutionary scale stood the angels, and above the angels was God Himself. Viewed this way, the British aristocracy was closer to God than, say, the Australian Aborigines were. By today's standards, the hubris of colonialism is simply shocking.

How "Evolution" Became a Dirty Word

In the early 20th century, the nascent field of anthropology turned against this **ethnocentric** notion of progress. Franz Boas (1858–1942), often called the "father of American anthropology," and his students rejected unilineal evolution as a valid way of studying the human condition. In large measure, this was because of the paradigm's racist overtones and the colonial excesses that it supported. A Jewish immigrant from Germany, Boas was quite familiar with exclusion and ethnocentrism.

Boas argued that each culture is unique and should be valued as such. He argued that cultures change in ways unique to themselves and that current evidence did not warrant sweeping generalizations. Instead, Boas argued in favour of **historical particularism.** He pointed out that, because cultural evolution was so complex and had taken so many diverse paths, there was no single line of progressive evolution and, consequently, cultures cannot be placed into a unilineal evolutionary scheme. Human institutions such as matrilineal descent, slavery, private property, or formal courts are associated with an array of other sociocultural features. Complex forms of kinship, for example, can accompany the simplest kinds of technology (as among Australian Aborigines).

Although Boas admitted to some degree of regularity in history, he believed that earlier researchers had exaggerated the patterns. And even if patterns did exist, Boas believed that the patient accumulation of ethnographic detail and historical facts must precede the construction of any generalities concerning human cultural evolution.

The Return of Evolution

Unilineal cultural evolution collapsed under the assault from Boas and his students. But research conducted under the paradigm of historical particularism eventually amassed sufficient data from ethnography and archaeology to show strong regularities in cultural evolution.

Within a decade after Boas's death—he died at lunch after presenting an anti-racism lecture at Columbia University—evolution paid another visit to the halls of anthropology. Although evolutionary thinking does not today dominate anthropological explanation, it does play a significant role in archaeology. Evolutionary thought has changed markedly over time, and several current paradigms compete for Darwin's mantle.

A complete description of those paradigms is beyond our scope, but before we consider explanations of world prehistory, we wish to point out three key differences between unilineal and modern evolutionism.

First, modern evolutionism contains none of the racist or moral overtones of 19th-century unilineal evolutionism. Contemporary evolutionism does not believe that differences between cultures are a product of differences in intellect or morality. Instead, as part of a larger materialist paradigm, modern evolutionism accentuates the role of ecological, demographic, and/or technological factors in conditioning how cultures change.

Second, contemporary evolutionary thinking recognizes that, if natural selection is at work on cultural phenomena, it operates in a far subtler manner than it does among animals. Natural selection depends on differential reproductive success for particular traits to become more prevalent. This means that plants or animals with a favoured trait survive and reproduce at a higher rate than those who lack the trait—among animals, by either attracting more mates or by providing more resources to their young. But whereas animals pass on most behavioural traits genetically, humans pass on critical behaviours through culture.

ethnocentric (also ethnocentrism) The attitude or belief that one's own cultural ways are superior to any other.

historical particularism The view that each culture is the product of a unique sequence of developments in which chance plays a major role in bringing about change.

Individual humans can also adapt to change, alter their behaviour, and adopt new technologies. Their genetic composition does not determine what "tools" they have to be successful in life. Although anthropology today is marked by considerable debate over the role of natural selection in cultural behaviour, anthropologists agree that (1) cultural behaviour is not genetic, and therefore (2) the transmission of cultural information from generation to generation does not depend directly on biological reproduction (although one may affect the other).

Third, although unilineal evolutionists argued over the details of the evolutionary sequence, they united in believing in a single immutable sequence. Modern evolutionism is not concerned with the evolutionary sequence of particular cultural behaviours like matrilineal kinship or monotheistic religions. The human past is vastly more complex than 19th-century scholars imagined it to be.

More than a century of archaeological research has amply demonstrated the intricate details that make up a particular historical sequence; this is the *specific* evolution of particular cultures. But modern evolutionary theory looks at prehistory to extract the "big picture," the *general* evolutionary pattern that characterized the deep human past. It is this long-term patterning that concerns us here.

An Evolutionary Sequence

In the rest of this chapter, we examine two major transitions in human cultural evolution—the origins of agriculture and the origins of the state. We begin by situating these transitions into a generalized historical sequence that illustrates some patterns in human cultural evolution (Table 15-2).

Prior to about 12,000 years ago, all our ancestors lived in hunting-and-gathering bands. Although few hunter-gatherer bands survive today, they were common in many parts of the world during the 19th century, surviving on wild plants and animals and often changing their camps several times throughout the year. Most settlements housed fewer than three dozen people, although larger aggregations occurred when resources were particularly abundant.

Hunting-and-gathering bands are *usually* egalitarian (refer to Chapter 13). They lack hereditary differences in social rank and are integrated on the basis of age and gender. Leadership is informal and temporary, based mostly on age, competence, and personal magnetism. The Great Basin Shoshone of the 19th century are a frequently cited example of bands, as are the Inuit (Eskimo), South African Bushmen, and Australian Aborigines.

Were it not for the domestication of plants and animals, the entire world would still be living a

TABLE 15-2 Summary of Differences among Bands, Tribes, Chiefdoms, and States

CHARACTERISTIC	BAND	TRIBE	CHIEFDOM	STATE
Subsistence	Foraging	Foraging, horticulture, pastoralism (herding)	Agriculture; pastoralists often incorporated within society.	Agriculture, industrial, pastoral separated as specialists.
Economic organization	Equal access to strategic resources through sharing and reciprocity	Reciprocity; limited redistribution of goods by charismatic leaders	Chief redistributes goods collected from lower-ranking people; society includes some non-food producers.	Elites control access to strategic resources like land and labour; includes many non-food producers such as specialists.
Political organization	Egalitarian; no permanent positions of authority	Egalitarian; temporary and limited roles of authority; competitive feasting to establish rank	Differences in status based on genealogical closeness to chief, who holds a permanent, inherited office.	State controlled by elites and run by administrative specialists; includes military and fiscal specialists.
Social organization	Based on actual and fictive kinship; major units are nuclear family and bands of flexible membership.	Kinship-based, egalitarian descent groups; less flexibility	Kinship important in determining rank; lineages are ranked in clans.	Class membership (elite or commoner) is most important; kinship and descent important within class.
Settlement pattern	Temporary camps; some seasonal settlement reoccupied.	Sedentary villages (temporary camps among pastoralists)	Sedentary villages of different sizes; ranked (chief's village has highest rank).	Hierarchy of settlements reflects administrative functions; may be cities.
Population density	Low	Low to medium	Medium to high	High

hunting-and-gathering lifestyle. But we know that agriculture came into being at several places over the past 10,000 years. Archaeologists often refer to agricultural crops as domesticated plants, because the plants are genetically manipulated versions of wild species that came to require human intervention for their continued survival. Modern maize, for example, would have a hard time propagating itself if humans stopped planting it.

It was largely with the advent of domesticated plants that **tribal societies** appeared. Characterized by larger and more sedentary settlements, tribal societies occur throughout the world and vary considerably in appearance. Although community size is generally larger than that of hunters and gatherers, autonomous village societies still lack hereditary differences in rank, and larger villages maintain no authority over smaller neighbouring communities. Although everyone in tribal society is equal at birth, considerable disparities in prestige can accrue during one's lifetime, and ritual privileges are often differentially distributed along gender lines. Early 20th-century examples include the Pueblo Indians of the American Southwest, communities in highland New Guinea, and many peoples of the Amazon Basin. Some hunting-and-gathering societies—ones that lived in environments that supported high population densities without recourse to agriculture—are classified as "tribal" as well (such as those along the Northwest Coast of North America, or the Hopewell culture of the midwestern United States; see Chapters 2, 13, and 14).

A third social form, ranked society (discussed in Chapter 13), sometimes evolved when the egalitarian ethic (which downplays success and prestige) gave way to the belief that individuals are inherently unequal at birth. Commonly, certain family groups are considered to have descended from esteemed ancestors, supernatural beings, or gods. The closer this relationship, the greater one's hereditary rank and power. Marrying wisely becomes a way to enhance the rank of your children.

In some societies, such as the Natchez (who lived along the lower Mississippi River at the time of European contact) and many African societies, smaller villages were subject to the powerful, hereditary leadership of the larger, stronger neighbouring communities. These societies—large-scale ranked societies with loss of village autonomy—are called chiefdoms. An example includes the prehistoric society of Moundville, which we discussed in Chapter 13.

Under certain conditions, **archaic states** evolved from competing chiefdoms. We use the term "archaic" to distinguish this ancient social form from modern industrial states, which are commonly governed by elected presidents or prime ministers. The term "state" refers to a form of political organization—not to be confused with its modern meaning as an entity within a nation.

Most archaic states operated as kingdoms, characterized by a strong and centralized government with a professional bureaucratic ruling class. The appearance of archaic states marks a major shift in human social organization, because these societies devalued the kinship bonds evident in chiefdoms, tribes, and bands. States maintained their authority through an established legal system and the power to wage war, levy taxes, and draft soldiers. Generally, states had populations numbering (at least) in the tens of thousands, and urban centres exhibited a high level of artistic and architectural achievement. A state religion was usually practised, even in areas of linguistic and ethnic diversity. The Classic Maya, Aztec, Inka, and ancient Egyptian societies are examples of archaic states.

One final term needs some attention: **civilization.** In common usage, "civilization" refers to behaviours that are ethnocentrically associated with proper behaviour and some definition of high culture. But in anthropological terms, no such value judgment is implied. Instead, "civilization" refers to characteristics often associated with the archaic state, such as writing and bureaucratic records, calendrical systems, and the construction of monumental architecture.

Patterns in the Evolutionary Sequence

This sequence tells us several things. First, we know that agriculture is a relatively recent phenomenon, developing only after the end of the Pleistocene

tribal societies A wide range of social formations that lie between egalitarian foragers and ranked societies (such as chiefdoms); tribal societies are normally horticultural and sedentary, with a higher level of competition than seen among nomadic hunter-gatherers.

archaic state A centralized political system found in complex societies, characterized by having a virtual monopoly on the power to coerce.

civilization A complex urban society with a high level of cultural achievement in the arts and sciences, craft specialization, a surplus of food and/or labour, and a hierarchically stratified social organization.

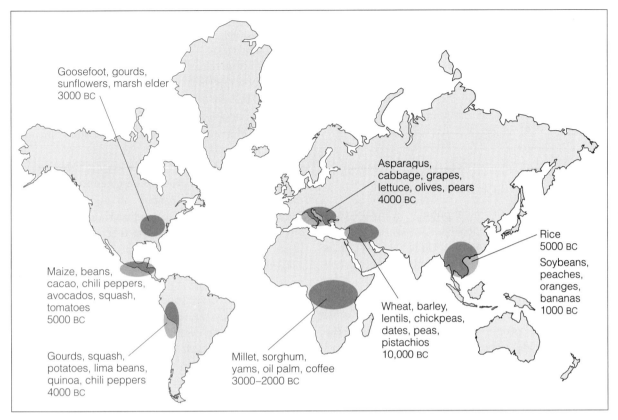

Figure 15-1 The major hearths of agriculture—places where various wild plants were independently domesticated—and the approximate dates that domestication occurred.

period (about 10,000 years ago). But once it appeared, agriculture spread rapidly throughout much of the world. The domestication of plants and animals was hardly a single event; instead, the process happened several times, in several different areas of the world. Figure 15-1 shows the major hearths of plant and animal domestication. These regions are all independent centres of domestication, unconnected to one another, although in many cases the plants and animals they produced eventually spread over much of the globe.

Note also that the shift from egalitarian to ranked society is associated with agriculture. Egalitarian societies are associated with hunting and gathering and **horticulture.** Chiefdoms and states tend to be associated with **intensive agriculture.**

Finally, we have learned that chiefdoms and archaic states appear even later in prehistory than agriculture, only in the past 5000 years or so, and they are always associated with high population densities. No hunter-gatherers live or lived in archaic states; no states are dependent on hunting and gathering for food.

In sum, a century of global archaeological research discerned some links among economy, social and political organization, and population density—links that will be well demonstrated as we explore the origins of agriculture and the origins of the archaic state.

Why Were Plants Domesticated?

Scholars of the 18th and 19th centuries were largely unconcerned with explaining the *process* of plant and animal domestication. They focused instead on historical questions, such as when did plant domestication

horticulture Cultivation using hand tools only and in which plots of land are used for a few years and then allowed to lie fallow.

intensive agriculture Cultivation using draft animals, machinery, or hand cultivation in which plots are used annually; often entails irrigation, land reclamation, and fertilizers.

begin, and did it come before or after the domestication of animals? This was, of course, a necessary step, because one cannot ask *why* something happened until you know roughly *when* and *how* it happened. But once archaeological data began to accumulate, archaeologists shifted their attention from the "what" and the "when" of plant and animal domestication to the "why."

The Unilineal Paradigm: Childe and Braidwood

The **oasis theory** was made popular in the 1940s by Australian–British archaeologist V. Gordon Childe (1892–1957). A prolific author, Childe was one of the first modern archaeologists to synthesize the archaeology of Europe and the Near East.

Childe knew that, as the Ice Age ended, the world's climate became warmer and drier. In desert areas, Childe argued, people and animals flocked to oases, such as the Nile River, in search of water and food. This association eventually produced a symbiotic relationship between animals and people. People drove away predators and fed animals their surplus grain. Animals became accustomed to humans and were gradually domesticated.

Childe thus assumed that people grew crops before they domesticated animals, but he was unclear about why they became agriculturalists. He simply suggested that people became familiar with the "nobler grasses"—ancient ancestors of modern wheat and barley—that grew on the banks of the Nile, where they thrived on alluvial soil enriched by annual flooding. Childe felt that it remained only for "some genius" to produce similar artificial conditions elsewhere through irrigation and begin to grow wheat and barley.

oasis theory Proposed by V. Gordon Childe, it argues that animal domestication arose as people, plants, and animals congregated around water sources during the arid years that followed the Pleistocene. In this scenario, agriculture arose because of "some genius" and preceded animal domestication.

hilly flanks theory Proposed by Robert Braidwood, it claims that agriculture arose in the areas where wild ancestors of domesticated wheat and barley grow, attributing agriculture's appearance to human efforts to continue to increase the productivity and stability of their food base, coupled with culture being "ready" to accept an agricultural lifeway.

Although Childe's explanation seemed plausible, the chronology for the Near East was sketchy, and no solid archaeological evidence for early food production was available. Shortly after World War II, Robert Braidwood (1907–2003) set out to search for that evidence. The hilly flanks of the mountains of southwestern Asia seemed a logical place to search because wild wheat, barley, and legumes grew there and wild cattle, sheep, and goats lived there.

So Braidwood set off for the foothills of Iraq and Turkey, directing excavations designed to test explanations regarding the origins of domestication. He obtained some of the first radiocarbon dates on early agriculture and, after learning that climate had been essentially stable during the period of animal and plant domestication, Braidwood rejected Childe's oasis theory.

In its place, Braidwood proposed a **hilly flanks theory,** which saw agriculture developing as a "logical outcome" of the evolutionary tendency to specialize. As foragers "settled in" after the Pleistocene, they became familiar with their plant and animal neighbours; eventually, this accumulated knowledge permitted them to cultivate rather than simply gather plants.

Although Childe and Braidwood disagreed about the "where" and "how" of plant domestication, both assumed that humanity continually seeks to improve its technology and subsistence. And, because they thought that plant domestication provided a more abundant and reliable economic base than foraging, they also assumed that all it took for agriculture to appear was the *idea* and the *capacity* (the necessary plants). Anyone, they thought, with the idea and capacity would switch from foraging to agriculture. In this regard, Childe and Braidwood still subscribed to a portion of the paradigm of unilineal evolution.

But their explanations ran afoul of both archaeological and ethnographic data. If the idea of agriculture is sufficient, then the transition from foraging to agriculture should be quick (at least in archaeological time). And yet nearly everywhere, that transition was slow. In the eastern woodlands of the United States, for example, native peoples grew squash, sunflower, marsh elder, and chenopods some 4000 years ago. Maize (known in North America as corn), an import from Mexico, appeared in the woodlands about 2000 years ago. But it was only 1100 years ago that a full-fledged agricultural economy based on maize appeared. Because they obviously had the idea of agriculture 4500 years ago and maize 2000 years ago, why didn't these people become full-time agriculturalists sooner?

Ethnographic research also turned up hunter-gatherers who knew about and understood agriculture, but who continued to hunt animals and gather. Ethnographer Richard Lee (University of Toronto) once asked /Xashe, a Ju/'hoansi man of Africa's Kalahari Desert, why he did not plant food. /Xashe's memorable response was, "Why should we plant when there are so many mongongos [edible nuts] in the world?"

The Materialist Paradigm: Population Pressure

Childe and Braidwood assumed that the idea for agriculture would be picked up by anyone who had it, but /Xashe reminds us that agriculture takes hard work. The forager who wants seeds simply picks and processes them; but the farmer must till the soil, plant the seeds, and later harvest, process, and probably store the seeds. Why would anybody take on the additional labour of agriculture?

In the 1960s, several archaeologists argued that agriculture was related to **population pressure** brought about by slow population growth. Lewis Binford (see Chapter 1) argued that people adopt domesticated plants *only when forced to do so.* In his **density-equilibrium model,** Binford rejected Braidwood's notion that agriculture developed simply because of the accumulation of knowledge. Rather than viewing agriculture as a chance to "move up the evolutionary scale," Binford proposed that agriculture happened when population growth outstrips an environment's **carrying capacity.** Population growth requires that some people move to more marginal environments, and it is these people who turn to agriculture to make up for the lack of high-ranked resources.

In framing this argument, Binford turned unilineal evolutionism on its head. Instead of agriculture being a step up in progress, it became the strategy implemented by the "losers," people who had to make marginal land productive—and who, in the end, needed to work harder. The unilineal evolutionists saw hunting and gathering as an onerous lifeway, with agricultural productivity providing a breakthrough. Binford's hypothesis suggested just the opposite. Who is right?

Is It Better to Farm or to Forage?

Binford assumed that some resources were collected more efficiently than others, but he lacked the data to back up this assumption. Bear in mind that the plants we know as the major agricultural plants—such as maize, wheat, millet, and rice—*did not exist* at the end of the Pleistocene. What did exist were their wild forerunners, but these were often substantially different from the domesticated plants of today.

The wild form of maize, for example, is southern Mexico's **teosinte,** a tall tropical grass with a small head of grains on it that is no bigger than your pinky. It looks nothing like the sweet corn you buy at the supermarket. Of all the wild plants that foragers in southern Mexico harvested, why did teosinte become a domesticated one?

The reason is that maize, and other plants that were eventually domesticated, has the latent genetic capacity to be modified. Human use of these plants over many generations—which included the intentional sowing of seeds with favourable characteristics (such as size)—constitutes natural selection. The result of this process is the vast maize fields of Iowa, the extensive rice terraces of Asia, the millet fields of Africa, and so on.

But in the beginning these domesticated plants were far more modest, and one wonders why hunter-gatherers would have bothered with them at all. To answer this question, we must consider a resource's **return rate:** the relationship between the amount of energy a resource provides measured against the amount of time it takes to procure and process (see "Looking Closer: Hunter-Gatherers as Optimal Foragers").

Return rates can be complicated by many factors, but experimental data show that large game generally

population pressure The effects of a population reaching carrying capacity.

density-equilibrium model Proposed by Binford, it attributes the origins of agriculture to population pressure in favourable environments that resulted in emigration to marginal lands, where agriculture was needed to increase productivity.

carrying capacity The number of people that a unit of land can support under a particular technology.

teosinte A plant native to southern Mexico; believed to be the wild ancestor of maize.

return rate The amount of energy acquired by a forager per unit of harvesting/processing time.

have high return rates, whereas seeds (including those of wild wheat, barley, and teosinte) have much lower rates. **Optimal foraging theory** predicts that, as high-return-rate resources (such as large game animals) become scarce, foragers add lower-return-rate resources (such as seeds) to their diet. Higher-return-rate resources can become scarce because of environmental change or because a human population has overexploited them. Ethnographic and experimental data suggest that people may have turned to the seeds of those plants that eventually became agricultural plants when high-ranked resources, such as large game, became scarce.

But many hunter-gatherers around the world expanded their diets to include a variety of plant resources—including native peoples of California and the Great Basin—yet they did not become agriculturalists (even though California is today one of the world's major agricultural regions). And when Steve Simms (Utah State University) and Ken Russell (1950–1992) conducted ethnoarchaeological research with Bedouins in Jordan, they found the return rate from cultivated wheat (which includes the cost of tilling the soil and sowing the seeds) was little different from the return rate of gathering wild wheat. So, what's the advantage of agriculture?

A Selectionist Perspective

The answer to this question may come from a third paradigm, one that focuses on the underlying process of natural selection.

David Rindos (1949–1996) argued that plant domestication is an example of **coevolution,** the result of natural selection operating simultaneously on both plants and the people using them. He argued that, because of some plants' genetic composition and because of how they must be harvested, the very act of harvesting them results in unintentional selection in such a way that the plants become dependent on humans for survival. And it is this side of the coevolutionary process that makes the plant species more productive, such that humans will in turn become more dependent on it: The humans and plants *coevolve.* This may happen, for example, when people plant seeds outside a plant's normal range. Eventually, the people and plants become mutually dependent: The people need the plants for food and the plants need the people to survive outside their normal range. So, whether humans become agriculturalists depends a lot on the genetic capacity of the plants at hand. Eventually, those agricultural plants may provide better return rates than the available wild plants. When that happens, people eschew the gathering of wild plants for domesticated ones.

Rindos ignored the impact of population growth or climate change. And he claimed that human intent doesn't matter, that humans "intended" to become agriculturalists as much as certain ant species "intended" to develop symbiotic relationships with fungi. As a Darwinian paradigm, the coevolutionary approach holds that if a particular behaviour, such as agriculture, increased the rate of survival of the young, then that behaviour would become more prevalent.

Another Look at the Environment

But humans foraged for hundreds of thousands of years before agriculture appeared in the early Holocene period. If Rindos is right, why didn't agriculture appear sooner?

Braidwood would have said that human culture was "not ready for it," but Peter Richerson (University of California, Davis), Robert Boyd (University of California, Los Angeles), and Robert Bettinger (University of California, Davis) argue that it was the environment that was not ready for it.

These scholars point out that the Pleistocene (the 2 million years preceding the Holocene) was an odd time in earth's climatic history. Thick glaciers covered vast parts of the globe and tied up a lot of the world's water supply. As you probably know, this means that sea level dropped. But sea level dropped because there was less water running into the ocean. And there was less water because the Pleistocene not only was colder than today, but also in many places was drier.

Additionally, the Pleistocene atmosphere contained less carbon dioxide (this is why, you will recall from Chapter 8, late Pleistocene radiocarbon dates are so far off from their calibrated calendar ages). Plants take in carbon dioxide through photosynthesis and release oxygen. Less carbon dioxide means that plants were

optimal foraging theory The idea that foragers select foods that maximize the overall return rate.

coevolution An evolutionary theory that changes in social systems are best understood as mutual natural selection among components rather than as a linear cause-and-effect sequence.

"asphyxiating" in the Pleistocene; consequently, plant productivity was lower. And, to make matters worse, climate was more variable during the Pleistocene than during the Holocene, making plants a less reliable source of food than animals before 10,000 years ago.

For these reasons, Richerson and his colleagues argue that agriculture *could not* have appeared before the Holocene. Rindos's process of coevolution could not have arisen until the Holocene, when plant exploitation could provide a sufficiently abundant and reliable food source. But Richerson adds that, by providing a reliable food source, agriculture caused human population to grow, and the ensuing population pressure forced neighbours to adopt agriculture as a way to increase food productivity (as Binford argued). As a result, agriculture quickly spread during the Holocene to most parts of the globe that could support it and where foraging did not provide higher return rates.

A Social Perspective

So far, each of the paradigms offered to explain the origins of agriculture has privileged the power of human intent and the conditions of environment, demography, and selection. But looking at what we know about agriculture around the world, we see another possibility. In some places, agriculture is indeed *preceded* by population growth—for example, in large sedentary communities. But in other places, such as southern Mexico (where maize was domesticated), sedentary villages appear a thousand or more years *after* plant domestication. And some regions that are suitable for agriculture, such as California, were occupied by hunting-and-gathering peoples until European contact, even though they were densely populated. Population and environment may not be the only relevant variables here.

Some archaeologists, such as Brian Hayden (Simon Fraser University), suggest that agriculture arose as a way to increase productivity so that certain individuals could garner prestige and power through competitive feasts and ostentatious displays of wealth in the form of exotic items obtained through trade (like the potlatch we described in Chapter 2). This increase in productivity, Hayden argues, was possible because new technologies such as nets, baskets, and grinding stones allowed hunter-gatherers to harvest resources such as fish and seeds efficiently, allowing people to create the food surpluses needed for competitive feasts. Hayden argues that efforts to increase productivity for these feasts led people to agriculture.

To support this explanation, Hayden points to another post-Pleistocene trend: the trade of exotic goods, such as carved shells, rare stones, and beads. These trade goods (along with exotic domesticated foods) may have figured in competitive feasts or other social displays of power. And Hayden suggests that this "food fight" theory explains why some of the earliest domesticates were not essential to subsistence, such as chili peppers, bottle gourds, and avocados.

The Origins of Agriculture in the Near East

Different paradigms clearly offer different explanations for the origins of agriculture, and each one makes some sense. To evaluate these alternatives, let's turn to the archaeology of the Near East, one of the world's major hearths of plant domestication.

In the Near East, agriculture originated in a broad arc of mountains in Israel, Jordan, Syria, Iraq, and Iran—sometimes called the **Fertile Crescent**—where wild wheat and barley still grow today. Although Braidwood saw no evidence for it, significant climate change occurred at the end of the Pleistocene. Based on data from palynology and other studies, we know that around 18,000 years ago the Near East was cooler and drier than it is today. Annual precipitation and temperature increased until about 13,500 B.P. but, between 13,000 and 11,600 B.P., the world saw a rapid return to cooler and drier but highly variable conditions during a climatic interval known as the **Younger Dryas.** After this time, climate returned to wetter and warmer conditions. And after 9000 B.P., the Near East became considerably more arid.

We can't tell exactly when intentional agriculture began, because it's difficult for paleoethnobotanists to distinguish wild wheat and barley from their early domesticated forms. The best evidence suggests that a full-time agricultural economy began about 10,000 to

Fertile Crescent   A broad arc of mountains in Israel, Jordan, Syria, Iraq, and Iran where wild wheat, barley, and other domesticated plants are found today.

Younger Dryas A climatic interval, 13,000 to 11,600 B.P., characterized by a rapid return to cooler and drier, but highly variable, climatic conditions.

Looking Closer
Hunter-Gatherers as Optimal Foragers

Behavioural ecology is the study of the evolutionary and ecological basis for human behaviour, and how such behaviour enables individuals to adapt to their environment. This perspective has been used to study the subsistence activities of hunter-gatherer societies in anthropology. Within the paradigm of behavioural ecology, individuals are seen as "strategists" who attempt to maximize material returns on their investments of time and labour. Maximum economic returns, usually measured in kcal/hr, are offset by the energy costs associated with searching for, capturing, and processing prey.

Optimal foraging theory (OFT) is a branch of behavioural ecology that defines the decision rules used by predators to achieve these maxi/min objectives. While OFT models were originally designed to examine the feeding behaviour of true predators (e.g., lions, birds, whales), grazing animals, and parasites, they have also been used to examine the foraging behaviour of humans. Not surprisingly, the use of OFT in anthropology has been criticized for ignoring the fact that humans select foods for symbolic as well as caloric reasons. OFT models also ignore the complexities of human social interaction, and its potential impact on foraging efficiency. Does behavioural ecology simplify human behaviour too much? Eric Alden Smith, an anthropologist who has used OFT to examine Inuit foraging strategies, doesn't think so. He argues that the approaches used in behavioural ecology are valid ways of reducing the complexities of human foraging behaviour to a first-order approximation.

During the 1970s Smith lived in the Inuit community of *Inujjuaq,* located on the eastern coast of Hudson Bay, where he studied the decision making of *Inujjuarmiut* Inuit foragers. The extent and movement of sea ice determines the frequencies and distributions of sea mammals in many regions of the Canadian Arctic. The Inujjuarmiut use their exten-

Figure 15-2 A beluga hunt.
Source: Kim Hill

sive knowledge of this sea ice environment of Hudson Bay to hunt a wide variety of birds, fish, and sea and land mammals. Individual hunters, or groups of between 2 and 15 hunters, harvest various animal species throughout the year. Smith was interested in determining what the optimal group sizes for different types of hunting should be. This is an important question because different group sizes have very different energy costs and energy returns. By way of illustration, foraging in groups can be more efficient when individuals are able to passively or actively share information about prey. Group foraging can also reduce variance in food capture rates because more people are searching for prey—simply put, the more you search, the more you find. However, return rates for foraging in groups begin to decline after the groups reach a certain size. Having more people may not necessarily increase the amount of food found—it only means that there are more mouths to feed.

So, just how big should a foraging group be? In an ideal world, foragers would know what the optimal group size was for each hunt type, and would have no problems joining such groups when they wanted to. In the world of OFT, however, things are rarely this simple. Let's look at two types of foragers that illustrate why this is so: "joiners" and "members." A joiner is someone who is considering joining a foraging group, while a member is someone who is already in a foraging group. OFT predicts that a joiner will decide to join a group as long as the energy return rates for doing so are greater than if s/he continued to forage alone. This is called the "joiner's rule." Once a group size reaches its optimum level, however, OFT predicts that members will begin excluding additional joiners or risk having their rates of energy return diminish. This is called the "member's rule." Not surprisingly, these two rules can create tension and conflict among individuals.

Smith collected information on all aspects of Inujjuarmiut hunting practices. Every time somebody from the community went out hunting, for example, he recorded the type of hunting they did, how many people were in the hunting party, how they knew each other, and the maximum per capita return rates (measured in kcal/hr). Smith then used OFT to derive the optimal group size for each hunt type practised by the Inujjuarmiut. Interestingly, the group sizes predicted by the OFT model were similar to those observed for most hunt types. Breathing-hole sealing and beluga whale hunting, however, had group sizes that exceeded the optimal sizes identified by OFT. Why might this be the case?

Smith points out that most OFT models treat individuals as self-interested agents. Inclusive fitness, on the other hand, sees natural selection as favouring those who take each other's interests into account. Smith observed that most Inuit hunting groups comprised individuals related to one another through kinship ties. If joiners and members were related to one another, then social tensions might be offset in groups that were growing beyond their optimal size. Although allowing younger, less experienced joiners into foraging groups would reduce energy gains in the short term, it would provide them with training that might actually increase energy gains over the long term. However, the Inujjuarmiut foraging groups associated with beluga whaling and breathing-hole sealing comprised individuals who were not that closely related. Instead, Smith thinks that these suboptimal hunting group sizes may partially reflect the fact that Inuit now live in settled communities rather than traditional camps.

During the 1950s and 1960s, the Canadian government moved Inuit groups such as the Inujjuarmiut into permanent settlements. Rather than the traditional camps of 50 to 60 individuals, Inuit soon found themselves living in communities of 600 to 1000 people. While living in such large numbers would have given members lots of joiners to choose from, it would have also made it difficult to control how many joiners might decide to participate in a hunt. Dawson once witnessed a beluga whale hunt while living in Arviat, Nunavut—an arctic community of about 2000 people. One evening, word got around the town that a pod of beluga whales had been sighted in a small bay. Chaos ensued as hunters piled into boats and roared off in search of the whales. A near disastrous collision between two boats made it evident to him that too many people had decided to take part in the hunt. Settlement life may result in other situations in which foraging groups of suboptimal size are formed.

While the application of OFT in anthropology has been criticized, it is nevertheless useful because it shows the evolutionary implications of small-group dynamics. How different are the tensions between Inuit joiners and members from those we often see in reality-based television shows such as *Survivor*? The complexities of small-group interactions are likely the seeds from which more complex societies are grown.

Looking Closer

What Happened to the Laetoli Hot Stuff! The Domestication of Peppers (*Capsicum* sp.) in the New World?

Plants were domesticated for use as condiments, as well as dietary staples, by human societies in the past. Canadian researchers are playing an important role in the development of methodological techniques that allow us to identify the presence of such plants in the archaeological record. Dr. J. Scott Raymond, of the University of Calgary, describes recent research, undertaken with national and international colleagues, that identifies one of the earliest uses of chili peppers in the New World.

In studies of the origins of agriculture, high-carbohydrate, staple crops such as corn, wheat, potatoes, rice, and sorghum have stolen the interest of most archaeologists, as if humans in the past lived by bread alone. Spices and condiments have received comparatively little attention. Thanks to the discovery that microscopic granules of starch are extremely durable and to the development of techniques for recovering these granules from ancient cooking pots and grinding stones, we now know that the earliest farmers in the American tropics were spicing up their meals with chili peppers.

It is hard to imagine Asian, African, or Mediterranean food without hot chili peppers, but before the European discovery of the Americas peppers were unknown to Old World cuisines. All of the many varieties of chili peppers cultivated around the world today trace their ancestry to five species of the genus *Capsicum,* all of which in their wild state occur in the tropical regions of South and Central America. Botanists have been aware

of this for many years, and with the advent of technology allowing DNA fingerprinting of plants, they are now able to identify the geographical loci of the species of wild peppers with some precision. Botanists, however, could not investigate the human role in the cultivation, domestication, and dispersal of chili peppers without the aid of archaeologists.

Even under the best conditions for preservation, plant remains are unlikely to survive in archaeological sites. In the warm, wet tropics, the natural habitat of chili peppers, conditions for the preservation of food remains are at their worst. Anything organic decays rapidly. The earliest village sites yet discovered in the Americas are in southwestern Ecuador. The size and permanence of the settlements that created these sites and their locations adjacent to prime farming land all indicate that agriculture was important; however, verification of that through the discovery of the remains of domesticated food plants has not been possible because of the poor conditions for preservation. The development of techniques for recovering and identifying microscopic bits of plants, noted above, promises a possible way out of this dilemma.

Excavations at Loma Alta, a 6000-year-old village site in Ecuador, have yielded thousands of fragments of pottery, including many from cooking pots with charred residues on the interior. Analysis of these residues led to the discovery of starch granules from domesticated chili peppers. The granules, as viewed through a microscope, are lenticular in shape with a flat central depression.

9000 B.P. Less intensive, but nonetheless intentional, cultivation may have begun much earlier. Following is what the evidence seems to show.

Natufian A cultural manifestation in the Levant (the southwest Fertile Crescent) dating from 14,500 to 11,600 B.P. and consisting of the first appearance of settled villages, trade goods, and possibly early cultivation of domesticated wheat, but lacking pottery.

Prior to 15,500 B.P., nomadic foragers occupied the southwest Fertile Crescent, an area known as the Levant (in Israel, Jordan, and Syria). They lived primarily along major waterways and the Mediterranean coast, hunting gazelle and taking a variety of plant foods. Soon, however, these nomadic folks became sedentary. The **Natufian** culture (ca. 14,500–11,600 B.P.) built round, semi-subterranean structures, 3 to

They are no more than 16 to 28 microns across, but double the size of granules from wild chili peppers. Starch is not abundant in chili peppers, but there is a small amount stored under the skin of a pepper. Analysis of grinding stones associated with the pottery and of associated soil sediments revealed more starch granules. Some of the granules from the grinding stones showed damage characteristic of ground or pounded starch, and some of the granules from the cooking pots were partially gelatinized from having been heated.

A bonus of having found starch granules from the carbonized residues of the cooking pots was that the residues could be directly dated through radiocarbon accelerator mass spectrometry, thereby revealing that the chili peppers were being cultivated and cooked from the time of the earliest occupation of Loma Alta. An additional bonus was that starch granules from other plants such as corn and manioc were discovered in the same residues, providing insight into the cuisine of the people who lived at Loma Alta.

Beyond the knowledge that societies were practising agriculture and cultivating spicy foods 6000 years ago in the tropics of Ecuador, the discovery of the starch granules of domesticated chili peppers tells us something about networks of contact in that long ago time. Wild chili peppers do not occur on the western side of the Andes. Therefore, the chili peppers cultivated at Loma Alta were domesticated elsewhere, possibly in Central America, but more likely across the Andes in the Amazon Basin. The picture that

Figure 15-3 Canadian researchers Ruth Dickau, Sonia Zarrilo, and Scott Raymond are feeling the heat from their research into the cultivation of chili peppers. The research is contributing to a greater understanding of the cultural and economic evolution of indigenous peoples of the Americas.

Source: Mike Drew/The Calgary Sun

is emerging is that throughout the American tropics, early in the Holocene, people were experimenting with the cultivation and domestication of plants and that the successful domesticates were dispersed over thousands of kilometres and across formidable geographical barriers via a complex network of social and economic interactions.

6 metres in diameter, with stone foundations and probably wood-and-brush upper walls and roof; an excavated example appears in Figure 15-4. Abundant remains of house mice suggest a continual source of fresh garbage at these sites, which, in turn, suggests that people were there year-round (this conclusion is supported by seasonality studies of gazelle teeth).

Natufian settlements were located in places where natural stands of wheat and barley were readily available. People harvested these wild cereals, as demonstrated by the plant macrofossils, grinding and pounding stones, and sickle sheen on flint blades. But the plant foods appear to be wild, not domesticated, forms.

The Younger Dryas climatic interval interrupted the Natufian lifeway about 13,000 B.P. Some villages were

Figure 15-4 A portion of a large house at the Natufian site of Ain Mallaha, Israel (in Hebrew, the site is called Eynan). Note the substantial postholes that suggest the house was covered by a large, heavy roof.

Source: Ofer Bar-Yosef

abandoned, and people returned to a more nomadic lifeway as plant foods became less abundant. Ofer Bar-Yosef (Harvard University) suggests that the Younger Dryas may have encouraged the now-large Natufian population to make land more productive by husbanding and later intentionally planting "wild" cereals. The extreme climatic variability of the Younger Dryas interval, however, probably made reliance on agriculture a risky venture.

After the Younger Dryas (ca. 11,600 B.P.), climate returned to the wetter, warmer, and more stable conditions that are conducive to the growth of cereals. Foragers returned to village life; but this time the villages were considerably larger, signalling a growth in population. We find these **Neolithic** sites in the mountains, within the natural range of wild wheat and barley. Away from the mountains, nomadic hunter-gatherers living in small, temporary settlements occupied the deserts.

Neolithic sites contain many large, oval dwellings, some containing two rooms. There were storage structures in each site as well, including large stone silos

Neolithic The ancient period during which people began using ground stone tools, manufacturing ceramics, and relying on domesticated plants and animals—literally, the "New Stone Age"—coined by Sir John Lubbock (in 1865).

and bins. Flotation has recovered copious amounts of carbonized seeds of barley, wheat, and other plants. We cannot be certain if these plants were cultivated, but they were an important part of Neolithic subsistence. Neolithic peoples still hunted gazelle, and they gathered various fruits and wild seeds.

With the return of a more benevolent climate about 11,600 years ago, habitats opened up that were conducive to agriculture. Bar-Yosef estimates that human population exploded at this time by more than 1000 percent. During the Younger Dryas, people developed the techniques that gave agriculture at least the return rate of gathering wild plants. By 9000 years ago, a growing population now required that the full productivity of agriculture be harnessed, and agricultural communities appeared.

Comparing the Paradigms

So, which explanation is right?

As we pointed out in Chapter 3, paradigms reflect particular perspectives on the world—elevating some variables and downplaying the importance of others. The paradigm channels researchers toward certain explanations and guides them away from others. But because human behaviour is complex, it is unlikely that any single paradigm will adequately capture the entire picture; each sees just one portion of the puzzle. A complete explanation for the origins of agriculture, or any aspect of human evolutionary history, probably requires input from several different paradigms. We can see how this works in the various explanations for the origins of agriculture.

Clearly, agriculture requires a working knowledge of plant foods. But the plants that would eventually be domesticated were being used at least 18,000 years ago; surely, foragers did not require *thousands* of years to understand that seeds produce plants. Unilineal evolutionists might have argued that these ancient hunters lacked the intelligence to understand plants sufficiently to be agriculturalists. But these were the same people who were capable of fine artistry and tool manufacture (as evidenced by Upper Paleolithic art and stone technology), and their hunting strategies required detailed understandings of animal behaviour. Certainly, these late Pleistocene foragers were every bit as intelligent as people today. Knowledge is necessary *but not sufficient* to explain the origins of agriculture.

As Childe suggested, climatic change also clearly has something to do with agriculture, although not in the way he thought. Foragers could not become agriculturalists until the environment was capable of supporting agriculture, and this may not have happened until the early Holocene. And the Younger Dryas clearly altered the Natufian lifeway, requiring that a former sedentary foraging population make the land more productive, through the cultivation of wild wheat and barley.

Did population pressure play a role? The earliest evidence for agriculture does not come from marginal areas (contrary to Binford's expectations), but from the homeland of wild wheat and barley. Evidence from Natufian settlements also suggests that population growth had caused some groups to become sedentary on choice localities that included stands of wild wheat and barley. By the beginning of the Neolithic, this expanded population may have congregated around these localities and created local population pressure on resources, requiring people to expand their diets and rely more heavily on plants. Because wheat and barley respond genetically (through selection) to human harvesting by becoming more abundant, their domestication was perhaps inevitable.

What about social processes? Did competitive feasting have anything to do with agriculture? Natufian settlements do provide archaeological evidence for trade—sea shells, some from as far away as the Atlantic Ocean, beads made of rare stone, and figurines carved in bone and stone. Many burials contain elaborate personal ornaments, including necklaces, belts, bracelets, and headdresses. It is possible that these ornaments indicate trade relations that, in turn, reflect the building of social alliances. But Natufian sites lack storage structures (which appear only in Neolithic sites). And wheat and barley were important to the diets of both, not peripheral "luxury" items. Natufian and Neolithic communities

were probably self-sufficient, and the need for alliances probably arose much later. However, it is likely that feasting and trade created alliances that were critical to survival when crops failed or animals migrated in the climatically uncertain world of the Younger Dryas. Agriculture may have helped make possible the feasts that, in turn, helped to form those social alliances.

Finally, what about human intentionality? Rindos claimed that human intentionality had nothing to do with agriculture and, at one level, this must be true: It's unlikely that a forager in the Levant woke up one morning 10,000 years ago and decided to become a farmer. But human intention must have played *some* role. The changes that occurred in the wild cereals suggest that humans *intended* to increase harvest productivity and efficiency, for example by saving the largest seeds for the next planting, by transporting plants to favoured localities, or by irrigating natural stands. They *intended* to forage as well as possible, and these intentions led them to agriculture.

Processes and conditions similar to those we've described for the Near East were also at work in Asia, Africa, and the Americas. We still have much to learn about the origins of agriculture. In this brief overview, we have tried to provide a feel for the paradigms archaeologists use to understand this research problem, how archaeological data can be used to evaluate hypotheses, and how most paradigms contribute some pieces to a research puzzle.

Why Did the Archaic State Arise?

We now turn to a second major transition in human cultural evolution, the origins of the archaic state. Some instances where archaic states arose are shown in Figure 15-5. Nearly every student of anthropology today lives in a state society, and some probably consider the state to be the "natural" form of human social and political organization. But not so long ago (in archaeological time), nobody lived in a state society. Evolutionarily speaking, states are simply the latest form of human organization (and probably not the last). How did they arise?

We first need to define what we mean by the archaic state. There are many definitions; we follow one proposed by Kent Flannery:

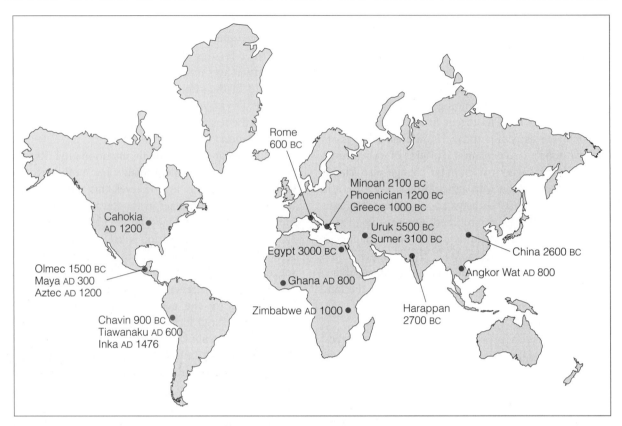

Figure 15-5 Major primary archaic states; these are places where state forms of political organization developed independently.

The state is a type of very strong, usually highly centralized government, with a professional ruling class, largely divorced from the bonds of kinship which characterize simpler societies. It is highly stratified and extremely diversified internally, with residential patterns often based on occupational specialization rather than blood or **affinal** relationships. The state attempts to maintain a monopoly of force, and is characterized by true law.

Not all archaic states fit this definition exactly, but it points out the salient aspects of most such political formations.

The archaic state is a complex form of sociopolitical organization. States generally have powerful economic structures and often a market system. An elite controls the state economy and maintains authority by laws and by privileged access to key goods, services, and ideology. Archaic states generally have populations numbering at least in the hundreds of thousands, and this population is often concentrated in large cities. Some people were specialists—potters, weavers, stone masons, and so on—who depended on the labour of others for subsistence (that is, they did not grow their own food). Archaic states are also known for a high level of artistic achievement, monumental architecture, and an "official" state religion.

Theories about the origin of the archaic state date from the 19th-century evolutionists. As with agriculture, unilineal evolutionists argued that "civilization" appeared when people were intellectually and morally prepared to enter into a social contract and to give up some of their liberties in exchange for benefits, such as protection in time of war. As with agriculture, this approach fails to explain why states originated where and when they did.

We know that the formation of archaic states did not depend on domesticated animals, metal tools, or wheeled transportation, because states appeared in places such as Mesoamerica where none of these

affinal   Relatives that one is related to by marriage, rather than blood.

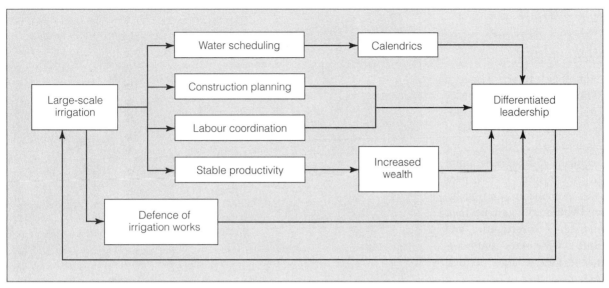

Figure 15-6 Schematic diagram of Wittfogel's irrigation hypothesis for the origin of the state.

existed prior to European contact. The first three explanations we'll present—which privilege irrigation, warfare, population growth, and environment—fall within the materialist paradigm. A fourth explanation focuses on the role of ideology and falls more within the postprocessual paradigm. As with the origins of agriculture, we believe that it's possible to reconcile these different views.

The Irrigation Hypothesis

In his influential book *Oriental Despotism* (1957), Karl Wittfogel (1896–1988) asserted that the mechanisms of large-scale irrigation were directly responsible for creating the archaic state. His **irrigation hypothesis** argued that irrigation systems require an extraordinary level of coordination above the individual farmer. How this works is shown in Figure 15-6. First, someone must construct the system, dig the channels, and build the dams and headgates. This requires organization above the household, because portions of the system benefit everyone, but not all portions benefit each individual household (for instance, the ones downstream from your home). Irrigation systems are inherently problematic, because people living upstream could take all the water, leaving nothing for those downstream. Wittfogel pointed out that this means that irrigation systems inherently require a level of continuing control above that of the individual farmers who benefit from it.

Wittfogel argued that the great Asian societies of China, India, and Mesopotamia followed a radically different evolutionary course than did the societies of western Europe and elsewhere. The particular forms of archaic states in the Orient evolved because of the conditions required by large-scale irrigation—the imposition of inordinately strong political controls to maintain the hydraulic works, the tendency for the ruling class to merge with the ruling bureaucracy, the close identification of the dominant religion with governmental offices, and the diminution of private property and economic initiative.

Wittfogel contended that, after a creative period in which the bureaucracy began, stagnation set in, corrupting power and creating a despotic and feudal system. He also saw the hydraulic society as an initial step toward totalitarianism (a German intellectual who spent time in a concentration camp for speaking out against the Nazis, Wittfogel was vehemently anti-fascist).

According to Wittfogel's theory, the state evolved in direct response to the demands of large-scale irrigation. The need for coordinated labour, massive construction, and so forth led to increased wealth and military strength and eventually to the powerful ruling bureaucracy that characterized state development.

irrigation hypothesis Proposed by Karl Wittfogel, it attributes the origin of the state to the administrative demands of irrigation.

The Warfare and Circumscription Hypothesis

Ethnologist Robert Carneiro (American Museum of Natural History) terms Wittfogel's irrigation hypothesis a "voluntaristic" theory, one requiring that "at some point in their history, certain peoples spontaneously, rationally, and voluntarily gave up their individual sovereignties and united with other communities to form a larger political unit deserving to be called a state." In this respect, Wittfogel's explanation is more in line with unilineal evolutionism—that is, people give up individual freedoms when they are ready to take the next "step" in cultural development. But by studying modern tribal societies and chiefdoms, Carneiro knew that autonomous political units never willingly surrender their sovereignty, and he saw no reason why they should have done so in the past.

Figure 15-7 A carving of a decapitated head from the 3500-year-old site of Cerro Sechín in Peru. The carving is one of 400 decorating a stone facade that forms the base of a platform mound. The facade is covered by images of warriors and the jumbled body parts of their victims. Some archaeologists believe this frieze commemorates a mythical or historical battle.
Source: Robert Kelly

Carneiro argues, instead, that egalitarian settlements transform into chiefdoms, and chiefdoms into states, only when coercive force is involved; warfare thus plays an especially pertinent role in the early stages of state development, as shown in Figure 15-7. Of course, some tribes might agree to cooperate in times of stress, but such federations are temporary and voluntarily dissolved once the crisis has passed. Carneiro's initial premise stipulates that political change of lasting significance arises only from coercive pressure. And warfare, he suggested, is the only mechanism powerful enough to impose bureaucratic authority on a large scale.

It is clear from the archaeological record, however, that warfare is considerably older and more widespread than the state. Because warfare does not invariably lead to archaic state formation, Carneiro adds that, though *necessary,* warfare is not *sufficient* in itself to account for the state. According to Carneiro, only in areas where agricultural land is at a premium—areas that are environmentally "circumscribed"—will warfare lead to state formation. Competition over land arose first where natural barriers—such as mountains, deserts, or seas—restricted the availability of arable land. The vanquished peoples had no place to flee and thus were required to submit to the expanding political units of the victors. A centralized political authority was needed to maintain a standing army as well as to control conquered populations.

In Carneiro's **warfare and circumscription hypothesis,** shown in Figure 15-8, the combination of population growth and circumscribed agricultural resources leads to increased warfare, which in turn fosters the centralized political organization characteristic of state-level complexity. He musters support for his hypothesis from the archaeology of initial archaic states near the Nile, the Tigris-Euphrates (Mesopotamia), the Indus Valley, and the valleys of Mexico and Peru—all of which evolved in areas of circumscribed agricultural land. Conversely, in areas where agricultural land was plentiful and not tightly

warfare and circumscription hypothesis Proposed by Robert Carneiro, it attributes the origin of the state to the administrative burden of warfare conducted for conquest as a request of geographic limits on arable land in the face of a rising population.

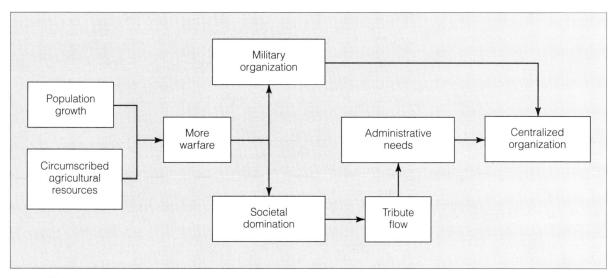

Figure 15-8 Schematic diagram of Carneiro's circumscription and warfare hypothesis for the origin of the state.

bounded—such as in northern Europe, central Africa, and the eastern woodlands of North America—states were quite late in developing, if they did at all.

A Multicausal Theory

Scientists often propose ideas before the data to evaluate them are available. This was certainly the case with Wittfogel's and Carneiro's explanations for the rise of the state. But over the past few decades, archaeologists have studied the origins of the state all over the world, in places such as Mesopotamia, the Indus Valley, Mesoamerica, China, and the Andes. From these studies we can see that neither irrigation nor circumscription and warfare alone account for all the archaeological data. In some places, irrigation exists without states; in others, states exist without irrigation agriculture. In some, warfare precedes state formation, but in others, it follows. As with agriculture, it is impossible to specify a single "prime mover" for states. No *single* condition is both *necessary* and *sufficient* to create an archaic state.

As we pointed out above, in studying the origins of any social institution it is important to differentiate between the *conditions* that generate cultural change and the *process* that actually creates the change. Drawing on three case studies—France, Japan (both during the Middle Ages), and the Inka—ethnologist Allen Johnson (UCLA) and archaeologist Timothy Earle (Northwestern University) searched for more general

conditions rather than specific factors. They concluded that three general *conditions* are necessary and sufficient for archaic states to form:

1. High population density that strains the food production system
2. A need for a system of integration (such as trade or irrigation)
3. The possibility that the economy could be controlled to permit the financing of regional institutions (such as a state religion) and to support a ruling class

Given these *conditions,* however, any number of specific *processes* can result in a state.

Figure 15-9 shows how these conditions might result in social change as population grows after agriculture. A growing population demands that land become more productive. Horticulturalists, such as Madagascar's Mikea (see Chapter 10), may use slash-and-burn farming, where a plot of land supports one to three harvests and is allowed to lie fallow for some time. As population grows, however, a family cannot switch their land because all available land is occupied. If there are no new fields, people must artificially fertilize land. The native peoples of northeastern North America did this with fish remains. In the Near East, people used manure from domesticated animals. Lacking domesticated animals, the Aztec collected the "night soil" from residents of large villages for use as fertilizer.

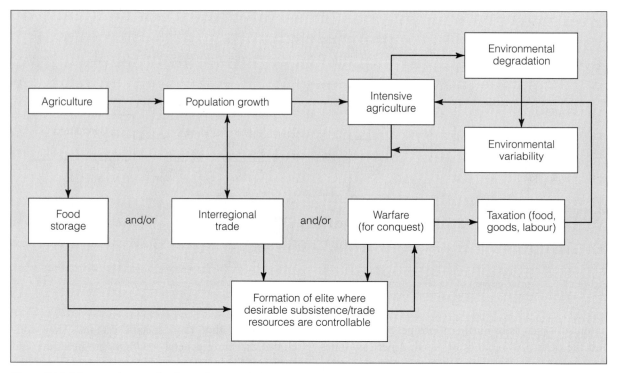

Figure 15-9 Schematic diagram of multicausal origins of the archaic state.

As the best arable land is used, some people are pushed to marginal lands (as Binford argued). Here they must develop intensive agriculture, using labour-intensive ways to make land more productive. This can entail canals that must be maintained as they fill with silt and debris. In mountainous regions, people build terraces along hillsides (as they did at Machu Picchu) to create flat, arable land where there had been only a steep hillside. The Aztec created **chinampas**— long, low islands in shallow lakes—by dredging soil from the lake bottom and piling it up. All of these require labour and, at some point, the system simply cannot produce more at a given level of technology.

So, what happens during an environmental calamity, when a severe drought, flood, or insect plague strikes?

Today, farmers in developed nations have insurance to buffer against disasters. In the past, horticulturalists also tried to buffer environmental fluctuations. The

Hopi and Zuni Indians in the American Southwest, for example, plant fields of maize in different environmental locations. They plant some on south-facing hillsides, others on hilltops, and still others on the valley floor. They know that, by putting their fields in different microenvironments, they increase the probability that at least one of those fields will survive. If one field is lost to drought, another might prosper; if insects attack one field, the others might be spared.

As population grows, the need for such buffering strategies increases. These include family-level decisions, such as field placement and long-term household food storage, but they also include group-level responses, such as interregional trade, conquest, or some sort of cooperative system of exchange, perhaps based on religious obligations. These group responses require a system of social integration. This is also the point at which the specific *processes* of state development can differ. States will have different histories and will take on different characters depending on whether trade, warfare, or religion is the primary "system of integration" (the theory's second condition).

At some point, the individuals who negotiate the relations between groups take on a special impor-

chinampas A form of intensive agriculture; low mounds the Aztec built by piling up sediments from the bottoms of shallow lakes and marshes to form islands of arable land.

tance. These middlemen could manipulate and exploit social ties—marriages and trade relations, primarily—between villages and centres in times of stress. They are individuals who, for whatever specific reason, hold sway over a productive resource by controlling territory and/or labour. A system of social integration therefore might create Johnson and Earle's third condition: the possibility that an individual or group could control the economy to permit the financing of regional institutions and to support a ruling class.

In times of stress, people living under high population densities compete for land and resources. Some unfortunates may petition those who control productive land for some of their stores, land, or protection. If those who control productive land do not share, they themselves could be attacked. By allowing others to migrate to their territory or share in their long-term stores, those on productive land buy security. And it appears that they did this by exacting tribute or taxation from the petitioners, which they then used to support an army as well as their entourage or court. By controlling key resources, some individuals become the "elite."

Such social systems, however, require an "explanation" that provides an account of why some people are elite and some are peasants. What role does ideology play in the origin of archaic states?

The Role of Ideology in State Formation

To this point, we have explored the *material conditions* that create archaic states. This is because processual research provided an understanding of how significant cultural change takes place when the technology and economic base changes. Subsistence-level change produces population growth that eventually requires new mechanisms to buffer fluctuations in the food base. This, in turn, cause shifts in social organization.

Ideological changes develop as a means to validate the new social organization—to explain why some people live in luxurious houses with servants and the best food, while others toil in the fields and inhabit more humble abodes.

By **ideology,** we mean the cultural, religious, or cosmological ideas that provide group members with a rationale for their existence. *Ideology masks the fact that one group is exploiting another.* Unilineal evolutionism, for example, was an ideology in the sense that it provided a justification for the domination of colonized lands by Western nations.

In archaic states, ideologies are often linked to religion, and here we see how the kinship links that tie the elite in chiefdoms to the population often become severed in states. In early states, the elite claimed that they were different from everyone else and that they deserved their lofty position because they were descended from the gods. If they considered themselves kin to the peasants, then this would mean that the peasants, too, were kin to the gods. Such a situation could undermine the elites' control of the region's resources. That archaic states often suffered internal warfare is evidence that people can sometimes see through the ideology.

Ideologies have a tendency to take on a life of their own, and here is where they can play a causal role in the development of states. As we pointed out in Chapter 14, humans see the world through their own cultural logic, a logic that is expressed as a particular symbolic system. This "cultural" world can provide its own engine of change. If kings are descended from the gods, then they should be all-powerful. If they are all-powerful, then shouldn't the entire world be under their rule? Possibly for this reason, states tend to be expansionist, eventually collapsing when they reach beyond their physical limits of control. Sometimes this expansion is militaristic, and sometimes it is based on religion (we saw a possible example of this in Chapter 14's discussion of the expansion of the Chavín culture in central Peru).

The Maya: A Case Study in State Formation

As we did with agriculture, let's take these abstract ideas and see how they help us understand a particular case, the lowland Maya of Central America. Figure 15-10 shows the location of some of the sites we mention below.

We have visited the Maya in previous chapters. Here we focus on the lowland Maya, who lived (and still live) in Mexico's Yucatan Peninsula, Belize, and portions of Guatemala and Honduras. Some occupied the Petén rain forest, and others lived on the more arid Yucatan Peninsula.

ideology A set of beliefs—often political, religious, or cosmological in nature—that rationalizes exploitative relations between classes or social groups.

Figure 15-10 A map of the lowland Maya region, with sites discussed in the text. Many other Maya sites exist in the lowlands, the Yucatan Peninsula, and the highlands to the east in Mexico, Guatemala, Honduras, and El Salvador.

By 5000 B.P., agriculture had begun in the highlands to the west of the lowland Maya region. Here the Maya grew maize, beans, squashes, pumpkins, chili peppers, amaranth, and cotton. As expected, population grew after a shift to full-time agriculture, and some people apparently moved into the lowland regions.

Evidence for human settlement of the lowland Maya region pre-agricultural is limited. This is partly due to the difficulty of finding small, ephemeral sites in a forest that is dense enough to hide large stone temples and partly due to the fact that Maya settlements destroyed earlier occupations. But current evidence suggests that few people lived in the area until maize horticulturalists moved there about 4000 years ago. Settlements from this time period lack any large public buildings, elaborate burials, or exotic trade items, suggesting that the early farmers were egalitarian.

ancestor worship A religion in which one's deceased ancestors serve as important intermediaries between the natural and supernatural.

The Middle Preclassic Period: Population Growth

During the Middle Preclassic Period (900–300 B.C.) population grew, emigrants arrived from other areas, and a lively trade developed in colourful feathers of tropical birds and animal skins. Archaeological surveys show that all major regions of the lowlands were occupied by sedentary, slash-and-burn horticulturalists by 500 B.C. This growth apparently approached the region's carrying capacity, for farmers were finding ways to make the land produce more food. In the swamps of Belize, for example, farmers built raised fields, much like the Aztec *chinampas* we described above. They also grew a greater variety of crops, including maize, but also beans, squash, tomatoes, chilies, ramon and cashew nuts, avocado, papaya, guava, and cacao (chocolate). Still, analyses of skeletal isotope data suggests that maize sometimes constituted only about 30 percent of the diet, and faunal data show that white-tailed deer, turtles, fish, and dogs were eaten.

The increase in population precipitated a change from more or less egalitarian communities to small chiefdoms. Some of these late Middle Preclassic period centres were quite large; Nakbé, for example, covered some 50 hectares. These centres contained large buildings and stone platforms, built with public labour. Previously, people were interred beneath the floors of houses but, during the Middle Preclassic, some individuals were buried within the stone platforms or the buildings themselves. Patricia McAnany (Boston University) suggests that these burials signal a shift to **ancestor worship,** a religion in which one's deceased ancestors serve as important intermediaries between the natural and supernatural. From ethnographic data, anthropologists know that ancestor worship tends to occur with restrictive claims on land, and the burials within the public structures may have served to justify a kin group's claim to territory. Thus, by the end of the Middle Preclassic period, groups exerted control over land just, as we might expect, at the time when all land was occupied.

The Late Preclassic Period: Formation of Chiefdoms

By the beginning of the Late Preclassic Period (300 B.C.–A.D. 250) a few sites, such as Altar de Sacrificios and Seibal, developed into towns of several thousand people, but no single centre emerged. The Maya built public buildings in these centres, some including the corbelled arch. (Arches with a keystone did not exist in the pre-contact New World; corbelled arches were made by piling stone blocks up, moving each layer in a little closer until the walls could be bridged with a lintel stone.) They also erected stelae using local hieroglyphic styles, and they participated in a lively trade in exotic goods, including polychrome pottery, jade, and obsidian.

Survey data suggest that the regional population grew again by some 350 percent during the Late Pre-classic Period, and people aggregated into a few large settlements. El Mirador, for example, covered some 15 square kilometres and contained more than 200 stone structures. One was a pyramid some 55 metres high; another was built atop a hill, with multiple tiers cut into the hillside. Others were large public buildings decorated with plaster and stone masks of deities. And at Nakbé and El Mirador, extensive stone causeways were built to traverse the swamps. These rose 4 metres high in places and were filled with crushed white stone.

Nonetheless, during most of the Late Preclassic, Maya political organization had no single centre. Instead, many small centres controlled the territory around themselves.

The Classic Period: State Formation

But this changed near the end of the Preclassic Period and during the Classic Period (A.D. 250–700), when the lowland Maya took on the characteristics of the archaic state. There is evidence for warfare in earlier times, but now it seems that Maya leaders wrestled for control over centres, as attested to by burned build-ings, fortifications such as palisades and moats, and mass burials of males with fractured bones—all of which first appear in the Late Preclassic. The causeways connected sites, suggesting alliances between the centres. Such evidence of supra-village control and coordination is a hallmark of the state.

During the Classic period these centres became solidified, albeit temporarily, as states. The sites of Tikal (tee-*call*) and Uaxactún (wah-shock-*toon*) became major centres, and others soon followed. Tikal, shown in Figure 15-11, would grow to cover 16 square kilometres and house some 80,000 people (larger than 16th-century London). It contained numerous stone public buildings, causeways, and pyramids with remarkably steep stairways leading to ceremonial chambers and astronomical observatories on their tops. Hieroglyphs became standardized across the southern Maya lowlands, suggesting the development of a common political culture and some kind of political interaction and coordination.

Survey data indicate that population continued to grow throughout the Classic Period. As many as 10 million people lived in the lowland Maya area—more than live there today. Moreover, this population was more concentrated. Many Preclassic centres were abandoned during the early Classic period, and their inhabitants moved into the large centres, such as Tikal. So, not only does the overall population increase, but also there is an *aggregation* of population during the Classic period in large centres.

Population growth and aggregation created new problems for the Maya as they exacerbated the local effects of drought and conquest. Stable isotope, macrobotanical, and faunal data suggest that the

Figure 15-11 A painting by Carlos Vierra (1915) of Tikal based on his imagining the site's appearance soon after its abandonment.
Source: San Diego Museum of Man, photo by Peter D. Harrison, Ca. 1993

commoners had an increasingly more monotonous diet of maize, while the elite continued to enjoy a more varied diet. And skeletal data show that males decreased in average height during the Classic period.

Producing enough food to feed the growing and aggregated population may have been difficult. Many of the centres were located next to *bajos*—low-lying areas that today are little more than swampy ground. Research by Vernon Scarborough and Nicholas Dunning (University of Cincinnati) suggests that in the past the *bajos* were shallow lakes that could have provided the Maya with freshwater. By 100 B.C., these *bajos* had filled with silt that washed in as slash-and-burn horticulture denuded the surrounding land of forest. As the *bajos* filled up, Late Preclassic centres relocated.

In Classic centres, and even in some Preclassic sites, Scarborough and Dunning found extensive water collection and control devices. The Maya modified natural gullies, runnels, and basins to channel runoff into small artificial reservoirs. Causeways and plazas were not just a way to keep one's feet out of the mud, but also were part of a system of water catchment and dams. At Tikal, the paved areas could capture some 900,000 cubic metres of water in a single season. Some of the catchment basins are positioned to provide water for fields surrounding the *bajos,* but direct evidence for irrigation is still lacking.

The large centres contained rectangular ballcourts, sunken stone-walled courtyards, sometimes with stone rings mounted high on the two long side walls; one is shown in Figure 15-12. The ballgame first appears in Preclassic sites and, although nobody knows exactly how the game was played, it likely involved driving a rubber ball through the stone rings without using hands or feet. This was more than just entertainment, because ballgame images depicted on polychrome pots and stone carvings clearly depict human sacrifice as part of the ritual "game." By the time of the Spanish conquest, the game was played throughout Mesoamerica with a new twist: The winning team and their supporters pursued the losers and their boosters to take their clothing and jewellery.

Commoners lived in compounds of stone-walled, thatch-roofed houses with above- and belowground storage structures. In the arid north, the belowground storage structures, called *chultuns,* probably were used to store water. Status differences are reflected in house compounds of different sizes and the presence of exotic goods such as jade and obsidian. Elite burials became more elaborate and contained exotics and labour-intensive items such as polychrome pottery.

The Maya also had an elaborate calendar (in fact, they had three; see "Looking Closer: How the Maya Reckoned Time"), and they marked the dates of events on the stelae that we have discussed in previous chapters. After years of hard work, Tatiana Proskouriakoff (1909–1985) and Yuri Knorosov (1922–1999) figured out how to read the glyphs. Using the stelae and other archaeological sources of information, we can piece together the shifting rivalries of Maya political life.

During much of the late Classic Period, the lowlands were divided into numerous centres that alternately competed and allied with one another to control stretches of land and to garner prestige. The

Figure 15-12 A ballcourt at the Maya site of Copán, Honduras. The stone rings are visible above the sloping left wall.

Source: American Museum of Natural History

glyphs carved on stelae and painted on pottery tell us the names of the *K'uhul Ajaw,* or "divine lord," who ruled over a Maya capital. For instance, the royal name of a 7th-century ruler of Palenque was K'inich Kan B'alam ("Great Sun-Snake Jaguar"); a 4th-century ruler of Tikal was Yax Nuun Ayiin ("First Crocodile"). Maya kings had some of the coolest names in prehistory!

But the Maya were not trying to be cool. The names were intended to reflect a king's divine status. Maya kings claimed to be descended from the gods; the stelae portrayed their lives and succession to the throne as repeating mythical events of the past. To reinforce Mayan ideology, the kings conducted rituals at auspicious times according to the ritual calendar to propitiate the gods. Without these rituals, the Maya believed, chaos would reign and the universe would collapse. Kings and their power were essential to the world's continuity. Power flowed from father to son or from brother to brother, and royal families were ranked in terms of their kinship distance from the king.

Seeing themselves as descended from the gods, these kings competed with one another to determine who was the greatest among them. In fact, David Webster (Pennsylvania State University) suggests that the Maya might have seen war as a way for Maya kings not only to subdue unruly neighbours but also to demonstrate their ability to quell the potential for chaos in the world. Warfare, the need to control subdued centres, and the need to reward those who supported the king in these endeavours produced the political hierarchy of the Maya in the Classic period. The stelae and other evidence on monumental architecture record the exploits of the elites. It is this hierarchy of power that makes Maya Classic centres archaic states.

We know that Maya courts were places of intrigue and backroom deals, perhaps like those in Medieval and Renaissance Europe, with lords and sublords plotting coups and competing for power. Iconography between A.D. 250 and 600 is replete with images of warfare; some sites show evidence of violent destruction, such as the toppling of stelae, and subsequent rebuilding.

This hieroglyphic evidence also tells us that, by A.D. 700, the internecine competition among the many small centres had reduced itself to a single rivalry between Tikal and Calakmul (kah-lock-*mool*). Each of these centres was allied with several smaller centres. These alliances were the result of centuries of warfare, with one centre eclipsing another only to be conquered by a former rival. Tikal and Caracol, for example, fought for 250 years. Caracol eventually eclipsed Tikal in A.D. 562 only to become an ally of Calakmul later (along with the centres of Naranjo and Dos Pilas). Tikal returned to power, allying itself with Palenque and other centres. Eventually, around A.D. 695, Tikal defeated Calakmul, captured its war effigy (a large jaguar carving), and may have killed its ruler, Jaguar Paw. These shifting alliances and changing centres of power were no different from those of Europe in the 16th through 19th centuries.

Conquered populations sent annual tribute to the royal court of the victor in the form of cotton, feathers, shells, jade, cacao, and possibly maize and labour. Much of the warfare was status-related. By dominating powerful neighbours, a king communicated his authority to his people. And by assisting that king, lesser nobles could earn privileges and acquire control over conquered resources that might permit them to move up in status.

No single Maya centre was ever able to maintain control over the entire lowlands; nor did any centre maintain control for many generations. Still, it appears that some tried. And in the act of trying, the Maya meet the definition of an archaic state.

So, What Explains the Origin of the Maya State?

All archaeologists who try to explain the origins of a *particular* state find it nearly impossible to put their finger on the single factor without which the state would not have formed. Instead, each explanation points to one or more important conditions. Carneiro's explanation focused on competition over land generated initially by population pressure, and some evidence supports this idea in the Maya case. Raised-field agriculture, occupation of virtually all land, the control of water, high population estimates, and human skeletal analyses all suggest that the Maya had reached the land's carrying capacity. And, in one sense, Maya land was circumscribed—by the ocean to the east, the dry Yucatan Peninsula to the north, and the highlands to the east and south (which witnessed their own population growth).

But the archaeological evidence also shows that the control of water played a role in determining where the centres were erected. Although it is unclear

Looking Closer
How the Maya Reckoned Time

The Maya were keen observers of astronomical events, and their rituals were governed by three precise calendars. The Maya did not invent these calendars, but they appear to have perfected them.

The first of these calendars was the Long Count. Figure 15-13 shows the two sides of a jade plaque that commemorates the ascent to the throne of one of Tikal's rulers, Zero-Moon-Bird (his name appears as one of the glyphs). On one side, Zero-Moon-Bird wears a jaguar headdress and tramples a captive underfoot. On the other is a series of glyphs. Look at them closely, and you will see that five of them have bars and/or dots to their left. These are calendar glyphs, and they date Zero-Moon-Bird's coronation.

The Maya used bars to symbolize five and dots to symbolize one (a stylized shell stood for zero). The Long Count dates an event by counting the number of days that have passed since "the beginning of time." The date is given in a series of units: Baktun are units of 144,000 days; katun, units of 7200 days; tun, 360 days; uinal, 20 days; and kin, 1 day. The number of each unit is denoted by the bars and dots. Looking at the figure, we see that the second glyph from the top—the baktun glyph—has one bar (indicating 5) and three dots (3) next to it for a total of 1,152,000 days (144,000 × 8). The next glyph down (the katun glyph) has 2 bars (10) and 4 dots (4), for a total of 100,800 days (7200 × 14); likewise there are 3 tun (1080 days), 1 uinal (20 days), and 12 kin (12 days). Archaeologists write Long Count dates as the series of units; in this case, 8.14.3.1.12. The total number of days is their sum: The event depicted occurred 1,253,912 days since the beginning of the calendar.

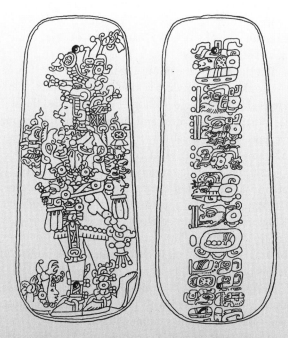

Figure 15-13 The front and back of the Leiden Plaque; on the back are glyphs that indicate the age of the event depicted on the front.

Source: © Peabody Museum, Harvard University

Although epigraphers debate it, many place the beginning of the Maya calendar at August 13, 3114 B.C. So the date in the Gregorian calendar is approximately

$$1,253,912/365 = 3435.37$$
$$3435.37 - 3114 = 321.37 \text{ A.D.}$$

We then subtract a year, because the Gregorian calendar implies a "0" year B.C. Count the days from the calendar's start date, and the glyph gives a date for Zero-Moon-Bird's coronation as September 17, A.D. 320.

whether the water was used to irrigate fields, this is less important than the level of organization and authority needed to construct the reservoirs and to apportion the water. So, in one sense, Wittfogel's "irrigation hypothesis" also plays a role here.

But both explanations can be subsumed under the more general scenario of Johnson and Earle. Recall that their explanation required three conditions: (1) stress on food resources created by high population density, (2) the need for an overarching system of

The second calendar is called the *tzolk'in,* or Sacred Almanac (shown in Figure 15-14). It is best envisioned as two cogged wheels, one with the numbers 1 through 13 on it, the other with 20 named days (such as "flint knife," "monkey," and "lizard"). This defines a sacred year of 260 days (13 × 20) with each day having a unique number–name combination.

The third calendar was the *haab,* or Vague Year, which consisted of 18 months of 20 days each, with 5 extra days added at the end. (The Maya were aware that the year was 365.25 days in length, but they did not use a leap year.) The Vague Year and the Sacred Almanac worked together to produce a cycle of 18,980 days. The exact same day—with the same number–name combination and Vague Year day—occurs only once every 52 years. The days when the 52-year cycle began over were critical to the Maya and required world renewal ceremonies.

The Maya recognized cycles of time, and a return to the beginning of time (or the end of time, some say), according to the Maya calendar, will occur on December 23, 2012.

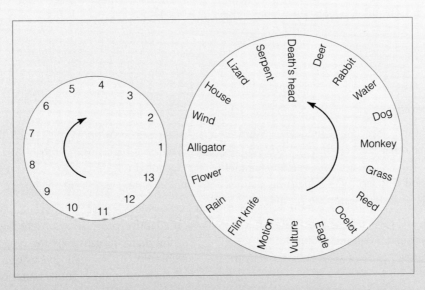

Figure 15-14 The Sacred Almanac. Each day has a name and a number. Envision the two wheels turning opposite to one another, and you can see that the current day is "1 alligator," tomorrow will be "2 wind," the day after tomorrow "3 house," and so on.

integration, and (3) opportunities for economic control. All of these characteristics are found among the Maya of the late Preclassic and Classic periods. The high population density places pressure on the agricultural economy and, in dry years, this pressure can be so severe that it leads to outright conflict. Warfare, as well as efforts to prevent it, requires a system of social integration, as do efforts to ensure the flow of trade goods, information, and rituals between allied centres. The large centres, however, had the ability to control labour and, hence, agricultural productivity and warfare. It is possible that, as one large centre gained the edge in authority, families moved to it and smaller centres gave their allegiance (and their labour) in return for protection. To maintain their positions of power, leaders of the large centres controlled the religion and calendrical rituals that provided a powerful integrating ideology for the Maya.

So when we examine the material and ideological fundamentals of Maya culture, we see that they satisfy each of Johnson and Earle's three conditions. As with the origins of agriculture, there is no single "prime mover" to account for the development of a particular archaic state, and various paradigms each contribute something to a final explanation.

Conclusion

We have only briefly discussed the origins of agriculture and the archaic state. The specific developmental sequences for each differ widely throughout the world, but the variables of population, environment, warfare, trade, and ideology all seem to play key roles in one or both of these cultural changes. The specific *processes* that gave rise to the transition differ from case to case, but the general *conditions* appear to be similar. Explanations that seek to attribute these major changes in human cultural evolution using single variables—such as knowledge, environment, irrigation, or warfare—seem to be less useful than ones that incorporate a number of variables and perspectives.

Human cultural behaviour and large-scale change in social and political organization are products of multiple variables that work in different combinations in different parts of the world. One of archaeology's tasks is to reconstruct these different, specific historical sequences. Another is to use these sequences to discover conditions that are both sufficient *and* necessary to account for major transitions in cultural evolution. In this chapter, we have recounted two instances in which archaeologists have tried to do precisely this.

Summary

- The 19th-century idea of unilineal evolution claimed that the differences among modern peoples resulted from differential progress various peoples had made toward "modernity"—which was defined as an upper-class, western European lifestyle.

- Living "primitives" were seen as providing evidence of the stages of human cultural evolution; for some scholars, "primitive" peoples were still "back in the Stone Age."

- Darwin did not actually use the term "evolution" in his revolutionary work *On the Origin of Species*, but he provided social Darwinists with a scientific explanation for why some peoples had not made progress, as well as the expectation that primitive peoples would all become extinct.

- Social Darwinism suggested that human progress depends on competition and, in the 19th century, this theory was used to justify global imperialism, racism, and the excesses of capitalism.

- American anthropology rejected unilineal cultural evolution, replacing it with historical particularism that sought to understand each culture within itself, not as a stage in human evolution.

- Archaeology's processual agenda, with its emphasis on adaptive processes, brought back an interest in evolutionary processes by focusing on the degree of regularity in human behaviour. Archaeological research does show some patterns in human cultural evolution; in particular, increasing population density is associated with major changes in economy and social/political organization.

- The origins of agriculture appear to have resulted from (1) climate changes at the end of the Pleistocene that were favourable for plant domestication, (2) population growth that caused foragers to take less efficient resources, including small seeds, and (3) the existence in some places of plants that responded to human foraging by becoming more productive.

- Archaic states appear to be a response to (1) population growth and the resultant need to intensify agriculture, (2) coordination of mechanisms of social integration, such as trade and ideology, and (3) the potential to control productive resources. The specific character and history of an archaic state, however, depends on the particular environmental situation, the importance of warfare versus trade, and the kind of ideology that supports the elite rulers.

- Archaeology uses specific historical sequences, constructed through a more humanistic approach to prehistory, to determine what conditions are necessary and sufficient to explain major cultural evolutionary transitions.

Additional Reading

CANADIAN RESOURCES

Hart, J. P., Asch-Sidell, Nancy, Scarry, C. M., and Crawford, G. W. (2002). The age of common beans (*Phaseolus vulgaris L.*) in the Northern Eastern Woodlands. *Antiquity, 76,* 292.

Matson, R. G., and Coupland, Gary. (1995). *The Prehistory of the Northwest Coast.* New York: Academic Press.

Rankin, Lisa. (2000). *Interpreting Long-term Trends in the Transition to Farming: Reconsidering the Nodwell Site, Ontario, Canada.* British Archaeological Reports S830. Oxford, UK: Hadrian Books Ltd.

OTHER RESOURCES

Coe, Michael, and Van Stone, Mark. (2001). *Reading the Maya Glyphs.* London: Thames and Hudson.

Harrison, Peter. (1999). *The Lords of Tikal: Rulers of an Ancient Maya City.* London: Thames and Hudson.

Price, T. Douglas (Ed.). (2000). *Europe's First Farmers.* Cambridge: Cambridge University Press.

Price, T. Douglas, and Gebauer, Anne Birgitte. (Eds.). (1995). *Last Hunters—First Farmers: New Perspectives on the Prehistoric Transition to Agriculture.* Santa Fe: School of American Research Press.

Sabloff, Jeremy. (1989). *The Cities of Ancient Mexico: Reconstructing a Lost World.* London: Thames and Hudson.

Schele, Linda, and Freidel, David. (1990). *A Forest of Kings: The Untold Story of the Ancient Maya.* New York: William Morrow.

Smith, Bruce. (1995). *The Emergence of Agriculture.* New York: Scientific American Library.

Toby, Susan. (2004). *Ancient Mexico and Central America.* London: Thames and Hudson.

Online Resources

COMPANION WEBSITE
Visit *http://www.archaeology1ce.nelson.com* to access a wide range of material to help you succeed in your introductory archaeology course. These include flashcards, Internet exercises, Web links, and practice quizzes.

RESEARCH ONLINE
WITH INFOTRAC COLLEGE EDITION
From the Student Companion Website, you can access the InfoTrac College Edition database, which offers thousands of full-length articles for your research.

16

Historical Archaeology and Industrial Archaeology: Insights into Canada's Rural, Urban, and Industrial Past

The Davis water wheel and flume, Williams Creek, British Columbia, 1868. Mining has played an important role in the history of Canada, and is one of the areas studied by industrial archaeology.

Source: NA-674, Glenbow Archives

Preview

Historical archaeology and industrial archaeology are somewhat unique because they often use written documents (texts) to aid in the interpretation of archaeological data. At first glance, this type of "text-aided archaeology" might seem to give archaeologists who work in these areas a bit of an edge over colleagues who study societies that lack writing systems. As we will see, however, this can be as much a curse as it is a blessing.

Historical archaeologists in Canada work primarily for government agencies, where they use documentary evidence in combination with archaeological information to record, interpret, conserve, and in some cases physically reconstruct important sites. The same is also true for industrial archaeologists, although they are far fewer in number.

In this chapter, we will examine some of the unique problems associated with text-aided archaeology, and show how historical archaeologists use the goals of both history and anthropological archaeology in their research. We will also look at how industrial archaeology is currently examining the origins of Canada's industrial landscape and its effect on the development of Canadian society.

Introduction

Historical archaeology and industrial archaeology are two important areas of our discipline that don't often get the attention they deserve. Historical archaeology is the study of Canada's colonial past, and it has tended to concentrate on the fur trade, which began soon after the arrival of Europeans in North America during the 16th century. Relationships were subsequently forged between European traders and First Nations peoples to aid in the acquisition of pelts from fur-bearing animals like the beaver (Figure 16-1). The fur trade has been a topic of great interest in Canada because it played an important role in shaping the development of Canada as a nation. It also dramatically changed the course of many First Nations and Inuit societies through the introduction of disease and European material goods.

Industrial archaeology is a specialized branch of historical archaeology that examines such things as the evolution of technology and how Canada's industrial heritage has shaped the course of rural and urban life. Until recently, most industrial archaeology has focused on the documentation and preservation of industrial sites that played a significant role in the development of transportation, manufacturing, and the extraction of primary resources like oil, coal, and forestry products (Figure 16-2). Industrial archaeologists are now beginning to address anthropological questions by examining these industries as **socio-technical systems.**

Historical archaeology suffers from somewhat of an identity crisis. Unlike their cousins who study societies that lacked well-developed systems of writing, historical archaeologists interpret artifacts using documents such as probates, diaries, catalogues, letters, and insurance claims. This is why historical archaeology is often referred to as **text-aided archaeology.** Documents

---

socio-technical system A means of understanding the interaction between people and technology in the workplace.

text-aided archaeology The use of written documents such as probates, shipping records, diaries, and catalogues to interpret artifacts recovered from historical sites.

437

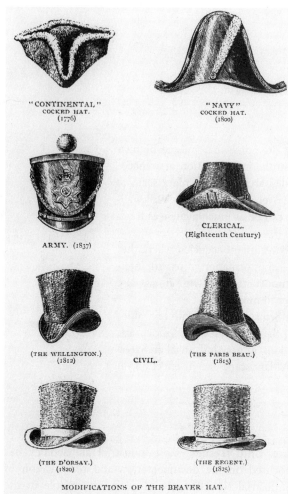

"CONTINENTAL"
COCKED HAT.
(1776)

"NAVY"
COCKED HAT.
(1800)

ARMY. (1837)

CLERICAL.
(Eighteenth Century)

(THE WELLINGTON.)
(1812)

CIVIL.

(THE PARIS BEAU.)
(1815)

(THE D'ORSAY.)
(1820)

(THE REGENT.)
(1825)

MODIFICATIONS OF THE BEAVER HAT.

Figure 16-1 Illustrations of various styles of beaver hat [ca. 1776–1825]. Beaver pelts were important commodities during the fur trade.

Source: NA-1532-4/Glenbow Archives

archaeology at all. In other words, what prevents historical archaeology from becoming the most expensive way in the world to learn something we already know? Answering this question requires that we examine the theoretical and methodological basis of historical archaeology.

Historical Archaeology: Is It History or Is It Anthropology?

Historical archaeology emerged as a discipline in the 1960s in North America, with the creation of *The Society for Historical Archaeology* along with its flagship journal, *Historical Archaeology*. Right from the beginning, however, archaeologists struggled to define this new area of study. Was historical archaeology unique in its use of both documentary and artifactual data? Not really, because archaeologists as far back as the 16th century had been using written documents *and* artifacts to study literate societies such as Ancient Greece and Rome. Other definitions focused on the *time depth* and *subject matter* of historical archaeology. James Deetz, for example, described historical archaeology as "the archaeology of the spread of European cultures throughout the world since the 15th century, and its impact on indigenous people." Such a characterization acknowledges the close association between historical archaeology and colonialism. However, studying the spread of European culture ignores the experiences of Africans and Asians, who came to the New World as slaves and immigrant workers (Figure 16-3). Adding to the confusion is the uncertain parentage of historical archaeology. Was it borne from history because of its use of historical documents, or from anthropology because of its utilization of artifacts to study human behaviour?

The discipline of history is often categorized as **particularizing,** meaning that detailed descriptions of historical events are emphasized instead of trying to establish general explanations for their occurrence. As we saw in Chapter 1, anthropology and archaeology went through a particularizing phase in the late 19th and early 20th centuries. Things changed, however, when scientific (generalizing) approaches became popular in the 1960s. Many historical archaeologists were caught up in this new movement because most were being trained in departments of anthropology, rather than history. These anthropologically trained

provide descriptions of past activities and events that are far more detailed than those usually obtained from archaeological data alone. Unlike pre-contact archaeology, many of the artifacts that historical archaeologists find are familiar because objects like tin cans, bottles, and nails continue to be used today, albeit in slightly different forms. Consequently, one might legitimately wonder why we do historical

particularizing Emphasizing detailed descriptions of historical events instead of trying to establish general explanations for their occurrence.

Figure 16-2 Canada's first oil field at Petrolia, Ontario, ca. 1862–1894.
Source: NA-302-9, Glenbow Archives

Figure 16-3 Chinese men on handcars, Canadian Pacific Railway, ca. 1866.
Source: NA-387-27, Glenbow Archives

archaeologists felt that historical archaeology should address such issues as defining human cultural adaptation and cultural evolution. But was archaeological theory up to the task of dealing with both documentary *and* artifactual evidence? If not, then new methods and theories, unique to historical archaeology, would have to be developed. Despite all of this hand wringing, it seems as though historical archaeology today is no closer to solving its identity crisis.

Lines of Inquiry in Historical Archaeology

Kathleen Deagan has defined five lines of inquiry that nicely define how historical archaeology is currently practised in Canada and the United States. These approaches can be particularizing or generalizing, depending on the nature of the research.

1. *Historical Supplementation: (Particularizing).* This is also referred to as the "handmaiden to history" approach—a line made famous in 1964 by archaeologist and author Noel Hume. Here, archaeology is used to supplement the documentary record of the past, and provide data for the reconstruction and restoration of historical sites. This approach is commonly used by government agencies, such as Parks Canada, that are concerned with documenting and preserving sites of national importance. This requires a particularistic approach to historical archaeology, and involves excavating, describing, and documenting features such as buildings for the purposes of preservation, reconstruction, and tourism. For example, fur trade posts—such as Fort William in Thunder Bay, Ontario, and Lower Fort Garry in Winnipeg, Manitoba—have been painstakingly reconstructed using information obtained by supplementing written records with archaeological data. Historians have also used archaeological data to balance out the more subjective and biased standard of written history.

2. *Reconstruction of Past Lifeways: (Particularizing).* This orientation uses archaeological data to examine historical events from a nondocumentary point of view. These approaches tend to focus on specific social groups or events where a written record may not exist. Rather than focus on the grandiose, this orientation is concerned with reconstructing the everyday conditions of the past. This is an especially effective way of looking at the social histories of women and disenfranchised and disadvantaged groups in Canada such as Asian immigrants and First Nations societies. This approach has also been used to examine how people adapted to relocation in new environments and integrated themselves into society. As we will see later in this chapter, archaeological studies of the homestead of Susanna Moodie in rural Ontario by Susan Jamieson (Trent University) provide an example of this type of approach.

3. *Processual Studies: (Generalizing).* Rather than investigate specific times, places, and social groups, this tactic investigates cultural processes as a means of addressing more general questions about human culture. Such approaches make use of the *hypothetical-deductive method,* where hypotheses are developed and tested against the archaeological and documentary record. Processual studies in historical archaeology have been used to examine acculturation, and the impact of European technology on indigenous peoples. Work by Clifford Hickey (University of Alberta), for example, suggests that the economic and social systems of the Copper Inuit in the Canadian Arctic were altered through the abandonment of a supply depot and ship by European explorers in search of the lost Franklin Expedition.

4. *Archaeological Science: (Generalizing).* Historical archaeology has played an important role in testing the basic principles of archaeological interpretation under controlled conditions. For example, well-dated objects such as headstones have been used to test the assumption that stylistic traits are normally distributed through time. This, of course, is the basis of the principle of *seriation.* Historical archaeology has also been used to validate the assumption that particular forms of human and cultural behaviour "pattern" archaeological data. The work of Stanley South, for example, has focused on defining patterns of refuse disposal that are characteristic of particular environmental circumstances, ethnic backgrounds, and cultural heritage. Others have examined how social status is reflected in the use of material culture. As we will see, the use of earthenware ceramics by 19th-century Métis women living in the Red River Settlement in Manitoba provides us with an excellent example of this type of approach.

5. *Cognitive Studies: (Generalizing).* Historical archaeologists have begun to adopt cognitive approaches that focus on the symbolic meaning of objects, and how architecture and material culture are used to communicate authority, ethnicity, status, and gender. Such studies

often focus on a **mindset**—a set of organizing principles that determine how people perceive the world around them. Prior to the mid eighteenth century, most people shared a *Medieval mindset* of the world. This consisted of an organic, disorganized, and informal view of the world. Houses, for example, were largely asymmetrical and unplanned because they were built according to need. This was eventually replaced by the *Georgian mindset,* which was more concerned with order, individuality, and hierarchy. Houses and landscapes became more symmetrical and ordered, and people ate from individual place settings rather than communal pots. In the United States, the work of James Deetz, Mark Leone, and Henry Glassie best typifies this approach. Later in this chapter, we will see how this orientation has been used by Greg Monks (University of Manitoba) and Scott Hamilton (Lakehead University) to study the architecture of historic fur trade forts in Canada.

The examples we will look at in this chapter suggest that no single overarching theoretical orientation characterizes historical archaeology in the early 21st century. Rather, it is best characterized as a hybridization of various goals and ideas. As we will see, Canadian historical archaeology can be *historical* and *anthropological; particularistic* and *generalizing; processual* and *postprocessual.* It is a way of pursuing questions that neither history nor archaeology could address alone. Now, let's look at some of the issues historical archaeologists face when using documentary evidence.

Integrating Data Sets: Working with Artifacts and Written Documents

Documentary Evidence and the Fallacy of the Written Word

The story is a common one, and something many of us working in archaeology have experienced. A reporter asks if they can write a story on an archaeological site you are excavating. You agree, and arrange to meet them at the site to show them around. You carefully explain the objectives of your research, show them some artifacts and cultural features, and offer some preliminary interpretations. A few days later the newspaper article appears, and you notice that certain facts have been left out, while others have been emphasized to make the story more interesting from the reporter's point of view. Few archaeologists we know have read such stories and giddily exclaimed, "That's exactly what I said . . . they got everything right!" The lesson to be learned here is that newspaper articles are like any other written document—they reflect the author's perception of the world, and not the actual world itself.

Written documents such as probates, wills, tax lists, and diaries were never intended by their authors to be used as data sources by historical archaeologists. Instead, they were produced for specific purposes, and to be read by a certain audience. Take our newspaper example, for instance. The articles that newspaper reporters write about archaeologists are generally considered human-interest stories. The purpose of such articles is to inform and entertain an audience of nonspecialists. An article on the same research project would have to be written for an entirely different audience if it were to be published in a peer-reviewed academic journal. Other factors exist that can bias the information contained in historical documents. While eyewitnesses often produce accounts of historical events, others are written using second-hand information. Under such circumstances, details might get altered in the same way that jokes are changed when told repeatedly. One must also keep in mind that written documents are biased toward the views of a small group of literate people. Indeed, much of the documentary evidence available to archaeologists was produced by upper-class males who by virtue of their gender and position in society had learned to read and write. One might wonder how well the views of such individuals matched those of women, the lower classes, aboriginal people, and slaves.

You might think that documents such as inventories and shipping manifests are free of such biases because they deal with numbers and objects rather than thoughts and feelings. However, a fascinating look into the world of smuggling in the pre-revolutionary United States reveals that this is not the case. Peter R. Schmidt and Stephen A. Mrozowski have

> **mindset** A set of organizing principles that determine how people perceive the world around them.

examined how smuggling was used by New England merchants in the 17th and 18th centuries to outwit the British in their attempts to regulate the importing of Dutch and French products into the United States (Figure 16-4). Excavations at several archaeological sites in Rhode Island revealed an abundance of such non-English items as French earthenware ceramics, French brandy bottles, and Dutch gin bottles. While these items were obviously smuggled, Schmidt and Mrozowski point out that evidence for this complex activity is sparse because of its highly secretive nature. Perpetrators saw smuggling as a justified act of resistance to British authority, and as a way of reducing economic hardships produced by the attempts of outsiders to regulate the marketplace. Schmidt and Mrozowski found that historical documents provided only a biased and partial account of these practices. Documents such as day books and store blotters, for example, contained some evidence for the categories and amounts of illegal goods that were available for purchase in the colonies. Letters from ship owners to agents told the same story, but from a perspective filled with the strategies and tactics of the smuggling trade. Such documents reveal that smugglers continually changed these tactics as British authorities increased their efforts to suppress trade in contraband.

So, it would seem that being able to read does not make one a historian any more than being able to pick up a shovel makes one an archaeologist. How does a historical archaeologist identify and control for the biases present in the documents she/he uses? The best way is to treat them as if they were artifacts. As we have seen in earlier chapters, artifacts found at archaeological sites occur in a particular context. This context can include where the artifact occurs in the stratigraphic column, its association with other artifacts and cultural features, and so on. Various *natural* and *cultural* site formation processes can introduce biases that can alter the context of the artifact, and affect our

Figure 16-4 Revenue Captain William Cooke seizes contraband gold landed from a French privateer, 1793.
Source: Captain WIliam Cooke Seizes Contraband by John Thompson (ID# 88229), courtesy of U.S. Department of Homeland Security

interpretations of it. Archaeologists need to understand the history of a site in order to control for such biases. In the same way, historical archaeologists use something called **historiography** to reconstruct the context or history of the documents they wish to use. Rather than study historic events directly, historiographers examine the changing interpretations of those events through the eyes of different individuals. Historiographers begin by examining the document *externally,* attempting to establish the authenticity of the source and whether or not its author can be *believed.* Primary sources written by eyewitnesses to events, for example, are usually more accurate than secondary sources where individuals have summarized things they did not experience first-hand. The researcher then examines the document *internally,* examining such factors as 1) the type and origin of the document, 2) the identity of the author, 3) the purpose of the document, 4) the time period when the document was written, 5) the length of time separating the event from when it was recorded in the document, 6) the presence of factual errors, 7) the veracity of information, 8) the multiplicity of documents, 9) the inconsistencies in style, and 10) the intended audience. This is usually accomplished by cross-referencing the document with other papers containing similar kinds of information. Rather than arrive at a true/false conclusion, however, evaluating the information contained in historical documents is still largely a subjective process based on common sense and on the researcher's intimate familiarity with the texts of a specific time period, geographic location, and social environment under study. Put simply, only through familiarity with the expected can one hope to recognize the unexpected.

Maps and Pictures—A Special Type of Documentary Evidence

The old saying that a picture is worth a thousand words aptly describes why maps and paintings, such as the one in Figure 16-5, are useful sources of documentary evidence, and why they are also subject to many of the same biases affecting written documents. Archaeologist Nancy Seasholes maintains that maps are important sources of information that can help one locate historical sites, define settlement patterns, and even examine topographic changes on the landscape. But these very same maps can also distort spatial reality through inaccuracies and information biases. Historical maps are evaluated in much the same way as historical documents—by considering why and for whom they were made.

Websites such as Google Earth provide us with a good example of how this works in the modern-day world. Using Google Earth allows us to generate maps that show just the locations of hotels, or car rental agencies, or shopping malls for any city in the world. These specialized maps are designed to selectively display only the spatial information that we want—everything else is left off the map. An archaeologist discovering one of our printed Google Earth maps a few thousand years from now might think that cities in the 21st century were dominated by specific types of service industries like hotels and restaurants! In the same way, a military map of Upper Canada produced during the War of 1812 might emphasize the location of garrisons, storehouses, artillery, and other locations of strategic importance, yet leave off private residences, stores, and public buildings. Likewise, directories might accurately depict the grids of streets running through a town, but leave buildings off the map. It is therefore important that the archaeologist understand the intended purpose of the map she/he is dealing with. Finally, it is important to take the skill and accuracy of the cartographer into account, as this can also affect the usefulness of historical maps for archaeological purposes.

Historical maps can be broken down into many different categories. Sometimes a historic event is deemed important enough that several maps are commissioned to document the same subject at the same time. These *comparable maps* can be combined to produce a more complete picture of an area during a specific time period. Real estate and insurance companies used *atlas maps* to determine property values and assess fire risks to buildings. Consequently, they can be an invaluable source of information when identifying the remains of buildings and other structures encountered during excavations. *Bird's-eye-view* maps were also very popular during the 19th century, and were used to produce a three-dimensional perspective of a town or city as if it were seen from the air. The

historiography The study of the practice of history, focuses on the narratives, interpretations, worldview, use of evidence, or method of presentation of other historians.

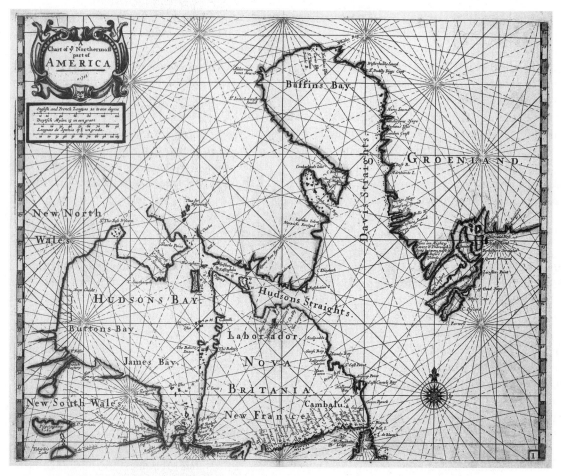

Figure 16-5 A historical map of the Hudson Bay Area, ca. 1700.

Source: NA-2295-1/Glenbow Archives

problem with these types of maps, however, is that buildings were occasionally portrayed as stylized versions of their actual appearance (Figure 16-6).

Archaeologists have used maps of Canada drawn by First Nations and Inuit groups to identify and locate trail systems, and to understand how indigenous societies perceived the landscapes they inhabited. The *Historic Atlas of Canada* has many indigenous maps from the 1700s and 1800s, most of which were drawn at the request of explorers such as David Thompson. These maps illustrate how cartography and the conceptualization of space can vary cross-culturally. The scale of many indigenous maps, for example, often varies according to the difficulty of the terrain and the corresponding time it takes to travel across it. Consequently, the scale used by the

author can vary within a single map sheet. This stands in vivid contrast to the topographic maps produced by the Centre for Topographic Information (Ottawa), which are drawn to standardized scales of either 1/50,000 or 1/250,000.

"Roughing It in the Bush": How Artifacts Illustrate Life in 19th-Century Canada

Once the validity of various maps and historical documents has been established, and assorted biases have been controlled for, how is this information integrated with archaeological data? At a very basic level, archaeological data can be used to supplement information contained in written documents. It can also be used to reconstruct the everyday lives of ordinary people at a

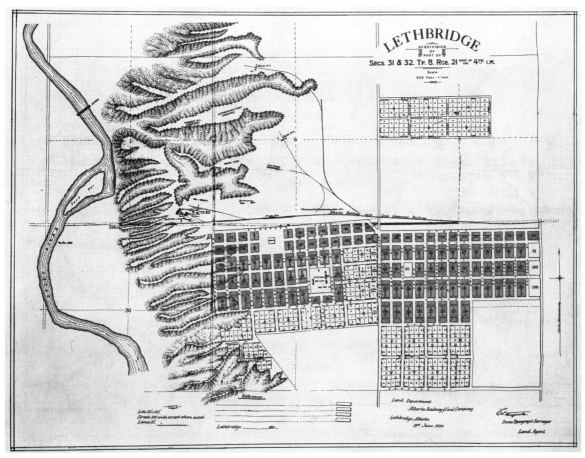

Figure 16-6 A bird's-eye-view historical map of the city of Lethbridge, Alberta, ca. 1890.

Source: NA-2529-1/Glenbow Archives

specific time and place (see Kathleen Deagan's characterization of historical archaeology above). Excavations by Trent University at the homestead of Susanna Moodie in Douro Township, Ontario, illustrate how this can be accomplished.

Susanna Moodie was born in 1803 in Suffolk, England, and from an early age she loved to write. The fact that she was able to publish many of her poems, stories, and articles is a testament to her skills as an author. Her life dramatically changed in 1830 when she met Lt. John Wedderburn Dunbar Moodie. They married in 1831 and emigrated to Canada a year later, following the birth of their first child. The Moodie family settled in Upper Canada, a British colony in what is now the province of Ontario, and lived on a half-cleared farm. They were soon forced to move into the "bush," however, after some bad investments required them to sell up. They remained there until

Susanna's husband took up the job of sheriff in the county of Hastings.

Life in 19th-century Upper Canada likely would have been difficult for someone of Susanna's social status. She documented many of her experiences in articles she wrote for local journals and ladies' magazines. However, the most thorough account of this period in Susanna Moodie's life is contained in her book *Roughing It in the Bush; Or, Life in Canada*. Published as a two-volume set in 1852, the book was so popular that it spawned a sequel the following year called *Life in the Clearings versus the Bush*. Both volumes contain honest and humorous descriptions of the challenges she faced while trying to forge a life in 19th-century rural Canada. Margaret Atwood's *The Journals of Susanna Moodie* is a collection of poetry inspired by Moodie's books, and illustrates how her work has influenced the Canadian literary landscape.

Looking Closer
Victorian Art and the Franklin Expedition

Art historian Constance Martin (Arctic Institute of North America) provides us with a fascinating example of how pictures and paintings can be used to convey a society's "sense of place" when tragic circumstances befall its members.

Images of the landscape and climate of the Arctic have long fascinated Europeans. In the years following 1818, when the British Admiralty renewed its quest for a Northwest Passage through the Canadian arctic archipelago, depictions of this strange northern world emerged in many 19th-century paintings and works of literature. Explorer-artists such as George Back and F. W. Beechey completed early paintings of the Canadian Arctic during their many voyages. Painting and drawing skills were encouraged by the Royal Society because of their use in surveying and navigation prior to the advent of photography. In many of these paintings, however, the Canadian Arctic was often transformed into images that were familiar to viewers; for example, icebergs were portrayed as gothic cathedrals, castles, or caverns. This gothic view of the Arctic, propagated by explorers' accounts of isolation, privation, starvation, and death, influenced writers of fiction and dramatic plays—such as Charles Dickens and

Wilkie Collins in their Christmas plays *The Frozen Deep* and *The Wreck of the Golden Mary*.

In 1847, Sir John Franklin led two ships, HMS *Erebus* and HMS *Terror*, into the Canadian Arctic and was never seen or heard from again. At the age of 60, Franklin himself was already a *relic* of the time of Trafalgar, when British Maritime Supremacy ruled the day. Dr. John Rae of the Hudson Bay Company discovered the fate of the 128 men of the Franklin Expedition while searching for them in 1854. Inuit travelling to the arctic coast told him of encountering the expedition in a state of anarchy and cannibalism. These reports of the moral collapse of a British Naval Expedition captured the attention of the average Victorian. Charles Dickens himself was even prompted to write several essays and plays in which he denounced Rae and his conclusions.

As information about the doomed expedition became public, Martin observed that artistic portrayals of the Canadian Arctic began to change. Instead of a gothic world of fantasy, the northern landscape was increasingly portrayed as a harsh and brutish place. By way of illustration, Edwin Landseer, in his painting *Man Proposes, God Disposes* (Figure 16-7), and Frederick Church, in *Iceberg*, both portray the broken masts of ships on

Conducting archaeological research at the Moodie homestead provided a unique opportunity for Trent University archaeologist Susan Jamieson to reconstruct 19th-century pioneer life in rural Ontario, using historical documents and early Canadian emigration literature. Excavations focused on the Moodie cabin, which appeared only as a shallow depression when the project was initially undertaken. While the homestead had been disturbed by 20th-century bulldozing and looting, it nevertheless yielded more than 20,000 artifacts. Many of these items were unlike those typically found in bush-lot homesteads. For example, hand-decorated and transfer-print ceramic plates, usually found in wealthier established residences, were recovered from the otherwise humble Moodie farmstead.

Such items likely reflect the social status of the Moodie family soon after their arrival in Upper Canada. However, several aspects of the assemblage support Susanna Moodie's accounts of the strained financial circumstances later experienced by her family. The faunal remains recovered from the site, for instance, contain high percentages of wild animal species such as eel, beaver, and raccoon. The remains of domestic animals recovered were also associated with low meat-yielding portions of carcasses. Such an assemblage is not something one would expect to see among upper-class English settlers. Instead, it suggests that, as times got harder, the Moodies relied more and more on local resources. Another interesting aspect of the assemblage was the recovery of drawn tube and wire-spun beads. Such items were commonly used to

Figure 16-7 Edwin Landseer's epic painting *Man Proposes, God Disposes,* capturing how the Victorian public may have perceived the Canadian Arctic following the Franklin disaster.

Source: Man proposes, God disposes, 1864, Landseer, Sir Edwin (1802-73)/Royal Holloway, University of London/The Bridgeman Art Library

ice-strewn shores. This "demonization" of the arctic landscape is perhaps best exemplified in Landseer's painting, which depicts the carcasses of Franklin sailors being devoured by bloodthirsty polar bears.

In its day, the Franklin disaster was a historic event that would have likely been comparable to the destruction of the space shuttles *Challenger* and *Columbia.* Such events can cause entire societies to question many of their core values. In the case of Victorian England, the failure of the expedition, coupled with charges of cannibalism, directly challenged cherished ideas about the discipline of British seamen and their ability to resist extreme conditions. These fears seem to have taken shape in the paintings and sketches of the Canadian Arctic.

barter with aboriginal people, and support Susanna Moodie's claims that the family had a close relationship with local First Nations groups. Thus, the artifacts recovered by Jamieson are useful because they add another dimension to Susanna Moodie's graphic literary depictions of pioneer life in Upper Canada (see Figure 16-8).

The Theoretical Dimensions of Historical Archaeology

As we have seen, working back and forth between historical documents and artifacts can provide a more complete picture of an event, or what life was like during a particular period in history. However, historical

archaeologists also use a variety of theoretical approaches to interpret their data. In the late 1970s, for example, Stanley South admonished historical archaeologists for being too particularistic and failing to employ the methods of processual archaeology in their research. Like Lewis Binford and his followers, South maintained that the artifacts found at historical sites were the static remains of *patterned* human behaviour. An English family travelling to Canada in the 19th century, for example, carried particular attitudes and modes of behaviour with them. These organizational behaviours were then reflected in the types and frequencies of the artifacts they discarded. Because all 19th-century English families shared particular modes of behaviour, South reasoned that the same categories of artifacts should occur in expected frequencies at other

Figure 16-8 A drawing of a goldfinch and thistle by Susanna Moodie. Although Susanna was not as interested in natural history as her sister was, drawing and painting were a welcome distraction from the rigours of pioneer life in Ontario.

Source: NL-15558/National Library of Canada

sites. South and other historical archaeologists have used this idea to define a number of artifact patterns or profiles that defined such behavioural modes. These include the "Carolina artifact pattern," the "Brunswick pattern," the "slave pattern," the "frontier pattern," the "fur trade pattern," the "incarceration pattern," and the "public interaction pattern."

The "frontier pattern," for example, was based on the idea that British colonial sites in urban and rural areas could be distinguished based on local circumstances. South observed that historical sites located in remote rural areas typically contain lower percentages of ceramics as compared with sites in more urban settings. This distinctive artifact pattern reflects the fact that frontier sites are located farther away from supply lines than are urban ones. As a result, it would have

Looking Closer
Historic Artifacts as Temporal Types

It is a truism in business that competition leads to innovation. Such innovations can mean more cost-effective and efficient manufacturing techniques, or improvements to the actual items themselves. Computers provide an excellent example of this. Dawson currently uses a sleek laptop computer. However, in his basement resides a ten-year-old "clunker" of a desktop that is far slower than his current computer and has a much smaller hard drive. Because his old computer was manufactured for a period of only three years, it would be an excellent index fossil for some future archaeologist to use. Cartridge casings and nails are artifacts that are ubiquitous to historical sites. Like computers, they also possess attributes that reflect innovations in manufacture that can be used to dateal historic sites.

Cartridge Casings

Expended firearm cartridges are found at many historical archaeology sites dating to the period following A.D. 1850. Before the invention of repeating rifles and chambered pistols, guns used a piece of flint attached to a spring-loaded lever to ignite the gunpowder. Rather than a bullet, these flint-lock rifles fired a small, round lead ball. Flintlock rifles were eventually replaced by guns that could be

fired repeatedly because bullets came pre-packed with gun powder in percussion caps. The most famous of these repeating firearms was the Colt revolver, invented by Samuel Colt in 1835–36.

Historical archaeologists usually identify two types of cartridge casings: *rim fire* and *centre fire* cartridges. Rim fire cartridges were manufactured between 1856 and 1868. Gunpowder was built right into the rim of these cartridges, so that a hammer striking its edge would ignite the charge. Centre fire cartridges eventually replaced rim fire cartridges after 1868. The hammer of the gun now struck the middle of the cartridge base (called a percussion cap), where the gunpowder was located. The presence/absence of a centrally located percussion cap is an attribute used to distinguish earlier rim fire from later centre fire cartridges. In addition, the base of the cartridge is usually stamped with the calibre or gauge of the gun, the manufacturer's name and/or initials, and sometimes a trade name. This information can be used to look up precise dates of manufacture and distribution in catalogues.

Nails

Like firearm cartridges, nails are also common at historical sites (Figure 16-9). While machines using bailing wire make the nails we buy today at hardware

been difficult to transport ceramics to remote locations without breaking them.

While many archaeologists have challenged the assumptions upon which these artifact profiles are based, South's work is an example of the *archaeological science* orientation defined earlier, and demonstrates how historical archaeologists have attempted to align themselves with the goals of anthropological archaeology.

Ideas in Things: The Meaning of Everyday Objects

The approach advocated by Stanley South is firmly rooted in a **materialist perspective,** which views artifacts as functioning solely to adapt people to their environments. The frontier artifact pattern, for example, predicts that people living in remote settings will forgo the finer things in life in favour of more practical items used to acquire food, clothing, and shelter. However, artifacts that defy functional explanations occasionally appear in frontier settings. Dawson participated in the excavation of an early 20th-century mission on Herschel Island in the western Canadian Arctic, where his team recovered pieces of the resident missionary's wedding china. What would compel someone to bring an impractical item like this to such a remote setting? When functional explanations don't seem to fit,

materialist perspective Views artifacts as functioning solely to adapt people to their environments.

stores, "old timey" nails were made the hard way—by hand.

Hand-forged nails were manufactured between A.D. 1600 and 1800, and are the earliest nails found on historical sites. They are tapered on four sides, and vary in thickness from head to point. Hand-forged nails were made by taking a sheet of iron and splitting it into narrow sections. These sections were then snapped off into smaller lengths, placed in a vice, and hammered on one end to create a flat head that was either square (rectangular headed) or circular (rose headed) in shape.

Machine-cut nails, made between 1790 and 1040, had handmade heads, while those manufactured between 1815 and 1840 had machined heads that were rectilinear to oval in shape.

Modern wire nails were invented in France in 1850. By 1855, wire nail production had been completely automated, although wire nails did not outnumber machine-cut nails until after the 1890s. Modern wire nails contain parallel striations under the head, which are produced by the die gripper used to hold the nail in place while the head was pressed.

Historical archaeology requires an almost encyclopedic knowledge of the manufacturing information associated with even the most mundane of objects— from cartridge casings and nails, to doorknobs and buttons. In fact, most historical archaeologists would probably have no trouble earning a little extra money on weekends at their local hardware store. Nevertheless, while it can be somewhat tedious spending hours poring over 18th- and 19th-century catalogues, being able to date an artifact to within a decade is something that pre-contact archaeologists can only dream about.

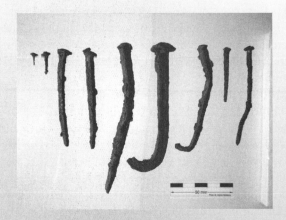

Figure 16-9 Examples of hand-wrought and machine-cut nails recovered from a historical site in the Canadian Arctic. Nails were useful items to the Inuit, and were either acquired through trade or scavenged from abandoned ships and fur trade posts.

Source: Dr. Peter Dawson

historical archaeologists often turn to the non-material dimensions of culture and attempt to understand the symbolic meanings of artifacts.

High Tea on the Canadian Prairies

The use of transfer-print ceramics by the *Hivernant* Métis of the Northwestern Plains provides an interesting example of this type of non-materialist approach in historical archaeology. During the 1980s, David Burley of Simon Fraser University conducted a series of excavations at Métis wintering sites in areas of Alberta, Saskatchewan, and Manitoba. Burley was surprised to discover that fragile earthenware ceramics, such as teacups and saucers, were consistently being recovered. Most had been produced by the Spode/Copeland Company of Staffordshire, England, and were adorned with patterns and pictures that would have seemed strange and unfamiliar to the Métis. The presence of these ceramics stuck out like a sore thumb in an assemblage that otherwise reflected a life of mobility and communal bison hunting. Burley wondered why a group of semi-sedentary bison hunters would have wanted to own such items when much more durable alternatives were available. The answer seems to be that the meanings of these objects were far more valuable to the Métis than their function.

Métis people were the progeny of European fur traders and their native wives. The Métis emerged as a distinct ethnic group during the 19th century, when they were active participants in the fur trade. Many worked as voyageurs, carters, and provisioners for the Hudson Bay Company (HBC) and its principal rival, the Northwest Company. Métis families hunted bison on the Plains, and the pemmican and hide robes that they produced were traded to various fur trade posts and settlements. Before the end of the 1870s, most Métis families had congregated below the confluence of the Red and Assiniboine rivers in southeastern Manitoba, in an area known as the Red River Settlement (Figure 16-10). During this time period, Hudson Bay Company policy decreed that English women were not allowed to live at fur trade posts. As a result, many officers and clerks had taken native wives—a practice initially encouraged by the HBC because the alliances they forged often resulted in new trading opportunities. By the 1820s, however, marriage to a native woman was no longer considered appropriate. Because Métis women were of mixed blood, they quickly became sought after as marriage partners.

A core group of Métis women were soon integrated into the social hierarchies of the Red River Settlement, where they were required to behave as "civilized" English ladies. Ceramic tea sets were important symbols of such behaviour. The Métis wives of company officers overtly displayed their china to visitors in cabinets, and used them according to the appropriate social protocols of British society. Such practices facilitated the assimilation of Métis wives into the upper ranks of the fur trade settlement. The social status of Métis women in Red River Society was usurped, however, when the HBC relaxed its policy regarding the presence of English women at its posts. The arrival of this new enclave of wives introduced an all-white social hierarchy to the Red River Settlement. Many Métis women now found themselves shunned—even those who had previously acquired high status. As the social positions of Métis women became increasingly contested, Burley argued that they intensified their use of ceramics to reinforce their gentrification through displays of social etiquette. But how did earthenware ceramics become so entrenched among poorer Métis bison hunters? In order to explain this, Burley turned to anthropological theories about human consumption.

Consumer behaviour is not unlike an infectious disease. Imagine that a household acquires a new item. In the suburban world of the 21st century, such an item could be a car, backyard deck, or a wide screen plasma television. Neighbouring households understand that such items signify status and wealth. As a result, they soon become "infected" with the idea of obtaining the same item. Once it has been acquired, the neighbouring household is "immunized" from the idea, but becomes a source of infection for other households. This process of "keeping up with the Joneses" ensures that everyone will eventually own the item—even if they don't have a use for it! Burley suggested that transfer-print ceramics had been spread from elite Métis women to wider Métis society in a similar way. As earthenware ceramics became more widely used, their meanings shifted away from visual displays of status and toward a shared form of material culture. Teacups and saucers remained focal points of social interaction, but the rigidly structured protocols of British "high tea" were replaced by informal Métis behaviours such as card playing and gossip. The social dimensions of transfer-print ceramics ensured that they soon became indispensable household items, and were owned by even the poorest Métis bison hunters.

BAKING BREAD.

Figure 16-10 A Métis camp near Pembina, en route to Red River, Manitoba (1859).
Source: NA-1406-26, Glenbow Museum

Historical documents indicate that Hudson Bay Company officials were justifiably puzzled by the use of ceramic tea sets among the Métis (Figure 16-11). HBC fur trader Alexander Ross, for example, couldn't understand why brigades of bison hunters would carry such fragile objects around with them. While Ross was unable to decode the social messages they contained, David Burley's innovative analysis reveals that these artifacts played an important role in mediating social interactions, defining status, and integrating people into society.

"Lawn and Order": Homes, Gardens, and Symbolism

Buildings, like earthenware ceramics, can also be imbued with meaning. Walk around any neighbourhood in Canada, and you'll see what we mean. People paint the exteriors of their houses different colours,

and put different types of plants in their gardens. Occasionally, they place gaudy ornaments on their lawns, like garden gnomes and those wooden cutouts of large-bottomed cartoon gardeners, perpetually bending over to extract unseen weeds. Clearly the occupants of such houses are trying to communicate something to passers-by. Is it just bad taste?

Just like in the best-selling book *The Da Vinci Code*, visual cues abound in the buildings, the ceramic place settings, and even the gardens explored by historical archaeologists. Archaeologists use architectural plans, illustrations, and written documents to decipher these codes. But what kind of information do these codes contain, and for what purpose was it being communicated?

Historical archaeologists such as James Deetz have demonstrated that social orders are often reinforced using material culture. Deetz has argued that the rise of individuality in American society, referred to earlier

Figure 16-11 A sample of some Spode Copeland ceramic design patterns found at Hivernant Métis sites.

Source: Photo courtesy of Fort Vancouver National Historic Site, National Park Service

in this chapter as the Georgian mindset, was reinforced through the segmentation of space in houses, creating more opportunities for people to isolate themselves from one another. Reproducing individuality was also achieved by replacing communal bowls and pots with individual place settings within the home. Even something as simple as gardening can be

ideology The ideas held by members of a society that relate to nature, time, and place.

used to surreptitiously communicate information about one's status.

Mark Leone is a historical archaeologist who has explored the use of visual cues in historical archaeology using the concept of **ideology.** The term "ideology" refers to the ideas held by members of a society that relate to nature, time, and place. According to Leone, these ideas "naturalize" inequalities among people by disguising the fact that the power individuals hold over others is arbitrary, and based in historical precedent. Ask yourself why the English put up with the antics of the Royal Family, and you'll see what I mean. Ideology's function is to use historical precedent to disguise the fact that the monarchy has no real power over citizens of the Commonwealth. The Royal Family has a long history and symbolizes the class-based social order of British society. Perpetuating this social order requires supporting the monarchy through state taxes, and so on. Historical archaeologist Mark Leone provides an interesting example of the naturalization of class using an example of what one might call "lawn and order."

Leone decided to investigate the garden of William Paca, one of the fathers of American Con-federation, who lived in Annapolis, Maryland in the 18th century. During the 1760s, Paca built a large mansion and accompanying garden. The garden was constructed using handbooks filled with detailed observations on such things as plant behaviour and weather patterns. They also promoted the aesthetics of garden layouts, showing how symmetry and terracing could be used to create illusions that made pathways seem longer than they actually were. But Leone argued that the garden also altered one's perception of society, as well. The highly ordered character of the plots, for example, reflected the hierarchical structure of the society in which Paca lived. According to Leone, William Paca's management and control over his garden "naturalized" the control he held over others by virtue of his social position in Anapolis society. Throughout much of his life, Paca vehemently fought for liberty and freedom—the very essence of the American Revolution. However, much of Paca's inherited wealth had been accumulated through use of slavery. Leone argues that Paca's highly ordered garden disguised his ethical dilemma by "naturalizing" the idea of order and hierarchy within his society.

"Big Brother" Architecture: Social Relations at a Canadian Fur Trade Fort

University of Manitoba archaeologist Greg Monks has used an approach similar to that of Leone and Deetz

Figure 16-12 View of Upper Fort Garry, Winnipeg, Manitoba.
Source: NA-354-13, Glenbow Archives

to decode social information contained within the architecture of a historic fur trade fort in Manitoba (Figure 16-12). Upper Fort Garry is located within the Red River Settlement we discussed previously. The fort was occupied between 1836 and 1881, and served both as an administrative centre and as an *instrument of thought* to the settlers who lived there.

Monks was interested in understanding Upper Fort Garry as a set of architectural symbols that were actively used by the Hudson Bay Company to regulate its authority over the economic and social lives of the Red River settlers. Even though the approach taken by Monks is decidedly cognitive, he used archival data in the form of illustrations, scale drawings, photographs, and written documents to form bridging arguments linking the fort's architecture to the motivations of historical agents like the officers and managers of the HBC.

The idea that the architecture of Upper Fort Garry contained recognizable symbols with clear cultural meanings is predicated on the assumption that they would have been intelligible to Red River settlers, who were of various ethnic and religious backgrounds. Those from Britain, France, and Upper and Lower Canada would have been familiar with the cultural schemata upon which the code was based because of their shared backgrounds. Visual cues and their meanings also would have been familiar to Métis and local native populations because of their familiarity with

Euro-Canadian culture through trade relations. Thus, while not everyone was inclined to accept the messages, all likely understood them.

Like people, buildings tend to communicate when they have something to say. So it is not surprising that the use of visual cues in the architecture of Upper Fort Garry was tied to rising economic and social tensions within the settlement. One of the most prominent exterior features of Upper Fort Garry, for example, was an imposing stone wall that enclosed the grounds. Such walls were usually erected for defensive purposes. However, Upper Fort Garry had been constructed *after* the Hudson Bay Company had merged with its chief rival, the Northwest Company. Some have suggested that the walls were built to protect the fort from flooding, but illustrations and plans reveal the presence of rifle holes. Also puzzling was the fact that the foundations upon which the wall rested were a mere 50 centimetres thick. This contributed to the collapse of a section of the wall in 1871, and suggests that it had been intended mainly for show. So just what was the Hudson Bay Company afraid of?

A definite social hierarchy existed in the Red River Settlement, and French-speaking Catholics like the Métis occupied the bottom rung of the ladder. What's more, social tensions were exacerbated whenever the Red River Settlement fell on hard times. The fact that settlers were told they could trade furs only with the Hudson Bay Company just made matters worse. In 1849, a Métis by the name of Guillaume Sayer and three other men were charged with illegally trading furs with Americans. While all were found guilty, no charges were laid because 377 armed Métis awaited the verdict outside the courthouse. The HBC felt its authority threatened whenever these types of conflicts occurred. Monks argues that it responded by demonstrating and reinforcing its authority through the architecture of the fort. Consequently, the "defensive" wall at Upper Fort Garry had been built to send a signal of HBC authority to unruly settlers that any attempts to upset economic and social relations would be resisted by force.

In addition to the exterior wall, Monks discovered other visual cues within the fort itself. While exterior paint was applied to residential buildings, for example, it was rarely used on non-residential buildings. Maps of the fort also revealed that buildings had been arranged along a north–south and east–west axis (Figure 16-13). This spatial patterning was based upon a medieval European social template seen elsewhere in

England's Royal Court, the houses of Parliament, and the seating of guests at a formal dinner. The Governor's house, located at the intersection of the two axes, occupies the same position as a ruling monarch would to a speaker in court, to a representative in parliament, and to the host of a formal dinner. Upon entering the fort, Monks argues that a visitor would have been immediately struck by this powerful symbolic message of supreme authority.

Many of the interpretations made by Monks are easily criticized because there is ultimately no way to demonstrate whether he is right or wrong. Nevertheless, his examination of Upper Fort Garry through communication theory provides a plausible explanation for some of the architectural anomalies that exist. Placing them within the economic and social context of the Red River Settlement reveals that architecture is like any other artifact. It can function as a source of encoded information providing insight into how individuals actively use material culture to influence social action.

"You Are What You Eat": Food as a Symbol of Social Status

Using architecture to reinforce your authority over others is easy when you live in a large fur trade fort like Upper Fort Garry. But many posts in remote areas of Canada consisted of a single building. As with the larger forts, hierarchical social structures existed that placed officers in charge of labourers. Not surprisingly, tensions existed between "management" and "staff" at these remote fur trade posts. The officers in charge were usually young Englishmen with little experience, and who rarely spoke the languages of the men who served under them.

Earlier in this chapter, we saw how material culture can be used to non-verbally communicate messages of status and authority. Under normal circumstances, fort officers would have used material culture to symbolically communicate their authority to their subordinates. Such items might have consisted of fine furniture, clothing, cutlery, and dinnerware. However, shipping such things to remote fur trade posts by canoe would have incurred huge costs. In some cases, the cost of transporting them would have far exceeded their monetary value. So, how did these officers assert their status and authority? Scott Hamilton, an archaeologist at Lakehead University, suggests that they used food.

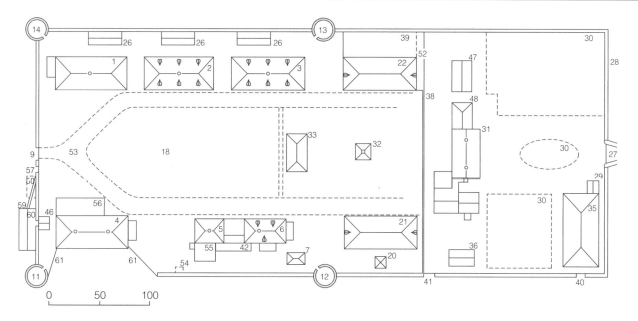

Figure 16-13 Plan of Upper Fort Garry in 1874.

Source: Monks, G. (1992). Architectural symbolism and non-verbal communication at Upper Fort Garry. *Historical Archaeology 26*(2), 52.

Fur-bearing animals were extremely important and highly valued by fur traders, but food was also imperative because the acquisition of furs was extremely labour intensive. Furs and trade goods, for example, were moved between posts and markets via an extensive canoe transportation system powered by voyageurs. Like an army that marches on its stomach, large quantities of food were necessary to feed such a large workforce. The meat of animals like bison, moose, and elk was the food that fur traders most favoured. However, the permanent nature of fur trade posts meant that the areas surrounding them were soon cleaned out of such animals. This forced hunters to move farther and farther afield. The creation of many small fur trade posts in remote locations in the boreal forests of northern Canada, triggered by intense competition between the HBC and the NWC, didn't make matters any easier. The provisioning of such posts was essential because of the absence of bison and the "scattered" distribution of resources in boreal forest environments.

Provisioning fur trade posts with food soon became an industry in and of itself. Métis and First Nations hunters intensively exploited bison on the Northern Plains. The meat was then made into pemmican—a mixture of dried and pulverized meat mixed with rendered fat and sometimes berries. Pemmican literally "fuelled" the summer canoe brigades used to transport goods and services because of its high nutritional value and long-term preservation capacity. Pemmican was supplemented with red meat derived from large ungulates such as moose, and waterfowl and fish. The success rates of bison hunts were highly variable, and this often created food shortages at remote fur trade posts. When times were good, definite food preferences were expressed among the men, with mammalian meat being preferred over fish. When food shortages occurred, most had to forgo the consumption of red meat in favour of fish. However, archaeological research has revealed that some individuals were able to retain access to most preferred foods when times were tough.

Hamilton worked from the old adage, "you are what you eat." He analyzed the faunal assemblages recovered from Nottingham House, a northern post established in 1802 by the HBC in the Lake Athabasca region of Alberta (Figure 16-14). Like many remote posts, Nottingham House consisted of a single building subdivided into four areas. The officer and the labourers occupied their own quarters, which were

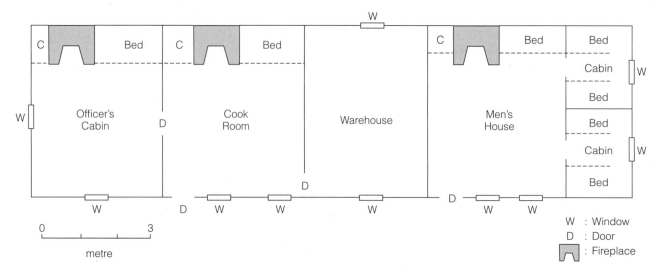

Figure 16-14 Plan of a wintering post likely modelled after Nottingham House.

Source: © HBC Archives, PAM.B.39/a/5b/1. E-mail: archives@gov.mb.ca

separated by two rooms used as a kitchen/mess and a warehouse. Excavation of this structure revealed two different patterns of refuse disposal. The officer's quarters contained very little refuse, suggesting that food remains had been removed from the building for deposition in a refuse pit. The labourers' quarters, on the other hand, contained larger quantities of bone that were discarded in the room rather than taken outside. We might expect to see such differences in refuse disposal, given the status differences between officers and their minions. However, Hamilton discovered real differences in the kinds of foods that these two groups of men were eating. Nottingham House's officer's quarters, for example, yielded much higher quantities of avian and mammalian bone fragments compared to fish. In contrast, the assemblage recovered from the labourers' quarters was clearly dominated by fish remains.

In lieu of expensive material goods, Hamilton suggests that the officer used his access to most preferred foods during times of scarcity as a means of reinforcing his authority and status within the fort. Hamilton argues that in doing so the officer was able to create a *new* kind of luxury good that could be used in place of more conventional items that he could not acquire due to the difficulties of transport. Hamilton's ideas are fascinating, and serve to reinforce the idea that material objects can exist as powerful symbols whose meanings can be manipulated for social purposes.

"Heavy Metal Bands": Material Culture and Social Change

The introduction of new technologies can have a transformative effect on human societies. Think about how the Internet has changed our society over the past decade. We can play games, conduct research, purchase items, and expand our social network of friends—all with the click of a button. While not all of these changes are positive, there is little doubt that the Internet has produced some fundamental economic and social changes in Euro-Canadian society. The new technologies brought to the New World by Europeans also had a transformative effect on the social and economic systems of indigenous peoples. Items like knives and containers made from metal represented more efficient and durable versions of objects they were already familiar with. Others, such as firearms and brass telescopes, had no parallel in aboriginal technology, and were completely new.

Historical archaeologists study the economic and social changes brought about by the introduction of trade goods, using theories derived from the fields of economics and political science. Approaches like Worlds Systems Analysis are grounded in Marxism, and examine how social inequalities emerge as capitalist economies develop and spread throughout the world. While social inequality is a feature of the capitalist economy we participate in, many of the indigenous societies encountered by Europeans were egalitarian. As we have seen in earlier chapters, leadership is not institutionalized in egalitarian societies, and concepts of private property and ownership are weakly developed. Many trade items were highly valued by indigenous people because they were both novel and useful. These items soon became symbols of status, creating inequalities among people that changed their societies forever. Inter-societal contact provided the catalyst for this process to occur.

In her book *Vectors of Death: The Archaeology of European Contact*, Anne Ramenovsky distinguishes between *sustained* and *incipient* forms of contact. Sustained contact involves the continuous presence of Europeans through the establishment of permanent settlements and colonies. Incipient contact, on the other hand, refers to "one-off" situations where European explorers briefly visit an area and, barring some unforeseen circumstance, return home after a few years. Traditionally, it was believed that most of the changes experienced by First Nations and Inuit societies, especially those associated with disease, were caused by the sustained presence of Europeans in the New World. However, Ramenovksy points out that incipient contact can produce changes that are just as profound.

The search for the Northwest Passage by British Naval Expeditions during the 19th century provides us with an excellent example of the economic and social effects that incipient contact can have. With the defeat of France and the subsequent exile of Napoleon Bonaparte from Europe, the British Admiralty found itself with a surplus of idle naval officers—all of whom remained in the employment of the Crown. These officers were put to work on a series of expeditions to the Canadian Arctic. Their main objective was the discovery of a Northwest Passage to the Pacific Ocean, and the trade routes that lay beyond.

This brought many of the British Navy's ships into areas occupied by such Central Arctic Inuit groups as the *Netsilingmiut, Iglulingmiut, Ookjulingmiut, Utkuhikjalik,* and the Copper Inuit. Historical documents suggest that direct contact with British explorers had little effect on Inuit societies because sailors and ships' captains often chose to completely dissociate themselves from native groups they encountered. If contact was made it was usually minimal, and for the purposes of acquiring food and geographical information. However, the abandoned ships and storage depots left behind by many of these expeditions would have been incredibly rich sources of materials like iron and other metals for any Inuit hunter lucky enough to stumble across them.

This situation seems to have occurred in the Canadian Arctic during the Franklin Era. Cliff Hickey, a researcher at the Canadian Circumpolar Institute, University of Alberta, has suggested that social relations among the Copper Inuit were transformed as a direct result of the abandonment of HMS *Investigator,* a vessel deployed by the British Admiralty in the search for Sir John Franklin in 1853 (Figure 16-15; see also "Looking Closer: Victorian Art and the Franklin Expedition" earlier in this chapter). The ship was deserted, along with a large storage depot, at her anchorage at Mercy Bay on northern Banks Island, in the Canadian Arctic. Copper Inuit living in the area had already made contact with the crew of the HMS *Investigator* during the spring of 1851, and they easily located the wrecked ship and her caches some years later, removing such items as exotic wood, smelted copper, glass, tin, and various textiles. A number of historic period Copper Inuit sites on Banks Island contain large quantities of items taken from the *Investigator* depot at Mercy Bay. Hickey has suggested that the sudden injection of so many exotic and valuable goods into the economic system of the Copper Inuit—a group numbering only between 800 and 900 people—would have threatened to undermine the egalitarian structure of their society.

Egalitarian societies work on the principle of *immediate return,* meaning that an individual receiving a gift is expected to return something to the giver of equal or greater value. The exotic items acquired from the *Investigator* and its depot, however, would have made it difficult for someone receiving such an item to adequately reciprocate. Hickey proposes that Copper Inuit compensated for this by: 1) increasing the circulation of traditional items made using local materials such as native copper, beached driftwood, soapstone, and caribou skins, and 2) re-defining formal exchange relationships to allow individuals to defer debt. This was done to quash the emergence of social inequalities between *gift-givers,* those individuals redistributing the impressive quantities of European goods they quarried from the Mercy Bay depot, and *gift-receivers,* those individuals traditionally obligated to immediately repay such gifts, but who may have become increasingly unable to do so. This had the effect of

Figure 16-15 HMS *Investigator* trapped in ice.

Source: T859 Critical Position of H.M.S. Investigator on the North Coast of Baring Island, August 20th 1851, drawn by Lieu. S. Gurney Cresswell, pub. 1854 by Day & Son and Ackermann & Co. (colour lithograph), English School, (19th century)/© Royal Geographical Society, British Library

making Copper Inuit trading partners something more important than primary kin, and making social groups more territorial. Many of the characteristics that make the Copper Inuit unique among other Inuit may also be tied to the *Investigator* materials. For example, the traditional concept of dividing the world along the lines of land and sea is much more strongly expressed among the Copper Inuit. Hickey attributes this to the terrestrial origin of many of the valued aboriginal commodities injected into the Copper Inuit economy to circumvent the effects of the *Investigator*'s goods.

Thus, while physical contacts between early European explorers and Inuit groups can be classified as incipient and ineffectual, the ships and caches they frequently left behind constituted a sustained European material presence in the Canadian Arctic. When Inuit groups encountered such materials, they appear to have been eagerly and rapidly incorporated into local and regional economic systems. This resulted in the small-scale modification of traditional subsistence–settlement systems, as these "heavy metal bands" began to incorporate stops at European caches and shipwrecks into their seasonal rounds. Hickey's ideas also suggest that social relations among some Inuit groups were at least partially transformed through contact with these European goods. This challenges assumptions that the Copper Inuit were largely pristine when first documented by

ethnographers because they were among the last to be directly affected by European contact.

Industrial Archaeology: Examining Canada's Industrial Heritage

Industrial archaeologists study the remains of large-scale structures associated with the industrial past for the purpose of understanding the processes of invention, innovation, and development during the early days of capitalism. Industrial archaeologists typically work with engineers and historians to record and preserve industrial heritage sites such as factories, mines, brickworks, railroads, and canals. They are also interested in understanding how these sites functioned within larger multi-scalar networks of production, exchange, and consumption.

Industrial archaeology has been described as the archaeology of the second millennium. But are the remains of industry old enough to be considered archaeological? In British Columbia, for example, sites more recent than 1846 are currently unprotected by provincial heritage legislation. The answer to this question is unequivocally yes, because all artifacts are reflections of patterned human behaviour—regardless of their age or cultural context. Using the methods of archaeology to study industrial sites provides a long-term perspective on human decision making and organizational behaviour in the workplace. More importantly, we live in a period where more and more human societies are being absorbed by capitalist economic systems. As labour-intensive and environmentally destructive industries relocate to the developing world, one might wonder how the lives of people living in these countries will be affected. Perhaps investigating the origins of industrial systems may provide us with some clue.

The Origins of Industrial Archaeology

Industrial archaeology first appeared during the 1960s in Great Britain—not surprising, since it was the birthplace of the Industrial Revolution. The first industrial archaeological society was founded in North America a decade later, and is based out of the Smithsonian Institution, in Washington D.C. The *Society for Industrial Archaeology*, as it is called, produces

Archaeological Ethics
Conserving a 16th-Century Basque Whaling Boat

Providing for the conservation of artifacts is an integral part of archaeological research. All archaeologists have an ethical responsibility to ensure that the objects they study are preserved for generations to come. This often requires allocating funds in research budgets for conservation practices. The recent discovery of a unique type of whaling boat at Red Bay, Labrador, illustrates why conservation is so vital in archaeological research.

During the 16th century, Basque whalers from northeastern Spain and southwestern France hunted whales each summer from dozens of whaling ports in southern Labrador. The most important of these was a port now known as Red Bay. Archaeologists have been conducting excavations at Red Bay since 1977, both on land and under the water.

Underwater archaeology is a fascinating area of study, and it has played an important role in the Red Bay Project. A number of remarkable finds have been made, including the discovery of three Basque whaling galleons, and four small whaling craft. The larger galleons were not used directly to hunt whales, but were anchored in harbours where they served as floating factories for processing whale oil. Instead, crews manning smaller boats called *chalupas* pursued, killed, and towed the whales. In 1978, archaeologists found a small eight-metre-long chalupa pinned underneath the collapsed starboard side of a sunken whaling galleon (Figure 16-16). Such a unique and remarkable find requires careful excavation, meticulous recording, and many specialized conservation techniques.

The chalupa's excellent state of preservation meant that archaeologists could learn a lot about Basque boat design, craftsmanship, and construction techniques. Studying the design of the boat would also shed light on how such watercraft were used in Basque whale-hunting practices. When the marine archaeologists had finished their recording of the find, objects conservators carefully packed up the boat for shipping to the main lab of the Canadian Conservation Institute in Ottawa.

Upon its arrival, the boat was carefully unpacked. Condition reports for each artifact were written, with accompanying photographs and sketches. The wooden surfaces of the boat were carefully cleaned with soft brushes. The wood was then soaked for several years in a tank containing a special mixture of water and a type of wax called polyethylene glycol (PEG), to help prevent the wood from cracking when it was later dried. A vacuum freeze-dryer was next used to dry the wood. Freeze drying prevents the wood from shrinkage. Longer pieces of planking were kept in a walk-in freezer for a period of 18 months. The conservators frequently weighed the objects as they were drying—a process that was completed when the weight no longer decreased.

Once the conservation process had been finished, the various pieces of the boat were ready for re-assembly. Re-assembling the chalupa provided archaeologists with a rare opportunity to retro-engineer a 16th-century boat using the actual keel, planks, thwarts, and gunnels. Each component was carefully numbered and recorded, and a series of maps, photos, and drawings of the individual pieces were produced. Composite drawings and small wooden models were then used to re-build the boat. Doing so placed the archaeologists in the shoes of ancient Basque boat builders, and provided many new insights into how such watercraft were constructed.

The preserved whaleboat can now form part of a much larger study of Basque whalers in Labrador. The Red Bay National Historic Site has been recognized for its historical value in understanding Canada's history, due, in part, to its commitment to the preservation of the site and its artifacts. On July 1, 1998, the reconstructed chalupa was returned to Red Bay for permanent display at the Red Bay NHS Visitor Centre.

Figure 16-16 The reconstructed chalupa whaleboat from Red Bay, a 16th-century Basque whaling station in Labrador.

Source: Rolf Hicker, Nature and Travel Stock Photography, www.hickerphoto.com

a peer-reviewed journal, and boasts more than 1800 members worldwide. The society and its members are dedicated to the preservation and study of industrial heritage. Sadly, no national organization for industrial archaeology currently exists in Canada. However, both Ontario (Ontario Society for Industrial Archaeology) and Quebec (Association Québecois pour le Patrimonie Industrial) have recently formed regional societies. This is likely because both provinces were centres of industrial development in Canada during the 19th century.

While industrial archaeologists use the same techniques as other historical archaeologists, the sites they work on are obviously quite different. For one thing, many of the structures they investigate are still standing. These include such objects as factory machinery, mining equipment, bridges, and canal systems. Techniques like remote sensing and excavation are used to analyze the parts that are buried, but these methods aren't much good for examining parts that still stick out of the ground. As a result, industrial archaeologists often work with engineers, architects, and planners to understand how standing structures were built, and establish whether they have been altered since their original construction. This type of interdisciplinary approach to recording structures also assists with understanding the socio-technical systems present at the site.

Interestingly, many industrial sites are seldom mentioned in the written histories of communities. So, rather than rely on probates and wills, industrial archaeologists instead use blueprints, photographs, operator's manuals, and parts catalogues to interpret their finds. Paintings also come in handy, as it was common practice for engineers to call upon artists to produce illustrations of structures before they were actually built. A watercolour of the Hamilton pump house in Ontario, commissioned by Thomas S. Scott, the chief architect for the federal department of public works, provided industrial archaeologist Dianne Newell with insights into the building's *intended* verses *actual* appearance. Newell discovered that a number of features that appear in the painting are missing from the actual pump house, including a flight of stairs leading to the main engine house.

In areas like Ontario and Quebec, the Industrial Revolution was fuelled by the invention of steam power. The associated risks of fire and explosion mean that insurance documents can be used as sources of descriptive information about industrial sites. Other sources of information can come from the former employees of the site itself. Such individuals can provide oral histories of the workplace under study, creating a personal and emotional link to the past. Students from the University of Lethbridge in Alberta, for example, interviewed former miners about selected buildings and features of the former Galt No. 8 mine, opened by the Canadian Pacific Railway in 1936 (Figure 16-17). When combined with archival documents, such personal accounts can provide insight into the everyday lives of working-class people of the recent past.

But there is also a dark side to industrial archaeology that can occasionally make field research extremely challenging. Dilapidated machinery and old mine shafts, for example, can pose a real threat to archaeologists, as can many of the toxic chemicals that were likely disposed of. Consequently, excavations at industrial sites in Canada have tended to focus on workers' residences rather than on production areas. Excavations are undertaken in such areas only if they have been properly cleaned via bioremediation or some other process for dealing with potentially hazardous materials.

Industrial Archaeology as Heritage Practice

Quite often, the objective of industrial archaeology is to document and preserve a particular site. These types of projects are expensive, however, and require a wide range of expertise. As a result, most are undertaken as joint partnerships between government organizations and local "friends"—engineers, technological historians, economic historians, and former employees who frequently volunteer their time and expertise. One of the most important first steps involves assessing the historical significance of the site so that resources can be allocated accordingly.

In England, where a great deal of industrial archaeology takes place, the level of significance determines the amount of architectural detail that will be recorded. A visual record of the exterior of a structure is collected if the site is of only local significance. In contrast, a site of national significance requires a full range of recording, from three-dimensional projections to interior and exterior photography, excavation, and detailed mapping. The advantages of this approach are

Figure 16-17 Entrance to Silver Creek Coal Mine, west of Cremona, Alberta. Mines like Silver Creek and Galt No. 8 in Lethbridge are an important part of Canadian economic and social history.
Source: NA-1929-1, Glenbow Archives

that it allows for limited archaeological resources (time and money) to be used more strategically.

In Canada, partnership arrangements are commonly used to assess, record, and preserve industrial sites. Such agreements are usually formed among Parks Canada, provincial and municipal government agencies, and local interest groups. Parks Canada uses what is called a *systems plan* to allocate time and money according to "themes" of potential national historical significance. These themes involve such areas as forestry, fisheries, energy development, manufacturing, and mining. Two sites in western Canada that have been developed by Parks Canada under its systems plan are the Gulf of Georgia Cannery at Stevenson, BC, and the McLean Saw Mill in Port Alberni, BC. Detailed assessments have been made at both sites, using mapping and partial excavation of features, because both are important in the province's history.

Dianne Newell and the late Ralph Greenhill, two of Canada's leading industrial archaeologists, undertook a large-scale study documenting many of Ontario's industrial sites from the 1840s and 1850s. Newell and Greenhill used field observations and documentary research to produce in-depth essays of such sites as the Rideau Canal, Peterborough lift locks, power sta-

tions, and early Grand Trunk Railway bridges and stations. Many of these sites had changed significantly in the short time between their conducting this research project and publishing the results. This drives home the need to enact measures to increase awareness of the historical significance of such sites, so that they might be protected for future generations.

Areas of Research in Industrial Archaeology

In addition to their recording skills, archaeologists can bring a unique perspective to industrial sites that elucidate aspects of human decision making, actions, and responses. If you've ever had a job, you know that the workplace is often wrought with tensions between management and staff. Historical documents generally provide only management's side of the story. Industrial archaeology, on the other hand, deals with the material culture of workers and skilled craftsmen, who have left no written record of their contributions to technological innovations. This addresses the important issue of "authorship"—and demonstrates the need to acknowledge who produced the individual elements of the industrial archaeological record, rather than simply who controlled them. This type of

In Her Own Words
Reflections on Industrial Archaeology

by Dianne Newell, Department of History, University of British Columbia

Figure 16-18 Dianne Newell, Professor of History, and Director, Peter Wall Institute for Advanced Studies, The University of British Columbia.

Source: Dianne Newell

In the early 1970s, I researched material history for Parks Canada in Ottawa and completed my master's degree in Canadian Studies. I also accidentally entered the ground floor of North American industrial archaeology (IA), a site-based approach to above-ground archaeology that con-

tributes to material history and heritage conservation. In 1973 the Parks Canada archaeology division spurned the inaugural meeting of the Smithsonian-based Society for Industrial Archaeology (SIA) in New York City, arguing that IA was not really "about" archaeology, so I got sent in their place. I had at least heard of the field. Kenneth Hudson in England had been writing engaging, well-illustrated books about British industrial history and archaeology; I encountered his work in my search for an intellectual framework for tackling my assigned research into breweries. I soon found myself not only meeting Hudson but also riding and leading the IA wave.

While at Parks Canada I organized an SIA field trip along the Rideau Canal, and later, while working at the Ontario Heritage Foundation in Toronto in 1975, another SIA tour, this time of Toronto and Hamilton. It seemed imperative to highlight for U.S. and Canadian colleagues the richness and diversity of Canada's industrial engineering and architectural remains. My encounters on those occasions with the late Ralph Greenhill led to our eventual co-authorship of *Survivals: Aspects of Industrial Archaeology in Ontario* (1989), which was (is?) the only published monograph on the field in Canada.

For me, the people as much as the content were important, especially once I began doctoral work in history at Western in 1975. I worked with

research often reveals patterns of domination and resistance. Industrial archaeologists in Britain, for example, have examined how workers in the textile and nail industries actively resisted attempts by owners and managers to automate their work through machinery. Many workers also refused to go along with attempts to centralize them in factories. Instead, they preferred the autonomy that "working at home" provided. Given that the Internet is starting to make home offices more attractive to employees in some

businesses, perhaps these same battles will re-emerge in the 21st century—only in reverse!

At present, industrial archaeology in Canada remains focused on industrial site preservation. Consequently, there is much unrealized potential for this type of research in this country (Figure 16-19).

Margaret Kennedy, an archaeologist at the University of Saskatchewan, has advocated the use of more social science–oriented approaches in industrial archaeology. Kennedy has conducted archaeological

exceptional "enthusiasts" and professionals—everyone from architects and heritage planners to labour historians, museum directors, engineering professors, and (even) archaeologists. It was extraordinary as a graduate student also to become president of the SIA, and then editor of its journal, IA (1978–83). Only a new field could have been open to the idea.

At the time, I was steeped in so-called "new history," thus committed to promoting the scholarly content of IA. A small, intense research symposium on IA and the human sciences I organized with Vance Packard Jr. on Martha's Vineyard in 1978, the papers of which I edited for publication by the SIA, was a modest attempt in this direction.

It was also during my doctoral years that I got my first taste of the international scene. I gave one of the keynote talks at the first Italian IA conference, held in Milan. The contacts I made with Marie Nisser (Sweden) and Neil Cossins (England), among others, and the chance to test my ideas in the pages of the conference publication swept me along into the academic meetings, fieldtrips, and collaborations of the newly formed international IA organization TICCIH (The International Committee for the Conservation of Industrial Heritage).

Becoming an academic in 1980 opened the doors to Canadian international scholarly conference and representation travel grants. This in turn made possible my membership on the TICCIH Board. I also could publish my IA scholarship (such as the paper on the persistence of ancient techniques in the petroleum fields of Ontario in a 1983 special issue of World Archaeology), sit on the boards of specialized journals and industrial museums, and initiate an undergraduate course in historical archaeology at my university, UBC. Most important was the BC Heritage Trust grant in archaeology that launched my IA study, with Art Roberts, a SFU geographer/archaeologist, of Canada's pacific salmon canning industry. Twenty years and almost four books later, aspects of this incredible topic still feed one stream of my scholarship.

Where does industrial archaeology stand today? Canada has never produced a dedicated community of IA practitioners, and among the founding countries of the field there has been little recent growth. The seventies and eighties in Western countries seemed unusually adventuresome in the humanities and social science disciplines, and certainly those were times more favourable for studying and preserving the industrial past. That said, many countries in South America and the former Soviet bloc seem keen to develop IA and establish comparative projects. This suggests that the artifacts and features of concern to industrial archaeologists are in some contexts symbolic not so much of an industrial past as of a repressive one.

research at several important industrial sites in western Canada. The following is a summary of the kinds of research questions that she feels industrial archaeologists should be pursuing:

- *Technology and adaptation.* Industries involved in the extraction of primary resources like oil, coal, gas, and lumber typically move in "boom" and "bust" cycles and operate in remote areas. Were existing technologies adapted for use in these new environments? When this was not possible, were homegrown solutions developed? Was the right equipment used for the job? Was the equipment considered state of the art for its day? How and why were particular technologies promoted and adapted?

- *The workplace.* Many industries in western Canada were highly dependent on immigrant labour during the 19th and early 20th centuries. Did these individuals express their ethnic identities and

Figure 16-19 Industrial archaeologists are interested in technology, the workplace, and how production was organized. In this picture, men are seen teeming crucible steel at Jessop's Brightside Steel Works, Sheffield.

Source: 'The Wealth of England: the Bessemer Process of Making Steel', 1895 (oil on canvas), Titcomb, William Holt Yates (1858-1930)/Kelham Island Industrial Museum, Sheffield, UK/The Bridgeman Art Library

maintain boundaries through material culture? Industrial sites were also contested environments where workers and management were frequently in conflict over wages and conditions in the workplace. Were things like amenities used as a form of social control? Kennedy points out lunchrooms were rare at early mining camps because such common areas provided opportunities for workers to share grievances. Did the spatial organization of the workplace reflect the use of surveillance as a means of enforcing control over workers?

■ *Site structure and management.* All industries were comprised of businesses that were highly competitive with one another. Was such competition overtly displayed through material culture? Kennedy explains that mining companies in western Canada were often located within plain sight of one another. In these situations, buildings were frequently painted bright colours that were easily visible to competitors. Production

efficiency also played a large role in remaining competitive. Were factories organized in order to maximize such things as efficiency and worker safety? What kind of impact did the presence of industry have on settlement patterns?

Let's look briefly at how the social science–oriented approaches outlined by Kennedy can be used to interpret an important industrial site in Ontario. As we will see, such sites can shed new light on the evolution of human decision making and organizational behaviour in industrial settings.

The Rideau Canal as a Socio-Technical System

Industrial archaeologists attempt to understand industrial sites as socio-technical systems, an approach that recognizes the interaction between people and technology in workplaces. An example would be a factory or hospital, where people are organized into technical groups or departments that use specialized machines like metal presses and MRI scanners. The

Rideau Canal in Ottawa can be viewed as a socio-technical system because it served as an organizing focus for labour, both in its construction and eventual use. In their excellent book *Survivals: Aspects of Industrial Archaeology in Ontario,* industrial archaeologists Dianne Newell and Ralph Greenhill provide a fascinating overview of the history of this remarkable feat of 19th-century engineering.

The Rideau Canal is the only surviving canal from the great era of nineteenth-century canal building in North America (Figure 16-20). The canal was originally built for strategic military purposes following the War of 1812. The canal system provided a means of transporting troops and artillery, via an inland waterway, from the ocean ports of Quebec City and Montreal to Kingston. Lieutenant-Colonel John By, who had been contracted to build the canal, immediately recognized the commercial advantages of transporting goods through an inland waterway. He therefore aggressively lobbied government officials to make the canals wide enough to accommodate steamers.

By's predictions turned out to be true, as commercial use of the finished canal quickly eclipsed that of the military. The construction of the canal began in 1826, and took six years to complete. Once it was finished, the canal covered a total distance of 123 miles and contained 52 dams and embankments and 47 large masonry locks with a lift of 437 ft. The artificial waterway was excavated by hundreds of workmen and covered a distance of 18 miles. The remaining 105 miles consisted of the natural courses of the Rideau and Cataroqui Rivers, and an extensive chain of lakes.

The Rideau Canal served as a focus for organizing labour throughout its construction. Various dams, for example, had to be built in order to regulate the level of water in the canal system during different seasons of the year. Perhaps the most impressive of these was the Jones Farm Dam—a masonry structure built from sandstone blocks measuring 6 ft × 4 ft × 18 in. thick. These immense blocks had to be quarried and hand-chiselled from a location six miles away, and transported to the construction site. Once there, more than 200 Irish and French Canadian labourers set the blocks in place. These men worked under incredibly harsh conditions of disease, hard labour, and loneliness in the remote swampy area where the dam was constructed. The contractors in charge of building the dam carefully coordinated the work of these dedicated stonemasons and labourers. The completed dam rose

Figure 16-20 Hand-operated locks at Jones Falls, as they appeared in 1980.

Source: J. Schwanke/Alamy

more than 60 ft in the air, making it double the size of any existing dam in North America at that time. The fact that the Jones Farm Dam remains standing today is a true testament to the skills of the men who constructed it.

The actual operation of the dam also required an organizational structure. As a boat approached the lock from the lower downstream level of the canal, technicians had to open a series of valves in the lower gates to let the water out of the lock. The operators then had to close the lower gates and open the upper gates in order to allow water to rise to the upstream level of the canal. Once this occurred, the upper gates were then opened, allowing the boat to continue upstream. As the lock was now set for a boat travelling in the opposite direction, the process was repeated. Swing bridges at various locations also had to be retracted so that larger ships could pass through the canal system without having their smokestacks damaged.

The Rideau Dam also had a profound effect on human and industrial settlement patterns. For instance, the canal was responsible for the steady growth of many towns and industries along its banks because it provided a cheap source of transportation, water, and waterpower. Many felt that the use of the canal for the transportation of commercial goods would drastically decline with the rise of the railways. The high costs of shipping bulky, low-value items by railway, however, ensured that this did not occur. The hydraulic systems used in the locks and dams could also be used to turn waterwheels. Therefore, many gristmills and sawmills located themselves at the base of locks to take advantage of this power source. The hydraulic systems of the locks were later used to generate hydroelectric power, which powered electric lights in various Ontario homes and businesses.

The Rideau Canal had a major transformative effect on industry and the lives of everyday citizens living in Ontario during the 19th and early 20th centuries. By the time Parks Canada assumed responsibility for the canal in 1972, many of the locks' hydraulic mechanisms were controlled by electrical systems. While this made the filling and draining of the locks more efficient, the canal system was more susceptible to oil leaks and power cuts. Parks Canada has since halted this trend toward electrification of the canal system, proving that new technologies aren't always the best way to increase efficiency.

Conclusion: The Future of Historical and Industrial Archaeology in Canada

We began this chapter by defining historical archaeology and industrial archaeology and exploring how they fit into the disciplines of archaeology and history. Both types of archaeology utilize documentary evidence and deal primarily with European material culture produced since the 15th century A.D. Both also utilize methods and theories derived from the disciplines of history and anthropological archaeology. So,

perhaps the best definition is that they both study the archaeology of modern life. Such a characterization might explain why the use of theory has sometimes been seen as unnecessary. Many of the objects that historical and industrial archaeologists find, for example, are instantly recognizable. Things like bottles, cans, coins, and nails all continue to be used today, albeit in varied forms. As a result, they *appear* to be easily and readily understandable. Theory seems needless in these situations. While the *function* of an object might be obvious, however, the symbolic meanings such items can convey are more difficult to get at. Look beyond function, and you find that everyday objects are often used to send powerful messages of ethnicity, gender, social position, and authority.

European material culture also appears to have had a remarkable transformative effect on indigenous societies in Canada and throughout the world. The desire to obtain such items drew many of these societies into the ever-expanding European capitalist system. Similar processes are at work today through globalization. So, perhaps the future of historical archaeology lies in using archaeology's unique long-term perspective to better understand the dynamics of this process.

In a similar way, industrial archaeology promises to shed new light on how industry has shaped "modern life" in Canada over the past 200 years. While industrial archaeology is a relatively new area within Canadian archaeology, it holds great potential for examining the contributions made by immigrants to the growth of Canada, the social organization of the workplace, how people travelled, and where they chose to live.

Both historical archaeology and industrial archaeology challenge the idea that artifacts have to be "old," and that Euro-Canadian history can be studied only by looking at documents and texts. It is ironic that most archaeologists working in Canada are of Euro-Canadian descent, yet much of their work addresses First Nations and Inuit history. Perhaps it is time that Euro-Canadians used the tools and theories of archaeology to develop an understanding of their own history, and the global nature of modern life.

Summary

- Historical archaeology examines the remains left behind by societies that also produced written accounts of their activities. Historical archaeologists integrate artifactual data with various types of documents, maps, and illustrations to interpret archaeological sites that cover the period since European contact in Canada.

- Many of the documents used by historical archaeologists were written with an intended audience in mind. They also frequently reflect the views of only a few literate individuals, and not those of everyone in society. Historical archaeologists, therefore, need to understand how the intended purpose of a document, as well as the gender, status, and worldview of the author, can bias the information documentary evidence contains.

- Historical archaeology has been criticized for being too particularistic and a-theoretical. After the 1960s, many historical archaeologists began to use the generalizing theories of anthropological archaeology. Many historical archaeologists are adopting postprocessual or humanistic approaches in their research. Examining the symbolic and social dimensions of architecture and everyday material objects, and how they were used to communicate authority, social status, ethnicity, and gender, are examples of this type of studies.

- Industrial archaeology uses artifacts and documentary evidence to study the remains of industry and infrastructure, including such things as factories, mines, railroads, canals, and bridges.

- Industrial archaeology has struggled to define itself in archaeology, because some feel that the remains of 19th-century industry are simply not "old" enough to be considered archaeological.

- However, factories, canal systems, and mines are socio-technical systems that influenced organizational behaviour in the workplace. Industries also transformed the landscape of Canada by extracting primary resources like coal and forestry products, influencing the location and growth of towns, and changing how goods and people were moved from place to place.

- Industrial archaeologists usually work with engineers, architects, and planners to preserve Canada's industrial heritage, and study industrialization as a long-term process.

- Right now government agencies and culture resource management companies do most of the historical and industrial archeology in Canada. There are few historical archaeologists working in departments of anthropology and archaeology at Canadian universities. It is hoped this will change in the years to come, as researchers begin to explore many exciting directions that historical and industrial archaeology have taken in other parts of the world.

Additional Reading

CANADIAN RESOURCES

Burley, D. (1989). Function, meaning and context: Ambiguities in ceramic use by the Hivernant Metis of the Northwestern Plains. *Historical Archaeology, 23*(1), 97–106.

Burley, D., Fladmark, K. R., and Hamilton, J. S. (1996). *Prophecy of the Swan: The Upper Peace River Fur Trade of 1794–1823.* Vancouver: UBC Press.

Gray, C. (1999). *Sisters in the Wilderness: The Lives of Susanna Moodie and Catharine Parr Trail.* Toronto: Viking Press.

Monks, G. (1992). Architectural symbolism and nonverbal communication at Upper Fort Garry. *Historical Archaeology, 26*(2), 37–55.

Newell, D., and Greenhill, R. (1989). *Survivals: Aspects of Industrial Archaeology in Ontario.* Erin, ON: Boston Mills Press.

OTHER RESOURCES

Beaudry, M. C. (Ed.). (1988). *Documentary Archaeology in the New World.* Cambridge: Cambridge University Press.

Orser, C. E. (1996). *Images of the Recent Past: Readings in Historical Archaeology.* Walnut Creek, CA: Alta Mira Press.

Online Resources

Visit Wilfrid Laurier University's field school in industrial archaeology at *http://www.as.wvu.edu/ihtia/IA_Fieldschool.htm*
Visit the Society for Industrial Archaeology at http://www.siahq.org/

COMPANION WEBSITE
Visit *http://www.archaeology1ce.nelson.com* to access a wide range of material to help you succeed in your introductory archaeology course. These include flashcards, Internet exercises, Web links, and practice quizzes.

RESEARCH ONLINE WITH INFOTRAC COLLEGE EDITION
From the Student Companion Website, you can access the InfoTrac College Edition database, which offers thousands of full-length articles for your research.

17 Archaeological Ethics and Indigenous Archaeology Exploring Ways to Protect, Respect, and Share Canada's Diverse Cultural Heritage

OUTLINE

Inuit Elders from across Nunavut inspect artifacts recovered from an archaeological site near the community of Arviat. Archaeologists are very concerned about the ethics of doing archaeology in the twenty-first century. Should artifacts such as these be returned to Inuit communities, or held in trust for communities in museums?

Source: Dr. Peter Dawson

Preview

I f you've read this far, you will have noticed that many of the chapters in this book contain short sections that deal with ethical issues in archaeology. In this chapter, we will examine archaeological ethics more closely, including how ethics are linked to heritage legislation and indigenous archaeology—both of which are important topics in 21st-century archaeology.

Introduction

Many national and international archaeological associations have developed *codes of conduct* that define how archaeology should be practised throughout the world. These guidelines cover everything from the protection of archaeological sites and artifacts, to consultation with **descendant communities** over the interpretation, care, and occasionally repatriation of items recovered from archaeological sites. We will discuss why archaeologists have devoted so much time and energy in recent years to the development and enforcement of these standards in Canada.

Most of the ethics statements adopted by archaeological associations acknowledge the impact that archaeology can have on indigenous societies. It is clear that these descendant communities are strongly connected to the sites and objects that archaeologists investigate. In colonial countries like Canada, Australia, the United States, and New Zealand, the vast majority of sites excavated by archaeologists tell the history of another cultural group. As a consequence, the descendants of these first peoples feel disenfranchised from the practice of interpreting their own past.

descendant community A society that has a demonstrable historical link to one in the past.

ethics Sets of standards that we use to guide our actions; often are borne out of societal norms that prescribe particular ways of behaving under certain circumstances.

Indigenous archaeology attempts to "de-colonize" the past by empowering indigenous societies to interpret their own unique histories. In Canada, this process involves the training of First Nations and Inuit archaeologists, the repatriation of human remains and culturally significant artifacts, and the development of collaborative research alliances between native and non-native communities. Not surprisingly, the issues of ethics and indigenous archaeology have occasionally been fractious ones. While the road ahead presents many challenges, all signs indicate that Canadian archaeology is moving in the right direction.

What Are Ethics?

Imagine that you catch your best friend cheating on a midterm exam. You know that your friend is upset over a recent break-up, and has had a hard time studying for the test. Do you accept this as an excuse and not tell the professor? Or do you tell the professor to be fair to others in the class (including yourself) who studied long and hard for the exam? We all confront these types of decisions at some point in our lives. They often cause us to reflect on the values we possess as individuals, and as members of society at large. **Ethics** are sets of standards that we use to guide our actions in these situations. They are often borne out of societal norms that prescribe particular ways of behaving under certain circumstances. We use the word "guide" because ethics define courses of action that you *should* follow rather than those that you are required to follow. This is a distinction that separates ethics from laws.

Alison Wylie is an archaeologist and philosopher who has spent a great deal of time grappling with the role of ethics in archaeology as a member of the Society for American Archaeology's (SAA) Ethics in Archaeology Committee. Wylie points out that "laws" set outer limits on what actions are deemed acceptable, while "ethics" more narrowly define how we conduct ourselves in everyday life. Take the salvaging of underwater shipwrecks, for example. The Ontario provincial government recently amended a law called the *Ontario Heritage Act* to limit scuba diver access to the *Edmund Fitzgerald,* a shipwreck made famous by Canadian songwriting icon Gordon Lightfoot. The *Edmund Fitzgerald* was an American bulk carrier that became one of the best-known shipping disasters in the Great Lakes (Figure 17-1). All hands were lost when the ship sank after encountering a storm in Lake Superior, on November 10, 1975, in Canadian waters northwest of Whitefish Point, Michigan. "We are very pleased that the Province has recognized the *Edmund Fitzgerald* as an important heritage site," said Ruth Hudson and Cheryl Rozman, who both lost close family members in this tragic event. "We are thankful that the site is protected from unauthorized visits, and we can now be at peace." Prior to the amendment of the *Ontario Heritage Act,* it was perfectly legal to dive this particular wreck and others like it. Given the sentiments expressed by the surviving relatives, however, would it have been moral and ethical for divers to do so? In this case, a law has been enacted to enforce a particular ethical position.

Consequentialist Ethics: How Our Actions Affect Others

Another way of looking at ethics is in terms of moral theory—specifically, how we justify our actions, and those of other individuals. **Consequentialist ethics** refer to moral theories where actions are judged as either "right" or "wrong" by the effects they have on the world at large, or on the happiness and well-being of others. *Agent-centred* and *agent-neutral* theories of consequentialism define who benefits or suffers from

the consequences of these actions. Agent-centred theories place the needs of the individual above the needs of others when making moral decisions about what action should be taken. In the case of the *Edmund Fitzgerald,* an agent-centred consequentialist might view diving the wreck as a "good" thing to do because she/he derives personal pleasure from the act of doing so. Agent-neutral theories, on the other hand, focus more on the consequences that an action might have on others. An agent-neutral consequentialist would see the act of diving the *Edmund Fitzgerald* as ethically "bad" because it causes pain and anguish for the relatives of those who died.

But who are the beneficiaries of "good" actions in archaeology? And who suffers the consequences of "bad" actions? Up until recently, many First Nations and Inuit would argue that the prime beneficiaries of archaeology have been the archaeologists themselves. Archaeological research in Canada, for example, has resulted in the publication of thousands of academic papers that have furthered the careers of many individuals, and contributed to the development of the discipline of archaeology itself. Sadly, First Nations and Inuit people have received little direct benefit from this research. Ethics statements drafted by organizations like the Canadian Archaeological Association are attempting to change this. Archaeologists in the 21st century recognize that they have a responsibility to preserve the archaeological record, disseminate information to the public, and involve First Nations and Inuit communities in the practice of archaeology in meaningful ways. From the perspective of moral theory, assuming these responsibilities reflects a shift away from forms of consequentialism that are *agent-centred* and toward forms that are more *agent-neutral.*

Deontological Ethics: Examining the Good Will in Actions

Some philosophers disagree with the idea that the morality of an action can be judged solely on its consequences. As an alternative, the 18th-century philosopher Immanuel Kant (1724–1804) offered up the idea

consequentialist ethics Moral theories where actions are judged as either "right" or "wrong" by the effects they have on the world at large, or on the happiness and well-being of others.

Figure 17-1 Painting of the *Edmund Fitzgerald*.

Source: Captain C. (Bud) Robinson

of **deontological ethics**—the view that human actions have an intrinsic quality that makes them right or wrong, regardless of consequences (Figure 17-2). Put another way, deontological approaches are concerned with the *good will* of actions, rather than the *good effects* they may have. An army officer, for example, might order his platoon to advance on an enemy position, even though he knows the consequences might mean certain death. The officer sees this as the correct choice because the nature of this action is derived from his inherent sense of duty.

From a deontological perspective, an archaeologist working in Canada might feel that she/he has a professional responsibility to excavate archaeological sites, and learn about the past, because it is part of our shared human heritage. When viewed in this light, the practice of archaeology could be seen as an act of good will—regardless of its consequences. Members of an indigenous group, however, might regard the same action as inherently wrong because of the destruction and harm they see it causing.

deontological ethics The view that human actions have an intrinsic quality that makes them right or wrong, regardless of consequences.

Virtue Ethics: Linking Trust and Obligation

Virtue ethics is a third type of moral theory that focuses on issues such as moral motivation, character, moral wisdom, and the role of trust in human relationships. Trust, in particular, is an issue in virtue

Figure 17-2 The 18th-century German philosopher Immanuel Kant.

Source: Portrait of Emmanuel Kant (1724-1804) (oil on canvas), German School, (18th Century)/Private Collection/The Bridgeman Art Library

ethics that has special relevance to archaeology. Moral philosopher Annette Baier explains that *trust* and *trustworthiness* are salient aspects of human interaction because society could not exist without them. The obligations outlined in the ethical statements adopted by archaeologists are often based upon trust. For example, members of the Canadian Archaeological Association must be trusted to follow each one of the guidelines outlined in the association's recently drafted statement of ethical principles. But how are *trust* and *obligation* linked?

Ethics statements define courses of action that *ought* to be followed. Unfortunately, there has been a tendency in archaeology to focus on ethics only during times of crisis; for example, when archaeologists are denied permission to excavate, or asked by a descendant community to return valuable artifacts. Because virtue ethics are *action-focused,* it requires that we adhere to our obligations at all times, and not only during moments of crisis. Deeds and not words link *trust* to *obligation* in archaeology. Therefore, earning the trust of indigenous communities requires that our actions always be viewed as responsible and respectful.

Ethics in Archaeology and Museum Studies

"Written in Earth"—Virtue Ethics in Action

Let's look at an example of how virtue ethics can work in archaeology. In 1991, the University of British Columbia's Museum of Anthropology decided it would set up an exhibition of pre-contact Northwest Coast art called "Written in Earth" (see Figure 17-3). The purpose of the exhibit was to showcase art objects recovered from archaeological sites on the south coast region of the province. Around the same time, a task force formed by the Association of First Nations (AFN) and the Canadian Museums Association (CMA) had developed an ethical policy stating that the inclusion of First Nations in museum work is important and essential in order to improve on interpretations of their histories and cultures. Wanting to abide by this principle, the organizers decided to enter into a partnership with local First Nations to jointly plan the exhibit. Earning the trust of these First

Figure 17-3 The Written in Earth exhibit was shown at the University of British Columbia's Museum of Anthropology.

Source: Courtesy of Museum of Anthropology, University of British Columbia

Nations communities required the organizers to find ways of translating the ethical policy outlined by the task force into actions.

The exhibit's organizers began by hiring a **Musqueam First Nations** researcher to consult with community members to solicit their opinions and concerns regarding the planned exhibit. The consultation process revealed that many people felt a strong physical, spiritual, and cultural connection to the archaeological materials that were to be displayed. For example, some individuals felt that it would be inappropriate to exhibit items that were of religious significance. The objectives of the exhibit were subsequently broadened to include the opinions of those consulted. In addition to showing what archaeological research can tell us about the age and stylistic development of pre-contact art on the Northwest Coast, the exhibit would now reflect on the significance of pre-contact

Musqueam First Nations Band The Musqueam people are a strong aboriginal community of more than 1000 members. Their traditional territory once occupied what is now Vancouver and its surrounding areas.

art to contemporary First Nations communities and examine the roles played by First Nations, archaeologists, and museums in caring for Canada's cultural heritage.

David Pokotylo and Margaret Holm from the University of British Columbia were involved in the planning of the exhibit, and have described just how challenging the process of trust building can be. Legal issues, for instance, had to be negotiated to establish who owned the objects on display. While government agencies and cultural institutions did not claim ownership of the artifacts, legislation in British Columbia made it clear that they were responsible for holding the objects in trust for First Nations. However, many of British Columbia's Native peoples have claimed that the rights to these materials should be turned over to them because the government has not looked after them in ways they consider appropriate. Archaeologists and First Nations also valued the objects differently. By way of illustration, archaeologists felt the value of certain artifacts would be increased if they were radiocarbondated. In contrast, First Nations saw the removal of small pieces from objects for dating as unnecessarily destructive, and argued that it would add little to the spiritual and cultural significance they held. The resolution of these issues took time, patience, and money. In the end, however, the actions of all involved increased the levels of trust among archaeologists, museum workers, and First Nations. It also resulted in a highly successful exhibition that has benefited everyone.

When Ethics Become Dilemmas: The Problem of Subsistence Digging

On the surface, behaving ethically as an archaeologist might seem pretty straightforward. All professional archaeologists, for example, condemn the looting of archaeological sites and the selling of antiquities on the open market. Looting is defined as the unlawful or unsanctioned removal of objects from an archaeological site. A great deal of information is lost when looters remove objects because their context and provenience within the site are rarely recorded. Mining a site for artifacts can also result in its complete destruction. Many of the artifacts that are sold end up in private collections, depriving others of opportunities to see and learn about them. These consequences make it easy to judge looting as "bad." But are there situations in which these seemingly unethical forms of behaviour might be justified?

Julie Hollowell is currently a Killam Postdoctoral Research Fellow at the University of British Columbia. Hollowell is an archaeologist who has studied a form of looting referred to as "subsistence digging" on St. Lawrence Island, in the Bering Strait. Since the early 1990s, the Yupik Eskimo families who live there have "mined" artifacts from many of the archaeological sites that dot the island. These include intricate bone and ivory carvings from the Old Bering Sea/Okvik period (ca. A.D. 1–700), Birnirk/Punuk period (ca. A.D. 500–1200), and Thule periods (ca. A.D. 900–1500). Finding such items is the equivalent of winning the lottery for many islanders, who sell them to antiquities dealers for high prices. Doing so is perfectly legal on St. Lawrence Island, but is it ethical?

On the surface, looting could be judged as unethical from both consequentialist and deontological perspectives. These actions have definite consequences because they destroy important information about the past, and deny future generations access to some truly remarkable objects. One could also see looting as an act of ill will on the part of St. Lawrence Islanders because they have a "duty" to protect their heritage. But Hollowell explains that their actions occur within a particular economic, social, and environmental context that needs to be taken into consideration *before* they can be judged.

Like many indigenous societies, the effects of European contact have economically disadvantaged the Yupik occupants of St. Lawrence Island. Therefore, the selling of artifacts provides Yupik individuals with a means of increasing their economic self-sufficiency. Such an economic justice argument could be used to excuse the practice of subsistence digging. Statements like, "Our ancestors left us these things so we could survive in a cash economy," and claims that "voices" occasionally told people where to find objects—and when to avoid objects that didn't want to be found, indicate that the Yupik Islanders see their actions as ethical. To them, the archaeological record is their rightful inheritance. Perhaps the antiquities dealers are the real villains here because they encourage subsistence digging by paying top dollar for artifacts. However, many dealers justify their actions by claiming that they are improving the lives of Yupik by purchasing the products of subsistence digging.

It seems as though a reasonable case could be made to support any or all of these positions, depending on your ethical point of view. Ambiguous situations like these often cause people to reflect and even question the merits of the codes they follow. According to Alison Wylie, ethical dilemmas arise when the existing standards upon which people operate are disrupted, as they are in the case of subsistence digging. Ethical dilemmas are resolved by developing new moral strategies that are made explicit in ethics statements.

Ethics statements provide leverage in justifying the practices we engage in. This is one of the reasons why lawyers, doctors, and engineers form professional associations and set standards of practice for their members to follow. Archaeologists are no different in this regard, and there are many international and national associations that one can join. Like anyone else in a society, archaeologists are expected to be trustworthy, honest, keep promises, and refrain from harming others. However, they carry the additional burden of following the responsibilities defined by their discipline.

Figure 17-4 Mode by which Memnon's head (currently in the British Museum) was removed by the famous Giovanni Belzoni (1778–1823), showman, engineer, explorer.

Source: Mode in which the young Memnon's head (now in the British Museum) was removed by G. Belzoni (lithograph), c. 1816, © Royal Geographical Society, London, UK/The Bridgeman Art Library

A History of Ethics in Archaeology

In the Beginning . . .

Concerns about the development of ethical principles in archaeology followed the professionalization of the discipline during the 19th century. Prior to this, archaeology had been the domain of the bored, wealthy, eccentric, and adventurous, and ethics were less of a concern. Such individuals included the famous circus strongman, engineer, and adventurer Giovanni Belzoni (A.D. 1778–1823). Belzoni was responsible for the looting of many tombs and temples in Egypt, including the great temple of Ramses II at Abu Simbel and the tombs of Amenhotep III, Ramses I, Merneptah, and Ay (Figure 17-4). Belzoni was able to put his considerable skills as an engineer to

work removing many large Egyptian statues and monuments from their original resting places to the exhibit halls of the British Museum, including the famous seated statues of Ramses II from Luxor. Even by 19th-century standards, many viewed the actions of Belzoni as unethical. Newly emerging professional archaeologists, for example, sought to distance themselves from individuals like Belzoni, whose methods were seen as crude, destructive, and unscientific.

Markets dealing in the trade of antiquities were also emerging in North America during the 19th century. Many Americans were becoming increasingly upset over the removal of artifacts from **Anasazi** sites by foreign archaeologists. Early Canadian archaeologists, such as David Boyle, expressed similar concerns about outsiders taking artifacts from Canada to other countries. These concerns likely explain why the predominant ethical principle championed by 19th-century archaeologists dealt with the preservation and protection of archaeological sites from looting, vandalism, and destruction. The creation of institutions in North America, like the Smithsonian Institution

Anasazi A Native American culture flourishing in southern Colorado, Utah, northern New Mexico, and Arizona from about AD 100, whose descendants are considered to include the present-day Pueblo peoples.

and the Canadian Institute, demonstrated that the public was interested in preserving archaeological remains. This interest led to the passing of heritage legislation in both countries that was aimed at protecting archaeological sites from destruction.

A Call for Professional Standards

The economic boom that followed the end of World War II required the enactment of even more stringent legislative measures. Infrastructure projects, such as the building of large dams in areas of Canada and the United States, were threatening archaeological sites at an unprecedented level. However, the demand for professional archaeologists outstripped their availability, because newly enacted heritage legislation required that the work be conducted professionally. As a result, professionally trained archaeologists were a hot commodity, and in high demand. Qualified individuals were needed to hold archaeological permits, and archaeologists became increasingly concerned about the importance of credentials within the discipline. In response, in 1960 the Society for American Archaeology (SAA) drafted a set of ethics statements. These statements defined the discipline of archaeology, emphasized the importance of using systematic collection methods in fieldwork, stressed the need to publish results, and advocated the idea that training should include a bachelor's degree, with a master's and Ph.D. preferable.

Unfortunately, the sheer volume of archaeological work during this time resulted in few published papers, and poor-quality site reports. The rights of descendant communities, and their unique connection to the archaeological record, were also being ignored. The existing standards upon which archaeologists operated were now seen as inadequate. In response, both national and international professional associations drafted new ethical statements. Let's look at some of the most important examples of these from the last 30 years.

Some Examples of Ethics Statements in Archaeology

The Society of Professional Archaeologists (SOPA) Code of Ethics (1976)

Members of the Society for American Archaeology (SAA) created this statement of ethics as a response to rapid increases in cultural resource management

(CRM) activity during the early post-war years. The aim of SOPA was to ensure that archaeological standards were maintained through professional accreditation. In this way, it didn't really function any differently than a medical association for doctors, or a bar association for lawyers. SOPA's ethics statement is broken down into three sections that outline the archaeologist's responsibility to the public, colleagues, and employers.

At the time, SOPA's code of ethics was somewhat revolutionary because it recognized the public's interest in, and right to know about, the results of archaeological research. The code instructed archaeologists to be sensitive to the wishes of communities whose cultural histories were subject to archaeological investigation. The standards of research performance adopted by SOPA also required archaeologists to assume responsibility for the curation and permanent storage of artifacts. Unfortunately, SOPA found itself at odds with the SAA, which viewed this professional code of ethics as applicable only to CRM archaeologists (most SAA members were university-based academic archaeologists).

The Vermillion Accord on Human Remains (1989)

The Vermillion Accord was adopted in 1989 in South Dakota by the World Archaeological Inter-Congress, and is unique in that it deals exclusively with the treatment of human remains. Not surprisingly, this highly sensitive issue is one of the most contested areas in archaeology and anthropology. The Accord consists of six ethics statements that call for respectful treatment of human remains by archaeologists and biological anthropologists. The Accord states that wishes of the dead, and the descendant communities to which they belong, should be followed whenever possible, reasonable, or lawful. Interestingly, the Vermillion Accord also acknowledges the scientific research value of skeletal, mummified, and other types of human remains. As a result, other statements in the accord focus on the importance of negotiating agreements among researchers and descendant communities as to the proper treatment of human remains while under study, and their eventual deposition. The Vermillion Accord views the concerns of ethics groups and scientists as equally legitimate, and it attempts to balance the ethical responsibilities of archaeologists against the protection of heritage resources and the desires of descendant communities.

World Archaeological Congress (WAC) First Code of Ethics (1990)

In addition to the rise of the CRM industry, the 1960s also saw a second important change in archaeology. Across North America, indigenous societies began to contest the excavation of archaeological sites, the removal of human remains for study, and the display of sensitive cultural artifacts in museums. In 1971, for example, Native protestors occupied the Southwest Museum in Los Angeles. The same year saw members of the American Indian Movement (AIM) protesting excavations at an archaeological site in Minnesota. The concerns of Native peoples were reflected in aboriginal newspapers like *Akwesasne Notes* and *Wasaja,* and in books written by indigenous authors such as Vine Deloria's *Custer Died for Your Sins.* In Canada, First Nations mobilized against cultural institutions—such as Calgary's Glenbow Museum over an exhibit held concurrently with the 1988 Winter Olympic Games called *The Spirit Sings.* The rise of Native activism happened about the same time that the civil rights movement was emerging in the 1960s, and it caused many archaeologists to re-think their ethics and core values. Specifically, these events forced archaeologists to address the question: Who owns the past? Rather than focus on professional standards as SOPA had done, WAC attempted to address the concerns of indigenous groups through the ethical code it developed. This is reflected in the title of the document: *First Code of Ethics: Members' Obligations to Indigenous Peoples.*

The code was drafted by a delegation of ten Maori from New Zealand who attended WAC's conference in Venezuela. It was then discussed and revised by indigenous societies from around the world. Once completed, the code was presented to the WAC executive, and adopted by council. The document consists of 15 guidelines, organized into "principles to abide by" and "rules to adhere to." These guidelines acknowledge the special meaning of indigenous cultural heritage, and the important relationship indigenous people have with places, object, artifacts, and human remains—regardless of legal ownership. Indigenous methodologies for interpretation, curation, management, and protection of cultural heritage are placed on equal footing with those of Western science. Furthermore, WAC's code of ethics stresses the importance of developing equitable partnerships and relationships with the indigenous peoples whose heritage is being investigated.

The Society for American Archaeology— Principles of Archaeological Ethics (1996)

The SAA's ethical statement came about because of a decision made by Prudence Rice, editor of the journal *Latin American Antiquity,* to publish no articles that made use of looted materials. This decision was enacted because some archaeologists felt that doing so would encourage the illegal trade in antiquities. In 1991, the SAA formed its own Ethics in Archaeology committee to review and update earlier ethical statements made by the society in 1960. These ethics statements had dealt mainly with issues of maintaining appropriate standards for methodology, and stressed the need to publish results and to adequately train young archaeologists. By 1996, the committee presented eight newly revised principles of ethics, which were subsequently adopted by the society. These principles addressed issues of stewardship; accountability; commercialization; public education; intellectual property; public reporting and outreach; records and preservation; and training and resources. The underlying premise of the SAA's ethics statement was that the past belonged to everyone. The archaeological record therefore needed to be collected, preserved, documented, and presented to a diverse public in ways that were intelligible and meaningful. The SAA ethics statement acknowledges that archaeologists carry this responsibility because they are most qualified to do so.

Canadian Archaeological Association (CAA)— Statement of Principles and Ethical Conduct Pertaining to Aboriginal Peoples (1997)

While SOPA and WAC are international institutions, the CAA is a national association of professional archaeologists working in Canada. The CAA's interest in developing a code of ethics stems from the fact that the archaeological record in Canada is largely comprised of the heritage of First Nations and Inuit societies. In other words, it is primarily someone else's heritage. Furthermore, most archaeologists in Canada work on sites that are located near aboriginal communities, or on lands that these communities control.

The CAA struck an Aboriginal Heritage Committee in 1992 to develop ethical principles that could be used to guide relations among archaeologists and indigenous societies in Canada. The CAA was also committed to protecting, preserving, and managing heritage resources in Canada, and ensuring that the highest possible standards were used when conducting archaeological research. In this way, the CAA's Ethics Statement attempts to combine the concern with maintaining professionalism and stewardship expressed by SOPA with the goals of recognizing the rights of indigenous peoples to be included in the practice of archaeology. The resulting document contains 12 principles that are divided into four categories: consultation, aboriginal involvement, sacred sites, and communication and interpretation.

The CAA statement of ethics is somewhat unique because it acknowledges the spiritual connection that many First Nations and Inuit people have with sites, objects, and features on the landscape. It also encourages the active participation of indigenous peoples in archaeological research. Due to Canada's size, politics and history tend to vary regionally. This is reflected in the CAA's Ethical Statement, which leaves some of the protocols for regional archaeologists and indigenous societies to establish.

Are All These Ethics Statements Saying the Same Thing?

Reading through these various codes of ethics makes most archaeology students wonder if they should be majoring in law or philosophy. It is not surprising that the content varies dramatically, given that specific professional associations produced them in different times and places. Robert Rosenwig of Yale University has analyzed the content of ethical statements in archaeology to examine how and why they differ. Because one of the purposes of this textbook is to compare the development of archaeology in Canada with that in the United States, let's look at what Rosenwig's analysis reveals about how the ethics statements made by the Canadian Archaeological Association differ from those of the Society for American Archaeology.

Rosenwig used something called **bibliometrics** to conduct his analysis. You've probably used this technique to search electronic databases for articles when writing course papers. Say you're looking for papers on the feeding habits of woodpeckers. You simply type in the terms "food," "habits," and "woodpecker" into a

bibliometric search engine, which then scans the titles, abstracts, and key words contained in a database of articles. Bibliometrics measures the strength of association among these terms to identify articles that would be of most interest to you.

For his analysis of archaeological ethics statements, Rosenwig used paired terms: "archaeology" and "native people"; "science" and "spiritual"; "law" and "native rights." Rosenwig's results indicate that the CAA's principles differed from those of the SAA in a number of interesting ways.

- The CAA's ethics statement makes more references to "native people" than to "archaeology." It also makes no reference to "law," and is the only ethics statement to use the term "spiritual."
- The SAA's ethics statement contains more references to "archaeology," "science," and "law," and makes little or no mention of "native rights" and "spirituality."

But what do these semantic differences really mean? In more general terms, the content of the CAA's ethics statement seems to focus more on how the archaeological community should interact with indigenous peoples. It also stresses the training of indigenous archaeologists, and places more emphasis on soliciting the opinions of First Nations and Inuit societies. In this way, the CAA's ethical statement more closely resembles those of the World Archaeological Congress (WAC). In contrast, the SAA's ethics statement bears more of a resemblance to that of SOPA because it emphasizes modes of professional conduct. The SAA statement does acknowledge that archaeology needs to be more inclusive, but while the CAA specifically identifies aboriginal peoples, the SAA defines the public in much broader terms.

Does the fact that the CAA's ethics statement focuses more on indigenous people make it "better" or more "ethical" than the SAA's set of statements? The answer is unequivocally no. These differences simply reflect the fact that archaeology in Canada and the United States has developed differently (see Chapter 1). Remember that the professionalization of archaeology occurred much later in Canada. Furthermore, the close proximity of First Nations communities to urban centres in Canada increased their contact with archaeologists. This may explain why the CAA's ethics statements place such an emphasis on involving

bibliometrics A set of methods used to study or measure texts and information, and the impact they have in various fields of study.

indigenous peoples in archaeology. Alison Wylie, who sat on the SAA's Committee on Ethics in Archaeology, offers another reason for why Native Americans are mentioned so few times in the SAA guidelines. In the United States, Black and Hispanic communities make up a much larger segment of the population. If the SAA were to focus on Native Americans, it would risk alienating these other descendant communities. In effect, the SAA's guidelines leave the door open for the inclusion of other groups.

Regardless of these differences, archaeologists on both sides of the border recognize that descendant communities need to be given a privileged position when studying the past through archaeology. As we have seen, this requires the development of trusting relationships (virtue ethics) with these communities, and ethics statements provide the guidelines for accomplishing this.

Heritage Legislation in Canada

While ethics serve as standards for guiding actions, laws place definite limits on what forms of action are acceptable. The development of legislation to protect archaeological sites from destruction can be traced back as far as 1797, when a proclamation issued by Peter Russell instructed "Her Majesty's Subjects" living in the New World to stop the practice of despoiling Mississauga Indian burying grounds and fishing areas, and that anyone caught doing so would be prosecuted. The scientific approaches used by Thomas Jefferson in his 18th-century archaeological investigations also helped to define the roles that archaeologists would eventually play in the management of the archaeological record. In the first decade of the 20th century, the government of the United States passed the *Antiquities Act of 1906*. This Act authorized the president to establish national monuments to protect sites on public land, and prevent their destruction at the hands of developers and looters. This meant that archaeologists now required permits in order to excavate. However, the Act did nothing to protect sites on privately owned land.

Instead of pursuing heritage legislation at the national level, as the Americans had done, the provinces and territories of Canada enacted regional laws to protect archaeological sites. One of the earliest was the *Archaeological and Historic Sites Protection Act*

of 1961, in the province of British Columbia. The passage of the act was achieved through the efforts of William Duff, a provincial anthropologist in British Columbia; Carl Borden, an archaeologist at the University of British Columbia (Figure 17-5); and Willard Ireland, a provincial archivist. The *Act* defined the various types of sites that were to be protected, including: 1) designated sites, 2) human burials, 3) rock art sites, and 4) virtually any other site found on Crown lands. The main part of the text read:

> No person shall knowingly destroy, deface, or otherwise alter, excavate, or dig up any Indian kitchen-midden, shell-heap, house pit, cave, or habitation site, or any cairn, mound, fortification, or other structure, or any other archaeological remain on Crown lands, whether designated as an archaeological site or not . . . .

Neil Ferris, a government archaeologist in the province of Ontario, has argued that restricting access to archaeological sites through heritage legislation has had two important effects in North America. First, it has allowed federal, provincial, and territorial governments to assert their ownership over heritage resources. Second, by excluding non-professionals, governments have granted professional archaeologists and museum officials privileged access to the archaeological record. This "privileged access" has been

Figure 17-5 Charles E. (Carl) Borden (1905–1978).

Source: Photo by Roy Carlson courtesy Museum of Archaeology and Ethnology, Simon Fraser University

reinforced through the enactment of various antiquities and historical preservation laws aimed at protecting archaeological sties.

Regional versus National Heritage Legislation

Surprisingly, Canada lags behind the United States in the enactment of heritage legislation at the national level. Currently, no coherent legal framework exists for protecting archaeological sites on lands and in waters controlled by the federal government. Instead, the provinces and territories control heritage legislation, with only a few notable exceptions. National Historic Sites, for example, are protected under the jurisdiction of **Parks Canada.** Although archaeological sites present along coastlines and ocean beds are unprotected by federal legislation, shipwrecks are protected under the *Canada Shipping Act.* Attempts were made to develop more comprehensive forms of heritage legislation during the 1980s, but they were often prevented because of disagreements with First Nations and Inuit groups over the ownership of archaeological resources. The *Government of Canada Archaeological Heritage Policy Framework (1990)* does, however, recognize the value of national-level legislation, stating:

> As our cultural heritage is a source of inspiration and knowledge, it is the policy of the Government of Canada to protect and manage archaeological resources .... By protecting and managing this resource through policy, legislation, and programs, the Government will achieve a general symmetry with international standards and provincial measures.

As of 2006, the major federal statutes applicable to archaeology in Canada include the Acts described below.

Canadian Environmental Assessment Act (2003)

The pace of development has been steadily quickening in many areas of Canada. It seems as though new pipelines, highways, and buildings are being planned and constructed at an almost continuous rate. Indus-

tries focusing on the extraction of primary resources like oil, gas, and forestry products are also leaving their mark upon the landscape. The *Canadian Environmental Assessment Act* is a federal statute that requires government departments to determine the impact that planned projects and activities might have on the surrounding environment. These environmental impact assessments also require that impacted areas are thoroughly searched for archaeological and paleontological sites.

Cultural Property Export and Import Act (1985)

The illicit trade of artifacts has always been a problem for those concerned with managing heritage resources. The rise of online auction and e-commerce sites in recent years has served to further increase the market for antiquities acquired through small-scale looting activities. Individuals engaged in these activities now have easy access to buyers from all over the world. The *Cultural Property Export and Import Act* prohibits the illicit import, export, and transfer of ownership of cultural property that is of importance to archaeology, prehistory, history, literature, art, or science. In other words, archaeological and other items on the controlled list are the property of the state, and cannot be exported.

Canada Historic Places Act (proposed)

The Government of Canada is considering legislation to establish a new *Canada Historic Places Act.* Over the past three years, government officials have been consulting with stakeholders regarding what the Act should contain. This bill would likely offer protection of all historic places on federal lands, as well as the protection of archaeological sites that lie on or below the surface of federal waters. It would also enforce guidelines and standards for artifact conservation, require owners to maintain historic buildings and properties, and require archeological impact assessments on government-owned lands slated for development. More extensive archaeological salvage work would then be compulsory if the impact assessments revealed that proposed development placed archaeological and historical sites at serious risk. Archaeologists doing this work would have to apply for permits from Parks Canada, with the expectation that a thorough report of the results would be produced, and that suitable storage space for the artifacts recovered would be provided. It has also been suggested that the

Parks Canada A Government of Canada agency that is mandated to protect and represent nationally significant examples of Canada's natural and cultural heritage and foster public understanding, appreciation, and enjoyment for present and future generations.

Canadian Museum of Civilization should manage an inventory of archaeological sites (location, contents, age, cultural affiliation, etc.). Access to this database would be restricted, to prevent the destruction of these sites through looting activities and other forms of vandalism.

Comparing Provincial and Territorial Legislation for Cultural Sites and Property

All provinces and territories in Canada have enacted legislation to protect from harm archaeological sites and historical places. While the regulations themselves don't vary much between regions, the ways in which they are implemented often do. This is partially due to differing levels of economic development experienced across the country. Provinces like Alberta, for example, have seen an exponential increase in oil and gas development in recent years. This has placed a huge strain on provincial government departments that manage cultural resources. In response, the processes that determine how regions are searched for archaeological sites, what sites are significant, and how much of a threatened site should be preserved or salvaged through excavation reflect attempts to balance the needs of industry against those of heritage resources. We might expect such processes to differ in provinces and territories where development is not as rampant.

Who Sets the Agenda?

Heritage legislation also varies among the provinces and territories because of their different histories, and the relative proportions of distinct ethnic groups. Take Quebec and Nunavut, for example. Quebec was founded by British Royal Proclamation in 1763, following the acquisition of Canada by the British as a result of the Treaty of Paris. Quebec is comprised primarily of francophone and anglophone peoples, with Inuit and First Nations making up a smaller segment of the population. Nunavut, on the other hand, was created on April 1, 1999, making it Canada's youngest territory. Approximately 30,000 people live in an area that covers roughly 1.9 million square kilometres. As of 2005, peoples of Inuit and First Nations descent make up 85 percent of the population. These differences likely explain why indigenous peoples play a much larger role in the regulation of archaeological permits and the management of cultural resources in Nunavut than they do in Quebec. In Nunavut, the

Inuit Heritage Trust is an Inuit organization established by and for the Inuit of Nunavut. The Trust is dedicated to the preservation, protection, and enrichment of Inuit cultural heritage and identity as embodied in Nunavut's archaeological sites, ethnographic resources, and traditional place names. The Trust's activities are based on the principle of respect for the traditional knowledge and wisdom of Elders. Inuit Heritage Trust oversees the issuing of archaeological permits and consults with communities about proposed archaeological research projects. In addition, it conducts archaeological field schools that provide mentoring opportunities for Inuit youth interested in archaeology.

What Is an Archaeological Object?

Most provincial and territorial heritage legislation defines archaeological objects in similar ways. They are usually classified as "items" that are: a) found on or under the *ground*, b) pertain to *human occupation*, and c) are *old*. Each of these features of the archaeological record, however, has distinctive connotations in different areas of Canada. Provinces and territories in coastal areas, or that abut sizable bodies of water, for example, have to deal with protection of archaeological sites that may be submerged in water, rather than just on or under the land. There is also some variation regarding the inclusion of prehistoric plant and animal remains in heritage legislation. In legal practice, the distinction between archaeology and paleontology is usually one that is more apparent than real. Even if most statutes don't treat the words "archaeology" and "paleontology" as synonymous, they nevertheless give them the same protection. This is the case for most national and regional laws, where archaeological and paleontological specimens are protected under the same regulations. Quebec is the only province where paleontology is specifically excluded from the laws' treatment of archaeology.

How Old Does It Have to Be?

The provinces and territories also differ in their ideas about *how old* an object has to be in order to be classified as a heritage resource. Some international laws specify objects must be 100 years of age or older to be considered "antiquities." In Canada, federal laws such as the *Canadian Cultural Property Export Control List* specify 75 years as the cutoff. Most provincial and territorial laws make no mention of how old an object must be to be considered "archaeological." Instead, they merely state that the items in question must have archaeological, prehistoric, historic, or heritage interest—but don't really define what that means.

Who Gets to Dig?

All provinces and territories have implemented thorough permitting procedures to regulate the research and excavation of archaeological sites. These permits are issued only to individuals who are deemed to be qualified. Many government offices now require at least a master's degree in archaeology, and some previous experience working in the provincial region or territory in which the permit is being sought. Once granted, archaeologists are obligated to satisfy a series of requirements. This usually involves the submission of interim and final reports on the work, a detailed catalogue of the artifacts recovered, submission of photographs and field notes, evaluation of significance, and recommendations for future protection measures.

Heritage Legislation and the Sensitive Issue of Human Remains

The treatment of human remains and burial goods is perhaps the most sensitive issue that archaeologists and museum officials face. Until recently, human remains and grave goods were treated as "abandoned property" by many judicial systems in North America. James Young, a professor of philosophy at the University of Victoria, has pointed out that the concepts of "lost" and "abandoned" property have important legal implications for determining who owns archaeological finds in the eyes of the law. When someone loses something, they usually don't give it up intentionally. In these cases, lost items are frequently returned to their rightful owners. In contrast, something that is abandoned *is* deliberately given up. Hence, someone finding abandoned property can usually lay claim without the original owner having any recourse to retrieve it. Classifying human remains as abandoned property has given some looters cause to seek legal claim to the objects they remove from archaeological sites. In one particular case in the United States, a pothunter launched a lawsuit to reclaim 2.5 tons of grave goods and skeletal remains from a historic Tunica cemetery in Louisiana so that he could sell them to the Peabody Museum.

The Repatriation of Human Remains

Human remains and burial goods are extremely important and deeply meaningful to many indigenous societies. Therefore, many native groups have requested that such items be removed from displays and storage areas in museums and universities, and returned to their communities. During the 1970s, for example, archaeologists working on Rose and Upernavik Islands, off the coast of Labrador, excavated 79 Thule Inuit cairn burials. These remains were analyzed at the University of Toronto before being finally housed at Memorial University in Newfoundland. During the 1990s, some Labrador Inuit were outraged to learn that the remains of their ancestors had been studied and held in a university laboratory for more than 20 years. Community leaders approached the Newfoundland government and demanded that the remains be returned to them for reburial. The provincial government agreed to the repatriation, and the remains and their associated artifacts were transported to Rose Island, off the Labrador coast. The remains were deposited inside a wooden frame, and then covered over with boulders and cobbles. The burial ceremony was conducted in Inuktitut and presided over by an Inuit elder.

Two key pieces of legislation in the United States have been enacted to address issues such as those raised by the Labrador Inuit, which relate to the ownership and treatment of human remains. The first was passed in 1989, and is called the *National Museum of the American Indian Act* (NMAIA). It called upon the Smithsonian Institution to inventory all of the human remains and grave goods it had in its possession, and arrange for their repatriation to Native American groups who could claim a direct historical connection to the remains. The second is the *Native American Graves Protection and Repatriation Act* (NAGPRA), passed by Congress in 1990. NAGPRA legislation goes beyond NMAIA because it requires all federally funded museums and institutions to repatriate native skeletal remains, funerary objects, and any other type of item that is seen as either sacred or of continuing historical and cultural interest to the descendant community. Under NAGPRA, museums and institutions are allowed to retain these items only with the express consent of their "true" Native American owners.

Legislation equivalent to NAGPRA has yet to emerge in Canada. The Canadian Archaeological

Figure 17-6 Inuit in front of their skin tent (*tupiq*), Okak, Labrador, 1896.

Source: Archives and Manuscripts, Queen Elizabeth II Library, Memorial University

Association's Statement of Principles for Ethical Conduct requires archaeologists to "acknowledge the cultural significance of human remains" and to "respect protocols governing . . . human remains," but it falls short of explicitly stating that the repatriation of human remains is the *only* appropriate action. In the absence of federal legislation, the issue of how human remains are treated in Canada is handled by provincial and territorial governments, and varies regionally. Provinces like British Columbia, for example, define human remains as "archaeological objects," which are therefore subject to the archeological permitting process.

In the province of Saskatchewan, the *Saskatchewan Heritage Property Act* considers burials that are not found in a recognized cemetery to be Crown property. Up until recently the Crown required the reburial of human remains. However, the Royal Saskatchewan Museum has developed a protocol with the Saskatchewan Indian Cultural Centre, the cultural arm of the Federation of Saskatchewan Indian Nations, which now permits the scientific study of human remains prior to repatriation.

In Ontario, burials are protected by the *Ontario Cemeteries Act (1990)*. Archaeologists have no role in determining what happens to the remains, and their scientific study is prohibited without the permission of a representative of the deceased. Instead, the owner of the land where the remains were discovered negotiates what will happen to them with the deceased's descendants. If the remains are of an indigenous person(s), then the First Nations community nearest the site of discovery decides this.

While legislation such as the *Ontario Cemeteries Act* is similar to NAGPRA, there is still a need for federal legislation relating to the treatment of human remains in Canada. Regional variation in policies makes it unclear as to who can rightfully claim ownership of burials and their contents—be they academic researchers, museums, or First Nations communities. The Assembly of First Nations and the Canadian Museums Association have written a task force report that strongly advocates the development of something that resembles NAGPRA in Canada. Such legislation would likely define practices of co-management, research, repatriation, and re-burial.

Developing New Repatriation Policies

In the absence of federal legislation, many Canadian institutions are working proactively with indigenous communities to develop their own repatriation policies for ethnographic and archaeological materials—including human burials. By way of illustration, a partnership between Nisichawayasihk (Nelson House) Cree First Nation and the Manitoba Museum was formed as part of the 1977 Northern Flood Agreement in the province of Manitoba. The partnership was designed to work out the recovery, analysis, and display of artifacts found within the Churchill River Diversion basin in northern Manitoba. Under this agreement, burials are excavated in cooperation with Elders from Nelson House, and the Manitoba Museum. The Elders view the excavations as ethical because they believe that the ancestors are allowing themselves to be discovered, so that adults and children in their community can learn about the past. Scientific analysis involving AMS dating and DNA analysis has been allowed by the Cree First Nation, with the understanding that the burials and grave goods will be eventually returned to Nelson House for re-interment.

Who Owns the Dead?

The Canadian Museum of Civilization (CMC) entered into a similar type of cooperative relationship with the Lakalzap Band Council from Greenville, British Columbia, during the 1980s. Human remains recovered from a Coast Tsimshian village on the Nass River were returned to band council for reburial after Dr. Jerome Cybulski, a Canadian Museum of Civilization physical anthropologist, had studied them.

Legislation like NAGPRA and the *Ontario Cemeteries Act* requires native groups to demonstrate their historical connection to the objects and human remains they lay claim to. Hence, the burden to prove cultural affiliation lies with the group seeking repatriation.

> **negotiated archaeology** Working directly with communities to educate archaeologists about the concerns of aboriginal people, and aboriginal people about the methods and goals of archaeology.

From a legal perspective, such proof often requires the "science" of archaeology. But the older something is, the more difficult it is to determine its relationship to contemporary peoples. If ties to a living community cannot be demonstrated, then archaeologists retain access to and care of those remains. Margaret Hanna, a curator with the Royal Saskatchewan Museum, has pointed out the irony of requiring First Nations to demonstrate genetic relatedness in order to repatriate their ancestors when museums are not required to do the same. To many indigenous peoples, the fact that they are related to burials—regardless of how old those remains are—is self-evident. Many view their relationship to ancestors through the shared experiences of living on the land, because the land and the people are seen as one and the same. They point out that aboriginal people were on the continent thousands of years before Europeans, and cite oral histories as proof of their connection to human remains and objects.

Proving ownership is at the heart of repatriation issues. Margaret Hanna has suggested that resolving these issues will require what might be best described as **negotiated archaeology.** This involves working directly with communities to educate archaeologists about the concerns of aboriginal people, and aboriginal people about the methods and goals of archaeology. Institutions in Canada such as the Manitoba Museum and the Royal Saskatchewan Museum are already practising negotiated archaeology.

Cultural Resource Management Archaeology: Balancing the Good with the Bad

The cultural resource management industry (CRM for short) is tied to the development of heritage legislation in North America. CRM archaeology can be *agency* driven, as is the case at Parks Canada, which is a government agency charged with managing heritage resources within the Canadian Parks system (see "In His Own Words: Marty Magne: A Parks Canada Archaeologist"). CRM archaeology can also be *industry* driven, and this type of archaeology emerged during a time of unparalleled economic prosperity following the end of World War II. During this time, nationwide programs of dam building required the development of government and university-based research programs to salvage archaeological sites that were threatened with destruction. In the United States, this resulted in the establishment of the Interagency Archaeological Salvage Program and the River Basin Survey Programs. Similar projects were also being carried out in Canada. Archaeologists at the University of Manitoba, for example, worked on the Winnipeg Floodway Project, the Grand Rapids Forebay Survey, and the Churchill Diversion Archaeology Project—all of which were archaeological salvage operations. The archaeological data generated by these three large projects shed new light on the culture history of the North-

Figure 17-7 A CRM archaeologist digs a test pit near the Wolverine mine, in Canada's Yukon Territory.

Source: Courtesy of Kate Peach

eastern Plains in Canada, and trained many young Canadian archaeologists. Soon, private archaeological consulting companies emerged to continue this type of work in other areas of the country.

In many cases, CRM archaeologists are the first line of defence in the preservation of archaeological resources. In Canada, the CRM industry has been around for about 25 years, and most professional archaeologists in Canada have spent at least some of their career working in this challenging area of archaeology. Heritage legislation in Canada requires that companies hire CRM archaeologists to determine and mitigate the impact that any proposed development might have on archaeological resources.

Typically, a team of archaeologists will begin by determining the *archaeological potential* of the area that has been slated for development. The archaeologists begin by consulting site databases to see if any archaeological sites have been previously reported in the area being developed. The area is then surveyed for archaeological sites by digging shovel tests at judgmentally determined intervals (Figure 17-7). If the area in question is a plowed field, surface collections of artifacts will be made. The archaeologists then use the background information and survey results to assess the impact that the proposed development will

have on heritage resources in the area, and make recommendations to provincial and territorial government archaeologists about what should be done to investigate potential impacts. If no sites are present, then clearance is given for the development to take place. If sites are present, then these recommendations usually require the development to be relocated to another area. This is almost always the preferred choice, as the archaeological sites are left intact. If relocation is not possible, then any sites under threat of destruction must be mitigated (salvaged) through methods such as excavation, surface collection, detailed mapping, documentary research, First Nations consultation, and monitoring.

The Good

Ron Williamson is an archaeologist who knows a great deal about the CRM business. He owns a successful consulting firm located in Toronto. Williamson participated in a discussion of the future of archaeology in Canada, with specific reference to CRM archaeology, during a Canadian Archaeology Association conference in 1998. Williamson pointed out many of the good things that CRM archaeology has done for the discipline. Funding for CRM archaeology in Canada,

In His Own Words
Marty Magne: A Parks Canada Archaeologist

Figure 17-8 Marty Magne, Manager of Cultural Resource Services in Parks Canada Agency's Western and Northern Service Centre.

Source: Dr. Marty Magne

As manager of cultural resource services in Parks Canada Agency's Western and Northern Service Centre, I oversee a staff of archaeologists and historians located in Calgary, Vancouver, and Victoria. As part of a 180-person professional services team, we provide cultural resource management (CRM) services to the National Parks and National Historic Sites throughout Alberta and British Columbia, and at times in Manitoba, Saskatchewan, Yukon, NWT, and Nunavut. We also work closely with National Historic Sites that are owned privately or by provinces, and we provide archaeological services to other federal government departments. This position requires advanced financial and human resource manage-

ment skills as well as excellent relationships with First Nations bands, cultural societies, museums, and provincial governments. In professional activities as an archaeologist I undertake research and maintain an international publication record in the areas of stone tool technology, Aboriginal rock art, pre-contact migrations, archaeological resource management, and the relevance of historical disciplines to ecological research. I am Adjunct Associate Professor at the University of Calgary, and I sit on thesis committees, deliver lectures, and provide advice to students and faculty.

My job is first and foremost that of a federal government manager within the Western and Northern Service Centre (WNSC) of Parks Canada. The WNSC has offices in Winnipeg, Calgary, and Vancouver, in which are based a suite of professional services in natural resource conservation, environmental assessment, cultural resources, social science, planning, presentation, finance, and human resources. My principal role is to assist the National Parks and National Historic Sites to manage their in situ archaeological and architectural resources and collections, including interpretive collections. My staff and I have strong working relationships with the diverse National Parks and National Historic Sites of Alberta and B.C., and we have sought opportunities to advance knowledge and understanding of CRM principles across the west. All told, we have approximately 4000 archaeological sites and 1 million artifacts on record from Alberta and British Columbia. My staff and I also play significant roles in the preparation of key accountability documents, in the form of management plans and commemorative integrity statements. The former are tabled in parliament and are thus of prime importance, while the latter are overviews of the key philosophical and physical elements of the reasons for a site's designation of national significance. These are followed by commemorative integrity evaluations, which provide an in-depth review of whether the national historic sites are under threat, whether their importance is being communicated to the Canadian public, and whether the CRM policy is being considered when management decisions will affect the site. Other sorts of management activities are equally critical. For example, in 2005–06 I led a nine-person multidisciplinary team that prepared a review of the status of the Parks Canada archaeological collection in holdings across the country. I am also active in consulting with First Nations communities to assist them in having places, persons, and events recognized as being of national significance, and most recently have been successful in working with the Kainaiwa from southern Alberta with respect to Aisinai'pi (Writing-on-Stone), and with the Upper Similkameen Indian Band in southern British Columbia with respect to the Upper Similkameen Cultural Landscape, a series of pictograph sites, rockshelters, ceremonial locations, and ochre sources. In fact my job has enabled me to work in various ways with 30 separate First Nation bands and Métis communities. Similarly, I am working actively with ethnocultural groups such as the Descendents of Black Pioneers in central Alberta and the Japanese community in southern Alberta. Since we are a federal agency we are involved with treaty negotiations in British Columbia, mainly in the preparation of "Parks and Protected Area" chapters of the draft treaties, but also because we curate collections of archaeological and ethnographic materials from traditional territories of many of the First Nations that are in the treaty process. This process led me to become a direct part of the negotiation team in one instance where we agreed to return ethnographic specimens to a treaty group upon finalization of the agreement.

In terms of research-oriented archaeology our most interesting projects arise either in the course of inventories when new National Parks are established, when National Parks seek to gain a better understanding of ecological history, or when aboriginal communities with whom we have cooperative management agreements wish to have their culture and history more completely represented. Our work in Gwaii Haanas National Park Reserve and Haida Heritage Site, in Haida Gwaii (Queen Charlotte Islands, British Columbia), has elements of all three of those. The inventory work, begun in 1991, has revealed nearly 800 aboriginal archaeological sites, extending to 10,550 years ago. The archaeological work has made pivotal contributions to understanding environmental change from post-glacial times about 13,500 years ago to the present, and the support and participation of the Haida has been absolutely essential to the success of the program. Here in Gwaii Haanas, we played important roles in the pole stabilization project for SGaang Gwaay (Anthony Island) World Heritage Site, which has protected some of the outstanding cultural resources of Canada and the world.

Parks Canada has the mandate to provide advice to other federal departments with respect to the management of archaeological resources on their lands. Unlike the United States, Canadian federal departments do not have professional archaeological staff to review development projects and provide recommendations on appropriate actions. This type of work leads to about 40 project referrals and report reviews per year in the areas I oversee, usually from the Department of Indian Affairs and Northern Development, but also from National Defence, Fisheries and Oceans, Transport, and Public Works and Government Services. I also played a major role in preparing the DND document *Contracting Manual for Land Archaeology* in 1999. The DND has published this document and is applying it across the country to guide its archaeological impact assessment and mitigation work.

for example, has actually increased during a time when funding for academic archaeology has sharply declined. As a result, archaeologists working in the private sector have been responsible for finding and investigating 80 percent of the 3000 sites that have been added to Ontario's sites database in recent years. In the previous six years alone, Williamson explains, three times the number of archaeological sites have been documented—due, in large part, to the efforts of CRM archaeology. This has substantially increased our understanding of the culture history of this province. While Williamson was speaking about Ontario, CRM archaeologists working in other provinces and territories have also made similar contributions.

One of the reasons why CRM archaeology has provided us with an abundance of new information is because construction projects are often located in areas that an academic archaeologist might not normally investigate due to limitations enforced by tightly focused research designs and more restricted logistical capacity. CRM archaeology has also focused our attention on small sites, which are not typically studied by mainstream academic archaeologists. Such sites occasionally consist of nothing more than a scatter of lithic debitage, pottery, bone, and fire-cracked rock. They likely represent overnight camps, or brief stops while travelling. Documenting these sites has provided us with a much more detailed understanding of past human uses of the landscape.

The CRM industry has also helped municipalities develop master plans of archaeological resources using geographic information systems (GIS). These systems have been used to determine the archaeological potential of areas before they are developed, based on such environmental parameters as slope, aspect, elevation, and distance to water. Although the use of predictive modelling in archaeology is somewhat controversial, GIS is also an effective means of managing existing archaeological sites so that they can be protected from future development.

Finally, Williamson explains that First Nations and Inuit communities have benefited from CRM archaeology because oral history and traditional land use mapping are now required for environmental and culture impact assessments in Canada. Elders are consulted to offer their expertise in locating and interpreting archaeological sites and culturally significant areas on the landscape. In addition, most CRM consulting firms employ First Nations and Inuit field assistants. While these activities provide much-needed employment for indigenous communities, they also expose young and old to the practice of archaeology.

The Bad

As with anything, there is also a downside to CRM archaeology. For example, CRM archaeology sometimes suffers from a credibility problem with clients and the general public because of a perceived lack of professionalism. As you can imagine, CRM archaeology can be an expensive proposition for developers, who must pay for all of the survey and mitigation work that is required by law. Companies that are forced to comply with heritage legislation are demanding to know why archaeology is relevant. Many are openly skeptical about the motives of CRM archaeologists, and wonder if they aren't simply taking advantage of the law and "digging for profit" when they make recommendations that require additional survey and excavation work. Some developers resent the fact that they are being forced to spend millions of dollars to preserve small sites consisting of a few scatters of artifacts— definitely not the kinds of archaeological sites that the public sees highlighted in television documentaries. It certainly doesn't help matters when the rates charged by CRM archaeology companies tend to vary considerably from firm to firm.

CRM archaeologists have also been criticized by their academic colleagues for not publishing the results of their findings in peer-reviewed journals, or presenting it at conferences organized by professional associations like the CAA and SAA. Many university-based archaeologists feel that this has created a "grey literature" of reports written for clients that they are unable to access. The demand for archaeological permit holders also means that young archaeologists are being placed in major decision-making positions within a few years of graduating. Many lack the experience that the archaeological establishment would have demanded 20 years ago for doing this type of work. Young CRM archaeologists take endless industrial safety and first-aid courses, but few are encouraged to upgrade their archaeology skills at post-secondary institutions to further their theoretical and methodological development. This is partially due to the fact that many CRM archaeologists are over-worked, as the companies they work for try to keep up with the blistering pace of development in many provinces in Canada. Neil Ferris feels that this has frozen Canadian archaeology into a position of not being able to change to meet the current needs and expectations of developers, and the public at large.

Most of the "bad" in CRM archaeology can be attributed to the "boom" and "bust" cycles under which most economies operate. Periods of rapid growth make it difficult to provide young permit holders with anything beyond on the job training, and the sheer volume of work can sometimes result in reports of varying quality. In contrast, "bust" cycles mean decreased employment opportunities that make it difficult for newly minted archaeologists to gain proper field experience.

The solutions to these problems may lie in the development of professional standards of practice that are followed by all CRM companies. For example, provincial and territorial-wide standards could be set for charge-out rates to clients, expected levels of accreditation, reporting quality, First Nations and Inuit involvement, and public education. Regardless of these growing pains, a great deal of "good" results from CRM archaeology. Countless sites have been saved that would have otherwise been destroyed. What's more, the industry will continue to grow as heritage legislation becomes increasingly stringent in the provinces and territories.

Indigenous Archaeology—Taking Ethics to Their Logical Conclusion

As we have seen, the statement of ethics adopted by the Canadian Archaeological Association makes aboriginal involvement in archaeology a priority. Indigenous archaeology is one of the ways this can be accomplished, and it represents a new and exciting direction. For the remainder of this chapter, we will examine what defines the practice of indigenous archaeology through the eyes of two generations of archaeologists who share a passion for making the practice of archaeology in Canada more inclusive.

Indigenous Archaeology and the Next Generation of Canadian Archaeologists

Natasha Lyons and Rudy Reimer/Yumaks are two young archaeologists who share a passion for indigenous archaeology in Canada. Lyons is Euro-Canadian, while Reimer/Yumks is a member of the Squamish First Nation, in British Columbia. In 2006, both archaeologists teamed up to organize a session at the annual meetings of the Canadian Archaeological Association. Their intentions were to define the practice of indigenous archaeology in Canada by bringing together archaeologists with similar interests from across the country. In "In Their Own Words: Indigenous Archaeology and Why It Is Important," Lyons and Reimer/Yumks present their view of indigenous archaeology, based on the dialogue that came to light through the session.

E. Leigh Syms Paves the Way for Indigenous Archaeology in Canada

Leigh Syms belongs to an earlier generation of archaeologists in Canada, who have often been criticized by younger colleagues for excluding indigenous peoples from the practice of archaeology (Figure 17-9). In Syms's case, nothing could be further from the truth. In fact, his career-long commitment to including First Nations in archaeology literally laid the foundation for the CAA's Statement of Principles and Ethical

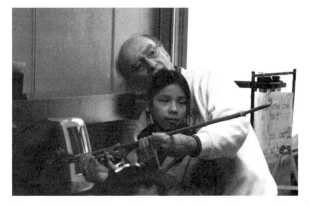

Figure 17-9 E. Leigh Syms demonstrating the techniques used in throwing an atlatl to a student from O pipon na pipwin Cree Nation (South Indian Lake) during a workshop in the community, 2005.
Source: © The Manitoba Museum, Winnipeg, MB

Archaeological Ethics
Protecting an Ancient Arctic Petroglyph Site in Northern Canada

 In most cases, governments enact heritage legislation to protect archaeological sites from destruction by Euro-Canadians (looters, developers, etc). Sometimes, however, important and unique sites are overlooked by national and international government agencies. As a result, archaeologists and indigenous communities often become strong advocates, and lobby governments and international organizations, such as UNESCO, to protect these significant sites from harm.

Carved into a soapstone ridge on a small island off Québec's northern coast is a mysterious 1500 year old gallery of faces, which archaeologists believe were made by people of the Dorset culture tradition. Dorset peoples lived in the Arctic for thousands of years before the arrival of modern Inuit and their Thule culture ancestors. Dorset peoples were renowned for their artistic talents. For example, archaeologists have discovered fantastic ivory and bone carvings of humans and animals, often morphing one into the other. The emphasis placed on human–animal transformation in Dorset art has led archaeologists to speculate that they may reflect the presence of a strong shamanistic tradition.

More than 170 mask-like faces and other symbols are carved into the rock at Qajartalik Island in Northern Québec (Nunavik) and similarities with the small ivory, antler, and bone carvings recovered at other Dorset site suggest that this location may have functioned as a place for spiritual/shamanic ceremonies (Figure 17.10). Archaeologists call carved stone images petroglyphs, and while these types of rock art sites have been found all over the world, Qajartalik Island contains the only major petroglyph site that has ever been discovered in the Canadian Arctic.

Consequently, archaeologists and government officials in the province of Québec have argued that the rock art images on Qajartalik Island should be protected as a UNESCO World Heritage Site.

Qajartalik Island is about a one-hour boat ride from Kangiqsujuaq, a small Inuit community of about 500 people. It has been the subject of study by several archaeologists—all of whom recognize its uniqueness. Many would like to see the area monitored and protected, with access to the site possibly restricted. In 2006, Louis Gagnon, a curator with the Avataq Cultural Institute, a non-profit group dedicated to projecting and promoting indigenous cultural heritage in the eastern arc-

Conduct. Leigh Syms began his professional career as a faculty member in the Department of Archaeology at Brandon University in Brandon, Manitoba. He later took up the position of Curator of Archaeology at the Manitoba Museum of Man and Nature (now called the Manitoba Museum)—a job he held until his retirement in 2004.

While at the Manitoba Museum, Syms actively promoted archaeology within, by, and for the aboriginal community. He set up an Aboriginal Museum Internship Program at the museum to train young aboriginal archaeologists. He has also spent a great deal of time consulting with First Nations communities about

petroglyphs Carved stone images.

tic, told CBC National Radio that "If you count how many faces, you can go as far as 170 faces and all of them are different, but they look from the same age." Gagnon added that "they were probably made at the same period. So, this is very, very special. We tried to understand why they were made like that—it means something. And especially as you cannot find other faces like that anywhere else in the North." (Tuesday, August 29, 2006 | 3:58 PM ET, CBC Arts).

The images are carved onto soapstone, which is very soft and easily damaged. Mary Piliqtuut, the mayor of Kangiqsujuaq, quickly dismissed inaccurate reports in several newspapers stating that vandals had intentionally damaged a few of the petroglyphs. Piliqtuut stressed that people living in the nearby Inuit community care about the carvings, and want to see them protected. Inuit express similar sentiments across the Canadian arctic, and see archaeological sites in areas that fall under their control as important heritage resources that need to be preserved for future generations.

In the case of the Qajartalik Island petroglyphs, archaeologists and other heritage activists have lobbied for the site to be protected, but the issue has been delayed by government negotiations over ownership of the Hudson Strait region of the Canadian Arctic. Canada has already introduced legislation protecting

Figure 17-10 A gallery of mysterious faces: 1500-year-old Dorset petroglyphs from Qajartalik Island, Nunavik, Canada.

Source: Courtesy of Journal Etudes/Inuit/Inuit Studes

significant petroglyph sites in other areas of the country. These include sites in Peterborough, Ontario, and Nanaimo, B.C. Hopefully, similar protection will soon be afforded to one of the Canadian Arctic's most fascinating heritage sites.

their concerns and needs regarding the stewardship of archaeological and ethnographic objects, and the repatriation of human remains and their accompanying grave goods. Syms's work has had an extremely positive effect within First Nations communities in Manitoba and Northern Ontario. After one of his presentations at an Urban Circle Training Centre, for example, an adult aboriginal student approached him and said, "Thanks so much for your presentation. I feel pride when I think of my ancestors now." Such statements demonstrate why the type of work that Syms is doing is so important. In "In His Own Words: A Career-Long Commitment to Indigenous Archaeology," Dr. Syms outlines some of his work and discusses why it is important that archaeologists pursue indigenous archaeology in Canada.

In Their Own Words
Indigenous Archaeology and Why It Is Important

by Natasha Lyons and Rudy Reimer/Yumks

Indigenous archaeology is an emerging focus of archaeology. It is a worldwide movement inspired by the call of indigenous peoples to represent their pasts, presents, and futures in ways they see appropriate. At times, these representations stand in contrast with Western academic interpretations of archaeology and, at a broader scale, Euro-Canadian ideology. Indigenous archaeology may be defined as an archaeology done by, with, or for indigenous peoples. A primary feature, according to leading Canadian practitioner George Nicholas, is a focus on collaborative and community-driven projects that lead to alternative interpretations of traditional archaeological practices. We concentrate here on developments in indigenous archaeology across Canada. We draw particularly from papers presented in a recent session called Emerging Discourses in Indigenous Archaeology in Canada, at the 2006 Annual Meetings of the Canadian Archaeological Association in Toronto. This session examined the nature, breadth, parallels, and divergences in approaches to the practice of indigenous archaeology in Canada.

Indigenous archaeology arose from a variety of circumstances and influences. Most notable was the dissatisfaction of aboriginal peoples and some archaeologists with processual archaeology. They felt that this paradigm objectified indigenous peoples and depicted them as homogenous and incapable of change, and they demanded the re-examination and at times re-writing of traditional archaeological interpretations. This critique led to lively debates in the discipline of archaeology about who has the right to represent indigenous peoples' interests, including that of their pasts.

Some of the outcomes of these debates have been the escalated attention to ethics in archaeology, the emergence of legal and moral frameworks for the treatment and repatriation of human and other cultural remains, such as NAG-PRA in the United States, as well as the rise of archaeological organizations with greater concern for indigenous interests, such as the World Archaeological Congress.

Indigenous worldviews and a range of archaeological theories influence indigenous archaeology. It does not adhere to a single view of looking at the archaeological record, nor is there a unifying doctrine for how it is done. Instead, practitioners aim to work within the traditional viewpoints of each particular aboriginal group. They seek to interpret the findings of the material record through multiple concepts and ideas of history, such as oral history and tradition, song and dance, language, place names, and direct landscape experience. For example, Gerry Oetelaar of the University of Calgary has been aided by Blackfoot (Niitsitapi) Elders in interpreting the patterning and arrangement of stone circles (tipi rings) on the Northern Plains using Niitsitapi conceptions of how people arranged space and socialized in camp life. Paul General of the Six Nations of southern Ontario and Gary Warrick of Wilfrid Laurier University have criticized how site significance is determined in Ontario and are currently re-framing this model in terms of *Haudensosaunee* cultural values. (*Haudensosaunee* means "people of the longhouse." It refers to the League of Peace and Power, and is comprised of five tribes: the Mohawks, the Oneidas, the Onondagas, the Cayugas, and the Senecas.)

Figure 17-11 Natasha Lyons and Rudy Reimer/Yumks.
Source: Courtesy of Natasha Lyons (both)

The methods used to practise indigenous archaeology also vary with each context. A central focus of all indigenous archaeologists is to "de-colonize" research practices and methodologies. This refers to the process of re-formulating archaeological practices in more culturally sensitive ways. There is a rapidly growing cohort of young archaeologists of aboriginal descent in Canada who are shaping how archaeology is done in their communities and beyond. Protocols and permits for doing indigenous archaeology have evolved particularly quickly in the cultural resource management (CRM) industry in British Columbia, due to political and legal pressure from First Nations toward government and industry. Many Nations in this province, such as the Squamish and Wet'sewet'en Nations, have developed their own protocols for doing archaeology in their territories.

The theoretical and methodological pluralism of indigenous archaeology makes the various practices difficult to compare across Canada. Some archaeologists who promote a more unified approach to archaeology based solely on the scientific method have criticized this pluralism. By contrast, Blackfoot archaeologist Eldon Yellowhorn of Simon Fraser University has called for an internalist archaeology that advocates telling history from a First Peoples' point of view. Others, like Cree archaeologist Evelyn Sigfried and Anishnaabe archaeologist Brandi George, are working to adapt their ways of knowing into their archaeological practices and to translate these to their non-aboriginal colleagues. We view these varying and sometimes divergent viewpoints and emphases as a healthy aspect of the emerging discourse and a venue where ethical practices can be defined and developed in indigenous archaeologies in Canada.

In His Own Words

A Career-Long Commitment to Indigenous Archaeology

by E. Leigh Syms

It is essential to find meaningful ways to involve First Nations, Inuit, and Métis peoples in archaeological research and interpretation. There are pragmatic reasons, such as the frequent need to have community support for research and interpretation. More importantly, there are the ethical, moral, and academic responsibilities to return the knowledge to the peoples whose heritage we are recovering, in a manner that is respectful and meaningful to them. There is the satisfaction of seeing the emerging awareness and pride in their ancient heritage and their developing concern and commitment to preserve this ancient heritage.

The future of much of the archaeological discovery, preservation, development, and interpretation will depend to a considerable degree upon Aboriginal involvement, since much of the record represents their heritage. In the province of Manitoba, it will be aboriginal people who will put pressure on governments and Crown corporations such as Manitoba Hydro to fund recovery and interpretation and will be the prime force to make funding available for the production of educational materials. An important role of the nonaboriginal archaeologists, then, is to develop among aboriginal peoples the awareness of the richness, excitement, and importance of their ancient heritage, to work with them on collaborative projects, and to be available to help them develop plans and activities to achieve their goals.

In order to develop an awareness of what archaeologists really do, I have met with numerous aboriginal groups. Over a thousand aboriginal students, teachers, and the public have been treated to archaeology at the Manitoba Museum through behind-the-scenes tours in the Archaeology Lab, training sessions for teachers from Northern Manitoba, and classroom workshops, some lasting most of the week, tours of adult aboriginal students in Native training programs such as Urban Circle Training Centre, and sessions with various groups such as the Elders cultural group at Stony Mountain Penitentiary. As a result of these activities they have become aware of their heritage, and many have dispelled their original stereotypes of archaeologists and have become supporters of archaeological activities and interpretations. It is necessary to keep in touch with the communities and to re-introduce programs for new teachers and principals on an ongoing basis.

In order to provide the opportunity for aboriginal peoples to become leaders in interpreting their archaeological heritage, the Aboriginal Archaeological Internship Program was developed in 1992 and 2002 at The Manitoba Museum. One of the first interns, Cree archaeologist Eva Linklater, compared oral traditions of the Elders with archaeological perspectives. Kevin Brownlee, who has gone on to replace me and become the first aboriginal curator at a major non-aboriginal museum, completed the latter program. Since his appointment, more First Nations people have been coming to the Archaeology Lab, and more aboriginal students are being employed through various contracts. The greater numbers of working aboriginal archaeologists also produce a critical social mass that provides a workplace comfort zone.

Currently, there is a surge in interest in the development of aboriginal educational materials.

Since Winnipeg is purported to have the fastest growing urban aboriginal population in Canada, various agencies are responding to address this trend. School divisions are scrambling to incorporate more aboriginal content into the curriculum, and some are mandating that teachers increase this content in their classes. The Aboriginal Curriculum Advisory staff for Winnipeg School Division #1 has been involved with specific schools and the Manitoba Museum to establish day-long workshops on how the museum galleries can be used to teach aboriginal content in the classroom.

Public-focused publications are needed to provide awareness and to be used as resource materials. A few have been produced and we are shifting to more colourful and appealing formats such as the limited edition but highly illustrated *Bruneau Lake Report* and the delightful children's booklet *Digging The Past*.

Recently, I agreed to help develop the content for and write the first three chapters of the new Grade 5 text *Peoples and Stories of Canada to 1867*, which briefly includes the entire archaeological record. We must work with the teachers, curriculum developers, and publishers to demonstrate the importance of archaeological knowledge.

As a result of the growing trend to learn about aboriginal heritage, there have been a number of requests for more knowledge. After programming with Grade 5 students at Opaskwiak Cree Nation school in The Pas, Manitoba, a local teacher contracted with an archaeologist to produce educational materials for her school. As aboriginal communities have become more aware of the potential of their ancient heritage, there has been a growing need to develop aboriginal professional archaeologists, to inform aboriginal educators about their heritage, and to plan cultural centres to interpret these materials.

The Manitoba Museum has developed a program whereby many recently recovered burial caches are studied and educational tabletop displays are made with replicas of the artifacts. The Elders agreed to these displays so that the young people would develop more pride in their past. These are tangible, visual expressions of outstanding accomplishments of the old ones. The children are so proud of these displays that they brought in toys such as Transformers to "protect" these artifacts at night. The elders as well as the teachers use these displays as teaching aids, adding to their own traditions.

One important aspect of recognizing archaeology as heritage is being sensitive to language use. In addition to using terms such as heritage, it is necessary to replace unacceptable or derogatory words with appropriate words. For example, "prehistoric" implies that the archaeological record is not part of history and aboriginal peoples have little history, all of which is tied into Euro-Canadian history; a preferable term is "pre-contact." Another term, "archaic," needs to be replaced by a term such as "intensive diversification," because the dictionary definition and general public perception of "archaic" means simplicity and backwardness.

There is much to be done to build bridges between archaeologists and aboriginal peoples. We have to remind ourselves that we are dealing with their heritage and to adapt our orientation to that focus. The results are better working relationships, enhanced opportunities to recover and interpret this great heritage, and seeing the satisfaction of large numbers of aboriginal peoples incorporating their ancient heritage.

Conclusion

The archaeological record is a non-renewable resource in Canada, and we all have an ethical responsibility to ensure its protection. But our ethical responsibilities also need to include finding ways to involve descendant communities in the joint management of these resources. The ethical principles adopted by the Canadian Archaeological Association, and the enactment of heritage legislation in Canada, provide us with a means of achieving this. However, they are clearly not enough. Archaeologists need to continue to gain the trust of the diverse communities that support their research. We need to find ways to make developers *want* to protect the sites they inadvertently threaten.

We need to make looters realize that everyone loses when artifacts are dug up and sold. Finally, we need to build long and lasting partnerships with indigenous societies that are meaningful and respectful, and encourage their participation in the practice of archaeology in Canada.

We hope that this textbook has increased your awareness of the importance of archaeology. Play an active role in your community as a steward of the archaeological record. Report looting activities to a provincial or territorial archaeologist. Speak out if you see that the activities of developers are threatening nearby sites, or people selling artifacts at flea markets, or over the Internet. We need your support if the past is to be protected for the future.

Summary

- Ethical codes of conduct have become an important part of doing archaeology in the 21st century. National and international associations of professional archaeologists have spent a great deal of time and energy developing such codes. They define acceptable practices, acknowledge obligations, and offer guidelines for dealing with a wide range of issues, including stewardship of the archaeological record, the repatriation of human remains and objects of cultural significance, and the involvement of descendant communities in archaeology.

- Subsistence digging and disputes over the ownership of human remains and archaeological objects sometimes "muddy" existing ethical statements in archaeology. As a result, ethical principles are never static, but are constantly being re-assessed within changing political and social climates.

- Some of the ethics codes developed by archaeologists emphasize the development of professional standards within the discipline, and the role of archaeologists as stewards of the archaeological record. Others, like that of the Canadian Archaeological Association, acknowledge the spiritual and cultural connection between archaeological sites and objects and Canada's indigenous peoples.

- Heritage legislation places absolute limits on what can and cannot be done with archaeological resources, and exacts penalties for those who break the law. Unlike the United States, there is currently no heritage legislation at the national level in Canada. Instead, heritage legislation is developed, enacted, and enforced by the provinces and territories.

- Provincial and territorial legislation has led to the development of the cultural resource management (CRM) industry in Canada. CRM archaeologists work with government and private-sector industries to assess the impact of proposed developments on archaeological sites. Most archaeology in Canada is currently being done by the CRM industry. Government permitting procedures require that CRM archaeologists are accredited professionals with extensive field experience in archaeology.

- Concern with ethics in archaeology has contributed to the development of indigenous archaeology. Indigenous archaeology is defined as archaeology by, for, and involving Aboriginal peoples.

■ Archaeologists of all ages and professional stripes are currently training young Aboriginal people in archaeology, addressing issues of the interpretation and ownership of archaeological objects and human remains through their research, and forming meaningful partnerships with First Nations and Inuit communities for collaborative archaeological projects.

Additional Reading

CANADIAN RESOURCES

Nicholson, Bev. (1996). Introduction. In B. Nicholson, D. Pokotylo, and R. Williamson (Eds.), *Statement of Principles for Ethical Conduct Pertaining to Aboriginal Peoples: A Report from the Aboriginal Heritage Committee* (pp. 3–6). Ottawa: Jointly sponsored by the Canadian Archaeological Association and the Department of Communications.

Rosenwig, Robert M. (1997). Ethics in Canadian archaeology: An international comparative analysis. *Canadian Journal of Archaeology, 21*(2), 99–114.

Rosenwig, Robert M. (2000). Ethics, archaeological resource management and federal legislation: A few thoughts for the direction of Canadian archaeology. *Canadian Journal of Archaeology, 24*(1–2), 176–178.

Ferris, Neal. (1998). "I don't think we're in Kansas anymore . . ." The rise of the archaeological consulting industry in Ontario. In P. Smith and D. Mitchell (Eds.), *Bringing Back the Past: Historical Perspectives on Canadian Archaeology* (Vol. 158, pp. 225–247). Ottawa: Museum of Civilization, Archaeological Survey of Canada, Mercury Series.

Ferris, Neal. (2003). Between colonial and indigenous archaeologies: Legal and extra-legal ownership of the archaeological past in North America. *Canadian Journal of Archaeology, 27*(2), 154–190.

Wylie, Alison. (1997). Contextualizing ethics: Comments on ethics in Canadian archaeology by Robert Rosenwig. *Canadian Journal of Archaeology, 21*(2), 115–120.

Wylie, Alison. (2000). Some reflections on the work of the SAA Committee for Ethics in Archaeology. *Canadian Journal of Archaeology, 24*(1–2), 151–158.

OTHER RESOURCES

Scarre, Chris, and Scarre, Geoffrey (Eds.). (2006). *The ethics of archaeology: Philosophical perspectives on archaeological practice.* Cambridge: Cambridge University Press.

Zimmerman, Larry, Vitelli, Karen, and Hollowell-Zimmer, Julie (Eds.). (2003). *Ethical Issues in Archaeology* (pp. 3–16). Walnut Creek, CA: Altamira Press.

Online Resources

The Canadian Archaeological Association (CAA) Statement of Principles for Ethical Conduct Pertaining sto Aboriginal Peoples: *http://www.canadianarchaeology.com/documents.lasso*

COMPANION WEBSITE

Visit *http://www.archaeology1ce.nelson.com* to access a wide range of material to help you succeed in your introductory archaeology course. These include flashcards, Internet exercises, Web links, and practice quizzes.

RESEARCH ONLINE
WITH INFOTRAC COLLEGE EDITION

From the Student Companion Website, you can access the InfoTrac College Edition database, which offers thousands of full-length articles for your research.

18 Archaeology's Future

OUTLINE

Students experience a virtual bobsled ride in a C.A.V.E. (computer automated virtual environment) at the University of Calgary. Archaeologists are currently exploring how computer technology can be utilized to study and digitally archive archaeological remains.

Source: Dr. Peter Dawson

Preview

Throughout this book, we have tried to paint a realistic picture of what North American archaeology is all about. We have often reached into the past to demonstrate how today's archaeology has evolved over the last 150 years. Now we will look forward to address two of the key challenges facing North American archaeology in the 21st century:

- How is archaeology relevant to the modern world?

- How should archaeologists share control over knowledge of the past?

- As we explore these related issues, we will probably find more questions than answers.

Introduction

We began this book by describing Kwäday Dän Ts'inchi, an important archaeological find that demonstrates the positive things that can happen when archaeologists and indigenous groups cooperatively investigate the past as equals. The ethical principles that lie behind the Kwäday Dän Ts'inchi case highlight even larger issues surrounding the role of archaeology in modern society. But before we consider those issues, we must first recap some key concepts from earlier chapters.

We have emphasized throughout this text the "big picture" of archaeology: the place of archaeological objects in the modern world. We discussed archaeology's contribution to the larger field of anthropology and the different ways that archaeologists think—the different paradigms that we use to reconstruct and explain the past.

We then focused on the particulars of archaeological fieldwork and analysis: how to find and excavate sites; how to date and analyze artifacts and dirt; and how to interpret the remains of plants, animals, and people themselves. You have seen how archaeologists can extract an enormous amount of information from broken, dirty bits of ancient objects to reconstruct ancient cultural behaviour—and archaeology is still a relatively young science, making progress each year.

The future promises *even greater* knowledge and understanding—achieved by methods that will be even more remarkable than those described in this text.

We then examined two major transitions in the human past: the beginnings of agricultural economies and the origins of the archaic state. Both transitions triggered major changes in world history, each with lasting repercussions—and both processes can be known only through archaeology. These examples served to show what archaeology can learn about the past and the contribution that archaeology makes to an understanding of world history. These two examples likewise demonstrated that the different paradigms of archaeology need *not* compete, but can provide complementary tools for reconstructing the past.

We examined historical archaeology and industrial archaeology, the particular methods available to understand the more recent past. Here we saw archaeology's special power to correct historical inaccuracies, to recover portions of history unrecorded in documents, and to bring new meaning to the present by re-evaluating the past.

Finally, we looked at ethics in archaeology, cultural resource management, and its link to laws that govern the preservation of cultural resources, which accounts for most of modern archaeology. We examined the rise of indigenous archaeology, and how First Nations and Inuit archaeologists are interpreting their own past. We also saw how heritage legislation protects the various *interests* in the past, and not just the objects themselves. These laws explicitly recognize that archaeologists are not the only ones interested in antiquity and that the past holds different meanings for different people.

And through the "Archaeological Ethics" boxes and Chapter 17, we discussed issues that reiterated a point first made in Chapter 1: archaeology in Canada and the United States is not just about the dead; it's also about the living. We will devote part of this final chapter to exploring the implications of that statement.

Virtually everyone cares about the past, to one degree or another. But people care about history for different reasons. We will always face important issues regarding (1) what is done with our knowledge of the past, (2) who gets to "tell the story," and (3) who controls access to data. We believe that archaeology plays several roles in the modern world and, although each of these functions can be beneficial, some soul-searching is required for professional archaeologists to understand and fulfill their responsibilities. We discuss some of these different roles below.

Archaeological Science: Pure or Applied?

Anthropology is conventionally perceived as a **pure science,** as the systematic pursuit of knowledge for its own sake. And it is true that anthropologists, like many other scientists, are commonly motivated more by intellectual curiosity than by the practical applications of what they learn. Anthropologists have traditionally looked for answers to the larger, holistic questions regarding the human condition: how, where, and when did humanity arise? What is the relative importance of nature versus nurture? How (and why) did the major social institutions evolve? These are large-scale questions about the basic nature of the human condition, issues without immediate practical application or "relevance."

But anthropologists have long attempted to apply their findings to practical ends—that is, to do **applied science.** During World War II, for instance, some anthropologists volunteered their services in the war effort. Several collaborated on "national character" studies—detailed memoranda on European and Asian countries that tried to characterize peoples who were either allies or enemies, or who lived in enemy-occupied territory. Working with knowledgeable people in the United States, these anthropologists eventually evolved their own research methods—the "cultures at a distance" approach—to generalize about countries inaccessible because of wartime conditions.

One of the best known of these studies was conducted by Ruth Benedict (1887–1948). At the time a recognized authority on American Indians, Benedict temporarily left her professorship at Columbia to join the Bureau of Overseas Intelligence of the U.S. War Department (1943–1946). She eventually took on a study of Japanese national character, providing information that would ultimately prove critical for the Allied forces occupying Japan during the post-war period.

Applied anthropology is now a huge field. Applied anthropologists evaluate domestic social programs, improve corporate working conditions, develop culturally appropriate methods of delivering health care or agricultural assistance programs, and devise and implement international development programs, to mention only a few areas. Some cultural resource management (CRM) archaeologists also see themselves as applied anthropologists.

Modern archaeology likewise attempts to apply its knowledge and insights to the modern world. In this chapter, we will present multiple examples of how applied archaeology (1) brings the *techniques* of archaeology to non-traditional venues, and (2) applies our knowledge of the human past to concrete economic or social problems.

The Garbage Project

Emil Haury (1904–1992) was the senior archaeologist at the University of Arizona for decades. A specialist in Southwestern prehistory, Haury continually taught

pure (basic) science Systematic research directed toward acquisition of knowledge for its own sake.

applied science Research to acquire the knowledge necessary to solve a specific, recognized problem.

his students that "if you want to know what is really going on in a community, look at its garbage."

Haury's earthy advice was not lost on his students and colleagues. In 1971, the University of Arizona launched a long-term, in-depth study of a community's garbage. But it must have surprised Haury when the Garbage Project decided to focus on the garbage of contemporary Tucson.

The Garbage Project was begun by William Rathje (then at the University of Arizona, now at Stanford University), a Harvard-trained archaeologist who had previously specialized in Maya archaeology. Through the Garbage Project, Rathje applied archaeological methods to the analysis of modern American society.

Rathje was dissatisfied with available research techniques for dealing with contemporary society, particularly the dependence on interviews and questionnaires, because, like many anthropologists, Rathje realized that they can be problematic. Respondents on questionnaires might lie or give answers that they think are truthful but actually are not.

Archaeologists, of course, have methods designed to reconstruct human behaviour from trash. Rathje reasoned, "Why can't we use these methods to study modern human behaviour?"

How Do Archaeologists Collect Trash?

Although it would eventually investigate community trash and landfills around the United States (Figure 18-1), Rathje's Garbage Project began in Tucson, Arizona in 1973. Garbage was picked up from randomly selected households, and a sampling design ensured that different socioeconomic neighbourhoods were included. Student volunteers from the University of Arizona sorted the garbage on special tables provided by Tucson's sanitation department. Student workers had appropriate inoculations and wore laboratory coats, surgical masks, and gloves. Students sorted

Figure 18-1 At California's Sunnyvale landfill, Garbage Project coordinators Bill Rathje (centre) and Wilson Hughes (to Rathje's left) search for newspapers to date a landfill sample.
Source: Courtesy Bill Rathje, photo by Jim Sugar

garbage items into about 150 categories—under the larger headings of food, drugs, sanitation products, amusement and educational items, communication, and pet-related products—and recorded the data on forms for computer processing. The principles of archaeological classification provided objective, repeatable categories of data retrieval. The Garbage Project has involved hundreds of students and 60 participating organizations, recording more than 2 million items from 15,000 household refuse samples from some 250,000 pounds of garbage.

In case you're wondering, courts have ruled that garbage is "abandoned property," meaning that rummaging through someone's trash is not a crime. Nonetheless, the Garbage Project uses various procedures to ensure the anonymity of individuals and households. Volunteers do not record information such as names or addresses, and nothing is saved (although aluminum is recycled); ultimately, the garbage goes to the landfill it was originally headed for.

The Archaeology of Us

The Garbage Project has studied a number of contemporary social issues, including alcohol consumption. Years ago, the Pima County Health Department conducted interviews with a sample of Tucson households to discover how much beer people drank in a week. The sample was carefully chosen using conventional sociological procedures, and informant anonymity was assured. Many took the health department's information as accurate measures of the rate of alcohol consumption in Tucson.

How did the questionnaires stack up against the material evidence—the beer bottles and cans that Rathje's volunteers recorded? It turned out that a large discrepancy existed between front-door answers given to interviewers and back-door behaviour reflected in the contents of the trash. Garbage cans don't lie, and the difference from the health department questionnaire's results were striking: The Garbage Project found significantly heavier beer consumption—in the form of more drinkers and higher rates of drinking—than was reported to the interviewers.

This should astound nobody. People drink more beer than they own up to. But the degree of distortion is noteworthy. The skewing, it turns out, correlates with socioeconomic factors. Low-income households typically distorted their interviews by reporting no beer consumption at all (low-income households may receive food stamps and, fearing the loss of support, they might lie on surveys). By contrast, middle-income respondents did admit to drinking beer, but they significantly underreported the amount they actually consumed. These individuals probably gave an honest, though inaccurate, estimate because they don't perceive themselves to be "beer drinkers." These findings actually provided future studies with a way to correct for this inevitable skewing in the data of health questionnaires.

The Garbage Project also analyzed trends in food discard. In 1918, the War Food Administration (one of the few precursors to Rathje's Garbage Project) collected food discard data for U.S. households. At the end of World War I, households discarded 25 to 30 percent of the total amount of solid food brought into the household. But the Garbage Project found a rate of only 10 to 15 percent. Refrigeration as well as food preservatives are probably the major causes of the decline in waste.

In the mid-1980s, Rathje found that, after the National Academy of Sciences published a report linking cancer and heart disease to a diet high in red meat, people in Tucson ate less red meat. And they also discarded twice as much fat from the red meat they did buy. Consumers were obviously trying to cut down on their fat intake. But at the same time, Rathje found an increase in consumers' use of processed meats, such as lunch meats, that contain non-separable fat. Even with a decline in red meat consumption, people's intake of fat actually *increased* because of the use of processed meat products—the exact opposite of the report's intended effect.

Myths about America's Landfills

Everyone knows that we produce a lot of trash. But it's hard to say how much we're producing and whether it's increasing or decreasing. Studies suggest that we create between 2 and 8 pounds of trash per person per day. Surprisingly, although the kinds of trash have changed—no one throws out bucketloads of ash and clinkers from coal-burning furnaces anymore—the amount generated per person has remained about the same over the last 80 years. The overall volume has increased, of course, because there are more people today (four times as many as in 1890).

Prior to the 1940s, many rural households disposed of trash in their own dumps—in a gully or along a river. In cities, garbage was used to create new land. The southern tip of Manhattan, for example, has been growing since the 17th century. Speculators would purchase the rights to a stretch of the East River, build piers, and then dump garbage between them. One enterprising builder acquired a ship, filled it with garbage, and then sank it between the piers (CRM archaeologists found it later). Eventually, the speculators created land that they then sold.

Formal landfills, however, did not appear on the landscape until the early 20th century. In fact, it was not until after 1945, when the country's rural population shifted to the industrial cities, that landfills became a significant feature on the American landscape. As in previous centuries, cities used these landfills to create usable space for development; New York's La Guardia airport, for example, sits on one.

Six decades later, more than 70 percent of U.S. garbage—180 million tons annually—goes into some 5,500 active landfills across the country. Landfills are the largest human-made structures in the world; some are many times the size of such massive prehistoric structures as Khufu's Pyramid near Cairo or the Temple of the Sun at Teotihuacan outside Mexico City. The 20th century's lasting monuments for posterity will be places like Staten Island's Fresh Kills landfill.

Even before rubble from the World Trade Center was deposited there, the landfill covered 3000 acres and rose to more than 150 feet in places—3 billion cubic feet of trash.

But space for landfills around large cities is rapidly dwindling; New York City, for example, trucks some of its garbage as far away as New Mexico. One reason is that old landfills were simply holes in the ground, while new landfills are complex places governed by a host of regulations and technologies designed to control toxic substances and methane gas. As a result, the national cost of U.S. garbage disposal is skyrocketing—$15 billion a year and rising. This means that North Americans need to know as much about landfills as possible.

But surprisingly, prior to Rathje's studies, little was known about what is actually in landfills and what actually happens there. Rathje argues that "if we are making such a large contribution to future generations, we should know exactly what we are bequeathing them. The only way to unlock these entombed secrets is to excavate." And so Rathje dug, and his research exposed a number of myths about landfills.

The Garbage Project used systematic archaeological methods to explore nine landfills across the United States, recovering about 12 metric tons of debris deposited between 1952 and 1989.

Landfills are generally covered with layers of earth on a set schedule, so they are conveniently stratified. And these strata can be chronologically ordered using newspapers and magazines. But the size of modern landfills did not allow Rathje to sample them with a trowel and dustpan. Instead, he used backhoe trenches (up to 25 feet deep) and a 3-foot-diameter auger equipped with steel teeth that can cut through anything, including a car chassis. Each auger load was hand-sorted, allowing the Garbage Project personnel to calculate what's in America's landfills.

Let's first consider what Americans *think* is in their landfills. The Garbage Project conducted several surveys, with startling results. Many people think disposable diapers, plastic bottles, and large appliances take up most space in landfills. But Rathje's excavations show that these three items *together* take up *less than 5 percent* of a landfill's volume. All kinds of plastics take up less than 15 percent of landfills. And the percentage volume of plastic is going down as manufacturers continually "lightweight" packaging—making milk jugs, for example, out of less and less plastic. The

volume of plastic is going up because the population is rising but, as a percentage of our trash, the much-maligned plastic container appears to be decreasing.

So, something else must be taking up the space. A survey conducted at an Audubon Society meeting concluded that fast-food containers, polystyrene foam cups and packaging, and disposable diapers constituted 70 to (an impossible) 115 percent of landfills, but Rathje shows that these products together take up *less than 3 percent* of a landfill's volume.

So, what's in landfills? What fills up the 3000 acres at Fresh Kills?

The largest component, it turns out, is *paper*—packaging, newspapers, telephone books, magazines, and mail order catalogues. Paper takes up *40 to 50 percent* of the volume in American landfills. Despite the growing commitment to local recycling programs, the amount of paper is steadily rising—up from 35 percent in 1970. The rest of a landfill consists of, in descending order of volume, construction/demolition debris, metals, plastics, other materials, food and yard waste, and glass.

And, here's the really bad news: Contrary to popular opinion, paper doesn't biodegrade in landfills. The Garbage Project has found 40-year-old newspapers, still fully readable (and some with 40-year-old hot dogs wrapped in them). Our landfills are constructed on the belief that the nasty stuff inside will decompose on its own, like some kind of monumental compost heap.

But very little in our landfills actually biodegrades. Compost heaps work only when we chop up the organics, add fluids, and regularly churn the whole batch. This doesn't happen in landfills: Nothing is chopped up, fluids are often prohibited, and debris is compacted, not churned. Methane production, a by-product of decomposition, ceases 15 to 20 years after a landfill is closed, indicating that decomposition has stopped. But Rathje's excavations show that after 20 years, from one-third to one-half of all organic materials are still recognizable. These remaining organics may eventually break down, but only after many more decades, if not longer.

Most of our knowledge about solid waste disposal and landfill design comes from laboratory experiments, but the inside workings of landfills—what actually happens—have remained almost entirely unknown. Plenty of federal policies regulate landfills, but usually government planners work with "logical assumptions" about what landfills "should" contain.

Rathje doesn't assume, he digs. If we are interested in finding sensible ways to dispose of our trash, we need to know *exactly* what is being thrown away and what happens to it after it enters a landfill. By applying some archaeological approaches, Rathje has learned that many of the long-held assumptions about America's garbage are just that—rubbish.

Forensic Archaeology

When Thomas was a first-year curator at the American Museum of Natural History (in the early 1970s), he received a telephone call from a Sergeant McTigue of the New York City bomb squad. At the time, McTigue was working a series of New York City subway bombings. Nearly a dozen such attacks had occurred, killing one person and injuring several others. McTigue suspected that a political protest group was behind the bombings, and he had even identified a prime suspect ("I know the creep who's doin' it.").

Before he could make an arrest, however, McTigue had to establish that, in fact, a crime had been committed. Otherwise, "the perp's lawyer will claim that it was a natural gas explosion, and we can't prove otherwise." To clinch his case, McTigue needed to produce parts of the actual detonating device that had triggered the explosion. Knowing this, McTigue kept sorting through the debris left by each underground explosion. But he never could find what he was looking for. So "the perps" remained free to bomb again, which they did with alarming regularity.

As he was investigating yet another ruined subway station, McTigue finally admitted to himself that he was a cop—trained in standard law enforcement techniques—and not an expert in sorting through trash and debris. But if he wasn't, who was? That's what archaeologists do, right?

That insight brought McTigue to Thomas's office. He explained the problem in simple terms: Suppose that he were to treat each crime scene as if it were an ancient archaeological site. What are the systematic, standardized techniques that archaeologists use to recover their data?

forensic archaeology The application of archaeological and bioarchaeological knowledge for legal purposes.

So McTigue and Thomas spent 3 hours working through Archaeology 101: how to establish a three-dimensional grid system and datum point, map surface finds, remove archaeological strata, and use sifters and flotation devices. They went over note taking, photography, and cataloguing. Armed with this new investigative strategy, McTigue said thanks and took off.

A few days later, there was the sergeant with his bomb squad on the 6 o'clock news. They were quickly yet efficiently digging and measuring, photographing and sifting the ruins of the latest subway bombing. Except for being a little older (and also heavily armed), the police looked no different from other novices on their first "dig class." After a week or two, Thomas got another call from Sergeant McTigue and, sure enough, they'd found the detonating device they were looking for. An arrest was quickly made, and New York's subway bombings came to an end.

This is an example of **forensic archaeology**—using established archaeological techniques to assist law enforcement agencies. It has become increasingly common in the past 20 years—although, as you will see, for some tragic reasons.

Archaeologists as Crimebusters

Today, several archaeological organizations regularly conduct seminars and workshops for law enforcement personnel. For 20 years, the Oklahoma City Police Academy has sent trainees to an archaeological field program, now taught by Kent Buehler of the Oklahoma Archeological Survey. There, police trainees learn how to read a soil profile, probe the ground to find subsurface pits, read topographic maps and soil reports, as well as how to find and map surface evidence. Through the use of mock crime scenes, trainees acquire basic identification skills, such as distinguishing human from animal bones, and they learn basic mapping and evidence-collection skills.

Protecting the Rights of the Dead

Archaeologists also work directly with investigative teams on crime scenes. In Louisville, Kentucky, for example, Phil DiBlasi (University of Louisville) has worked on several cases involving violations of cemetery laws.

Louisville's Eastern Cemetery was established in 1843, although it was probably used for burials before then. The wealthy of Louisville were buried there along with slaves and the indigent. In the 1980s, the cemetery's backhoe operator routinely encountered bones when digging a grave, and he was just as routinely told to "get rid of them" when he brought them to the cemetery owners.

But the reuse of graves, even ones that are more than a century old, is illegal in Kentucky, where your grave is yours forever. The backhoe operator's conscience began to bother him, and he finally blew the whistle.

Kentucky's attorney general at the time was Fred Cowan, whose brother was an archaeologist. Cowan quickly saw that archaeological documentation was needed to create evidence for prosecution and, for assistance, he called upon the University of Louisville's Archaeology Program, run by DiBlasi.

Grave plots in the cemetery were roughly 40 square feet in size. By taking the total cemetery area, subtracting the square footage allotted to roads and buildings, and dividing by 40, DiBlasi calculated the maximum number of burials the cemetery could hold. Comparing that figure with the cemetery's records, he found that the cemetery had exceeded its capacity many years ago.

To confirm this, DiBlasi used shallow backhoe trenches, such as those shown in Figure 18-2, to show that virtually all areas of the cemetery, even those lacking headstones, contained rectangular east–west-oriented pits that were most likely graves. Grave plots that still-living people had purchased were opened to see if someone was already occupying the gravesite. In every single case, DiBlasi found at least one person (and sometimes as many as three people) already in a grave. Using coffin hardware as time-markers, DiBlasi showed that grave reuse had begun by at least 1858. His standard archaeological information—plan views, stratigraphies, photographs, and artifact dating—were important in the effort to prosecute the cemetery's operators.

DiBlasi has since worked on a number of other historical cemeteries, collecting crime scene evidence and showing that graves allegedly removed during previous construction projects were never actually moved. In one case, DiBlasi found unmarked grave pits in the African-American section of a cemetery, and, at their bottoms, coffin nails and fragments of delicate burial cloths lying in situ, but no sign of a body. This, DiBlasi argued, corroborated local oral histories that

Figure 18-2 University of Louisville archaeologist Phil DiBlasi (in trench) uses a backhoe trench to expose unmarked grave pits at a paupers' cemetery.
Source: Robert Kelly

describe how this section of the cemetery was routinely robbed of cadavers in the 19th and early 20th centuries—most likely by local medical students and faculty.

The Archaeology of Mass Disasters

As archaeologists become increasingly involved with criminal investigations domestically, they are also increasingly involved with international investigations. These are sad cases, as they involve people who were lost in war, massacres, and assassinations. Professional archaeologists have joined investigatory teams to recover MIAs in Vietnam, excavate mass graves of missing persons in South and Central America, and work with United Nations investigatory teams to collect data for tribunals and courts from massacre sites in Croatia, El Salvador, and Rwanda. We'll just look at the last of these.

The violence in Rwanda began in April 1994, shortly after Rwandan president Juvenal Habyarimana was killed in an airline crash (allegedly caused by a missile). An ethnic war broke out between the Hutus and Tutsis and, within months, more than 500,000 people were slaughtered. Many were rumoured to be civilians, including women and children who were mercilessly clubbed, burned, or macheted to death. Seeking to determine whether the deaths resulted from civil war or genocide, United Nations investigators authorized archaeological investigations at key sites in central Rwanda.

In His Own Words
A Day in the Life—Forensic Anthropology in Canada

by Mark Skinner, Simon Fraser University

Yesterday we got another forensic case to try to solve. At Simon Fraser University we have been offering this service to the community for more than 30 years. The excitement never goes away. The body was found decomposing on the edge of a lake and labelled "JAM"—for the "J"th unidentified adult male processed by a particular hospital morgue; clothing is simply sweats. There are a lot of insect larvae in the very short hair on the scalp, which will be studied by a forensic entomologist to determine elapsed time since death. We have now cleaned the skull and pelvis. This is Maria's case and I supervise her doctoral studies in forensic osteology. She has studied those parts of the skull affected by sexual hormones and muscle markings and it seems to be a mix of male and female traits; her study of the pelvis shows that, despite very pronounced muscle markings, this individual is a female about 30 to 50 years old. The jaws show a lot of dental work, which will be studied later by a forensic odontologist. She seems to have fallen on bad times in the years before her death; her fillings are falling apart, she has terribly crowded teeth, and has bad cavities in some of her anterior teeth. Her nose is badly broken but healed. The back of her skull is recently smashed into half a dozen small fragments still held in place by a layer of soft tissue. There is a small, crescent-shaped divot on the left side of her head. This is probably, but not certainly yet, a case of homicide. A pathologist will also examine the remains. Will she be identified? Probably. DNA will be extracted from one of her less-decomposed teeth or a piece of dense bone. Once the team of forensic scientists has built up a picture of when she died, her stature, her personal history such as dental work and medical procedures, and the record of missing persons has been checked, her identity may become clear. Confirmation of her identity will be obtained, it is hoped, by matching the body's nuclear DNA with that from some antemortem tissue of the victim such as a cervical smear or hair from a brush; or, failing that, matching her DNA with that of several relatives. For example, if DNA from a sibling, child, and parent can be obtained, in all likelihood she can be identified with a great deal of confidence. Will someone be charged in her death? Probably. It might take years, but the police in Canada never give up on a homicide case.

Practitioners of this specialty, called forensic anthropology, usually have specialized at the graduate level in osteology and received a wide variety of essential and related instruction in topics ranging from comparative anatomy to geographical information systems, archaeology, terminal ballistics and tool marks, criminal justice, scene of crime procedures, and many others. In some ways the students are self-taught, as they pick their own areas of specialization and pursue these at the graduate level. Most students seek a university appointment as a professor and researcher in biological anthropology, specializing, both in terms of teaching and casework, in forensics. A history of Canadian forensic anthropology has just been written (Skinner and Bowie, in press). It tells how

One such excavation took place at Home St. Jean, where an estimated 4000 to 6000 people were killed. The Midwest Archeological Center, a branch of the National Park Service, assisted in the investigations at the massacre site. Working with forensic specialists, the archaeological team first mapped and photographed the site. They mapped the locations of sur-face skeletal materials, numbering each item and collecting it for analysis. Through this process, the team discovered six potential mass graves and began working on the largest. Once the stratigraphy was determined through hand excavation of several test trenches, the overburden was removed with a backhoe. The archaeologists then exposed human remains

most of us got into this kind of work, current practices, and training opportunities.

Another way to get involved is to work internationally. Once a student has obtained the basics of forensic anthropology and forensic archaeology and knows the bones of the human body thoroughly—including variation due to age, sex, occupation, life history, disease, and so on—such students are very useful to organizations that deal with mass disasters and mass graves. Deployment may be for just a few weeks or may span several years. Canadian students have worked for the United Nations Volunteer (UNV) program in East Timor, for the International Criminal Tribunal for the Former Yugoslavia (ICTY), Physicians for Human Rights (PHR) in many countries, the Guatemalan Forensic Anthropology Team, and the International Commission on Missing Persons in Bosnia and Herzegovina. In 2004, several Canadians worked on the victims of Hurricane Katrina and the Boxing Day Tsunami. Opportunities continue to occur.

Some worry about the emotional distress of working on recently deceased individuals. Most of us started working with ancient bones, then graduated to dry recent skeletons with a bit of soft tissue. Ultimately, some of us have had to deal with bodies in every stage of decomposition, from fresh to frankly awful. But these are natural processes, and most forensic scientists forget the negative parts and are intellectually engaged by the puzzles of who the individuals they are studying were and how they died. Finally, those of us fortunate in this world to grow up in democracies like Canada know that to preserve this precious heritage we have to catch the bad guys, be they murderers in our own communities or despots in other countries.

Figure 18-3 July 11, 2005—10th anniversary reburial at Potocari of victims of the fall of Srebrenica. In the course of only 10 days in 1995 about 7500 Muslim males were killed, secretly buried, and then relocated to clandestine secondary graves where the remains were badly commingled. These individuals were located and identified by joint cooperation between the Federation Commission of Missing Persons (Bosnia I Herzegovina) and the International Commission on Missing Persons.

Source: Courtesy of Mark Skinner, Simon Fraser University

by standard archaeological procedures and photographed, mapped, and removed them from the grave.

The archaeologists recovered several hundred sets of remains using these procedures, making this one of the largest exhumations ever conducted in the investigation of human rights violations. Autopsies were conducted to determine sex, age, kind of trauma, and cause of death. Decomposition is rapid in tropical environments, and many of the identifications were made using the techniques discussed in Chapter 12.

Cut marks on bones showed that many individuals were killed by machetes from behind, as if they were fleeing their attackers; cut marks on the bones of hands and forearms showed that some people were unmercifully macheted to death, their arms raised in a desperate effort to ward off the blows. These were clearly unarmed civilians, murdered as part of a program of genocide. The meticulous archaeological documentation provided critical evidence for the United Nations tribunal, which quickly handed down numerous indictments.

Archaeologists are playing an increasingly important role in the investigation and documentation of human rights abuses. In fact, as we write this, teams are at work uncovering mass graves in Iraq that could contain over 300,000 bodies of people whose deaths were allegedly ordered by Saddam Hussein.

Archaeology and the World Trade Center

The story is all too well known: On September 11, 2001, two airplanes piloted by al-Qaeda terrorists slammed into the 110-storey World Trade Center towers. Within hours, the towers and neighbouring buildings collapsed into a massive pile of concrete and twisted steel. Rescue efforts, which had begun even before the towers collapsed, continued for days afterward.

Emotionally taxing as the attack was, cleanup efforts had to begin immediately—and they continued, around the clock, for the next seven months. The steel girders were recycled, but the rest of the debris—over 1.7 million tons—was hauled off in a continuous stream of trucks to the Hudson River. Here the debris was loaded onto barges and taken to the Fresh Kills landfill on Staten Island (the same landfill that Rathje had sampled years before).

This was no ordinary cleanup operation. Besides the sheer enormity of the task, the massive rubble pile was the world's largest crime scene. The debris had to be manually searched for the remains of victims, as well as for personal effects that could help identify people whose bodily remains might have simply vanished. The debris was run through sorters to remove large objects, then it was spread out on the ground and manually searched with rakes. Later, a conveyor belt operation sped up the search.

Within days of the disaster, Brooklyn College archaeologist Sophia Perdikaris put out an informal call to archaeologists for assistance. She recognized that although archaeologists usually deal with ancient artifacts, they are also skilled at finding small things in a vast matrix of dirt and rock, at recognizing and identifying fragments of human bone, and at recognizing broken fragments of objects for what they used to be.

Overwhelmed by the response, she asked the Society for American Archaeology for help. The society set up an online registrar and within a week had over 300 individuals and organizations prepared to volunteer at the landfill. The FBI declined to take advantage of this resource, because they were already overwhelmed with police and fire personnel who had the appropriate clearance and hazardous materials training.

Nonetheless, this effort, and his personal experience with the World Trade Center disaster, inspired archaeologist Richard Gould (Brown University) to develop a volunteer archaeological unit designed to assist at disaster scenes (see "In His Own Words: Disaster Archaeology," by Richard Gould). Most archaeological excavations are pretty happy affairs, with plenty of banter and good-natured ribbing. Gould shows us that the archaeology of disasters is quite different.

Rediscovering Ancient Technology

There are also more cheerful applications of archaeology. So far, we've been looking at the utility of archaeological methods to modern problems. But the more traditional goal of archaeology—knowledge about the past—can also be applied to current problems.

For example, some archaeologists have found ways to harness ancient technologies to benefit modern populations. Ancient techniques for growing and storing foodstuffs have often fallen into disuse and been forgotten. Yet some of these techniques were developed in places ill-suited for agriculture and might be of value to modern populations coping with strained agricultural systems.

Throughout the world, peasant populations use increasingly marginal land as populations expand and as wealthier farmers and corporations claim exclusive use of prime farmland. In addition, intensive agricultural practices sometimes lead to severe degradation of soil and water, making even highly desirable farmland less productive.

Throughout Peru and Bolivia we find ample evidence of vast expanses of former croplands during pre-Hispanic times that are all but abandoned today. Between 50 and 75 percent of the ancient Inka agricultural terraces are no longer in use. Some archaeologists suggest that, along the Peruvian coastline, up to 40 percent more farmland was irrigated in preconquest times than today.

Some pre-Hispanic technologies have been completely forgotten; in other places, practices such as sunken gardens in dry coastal areas of high groundwater and systems of raised fields in waterlogged areas in the Amazon Basin (similar to the *chinampas* we discussed in Chapter 15) are used today only on a limited basis.

Several teams of archaeologists have been studying these ancient Andean agricultural systems with an eye toward reintroducing selected aspects of these technologies, as shown in Figure 18-4. Working from aerial photographs of the Lake Titicaca area along the Peru–Bolivia border, Clark Erickson (University of Pennsylvania) identified a series of ancient raised fields along the lake's margin.

Subsequent archaeological excavations revealed that, starting about 3000 years ago, farmers dug a series of parallel canals and piled the earth between them to form long, low mounds roughly 3 feet high, 15 to 30 feet wide, and up to 300 feet long. These artificial canals provided moisture during drought periods, and the organic-rich muck periodically dredged from the canals fertilized the fields (reducing the need for

fallow periods between plantings). Pollen analysis showed that ancient farmers grew potatoes and quinoa (a high-altitude, protein-rich grain) on these fields. We now know, in fact, that these farmers had created more than 200,000 acres of these raised agricultural platforms on the low-lying land near Lake Titicaca.

Experiments based on the archaeological findings show that the water in the canals running between the raised surfaces also served as heat sinks. Collecting warmth during the day and slowly releasing it at night, the canals kept temperatures around the crops about 2° higher than in the surrounding area, both reducing frost damage and extending the length of the growing season—an important attribute at Titicaca's elevation of 3800 metres (12,500 feet).

Modern agricultural technology has damaged the delicate highland environment. Although Erickson does not advocate a naïve "turning back of the clock," he does believe that ancient methods of agriculture provide viable alternatives for rural development. For instance, experimental raised-field farming provides twice the potato yield versus plots using conventional (modern) techniques.

The ancient technology also appears to be cost effective. Several agribusiness experiments in this area,

Figure 18-4 Quechua farmers from the Andean community of Huatta reconstructing raised-field patterns in the seasonally flooded plain around Lake Titicaca (Peru). This reconstructed agricultural system is based on both indigenous knowledge systems and intensive archaeological research on ancient field patterns. The retaining wall and platform (at left) are made of sod blocks, and the archaeologically excavated canal appears on the right.

Source: Clark Erikson

In His Own Words
Disaster Archaeology

by Richard A. Gould, Professor of Anthropology, Brown University

Archaeologists use their skills only to study past human cultures, or so it seemed to me until October 6, 2001. That was the day I first saw the World Trade Center disaster scene. What I found there that day and on subsequent visits to the site and its surroundings changed my outlook toward archaeology and many other things.

As I walked the streets and alleys east of Ground Zero, I encountered fragmented human remains scattered in the gritty, grey matrix of ash and pulverized building materials that covered the fire escapes, sidewalks, and dumpster tops of lower Manhattan. This initial encounter was followed by repeated visits to the area, reports to the authorities, and a rooftop survey with Brooklyn College archaeologist Sophia Perdikaris. The aftermath of this appalling disaster was initially marked by feelings of inadequacy, followed by a realization that archaeological skills could help the healing process for the victims' families and friends. By locating, recording, and recovering human remains and personal effects using archaeological methods and entering this evidence in a chain of custody, we could help victims' families and friends cope with their terrible loss.

Following a workshop at Brown University that brought together archaeologists and police, fire, and emergency-services professionals, we began recruiting and training volunteers. Our team was eventually invited by the New York City Office of the Chief Medical Examiner to perform forensic recoveries at a location next to Ground Zero, in March of 2002. By then, few remains were left undisturbed by the city's cleanup efforts, so our results were disappointing. But later, the NYC Fire Department's "Phoenix Unit" found human remains across lower Manhattan—including the specific localities I had reported earlier and at the location where we performed our trial excavations.

The lessons from this experience guided further training. Eventually, we created a volunteer unit that included safety, medical, and public affairs experts, which we dubbed Forensic Archaeology Recover (FAR). We trained and prepared in a variety of ways based on advice from different agencies in Rhode Island. But we never expected what happened next.

Shortly after 11 p.m. on February 20, 2003, a fast-moving fire devastated The Station Nightclub in West Warwick, Rhode Island, killing 100 people and leaving others horribly burned. Almost exactly one year after our deployment to the WTC, our volunteer team was activated by the Rhode Island State Fire Marshall's Office and was at the disaster scene by February 26.

often directed at producing cash rather than subsistence crops, required huge investments in capital. In contrast, projects involving ancient technologies used human labour to produce subsistence products and eliminated the need to import seed, chemicals, and machinery.

Erickson is cautiously optimistic when evaluating the results of these experiments. Some communities participate freely, others do not. Some began the experiment but then abandoned it. The reintroduced technology seems to work best for family-based agricultural fields, with more resistance turning up in community-owned fields. And, of course, the modern sociopolitical situation is different from that of the past, when agricultural technology and productivity were controlled by the Andean state. Today, the failure to adopt or continue raised-field agriculture may not be due to problems in technology, but rather to sociopolitical constraints.

Some argue that, if we do not make archaeology relevant to the modern world, then the modern

Although it was a much smaller scale than the WTC disaster, the West Warwick nightclub fire presented FAR with technical and emotional challenges that went beyond anything we experienced in New York. Twenty-two FAR volunteers responded.

The medical examiner's staff had already recovered and identified the fire's victims. Our initial task was to recover, record, and enter as evidence hundreds of personal items for the R. I. State Medical Examiner's Office to repatriate to the victims' families. The winter conditions required that we dry-sieve the frozen remains. At the request of the fire marshal, we also watched for specific items related to the investigation. While maintaining its primary humanitarian activities, FAR also came to play an increasingly investigative role.

The work took place within a limited area surrounded by a chain-link fence covered with flowers, photographs, and messages. Hundreds of mourners, survivors, and the media viewed our activities through the fence. It was like working in a fish bowl, but the FAR team remained focused on the archaeological tasks. This in itself did much to comfort and reassure those watching, as I learned by speaking with my own friends, several of whom lost relatives or close friends in the fire. It was trying at times, for myself and other members of the team, but it taught us that victims' families and friends find it reassuring to know that there are people willing to engage in this kind of recovery effort on their behalf.

Disaster scenes are always complex and chaotic. Archaeology can bring a degree of order out of chaos to comfort the people affected and to help to understand the circumstances of the disaster.

FAR is continuing to train and to recruit new team members—hoping, of course, that nothing like these disasters happens again. This sort of work is not for everyone. We have found, however, that with people who combine their skills and dedication in the way that FAR has done, it is possible. As I watched the FAR volunteers at work, I experienced pride and elation at their efforts while sharing the sense of loss that comes with these kinds of disasters. Perhaps we, as archaeologists and as members of our respective communities, need closure, too. Now I think we know how to find it.

world will find itself able to get along without archaeology. In this section, we have discussed some examples of how archaeological techniques and knowledge can shed light on modern problems and improve the lives of living peoples. These are cases of archaeologists trying to meet one of its challenges in the 21st century.

Another use of archaeology is perhaps less directly, but no less significantly, pragmatic. Increasingly, archaeologists are incorporating the public into research programs through the active participation of interested members and through public education programs.

Archaeologists are also exploring how computer gaming technology can be used to excite public interest in archaeology, as well as provide a high tech means to preserve important historic sites. We examine this facet of modern archaeology in the next section.

Xbox Archaeology: Computer Modelling the Past

If you've ever played a video game, you know that computer graphics can be amazingly realistic. You can make objects like cars, boats, tanks, and spaceships zoom around virtual worlds where they seem to obey all the laws of physics—they speed up, slow down, and of course crash and explode. Archaeologists are becoming increasingly interested in putting computer technology to work in their research. Many are intrigued with the idea that it might be possible to reconstruct an artifact, house, or ancient city, with technology similar to that currently being used to create the most advanced computer games.

Using Computers in Archaeology— A History

Computer modelling has a surprisingly long history in archaeology, with some of the earliest attempts at computer reconstruction dating back to the early 1980s. Even though computers were pretty primitive back then, pioneering projects such as John Woodwark's recreation of the temple precinct of Roman Bath for the BBC (British Broadcasting Corporation) demonstrated that computer reconstructions of archaeological sites were possible, and that they could be used to capture the attention of the public. Limitations in software and computing power at the time meant that these reconstructions were often very crude. However, technology is a moving target. Nowadays, the development of more powerful desktop computers allows us to create incredibly sophisticated and realistic models of archaeological sites. Recent examples include reconstructions of the temple site at Phimai, Thailand, by Dr. Richard Levy, of the University of Calgary. The

surfaces of objects can be "digitally painted" with textures and colours, and the interiors of buildings illuminated with light—all of which creates a photo-realistic image of the site environment. Using a technique known as particle tracing, researchers have even been able to simulate the effects of environmental factors such as candle smoke, fog, and dust!

Another breakthrough in archaeological computing has been the development of virtual reality applications that allow the user to navigate through the model so that it can be explored from different vantage points. Virtual reality can be either immersive or non-immersive, depending on the delivery mechanism. Non-immersive environments are delivered through a PC where the user navigates around the virtual world using a mouse. VRML (virtual reality markup language) enables these models to be placed on the Internet, where a wider audience can experience them. Immersive environments, on the other hand, use high-end computing power to generate real-time complex moving models, and require head-mounted displays (HMDs) or Cave Automated Virtual Environments (CAVEs). CAVEs, in particular, can produce sensory experiences that are startlingly realistic. Essentially, the CAVE is a small room with a number of display screens in a wraparound configuration, which create an immersive environment for one or more people. Wearing a pair of shutter-glasses, the user navigates around an environment whose size exceeds that of the physical projection room (Figure 18-5).

Figure 18-5 Viewers experience the inside of a pre-contact Inuit dwelling at the CAVE in the Schlumberger iCentre at the Calgary Centre for Innovative Technology (CCIT), University of Calgary.
Source: Dr. Peter Dawson

Virtual Environments: A Tool for Preserving Cultural Heritage

Many important historic sites are falling into disrepair due to centuries of neglect. Others have been only partially restored because of the expense of restoration work. The temple site at Phimai is considered the most important Khmer monument in Thailand, and like Head-Smashed-In Buffalo Jump in Alberta, it is listed as a UNESCO World Heritage Site. Located 60 kilometres south of the modern capital of Nakhon Ratchasima (Korhat), Phimai was a centre of royal patronage for such rulers as Suryavarman II (A.D. 1113–1150) and Kauavarymam VII (A.D. 1181–1219). The site contains numerous reconstructed temples, libraries, and ancillary structures, all of which were first documented in 1901. The Thailand Fine Arts Department, under the auspices of Prince Yachai Chitrabongse, began reconstruction of the site in 1964, a process that took five years to complete. However, because of centuries of neglect, many of the galleries and naves remain in a state of partial ruin.

One of the advantages of using computers to do restoration work at archaeological sites is that they provide a non-invasive environment for testing various reconstruction scenarios. Using information about how other temple complexes in Thailand were constructed has allowed Richard Levy to show how the site at Phimai may have appeared when it was occupied during the 12th century (Figure 18-6). Because the computer model can be altered at any time, archaeologists and art historians can better prepare for future reconstruction efforts by trying out alternative architectural interpretations in the virtual world. Analyzing the structures in virtual space also means that architects and curators can predict what areas of the site might require repair, as well as identify areas in imminent danger of collapse. For good reasons, reconstructions of ruined structures at archaeological sites are often undertaken to make them safer for tourists. In the process, however, existing remains are often destroyed. Unlike an actual reconstruction, virtual reconstructions leave the site intact. Visiting a virtual reconstruction on the Internet can further protect the actual site from destruction by reducing the pressures of excessive visitation. As sites become increasingly unsafe, or inaccessible, because of unstable political situations in certain countries, virtual models may end up as the only means by which the public can experience certain historical sites.

Figure 18-6 The completed computer reconstruction of the temple site at Phimai, Thailand.
Source: Dr. Richard M. Levy

Computer modelling may some day help archaeologists address many of the issues raised in the previous chapter about the "ownership" of archaeological objects. As we saw, certain First Nations and Inuit communities are demanding the return of human remains and other objects that they consider sacred from institutions such as museums. Archaeologists are concerned that returning these items means they will no longer be available for study. Technologies such as laser scanning allow archaeologists to scan objects in 3D and construct highly accurate models, which can be either mounted in Web pages or used to create actual replicas made from plastic or plaster. This would make them available for further scientific study in the years following their repatriation.

By utilizing a portal on the Internet, archaeological sites and their artifacts can be presented as interactive websites, hosting a variety of media. Streaming audio, video, QuickTime VR, and Virtual 3D worlds can be placed on a website or a CD-ROM, creating environments that can serve to educate the public on the importance of archaeological sites as cultural resources. As a repository for cultural heritage, these interactive worlds could aid communities in their preservation of traditional skills, myths, music, and knowledge of the biophysical world.

Virtual Environments: An Educational Tool for Exploring Time

As an educational laboratory, a virtual world offers a framework for understanding the development of cultures from the past. Data acquired on a site's historical, archaeological, and geological past, for example, can be placed into a 3D interactive database and indexed according to its place in time. Rather than a single structure isolated from context, the presence of other buildings, as seen in the Phimai reconstruction, can help clarify a story about life in an earlier age. The virtual world also offers a unique opportunity to understand the environmental context of a site. Within this database a "virtual time machine" can be created that can turn back the clock to consider the action of geological forces and disturbances that shaped the land. Furthermore, early human settlement patterns, mapped over time, could be used to reveal the connection between site context and artifact. Terrain, geographical features, and the relative location to other population centres and transportation routes

can all be linked to the archaeological site under study.

In retelling a story about life in an early hunting community, for instance, the site can be recreated complete with residents, known as *avatars*. In Hindu philosophy, an avatar most commonly refers to the incarnation (bodily manifestation) of a higher being (deva), or the Supreme Being (God) onto planet Earth. Avatars are usually represented in the form of two or three-dimensional graphical representations of humanoids (or other graphical or text-based avatars). Some, but not all, virtual worlds allow for multiple users. Avatars can also be used as virtual tour guides at computer-reconstructed sites such as Phimai. Avatars could offer the viewer explanations on how certain types of artifacts were made and used by the occupants of a site. A virtual experience as an introduction to the site can help guide the public on how to interpret visible remnants of earlier human activity. It all sounds like something out of science fiction, but popular computer games such as *Second Life* and *The Syms* demonstrate that these types of approaches are currently achievable and could be used in archaeology.

Addressing Concerns Regarding How the Past Is Represented

While computer modelling and virtual reality hold great promise as tools for use in archaeology, there are a number of caveats that must be taken into consideration. First, the technical expertise required for computer modeling projects often necessitates collaboration between computer specialists and archaeologists. Although many such partnerships have been fruitful, both parties need to be aware of the limitations imposed by computer technology and archaeological data.

A number of researchers have also expressed serious concerns about the potential for misrepresenting the past through computer modelling. For the most part, archaeologists deal with "fuzzy" data sets that are frequently difficult for computer modellers to deal with. While archaeologists may want to emphasize the uncertainty of the past and stress the importance of multi-vocality in archaeological interpretation, computer modellers require single explanations for where doorways were placed and how walls were constructed. The problem then becomes, "How does one portray uncertainty in computer models?" In response, some researchers have experimented with "pink cement" and different degrees of opacity as a means of drawing attention to areas of the model that archaeologists may be unsure about.

The second problem relates to the first, because our inability to deal with fuzzy data can result in "fudge factors" that, while extremely realistic, can convey authority where none might exist. After all, we live in an image-hungry world in which the public has become increasingly used to visually striking computer images in video games and movies. Members of the public also accept the premise that computers make research more accurate and precise. Consequently, the use of computers to meet the public demand for archaeological reconstructions that are evermore realistic and exciting can create the impression that archaeologists know more about the past than they actually do.

While these are certainly justifiable concerns, it is important to note that reconstruction based on incomplete data has been a part of archaeological interpretation since the Renaissance. Throughout history, drawings and models have been important vehicles for considering how human societies in the past built their monuments. Like the intricate wooden models built by Renaissance architects such as Donato Bramante, Sabastiano Serlio, Andrea Palladio, and Jacopo Barozzi da Vignola, virtual reconstructions can be used to kindle similar excitement and interest in archaeology. This makes them powerful tools for soliciting public support for the preservation and excavation of archaeological sites. VR modelling also provides an interactive space for exploring possible arrangements of architectural elements, and their effect on how buildings of the past may have been experienced by their inhabitants. Let's look at two examples of how computer modelling can be used as a tool for archaeological research.

Building a 3D Computer Model of a Thule Whalebone House

As we saw in Chapter 14, Canada's Inuit people are descended from Thule culture peoples, who left their Alaskan homeland sometime during the 12th century. These Thule pioneers embarked on an epic journey that took them through the Canadian Arctic Archipelago. In Alaska, Thule people constructed semi-subterranean houses from driftwood, whalebone, hide, and

sod. In comparison, the islands of the Canadian Arctic were relatively driftwood-free. As a response, Thule migrants developed a new type of architecture that is almost entirely unique in the world. They built their houses from the bones of large baleen whales known as bowheads (*Balaenae mysticetus*). These massive bones were obtained from whales that were either hunted in the open water using kayaks and small open-decked skin boats called *umiaqs,* or from the carcasses of long-dead whales that had beached themselves over the centuries.

Thule whalebone houses have always fascinated archaeologists. Therkel Mathiassen, a Danish archaeologist who first defined Thule culture during the 1920s, was perhaps the first to speculate on how they were built. Eighty years later, we still know relatively little about how these enigmatic houses were constructed. This is partly because Thule people had stopped building them by the 16th century, meaning that no European had ever seen one intact. What we do know has been learned from archaeological excavations of collapsed structures. A pit was first dug out of the ground with a semi-subterranean entrance passage. A flagstone floor and rear sleeping platform were then installed. Next, a framework of whalebone was erected over the house pit and entrance passage, and covered with hide, stone, and blocks of sod.

Using whalebone as a construction material would have been extremely challenging for Thule builders. Elements with the best spanning potential, such as jawbones, are extremely heavy and unusually shaped. It seems likely that whalebones most suited to house construction were almost always in short supply. The late Allan McCartney, one of arctic archaeology's most important researchers, once estimated that the average Thule house must represent close to 20 whales' worth of bone. Given the logistical difficulties and dangers of hunting whales often greater than 13 metres in length, this would have represented quite an achievement! It seems more likely that Thule architects used elements acquired through active hunting and the scavenging of whalebone from natural stranding locations and abandoned houses.

Without a doubt, the best way to learn about how anything was built is to try building it from scratch. Over the years, archaeologists have attempted to reconstruct everything from Egyptian pyramids to Neolithic villages—with varying degrees of success.

However, reconstructing a Thule whalebone house presents a unique set of challenges. For example, it is impossible to acquire enough whalebone elements to build such a dwelling in real life. Peter Dawson and Richard Levy, from the University of Calgary, decided that many of these issues could be addressed if they built their own Thule house in a virtual world.

Such an enterprise would require assembling digital models of the various elements in a bowhead whale skeleton that were important in Thule architecture. Luckily, the New England Aquarium in Boston, Massa-

chusetts, had a massive North Atlantic right whale (*Eubalaena glacialis*) skeleton on display in a large gallery. The skeleton was fully articulated and suspended from the roof of the gallery using heavy-gauge wires. While this whale was not the same species as those hunted by Thule groups (the bowhead whale, *Balaena mysticetus*), the skeleton was similar enough in size and morphology that it was a suitable analogue.

Dawson and Levy then used a CYRAX-2500 laser scanner to scan the whale skeleton (Figure 18-7). The laser scanner works on a similar principle to the scan-

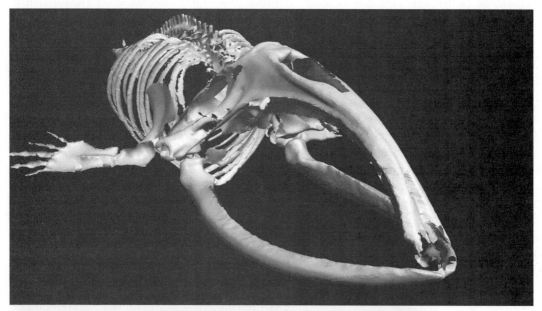

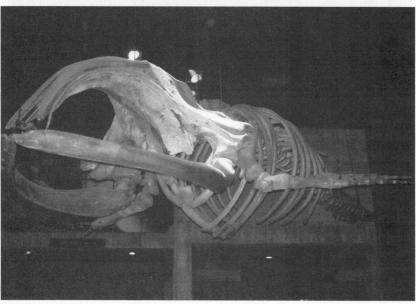

Figure 18-7 The whale skeleton at the New England Aquarium (a), and the digital whale skeleton constructed from the laser scanning data (b).

Source: Dr. Peter Dawson (both)

ner you use with your home or school computer. The difference is that a laser scanner casts a fan of millions of points of laser light, which are spaced so closely together that they can capture the shape of an object in three dimensions. These objects are rendered as "point clouds." In this case, the point clouds were individual elements within the whale skeleton. The fact that the skeleton was articulated meant that some elements would occlude others during the scanning process. However, it was possible to extrapolate from other areas of the skeleton to account for any missing data. Unlike Thule architects, who would have had limited access to whale bones like mandibles and maxillae, we (Dawson and Levy) now had the luxury of reproducing as many of each type of element as we wanted for use in our virtual reconstruction!

A detailed architectural plan of a well-preserved Thule whalebone house from Bathurst Island, Nunavut, recorded by Dawson, was then selected. The plans had been drafted using AutoCAD software, and showed the shape and dimensions of the house pit and entrance tunnel, and the placement of elements within the collapsed roof frame. This map served as a template upon which the digitized skeletal elements where placed. Dawson and Levy then began the process of experimenting with how the roof frame had been assembled.

The experience of building a three-dimensional model of a Thule whalebone house in a virtual world provided Dawson and Levy with a deeper appreciation of the challenges faced by Thule architects (Figure 18-8). They were able to discern four basic design principles that were regularly employed. First, the difficulties of spanning the house pit meant that building techniques needed to be developed that maximized the spanning potential of elements whenever possible. As a result, upper jawbones (maxillae) were likely left attached to skulls. Dawson and Levy were also able to determine that placing long, slender elements such as maxillae inside the house pit ensured that the full length of the element was used to span the largest possible space. In addition, this made the elements more vertical, reducing lateral thrust at the base of the frame. While canting elements upward reduces the amount of floor area, it improves the amount of headroom toward the edges of the structure. This has the effect of actually increasing the amount of usable space within the dwelling. Finally, Dawson and Levy

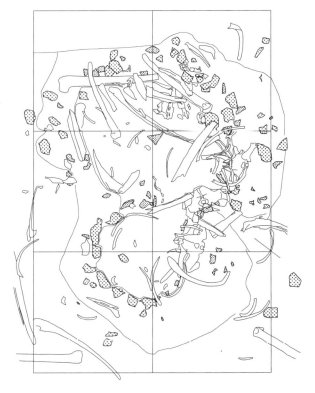

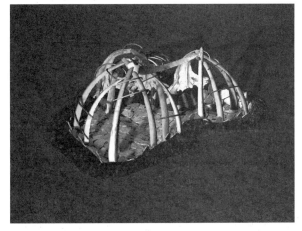

Figure 18-8 2D plan view of collapsed Thule house ruin (a), and the completed computer reconstruction—minus sod and hide coverings (b).

Source: Dr. Peter Dawson and Dr. Richard Levy (both)

discovered that trying to design a roof frame to fit a house pit of a particular size and shape was extremely difficult. The computer reconstruction revealed that it is far more efficient to experiment with possible roof frame configurations first, using elements at hand, and then excavate a house pit to fit the dimensions of the best design. It would not have been possible to gain any of these insights using simple two-dimensional site plans.

Simulating Environmental Effects

Computer models offer archaeologists an excellent way of communicating research to the general public, but can they also be used as tools for research? As we have seen, being able to visualize archaeological data in three dimensions can provide new insights into precontact construction practices. It can also give users an impression of the spaces within, because environmental factors like light, shadow, and smoke can be simulated. How light is distributed within a dwelling is something that archaeologists rarely think about. However, it was likely an important factor in determining where certain types of activities might have taken place within the dwelling.

Take the whalebone house computer model, for example. The arctic world is somewhat unique because it experiences extreme seasonal variations in daylight and darkness. The community of *Iqaluit* on Baffin Island receives 24 hours of daylight in June, and 6 hours per day in December. Grise Fiord, the most northerly community in the Canadian Arctic, experiences 24 hours of daylight in June and round the clock darkness in December. During the months of darkness, household duties such as cooking, sewing, and tool making/repair would have had to be done by lamplight in Thule dwellings. The stone lamps used by Inuit are called *qulliqs*. They were manufactured from stone or clay, and ranged from 60 to 135 centimetres in length. The standard fuel for a *qulliq* was seal or whale oil, which was used to soak a wick made of moss.

Hypothetically, the low levels of light put out by a *qulliq* lamp would have made intricate tasks like sewing and carving extremely difficult. Sewing durable, waterproof clothing from hide would have been essential to the survival and livelihood of Thule families. The recovery of sewing equipment, such as needle cases, thimbles, cutting boards, and *ulu* knives, indicates that hide clothing was being sewn inside Thule houses during the winter months. Tools and other objects, often displaying impressive levels of craftsmanship, have also been found inside the ruins of Thule winter dwellings. Just how much light would have been available for these complex tasks?

In order to answer this question, Dawson and Levy conducted lighting experiments with replicas of *qulliq* lamps (Figure 18-9). Using lard as a fuel substitute for sea mammal oil, and cotton as a replacement for the moss wick, they fired up the experimental lamp. An illuminance meter was then used to measure the amount of light emitted at different distances from the lamp. Results indicated the experimental *qulliq* lamp produced as much light as a 15-watt light bulb—not a lot of light.

Architects put a lot of time and thought into how buildings should be illuminated. The reflectivity of

Figure 18-9 Experimenting with reconstructed *qulliq* lamps.
Source: Dr. Peter Dawson

Figure 18-10 How the interior of a Thule whalebone house might have appeared to its occupants under *qulliq* lamplight.

Source: Dr. Peter Dawson and Richard Levy

surfaces like walls, floors, and furnishings can affect how the inside of a room appears. **Luminance** is a measure of how bright or dark a surface is perceived to be by the human eye. **Illuminance,** on the other hand, measures how much energy has fallen on the surface. Lighting specialists use these measures to determine how much light should be used in rooms that serve different functions. Once the amount of light produced by the lamp had been established, Dawson and Levy used this value to illuminate the interior of the Thule house model. Dawson and Levy assumed 15-percent reflectivity for surfaces in the structure, because lamp soot would have likely coated floors, walls, and the sleeping platform. The light source was placed on one side of the sleeping platform, in accordance with archaeological and ethnographic observations of lamp placement in other Thule and his-

toric Inuit dwellings. This provided an impression of how the inside of a Thule whalebone house might have appeared to its occupants (Figure 18-10).

A computer program called Lightscape was then used to produce a colour rendering of the interior of the house using illuminance. Illuminance is a function of distance from the light source, and therefore is useful for gauging how much light would have been available for activities in different areas of the dwelling. In Figure 18-11, all interior surfaces are coloured according to their illumination valued (lx), from red (high) through the floor spectrum to blue (low).

luminance A measure of how bright or dark a surface is perceived to be by the human eye.

illuminance A measure of how much energy has fallen on a surface.

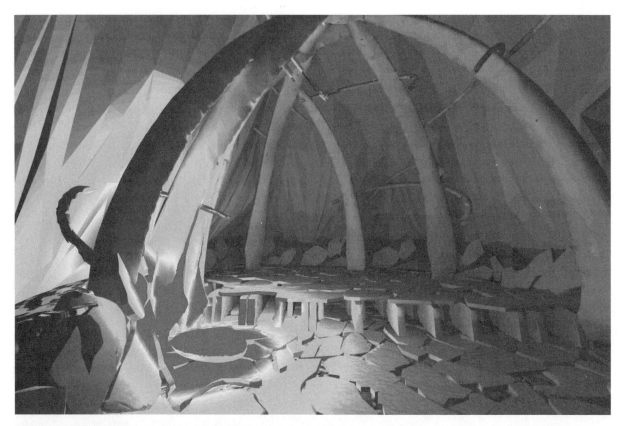

Figure 18-11 A photometric rendering of the house interior, mapping illuminance levels. Illuminance measures how much energy has fallen on the surface of the floor, sleeping platform, and walls of the dwelling.

Source: Dr. Peter Dawson and Richard Levy

The photometric map indicates that the interiors of Thule winter houses were likely pretty dark places. To put this into a context, Dawson and Levy compared the illuminance values for the model to Western architectural standards for lighting used by architects when designing houses, factories, and office towers. The levels of light recommended by these standards are generally dictated by the needs of the visual task. This includes such factors as details of the activity, the contrast between task and background, the age and condition of the eye, and the importance of speed and accuracy when performing the task. Typically, the more light available, the easier it is to carry out a specific activity. Table 18-1 presents the recommended light levels for a series of generalized tasks. Interest-

ingly, difficult and prolonged visual tasks with objects of low brightness and contrast have recommended light levels that far exceed those generated in Dawson and Levy's experimental lighting simulation. Furthermore, the light levels suggested for detailed close-up work, where speed and accuracy are not as essential, are found only within about a metre of the lamp.

These results have interesting implications for understanding the spatial organization of activity areas within arctic winter dwellings. If artifact distributions were projected inside the illuminated virtual model, for example, we might expect those associated with carving and sewing tasks to cluster closely around the lamp. Alternatively, the low levels of light may have encouraged individuals to depend more on

TABLE 18-1 Recommended Light Levels for Generalized Tasks

TASK CONDITION	LIGHT LEVEL	(FOOTCANDLES [fc])	TYPE OF LIGHTING
Very difficult and prolonged visual tasks with objects of low brightness contrast. High speed and extreme accuracy required	100 or more	Supplementary	Special fixtures such as desk
Small detail, fair contrast, close work, speed not essential	50 or more	Supplementary	
Prolonged reading, assembly, general office, ordinary bench or laboratory work	25 or more		Local lighting and ceiling fixtures directly overhead
Occasional reading. Washrooms, power plants, waiting rooms and kitchens	10 or more		General lighting
No detail vision necessary. Stairways or supply houses	5 or more		General or supplementary lighting

Source: From *Human Factors Design Handbook: Information and Guidelines for the Design of Systems, Facilities, Equipment, and Products for Human Use.* Wesley Woodson. 2nd ed. New York: McGraw-Hill, 1992.

haptic (touch) sensory information than they did on sight when performing tasks that would normally require high levels of visual acuity. Rather than rely on vision alone, it seems logical to assume that peoples living in different times and places would have developed ratios of sensation that were uniquely suited to the environments in which they lived. Using computer models may provide archaeologists with a means of further exploring how people may have experienced past environments.

Conclusion

In this chapter, we have looked at the role of archaeology in the future. We examined some ways in which archaeology can be of pragmatic value—by using archaeological techniques to understand modern garbage, gather the data needed to bring criminals to justice, and reconstruct archaeological sites and artifacts using laser scanners and VR computing technology.

Perhaps even more important, however, will be archaeology's role in knocking down the walls that so often divide people of the world. Archaeology can do this in part by the information that it gathers. Archaeology can show, for example, how different environmental and historical circumstances work together to create the diversity of human societies. In so doing, archaeology proves that unilineal evolution and the racist assumptions that stand behind it are wrong. But archaeology also contributes not only by *what* it learns about the past, but *how* it goes about learning it—the way in which it incorporates different perspectives, attitudes, and concerns of descendant communities and other stakeholders in the past.

Archaeology, as we have said, is not just about the dead; it's also about the living. And, it turns out, archaeology is not just about the past; it's also about the future.

In His Own Words

Laser Scanning Technology: Imaging a Building or a Scratch on a Sword

by Richard Levy

In the last decade the use of laser scanning technology has emerged as an important tool in historical preservation and archaeological investigations. In the past, creating a three-dimensional model of a site or object from field measurements would be a time-consuming task (Figure 18-12). Often, many weeks of data collection would be needed to reconstruct the plan of a single site or building. Today, laser scanning technology offers the archaeologist accuracy and speed in data collection on objects as small as a coin and as large as an entire city.

Technology used in engineering and manufacturing relies on the accuracy of a laser beam to collect millions of surface points needed in reconstructing the shape of an object. For terrestrial surveys, time-of-flight laser scanners use a pulse reflected off the surface of the object. The time recorded for this path can be used to determine the location of a point on the surface of the object under study. This type of scanner can operate up to several hundred metres and provides a point accuracy of about 5 millimetres. Another type of scanner, phase based, uses a two-frequency modulated laser beam to capture data at a distance of less than 100 metres (range) at a 10-millimetre accuracy. The advantage of this type of scanner is its very high speed of data collection, perfect for an initial survey. For archaeologists focused on small objects, where high detail is needed, short- to medium-range scanners can achieve resolutions of less than .04 millimetres. In using a laser reflected from the surface of the scanned object, each scan line is observed by a single frame of a specifically designed camera. The contour of the surface is derived from the shape of the image of each reflected scan line. With this type of scanner it is not unusual to employ turntables that rotate the object during the scanning process to facilitate the data capture process for small statues and pieces of pottery. Higher-resolution scanners operating at short range can achieve resolutions as small as 50 to 100 μm, which can reveal a detail as small as a scratch on a coin or metal sword. In addition, many laser scanners can capture the colour of an object. This information is saved as either a digital image or three colour bands: red, green, and blue. These 3D images can be used to define an object's shape and appearance.

Data Conversion

Once the laser scanner captures data, computer software is needed to convert the millions of point measurements into a 3D object. Even for a relatively small object, a 3D array of points, or point cloud, requires postprocessing if it is to be useful in measuring and reconstructing a site or object. Using software employed in surveying and reverse engineering, these point clouds containing millions of points can be converted into a 3D mesh that can be studied in most CAD programs (computer aided design). Improved computer graphics make it possible to view these massive data files without the high-end graphic workstations needed just a few years ago.

Research and Preservation

As a research tool, having an accurate virtual copy of an artifact that can be shared over the Internet offers academics and scholars the opportunity to test hypotheses using a data set that is not constrained by the cost of travel to distant locations to acquire. Using a virtual testing approach, the researcher can examine artifacts, take critical measurements, and perform statistical analyses. For example, a series of cross-sections obtained by scanning clay pots over the course of an excavation can be used to help classify and date objects. As a method for architectural preservation and conservation, laser scanning offers an important tool for acquiring data on ancient and historical sites and buildings. Efforts to preserve and document San Francisco City Hall, the Statue of Liberty, Chartres Cathedral, and the Coliseum in Rome are among the projects in which laser scanners have been used to capture virtual representations. In recent years laser scanning has contributed to the construction of accurate 3D models that can serve as an armature for judging future preservation efforts. For the public, the ability to tour these sites from their desktop computer will open up a new window to the world of archaeology and architectural history.

Figure 18-12 Virtual snow goggles from Arviat, Nunavut. This accurate 3D model of an artifact recovered from a nearby archaeological site was created using laser scanning, and can be rotated three dimensionally, allowing inspection from every angle.

Source: Dr. Peter Dawson and Richard Levy (both)

Summary

- One way or another, virtually all archaeological research depends on public support. Particularly within the last two decades, responsible archaeologists have recognized the importance of returning to the public some of the benefits and insights— that is, the archaeological knowledge.

- Although archaeology is conventionally perceived as a "pure" science, many archaeologists are finding ways to apply the techniques of archaeology to new problems, such as the analysis of contemporary garbage and landfills to help solve the nation's trash problem.

- Others are involved in forensic archaeology, working with law enforcement officials, providing training in the recovery and analysis of material remains, and generating firsthand evidence to be presented in courts of law; others use archaeology to recover ancient technologies that benefit developing nations.

- Virtual reality, computer modelling, and laser scanning offer archaeologists with a means of reconstructing archaeological sites and visualizing archaeological data in new and exciting ways.

- Computer reconstructions of archaeological sites and artifacts can be used as a high-tech means of heritage preservation. Important sites can be reconstructed in non-invasive ways. Computer reconstructions can be placed in virtual worlds where visitors, from the comfort of their own desktop computers, can explore them. Images of artifacts can be captured in 3D and used for archival and research purposes.

- Computer modelling is an exciting way to gain the interest of the general public. However, archaeologists need to be aware of the limitations caused by data gaps when engaged in computer reconstruction work. If not, then they may leave a virtual visitor with the impression that more is known about a structure than is actually the case.

- The future of archaeology depends on our ability to engage the public in archaeological research. This can be done through Web-based presentations of archaeological data, as well as public education and outreach programs.

Additional Reading

CANADIAN RESOURCES

Dawson, Peter, Levy, Richard, Gardner, Donald, and Walls, M. (2007). Simulating the behavior of light inside Arctic dwellings: Implications for assessing the role of vision in task performance. *World Archaeology, 39*(3), 17–35.

Dawson, Peter, and Levy, Richard M. (2005). Constructing a 3D computer model of a Thule whalebone house using laser scanning technology. *Journal of Field Archaeology, 30,* 443–455.

Levy, Richard, Dawson, Peter, and Arnold, Charles (2004). Reconstructing traditional Inuit house forms using 3 dimensional interactive computer modeling. *Visual Studies, 1,* 26–35.

OTHER RESOURCES

Brown, Michael F. (2003). *Who Owns Native Culture?* Cambridge: Harvard University Press.

Koff, Clea. (2004). *The Bone Woman: A Forensic Anthropologist's Search for Truth in the Mass Graves of Rwanda, Bosnia, Croatia, and Kosovo.* New York: Random House.

Layton, Robert (Ed.). (1989). *Who Needs the Past? Indigenous Values and Archaeology.* One World Archaeology Series. London: Unwin Hyman.

Lynott, Mark J., and Wylie, Alison (2000). *Ethics in American Archaeology: Challenges for the 1990s* (2nd ed.) Washington, DC: Society for American Archaeology.

Watkins, Joe. (2000). *Indigenous Archaeology: American Indian Values and Scientific Practice.* Walnut Creek, CA: Altamira Press.

Zimmerman, Larry. (2003). *Presenting the Past.* Walnut Creek, CA: Altamira Press.

Zimmerman, Larry J., Vitelli, Karen D., and Hollowell-Zimmer, Julie. (Eds.). (2003). *Ethical Issues in Archaeology.* Walnut Creek, CA: Altamira Press.

Online Resources

COMPANION WEBSITE

Visit *http://www.archaeology1ce.nelson.com* to access a wide range of material to help you succeed in your introductory archaeology course. These include flashcards, Internet exercises, Web links, and practice quizzes.

RESEARCH ONLINE
WITH INFOTRAC COLLEGE EDITION

From the Student Companion Website, you can access the InfoTrac College Edition database, which offers thousands of full-length articles for your research.

Glossary

A horizon The upper part of a soil, where active organic and mechanical decomposition of geological and organic material occurs.

absolute date A date expressed as specific units of scientific measurement, such as days, years, centuries, or millennia; absolute determinations attempting to pinpoint a discrete, known interval in time.

accelerator mass spectrometry (AMS) A method of radiocarbon dating that counts the proportion of carbon isotopes directly (rather than using the indirect Geiger counter method), thereby dramatically reducing the quantity of datable material required.

achieved status Rights, duties, and obligations that accrue to a person by virtue of what they accomplished in their life.

adaptive perspective A research perspective that emphasizes technology, ecology, demography, and economics in the definition of human behaviour.

aeolian A geomorphic process whereby soil-forming material is transported and deposited by wind.

affinal Relatives that one is related to by marriage, rather than blood.

alluvial sediments Sediments transported by flowing water.

Americanist archaeology The brand of archaeology that evolved in close association with anthropology in the Americas. It is practised throughout the world.

analogy Noting similarities between two entities and inferring from that similarity that an additional attribute of one (the ethnographic case) is also true of the other (the archaeological case).

Anasazi A Native American culture flourishing in southern Colorado, Utah, northern New Mexico, and Arizona from about A.D. 100, whose descendants are considered to include the present-day Pueblo peoples.

ancestor worship A religion in which one's deceased ancestors serve as important intermediaries between the natural and supernatural.

androcentric A perspective that focuses on what men do in a society, to the exclusion of women.

anthropology The study of all aspects of humankind—biological, cultural, and linguistic, extant and extinct—employing an all-encompassing holistic approach.

antiquarian Originally, someone who studied antiquities (that is, ancient objects) largely for the sake of the objects themselves—not to understand the people or culture that produced them.

appendicular skeleton All parts of an animal excluding the axial skeleton.

applied science Research to acquire the knowledge necessary to solve a specific, recognized problem.

arbitrary level The basic vertical subdivision of an excavation square; used only when easily recognizable "natural" strata are lacking and when natural strata are more than 10 centimetres thick.

archaeofauna The animal bones recovered from an archaeological site

archaeological context Once artifacts enter the ground, they are part of the archaeological context, where they can continue to be affected by human action, but where they also are affected by natural processes.

archaeological record The documentation of artifacts and other material remains, along with their contexts recovered from archaeological sites.

archaeological site Any place where material evidence exists about the human past. Usually, "site" refers to a concentration of such evidence.

archaeology The study of the past through the systematic recovery and analysis of material remains.

archaic state A centralized political system found in complex societies, characterized by having a virtual monopoly on the power to coerce.

argilliturbation A natural formation process in which wet/dry cycles in clay-rich soils push artifacts upward as the sediment swells and then moves them down as cracks form during dry cycles.

argon-argon dating A high-precision method for estimating the relative quantities of argon-39 to argon-40 gas; used to date volcanic ashes that are between 500,000 and several million years old.

ascribed status Rights, duties, and obligations that accrue to a person by virtue of their parentage; ascribed status is inherited.

assemblage A collection of artifacts of one or several classes of materials (stone tools, ceramics, bones) that comes from a defined context, such as a site, feature, or stratum.

atlatl A spear thrower made from antler, bone, or wood and used to launch stone-tipped spears.

axial skeleton The head, mandibles, vertebrae, ribs, sacrum, and tail of an animal skeleton.

B horizon A layer found below the A horizon, where clays accumulate that are transported downward by water.

band A residential group composed of a few nuclear families, but whose membership is neither permanent nor binding.

berdaches Among Plains Indian societies, men who elected to live life as women; they were recognized by their group as a third gender.

bibliometrics A set of methods used to study or measure texts and information, and the impact they have in various fields of study.

bilateral descent A kinship system in which relatives are traced equally on both the mother's and father's side.

bilocal residence A cultural practice in which a newly married couple may live in either the village of the groom or the village of the bride.

bioarchaeology The study of the human biological component evident in the archaeological record.

biological anthropology A subdiscipline of anthropology that views humans as biological organisms; also known as *physical anthropology.*

bone collagen The organic component of bone.

bonebed Archaeological and paleontological sites consisting of the remains of a large number of animals, often of the same species, and often representing a single moment in time—a mass kill or mass death.

bridging arguments Logical statements linking observations on the static archaeological record to the dynamic behaviour or natural processes that produced it.

bundle burial Burial of a person's bones, bundled together, after the flesh has been removed or allowed to decay off the bones.

burial population A set of human burials that come from a limited region and a limited time period. The more limited the region and the time period, the more accurate will be inferences drawn from analysis of the burials.

C horizon A layer found below the B horizon that consists of the unaltered or slightly altered parent material; bedrock lies below the C horizon.

cargo system Part of the social organization found in many Central American communities in which a wealthy individual is named to carry out and bear the cost of important religious ceremonies throughout the year.

caries Cavities.

carrying capacity The number of people that a unit of land can support under a particular technology.

channel flake The longitudinal flake removed from the faces of Folsom and Clovis projectile points to create the flute.

charnel house A structure used by eastern North Americans to lay out the dead where the body would decompose. The bones would later be gathered and buried or cremated.

chiefdom A regional polity in which two or more local groups are organized under a single chief (who is the head of a ranked social hierarchy). Unlike autonomous bands and villages, chiefdoms consist of several more or less permanently aligned communities or settlements.

chinampas A form of intensive agriculture; low mounds the Aztec built by piling up sediments from the bottoms of shallow lakes and marshes to form islands of arable land.

civilization A complex urban society with a high level of cultural achievement in the arts and sciences, craft specialization, a surplus of food and/or labour, and a hierarchically stratified social organization.

clans A group of matri- or patrilineages who see themselves as descended from a (sometimes mythical) common ancestor.

classical archaeology The branch of archaeology that studies the "classical" civilizations of the Mediterranean, such as Greece and Rome, and the Near East.

Clovis The earliest well-established Native American culture, distributed throughout much of North America and dating 10,900 to 11,200 B.C.

codices Maya texts, long strips of paper, many metres in length when unfolded, made of the pounded inner bark of certain trees; these texts helped analysts interpret Maya hieroglyphics on stelae.

coevolution An evolutionary theory that changes in social systems are best understood as mutual natural selection among components rather than as a linear cause-and-effect sequence.

cognitive archaeology The study of all those aspects of ancient culture that are the product of the human mind: the perception, description, and classification of the universe; the nature of the supernatural; the principles, philosophies, ethics, and values by which human societies are governed; and the ways in which aspects of the world, the supernatural, or human values are conveyed in art.

colluvial sediments Sediments deposited primarily through the action of gravity on geological material lying on hillsides.

comparative collection A skeletal collection of modern fauna of both sexes and different ages used to make identifications of archaeofaunas.

comparative method In Enlightenment philosophy, the idea that the world's existing peoples reflect different stages of human cultural evolution.

component An archaeological construct consisting of a stratum or set of strata that are presumed to be culturally homogeneous; a set of components from various sites in a region will make up a phase.

conjunctive approach As defined by Walter W. Taylor, using functional interpretations of artifacts and their contexts to reconstruct daily life of the past.

consequentialist ethics Moral theories where actions are judged as either "right" or "wrong" by the effects they have on the world at large, or on the happiness and well-being of others.

coprolite Desiccated feces, often containing macrobotanical remains, pollen, and the remains of small animals.

core A piece of stone that is worked ("knapped"). Cores sometimes serve merely as sources for raw materials; they also can serve as functional tools.

cosmology The study of the origin, large-scale structure, and future of the universe. A cosmological explanation demonstrates how the universe developed—both the totality and its constituent parts—and also describes what principles keep it together.

cribra orbitalia A symptom of iron deficiency anemia in which the bone of the upper eye sockets takes on a spongy appearance.

cryoturbation A natural formation process in which freeze/thaw activity in a soil selectively pushes larger artifacts to the surface of a site.

cultural anthropology A subdiscipline of anthropology that emphasizes nonbiological aspects: the learned social, linguistic, technological, and familial behaviours of humans.

cultural disturbance processes Human behaviours that modify artifacts in their archaeological context; for instance, digging pits, hearths, canals, and houses.

cultural materialism A research paradigm that takes a scientific approach and that emphasizes the importance of material factors—such as environment, population density, subsistence, and technology—in understanding change and diversity in human societies.

culture An integrated system of beliefs, traditions, and customs that govern or influence a person's behaviour. Culture is learned, shared by members of a group, and based on the ability to think in terms of symbols.

culture history The kind of archaeology practised mainly in the early to mid-twentieth century; it "explains" differences or changes over time in artifact frequencies by positing the diffusion of ideas between neighbouring cultures or the migration of a people who had different mental templates for artifact styles.

data Relevant observations made on objects that then serve as the basis for study and discussion.

datum point The zero point, a fixed reference used to keep control on a dig; usually controls both the vertical and horizontal dimensions of provenience.

de Vries effects Fluctuations in the calibration curve produced by variations in the atmosphere's carbon-14 content; these can cause radiocarbon dates to calibrate to more than one calendar age.

deconstruction Efforts to expose the assumptions behind the alleged objective and systematic search for knowledge. A primary tool of postmodernism.

deductive reasoning Reasoning from theory to account for specific observational or experimental results.

deflation A geologic process whereby fine sediment is blown away by the wind and larger items—including artifacts—are lowered onto a common surface and thus become recognizable sites.

density-equilibrium model Proposed by Binford, it attributes the origins of agriculture to population pressure in favourable environments that resulted in emigration to marginal lands, where agriculture was needed to increase productivity.

deontological ethics The view that human actions have an intrinsic quality that makes them right or wrong, regardless of consequences.

descendant community A society that has a demonstrable historical link to one in the past.

direct acquisition A form of trade in which a person/group goes to the source area of an item to procure the raw material directly or to trade for it or finished products.

domestic economy The organization of reproduction and basic production, exchange, and consumption within camps, houses, apartments, or other domestic settings.

dosimeter A device to measure the amount of gamma radiation emitted by sediments. It is normally buried in a stratum for a year to record the annual dose of radiation. Dosimeters are often a short length of pure copper tubing filled with calcium sulphate.

down-the-line trade An exchange system in which goods are traded outward from a source area from group to group, resulting in a steady decline in the item's abundance in archaeological sites farther from the source.

eburnation A sign of osteoarthritis in which the epiphyses of long bones are worn smooth, causing them to take on a varnish-like appearance.

ecofact Plant or animal remains found in an archaeological site.

egalitarian societies Social systems that contain roughly as many valued positions as there are persons capable of filling them; in egalitarian societies, all people have nearly equal access to the critical resources needed to live.

electron spin resonance A trapped charge technique used to date tooth enamel and burned stone tools; it can date teeth that are beyond the range of radiocarbon dating.

element In faunal analysis, a specific skeletal part of the body—for example, humerus or sternum.

enamel hypoplasias Horizontal linear defects in tooth enamel indicating episodes of physiological stress.

enculturation The process whereby individuals learn their culture.

energy dispersive x-ray fluorescence (XRF) An analytical technique that uses obsidian's trace elements to "fingerprint" an artifact and trace it to its geologic source.

Enlightenment A Western philosophy that advocated ideas of linear progress, absolute truth, science, rational planning of ideal social orders, and the standardization of knowledge. It held that rational thought was the key to progress; that science and technology would free people from the oppression of historical traditions of myth, religion, and superstition; and that the control of nature through technology would permit the development of moral and spiritual virtues.

epiphyses The ends of bones that fuse to the main shaft or portion of bone at various ages; most bones are fused by age 25. This fact can be used to age skeletons of younger individuals.

ethics Sets of standards that we use to guide our actions; often are borne out of societal norms that prescribe particular ways of behaving under certain circumstances.

ethnoarchaeology The study of contemporary peoples to determine how human behaviour is translated into the archaeological record.

ethnocentric (also ethnocentrism) The attitude or belief that one's own cultural ways are superior to any other.

ethnographers Anthropologists who study one culture and write detailed descriptions of that culture's traditions, customs, religion, social and political organization, and so on.

ethnographies The descriptions of cultures written by ethnographers.

ethnology That branch of anthropology dealing chiefly with the comparative study of cultures.

exotics Material culture that was not produced locally and/or whose raw material is not found locally.

experimental archaeology Experiments designed to determine the archaeological correlates of ancient behaviour; may overlap with both ethnoarchaeology and taphonomy.

faunal In archaeology, animal bones in archaeological sites.

faunal analysis Identification and interpretation of animal remains from an archaeological site.

faunalturbation A natural formation process in which animals, from large game to earthworms, affect the distribution of material within an archaeological site.

feature The nonportable evidence of technology; usually fire hearths, architectural elements, artifact clusters, garbage pits, soil stains, and so on.

Fertile Crescent A broad arc of mountains in Israel, Jordan, Syria, Iraq, and Iran where wild wheat, barley, and other domesticated plants are found today.

fining upward sequence A layer of sediment that includes coarser materials (usually sand) at the bottom and finer materials (usually clays) at the top.

flake A thin, sharp sliver of stone removed from a core during the knapping process.

floralturbation A natural formation process in which trees and other plants affect the distribution of artifacts within an archaeological site.

flotation The use of fluid suspension to recover tiny burned plant remains and bone fragments from archaeological sites.

flute Distinctive channel on the faces of Folsom and Clovis projectile points formed by removal of one or more flakes from the point's base.

forensic archaeology The application of archaeological and bioarchaeological knowledge for legal purposes.

formal analogies Analogies justified by similarities in the formal attributes of archaeological and ethnographic objects and features.

formation processes The ways in which human behaviours and natural actions operate to produce the archaeological record.

full-coverage survey Performing 100-percent coverage of a large region; used where topography and archaeological remains make it feasible and where the relationships between specific sites (as opposed to types of sites) are the subject of interest.

functional type A class of artifacts that performed the same function; these may or may not be temporal and/or morphological types.

gender ideology The culturally prescribed values assigned to the task and status of men and women; values can vary from society to society.

gender role The culturally prescribed behaviour associated with men and women; roles can vary from society to society.

gene A unit of the chromosomes that controls inheritance of particular traits.

general systems theory An effort to describe the properties by which all systems, including human societies, allegedly operated. Popular in processual archaeology of the late 1960s and 1970s.

geoarchaeology The field of study that applies the concepts and methods of the geosciences to archaeological research.

geographic information system (GIS) A computer program for storing, retrieving, analyzing, and displaying cartographic data.

geomorphology The geological study of landforms and landscapes, for instance, soils, rivers, hills, sand dunes, deltas, glacial deposits, and marshes.

georeferenced Data that are input to a GIS database using a common mapping reference—for example, the UTM grid—so that all data can be spatially analyzed.

glacial till The mixture of rock and earth pushed along the front and sides of a glacier.

global positioning system Hand-held devices that use triangulation from radio waves received from satellites to determine your current position in terms of either the UTM grid or latitude and longitude.

gravilturbation A natural formation process in which artifacts are moved downslope through gravity, sometimes assisted by precipitation runoff.

ground-penetrating radar A remote sensing technique in which radar pulses directed into the ground reflect back to the surface when they strike features or interfaces within the ground, showing the presence and depth of possible buried features.

haplogroup Genetic lineages defined by similar genes at a locus on a chromosome.

Harris lines Horizontal lines near the ends of long bones indicating episodes of physiological stress.

heat-treatment A process whereby the flintknapping properties of stone tool raw material are improved by subjecting the material to heat.

high-level (or general) theory Theory that seeks to answer large "why" questions.

hilly flanks theory Proposed by Robert Braidwood, it claims that agriculture arose in the areas where wild ancestors of domesticated wheat and barley grow, attributing agriculture's appearance to human efforts to continue to increase the productivity and stability of their food base, coupled with culture being "ready" to accept an agricultural lifeway.

historical particularism The view that each culture is the product of a unique sequence of developments in which chance plays a major role in bringing about change.

historiography The study of the practice of history, focuses on the narratives, interpretations, worldview, use of evidence, or method of presentation of other historians.

Holocene The post-Pleistocene geological epoch that began about 10,000 radiocarbon years ago and continues today.

Hopewell Interaction Sphere The common set of symbols found in the midwestern United States between 200 B.C. and A.D. 400.

Hopewell A cultural tradition found primarily in the Ohio River Valley and its tributaries, dating from 200 B.C.–A.D. 400. Hopewell societies engaged in hunting and gathering and in some horticulture of indigenous plants. They are known for their mortuary rituals, which included charnel houses and burial mounds; some central tombs contained exotics.

They also constructed geometric earthworks as ceremonial enclosures and effigy mounds.

horticulture Cultivation using hand tools only and in which plots of land are used for a few years and then allowed to lie fallow.

humanism A doctrine, attitude, or way of life that focuses on human interests and values. In general, a humanistic approach tends to reject a search for universals and stress instead the importance of the individual's lived experience.

hypothesis A proposition proposed as an explanation of some phenomena.

iconography Art forms or writing systems (such as Egyptian or Maya hieroglyphics) that symbolically represent ideas about religion or cosmology.

ideational perspective The research perspective that defines ideas, symbols, and mental structures as driving forces in shaping human behaviour.

ideology The ideas held by members of a society that relate to nature, time, and place.

ideology A set of beliefs—often political, religious, or cosmological in nature—that rationalizes exploitative relations between classes or social groups.

illuminance A measure of how much energy has fallen on a surface.

in situ From Latin, meaning "in position"; the place where an artifact, ecofact, or feature was found during excavation or survey.

index fossil concept The idea that strata containing similar fossil assemblages are of similar age. This concept enables archaeologists to characterize and date strata within sites using distinctive artifact forms that research shows to be diagnostic of a particular period of time.

inductive reasoning Working from specific observations to more general hypotheses.

infrastructure In cultural materialism, the elements most important to satisfying basic human survival and well-being—food, shelter, reproduction, health—which are assumed to lie at the causal heart of every sociocultural system.

instrumental neutron activation analysis (INAA) An analytical technique that determines the trace element composition of the clay used to make a pot to identify the clay's geologic source.

intensive agriculture Cultivation using draft animals, machinery, or hand cultivation in which plots are used annually; often entails irrigation, land reclamation, and fertilizers.

irrigation hypothesis Proposed by Karl Wittfogel, it attributes the origin of the state to the administrative demands of irrigation.

kill sites Places where animals were killed in the past.

kinship Socially recognized network of relationships through which individuals are related to one another by ties of descent (real or imagined) and marriage.

kiva A Pueblo ceremonial structure that is usually round (but may be square or rectangular) and semi-subterranean. They appear in early Pueblo sites and perhaps even in the earlier (pre-A.D. 700) pithouse villages.

Koshare An English rendering of a Keresan (one of the Pueblo Indian languages) word that refers to ritual clowns in Rio Grande Pueblo society.

krotovina A filled-in animal burrow.

landscape archaeology The study of ancient human modification of the environment.

law of superposition The geological principle stating that, in any pile of sedimentary rocks that have not been disturbed by folding or overturning, each bed is older than the layers above and younger than the layers below; also known as Steno's law.

Libby half-life The time required for half of the carbon-14 available in an organic sample to decay; the standard is 5,568 years, although it is known that the half-life is closer to 5,730 years.

linguistic anthropology A subdiscipline of anthropology that focuses on human language: its diversity in grammar, syntax, and lexicon; its historical development; and its relation to a culture's perception of the world.

lipids Organic substances—including fats, oils, and waxes—that resist mixing with water; found in both plant and animal tissues.

lithic reduction sequence A series of stages used by a flint knapper to sequentially remove flakes for the purposes of creating a finished tool.

living floors A distinct buried surface on which people lived.

long bone cross-sections Cross-sections of the body's long bones (arms and legs) used to analyze bone shape and reconstruct the mechanical stresses placed on that bone—and hence activity patterns.

low-level theories The observations and interpretations that emerge from hands-on archaeological field and labwork.

luminance A measure of how bright or dark a surface is perceived to be by the human eye.

macrobotanical remains Readily recognizable plant parts.

Magdalenian The last major culture of the European Upper Paleolithic period (ca. 16,000–10,000 B.C.); named after the rockshelter La Madeleine, in southwestern France. Magdalenian artisans crafted intricately carved tools of reindeer bone and antler; this was also the period during which Upper Paleolithic cave art in France and Spain reached its zenith.

mano A fist-sized, round, flat, hand-held stone used with a metate for grinding foods.

marker bed An easily identified geologic layer whose age has been independently confirmed at numerous locations and whose presence can therefore be used to date archaeological and geological sediments.

materialist perspective Views artifacts as functioning solely to adapt people to their environments.

matrilineage Individuals who share a line of matrilineal descent.

matrilineal descent A unilineal descent system in which ancestry is traced through the female line.

matrilocal residence A cultural practice in which a newly married couple live in the bride's village of origin; it is often associated with matrilineal descent.

matrix-sorting The hand-sorting of processed bulk soil samples for minute artifacts and ecofacts.

mean ceramic date A statistical technique for combining the median age of manufacture for temporally significant pottery types to estimate the average age of a feature or site.

metate A large, flat stone used as a stationary surface upon which seeds, tubers, and nuts are ground with a mano.

microwear Minute, often microscopic evidence of use damage on the surface and working edge of a flake or artifact; it can include striations, pitting, microflaking, and polish.

midden Refuse deposit resulting from human activities, generally consisting of sediment; food remains such as charred seeds, animal bone, and shell; and discarded artifacts.

middle-level (or middle-range) theory Hypothesis that links archaeological observations with the human behaviour or natural processes that produced them.

mindset A set of organizing principles that determine how people perceive the world around them.

minimum number of individuals (MNI) The smallest number of individuals necessary to account for all identified bones.

Mississippian A widespread cultural tradition across much of the eastern United States from A.D. 800–1500. Mississippian societies engaged in intensive village-based maize horticulture and constructed large, earthen platform mounds that served as substructures for temples, residences, and council buildings.

mitochondrial DNA (mtDNA) Genetic material found in the mitochondria of cells; it is inherited only from the mother and appears to mutate at a rate of 2–4 percent per 1 million years.

moieties Two groups of clans that perform reciprocal ceremonial obligations for one another; moieties often intermarry.

molecular archaeology The use of genetic information in ancient human remains to reconstruct the past.

molecular clock Calculations of the time since divergence of two related populations using the presumed rate of mutation in mtDNA and the genetic differences between the two populations.

morphological type A descriptive and abstract grouping of individual artifacts whose focus is on overall similarity rather than function or chronological significance.

mortality profiles Charts that depict the various ages at death of a burial population.

multiple working hypotheses A set of hypotheses that are rested against the empirical record from the simplest to the most complex.

Musqueam First Nations Band The Musqueam people are a strong aboriginal community of more than 1000 members. Their traditional territory once occupied what is now Vancouver and its surrounding areas.

Natufian A cultural manifestation in the Levant (the southwest Fertile Crescent) dating from 14,500 to 11,600 BP and consisting of the first appearance of settled villages, trade goods, and possibly early cultivation of domesticated wheat, but lacking pottery.

natural level A vertical subdivision of an excavation square that is based on natural breaks in the sediments (in terms of colour, grain size, texture, hardness, or other characteristics).

natural selection The process through which some individuals survive and reproduce at higher rates than others because of their genetic heritage; leads to the perpetuation of certain genetic qualities at the expense of others.

Neanderthals (or Neandertals) An early form of humans who lived in Europe and the Near East about 300,000 to 30,000 years ago; biological anthropologists debate whether Neanderthals were in the direct evolutionary line leading to *Homo sapiens*.

negotiated archaeology Working directly with communities to educate archaeologists about the concerns of aboriginal people, and aboriginal people about the methods and goals of archaeology.

Neolithic The ancient period during which people began using ground stone tools, manufacturing ceramics, and relying on domesticated plants and animals—literally, the "New Stone Age"—coined by Sir John Lubbock (in 1865).

new archaeology An approach to archaeology that arose in the 1960s emphasizing the understanding of underlying cultural processes and the use of the scientific method; today's version of the "new archaeology" is sometimes called processual archaeology.

non-site archaeology Analysis of archaeological patterns manifested on a scale of kilometres or hectares, rather than of patterns within a single site.

nuclear DNA Genetic material found in a cell's nuclei; this material is primarily responsible for an individual's inherited traits.

number of identified specimens (NISP) The raw number of identified bones (specimens) per species; a largely outmoded way of comparing archaeological bone frequencies.

oasis theory Proposed by V. Gordon Childe, it argues that animal domestication arose as people, plants, and animals congregated around water sources during the arid years that followed the Pleistocene. In this scenario, agriculture arose because of "some genius" and preceded animal domestication.

objectivity The attempt to observe things as they actually are, without prejudging or falsifying observations in light of some preconceived view of the world—reducing subjective factors to a minimum.

old wood problem A potential problem with radiocarbon (or tree-ring) dating in which old wood has been scavenged and reused in a later archaeological site; the resulting date is not a true age of the associated human activity.

optimal foraging theory The idea that foragers select foods that maximize the overall return rate.

oracle A shrine in which a deity reveals hidden knowledge or divine purpose.

osteoarthritis A disorder in which the cartilage between joints wears away, often because of overuse of the joint, resulting in osteophytes and eburnation.

osteology The study of bone.

osteophyte A sign of osteoarthritis in which bones develop a distinct "lipping" of bone at the point of articulation.

paleodemography The study of ancient demographic patterns and trends.

paleoethnobotanist An archaeologist who specializes in recovering and identifying plant remains from ancient contexts, focusing on the world of plant–people interactions.

paleopathology The study of ancient disease.

paleosol Old (fossil) soils formed over long periods of time that are buried underneath either sediments or volcanic ash.

palynology The technique through which the fossil pollen grains and spores from archaeological sites are studied.

paradigm The overarching framework, often unstated, for understanding a research problem. It is a researcher's "culture."

Parks Canada A Government of Canada agency that is mandated to protect and represent nationally significant examples of Canada's natural and cultural heritage and foster public understanding, appreciation, and enjoyment for present and future generations.

participant observation The primary strategy of cultural anthropology in which data are gathered by questioning and observing people while the observer lives in their society.

particularizing Emphasizing detailed descriptions of historical events instead of trying to establish general explanations for their occurrence.

patrilineage Individuals who share a line of patrilineal descent.

patrilineal descent A unilineal descent system in which ancestry is traced through the male line.

patrilocal residence A cultural practice in which a newly married couple live in the groom's village of origin; it is often associated with patrilineal descent.

period A length of time distinguished by particular items of material culture, such as house form, pottery, or subsistence.

petroglyphs Carved stone images.

petrographic analysis An analytical technique that identifies the mineral composition of a pot's temper and clay through microscopic observation of thin sections.

phase An archaeological construct possessing traits sufficiently characteristic to distinguish it from other units similarly conceived; spatially limited to roughly a locality or region and chronologically limited to the briefest interval of time possible.

photosynthetic pathways The specific chemical process through which plants metabolize carbon; the three major pathways discriminate against carbon-13 in different ways, therefore similarly aged plants that use different pathways can produce different radiocarbon ages.

phytoliths Tiny silica particles contained in plants. Sometimes these fragments can be recovered from archaeological sites, even after the plants themselves have decayed.

pithouse A semi-subterranean structure with a heavy log roof, covered with sod.

Pleistocene A geologic period from 2 million to 10 thousand years ago, which was characterized by multiple periods of extensive glaciation.

plow zone The upper portion of a soil profile that has been disturbed by repeated plowing or other agricultural activity.

political economy The organization of reproduction, production, exchange, and consumption within and between bands, villages, chiefdoms, states, and empires.

political organization A society's formal and informal institutions that regulate a population's collective acts.

pollen diagram A chart showing the changing frequencies of different identified pollens through time from samples taken from archaeological or other sites.

population pressure The effects of a population reaching carrying capacity.

porotic hyperostosis A symptom of iron deficiency anemia in which the skull takes on a porous appearance.

postmodernism A paradigm that rejects grand historical schemes in favour of humanistic approaches that appreciate the multiple voices of history. It seeks to see how colonialism created our vision of the world we occupy today; it eschews science and argues against the existence of objective truth.

postprocessual paradigm A paradigm that focuses on humanistic approaches and rejects scientific objectivity; it sees archaeology as inherently political and is more concerned with interpreting the past than with testing hypotheses. It sees change as arising largely from interactions between individuals operating within a symbolic and/or competitive system.

potassium-argon dating An absolute dating technique that monitors the decay of potassium (K-40) into argon gas (Ar-40).

potlatch Among nineteenth-century Northwest Coast Native Americans, a ceremony involving the giving away or destruction of property in order to acquire prestige.

potsherd Fragment of pottery.

principle of infrastructural determinism Argument that the infrastructure lies at the causal heart of every sociocultural system, that human society responds to factors that directly affect survival and well-being, and that such responses determine the rest of the sociocultural system.

principle of uniformitarianism The principle asserting that the processes now operating to modify the earth's surface are the same processes that operated long ago in the geological past.

processual paradigm The paradigm that explains social, economic, and cultural change as primarily the result of adaptation to material conditions; external conditions (for example, the environment) are assumed to take causal priority over ideational factors in explaining change.

projectile points Arrowheads, dart points, or spear points.

proton precession magnetometer A remote sensing technique that measures the strength of magnetism between the earth's magnetic core and a sensor controlled by the archaeologist. Magnetic anomalies can indicate the presence of buried walls or features.

provenience An artifact's location relative to a system of spatial data collection.

pubic symphysis Where the two halves of the pelvis meet in the groin area; the appearance of its articulating surface can be used to age skeletons.

pure (basic) science Systematic research directed toward acquisition of knowledge for its own sake.

ranked societies Social systems in which a hierarchy of social status has been established, with a restricted number of valued positions available; in ranked societies, not everyone has the same access to the critical resources of life.

reclamation processes Human behaviours that result in artifacts moving from the archaeological context back to the systemic context; for example, scavenging beams from an abandoned structure to use them in a new one.

relational analogies Analogies justified on the basis of close cultural continuity between the archaeological and ethnographic cases or similarity in general cultural form.

relative dates Dates expressed relative to one another (for instance, earlier, later, more recent, and so forth) instead of in absolute terms.

religion A specific set of beliefs about one's relation to the supernatural; a society's mechanism for relating supernatural phenomena to the everyday world.

remote sensing The application of methods that employ some form of electromagnetic energy to detect and measure characteristics of an archaeological target.

reservoir effect When organisms take in carbon from a source that is depleted of or enriched in ^{14}C relative to the atmosphere; such samples may return ages that are considerably older or younger than they actually are.

return rate The amount of energy acquired by a forager per unit of harvesting/processing time.

reuse processes Human behaviours that recycle and reuse artifacts before the artifact enters an archaeological context.

reverse stratigraphy The result when one sediment is unearthed by human or natural actions and moved elsewhere, whereby the latest material will be deposited on the bottom of the new sediment, and progressively earlier material will be deposited higher and higher in the stratigraphy.

ritual A succession of discrete behaviours that must be performed in a particular order under particular circumstances.

rockshelter A common type of archaeological site, consisting of a rock overhang that is deep enough to provide shelter but not deep enough to be called a cave (technically speaking, a cave must have an area of perpetual darkness).

sample fraction The percentage of the sample universe that is surveyed. Areas with a lot of variability in archaeological remains require larger sample fractions than do areas of low variability.

sample units Survey units of a standard size and shape used to obtain the sample, determined by the research question and practical considerations.

sample universe The region that contains the statistical population and that will be sampled. Its size and shape are determined by the research question and practical considerations.

sciatic notch The angled edge of both halves of the posterior (rear) side of the pelvis; measurement of this angle is used to determine sex in human skeletons. Although its width varies among populations, narrow notches indicate a male and wider notches indicate a female.

science The search for universals by means of established scientific methods of inquiry.

scientific reasoning Accepted principles and procedures for the systematic pursuit of secure knowledge. Established scientific procedures involve the following steps: define a relevant problem; establish one or more hypotheses; determine the empirical implications of the hypotheses; collect appropriate data through observation and/or experimentation; compare these data with the expected implications; and revise and/or retest hypotheses as necessary.

seasonal round Hunter-gatherers' pattern of movement between different places on the landscape timed to the seasonal availability of food and other resources.

seasonality An estimate of the time of year during which a particular archaeological site was occupied.

seriation A relative dating method that orders artifacts based on the assumption that one cultural style slowly replaces an earlier style over time; with a master seriation diagram, sites can be dated based on their frequency of several artifact (for instance, ceramic) styles.

shaman One who has the power to contact the spirit world through trance, possession, or visions. On the basis of this ability, the shaman invokes, manipulates, or coerces the power of the spirits for socially recognized ends—both good and ill.

shell midden The remnants of shellfish collecting; some shellfish middens can become many metres thick.

shovel-testing A sample survey method used in regions where rapid soil buildup obscures buried archaeological remains; it entails digging shallow, systematic pits across the survey unit.

sipapu A Hopi word that loosely translates as "place of emergence." The original sipapu is the place where the Hopi are said to have emerged into this world from the underworld. Sipapus are also small pits in kivas through which communication with the supernatural world takes place.

site formation The human and natural actions that work together to create an archaeological site.

size classes A categorization of faunal remains, not to taxon, but to one of five categories based on body size.

slash-and-burn A horticultural method used frequently in the tropics wherein a section of forest is cut, dried, and then burned, thus returning nutrients to the ground. This permits a plot of land to be farmed for a limited number of years.

Smithsonian number A unique catalogue number given to U.S. sites; it consists of a number (the state's position alphabetically), a letter abbreviation of the county, and the site's sequential number within the county.

social Darwinism The extension of the principles of Darwinian evolution to social phenomena; it implies that conflict between societies and between classes of the same society benefits humanity in the long run by removing "unfit" individuals and social forms. Social Darwinism assumed that unfettered economic competition and warfare were primary ways to determine which societies were "fittest."

social organization The rules and structures that govern relations within a group of interacting people. Societies are divided into social units (groups) within which are recognized social positions (statuses), with appropriate behaviour patterns prescribed for these positions (roles).

socio-technical system A means of understanding the interaction between people and technology in the workplace.

soil resistivity survey A remote sensing technique that monitors the electrical resistance of soils in a restricted volume near the surface of an archaeological site; buried walls or features can be detected by changes in the amount of resistance registered by the resistivity meter.

Southeastern Ceremonial Complex An assortment of ceremonial objects that occurs in the graves of high-status Mississippian individuals. Ritual exchange of these artifacts crosscut the boundaries of many distinctive local cultures.

space–time systematics The delineation of patterns in material culture through time and over space. These patterns are what the archaeologist will eventually try to explain or account for.

statistical population A set of counts, measurements, or characteristics about which relevant inquiries are to be made. Scientists use the term "statistical population" in a specialized way (quite different from "population" in the ordinary sense).

statistical sampling The principles that underlie sampling strategies that provide accurate measures of a statistical population.

status The rights, duties, privileges, powers, liabilities, and immunities that accrue to a recognized and named social position.

stelae Stone monuments erected by Maya rulers to record their history in rich images and hieroglyphic symbols. These symbols can be read and dated.

strata (singular, "stratum") More or less homogeneous or gradational material, visually separable from other levels by a discrete change in the character of the material—texture, compactness, colour, rock, organic content—and/or by a sharp break in the nature of deposition.

stratified random sample A survey universe divided into several sub-universes that are then sampled at potentially different sample fractions.

structuralism A paradigm holding that human culture is the expression of unconscious modes of thought and reasoning, notably binary oppositions. Structuralism is most closely associated with the work of the French anthropologist Claude Levi-Strauss.

structure The behaviour that supports choices made at the level of the infrastructure, including the organization of reproduction, production, exchange, family structure, division of labour, age and sex roles, political units, social organization, and warfare.

superstructure A group's values, aesthetics, rules, beliefs, religions, and symbols, which can be behaviourally manifested as art, music, dance, literature, advertising, religious rituals, sports, games, hobbies, and even science.

symbol An object or act (verbal or nonverbal) that, by cultural convention, stands for something else with which it has no necessary connection.

sympathetic magic Rituals in which doing something to an image of an object produces the desired effect in the real object.

systematic regional survey A set of strategies for arriving at accurate descriptions of the range of archaeological material across a landscape.

systemic context A living behavioural system wherein artifacts are part of the ongoing system of manufacture, use, reuse, and discard.

taphonomy The study of how organisms become part of the fossil record; in archaeology it primarily refers to the study of how natural processes produce patterning in archaeological data.

taxon In faunal analysis, the classification of a skeletal element to a taxonomic category—species, genus, family, or order.

temper Material added to clay to give a ceramic item strength.

temporal type A morphological type that has temporal significance; also known as a time-marker or index fossil.

teosinte A plant native to southern Mexico; believed to be the wild ancestor of maize.

terminus post quem (TPQ) The date after which a stratum or feature must have been deposited or created.

test excavation A small initial excavation to determine a site's potential for answering a research question.

testability The degree to which one's observations and experiments can be reproduced.

text-aided archaeology The use of written documents such as probates, shipping records, diaries, and catalogues to interpret artifacts recovered from historical sites.

The Canadian Institute An organization, founded in 1849 by Sir Sandford Fleming, dedicated to the advancement of science. It exists today as the Royal Canadian Institute, and is the oldest scientific society in Canada.

theory An explanation for observed, empirical phenomena. It is empirical and seeks to explain the relationships between variables; it is an answer to a "why" question.

thermoluminescence A trapped charge dating technique used on ceramics and burnt stone artifacts—anything mineral that has been heated to more than 500°C.

time-markers Similar to index fossils in geology; artifact forms that research shows to be diagnostic of a particular period of time.

total station A device that uses a beam of light bounced off a prism to determine an artifact's provenience; it is accurate to +/– 3 millimetres.

totem A natural object, often an animal, from which a lineage or clan believes itself to be descended and/or with which lineage or clan members have special relations.

trade language A language that develops among speakers of different languages to permit economic exchanges.

trait list A simple listing of a culture's material and behavioural characteristics, for example, house and pottery styles, foods, degree of nomadism, particular rituals, or ornaments. Trait lists were used primarily to trace the movement of cultures across a landscape and through time.

trapped charge dating Forms of dating that rely upon the fact that electrons become trapped in minerals' crystal lattices as a function of background radiation; the age of the specimen is the total radiation received divided by the annual dose of radiation.

tree-ring dating (dendrochronology) The use of annual growth rings in trees to assign calendar ages to ancient wood samples.

tribal societies A wide range of social formations that lie between egalitarian foragers and ranked societies (such as chiefdoms); tribal societies are normally horticultural and sedentary, with a higher level of competition than seen among nomadic hunter-gatherers.

type A class of archaeological artifacts defined by a consistent clustering of attributes.

typology The systematic arrangement of material culture into types.

unilineal cultural evolution The belief that human societies have evolved culturally along a single developmental trajectory. Typically, such schemes depict Western civilization as the most advanced evolutionary stage; anthropology rejects this idea.

Upper Paleolithic The last major division of the Old World Paleolithic, beginning about 40,000 years ago and lasting until the end of the Pleistocene (ca. 10,000 B.C.).

vision quest A ritual in which an individual seeks visions through starvation, dehydration, and exposure; considered in some cultures to be a way to communicate with the supernatural world.

warfare and circumscription hypothesis Proposed by Robert Carneiro, it attributes the origin of the state to the administrative burden of warfare conducted for conquest as a request of geographic limits on arable land in the face of a rising population.

water-screening A sieving process in which deposit is placed in a screen and the matrix washed away with hoses; essential where artifacts are expected to be small and/or difficult to find without washing.

wickiup A conical structure made of poles or logs laid against one another that served as fall and winter homes among the prehistoric Shoshone and Paiute.

wood rats (also pack rats) Rodents that build nests of organic materials and thus preserve a record, often for thousands of years, of changing plant species within the local area of the nest.

Younger Dryas A climatic interval, 13,000 to 11,600 BP, characterized by a rapid return to cooler and drier, but highly variable, climatic conditions.

zooarchaeologist (also faunal analyst) An individual who studies the faunal (animal) remains recovered from archaeological sites.

Bibliography

The following chapter-by-chapter bibliography contains the specific references used in each chapter as well as some additional references that can provide the student with more in-depth reading on particular subjects. We've arranged this bibliography by chapter specifically so that the student would be able to more easily locate additional readings on a particular subject. Where direct quotes have been used, their source is indicated here at the end of the appropriate entry.

Chapter 1

Babcock, Barbara A., and Nancy J. Parezo. 1988. *Daughters of the Desert: Women Anthropologists and the Native American Southwest 1880–1980.* Albuquerque: University of New Mexico Press.

Beattie, Owen, Brian Apland, Erik W. Blake, James A. Cosgrove, Sarah Gaunt, Sheila Grur, Alexander P. Macki, Kjerstin E. Mackie, Dan Stran Thof, Valerie Thorp, and Peter Troffe. 2000. The Kwäday Dän Ts'inchi discovery from a glacier in British Columbia. *Canadian Journal of Archaeology* 24: 129–147.

Benedict, Jeff. 2002. *No Bone Unturned: The Adventures of a Top Smithsonian Forensic Scientist and The Legal Battle for America's Oldest Skeletons.* New York: HarperCollins.

Binford, Lewis R. 1962. Archeology as anthropology. *American Antiquity* 28: 217–225.

———. 1964. A consideration of archaeological research design. *American Antiquity* 29: 425–441.

———. 1965. Archaeological systematics and the study of cultural process. *American Antiquity* 31: 203–210.

———. 1968. Archeological perspectives. In Sally R. Binford and Lewis R. Binford (Eds.), *New Perspectives in Archeology* (pp. 5–32). Chicago: Aldine.

———. 1972. *An Archaeological Perspective.* New York: Seminar Press.

———(Ed.). 1977. *For Theory Building in Archaeology.* New York: Academic Press.

———. 1983a. *In Pursuit of the Past: Decoding the Archaeological Record.* London: Thames and Hudson ("In His Own Words" text quoted from pp. 19, 23).

———(Ed.). 1983b. *Working at Archaeology.* New York: Academic Press.

———. 1989. *Debating Archaeology.* San Diego: Academic Press.

———. 2001. Constructing Frames of Reference: An Analytical Method for Archaeological Theory Building Using Ethnographic and Environmental Data Sets. Berkeley: University of California Press.

Binford, Sally R., and Lewis R. Binford (Eds.). 1968. *New Perspectives in Archeology.* Chicago: Aldine.

Brigham, Clarence S. 1937. Clarence Bloomfield Moore. *Proceedings of the American Antiquarian Society* (1936) 46: 13–14.

Brown, Ian W. 1978. James Alfred Ford: The man and his works. Southeastern Archaeological Conference, Special Publication no. 4.

Caldwell, Joseph. 1959. The new American archaeology. *Science* 129(3345): 303–307.

Cannon, Aubrey. 1989. The historical dimension in mortuary expressions of status and sentiment. *Current Anthropology* 30: 437–458.

Chatters, James C. 2001. *Ancient Encounters: Kennewick Man and the First Americans.* New York: Simon and Schuster.

Claassen, Cheryl (Ed.). 1994. *Women in Archaeology.* Philadelphia: University of Pennsylvania Press.

Daniel, Glyn. 1976. *A Hundred and Fifty Years of Archaeology.* Cambridge: Harvard University Press.

———(Ed.). 1981. *Towards a History of Archaeology.* New York: Thames and Hudson.

Davis, Mary B. (Comp.). 1987. Field Notes of Clarence B. Moore's Southeastern Archaeological Expeditions, 1891–1918: A Guide to the Microfilm Edition.

Bronx, NY: Huntington Free Library, Museum of the American Indian.

Deagan, Kathleen. 1973. Mestizaje in colonial St. Augustine. *Ethnohistory* 20: 55–65.

———. 1978a. Cultures in transition: Fusion and assimilation among the Eastern Timucua. In Jerald Milanich and Samuel Proctor (Eds.), *Tacachale: Essays on the Indians of Florida and Southeastern Georgia During the Historic Period* (pp. 89–119). Gainesville: University Press of Florida.

———. 1978b. The material assemblage of 16th century Spanish Florida. *Historical Archaeology* 12: 25–50.

———. 1980. Spanish St. Augustine: America's first "melting pot." *Archaeology* 33(5): 22–30.

———. 1981. Downtown survey: The discovery of 16th century St. Augustine in an urban area. *American Antiquity* 46: 626–634.

———. 1982. Avenues of inquiry in historical archaeology. In Michael B. Schiffer (Ed.), *Advances in Archaeological Method and Theory*. Vol. 5 (pp. 151–177). New York: Academic Press ("In Her Own Words" text quoted from pp. 170–171).

———. 1983. *Spanish St. Augustine: The Archaeology of a Colonial Creole Community*. New York: Academic Press.

———. 1987. Artifacts of the Spanish Colonies of Florida and the Caribbean, 1500–1800, vol. 1, *Ceramics, Glassware, and Beads*. Washington, DC: Smithsonian Institution Press.

———. 1988. Neither history nor prehistory: The questions that count in historical archaeology. *Historical Archaeology* 22: 7–12.

———. 1991. Historical archaeology's contributions to our understanding of early America. In Lisa Falk (Ed.), *Historical Archaeology in Global Perspective* (pp. 97–112). Washington, DC: Smithsonian Institution Press.

———(Ed.). 1995. *Puerto Real: The Archaeology of a Sixteenth-Century Spanish Town in Hispaniola*. Gainesville: University Press of Florida.

———. 1996. Colonial transformation: Euro-American cultural genesis in the early Spanish-American colonies. *Journal of Anthropological Research* 52: 135–160.

Deagan, Kathleen, and José María Cruxent. 2002a. *Archaeology at La Isabela: America's First European Town*. New Haven: Yale University Press.

———. 2002b. *Columbus's Outpost Among the Tainos*. New Haven: Yale University Press.

Dunnell, Robert C. 1979. Trends in current Americanist archaeology. *American Journal of Archaeology* 83: 437–449.

———. 1986. Five decades of American archaeology. In David J. Meltzer, Don D. Fowler, and Jeremy A. Sabloff (Eds.), *American Archaeology Past and Future: A Celebration of the Society for American Archaeology 1935–1985* (pp. 23–49). Washington, DC: Smithsonian Institution Press.

Ferric, Helke. 2001. An interview with Richard S. MacNeish. *Current Anthropology* 42: 715–735.

Ford, James Alfred. 1949. Cultural dating of prehistoric sites in the Virú Valley, Peru. Pt. 2 of "Surface survey of the Virú Valley, Peru" by James Alfred Ford and Gordon R. Willey. *Anthropological Papers of the American Museum of Natural History* 43(1). New York.

———. 1952. Measurements of some prehistoric design developments in the southeastern states. *Anthropological Papers of the American Museum of Natural History* 44(3). New York ("In His Own Words" text quoted from pp. 317–318).

———. 1954. The type concept revisited. *American Anthropologist* 56: 42–54.

———. 1957. *A quantitative method for deriving cultural chronology. Pan American Union, Technical Manual, I.* (Reprinted as University of Missouri, Museum of Anthropology, Museum Brief, no. 9.)

———. 1962. *A quantitative method for deriving cultural chronology.* Washington, DC: Pan American Union, Technical Manual, I.

———. 1969. A comparison of formative cultures in the Americas: Diffusion or the psychic unity of man? *Smithsonian Contributions to Anthropology,* Vol. 2. Washington, DC.

Ford, James Alfred, and Clarence H. Webb. 1956. Poverty Point, a late Archaic site in Louisiana. *Anthropological Papers of the American Museum of Natural History* 46(1): 1–140. New York.

Ford, James Alfred, and Gordon R. Willey. 1941. An interpretation of the prehistory of the eastern United States. *American Anthropologist* 43: 325–363.

Grayson, Donald K. 1983. *The Establishment of Human Antiquity.* New York: Academic Press.

Hayden, Brian, and Aubrey Cannon. 1982. The corporate group as an archaeological unit. *Journal of Anthropological Archaeology* 1: 132–158.

Irwin-Williams, Cynthia. 1990. Women in the field: The role of women in archaeology before 1960. In G. Kass-Simon and Patricia Farnes (Eds.), *Women of Science: Righting the Record* (pp. 1–41). Bloomington: Indiana University Press.

Jenness, Stewart E. (Ed.). 1995. *Arctic Odyssey: The Diary of Diamond Jenness, Ethnologist with the Canadian Arctic Expedition Northern Alaska and Canada, 1913–1916*. Hull, QC: Canadian Museum of Civilization.

Kelley, Jane, and Ronald Williamson. 1996. The positioning of archaeology within anthropology: A Canadian historical perspective. *American Antiquity* 61: 5–20.

Kidder, Alfred V. 1924. *An Introduction to the Study of Southwestern Archaeology*. New Haven: Yale University Press.

———. 1928. *The present state of knowledge of American history and civilization prior to 1492* (pp. 749–753). Paris: International Congress of History, Oslo ("In His Own Words" text quoted from p. 753).

———. 1960. Reminiscences in Southwest archaeology, I. *Kiva* 25: 1–32.

Kidder, Alfred V., and Samuel J. Guernsey. 1921. Basketmaker caves of northeastern Arizona. *Papers of the Peabody Museum of American Archaeology and Ethnology* 8(2). Cambridge, MA.

Kidder, Alfred V., Jesse D. Jennings, and Edwin M. Shook. 1946. *Excavations at Kaminaljuyu, Guatemala*. Washington, DC: Carnegie Institution of Washington Publication no. 561. Washington, DC.

Killan, Gerald. 1983. *David Boyle: From Artisan to Archaeologist*. Toronto: University of Toronto Press.

———. 1998. Towards a scientific archaeology: Daniel Wilson, David Boyle, and the Canadian Institute 1852–96. In *Bringing Back the Past: Historical Perspectives on Canadian Archaeology*, vol. Mercury Series Canadian Archaeological Survey Paper 158. P. J. Smith and D. Mitchell (Eds.), pp. 15–24. Ottawa: Canadian Museum of Civilization.

Lamberg-Karlovsky, C. C. (Ed.). 1989. *Archaeological Thought in America*. Cambridge: Cambridge University Press.

Levine, Mary Ann. 1994. Creating their own niches: Career styles among women in Americanist archaeology between the wars. In Cheryl Claassen (Ed.), *Women in Archaeology* (pp. 9–40). Philadelphia: University of Pennsylvania Press.

MacNeish, Richard. 1999. My life in Canadian archaeology. In *Bringing Back the Past: Historical Perspectives on Canadian Archaeology*, vol. Mercury Series Canadian Archaeological Survey Paper 158. P. J. S. a. D. Mitchell (Eds), pp. 61–77. Ottawa: Canadian Museum of Civilization.

Moore, Clarence B. 1905. Certain aboriginal remains of the Black Warrior River. *Journal of the Academy of Natural Sciences of Philadelphia*. Second Series, 13: 123–244.

———. 1907. Moundville revisited. *Journal of the Academy of Natural Sciences of Philadelphia*. Second Series, 13: 337–405.

Nelson, Nels C. 1909. Shellmounds of the San Francisco Bay region. *University of California Publications in American Archaeology and Ethnology* 7(4): 310–356.

———. 1914. Pueblo ruins of the Galisteo Basin, New Mexico. *Anthropological Papers of the American Museum of Natural History* 15(1). New York.

Noble, William. C. 1972. One hundred and twenty-five years of archaeology in the Canadian provinces. *Canadian Archaeological Association Bulletin* 4(1972).

Parezo, Nancy J. (Ed.). 1993. *Hidden Scholars: Women Anthropologists and the Native American Southwest*. Albuquerque: University of New Mexico Press.

Richling, Bernard. 1989. Diamond Jenness and the National Museum of Canada. *Curator* 33: 245–260.

Smith, Pamela Jane, and Donald Mitchell. 1998. *Bringing back the past: Historical perspectives on Canadian archaeology. Mercury series*. Hull, QC: Canadian Museum of Civilization.

Taylor, Walter W. 1948. A study of archeology. *American Anthropological Association, Memoir*, 69.

———. 1954. Southwestern archaeology, its history and theory. *American Anthropologist* 56: 561–570.

———. 1972. Old wine and new skins: A contemporary parable. In Mark P. Leone (Ed.), *Contemporary Archaeology* (pp. 28–33). Carbondale: Southern Illinois University Press.

Tester, Frank J., and Peter Keith Kulchyski. 1994. *Tammarniit (mistakes): Inuit relocation in the Eastern Arctic, 1939–63*. Vancouver: UBC Press.

Trigger, Bruce G. 1980. Archaeology and the image of the American Indian. *American Antiquity* 45: 662–676.

———. 1999. *A History of Archaeological Thought.* 2nd ed. Cambridge: Cambridge University Press.

———. 2006. *A History of Archaeological Thought.* Cambridge: Cambridge University Press.

Victor, Katharine L., and Mary C. Beaudry. 1992. Women's participation in American prehistoric and historical archaeology: A comparative look at the journals *American Antiquity* and *Historical Archaeology.* In Cheryl Claassen (Ed.), Exploring gender through archaeology: Selected papers from the 1991 Boone Conference. *Monographs in World Archaeology,* no. 11 (pp. 11–21). Madison, WI: Prehistory Press.

Wardle, H. Newell. 1956. Clarence Bloomfield Moore (1852–1936). *Bulletin of the Philadelphia Anthropological Society* 9(2): 9–11.

Watson, Patty Jo. 1973. The future of archeology in anthropology: Cultural history and social science. In Charles L. Redman (Ed.), *Research and Theory in Current Archeology* (pp. 113–124). New York: Wiley.

Wauchope, Robert. 1965. (Obituary of) Alfred Vincent Kidder, 1885–1963. *American Antiquity* 31(2, pt. 1): 149–171.

Webb, Clarence H. 1968. (Obituary of) James Alfred Ford, 1911–1968. *Texas Archaeological Society Bulletin* 38: 135–146.

White, Nancy M., Lynne P. Sullivan, and Rochelle A. Marrinan. 1999. *Grit-Tempered: Early Women Archaeologists in the Southeastern United States.* Knoxville: University of Tennessee Press.

Willey, Gordon R. 1967. (Obituary of) Alfred Vincent Kidder. *National Academy of Sciences Biographical Memoirs.* Vol. 39 (pp. 292–322). New York: Columbia University Press.

———. 1969. (Obituary of) James Alfred Ford, 1911–1968. *American Antiquity* 34: 62–71.

Willey, Gordon R., and Jeremy A. Sabloff. 1993. *A History of American Archaeology.* 3rd ed. New York: Freeman.

Williams, Barbara. 1981. *Breakthrough: Women in Archaeology.* New York: Walter.

Williamson, Ronald, and Michael Bisson. 2006. *The Archaeology of Bruce Trigger: Theoretical Empiricism.* Montreal and Kingston: McGill–Queen's University Press.

Wissler, Clark. 1914. A pioneer student of Ancient America (Bandelier obituary). *El Palacio* 1(6, 7): 8.

———. 1917. The new archaeology. *The American Museum Journal* 17(2): 100–101.

Woodbury, Richard B. 1954. Review of *A Study of Archeology* by Walter W. Taylor. *American Antiquity* 19: 292–296.

———. 1960. Nels C. Nelson and chronological archaeology. *American Antiquity* 25: 400–401.

———. 1973. *Alfred V. Kidder.* New York: Columbia University Press.

———. 1993. *Sixty Years of Southwestern Archaeology: A History of the Pecos Conference.* Albuquerque: University of New Mexico Press.

Wright, James V. 1978. Trends and consequences in Canadian prehistory. *Canadian Journal of Archaeology* 2: 59–78.

Chapter 2

Atwater, Caleb. 1820. Description of the antiquities discovered in the state of Ohio and other western states. *Archaeologia Americana: Transactions and Collections of the American Antiquarian Society* 1: 105–267.

Baldwin, J. D. 1872. *Ancient America.* New York: Harper.

Bell, James A. 1994. *Reconstructing Prehistory: Scientific Method in Archaeology.* Philadelphia: Temple University Press.

Benedict, Ruth. 1948. Anthropology and the humanities. *American Anthropologist* 50: 585–593.

Boas, Franz. [1888] 1940. *Race, Language and Culture.* New York: Macmillan.

Carrithers, Michael. 1990. Is anthropology art or science? *Current Anthropology* 31: 263–282.

———. 1992. *Why Humans Have Culture: Explaining Anthropology and Social Diversity.* Oxford: Oxford University Press.

Cerroni-Long, E. L. 1996. Human science. *Anthropology Newsletter* 37(1): 50, 52.

Deetz, James. 1983. Scientific humanism and humanistic science: A plea for paradigmatic pluralism in historical archaeology. *Geoscience and Man* 23: 27–34.

de Laguna, Frederica. 1957. Some problems of objectivity in ethnology. *Man* 57: 179–182.

Esber, George S. 1987. Designing Apache homes with Apaches. In Robert W. Wulff and Shirley J. Fiske (Eds.), *Anthropological Praxis: Translating Knowledge into Action* (pp. 187–196). Boulder: Westview Press.

Feder, Kenneth L. 1995. *Frauds, Myths, and Mysteries: Science and Pseudoscience in Archaeology.* 2nd ed. Mountain View, CA: Mayfield.

Flannery, Kent V. 1967. Culture history vs. cultural process: A debate in American archaeology. *Scientific American* 217(2): 119–121.

———. 1973. Archeology with a capital S. In Charles L. Redman (Ed.), *Research and Theory in Current Archeology* (pp. 47–53). New York: Wiley and Sons.

Fotiadis, M. 1994. What is archaeology's "mitigated objectivism" mitigated by? Comments on Wylie. *American Antiquity* 59: 545–555.

Fox, Richard G. (Ed.). 1991. *Recapturing Anthropology: Working in the Present.* Santa Fe: School of American Research Press.

Geertz, Clifford. 1973. *The Interpretation of Cultures.* New York: Basic Books.

———. 1983. *Local Knowledge: Further Essays in Interpretive Anthropology.* New York: Basic Books.

Harris, Marvin. 1968. *The Rise of Anthropological Theory.* New York: Thomas Y. Crowell.

———. 1985. *Good to Eat: Riddles of Food and Culture.* New York: Simon and Schuster.

———. 1991. Anthropology: Ships that crash in the night. In Richard Jessor (Ed.), *Perspectives on Social Science: The Colorado Lectures* (pp. 70–114). Boulder: Westview Press.

Hill, Jane. 1995. Science in anthropology: A perspective from linguistic anthropology. *Anthropology Newsletter* 36(7): 20.

Horgan, John. 1996. *The End of Science: Facing the Limits of Knowledge in the Twilight of the Scientific Age.* Reading, MA: Addison-Wesley.

Jefferson, Thomas. 1787. *Notes on the state of Virginia.* London: John Stockdale (reprinted Chapel Hill: University of North Carolina Press, 1954).

Keesing, Roger. 1981. *Cultural Anthropology: A Contemporary Perspective.* New York: Holt, Rinehart, and Winston.

Kelley, Jane Holden, and Marsha P. Hanen. 1988. *Archaeology and the Methodology of Science.* Albuquerque: University of New Mexico Press.

Kemeny, John G. 1959. *A Philosopher Looks at Science.* New York: Van Nostrand Reinhold.

Kroeber, Alfred, and Clyde Kluckholn. 1952. Culture: A critical review of concepts and definitions. *Papers of the Peabody Museum of American Archaeology and Ethnology* 47(1). Cambridge, MA.

Kuznar, Lawrence. 1997. *Reclaiming a Scientific Anthropology.* Walnut Creek, CA: AltaMira.

Lamberg-Karlovsky, C. C. (Ed.). 1989. *Archaeological Thought in America.* Cambridge: Cambridge University Press.

Mcgee, R. Jon, and Richard L. Williams. 2004. *Anthropological Theory: An Introductory History.* 3rd ed. New York: McGraw Hill.

McGhee, Robert. 1977. Who owns prehistory? The Bering land bridge dilemma. *Canadian Journal of Archaeology* 13: 13–20.

———. 2004. Between racism and romanticism, scientism and spiritualism: The dilemmas of New World Archaeology. In B. Kooyman and J. Kelley, *Archaeology on the Edge, New Perspectives from the Northern Plains.* Calgary: Occasional Paper #4, Canadian Archaeological Association.

Meltzer, David J. 1998. Introduction. In *Ancient Monuments of the Mississippi Valley* [reprint of 1848 publication] (pp. 1–95). Washington, DC: Smithsonian Institution Press.

Morell, Virginia. 1993. Anthropology: Nature–culture battleground. *Science* 261: 1798–1802.

———. 1994. An anthropological culture shift. *Science* 264: 20–22.

Nicholson, B., D. Pokotylo, and R. Williamson. 1996. *Canadian Archaeological Association Statement of Principles for Ethical Conduct Pertaining to Aboriginal Heritage Committee: A Report to the Aboriginal Heritage Committee.* Canadian Archaeological Association and the Department of Canadian Heritage.

Peacock, James. 1994. Challenges facing the discipline. *Anthropology Newsletter* 35(9): 1, 5.

Phillips, Philip. 1955. American archaeology and general anthropological theory. *Southwestern Journal of Anthropology* 11: 246–250 (quote from p. 246).

Rowe, John Howland. 1965. The renaissance foundations of anthropology. *American Anthropologist* 67: 1–20.

Salmon, Merrilee H. 1982. *Philosophy and Archaeology.* New York: Academic Press.

Salmon, Merrilee H., and Wesley C. Salmon. 1979. Alternative models of scientific explanation. *American Anthropologist* 81: 61–74.

Spector, Janet. 1993. *What This Awl Means: Feminist Archaeology at a Wahpeton Dakota Village.* St. Paul, MN: Minnesota Historical Society Press (quotes from pp. 15, 65, 89, 121; "In Her Own Words" text quoted from pp. 19–29).

Squier, Ephraim G., and Edwin H. Davis. 1998 [1848]. *Ancient Monuments of the Mississippi Valley,* edited and with an introduction by David J. Meltzer. Washington: Smithsonian Institution Press.

Thomas, Cyrus. 1894. *Report on the Mound Explorations of the Bureau of Ethnology.* Washington, DC: Smithsonian Institution.

Tylor, Edward Burnett. 1871. *Primitive Culture.* Vols. 1 and 2. London: Murray (quote from p. 1).

U'mista Culture Centre. 1983. *Box of Treasures.* Film. Directed by Dennis Wheeler, narrated by Gloria Cranmer Webster. Alert Bay, Canada: U'mista Cultural Centre.

Walens, Stanley. 1981. *Feasting with Cannibals: An Essay on Kwakiutl Cosmology.* Princeton: Princeton University Press.

Watson, Patty Jo. 1995. Archaeology, anthropology, and the culture concept. *American Anthropologist* 97: 683–694.

Webster, Gloria Cranmer. 1991. The contemporary potlatch. In Aldona Jonaitis (Ed.), *Chiefly Feasts: The Enduring Kwakiutl Potlatch* (pp. 227–250). Seattle: University of Washington Press; New York: American Museum of Natural History.

White, Leslie A. 1949. *The Science of Culture.* New York: Grove Press.

———. 1959. *The Evolution of Culture.* New York: McGraw-Hill.

———. 1975. *The Concept of Cultural Systems.* New York: Columbia University Press.

Willey, Gordon R., and Philip Phillips. 1958. *Method and Theory in American Archaeology.* Chicago: University of Chicago Press.

Wylie, Alison. 2002. *Thinking from Things: Essays on the Philosophy of Archaeology.* Berkeley: University of California Press.

Chapter 3

Babcock, Barbara A. 1982. Ritual undress and the comedy of self and other: Bandelier's *The Delight Makers.* In Jay Ruby (Ed.), *A Crack in the Mirror: Reflexive Perspectives in Anthropology* (pp. 187–203). Philadelphia: University of Pennsylvania Press.

Bamforth, Douglas B., and Albert C. Spaulding. 1982. Human behavior, explanation, archaeology, history, and science. *Journal of Anthropological Archaeology* 1: 179–195.

Bandelier, Adolph. 1883. A visit to the aboriginal ruins in the Valley of the Rio Pecos. *Papers of the Archae-*

ological Institute of America (American Series) 1(2): 34–133.

———. 1890. Final report of investigations among the Indians of the Southwestern United States, carried on mainly in the years from 1880 to 1885, Part I. *Papers of the Archaeological Institute of America* (American Series III). Cambridge, MA.

———. 1892. Final report of investigations among the Indians of the Southwestern United States, carried on mainly in the years from 1880 to 1885, Part II. *Papers of the Archaeological Institute of America* (American Series IV). Cambridge, MA.

———. 1966. *The Southwestern Journals of Adolph F. Bandelier, 1880–1882.* Edited and annotated by Charles H. Lange and Carroll Riley. Albuquerque: University of New Mexico Press.

———. 1971 [1890]. *The Delight Makers: A Novel of Prehistoric Pueblo Indians.* San Diego: Harcourt Brace Jovanovich ("Looking Closer" text quoted from pp. 3–4, 485–489).

———. 1975. *The Southwestern Journals of Adolph F. Bandelier, 1885–1888.* Edited and annotated by Charles H. Lange, Carroll Riley, and Elisabeth M. Lange. Albuquerque: University of New Mexico Press.

Bandelier, Adolph, and Edgar L. Hewett. 1937. *Indians of the Rio Grande Valley.* Albuquerque: University of New Mexico Press.

Bapty, Ian, and Tim Yates (Eds.). 1990. *Archaeology After Structuralism: Post-Structuralism and the Practice of Archaeology.* London: Routledge.

Binford, Lewis R. 1983. *In Pursuit of the Past: Decoding the Archaeological Record.* London: Thames and Hudson.

———. 1989a. Science to seance, or processual to "post-processual" archaeology. In *Debating Archaeology* (pp. 27–40). San Diego: Academic Press.

———. 1989b. Review of Hodder, Reading the Past: Current Approaches to Interpretation in Archaeology. In *Debating Archaeology* (pp. 69–71). San Diego: Academic Press.

Bingham, Hiram. 1914. Bandelier. *The Nation* 98(2543, March 26): 328–329.

Bintliff, John. 1991. Post-modernism, rhetoric, and scholasticism at TAG: The current state of British archaeological theory. *Antiquity* 65: 274–278.

Clarke, David L. 1968. *Analytical Archaeology.* London: Methuen.

————. 1972. Archaeology: The loss of innocence. *Antiquity* 47: 6–18.

Clifford, James. 1988. The Predicament of Culture: Twentieth Century Ethnography, Literature, and Art. Cambridge: Harvard University Press.

Clifford, James, and George E. Marcus (Eds.). 1986. *Writing Culture: The Poetics and Politics of Ethnography.* Berkeley: University of California Press.

Daniel, Glyn. 1991. Post-processual developments in Anglo-American archaeology. *Norwegian Archaeological Review* 24: 65–76.

————. 1995. Expanding middle-range theory. *Antiquity* 69: 449–458.

Dark, K. R. 1995. *Theoretical Archaeology.* Ithaca: Cornell University Press.

Gibbon, Guy. 1989. *Explanation in Archaeology.* Oxford: Basil Blackwell.

Habermas, J. 1987. *The Philosophical Discourse of Modernity.* Oxford: Oxford University Press.

Hagelberg, Erika. 1993, August/September. DNA from archaeological bone. *The Biochemist,* pp. 17–22.

Hammond, George P., and Edgar F. Goad. 1949. *A Scientist on the Trail: Travel Letters of A. F. Bandelier, 1880–1881.* Berkeley, CA: Quivira Society.

Harris, Marvin. 1979. *Cultural Materialism: The Struggle for a Science of Culture.* New York: Random House.

————. 1985. *Good to Eat: Riddles of Food and Culture.* New York: Simon and Schuster.

————. 1994. Cultural materialism is alive and well and won't go away until something better comes along. In R. Borofsky (Ed.), *Assessing Cultural Anthropology* (pp. 62–76). New York: McGraw-Hill.

Harris, Marvin, and Eric B. Ross (Eds.). 1987. *Food and Evolution: Toward a Theory of Human Food Habits.* Philadelphia: Temple University Press.

Harvey, David. 1989. The Condition of Postmodernity: An Enquiry into the Origins of Cultural Change. Cambridge, MA: Blackwell.

Harvey, Oliver. 2000. Ghouls dig up war heroes. *The Sun* [London], 11 November, 2000.

Hassan, I. 1985. The culture of postmodernism. *Theory, Culture and Society* 2: 119–132.

Hegmon, Michelle. 2003. Setting theoretical egos aside: Issues and theory in North American archaeology. *American Antiquity* 68: 213–244.

Henderson, Julian (Ed.). 1989. *Scientific Analysis in Archaeology and Its Interpretation.* Los Angeles: UCLA Institute of Archaeology.

Hill, James N. 1991. Archaeology and the accumulation of knowledge. In Robert W. Preucel (Ed.), *Processual and Postprocessual Archaeologies: Multiple Ways of Knowing the Past* (pp. 42–53). Center for Archaeological Investigations, Occasional Paper, no. 10. Carbondale: Southern Illinois University.

Hobbs, Hulda R. 1940, June. Bandelier in the Southwest. *El Palacio* 47: 121–136.

Hodder, Ian. 1982a. *Symbols in Action: Ethnoarchaeological Studies of Material Culture.* Cambridge: Cambridge University Press.

————(Ed.). 1982b. *Symbolic and Structural Archaeology.* Cambridge: Cambridge University Press.

————. 1985. Postprocessual archaeology. In Michael B. Schiffer (Ed.), *Advances in Archaeological Method and Theory.* Vol. 8 (pp. 1–26). Orlando, FL: Academic Press.

————. 1986. *Reading the Past: Current Approaches to Interpretation in Archaeology.* Cambridge: Cambridge University Press.

————. 1989a. Post-modernism, post-structuralism and post-processual archaeology. In Ian Hodder (Ed.), *The Meaning of Things.* One World Archaeology, no. 6 (pp. 64–78). London: Unwin Hyman.

————. 1989b. Writing archaeology: Site reports in context. *Antiquity* 63: 268–274.

————. 1990. Archaeology and the post-modern. *Anthropology Today* 6(5): 13–15.

————. 1991a. Postprocessual archaeology and the current debate. In Robert W. Preucel (Ed.), *Processual and Postprocessual Archaeologies: Multiple Ways of Knowing the Past* (pp. 30–41). Center for Archaeological Investigations, Occasional Paper, no. 10. Carbondale: Southern Illinois University.

————. 1991b. Interpretive archaeology and its role. *American Antiquity* 56: 7–18.

————. 1995. *Theory and Practice in Archaeology.* London: Routledge.

————. 1999. *The Archaeological Process: An Introduction.* Oxford: Blackwell.

————. (Ed.). 2001. *Archaeological Theory Today.* Oxford: Blackwell.

————. 2006. Triggering post-processual archaeology and beyond. In R. Williamson and M. Bisson, *The Archaeology of Bruce Trigger: Theoretical Empiricism.* Montreal: Queen's University Press.

Hodge, Frederick Webb. 1914. Bandelier obituary. *American Anthropologist* 16: 349–358.

———. 1932. Biographical sketch and bibliography of Adolphe Francis Alphonse Bandelier. *New Mexico Historical Review* 7: 353–370.

Johnson, Matthew. 1999. *Archaeological Theory: An Introduction.* Oxford: Blackwell.

Knapp, A. Bernard. 1996. Archaeology without gravity: Postmodernism and the past. *Journal of Archaeological Method and Theory* 3: 127–158.

Lange, Charles H., and Carroll L. Riley. 1996. *Bandelier: The Life and Adventures of Adolph Bandelier.* Salt Lake City: University of Utah Press.

Lyotard, Jean François. 1984. *The Postmodern Condition: A Report on Knowledge.* Translated by G. Bennington and B. Massumi. Minneapolis: University of Minnesota Press.

Marcus, George E., and Michael M. J. Fischer. 1986. *Anthropology as Cultural Critique: An Experimental Moment in the Human Sciences.* Chicago: University of Chicago Press.

McGhee, Robert. 1976. *The Burial at L'Anse-Amour.* Ottawa: National Museum of Man.

Miller, Daniel, and Christopher Tilley (Eds.). 1984. *Ideology, Power and Prehistory.* Cambridge: Cambridge University Press.

Mithen, Steven. 1989. Evolutionary theory and postprocessual archaeology. *Antiquity* 63: 483–494.

Pinsky, Valerie, and Alison Wylie (Eds.). 1995. Critical Traditions in Contemporary Archaeology: Essays in the Philosophy, History and Socio-Politics of Archaeology. Albuquerque: University of New Mexico Press.

Preucel, R. W. (Ed.). 1991. *Processual and Postprocessual Archaeologies: Multiple Ways of Knowing the Past.* Center for Archaeological Investigations, Occasional Paper, no. 10. Carbondale: Southern Illinois University.

———. 1995. The postprocessual condition. *Journal of Archaeological Research* 3: 147–175.

Price, Barbara J. 1982. Cultural materialism: A theoretical review. *American Antiquity* 47: 709–741.

Radin, Paul. 1942. The Unpublished Letters of Adolphe F. Bandelier Concerning the Writing and Publication of The Delight Makers. El Paso: Carl Hertzog.

Rosenau, Pauline Marie. 1992. *Post-Modernism and the Social Sciences: Insights, Inroads, and Intrusions.* Princeton: Princeton University Press.

Sabloff, Jeremy A., Lewis R. Binford, and Patricia A. McAnany. 1987. Understanding the archaeological record. *Antiquity* 61: 203–209.

Saunders, Nicholas. 2002. Excavating memories: Archaeology and the Great War, 1914–2001. *Antiquity* 76: 101–108.

———. 2003. *Trench Art: Materialities and Memories of War.* Oxford: Berg Press.

Shanks, Michael, and Christopher Tilley. 1987a. *Reconstructing Archaeology: Theory and Practice.* Cambridge: Cambridge University Press.

———. 1987b. *Social Theory and Archaeology.* Albuquerque: University of New Mexico Press.

———. 1992. Re-Constructing Archaeology: Theory and Practice. 2nd ed. London: Routledge.

Sherratt, Andrew. 1993. The relativity of theory. In Norman Yoffee and Andrew Sherratt (Eds.), *Archaeological Theory: Who Sets the Agenda?* (pp. 119–130). Cambridge: Cambridge University Press.

Skibo, James M., William H. Walker, and Axel E. Nielsen (Eds.). 1995. *Expanding Archaeology.* Salt Lake City: University of Utah Press.

Spaulding, Albert C. 1968. Explanation in archeology. In Sally R. Binford and Lewis R. Binford (Eds.), *New Perspectives in Archeology* (pp. 33–39). Chicago: Aldine.

———. 1985. Fifty years of theory. *American Antiquity* 50: 301–308.

Tilley, Christopher. 1990. *Reading Material Culture.* Oxford: Blackwell.

Trigger, Bruce. 2006. *A History of Archaeological Thought.* Cambridge: Cambridge University Press.

Watson, Patty Jo. 1973. The future of archeology in anthropology: Cultural history and social science. In Charles L. Redman (Ed.), *Research and Theory in Current Archeology* (pp. 113–124). New York: Wiley.

———. 1986. Archaeological interpretation, 1985. In David J. Meltzer, Don D. Fowler, and Jeremy A. Sabloff (Eds.), *American Archaeology Past and Future: A Celebration of the Society for American Archaeology 1935–1985* (pp. 439–457). Washington, DC: Smithsonian Institution Press.

White, Leslie (Ed.). 1940. *Pioneers in American Anthropology: The Bandelier-Morgan Letters, 1873–1883.* Albuquerque: Coronado Cuarto Centennial Publ., 1540–1940 (quotes from pp. 212–213).

Wilk, Richard. 1985. The ancient Maya and the political present. *Journal of Anthropological Research* 41: 307–326.

Wissler, Clark. 1914. A pioneer student of Ancient America (Bandelier obituary). *El Palacio* 1 (6, 7): 8.

Wolf, Eric R. 1982. *Europe and the People without History*. Berkeley: University of California Press.

Wylie, Alison. 1992. The interplay of evidential constraints and political interests: Recent archaeological research on gender. *American Antiquity* 57: 15–35.

———. 1994. On "capturing facts alive in the past" (or present): Response to Fotiadis and to Little. *American Antiquity* 59: 556–560.

Yoffee, Norman, and Andrew Sherratt (Eds.). 1993a. *Archaeological Theory: Who Sets the Agenda?* Cambridge: Cambridge University Press.

———. 1993b. Introduction: The sources of archaeological theory. In Norman Yoffee and Andrew Sherratt (Eds.), *Archaeological Theory: Who Sets the Agenda?* (pp. 1–9). Cambridge: Cambridge University Press.

Chapter 4

Ammerman, A. J. 1981. Surveys and archaeological research. *Annual Review of Anthropology* 10: 63–88.

Binford, Lewis R. 1964. A consideration of archaeological research design. *American Antiquity* 29: 425–441.

Blanton, Richard E. 1978. *Monte Albán: Settlement Patterns at the Ancient Zapotec Capital*. New York: Academic Press.

Borden, Charles E. 1952. A uniform site designation scheme for Canada. In *Anthropology in British Columbia,* vol. no. 3 (pp. 44–48). British Columbia Provincial Museum: Department of Education.

Davis, Hester A. 1991. Avocational archaeology groups: A secret weapon for site protection. In George S. Smith and John E. Ehrenhard (Eds.), *Protecting the Past* (pp. 175–180). Boca Raton, FL: CRC Press. ("Archaeological Ethics" text quoted from this work.)

Dillon, Brian D. (Ed.). 1989. *Practical Archaeology: Field and Laboratory Techniques and Archaeological Logistics*. Archaeological Research Tools 2. Los Angeles: Institute of Archaeology, UCLA.

Dunnell, Robert C., and William S. Dancey. 1983. The siteless survey: A regional scale data collection strategy. In Michael B. Schiffer (Ed.), *Advances in Archeological Method and Theory*. Vol. 6 (pp. 267–287). New York: Academic Press.

Ebert, James. 1992. *Distributional Archaeology*. Albuquerque: University of New Mexico Press.

Fedje, Daryl W. and Rolf W. Mathewes. 2005. *Human History and Environment from the Time of Loon to the Time of the Iron People*. Vancouver: UNB Press.

Fedje, Daryl W., and Tina Christian. 1999. Modeling paleo-shorelines and locating Early Holocene coastal sites in Haida Gwaii. *American Antiquity* 64: 635–652.

Fish, Suzanne K., and Stephen A. Kowalewski (Eds.). 1990. *The Archaeology of Regions: A Case for Full-Coverage Survey*. Washington, DC: Smithsonian Institution Press.

Fletcher, Roland. 1977. Settlement studies. In David L. Clarke (Ed.), *Spatial Archaeology* (pp. 47–162). New York: Academic Press.

Foley, Robert. 1981. Off-site archaeology: An alternative approach for the short-sited. In Ian Hodder, Glynn Isaac, and Norman Hammond (Eds.), *Pattern of the Past: Studies in Honour of David Clarke* (pp. 157–183). Cambridge: Cambridge University Press.

Frison, George C. 1984. Avocational archaeology: Its past, present, and future. In E. L. Green (Ed.), *Ethics and Values in Archaeology* (pp. 184–193). New York: Free Press.

Hester, Thomas R., Harry J. Shafer, and Kenneth L. Feder. 1997. *Field Methods in Archaeology*. 7th ed. Mountain View, CA: Mayfield.

Hyslop, John. 1984. *The Inka Road System*. Orlando: Academic Press.

Judge, W. James, James I. Ebert, and Robert K. Hitchcock. 1975. Sampling in regional archaeological survey. In James W. Mueller (Ed.), *Sampling in Archaeology* (pp. 82–123). Tucson: University of Arizona Press.

Kelly, Robert. 2001. Prehistory of the Carson Desert and Stillwater Mountains, Nevada: Environment, Mobility, and Subsistence. *University of Utah Anthropological Papers* 123. Salt Lake City.

Kowalewski, Stephen A. 1990a. Merits of full-coverage survey: Examples from the Valley of Oaxaca, Mexico. In Suzanne K. Fish and Stephen A. Kowalewski (Eds.), *The Archaeology of Regions: A Case for Full-Coverage Survey* (pp. 33–85). Washington, DC: Smithsonian Institution Press.

———. 1990b. Scale and complexity: Issues in the archaeology of the Valley of Oaxaca. In Joyce Marcus (Ed.), *Debating Oaxaca Archaeology*. Museum of Anthropology, University of Michigan Anthropological Papers 84: 207–270. Ann Arbor.

Lekson, Stephen H. 1986. *Great Pueblo Architecture of Chaco Canyon.* Albuquerque: University of New Mexico Press.

Lewarch, Dennis E., and Michael J. O'Brien. 1981. The expanding role of surface assemblages in archaeological research. In Michael B. Schiffer (Ed.), *Advances in Archaeological Method and Theory.* Vol. 4 (pp. 297–342). New York: Academic Press.

McManamon, Francis P. 1984. Discovering sites unseen. In Michael B. Schiffer (Ed.), *Advances in Archaeological Method and Theory.* Vol. 7 (pp. 223–292). New York: Academic Press.

Morris, Craig, and Adriana von Hagen. 1993. *The Inka Empire and Its Andean Origins.* New York: Abbeville Press.

Mueller, James W. 1974. The use of sampling in archaeological survey. *Society for American Archaeology Memoir* 28.

———(Ed.). 1975. *Sampling in Archaeology.* Tucson: University of Arizona Press.

Murra, John V. 1994. John Hyslop, 1945–1993. *Andean Past* 4: 1–7.

Noble, David Grant (Ed.). 1984. *New Light on Chaco Canyon.* Santa Fe: School of American Research Press.

Parsons, Jeffrey R. 1990. Critical reflections on a decade of full-coverage regional survey in the Valley of Mexico. In Suzanne K. Fish and Stephen A. Kowalewski (Eds.), *The Archaeology of Regions: A Case for Full-Coverage Survey* (pp. 7–31). Washington, DC: Smithsonian Institution Press.

Peck, Mary. 1994. *Chaco Canyon: A Center and Its World.* Santa Fe: Museum of New Mexico Press.

Plog, Stephen, Fred Plog, and Walter Wait. 1978. Decision making in modern surveys. In Michael B. Schiffer (Ed.), *Advances in Archaeological Method and Theory.* Vol. 1 (pp. 383–421). New York: Academic Press.

Rossignol, Jacqueline, and LuAnn Wandsnider (Eds.). 1992. *Space, Time, and Archaeological Landscapes.* New York: Plenum Press.

Sebastian, Lynne. 1992. *The Chaco Anasazi: Sociopolitical Evolution in the Prehistoric Southwest.* Cambridge: Cambridge University Press.

Steward, Julian H. 1938. Basin–plateau aboriginal sociopolitical groups. Washington, DC: *Bureau of American Ethnology Bulletin* 120.

Tainter, Joseph A. 1983. Settlement behavior and the archaeological record: Concepts for the definition of "archaeological site." *Contract Abstracts and CRM Archaeology* 3(2): 130–132.

Thomas, David Hurst. 1969. Great Basin hunting patterns: A quantitative method for treating faunal remains. *American Antiquity* 34(4): 392–401.

———. 1972a. A computer simulation model of Great Basin Shoshonean subsistence and settlement patterns. In David L. Clarke (Ed.), *Models in Archaeology* (pp. 671–704). London: Methuen.

———. 1972b. Western Shoshone ecology: Settlement patterns and beyond. In Don D. Fowler (Ed.), Great Basin Cultural Ecology, a Symposium. *Desert Research Institute Publications in the Social Sciences* 8: 135–153.

———. 1973. An empirical test for Steward's model of Great Basin settlement patterns. *American Antiquity* 38(2): 155–176.

———. 1978. The awful truth about statistics in archaeology. *American Antiquity* 43(2): 231–244.

———. 1983a. The archaeology of Monitor Valley: 1. Epistemology. *Anthropological Papers of the American Museum of Natural History* 58(1): 1–194.

———. 1983b. The archaeology of Monitor Valley: 2. Gatecliff Shelter. *Anthropological Papers of the American Museum of Natural History* 59(1): 1–552.

———. 1987. The archaeology of Mission Santa Catalina de Guale: 1. Search and discovery. *Anthropological Papers of the American Museum of Natural History* 63(2): 47–161.

———. 1988. The archaeology of Monitor Valley: 3. Survey and additional excavation. *Anthropological Papers of the American Museum of Natural History* 66(2): 131–633.

Thomas, David Hurst, and Robert L. Bettinger. 1976. Prehistoric piñon ecotone settlements of the upper Reese River Valley, central Nevada. *Anthropological Papers of the American Museum of Natural History* 53(3): 263–366.

Vivian, R. Gwinn. 1990. *The Chacoan Prehistory of the San Juan Basin.* San Diego: Academic Press.

Williams, Leonard, David Hurst Thomas, and Robert Bettinger. 1973. Notions to numbers: Great Basin settlements as polythetic sets. In Charles L. Redman (Ed.), *Research and Theory in Current Archeology* (pp. 215–237). New York: Wiley.

Chapter 5

Abbott, James T., and Charles D. Frederick. 1990. Proton magnetometer investigations of burned rock middens in West-Central Texas: Clues to formation processes. *Journal of Archaeological Science* 17: 535–545.

Aldenderfer, Mark, and Herbert Maschner (Eds.). 1996. *Anthropology, Space, and Geographic Information Systems.* New York: Oxford University Press.

Allen, K. M. S., S. W. Green, and E. B. W. Zubrow (Eds.). 1990. *Interpreting Space: GIS and Archaeology.* London: Taylor and Francis.

Ambler, J. Richard. 1989. *The Anasazi: Prehistoric People of the Four Corners Region.* 4th ed. Flagstaff: Museum of Northern Arizona Press.

Avery, T. E., and T. R. Lyons. 1981. *Remote Sensing: Aerial and Terrestrial Photography for Archaeologists.* Washington, DC: National Park Service, Supplement 7.

Bevan, Bruce W. 1983. Electromagnetics for mapping buried earth features. *Journal of Field Archaeology* 10: 47–54.

Bevan, Bruce W., and J. Kenyon. 1975. Ground-penetrating radar for historical archaeology. *MASCA Newsletter* 11(2): 2–7.

Boyd, Mark, F., Hale G. Smith, and John W. Griffin. 1951. *Here They Once Stood: The Tragic End of the Apalachee Missions.* Gainesville: University of Florida Press.

Brody, J. J. 1990. *The Anasazi: Ancient Indian People of the American Southwest.* New York: Rizzoli.

Brumley, John H. 1988. *Medicine Wheels on the Northern Plains: A Summary and Appraisal.* [Edmonton], AB: Alberta Culture and Multiculturalism, Historical Resources Division.

Carr, Christopher. 1977. A new role and analytical design for the use of resistivity surveying in archaeology. *Mid-Continental Journal of Archaeology* 2: 161–193.

———. 1982. Handbook on Soil Resistivity Surveying: Interpretation of Data from Earthen Archaeological Sites. Evanston, IL: Center for American Archeology Press.

Clark, Anthony. 1990. *Seeing Beneath the Soil: Prospecting Methods in Archaeology.* London: Batsford.

Conyers, Lawrence B. 1995. The use of ground-penetrating radar to map the buried structures and landscape of the Cerén site, El Salvador. *Geoarchaeology* 10: 275–299.

Cordell, Linda S. 1984. *Prehistory of the Southwest.* Orlando, FL: Academic Press.

Crown, Patricia L., and W. James Judge (Eds.). 1991. *Chaco and Hohokam: Prehistoric Regional Systems in the American Southwest.* Santa Fe: School of American Research Press.

Crumley, Carole. 1994. Historical ecology: A multidimensional ecological orientation. In C. Crumley (Ed.), *Historical Ecology: Cultural Knowledge and Changing Landscapes.* (pp. 1–16). Santa Fe: School of American Research Press (quote from p. 6).

Deuel, Leo. 1969. Flights into Yesterday: The Story of Aerial Archaeology. New York: St. Martin's Press.

Donoghue, D. N. M. 2001. Remote sensing. In D. Brothwell and A. Pollard (Eds.), *Handbook of Archaeological Sciences* (pp. 555–564). Chichester, England: John Wiley and Sons.

Ebert, James I. 1984. Remote sensing applications in archaeology. In Michael B. Schiffer (Ed.), *Advances in Archaeological Method and Theory.* Vol. 7 (pp. 293–362). New York: Academic Press.

Eddy, Frank, Dale R. Lightfoot, Eden A. Welker, Layne L. Wright, and Dolores C. Torres. 1996. Air photographic mapping of San Marcos Pueblo. *Journal of Field Archaeology* 23: 1–13.

Eddy, John A. 1977. Probing the mystery of the medicine wheels. *National Geographic* 151: 140–147.

Ehrenberg, Ralph E. 1987. Scholars' Guide to Washington, DC for Cartography and Remote Sensing Imagery. Washington, DC: Smithsonian Institution Press.

Gabriel, Kathryn. 1991. *Roads to Center Place: A Cultural Atlas of Chaco Canyon and the Anasazi.* Boulder: Johnson Books.

Garrison, Ervan G., James G. Baker, and David Hurst Thomas. 1985. Magnetic prospection and the discovery of Mission Santa Catalina de Guale, Georgia. *Journal of Field Archaeology* 12: 299–313.

Good, Diane L. 1989. Birds, beads and bells: Remote sensing of a Pawnee sacred bundle. *Kansas State Historical Society, Anthropological Series,* no. 15.

Goodman, Dean. 1994. Ground-penetrating radar simulation in engineering and archaeology. *Geophysics* 59: 224–232.

Harp, Elmer, Jr. 1975. *Photography in Archaeological Research.* Albuquerque: University of New Mexico Press.

Harris, Jason C. 2005. Oilfield visual impact mitigation—Innovation in regulation compliance. Unpublished paper presented at *Tools of the Trade—Methods, Techniques, and Innovative Approaches to Archaeology: Chacmool Archaeology Conference 2005*. Calgary, AB: Chacmool Archaeological Association.

Johnston, R. B. 1961. Archaeological application of the proton magnetometer in Indiana (U.S.A.). *Archaeometry* 4: 71–72.

Kantner, John. 1997. Ancient roads, modern mapping: Evaluating prehistoric Chaco Anasazi roadways using GIS technology. *Expedition Magazine* 39: 4962.

———. 2004. Geographical approaches for reconstructing past human behavior from prehistoric roadways. In M. F. Goodchild and D. G. Janelle (Eds.), *Spatially Integrated Social Sciences: Examples in Best Practice* (pp. 323–344). Oxford: Oxford University Press.

Kehoe, Alice Beck, and Thomas F. Kehoe. 1979. *Solstice-Aligned Boulder Configurations in Saskatchewan. Mercury Series*. Ottawa: National Museum of Canada.

Kvamme, Kenneth L. 1989. Geographic information systems in regional archaeological research and data management. In M. B. Schiffer (Ed.), *Archaeological Method and Theory*. Vol. 1 (pp. 139–204). Tucson: University of Arizona Press.

Lister, Robert H., and Florence C. Lister. 1981. *Chaco Canyon: Archaeology and Archaeologists*. Albuquerque: University of New Mexico Press.

Lyons, T. R., and T. E. Avery. 1984. *Remote Sensing: A Handbook for Archaeologists and Cultural Resource Managers*. Washington, DC: National Park Service.

Martin, William A., James E. Bruseth, and Robert J. Huggins. 1991. Assessing feature function and spatial patterning of artifacts with geophysical remote-sensing data. *American Antiquity* 56: 701–720.

Morris, Craig. 1995. Airborne archeology. *Natural History* 104(12): 70–72.

Parrington, Michael. 1983. Remote sensing. *Annual Review of Anthropology* 12: 105–124.

Riley, D. N. 1987. *Air Photography and Archaeology*. London: Duckworth.

Sabins, Floyd F., Jr. 1996. *Remote Sensing: Principles and Interpretation*. 3rd ed. New York: W. H. Freeman.

Sanders, John, and Peggy Sanders. 1986. Archaeological Graphic Services remote mapping system. *Advances in Computer Archaeology* 3: 40–55.

Scollar, Irwin, A. Tabbagh, A. Hesse, and I. Herzóg (Eds.). 1990. *Archaeological Prospecting and Remote Sensing*. Cambridge: Cambridge University Press.

Shapiro, Gary. 1984. A soil resistivity survey of 16th-century Puerto Real, Haiti. *Journal of Field Archaeology* 11: 101–110.

———. 1987. Archaeology at San Luis: Broad-scale testing, 1984–1985. *Florida Archaeology*, no. 3.

Sheets, Payson D. 2002. *Before the Volcano Erupted: The Ancient Cerén Village in Central America*. Austin: University of Texas Press.

Sheets, Payson D., and Donald K. Grayson (Eds.). 1979. *Volcanic Activity and Human Ecology*. New York: Academic Press.

Sheets, Payson D., and Brian R. McKee (Eds.). 1994. *Archaeology, Volcanism, and Remote Sensing in the Arenal Region, Costa Rica*. Austin: University of Texas Press.

Sheets, Payson D., and Tom Sever. 1988, November/December. High-tech wizardry. *Archaeology* 41(6): 28–35.

Snead, J., and Preucel, R. 1999. The ideology of settlement: Ancestral Keres landscapes in the northern Rio Grande. In W. Ashmore and A. B. Knapp (Eds.), *Archaeologies of Landscape: Contemporary Perspectives* (pp. 169–197). Oxford: Blackwell Publishers.

Steponaitis, Vincas P., and J. P. Brain. 1976. A portable differential proton magnetometer. *Journal of Field Archaeology* 3: 455–463.

Thomas, David Hurst. 1993. The archaeology of Mission Santa Catalina de Guale: Our first 15 years. In Bonnie G. McEwan (Ed.), *The Missions of La Florida* (pp. 1–34). Gainesville: University Press of Florida.

Ubelaker, Douglas. 1990. Review of "Birds, beads and bells: Remote sensing of Pawnee sacred bundle" by Diane L. Good. *Plains Anthropologist* 35: 213–214.

von Frese, R. R. B., and V. E. Noble. 1984. Magnetometry for archaeological exploration of historical sites. *Historical Archaeology* 18(2): 38–53.

Wescott, Konnie L., and R. Joe Brandon (Eds.). 1999. *Practical Applications of GIS for Archaeologists: A Predictive Modeling Kit*. London: Taylor and Francis.

Wescott, Konnie L., and James A. Kuiper. 1999. Using a GIS to model prehistoric site distributions in the

Upper Chesapeake Bay. In Konnie Wescott and R. Joe Brandon (Eds.), *Practical Applications of GIS for Archaeologists: A Predictive Modeling Kit* (pp. 59–72). London: Taylor and Francis.

Weymouth, John W. 1986. Geophysical methods of archaeological site surveying. In Michael B. Schiffer (Ed.), *Advances in Archaeological Method and Theory.* Vol. 9 (pp. 311–395). Orlando, FL: Academic Press.

Weymouth, John W., and Robert Huggins. 1985. Geophysical surveying of archaeological sites. In George R. Rapp, Jr., and J. Gifford (Eds.), *Archaeological Geology* (pp. 191–235). New Haven: Yale University Press.

Wheatley, David, and Mark Gillings. 2002. *Spatial Technology and Archaeology: The Archaeological Applications of GIS.* London: Taylor and Francis.

Willey, Gordon R. 1953. Prehistoric Settlement Patterns in the Virú Valley, Peru. *Bureau of American Ethnology, Bulletin* 155. Washington, DC.

Wynn, J. C. (Ed.). 1986. Special issue: Geophysics in archaeology. *Geophysics* 51: 533–639.

Zeanah, David. 2004. Sexual division of labor and central place foraging: A model for the Carson Desert of western Nevada. *Journal of Anthropological Archaeology* 23: 1–12.

Zeanah, D. W., J. A. Carter, D. P. Dugas, R. G. Elston, and J. E. Hammett. 1995. *An Optimal Foraging Model of Hunter-Gatherer Land Use in the Carson Desert.* Report in partial fulfillment of U.S. Fish and Wildlife Service Contract # 14-48-0001-93015(DB) prepared for U.S. Fish and Wildlife Service and U.S. Department of the Navy.

Chapter 6

Bird, Junius. 1980. Comments on sifters, sifting, and sorting procedures. In Martha Joukowsky, *A Complete Manual of Field Archaeology* (pp. 165–170). Englewood Cliffs, NJ: Prentice Hall.

Beattie, Owen, Brian Apland, Erik W. Blake, James A. Cosgrove, Sarah Gaunt, Sheila Grur, Alexander P. Macki, Kjerstin E. Mackie, Dan Stran Thof, Valerie Thorp, and Peter Troffe. 2000. The Kwaday Dan Tsinchi discovery from a glacier in British Columbia. *Canadian Journal of Archaeology* 24: 129–147.

Collis, John. 2001. *Digging Up the Past: An Introduction to Archaeological Excavation.* Phoenix Mills, UK: Sutton Publishing.

Dancey, William S. 1981. *Archaeological Field Methods: An Introduction.* Minneapolis: Burgess.

Daugherty, Richard, and Ruth Kirk. 1976. Ancient Indian village where time stood still. *Smithsonian* 7(2): 68–75.

Dibble, Harold L. 1987. Measurement of artifact provenience with an electronic theodolite. *Journal of Field Archaeology* 14: 249–254.

Fladmark, Knud R. 1978. *A Guide to Basic Archaeological Field Procedures.* Burnaby, BC: Department of Archaeology, Simon Fraser University.

———. 2006. *A Guide to Basic Archaeological Field Procedures.* Burnaby, BC: Simon Fraser University Archaeology Press.

Folsom, Franklin. 1992. *The Black Cowboy.* Niwot, CO: Roberts Rinehart.

Fowler, Brenda. 2001. *Iceman: Uncovering the Life and Times of a Prehistoric Man Found in an Alpine Glacier.* Chicago: University of Chicago Press.

Joukowsky, Martha. 1980. *A Complete Manual of Field Archaeology: Tools and Techniques of Field Work for Archaeologists.* Englewood Cliffs, NJ: Prentice Hall.

Kirk, Ruth, and Richard Daugherty. 1974. *Hunters of the Whale.* New York: William Morrow.

Lock, Gary. 2003. *Using Computers in Archaeology: Towards Virtual Pasts.* London: Routledge.

Loud, Lewellyn L., and Mark R. Harrington. 1929. Lovelock Cave. *University of California Publications in American Archaeology and Ethnology* 25: 1–183.

McMillon, Bill. 1991. *The Archaeology Handbook: A Field Manual and Resource Guide.* New York: John Wiley and Sons.

Meltzer, David. 1993. *Search for the First Americans.* Washington, DC: Smithsonian Institution Press.

Ogilvie, Bob. 1996. *Archaeology in Nova Scotia: Protecting Archaeological and Historical Sites and Artifacts.* Halifax: Nova Scotia Museum.

Pendleton, Michael W. 1983. A comment concerning testing flotation recovery rates. *American Antiquity* 48: 615–616.

Percy, George. 1976. The use of a mechanical earth auger at the Torreya Site, Liberty County, Florida. *Florida Anthropologist* 29(1): 24–32.

Purdy, Barbara A. 1996. *How to Do Archaeology the Right Way.* Gainesville: University Press of Florida.

Rick, John W. 1996. Total stations in archaeology. *Bulletin of the Society for American Archaeology* 14(4): 24–27.

Samuels, Steven. (Ed.). 1991a. *Ozette Archaeological Research Reports,* vol. 1, *House Structure and Floor Midden.* Pullman, WA: Washington State University and National Park Service, Pacific Northwest Regional Office.

———(Ed.). 1991b. *Ozette Archaeological Research Reports,* vol. 2, *Fauna.* Pullman, WA: Washington State University and National Park Service, Pacific Northwest Regional Office.

South, Stanley. 1994. The archaeologist and the crew: From the mountains to the sea. In Stanley South (Ed.), *Pioneers in Historical Archaeology: Breaking New Ground* (pp. 165–187). New York: Plenum Press.

Struever, Stuart. 1968. Flotation techniques for the recovery of small-scale archaeological remains. *American Antiquity* 33: 353–362.

Wagner, Gail E. 1982. Testing flotation recovery rates. *American Antiquity* 47: 127–132.

Watson, Patty Jo. 1974. Flotation procedures used on Salts Cave sediments. In Patty Jo Watson (Ed.), *Archeology of the Mammoth Cave Area* (pp. 107–108). New York: Academic Press.

———. 1976. In pursuit of prehistoric subsistence: A comparative account of some contemporary flotation techniques. *Midcontinental Journal of Archaeology* 1: 77–100.

Yarnell, Richard A. 1974. Intestinal contents of the Salts Cave mummy and analysis of the initial Salts Cave flotation series. In Patty Jo Watson (Ed.), *Archaeology of the Mammoth Cave Area* (pp. 109–112). New York: Academic Press.

———. 1982. Problems of interpretation of archaeological plant remains of the Eastern Woodlands. *Southeastern Archaeology* 1(1): 1–7.

Chapter 7

Browman, David L., and Douglas R. Givens. 1996. Stratigraphic excavation: The first "new archaeology." *American Anthropologist* 98: 1–17.

Davis, Jonathan O. 1978. Quaternary tephrochronology of the Lake Lahontan area. *Nevada Archaeological Survey Research Paper,* no. 7.

Davis, Jonathan. 1983. Geology of Gatecliff Shelter: Sedimentary facies and Holocene climate. In "The archaeology of Monitor Valley: 2. Gatecliff Shelter" by David Hurst Thomas. *Anthropological Papers of the American Museum of Natural History* 59(1): 64–87.

Dibble, Harold, Philip Chase, Shannon McPherron, and Alain Tuffreau. 1992. Testing the reality of a "living floor" with archaeological data. *American Antiquity* 62: 629–651.

Ellis, Florence Hawley. 1983. Foreword to Stephen H. Lekson (Ed.), The Architecture and Dendrochronology of Chetro Ketl, Chaco Canyon, New Mexico. *Reports of the Chaco Center,* no. 6. Albuquerque: Division of Cultural Research, National Park Service.

Feibel, C. S., N. Agnew, B. Latimer, M. Demas, F. Marshall, S. A. C. Waane, and P. Schmid, 1996. A new look at the Laetoli hominid footprints: A preliminary report on the conservation and scientific restudy. *Evolutionary Anthropology* 4: 149–154.

Frisbie, Theodore R. 1975. A biography of Florence Hawley Ellis and bibliography of Florence Hawley Ellis. In Theodore R. Frisbie (Ed.), Collected Papers in Honor of Florence Hawley Ellis. *Papers of the Archaeological Society of New Mexico* 2: 1–11, 12–21.

———. 1991. Florence Hawley Ellis, 1906–1991. *Kiva* 57(1): 93–97.

Greenfield, Jeanette. 1989. *The Return of Cultural Treasures.* Cambridge: Cambridge University Press.

Harris, E. 1989. *Principles of Archaeological Stratigraphy.* 2nd ed. New York: Academic Press.

Hawley, Florence M. 1934. The significance of the dated prehistory of Chetro Ketl, Chaco Canyon, New Mexico. *University of New Mexico Bulletin,* Monograph Series 1(1). Albuquerque: University of New Mexico Press.

———. 1937. Reversed stratigraphy. *American Antiquity* 4: 297–299.

Hay, Richard I., and Mary D. Leakey. 1982. The fossil footprints of Laetoli. *Scientific American* 246(2): 50–57.

Herz, Norman, and Ervan Garrison. 1998. *Geological Methods for Archaeology.* Oxford: Oxford University Press.

Holliday, Vance T. (Ed.). 1992. *Soils in Archaeology: Landscape Evolution and Human Occupation.* Washington, DC: Smithsonian Institution Press.

Kooyman, Brian, L. V. Hills, P. McNeil, and S. Tolman. 2006. Late Pleistocene horse hunting at the Wally's Beach Site (DhPg-8), Canada. *American Antiquity* 71: 101–121.

McNeil, Paul, L. V. Hills, B. Kooyman, and Shayne M. Tolman. 2005. Mammoth tracks indicate a declining Late Pleistocene population in Southwestern Alberta, Canada. *Quaternary Science Review* 24: 1253–1259.

Leakey, Mary, and J. M. Harris (Eds.). 1987. *Laetoli: A Pliocene Site in Northern Tanzania.* Oxford: Clarendon Press.

Rapp, George, and John A. Gifford (Eds.). 1985. *Archaeological Geology.* New Haven: Yale University Press.

Schiffer, Michael B. 1972. Archaeological context and systemic context. *American Antiquity* 37: 156–165.

———. 1976. *Behavioral Archeology.* New York: Academic Press.

———. 1987. *Formation Processes of the Archaeological Record.* Albuquerque: University of New Mexico Press.

Steen-McIntyre, Virginia. 1985. Tephrochronology and its application to archaeology. In George Rapp, Jr., and John A. Gifford (Eds.), *Archaeological Geology* (pp. 265–302). New Haven: Yale University Press.

Stein, Julie K. 1987. Deposits for archaeologists. In Michael B. Schiffer (Ed.), *Advances in Archaeological Method and Theory.* Vol. 11 (pp. 337–395). New York: Academic Press.

———(Ed.). 1992. *Deciphering a Shell Midden.* San Diego: Academic Press.

Straus, Lawrence G. 1990. Underground archaeology: Perspectives on caves and rockshelters. In M. B. Schiffer (Ed.), *Archaeological Method and Theory.* Vol. 2 (pp. 255–304). Tucson: University of Arizona Press.

Thomas, David Hurst. 1983. The archaeology of Monitor Valley: 2. Gatecliff Shelter. *Anthropological Papers of the American Museum of Natural History* 59 (part 1). New York (quote is from pp. 55–56).

Tuttle, Russell, D. Webb, E. Weidl, and M. Baksh. 1990. Further progress on the Laeotoli trails. *Journal of Archaeological Science* 17: 347–362.

Waters, Michael R. 1992. *Principles of Geoarchaeology: A North American Perspective.* Tucson: University of Arizona Press (quotes from pp. 3, 7, 11).

Chapter 8

Aitken, M. J. 1989. Luminescence dating: A guide for non-specialists. *Archaeometry* 31: 147–159.

———. 1990. *Science-Based Dating in Archaeology.* London: Longman.

Baillie, M. G. L. 1995. *A Slice Through Time: Dendrochronology and Precision Dating.* London: Batsford.

Banning, E. B., and L. A. Pavlish. 1978. Direct detection in radiocarbon dating. *Journal of Field Archaeology* 5: 480–483.

Bannister, Bryant. 1962. The interpretation of tree-ring dates. *American Antiquity* 27: 508–514.

———. 1970. Dendrochronology. In Don Brothwell and Eric Higgs (Eds.), *Science in Archaeology: A Survey of Progress and Research.* 2nd ed. (pp. 191–205). New York: Praeger.

Bannister, Bryant, and William J. Robinson. 1975. Tree-ring dating in archaeology. *World Archaeology* 7: 210–225.

Beck, Charlotte (Ed.). 1994. *Dating in Exposed and Surface Contexts.* Albuquerque: University of New Mexico Press.

Bennett, C. L., R. P. Beukens, M. R. Clover, H. E. Gove, R. B. Liebert, A. E. Litherland, K. H. Purser, and W. E. Sondheim. 1977. Radiocarbon dating using electrostatic accelerators: Negative ions provide the key. *Science* 198: 508–510.

Berger, R. 1979. Radiocarbon dating with accelerators. *Journal of Archaeological Science* 6: 101–104.

Binford, Lewis R. 1962. A new method of calculating dates from kaolin pipe stem samples. *Southeastern Archaeological Conference Newsletter* 9(2): 19–21.

———. 1972. The "Binford" pipe stem formula: A return from the grave. *The Conference on Historic Site Archaeology Papers* 6: 230–253.

Bowman, Sheridan. 1990. *Radiocarbon Dating.* Berkeley: University of California Press.

———. 1994. Using radiocarbon: An update. *Antiquity* 68: 838–843.

Braun, David P. 1985. Absolute seriation: A time-series approach. In Christopher Carr (Ed.), *For Concordance in Archaeological Analysis: Bridging Data Structure, Quantitative Technique, and Theory* (pp. 509–539). Kansas City, MO: Westport.

Browman, David L. 1981. Isotopic discrimination and correction factors in radiocarbon dating. In Michael B. Schiffer (Ed.), *Advances in Archaeological Method and Theory.* Vol. 6 (pp. 241–295). New York: Academic Press.

Chaffee, Scott D., Marian Hyman, Marvin W. Rowe, Nancy J. Coulam, Alan Schroedl, and Kathleen Hogue. 1994. Radiocarbon dates on the All American Man pictograph. *American Antiquity* 59: 769–781.

Chase, A. F., D. Z. Chase, and H. W. Topsey. 1988. Archaeology and the ethics of collecting. *Archaeology* 41(1): 56–60, 87.

Creel, Darrell, and Austin Long. 1986. Radiocarbon dating of corn. *American Antiquity* 51: 826–837.

Dale, W. S. A. 1987. The shroud of Turin: Relic or icon? In H. H. Andersen and S. T. Picraux (Eds.), Nuclear Instruments and Methods in Physics Research: Section B, Beam Interactions with Materials and Atoms. *Proceedings of the Fourth International Symposium on Accelerator Mass Spectrometry* B29: 187–192.

Deagan, Kathleen. 1983. *Spanish St. Augustine: The Archaeology of a Colonial Creole Community.* New York: Academic Press.

Dean, Jeffery S. 1978. Independent dating in archaeological analysis. In Michael B. Schiffer (Ed.), *Advances in Archaeological Theory and Method.* Vol. 1 (pp. 223–255). New York: Academic Press.

de Vries, Hessel L. 1958. Variation in concentration of radiocarbon with time and location on earth. *Proceedings Koninlijke Nederlandse Akademie Wetenschappen* B, 61: 94–102.

Douglass, Andrew Ellicott. 1929. The secret of the Southwest solved by talkative tree rings. *National Geographic* 56(6): 736–770.

Drennan, Robert D. 1976. A refinement of chronological seriation using nonmetric multidimensional scaling. *American Antiquity* 41: 290–302.

Dunnell, Robert C. 1970. Seriation method and its evaluation. *American Antiquity* 35: 305–319.

Feathers, James. 2003. Use of luminescence dating in archaeology. *Measurement Science and Technology* 14: 1493–1509.

Fleming, Stuart. 1977. *Dating Techniques in Archaeology.* New York: St. Martin's Press.

———. 1979. *Thermoluminescence Techniques in Archaeology.* New York: Oxford University Press.

Fritts, H. C. 1976. *Tree Rings and Climate.* New York: Academic Press.

Fullagar, R. L. K., D. M. Price, and L. M. Head. 1996. Early human occupation of northern Australia: Archaeology and thermoluminescence dating of Jinmium rockshelter, Northern Territory. *Antiquity* 70: 751–773.

George, Jane. 1999. Keen-eyed archeologist spots stolen Inuit figurines. *Nunatsiaq News.*

Gove, H. E. 1987. Turin workshop on radiocarbon dating the Turin shroud. *Nuclear Instruments and Methods in Physics Research* B29(1, 2): 193–195.

Grün, R. 1999. Trapped charge dating (ESR, TL, OSL). In D. Brothwell and A. Pollard (Eds.), *Handbook of Archaeological Sciences* (pp. 47–62). Chichester, England: John Wiley and Sons.

Haas, Herbert, James Devine, Robert Wenke, Mark Lehner, Willy Wolfli, and George Bonani. 1987. Radiocarbon chronology and the historical calendar in Egypt. In Oliver Aurenche, Jacques Evin, and Francis Hours (Eds.), Chronologies in the Near East: Relative Chronologies and Absolute Chronology 16,000–4,000 BP (pp. 585–606). *British Archaeology Reports International Series* 379. Oxford, England.

Harrington, Jean C. 1954. Dating stem fragments of seventeenth and eighteenth century clay tobacco pipes. *Quarterly Bulletin: Archaeological Society of Virginia* 9(1).

Hedges, R. E. M., and J. A. J. Gowlett. 1986. Radiocarbon dating by accelerator mass spectrometry. *Scientific American* 254(1): 100–107.

Heighton, Robert F., and Kathleen A. Deagan. 1972. A new formula for dating kaolin clay pipestems. *The Conference on Historic Site Archaeology Papers* 6(2): 220–229.

Hu, Q., P. E. Smith, N. M. Evensen, and D. York. 1994. Lasing in the Holocene: Extending the 40Ar-39Ar laser probe method into the 14C age range. *Earth and Planetary Science Letters* 123: 331–336.

Irving, W. N., and C. R. Harrington. 1973. Upper Pleistocene radiocarbon dated artifacts from the Northern Yukon. *Science, New Series* 179: 335–340.

Jull, A. J. T., D. J. Donahue, and P. E. Damon. 1996. Factors affecting the apparent radiocarbon age of textiles: A comment on "Effects of fires and biofractionation of carbon isotopes on results of radiocarbon dating of old textiles: The shroud of Turin" by D. A. Kouznetsov et al. *Journal of Archaeological Science* 23: 157–160.

Kouznetsov, Dmitri A., Andrey A. Ivanov, and Pavel R. Veletsky. 1996. Effects of fires and biofractionation of carbon isotopes on results of radiocarbon dating of old textiles: The shroud of Turin. *Journal of Archaeological Science* 23: 109–121.

Litherland, A. E., and L. A. Pavlish (Eds.). 2003. Physics and archaeometry, 2003, Special issue, *Physics in Canada* Vol. 59, No. 5 (Sept–Oct).

Long, A., and Bruce Rippeteau. 1974. Testing contemporaneity and averaging radiocarbon dates. *American Antiquity* 39: 205–215.

Loy, Thomas H., D. Rhys Jones, E. Nelson, Betty Meehan, John Vogel, John Southon, and Richard Cosgrove. 1990. Accelerator radiocarbon dating of human blood proteins in pigments from Late Pleistocene art sites in Australia. *Antiquity* 64: 110–116.

MacNeish, R. S. 1952. Iroquoian pottery types: A technique for the study of Iroquois prehistory. *Bulletin (National Museum of Canada)*.

Marquardt, William H. 1978. Advances in archaeological seriation. In Michael B. Schiffer (Ed.), *Advances in Archaeological Method and Theory*. Vol. 1 (pp. 257–314). New York: Academic Press.

Mazess, Richard B., and D. W. Zimmermann. 1966. Pottery dating from thermoluminescence. *Science* 152(3720): 347–348.

McDougall, I. 1990. Potassium-argon dating in archaeology. *Science Progress* 74: 15–30.

McNutt, Charles H. 1973. On the methodological validity of frequency seriation. *American Antiquity* 38: 45–60.

Messenger, Phyllis (Ed.). 1989. *The Ethics of Collecting Cultural Property: Whose Culture? Whose Property?* Albuquerque: University of New Mexico Press.

Michels, Joseph W. 1973. *Dating Methods in Archaeology*. New York: Seminar Press.

Nelson, D. E., Richarn Morlan, J. S. Voyel, J. R. Southon, and C. R. Harrington. 1986. New dates on Northern Yukon artifacts: Holocene, not Upper Pleistocene. *Science, New Series* 232: 749–751.

Nelson, Nels. 1916. Chronology of the Tano Ruins, New Mexico. *American Anthropologist* 18: 159–180 (Table 8-1 is from p. 166).

Orser, Charles E., Jr., and Brian M. Fagan. 1995. *Historical Archaeology*. New York: HarperCollins.

Ralph, Elizabeth K., and Mark C. Han. 1966. Dating of pottery by thermoluminescence. *Nature* 210(5033): 245–247.

———. 1969. Potential of thermoluminescence in supplementing radiocarbon dating. *World Archaeology* 1: 157–169.

Renfrew, Colin. 1979. *Problems in European Prehistory*. Edinburgh: Edinburgh University Press.

Roberts, R. G., M. Bird, J. Olley, R. Galbraith, E. Lawson, G. Laslett, H. Yoshida, R. Jones, R. L. K. Fullagar, G. Jacobsen, and Q. Hua. 1998. Optical and radiocarbon dating at Jinmium rock shelter in northern Australia. *Nature* 393: 358–362.

Rouse, Irving. 1967. Seriation in archaeology. In Carrol L. Riley and Walter W. Taylor (Eds.), *American Historical Anthropology: Essays in Honor of Leslie Spier* (pp. 153–195). Carbondale: Southern Illinois University Press.

South, David B. 1972. Mean ceramic dates, median occupation dates, red ant hills and bumble bees: Statistical confidence and correlation. *The Conference on Historic Site Archaeology Papers* 6: 164–174.

South, Stanley A. 1977. *Method and Theory in Historical Archeology*. New York: Academic Press (Table 8-4 is from p. 220).

Stafford, T. W., Jr., A. J. T. Jull, T. H. Zabel, D. J. Donahue, R. C. Duhamel, K. Brendel, C. V. Haynes, Jr., J. L. Bischoff, L. A. Payen, and R. E. Taylor. 1984. Holocene age of the Yuha burial: Direct radiocarbon determinations by accelerator mass spectrometry. *Nature* 308: 446–447.

Stahle, David W., and Daniel Wolfman. 1985. The potential for archaeological tree-ring dating in eastern North America. In Michael B. Schiffer (Ed.), *Advances in Archaeological Method and Theory*. Vol. 8 (pp. 279–302). New York: Academic Press.

Staley, David P. 1993. The antiquities market. *Journal of Field Archaeology* 20: 347–355.

Stallings, W. S., Jr. 1939. Dating prehistoric ruins by tree-rings. *Laboratory of Anthropology Bulletin* 8. Santa Fe, NM.

Stuckenrath, R. 1977. Radiocarbon: Some notes from Merlin's diary. *Annals of the New York Academy of Science* 288: 181–188.

Stuiver, Minze, and Paula J. Reimer. 1993. Extended 14C database and revised CALIB 3.0 14C age calibration program. *Radiocarbon* 35: 215–230.

Stuiver, Minze, and Hans E. Suess. 1966. On the relationship between radiocarbon dates and true sample ages. *Radiocarbon* 8: 534–540.

Suess, Hans E. 1955. Radiocarbon concentration in modern wood. *Science* 122: 415–417.

Swisher, C. C., III, G. H. Curtis, T. Jacob, A. G. Getty, and A. Suprijo Widasmoro. 1994. Age of the earliest known hominids in Java, Indonesia. *Science* 263: 1118–1121.

Taylor, R. E. 1985. The beginnings of radiocarbon dating in American antiquity: A historical perspective. *American Antiquity* 50: 309–325.

———. 1987a. AMS 14-C dating of critical bone samples: Proposed protocol and criteria for evaluation. In H. H. Andersen and S. T. Picraux (Eds.), Nuclear Instruments and Methods in Physics Research: Section B, Beam Interactions with

Materials and Atoms. *Proceedings of the Fourth International Symposium on Accelerator Mass Spectrometry,* B29: 159–163. Ontario, Canada.

———. 1987b. Radiocarbon Dating: An Archaeological Perspective. New York: Academic Press.

Taylor, R. E., and M. J. Aitken (Eds.). 1997. *Chronometric Dating in Archaeology.* New York: Plenum Press.

Taylor, R. E., Austin Long, and Renee S. Kra (Eds.). 1992. *Radiocarbon After Four Decades: An Interdisciplinary Perspective.* New York: Springer-Verlag.

Turnbaugh, William, and Sarah Peabody Turnbaugh. 1977. Alternative applications of the mean ceramic date concept for interpreting human behavior. *Historical Archaeology* 11: 90–104.

Valladas, H., H. Cachier, P. Maurice, F. Bernaldo de Quiro, J. Clottes, V. Cabrera Valdés, P. Uzquiano, and M. Arnold. 1992. Direct radiocarbon dates for prehistoric paintings at the AltaMira, El Castillo and Niaux caves. *Nature* 357: 68–70.

van der Merwe, Nikolaas J. 1982. Carbon isotopes, photosynthesis, and archaelogy. *American Scientist* 70: 596–606.

van der Plicht, Johannes. 1993. The Groningen radiocarbon calibration program. *Radiocarbon* 35(1): 231–237.

Wendorf, Fred, R. Schild, A. E. Close, D. J. Donahue, A. J. T. Jull, T. H. Zabel, H. Więclowska, M. Kobusiewicz, B. Issawi, N. el Hadidi, and H. Haas. 1984. New radiocarbon dates on the cereals from Wadi Kubbaniua. *Science* 225: 645–646.

Wendorf, Fred, R. Schild, N. el Hadidi, A. E. Close, M. Kobusiewicz, H. Więclowska, B. Issawi, and H. Haas. 1979. The use of barley in the Egyptian late Paleolithic. *Science* 205: 1341–1347.

Willis, E. H. 1969. Radiocarbon dating. In Don Brothwell and Eric Higgs (Eds.), *Science in Archaeology* (pp. 46–57). London: Thames and Hudson.

Wintle, Ann G. 1996. Archaeologically relevant dating techniques for the next century. *Journal of Archaeological Science* 23: 123–138.

Chapter 9

Adams, William Y. 1988. Archaeological classification: Theory versus practice. *Antiquity* 62: 40–56.

Adams, William Y., and Ernest W. Adams. 1991. *Archaeological Typology and Practical Reality: A Dialectical Approach to Artifact Classification and Sorting.* Cambridge: Cambridge University Press.

Binford, Lewis R. 1973. Interassemblage variability—The Mousterian and the "functional" argument. In Colin Renfrew (Ed.), *The Explanation of Culture Change: Models in Prehistory* (pp. 227–254). London: Duckworth.

Cordell, Linda. 1984. *Prehistory of the Southwest.* New York: Academic Press.

Cronyn, J. M. 1990. *The Elements of Archaeological Conservation.* London: Routledge.

Deller, Brian D., and Christoper J. Ellis. 1990. Paleo-Indians. In C. J. Ellis and N. Ferris (Eds.), *The Archaeology of Southern Ontario to A.D. 1650, Occasional Publication of the London Chapter, OAS Number 5* (pp. 37–64).

———. 1992. Thedford II: A Paleo-Indian Site in the Ausable River Watershed of Southwestern Ontario. *Memoirs: Museum of Anthropology, University of Michigan No. 24.* Ann Arbor.

Dunnell, Robert C. 1971. *Systematics in Prehistory.* New York: Free Press.

———. 1986. Methodological issues in Americanist artifact classification. In Michael B. Schiffer (Ed.), *Advances in Archaeological Method and Theory.* Vol. 9 (pp. 149–207). New York: Academic Press.

Ford, James. 1954. The type concept revisited. *American Anthropologist* 56: 42–54.

Griset, Suzanne (Ed.). 1986. Pottery of the Great Basin and adjacent areas. *University of Utah Anthropological Papers,* no. 111.

Haury, Emil W. 1950. *The Stratigraphy and Archaeology of Ventana Cave, Arizona.* Albuquerque: University of New Mexico Press; Tucson: University of Arizona Press (quote from p. 329).

Klejn, L. S. 1982. Archaeological typology. Translated by P. Dole. *British Archaeological Reports, International Series,* no. 153. Oxford, England.

Krieger, Alex D. 1944. The typological concept. *American Antiquity* 9: 271–288.

Lyman, R. Lee, and Michael O'Brien. 2003. *W. C. McKern and the Midwestern Taxonomic Method.* Tuscaloosa: University of Alabama Press.

Lyman, R. Lee, Michael O'Brien, and Robert C. Dunnell (Eds.). 1997. *Americanist Culture History: Fundamentals of Time, Space, and Form.* New York: Plenum Press.

Park, R. W., and D. Stenton. 1978. *Ancient Harpoon Heads of Nunavut: An Illustrated Guide.* Ottawa: Parks Canada.

Rouse, Irving. 1960. The classification of artifacts in archaeology. *American Antiquity* 25: 313–323.

Spaulding, Albert C. 1953. Statistical techniques for the discovery of artifact types. *American Antiquity* 18: 305–313.

———. 1960. The dimensions of archaeology. In G. E. Dole and R. L. Carneiro (Eds.), *Essays in the Science of Culture in Honor of Leslie A. White* (pp. 437–456). New York: Thomas Y. Crowell.

———. 1977. On growth and form in archaeology: Multivariate analysis. *Journal of Anthropological Research* 33: 1–15.

Spier, Leslie. 1917. An outline for a chronology of Zuñi ruins. *Anthropological Papers of the American Museum of Natural History* 18(3): 207–331.

———. 1931. N. C. Nelson's stratigraphic technique in the reconstruction of prehistoric sequences in southwestern America. In S. A. Rice (Ed.), *Methods in Social Science* (pp. 275–283). Chicago: University of Chicago Press.

Steward, Julian H. 1954. Types of types. *American Anthropologist* 56: 54–57.

Sutton, Mark Q., and Brooke S. Arkush. 1996. *Archaeological Laboratory Methods: An Introduction.* Dubuque, IA: Kendall/Hunt Publishing.

Thomas, David Hurst. 1981. How to classify the projectile points from Monitor Valley, Nevada. *Journal of California and Great Basin Anthropology* 3: 7–43.

Whallon, Robert E., Jr., and James A. Brown (Eds.). 1982. *Essays on Archaeological Typology.* Evanston, IL: Center for American Archaeology Press.

Willey, Gordon R., and Philip Phillips. 1958. *Method and Theory in American Archaeology.* Chicago: University of Chicago Press (quote is from p. 22).

Wissler, Clark. 1926. *The Relation of Nature to Man in Aboriginal America.* New York: Oxford University Press.

Chapter 10

Agenbroad, Larry. 1978. *The Hudson-Meng Site: An Alberta Bison Kill in the Nebraska High Plains.* Washington, DC: University Press of America.

Andrefsky, William. 1998. *Lithics: Macroscopic Approaches to Analysis.* Cambridge: Cambridge University Press.

Behrensmeyer, Anna K., and Susan M. Kidwell. 1985. Taphonomy's contributions to paleobiology. *Paleobiology* 1: 105–119.

Binford, Lewis R. 1967. Smudge pits and hide smoking: The use of analogy in archaeological reasoning. *American Antiquity* 32: 1–12.

———(Ed.). 1977. *For Theory Building in Archaeology.* New York: Academic Press.

———. 1978a. Dimensional analysis of behavior and site structure: Learning from an Eskimo hunting stand. *American Antiquity* 43: 330–361.

———. 1978b. *Nunamiut Ethnoarchaeology.* New York: Academic Press.

———. 1980. Willow smoke and dogs' tails: Hunter-gatherer settlement systems and archaeological site formation. *American Antiquity* 45: 4–20.

———. 1982. The archaeology of place. *Journal of Anthropological Archaeology* 1: 5–31.

———. 1983. *In Pursuit of the Past: Decoding the Archaeological Record.* London: Thames and Hudson ("In His Own Words" text quoted from pp. 98, 100–101).

———. 1986. An Alyawara day: Making men's knives and beyond. *American Antiquity* 51: 547–562.

Binford, Lewis R., and James F. O'Connell. 1984. An Alyawara day: The stone quarry. *Journal of Anthropological Research* 40: 406–432.

Brandt, Steve A., and Kathryn Weedman. 1997. The ethnoarchaeology of hideworking and flaked stone-tool use in southern Ethiopia. In K. Fukui, E. Kuimoto, and M. Shigeta (Eds.), *Ethiopia in Broader Perspective: Papers of the XIIth International Conference of Ethiopian Studies* (pp. 351–361). Kyoto: Shokado Book Sellers.

Buck, Bruce A. 1982. Ancient technology in contemporary surgery. *The Western Journal of Medicine* 136: 265–269.

Chaplin, R. E. 1971. *The Study of Animal Bones from Archaeological Sites.* New York: Seminar Press.

Coles, John M. 1973. *Archaeology by Experiment.* New York: Scribner's.

Cotterell, Brian, and Johan Kamminga. 1990. *Mechanics of Pre-Industrial Technology.* Cambridge: Cambridge University Press.

Crabtree, Don E. 1966. A stoneworker's approach to analyzing and replicating the Lindenmeier Folsom. *Tebiwa* 9: 3–39.

———. 1968. Mesoamerican polyhedral cores and prismatic blades. *American Antiquity* 33: 446–478.

———. 1979. Interview. *Flintknappers' Exchange* 2 (1): 29–33 ("Looking Closer" text quoted from p. 30).

David, Nicholas, and Carol Kramer. 2001. *Ethnoarchaeology in Action.* Cambridge: Cambridge University Press.

Dawson, P. 1995. Unsympathetic users: An ethnoarchaeological examination of Inuit responses to the changing nature of the built environment. *Arctic* 28(2), 71–80.

———. 2003. Examining the impact of Euro-Canadian architecture on Inuit families living in Arctic Canada. In J. Hanson (Ed.), *Proceedings: Space Syntax: 4th International Symposium* (pp. 21.1–21.16). Volume 1 of 2. The Space Syntax Laboratory, Bartlett School of Graduate Studies, University College London.

———. 2004. *Inuit Space Use in Euro-Canadian Houses.* Ottawa: Canada Mortgage and Housing Corporation.

———. 2006. The relationship between "house form" and "culture" in Inuit society. *Etudes/Inuit Studies* 30(2).

Efremov, I. A. 1940. Taphonomy: A new branch of paleontology. *Pan-American Geologist* 74(2): 81–93.

Flenniken, J. Jeffrey. 1978. Reevaluation of the Lindenmeier Folsom: A replication experiment in lithic technology. *American Antiquity* 43: 473–480.

———. 1981. Replicative systems analysis: A model applied to the vein quartz artifacts from the Hoko River site. *Laboratory of Anthropology Reports of Investigations,* no. 59. Pullman: Washington State University.

———. 1984. The past, present, and future of flintknapping: An anthropological perspective. *Annual Review of Anthropology* 13: 187–203.

Frison, George C. 1989. Experimental use of Clovis weaponry and tools on African elephants. *American Antiquity* 54: 766–784.

Gamble, C. S., and W. A. Boismier (Eds.). 1991. *Ethnoarchaeological Approaches to Mobile Campsites.* Ann Arbor: International Monographs in Prehistory.

Gifford, Diane P. 1981. Taphonomy and paleoecology: A critical review of archaeology's sister disciplines. In Michael B. Schiffer (Ed.), *Advances in Archaeological Method and Theory.* Vol. 4 (pp. 365–438). New York: Academic Press.

Gordon, R. 2002. *Head-Smashed-In Buffalo Jump.* Calgary: Fifth House.

Graham, Martha. 1994. Mobile Farmers: An Ethnoarchaeological Approach to Settlement Organization Among the Rarámuri of Northwestern Mexico.

International Monographs in Prehistory, Ethnoarchaeological Series 3. Ann Arbor, Michigan.

Grayson, Donald K. 1986. Eoliths, archaeological ambiguity, and the generation of "middle-range" research. In David J. Meltzer, Don D. Fowler, and Jeremy A. Sabloff (Eds.), *American Archaeology Past and Future: A Celebration of the Society of American Archaeology 1935–1985* (pp. 77–133). Washington, DC: Smithsonian Institution Press.

Gryba, Eugene M. 1988. A Stone Age pressure method of Folsom fluting. *Plains Anthropologist* 33: 53–66.

Hayden, Brian. 1979. Palaeolithic Reflections: Lithic Technology and Ethnographic Excavation Among Australian Aborigines. Atlantic Highlands, NJ: Humanities Press.

———. 1987. Lithic Studies Among the Contemporary Highland Maya. Tucson: University of Arizona Press.

Hayden, Brian, and Aubrey Cannon. 1984. The structure of material systems: Ethnoarchaeology in the Maya highlands. *Society for American Archaeology Papers,* no. 3.

Henry, Donald O., and George H. Odell (Eds.). 1989. Alternative Approaches to Lithic Analysis. *Archaeological Papers of the American Anthropological Association,* no. 1. Washington, DC: American Anthropological Association.

Hill, Andrew. 1979a. Butchery and natural disarticulation: An investigatory technique. *American Antiquity* 44: 739–744.

———. 1979b. Disarticulation and scattering of mammal skeletons. *Paleobiology* 5: 261–274.

Hill, Andrew, and Anna Kay Behrensmeyer. 1984. Disarticulation patterns of some modern East African mammals. *Paleobiology* 10: 366–376.

Hodder, Ian. 1982. *Symbols in Action.* Cambridge: Cambridge University Press.

———. 1987. The meaning of discard: Ash and domestic space in Baringo. In S. Kent (Ed.), *Method and Theory in Activity Area Research* (pp. 424–448). New York: Columbia University Press.

Holly, Gerald A., and Terry A. Del Bene. 1981. An evaluation of Keeley's "Microwear approach." *Journal of Archaeological Science* 8: 337–352.

Keeley, Lawrence H. 1974. Technique and methodology in microwear studies: A critical review. *World Archaeology* 5: 323–336.

———. 1980. *Experimental Determination of Stone Tool Uses: A Microwear Analysis.* Chicago: University of Chicago Press.

Keeley, Lawrence H., and M. H. Newcomer. 1977. Microwear analysis of experimental flint tools: A test case. *Journal of Archaeological Science* 4: 29–62.

Kelly, Robert, Lin Poyer, and Bram Tucker. 2004. Mobility and houses in southwestern Madagascar: Ethnoarchaeology among the Mikea and their neighbors. In F. R. Sellet, R. Greaves, and P. L. Yu (Eds.), *Archaeology and Ethnoarchaeology of Mobility.* Gainesville: University Press of Florida (forthcoming).

Kelly, Robert, Jean-François Rabedimy, and Lin A. Poyer. 1999. The Mikea of southwestern Madagascar. In R. B. Lee and R. Daly (Eds.), *The Cambridge Encyclopedia of Hunter-Gatherers* (pp. 215–219). Cambridge: Cambridge University Press.

Koch, Christopher P. (Ed.). 1989. *Taphonomy: A Bibliographic Guide to the Literature.* Orono, ME: Center for the Study of the First Americans.

Kooyman, B. 2006. Boundary theory as a means of understanding social space in archaeological sites. *Journal of Anthropological Archaeology* 25: 424–435.

Kosso, P. 1991. Method in archaeology: Middle-range theory as hermeneutics. *American Antiquity* 56: 621–627.

Kramer, Carol. 1997. *Pottery in Rajasthan: Ethnoarchaeology in Two Indian Cities.* Washington, DC: Smithsonian Institution Press.

Kroeber, Theodora. 1961. *Ishi in Two Worlds: A Biography of the Last Wild Indian in North America.* Berkeley: University of California Press.

Lehner, Mark. 1997. *The Complete Pyramids: Solving the Ancient Mysteries.* London: Thames and Hudson.

Longacre, William A. (Ed.). 1991. *Ceramic Ethnoarchaeology.* Tucson: University of Arizona Press.

Longacre, William A., and James M. Skibo (Eds.). 1994. *Kalinga Ethnoarchaeology: Expanding Archaeological Method and Theory.* Washington, DC: Smithsonian Institution Press.

Moss, Emily. 1983. The Functional Analysis of Flint Implements—Pincevent and Pont d'Ambon: Two Case Studies from the French Final Palaeolithic. *British Archaeological Reports, International Series,* no. 177.

Nelson, Margaret. 1999. *Mimbres During the Twelfth Century: Abandonment, Continuity, and Reorganization.* Tucson: University of Arizona Press.

Newcomer, M. H., and L. H. Keeley. 1979. Testing a method of microwear analysis with experimental flint tools. In Brian Hayden (Ed.), *Lithic Use-Wear Analysis* (pp. 195–205). New York: Academic Press. (Data for Table 10-1 from this publication's Table 1.)

O'Connell, James F. 1995. Ethnoarchaeology needs a general theory of behavior. *Journal of Archaeological Research* 3: 205–255.

Odell, George Hanley (Ed.). 1996. *Stone Tools: Theoretical Insights into Human Prehistory.* New York: Plenum Press.

Odell, George Hanley, and F. Odell-Vereecken. 1980. Verifying the reliability of lithic use-wear assessments by "blind tests": The low power approach. *Journal of Field Archaeology* 7: 87–120.

Perkins, D., Jr., and P. Daly. 1968. A hunter's village in Neolithic Turkey. *Scientific American* 219(5): 96–106.

Pope, Saxton T. 1974. Hunting with Ishi—The last Yana Indian. *Journal of California Anthropology* 1: 152–173.

Poyer, Lin, and Robert Kelly. 2000. Mystification of the Mikea: Constructions of foraging identity in southwest Madagascar. *Journal of Anthropological Research* 56: 163–185.

Raab, L. Mark, and Albert C. Goodyear. 1984. Middle-range theory in archaeology: A critical review of origins and applications. *American Antiquity* 49: 255–268.

Saitta, Dean J. 1992. Radical archaeology and middle-range methodology. *Antiquity* 66: 886–897.

Scheper-Hughes, Nancy. 2002. Ishi's brain, Ishi's ashes: Anthropolology and genocide. *Anthropology Today* 17(1): 12–18.

———. 2003. Ishi's ashes: Anthropology and genocide. In K. Kroeber (Ed.), *Ishi in Three Centuries* (pp. 99–131). Lincoln: University of Nebraska Press.

Schick, Kathy, and Nicholas Toth. 1993. *Making Silent Stones Speak: Human Evolution and the Dawn of Technology.* New York: Touchstone.

Schiffer, Michael B., James M. Skibo, Tamara C. Boelke, Mark A. Neupert, and Meredith Aronson. 1994. New perspectives on experimental archaeology: Surface treatments and thermal response of the clay cooking pot. *American Antiquity* 59: 197–217.

Semenov, Sergei. 1964. *Prehistoric Technology.* Translated by M. W. Thompson. London: Cory, Adams, and MacKay.

Shea, John J. 1987. On accuracy and relevance in lithic use-wear analysis. *Lithic Technology* 16(2–3): 44–50.

Sheets, Payson D. 1987. Dawn of a new Stone Age in eye surgery. In Robert J. Sharer and Wendy Ashmore (Eds.), *Archaeology: Discovering Our Past* (pp. 230–231). Mountain View, CA: Mayfield Publishing.

Stahl, Ann B. 1995. Has ethnoarchaeology come of age? *Antiquity* 69: 404–407.

Starn, Orin. 2003. *Ishi's Brain: In Search of the Last "Wild" Indian.* San Francisco: W. W. Norton and Company.

Tindale, Norman B. 1985. Australian aboriginal techniques of pressure-flaking stone implements: Some personal observations. In Mark G. Plew, James C. Woods, and Max G. Pavesic (Eds.), *Stone Tool Analysis: Essays in Honor of Don E. Crabtree* (pp. 1–33). Albuquerque: University of New Mexico Press.

Todd, Lawrence C., and David Rapson. 1999. Formational analysis of bison bonebeds and interpretation of Paleoindian subsistence. In J-P. Brugal, F. David, J. G. Enloe, and J. Jaubert (Eds.), *Le Bison: Gibier et Moyen de Subsistance des hommes du Paléolithique aux Paléoindiens des Grandes Plains* (pp. 479–499). Antibes, France: Association pour la promotion et la diffusion des Connaissance Archéologiques.

Trigger, Bruce G. 1981. Archaeology and the ethnographic present. *Anthropologica* 23: 3–17.

———. 1995. Expanding middle-range theory. *Antiquity* 69: 449–458.

Tringham, Ruth, G. Cooper, G. Odell, R. Voiytek, and A. Whitman. 1974. Experimentation in the formation of edge damage: A new approach to lithic analysis. *Journal of Field Archaeology* 1: 171–196.

Tunnell, C. 1977. Fluted projectile point production as revealed by lithic specimens from the Adair-Steadman site in northwest Texas. In Eileen Johnson (Ed.), Paleoindian Lifeways. Lubbock: West Texas Museum Association, Texas Tech University. *The Museum Journal* 17: 140–168.

Vaughan, Patrick C. 1985. *Use-Wear Analysis of Flaked Stone Tools.* Tucson: University of Arizona Press.

Weedman, Kathryn. 2002. On the spur of the moment: Effects of age and experience on hafted stone scraper morphology. *American Antiquity* 67: 731–744.

White, Theodore E. 1953. A method of calculating the dietary percentage of various food animals utilized by aboriginal peoples. *American Antiquity* 18: 396–398.

———. 1954. Observations on the butchering technique of some aboriginal peoples, nos. 3, 4, 5, and 6. *American Antiquity* 19: 254–264.

Whittaker, John C. 1994. *Flintknapping: Making and Understanding Stone Tools.* Austin: University of Texas Press.

Wilshusen, Richard H., and Glenn D. Stone. 1990. An ethnoarchaeological perspective on soils. *World Archaeology* 22: 104–114.

Wylie, Alison. 1985. The reaction against analogy. In M. B. Schiffer (Ed.), *Advances in Archaeological Method and Theory.* Vol. 8 (pp. 63–112). New York: Academic Press.

Yellen, John E. 1976. Settlement patterns of the !Kung: An archaeological perspective. In R. B. Lee and I. DeVore (Eds.), *Kalahari Hunter-Gatherers* (pp. 47–72). Cambridge: Harvard University Press.

———. 1977. *Archaeological Approaches to the Present: Models for Reconstructing the Past.* New York: Academic Press.

Chapter 11

Adams, Karen R., and Robert E. Gasser. 1980. Plant microfossils from archaeological sites: Research considerations and sampling techniques and approaches. *The Kiva* 45: 293–300.

Betancourt, Julio L., Thomas R. Van Devender, and Paul S. Martin (Eds.). 1990. *Packrat Middens: The Last 40,000 Years of Biotic Change.* Tucson: University of Arizona Press.

Billman, B. R., P. M. Lambert, and B. L. Leonard. 2000. Cannibalism, warfare, and drought in the Mesa Verde region during the twelfth century AD. *American Antiquity* 65: 145–178.

Binford, Lewis R. 1978. *Nunamiut Ethnoarchaeology.* New York: Academic Press.

———. 1981. *Bones: Ancient Men and Modern Myths.* New York: Academic Press.

Brewer, Douglas J. 1992. Zooarchaeology: Method, theory, and goals. In M. B. Schiffer (Ed.), *Archaeological Method and Theory.* Vol. 4 (pp. 195–244). Tucson: University of Arizona Press.

Brothwell, D., and A. Pollard (Eds.). 2001. *Handbook of Archaeological Sciences.* Chichester, England: John Wiley and Sons.

Bryant, Vaughn M., Jr., and Stephen A. Hall. 1993. Archaeological palynology in the United States: A critique. *American Antiquity* 58: 277–286.

Bryant, Vaughn M., Jr., and Richard G. Holloway. 1983. The role of palynology in archaeology. In Michael B. Schiffer (Ed.), *Advances in Archaeological Method and Theory.* Vol. 6 (pp. 191–224). New York: Academic Press.

Cannon, Aubrey, and Dongya Y. Yang. 2006. Early storage and sedentism on the Pacific Northwest Coast: Ancient DNA analysis of salmon remains from Namu, British Columbia. *American Antiquity* 71(1): 123–141.

Crabtree, Pam J. 1990. Zooarchaeology and complex societies: Some uses of faunal analysis for the study of trade, social status, and ethnicity. In M. B. Schiffer (Ed.), *Archaeological Method and Theory.* Vol. 2 (pp. 155–205). Tucson: University of Arizona Press.

Cummings, Linda Scott. 2001. Phytolith analysis. In R. L. Kelly (Ed.), Prehistory of the Carson Desert and Stillwater Mountains: Environment, Mobility, and Subsistence in a Great Basin Wetland (pp. 251–252). *University of Utah Anthropological Papers* 123. Salt Lake City.

Dincauze, Dena. 2000. *Environmental Archaeology: Principles and Practice.* Cambridge: Cambridge University Press.

Dongoske, K. E., D. L. Martin, and T. J. Ferguson. 1999. Critique of the claim of cannibalism at Cowboy Wash. *American Antiquity* 65: 179–190.

Evershed, R. P., S. N. Dudd, M. J. Collins, O. E. Craig, and R. J. Sokal. 2001. Lipids in archaeology. In D. Brothwell and A. Pollard (Eds.), *Handbook of Archaeological Sciences* (pp. 331–350). Chichester, England: John Wiley and Sons.

Faegri, K., P. E. Kaland, and K. Krzywinski. 1989. *Textbook of Pollen Analysis.* 4th ed. New York: Wiley.

Frison, George C., and Dennis Stanford. 1982. *The Agate Basin Site: A Record of the Paleoindian Occupation of the Northwestern High Plains.* New York: Academic Press.

Gilbert, B. Miles. 1980. *Mammalian Osteology.* Laramie, WY: Modern Printing.

Gilbert, Robert I., Jr., and James H. Mielke (Eds.). 1985. *The Analysis of Prehistoric Diets.* Orlando, FL: Academic Press.

Grayson, Donald K. 1984. *Quantitative Zooarchaeology: Topics in the Analysis of Archaeological Faunas.* Orlando, FL: Academic Press.

Harper, K. T., and G. M. Alder. 1970. Appendix I: The macroscopic plant remains of the deposits of Hogup Cave, Utah, and their paleoclimatic implications. In C. Melvin Aikens, Hogup Cave. *University of Utah Anthropological Papers* 93: 215–240.

Hastorf, Christine A., and Sissel Johannessen. 1991. Understanding changing people/plant relationships in the prehispanic Andes. In Robert W. Preucel (Ed.), Processual and Postprocessual Archaeologies: Multiple Ways of Knowing the Past (pp. 140–155). *Center for Archaeological Investigations, Occasional Paper, no.* 10. Southern Illinois University at Carbondale

Hastorf, Christine A., and Virginia S. Popper (Eds.). 1988. *Current Paleoethnobotany: Analytical Methods and Cultural Interpretations of Archaeological Plant Remains.* Chicago: University of Chicago Press.

Hather, Jon G. (Ed.). 1994. *Tropical Archaeobotany: Applications and New Developments.* London: Routledge.

Haury, Emil W., E. B. Sayles, and William W. Wasley. 1959. The Lehner mammoth site, southeastern Arizona. *American Antiquity* 25: 2–30.

Hill, Matthew G. 2001. *Paleoindian Diet and Subsistence Behavior on the Northwestern Great Plains of North America.* PhD dissertation, University of Wisconsin, Madison. (Table 11-1 is from p. 55.)

———. 2005. *Paleoindian Diet and Subsistence Behavior on the Northwestern Great Plains.* Boulder: University Press of Colorado.

Holden, T. G. 2001. Dietary evidence from the coprolites and the intestinal contents of ancient humans. In D. Brothwell and A. Pollard (Eds.), *Handbook of Archaeological Sciences* (pp. 403–414). Chichester, England: John Wiley and Sons.

Kantner, J. 1999a. Anasazi mutilation and cannibalism in the American southwest. In L. R. Goldman (Ed.), *The Anthropology of Cannibalism* (pp. 75–104). Westport: Bergin and Garvey.

———. 1999b. Survival cannibalism or sociopolitical intimidation? Explaining perimortem mutilation in the American southwest. *Human Nature* 10: 1–50.

Kuckelman, K. A., R. R. Lightfoot, and D. L. Martin. 2002. The bioarchaeology and taphonomy of violence at Castle Rock and Sand Creek Pueblos, southwestern Colorado. *American Antiquity* 67: 486–511.

Lambert, P. M., B. L. Leonard, B. R. Billman, R. A. Marlar, M. E. Newman, and K. J. Reinhard. 2000.

Response to critique of the claim of cannibalism at Cowboy Wash. *American Antiquity* 65: 397–403.

Leroi-Gourhan, Arlette. 1975. The flowers found with Shanidar IV, a Neanderthal burial in Iraq. *Science* 190: 562–564.

Lyman, R. Lee. 1994. *Vertebrate Taphonomy.* Cambridge: Cambridge University Press.

Malainey, Mary E., R. Przybylski, and B. L. Sherriff. 1999a. Identifying the former contents of late pre-contact period pottery vessels from western Canada using gas chromatography. *Journal of Archaeological Science* 26: 425–438.

———. 1999b. The fatty acid composition of native food plants and animals of western Canada. *Journal of Archaeological Science* 26: 83–94.

———. 1999c. The effects of thermal and oxidative decomposition on the fatty acids composition of food plants and animals of western Canada: Implications for the identification of archaeological vessel residues. *Journal of Archaeological Science* 26: 95–103.

Marlar, R. A., B. L. Leonard, B. R. Billman, P. M. Lambert, and J. E. Marlar. 2000, September. Biochemical evidence of cannibalism at a prehistoric site in southwestern Colorado. *Nature* 7: 74–78.

Mehringer, Peter J., and Vance Haynes. 1965. The pollen evidence for the environment of early man and extinct mammals at the Lehner mammoth site, southeastern Arizona. *American Antiquity* 31: 17–23.

Miksicek, Charles H. 1987. Formation processes of the archaeobotanical record. In Michael B. Schiffer (Ed.), *Advances in Archaeological Method and Theory.* Vol. 10 (pp. 211–247). New York: Academic Press.

Miller, George. 1979. *An Introduction to the Ethnoarchaeology of the Andean Camelids.* PhD diss., University of California, Berkeley.

Miller, George, and Richard Burger. 1995. Our father the cayman, our dinner the llama: Animal utilization at Chavín de Huántar, Peru. *American Antiquity* 60: 421–458.

———. 2000. Ch'arki at Chavín: Ethnographic models and archaeological data. *American Antiquity* 65: 573–576.

Minnis, Paul E. 1981. Seeds in archaeological sites: Sources and some interpretive problems. *American Antiquity* 46: 143–152.

Monks, Gregory G. 1981. Seasonality studies. In Michael B. Schiffer (Ed.), *Advances in Archaeologi-*

cal Method and Theory. Vol. 4 (pp. 177–240). New York: Academic Press.

Moore, P. D., J. A. Webb, and M. E. Collinson. 1991. *Pollen Analysis.* Oxford: Blackwell Scientific.

Olsen, Stanley J. 1960. Post-cranial skeletal characters of Bison and Bos. *Papers of the Peabody Museum of American Archaeology and Ethnology* 35(4).

———. 1964. Mammal remains from archaeological sites, part 1: Southeastern and southwestern United States. *Papers of the Peabody Museum of American Archaeology and Ethnology* 61(1).

———. 1968. Fish, amphibian, and reptile remains from archaeological sites, part 1: Southeastern and southwestern United States. *Papers of the Peabody Museum of American Archaeology and Ethnology* 61(2).

———. 1973. Mammal remains from archaeological sites, part 1: Southeastern and southwestern United States. *Papers of the Peabody Museum of Archaeology and Ethnology* 56(1).

Pearsall, Deborah M. 2000. *Paleoethnobotany: A Handbook of Procedures.* New York: Academic Press.

Piperno, Dolores R. 1987. *Phytolith Analysis: An Archaeological and Geological Perspective.* San Diego: Academic Press.

Rapp, George, and Susan C. Mulholland (Eds.). 1992. *Phytolith Systematics: Emerging Issues.* New York: Plenum Press.

Reitz, Elizabeth J., and C. Margaret Scarry. 1985. Reconstructing historic subsistence with an example from sixteenth-century Spanish Florida. *Society of Historical Archaeology, Special Publication Series,* no. 3.

Reitz, Elizabeth, and Elizabeth Wing. 1999. *Zooarchaeology.* Cambridge: Cambridge University Press.

Rhode, David. 2001. Macrobotanical remains. In R. L. Kelly (Ed.), Prehistory of the Carson Desert and Stillwater Mountains: Environment, Mobility, and Subsistence in a Great Basin Wetland (pp. 254–262). *University of Utah Anthropological Papers* 123. Salt Lake City.

———. 2004. Coprolites from Hidden Cave, revisited: Evidence for occupation history, diet, and gender. *Journal of Archaeological Science* 30: 909–922.

Rovner, Irwin. 1983. Plant opal phytolith analysis: Major advances in archaeobotanical research. In Michael B. Schiffer (Ed.), *Advances in Archaeological Method and Theory.* Vol. 6 (pp. 225–266). New York: Academic Press.

Smith, P., and M. Wilson. 2001. Blood residues in archaeology. In D. Brothwell and A. Pollard (Eds.), *Handbook of Archaeological Sciences* (pp. 313–322). Chichester, England: John Wiley and Sons.

Sobolik, Kristin. 2003. *The Archaeologist's Toolkit*, vol. 5, *Archaeobiology.* Walnut Creek, CA: AltaMira Press.

Solecki, Ralph S. 1971. *Shanidar: The First Flower People.* New York: Knopf.

Sommer, Jeffrey. 1999. The Shanidar IV "Flower Burial": A Reevaluation of Neanderthal Burial Ritual. *Cambridge Archaeological Journal* 9: 127–137.

Speller, C. F., D. Y. Yang, and B. Hayden. 2005. Ancient DNA investigations of prehistoric salmon resource utilization at Keatley Creek, British Columbia, Canada. *Journal of Archaeological Science* 32: 1378–1389.

Stahl, Peter. 1999. Structural density of domesticated South American camelid skeletal elements and the archaeological investigation of prehistoric Andean ch'arki. *Journal of Archaeological Science* 26: 1347–1368.

Sutton, Mark Q., Minnie Malik, and Andrew Ogram. 1996. Experiments on the determination of gender from coprolites by DNA analysis. *Journal of Archaeological Science* 23: 263–267.

Turner, C. G., II, and J. A. Turner. 1999. *Man Corn: Cannibalism and Violence in the Prehistoric American Southwest.* Salt Lake City: University of Utah Press.

Valdez, Lidio. 2000. Ch'arki consumption in the ancient central Andes: A cautionary note. *American Antiquity* 65: 567–572.

White, T. D. 1992. *Prehistoric Cannibalism at Mancos 5MTUMR-2346.* Princeton: Princeton University Press.

Wigand, Peter. 2001. Pollen. In R. L. Kelly (Ed.), *Prehistory of the Carson Desert and Stillwater Mountains: Environment, Mobility, and Subsistence in a Great Basin Wetland* (pp. 252–254). *University of Utah Anthropological Papers* 123. Salt Lake City.

Wigand, Peter, and Cheryl Nowak. 1992. Dynamics of northwest Nevada plant communities during the last 30,000 years. In C. A. Hall, V. Doyle-Jones, and B. Widawski (Eds.), *The History of Water: Eastern Sierra Nevada, Owens Valley, White-Inyo Mountains* (pp. 40–62). White Mountain Research Station Symposium 4.

Yang, D. Y., J. R. Woiderski, and J. C. Driver. 2005. DNA analysis of archaeological rabbit remains from the American Southwest. *Journal of Archaeological Science* 32: 567–578.

Yang, Dongya Y., and Kathy Watt. 2005. Contamination controls when preparing archaeological remains for ancient DNA analysis. *Journal of Archaeological Science* 32(3): 331–336.

Chapter 12

Benditt, J. 1989. Molecular archaeology: DNA from a 7,000-year-old brain opens new vistas in prehistory. *Scientific American* 261: 25–26.

Brooks, Sheilagh, Michele Haldeman, and Richard Brooks. 1988. *Osteological Analyses of the Stillwater Skeletal Series, Stillwater Marsh, Churchill County, Nevada.* U.S. Fish and Wildlife Service Cultural Resource Series Number 2.

Brown, Terence A., and Keri A. Brown. 1992. Ancient DNA and the archaeologist. *Antiquity* 66: 10–23.

Buikstra, Jane E., and Della C. Cook. 1980. Paleopathology: An American account. *Annual Review of Anthropology* 9: 433–470.

Buikstra, Jane E., and L. Konigsberg. 1985. Paleodemography: Critiques and controversies. *American Anthropologist* 87: 316–333.

Cann, Rebecca, Mark Stoneking, and Alan C. Wilson. 1987. Mitochrondrial DNA and human evolution. *Nature* 325: 31–36.

DeNiro, Michael J. 1987. Stable isotopy and archeology. *American Scientist* 75: 182–191.

DeNiro, Michael J., and S. Epstein. 1981. Influence of diet on the distribution of nitrogen isotopes in animals. *Geochimica de Cosmochimica Acta* 45: 341–351.

Dillehay, Tom D. 1989. *Monte Verde: A Late Pleistocene Settlement in Chile, Vol. 1, Paleoenvironment and Site Context.* Washington, DC: Smithsonian Institution Press.

———. 1997. *Monte Verde: A Late Pleistocene Settlement in Chile, Vol. 2, The Archaeological Context and Interpretation.* Washington, DC: Smithsonian Institution Press.

Doran, Glen H., David N. Dickel, William E. Ballinger, Jr., O. Frank Agee, Philip J. Laipis, and William W. Hauswirth. 1986. Anatomical, cellular and molecular analysis of 8,000-yr-old human brain tissue from the Windover archaeological site. *Nature* 323: 803–806.

Eshleman, Jason A., Ripan S. Mahli, and David Glenn Smith. 2003. Mitochondrial DNA studies of Native

Americans: Conceptions and misconceptions of the population prehistory of the Americas. *Evolutionary Anthropology* 12: 7–18.

Ezzo, Joseph A., Clark Spencer Larsen, and James H. Burton. 1995. Elemental signatures of human diets from the Georgia Bight. *American Journal of Physical Anthropology* 98: 471–481.

Gill-Robinson, H., J. Elias, F. Bender, T. Allard, and R. Hoppa. 2006. Using imaging analysis software to create a physical skull model for the facial reconstruction of a wrapped Akhmimic mummy. *Journal of Computing and Information Technology—CIT* 14(1): 45–51.

Goodman, Alan, and George Armelagos. 1988. Infant and childhood morbidity and mortality risks in archaeological populations. *World Archaeology* 21: 225–243.

Herrmann, Bernd, and Susanne Hummell (Eds.). 1994. *Ancient DNA: Recovery and Analysis of Genetic Material from Paleontological, Archaeological, Museum, Medical, and Forensic Specimens.* New York: Springer-Verlag.

Horai, Satoshi, Rumi Kondo, Yuko Nakagawa-Hattori, Seiji Hayashi, Shunro Sonoda, and Kazuo Tajima. 1993. Peopling of the Americas, founded by four major lineages of mitochondrial DNA. *Molecular Biological Evolution* 10(1): 23–47.

Huss-Ashmore, Rebecca, Alan H. Goodman, and George J. Armelagos. 1982. Nutritional inference from paleopathology. In Michael B. Schiffer (Ed.), *Advances in Archaeological Method and Theory.* Vol. 5 (pp. 395–474). New York: Academic Press.

Hutchinson, Dale, and Clark Spencer Larsen. 1988. Determination of stress episode duration from linear enamel hypoplasias: A case study from St. Catherines Island, Georgia. *Human Biology* 60: 93–110.

———. 1995. Physiological stress in the prehistoric Stillwater Marsh: Evidence of enamel defects. In C. S. Larsen and R. L. Kelly (Eds.), Bioarchaeology of the Stillwater Marsh: Prehistoric Human Adaptation in the Western Great Basin (pp. 81–95). *Anthropological Papers of the American Museum of Natural History,* Number 77. New York.

Katzenberg, M. Anne, Henry P. Schwarcz, Martin Knyf, and F. Jerome Melbye. 1995. Stable isotope evidence for maize horticulture and paleodiet in southern Ontario, Canada. *American Antiquity* 60: 335–350.

Kelly, Robert. 2003. Maybe we do know when people came to North America; and what does it mean if we do? *Quaternary International* 109–110: 133–145.

Konigsberg, Lyle W., and Jane E. Buikstra. 1995. Regional approaches to the investigation of past human biocultural structure. In Lane Anderson Beck (Ed.), *Regional Approaches to Mortuary Analysis* (pp. 191–219). New York: Plenum Press.

Larsen, Clark Spencer. 1987. Bioarchaeological interpretations of subsistence economy and behavior from human skeletal remains. In Michael B. Schiffer (Ed.), *Advances in Archaeological Method and Theory.* Vol. 10 (pp. 339–445). Orlando, FL: Academic Press.

———. 1995. Biological changes in human populations with agriculture. *Annual Review of Anthropology* 24: 185–213.

Larsen, Clark Spencer, and Robert L. Kelly (Eds.). 1995. Bioarchaeology of the Stillwater Marsh: Prehistoric human adaptation in the Western Great Basin. *Anthropological Papers of the American Museum of Natural History,* Number 77.

Larsen, Clark Spencer, Christopher B. Ruff, and Robert L. Kelly. 1995. Structural analysis of the Stillwater postcranial human remains: Behavioral implications of articular joint pathology and long bone diaphyseal morphology. In C. S. Larsen and R. L. Kelly (Eds.), Bioarchaeology of the Stillwater Marsh: Prehistoric Human Adaptation in the Western Great Basin (pp. 107–133). *Anthropological Papers of the American Museum of Natural History,* Number 77. New York.

Martin, Debra L., Alan H. Goodman, and George J. Armelagos. 1985. Skeletal pathologies as indicators of quality and quantity of diet. In Robert I. Gilbert and James H. Mielke (Eds.), *The Analysis of Prehistoric Diets* (pp. 227–279). Orlando: Academic Press.

Meltzer, David J. 1989. Why don't we know when the first people came to North America? *American Antiquity* 54(3): 471–490.

———. 1995. Clocking the First Americans. *Annual Review of Anthropology* 24: 21–45.

Nei, Masatoshi. 1992. Age of the common ancestor of human mitochondrial DNA. *Molecular Biology and Evolution* 9(6): 1176–1178.

Ortner, Donald J., and Walter G. J. Putschar. 1985. *Identification of Pathological Conditions in Human*

Skeletal Remains. Washington, DC: Smithsonian Institution Press.

Pääbo, Svante. 1993, November. Ancient DNA: Genetic information that had seemed lost forever turns out to linger in the remains of long-dead plants and animals. *Scientific American,* pp. 87–92.

Pfeiffer, S., and R. F. Williamson. 1991. *Snake Hill: An Investigation of a Military Cemetery from the War of 1812.* Toronto: Dundurn Press.

Powell, J., and W. A. Neves. 1999. Craniofacial morphology of the first Americans: Pattern and process in the peopling of the new world. *Yearbook of Physical Anthropology* 42: 153–188.

Powell, Mary Lucas. 1985. The analysis of dental wear and caries for dietary reconstructions. In R. I. Gilbert, Jr., and J. H. Mielke (Eds.), *The Analysis of Prehistoric Diets* (pp. 307–338). Orlando: Academic Press.

Price, T. Douglas (Ed.). 1989. *The Chemistry of Prehistoric Human Bone.* Cambridge: Cambridge University Press.

Rogers, Juliet, and Tony Waldron. 1989. Infections in paleopathology: The basis of classification according to most probable cause. *Journal of Archaeological Science* 16: 611–625.

Rothschild, Bruce M., and Larry D. Martin. 1993. *Palaeopathology: Disease in the Fossil Record.* Boca Raton, FL: CRC Press.

Sahlins, Marshall. 1968. Notes on the original affluent society. In Richard Lee and Irven DeVore (Eds.), *Man the Hunter* (pp. 85–89). Chicago: Aldine.

Schoeninger, Margaret. 1995. Dietary reconstruction in the prehistoric Carson Desert: Stable carbon and nitrogen isotopic analysis. In C. S. Larsen and R. L. Kelly (Eds.), Bioarchaeology of the Stillwater Marsh: Prehistoric Human Adaptation in the Western Great Basin (pp. 96–106). *Anthropological Papers of the American Museum of Natural History,* Number 77. New York.

Seielstad, Mark, Nadira Yuldasheva, Nadia Singh, Peter Underhill, Peter Oefner, Peidong Shen, and R. Spencer Wells. 2003. A novel Y-chromosome variant puts an upper limit on the timing of first entry into the Americas. *American Journal of Human Genetics* 73: 700–705.

Stone, Anne C., and Mark Stoneking. 1993. Ancient DNA from a Pre-Columbian Amerindian population. *American Journal of Physical Anthropology* 92: 463–471.

Stoneking, Mark. 1994. In defense of "Eve": A response to Templeton's critique. *American Anthropologist* 96(1): 131–141.

Szathmary, Emöke J. E. 1993. Genetics of aboriginal North Americans. *Evolutionary Anthropology* 1(6): 202–220.

Templeton, Alan R. 1993. The "Eve" hypotheses: A genetic critique and reanalysis. *American Anthropologist* 95: 51–72.

———. 1994. "Eve": Hypothesis compatibility versus hypothesis testing. *American Anthropologist* 96: 141–147.

Torroni, Antonio, Theodore G. Schurr, Chi-Chuan Yang, Emöke J. E. Szathmary, Robert C. Williams, Moses S. Schanfield, Gary A. Troup, William C. Knowler, Dale N. Lawrence, Kenneth M. Weiss, and Douglas C. Wallace. 1991. Native American mitochondrial DNA analysis indicates that the Amerind and the Nadene populations were founded by two independent migrations. *Genetics* 130: 153–162.

Turner, Christy G., II. 1979. Dental anthropological indications of agriculture among the Jomon people of central Japan, pt. 10: Peopling of the Pacific. *American Journal of Physical Anthropology* 51: 619–636.

Verano, John W., and Douglas H. Ubelaker (Eds.). 1992. *Disease and Demography in the Americas.* Washington, DC: Smithsonian Institution Press.

Walker, Phillip L. 1986. Porotic hyperostosis in a marine-dependent California Indian population. *American Journal of Physical Anthropology* 69: 345–354.

Whitehorn, J. 1991. Fort Erie and U.S. operations on the Niagara Frontier, 1884. In S. Pfeiffer and R. F. Williamson (Eds.), *Snake Hill: An Investigation of a Military Cemetery from the War of 1812* (pp. 25–61). Toronto: Dundurn Press.

Williamson, R. (1991). Introduction. In S. Pfeiffer and R. F. Williamson (Eds.), *Snake Hill: An Investigation of a Military Cemetery from the War of 1812* (pp. 21–25). Toronto: Dundurn Press.

Williamson, R., and Susan Pfeiffer. 1991. Conclusions. In S. Pfeiffer and R. F. Williamson (Eds.), *Snake Hill: An Investigation of a Military Cemetery from the War of 1812* (pp. 295–303). Toronto: Dundurn Press.

Chapter 13

Alkire, William. 1977. *An Introduction to the Peoples and Cultures of Micronesia.* 2nd ed. Menlo Park, CA: Cummings.

Bacus, Elisabeth A., Alex W. Barker, Jeffrey D. Bonevich, Sandra L. Dunavan, J. Benjamin Fitzhugh, Debra L. Gold, Nurit S. Goldman-Finn, William Griffin, and Karen M. Mudar (Eds.). 1993. *A Gendered Past: A Critical Bibliography of Gender in Archaeology.* Technical Report 25. Ann Arbor: University of Michigan, Museum of Anthropology.

Bailey, Robert C., and Robert Aunger. 1989. Hunters vs. archers: Variation in women's subsistence strategies in the Ituri Forest. *Human Ecology* 17: 273–297.

Beck, Lane Anderson (Ed.). 1995. *Regional Approaches to Mortuary Analysis.* New York: Plenum Press.

Chapdelaine, Claude, Jean-Francois Millaire, and Greg Kennedy. 2001. Compositional analysis and provenance study of spindle whorls from the Moche site, North Coast of Peru. *Journal of Archaeological Science* 28: 795–806.

Claassen, Cheryl (Ed.). 1992. Exploring gender through archaeology: Selected papers from the 1991 Boone Conference. *Monographs in World Archaeology,* no. 11. Madison, WI: Prehistory Press.

Cobb, Charles R. 1993. Archaeological approaches to the political economy of nonstratified societies. In M. B. Schiffer (Ed.), *Archaeological Method and Theory.* Vol. 5 (pp. 43–100). Tucson: University of Arizona Press.

Conkey, Margaret W., and Janet Spector. 1984. Archaeology and the study of gender. In Michael B. Schiffer (Ed.), *Advances in Archaeological Method and Theory.* Vol. 7 (pp. 1–38). Orlando, FL: Academic Press.

Costin, Cathy Lynne, and Timothy Earle. 1989. Status distinction and legitimation of power as reflected in changing patterns of consumption in late prehispanic Peru. *American Antiquity* 54: 691–714.

Dawson, Peter, and A. Kate Peach. 2004. Redefining the northern limits of the Devils Lake–Sourisford burial complex: New evidence from the Pas, Manitoba. *Manitoba Archaeology Journal* 12(21): 55–71.

DeNiro, Michael J., and Margaret J. Schoeniger. 1983. Stable carbon and nitrogen isotope ratios of bone collagen: Variations within individuals, between sexes, and within populations raised on monotonous diets. *Journal of Archaeological Science* 10: 199–203.

Descantes, Christophe, Hector Neff, Michael D. Glascock, and William R. Dickinson. 2001. Chemical characterization of Micronesian ceramics through instrumental neutron activation analysis: A preliminary provenance study. *Journal of Archaeological Science* 28: 1185–1190.

Dickinson, W. R., and R. Shutler, Jr. 2000. Implications of petrographic temper analysis for Oceanic prehistory. *Journal of World Prehistory* 14: 203–266.

Ember, Melvin. 1973. An archaeological indicator of matrilocal versus patrilocal residence. *American Antiquity* 38: 177–182.

Ember, Melvin, and Carol Ember. 1995. Worldwide cross-cultural studies and their relevance for archaeology. *Journal of Archaeological Research* 30: 69–94.

Enloe, James. 2003. Food sharing past and present: Archaeological evidence for economic and social interactions. *Before Farming* 1: 1–23.

Enloe, James, and Francine David. 1992. Food sharing in the Paleolithic: Carcass refitting at Pincevent. In J. L. Hofman and J. G. Enloe (Eds.), *Piecing Together the Past: Applications of Refitting Studies in Archaeology* (pp. 296–315). British Archaeological Reports International Series 578. Oxford.

Fitzpatrick, Scott M., William R. Dickinson, and Geoffrey Clark. 2003. Ceramic petrography and cultural interaction in Palau, Micronesia. *Journal of Archaeological Science* 30: 1175–1184.

Galloway, Patricia (Ed.). 1989. *The Southeastern Ceremonial Complex: Artifacts and Analysis.* Lincoln: University of Nebraska Press.

Gargett, R., and B. Hayden. 1991. Site structure, kinship, and sharing in Aboriginal Australia: Implications for archaeology. In E. M. Kroll and T. D. Price (Eds.), *The Interpretation of Archaeological Spatial Patterning* (pp. 11–32). New York: Plenum Press.

Gero, Joan M. 1985. Socio-politics and the woman-at-home ideology. *American Antiquity* 50: 342–350.

———. 1991. Genderlithics: Women's roles in stone tool production. In Joan M. Gero and Margaret W. Conkey (Eds.), *Engendering Archaeology: Women and Prehistory* (pp. 163–193). Oxford: Basil Blackwell.

Gero, Joan M., and Margaret W. Conkey (Eds.). 1991. *Engendering Archaeology: Women and Prehistory.* Oxford: Basil Blackwell.

Gibson, Alex M., and Ann Woods. 1990. *Prehistoric Pottery for the Archaeologist.* Leicester, England: Leicester University Press.

Goodenough, Ward H. 1965. Rethinking "status" and "role": Toward a general model of the cultural organization of social relationships. In Michael Banton (Ed.), *The Relevance of Models for Social Anthropology* (pp. 1–24). *Association for Social Anthropology Monographs,* no. 1. New York: Praeger.

Griffin, James B., A. A. Gordus, and G. A. Wright. 1969. Identification of the sources of Hopewellian obsidian in the Middle West. *American Antiquity* 34: 1–14.

Hastorf, Christine. 1991. Gender, space and food in prehistory. In Joan Gero and Margaret Conkey (Eds.), *Engendering Archeology: Women and Prehistory* (pp. 132–158). Oxford: Basil Blackwell.

Hatch, James W., Joseph W. Michels, Christopher M. Stevenson, Barry E. Scheeta, and Richard A. Geidel. 1988. Hopewell obsidian studies: Behavioral implications of recent sourcing and dating research. *American Antiquity* 55: 461–479.

Houston, S. D., and P. A. McAnany. 2003. Bodies and blood: Critiquing social construction in Maya archaeology. *Journal of Anthropological Archaeology* 22: 26–41.

Hughes, Richard E. 2005. The sources of Hopewell obsidian: Thirty years after Griffin. In Douglas K. Charles and Jane E. Buikstra (Eds.), *Recreating Hopewell.* Gainesville: University Press of Florida (forthcoming).

Jackson, Ed, and Susan Scott. 2003. Patterns of elite faunal utilization at Moundville, Alabama. *American Antiquity* 69: 552–572.

Jamieson, Susan. 1992. Regional interaction and Ontario Iroquois evolution. *Canadian Journal of Archaeology* 16: 70–81.

———. 1994. Comment on Williamson and Robertson's "Peer politics beyond the periphery: Early and Middle Iroquoian regional interaction." *Ontario Archaeology* 58: 45–46.

Joyce, Rosemary. 1995. The construction of gender in Classic Maya monuments. In Rita Wright (Ed.), *Gender and Archaeology* (pp. 167–195). Philadelphia: University of Pennsylvania Press.

Knight, Vernon, J., Jr. 1998. Moundville as a diagrammatic ceremonial center. In V. J. Knight, Jr., and V. Steponaitis (Eds.), *Archaeology of the Moundville Chiefdom* (pp. 44–62). Washington, DC: Smithsonian Institution Press.

Knight, Vernon, J., Jr., and Vincas Steponaitis. 1998. *Archaeology of the Moundville Chiefdom.* Washington, DC: Smithsonian Institution Press.

Mills, Barbara. 1999. Recent research on Chaco: Changing views on economy, ritual, and society. *Journal of Archaeological Research* 10: 65–117.

Nelson, Sarah M. 1995. *Gender in Archaeology: Analyzing Power and Prestige.* Walnut Creek, CA: AltaMira Press.

Orton, Clive, Paul Tyers, and Alan Vince. 1993. *Pottery in Archaeology.* Cambridge: Cambridge University Press.

O'Shea, John M. 1984. *Mortuary Variability: An Archaeological Investigation.* Orlando: Academic Press.

Parker Pearson, Michael. 1982. Mortuary practices, society and ideology: An ethnoarchaeological study. In Ian Hodder (Ed.), *Symbolic and Structural Archaeology* (pp. 99–113). Cambridge: Cambridge University Press.

———. 1995. Return of the living dead: Mortuary analysis and the new archaeology revisited. *Antiquity* 69: 1046–1048.

Peebles, Christopher S. 1971. Moundville and surrounding sites: Some structural considerations of mortuary practices II. In James A. Brown (Ed.), Approaches to the Social Dimensions of Mortuary Practices. *Society for American Archaeology Memoir* 25: 68–91.

———. 1977. Biocultural adaptation in prehistoric America: An archeologist's perspective. In Robert L. Blakely (Ed.), Biocultural Adaptation in Prehistoric America (pp. 115–130). *Southern Anthropological Society Proceedings,* no. 11. Athens: University of Georgia Press.

———. 1981. Archaeological research at Moundville: 1840–1980. *Southeastern Archaeological Conference Bulletin* 24: 77–81.

———. 1987. Moundville from 1000 to 1500 AD as seen from 1840 to 1985 AD. In Robert D. Drennan and Carlos A. Uribe (Eds.), *Chiefdoms in the Americas* (pp. 21–41). Lanham, MD: University Press of America.

Peebles, Christopher S., and Susan M. Kus. 1977. Some archaeological correlates of ranked societies. *American Antiquity* 42: 421–448.

Peregrine, Peter. 2000. Matrilocality, corporate strategy, and the organization of production in the Chacoan world. *American Antiquity* 66: 36–46.

Powell, Mary L. 1988. *Status and Health in Prehistory: A Case Study of the Moundville Chiefdom.* Washington, DC: Smithsonian Institution Press.

———. 1991. Rank, status and health in the Mississippian chiefdom at Moundville. In Mary L. Powell, Patricia S. Bridges, and Ann Marie Wagner Mires (Eds.), *What Mean These Bones? Studies in Southeastern Bioarchaeology* (pp. 22–51). Tuscaloosa: University of Alabama Press.

Price, T. Douglas, and Gary M. Feinman (Eds.). 1995. *Foundations of Social Inequality.* New York: Plenum Press.

Renfrew, Colin, and Stephen Shennan (Eds.). 1982. *Ranking, Resource and Exchange.* Cambridge: Cambridge University Press.

Rice, Prudence M. 1987. *Pottery Analysis: A Sourcebook.* Chicago: University of Chicago Press.

———. 1991. Women and prehistoric pottery production. In D. Walde and N. Willows (Eds.), *The Archaeology of Gender* (pp. 436–443). Calgary: Archaeological Association of the University of Calgary.

———. 1996a. Recent ceramic analysis: 1. Function, style, and origins. *Journal of Archaeological Research* 4: 133–163.

———. 1996b. Recent ceramic analysis: 2. Composition, production, and theory. *Journal of Archaeological Research* 4: 165–202.

Schillaci, Michael, and Christopher Stojanowski. 2000. Postmarital residence and population structure at Pueblo Bonito. *American Journal of Physical Anthropology* supplement 30: 271.

———. 2002. A reassessment of matrilocality in Chacoan culture. *American Antiquity* 67: 343–356.

Schoeninger, Margaret J., and Christopher Peebles. 1981. Notes on the relationship between social status and diet at Moundville. *Southeastern Archaeological Conference Bulletin* 24: 96–97.

Schoeninger, Margaret J., and Mark Schurr. 1999. Human subsistence at Moundville: The stable isotope data. In V. J. Knight, Jr., and V. Steponaitis (Eds.), *Archaeology of the Moundville Chiefdom* (pp. 120–132). Washington, DC: Smithsonian Institution Press.

Sinopoli, Carla. 1991. *Approaches to Archaeological Ceramics.* New York: Plenum Press.

Smith, Bruce D. (Ed.). 1990. *The Mississippian Emergence.* Washington, DC: Smithsonian Institution Press.

Steponaitis, Vincas P. 1983. *Ceramics, Chronology, and Community Patterns: An Archaeological Study at Moundville.* New York: Academic Press.

Syms, L. 1979. The Devils Lake–Sourisford burial complex on the Northeastern Plains. *Plains Anthropologist* 24(86): 283–308.

Waring, A. J., Jr., and Preston Holder. 1945. A prehistoric ceremonial complex in the southeastern United States. *American Anthropologist* 47: 1–34.

Wason, Paul K. 1994. *The Archaeology of Rank.* Cambridge: Cambridge University Press.

Webb, William S. 1974 [1946]. *Indian Knoll.* Knoxville: University of Tennessee Press (quote from p. 330).

Welch, Paul D., and C. Margaret Scarry. 1995. Status-related variation in foodways in the Moundville chiefdom. *American Antiquity* 60: 397–419.

Williamson, Ron F., and David Robertson. 1994. Peer politics beyond the periphery: Early and Middle Iroquoian regional interaction. *Ontario Archaeology* 58: 27–44.

Wright, Rita (Ed). 1996. *Gender and Archaeology.* Philadelphia: University of Pennsylvania Press.

Wylie, Alison. 1992. The interplay of evidential constraints and political interests: Recent archaeological research on gender. *American Antiquity* 57: 15–35.

Chapter 14

Anyon, Roger, T. J. Ferguson, Loretta Jackson, Lillie Lane, and Philip Vicenti. 1997. Native American oral tradition and archaeology: Issues of structure, relevance, and respect. In Nina Swidler, Kurt E. Dongoske, Roger Anyon, and Alan S. Downer (Eds.), *Native Americans and Archaeologists: Stepping Stones to Common Ground* (pp. 77–87). Walnut Grove, CA: AltaMira.

Bahn, Paul. 1998. *The Cambridge Illustrated History of Prehistoric Art.* Cambridge: University of Cambridge Press.

Bender, Barbara. 1993. Cognitive archaeology and cultural materialism. *Cambridge Archaeological Journal* 3: 257–260.

Burger, Richard L. 1992. *Chavín and the Origins of Andean Civilization.* London: Thames and Hudson.

Conrad, Geoffrey W. 1981. Cultural materialism, split inheritance, and the expansion of ancient Peruvian empires. *American Antiquity* 46: 3–26.

Conrad, Geoffrey W., and Arthur A. Demarest. 1984. *Religion and Empire: The Dynamics of Aztec and Inca Expansionism.* Cambridge: Cambridge University Press.

D'Altroy, Terence N. 1992. *Provincial Power in the Inka Empire.* Washington, DC: Smithsonian Institution Press.

D'Andrade, Roy G. 1995. *The Development of Cognitive Anthropology.* Cambridge: Cambridge University Press.

Dawson, Peter. 2001. Interpreting variability in Thule Inuit architecture: A case study from the Canadian High Arctic. *American Antiquity* 66(3): 453–471.

Dawson, Peter, and Richard Levy. 2006. Constructing a 3D computer model of a Thule whalebone house using laser scanning technology. *Journal of Field Archaeology* 30: 443–455.

Echo-Hawk, Roger. 2000. Ancient history in the New World: Integrating oral traditions and the archaeological record in deep time. *American Antiquity* 65: 267–290.

Fienup-Riordan, Anne. 1994. *Boundaries and Passages.* Norman and London: University of Oklahoma Press.

Flannery, Kent V., and Joyce Marcus. 1993. Cognitive archaeology. *Cambridge Archaeological Journal* 3: 260–270.

Grossett, C., and Suluk, L. 2007. Righting the map: Mapping Inuit place names. *International Federation of Landscape Architects* 1.

Hall, Robert L. 1977. An anthropocentric perspective for eastern United States prehistory. *American Antiquity* 42: 499–518.

———. 1997. *An Archaeology of the Soul: North American Indian Belief and Ritual.* Urbana: University of Illinois Press.

Kehoe, Alice B., and Thomas F. Kehoe. 1973. Cognitive models for archaeological interpretation. *American Antiquity* 38: 150–154.

Laming-Emperaire, Annette. 1962. *La signification de l'art rupestre Paléolithique.* Paris: Picard.

Lathrap, Donald W. 1973. Gifts of the cayman: Some thoughts on the subsistence basis of Chavín. In Donald W. Lathrap and Jody Douglas (Eds.), *Variation in Anthropology* (pp. 91–105). Urbana: Illinois Archaeological Survey.

———. 1977. Our father the cayman, our mother the gourd: Spinden revisited, or a unitary model for the emergence of agriculture in the New World. In Charles A. Reed (Ed.), *Origins of Agriculture* (pp. 713–751). The Hague: Mouton.

———. 1985. Jaws: The control of power in the early nuclear American ceremonial center. In C. B. Donnan (Ed.), *Early Ceremonial Architecture in the Andes* (pp. 241–267). Washington, DC: Dumbarton Oaks Research Library and Collection.

Leroi-Gourhan, André. 1968. *The Art of Prehistoric Man in Western Europe.* London: Thames and Hudson.

———. 1980. *Treasures of Prehistoric Art.* Translated from the French by Norbert Guterman. New York: Harry H. Abrams.

———. 1982. *The Dawn of European Art: An Introduction to Palaeolithic Cave Painting.* Cambridge: Cambridge University Press.

Lewis-Williams, David. 2002. *The Mind in the Cave.* London: Thames and Hudson.

Lowenstein, Tom. 1993. *Ancient Land, Sacred Whale: The Inuit Hunt and Its Rituals.* London: Bloomsbury.

Marcus, Joyce, and Kent Flannery. 1996. *Zapotec Civilization.* London: Thames and Hudson.

Mason, Ronald. 2000. Archaeology and Native North American oral traditions. *American Antiquity* 65: 239–266.

Maxwell, Moreau S. 1985. *Prehistory of the Eastern Arctic.* New York: Academic Press.

McCartney, Allan. 1980. The nature of Thule Eskimo whale use. *Arctic* 33: 517–541.

Mithen, Steven. 1995. Palaeolithic archaeology and the evolution of mind. *Journal of Archaeological Research* 3: 305–332.

Renfrew, Colin. 1982. *Towards an Archaeology of the Mind: An Inaugural Lecture Delivered Before the University of Cambridge on 30 November 1982.* Cambridge: Cambridge University Press.

———. 1993. Cognitive archaeology: Some thoughts on the archaeology of thought. *Cambridge Archaeological Journal* 3: 248–250.

Renfrew, Colin, and Ezra B. W. Zubrow (Eds.). 1994. *The Ancient Mind: Elements of Cognitive Archaeology.* Cambridge: Cambridge University Press.

Sheppard, W. L. 1998. Population movements, interaction, and legendary geography. *Arctic Anthropology* 35(2): 147–166.

Steinbring, Jack. 1998. Aboriginal rock painting sites in Manitoba. *Manitoba Archaeology Journal* 8(1,2): 153.

Valladas, Hélène. 2003. Direct radiocarbon dating of prehistoric cave paintings by accelerator mass spectrometry. *Measurement Science and Technology* 14: 1487–1492.

Von Hagen, Adriana, and Craig Morris. 1998. *The Cities of the Ancient Andes.* London: Thames and Hudson.

Whiteley, Peter. 2002. Archaeology and oral tradition: The scientific importance of dialogue. *American Antiquity* 67: 405–415.

Chapter 15

Bar-Yosef, Ofer. 1998. The Natufian Culture in the Levant, threshold to the origins of agriculture. *Evolutionary Anthropology* 6: 159–177.

Bar-Yosef, Ofer, and R. H. Meadow. 1995. The origins of agriculture in the Near East. In T. Douglas Price and Anne B. Gebauer (Eds.), *Last Hunters, First Farmers: New Perspectives on the Prehistoric Transition to Agriculture* (pp. 39–94). Santa Fe: School of American Research Press.

Bender, Barbara. 1978. Gatherer-hunter to farmer: A social perspective. *World Archaeology* 10: 204–222.

Bettinger, Robert L. 1991. *Hunter-Gatherers: Archaeological and Evolutionary Theory.* New York: Plenum Press.

Binford, Lewis R. 1968. Post-Pleistocene adaptations. In Sally R. Binford and Lewis R. Binford (Eds.), *New Perspectives in Archeology* (pp. 313–341). Chicago: Aldine.

Blanton, Richard E., Stephen A. Kowalewski, Gary Feinman, and Jill Appel. 1981. *Ancient Mesoamerica: A Comparison of Change in Three Regions.* Cambridge: Cambridge University Press.

Boserup, Ester. 1965. *Conditions of Agricultural Growth: The Economics of Agrarian Change Under Population Pressure.* Chicago: Aldine.

Boyd, Robert, and Peter J. Richerson. 1985. *Culture and the Evolutionary Process.* Chicago: University of Chicago Press.

Braidwood, Robert J. 1959. Archeology and the evolutionary theory. In B. J. Meggers (Ed.), *Evolution and Anthropology: A Centennial Appraisal* (pp. 76–89). Washington, DC: Anthropological Society of Washington.

Carmichael, David L., Jane Hubert, Brian Reeves, and Audhild Schanche (Eds.). 1994. *Sacred Sites, Sacred Places.* One World Archaeology, Vol. 23. London: Routledge.

Carneiro, Robert L. 1970. A theory of the origin of the state. *Science* 169: 733–738 (quote is from p. 734).

———. 1988. The circumscription theory: Challenge and response. *American Behavioral Scientist* 31: 497–511.

Childe, V. Gordon. 1951. *Man Makes Himself.* New York: New American Library.

Coe, Michael. 1996. *The Maya.* 6th ed. London: Thames and Hudson.

Cohen, Mark Nathan. 1977. *The Food Crisis in Prehistory: Overpopulation and the Origins of Agriculture.* New Haven: Yale University Press.

———. 1981. The ecological basis of new world state formation: General and local model building. In Grant D. Jones and Robert R. Kautz (Eds.), *The Transition to Statehood in the New World* (pp. 105–122). Cambridge: Cambridge University Press.

Cowan, C. Wesley, and Patty Jo Watson (Eds.). 1992. *The Origins of Agriculture: An International Perspective.* Washington, DC: Smithsonian Institution Press.

Cowgill, George L. 1975a. On the causes and consequences of ancient and modern population changes. *American Anthropologist* 77: 505–525.

———. 1975b. Population pressure as a non-explanation. In A. Swelund (Ed.), Population Studies in Archaeology and Biological Anthropology: A Symposium (pp. 127–131). *Society for American Archaeology Memoir*, no. 33. Washington, DC.

———. 1988. Comment on "Ecological theory and cultural evolution in the Valley of Oaxaca" by William T. Sanders and Deborah L. Nichols. *Current Anthropology* 29: 54–55.

Darwin, Charles. 1958 [1859]. *The Origin of Species.* New York: The New American Library.

Demarest, Arthur A. 1989. Ideology and evolutionism in American archaeology: Looking beyond the economic base. In C. C. Lamberg-Karlovsky (Ed.), *Archaeological Thought in America* (pp. 89–102). Cambridge: Cambridge University Press.

Demarest, Arthur A., and Geoffrey W. Conrad (Eds.). 1992. *Ideology and Pre-Columbian Civilizations.* Santa Fe: School of American Research Press.

Diamond, Jared. 1988. The golden age that never was. *Discover* 9(12): 70–79.

Dunnell, Robert C. 1980. Evolutionary theory and archaeology. In Michael B. Schiffer (Ed.), *Advances in Archaeological Method and Theory.* Vol. 3 (pp. 35–99). New York: Academic Press.

———. 1989. Aspects of the application of evolutionary theory in archaeology. In C. C. Lamberg-

Karlovsky (Ed.), *Archaeological Thought in America* (pp. 35–49). Cambridge: Cambridge University Press.

Durham, William. 1981. Overview: Optimal foraging analysis in human ecology. In Bruce Winterhalder and Eric Alden Smith (Eds.), *Hunter-Gatherer Foraging Strategies: Ethnographic and Archaeological Analyses* (pp. 218–232). Chicago: University of Chicago Press.

———. 1990. Advances in evolutionary culture theory. *Annual Review of Anthropology* 19: 187–210.

———. 1992. Applications of evolutionary culture theory. *Annual Review of Anthropology* 21: 331–355.

Earle, Timothy K. (Ed.). 1991. *Chiefdoms: Power, Economy, and Ideology.* Cambridge: Cambridge University Press.

Earle, Timothy K., Terence D'Altroy, Cathy LeBlanc, Christine Hastorf, and Terry Levine. 1980. Changing settlement patterns in the Yanamarca Valley, Peru. Los Angeles: Institute of Archaeology, University of California, *Journal of New World Archaeology* 4(1).

Ehrenreich, Robert M., Carole L. Crumley, and Janet E. Levy (Eds.). 1995. Heterarchy and the analysis of complex societies. *Archeological Papers of the American Anthropological Association,* no. 6. Washington, DC.

Fedick, Scott L. 1995. Indigenous agriculture in the Americas. *Journal of Archaeological Research* 3: 257–303.

Flannery, Kent V. 1965. The ecology of early food production in Mesopotamia. *Science* 147: 1247–1255.

———. 1966. The postglacial "readaptation" as viewed from Mesoamerica. *American Antiquity* 31: 800–805.

———. 1969. Origins and ecological effects of early domestication in Iran and the Near East. In P. J. Ucko and G. W. Dimbleby (Eds.), *The Domestication and Exploitation of Plants and Animals* (pp. 73–100). Chicago: Aldine.

———. 1972. The cultural evolution of civilizations. *Annual Review of Ecology and Systematics* 3: 399–426. (Quote is from pp. 403–404).

———. 1973. The origins of agriculture. *Annual Review of Anthropology* 2: 271–310.

Fried, Morton H. 1967. *The Evolution of Political Society.* New York: Random House.

Fritz, Gayle J. 1990. Multiple pathways to farming in precontact eastern North America. *Journal of World Prehistory* 4: 387–435.

Harner, Michael J. 1970. Population pressure and the social evolution of agriculturalists. *Southwestern Journal of Anthropology* 26: 67–86.

Harris, David R. 1972. The origins of agriculture in the tropics. *American Scientist* 60: 180–193.

———. 1994. Agricultural origins, beginnings and transitions: The quest continues. *Antiquity* 69: 873–877.

Harris, David R., and Gordon C. Hillman (Eds.). 1989. *Foraging and Farming: The Evolution of Plant Exploitation.* London: Unwin Hyman.

Harrison, Peter D. 1981. Some aspects of preconquest settlement in southern Quintana Roo, Mexico. In Wendy Ashmore (Ed.), *Lowland Maya Settlement Patterns* (pp. 259–286). Albuquerque: University of New Mexico Press.

Hawkes, Kristen, and James F. O'Connell. 1985. Optimal foraging models and the case of the !Kung. *American Anthropologist* 87: 401–405.

Hawkes, Kristen, James F. O'Connell, and N. Blurton Jones. 1987. Hardworking Hadza grandmothers. In R. Foley and V. Standen (Eds.), *Comparative Socioecology of Mammals and Man* (pp. 341–366). London: Basil Blackwell.

Hayden, Brian. 1990. Nimrods, piscators, pluckers, and planters: The emergence of food production. *Journal of Anthropological Archaeology* 9: 31–69.

———. 1995. A new overview of domestication. In T. Douglas Price and Anne B. Gebauer (Eds.), *Last Hunters, First Farmers: New Perspectives on the Prehistoric Transition to Agriculture* (pp. 273–300). Santa Fe: School of American Research Press.

Hill, Kim, and Kristen Hawkes. 1983. Neotropical hunting among the Aché of eastern Paraguay. In R. Hames and W. Vickers (Eds.), *Adaptive Responses of Native Amazonians* (pp. 139–188). New York: Academic Press.

Houston, S. D. 2000. Into the minds of ancients: Advances in Maya glyph studies. *Journal of World Prehistory* 14: 121–201.

Houston, S. D., and Patricia McAnany. 2003. Bodies and blood: Critiquing social construction in Maya archaeology. *Journal of Anthropological Archaeology* 22: 26–41.

Johnson, Allen W., and Timothy Earle. 1987. *The Evolution of Human Societies: From Foraging Group to Agrarian State.* Stanford: Stanford University Press.

Keegan, William F. 1986. The optimal foraging analysis of horticultural production. *American Anthropologist* 88: 92–107.

Kelly, Robert L. 1995. *The Foraging Spectrum.* Washington, DC: Smithsonian Institution Press.

Lee, Richard B. 1979. *The !Kung San: Men, Women and Work in a Foraging Society.* Cambridge: Cambridge University Press (quote is from the frontispiece).

Lee, Richard B., and Irven DeVore (Eds.). 1968. *Man the Hunter.* Chicago: Aldine.

Lees, Susan H. 1994. Irrigation and society. *Journal of Archaeological Research* 2: 361–378.

Lubbock, Sir John. 1865. *Pre-Historic Times, As Illustrated by Ancient Remains, and the Manners and Customs of Modern Savages.* London: Williams and Norgate.

Manzanilla, Linda. 2001. State formation in the New World. In Gary Feinman and T. Douglas Price (Eds.), *Archaeology at the Millennium: A Sourcebook* (pp. 381–414). New York: Kluwer Academic/Plenum.

Marcus, Joyce. 1992. *Mesoamerican Writing Systems: Propaganda, Myth, and History in Four Ancient Civilizations.* Princeton: Princeton University Press.

———. 2003. Recent Advances in Maya Archaeology. *Journal of Archaeological Research* 11: 71–148.

Matson, R. G., and G. Coupland. 1995. *Prehistory of the Northwest Coast.* New York: Academic Press.

McAnany, Patricia. 1995. *Living with the Ancestors: Kinship and Kingship in Ancient Maya Society.* Austin: University of Texas Press.

Morgan, Lewis Henry. 1974 [1877]. *Ancient Society.* Edited with an introduction and annotations by Eleanor Leacock. Gloucester, MA: Peter Smith.

O'Connell, James F., and Kristen Hawkes. 1981. Alyawara plant use and optimal foraging theory. In Bruce Winterhalder and Eric Alden Smith (Eds.), *Hunter-Gatherer Foraging Strategies: Ethnographic and Archaeological Analyses* (pp. 99–125). Chicago: University of Chicago Press.

Richerson, Peter J., Robert Boyd, and Robert Bettinger. 2001. Was agriculture impossible during the Pleistocene but mandatory during the Holocene? A climate change hypothesis. *American Antiquity* 66: 387–411.

Rindos, David. 1984. *The Origins of Agriculture: An Evolutionary Perspective.* Orlando, FL: Academic Press.

Sahlins, Marshall D., and Elman R. Service. 1960. *Evolution and Culture.* Ann Arbor: University of Michigan Press.

Scarborough, Vernon. 1994. Maya water management. *National Geographic Research and Exploration* 10(2): 184–199.

Service, Elman. 1971. *Primitive Social Organization: An Evolutionary Perspective.* 2nd ed. New York: Random House.

———. 1975. *Origins of the State and Civilization: The Process of Cultural Evolution.* New York: Norton.

Simms, Steven, and Kenneth Russell. 1997. Bedouin hand harvesting of wheat and barley: Implications for early cultivation in southwestern Asia. *Current Anthropology* 38: 696–702.

Smith, Bruce D. 1992. *Rivers of Change: Essays on Early Agriculture in Eastern North America.* Washington, DC: Smithsonian Institution Press.

———. 2001. The transition to food production. In Gary Feinman and T. Douglas Price (Eds.), *Archaeology at the Millennium: A Sourcebook* (pp. 199–230). New York: Kluwer Academic/Plenum.

Smith, E. A. 1985. Inuit foraging groups: Some simple models incorporating conflicts of interest, relatedness, and central place sharing. *Ethnology and Sociobiology* 6: 27–47.

———. 1991. *Inujjuamiut Foraging Strategies: Evolutionary Ecology of an Arctic Hunting Economy.* New York: Aldine de Gruyter.

Smith, Eric Alden, and Bruce Winterhalder (Eds.). 1992. *Evolutionary Ecology and Human Behavior.* New York: Aldine de Gruyter.

Spencer, Charles. 1990. On the tempo and mode of state formation: Neoevolutionism reconsidered. *Journal of Anthropological Archaeology* 9: 1–30.

Tallbull, William. 1994. Archaeological sites or sacred places? Native American perspective. In David Hurst Thomas, *Exploring Ancient Native America* (pp. 238–239). New York: Macmillan.

Tylor, Edward Burnett. 1889. On a method of investigating the development of institutions, applied to laws of marriage and descent. *Journal of the Royal Anthropological Institute* 18: 245–272 (quote is from p. 269).

Upham, Steadman (Ed.). 1990. *The Evolution of Political Systems: Sociopolitics in Small-Scale Sedentary Societies.* Cambridge: Cambridge University Press.

Webster, D. 2000. The not so peaceful civilization: A review of Maya war. *Journal of World Prehistory* 14: 65–119.

Winterhalder, Bruce, and Eric Alden Smith (Eds.). 1981. *Hunter-Gatherer Foraging Strategies: Ethno-*

graphic and Archaeological Analyses. Chicago: University of Chicago Press.

Wittfogel, Karl A. 1957. *Oriental Despotism: A Comparative Study of Total Power.* New Haven: Yale University Press.

Wright, Henry T. 1986. The evolution of civilizations. In David J. Meltzer, Don D. Fowler, and Jeremy A. Sabloff (Eds.), *American Archaeology Past and Future: A Celebration of the Society for American Archaeology 1935–1985* (pp. 323–365). Washington, DC: Smithsonian Institution Press.

Chapter 16

Armstrong, D. 2001. Attaining the full potential of historical archaeology. *Historical Archaeology* 35(2): 9–13.

Beaudry, M. C. 1988. Words for things: Linguistic analysis of probate inventories. In M. C. Beaudry (Ed.), *Documentary Archaeology in the New World* (pp. 51–67). Cambridge: Cambridge University Press.

———(Ed.). 1988. *Documentary Archaeology in the New World.* Cambridge: Cambridge University Press.

Brumbach, H. J. 1985. The recent fur trade in Northwestern Saskatchewan. *Historical Archaeology* 19(2): 19–39.

Burley, D. 1989. Function, meaning and context: Ambiguities in ceramic use by the Hivernant Metis of the Northwestern Plains. *Historical Archaeology* 23(1): 97–106.

Burley, D., K. R. Fladmark, and J. S. Hamilton. 1996. *Prophecy of the Swan: The Upper Peace River Fur Trade of 1794–1823.* Vancouver: UBC Press.

Casella, E. C. 2005. Social workers. In E. C. Casella and J. Symonds (Eds.), *Industrial Archaeology: Future Directions* (pp. 3–33). New York: Springer.

Casella, E. C., and J. Symonds (Eds.). 2005. *Industrial Archaeology: Future Directions.* New York: Springer.

Casella, E. C. a. J. S. 2005. Introduction. In E. C. a. J. S. Casella (Ed.), *Industrial Archaeology: Future Directions* (pp. xi–xiii). New York: Springer.

Cleland, C. E. 1992. From ethnohistory to archaeology: Ottawa and Ojibwa band territories of the Northern Great Lakes. In B. J. Little (Ed.), *Text-Aided Archaeology* (pp. 97–103). CRC Press.

Cossons, S. N. 2005. New directions in industrial archaeology. In E. C. Casella and J. Symonds (Eds.),

Industrial Archaeology: Future Directions (pp. ix–xi). New York: Springer.

Cranstone, D. 2005. After industrial archaeology? In E. C. a. J. S. Casella (Ed.), *Industrial Archaeology: Future Directions* (pp. 77–95). New York: Springer.

Deagan, K. 1982. Avenues of inquiry in historical archaeology. In C. E. Orser (Ed.), *Images of the Recent Past: Readings in Historical Archaeology* (pp. 16–42). Walnut Creek, CA: AltaMira Press.

Drouin, P. 1987. *Archaeological Activities at Sir George-Etienne Cartier National Historic Park* (Vol. 257). Ottawa: Parks Canada

Gray, C. 1999. *Sisters in the Wilderness: The Lives of Susanna Moodie and Catharine Parr Trail.* Toronto: Viking Press.

Hamilton, J. S. 1990. Fur Trade Social Inequality and the Role of Non-Verbal Communication. Unpublished PhD Dissertation: Simon Fraser University.

Hamilton, S. 1993. Over-hunting and local extinctions: Socioeconomic implication of fur trade subsistence. In C. E. Orser (Ed.), *Images of the Recent Past: Readings in Historical Archaeology* (pp. 416–437). Walnut Creek, CA: AltaMira Press.

Hanna, M. 2005. The changing legal and ethical context of archaeological practice in Canada, with special reference to the repatriation of human remains. *Journal of Museum Ethnography* 17: 141–151.

Hickey, C. 1984. An examination of processes of culture change among nineteenth century Copper Inuit. *Etudes/Inuit Studies* 8(1): 13–34.

Hudson, K. 1979. *World Industrial Archaeology.* Cambridge [Eng.]; New York: Cambridge University Press.

Jamieson, S. 1992. Trent University— Final season at the Moodie farmstead. In P. Storck (Ed.), *Annual Archaeological Report, Ontario* (Vol. 3, pp. 62–64). Toronto: The Ontario Heritage Foundation.

Kennedy, M. 1995. Industrial archaeology in Western Canada. *Manitoba Archaeology Journal* 5(2): 86–104.

Leone, M. P. 1984. Interpreting ideology in historical archaeology: Using the rules of perspective in the William Paca Garden in Annapolis, Maryland. In C. E. Orser (Ed.), *Images of the Recent Past: Readings in Historical Archaeology* (pp. 368–371). Walnut Creek, CA: AltaMira Press.

Little, B. J. (Ed.). 1992. *Text-Aided Archaeology.* Boca Raton, FL: CRC Press.

Lunn, K. 1985. Fort Prince of Wales National Historic Site/Park and Cape Merry National Historic Site. *Manitoba Archaeology Quarterly* 9(3): 56–84.

McAleese, K. 1998. The reinterment of the Thule Inuit burials and associated artefacts—Ider-14 Rose Island, Saglek Bay, Labrador. *Etudes/Inuit Studies* 22(2): 41–52.

McGuire, R., and P. Reckner. 2005. Building a working class archaeology: The Colorado coal field war project. In E. C. Casella and J. Symonds (Eds.), *Industrial Archaeology: Future Directions* (pp. 217–243). New York: Springer.

Monks, G. 1992. Architectural symbolism and non-verbal communication at Upper Fort Garry. *Historical Archaeology* 26(2): 37–55.

Morgan, E. D., C. Edwards, and S. A. Pepper. 1992. Analysis of the fatty debris from the wreck of a Basque whaling ship at Red Bay, Labrador. *Archaeometry* 34(1): 129–133.

Mrozowski, S. A. 1988. For gentlemen of capacity and leisure: The archaeology of colonial newspapers. In M. C. Beaudry (Ed.), *Documentary Archaeology in the New World* (pp. 184–192). Cambridge: Cambridge University Press.

Newell, D., and R. Greenhill. 1989. *Survivals: Aspects of Industrial Archaeology in Ontario.* Erin, ON: Boston Mills Press.

Orser, C. E. 1996. *Images of the Recent Past: Readings in Historical Archaeology.* Walnut Creek, CA: AltaMira Press.

Palmer, M. 2005. Industrial archaeology: Constructing a frame of reference. In E. C. Casella and J. Symonds (Eds.), *Industrial Archaeology: Future Directions* (pp. 59–77). New York: Springer.

Ray, A. J. 1974. *Indians in the Fur Trade: Their Role as Trappers, Hunters, and Middlemen in the Lands Southwest of Hudson Bay, 1660–1870.* Toronto; Buffalo: University of Toronto Press.

Schmidt, P. R. a. S. M. 1988. Documentary insights into the archaeology of smuggling. In M. C. Beaudry (Ed.), *Documentary Archaeology in the New World* (pp. 32–43). Cambridge: Cambridge University Press.

Seasholes, N. 1988. On the use of historic maps. In M. C. Beaudry (Ed.), *Documentary Archaeology in the New World* (pp. 92–119). Cambridge: Cambridge University Press.

South, S. A. 1977. *Method and Theory in Historical Archeology.* New York: Academic Press.

Stewart, J. 1995. Reburial of the Red Bay wreck as a form of preservation and protection of the historic resource. *Material Issues in Art and Archaeology–Pittsburgh* 4(352): 791–805.

Stone, G. W. 1988. Artifacts are not enough. In M. C. Beaudry (Ed.), *Documentary Archaeology in the New World* (pp. 68–79). Cambridge: Cambridge University Press.

Symonds, J. 2005. Experiencing industry: Beyond machines and history of technology. In E. C. a. J. S. Casella (Ed.), *Industrial Archaeology: Future Directions* (pp. 33–59). New York: Springer.

Trinder, B. S. 1992. *The Blackwell encyclopedia of industrial archaeology.* Oxford, UK; Cambridge, MA: Blackwell.

Tuck, J. A. 1978. A 16th century Spanish Basque whaling station in Labrador. *Research Reports–National Geographic Society* 19: 565–572.

———. 1981. A 16th century whaling station in Labrador. *Scientific American* 245(5): 180–190.

———. 1982. A 16th century whaling station at Red Bay, Labrador. In G. M. Story (Ed.), *Early European Settlement and Exploitation in Atlantic Canada: Selected Papers.* St. John's: Memorial University of Newfoundland.

———. 1986. Excavations at Red Bay Labrador: 1986. *Archaeology in Newfoundland and Labrador* 7: 213–237.

———. 1987. The world's first oil boom. *Archaeology* 40(1): 50–55.

Chapter 17

Asch, Michael. 1997. Cultural property and the question of underlying title. In G. P. Nicholas and T. Andrews (Eds.), *At a Crossroads: Archaeology and First Peoples in Canada* (pp. 266–271). Burnaby, BC: Archaeology Press, Department of Archaeology Simon Fraser University.

Bass, George F. 2003. The ethics of shipwreck archaeology. In L. Zimmerman, J. K. D. Vitelli, and J. Hollowell-Zimmer (Eds.), *Ethical Issues in Archaeology* (pp. 57–70). Walnut Creek, CA: Altimira Press.

Bergman, C., and J. Doersauk. 2003. Culture resource management and the business of archaeology. In L. Zimmerman, J. K. D. Vitelli, and J. Hollowell-Zimmer (Eds.), *Ethical Issues in Archaeology* (pp. 85–98). Walnut Creek, CA: Altimira Press.

Bray, Tamara L. 1996. Repatriation, power relations and the politics of the past. *Antiquity* 70(268): 440–444.

Brownlee, Kevin, and E. Leigh Syms. 1999. *Kayasochi kikawenow = Our Mother from Long Ago: An Early Cree Woman and Her Personal Belongings from Nagami Bay, Southern Indian Lake.* Winnipeg: Manitoba Museum of Man and Nature.

Burley, David V. 1994. A never ending story: Historical developments in Canadian archaeology and the quest for federal heritage legislation. *Canadian Journal of Archaeology* 18: 77–98.

Canadian Archaeological Association. 1996. *Statement of Principles of Ethical Conduct Pertaining to Aboriginal Peoples.* From http://www.canadianarchaeology.ca/ethical.lasso.

Champe, John L., Douglas S. Byers, Clifford Evans, A. K. Guthe, Henry W. Hamilton, Edward B. Jelks, Clement W. Meighan, Sigfus Olafson, George I. Quimby, Watson Smith, and Fred Wendorf. 1961. Four Statements for Archaeology. *American Antiquity* 27(2): 137–138.

Chodkiewiez, J. L., and Jennifer Brown. 1999. *First Nations and Hydroelectric Development in Northern Manitoba: The Northern Flood Agreement, Issues and Implications.* Winnipeg: Centre for Rupert's Land Studies, University of Winnipeg.

Colwell-Chan P. C., and T. J. Ferguson. 2006. Trust and archaeological practice: Toward a framework of virtue ethics. In C. Scarre and G. Scarre (Eds.), *The Ethics of Archaeology: Philosophical Perspectives on Archaeological Practice* (pp. 115–131). Cambridge: Cambridge University Press.

Croarke, L., and Gary Warrick. 2006. Stewardship gone astray: Ethics and the SAA. In C. Scarre and G. Scarre (Eds.), *The Ethics of Archaeology: Philosophical Perspectives on Archaeological Practice* (pp. 146–163). Cambridge: Cambridge University Press.

Davis, Hester A. 1982. Professionalism in archaeology. *American Antiquity* 47(2): 158–163.

Erasmus, Georges, and Renâe Dussault. 1996. *Report of the Royal Commission on Aboriginal Peoples.* Ottawa: The Commission: Available by mail from Canada Communication Group—Pub.

Ferris, Neal. 1998a. *Current Issues in the Governance of Archaeology in Canada.* Paper presented at the CAA 1998: Warning—Steep Grade Ahead: Current Directions in Canadian Archaeology. From http://www.canadianarchaeology.com/1998plenary/ferris.lasso.

———. 1998b. "I don't think we're in Kansas anymore...": The rise of the archaeological consulting industry in Ontario. In P. Smith and D. Mitchell (Eds.), *Bringing Back the Past: Historical Perspectives on Canadian Archaeology* (Vol. 158, pp. 225–247). Ottawa: Museum of Civilization, Archaeological Survey of Canada, Mercury Series.

———. 2003. Between colonial and indigenous archaeologies: Legal and extra-legal ownership of the archaeological past in North America. *Canadian Journal of Archaeology* 27(2): 154–190.

Goldstein, Lynne, and Keith Kintigh. 1990. Ethics and the reburial controversy. *American Antiquity* 55(3): 585–591.

Government of Saskatchewan. 1980. *An Act to Provide for the Preservation, Interpretation and Development of Certain Aspects of Heritage Property in Saskatchewan.* Heritage Property Regulations, chapter H-2.2 (1980).

Hanna, Margaret. 2005. The changing legal and ethical context of archaeological practice in Canada, with special reference to repatriation. *Journal of Museum Ethnography* 17: 141–151.

Henderson, James, Y. Youngblood, M. L. Benson, and Findlay Ian. 2000. *Aboriginal Tenure in the Constitution of Canada.* Scarborough: Carswell Legal Publications.

Hill, T., and T. Nicks. 1992. Turning the page: Forging a new partnership between museums and First Peoples in Canada. *Journal of Museum Ethnography* 6: 39–64.

Hollowell, J. 2006. Moral arguments on subsistence digging. In C. Scarre and G. Scarre (Eds.), *The Ethics of Archaeology: Philosophical Perspectives on Archaeological Practice* (pp. 69–96). Cambridge: Cambridge University Press.

Holm, M., and D. Pokotylo. 1997. From policy to practice: A case study in collaborative exhibits with First Nations. *Canadian Journal of Archaeology* 21(1): 33–44.

Hoppa, Robert D., Laura Allingham, Kevin Brownlee, Linda Larcombe, and Gregory Monks. 2005. An analysis of two late archaic burials from Manitoba: The Eriksdale Site (EfL 1-1). *Canadian Journal of Archaeology* 29(2): 234–266.

Lackey, Douglas. 2006. Ethics and Native American reburials: A philosopher's view of two decades of NAGPRA. In C. Scarre and G. Scarre (Eds.), *The Ethics of Archaeology: Philosophical Perspectives on*

Archaeological Practice (pp. 163–180). Cambridge: Cambridge University Press.

Lynott, Mark J. 2003. The development of ethics in archaeology. In L. J. Zimmerman, K. Vitelli, and J. Hollowell-Zimmer (Eds.), *Ethical Issues in Archaeology* (pp. 17–30). Walnut Creek, CA: Altimira Press.

Lynott, Mark J., and Alison Wylie. 1995. *Ethics in American Archaeology: Challenges for the 1990s.* Washington, DC: Society for American Archaeology.

McGhee, Robert. 1989. Who owns prehistory? The Bering land bridge dilemma. *Canadian Journal of Archaeology* 13: 13–20.

Monks, Greg. *Smith Winternberg Award Winner E. Leigh Syms.* From www.canadianarchaeology.com/awards/syms/lasso.

Nicholson, B. 1996. Introduction. In B. Nicholson, D. Pokotylo, and R. Williamson (Eds.), *Statement of Principles for Ethical Conduct Pertaining to Aboriginal Peoples: A Report from the Aboriginal Heritage Committee* (pp. 3–6). Ottawa: Jointly sponsored by the Canadian Archaeological Association and the Department of Communications.

Nicholson, B., D. Pokotylo, and R. Williamson. 1996. *Statement of Principles for Ethical Conduct Pertaining to Aboriginal Peoples: A Report from the Aboriginal Heritage Committee.* Ottawa: Jointly sponsored by the Canadian Archaeological Association and the Department of Communications.

Powell, L., E. Garcia, and A. Hendriks. 1993. Ethics and ownership of the past: The reburial and repatriation controversy. *Archaeological Method and Theory* 5: 1–42.

Rosenwig, Robert M. 1997. Ethics in Canadian archaeology: An international comparative analysis. *Canadian Journal of Archaeology* 21(2): 99–114.

———. 2000. Ethics, archaeological resource management and federal legislation: A few thoughts for the direction of Canadian Archaeology. *Canadian Journal of Archaeology* 24(1–2): 176–178.

Singleton, T., and C. Orser Jr. 2003. Descendant communities: Linking people in the present to the past. In L. J. Zimmerman, K. Vitelli, and J. Hollowell-Zimmer (Eds.), *Ethical Issues in Archaeology* (pp. 143–152). Walnut Creek, CA: Altimira Press.

Society for American Archaeology (SAA). 2005, December. *Principles of Archaeological Ethics.* From http://www.saa.org/aboutSAA/committees/ethics/principles.html.

Syms, E. Leigh. 1997. Archaeological Native internships at the Manitoba Museum of Man and Nature. In G. Nicholas and T. Andrews (Eds.), *At a Crossroads: Archaeology and First Peoples in Canada.* Burnaby, BC: Archaeology Press, Department of Archaeology Simon Fraser University.

Trigger, Bruce G. 1980. Archaeology and the image of the American Indian. *American Antiquity* 46(4): 662–676.

Williamson, R. 2000. Trends and issues in consulting archaeology. *Canadian Journal of Archaeology* 24(1–2): 158–161.

World Archaeological Congress (WAC). 1989. *Vermillion Accord on Human Remains.* From http://www.wac.uct.ac.za/archive/content/vermillion.accord.hml.

———. 1990. *First Code of Ethics.* From www.wac.uct.ac.za/archive/content/ethics.html.

Wylie, Alison. 1996. Ethical dilemmas in archaeological practice: Looting, repatriation, stewardship, and the (trans) formation of disciplinary identity. *Perspectives on Science* 4: 154–194.

———. 1997. Contextualizing ethics: Comments on ethics in Canadian Archaeology by Robert Rosenwig. *Canadian Journal of Archaeology* 21(2): 115–120.

———. 2000. Some reflections on the work of the SAA Committee for Ethics in Archaeology. *Canadian Journal of Archaeology* 24(1–2): 151–158.

———. 2003. On ethics. In L. Zimmerman, K. Vitelli, and J. Hollowell-Zimmer (Eds.), *Ethical Issues in Archaeology* (pp. 3–16). Walnut Creek, CA: AltaMira Press.

Yellowhorn, Elden. 1998. *The Evolving Relationship Between Archaeologists and First Nations.* Paper presented at the CAA 1998: Warning—Steep Grade Ahead: Current Directions in Canadian Archaeology. From http://www.canadianarchaeology.com/1998plenary/1998plenary.lasso.

Young, James O. 2006. Cultures and the ownership of archaeological finds. In C. Scarre and G. Scarre (Eds.), *The Ethics of Archaeology: Philosophical Perspectives on Archaeological Practice* (pp. 15–32). Cambridge: Cambridge University Press.

Chapter 18

Addison, A. C. 2000. *Virtual Heritage—Technology in the Service of Culture.* Paper presented at the Proceedings of the 2001 Conference on Virtual Reality, Archaeology and Cultural Heritage, Glyfada, Greece.

Arden, H. 1989. Who owns our past? *National Geographic Magazine* 175(3): 376–392.

Arnold, Bettina. 1992, July/August. The past as propaganda. *Archaeology* 45(4): 30–37.

Bray, Tamara L., and Thomas W. Killion (Eds.). 1994. *Reckoning with the Dead: The Larsen Bay Repatriation and the Smithsonian Institution.* Washington, DC: Smithsonian Institution Press.

Brear, Holly. 1995. *Inherit the Alamo: Myth and Ritual at an American Shrine.* Austin: University of Texas Press (quote is from p. 146).

Butler, V. L. and M. G. Delacorte. 2004. Doing zooarchaeology as if it mattered: Use of faunal data to address current issues in fish conservation biology in Owens Valley, California. In R. L. Lyman and K. Cannon (Eds.), *Zooarchaeology and Conservation Biology.* Salt Lake City: University of Utah Press (forthcoming).

Carney, Heath J., Michael W. Binford, Alan L. Kolata, Ruben R. Marin, and Charles R. Goldman. 1993. Nutrient and sediment retention in Andean raised-field agriculture. *Nature* 364: 131–133.

Colley, S., S. Todd, and N. Campling. 1988. 3D computer graphics for archaeological data exploration: An example from Saxon, Southampton. *Journal of Archaeological Science* 15: 99–106.

Connor, Melissa. 1996. The archaeology of contemporary mass graves. *Bulletin of the Society for American Archaeology* 14(4): 6, 31.

Crowell, Aron L., Amy F. Steffian, and Gordon L. Pullar (Eds.). 2001. *Looking Both Ways: Heritage and Identity of the Alutiiq People.* Fairbanks: University of Alaska Press.

Dawson, Peter. 2001. Interpreting variability in Thule Inuit architecture: A case study from the Canadian High Arctic. *American Antiquity* 66(3): 453–470.

Dawson, Peter, Richard Levy, Donald Gardner, and M. Walls. 2007. Simulating the behavior of light inside Arctic dwellings: Implications for assessing the role of vision in task performance. *World Archaeology* 39(3): 17–35.

Dawson, Peter, and Richard Levy. 2005a. Constructing a 3D computer model of a Thule whalebone house using laser scanning technology. *Journal of Field Archaeology* 30: 443–455.

———. 2005b. Using computer modeling and virtual reality to explore the ideological dimensions of Thule whalebone architecture in Arctic Canada. *Internet Archaeology,* Issue 18, Winter. http://intarch.ac.uk/.

———. 2006. Using 3D computer models of Inuit architecture as visualization tools in archaeological interpretation: Two case studies from the Canadian Arctic. In *Dynamics of Northern Societies.* Proceedings of the SILA/NABO Conference on Arctic and North Atlantic Archaeology, Copenhagen, May 10th–14th, 2004, edited by Jette Arneborg and Bjarne Gronnow–PNM, Publications from the National Museum, *Studies in Archaeology and History,* Vol. 10. Copenhagen 2006: 415 pp.

Deloria, Vine, Jr. 1992a. Indians, archaeologists, and the future. *American Antiquity* 57: 595–598.

———. 1992b. Afterword. In Alvin M. Josephy, Jr. (Ed.), *America in 1492: The World of the Indian Peoples Before the Arrival of Columbus* (pp. 429–443). New York: Knopf.

———. 1993. Sacred lands. *Winds of Change* 8(4): 30–37.

———. 1995. *Red Earth, White Lies: Native Americans and the Myth of Scientific Fact.* New York: Scribner's.

Eddy, John A. 1974. Astronomical alignment of the Big Horn medicine wheel. *Science* 184: 1035–1043.

———. 1977. Medicine wheels and Plains Indian astronomy. In Anthony F. Aveni (Ed.), *Native American Astronomy* (pp. 147–169). Austin: University of Texas Press.

Erickson, Clark L. 1988. Raised field agriculture in the Lake Titicaca Basin: Putting ancient agriculture back to work. *Expedition* 30(3): 8–16.

———. 1992a. Applied archaeology and rural development: Archaeology's potential contribution to the future. *Journal of the Steward Anthropological Society* 20(1, 2): 1–16.

———. 1992b. Prehistoric landscape management in the Andean highlands: Raised field agriculture and its environmental impact. *Population and Environment* 13(4): 285–300.

———. 1993. The social organization of prehispanic raised field agriculture in the Lake Titicaca Basin. In V. L. Scarborough and B. L. Isaac (Eds.), *Research in Economic Anthropology: Economic Aspects of Water Management in the Prehistoric New World.* Supplement 7: 369–426. Greenwich, CT: JAI Press.

————. 1995. Archaeological methods for the study of ancient landscapes of the Llanos de Mojos in the Bolivian Amazon. In Peter W. Stahl (Ed.), *Archaeology in the Lowland American Tropics: Current Analytical Methods and Applications* (pp. 66–95). Cambridge: Cambridge University Press.

————. 2003. Agricultural landscapes as world heritage: Raised field agriculture in Bolivia and Peru. In Jeanne-Marie Teutonico and Frank Matero (Eds.), *Managing Change: Sustainable Approaches to the Conservation of the Built Environment* (pp. 181–204). Oxford: Getty Conservation Institute and Oxford University Press.

Ferguson, T. J. 1996. Native Americans and the practice of archaeology. *Annual Review of Anthropology* 25: 63–79.

Ford, Richard I. 1973. Archeology serving humanity. In Charles L. Redman (Ed.), *Research and Theory in Current Archeology* (pp. 83–93). New York: Wiley.

Forte, M., and A. Silotti. 1997. *Virtual Archaeology: Great Discoveries Brought to Life through Virtual Reality.* London: Thames and Hudson.

Fowler, Don. 1987. Uses of the past: Archaeology in the service of the state. *American Antiquity* 52: 229–248.

Gillings, M. 2005. The real, the virtually real, and the hyperreal: The role of VR in archaeology. In S. Smiles, Moser (Ed.), *Envisioning the Past: Archaeology and the Image:* Blackwell Pubishing Ltd.

Green, Ernestine L. (Ed.). 1984. *Ethics and Values in Archaeology.* New York: Free Press.

Greenburg, D. W. 1929. Sheridan's historic settings. *The Midwest Review* 7(10): 50–69ff, 71, 90 (quote describing Red Plume's vision from p. 66).

Greenlee, Bob. 1995. *Life Among the Ancient Ones: Two Accounts of an Anasazi Archaeological Research Project.* Boulder: Hardscrabble Press.

Grey, Don. 1963. Big Horn medicine wheel site, 48BH302. *Plains Anthropologist* 8: 27–40.

Kay, C. E. and R. T. Simmons (Eds.). 2002. *Wilderness and Political Ecology: Aboriginal Influences and the Original State of Nature.* Salt Lake City: University of Utah Press.

Klesert, Anthony L. 1992. A view from Navajoland on the reconciliation of anthropologists and Native Americans. *Human Organization* 51: 17–22.

Klesert, Anthony L., and Alan S. Downer (Eds.). 1990. Preservation on the reservation: Native Americans, Native American lands and archaeology. *Navajo Nation Papers in Anthropology,* no. 26.

Klesert, Anthony L., and Shirley Powell. 1993. A perspective on ethics and the reburial controversy. *American Antiquity* 58: 348–354.

Kolata, Alan L., and Charles Ortloff. 1989. Thermal analysis of Tiwanaku raised field systems in the Lake Titicaca Basin of Bolivia. *Journal of Archaeological Science* 16: 233–263.

Lauwerier, R. C. G. M., and I. Plug (Eds.). 2004. *The Future from the Past: Archaeozoology in Wildlife Conservation and Heritage Management.* Oxford: Oxbow Books.

Levoy, M. 2000. *The Digital Michelangelo Project: 3D Laser Scanning of Large Status.* Paper presented at the Proceedings, SIGGRAPH 2000, New Orleans, Louisiana, USA, July 23–28.

Levy, Richard, and Peter Dawson. 2006a. From laser scanning to virtual reality: The art and science of archaeological reconstructions. *IEEE Computer Graphics.*

————. 2006b. 3D imaging as a tool in the computer reconstruction of a Thule whalebone house. *IEEE MultiMedia* 13(2): 78–83.

Levy, Richard, Peter Dawson, and Charles Arnold. 2004. Reconstructing traditional Inuit house forms using 3-dimensional interactive computer modeling. *Visual Studies* 1: 26–35.

Lipe, William D. 1995. The archeology of ecology. *Federal Archaeology* 8(1): 8–13.

Long, William R. 1993, August 24. Old canals carry hope to Andes. *Los Angeles Times.*

Mansfield, Victor N. 1980. The Bighorn Medicine Wheel as a site for the vision quest. *Archaeoastronomy Bulletin* 3(2): 26–29.

Meighan, Clement. 1992. Some scholars' views on reburial. *American Antiquity* 57: 704–710.

Nicholas, Lynn H. 1994. *The Rape of Europe: The Fate of Europe's Treasures in the Third Reich and the Second World War.* New York: Knopf.

Ovenden, Michael W., and David A. Rodger. 1981. Megaliths and medicine wheels. In Michael Wilson, Kathie L. Road, and Kenneth J. Hardy (Eds.), Megaliths to Medicine Wheels: Boulder Structures in Archaeology. *Proceedings of the Eleventh Annual Chacmool Conference* (pp. 371–386). Calgary: The Archaeological Association of the University of Calgary.

Powell, Shirley, Christiana Elnora Garza, and Aubrey Hendricks. 1993. Ethics and ownership of the past: The reburial and repatriation controversy. In

Michael B. Schiffer (Ed.), *Archaeological Method and Theory.* Vol. 5 (pp. 1–42). Tucson: University of Arizona Press.

Rathje, William L. 1984. The garbage decade. *American Behavioral Scientist* 28(1): 9–29.

———. 1991. Once and future landfills. *National Geographic* 25(May): 116–134 (quote from p. 120).

Rathje, William, and Cullen Murphy. 2001. *Rubbish! The Archaeology of Garbage.* Tucson: University of Arizona Press.

Rathje, William L., W. W. Hughes, D. C. Wilson, M. K. Tani, G. H. Archer, R. G. Hunt, and T. W. Jones. 1992. The archaeology of contemporary landfills. *American Antiquity* 57: 437–447.

Riding In, James. 1992. With ethics and morality: A historical overview of imperial archaeology and American Indians. *Arizona State Law Journal* 24(1): 11–34.

Swidler, Nina, Kurt E. Dongoske, Roger Anyon, and Alan S. Downer (Eds.). 1997. *Native Americans and Archaeologists: Stepping Stones to Common Ground.* Walnut Creek, CA: AltaMira Press.

Photo and Illustration Credits

Chapter 1 **1:** Sarah Gaunt–CAFN; **3:** Yukon Government Heritage Branch; **6:** Dr. Peter Dawson; **8:** American Museum of Natural History; **13:** Diamond Jenness at Bernard Harbour, Northwest Territories (Nunavut) © Canadian Museum of Civilization, George H Wilkins, July 1916, 51236; **14:** Faith Kidder Fuller; **16:** American Museum of Natural History and Junius Bird; **18:** Denver Museum of Nature and Science; **19:** Courtesy of Walter W Taylor; **20:** Courtesy of Lewis R Bingford, photo by Grant Spearman; **23:** Courtesy of McGill University; **25:** Paul Ewonus, Department of Anthropology, McMaster University

Chapter 2 **28:** Dr. Peter Dawson; **36:** American Museum of Natural History; **41: top** Ohio Historical Society; **bottom** Peabody Museum, Harvard University; **45:** From Squier, E. G. and Davis, E. H., (1848). Ancient Monuments of the Mississippi Valley. Smithsonian Contributions to Knowledge, (1), Washington, DC; **46:** Wiley, G., and J. Sabloff, 1980. A History of American Archaeology, 2nd ed. San Francisco: W. H. Freeman and Company; **50:** American Museum of Natural History; **54:** American Museum of Natural History, drawing by Diana Salles

Chapter 3 **57:** Courtesy of FMA Heritage Resources Consultants Inc.; **60:** American Museum of Natural History, photo by Dennis O'Brien; **62:** University of Wyoming, Frison Institute; **63:** Robert Kelly, photo by Jim Yount; **72:** Charles & Josette Lenars/Corbis Canada; **74:** Stuart Rome, Drexel University; **76:** David H. Thomas; **81:** Dr. Jerimy J Cunningham

Chapter 4 **87:** Courtesy of Dr Marty Magne; **91:** American Museum of Natural History; **95:** Dr Claude Chapdelaine, Département d'Anthropologie, Université de Montréal; **96:** Robert Kelly; **97:** American Museum of Natural History; photo by Dennis O'Brien; **98:** Robert Kelly, "Prehistory of the Carson Desert and Stillwater Mountains," University of Utah Anthropological Papers, No. 123, 2001; **103:** Courtesy of Dr. Marty Magne; **104:** Charles A. Lindbergh, courtesy of the School of American Research; **107:** Robert Kelly, "Prehistory of the Carson Desert and Stillwater Mountains," University of Utah Anthropological Papers, No. 123, 2001; **110:** Robert Kelly; **111:** American Museum of Natural History; **113:** Donalee Deck, Parks Canada; **114:** American Museum of Natural History; photo by Dennis O'Brien; **115:** David H Thomas

Chapter 5 **120:** Photo courtesy of Laboratory of Anthropology, University of Manitoba; **126:** Courtesy of the University Press of Florida; **127:** American Museum of Natural History, photo by Dennis O'Brien; **128:** Courtesy American Museum of Natural History; **130:** Payson Sheets; **131:** Payson Sheets; **133:** J M Maillol, Department of Geology/Geophysics, University of Calgary; **136:** Wescott and Kuiper and Taylor & Francis Publishing; **137:** David Zeanah; **139:** C. Jason Harris; **140:** Snead, J., and Preucel, R. "The Ideology of Settlement: Ancestral Keres Landscapes in the Northern Rio Grande." In W. Ashmore and A. B. Knapp (Eds.), *Archaelogies of Landscape: Contemporary Perspectives* (pp. 169–197). Oxford: Blackwell Publishers

Chapter 6 **143:** Julie Ross; **146:** Robert Kelly; **147:** Denver Museum of Nature and Science; **148: left** National Museum of the American Indian; **right** Ruth Kirk; **149:** South Tyrol Museum of Archaeology; **152:** Courtesy American Museum of Natural History; **156:** Robert Kelly; **160:** Robert Kelly; **161:** Patty Jo Watson; **163:** Julie Ross

Chapter 7 **166:** Paul E McNeil; **169:** top Paul E McNeil; botom McNeil et al. (2005). "Mammoth tracks indicate a declining Late Pleistocene population in southwestern Alberta, Canada", Quaternary Science Reviews, 24(10–11), 1254; **172:** Dr. Gerald A Oetelaar, Department of Archaeology, University of Calgary; **179:** Dr Andrea Freeman; **184:** Shannon McPherron

Chapter 8 **190:** Canadian Museum of Civilization, J433; **193:** American Museum of Natural History; **194:** American Museum of Natural History; photo by Craig Chesek; **197:** American Museum of Natural History; **199:** Canadian Museum of Civilization, J1018; **209:** Canadian Museum of Civilization; S91-923; **211:** Dr W E (Liam) Kieser, University of Toronto; **213:** Ofer Bar-Yosef; **215:** James Ahern; **217:** Charles & Josette Lenars/Corbis Canada; **219:** Werner Forman/Art Resource, NY; **221:** American Museum of Natural History

Chapter 9 **225:** Dr Peter Dawson; **229:** American Museum of Natural History; **231:** Arctic Institute of North America; **234:** Ellis, Chris, and Deller, D. Brian. (1990), "Paleo-Indians" in *The Archaeology of Southern Ontario to A.D. 1650*, Ellis, C, and Ferris, N (Eds.). Occasional Publication of the London

Chapter, OAS Number 5; **235** Ellis, Chris, and Deller, D. Brian. (1990), "Paleo-Indians" in *The Archaeology of Southern Ontario to A.D. 1650,* Ellis, C, and Ferris, N (Eds.). Occasional Publication of the London Chapter, OAS Number 5; **240:** From L. Cordell, *Prehistory of the Southwest,* 1984. Reprinted by permission of Elsevier; **242:** Courtesy of David Blower; **244: bottom** American Museum of Natural History; **248:** Donald R. Tuohy/ Nevada State Museum

Chapter 10 **251:** Dr Peter Dawson; **256:** Robert Kelly; **257:** Steven Brandt/Kathryn Weedman; **260:** Diane Gifford-Gonzalez, photo by Michael J. Mehlman; **261:** Lawrence C. Todd; **265:** Caroline Commins/Alamy; **267: left** James Wood; **right** American Museum of Natural History; **271:** Doug Bamforth; **276:** Robert Kelly; **279:** Dr Peter Dawson; **282:** Margaret Nelson

Chapter 11 **285:** Frederick Arthur Verner, "The Stampede", 1883, oil on canvas, Collection of Glenbow Museum, Calgary, Canada, 55.28; **288:** University of Wyoming, Frison Institute; **292:** Matt Hill; **294:** Dr Ariane Burke; **296:** Dr Brian Hayden; **297:** K R Fladmark; **301:** Robert Kelly; **303:** Ralph Solecki; **305:** Susan Mulholland; **306:** Steve Jackson; **308:** Sandra Peacock; **311:** Robert Kelly

Chapter 12 **316: left** Military & Historical Image Bank; **right** Courtesy of Archaeological Services, Inc.; **319:** Courtesy of Richard W Roeller; **325:** Images courtesy of Akhmim Mummy Studies Consortium and Pinnacle Health System, Harrisburg, Pennsylvania; **326:** Clark Larsen; **327:** Clark Larsen; **330:** Dorothy Lippert; **338** Tom Dillehay; **340:** Smithsonian Institution, photo by Chip Clark; **343:** Dr. Dongya Yang, Department of Archaeology, Simon Fraser University

Chapter 13 **346:** Laurel Culture Burial Mound © Canadian Museum of Civilization, 71-2530; **351:** William S. Webb Museum of Anthropology; **352:** Barry Hewlett; **360:** Robert Kelly; **362:** The University of Alabama, Moundville Archaeological Park; **363: top** From *Archaeology of the Moundville Chiefdom,* edited by Vernon James Knight, Jr. and Vincas P. Steponaitis, published by the Smithsonian Institute Press, Washington, DC; copyright © 1998 by the Smithsonian Institution. Used by permission of the publisher; **bottom** American Museum of Natural History; **369:** University of Alberta; **375:** From Chapdelaine, Millaire, and Kennedy, 2001. "Compositional Analysis and Provenance Study of Spindle Whorls from the Moche Site, North Coast of Peru", Journal of Archaeological Science 28

Chapter 14 **378:** All Canada Photos/Alamy; **381:** Robert Kelly; **383:** Dr Peter Dawson; **385L** American Museum of Natural History; **386:** American Museum of Natural History; **387:** Robert Kelly; **391:** Dr Peter Dawson; **393:** American Museum of Natural History; **400:** Charles & Josette Lenars/Corbis Canada

Chapter 15 **403:** Historical Picture Archive/Corbis Canada; **416:** Kim Hill; **419:** Mike Drew/The Calgary Sun; **420:** Ofer Bar-Yosef; **424:** Robert Kelly; **429:** San Diego Museum of Man, photo by Peter D. Harrison, Ca. 1993; **430:** American Museum of Natural History; **432:** Peabody Museum, Harvard University

Chapter 16 **436:** NA-674/Glenbow Archives; **438:** NA-1532-4/Glenbow Archives; **439: top** NA-302-9, Glenbow Archives; **bottom** NA-387-27, Glenbow Archives; **442:** *Captain William Cooke Seizes Contraband* by John Thompson (ID# 88229), courtesy of U.S. Department of Homeland Security; **444:** NA-2295-1/Glenbow Archives; **445:** NA-2529-1/Glenbow Archives; **447:** Man proposes, God disposes, 1864, Landseer, Sir Edwin (1802-73)/Royal Holloway, University of London/The Bridgeman Art Library; **448:** NL-15558/National Library of Canada; **449:** Dr Peter Dawson; **451:** NA-1406-26/Glenbow Museum; **452:** Photo courtesy of Fort Vancouver National Historic Site, National Park Service; **453:** NA-354-13/Glenbow Archives; **458:** T859 *Critical Position of H.M.S. Investigator on the North Coast of Baring Island,* August 20th 1851, drawn by Lieu. S. Gurney Cresswell, pub. 1854 by Day & Son and Ackermann & Co. (colour lithograph), English School, (19th century), © Royal Geographical Society, British Library; **459:** Rolf Hicker, Nature and Travel Stock Photography, ; **461:** NA-1929-1/Glenbow Archives; **462:** Dianne Newell; **464:** *The Wealth of England: the Bessemer Process of Making Steel,* 1895 (oil on canvas), Titcomb, William Holt Yates (1858-1930)/Kelham Island Industrial Museum, Sheffield, UK/The Bridgeman Art Library; **465:** J Schwanke/Alamy

Chapter 17 **469:** Dr Peter Dawson; **472: top** Captain C. (Bud) Robinson; **bottom** Portrait of Emmanuel Kant (1724-1804) (oil on canvas), German School, (18th century)/Private Collection/The Bridgeman Art Library; **473:** Courtesy of Museum of Anthropology, University of British Columbia; **475:** Mode in which the young Memnon's head (now in the British Museum) was removed by G Belzoni (lithograph), c.1816, © Royal Geographical Society, London, UK /The Bridgeman Art Library; **479:** Photo by Roy Carlson courtesy Museum of Archaeology and Ethnology, Simon Fraser University; **483:** Archives and Manuscripts, Queen Elizabeth II Library, Memorial University; **485:** Courtesy of Kate Peach; **486:** Dr Marty Magne; **489:** The Manitoba Museum, Winnipeg, MB; **491:** Courtesy of Journal Etudes/Inuit/Inuit Studies; **493:** Courtesy of Natasha Lyons

Chapter 18 **498:** Dr Peter Dawson; **501:** Courtesy Bill Rathje, photo by Jim Sugar; **505:** Robert Kelly; **507:** Courtesy of Mark Skinner, Simon Fraser University; **509:** Clark Erikson; **512:** Dr Peter Dawson; **513:** Dr Richard M Levy; **516:** Dr Peter Dawson; **517:** Dr Peter Dawson and Dr. Richard M Levy; **518:** Dr Peter Dawson; **519:** Dr Peter Dawson and Dr. Richard M Levy; **520:** Dr Peter Dawson and Dr. Richard M Levy; **523:** Dr Peter Dawson and Dr. Richard M Levy.

Index